INCOSE SYSTEMS ENGINEERING HANDBOOK

系统工程手册 原书第5版

系统生命周期流程和活动指南

国际系统工程委员会（INCOSE） ◎编著

张新国◎译

国际系统工程委员会（INCOSE）编写的《系统工程手册》为系统工程师所从事的关键流程活动提供说明。本手册的目标读者是新的系统工程师、需要从事系统工程的非系统工程专业的工程师或需要进行参考的有经验的系统工程师。本手册描述了每个系统工程流程活动在可承受性和性能设计背景中的必需性方面的内容。

本书为中英文对照版。

Copyright © 2025 John Wiley & Sons, Inc.. All Rights Reserved.

This translation published under license. Authorized translation from the English language edition, entitled INCOSE SYSTEMS ENGINEERING HANDBOOK, ISBN 9781119814290, by INCOSE, Published by John Wiley & Sons, Inc. No part of this book may be reproduced in any form without the written permission of the original copyrights holder.

This edition is authorized for sale in the World.

此版本经授权在全球范围内销售。

北京市版权局著作权合同登记　图字：01-2024-0173 号。

图书在版编目（CIP）数据

系统工程手册：系统生命周期流程和活动指南：原书第 5 版：汉英对照 / 国际系统工程委员会（INCOSE）编著；张新国译. —— 北京：机械工业出版社，2025.8. —— ISBN 978-7-111-78687-0

Ⅰ.N945-62

中国国家版本馆CIP数据核字第20258MT519号

机械工业出版社（北京市百万庄大街22号　邮政编码：100037）
策划编辑：廖　岩　　　　　责任编辑：廖　岩　戴思杨
责任校对：张爱妮　张亚楠　　责任印制：任维东
北京科信印刷有限公司印刷
2025年8月第1版第1次印刷
170mm×242mm·64印张·3插页·1042千字
标准书号：ISBN 978-7-111-78687-0
定价：398.00元

电话服务　　　　　　　　　网络服务
服务电话：010-88361066　　机 工 官 网：www.cmpbook.com
　　　　　010-88379833　　机 工 官 博：weibo.com/cmp1952
　　　　　010-68326294　　金 书 网：www.golden-book.com
封底无防伪标均为盗版　　　机工教育服务网：www.cmpedu.com

译者序

《系统工程手册》（*Systems Engineering Handbook*）是国际系统工程委员会（INCOSE）在系统工程领域发布的知识体系中的核心内容，在过去的近30年里，先后经历了十多次修订，广泛地采纳INCOSE利益相关方的建议并扩大作者群体，不断地结合工程应用的发展扩充系统工程流程域的方法。直至2006年6月发布的3.0版，成为基于国际通行的系统工程标准ISO/IEC 15288的首个版本，并在此后与ISO/IEC/IEEE 15288标准共同演进，其目的是为广泛的工业界遵循国际标准提供丰富的流程和方法的指南。

本次翻译的《系统工程手册》5.0版，是继2015年修订的4.0版之后，于2023年更新的最新版本。从2006年的3.0版到2015年的4.0版，间隔近9年的时间，这次的5.0版与4.0版又间隔8年。如果说前一次的9年时间是传统系统工程向复杂系统工程转型发展最关键的时期，也是全球航空航天与防务领域从传统的基于文档的系统工程到基于模型的系统工程的转型期，那么这一次所经历的8年时间则是基于模型的系统工程在更多领域和更大范围从基本原理到方法、工具全面应用和深入实践的时期。本次更新的5.0版也是依据全球系统工程在数字技术和基于模型的技术支持下实现转型的过程中亟待加强和补充的系统工程知识而进行的修订和完善，主要体现在以下几个方面。

第一，与开放的、持续演进的《系统工程知识体指南》（SEBoK）融合。

《系统工程手册》5.0版在可行的范围内与《系统工程知识体指南》（SEBoK, 2024）一致，在很多地方，本手册为读者揭示了SEBoK中相关主题的更为详细的适用范围。

SEBoK是一个关于系统工程信息的大纲，基于开源、众创和共享的进化方式，类似系统工程领域的维基百科。从SEBoK近年的版本更新速度可以看出，全球系统工程知识体的开放、共享和演进达到了空前的程度。在这一背景下，5.0版融合SEBoK最新发展，按照系统工程理论基础、系统工程流程、生命周期分析和方法、剪裁和应用、系统工程实践和案例研究六大部分对手册整体结构进行了重要调整，使得系统工程学科知识体系的完整性和系统性更强，凸显了系统工程学科近年来的快速演进与成熟。

第二，系统工程理论基础趋向系统学（Systemology）统一框架。

《系统工程手册》4.0版首次加入系统科学和系统思维，回归了系统工程的方法论之根。系统科学主要研究系统基础知识域，包括系统（工程系统）群、复杂性、涌现性、系统类型等。系统科学打破了传统科学中的"解析研究方法"的局限性，即"一个实体在物质上或概念上可以被分解为多个部分并由其各部分复原整体"——这一"经典"科学的基本原理，从而揭示了系统科学这一新科学范式更为关注系统的开放性、涌现性和演进性，为独立于元素类型或应用的所有系统类型提供了理论基础。

系统思维是系统工程的思考方式。系统思维的主要任务是识别系统主要形式和功能，形式是指系统是如何组成的（由多少个部分组成的，以及它们的相互关系），功能是指系统要做什么，它们是系统最根本的两个要素。系统思维基于系统科学中的系统概念、系统原理与特征模式、系统表达等重要内容。系统概念需要使用系统思维的方法，与系统原理与特征模式建立相关性，其中，系统原理与特征模式是系统思维形成的基础，而系统表达则是系统思维的应用。系统的形式化表达高于自然语言表达，是基于模型的系统工程和数字工程的关键使能要素，起始于系统的概念建模和逻辑建模。

近年来，系统学的提出极大促进了系统工程的基础科学原理的发展。系统学是关于系统的主要研究领域（哲学、科学、工程和实践）的知识统一体，期望通过建立统一框架综合传统各个研究领域对系统的独立研究。基于系统学框架，5.0版首次提出了系统科学、系统思维和系统工程三者的关系，从而为系统工程为什么（Why）、做什么（What）和如何做（How）的原则提供支撑。值得一提的是，5.0版还新增了关于不确定性、认知偏差、系统工程原则和系统工程启发式方法等系统工程基础部分的最新发展。

第三，系统生命周期流程体系坚持正向设计的观点。

正向设计是系统工程流程体系的核心观点。《系统工程手册》4.0版在流程上的显著变化是将系统工程的起点从利益相关方需要上升到业务或任务需要，指明了需求工程是正向设计的源头，是后续的系统架构、设计、验证、确认的根本。再者，4.0版将"架构设计流程"拆分为"架构定义流程"与"设计定义流程"，凸显了架构和设计活动的不同且互补的观念。系统架构是更加抽象的、面向概念的、全局的，聚焦于达成任务的运行概念（OpsCon）和系统及系统元素的高层级结构，有效的架构应尽可能独立于设计，以在设计权衡空间中有最大的灵活性，它要聚焦于"做什么"，而不是"如何做"（属于设计流程的工作）。系统架构流程开发架构视角，并开发候选架构的模型和视图，通过对系统从需求到功能架构、逻辑架构，再到物理架构，以及对系统功能、行为和结构的映射，实现系统需求和架构实体向系统元素划分、对准和分配的正向设计，并建立系统设计与全生命周期演进的指导原则。

5.0 版在此基础上进一步调整了手册中协议流程组、项目使能流程组、技术管理流程组和技术流程组的逻辑顺序，与 ISO/IEC/IEEE 15288: 2023 保持一致。这一变化更加强调了组织间的协议流程是工程系统生命周期的起点，也是系统正向设计中需求工程的起点，希望引起系统工程实践者对协议流程的重视。同时，5.0 版新增了系统工程分析方法的最新发展，例如架构框架（Architecture Framework）、模式（Patterns）等。

第四，丰富了系统工程剪裁、应用和实践的内容。

《系统工程手册》5.0 版面向系统工程的有效实践，给出了绿地（Greenfield）/棕地（Brownfield）系统、基于商用货架产品（COTS）的系统、软件密集型系统、赛博物理系统（Cyber-Physical System）、物联网（Internet of Things）/大数据驱动的系统、服务系统和复杂组织体系（Enterprise）等多个系统类型的系统工程流程剪裁应用的考虑因素与建议。5.0 版同时进一步完善了系统工程在特定产品行业或领域（油气、电力和能源等 10 类）的应用，介绍了各产品行业或领域中系统工程特定的术语、概念、活动、方法和实践。

5.0 版还介绍了 INCOSE 系统工程胜任力框架，从核心、专业、技术、管理和综合五个方面丰富了系统工程从业人员胜任力的内涵，该框架与《INCOSE 系统工程胜任力评估指南》（2022）一起可用于系统工程从业人员招聘、评估、培训和提升等用途。

第五，数字工程、人工智能已成为系统工程未来发展的新趋势。

经过过去 8 年的从基于文档到基于模型的范式转型，基于模型的系统工程的有关流程、方法和工具已日趋成熟，且在众多产品行业/领域得到应用和推广。在这一背景环境下，伴随技术的迅猛发展，数字工程（Digital Engineering）被提出并作为基于模型的系统工程未来发展的新趋势。数字工程被定义为一种综合的数字式实施方法，使用系统数据和模型的权威来源作为跨学科的连续统一

译者序

体,支持系统从概念到退役的生命周期活动。基于模型的系统工程是数字工程的核心元素之一。数字系统模型是系统的数字表达,它综合了权威的基于模型的系统工程和其他数字工程技术数据及相关制品,定义了整个系统生命周期中系统的所有方面,构成了系统生命周期演进的权威真相源,是系统生命周期数字孪生和数字线索的底层逻辑。

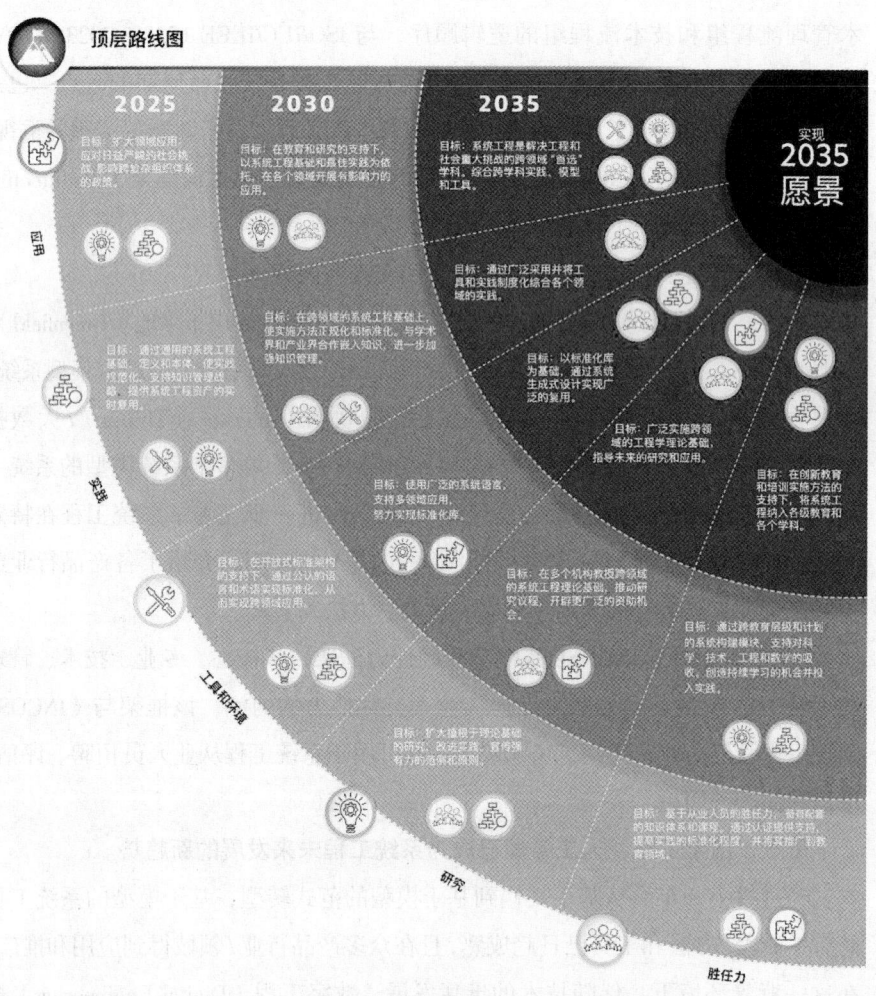

图 00.1　INCOSE 系统工程 2035 愿景路线图

译者序

人工智能（Artificial Intelligence）技术的发展为系统工程带来了新的机遇和挑战。INCOSE 于 2019 年首次提出"AI4SE"和"SE4AI"的概念，表示了未来系统工程和人工智能的双向转型。AI4SE 应用增强智能（Augmented Intelligence）和机器学习（Machine Learning）技术改进过去由人手动驱动的系统工程实践，提升模型构建等活动的规模和效率。SE4AI 则将系统工程方法应用于基于学习的系统的设计和运行。

最后回到 INCOSE 发布的 2035 愿景路线图上（见图 00.1），它对系统工程的未来演进路径进行了表达，涵盖了研究、工具和环境、实践、应用、胜任力等多个方面，勾勒出未来系统工程的发展趋势。总的来说，5.0 版本无疑是更具有全面性、时效性和实用性的。

这次《系统工程手册》5.0 版的翻译团队具有非常大的变化，包括来自清华大学（李乐飞、关若曦、郭孟宇、玉龙）、北京航空航天大学（高星海、常创业）、中国航空研究院（王乾、袁家骏）等学术界和工业界的系统工程研究与实践者组成的联合翻译和校对团队。更重要的是这支团队的主要成员经历了近十年基于模型的系统工程的基础理论研究和工程实践应用的探索，因此，对于一些新的和重要的术语、概念的语义、内涵及其外延的把握都具有较高的水准和理解力，从而保证了 5.0 版的翻译质量较 4.0 版又有较大的提升。

最后，感谢 INCOSE 及北京（中国）分会所给予的信任和支持，在此特别对清华大学郭孟宇以及机械工业出版社编辑团队在本次翻译、校对、版本管理、过程控制等工作中付出的努力，表示衷心的感谢。

张新国
2025 年 1 月

SYSTEMS ENGINEERING HANDBOOK

A GUIDE FOR SYSTEM LIFE CYCLE PROCESSES AND ACTIVITIES

FIFTH EDITION

INCOSE-TP-2003–002-05
2023

Prepared by:
International Council on Systems Engineering (INCOSE)

7670 Opportunity Rd, Suite 220
San Diego, CA, USA 92111-2222

Compiled and Edited by:
DAVID D. WALDEN, ESEP — EDITOR-IN-CHIEF — AMERICAS SECTOR
THOMAS M. SHORTELL, CSEP — DEPUTY EDITOR-IN-CHIEF — AMERICAS SECTOR

GARRY J. ROEDLER, ESEP — EDITOR — AMERICAS SECTOR
BERNARDO A. DELICADO, ESEP — EDITOR — EMEA SECTOR
ODILE MORNAS, ESEP — EDITOR — EMEA SECTOR
YIP YEW-SENG, CSEP — EDITOR — ASIA OCEANIA SECTOR
DAVID ENDLER, ESEP — EDITOR — EMEA SECTOR

系统工程手册

系统生命周期流程和活动指南

第 5 版

INCOSE-TP-2003—002-05
2023

编著：

国际系统工程委员会（INCOSE）
7670 Opportunity Rd, Suite 220
San Diego, CA, USA 92111-2222

编撰：

DAVID D. WALDEN, ESEP — 主编 — 美洲区
THOMAS M. SHORTELL, CSEP — 副主编 — 美洲区
GARRY J. ROEDLER, ESEP — 编辑 — 美洲区
BERNARDO A. DELICADO, ESEP — 编辑 — 欧洲/中东/非洲区
ODILE MORNAS, ESEP — 编辑 — 欧洲/中东/非洲区
YIP YEW-SENG, CSEP — 编辑 — 亚洲/大洋洲区
DAVID ENDLER, ESEP — 编辑 — 欧洲/中东/非洲区

WILEY

INCOSE NOTICES

This International Council on Systems Engineering (INCOSE) Technical Product was prepared by the INCOSE Systems Engineering Handbook Team. It is approved by the INCOSE Technical Operations Leadership for release as an INCOSE Technical Product.

Copyright ©2023 by INCOSE, subject to the following restrictions:

Author Use: Authors have full rights to use their contributions in a totally unfettered way with credit to the INCOSE technical source, except as noted in the following text. Abstraction is permitted with credit to the source.

INCOSE Use: Permission to reproduce and use this document or parts thereof by members of INCOSE and to prepare derivative works from this document for INCOSE use is granted, with attribution to INCOSE and the original author (s) where practical, provided this copyright notice is included with all reproductions and derivative works. Content from ISO/IEC/IEEE 15288 and ISO/IEC TR 24748-1 is used by permission and is not to be reproduced other than as part of this total document.

External Use: This document may not be shared or distributed to any non-INCOSE third party. Requests for permission to reproduce this document in whole or in part, or to prepare derivative works of this document for external and/or commercial use should be addressed to the INCOSE Central Office, 7670 Opportunity Road, Suite 220, San Diego, CA 92111-2222, USA.

Electronic Version Use: Any electronic version of this document is to be used for personal, professional use only and is not to be placed on a non-INCOSE sponsored server for general use.

Any additional use of these materials must have written approval from the INCOSE Central.

General Citation Guidelines: References to this handbook should be formatted as follows, with appropriate adjustments for formally recognized styles:

INCOSE SEH (2023) . *Systems Engineering Handbook: A Guide for System Life Cycle Process and Activities* (5th ed.) . D. D. Walden, T. M. Shortell, G. J. Roedler, B. A. Delicado, O. Mornas, Yip Y. S., and D. Endler (Eds.) . San Diego, CA: International Council on Systems Engineering. Published by John Wiley & Sons, Inc.

INCOSE 声明

本国际系统工程委员会（INCOSE）技术产品由 INCOSE 系统工程手册团队编制。经 INCOSE 技术运营领导层批准，作为 INCOSE 技术产品发行。

版权 ©2023 归 INCOSE 所有，但受下列限制：

作者的使用权：说明源自 INCOSE 技术文献，作者有权不受任何约束地使用他们的著作，除非下文另有说明。说明源自 INCOSE，允许摘录。

INCOSE 的使用权：允许 INCOSE 成员复制和使用本文件或其部分内容，允许从本文件中编制衍生文献以便 INCOSE 使用，在可行时，应说明 INCOSE 和原作者的贡献，须将本版权声明包含在复制和衍生文献中。ISO/IEC/IEEE 15288 和 ISO/IEC TR 24748-1 的内容经允许后方可使用，除作为本文件的一部分外，不得复制。

外部使用权：本文件不得共享或分发给任何非 INCOSE 的第三方。如有为了外部和/或商业用途而复制全部或部分本文件以及编制本文件的衍生文献的请求，需联系 INCOSE 行政办公室（地址：7670 Opportunity Road, Suite 220, San Diego, CA92111-2222, USA）。

电子版的使用权：本文件的任何电子版仅用于个人专业用途，不得为一般用途放置在非 INCOSE 所拥有的服务器中。

这些资料的任何额外使用必须经过 INCOSE 行政办公室的书面批准。

一般引用指南：本手册的参考文献按照如下方式编排格式，并按正式认可的风格做适当调整：

INCOSE SEH（2023）. 系统工程手册：系统生命周期流程和活动指南（第 5 版）. D. D. Walden, T. M. Shortell, G. J. Roedler, B. A. Delicado, O. Mornas, Yip Y. S., and D. Endler（Eds.）. 加州圣迭戈：国际系统工程委员会。由 John Wiley & Sons 公司出版。

HISTORY OF CHANGES

Revision	Revision date	Change description and rationale
Original	Jun 1994	Draft *Systems Engineering Handbook* (SEH) created by INCOSE members from several defense/aerospace companies—including Lockheed, TRW, Northrop Grumman, Ford Aerospace, and the Center for Systems Management—for INCOSE review.
1.0	Jan 1998	Initial SEH release approved to update and broaden coverage of SE process. Included broad participation of INCOSE members as authors. Based on Interim Standards EIA 632 and IEEE 1220.
2.0	Jul 2000	Expanded coverage on several topics, such as functional analysis. This version was the basis for the development of the Certified Systems Engineering Professional (CSEP) exam.
2.0A	Jun 2004	Reduced page count of SEH v2 by 25% and reduced the US DoD-centric material wherever possible. This version was the basis for the first publicly offered CSEP exam.
3.0	Jun 2006	Significant revision based on ISO/IEC 15288:2002. The intent was to create a country- and domain-neutral handbook. Significantly reduced the page count, with elaboration to be provided in appendices posted online in the INCOSE Product Asset Library (IPAL).
3.1	Aug 2007	Added detail that was not included in SEH v3, mainly in new appendices. This version was the basis for the updated CSEP exam.
3.2	Jan 2010	Updated version based on ISO/IEC/IEEE 15288:2008. Significant restructuring of the handbook to consolidate related topics.
3.2.1	Jan 2011	Clarified definition material, architectural frameworks, concept of operations references, risk references, and editorial corrections based on ISO/IEC review.
3.2.2	Oct 2011	Correction of errata introduced by revision 3.2.1.
4.0	Jul 2015	Significant revision based on ISO/IEC/IEEE 15288:2015, inputs from the relevant INCOSE working groups (WGs), and to be consistent with the Guide to the Systems Engineering Body of Knowledge (SEBoK).
5.0	Jul 2023	Significant revision based on ISO/IEC/IEEE 15288:2023 and inputs from the relevant INCOSE working groups (WGs). Significant restructuring of the handbook based inputs from INCOSE stakeholders.

变更历史

修订版本	修订日期	变更说明及原因
原版	1994 年 6 月	系统工程手册（SEH）草案由几家来自防务/航空航天公司的 INCOSE 成员创建——包括 Lockheed、TRW、Northrop Grumman、Ford Aerospace 和系统管理中心——以供 INCOSE 审查
1.0	1998 年 1 月	SEH 的初始发布版本经批准后更新和扩展系统工程流程的范围。INCOSE 成员广泛参与并成为作者。基于暂行标准 EIA 632 和 IEEE 1220
2.0	2000 年 7 月	扩展几个主题的范围，如功能分析。此版本是发展注册系统工程专业人员（CSEP）考试的基础
2.0A	2004 年 6 月	将 SEH v2 的页数减少 25%，并且尽可能减少以美国国防部为中心的材料。此版本是首次公开提供的 CSEP 考试的基础
3.0	2006 年 6 月	基于 ISO/IEC 15288:2002 的重要修订。目的是创造出对国家和领域都中立的手册。大幅减少页数，同时在 INCOSE 产品资产库（IPAL）在线公布的附录中提供详细阐述
3.1	2007 年 8 月	增加在 SEH v3 中没有包含的细节，主要是在新的附录中。此版本是更新的 CSEP 考试的基础
3.2	2010 年 1 月	基于 ISO/IEC/IEEE 15288:2008 的更新版本。对手册大幅度重新建构以巩固相关主题
3.2.1	2011 年 1 月	基于 ISO/IEC 的评审澄清：定义资料、架构框架、运行方案的引用、风险的引用以及编辑性的更正
3.2.2	2011 年 10 月	修正 3.2.1 版本推出的勘误表
4.0	2015 年 7 月	基于 ISO/IEC/IEEE 15288:2015 进行大幅修订，有相关 INCOSE 工作组（WGs）的输入，并与《系统工程知识体指南》相一致
5.0	2023 年 7 月	根据 ISO/IEC/IEEE 15288:2023 和相关 INCOSE 工作组（WGs）的意见进行了重大修订。根据 INCOSE 利益相关方的意见，对手册结构进行重大调整

PREFACE

The objective of the International Council on Systems Engineering (INCOSE) *Systems Engineering Handbook* (SEH) is to describe key Systems Engineering (SE) process activities. The intended audience is the SE practitioner. When the term "SE practitioner" is used in this handbook, it includes the new SE practitioner, a product engineer, an engineer in another discipline who needs to perform SE, or an experienced SE practitioner who needs a convenient reference.

The descriptions in this handbook show what each SE process activity entails, in the context of designing for required performance and life cycle considerations. On some projects, a given activity may be performed very informally; on other projects, it may be performed very formally, with interim products under formal configuration control. This document is not intended to advocate any level of formality as necessary or appropriate in all situations. The appropriate degree of formality in the execution of any SE process activity is determined by the following:

The need for communication of what is being done (across members of a project team, across organizations, or over time to support future activities)

The level of uncertainty

The degree of complexity

The consequences to human welfare

On smaller projects, where the span of required communications is small (few people and short project life cycle) and the cost of rework is low, SE activities can be conducted very informally and thus at low cost. On larger projects, where the span of required communications is large (many teams that may span multiple geographic locations and organizations and long project life cycle) and the cost of failure or rework is high, increased formality can significantly help in achieving project opportunities and in mitigating project risk.

In a project environment, work necessary to accomplish project objectives is considered "in scope"; all other work is considered "out of scope." On every project, "thinking" is always "in scope." Thoughtful tailoring and intelligent application of the SE processes described in this handbook are essential to achieve the proper balance between the risk of missing project technical and business objectives on the one hand and process paralysis on the other hand. Part IV provides tailoring and application guidance to help achieve that balance.

前言

国际系统工程委员会（INCOSE）《系统工程手册》（SEH）的目的是描述关键的系统工程（SE）流程活动。目标读者是系统工程从业人员。当本手册中使用术语"系统工程从业人员"时，其包括新的系统工程从业人员、产品工程师、需要实施系统工程的其他学科的工程师，或一个需要方便的参考的有经验的系统工程从业人员。

本手册中的描述内容指明在所要求的性能和生命周期考虑的设计背景环境中每个系统工程流程活动的必要性。在某些项目中，可能以很不正式的方式实施某一给定活动；而在其他项目中，却非常正式地实施，并且中间过渡产品都处于正式的构型控制之中。本文件的意图不是提倡在所有情况下任何正式程度都是必须或合适的，实施任何系统工程流程活动的适当正式程度取决于：

需要沟通正在做什么（项目团队成员之间、组织之间或随着时间而支持未来活动）

不确定性的等级

复杂性的程度

人类福祉的结果

在比较小的项目中，要求沟通的跨度小（人员少且项目生命周期短），返工成本低，因而系统工程活动可非常不正式地执行，因而成本低。在比较大的项目中，所需沟通的跨度大（许多团队可能跨越多重地理位置和组织且项目生命周期长）且失败或返工成本高，因而提高正式程度可极大地帮助增加实现项目的机会和减轻项目风险。

在项目环境中，完成项目目标所需的工作属于"范围内"；所有其他工作属于"范围外"。对于每个项目而言，"思考"总是在"范围内"。将本手册所述的系统工程流程进行深思熟虑的剪裁和颇具智慧的应用，对于错失项目技术和业务目标的风险与流程瘫痪之间取得适当平衡是根本性的。第四部分提供了剪裁准则，以帮助达到这种平衡。

APPROVED FOR THE INCOSE SEH FIFTH EDITION

Christopher D. Hoffman, CSEP, INCOSE Technical Director, January 2021-January 2023

Olivier Dessoude, INCOSE Technical Director, January 2023-January 2025

Theodore J. Ferrell, INCOSE Assistant Director, Technical Review, January 2021-January 2023

Krystal Porter, INCOSE Assistant Director, Technical Review, January 2023-January 2025

Lori F. Zipes, ESEP, INCOSE Assistant Director, Technical Information, January 2022-January 2024

Tony Williams, ESEP, INCOSE Assistant Director, Product Champion, January 2022-January 2025

国际系统工程委员会《系统工程手册》(第5版)审批

Christopher D. Hoffman, CSEP, INCOSE 技术总监,2021 年 1 月—2023 年 1 月

Olivier Dessoude, INCOSE 技术总监,2023 年 1 月—2025 年 1 月

Theodore J. Ferrell, INCOSE 助理总监,技术评审,2021 年 1 月—2023 年 1 月

Krystal Porter, INCOSE 助理总监,技术评审,2023 年 1 月—2025 年 1 月

Lori F. Zipes, ESEP, INCOSE 助理总监,技术信息,2022 年 1 月—2024 年 1 月

Tony Williams, ESEP, INCOSE 助理总监,产品冠军,2022 年 1 月—2025 年 1 月

HOW TO USE THIS HANDBOOK

PURPOSE

This handbook defines the "state-of-the-good-practice" for the discipline of Systems Engineering (SE) and provides an authoritative reference to understand the SE discipline in terms of content and practice.

APPLICATION

This handbook is consistent with ISO/IEC/IEEE 15288 (2023), *Systems and software engineering—System life cycle processes*, hereafter referred to as ISO/IEC/IEEE 15288, to ensure its usefulness across a wide range of application domains for engineered systems and products, as well as services. ISO/IEC/IEEE 15288 is an international standard that provides system life cycle process outcomes, activities, and tasks, whereas this handbook further elaborates on the activities and practices necessary to execute the processes.

This handbook is also consistent with the *Guide to the Systems Engineering Body of Knowledge*, hereafter referred to as the SEBoK (2023), to the extent practicable. In many places, this handbook points readers to the SEBoK for more detailed coverage of the related topics, including a current and vetted set of references. The SEBoK also includes coverage of "state-of-the-art" in SE.

For organizations that do not follow the principles of ISO/IEC/IEEE 15288 or the SEBoK to specify their life cycle processes, this handbook can serve as a reference to practices and methods that have proven beneficial to the SE community at large and that can add significant value in new domains, if appropriately selected, tailored, and applied. Part IV provides top-level guidance on the application of SE in selected product sectors and domains.

Before applying this handbook in a given organization or on a given project, it is recommended that the tailoring guidelines in Part IV be used to remove conflicts with existing policies, procedures, and standards already in use within an organization. Not every process will apply universally. Careful selection from the material is recommended. Reliance on process over progress will not deliver a system. Processes and activities in this handbook do not supersede any international, national, or local laws or regulations.

如何使用本手册

目的

本手册定义了系统工程（SE）学科的"最佳实践"，为了解系统工程学科的内容和实践提供了权威参考。

适用性

本手册与 ISO/IEC/IEEE 15288（2023）系统和软件工程—系统生命周期流程（以下简称 ISO/IEC/IEEE 15288）保持一致，以确保其适用于工程系统和产品以及服务的广泛应用领域。ISO/IEC/IEEE 15288 是一项提供系统生命周期流程结果、活动和任务的国际标准，而本手册则进一步阐述了执行流程所需的活动和实践。

本手册还在可行的范围内与《系统工程知识体指南》[以下简称 SEBoK（2023）]保持一致。在许多地方，本手册都将读者引向 SEBoK，以了解相关主题的更详细内容，包括一套最新的、经过审核的参考文献。SEBoK 还涵盖了系统工程中的"最新"内容。

对于那些不按照 ISO/IEC/IEEE 15288 或 SEBoK 原则来指定其生命周期流程的组织，本手册可作为其实践和方法的参考，这些实践和方法已被证明对整个系统工程领域有益，而且如果选择、调整和应用得当，还能为新领域带来巨大价值。第四部分为系统工程在选定产品部门和领域方面的应用提供了顶层指导。

特定组织或特定项目中应用本手册之前，建议使用第四部分中的剪裁指南来消除与组织内已在使用的现有政策、程序和标准之间的冲突，并非每个流程都适用于所有情况。建议从材料中仔细选择。依赖于流程而不是进度，是无法实现系统的。本手册中的流程和活动并不取代任何国际、国家或地方法律法规。

HOW TO USE THIS HANDBOOK

USAGE

This handbook was developed to support the users and use cases shown in Table 0.1. Primary users are those who will use the handbook directly. Secondary users are those who will typically use the handbook with assistance from SE practitioners. Other users and use cases are possible.

TABLE 0.1   Handbook users and use cases

User	Type	Use cases
Seasoned SE Practitioner. Those who need to reinforce, refresh, and renew their SE knowledge	Primary	• Adapt or refer to handbook to suit individual applicability • Explore good practices • Identify blind spots or gaps by providing a good checklist to ensure necessary coverage • References to other sources for more in-depth understanding
Novice SE Practitioner: Those who need to start using SE	Primary	• Support structured, coherent, and comprehensive learning • Understand the scope (breadth and depth) of systems thinking and SE practices
INCOSE Certification: Systems Engineering Professional (SEP) certifiers and those being certified	Primary	• Define body of knowledge for SEP certification • Form the basis of the SEP examination
SE Educators: Those who develop and teach SE courses, including universities and trainers	Primary	• Support structured, coherent, and comprehensive learning • Suggest relevant SE topics to trainers for their course content • Serve as a supplemental teaching aid
SE Tool Providers/Vendors: Those who provide tools and methods to support SE practitioners	Primary	• Suggest tools, methods, or other solutions to be developed that help practitioners in their work
Prospective SE Practitioner or Manager: Those who may be interested in pursuing a career in SE or who need to be aware of SE practices	Secondary	• Provide an entry level survey to understand what SE is about to someone who has a basic technical or engineering background
Interactors: Those who perform in disciplines that exchange (consume and/or produce) information with SE practitioners	Secondary	• Understand basic terminologies, scope, structure, and value of SE • Understand the role of the SE practitioner and their relationship to others in a project or an organization

INCOSE SEH original table created by Yip. Usage per the INCOSE Notices page. All other rights reserved.

使用

本手册旨在为表 0.1 所示的用户和用例提供支持。主要用户是指直接使用本手册的用户。次要用户是指通常在系统工程从业人员的协助下使用本手册的用户。其他用户和用例也是可能的。

表 0.1　手册用户和用例

用户	类型	用例
经验丰富的系统工程从业人员。需要巩固、温习和更新系统工程知识的人	主要	• 调整或参考手册，以适合个人的适用性探索良好实践 • 通过提供一个良好的核对表来确定盲点或差距，以确保必要的覆盖范围 • 参考其他资料来源，以加深理解
系统工程新手：需要开始使用系统工程的人员	主要	• 支持结构化、连贯和全面的学习 • 了解系统思维和系统工程实践的范围（广度和深度）
INCOSE 认证：系统工程专业人员（SEP）认证者和正在接受认证者	主要	• 确定 SEP 认证的知识体系 • 构成 SEP 考试的基础
系统工程教育工作者：开发和教授系统工程课程的人员，包括大学和培训师	主要	• 支持结构化、连贯和全面的学习 • 为培训师的课程内容建议相关的系统工程主题 • 作为辅助教学工具
系统工程工具提供商/供应商：提供工具和方法以支持系统工程从业人员的机构	主要	• 建议开发有助于从业人员工作的工具、方法或其他解决方案
未来的系统工程从业人员或管理人员：有兴趣从事系统工程职业或需要了解系统工程实践	次要	• 提供入门级综述，让有基本技术或工程背景的人了解系统工程的内容
互动者：与系统工程从业人员交换（消费和/或产生）信息的学科从业人员	次要	• 了解系统工程的基本术语、范围、结构和价值 • 了解系统工程从业人员的角色及其与项目或组织中其他人的关系

INCOSE SEH 原始表由 Yip 创建。按照 INCOSE 通知页使用。版权所有。

ORGANIZATION AND STRUCTURE

As shown in Figure 0.1, this handbook is organized into six major parts, plus appendices.

Systems Engineering Introduction (Part I) provides foundational SE concepts and principles that underpin all other parts. It includes the what and why of SE and why it is important, key definitions, systems science and systems thinking, and SE principles and concepts.

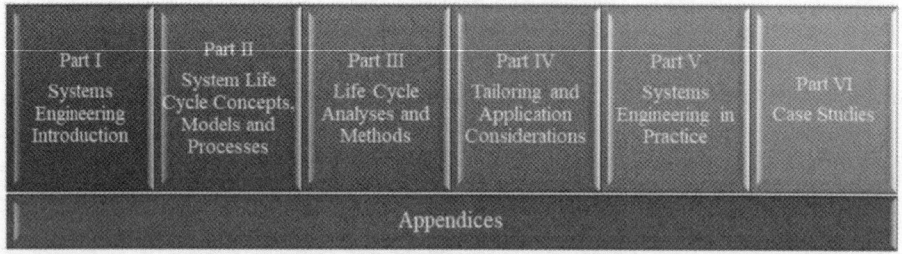

FIGURE 0.1 Handbook structure. INCOSE SEH original figure created by Mornas. Usage per the INCOSE Notices page. All other rights reserved.

System Life Cycle Concepts, Models, and Processes (Part II) describes an informative life cycle model with six stages: concept, development, production, utilization, support, and retirement. It also describes a set of life cycle processes to support SE consistent with the four process groups of ISO/IEC/IEEE 15288: Agreement Processes, Organizational Project Enabling Processes, Technical Management Processes, and Technical Processes.

Life Cycle Analyses and Methods (Part III) describes a set of quality characteristics approaches that need to be considered across the system life cycle. This part also describes methods that can apply across all processes, reflecting various aspects of the concurrent, iterative, and recursive nature of SE.

Tailoring and Application Considerations (Part IV) describes information on how to tailor (adapt and scale) the SE processes. It also introduces various considerations to view and apply SE: SE methodologies and approaches, system types, and project sectors and domains.

Systems Engineering in Practice (Part V) describes SE competencies, diversity, equity, and inclusion, SE relationship to other disciplines, SE transformation, and insight into the future of SE.

组织和结构

如图 0.1 所示，本手册分为六大部分和附录。

系统工程介绍（第一部分）提供了作为所有其他部分基础的系统工程基本概念和原则。它包括系统工程是什么、为什么、为什么重要、关键定义、系统科学和系统思维，以及系统工程的原则和概念。

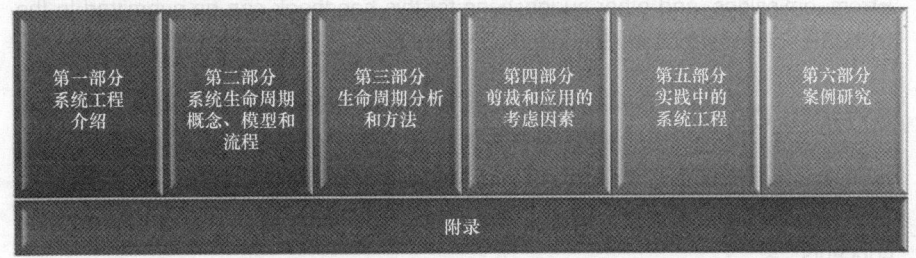

图 0.1 手册结构。INCOSE SEH 原始图由 Mornas 创建。按照 INCOSE 通知页使用。版权所有。

系统生命周期概念、模型和流程（第二部分）描述了一个包含六个阶段的翔实的生命周期模型：概念、开发、生产、使用、支持和退役。它还描述了一套支持系统工程的生命周期流程，与 ISO/IEC/IEEE 15288 的四个流程组一致：协议流程、组织项目使能流程、技术管理流程和技术流程。

生命周期分析和方法（第三部分）介绍了一系列需要在整个系统生命周期中加以考虑的质量特性方法。这部分还介绍了可适用于所有流程的方法，反映了系统工程的并行、迭代和递归性质的各个方面。

剪裁和应用的考虑因素（第四部分）介绍了如何定制（调整和扩展）系统工程流程的信息。它还介绍了看待和应用系统工程的各种考虑因素：系统工程方法论和实施途径、系统类型以及项目部门和领域。

实践中的系统工程（第五部分）介绍了系统工程的胜任力，多样性、公平性和包容性，系统工程与其他学科的关系，系统工程的转型以及对系统工程未来的见解。

HOW TO USE THIS HANDBOOK

Case Studies (Part VI) describes several case studies that are used throughout the handbook to reinforce the SE principles and concepts.

Appendix A contains a list of references used in this handbook. Appendices B and C provide a list of acronyms and a glossary of SE terms and definitions, respectively. Appendix D provides an N 2 diagram of the SE life cycle processes showing an example of the dependencies that exist in the form of shared inputs or outputs. Appendix E provides a list of all the typical inputs/outputs identified for each SE life cycle process. Appendix F acknowledges the various contributors to this handbook. Errors, omissions, and other suggestions for this handbook can be submitted to the INCOSE using instructions found in Appendix G.

SYMBOLOGY

As described in Section 2.3.1.2, SE is a concurrent, iterative, and recursive process. The following symbology is used throughout this handbook to reinforce these concepts

Concurrency is indicated by the parallel lines.
Iteration is indicated by the circular arrows.

Recursion is indicated by the down and up arrows.

TERMINOLOGY

One of the SE practitioner's first and most important responsibilities on a project is to establish nomenclature and terminology that support clear, unambiguous communication and definition of the system and its elements, functions, operations, and associated processes. Further, to promote the advancement of the field of SE throughout the world, it is essential that common definitions and understandings be established regarding general methods and terminology that in turn support common processes. As more SE practitioners accept and use common terminology, SE will experience improvements in communications, understanding, and, ultimately, productivity.

The glossary of terms used throughout this book (see Appendix C) is based on the definitions found in ISO/IEC/IEEE 15288; ISO/IEC/IEEE 24765 (2017) ; and the SEBoK.

案例研究（第六部分）介绍了本手册中的几个案例研究，以强化系统工程的原则和概念。

附录 A 包含本手册中使用的参考文献列表。附录 B 和 C 分别提供了首字母缩写列表和系统工程术语表及定义。附录 D 提供了系统工程生命周期流程的 N^2 图，以共享输入或输出的形式举例说明存在的依赖关系。附录 E 列出了每个系统工程生命周期流程的所有典型输入/输出。附录 F 感谢为本手册做出贡献的各位人士。对于本手册的错误、遗漏和其他建议，可以根据附录 G 中的说明提交给 INCOSE。

符号

如第 2.3.1.2 节所述，系统工程是一个并行、迭代和递归的流程。本手册使用以下符号来强化这些概念。

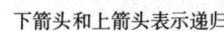
并行由平行线表示。
循环箭头表示迭代。

下箭头和上箭头表示递归。

术语

系统工程从业人员在项目中的首要和最重要的职责之一就是建立术语和术语表，以支持系统及其元素、功能、运行和相关流程的清晰、明确的交流和定义。此外，为了促进全世界系统工程领域的发展，必须就一般方法和术语建立共同的定义和理解，进而支持共同的流程。随着越来越多的系统工程从业人员接受并使用通用术语，系统工程将在交流、理解以及最终生产力方面得到改善。

本书使用的术语表（见附录 C）基于 ISO/IEC/IEEE 15288、ISO/IEC/IEEE 24765（2017）和 SEBoK 中的定义。

CONTENTS

1 Systems Engineering Introduction··2
   1.1 What Is Systems Engineering?···2
   1.2 Why Is Systems Engineering Important?······································14
   1.3 Systems Concepts··22
        1.3.1 System Boundary and the System of Interest (SoI)············24
        1.3.2 Emergence···26
        1.3.3 Interfacing Systems, Interoperating Systems, and Enabling Systems··28
        1.3.4 System Innovation Ecosystem···32
        1.3.5 The Hierarchy within a System···36
        1.3.6 Systems States and Modes···38
        1.3.7 Complexity···42
   1.4 Systems Engineering Foundations···44
        1.4.1 Uncertainty··44
        1.4.2 Cognitive Bias···48
        1.4.3 Systems Engineering Principles···48
        1.4.4 Systems Engineering Heuristics···56
   1.5 System Science and Systems Thinking··60

2 System Life Cycle Concepts, Models, and Processes···························72
   2.1 Life Cycle Terms and Concepts··72
        2.1.1 Life Cycle Characteristics··72
        2.1.2 Typical Life Cycle Stages···76
        2.1.3 Decision Gates··82
        2.1.4 Technical Reviews and Audits··86

目录

1 系统工程介绍 ·· 3
  1.1 什么是系统工程？ ··· 3
  1.2 系统工程为什么很重要？ ··· 15
  1.3 系统的概念 ·· 23
    1.3.1 系统边界和所感兴趣之系统（SoI） ·························· 25
    1.3.2 涌现性 ··· 27
    1.3.3 接口系统、互操作系统和使能系统 ····························· 29
    1.3.4 系统创新生态 ·· 33
    1.3.5 系统内的层级结构 ·· 37
    1.3.6 系统状态和模式 ··· 39
    1.3.7 复杂性 ··· 43
  1.4 系统工程基础 ··· 45
    1.4.1 不确定性 ··· 45
    1.4.2 认知偏差 ··· 49
    1.4.3 系统工程原则 ·· 49
    1.4.4 系统工程启发式方法 ··· 57
  1.5 系统科学和系统思维 ·· 61

2 系统生命周期概念、模型和流程 ·· 73
  2.1 生命周期术语和概念 ·· 73
    2.1.1 生命周期特征 ·· 73
    2.1.2 典型生命周期阶段 ·· 77
    2.1.3 阶段门 ··· 83
    2.1.4 技术评审和审核 ··· 87

CONTENTS

2.2 Life Cycle Model Approaches 92
    2.2.1 Sequential Methods 96
    2.2.2 Incremental Methods 102
    2.2.3 Evolutionary Methods 104
2.3 System Life Cycle Processes 110
    2.3.1 Introduction to the System Life Cycle Processes 110
        2.3.1.1 Format and Conventions 114
        2.3.1.2 Concurrency, Iteration, and Recursion 116
    2.3.2 Agreement Processes 122
        2.3.2.1 Acquisition Process 124
        2.3.2.2 Supply Process 134
    2.3.3 Organizational Project-Enabling Processes 142
        2.3.3.1 Life Cycle Model Management Process 142
        2.3.3.2 Infrastructure Management Process 152
        2.3.3.3 Portfolio Management Process 160
        2.3.3.4 Human Resource Management Process 170
        2.3.3.5 Quality Management Process 178
        2.3.3.6 Knowledge Management Process 186
    2.3.4 Technical Management Processes 198
        2.3.4.1 Project Planning Process 200
        2.3.4.2 Project Assessment and Control Process ... 212
        2.3.4.3 Decision Management Process 222
        2.3.4.4 Risk Management Process 232
        2.3.4.5 Configuration Management Process 250
        2.3.4.6 Information Management Process 260
        2.3.4.7 Measurement Process 268
        2.3.4.8 Quality Assurance Process 282

2.2 生命周期模型方法 ... 93
2.2.1 顺序方法 ... 97
2.2.2 增量方法 ... 103
2.2.3 演进方法 ... 105
2.3 系统生命周期流程 ... 111
2.3.1 系统生命周期流程介绍 ... 111
2.3.1.1 格式和约定 ... 115
2.3.1.2 并行、迭代和递归 ... 117
2.3.2 协议流程 ... 123
2.3.2.1 采办流程 ... 125
2.3.2.2 供应流程 ... 135
2.3.3 组织项目使能流程 ... 143
2.3.3.1 生命周期模型管理流程 ... 143
2.3.3.2 基础设施管理流程 ... 153
2.3.3.3 项目组合管理流程 ... 161
2.3.3.4 人力资源管理流程 ... 171
2.3.3.5 质量管理流程 ... 179
2.3.3.6 知识管理流程 ... 187
2.3.4 技术管理流程 ... 199
2.3.4.1 项目计划流程 ... 201
2.3.4.2 项目评估和控制流程 ... 213
2.3.4.3 决策管理流程 ... 223
2.3.4.4 风险管理流程 ... 233
2.3.4.5 构型配置管理流程 ... 251
2.3.4.6 信息管理流程 ... 261
2.3.4.7 测量流程 ... 269
2.3.4.8 质量保证流程 ... 283

2.3.5 Technical Processes ··· 290
    2.3.5.1 Business or Mission Analysis Process ·················· 296
    2.3.5.2 Stakeholder Needs and Requirements Definition Process ·· 308
    2.3.5.3 System Requirements Definition Process ··············· 324
    2.3.5.4 System Architecture Definition Process ················· 342
    2.3.5.5 Design Definition Process ································· 362
    2.3.5.6 System Analysis Process ································· 376
    2.3.5.7 Implementation Process ··································· 386
    2.3.5.8 Integration Process ··· 392
    2.3.5.9 Verification Process ··· 402
    2.3.5.10 Transition Process ··· 418
    2.3.5.11 Validation Process ··· 426
    2.3.5.12 Operation Process ··· 446
    2.3.5.13 Maintenance Process ····································· 450
    2.3.5.14 Disposal Process ·· 458

3 Life Cycle Analyses and Methods ································· 464
3.1 Quality Characteristics and Approaches ····················· 464
    3.1.1 Introduction to Quality Characteristics ······················· 464
    3.1.2 Affordability Analysis ·· 466
    3.1.3 Agility Engineering ··· 482
    3.1.4 Human Systems Integration ··································· 488
    3.1.5 Interoperability Analysis ·· 500
    3.1.6 Logistics Engineering ··· 502
    3.1.7 Manufacturability/Producibility Analysis ····················· 510
    3.1.8 Reliability, Availability, Maintainability Engineering ······· 514

2.3.5 技术流程 ... 291
- 2.3.5.1 业务或任务分析流程 ... 297
- 2.3.5.2 利益相关方需要和需求定义流程 ... 309
- 2.3.5.3 系统需求定义流程 ... 325
- 2.3.5.4 系统架构定义流程 ... 343
- 2.3.5.5 设计定义流程 ... 363
- 2.3.5.6 系统分析流程 ... 377
- 2.3.5.7 实施流程 ... 387
- 2.3.5.8 综合流程 ... 393
- 2.3.5.9 验证流程 ... 403
- 2.3.5.10 转移流程 ... 419
- 2.3.5.11 确认流程 ... 427
- 2.3.5.12 运行流程 ... 447
- 2.3.5.13 维护流程 ... 451
- 2.3.5.14 处置流程 ... 459

3 生命周期分析和方法 ... 465
3.1 质量特性和实施方法 ... 465
- 3.1.1 质量特性介绍 ... 465
- 3.1.2 可承受性分析 ... 467
- 3.1.3 敏捷工程 ... 483
- 3.1.4 人与系统综合 ... 489
- 3.1.5 互操作性分析 ... 501
- 3.1.6 后勤工程 ... 503
- 3.1.7 可制造性/可生产性分析 ... 511
- 3.1.8 可靠性、可用性、可维护性工程 ... 515

		3.1.9	Resilience Engineering	526
		3.1.10	Sustainability Engineering	540
		3.1.11	System Safety Engineering	542
		3.1.12	System Security Engineering	556
		3.1.13	Loss-Driven Systems Engineering	562
	3.2	Systems Engineering Analyses and Methods		562
		3.2.1	Modeling, Analysis, and Simulation	564
		3.2.2	Prototyping	588
		3.2.3	Traceability	590
		3.2.4	Interface Management	594
		3.2.5	Architecture Frameworks	606
		3.2.6	Patterns	614
		3.2.7	Design Thinking	624
		3.2.8	Biomimicry	626
4	Tailoring and Application Considerations			630
	4.1	Tailoring Considerations		630
	4.2	SE Methodology/Approach Considerations		640
		4.2.1	Model-Based SE	642
		4.2.2	Agile Systems Engineering	648
		4.2.3	Lean Systems Engineering	656
		4.2.4	Product Line Engineering (PLE)	662
	4.3	System Types Considerations		670
		4.3.1	Greenfield/Clean Sheet Systems	672
		4.3.2	Brownfield/Legacy Systems	674
		4.3.3	Commercial-off-the-Shelf (COTS)-Based Systems	676
		4.3.4	Software-Intensive Systems	682

  3.1.9 强韧性工程 527
  3.1.10 可持续性工程 541
  3.1.11 系统安全工程 543
  3.1.12 系统安保工程 557
  3.1.13 损失驱动的系统工程 563
 3.2 系统工程分析和方法 563
  3.2.1 建模、分析和仿真 565
  3.2.2 原型开发 589
  3.2.3 可追溯性 591
  3.2.4 接口管理 595
  3.2.5 架构框架 607
  3.2.6 模式 615
  3.2.7 设计思维 625
  3.2.8 仿生学 627

4 剪裁和应用的考虑因素 631
 4.1 剪裁考虑因素 631
 4.2 系统工程方法论/实施方法考虑因素 641
  4.2.1 基于模型的系统工程 643
  4.2.2 敏捷系统工程 649
  4.2.3 精益系统工程 657
  4.2.4 产品线工程（PLE） 663
 4.3 系统类型考虑因素 671
  4.3.1 绿地/全新的系统 673
  4.3.2 棕地/遗留的系统 675
  4.3.3 基于商用货架产品（COTS）的系统 677
  4.3.4 软件密集型系统 683

		4.3.5	Cyber-Physical Systems (CPS)	684

- 4.3.5 Cyber-Physical Systems (CPS) ··················· 684
- 4.3.6 Systems of Systems (SoS) ·········· 688
- 4.3.7 Internet of Things (IoT)/Big Data-Driven Systems ········· 700
- 4.3.8 Service Systems ············ 702
- 4.3.9 Enterprise Systems ············ 706

4.4 Application of Systems Engineering for Specific Product Sector or Domain Application ·········· 714

- 4.4.1 Automotive Systems ··········· 716
- 4.4.2 Biomedical and Healthcare Systems ············ 724
- 4.4.3 Commercial Aerospace Systems ············ 730
- 4.4.4 Defense Systems ············ 734
- 4.4.5 Infrastructure Systems ············ 736
- 4.4.6 Oil and Gas Systems ············ 742
- 4.4.7 Power & Energy Systems ············ 744
- 4.4.8 Space Systems ············ 750
- 4.4.9 Telecommunication Systems ············ 754
- 4.4.10 Transportation Systems ············ 758

5 Systems Engineering in Practice ············ 762

5.1 Systems Engineering Competencies ············ 762

- 5.1.1 Difference between Hard and Soft Skills ············ 764
- 5.1.2 System Engineering Professional Competencies ············ 768
- 5.1.3 Technical Leadership ············ 768
- 5.1.4 Ethics ············ 770

5.2 Diversity, Equity, and Inclusion ············ 774

5.3 Systems Engineering Relationships to Other Disciplines ············ 776

- 5.3.1 SE and Software Engineering (SWE) ············ 778

4.3.5 赛博物理系统（CPS） ·················· 685
4.3.6 体系（SoS） ························· 689
4.3.7 物联网/大数据驱动的系统 ············· 701
4.3.8 服务系统 ·························· 703
4.3.9 复杂组织体系系统 ·················· 707
4.4 系统工程在特定产品行业或领域的应用 ······· 715
4.4.1 汽车系统 ·························· 717
4.4.2 生物医学和医疗卫生系统 ············· 725
4.4.3 商业航空航天系统 ··················· 731
4.4.4 防务系统 ·························· 735
4.4.5 基础设施系统 ······················ 737
4.4.6 油气系统 ·························· 743
4.4.7 电力和能源系统 ····················· 745
4.4.8 空间系统 ·························· 751
4.4.9 电信系统 ·························· 755
4.4.10 运输系统 ························· 759

5 实践中的系统工程 ··························· 763
5.1 系统工程胜任力 ························· 763
5.1.1 硬技能和软技能的区别 ················ 765
5.1.2 系统工程专业胜任力 ·················· 769
5.1.3 技术领导力 ························ 769
5.1.4 道德 ····························· 771
5.2 多样性、公平性和包容性 ···················· 775
5.3 系统工程与其他专业的关系 ················· 777
5.3.1 系统工程和软件工程（SWE） ············ 779

    5.3.2 SE and Hardware Engineering (HWE) 782

    5.3.3 SE and Project Management (PM) 784

    5.3.4 SE and Industrial Engineering (IE) 790

    5.3.5 SE and Operations Research (OR) 794

  5.4 Digital Engineering 798

  5.5 Systems Engineering Transformation 802

  5.6 Future of SE 804

6 Case Studies 808

  6.1 Case 1: Radiation Therapy—the Therac-25 808

  6.2 Case 2: Joining Two Countries—the Øresund Bridge 812

  6.3 Case 3: Cybersecurity Considerations in Systems Engineering—the Stuxnet Attack on a Cyber-Physical System 820

  6.4 Case 4: Design for Maintainability—Incubators 824

  6.5 Case 5: Artificial Intelligence in Systems Engineering—Autonomous Vehicles 828

  6.6 Other Case Studies 834

Appendix A: References 836

Appendix B: Acronyms 872

Appendix C: Terms and Definitions 890

Appendix D: N^2 Diagram of Systems Engineering Processes 900

Appendix E: Input/Output Descriptions 906

Appendix F: Acknowledgments 934

Appendix G: Comment Form 940

Index 942

  5.3.2 系统工程和硬件工程（HWE） 783

  5.3.3 系统工程和项目管理（PM） 785

  5.3.4 系统工程和工业工程（IE） 791

  5.3.5 系统工程和运筹学（OR） 795

 5.4 数字工程 799

 5.5 系统工程转型 803

 5.6 系统工程的未来 805

6 案例研究 809

 6.1 案例1：放射治疗——THERAC-25 809

 6.2 案例2：连接两个国家——厄勒海峡大桥 813

 6.3 案例3：系统工程中的网络安全考虑——对赛博物理系统的STUXNET攻击 821

 6.4 案例4：可维护性设计——保育箱 825

 6.5 案例5：系统工程中的人工智能——自动驾驶汽车 829

 6.6 其他案例研究 835

附录A：参考文献 836

附录B：首字母缩写词 873

附录C：术语和定义 891

附录D：系统工程流程的N^2图 901

附录E：输入/输出描述 907

附录F：致谢 935

附录G：意见表 941

索引 943

LIST OF FIGURES

FIGURE 1.1   Acceleration of design to market life cycle has prompted development of more automated design methods and tools ············ 16
FIGURE 1.2   Cost and schedule overruns correlated with SE effort ······················ 16
FIGURE 1.3   Project performance versus SE capability ···································· 20
FIGURE 1.4   Life cycle costs and defect costs against time ································ 20
FIGURE 1.5   Emergence ·· 28
FIGURE 1.6   System innovation ecosystem pattern ·· 34
FIGURE 1.7   Hierarchy within a system ·· 38
FIGURE 1.8   An architectural framework for the evolving the SE discipline ············ 62
FIGURE 2.1   System life cycle stages ·· 74
FIGURE 2.2   Generic life cycle stages compared to other life cycle viewpoints ······ 76
FIGURE 2.3   Criteria for decision gates ·· 84
FIGURE 2.4   Relationship between technical reviews and audits and the technical baselines ·· 90
FIGURE 2.5   Concepts for the three life cycle model approaches ···························· 94
FIGURE 2.6   The SE Vee model ·· 100
FIGURE 2.7   The Incremental Commitment Spiral Model (ICSM) ························ 104
FIGURE 2.8   DevSecOps ·· 108
FIGURE 2.9   Asynchronous iterations and increments across agile mixed discipline engineering ·· 108
FIGURE 2.10 System life cycle processes per ISO/IEC/IEEE 15288 ···················· 112
FIGURE 2.11 Sample IPO diagram for SE processes ·· 116
FIGURE 2.12 Concurrency, iteration, and recursion ·· 118
FIGURE 2.13 IPO diagram for the Acquisition process ·· 126

图目录

图 1.1 从设计到市场生命周期的加速促进了更多自动化设计方法和工具的发展 17

图 1.2 超支成本和延期进度与系统工程工作的相关性 17

图 1.3 项目绩效与系统工程能力的对比 21

图 1.4 生命周期成本和缺陷成本与时间的对比 21

图 1.5 涌现 29

图 1.6 系统创新生态模式 35

图 1.7 一个系统内的层级结构 39

图 1.8 一个系统工程学科演进的架构框架 63

图 2.1 系统生命周期阶段 75

图 2.2 一般生命周期与其他生命周期视角比较 77

图 2.3 决策门准则 85

图 2.4 技术评审、审核和技术基线间的关系 91

图 2.5 三种生命周期模型实施方法的概念 95

图 2.6 系统工程 V 模型 101

图 2.7 增量承诺螺旋模型（ICSM） 105

图 2.8 开发安保运行 109

图 2.9 敏捷混合学科工程的异步迭代和增量 109

图 2.10 依据 ISO/IEC/IEEE 15288 的系统生命周期流程 113

图 2.11 系统工程流程的 IPO 图 117

图 2.12 并行、迭代和递归 119

图 2.13 采办流程的 IPO 图 127

LIST OF FIGURES

FIGURE 2.14	IPO diagram for the Supply process	136
FIGURE 2.15	IPO diagram for Life Cycle Model Management process	144
FIGURE 2.16	IPO diagram for Infrastructure Management process	154
FIGURE 2.17	IPO diagram for Portfolio Management process	162
FIGURE 2.18	Requirements across the portfolio, program, and project domains	170
FIGURE 2.19	IPO diagram for Human Resource Management process	172
FIGURE 2.20	IPO diagram for the Quality Management process	180
FIGURE 2.21	QM Values and Skills Integration	188
FIGURE 2.22	IPO diagram for Knowledge Management process	190
FIGURE 2.23	IPO diagram for Project Planning process	202
FIGURE 2.24	The breakdown structures	212
FIGURE 2.25	IPO diagram for Project Assessment and Control process	214
FIGURE 2.26	IPO diagram for the Decision Management process	226
FIGURE 2.27	IPO diagram for Risk Management process	234
FIGURE 2.28	Level of risk depends upon both likelihood and consequence	242
FIGURE 2.29	Intelligent management of risks and opportunities	244
FIGURE 2.30	Typical relationship among the risk categories	248
FIGURE 2.31	IPO diagram for Configuration Management process	254
FIGURE 2.32	IPO diagram for Information Management process	264
FIGURE 2.33	IPO diagram for Measurement process	272
FIGURE 2.34	Integration of Measurement, Risk Management, and Decision Management processes	276
FIGURE 2.35	Relationship of product-oriented measures	280
FIGURE 2.36	TPM monitoring	282
FIGURE 2.37	IPO diagram for the Quality Assurance process	284

图 2.14	供应流程的 IPO 图	137
图 2.15	生命周期模型管理流程的 IPO 图	145
图 2.16	基础设施管理流程的 IPO 图	155
图 2.17	项目组合管理流程的 IPO 图	163
图 2.18	跨项目组合、项目集和项目领域的需求	171
图 2.19	人力资源管理流程的 IPO 图	173
图 2.20	质量管理流程的 IPO 图	181
图 2.21	质量管理价值观和技能的综合	189
图 2.22	知识管理流程的 IPO 图	191
图 2.23	项目计划流程的 IPO 图	203
图 2.24	分解结构	213
图 2.25	项目评估和控制流程的 IPO 图	215
图 2.26	决策管理流程的 IPO 图	227
图 2.27	风险管理流程的 IPO 图	235
图 2.28	取决于可能性和后果的风险等级	243
图 2.29	风险和机会的智能管理	245
图 2.30	风险类别之间的典型关系	249
图 2.31	构型配置管理流程的 IPO 图	255
图 2.32	信息管理流程的 IPO 图	265
图 2.33	测量流程的 IPO 图	273
图 2.34	测量、风险管理和决策管理流程的综合	277
图 2.35	以产品为导向的测度间的关系	281
图 2.36	技术性能测度监控	283
图 2.37	质量保证流程的 IPO 图	285

XLI

LIST OF FIGURES

FIGURE 2.38   Technical Processes in context 294
FIGURE 2.39   IPO diagram for Business or Mission Analysis process 298
FIGURE 2.40   IPO diagram for Stakeholder Needs and Requirements
               Definition process 310
FIGURE 2.41   IPO diagram for System Requirements Definition process 328
FIGURE 2.42   IPO diagram for System Architecture Definition process 346
FIGURE 2.43   Core architecture processes 356
FIGURE 2.44   IPO diagram for Design Definition process 364
FIGURE 2.45   Taxonomy of system analysis dimensions 380
FIGURE 2.46   IPO diagram for System Analysis process 380
FIGURE 2.47   IPO diagram for Implementation process 388
FIGURE 2.48   IPO diagram for Integration process 394
FIGURE 2.49   IPO diagram for Verification process 404
FIGURE 2.50   Verification per level 414
FIGURE 2.51   IPO diagram for Transition process 420
FIGURE 2.52   IPO diagram for Validation process 428
FIGURE 2.53   Validation per level 438
FIGURE 2.54   IPO diagram for Operation process 446
FIGURE 2.55   IPO diagram for Maintenance process 452
FIGURE 2.56   IPO diagram for Disposal process 460
FIGURE 3.1   Quality characteristic approaches across the life cycle 466
FIGURE 3.2   System operational effectiveness 472
FIGURE 3.3   Cost versus performance 474
FIGURE 3.4   Life cycle cost elements 478
FIGURE 3.5   HSI technology, organization, people within an environment ... 492
FIGURE 3.6   Interaction between system, environment, operating conditions,
               and failure modes and failure mechanisms 516

图 2.38　背景环境中的技术流程 ··295
图 2.39　业务或任务分析流程的 IPO 图 ·····································299
图 2.40　利益相关方需要和需求定义流程的 IPO 图 ·····················311
图 2.41　系统需求定义流程的 IPO 图 ···329
图 2.42　系统架构定义流程的 IPO 图 ···347
图 2.43　核心架构流程 ··357
图 2.44　设计定义流程的 IPO 图 ··365
图 2.45　系统分析维度分类 ··381
图 2.46　系统分析流程的 IPO 图 ··381
图 2.47　实施流程的 IPO 图 ···389
图 2.48　综合流程的 IPO 图 ···395
图 2.49　验证流程的 IPO 图 ···405
图 2.50　逐层验证 ··415
图 2.51　转移流程的 IPO 图 ···421
图 2.52　确认流程的 IPO 图 ···429
图 2.53　逐层确认 ··439
图 2.54　运行流程的 IPO 图 ···447
图 2.55　维护流程的 IPO 图 ···453
图 2.56　处置流程的 IPO 图 ···461
图 3.1　跨生命周期的质量特性实施方法 ····································467
图 3.2　系统运行效能 ··473
图 3.3　成本与性能的对比 ···475
图 3.4　生命周期成本元素 ···479
图 3.5　环境中的 HSI 技术、组织、人员 ···································493
图 3.6　系统、环境、运行条件以及故障模式和故障机制之间的相互作用 ···517

LIST OF FIGURES

FIGURE 3.7	Timewise values of notional resilience scenario parameters	536
FIGURE 3.8	Schematic view of a generic MA&S process	566
FIGURE 3.9	System development with early, iterative V&V and integration, via modeling, analysis, and simulation	570
FIGURE 3.10	Illustrative model taxonomy (non-exhaustive)	576
FIGURE 3.11	Model-based integration across multiple disciplines using a hub-and-spokes pattern	586
FIGURE 3.12	Multidisciplinary MA&S coordination along the life cycle	588
FIGURE 3.13	Sample N-squared diagram	602
FIGURE 3.14	Sample coupling matrix showing: (a) Initial arrangement of aggregates; (b) final arrangement after reorganization	604
FIGURE 3.15	Unified Architecture Method	608
FIGURE 3.16	Enterprise and product frameworks	610
FIGURE 3.17	S*Pattern class hierarchy	622
FIGURE 3.18	Examples of natural systems applications and biomimicry	626
FIGURE 4.1	Tailoring requires balance between risk and process	632
FIGURE 4.2	IPO diagram for Tailoring process	634
FIGURE 4.3	SE life cycle spectrum	650
FIGURE 4.4	Agile SE life cycle model	652
FIGURE 4.5	Feature-based PLE factory	666
FIGURE 4.6	Schematic diagram of the operation of a Cyber-Physical System	686
FIGURE 4.7	The relationship between Cyber-Physical Systems (CPS), Systems of Systems (SoSs), and an Internet of Things (IoT)	688
FIGURE 4.8	Example of the systems and systems of systems within a transport system of systems	690
FIGURE 4.9	Service system conceptual framework	704

图 3.7　名义韧性场景参数的时间值 ………………………………………537

图 3.8　通用 MA&S 流程示意图 …………………………………………567

图 3.9　通过建模、分析和仿真，进行早期迭代 V&V 和综合的系统开发 …571

图 3.10　说明性模型分类（非详尽）……………………………………577

图 3.11　利用"枢纽—辐条"模式实现基于模型的跨学科综合 ………587

图 3.12　生命周期内的多学科 MA&S 协同 ……………………………589

图 3.13　N^2 图示例 …………………………………………………………603

图 3.14　耦合矩阵示例显示：（a）聚合体的初始排列；（b）重组后的最终排列 ……………………………………………………………605

图 3.15　统一架构方法 ……………………………………………………609

图 3.16　复杂组织体系和产品框架 ………………………………………611

图 3.17　S* 模式中类的层级结构 …………………………………………623

图 3.18　自然系统应用和仿生学示例 ……………………………………627

图 4.1　剪裁要求风险和流程之间的平衡 ………………………………633

图 4.2　剪裁流程的 IPO 图 ………………………………………………635

图 4.3　系统工程生命周期谱系 …………………………………………651

图 4.4　敏捷的系统工程生命周期模型 …………………………………653

图 4.5　基于特征的产品线工程工厂 ……………………………………667

图 4.6　赛博物理系统运行示意图 ………………………………………687

图 4.7　赛博物理系统、体系、物联网之间的关系 ……………………689

图 4.8　运输体系内的系统及体系的示例 ………………………………691

图 4.9　服务系统概念框架 ………………………………………………705

LIST OF FIGURES

FIGURE 4.10   Organizations manage resources to create enterprise value ········ 708

FIGURE 4.11   Individual competence leads to organizational, system, and operational capability ···················· 710

FIGURE 4.12   Enterprise state changes through work process activities ············· 714

FIGURE 5.1   The "T-shaped" SE practitioner ···················· 764

FIGURE 5.2   Technical leadership is the intersection of technical expertise and leadership skills ···················· 770

FIGURE 5.3   Categorized dimensions of diversity ···················· 776

FIGURE 5.4   The intersection between PM and SE ···················· 786

FIGURE 5.5   IE and SE relationships ···················· 792

FIGURE 6.1   Timeline of vehicle impact ···················· 832

FIGURE D.1   Input/output relationships between the various SE processes ········ 904

图 4.10 组织管理资源以创建复杂组织体系价值 ············ 709

图 4.11 个人胜任力产生组织的、系统的以及运行的能力 ············ 711

图 4.12 通过工作流程活动改变复杂组织体系状态 ············ 715

图 5.1 "T形"系统工程从业人员 ············ 765

图 5.2 技术领导力是技术专长与领导技能的交集 ············ 771

图 5.3 多样性的分类维度 ············ 777

图 5.4 项目管理和系统工程的交集 ············ 787

图 5.5 工业工程和系统工程的关系 ············ 793

图 6.1 车辆碰撞时间轴 ············ 833

图 D.1 系统工程流程的输入/输出关系 ············ 905

LIST OF TABLES

TABLE 1.1	SE standards and guides	8
TABLE 1.2	SE return on investment	18
TABLE 1.3	Examples for systems interacting with the SoI	30
TABLE 1.4	Sources of system uncertainty	46
TABLE 1.5	Common cognitive biases	50
TABLE 1.6	SE principles and subprinciples	54
TABLE 2.1	Representative technical reviews and audits	88
TABLE 2.2	Life cycle model approach characteristics	94
TABLE 2.3	Eight Attributes of a Quality Management Culture	186
TABLE 2.4	Partial list of decision situations (opportunities) throughout the life cycle	222
TABLE 2.5	Measurement benefits	270
TABLE 2.6	Measurement references for specific measurement focuses	274
TABLE 2.7	Requirement statement characteristics	336
TABLE 2.8	Requirement set characteristics	338
TABLE 2.9	Requirement attributes	340
TABLE 3.1	Quality Characteristic approaches	468
TABLE 3.2	HSI perspective descriptions	498
TABLE 3.3	Resilience considerations	534
TABLE 3.4	Implementation process breakout	560
TABLE 4.1	Considerations of greenfield and brownfield development efforts	674
TABLE 4.2	Considerations for COTS-based development efforts	680
TABLE 4.3	SoS types	692
TABLE 4.4	Impact of SoS considerations on the SE processes	694

表目录

表 1.1　系统工程标准和指南 9
表 1.2　系统工程投资回报率 19
表 1.3　与 SoI 交互的系统示例 31
表 1.4　系统不确定性来源 47
表 1.5　常见的认知偏差 51
表 1.6　系统工程原则和次级原则 55
表 2.1　典型技术评审和审核 89
表 2.2　生命周期模型实施方法特点 95
表 2.3　质量管理文化的八个特征 187
表 2.4　系统生命周期中常见的决策情况（机会）的部分列表 223
表 2.5　测量的益处 271
表 2.6　特定测量关注点的测量参考 275
表 2.7　需求声明特征 337
表 2.8　需求集特征 339
表 2.9　需求属性 341
表 3.1　质量特性实施方法 469
表 3.2　HSI 观点描述 499
表 3.3　强韧性考虑因素 535
表 3.4　实施流程分解讨论 561
表 4.1　绿地和棕地开发工作的考虑因素 675
表 4.2　基于商用货架产品的开发工作的考虑因素 681
表 4.3　体系的类型 693
表 4.4　体系考虑因素对系统工程流程的影响 695

LIST OF TABLES

TABLE 4.5 Comparison of automotive, aerospace/defense, and consumer electronics domains ··718

TABLE 4.6 Representative organizations and standards in the automotive industry ··722

TABLE 4.7 Infrastructure and SE definition correlation ··738

TABLE 5.1 Differences between the hard skills and soft skills ·····························766

TABLE 5.2 Technical leadership model ··772

表 4.5 汽车、航空航天/防务和消费者电子设备产品领域的比较 ……………719
表 4.6 汽车产业的代表性组织和标准 ……………………………………723
表 4.7 基础设施与系统工程定义的相关性 ………………………………739
表 5.1 硬技能和软技能的差异 ……………………………………………767
表 5.2 技术领导力模型 ……………………………………………………773

1 SYSTEMS ENGINEERING INTRODUCTION

1.1 WHAT IS SYSTEMS ENGINEERING?

Systems Engineering (SE)

Our world and the systems we engineer continue to become more complex and interrelated. SE is an integrative approach to help teams collaborate to understand and manage systems and their complexity and deliver successful systems. The SE perspective is based on systems thinking—a perspective that sharpens our awareness of wholes and how the parts within those wholes interrelate (incose.org, *About Systems Engineering*). SE aims to ensure the pieces work together to achieve the objectives of the whole. SE practitioners work within a project team and take a holistic, balanced, life cycle approach to support the successful completion of system projects (INCOSE Vision 2035, 2022). SE has the responsibility to realize systems that are *fit for purpose*, namely that systems accomplish their intended purposes and be resilient to effects in real-world operation, while minimizing unintended actions, side effects, and consequences (Griffin, 2010).

Definition of SE

INCOSE Definitions (2019) and ISO/IEC/IEEE 15288 (2023) define:

Systems Engineering is a transdisciplinary and integrative approach to enable the successful realization, use, and retirement of engineered systems, using systems principles and concepts, and scientific, technological, and management methods.

INCOSE Definitions (2019) elaborates:

SE focuses on:

- establishing, balancing and integrating stakeholders' goals, purpose and success criteria, and defining actual or anticipated stakeholder needs, operational concepts, and required functionality, starting early in the development cycle;

INCOSE Systems Engineering Handbook: A Guide for System Life Cycle Processes and Activities, Fifth Edition.

Edited by David D. Walden, Thomas M. Shortell, Garry J. Roedler, Bernardo A. Delicado, Odile Mornas, Yip Yew-Seng, and David Endler.

© 2023 John Wiley & Sons Ltd. Published 2023 by John Wiley & Sons Ltd.

1 系统工程介绍

1.1 什么是系统工程？

系统工程（SE）

我们的世界和我们设计的系统不断变得更加复杂和相互关联。系统工程是一种综合的方法，可以帮助团队合作理解和管理系统及其复杂性，并交付成功的系统。系统工程看问题的角度是基于系统思维，其增强了我们对整体以及这些整体中各部分如何相互关联的认识（incose.org，关于系统工程）。系统工程旨在确保各部分协同工作，以实现整体目标。系统工程实践者在项目团队中工作，并采取整体的、平衡的生命周期方法来支持系统项目的成功完成（INCOSE 愿景 2035，2022）。系统工程的责任是实现适合目的的系统，即系统能够实现预期目的，对现实世界运行中的影响具有韧性，同时最大限度地减少非预期的动作、副作用和后果（Griffin，2010）。

系统工程的定义

INCOSE 定义（2019）和 ISO/IEC/IEEE 15288（2023）定义：

系统工程是一种跨学科的综合实施方法，旨在利用系统原理和概念以及科学的、技术的和管理的方法，使工程系统能够成功实现、使用和退役。

系统工程聚焦于：

INCOSE 定义（2019）阐明：

- 从开发周期的早期开始，建立、平衡和综合利益相关方的目标、目的和成功准则，并定义实际或预期的利益相关方需要、运行概念和所需功能；

SYSTEMS ENGINEERING INTRODUCTION

- establishing an appropriate life cycle model, process approach and governance structures, considering the levels of complexity, uncertainty, change, and variety;
- generating and evaluating alternative solution concepts and architectures;
- baselining and modeling requirements and selected solution architecture for each stage of the endeavor;
- performing design synthesis and system verification and validation;
- while considering both the problem and solution domains, taking into account necessary enabling systems and services, identifying the role that the parts and the relationships between the parts play with respect to the overall behavior and performance of the system, and determining how to balance all of these factors to achieve a satisfactory outcome.

SE provides facilitation, guidance, and leadership to integrate the relevant disciplines and specialty groups into a cohesive effort, forming an appropriately structured development process that proceeds from concept to development, production, utilization, support, and eventual retirement.

SE considers both the business and the technical needs of acquirers with the goal of providing a quality solution that meets the needs of users and other stakeholders, is fit for the intended purpose in real-world operation, and avoids or minimizes adverse unintended consequences.

The goal of all SE activities is to manage risk, including the risk of not delivering what the acquirer wants and needs, the risk of late delivery, the risk of excess cost, and the risk of negative unintended consequences. One measure of utility of SE activities is the degree to which such risk is reduced. Conversely, a measure of acceptability of absence of a SE activity is the level of excess risk incurred as a result.

Definitions of System

While the concepts of a system can generally be traced back to early Western philosophy and later to science, the concept most familiar to SE practitioners is often traced to Ludwig von Bertalanffy (1950, 1968) in which a system is regarded as a "whole" consisting of interacting "parts."

INCOSE Definitions (2019) and ISO/IEC/IEEE 15288 (2023) define:

A **system** is an arrangement of parts or elements that together exhibit behavior or meaning that the individual constituents do not.

- 考虑到复杂性、不确定性、变化和多样性的程度，建立合适的生命周期模型、流程实施方式和治理结构；
- 生成和评估备选解决方案概念和架构；
- 为每个阶段的需求和选定的解决方案架构建立基线和建模；
- 开展设计综合和对系统的验证和确认；
- 在考虑问题域和解决方案域的同时，也要考虑必要的使能系统和服务，识别各部分以及各部分之间的关系在系统整体行为和性能方面所起的作用，并确定如何平衡这些因素以达成满意的结果。

系统工程提供促进、指导和领导力，将相关学科和专业的团队整合到一个一致连贯的努力中，形成一个合适的、结构化的开发流程，覆盖从概念到开发、生产、使用、支持直至最终退役。

系统工程同时考虑采办方的业务和技术需要，目的是提供满足用户和其他利益相关方需要的高质量解决方案，适合现实世界运行中的预期目的，避免或尽量减少负面的、非预期的后果。

所有系统工程活动的目标都是管理风险，包括未按采办方期望和需要交付的风险、延迟交付的风险、成本超支的风险以及负面非预期后果带来的风险。对系统工程活动效用的一种衡量是此类风险降低的程度。相反，对系统工程活动缺失的可接受性可以通过其带来的过度风险程度来衡量。

系统的定义

虽然系统的概念通常可以追溯到早期的西方哲学和后来的西方科学，但系统工程实践者最熟悉的系统概念往往可以追溯到 Ludwig von Bertalanffy（1950，1968），系统被视为一个由相互作用的"部分"组成的"整体"。

INCOSE 定义（2019）和 ISO/IEC/IEEE 15288（2023）定义：

系统是对其组成部分或元素的编排，这些组成部分或元素共同表现出个体所不具备的行为或意义。

SYSTEMS ENGINEERING INTRODUCTION

A system is sometimes considered as a product or as the services it provides.

In practice, the interpretation of its meaning is frequently clarified using an associative noun (e.g., medical system, aircraft system). Alternatively, the word "system" is substituted simply by a context-dependent synonym (e.g., pacemaker, aircraft), though this potentially obscures a system principles perspective.

A complete system includes all of the associated equipment, facilities, material, computer programs, firmware, technical documentation, services, and personnel required for operations and support to the degree necessary for self-sufficient use in its intended environment.

INCOSE Definitions (2019) elaborates:

Systems can be either physical or conceptual, or a combination of both. Systems in the physical universe are composed of matter and energy, may embody information encoded in matter-energy carriers, and exhibit observable behavior. Conceptual systems are abstract systems of pure information, and do not directly exhibit behavior, but exhibit "meaning." In both cases, the system's properties (as a whole) result, or emerge, from:

a) the parts or elements and their individual properties,

b) the relationships and interactions between and among the parts, the system, other external systems (including humans), and the environment.

SE practitioners are especially interested in systems which have or will be "systems engineered" for a purpose. Therefore, INCOSE Definitions (2019) defines:

An **engineered system** is a system designed or adapted to interact with an anticipated operational environment to achieve one or more intended purposes while complying with applicable constraints.

"Engineered systems" may be composed of any or all of the following elements: people, products, services, information, processes, and/or natural elements.

Origins and Evolution of SE

Aspects of SE have been applied to technical endeavors throughout history. However, SE has only been formalized as an engineering discipline beginning in the early to middle of the twentieth century (INCOSE Vision 2035, 2022). The term "systems engineering" dates to Bell Telephone Laboratories in the early 1940s (Fagen, 1978; Hall, 1962; Schlager, 1956). Fagen (1978) traces the concepts of SE within the Bell System back to early 1900s and describes major applications of SE during World War II. The British used multidisciplinary teams to analyze their air defense system in the 1930s (Martin, 1996). The RAND

系统有时被视为产品或其提供的服务。

在实践中，对系统含义的解释经常使用关联名词（例如，医疗系统、航空器系统）进行澄清。有时，会将"系统"一词简单地替换为与上下文相关的同义词（例如，心脏起搏器、飞机），尽管这样会模糊系统原理的观点。

一个完整的系统包括在预期的环境中能够达到独立自主运行和支持所需程度的相关设备、设施、物料、计算机程序、固件、技术文档、服务和人员。

INCOSE 定义（2019）阐明：

系统可以是物理的或概念的，也可以是两者相结合。物理宇宙中的系统由物质和能量组成，可能嵌入物质—能量载体中编码的信息，并表现出可观察的行为。概念系统是纯信息的抽象系统，并不直接表现出行为，而是表现出"意义"。在这两种情况下，系统的属性（作为一个整体）是由以下因素产生或涌现而来：

a）组成部分或元素及其个体的属性；

b）组成部分、系统、其他外部系统（包括人员）和环境之间的关系和相互作用。

系统工程实践者尤其对已经或将要为某一目的进行"系统工程"的系统感兴趣。因此，INCOSE 定义（2019）定义：

工程系统是一个设计或改造为与预期运行环境交互的系统，以实现一个或多个预期目的，同时遵守适用的约束。

"工程系统"可由以下任何或所有元素组成：人员、产品、服务、信息、流程和/或自然元素。

系统工程的起源与演变

系统工程的各个方面在历史上一直被应用于技术工作。然而，系统工程只是在20世纪初至中期才正式成为一门工程学科（INCOSE 愿景2035，2022）。"系统工程"一词可追溯到20世纪40年代初的贝尔电话实验室（Fagen，1978；Hall，1962；Schlager，1956）。Fagen（1978）追溯了20世纪初在贝尔内部的系统工程的概念，并描述了系统工程在第二次世界大战期间的主要应用。20世纪30年代，英国使用多学科团队分析他们的防空系统（Martin，1996）。兰德公司由美国空军于1946年成立，并宣布创建了"系统分析"。Hall（1962）

SYSTEMS ENGINEERING INTRODUCTION

Corporation was founded in 1946 by the United States Air Force and claims to have created "systems analysis." Hall (1962) asserts that the first attempt to teach SE as we know it today came in 1950 at MIT by Mr. Gilman, Director of Systems Engineering at Bell. TRW (now a part of Northrop Grumman) claims to have "invented" SE in the late 1950s to support work with ballistic missiles. Goode and Machol (1957) authored the first book on SE in 1957. In 1990, a professional society for SE, the National Council on Systems Engineering (NCOSE), was founded by representatives from several US corporations and organizations. As a result of growing involvement from SE practitioners outside of the US, the name of the organization was changed to the International Council on Systems Engineering (INCOSE) in 1995 (incose.org, *History of Systems Engineering*; Buede and Miller, 2016).

With the introduction of the international standard ISO/IEC 15288 in 2002, the discipline of SE was formally recognized as a preferred mechanism to establish agreement for the creation of products and services to be traded between two or more organizations—the supplier(s) and the acquirer(s). This handbook builds upon the concepts in the latest edition of ISO/IEC/IEEE 15288 (2023) by providing additional context, definitions, and practical applications.

Table 1.1 provides a list of key SE standards and guides related to the content of this handbook.

TABLE 1.1   SE standards and guides

Reference	Title
ISO/IEC/IEEE 15026	Systems and software engineering—Systems and software assurance (Multi-part standard)
ISO/IEC/IEEE 15288	Systems and software engineering—System life cycle processes
IEEE/ISO/IEC 15289	Systems and software engineering—Content of life cycle information items(documentation)
ISO/IEC/IEEE 15939	Systems and software engineering—Measurement process
ISO/IEC/IEEE 16085	Systems and software engineering—Life cycle processes—Risk management
ISO/IEC/IEEE 16326	Systems and software engineering—Life cycle processes—Project management
ISO/IEC/IEEE 21839	Systems and software engineering—System of systems (SoS) considerations in life cycle stages of a system

称，我们今天所知的系统工程的第一次教学尝试是 1950 年贝尔公司的系统工程总监吉尔曼先生在麻省理工学院开展的。TRW（现为诺斯罗普·格鲁曼公司的一部分）称在 20 世纪 50 年代末"发明"了系统工程以支持弹道导弹相关的工作。Goode 和 Machol（1957）于 1957 年撰写了第一本关于系统工程的书。1990 年，由多家美国公司和组织的代表成立了系统工程专业协会，即国家系统工程委员会（NCOSE）。由于美国以外的系统工程实践者越来越多地参与进来，该组织于 1995 年更名为国际系统工程委员会（INCOSE）（incose.org，系统工程历史；Buede 和 Miller，2016）。

随着 2002 年国际标准 ISO/IEC 15288 的引入，系统工程学科正式成为在两个或多个组织（供应商和采办方）之间建立关于产品和服务的交易协议时所公认的首选机制。本手册在最新版 ISO/IEC/IEEE 15288（2023）中的概念的基础上，提供了更多的背景知识、定义和实际应用。

表 1.1 列出了与本手册内容相关的主要的系统工程标准和指南。

表 1.1 系统工程标准和指南

编号	标题
ISO/IEC/IEEE 15026	系统和软件工程——系统和软件保证（多部分标准）
ISO/IEC/IEEE 15288	系统和软件工程——系统生命周期流程
IEEE/ISO/IEC 15289	系统和软件工程——系统和软件生命周期流程信息产品的内容（文件）
ISO/IEC/IEEE 15939	系统和软件工程——测量流程
ISO/IEC/IEEE 16085	系统和软件工程——生命周期流程——风险管理
ISO/IEC/IEEE 16326	系统和软件工程——生命周期流程——项目管理
ISO/IEC/IEEE 21839	系统和软件工程——系统生命周期各阶段的体系考虑因素

SYSTEMS ENGINEERING INTRODUCTION

(Continued)

Reference	Title
ISO/IEC/IEEE 21840	Systems and software engineering—Guidelines for the utilization of ISO/IEC/IEEE 15288 in the context of system of systems (SoS)
ISO/IEC/IEEE 21841	Systems and software engineering—Taxonomy of systems of systems
ISO/IEC/IEEE 24641	Systems and software engineering—Methods and tools for model-based systems and software engineering
ISO/IEC/IEEE 24748-1	Systems and software engineering—Life cycle management—Part 1: Guidelines for life cycle management
ISO/IEC/IEEE 24748-2	Systems and software engineering—Life cycle management—Part 2: Guidelines for the application of ISO/IEC/IEEE 15288
ISO/IEC/IEEE 24748-4	Systems and software engineering—Life cycle management—Part 4: Systems engineering planning
ISO/IEC/IEEE 24748-6	Systems and software engineering—Life cycle management—Part 6: System integration engineering
ISO/IEC/IEEE 24748-7	Systems and software engineering—Life cycle management—Part 7: Application of systems engineering on defense programs
ISO/IEC/IEEE 24748-8 / IEEE 15288-2	Systems and software engineering—Life cycle management—Part 8: Technical reviews and audits on defense programs
ISO/IEC/IEEE 24765	Systems and software engineering—Vocabulary
ISO/IEC/IEEE 26550	Software and systems engineering—Reference model for product line engineering and management
ISO/IEC/IEEE 26580	Software and systems engineering—Methods and tools for the feature-based approach to software and systems product line engineering
ISO/IEC/IEEE 29148	Systems and software engineering—Life cycle processes—Requirements engineering
ISO/IEC/IEEE 42010	Systems and software engineering—Architecture description
ISO/IEC/IEEE 42020	Software, systems and enterprise—Architecture processes

（续）

编号	标题
ISO/IEC/IEEE 21840	系统和软件工程——在体系背景环境下使用 ISO/IEC/IEEE 15288 的指南
ISO/IEC/IEEE 21841	系统和软件工程——体系分类
ISO/IEC/IEEE 24641	系统和软件工程——基于模型的系统和软件工程的方法和工具
ISO/IEC/IEEE 24748–1	系统和软件工程—生命周期管理——第 1 部分：生命周期管理指南
ISO/IEC/IEEE 24748–2	系统和软件工程—生命周期管理——第 2 部分：ISO/IEC/IEEE 15288 应用指南
ISO/IEC/IEEE 24748–4	系统和软件工程—生命周期管理——第 4 部分：系统工程计划
ISO/IEC/IEEE 24748–6	系统和软件工程—生命周期管理——第 6 部分：系统集成工程
ISO/IEC/IEEE 24748–7	系统和软件工程—生命周期管理——第 7 部分：防务项目中的系统工程应用
ISO/IEC/IEEE 24748–8 / IEEE 15288–2	系统和测试工程——第 8 部分：防务项目的技术评审和审核
ISO/IEC/IEEE 24765	系统和软件工程——词汇
ISO/IEC/IEEE 26550	软件和系统工程——产品线工程和管理的参考模型
ISO/IEC/IEEE 26580	系统和软件工程——软件和系统产品线工程的基于特征的实施方法的方法和工具
ISO/IEC/IEEE 29148	系统和软件工程—生命周期管理——需求工程
ISO/IEC/IEEE 42010	系统和软件工程——架构描述
ISO/IEC/IEEE 42020	软件、系统和复杂组织体系——架构流程

SYSTEMS ENGINEERING INTRODUCTION

(Continued)

Reference	Title
ISO/IEC/IEEE 42030	Software, systems and enterprise—Architecture evaluation framework
ISO/IEC 29110	Systems and Software Engineering Standards and Guides for Very Small Entities (VSEs) (Multi-part set)
ISO/IEC 31000	Risk management
ISO/IEC 31010	Risk management—Risk assessment techniques
ISO/IEC 33060	Process assessment—Process assessment model for system life cycle processes
ISO/PAS 19450	Automation systems and integration—Object-Process Methodology (OPM)
ISO 10007	Quality management—Guidelines for configuration management
ISO 10303-233	Industrial automation systems and integration—Product data representation and exchange—Part 233: Application protocol:Systems engineering
NIST SP 800-160 Vol. 1	Systems Security Engineering: Considerations for a Multidisciplinary Approach in the Engineering of Trustworthy Secure Systems
NIST SP 800-160 Vol. 2	Developing Cyber-Resilient Systems: A Systems Security Engineering Approach
OMG SysML™	OMG Systems Modeling Language
SEBoK Guide to the	Systems Engineering Body of Knowledge (SEBoK)
SAE-EIA 649C Configuration Management Standard	
SAE 1001	Integrated Project Processes for Engineering a System (Note: Replaced ANSI/EIA 632)
ANSI/AIA.A G.043B	Guide to the Preparation of Operational Concept Documents
CMMI	CMMI® V2.0

INCOSE SEH original table created by Mornas, Roedler, and Walden. Usage per the INCOSE Notices page. All other rights reserved.

（续）

编号	标题
ISO/IEC/IEEE 42030	软件、系统和复杂组织体系——架构评估框架
ISO/IEC 29110	极小实体的系统和软件工程标准和指南（多部分集合）
ISO/IEC 31000	风险管理
ISO/IEC 31010	风险管理——风险评估技术
ISO/IEC 33060	流程评估——系统生命周期流程的流程评估模型
ISO/PAS 19450	自动化系统和集成——对象—过程方法论（OPM）
ISO 10007	质量管理——构型配置管理的指南
ISO 10303-233	工业自动化系统和综合——产品数据表示和交换——第233部分：应用协议：系统工程
NIST SP 800-160 Vol. 1	系统安保工程：可信安保系统工程中的多学科实施方法考虑因素
NIST SP 800-160 Vol. 2	开发赛博—韧性系统：一种系统安保工程实施方法
OMG SysML™	对象管理组（OMG）的系统建模语言（SysML™）
SEBoK	系统工程知识体指南
SAE-EIA 649C	
SAE 1001	工程化系统的集成项目流程（注：替代 ANSI/EIA 632）
ANSI/AIA.A G.043B	运行概念文档准备指南
CMMI	CMMI®V2.0

INCOSE SEH 原始表由 Mornas、Roedler 和 Walden 创建。根据 INCOSE 通知页使用。版权所有。

SYSTEMS ENGINEERING INTRODUCTION

1.2 WHY IS SYSTEMS ENGINEERING IMPORTANT?

The purpose of SE is to conceive, develop, produce, utilize, support, and retire the right product or service within budget and schedule constraints. Delivering the right product or service requires a common understanding of the current system state and a common vision of the system's future states, as well as a methodology to transform a set of stakeholder needs, expectations, and constraints into a solution. The right product or service is one that accomplishes the required service or mission. A common vision and understanding, shared by acquirers and suppliers, is achieved through application of proven methods that are based on standard approaches across people, processes, and tools. The application of these methods is continuous throughout the system's life cycle.

SE is particularly important in the presence of complexity (see Section 1.3.7). Most current systems are formed by integrating commercially available products or by integrating independently managed and operated systems to provide emergent capabilities which increase the level of complexity (see Sections 4.3.3 and 4.3.6). This increased reliance on off-the-shelf and systems of systems has significantly reduced the time from concept definition to market availability of products. Over the years between 1880 and 2000, average 25% market penetration has been reduced by more than a factor of four as illustrated in Figure 1.1.

In response to complexity and compressed timelines, SE methods and tools have become more adaptable and efficient. Introduction of agile methods (see Section 4.2.2) and SE modeling language standards such the Systems Modeling Language (SysML) have allowed SE practitioners to manage complexity and increase the implementation of a common system vision (see bottom of Figure 1.1). Model Based SE (MBSE) methods adoption continues to grow (see Section 4.2.1), particularly in the early conceptual design and requirements analysis (SEBOK, *Emerging Topics*). MBSE research literature continues to report on the increased productivity and quality of design and promises further progression toward a digital engineering (DE) approach, where data is transparent and cooperation optimized across all engineering disciplines. Standards organizations are updating or developing new approaches that take DE into consideration. SE will have to address this new digital representation of the system as DE becomes the way of doing business (see Section 5.4). The rapid evolution and introduction of Artificial Intelligence (AI) and Machine Learning (ML) into SE further increases complexity of verifiability, safety, and trust of self-learning and evolving systems.

1.2 系统工程为什么很重要？

系统工程的目的是在预算和进度约束范围内构思、开发、生产、使用、支持和退役正确的产品或服务。提供正确的产品或服务需要对系统当前状态有共同的理解、对系统的未来状态有共同的愿景，以及能够将众多利益相关方的需要、期望和约束转化为解决方案的方法论。正确的产品或服务能够完成所需的服务或任务。采办方和供应商共同的愿景和理解是通过在人员、流程和工具之间应用已被证明有效的标准化的方法来实现的。这些方法的应用在整个系统的生命周期中是持续的。

系统工程在复杂性面前显得尤为重要（见 1.3.7 节）。当前大多数系统是通过综合可以在市场上购买的商用货架产品或可以独立管理和运行的系统来提供涌现的能力，这提升了复杂性等级（见 4.3.3 节和 4.3.6 节）。这种对货架商品和体系的日益依赖大大缩短了产品从概念定义到上市所需的时间。在 1880 年至 2000 年间，平均 25% 的市场渗透所需的时间下降了四分之一以上，如图 1.1 所示。

在应对复杂性和时间周期压缩方面，系统工程方法和工具更具适应性和效率。敏捷方法（见 4.2.2 节）和系统工程建模语言标准如系统建模语言（SysML）的引入，使系统工程实践者能够管理复杂性并加速共同的系统愿景的实现（见图 1.1 的底部）。基于模型的系统工程（MBSE）方法的采用，尤其是在早期概念设计和需求分析中（SEBOK，新兴主题）的采用持续增长（见 4.2.1 节）。基于模型的系统工程的研究文献不断报告设计效率和设计质量的提高，并预示着向数字工程（DE）方法的进一步发展，其中数据是透明的，所有工程学科的协同合作可以得到优化。标准组织正在考虑纳入数字工程以更新已有的方法或开发新的方法。随着数字工程成为业务运行的方式，系统工程将需要应对系统的这种新的数字表达形式（见 5.4 节）。人工智能（AI）和机器学习（ML）的快速发展及其在系统工程中的引入进一步增加了有关可验证性、安全性，以及自学习和自进化系统信任度的复杂性。

SYSTEMS ENGINEERING INTRODUCTION

The overall value of SE has been the subject of studies and papers from many organizations since the introduction of SE. A 2013 study was completed at the University of South Australia to quantify the return on investment (ROI) of SE activities on overall project cost and schedule (Honour, 2013). Figure 1.2 compares the total SE effort with cost compliance (left figure) and schedule performance (right figure). In both graphs, increasing the percentage of SE within the project results in better success up to an optimum level, above which SE ROI is diminished above those total program expenditure levels due to increased unwarranted processes. Study data shows that SE effort had a significant, quantifiable effect on project success, with correlation factors as high as 80%. Results show that the optimum level of SE effort for a normalized range of 10% to 14% of the total project cost.

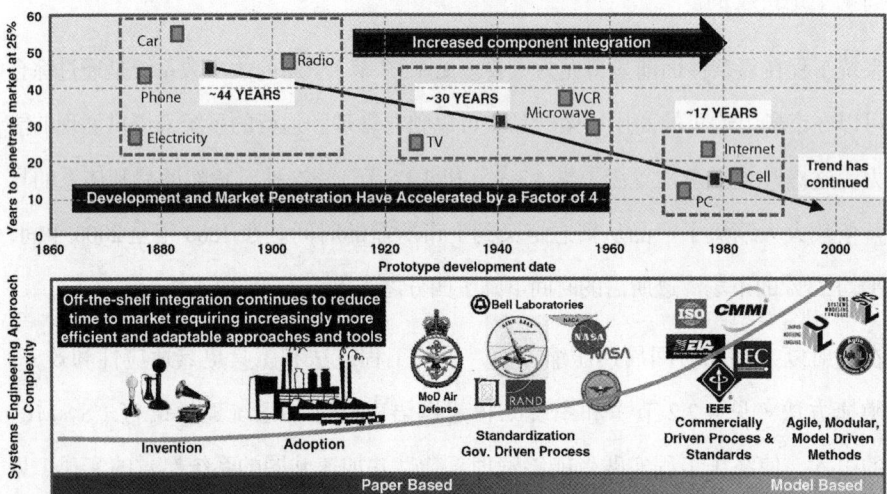

FIGURE 1.1   Acceleration of design to market life cycle has prompted development of more automated design methods and tools. INCOSE SEH original figure created by Amenabar. Usage per the INCOSE Notices page. All other rights reserved.

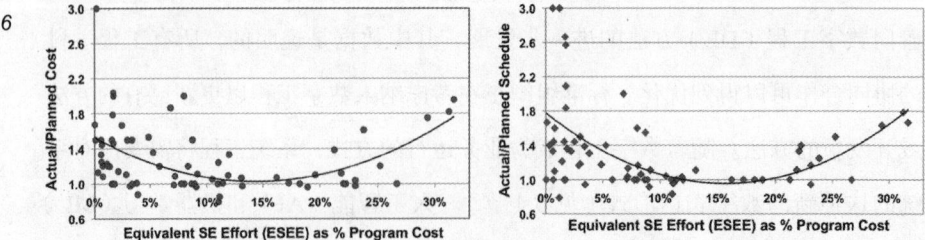

FIGURE 1.2   Cost and schedule overruns correlated with SE effort. From Honour (2013) with permission from University of South Wales. All other rights reserved.

自引入系统工程以来，对系统工程全面的价值衡量一直是许多组织研究和论文的主题。2013 年，南澳大利亚大学完成了一项研究，以量化系统工程活动在项目总体成本和进度方面的投资回报（ROI）（Honor，2013）。图 1.2 比较了系统工程总工作量与成本符合性（左图）和进度表现（右图）。两张图都展示出，增加系统工程在项目中的百分比直到一个最优水平可使项目获得更大的成功，超过该水平，由于增加了不需要的流程，系统工程在项目总支出水平中的投资回报率将降低。研究数据表明，系统工程努力对项目成功有着显著的、可量化的影响，相关性高达 80%。结果表明，进行标准化处理后的系统工程投入的最优占比为总体项目成本的 10%~14%。

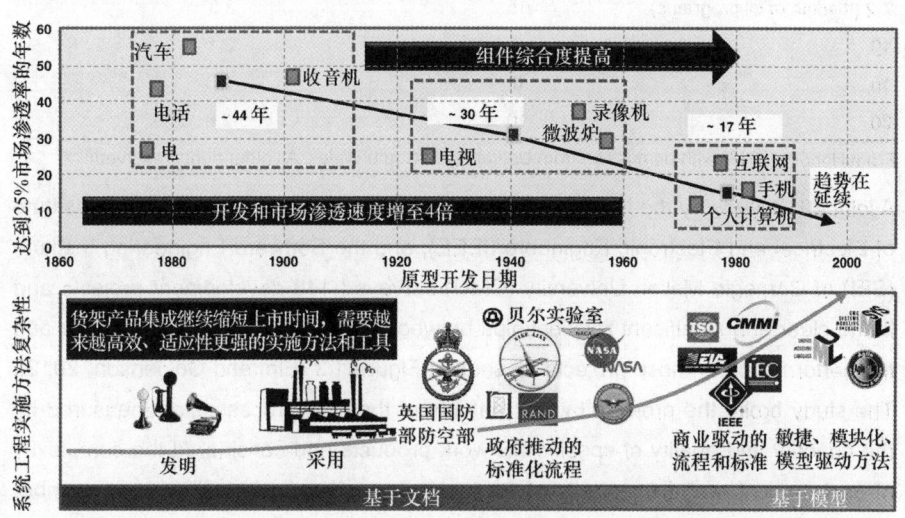

图 1.1 从设计到市场生命周期的加速促进了更多自动化设计方法和工具的发展。INCOSE SEH 原始图由 Michael Krueger 创建。按照 INCOSE 通知页使用。版权所有。

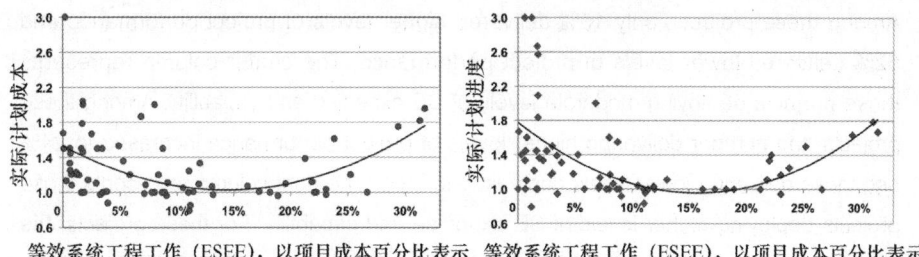

图 1.2 超支成本和延期进度与系统工程工作的相关性。源自 Honour（2013），经南威尔士大学许可。版权所有。

SYSTEMS ENGINEERING INTRODUCTION

The ROI of adding additional SE activities to a project is shown in Table 1.2, and it varies depending on the level of SE activities already in place. If the project is using no SE activities, then adding SE carries a 7:1 ROI; for each cost unit of additional SE, the project total cost will reduce by 7 cost units. At the median level of the projects interviewed, additional SE effort carries a 3.5:1 ROI.

TABLE 1.2 SE return on investment

Current SE effort (% of program cost)	Average cost overrun (%)	ROI for additional SE effort (cost reduction $ per $ SE added)
0	53	7.0
5	24	4.6
7.2 (median of all programs)	15	3.5
10	7	2.1
15	3	-0.3
20	10	-2.8

From Honour (2013) with permission from University of South Wales. All other rights reserved.

A joint 2012 study by the National Defense Industrial Association (NDIA), the Institute of Electrical and Electronic Engineers (IEEE), and the Software Engineering Institute (SEI) of Carnegie Mellon University (CMU) surveyed 148 development projects and found clear and significant relationships between the application of SE activities and the performance of those projects as seen in Figure 1.3 (Elm and Goldenson, 2012). The study broke the projects by the maturity of their SE processes as measured by the quantity and quality of specific SE work products and considered the complexity of each project and the maturity of the technologies being implemented (n=number of projects). It also assessed the levels of project performance, as measured by satisfaction of budget, schedule, and technical requirements. The left column represents those projects deploying lower levels of SE expertise and capability. Among these projects, only 15% delivered higher levels of project performance and 52% delivered lower levels of project performance. The center column represents those projects deploying moderate levels of SE expertise and capability. Among these projects, the number delivering higher levels of project performance increased to 24% and those delivering lower levels decreased to 29%. The right column represents those projects deploying higher levels of SE expertise and capability. For these projects, the number delivering higher levels of project performance increased substantially to 57%, while those delivering lower levels decreased to 20%. As Figure 1.3 shows, well-applied SE increases the probability of successfully developing an engineered system.

表 1.2 展示了向项目中添加额外系统工程活动的投资回报率，它随着已经投入的系统工程活动成本水平不同而改变。如果项目中还没有开展系统工程活动，那么增加系统工程会带来 7:1 的投资回报率；对于每增加一个单位成本的系统工程投入，项目总成本将减少 7 个单位。在调研的所有项目中，对于已投入的系统工程成本水平为中位数的项目，额外的系统工程努力会带来 3.5:1 的投资回报率。

表 1.2 系统工程投资回报率

当前的系统工程工作（占项目成本的百分比）	平均成本超支（百分比）	额外的系统工程工作的 ROI（增加每单位系统工程工作带来的成本下降值）
0	53	7.0
5	24	4.6
7.2（所有项目的中值）	15	3.5
10	7	2.1
15	3	−0.3
20	10	−2.8

源自 Honour（2013），经南威尔士大学许可。版权所有。

2012 年，美国国防工业协会（NDIA）、电气与电子工程师协会（IEEE）和卡内基梅隆大学（CMU）软件工程学院（SEI）联合开展了一项研究，调查了 148 个开发项目，发现系统工程活动的应用与这些项目的绩效之间存在着明确而显著的关系，如图 1.3 所示（Elm 和 Goldenson，2012）。该研究通过具体的系统工程工作产品的数量和质量来衡量所调查项目中系统工程流程的成熟度，同时考虑了每个项目的复杂性和技术实现的成熟度对项目进行分组（n= 项目数量）。该研究通过预算、进度和技术需求的满足度的衡量评估了项目绩效水平。柱状图中左边的立柱表示运用了较低水平系统工程专业知识和能力的项目。在这些项目中，只有 15% 的项目绩效水平较高，52% 的项目绩效水平较低。中间的立柱表示运用了中等水平系统工程专业知识和能力的项目。在这些项目中，绩效水平较高的项目数量增加到 24%，绩效水平较低的项目数量减少到 29%。右边的立柱表示运用了更高水平系统工程专业知识和能力的项目。对于这些项目，绩效水平较高的项目数量大幅增加到 57%，而那些交付绩效水平较低的项目数量降低到 20%。如图 1.3 所示，系统工程的良好应用可以提高成功开发工程系统的可能性。

SYSTEMS ENGINEERING INTRODUCTION

A 1993 Defense Acquisition University (DAU) statistical analysis on US Department of Defense (DoD) projects examined spent and committed life cycle cost (LCC) over time (DAU, 1993). As illustrated notionally in Figure 1.4, an important result from this study is that by the time approximately 20% of the actual costs have been accrued, over 80% of the total LCC has already typically been committed. Figure 1.4 also shows that it is less costly to fix or address issues if they are identified early. Good SE practice is the means by which the issues are identified and ensures that the understanding obtained is applied as appropriate during the life cycle, thus reducing technical debt.

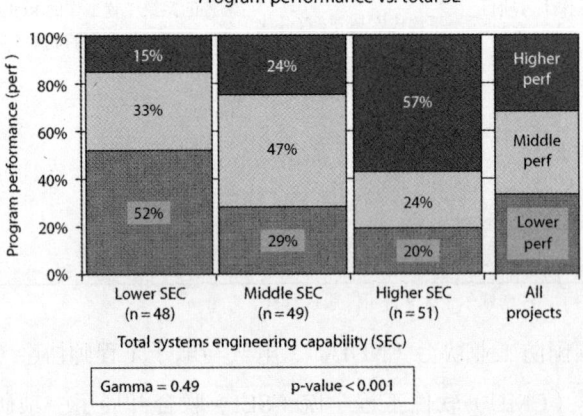

FIGURE 1.3 Project performance versus SE capability. From Elm and Goldenson (2012) with permission from Carnegie Mellon University. All other rights reserved.

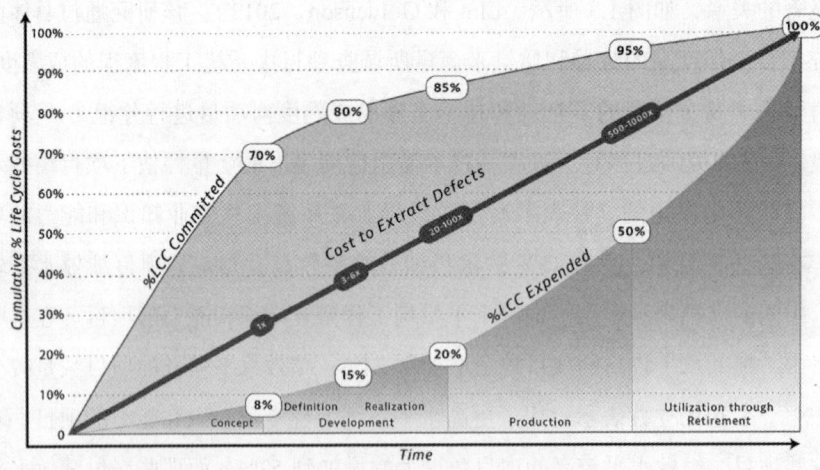

FIGURE 1.4 Life cycle costs and defect costs against time. INCOSE SEH original figure created by Walden derived from DAU (1993). Usage per the INCOSE Notices page. All other rights reserved.

系统工程介绍

1993年国防军需大学（DAU）对美国国防部（DoD）项目进行的统计分析调查了随时间分布的全生命周期成本（LCC）花费比例和由于缺陷带来的成本比例（DAU, 1993）。正如图1.4所示，这项研究的一个重要结论是，当实际花费发生接近20%的时候，已经造成了80%的全生命周期成本。图1.4还展示，如果及早发现问题，修复或处理问题的成本更低。良好的系统工程实践是识别问题的手段，并确保在生命周期内适当地应用所获得的理解，从而减少技术债务。

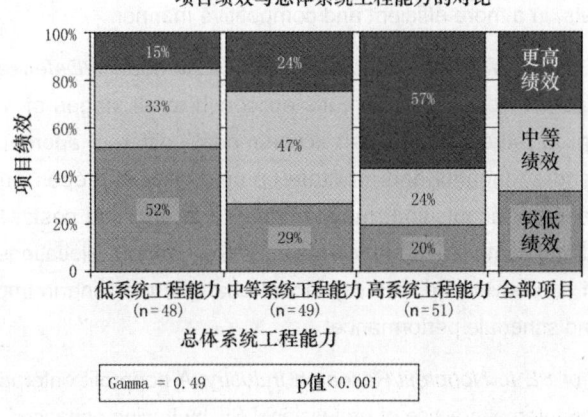

图1.3　项目绩效与系统工程能力的对比。源自 Elm 和 Goldenson（2012），经卡内基梅隆大学许可。版权所有。

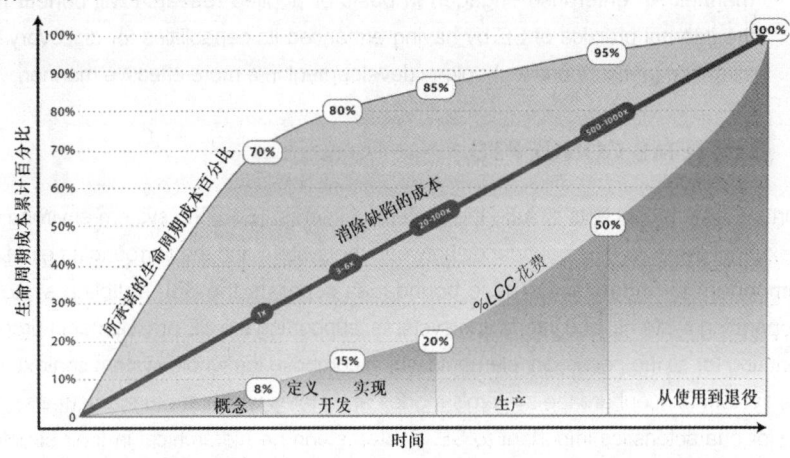

图1.4　生命周期成本和缺陷成本与时间的对比。INCOSE SEH 原始图由 Walden 根据 DAU（1993）创建。根据 INCOSE 通知页使用。版权所有。

SYSTEMS ENGINEERING INTRODUCTION

INCOSE maintains value proposition statements (INCOSE Value Strategic Initiative Report, 2021) as tailored to different areas and industries. Areas covered include individual INCOSE membership, organizational INCOSE membership, INCOSE SE certification, and the discipline of SE. Industries include commercial, government, and nonprofit organizations. A sample of these findings includes:

- *Value of SE to the Commercial/Market-Driven Industry*: Companies and other enterprises in commercial industry will benefit from the internal practice of professional SE by having enhanced their capability for the development of innovative products and services for distribution in both mature and immature markets, in a more efficient and competitive manner.

- *Value of SE to Government/Infrastructure/Aerospace/Defense Industry*: SE provides a tailorable, systematic approach to all stages of a project, from concept to retirement. SE can accommodate different approaches including agile and sequential and facilitate commonality and open architectures to ensure lower acquisition, maintenance, and upgrade costs. By confirming correct and complete requirements and requirements allocations, the resulting design has fewer and less significant changes resulting in improved overall cost and schedule performance.

- *Value of SE to Nonprofit/Research Industry*: A nonprofit enterprise will benefit from the internal practice of professional SE by having enhanced their capability for the development of innovative client services in a more efficient and effective manner. An enterprise engaged in basic or applied research will benefit from the internal practice of SE by having enhanced its capabilities for discovery and invention that supports technology development in a more effective manner.

1.3 SYSTEMS CONCEPTS

Important system concepts include the system of interest (SoI), the system environment, and external systems. The boundaries between the system and the surrounding elements are important to understand. These boundaries separate the SoI, enabling systems, interoperating systems, and interfacing systems, supporting the SE practitioner in properly accounting for all the necessary elements which comprise the whole system context. Part of the system concept are the system's modes and states which are fundamental system behavior characteristics important to SE. Systems can be hierarchical in their structural organization, or they can be complex where hierarchy is not always present. The system concepts encompass all types of systems structures and support the SE practitioner with a framework in which to engineer a system.

INCOSE 维持关于系统工程价值主张的声明（INCOSE 价值战略性倡议报告，2021），并将其剪裁定制到不同的领域和行业。这些领域包括 INCOSE 个人会员、INCOSE 组织会员、INCOSE 系统工程认证和系统工程学科。行业包括商业、政府和非营利组织。报告中的发现包括：

- 系统工程对商业/市场驱动行业的价值：商业领域的公司和其他复杂组织体系将受益于专业系统工程的内部实践。这些实践提高了他们开发创新型产品的能力以及在成熟的和未成熟的市场中销售服务的能力，使得这样的产品开发和服务更加高效和具有竞争力。

- 系统工程对政府/基础设施/航空航天/国防工业的价值：系统工程为项目从概念到退役的所有阶段提供了一种可剪裁的、系统的实施方法。系统工程可以适应不同的方法，包括敏捷方法和顺序式的方法，并利用共用性和开放式架构来确保更低的采办、维护和升级成本。通过确定正确和完整的需求以及需求分配使设计变更更少且变更带来的影响更小，从而改善项目整体的成本和进度表现。

- 系统工程对非营利组织和研究行业的价值：非营利组织将受益于专业系统工程的内部实践。这些实践提高了他们以更高效率和更加有效的方式开发创新型客户服务的能力。从事基础研究和应用研究的组织将从系统工程的内部实践中受益。这些实践使他们增强了探索发现和发明创造的能力，以更加有效的方式支撑技术发展。

1.3 系统的概念

重要的系统概念包括所感兴趣之系统（SoI）、系统环境和外部系统。理解系统和周围元素之间的边界很重要。这些边界分隔了 SoI、使能系统、互操作系统和接口系统，支持系统工程实践者正确处理构成整个系统背景环境的所有必要元素。系统的模式和状态是系统概念的组成部分，是系统工程中的重要概念，它是系统的基本行为特征。系统的结构组织可以是分层的，也可以是复杂但不分层的。系统概念涵盖了所有类型的系统结构，并为系统工程实践者提供了一个工程化系统的框架。

SYSTEMS ENGINEERING INTRODUCTION

1.3.1 System Boundary and the System of Interest (SoI)

General System Concepts An external view of a system must introduce elements that specifically do not belong to the system but do interact with the system. This collection of elements is called the *system environment or context* and can include the users (or operators) of the system. It is important to understand that the system environment or context is not limited to the operating environment, but also includes external systems that interface with or support the system at any time of the life cycle.

The internal and external views of a system give rise to the concept of a *system boundary*. In practice, the system boundary is a "line of demarcation" between the system under consideration, called the system of interest (SoI), and its greater context. It defines what belongs to the system and what does not. The system boundary is not to be confused with the subset of elements that interact with the environment.

The *functionality* of a system is typically expressed in terms of the interactions of the system with its operating environment, especially the users. When a system is considered as an integrated combination of interacting elements, the functionality of the system derives not just from the interactions of individual elements with the environmental elements but also from how these interactions are influenced by the organization (interrelations) of the system elements. This leads to the concept of system architecture, which ISO/IEC/IEEE 42020 (2019) defines as:

Fundamental concepts or properties of an entity in its environment and governing principles for the realization and evolution of this entity and its related life cycle processes.

This definition speaks to both the internal and external views of the system and shares the concepts from the definitions of a system (see Section 1.1).

Scientific Terminology Related to System Concepts In general, engineering can be regarded as the practice of creating and sustaining systems, services, devices, machines, structures, processes, and products to improve the quality of life—getting things done effectively and efficiently. The repeatability of experiments demanded by science is critical for delivering practical engineering solutions that have commercial value. Engineering in general, and SE in particular, draw heavily from the terminology and concepts of science.

An *attribute* of a system (or system element) is an observable characteristic or property of the system (or system element). For example, among the various attributes of an aircraft is its air speed. Attributes are represented symbolically by variables. Specifically, a *variable* is a symbol or name that identifies an attribute. Every variable has a domain, which could be but is not necessarily measurable. A *measurement* is the outcome of a process in which the SoI interacts with an observation system under specified conditions. The outcome of a measurement is the assignment of a *value* to a variable. A system is in a state when the values assigned to its attributes remain constant or steady for a meaningful period of time (Kaposi and Myers, 2001). In SE and software

1.3.1 系统边界和所感兴趣之系统（SoI）

一般系统概念 系统的外部视图必须引入不属于系统但与系统交互的元素。这些元素的集合被称为系统环境或系统的背景环境，并可包括系统的用户（或操作员）。重要的是要理解，系统环境或系统的背景环境不仅限于运行环境，还包括在生命周期的任何时候与系统有接口关系的或支持系统的外部系统。

系统的内部和外部视图产生了系统边界的概念。实际上，系统边界是所考虑的系统（即所感兴趣之系统，SoI）与其更大背景环境之间的"分界线"。它定义了什么属于该系统，什么不属于该系统。系统边界不能与和环境交互的系统元素子集相混淆。

系统的功能通常以系统与其运行环境的交互（尤其是用户）来表述。当一个系统被视为相互作用的元素综合体时，系统的功能不仅源于各元素与环境元素的相互作用，还来自于这些相互作用如何受到系统元素的组织（相互关系）的影响。这引出了系统架构的概念，ISO/IEC/IEEE 42020（2019）将系统架构定义为：

一个实体在其环境中的基本概念或属性，以及该实体及其相关生命周期流程的实现和演进的指导原则。

这个定义是同时对系统的内部和外部视图而言的，也共享了系统定义中的概念（见 1.1 节）。

与系统概念相关的科学术语 一般来说，工程可以被视为创建和维持系统、服务、设备、机器、结构、流程和产品的实践，以提高生活质量——使做事更加高效及有效。科学要求的实验重复性对于提供具有商业价值的实际工程解决方案至关重要。一般来说，工程学，尤其是系统工程，大量借鉴了科学的术语和概念。

系统（或系统元素）的属性是系统（或系统元素）的可观察的特征或性质。例如，在航空器的各种属性中，有一个是它的空速。属性由变量来进行符号性表示。具体来说，变量是标识属性的符号或名称。每个变量都有一个域，它可以是可测量的，但并不要求一定可测。测量是 SoI 与观测系统在一定条件下交互作用的结果。测量的结果是为变量赋予一个数值。当系统的属性值在一个有意义的时间段内保持恒定或稳定，则称系统处于某个状态（Kaposi 和 Myers，2001）。在系统工程和软件工程中，系统元素（例如软件对象）除了属性外，还有流

engineering, the *system elements* (e.g., software objects) have *processes* (e.g., operations) in addition to attributes. These have the binary logical values of being either *idle or executing*. A complete description of a system state therefore requires values to be assigned to both attributes and processes. *Dynamic behavior* of a system is the time evolution of the system state. *Emergent behavior* is a behavior of the system that cannot be understood exclusively in terms of the behavior of the individual system elements. See Section 1.3.2 for further information on emergent behavior and Section 1.3.6 for more information on states and modes.

The key concept used for problem solving is the *black box/white box* (also known as *opaque box/transparent box*) system representation. The *black box (opaque box)* representation is based on an external view of the system (attributes). The *white box (transparent box)* representation is based on an internal view of the system (attributes and structure of the elements). Both representations are useful to the SE practitioner and there must be an understanding of the relationship between the two. A system, then, is represented by the external attributes of the system, its internal attributes and structure, and the interrelationships between these that are governed by the laws of science.

1.3.2 Emergence

Emergence describes the phenomenon that whole entities exhibit properties which are meaningful only when attributed to the whole, not to its elements. Every model of human activity system exhibits properties as a whole entity that derive from its element activities and their structure, but cannot be reduced to them (Checkland, 1999). Emergence is a fundamental property of all systems (Sillitto and Dori, 2017). According to Rousseau et al. (2018), emergence derives from the systems science concept of "properties the system has but the elements by themselves do not."

System elements interact between themselves and can create desirable or undesirable phenomena called *emergent properties* such as inhibition, interference, resonance, or reinforcement of any property. Emergent properties can also result from the interaction between the system and its environment. Many engineering disciplines include emergence as a property. For example, system safety (Leveson, 1995) and resilience (Rasoulkahni, 2018) are examples of emergent properties of engineered systems (see Sections 3.1.11 and 3.1.9, respectively).

Definition of the architecture of the system includes an analysis of interactions between system elements in order to reinforce desirable and prevent undesirable emergent properties. According to Rousseau et al. (2019), the systemic virtue of emergent properties are used during systems architecture and design definition to highlight necessary derived functions and internal physical or environmental constraints (see Sections 2.3.5.4 and 2.3.5.5, respectively). Corresponding derived requirements should be added to system requirements baseline when they impact the SoI.

程（例如操作）。这些流程有二进制的逻辑值表达它们是在空闲还是正在执行。因此，系统状态的完整描述需要同时为属性和流程赋值。系统的动态行为是系统状态随时间的演进。涌现行为是无法仅从单个系统元素的行为来理解的系统行为。有关涌现行为的更多信息，请参见 1.3.2 节；有关状态和模式的更多信息，请参见 1.3.6 节。

系统的黑盒/白盒（也称为不透明盒/透明盒）表示是解决问题时使用的关键概念。系统的黑盒（不透明盒）表示基于系统（属性）的外部视图。白盒（透明盒）表示基于系统的内部视图（属性和元素的结构）。这两种表述对系统工程实践者都很有用，必须理解两者之间的关系。因此，一个系统由系统的外部属性、内部属性和结构以及这些属性和结构之间的相互关系来表示，这样的相互关系由科学法则所支配。

1.3.2 涌现性

涌现性描述了这样一种现象，即实体整体表现出的属性只有归属于整体才有意义，而对于系统的元素没有意义。人类活动系统的每一个模型都表现为一个整体的属性，这些属性源于但不能简化为系统元素的活动和结构（Checkland，1999）。涌现性是所有系统的基本属性（Sillitto 和 Dori，2017）。根据 Rousseau 等（2018），涌现性源自"系统具有，但系统的元素本身没有的属性"这一系统科学概念。

系统元素之间相互作用，可以造成想要的或不想要的现象，称为涌现属性，如抑制、干涉、共振或任何属性的强化。涌现属性也可以源于系统与其环境之间的相互作用。许多工程学科包含涌现属性。例如，系统安全性（Leveson，1995）和韧性（Rasoulkahni，2018）是工程系统涌现属性的例子（分别见 3.1.11 和 3.1.9 节）。

定义系统架构包括对系统元素之间交互的分析，以增强需要的涌现属性和避免不想要的涌现属性。根据 Rousseau 等（2019）的研究，在系统架构和设计定义期间使用涌现属性的系统性优点，以突出必要的派生功能和内部物理或环境约束（分别参见 2.3.5.4 和 2.3.5.5 节）。当它们影响 SoI 时，应将相应的派生需求添加到系统需求基线中。

SYSTEMS ENGINEERING INTRODUCTION

Calvo-Amodio and Rousseau (2019) explain how emergence applies to systems in which complexity is dominant. Complexity dominance, they say, encourages us to consider the significance of the difference between kinds of complexity and degrees of complexity systems have. Doing so enables the SE practitioner to use variety engineering to manage complexity accordingly.

Figure 1.5 illustrates how the interaction between elements can result in emergent properties in any kind of system. This figure illustrates the basic rules of emergence. First, individual elements cannot exhibit higher-level system emergence. Second, two or more elements are required for emergence. Finally, emergence occurs at a level above the individual elements.

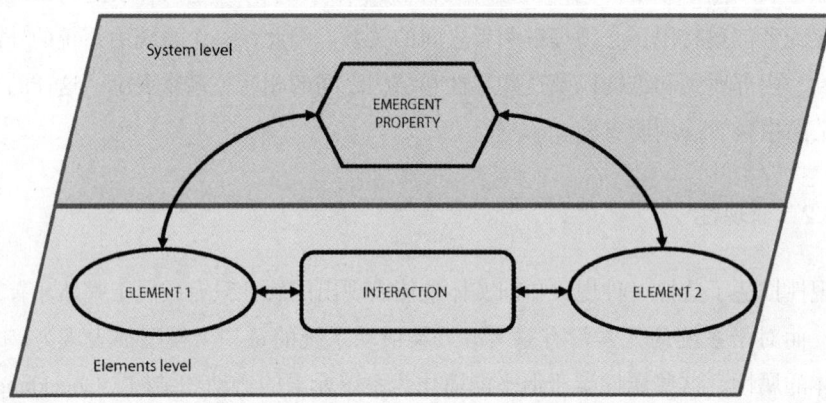

FIGURE 1.5 Emergence. INCOSE SEH original figure created by Jackson. Usage per the INCOSE Notices page. All other rights reserved.

1.3.3 Interfacing Systems, Interoperating Systems, and Enabling Systems

External systems are systems beyond (or outside of) the SoI boundary. *Interfacing systems* are external systems that share an interface (e.g., physical, material, energy, data/information) with the SoI. Typically, humans also interface with the SoI throughout the SoI's life cycle stages. Interoperating systems are interfacing systems that interface with the SoI in its operational environment to perform a common function that supports the SoI's primary purpose. The set of SoI and interoperating systems can be seen as a system of systems (see Section 4.3.6). *Enabling systems* are external systems that facilitate the life cycle activities of the SoI but are not a direct element of the operational environment. The enabling systems provide services that are needed by the SoI during one or more life cycle stages. Some enabling systems share an interface with the SoI and some do not. Examples of enabling systems include collaboration development systems, production systems, and logistics support systems. Table 1.3 gives examples of these types of external systems.

Calvo-Amodio 和 Rousseau（2019）解释了涌现性如何应用于复杂性所主导的系统。他们说，复杂性的主导地位鼓励我们考虑不同系统的复杂性和复杂性程度差异的重要性。这样，系统工程实践者就能利用各类工程来相应地管理复杂性。

图 1.5 说明了元素之间的相互作用如何在任何类型的系统中产生涌现属性。这幅图说明了涌现性的基本规则。首先，个体元素不能表现出更高层次的系统涌现性。其次，涌现性需要两个或多个元素。最后，涌现性发生在个体元素之上的层级。

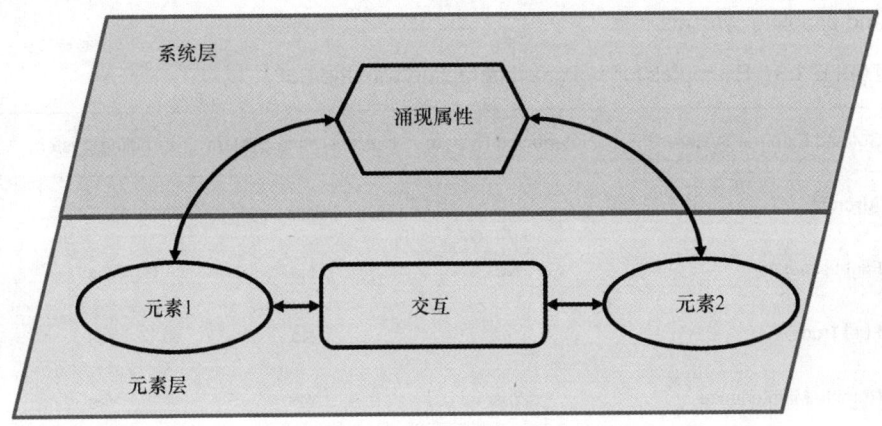

图 1.5 涌现。INCOSE SEH 原始图由 Jackson 创建。根据 INCOSE 通知页使用。版权所有。

1.3.3 接口系统、互操作系统和使能系统

外部系统是指超出 SoI 边界（或在边界以外）的系统。接口系统是与 SoI 共享接口（例如，物理的、物质的、能量的、数据/信息）的外部系统。通常，人员也会在 SoI 的整个生命周期与其交互。互操作系统是指在 SoI 运行环境中与 SoI 连接的接口系统，它们执行共同的功能以支持 SoI 的主要目的。SoI 和互操作系统的集合可被视为体系（系统之系统）（见 4.3.6 节）。使能系统是促进 SoI 生命周期活动的外部系统，但不是 SoI 运行环境的直接元素。使能系统提供 SoI 在一个或多个周期阶段所需的服务。一些使能系统与 SoI 有接口，而另一些则没有。使能系统的例子包括协作开发系统、生产系统和后勤支持系统。表 1.3 给出了这些类型外部系统的示例。

SYSTEMS ENGINEERING INTRODUCTION

During the life cycle stages for an SoI, it is necessary to concurrently consider interfacing, interoperating, and enabling systems along with the SoI. Otherwise, important requirements may not be identified, which will lead to significant costs in the further course of system development. Typical pitfalls include assuming that a new enabling system will come online in time to support the development of the SoI or that an existing enabling system will be available for the duration of the life cycle of the SoI. A delay in an enabling system coming online or the loss of an existing enabling system can lead to significant issues with the development and deployment of the SoI. In addition, horizontal and vertical integration considerations (see Section 2.3.5.8) may arise from the system context represented by interfacing, interoperating, and enabling systems.

TABLE 1.3   Examples for systems interacting with the SoI

SoI and External Systems	Interfacing System	Interoperating System	Enabling System
Aircraft			
Flight simulator	No	No	Yes
Fuel Truck	Yes	No	Yes
Remote Maintenance	Yes	Yes	Yes
Communication system	Yes	Yes	No
Runway	Yes	No	No
Automobile			
SE Tool	No	No	Yes
Car carrier	Yes	No	Yes
Diagnosis system	Yes	Yes	Yes
Parking assistant	Yes	Yes	No
Windshield snow cover	Yes	No	No

INCOSE SEH original table created by Endler. Usage per the INCOSE Notices page. All other rights reserved.

在 SoI 的生命周期中，有必要同时考虑 SoI 的接口、互操作和使能系统。否则，可能无法识别重要的需求，这将导致在系统接下来的开发中产生显著的成本。典型陷阱包含假设一个新的使能系统将及时上线，以支持 SoI 的开发，或者现有的使能系统将在 SoI 的生命周期内可用。使能系统上线的延迟或现有使能系统的缺失可能导致 SoI 的开发和部署出现重大问题。此外，横向和纵向综合的考虑（见 2.3.5.8 节）可能来自接口、互操作和使能系统所代表的系统背景环境。

表 1.3　与 SoI 交互的系统示例

所感兴趣之系统和外部系统	接口系统	互操作系统	使能系统
飞机			
飞行模拟器	No	No	Yes
加油车	Yes	No	Yes
远程维护	Yes	Yes	Yes
通信系统	Yes	Yes	No
跑道	Yes	No	No
汽车			
系统工程工具	No	No	Yes
汽车运载工具	Yes	No	Yes
诊断系统	Yes	Yes	Yes
停车助手	Yes	Yes	No
挡风玻璃防雪罩	Yes	No	No

INCOSE SEH 原始表由 Endler 创建。根据 INCOSE 通知页使用。版权所有。

31

SYSTEMS ENGINEERING INTRODUCTION

1.3.4 System Innovation Ecosystem

Sections 1.3.1 and 1.3.3 describe the system boundary and external systems in the overall context of the SoI. This section focuses on learning. Over single, and eventually multiple life cycles, engineered system innovation may be viewed as a form of group learning by "ecosystems" composed of individuals, teams, enterprises, supply chains, markets, and societies. Effective innovation requires effective learning and adaptation at a group level across these ecosystems and brings related challenges. To represent, plan, analyze, and improve such performance, the neutral descriptive System Innovation Ecosystem Pattern has been found to be useful (Schindel and Dove, 2016) (Schindel, 2022b). Figure 1.6 provides a high-level view of that multiple-layered descriptive model, further discussed as a formal pattern in Section 3.2.6.

Figure 1.6 identifies three top-level system boundaries:

1. **System 1 – The Engineered System** may be a product developed for a market, a defense system created under contract, a service-providing system, or other system subject to SE life cycle management. It is shown in its larger environment, the Life Cycle Project Management System (System 2). System 1 examples include Medical Devices, Aircraft, Consumer Packaged Goods, and Gas Turbine Engines. This system is typically referred to as the engineered SoI in this handbook.

2. **System 2 – The Life Cycle Project Management System** provides the environment of System 1 over its life cycle, including the life cycle management processes responsible for System 1—described in Part II. System 2, a socio-technical system of people, processes, and facilities, is responsible to learn about System 1 and its environment, and to effectively apply that learning in the life cycle management by System 2. System 2 examples include System Requirements Definition Processes, Verification Processes, Product Manufacturing Processes, Product Distribution Processes, Product Sustainment Systems, Product Life Cycle Management (PLM) Information Systems, and Product Digital Twin Systems.

3. **System 3 – The Enterprise Process and Innovation System** contains System 2 and is responsible for learning about and improving System 2. In that sense, System 3 includes formal life cycle management for the processes of System 2. System 3 contains the "organizational change management" for advancing and adapting System 2 as a recognized formal system in its own right. System 3 examples include Product Life Cycle Management Processes, Program and Project Configuration and Tailoring Processes, Engineering Recruitment, Education, and Advancement Processes, Product Development Methodology Descriptions, Engineering Automation Tooling Acquisition and Development, Development Process Performance Analysis Systems, Regulatory Authorities, Engineering Professional Societies, and Engineering Facilities Construction and Acquisition.

1.3.4 系统创新生态

1.3.1 和 1.3.3 节描述了系统边界和 SoI 总体背景环境中的外部系统。本节重点介绍学习。在单个乃至多个生命周期内，工程系统创新可以被视为由个人、团队、复杂组织体系、供应链、市场和社会组成的"生态系统"的一种群体学习形式。有效的创新需要在这些生态系统的群体层级进行有效的学习和适应，这也带来了相关挑战。为了表示、计划、分析和改进此类绩效，中性描述性的系统创新生态模式非常有用（Schindel 和 Dove，2016）（Schindel，2022b）。图 1.6 提供了这种多层描述模型的高阶视图，并将在 3.2.6 节中作为形式化的模式进一步讨论。

图 1.6 确定了三个顶层系统边界：

1. **系统 1 工程系统**可以是为市场开发的产品、根据合同创建的防务系统、提供服务的系统或受系统工程生命周期管理的其他系统。它显示在更大的环境中，即生命周期项目管理系统（系统 2）之中。系统 1 的例子包含医疗设备、航空器、消费品和燃气涡轮发动机。这样的系统在本手册中通常被称为工程的 SoI。

2. **系统 2 生命周期项目管理系统**提供系统 1 在其生命周期内的环境，包括负责系统 1 的生命周期管理流程——在本手册的第二部分进行描述。系统 2 是一个由人员、流程和设施组成的社会技术系统，负责认识系统 1 及其环境，并基于系统 2 将这样的认识有效地应用于系统 1 的生命周期管理。系统 2 的例子包含系统需求定义流程、验证流程、产品制造流程、产品配送流程、产品维护系统、产品生命周期管理（PLM）信息系统和产品数字孪生系统。

3. **系统 3 复杂组织体系流程和创新系统**包含系统 2，负责认识和改进系统 2。从这个意义上说，系统 3 包括对系统 2 生命周期流程的形式化管理。系统 3 包含"组织变革管理"，以推动和调整系统 2，使其成为公认的形式化系统。系统 3 的例子包含产品生命周期管理流程、计划和项目的配置以及剪裁流程、工程招聘、教育培训和晋升流程、产品开发方法描述、工程自动化工具采办和开发、开发流程绩效分析系统、监管机构、工程专业协会和工程设施建造和采办。

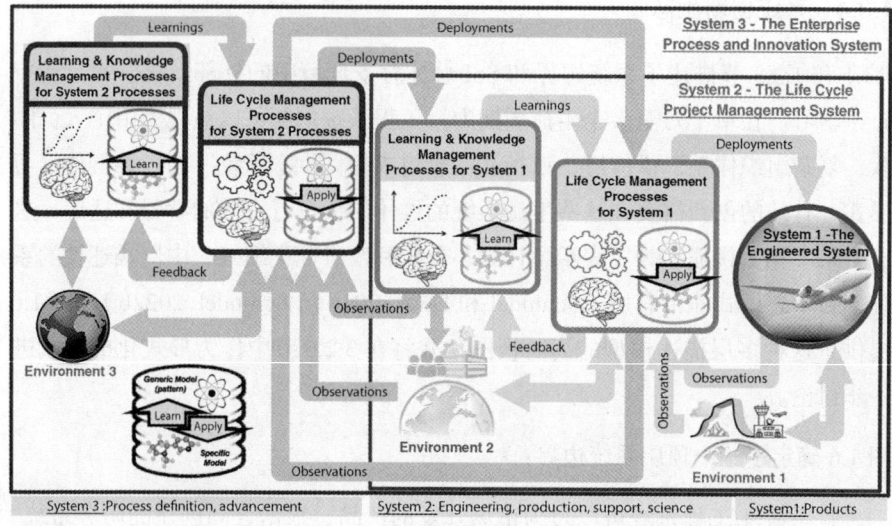

FIGURE 1.6 System innovation ecosystem pattern. From Schindel and Dove (2016) and Schindel (2022b). Used with permission. All other rights reserved.

The System Innovation Ecosystem Pattern emphasizes the learning and execution aspects of the enterprise ecosystem and directly integrates the SE life cycle processes described in Part II of this Handbook. Those processes are applied to two different managed SoIs (System 1 and System 2) and explicate the processes of learning versus application in each of the SE life cycle processes, along with how, and how effectively, execution is coupled with prior learning. The (configurable) System Innovation Ecosystem Pattern intentionally describes any engineering environment, whether effective in its learning and adaptation or not. It is intended as a descriptive, not prescriptive, reference model that can be used to plan and analyze any engineering and life cycle management ecosystem. So, while the "learned models" shown inside System 2 describe knowledge of System 1 (The Engineered System), the models shown inside System 3 describe knowledge of System 2 (The Life Cycle Project Management System).

The formal System Innovation Ecosystem Pattern includes the ability to be configured specific to a local enterprise, project, or supply chain, and for use to plan a series of migration increments representing advancing System 2 capabilities. For more details, refer to Section 3.2.6 and the INCOSE S*Patterns Primer (2022).

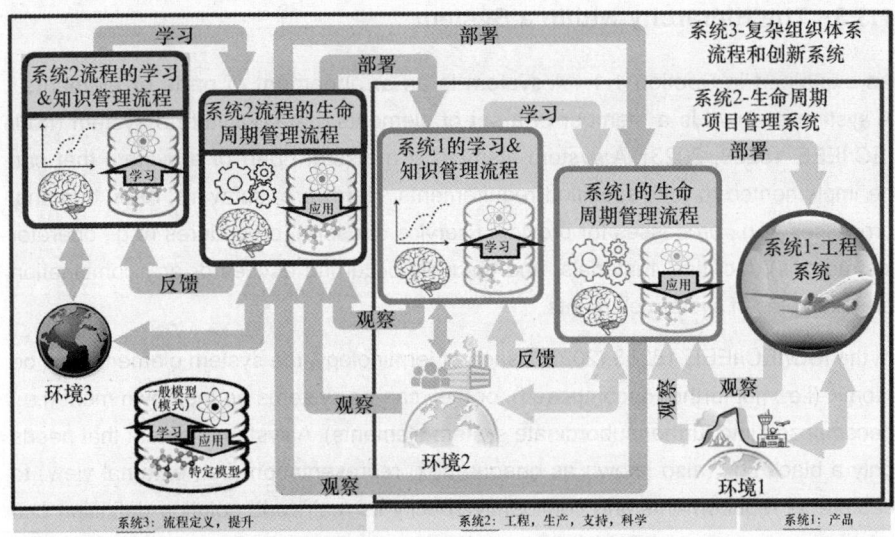

图 1.6　系统创新生态模式。源自 Schindel 和 Dove（2016）。经许可后使用。版权所有。

系统创新生态模式强调复杂组织体系生态的学习和执行方面，并直接集成了本手册第二部分中描述的系统工程生命周期流程。这些流程应用于两个不同的受管理的 SoI（系统 1 和系统 2），并阐述了在每个系统工程生命周期流程中，认识与应用的流程，以及如何有效地将执行与之前的认识相结合。（可配置的）系统创新生态模式有意描述任何工程环境，无论其学习和适应是否有效。它旨在作为一种描述性而非规定性的参考模型，可以用于计划和分析任何工程和生命周期管理生态。因此，系统 2 中显示的"学习模型"描述了系统 1（工程系统）的知识，系统 3 中显示的模型描述了系统 2（生命周期项目管理系统）的知识。

形式化的系统创新生态模式包括针对复杂组织体系、项目或供应链进行本地化配置的能力，以及用于计划一系列迁移增量以表示系统 2 升级的能力。更多详细信息，请参阅 3.2.6 节和《INCOSE S* 模式入门指南》（2022）。

SYSTEMS ENGINEERING INTRODUCTION

1.3.5 The Hierarchy within a System

As explained in Section 1.1, "A system is an arrangement of parts or elements." A *system element* is a member of a set of elements that constitute a system (ISO/IEC/IEEE 15288, 2023). A system element is a discrete part of a system that can be implemented to fulfil specified requirements. Hardware, software, data, humans, processes (e.g., processes for providing service to users), procedures (e.g., operator instructions), facilities, materials, and naturally occurring entities or any combination are examples of system elements.

In the ISO/IEC/IEEE 15288 (2023) usage of terminology, the system elements can be atomic (i.e., not further decomposed), or they can be systems on their own merit (i.e., decomposed into further subordinate system elements). A system element that needs only a black box (also known as opaque box) representation (i.e., external view) to capture its requirements and confidently specify its real-world solution definition can be regarded as atomic. Decisions to make, buy, or reuse the element can be made with confidence without further specification of the element.

One of the challenges of system definition is to understand what level of detail is necessary to define each system element and the interrelations between elements. The integration of the system elements must establish the relationship between the effects that organizing the elements has on their interactions and how these effects enable the system to achieve its purpose. One approach to defining the elements of a system and their interrelations is to identify a complete set of distinct system elements with regard only to their relation to the whole (system) by suppressing details of their interactions and interrelations. These considerations lead to the concept of hierarchy within a system. This is referred to as a *partitioning* of the system and the end result is called a *Product Breakdown Structure* (PBS) (see Section 2.3.4.1). As stated above, each element of the PBS can be either atomic or it can be at a higher level that could be viewed as a system itself. At any given level, the elements are grouped into distinct subsets of elements subordinated to a higher-level system, as illustrated in Figure 1.7. Thus, hierarchy within a system is an organizational representation of system structure using a partitioning relation.

The art of defining a hierarchy within a system relies on the ability of the SE practitioner to strike a balance between clearly and simply defining span of control and resolving the structure of the SoI into a complete set of system elements that can be implemented with confidence. Urwick (1956) suggested a possible heuristic for span of control, recommending that decomposition of any object in a hierarchy be limited to no more than seven subordinate elements, plus or minus two (7 +/−2).

1.3.5 系统内的层级结构

如 1.1 节所述,"系统是组成部分或元素的编排"。系统元素是构成系统的元素集合中的成员(ISO/IEC/IEEE 15288,2023)。系统元素是系统离散的组成部分,它可以被实现以满足特定需求。硬件、软件、数据、人员、流程(例如,向用户提供服务的流程)、程序(例如,操作说明)、设施、物料和自然存在的实体或它们的任意组合都是系统元素的例子。

在 ISO/IEC/IEEE 15288(2023)的术语使用中,系统元素可以是原子级的(即不可再被进一步分解),也可以是基于自己特质的系统(即可被进一步分解为次级系统元素)。仅需要黑盒表达形式(外部视图)捕获其需求,并有信心地指定其现实解决方案定义的系统元素可被认为是原子的。可以有信心地做出制造、购买、复用元素的决策而无须进一步的元素规范。

系统定义的挑战之一是理解什么样的详细程度对于定义每一个系统元素以及元素之间的关系而言是必要的。系统元素的综合必须确定组织方式对其相互作用的影响,以及这些影响如何使系统实现其目的。定义系统元素及其相互关系的一种途径是,通过隐藏其相互作用和相互关系的细节,仅就其与整体(系统)的关系确定由不同系统元素构成的完整集合。这样的考量引出了系统内部的层级结构的概念。这被称为系统的划分,最终的结果称为产品分解结构(PBS)(见 2.3.4.1 节)。如上所述,PBS 的每个元素可以是原子级的,也可以是更高的层级以至于其自身可以被视作一个系统。在任何给定的层级上,元素被分组为从属于更高层级系统的不同元素子集,如图 1.7 所示。因此,系统内部的层级结构是使用划分关系对系统结构的组织化表示。

定义一个系统内的层级结构的艺术依赖于系统工程实践者的能力——在清晰且简单地定义控制范围与分解 SoI 结构为有信心地实施系统元素完整集合之间达成平衡。Urwick(1956)提出了一种确定控制范围的可行的启发式方法,建议将层级结构中任何对象的分解限制为不超过七个从属元素,加上或减去两个(7 ± 2)。

SYSTEMS ENGINEERING INTRODUCTION

Others have also found this heuristic to be useful in other contexts (Miller, 1956). A level of design with too few subordinate elements is unlikely to have a distinct design activity. In this case, both design and verification activities may contain redundancy. In case of too many subordinate elements, it may be difficult to manage all the interfaces between the subordinate elements. In practice, the nomenclature and depth of the hierarchy can and should be adjusted to fit the nature of the system and the community of interest.

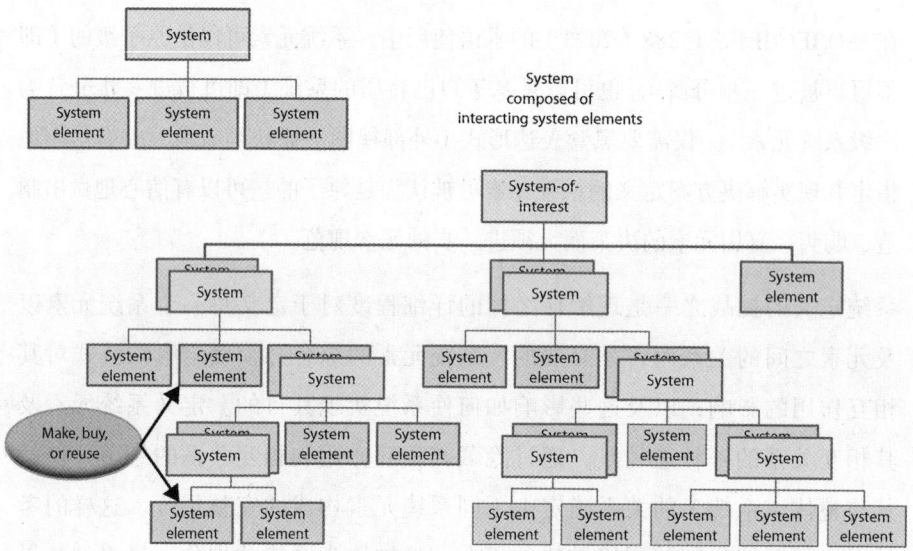

FIGURE 1.7   Hierarchy within a system. From ISO/IEC/IEEE 15288 (2023). Used with permission. All other rights reserved.

The interrelationships of system elements at a given architecture level of decomposition can be referred to as the horizontal view of the system. The horizontal view also includes requirements; integration, verification, or validation activities and results; various other related artifacts; and external elements. How the horizontal elements, activities, results, and artifacts are derived from or lead to higher-level systems and lower-level system element can be referred to as the vertical view of the system.

1.3.6   Systems States and Modes

States and modes are two related concepts that are used for defining and modeling system functional architectures and for modeling and managing system behaviors.

其他人也发现这种启发式方法在其他情况下也很有用（Miller，1956）。当一个层级的设计包含过少的次级元素时，不太可能开展有差异的设计活动。这种情况下，设计和验证活动也许都将包含冗余。当设计包含过多的次级元素时，管理这些次级元素之间所有的接口也许很困难。在实践中，层级结构的命名法和深度可以而且应该进行调整，以适应系统的本质和利益共同体。

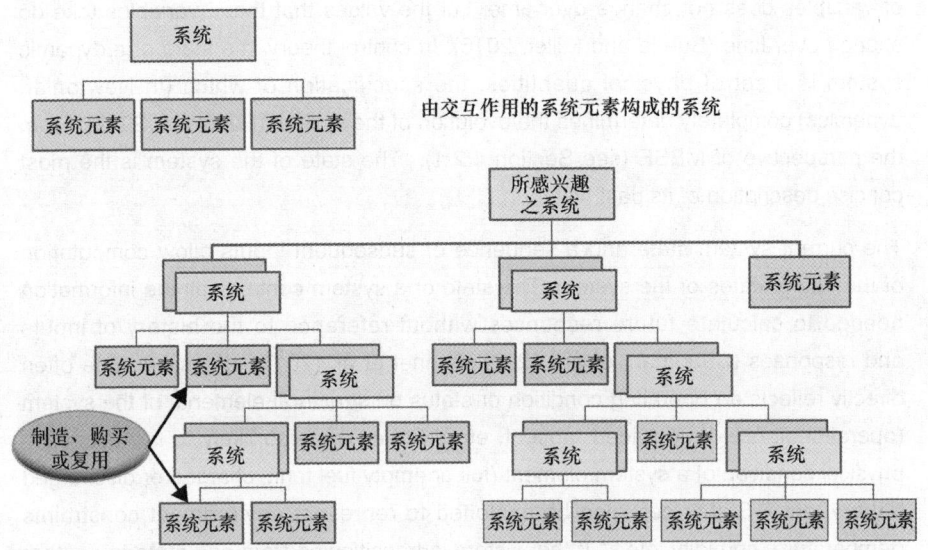

图1.7　一个系统内的层级结构。源自 ISO/IEC/IEEE 15288（2023）。经许可后使用。版权所有。

在给定的架构分解层级上，系统元素的相互关系可以称为系统的水平视图。水平视图也包括需求；综合、验证或确认活动和结果；各种其他相关的制品；以及外部元素。水平元素、活动、结果和制品如何派生自或引出高层级系统以及低层级系统元素，可以被称为系统的垂直视图。

1.3.6　系统状态和模式

状态和模式是两个相关的概念，用于系统功能架构的定义和建模，以及系统行为的建模和管理。

A *state* can be defined as:

An observable and measurable ... attribute used to characterize the current configuration, status, or performance-based condition of a System or Entity. (Wasson, 2016)

States are snapshots of a set of variables or measurements needed to describe fully the system's capabilities to perform the system's functions. *State variables* are the multidimensional list of variables that determine the state of the system. The list of variables does not change over time, but the values that these variables take do change over time (Buede and Miller, 2016). In control theory, the state of a dynamic system is a set of physical quantities, the specification of which (in Newtonian dynamics) completely determines the evolution of the system (Friedland, 2012). From the perspective of MBSE (see Section 4.2.1), "The state of the system is the most concise description of its past history."

The current system state and a sequence of subsequent inputs allow computation of the future states of the system. The state of a system contains all the information needed to calculate future responses without reference to the history of inputs and responses (Chapman, et al., 1992). Bonnet et al. (2017) states, "A state often directly reflects an operating condition or status on structural elements of the system (operational, failed, degraded, absent, etc.). States are also likely to represent the physical condition of a system element (full or empty fuel tank, charged or discharged battery, etc.). States can also be exploited to represent environment constraints (temperature, humidity, etc.)." If the system is transitioning from one state to another as time progresses, then time is one of the key attributes of the system. To monitor the system and manage it, the manager observes a state variable that is comprised of the appropriate collection of the system's attributes (Shafaat and Kenley, 2020).

A *mode* can be defined as:

A distinct operating capability of the system during which some or all of the system's functions may be performed to a full or limited degree. (Buede and Miller, 2016)

For a personal computer, examples of modes are "off," "on," "waking up," "waiting," "reading from disk," "writing to disk," "computing," "printing," and, of course, "down" (Wymore, 1993). Modes are part of the system functional architecture and can be derived by affinity analysis of system use cases (Wasson, 2016). Various perspectives can be used to define the distinct operating modes of a system (Bonnet, et al., 2017), such as:

状态可定义为：

可观察和可测量的……属性，用于特征化系统或实体的当前构型、状况或基于表现的状况。（Wasson，2016）

状态是一组变量或测度的快照，需要这些变量或测度来全面描述系统执行系统功能的能力。状态变量是确定系统状态的多维变量列表。变量列表不会随时间变化，但这些变量的值会随时间变化（Buede 和 Miller，2016）。在控制理论中，动态系统的状态是一组物理量，这些物理量的具体取值（在牛顿力学中）可以完全地决定系统的演进（Friedland，2012）。从基于模型的系统工程的视角来看（见 4.2.1 节）"系统的状态是对其过去历史最简洁的描述"。

通过当前的系统状态和一系列后续输入，可以计算出系统的未来状态。系统的状态包含计算未来响应所需的所有信息，无须参考历史的输入和响应（Chapman 等，1992）。Bonnet 等（2017）指出："状态通常直接反映运行状态或系统结构元素的状况（运行、故障、降级、缺失等），状态也可能表示系统元素的物理状态（油箱满或空、电池充电或放电等），状态也可以用来表示环境约束（温度、湿度等）。"如果系统随着时间的推移从一种状态转移到另一种状态，则时间是系统的关键属性之一。管理者通过观察由合适的系统属性集合组成的状态变量来监视和管理系统（Shafaat 和 Kenley，2020）。

模式可定义为：

系统的一种独特的运行能力，在此期间，系统的部分或全部功能可以完全或有限程度地执行。（Buede 和 Miller，2016）

对于个人计算机，模式的例子有"关闭""打开""唤醒""等待""从磁盘读取""写入磁盘""计算""打印"，当然还有"宕机"（Wymore，1993）。模式是系统功能架构的一部分，可以结合系统用例的分析来获得（Wasson，2016）。可以使用多种视角来定义系统不同的运行模式（Bonnet 等，2017），例如：

SYSTEMS ENGINEERING INTRODUCTION

- the phases of mission operations (taxiing, taking-off, cruising, landing, etc.),
- the system operating conditions (connected, autonomous, etc.),
- the specific conditions in which the system is used (test, training, maintenance, etc.).

Transitioning from one mode to another is the result of decisions made by the system itself, its users, or external actors in order to adapt to new needs or new contexts (Bonnet, et al., 2017). Decisions that result in the system transitioning from one mode to another are typically based on the observed values of the state variables. When using models to depict system behavior, mode transitions are often based on triggering events that meet specified entry and exit criteria (Wasson, 2016).

1.3.7 Complexity

Systems engineering practitioners encounter a number of systems with simple, complicated, and complex characteristics. Many traditional systems engineering approaches and techniques work well for simple and complicated systems but do not handle complexity in systems (i.e., complex systems) well. Conversely, approaches and techniques that handle complexity well are also used in some complicated system contexts, especially when complex characteristics exist in some aspects of the system. Thus, care must be used to ensure the SE approaches and techniques for the SoI are appropriate and tailored for the type of system, especially with respect to its complexity. Complex systems are defined in the INCOSE publication "A Complexity Primer for Systems Engineers" (INCOSE Complexity Primer, 2021). A complex system has elements, the relationship between the states of which are weaved together so that they are not fully comprehended, leading to insufficient certainty between cause and effect. Complicated systems are less challenging. A complicated system has elements, the relationship between the states of which can be unfolded and comprehended, leading to sufficient certainty between cause and effect. Systems can also be simple. A simple system has elements, the relationship between the states of which, once observed, are readily comprehended. Complex systems can provide beneficial solutions yet also contain challenging characteristics. Complexity can result in positive behavior, such as self-organization and virtuous cycles of activity. However, intricate networks of evolving cause-and-effect relationships can lead to novel, nonlinear, and counterintuitive dynamics over time, resulting in suboptimal system operation, unintended consequences, and system obsolescence. The INCOSE Complexity Primer identifies 14 distinguishing characteristics that define complexity in a system. These characteristics provide insights into complexity, realizing that systems are not wholly complex: they are typically complex in some characteristics and complicated or even simple in others.

- 任务行动的阶段（滑行、起飞、巡航、着陆等）；
- 系统运行状况（已连接、自主运行等）；
- 系统的特定使用状况（测试、培训、维护等）。

从一种模式转移到另一种模式是系统自身、用户或外部参与者为了适应新需要或适应新的背景环境而做出的决定的结果（Bonnet 等，2017）。导致系统从一种工作模式转移到另一种模式的决策通常是基于状态变量的观测值做出的。当使用模型描述系统行为时，模式的转移通常基于满足特定进入和退出准则的触发事件（Wasson，2016）。

1.3.7 复杂性

系统工程实践者会遇到许多具有简单、繁杂和复杂特征的系统。许多传统的系统工程方法和技术适用于简单和繁杂的系统，但不能很好地处理系统（即复杂系统）中的复杂性。相反，能够很好地处理复杂性的方法和技术也适用于一些繁杂的系统，尤其是当系统的某些方面存在复杂特征时。因此，必须小心确保系统工程方法和技术对 SoI 来说是合适的，并且根据系统的类型进行了剪裁，尤其是要考虑系统的复杂性。复杂系统在 INCOSE 出版物《系统工程师的复杂性入门指南》（INCOSE 复杂性入门指南，2021）中有定义。复杂系统的元素状态之间的关系交织在一起，以至于无法完全理解，导致因果之间的确定性不足。繁杂系统的本质挑战性较小。一个繁杂系统的元素状态之间的关系是可以展开和理解的，从而在因果之间形成足够的确定性。系统也可以是简单的。一个简单系统的元素状态之间的关系一旦被观察到，就能被迅速理解。复杂系统可以提供有益的解决方案，但也包含具有挑战性的特征。复杂性可以导致正向的行为，例如自组织和活动的良性循环。然而，随着时间的推移，错综复杂的因果关系网络可能会产生全新的、非线性和反直觉的动态变化，导致系统的次优运行，造成不希望的后果和系统的淘汰。《INCOSE 复杂性入门指南》明确了定义系统复杂性的 14 个显著特征。这些特征提供了对复杂性的洞察，认识到系统并不完全是复杂的：它们在某些特征上通常是复杂的，而在另一些特征上则是繁杂甚至是简单的。

SYSTEMS ENGINEERING INTRODUCTION

Traditional SE process for complicated systems takes a reductionist approach, whereby the problem is procedurally broken down into its parts (i.e., decomposition), solved, and reassembled to form the whole solution. This approach works well for complicated problems, where fixed, deterministic, or predictable patterns of behavior are required. However, these processes often do not perform well in complex environments, such as the challenges involved in designing autonomous vehicles or other socio-technical systems. A fundamentally different approach is required to understand the unexpected emergent interaction between the parts in the context of the whole through iterative exploration and adaptation (Snowden and Boone, 2007).

SE for complex systems requires a balance of linear, procedural methods for sorting through complicated and intricate tasks (e.g., systematic activity) and holistic, nonlinear, iterative methods for harnessing complexity (e.g., systems thinking). Complexity is not antithetical to simplicity, as even relatively simple systems can generate complex behavior. The INCOSE Complexity Primer provides guidance in the methods, approaches, and tools that may benefit complex systems engineering.

1.4 SYSTEMS ENGINEERING FOUNDATIONS

1.4.1 Uncertainty

There is uncertainty associated with much of the systems information and measurement data we use. This section provides a brief summary of the two major types of uncertainty, the sources of systems uncertainty, and decision making under uncertainty.

Types of Uncertainty. There are two types of uncertainties: epistemic and aleatory. In SE, *epistemic uncertainty* is due to our lack of knowledge about the potential demand for a new system and how a technology, system, or process will perform in the future, for example, the knowledge gap about key value attribute or about the acquirer's preferences. *Aleatory uncertainty* is uncertainty due to randomness. If a technology, system, or process can perform a function, there will be always some inherent randomness in every performance measurement. Our system requirements process, and development decisions focus on reducing epistemic uncertainty (overcoming our lack of knowledge), but we can never completely reduce aleatory uncertainty in our development or operational measurement of system performance.

Sources of Uncertainty and Risk. There are many sources of epistemic uncertainty that impact SE in the system life cycle. Table 1.4 provides a partial list of some of the major uncertainties that confront project managers and SE practitioners and describes some of the implications for SE.

针对繁杂系统的传统系统工程流程采用简化的方法，即按程序将问题拆解为它的组成部分（即分解），解决各个组成部分，然后重新组合，形成整体解决方案。这种方法适用于需要固定的、确定性的或可预测的行为模式的繁杂问题。然而，这些流程在复杂的环境中往往表现不佳，例如设计自动驾驶汽车或其他社会技术系统所涉及的挑战。需要一种从根本上不同的方法，来在迭代探索和适应中理解整体环境组成部分之间的不希望的涌现交互（Snowden 和 Boone，2007）。

针对复杂系统的系统工程需要在线性、程序化应对错综复杂的任务的方法（如系统活动）和应对复杂性的整体的、非线性、迭代的方法（如系统思维）之间取得平衡。复杂性并不是简单性的对立面，因为即使是相对简单的系统也可以生成复杂的行为。《INCOSE 复杂性入门指南》在方法、实施方法和工具方面提供了指导，这些可能有益于复杂系统工程。

1.4 系统工程基础

1.4.1 不确定性

我们使用的许多系统的信息和测量项数据都存在不确定性。本节简要总结两种主要的不确定性、系统不确定性的来源和不确定性下的决策过程。

不确定性的类型。有两种类型的不确定性：认知不确定性和偶然不确定性。在系统工程中，认知不确定性源自于我们对新系统的潜在需求以及技术、系统或流程的未来表现缺乏了解，例如，缺乏对关键数值属性或采办方偏好的知识。偶然不确定性是由于随机性而产生的不确定性。如果技术、系统或流程可以执行某个功能，那么在每个性能测度中总会存在一些固有的随机性。我们的系统需求流程和开发决策侧重于减少认知不确定性（克服我们知识的缺乏），但我们永远无法彻底减少系统性能开发或运行测量过程中的偶然不确定性。

不确定性和风险的来源。在系统生命周期中影响系统工程的认知不确定性的来源有很多。表 1.4 部分列出了项目经理和系统工程实践者面临的一些主要不确定性，并描述了对系统工程造成的部分影响。

SYSTEMS ENGINEERING INTRODUCTION

TABLE 1.4 Sources of system uncertainty

Sources of Uncertainty	Major Questions	Potential Uncertainties
Business	Will political, economic, labor, social, technological, environmental, legal or, other factors adversely affect the business environment?	Changes in political viewpoint (e.g., elections) Economic disruptions (e.g., recession). Global disruptions (e.g., supply chain). Changes to laws and regulations. Disruptive technologies. Adverse publicity.
Market	Will there be a market if the product or service works?	User and consumer demand. Threats from competitors (quality and price) and adversaries (e.g., hackers and terrorists). Continuing stakeholder support.
Management	Does the organization have the people, processes, and culture to manage a major system?	Organization culture. SE and management experience and expertise. Mature baselining processes (technical, cost, schedule). Reliable cost estimating processes.
Performance (Technical)	Will the product or service meet the required desired performance?	Defining future requirements in dynamic environments. Understanding of the technical baseline. Technology maturity to meet performance. Adequate modeling, simulation, test, and evaluation capabilities to predict and evaluate performance. Availability of enabling systems needed to support use.
Schedule	Can the system that provides the product or service be delivered on time?	Concurrency in development. Impact of uncertain events on schedule. Time and budget to resolve technical and cost risks.
Development and Production Cost	Can the system be delivered within the budget? Will the cost be affordable?	Changes in missions. Technology maturity. Hardware and software development processes. Industrial/supply chain capabilities. Production facilities capabilities and processes.
Operations and Support Cost	Can the owner afford to operate and support the system? Will the cost be affordable?	Increasing operations and support (e.g., resource or environmental) costs. Resiliency of the design to new missions and tasks. Changes in maintenance or logistics strategy/needs.
Sustainability	Will the system provide sustainable future value?	Availability of future resources and impact on the natural environment.

INCOSE SEH original table created by Jackson and Parnell derived from Parnell (2016). Usage per the INCOSE Notices page. All other rights reserved.

Decisions Under Uncertainty

As can be seen from Table 1.4, uncertainties impact every SE decision process. Taking decisions before having enough knowledge is potentially very risky. Key decisions that have a strong impact on the solution require reducing uncertainty by closing the knowledge gap to an appropriate level. However, SE practitioners must be able to make decisions under uncertainty and should record a corresponding risk with those decisions (see Sections 2.3.4.3 and 2.3.4.4).

表 1.4　系统不确定性来源

不确定性来源	主要问题	潜在不确定性
业务	政治、经济、劳动力、社会、技术、环境、法律或其他因素是否会对业务环境产生不利影响？	政治观点的变化（如选举）。经济混乱（如经济衰退）。全球中断（如供应链）。法律法规的变化。颠覆性技术。负面宣传。
市场	如果产品或服务有效，会有市场吗？	用户和消费者的需求。源自竞争对手（质量和价格）和敌方（如黑客和恐怖分子）的威胁。利益相关方的持续支持。
管理	组织是否拥有管理重要系统的人员、流程和文化？	组织文化。系统工程管理经验和专业知识。成熟的基线流程（技术、成本、进度）。可靠的成本估算流程。
性能（技术的）	产品或服务能否达到所需的预期性能？	在动态环境中确定未来需求。了解技术基线。满足性能需求的技术成熟度。充分的建模、仿真、测试和评估能力，以预测和评估性能。
进度	提供产品或服务的系统能否按时交付？	支持使用所需的使能系统的可用性。开发过程中的并行。不确定事件对进度的影响。解决技术和成本风险所需的时间和预算。
开发和生产成本	能否在预算范围内交付系统？成本是否可以承受？	任务的变化。技术成熟度。硬件和软件开发流程。工业/供应链能力。生产设施能力和流程。
运行和支持成本	所有者是否能够负担该系统的运行和支持？成本是否可以承受？	运行和支持（如资源或环境的）成本的增加。设计对新任务和工作的适应能力。维护或后勤战略/需要的变化。
可持续性	该系统能否提供可持续的未来价值？	未来资源的可用性和对自然环境的影响。

INCOSE SEH 原始表由 Jackson 和 Parnell 根据 Parnell（2016）创建。根据 INCOSE 通知页使用。版权所有。

不确定性下的决策

从表 1.4 中可以看出，不确定性影响每个系统工程决策流程。在拥有足够的知识之前做出决策可能有很大的风险。对解决方案有重大影响的关键决策需要通过将知识差距缩小到适当的水平来减少不确定性。然而，系统工程实践者必须能够在不确定的情况下做出决策，并应记录这些决策的相应风险（见 2.3.4.3 节和 2.3.4.4 节）。

SYSTEMS ENGINEERING INTRODUCTION

1.4.2 Cognitive Bias

SE practitioners need to obtain information from stakeholders throughout the system life cycle. SE practitioners and stakeholders (individual or groups) are subject to cognitive biases when interpreting uncertain information. The best defense from cognitive biases is understanding what they are and how they can be avoided and setting up organizational projects to obtain unbiased assessments. Cognitive biases are mental errors in judgment under uncertainty caused by our simplified information processing strategies (sometimes called heuristics) and are consistent and predictable (Tversky and Kahneman, 1974). There are many lists of cognitive biases, including one that lists 50 sources (Hallman, 2022). Cognitive biases can affect both individual and teams of SE practitioners (McDermott, et al., 2020). Cognitive biases can contribute to incidents, failures, or disasters as a result of distorted decision making and can lead to undesirable outcomes. Cognitive biases are included in a field called Behavioral Decision-Making. Table 1.5 lists some of the most common cognitive biases.

For major systems decisions, more formal methods are required to avoid cognitive biases. Both Tversky and Kahneman (1974) and Thaler and Sunstein (2008) describe mitigation methods suitable to different environments. The most effective methods are external group methods. For example, NASA (2003) recommends the Independent Technical Authority (ITA) to warn decision makers of the potential for failure. The ITA must be both financially and organizationally independent of the project manager. Another method, adopted by the aviation industry, is called the Crew Resource Management (CRM) method. With the CRM method, all crew members, including the co-pilot, are responsible for warning the pilot of imminent danger.

1.4.3 Systems Engineering Principles

SE is a relatively young discipline. The emergence of a set of SE principles has occurred over the past 30 years within the discipline. In reviewing various published SE principles, a set of criteria emerged for SE principles. SE principles cover broad application within the practice; they are not constrained to a particular system type, to the system development or operational context, or to a particular life cycle stage. SE principles transcend these system characteristics and inform a worldview of the discipline. Thus, a SE principle:

- transcends a particular life cycle model or stage,
- transcends system types,

1.4.2 认知偏差

系统工程实践者需要在整个系统生命周期中从利益相关方处获取信息。系统工程实践者和利益相关方（个体或团体）在理解不确定信息时会遇到认知偏差。防止认知偏差的最好方法是了解认知偏差是什么以及如何避免它们，并设立组织项目以获得无偏评估。认知偏差是指由于我们简化的信息处理策略（有时被称为启发式方法）导致的在不确定性条件下做出的判断中的认知错误，这样的错误是一致的和可预测的（Tversky 和 Kahneman，1974）。有关认知偏差的列表有很多，其中一个列出了 50 个来源（Hallman，2022）。认知偏差会影响系统工程实践者的个体和团队（McDermott 等，2020）。认知偏差会导致扭曲的决策过程进而造成意外、失败或灾难，导致不想要的结果。认知偏差是行为决策领域中的概念。表 1.5 列出了一些最常见的认知偏差。

对于主要的系统决策，需要更多的形式化的方法来避免认知偏差。Tversky 和 Kahneman（1974）以及 Thaler 和 Sunstein（2008）都描述了适合不同环境的避免认知偏差的方法。最有效的方法是外部群体方法。例如，NASA（2003）建议利用独立技术权威（ITA）来提醒决策者失败的可能性。ITA 必须在财务和组织上独立于项目经理。航空业采用的方法是机组资源管理（CRM）方法。使用 CRM 方法，包括副驾驶在内的所有机组成员都有职责向飞行员发出关于即将发生的危险的警告。

1.4.3 系统工程原则

系统工程是一门相对年轻的学科。在过去的 30 年里，学科内出现了一系列系统工程的原则。在回顾各种已发布的系统工程原则时，浮现出了一套系统工程原则的标准。系统工程原则在实践中的广泛应用；不局限于特定的系统类型，不局限于系统的开发或运行场景，也不局限于特定生命周期阶段。系统工程原则超越了这些系统特征，并形成了系统工程学科的世界观。因此，系统工程原则：

- 超越特定的生命周期模型或阶段；
- 超越系统类型；

SYSTEMS ENGINEERING INTRODUCTION

- transcends a system context,
- informs a world view on SE,
- is not a "how to" statement,
- is supported by literature or widely accepted by the community (i.e., has proven successful in practice across multiple organizations and multiple system types),
- is focused, concise, and clearly worded.

SE principles are a form of guidance proposition which provide guidance in application of the SE processes and a basis for the advancement of SE. SE has many kinds of guidance propositions that can be classified by their sources, e.g., heuristics (derived from practical experience as discussed in Section 1.4.4), conventions (derived from social agreements), values (derived from cultural perspectives), and models (based on theoretical mechanisms). Although these all support purposeful judgment or action in a context, they can vary greatly in scope, authority, and conferred capability. They can all be refined, and as they mature, they gain in their scope, authority, and capability, while the set becomes more compact. A key moment in their evolution occurs with gaining insight into why they work, at which point they become principles. Principles can have their origins associated in referring to them as "heuristic principles," "social principles," "cultural principles," and "scientific principles," although in practice it is usually sufficient to just refer to them as SE principles. SE principles are derived from principles of these various origins providing a diverse set of transcendent principles based on both practice and theory.

TABLE 1.5 Common cognitive biases

Cognitive Bias	Description	Implication for the SE Practitioner.
Framing	How we ask the question or describe the decision matters.	Carefully word questions and problem description to avoid influencing the response.
Representativeness	People draw conclusions based on representative characteristics and often ignore relevant facts or the base rates.	Discuss the relevant facts and data before requesting a judgment about an uncertainty or risk. Use Bayes Law to update our beliefs after we receive new data. Teams that reflect Diversity, Equity, and Inclusion principles can help reduce the bias for the team (see Section 5.2).
Availability	We place too much weight on vivid, striking, and recent events.	Ask about the relevant facts and data before requesting a judgment about an uncertainty or risk. Design systems to provide the relevant data.

- 超越系统背景环境；

- 描述系统工程的世界观；

- 不是关于"如何做"的陈述；

- 有文献支持或被系统工程界广泛接受（即在多个组织和多种系统的实践中被证明是成功的）；

- 重点突出、简洁、措辞清晰。

系统工程原则以一种指导性命题的形式，为系统工程流程的应用提供指导，并为系统工程的发展奠定基础。系统工程有很多指导性命题，可以根据其来源进行分类，例如启发式（源自实践经验，正如1.4.4节所述）、约定（源自社会协议）、价值观（源自文化视角）和模型（基于理论机制）。虽然这些都支持在背景环境中有目的的判断或行动，但它们在范围、权威和赋予的能力上可以有很大差异。它们都可以被细化，随着它们的成熟，它们的范围、权威和能力都会增加，同时这些原则的集合将变得更加精简。它们演进中的关键点是深入了解它们为什么起作用，它们在哪个点上可以成为原则。原则可以结合它们的来源将其称为"启发式原则"、"社会原则"、"文化原则"和"科学原则"，然而在实践中，通常仅将其称为系统工程原则就足够了。系统工程原则具有多种的来源，提供了一套基于实践和理论的多样的卓越原则。

表 1.5　常见的认知偏差

认知偏差	描述	对系统工程实践者的启示
框定	我们如何提出问题或描述决策很重要。	仔细措辞问题和问题描述，避免影响回答。
代表性	人们根据具有代表性的特征得出结论，往往忽略了相关事实或基比率。	在要求对不确定性或风险做出判断之前，先讨论相关事实和数据。在收到新数据后，使用贝叶斯定律更新我们的观点。体现多元化、公平和包容原则的团队有助于减少团队的偏差（见5.2节）。
可用性	我们过于看重生动的、引人注目的近期事件。	在要求对不确定性或风险做出判断之前，询问相关事实和数据。设计提供相关数据的系统。

SYSTEMS ENGINEERING INTRODUCTION

(Continued)

Cognitive Bias	Description	Implication for the SE Practitioner.
Anchoring	The initial estimate affects the final estimates.	Never begin by asking about the expected outcome. Instead obtain information about the worst or best outcomes first to understand the range of outcomes.
Motivational	When making probability judgments, people have incentives to provide estimates that will benefit themselves	Understand the potential bias of an individual providing an assessment. For example, a technology developer has an incentive to overestimate technology readiness if a more conservative estimate could result in loss of funding.
Optimism	We overestimate the likelihood of good outcomes and underestimate the likelihood bad outcomes.	Seek data on similar bad outcomes. Obtain assessments from experts not involved in the decision.
Confirmation	We seek or put more weight on data that confirms our beliefs.	Actively seek data that would disprove our current belief in all tests and evaluations.
Group Think	A group of people make irrational or unsound decisions to suppress dissent and maintain group harmony.	Seek dissenting opinions inside the group and seek outside assessments.
Authority	We trust and are more often influenced by the opinions of people in positions of authority	Assess the opinion independent of the source.
Rankism	Assumption that person of higher rank is always correct in decisions	Seek to determine correct decision

INCOSE SEH original table created by Jackson and Parnell. Usage per the INCOSE Notices page. All other rights reserved.

In addition, SE principles differ from systems principles in important ways (Watson, et al., 2019). System principles address the behavior and properties of all kinds of systems, looking at the scientific basis for a system and characterizing this basis in a system context via specialized instances of a general set of system principles. SE principles build on systems principles that are general for all kinds of systems (Rousseau, 2018) (Watson, 2020) and for all kinds of human activity systems (Senge, 1990) (Calvo-Amodio and Rousseau, 2019).

（续）

认知偏差	描述	对系统工程实践者的启示
锚定	初步估计会影响最终估计。	切忌一开始就询问预期结果。而是先获取最坏或最好结果的信息，以了解结果的范围。
动机的	在进行概率判断时，人们有动机提供对自己有利的估计值。	了解提供评估的个人可能存在的偏差。例如，如果技术准备度的评估过于保守可能导致资金损失，技术开发人员就有动机进行高估。
乐观	我们高估了好结果的可能性，低估了不好结果的可能性。	查找类似不好结果的数据。获取未参与决策的专家的评估意见。
确认	我们寻求或更看重能证实我们观点的数据。	在所有测试和评估中，积极寻求能够推翻我们当前观点的数据。
团队思考	一群人做出不合理或不稳妥的决策，以压制分歧和维持群体和谐。	在团队内部征求不同意见，并寻求外部评估。
权威	我们更信任权威人士的意见，也更容易受其影响。	独立于信息来源评估意见。
等级主义	假设上级的决策总是正确的。	力求做出正确的决策。

INCOSE SEH 原始表由 Jackson 和 Parnell 创建。根据 INCOSE 通知页使用。版权所有。

此外，系统工程原则在一些重要方面不同于系统原理（Watson 等，2019）。系统原理阐述了各种系统的行为和属性，研究系统的科学基础，并通过系统原理的一般集合的特殊实例在系统背景环境中描述了该基础。系统工程原则建立在系统原理的基础上，这样的系统原理适用于各种系统（Rousseau，2018）（Watson，2020）和各种人类活动系统（Senge，1990）（Calvo-Amodio 和 Rousseau，2019）。

SYSTEMS ENGINEERING INTRODUCTION

INCOSE compiled an early list of principles consisting of 8 principles and 61 subprinciples in 1993 (Defoe, 1993). These early principles were important considerations recognized in practice for the success of system developments and ultimately became the basis for the SE processes. These early principles were focused on particular aspects of the SE process and particular life cycle stages. The INCOSE work on SE principles considered these earlier sources and compiled a set of SE principles that are transcendent. The INCOSE SE Principles (2022) documents each SE principle with a description, evidence that supports the principle (e.g., observable evidence of the application, proof from scientific evidence), and implications in SE practice for application of the principle. There are presently 15 SE principles and 20 subprinciples as shown in Table 1.6.

TABLE 1.6 SE principles and subprinciples

---

1 SE in application is specific to stakeholder needs, solution space, resulting system solution(s), and context throughout the system life cycle.

2 SE has a holistic system view that includes the system elements and the interactions amongst themselves, the enabling systems, and the system environment.

3 SE influences and is influenced by internal and external resources, and political, economic, social, technological, environmental, and legal factors.

4 Both policy and law must be properly understood to not over-constrain or under-constrain the system implementation.

5 The real system is the perfect representation of the system.

6 A focus of SE is a progressively deeper understanding of the interactions, sensitivities, and behaviors of the system, stakeholder needs, and its operational environment.

Sub-Principle 6(a): Mission context is defined based on the understanding of the stakeholder needs and constraints

Sub-Principle 6(b): Requirements and models reflect the understanding of the system

Sub-Principle 6(c): Requirements are specific, agreed to preferences within the developing organization

Sub-Principle 6(d): Requirements and system design are progressively elaborated as the development progresses

Sub-Principle 6(e): Modeling of systems must account for system interactions and couplings

Sub-Principle 6(f): SE achieves an understanding of all the system functions and interactions in the operational environment

Sub-Principle 6(g): SE achieves an understanding of the system's value to the system stakeholders

Sub-Principle 6(h): Understanding of the system degrades during operations if system understanding is not maintained

7 Stakeholder needs can change and must be accounted for over the system life cycle.

8 SE addresses stakeholder needs, taking into consideration budget, schedule, and technical needs, along with other expectations and constraints.

Sub-Principle 8(a): SE seeks a best balance of functions and interactions within the system budget, schedule, technical, and other expectations and constraints

9 SE decisions are made under uncertainty accounting for risk.

10 Decision quality depends on knowledge of the system, enabling system(s), and interoperating system(s) present in the decision making process.

1993 年，INCOSE 编制了一份早期原则清单，其中包括 8 项原则和 61 项次级原则（Defoe，1993）。这些早期原则是系统开发成功的重要考虑因素，最终成为系统工程流程的基础。这些早期原则侧重于系统工程的特定方面和特定的生命周期阶段。INCOSE 在这些早期原则的基础上持续研究，进而编制了一套卓越的系统工程原则。INCOSE 系统工程原则（2022）记录了每项系统工程原则，包括描述、原则的支撑证据（例如，应用的可观察证据、来自科学证据的证明），以及系统工程实践中应用原则带来的影响。如表 1.6 所示，目前有 15 个系统工程原则和 20 个次级原则。

表 1.6 系统工程原则和次级原则

1 系统工程在应用中关注系统全生命周期中的利益相关方的需要、解决方案空间、所产生的系统解决方案，以及系统背景环境。

2 系统工程具有整体系统观，包括系统要素及其之间的相互作用、使能系统和系统环境。

3 系统工程与内部和外部资源，政治、经济、社会、技术、环境和法律因素产生相互影响。

4 必须正确理解政策和法律，以免对系统的实施造成过多或过少的限制。

5 真实系统是系统的完美呈现。

6 系统工程的一个重点是逐步加深对系统的相互作用、敏感性和系统行为、利益相关方的需要及其运行环境的理解。

次级原则 6（a）：在了解利益相关方的需要和约束的基础上确定任务背景环境

次级原则 6（b）：需求和模型反映对系统的理解

次级原则 6（c）：需求是具体的，体现开发组织内部的一致性偏好

次级原则 6（d）：需求和系统设计随着开发工作的进行而逐步完善

次级原则 6（e）：系统建模必须考虑到系统的相互作用和耦合作用

次级原则 6（f）：系统工程实现对运行环境中的所有系统功能和相互作用的理解

次级原则 6（g）：系统工程实现对系统对利益相关方的价值的理解

次级原则 6（h）：如果不保持对系统的了解，在运行期间对系统的了解就会减少

7 利益相关方的需要会发生变化，必须在系统生命周期内加以考虑。

8 系统工程在考虑预算、进度和技术需要以及其他期望和限制的情况下，满足利益相关方的需要。

次级原则 8（a）：系统工程在系统预算、进度、技术及其他预期和限制条件的范围内，寻求功能和交互的最佳平衡

9 系统工程在考虑风险的不确定情况下做出决策。

10 决策质量取决于决策过程中对系统、使能系统和互操作系统的了解。

SYSTEMS ENGINEERING INTRODUCTION

(Continued)

11 SE spans the entire system life cycle.
   Sub-Principle 11(a): SE obtains an understanding of the system
   Sub-Principle 11(b): SE defines the mission context (system application)
   Sub-Principle 11(c): SE models the system
   Sub-Principle 11(d): SE designs and analyzes the system
   Sub-Principle 11(e): SE tests the system
   Sub-Principle 11(f): SE supports the production of the system
   Sub-Principle 11(g): SE supports operations, maintenance, and retirement
12 Complex systems are engineered by complex organizations.
13 SE integrates engineering and scientific disciplines in an effective manner.
14 SE is responsible for managing the discipline interactions within the organization.
15 SE is based on a middle range set of theories.
   Sub-Principle 15 (a): SE has a systems theory basis
   Sub-Principle 15 (b): SE has a physical logical basis specific to the system
   Sub-Principle 15 (c): SE has a mathematical basis
   Sub-Principle 15 (d): SE has a sociological basis specific to the organization

From INCOSE SE Principles (2022). Usage per the INCOSE Notices page. All other rights reserved.

20 These principles provide a start in defining a transcendent disciplinary basis for SE. Application of the principles aids in determining a system life cycle model, implementing SE processes, and defining organizational constructs to help the SE practitioner successfully develop and sustain the SoI.

1.4.4 Systems Engineering Heuristics

Summary Heuristics provide a way for an established profession to pass on its accumulated wisdom. This allows practitioners to gain insights from what has been found to work well in the past, and apply the lessons learned. Heuristics usually take the form of short expressions in natural language. These can be memorable phrases encapsulating shortcuts, "rules of thumb," or "words of the wise," giving general guidelines on professional conduct or rules, advice, or guidelines on how to act under specific circumstances. Heuristics usually do not express all there is to know, yet they can act as a useful entry point for learning more. At their best, heuristics can act as aids to decision making, value judgments, and assessments.

Interest in SE heuristics currently centers on their use in two contexts: (1) encapsulating engineering knowledge in an accessible form, where the underlying practice is widely accepted and the underlying science understood, and (2) overcoming the limitations of more analytical approaches, where the science is still of limited use. This is especially applicable as we extend the practice of SE to providing solutions to inherently complex, unbounded, ill-structured, or very difficult problems.

（续）

11 系统工程跨越整个系统生命周期。
次级原则 11（a）：系统工程取得对系统的了解
次级原则 11（b）：系统工程确定任务背景环境（系统应用）
次级原则 11（c）：系统工程对系统建模
次级原则 11（d）：系统工程设计和分析系统
次级原则 11（e）：系统工程测试系统
次级原则 11（f）：系统工程支持系统的生产
次级原则 11（g）：系统工程支持运行、维护和退役
12 复杂的系统由复杂的组织来实现。
13 系统工程以有效的方式整合工程和科学学科。
14 系统工程负责管理组织内的学科交互。
15 系统工程基于一套中等范围的理论集合。
次级原则 15（a）：系统工程基于系统理论
次级原则 15（b）：系统工程以特定系统的物理逻辑为基础
次级原则 15（c）：系统工程具有数学基础
次级原则 15（d）：系统工程以特定组织的社会学为基础

源自 INCOSE 系统工程原则（2022）。根据 INCOSE 通知页使用。版权所有。

这些原则为定义系统工程的跨学科基础提供了一个起点。这些原则的应用有助于确定系统生命周期模型，实施系统工程流程，并定义组织结构，以帮助系统工程实践者成功开发和维持 SoI。

1.4.4 系统工程启发式方法

总结 启发式方法为一个已确立的专业提供了一种传递其积累的智慧的方式。这使得实践者能够从过去所发现的行之有效的方法中获得见解，并应用所学到的经验教训。启发式方法通常采用自然语言中的简短表达形式。它们通过简化形成容易记忆的短语，它们可以是"经验法则"或"智者之言"，给出专业行为的一般指导原则或规则、建议或在特定情况下如何行动的指导原则。启发式方法通常不能表达所有需要知道的内容，但它们可以作为一个继续学习的切入点。在最好的情况下，启发式方法可以作为决策、价值判断和评估的辅助手段。

目前，人们对系统工程启发式方法的兴趣集中在两种应用场景：（1）将广泛接受的实践经验和已被理解的科学原理封装成便于应用的工程知识；（2）在科学应用受限的情况下，用来克服解析方法带来的限制。这在我们将系统工程的实践推广到对固有复杂的、无边界的、结构不稳定的和十分复杂的问题的求解时，尤其有效。

SYSTEMS ENGINEERING INTRODUCTION

Background Engineering first emerged as a series of skills acquired while transforming the ancient world, principally through buildings, cities, infrastructure, and machines of war. Since then, mankind has sought to capture the knowledge of "how to" to allow each generation to learn from its predecessors, enabling more complex structures to be built with increasing confidence while avoiding repeated real-world failures. For example, early cathedral builders encapsulated their knowledge in a small number of "rules of thumb," such as "maintain a low center of gravity" and "put 80% of the mass in the pillars." Designs were conservative, with large margins. When the design margins were exceeded (e.g., out of a desire to build higher and more impressive structures), a high price was sometimes paid, with the collapse of a roof, a tower, or even a whole building. From such failures, new empirical rules emerged. Much of this took place before the science behind the strength of materials or building secure foundations was understood. Only in recent times have computer simulations revealed the contribution toward certain failures played by such dynamic effects as wind shear on tall structures.

Since then, engineering and applied sciences have co-evolved: with science providing the ability to predict and explain performance of engineered artefacts with greater assurance and engineering developing new and more complex systems, requiring new scientific explanations and driving research agendas. In the modern era, complex and adaptive systems are being built which challenge conventional engineering sciences, and we are turning to social and behavioral sciences, management sciences, and increasingly systems science to deal with some of the new forms of complexity involved and guide the profession accordingly.

Current Use Renewed interest in the application of heuristics to the field of SE stems from the seminal work of Maier and Rechtin (2009), and their book remains the best single published source of such knowledge. Their motivation was to provide guidance for the emerging role of system architect as the person (or team) responsible for coordinating engineering effort toward devising solutions to complex problems and overseeing their implementations. They observed that it was in many cases better to apply heuristics than attempt detailed analysis. The reason for this is the number of variables involved and the complexity of the interactions between stakeholders, internal dynamics of system solutions, and the organizations responsible for their realization. Some examples of SE heuristics are:

- ***Don't assume that the original statement of the problem is necessarily the best, or even the right one.*** This has to be handled with tact and respect for the user, but experience shows that failure to reach mutual understanding early on is a fundamental cause of failure, and strong relationships forged in the course of doing such coordination with stakeholders can pay off when solving more difficult issues which might arise later on.

背景 工程学最初主要是在建筑、城市、基础设施和战争机器等方面改造古代世界时获得的一系列技能。自那时以来，人类一直在寻求获取有关"如何做"的知识，让每一代人都能向上一代学习，从而能够更加自信地建造更复杂的结构，同时避免现实世界中的重复失败。例如，早期的大教堂建造者将他们的知识概括为少量的"经验法则"，如"保持较低的重心"和"将80%的质量放在柱子上"。设计是保守的，预留很大的设计余量。当超出设计余量时（例如，出于建造更高、更令人印象深刻的建筑的愿望），有时会付出高昂的代价，导致屋顶、塔楼甚至整个建筑倒塌。从这些失败中，出现了新的经验规则。很多这样的法则都是在材料强度或建筑安全基础等背后的科学诞生之前就被总结出来了。直到最近，计算机模拟才揭示了风剪切等动态效应对高层建筑某些事故的影响。

从那时起，工程和应用科学共同发展：科学提供了更精准的预测和解释工程制品性能的能力，工程开发了新的、更复杂的系统，需要新的科学解释并推动研究进程。在现代，复杂和自适应系统正在被大量建造出来，这对传统工程科学提出了挑战，我们正在转向使用社会和行为科学、管理科学，以及越来越多的系统科学，以应对所涉及的一些新形式的复杂性，并相应地为同行提供指导。

目前的应用 Maier 和 Rechtin（2009）的开创性工作使人们对系统工程领域启发式方法的应用产生新的兴趣。他们的书仍然是此类知识的最佳的单一来源。他们的动机是为系统架构师这一新兴角色提供指导，系统架构师可以是个人或团队，负责协调工程工作以设计复杂问题的解决方案并监督其实施。他们观察到，在许多情况下，应用启发式方法比尝试开展详细分析更好。原因包括涉及的变量数量过多，与利益相关方的交互过于复杂，系统解决方案内部的变动因素以及负责方案实现的组织。系统工程启发式方法的一些示例包括：

- *不要认为问题的原始陈述必然是最好的，甚至是正确的*。这必须以得体和尊重用户的态度来处理，但经验表明，早期共识达成的失败是造成结果失败的根本原因之一，在与利益相关方协调过程中建立的牢固关系可以在解决以后可能出现的更困难的问题时获得回报。

SYSTEMS ENGINEERING INTRODUCTION

- ***In the early stages of a project, unknowns are a bigger issue than known problems.*** Sometimes developing a clear understanding of the environment, all of the stakeholders, and the ramifications of possible solutions uncovers many unanticipated issues.

- ***Model before build, wherever possible.*** System Science postulates "The only complete model of the system in its environment is the system in its environment," which leads into using evolutionary life cycles, rapid deployment of prototypes, agile life cycles, and so on. This heuristic opens a door into twenty-first-century systems.

A repository of heuristics can act as a knowledge base, especially if media (such as video clips or training materials) or even interactive media (to encourage discussion and feedback) are included. A heuristics repository should link to other established knowledge sources and be tagged with other metadata to allow flexible retrieval. It should be organized to reflect accepted areas of SE competency and allow users to assemble a personal set of heuristics most meaningful to them, being relevant to their professional or personal sphere of activity.

1.5 SYSTEM SCIENCE AND SYSTEMS THINKING

This section considers the nature and relationship between systems science and systems thinking and describes how they relate to SE.

Relationship between Systems Science, Systems Thinking, and SE

The association of concepts such as system, boundary, relationships, environment/context, hierarchy, emergence, communication, and control, among others, when interrelated with purpose, gives rise to a *systems worldview* (Rousseau, et al., 2018). Interrelating concepts with purpose changes how we investigate and reason about things, producing systems thinking. Systems thinking enables us to recognize systems patterns across different phenomena, problem contexts, and disciplines. Studying these patterns has produced the systems sciences of General System Theory, Cybernetics, and Complexity Theory and their related systems methodologies, models, and methods. The application of systems thinking and systems science concepts, principles, methodologies, models, and methods in engineering is one of the bases for the practice of SE. Applying SE, and reflecting on the results, help us improve systems science and systems thinking, further enhancing our ability to design and intervene in complex systems—a virtuous cycle. Through this virtuous cycle, we develop principles to better our SE applications (Rousseau, et al., 2022).

- ***在项目的早期阶段，比已知的问题更棘手的是那些未知的事情。*** 有时，对环境、所有利益相关方以及可能的解决方案的后果建立清晰的理解，就会发现许多意想不到的问题。
- ***尽量在建造之前建模。*** 系统科学假设"系统在其环境中的唯一完整模型是其环境中的系统"，这指向进化式生命周期、快速部署的原型、敏捷的生命周期等的使用。这种启发式方法打开了进入 21 世纪系统的大门。

启发式方法库，特别是如果包括媒体（如视频剪辑或培训材料）甚至互动媒体（以鼓励讨论和反馈）的话可以作为一个知识库。启发式方法库应该链接到其他已建立的知识源，并使用其他元数据进行标记，以允许灵活的检索。它的组织应反映系统工程胜任力的公认领域，并允许用户收集对他们最有意义的个人启发式方法集，以使其与他们的职业或个人兴趣相关联。

1.5 系统科学和系统思维

本节讨论系统科学和系统思维的本质和它们之间的关系，并描述了它们如何与系统工程相关联。

系统科学、系统思维和系统工程之间的关系

当与目的相关时，系统、边界、关系、环境/背景环境、层级结构、涌现性、通信和控制以及其他的一些概念联合起来产生了系统世界观（Rousseau 等，2018）。将概念与目的关联起来改变了我们对事物的研究和推理方式，产生了系统思维。系统思维使我们能够跨越不同现象、问题背景和学科从而识别系统的模式。研究这些模式产生了一般系统论、控制论和复杂性理论等系统科学及其相关的系统方法论、模型和方法。系统思维和系统科学概念、原理、方法论、模型和方法在工程中的应用是系统工程实践的基础之一。应用系统工程并反思其结果，有助于我们改进系统科学和系统思维，进一步增强我们设计和干预复杂系统的能力，这是一个良性循环。通过这一良性循环，我们开发原则，以更好地应用系统工程（Rousseau 等，2022）。

SYSTEMS ENGINEERING INTRODUCTION

Figure 1.8 depicts this virtuous cycle as a multifaceted and purposeful activity to deliver elegant solutions to complex problems, supported by principles that guide why, what, and how we do SE. To connect our purpose to our actions, we adopt a systemic approach, because complexity and elegance are both systems phenomena. Our systemic approach is of course guided by our systems principles. The kinds and relationships of principles, as well as how they inform and are informed by SE practice, is depicted in Figure 1.8. We select and organize these based on our intentions as expressed by our motivational principles. We use our transdisciplinary principles to select and organize our technique principles. In this way, the systemic relationships between our principles support how our principles guide the systemic relationships between our purpose, approach, and practice. The systemic roles our principles play in our discipline thus support the systematic evolution of our value in society.

The success of SE applications reinforces the credibility of the systems worldview which in turn enhances the SE practitioner's ability to conceptualize why a solution is needed, how a solution can be conceptualized, and what tools and/or methods to use to solve complex problems and achieve elegant solutions.

Systems Science

Questions about the nature of systems, organization, and complexity are not specific to the modern age. As Warfield (2006) put it:

Virtually every important concept that backs up the key ideas emergent in systems literature is found in ancient literature and in the centuries that follow.

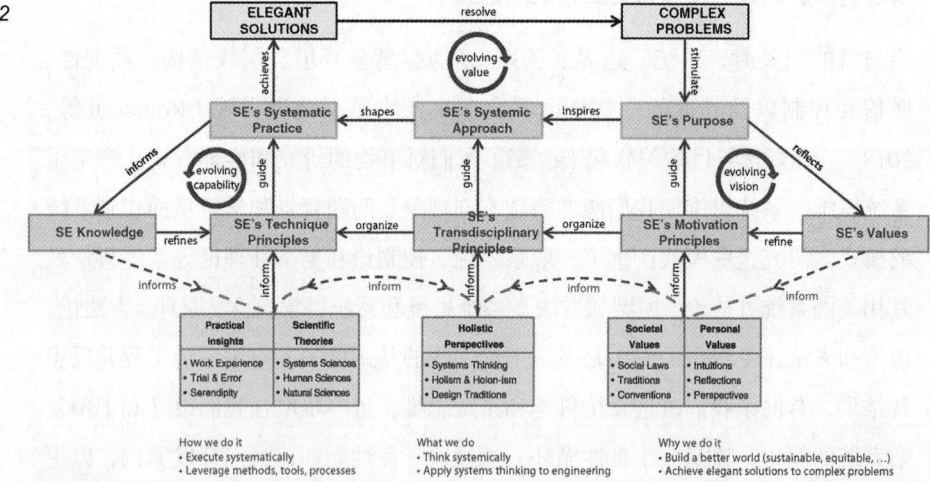

FIGURE 1.8 An architectural framework for the evolving the SE discipline. From Rousseau, et al. (2022). Used with permission. All other rights reserved.

系统工程介绍

图 1.8 将这种良性周期描述为一种多方面的、有目的的活动，旨在为复杂的问题提供优雅的解决方案，并为我们为什么、做什么和如何开展系统工程提供原则性指导。为了将我们的目标与我们的行动联系起来，我们采用了系统性方法，因为复杂性和优雅都是系统的现象。当然，我们的系统性方法是以我们的系统原则为指导的。图 1.8 描述了原则的种类和关系，以及它们如何影响系统工程和如何被系统工程所影响。我们根据我们的动机原则所表达的意图来选择和组织这些内容。我们使用跨学科的原则来选择和组织我们的技术原则。这样，我们的原则之间的系统性关系支持我们的原则如何指导我们的目标、实施方法和实践之间的系统性关系。因此，我们的原则在我们的学科中所起的系统性作用支持了我们的社会价值的系统性演变。

系统工程应用的成功增强了系统世界观的可信性，进而增强了系统工程实践者的能力，以构思为什么需要解决方案，如何构思解决方案，以及使用什么工具和/或方法来解决复杂问题并获得优雅的解决方案。

系统科学

关于系统、组织本质和复杂性本质的问题并不是现代所特有的。正如 Warfield（2006）所言：

事实上，用来证实系统文献中出现的关键观点的每一个重要概念，在古代及其后续几个世纪中的文献中都能找到。

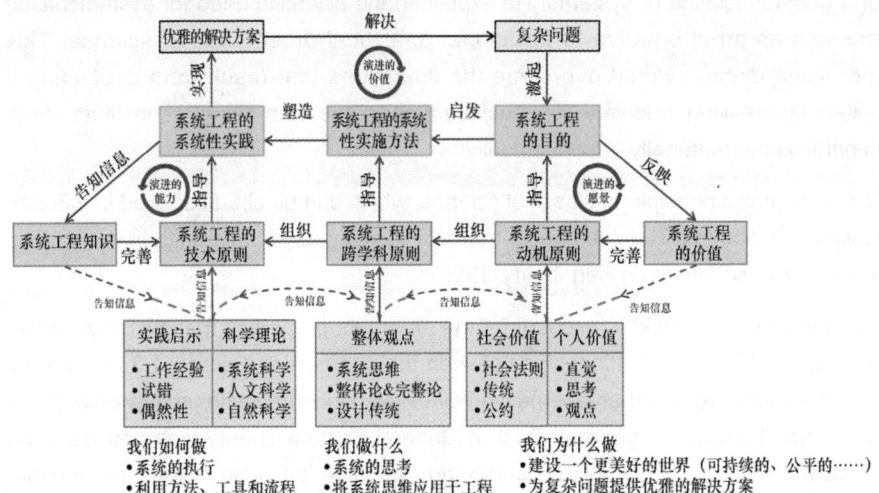

图 1.8 一个系统工程学科演进的架构框架。源自 Rousseau 等（2022）。经许可后使用。版权所有。

SYSTEMS ENGINEERING INTRODUCTION

Systems science can be defined as a transdisciplinary approach interested in understanding all aspects of systems with the goals of (1) identifying, exploring, and understanding patterns of behavior crossing disciplinary fields and areas of application, and (2) establishing a general theory applicable to all types of systems whether physical, natural, engineered, or social. Attempts to establish a systems science have taken on both reductionist and holistic forms, and both are valuable. For instance, a clock is a system, but its workings can be explained through reductionism. On the other hand, a holistic approach helps us understand why we need clocks, how clocks exist (operate/sustain/degrade) in their environment throughout their life cycle, and how the esthetics of their design evolve over time. Both the reductionist and the holistic approaches to explanation involve systemic arguments but each starts from different directions—bottom-up and outside-in. Complexity Theory has had some success developing a science of systems using a reductionist approach. Agent-based modeling, pioneered at the Santa Fe Institute, works from the "bottom-up" and seeks to explain the behavior of whole systems in terms of the rules of interaction of the "agents" that constitute the system.

Where reductionist (traditional) methods prove unsuccessful, systems science relies on the holistic approach. A holistic approach is adept at connecting and contextualizing systems, system elements, and their environments to understand difficult to explain patterns of organized complexity. This was the approach taken by Ludwig von Bertalanffy in developing General System Theory and Norbert Wiener in developing Cybernetics. The biologist von Bertalanffy was one of the first to argue for a general science of systems. He explained the scientific need for systemsbased research as an alternative to traditional analytical procedures in science. This alternative method would overcome the limitations that result from explaining a system by breaking it down to its constituent parts and then being reconstituted from its parts, either materially or conceptually:

This is the basic principle of classical science, which can be circumscribed in different ways: resolution into isolable causal trains or seeking for atomic units in the various fields of science, etc. (von Bertalanffy, 1969)

This makes it impossible to account for the emergent properties that systems display as a result of the interrelationships between their parts (see Section 1.3.2). Instead, von Bertalanffy promoted an alternative worldview concerned with the laws that apply to systems behavior in general. Such a General System Theory was possible, von Bertalanffy thought, and would be particularly valuable, because of the large number of parallelisms that appear across systems independent of the types and quantities of system elements in the systems:

*系统科学*可以定义为一种跨学科的实施方法，旨在理解系统的所有方面，其目标是：（1）识别、探索和理解跨学科领域和应用领域的行为模式；（2）建立适用于所有系统类型的一般理论，无论是物理的、自然的、工程的还是社会的系统。建立系统科学的尝试既有还原论的形式，也有整体论的形式，两者都很有价值。例如，时钟是一个系统，但它的工作原理可以用还原论来解释。另一方面，整体论的方法有助于我们理解为什么我们需要时钟，时钟在其整个生命周期的环境中是如何存在的（运行/维持/降级），以及设计的美学是如何随着时间的推移而演变的。还原论和整体论的方法都涉及系统性的争论，但每一种都从不同的方向开始，自下而上和自外而内。复杂性理论已经成功地运用还原论的方法发展了一门系统的科学。圣达菲学院首创的基于代理的建模从"自下而上"开始，试图通过构成系统的代理的交互规则来解释整个系统的行为。

当还原论（传统）方法被证明不成功时，系统科学依赖于整体论方法。整体论方法擅长将系统、系统元素及其环境连接起来并加以语境化，以理解难以解释的有组织复杂性模式。这是 Ludwig von Bertalanffy 发展一般系统理论和 Norbert Wiener 发展控制论时使用的方法。生物学家 von Bertalanfy 是最早主张一般系统科学的人之一。他解释了基于系统的研究作为传统科学分析方法替代的科学需要。这种替代方法无论是从物质上还是从概念上都将克服通过将系统分解为组成部分然后再组合起来解释系统的局限性：

这是经典科学的基本原则，可以以不同的方式加以限定：分解成可孤立的因果链，或在各个科学领域寻找原子单位等（von Bertalanffy，1969）。

这使得我们无法解释系统因其各部分之间的相互关系而展现的涌现属性（见 1.3.2 节）。相反，von Bertalanffy 提出了另一种与适用于系统行为的一般规律有关的世界观。von Bertalanffy 认为，一般系统论是可能的，而且将特别有价值，因为系统中出现了大量独立于系统类型和系统中元素数量的类似的现象：

SYSTEMS ENGINEERING INTRODUCTION

Thus, there exist models, principles, and laws that apply to generalized systems or their subclasses, irrespective of their particular kind, the nature of their component elements, and the relations or 'forces' between them. It seems legitimate to ask for a theory, not of systems of a more or less special kind, but of universal principles applying to systems in general. In this way we postulate a new discipline called General System Theory. (von Bertalanffy, 1971)

The study of general systems was to focus on such principles as:

growth, regulation, hierarchical order, equifinality, progressive differentiation, progressive mechanization, progressive centralization, closed and open systems, competition, evolution toward higher organization, teleology, and goal-directedness. (Hammond, 2003)

The systems sciences, including General Systems Theory, Cybernetics, and Complexity Theory, seek to provide key foundational concepts to build a common language and intellectual foundations to make rigorous systems theories and tools accessible to practitioners. Where they succeed, they can serve as the foundation for a meta-discipline such as SE, transdisciplinary in nature, that unifies scientific and engineering practices. SE, informed by systems science, would be in a powerful position to enhance its theory and practice in ways that would make it applicable to the most complex of systems.

Finally, identifying SE's principles and heuristics can offer a useful approach to categorize systems-related knowledge and to focus research efforts. Systems principles and heuristics are special cases of guiding propositions. A guiding proposition provides guidance for purposeful judgment or action in a context and offers a wider perspective to that of a principle or a heuristic. Guiding propositions vary in (1) scope—the range of SE contexts they work, (2) authority—how compelling they are, and (3) capability—how predictable the outcomes of applying them are (Rousseau, et al., 2022). Readers can consult details on SE Principles in Section 1.4.3 and details on SE Heuristics in Section 1.4.4.

Systems Thinking Divergences

Systems thinking is a key enabler of SE. It is one of the core competencies defined in INCOSE SE Competency Framework (2018). Systems thinking applies the properties, concepts, and principles of systems to the given situation as a framework for curiosity—to get insight and understanding about the situation.

因此，存在适用于一般系统或其子类的模型、原则和定律，而不管它们的特定类型、组件元素的性质以及它们之间的关系或"力"。提出一种作用于一般系统的普适原则而不是某种特殊的系统理论看上去是合理的。这样，我们建立了一门新的叫作一般系统论的学科。（von Bertalanffy，1971）

一般系统研究的重点是以下原则：

增长、规则、层级结构的秩序、公平性、渐进分化、渐进机械化、渐进集中、封闭和开放系统、竞争、向更高组织的演进、目的论和目标导向。（Hammond，2003）

系统科学，包括一般系统论、控制论和复杂性理论，旨在提供关键的基础概念，以建立共同的语言和知识基础，为实践者提供严谨的系统理论和工具。如果他们成功了，他们可以作为元学科（如系统工程）的基础，这是一门跨学科的学科，将科学和工程实践统一起来。系统工程受系统科学的影响，将处在一个强有力的地位，以加强其理论和实践，使其适用于最复杂的系统。

最后，确定系统工程的原则和启发式方法可以提供一种有用的实施方法来对系统相关知识进行分类并集中研究精力。系统原理和启发式方法是指导性命题的特例。指导性命题为背景环境中有目的的判断或行动提供了指导，并为原则或启发式方法提供了更广阔的视角。指导性命题在以下方面有所不同：（1）范围，它们在系统工程中发挥作用的范围；（2）权威性，它们有多使人信服；（3）能力，应用它们的结果的可预测性有多强（Rousseau 等，2022）。读者可以参考1.4.3 节中关于系统工程原则的详细信息，以及 1.4.4 节中关于系统工程启发式方法的详细信息。

系统思维的差异

系统思维是系统工程的关键使能项。它是 INCOSE 系统工程胜任力框架（2018）中定义的核心胜任力之一。系统思维将系统的属性、概念和原则应用于给定的情况作为一个框架，以获得对情况的洞察和理解。

SYSTEMS ENGINEERING INTRODUCTION

There needs to be a balance between the being systematic with the application of SE processes (as described in Part II) and being systemic, applying systems thinking to drive these processes. As SE practitioners, it is vital to possess the knowledge and skills necessary to perform holistic analysis and guide systemic intervention. Systems thinking lacks a unified definition; however, the following captures the nature of systems thinking and some key ideas:

Systems thinking is a field characterized by a baffling array of methods and approaches. We posit that underlying all, however, are four universal rules called DSRP (distinctions, systems, relationships, and perspectives). We make distinctions between and among things and ideas, each implying the existence of another. We identify systems, which are composed of parts and wholes. We recognize relationships composed of actions and reactions. We take perspectives consisting of a point (from which we see) and a view (that which is seen). (Cabrera, et al., 2015)

24 This definition incorporates aspects of complex problem situations, such as "distinctions" and "perspectives," which it is essential to take account of, but which systems science may never be able to incorporate into its scientific models.

Based on the pioneering work of Ludwig von Bertalanffy in General System Theory, Norbert Wiener in Cybernetics, Jay Forrester in System Dynamics, Peter Checkland in Soft Systems Thinking, and others, a variety of systems methodologies, models, and methods have been formalized to perform systemic analyses and interventions. The SE practitioner can take advantage of this diversity providing they are aware of what the different methodologies, models, and methods do well, and what they are less good at. To assist systems thinking practitioners in selecting the most appropriate systems approaches, Jackson and Keys (1984) offered an initial classification of systems methodologies, the Systems of Systems Methodologies (SOSM), according to their strengths in addressing the complexity of systems and in reconciling divergences among stakeholder viewpoints. Jackson (2019) has since updated the SOSM, to reflect developments in Complexity Theory, by incorporating lessons from the Cynefin framework (Kurtz and Snowden, 2003). This use of different systems approaches in informed combinations, according to their strengths and weaknesses and the nature of the problem situation, is called Critical Systems Thinking (CST) (Jackson, 2003, 2019). CST is a multi-perspectival, multi-methodological, and multi-method approach.

While most of the prominent systems thinking approaches are rooted and/or contextualized within the management sciences, these approaches apply equally to SE practice. This is because the problems faced by SE practitioners, such as the need to incorporate cultural, social, political, and project management perspectives into systems models and other SE tasks, are common to the management sciences.

需要在系统化地应用系统工程流程（如第二部分所述）与系统化地应用系统思维来驱动系统工程流程之间取得平衡。作为系统工程实践者，拥有进行整体分析和指导系统性干预所需的知识和技能至关重要。系统思维缺乏统一的定义；然而，以下内容描述了系统思维的本质和一些关键思想：

系统思维领域包含了一系列令人困惑的方法和实施方法。然而，我们认为，所有这些背后都有四条被称为 DSRP（区分、系统、关系和观点）的普遍规则。事物和思想相互依存，我们对它们进行区分。我们识别由部分和整体组成的系统。我们认识由行动和反应组成的关系。我们采取由视角（我们从哪里看）和视图（我们看到了什么）构成的透视法。（Cabrera 等，2015）

这一定义包含了复杂问题的各个方面，如"区分"和"透视"，这是必须考虑的，但系统科学可能永远无法将其纳入其科学模型。

基于 Ludwig von Bertalanffy 关于一般系统论的、Norbert Wiener 关于控制论的、Jay Forrester 关于系统动力学的、Peter Checkland 关于软系统思维的以及其他的开创性工作，各种各样的系统方法论、模型和方法已成形，以执行系统性分析和干预。系统工程实践者可以利用这种多样性，前提是他们知道不同的方法论、模型和方法擅长做什么，以及不擅长做什么。为了帮助系统思维的实践者选择最合适的系统方法论，Jackson 和 Keys（1984）根据在应对系统复杂性和调解利益相关方视角分歧方面的优势，建立了初始的系统方法论分类体系，即系统方法论体系（SOSM）。自那以后，Jackson（2019）通过吸收 Cynefin 框架（Kurtz 和 Snowden，2003）的经验，更新了系统方法论体系，以反映复杂性理论的发展。根据不同系统实施方法的优缺点和问题情况的性质，综合使用不同的系统方法，这被称为批判性系统思维（CST）（Jackson，2003，2019）。批判性系统思维是一种多视角、多方法论和多方法的实施途径。

虽然大多数重要的系统思维方法都植根于管理科学，和/或在管理科学中讨论，但这些方法同样适用于系统工程实践。这是因为系统工程实践者面临的问题和管理科学面临的问题是相同的，如需要将文化、社会、政治和项目管理视角纳入系统模型和其他系统工程任务中。

SYSTEMS ENGINEERING INTRODUCTION

According to Jackson (2019), systems methodologies translate hypotheses about the nature of problem situations, and how they can be improved, into practical action. There are a number of systems methodologies available, for example, system dynamics, the viable system model, soft systems methodology, and critical systems heuristics. Each is based upon different assumptions about the world and how best to intervene in it. Together, these methodologies can recognize and respond to the range of issues encountered during the exploration of complex problem situations. These systems approaches can then be used, individually or in combination, in the problem situation. When the systems approaches are used in combination, the weighting of each system approach in the hybrid solution will be tailored based on the technical, organizational, cultural, and political factors within the organization and the relative dominance of those factors. According to systems thinkers, if SE can embrace the full range of systems methodologies, models, and methods, it will be in a much better position to tackle the hyper-complexity plaguing projects, organizations, and society in the contemporary world.

根据 Jackson（2019），系统方法论将关于问题情况的本质和如何改进的推测转化为实际行动。有许多可用的系统方法论，例如，系统动力学、可行的系统模型、软系统方法论和批判性系统启发式方法。每种方法建立在对世界的不同假设以及如何最好地干预世界的假设基础上。这些方法加在一起，可以用于识别在复杂问题情况探索中遇到的难题并做出响应。然后，这些系统方法可以在问题情景中单独使用或合并使用。当合并使用系统方法时，每种方法的应用权重将根据组织内的技术、组织、文化和政治因素以及这些因素的相对主导地位进行调整。根据系统思想家的说法，如果系统工程可以采用全域的系统方法论、模型和方法，那么它将能够更好地解决困扰当前世界的项目、组织和社会中的高度复杂的问题。

2 SYSTEM LIFE CYCLE CONCEPTS, MODELS, AND PROCESSES

2.1 LIFE CYCLE TERMS AND CONCEPTS

The overall purpose of Systems Engineering (SE) is to enable successful realization of the system while optimizing among competing stakeholder objectives. One way in which realization is managed is by breaking the overall effort into transformational steps, or stages, then checking for satisfactory fulfillment of system characteristics at the end of each stage, as well as checking whether risk is acceptable and the system is ready to enter other stages. Stages do not need to be executed sequentially or singularly. They can be executed multiple times as needed, and often in parallel. The critical feature of this approach is that progress is gated by specific decision points, generally called decision gates. By analogy with the stages that living things go through, called a life cycle, the set of stages for a system is termed a system life cycle. In summary, engineered systems progress in some manner through a set of stages, conceptually forming a system life cycle, with decision gates determining the completion of one stage and start of another. This part of the SE Handbook gives details for each of these parts of the system life cycle concept, as well as pointing out the role of the SE practitioner throughout a system's life cycle. Further details can be found in ISO/IEC/IEEE 24748–1 (2018).

2.1.1 Life Cycle Characteristics

As the introduction states, life cycles are defined in terms of the stages that mark progress in achieving the system characteristics. A commonly encountered set of life cycle stages is shown in Figure 2.1. These stages are also shown in ISO/IEC/IEEE 15288 (2023) and in ISO/IEC/IEEE 24748–1 (2018).

System life cycle stages can be entered based on the needs of the SoI or any system element. Stages can be entered into as many times as needed. Stages often are not sequential and can occur concurrently or as needed. Stages can overlap and stages can be entered at any point in the life cycle. The retirement stage does not require the entire SoI to be retired, it can be any system element, and retirement does not need to be in the order the systems are delivered.

INCOSE Systems Engineering Handbook: A Guide for System Life Cycle Processes and Activities, Fifth Edition.

Edited by David D. Walden, Thomas M. Shortell, Garry J. Roedler, Bernardo A. Delicado, Odile Mornas, Yip Yew-Seng, and David Endler.

© 2023 John Wiley & Sons Ltd. Published 2023 by John Wiley & Sons Ltd.

2 系统生命周期概念、模型和流程

2.1 生命周期术语和概念

系统工程的总体目的是使系统能够成功实现,同时在相互竞争的利益相关方目标之间进行优化。管理实现的一种方法是将总体工作分解为转换的步骤或阶段,然后在每个阶段结束时检查系统特性是否得到满意的实现,以及检查风险是否可以接受,系统是否准备好进入其他阶段。阶段不需要按严格的顺序或单独执行。它们可以根据需要多次执行,而且通常是并行执行的。这种方法的关键特征是,进度由特定的决策点控制,通常被称为决策门。类比生物所经历的阶段称之为生命周期,系统的多个阶段被称为系统生命周期。总之,工程系统以某种方式通过多个阶段的发展,从概念上形成系统生命周期,决策门决定一个阶段的完成和另一个阶段的开始。系统工程手册的这一部分详细介绍了系统生命周期概念的每一部分,并指出了系统工程实践者在整个系统生命周期中的作用。更多内容请参见 ISO/IEC/IEEE 24748–1(2018)。

2.1.1 生命周期特征

正如引言所述,生命周期阶段是以系统特性实现为标志来定义阶段进展的。图 2.1 展示了一组常见的生命周期阶段。ISO/IEC/IEEE 15288(2023)和 ISO/IEC/IEEE 24748–1(2018)中也展示了这些阶段。

可以根据 SoI 或系统元素的需要进入系统生命周期阶段。根据需要可以多次进入一个阶段。阶段通常不是顺序的,可以同时发生或根据需要发生。阶段可以重叠,并且可以在生命周期的任何时候进入一个阶段。退役阶段不需要整个 SoI 退役,也可以是任何系统元素,退役不需要按照系统交付的顺序进行。

SYSTEM LIFE CYCLE CONCEPTS, MODELS, AND PROCESSES

Concept	Concept		Upgrade Concept	
Development	Development		Upgrade Development	
Production		Production		Upgrade Production
Utilization			Utilization	
Support			Support	
Retirement			Retirement	

FIGURE 2.1 System life cycle stages. INCOSE SEH original figure created by Yokell. Usage per the INCOSE Notices page. All other rights reserved.

Typically, life cycle stages have both entry and exit decision gates. The entry decision gate is intended to help ensure that the entry criteria are met and the resources needed for the stage are available. The exit decision gate is intended to help ensure that the objectives of the stage have been achieved and the risk of going forward is acceptable. Decision gates are discussed in more detail in Section 2.1.3.

Figure 2.2 compares the generic life cycle stages to other life cycle viewpoints. Typical decision gates are represented along the bottom.

Major system elements may have their own life cycles. These life cycles have to be managed so that an integrated SoI is achieved and used over a span of time. When the SoI is, or is part of, an SoS (see Section 4.3.6), the influences from the evolution of the SoS need to be considered in the life cycle of the SoI. Each constituent system of the SoS has its own life cycle. Further, enabling systems (see Section 1.3.3) also have their own life cycles, which must be integrated with that of the SoI.

Requirements must be flowed down to the elements to be integrated and the decision gates should support progressive integration into the final SoI in a timely manner to help ensure that the elements can be progressively integrated. The decision gates associated with the various life cycle models should be synchronized, whatever the types of system element or parts of the life cycle are involved to support progressive integration into the final SoI.

Note that the above figures are notional and do not attempt to scale the relative time spans of the stages. For example, a system could move from initial concept to a fielded system in a few years, then remain in utilization, being supported and possibly upgraded, for decades (e.g., jet aircraft, nuclear power facility, day care nursery). A different system could have a series of development efforts, each resulting in relatively short periods of utilization and retirement (e.g., mobile phone, consumer electronics). While that is of interest from a programmatic viewpoint, it is secondary to the rationale of breaking the life cycle into stages to allow decisions to be made at key points.

系统生命周期概念、模型和流程

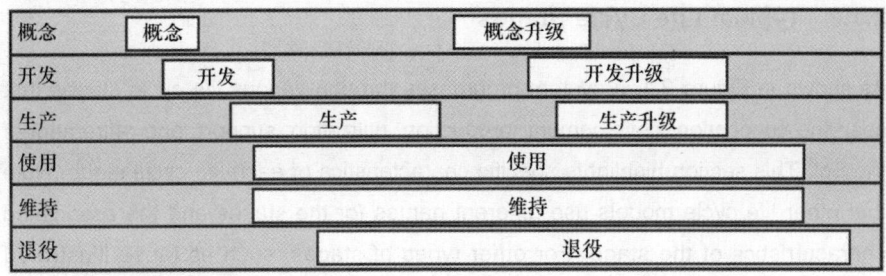

图 2.1　系统生命周期阶段。INCOSE SEH 原始图由 Yokell 创建。根据 INCOSE 通知页使用。版权所有。

通常，生命周期阶段既有进入决策门，也有退出决策门。进入决策门旨在帮助确保符合进入标准，并且该阶段所需的资源可用。退出决策门旨在帮助确保该阶段的目标已经实现，并且前进的风险是可以接受的。2.1.3 节详细讨论了决策门。

图 2.2 将一般生命周期阶段与其他生命周期视角进行了比较。典型的决策门在底部表示。

主要系统元素可能有自己的生命周期。必须管理这些生命周期，使得在一段时间内实现和使用综合后的 SoI。当 SoI 是体系或体系的一部分（见 4.3.6 节）时，需要在 SoI 的生命周期中考虑体系演进的影响。体系的每个成员系统都有自己的生命周期。此外，使能系统（见 1.3.3 节）也有自己的生命周期，必须与 SoI 的生命周期综合。

需求必须向下传递到需要综合的元素，决策门应及时支持元素逐步综合到最终 SoI 中。无论涉及何种类型的系统元素或生命周期的何种部分，与各种生命周期模型相关的决策门应同步，以实现逐步综合到最终的 SoI 中。

请注意，图 2.1 只是示意性的，并不标识各个阶段的相对时间跨度。例如，一个系统可以在几年内从最初的概念转变为实际的系统，然后在数十年内继续使用、支持保障并可能升级（例如，喷气式飞机、核电设施、日托幼儿园）。另一类不同的系统可能会有一系列的开发工作，每个只有相对较短的使用和退役时间（例如，移动电话、消费类电子产品）。从计划的角度来看，这一点固然重要，但对于将生命周期划分为若干阶段，以便在关键时刻做出决策来说，这一点是次要的。

SYSTEM LIFE CYCLE CONCEPTS, MODELS, AND PROCESSES

2.1.2 Typical Life Cycle Stages

As shown in Figure 2.1, a system progresses through various life cycle stages that span the conception, development, production, utilization, support, and retirement of the SoI. This section highlights specific characteristics of each life cycle stage. Note that other life cycle models use different names for the stages and the associated characteristics of the stage. For other types of stages, such as those illustrated in Figure 2.2, the discussion here needs to be adapted as appropriate. Additional discussion of life cycle stage characteristics is in ISO/IEC/IEEE 24748–1 (2018).

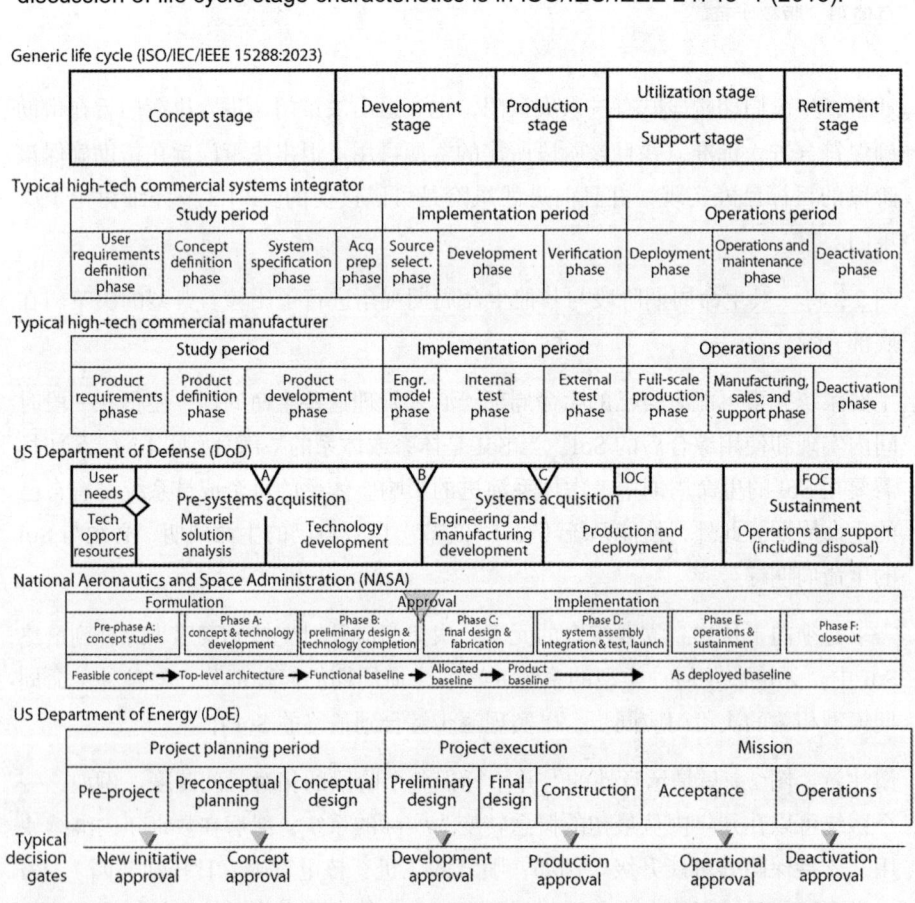

FIGURE 2.2 Generic life cycle stages compared to other life cycle viewpoints. Derived from Forsberg, et al. (2005) with permission from John Wiley & Sons. All other rights reserved.

2.1.2 典型生命周期阶段

如图 2.1 所示，一个系统要经历概念、开发、生产、使用、支持和退役的各个生命周期阶段。本节重点介绍每个生命周期阶段的具体特征。需要注意，其他生命周期模型对阶段和阶段的相关特征使用了不同的名称。对于其他类型的阶段，例如图 2.2 中所示，此处的讨论需要适当调整。ISO/IEC/IEEE 24748–1（2018）对生命周期阶段特征进行了补充讨论。

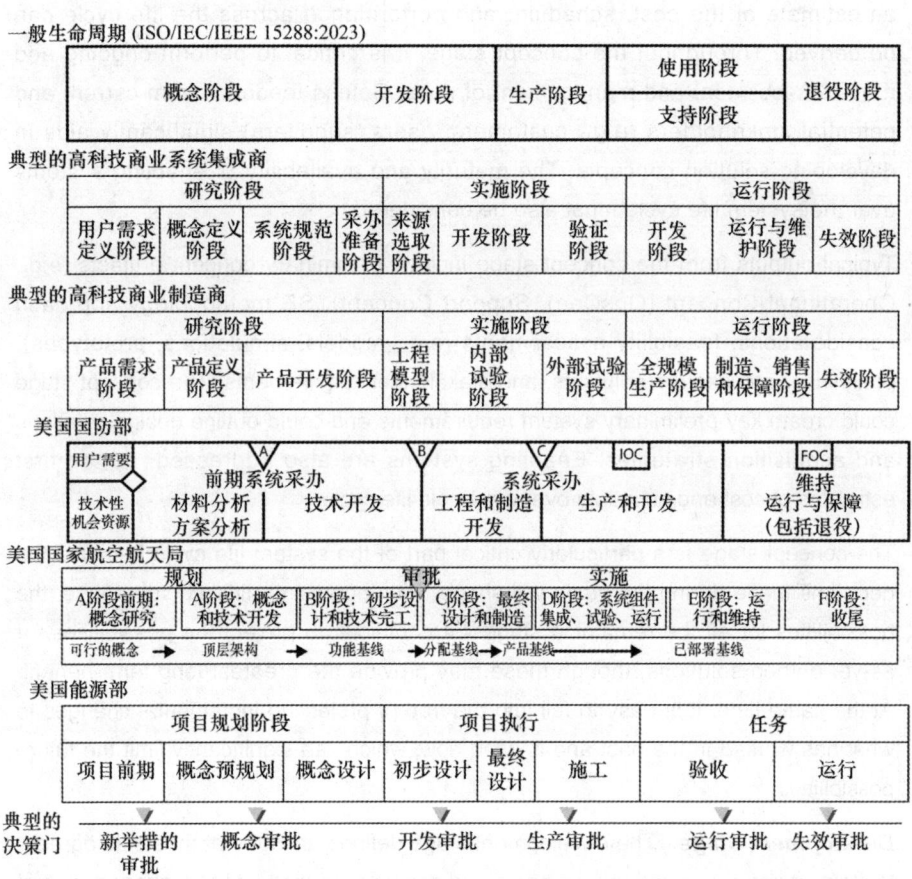

图 2.2　一般生命周期与其他生命周期视角比较。源自 Forsberg 等（2005），经 John Wiley & Sons 许可。版权所有。

SYSTEM LIFE CYCLE CONCEPTS, MODELS, AND PROCESSES

Concept Stage The concept stage can include exploratory research and begins with recognition of a need for a new or modified mission or business capability. Unless the solution is immediately at hand, which is the first thing to analyze, new potential solutions will need to be sought. Exploration needs to address both short- and long-range factors, including technical, economic, market, and resource considerations, including human resources. Surveys, trade-off studies, business or mission analyses, and other means of exploring the solution space are used. It is key that the problem space is clearly defined (existing issue or new opportunity), the solution space is characterized, business or mission requirements, and stakeholder needs and requirements are identified. From this, an estimate of the cost, schedule, and performance across the life cycle can be derived. Throughout the concept stage, it is critical to perform ongoing and robust assessment and management of risks. Getting feedback from current and potential stakeholders (e.g., customers, users, suppliers) significantly aids in developing solution concepts. The maturity and availability of enabling systems over the system life cycle must also be considered.

Typical outputs from the concept stage include preliminary concept artifacts (e.g., Operational Concept (OpsCon), Support Concept), SE methodology approach considerations, feasibility assessments (e.g., models, simulations, prototypes), preliminary architecture solutions, and stakeholder requirements. The concept stage could create key preliminary system requirements and could outline design solutions and acquisition strategies. Enabling systems are also addressed, as are first estimates of cost and schedule over the whole life cycle.

The concept stage is a particularly critical part of the system life cycle because the decisions made during the stage will shape, with increasing difficulty to change, the possibilities for all the remaining stages. It is difficult to project the possibilities for as-yet untried solutions, though these may provide the greatest long-term benefit. At the same time, it is easy to fall into the trap of projecting incremental changes to what has worked in the past and is used now, which can significantly limit the future possibilities.

Development Stage The development stage defines an SoI that meets its agreed-to stakeholder needs and requirements and can be produced, utilized, supported, and retired. System analyses, including trade-off analysis, as well as further modeling, simulation, and prototyping are performed to achieve system balance and to optimize the design for key parameters.

概念阶段　概念阶段可以包括探索性研究，并从认识到需要新的或改进的任务或业务能力开始。除非已有现成的解决方案（这是首先要分析的），否则就需要寻求新的潜在解决方案。探索需要解决短期和长期的因素，包括技术、经济、市场和资源方面的考虑，包括人力资源。可以使用调查、权衡研究、业务或任务分析以及探索解决方案空间的其他方法。明确定义问题空间（现有问题或新机会）、描述解决方案空间、确定业务或任务需求以及确定利益相关方需要和需求是关键。由此，可以得出整个生命周期的成本、进度和绩效水平估算。在整个概念阶段，对风险进行持续、稳健的评估和管理至关重要。从当前和潜在的利益相关方（如客户、用户、供应商）获得反馈，可以极大地帮助开发解决方案概念。还必须考虑整个系统生命周期内使能系统的成熟度和可用性。

概念阶段的典型输出包括初步概念制品（例如，运行概念、支持概念）、系统工程方法论实施方法的考虑、可行性评估（例如，模型、仿真、原型）、初步架构解决方案和利益相关方需求。概念阶段可以创建关键的初步系统需求，并概要地设计解决方案和采办策略。此外，还需要讨论使能系统，以及整个生命周期内成本和进度的初步估计。

概念阶段是系统生命周期中一个特别关键的部分，因为在该阶段所做的决策将决定所有后续阶段的可能性，并且后续阶段改变的难度越来越大。很难预测尚未尝试过的解决方案的可能性，尽管这些可能提供最大的长期效益。与此同时，也很容易陷入这样一个陷阱，即对过去行之有效、现在正在使用的东西进行渐进式改革，这会极大地限制未来的可能性。

开发阶段　开发阶段将定义 SoI，以满足所约定的利益相关方需要和需求，并且可以生产、使用、支持和退役。进行系统分析，包括权衡分析，以及进一步建模、仿真和原型设计，以实现系统平衡并优化关键参数的设计。

SYSTEM LIFE CYCLE CONCEPTS, MODELS, AND PROCESSES

The main aspect of the development stage is to mature the system concepts and stakeholder needs and requirements into an engineering baseline that can be produced, utilized, and supported over the desired span of its useful life, and finally retired in a responsible manner. The goal is not perfection, but rather to adequately meet the stakeholder needs and requirements in a manner that is supportable. The engineering baseline includes system requirements, architecture, design, documentation, and plans for subsequent stages. Outputs can include an SoI prototype, enabling system requirements (or the enabling systems themselves), plans for integration, verification, validation, transition, acquisition, logistics support, risk management, staffing and training, and detailed cost estimates and schedules for future stages. These outputs can occur incrementally, supporting a phased realization of the SoI, especially for complex systems.

Production Stage The production stage begins with approval to translate the baselines of the development stage into an actual system, or those parts of the SoI where approval is given (which is not uncommon for a complex system). The approval includes the enabling systems and must address all areas of the baseline. In this stage, the SoI becomes reality, is qualified for use, and is ready for installation and transition under the utilization stage. The outputs of this stage are the realized portions of the SoI (with its enabling systems) as well as the documentation that will go forward for use in the utilization, support, and retirement stages.

Utilization Stage The utilization stage begins with the transition to use of a system, or the parts of a system approved for use. This includes any enabling systems that will support use of the system being used in its intended environment to provide its intended capabilities. Product modifications are often introduced throughout the utilization stage, which generally is much longer than the other stages. Such changes can remedy deficiencies, enhance the capabilities, or extend the life of the system. Throughout, it is critical to maintain documentation from prior stages, as well as to ensure that Technical Management Processes, such as Configuration Management and Risk Management, and SE support remain in place and are robustly applied. The utilization stage proceeds in parallel with the support stage and ends, possibly by steps for different parts of the SoI, with the retirement stage.

Support Stage The support stage begins with provisioning of support for the SoI's utilization. Planning and acquisition actions for the system support are often taken before utilization is allowed to start. In this stage, deficiencies and failures are noted and used as the basis for either remediation of the problems, or to build a case for evolutionary modification. Modifications may be proposed to resolve supportability problems, to reduce operational costs, or to extend the life of a system. These changes require SE assessments to avoid loss of system capabilities while under operation, or violation of non-performance related requirements. The support stage ends when a decision is made that the system is at the end of its useful life or that it should no longer be supported.

系统生命周期概念、模型和流程

开发阶段的主要方面是将系统概念和利益相关方的需要和需求演进为工程实现的基线，该基线可在其预期有效生命阶段内生产、使用和支持保障，并最终以负责任的方式退役。本阶段的目标不是完美，而是以可支持的方式充分满足利益相关方的需要和需求。工程基线包括系统需求、架构、设计、文档和后续阶段的计划。输出可以包括 SoI 原型、使能系统需求（或使能系统本身）、综合、验证、确认、转移、采办、后勤支持、风险管理、人员配备和培训计划，以及未来阶段的详细成本估算和时间表。这些输出可以逐步进行，支持 SoI 的分阶段实现，尤其是对于复杂系统。

生产阶段 生产阶段从批准将开发阶段的基线转换为实际系统开始，或 SoI 中部分获得批准开始（对于复杂系统来说，这并不少见）。批准包括使能系统，必须解决基线的所有领域。在此阶段，SoI 被实现，具备使用资格，并准备在使用阶段进行安装和转移。该阶段的输出是 SoI 已实现的部分（及其使能系统）以及将在使用、支持和退役阶段使用的文档。

使用阶段 使用阶段从系统转移并使用或批准的系统部件使用开始，包括支持在其预期环境中使用系统以提供其预期功能的任何使能系统。产品变更通常在整个使用阶段产生，这个阶段比其他阶段长得多。此类变更可以弥补缺陷、增强能力或延长系统生命。在整个阶段中，维护前几个阶段的文档以及确保技术管理流程（如构型配置管理和风险管理）和系统工程支持随时就位并得到有效应用至关重要。使用阶段与支持阶段并行，最后可能按 SoI 不同部分的步骤与退役阶段一起结束。

支持阶段 支持阶段从为 SoI 的使用提供支持开始。在允许开始使用之前，通常会对系统支持进行计划和采办行动。在此阶段，需要记录缺陷和故障，并将其作为问题进行补救，或作为系统改进的用例。这时可能会提出改进，以解决可保障性问题、降低运营成本或延长系统生命。这些更改需要系统工程评估，以避免在运行时丧失系统能力，或损害非性能需求。当决定系统的使用生命结束或不再需要支持时，支持阶段结束。

Retirement Stage The retirement stage is where the system or a system element and its related services are removed from operation. SE activities in this stage are primarily focused on ensuring that disposal requirements, which can be extensive, are satisfied. However, it is often of value to ensure that documentation generated during at least the utilization and support stages is archived. That information can be invaluable when belated recognition arises that there is a need for new system.

Planning for retirement is part of the system definition during the concept and development stages. Experience has repeatedly demonstrated the consequences when system retirement is not considered from the outset. Early in the twenty-first century, many countries have changed their laws to hold the developer of a SoI accountable for proper end-of-life disposal of the system.

2.1.3 Decision Gates

It is good practice to have risk-managing decision points that occur at the beginning and end of each stage. This approach ensures that progress is gated by specific decision points that are clearly visible. These decision points help ensure the readiness to proceed with a stage and that the stage accomplishes is objective as it finishes. They often take place within the context of "project milestones," "project reviews," or "milestone reviews." Key is to help ensure that decisions are clearly made and documented and that they relate directly to the criteria established to begin or end a particular stage of a system's life cycle. Note that some approaches, such as agile (see Section 4.2.2), accomplish their decision points in a different cadence and tend to avoid the terms "milestones" and "decision gates." In agile development, frequent interaction with stakeholders can change the frequency (more frequent) and scope (smaller scope), and formality (less formal) of decision gates.

Typical goals of decision gates are to confirm that:

- increase in system maturity is within the defined threshold;
- the project deliverables satisfy the business case;
- the resources are sufficient to for the stage and subsequent stages;
- unresolved issues that need to be addressed in that stage are addressed; and
- overall risk for proceeding forward in the system life cycle is acceptable.

As shown in Figure 2.3, decision criteria can also include stage entry/exit criteria, entry/exit criteria from other stages, and risk assessment. Figure 2.3 shows the following cases:

退役阶段 退役阶段是系统或系统元素及其相关服务停止运行的阶段。本阶段的系统工程活动主要集中于确保满足广泛的退役处置需求。然而，至少确保在使用和支持阶段生成的文档得到存档也很有价值。当后续认识到需要开发新系统时，这些信息可能是非常宝贵的。

退役计划是概念和开发阶段进行系统定义的一部分。经验一再表明，如果一开始没有考虑系统退役，后果将不堪设想。在 21 世纪早期，许多国家已经修改了法律，要求 SoI 的开发人员对系统的合理报废处置负责。

2.1.3 阶段门

在每个阶段的开始和结束时都有风险管理决策点，这是一种很好的做法。这种方法确保进度由清晰可见的特定决策点决定。这些决策点有助于确保准备好进行某个阶段，并且该阶段在完成时是客观的。它们通常在"项目里程碑"、"项目评审"或"里程碑评审"的背景下进行。决策门的关键是确保明确制定和记录决策，并确保决策与为开始或结束特定系统生命周期阶段而制定的标准直接相关。请注意，一些方法，如敏捷方法（见 4.2.2 节），倾向于避免术语"里程碑"和"决策门"，而以不同的节奏完成其决策点。在敏捷开发中，与利益相关方的频繁交互可以改变决策门的频率（更频繁）和范围（更小范围），以及形式（较不形式化）。

决策门的典型目标是确认：

- 系统成熟度提高到了规定的阈值内；
- 项目交付物满足业务用例；
- 该阶段和后续阶段的资源充足；
- 解决了该阶段需要解决的问题；
- 在系统生命周期中继续前进的总体风险是可以接受的。

如图 2.3 所示，决策标准还可以包括阶段进入/退出准则、其他阶段的进入/退出准则和风险评估。图 2.3 展示了以下情况：

SYSTEM LIFE CYCLE CONCEPTS, MODELS, AND PROCESSES

- the entry criteria are met, but the start of the stage is delayed;
- when the entry criteria are met, the decision to start the stage is made;
- although the entry criteria are not met, the stage is started;
- although the exit criteria are met, the decision to end the stage is delayed;
- when the exit criteria are met, the decision to end the stage is made;
- the decision to end the stage is made before the exit criteria are met.

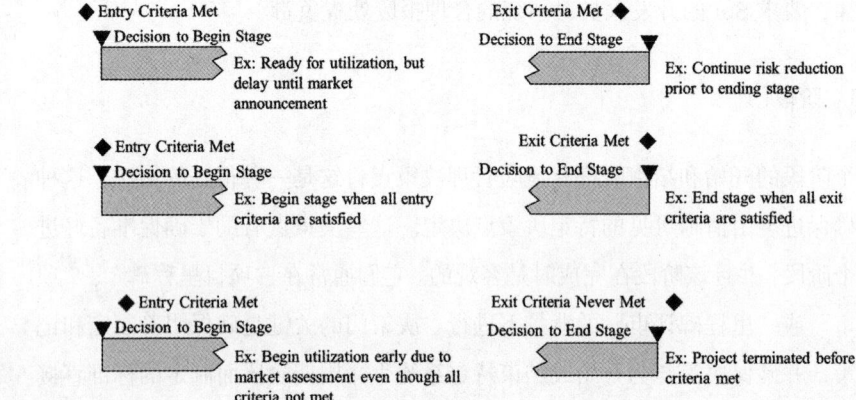

FIGURE 2.3 Criteria for decision gates. INCOSE SEH original figure created by Yokell. Usage per the INCOSE Notices page. All other rights reserved.

At each decision gate, the options can include:

- Begin subsequent stage or stages;
- Continue this stage, possibly after some reformulation;
- Go to or restart a preceding stage;
- Hold the project activity;
- Terminate the project.

The option selected depends on the quality of the results of the effort so far (based on the answers to the exit questions) plus the risk of moving forward (based on the answers to the entrance questions). Stages do not need to be sequential. Transitions often occur, but it is common to have stages occurring concurrently. In complex systems, the decision can also be more differentiated. For example: move part of the effort forward; hold on some; and terminate or reform others.

系统生命周期概念、模型和流程

- 符合进入准则，但阶段开始延迟；
- 当符合进入准则时，决定开始该阶段；
- 尽管未达到进入准则，但该阶段已开始；
- 虽然符合退出准则，但结束该阶段的决定被推迟；
- 当满足退出准则时，决定结束该阶段；
- 在满足退出准则之前，决定结束该阶段。

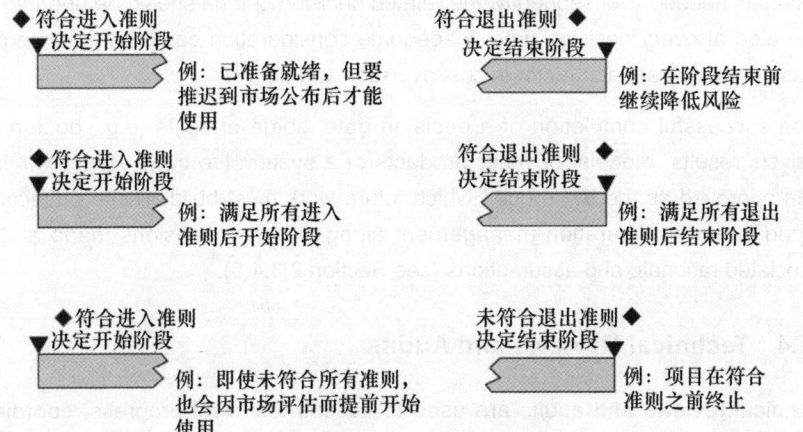

图 2.3 决策门准则。INCOSE SEH 原始图由 Yokell 创建。根据 INCOSE 通知页使用。版权所有。

在每个决策门，选项可以包括：

- 开始后续阶段；
- 继续这一阶段，可能在进行一些调整之后；
- 进入或重新启动前一阶段；
- 暂停项目活动；
- 终止项目。

决策的选择取决于迄今为止的工作结果的质量（基于阶段退出问题的结果）加上继续前进的风险（基于下阶段进入问题的结果）。阶段不需要是连续的。转换经常发生，但更常见的是阶段同时发生。在复杂系统中，决策也可以进行区分，例如：部分工作向前进入下阶段，部分工作保持当前阶段，终止或改进其他部分。

SYSTEM LIFE CYCLE CONCEPTS, MODELS, AND PROCESSES

Decision gate approval follows review by qualified experts, involved stakeholders, and management. Approval should be based on evidence of compliance to the criteria of the review. Balancing the formality and frequency of decision gates is seen as a critical success factor for all SE process areas. The consequences of conducting a superficial review, omitting a critical discipline, or skipping a decision gate are usually long-term and costly.

It is important to note that there may be significant changes in the project's environment. This may impact the project's business case, system scope, or resources needed. Consequently, the related decision criteria should be updated and evaluated at every decision gate. Inadequate consideration can set up subsequent failures—usually a major factor in cost overruns and delays.

Upon successful completion of a decision gate, some artifacts (e.g., documents, analysis results, models, or other products of a system life cycle stage) will have been approved as the basis upon which future work must build. These artifacts are placed under configuration management along with the decisions made and the associated rationale and assumptions (see Section 2.3.4.5).

2.1.4 Technical Reviews and Audits

Technical reviews and audits are used to assess technical progress, coordinate activities, and determine the technical status of a system of interest (SoI). According to ISO/IEC 24748-8 / IEEE 15288-2 (2014):

A technical review is "a series of systems engineering activities conducted at logical transition points in a system life cycle, by which the progress of a [project] is assessed relative to its technical requirements using a mutually agreed-upon set of criteria" and

An audit is "a detailed review of processes, product definition information, documented verification of compliance with requirements, and an inspection of products to confirm that products have achieved their required attributes or conform to released product configuration definition information."

The technical reviews and audits to be performed occur throughout the system life cycle and should be captured in the project's Systems Engineering Management Plan (SEMP) and reflected in the project's schedule (see Section 2.3.4.1). They may be part of a decision gate review (see Section 2.1.3). A representative set of technical reviews and audits are listed in Table 2.1. They should be tailored for the needs of the project and the methodologies being used. ISO/IEC/IEEE 24748-1 (2018), Annex F and ISO/IEC 24748-8 / IEEE 15288-2 (2014) provide useful guidance for the planning and tailoring of reviews to the needs of the project and its stakeholders.

决策门在有资格的专家、参与的利益相关方和管理层进行评审之后批准。批准应基于符合评审准则的证据。平衡决策门的形式和决策频率是所有系统工程流程领域的关键成功因素。进行草率的评审、忽略关键准则或跳过决策门的后果通常是长期且代价高昂的。

需要注意的是，项目环境可能会发生重大变化。这可能会影响项目的业务用例、系统范围或所需的资源。因此，应在每个决策门更新和评估相关决策准则。考虑不足可能导致后续失败，这通常是导致成本超支和进展延迟的主要因素。

成功完成决策门后，一些制品（例如，文档、分析结果、模型或系统生命周期阶段的其他产品）将被批准作为必须为未来工作构建的基础。这些制品与所做的决策以及相关的基本原理和假设都将一起被纳入构型配置管理之内（参见 2.3.4.5 节）。

2.1.4 技术评审和审核

技术评审和审核用于评估技术进步、协调活动和确定 SoI 的技术状态。根据 ISO/IEC 24748–8/IEEE 15288–2（2014）：

技术评审是"在系统生命周期的逻辑转换点进行的一系列系统工程活动，通过这些活动，使用一套经过协商的准则，针对其技术要求，评估 [项目] 的进度"。

审核是"对流程、产品定义信息的详细评审，对需求符合性的文档化验证，以及对产品的检查，以确认产品已达到所需满足的属性或符合所发布的产品构型定义信息"。

在整个系统生命周期内进行的技术评审和审核应包含在项目的系统工程管理计划（SEMP）中，并反映在项目进度表中（见 2.3.4.1 节）。它们可能是决策门评审的一部分（见 2.1.3 节）。表 2.1 中列出了一组具有代表性的技术评审和审核。它们应根据项目的需要和所使用的方法进行调整。ISO/IEC/IEEE 24748–1（2018）、附录 F 和 ISO/IEC 24748–8/IEEE 15288–2（2014）为计划和调整评审以满足项目及其利益相关方的需要提供了有用的指导。

SYSTEM LIFE CYCLE CONCEPTS, MODELS, AND PROCESSES

Figure 2.4 depicts the relationship between these reviews and audits identified in ISO/IEC 24748–8 / IEEE 15288–2 (2014) and the typical technical baselines across the system life cycle applicable for a sequential life cycle model. This depiction will vary significantly for incremental life cycle models.

TABLE 2.1   Representative technical reviews and audits

Defense Projects per ISO/IEC/IEEE 24748-8/IEEE 15288–2 (2014)	Space Projects per NASA (2007b)	Incremental Commitment Spiral Model per Boehm, et al. (2014)
Alternative Systems Review (ASR)	Mission Concept Review (MCR)	
System Requirements Review (SRR)	System Requirements Review (SRR)	
System Functional Review (SFR)	Mission Definition Review (MDR)	
	System Definition Review (SDR)	
Preliminary Design Review (PDR)	Preliminary Design Review (PDR)	Exploration Commitment Review (ECR)
Critical Design Review (CDR)	Critical Design Review (CDR)	Valuation Commitment Review (VCR)
	System Integration Review (SIR)	Foundation Commitment Review (FCR)
Test Readiness Review (TRR)	Operational Readiness Review (ORR)	Development Commitment Review $_n$ (DCR $_n$)
Functional Configuration Audit (FCA)	Flight Readiness Review (FRR)	Operations Commitment Review$_n$ (OCR $_n$)
System Verification Review (SVR)	Mission Readiness Review (MRR)	
Production Readiness Review (PRR)	Post-Launch Assessment Review (PLAR)	
Physical Configuration Audit (PCA)	Critical Events Readiness Review (CERR)	
	Post-Flight Assessment Review (PFAR)	
	Decommissioning Review (DR)	
	Disposal Readiness Review (DRR)	

INCOSE SEH original table created by Walden. Usage per the INCOSE Notices page. All other rights reserved.

Technical reviews and audits provide an opportunity to assess the following:

- The SoI is meeting its requirements
- The SoI is meeting stakeholder expectations, internal and external
- The SoI will have acceptable quality characteristics (QCs)
- The SoI is at an appropriate level of maturity
- The SoI is at an acceptable level of risk
- There is a clear path toward verifying and validating the SoI and its elements

图 2.4 描述了 ISO/IEC 24748-8/IEEE 15288-2（2014）中确定的评审和审核活动，与适用于顺序生命周期模型的整个系统生命周期的典型技术基线之间的关系。对于增量生命周期模型，这种描述会有很大的不同。

表 2.1　典型技术评审和审核

国防项目依据 ISO/IEC/IEEE 24748-8/IEEE 15288-2（2014）	太空项目依据 NASA（2007b）	增量承诺螺旋模型依据 Boehm 等（2014）
	任务概念评审	
备选系统评审	任务定义评审	
系统需求评审	系统定义评审	
系统功能评审	系统综合评审	
初步设计评审	运行准备度评审	探索承诺评审
关键设计评审	飞行准备度评审	估值承诺评审
测试准备度评审	任务准备度评审	基础承诺评审
功能构型配置审核	发射后评估评审	开发承诺评审
系统验证评审	关键事件准备度评审	运行承诺评审
生产准备度评审	飞行后评估评审	
物理构型配置审核	停用评审	
	处置准备度评审	

INCOSE SEH 原始表由 Walden 创建。根据 INCOSE 通知页使用。版权所有。

技术评审和审核提供了评估以下内容的机会：

- SoI 符合其需求
- SoI 满足了利益相关方的内部和外部期望
- SoI 将具有可接受的质量特性（QCs）
- SoI 处于适当的成熟度水平
- SoI 处于可接受的风险水平
- 有明确的途径来验证和确认 SoI 及其元素

SYSTEM LIFE CYCLE CONCEPTS, MODELS, AND PROCESSES

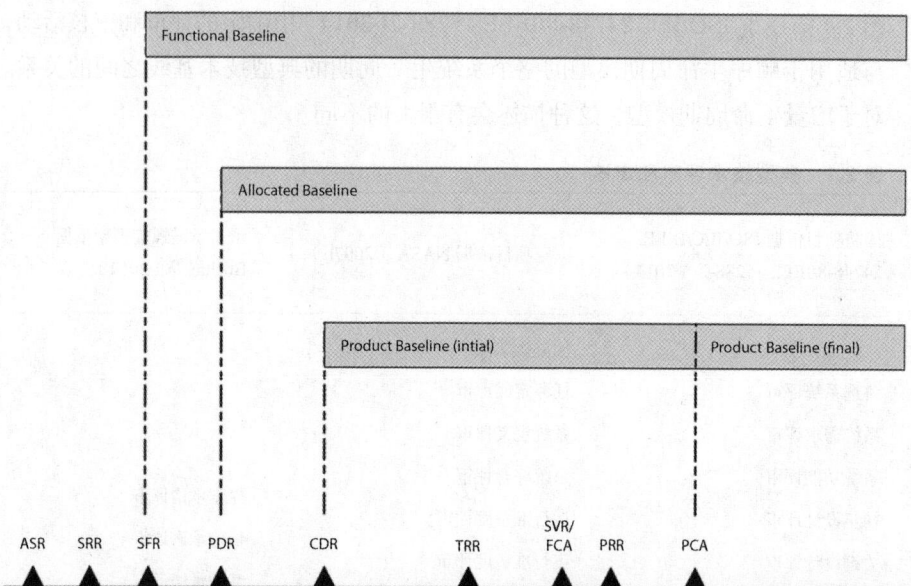

FIGURE 2.4 Relationship between technical reviews and audits and the technical baselines. From ISO/IEC 24748–8 / IEEE 15288–2 (2014). Used with permission. All other rights reserved.

Good practices for technical reviews and audits include:

- Plan the review or audit, including getting concurrence on a mutually agreeable location and date
- Application of multiple instances of the reviews and audits, both at multiple levels of the systems hierarchy and during each increment or iteration
- Elimination of unnecessary reviews or audits
- Establish clear entry and exit criteria for each review and audit
- Establish roles and responsibilities for the preparation, conduct, and acceptance of each review
- Make the reviews be risk-driven (risk is at an acceptable level) or event-driven (the entry criteria has been satisfied), not schedule-driven (must happen on a certain date)
- Consider "dry-runs" to make the review as efficient as possible

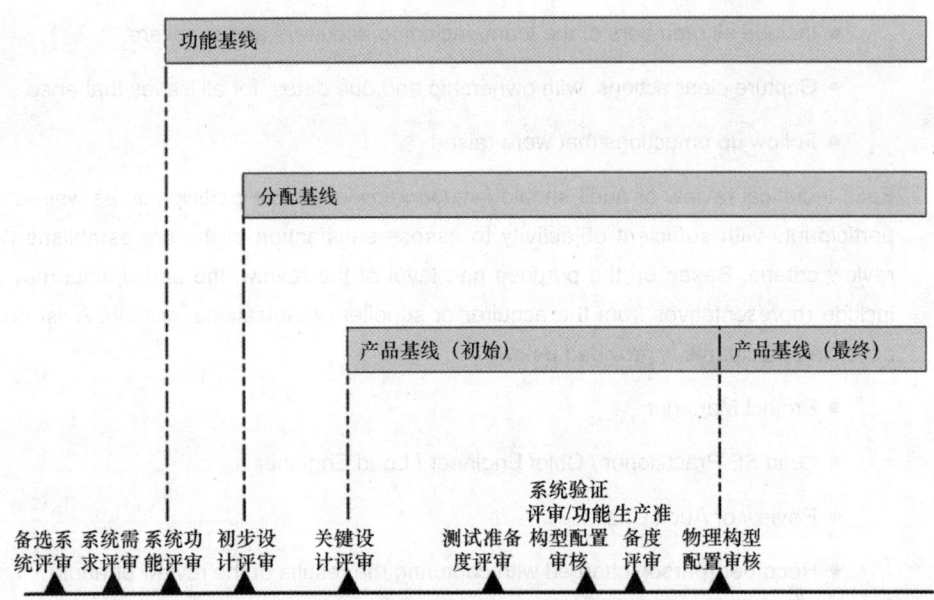

图 2.4 技术评审、审核和技术基线间的关系。源自 ISO/IEC 24748–8 / IEEE 15288–2（2014）。经许可后使用。版权所有。

技术评审和审核的好的实践做法包括：

- 计划评审或审核，包括在双方同意的地点和日期

- 在系统层级结构的多个层次上以及在每个增量或迭代期间，开展多个评审和审核

- 消除不必要的评审或审核

- 为每次评审和审核制定明确的进入和退出准则

- 确定准备、执行和接受每次评审的角色和职责

- 使评审由风险驱动（风险处于可接受的水平）或事件驱动（已满足进入准则），而非计划驱动（必须在特定日期进行）

- 考虑"试运行"，使评审尽可能高效

SYSTEM LIFE CYCLE CONCEPTS, MODELS, AND PROCESSES

- Include subject matter experts (SMEs) and independent reviewers
- Include all members of the team, including acquirers and suppliers
- Capture clear actions, with ownership and due dates, for all issues that arise
- Follow up on actions that were raised

Each technical review or audit should include knowledgeable participants as well as participants with sufficient objectivity to assess satisfaction of the pre-established review criteria. Based on the purpose and level of the review, the participants may include representatives from the acquirer or supplier organizations, or both. A list of possible participants is provided below:

- Project Manager
- Lead SE Practitioner / Chief Engineer / Lead Engineer
- Review or Audit Chair
- Recorder (person charged with capturing the results of the review or audit)
- Acquirer Representative(s)
- Supplier Representative(s)
- Project Verification and Validation Lead
- Other Technical Leads

2.2 LIFE CYCLE MODEL APPROACHES

Section 2.1 introduces the concept of life cycle stages. The life cycle models are thus the framework within which the individual life cycle stages and transitions between them are planned and implemented. There are many different life cycle models, each suitable for different situations. A common way to differentiate them is to divide the life cycle model approaches into three groups: sequential, incremental, and evolutionary. Figure 2.5 provides the general concept for each of these approaches, and Table 2.2 summarizes their distinguishing characteristics.

ISO/IEC/IEEE 24748–1 (2018) provides further information on sequential (identified as "once-through"), incremental, and evolutionary life cycle model approaches. Sections 2.2.1 to 2.2.3 elaborate on how these approaches can be applied to manage the work within each life cycle stage.

- 包括主题专家（SMEs）和独立评审员
- 包括团队的所有成员，包括采办方和供应商
- 针对出现的所有问题，捕获明确的行动，包括责任人和截止时间
- 跟进提出的行动

每次技术评审或审核应包括具有足够知识的参与者以及具有足够客观性的参与者，以评估预先制定的评审准则的满足度。根据评审的目的和层级，参与者可能包括采办方或供应商组织的代表，或两者都参加。可能的参与者名单如下：

- 项目经理
- 首席系统工程师 / 总工程师 / 首席工程师
- 评审或审核主席
- 记录员（负责记录评审或审核结果的人员）
- 采办方代表
- 供应商代表
- 项目验证和确认负责人
- 其他技术负责人

2.2 生命周期模型方法

2.1节介绍了生命周期阶段的概念。因此，生命周期模型是计划和实施各个生命周期阶段及其之间转换的框架。有许多不同的生命周期模型，每种模型适用于不同的情况。区分它们的一种常见方法是将生命周期模型方法分为三组：顺序、增量和演进。图2.5给出了每种方法的一般概念，表2.2总结了它们的区别特征。

ISO/IEC/IEEE 24748–1（2018）提供了关于顺序（被认为是"一次性"）、增量和演进生命周期模型方法的进一步信息。2.2.1至2.2.3节详细说明了如何应用这些方法来管理每个生命周期阶段内的工作。

SYSTEM LIFE CYCLE CONCEPTS, MODELS, AND PROCESSES

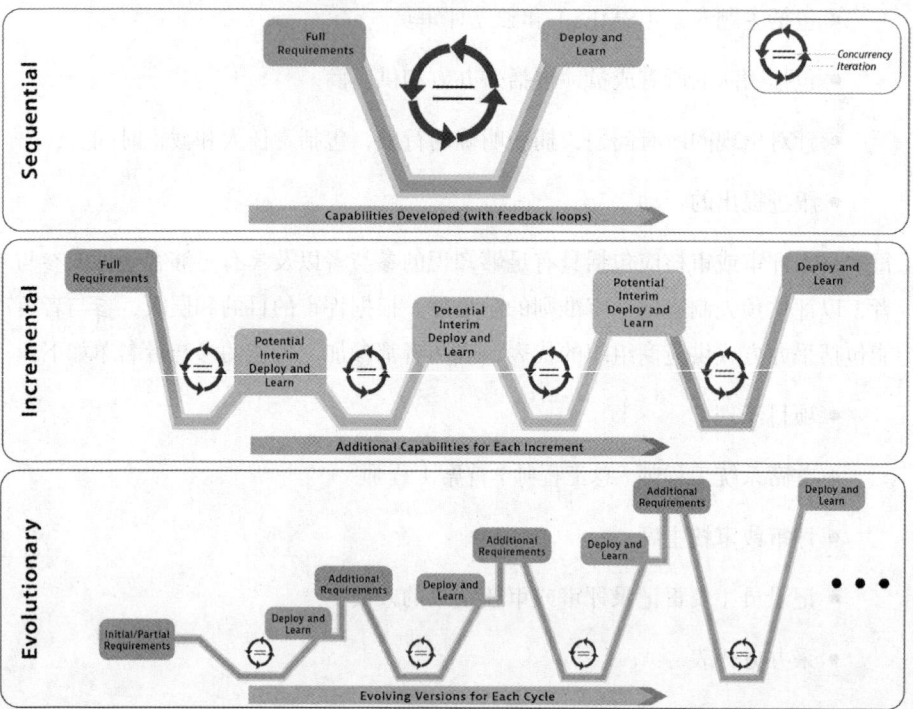

FIGURE 2.5 Concepts for the three life cycle model approaches. INCOSE SEH original figure created by Endler. Usage per the INCOSE NOTICES page. All other rights reserved.

TABLE 2.2 Life cycle model approach characteristics

Life cycle approach	Requirement set at start	Planned iterations	Multiple deployments
Sequential	Full	Single	No
Incremental	Full	Multiple	Potential
Evolutionary	Partial	Multiple	Typically

INCOSE SEH original table created by Endler derived from ISO/IEC/IEEE 24748-1 (2018). Usage per the INCOSE Notices page. All other rights reserved.

There are many factors that help determine which life cycle models are suitable for a specific system or project. Clause 6 of ISO/IEC/IEEE 24748-1 (2018) provides informational considerations that may influence the selection and adaptation of life cycle model, including:

系统生命周期概念、模型和流程

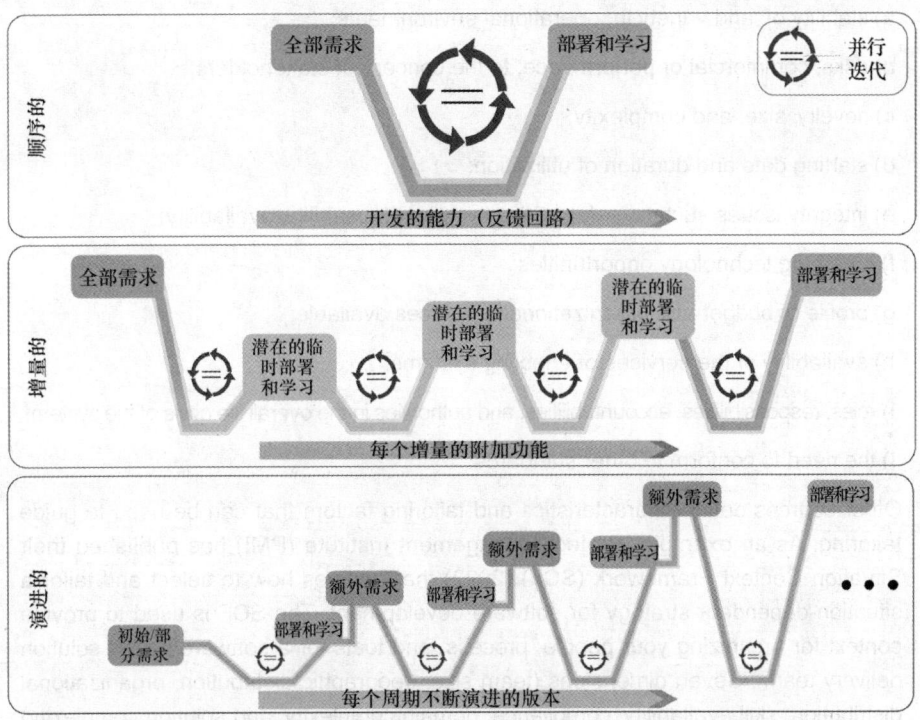

图 2.5　三种生命周期模型实施方法的概念。INCOSE SEH 原始图由 Endler 创建。根据 INCOSE 通知页使用。版权所有。

表 2.2　生命周期模型实施方法特点

生命周期实施方法	开始时需求集	计划的迭代次数	多次部署
顺序的	全部	一次	无
增量的	全部	多次	可能的
演进的	部分	多次	典型的

INCOSE SEH 原始表由 Endler 创建，源自 ISO/IEC/IEEE 24748-1（2018）。根据 INCOSE 通知页使用。版权所有。

有许多因素有助于确定哪些生命周期模型适用于特定的系统或项目。ISO/IEC/IEEE 24748–1（2018）第 6 条提供了可能影响生命周期模型选择和调整的信息考量，包括：

SYSTEM LIFE CYCLE CONCEPTS, MODELS, AND PROCESSES

a) stability of, and variety in, operational environments;

b) risks, commercial or performance, to the concern of stakeholders;

c) novelty, size, and complexity;

d) starting date and duration of utilization;

e) integrity issues such as safety, security, privacy, usability, availability;

f) emerging technology opportunities;

g) profile of budget and organizational resources available;

h) availability of the services of enabling systems;

i) roles, responsibilities, accountabilities, and authorities in the overall life cycle of the system;

j) the need to conform to other standards.

Other sources define characteristics and tailoring factors that can be used to guide tailoring. As an example, Project Management Institute (PMI) has published their Situation Context Framework (SCF) (2022) that "defines how to select and tailor a situation-dependent strategy for software development. The SCF is used to provide context for organizing your people, process, and tools for a software-based solution delivery team." Seven dimensions (team size, geographic distribution, organizational distribution, skill availability, compliance, domain complexity, and solution complexity) with scaling factors in each dimension are defined within this framework.

As there is no universal approach, it is recommended that each organization continuously questions itself as to which approach, or combination of approaches, is most suitable. Part IV of this handbook addresses tailoring and application considerations in more detail.

2.2.1 Sequential Methods

The sequential approach is focused on the general flow of the processes with feedback loops, but a single delivery. Sequential life cycle models break down SE activities into linear sequential stages, where each stage depends on the deliverables of the previous stages, along with feedback from subsequent stages.

On projects where it is necessary to coordinate large teams of people working in multiple companies, sequential approaches provide an underlying framework to provide discipline to the life cycle processes. Sequential life cycle models are characterized by a systematic approach that adheres to specified processes as the system moves through a series of representations from requirements through design to finished product. Specific attention is given to the completeness of documentation, traceability from requirements, and verification of each representation after the fact.

a）运行环境的稳定性和多样性；

b）利益相关方关注的商业或绩效风险；

c）新奇性、规模和复杂性；

d）使用开始日期和持续时间；

e）完整性问题，如安全、安保、隐私、易用性、可用性；

f）新兴技术机会；

g）可用预算和组织资源概况；

h）使能系统服务的可用性；

i）系统整个生命周期中的角色、职责、责任和权限；

j）符合其他标准的需要。

其他来源定义了可用于指导剪裁的特征和剪裁因素。例如，项目管理协会（PMI）发布了他们的情境背景框架（SCF）（2022），该框架"定义了如何选择和定制与情境相关的软件开发战略。SCF用于为基于软件的解决方案交付团队提供组织人员、流程和工具的背景"。在该框架中定义了七个维度（团队规模、地理分布、组织分布、技能可用性、符合性、领域复杂性和解决方案复杂性），每个维度都有比例因子。

由于没有通用的方法，建议每个组织不断审视哪种方法或方法的组合最合适。本手册第四部分更详细地介绍了剪裁和应用的注意事项。

2.2.1 顺序方法

顺序方法侧重于具有反馈回路的流程，但只进行一次。顺序生命周期模型将系统工程活动分解为线性顺序阶段，其中每个阶段取决于前几个阶段的可交付成果以及后续阶段的反馈。

对于需要协调多个公司工作人员的大型团队项目，顺序方法提供了一个基本框架，为生命周期流程提供规律。顺序生命周期模型的特点是，系统从需求到设计再到最终产品的一系列陈述中，遵循特定流程的系统方法。其特别注意文档的完整性、需求的可追溯性以及基于事实对每个陈述的验证。

SYSTEM LIFE CYCLE CONCEPTS, MODELS, AND PROCESSES

The strengths of sequential life cycle models are predictability, stability, repeatability, and high assurance. Process improvement focuses on increasing process capability through standardization, measurement, and control. These models rely on "master plans" to anchor their processes and provide project-wide communication. Historical data is usually carefully collected and maintained as inputs to future planning to make projections more accurate (Boehm and Turner, 2004).

The waterfall model, introduced by Royce (1970), was used to characterize the advantages and disadvantages of sequential approaches. The waterfall model has been used successfully in the manufacturing and construction industries, where the highly structured physical environments meant that design changes became prohibitively expensive much sooner in the development process. In addition, safety-critical products, such as the Therac-25 medical equipment (see the case study in Section 6.1), can only meet modern certification standards by following a thorough, documented set of plans and specifications. Such standards mandate strict adherence to process and specified documentation to achieve safety or security.

The SE Vee model (named due to its shape representing the letter "V" in the English language), introduced in Forsberg and Mooz (1991), described in Forsberg, et al. (2005), and shown in Figure 2.6, is another example of a sequential approach used to visualize key areas for SE focus, associating each development stage with a corresponding testing stage. The Vee highlights the need for continuous validation with the stakeholders, the need to define verification plans during requirements development, and the importance of continuous risk and opportunity assessment.

There are several variations of the Vee model. Typically, the "left" side of the Vee is called system definition and the "bottom" and "right" side of the Vee are called system realization. In the Vee model, time and system maturity conceptually proceed from left to right (down the left side of the Vee and up the right side of the Vee). However, all the system life cycle processes are performed concurrently and iteratively at each level of the system hierarchy and all the system life cycle processes are recursively applied at each level of the system hierarchy (see Section 2.3.1.2). One of the strengths of the Vee model is its depiction of the relationships between the left and right sides of the Vee.

顺序生命周期模型的优点是可预测性、稳定性、可重复性和高把握性。流程改进的重点是通过标准化、测量和控制来提高流程能力。这些模型依靠"主计划"来确定其流程，并提供项目范围内的沟通。通常会仔细收集和维护历史数据，作为未来计划的输入，以使预测更加准确（Boehm 和 Turner，2004）。

Royce（1970）引入的瀑布模型可用于描述顺序方法的优缺点。瀑布模型已成功应用于制造业和建筑业，在这些行业中，高度结构化的物理环境意味着设计更改在开发流程中很快就会变得昂贵到令人望而却步。此外，安全关键型产品，如 Therac-25 医疗设备（见 6.1 节中的案例研究），只有遵循一套完整的、有文档记录的计划和规范，才能满足现代认证标准。这些标准要求严格遵守流程和规定的文档，以实现安全或安保。

Forsberg 和 Mooz（1991）引入的系统工程 V 模型（因其形状代表英语中的字母"V"而得名）在 Forsberg 等（2005）描述中（见图 2.6）是用于可视化系统工程关键领域的顺序方法的另一个例子，将每个开发阶段与相应的测试阶段相关联。V 模型强调了与利益相关方进行连续验证的必要性，在需求开发期间定义验证计划的必要性，以及持续的风险和机会评估的重要性。

V 模型有几种变体。通常，V 的"左侧"称为系统定义，V 的"底部"和"右侧"称为系统实现。在 V 模型中，时间和系统成熟度在概念上从左到右发展（从 V 的左侧向下，从 V 的右侧向上）。然而，所有系统生命周期流程都是在系统层次结构的每个层级上并行和迭代执行的，所有系统生命周期流程都是在系统层次结构的每个层级上递归应用的（参见 2.3.1.2 节）。V 模型的一个优点是它描述了 V 左右两侧之间的关系。

SYSTEM LIFE CYCLE CONCEPTS, MODELS, AND PROCESSES

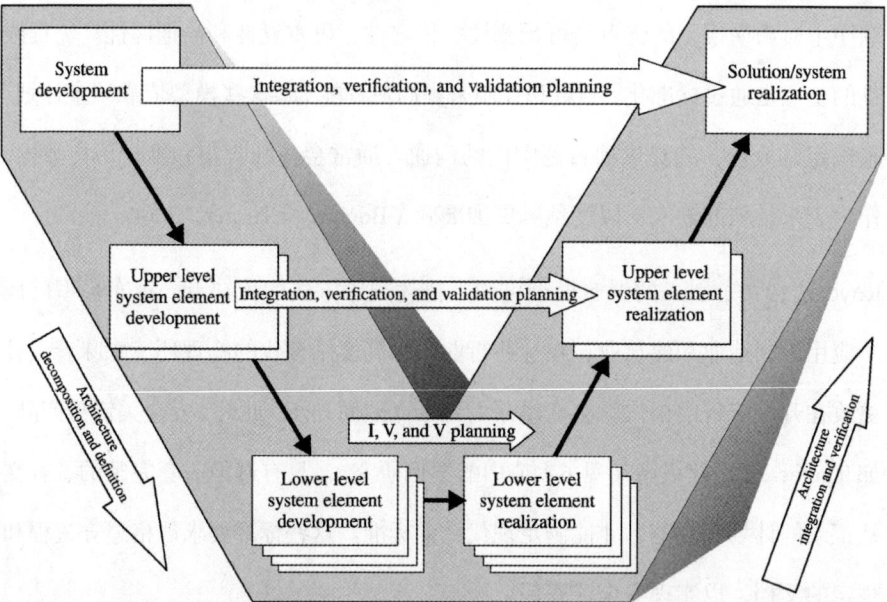

FIGURE 2.6   The SE Vee model. From Forsberg, et al. (2005) with permission from John Wiley & Sons. All other rights reserved.

The left side of the Vee depicts the evolving baseline from stakeholder requirements, to system requirements, to the identification of a system architecture, to definition of elements that will comprise the final system. The development team then can move from the highest level of the system requirements down to the lowest level of detail. Risk and opportunity management investigations address development options to provide assurance that the baseline performance being considered can indeed be achieved and to initiate alternate concept studies at the lower levels of detail to determine the best approach. Stakeholder discussions (in-process validation) occur to ensure that the proposed baselines are acceptable to the organization, customer, user, and other stakeholders. Changes to enhance system performance or to reduce risk or cost are welcome for consideration, but after baselining these must go through formal change control, since others may be building on previously defined and released design decisions. The bottom of the Vee depicts either the recursive application of the systems life cycle processes at the next level of the system hierarchy or the implementation of atomic system elements (see Section 1.3.5). The broadening at the base of the figure shows the growth in the number of system elements. Note that system elements can also be bought or reused. The right side of the Vee depicts the evolving baseline of system elements that are implemented, integrated, verified, and validated. In each stage of the system life cycle, the SE processes iterate to ensure that a concept or design is feasible and that the stakeholders remain supportive of the solution as it evolves.

系统生命周期概念、模型和流程

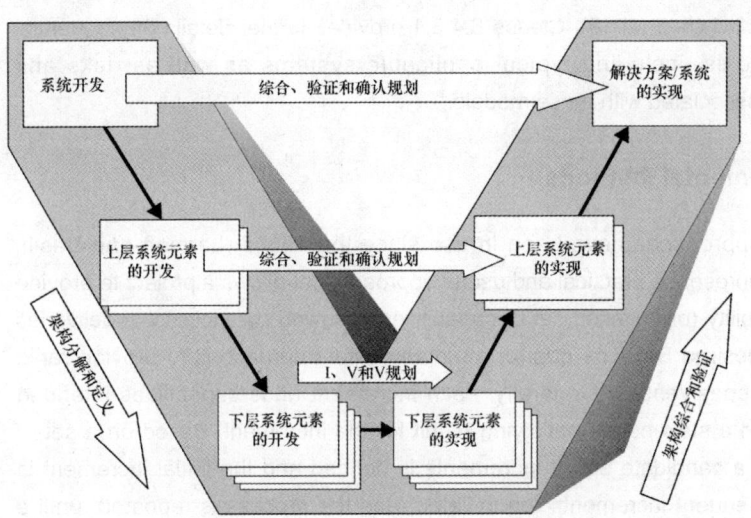

图 2.6　系统工程 V 模型。源自 Forsberg 等（2005），经 John Wiley & Sons. 许可。版权所有。

V 的左侧描述了从利益相关方需求到系统需求，到系统架构的确定，再到构成最终系统的元素的定义不断演进的基线。然后，开发团队可以从系统需求的最高层级向下移动到细节的最低层级。风险和机会管理研究可以提供开发的可选项，以确保所考虑的基线绩效确实能够实现，并通过在更低层级的概念研究中提供详细方案，以确定最佳实现方法。利益相关方的讨论（流程中确认）旨在确保所提的基线是组织、客户、用户和其他利益相关方可以接受的。为提高系统性能或降低风险或成本而进行的更改都是欢迎的，但在基线化之后，这些更改必须经过正式的更改控制，因为其他更改可能基于先前定义和发布的设计决策。V 的底部描述了系统生命周期流程在系统层次结构的下一个层次的递归应用或原子级系统元素的实现（见 1.3.5 节）。图底部的加宽展示了系统元素数量的增长。请注意，系统元素也可以购买或重用。V 右侧描述了已实施、综合、验证和确认的系统元素的演进基线。在系统生命周期的每个阶段，系统工程流程都会迭代，以确保概念或设计是可行的，并且利益相关方在解决方案开发流程中仍然支持该解决方案。

SYSTEM LIFE CYCLE CONCEPTS, MODELS, AND PROCESSES

36   ISO/IEC/IEEE 24748–2 (2018), Clause 6.4.3.1 provides further details on sequential life cycle models, including typical applicable systems as well as risks and opportunities associated with these models.

2.2.2   Incremental Methods

Incremental approaches have been in use since the 1960s (Larman and Basili, 2003). They represent a practical and useful approach that allows a project to provide an initial capability (or a limited set of capabilities) followed by successive deliveries to reach the desired SoI. The goal of an incremental approach is to provide rapid value and responsiveness. Generally, each increment adds capabilities intended to converge on a stakeholder satisfying result for the increment. Based on a set of requirements, a candidate set of increments is defined and the initial increment is initiated. Subsequent increments are initiated, and the process is repeated, until a complete system is deployed or until the organization decides to terminate the effort. Intermediate increments can potentially be deployed to support learning.

37   An incremental approach works well when an organization intends to market new versions of a product at planned intervals. Typically, the capabilities of the final delivery are known at the beginning. However, as there is significant technical risk, the development of the capabilities is performed incrementally to allow for the latest technology insertion or potential changes in needs or requirements. A core part of the planning process for an incremental approach establishes the cycle times for increments. Increments are beneficially timed in development projects to accommodate coordinated events such as integration testing and evaluation, capability deployment, experimental deployment, or release to production. Iteration cycles are beneficially timed to minimize rework cost as a project learns experimentally and empirically. Project planning and management often benefit from a constant cadence among increments.

One example of an incremental approach is the Incremental Commitment Spiral Model (ICSM) (Boehm, et al., 2014), which extends the classic Spiral Model for software introduced in Boehm (1987) for SE. A view of the ICSM is shown in Figure 2.7. In the ICSM, each increment addresses requirements and solutions concurrently, rather than sequentially. ICSM also considers products and processes; hardware, software, and human aspects; and business case analyses of alternative product configurations or product line investments. The stakeholders consider the risks and risk mitigation plans and decide on a course of action. If the risks are acceptable and covered by risk mitigation plans, the project proceeds into the next spiral (increment).

ISO/IEC/IEEE 24748–2（2018）第 6.4.3.1 条提供了顺序生命周期模型的进一步详细信息，包括典型的适用系统以及与这些模型相关的风险和机会。

2.2.2 增量方法

自 20 世纪 60 年代以来，增量方法（Larman 和 Basili，2003）一直被使用。它们代表了一种实用的方法，允许项目提供初始能力（或有限的能力集），然后连续交付，以达到所需的 SoI。增量方法的目标是提供快速的价值和响应能力。一般来说，每个增量都会添加一些功能，旨在汇聚到一个利益相关方满意的增量结果上。根据一组需求，定义一组候选增量，并定义初始增量。随后启动增量，并重复该流程，直到部署了完整的系统或组织决定终止工作。可以部署中间增量来辅助学习。

当组织打算按计划的时间间隔推广产品的新版本时，增量方法很有效。通常，最终交付的能力在一开始就知道了。然而，由于存在重大的技术风险，能力的开发以增量的方式进行，以允许最新的技术嵌入或需要和需求的潜在变化。增量方法的计划流程的核心部分是确定增量的周期时间。增量在开发项目中被给予有利的时间安排，以适应需要协调的事件，如综合测试和评估、能力部署、实验部署或投产。当项目通过实验和经验学习时，迭代周期对项目进行是有利的，以最小化返工成本。项目计划和管理通常受益于增量之间的恒定节奏。

增量方法的一个示例是增量承诺螺旋模型（ICSM）（Boehm 等，2014），它扩展了 Boehm（1987）针对系统工程引入的软件的经典螺旋模型。ICSM 视图如图 2.7 所示。在 ICSM 中，每个增量同时处理需求和解决方案，而不是按顺序处理。ICSM 还考虑产品和流程；硬件、软件和人员方面；以及备选产品构型或产品线投资的业务用例分析。利益相关方考虑风险和风险缓解计划，并决定行动方案。如果风险可以接受并被风险缓解计划覆盖，项目将进入下一个螺旋（增量）。

SYSTEM LIFE CYCLE CONCEPTS, MODELS, AND PROCESSES

ISO/IEC/IEEE 24748–2 (2018), Clause 6.4.3.2 provides further details on incremental life cycle models, including typical applicable systems as well as risks and opportunities associated with these models.

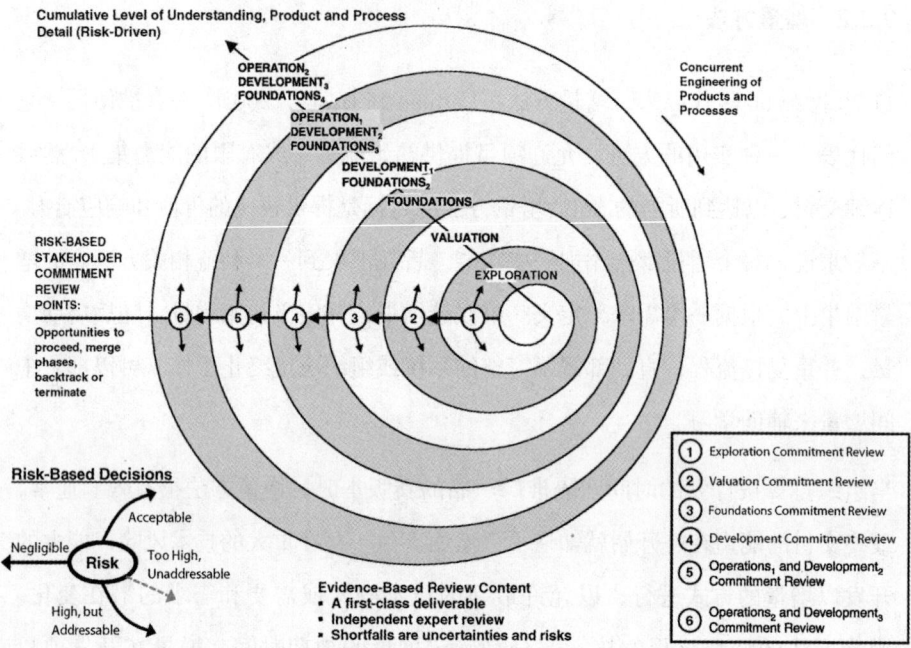

FIGURE 2.7 The Incremental Commitment Spiral Model (ICSM). From Boehm, et al. (2014) with permission from Pearson Education. All other rights reserved.

2.2.3 Evolutionary Methods

In the sequential and incremental approaches described previously, the full set of required capabilities of the final system is assumed to be mostly known at the start of the effort. In some cases, especially in novel systems, the final system requirements may be unknown or only partially known. An evolutionary approach provides the adaptability and flexibility needed for the development in these situations. For example, the high-temperature tiles of the NASA space shuttle were developed using an evolutionary approach (Forsberg, 1995). An evolutionary approach is often used in research and development (R&D) projects and SoS developments. Software development efforts are increasingly using agile methods, which are a type of evolutionary development.

ISO/IEC/IEEE 24748-2（2018）第 6.4.3.2 条提供了增量生命周期模型的进一步详细信息，包括典型的适用系统以及与这些模型相关的风险和机会。

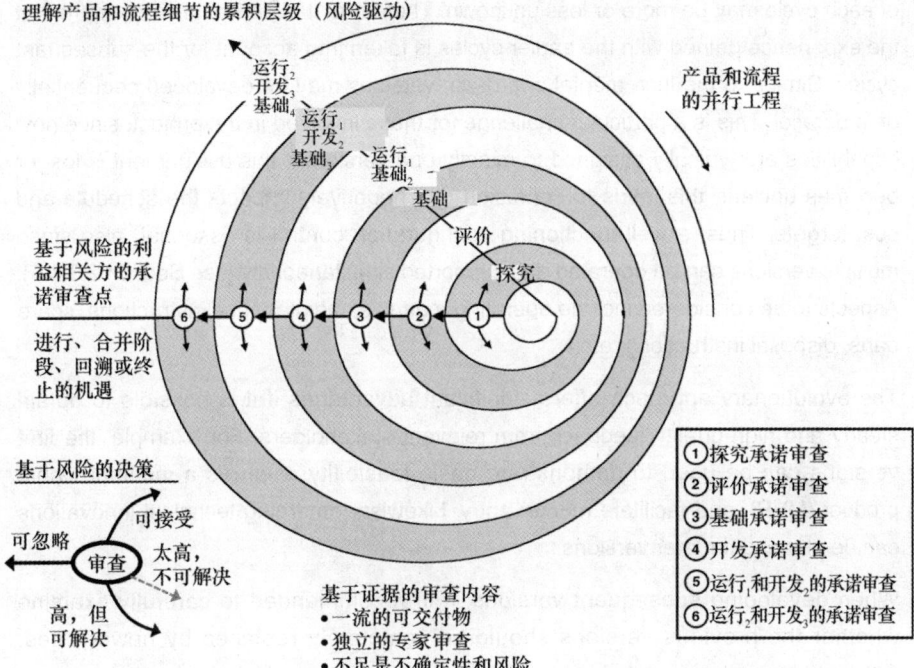

图 2.7　增量承诺螺旋模型（ICSM）。源自 Boehm 等，经 Pearson Education 许可。版权所有。

2.2.3　演进方法

在前面描述的顺序和增量方法中，假设最终系统的全部所需功能在工作开始时基本已知。在某些情况下，尤其是在新型系统中，最终系统需求可能未知或仅部分已知。演进方法提供了在这些情况下开发所需的适应性和灵活性。例如，美国宇航局航天飞机的高温瓷砖是采用演进方法开发的（Forsberg，1995）。演进方法通常用于研究与开发（R&D）项目和体系开发。软件开发工作越来越多地使用敏捷方法，这也是一种演进开发。

In evolutionary approaches, cycles are typically planned on a regular periodic basis, each resulting in a deployable version. The requirements for the SoI are typically only partially known and are increasingly refined with each cycle. At the beginning, the goal of each cycle may be more or less unknown. Therefore, it is particularly important that the experience gained with the earlier cycles is taken into account for the subsequent cycles. Similar to the incremental approach, versions may be developed sequentially or in parallel. This is a particular challenge for those involved in the project, since new capabilities are typically assigned to exactly one version. If this assignment is lost or becomes unclear, this leads to confusion and negatively impacts the schedule and cost targets. Thus, a well-functioning configuration control is essential, also since multiple versions can be operated and supported simultaneously (see Section 2.3.4.5). Aspects to be considered include operating manuals, maintenance instructions, spare parts, disposal instructions, etc.

The evolutionary approach offers significant advantages if it is possible to obtain steady and high-quality feedback from relevant stakeholders. For example, the first versions can be used to demonstrate basic feasibility, such as a minimal viable product (MVP), and facilitate market entry. Likewise, emerging technical innovations can be planned for later versions.

When developing subsequent versions, it is recommended to carefully examine whether the previous versions should be completely replaced by newer ones. Alternatively, subsequent versions can be developed such that a partial or even complete upgrade of the previous versions to the new version is possible. For this, it is necessary that these things are considered during the early cycles. Criteria such as adaptability, flexibility, and modularity should be carefully considered to enable the long-term evolution of the system. Decisions should be made in the context of life cycle cost (see Section 3.1.2).

An example of an evolutionary approach is DevOps (a blend of the terms and concepts for "development" and "operations"). The goal of DevOps is to provide continuous integration of the system and continuous delivery of capabilities. DevOps is typically characterized by three key principles: shared ownership, workflow automation, and rapid feedback. DevSecOps (a blend of "development," "security," and "operations"), shown in Figure 2.8, integrates security practices into DevOps. In DevSecOps, each delivery team is responsible and empowered to pick appropriate security means.

ISO/IEC/IEEE 24748–2 (2018), Clause 6.4.3.4 provides further details on evolutionary life cycle models, including typical applicable systems as well as risks and opportunities associated with these models.

在演进方法中，周期通常按固定期段进行计划，每个周期都会产生一个可部署的版本。SoI 的需求通常仅部分已知，并且随着每个周期不断完善。一开始，每个周期的目标可能或多或少是未知的。因此，特别重要的是，在随后的周期中需要考虑从先前周期中获得的经验。与增量方法类似，版本可以顺序开发或并行开发。这对于参与项目的人员来说是一个特殊的挑战，因为新功能通常只分配给一个版本。如果此任务丢失或变得不清楚，则会导致混淆，并对进度和成本目标产生负面影响。因此，功能完善的版本控制至关重要，因为可以同时运行和支持多个版本（见 2.3.4.5 节）。需要考虑的方面包括操作手册、维护说明、备件、处置说明等。

如果有可能从利益相关方那里获得稳定和高质量的反馈，则演进方法具有显著优势。例如，第一个版本可用于证明基本的可行性，如最小可行产品（MVP），并促进市场进入。同样，新出现的技术创新也可以在以后的版本中进行计划。

在开发后续版本时，建议仔细检查是否应将以前的版本完全替换为新版本。或者，可以开发后续版本，以便可以将之前的版本部分甚至全部升级到新版本。为此，有必要在周期早期时考虑这些因素。应仔细考虑适应性、灵活性和模块化等标准，以实现系统的长期发展。应在生命周期成本的背景下做出决策（见 3.1.2 节）。

演进方法的一个例子是 DevOps（混合了"开发"和"运行"的术语和概念）。DevOps 的目标是提供系统的持续综合和能力的持续交付。DevOps 通常有三个关键原则：共享所有权、工作流自动化和快速反馈。DevSecOps（支持"开发"、"安保"和"运行"），如图 2.8 所示，将安保实践综合到 DevOps 中。在 DevSecOps 中，每个交付团队都有职责并有权选择适当的安保手段。

ISO/IEC/IEEE 24748–2（2018）第 6.4.3.4 条提供了演进生命周期模型的进一步详细信息，包括典型的适用系统以及与这些模型相关的风险和机会。

SYSTEM LIFE CYCLE CONCEPTS, MODELS, AND PROCESSES

Figure 2.9 is an example of a mixed approach (both incremental and evolutionary). This figure shows the agile mixed-discipline approach employed by Rockwell Collins in the development of military radios (Dove, et al., 2017). Teams working on electronic-board hardware, firmware, and software have different timings for hardware increments and firmware and software epics (versions). The teams accomplish integrated work-in-process testing with the latest increments and versions from each of the disciplines.

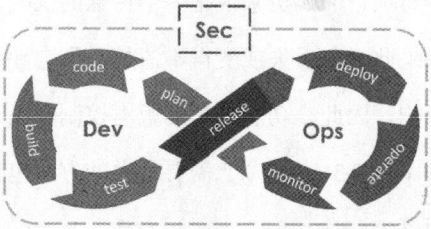

FIGURE 2.8 DevSecOps INCOSE SEH original figure created by working on electronic-board hardware, firmware, D'Souza derived from Banach (2019) and Anx (2021). Usage per the and software have different timings for hardware.

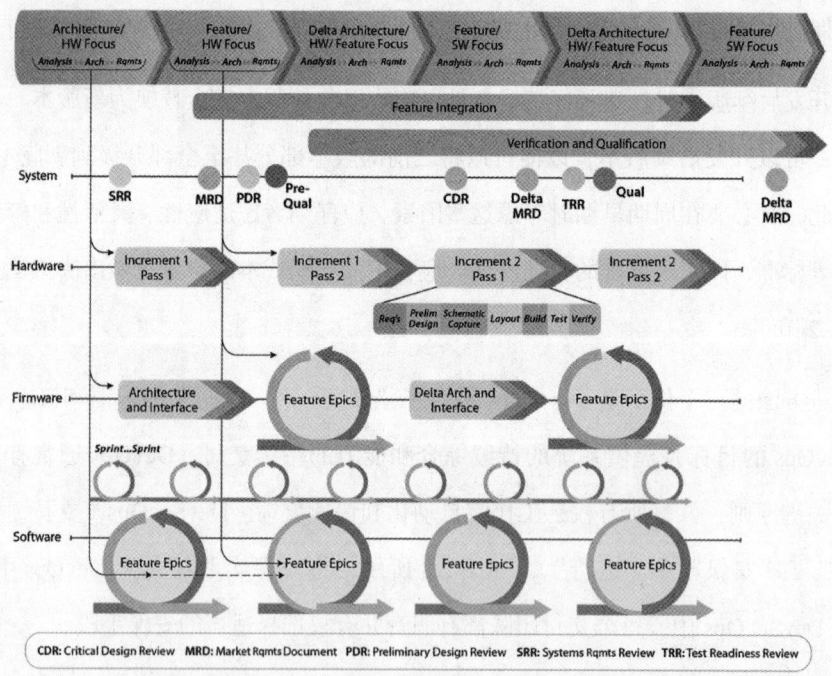

FIGURE 2.9 Asynchronous iterations and increments across agile mixed discipline engineering. From Dove, et al. (2017). Used with permission. All other rights served.

图 2.9 是混合方法的一个示例（增量方法和演进方法）。此图展示了罗克韦尔柯林斯公司在军用无线电开发中采用的敏捷混合学科方法（Dove 等，2017）。从事电子板硬件、固件和软件工作的团队对于硬件增量以及固件和软件 EPIC（版本）有不同的计时安排。团队使用每个学科的最新增量和版本完成综合的在制品测试。

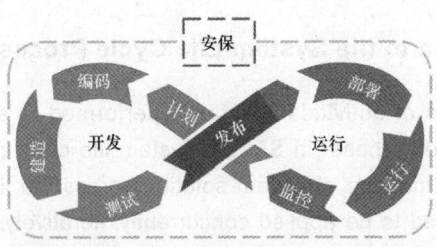

图 2.8 开发安保运行。INCOSE SEH 原始图由 D'Souza 创建，源自 Banach（2019）和 Anx（2021）。根据 INCOSE 通知页使用。

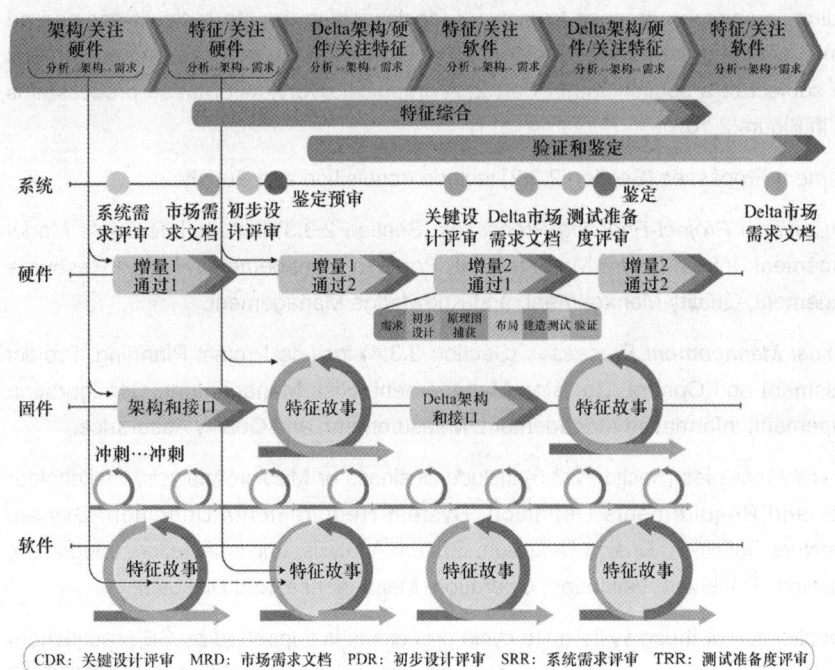

图 2.9 敏捷混合学科工程的异步迭代和增量。源自 Dove 等（2017）。经许可后使用。版权所有。

SYSTEM LIFE CYCLE CONCEPTS, MODELS, AND PROCESSES

All these life cycle approaches are supported by the processes defined in ISO/IEC/IEEE 15288 (2023) and this handbook. The life cycle model should be chosen so that it is sufficiently adaptable and flexible. Section 4.1 provides more information on tailoring life cycle models.

2.3 SYSTEM LIFE CYCLE PROCESSES

2.3.1 Introduction to the System Life Cycle Processes

A process is a series of activities and tasks performed to achieve one or more outcomes for a stated purpose. In SE, the system life cycle processes are one of the enablers to help manage a system solution across the life cycle stages. The processes are intended to be applied concurrently, iteratively, and recursively with other enablers (e.g., tools, technology) throughout the stages of the life cycle (see Section 2.3.1.2).

ISO/IEC/IEEE 15288 (2023) identifies four process groups for the system life cycle, providing "a common process framework for describing the life cycle of engineered systems, adopting a Systems Engineering approach." Each of these process groups is the subject of a section within Part 2. A graphical overview of these processes is given in Figure 2.10:

Agreement Processes (Section 2.3.2) include Acquisition and Supply.

Organizational Project-Enabling Processes (Section 2.3.3) include Life Cycle Model Management, Infrastructure Management, Portfolio Management, Human Resource Management, Quality Management, and Knowledge Management.

Technical Management Processes (Section 2.3.4) include Project Planning, Project Assessment and Control, Decision Management, Risk Management, Configuration Management, Information Management, Measurement, and Quality Assurance.

Technical Processes (Section 2.3.5) include Business or Mission Analysis, Stakeholder Needs and Requirements Definition, System Requirements Definition, System Architecture Definition, Design Definition, System Analysis, Implementation, Integration, Verification, Transition, Validation, Operation, Maintenance, and Disposal.

The application of these system life cycle processes is supported by SE practitioners having the relevant competencies. The competencies are defined in the INCOSE Systems Engineering Competency Framework (SECF) (2018). Note that the professional competencies (see Section 5.1.2) generally apply to all the processes.

Note: Acronyms for the process names are provided in Appendix D.

ISO/IEC/IEEE 15288（2023）和本手册中定义的流程支持所有这些生命周期方法。应选择生命周期模型，使其具有足够的适应性和灵活性。4.1 节提供了有关剪裁生命周期模型的更多信息。

2.3 系统生命周期流程

2.3.1 系统生命周期流程介绍

流程是为实现一个或多个既定目的而执行的一系列活动和任务。在系统工程中，系统生命周期流程是帮助跨生命周期阶段管理系统解决方案的使能因素之一。这些流程旨在在整个生命周期的各个阶段与其他使能项（如工具、技术）并行、迭代和递归地应用（见 2.3.1.2 节）。

ISO/IEC/IEEE 15288（2023）确定了系统生命周期的四个流程组，提供了"采用系统工程方法描述工程系统生命周期的通用流程框架"。这些流程组中的每一个都是第二部分中一节的主题。图 2.10 给出了这些流程的图形化概述：

协议流程（2.3.2 节）包括采办和供应。

组织项目使能流程（2.3.3 节）包括生命周期模型管理、基础设施管理、项目组合管理、人力资源管理、质量管理和知识管理。

技术管理流程（2.3.4 节）包括项目计划、项目评估和控制、决策管理、风险管理、构型配置管理、信息管理、测量和质量保证。

技术流程（2.3.5 节）包括业务或任务分析、利益相关方需要和需求定义、系统需求定义、系统架构定义、设计定义、系统分析、实施、综合、验证、转移、确认、运行、维护和处置。

具有相关胜任力的系统工程实践者支持这些系统生命周期流程的应用。胜任力在 INCOSE 系统工程胜任力框架（SECF）（2018）中定义。请注意，专业胜任力（见 5.1.2 节）通常适用于所有流程。

注：附录 D 中提供了流程名称的首字母缩略词。

SYSTEM LIFE CYCLE CONCEPTS, MODELS, AND PROCESSES

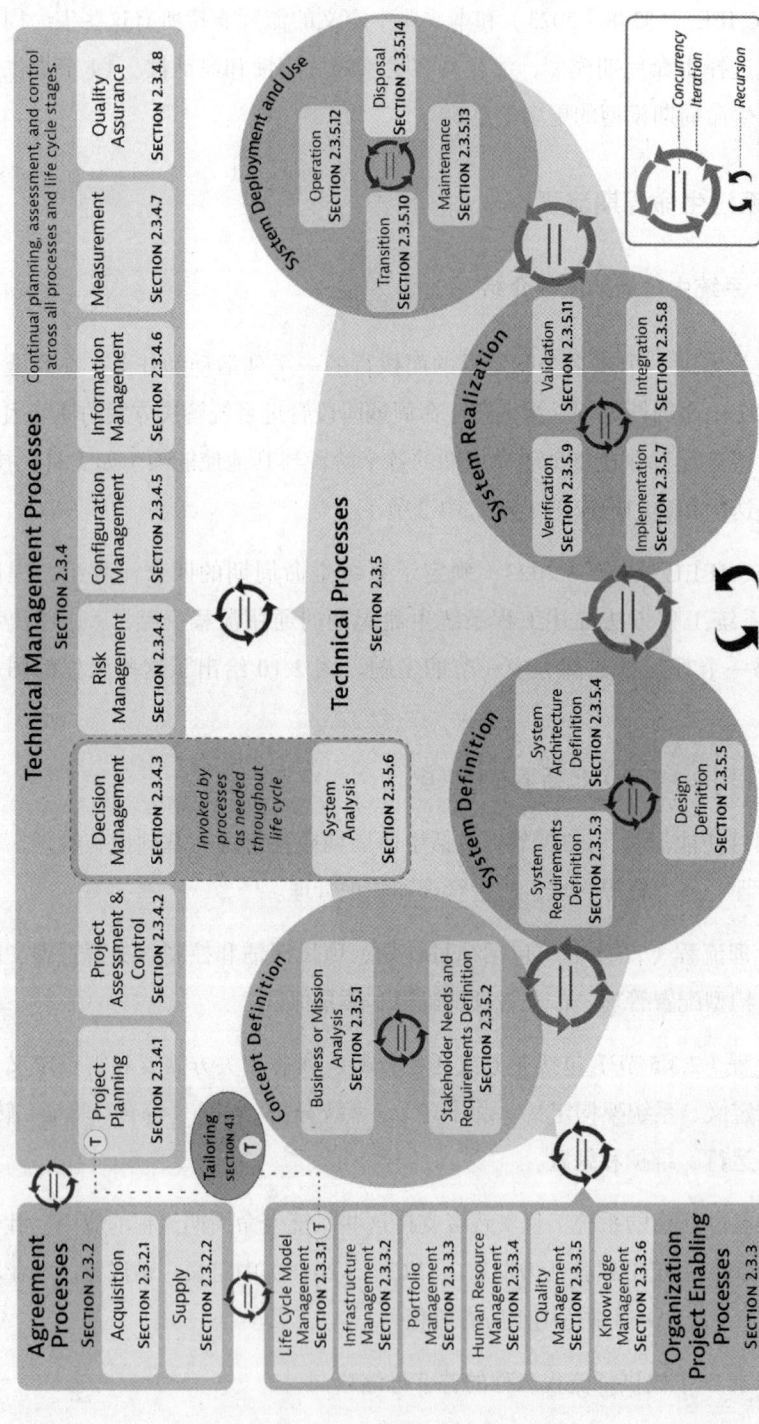

FIGURE 2.10 System life cycle processes per ISO/IEC/IEEE 15288. INCOSE SEH original figure created by Roedler and Walden. Usage per the INCOSE Notices page. All other rights reserved.

系统生命周期概念、模型和流程

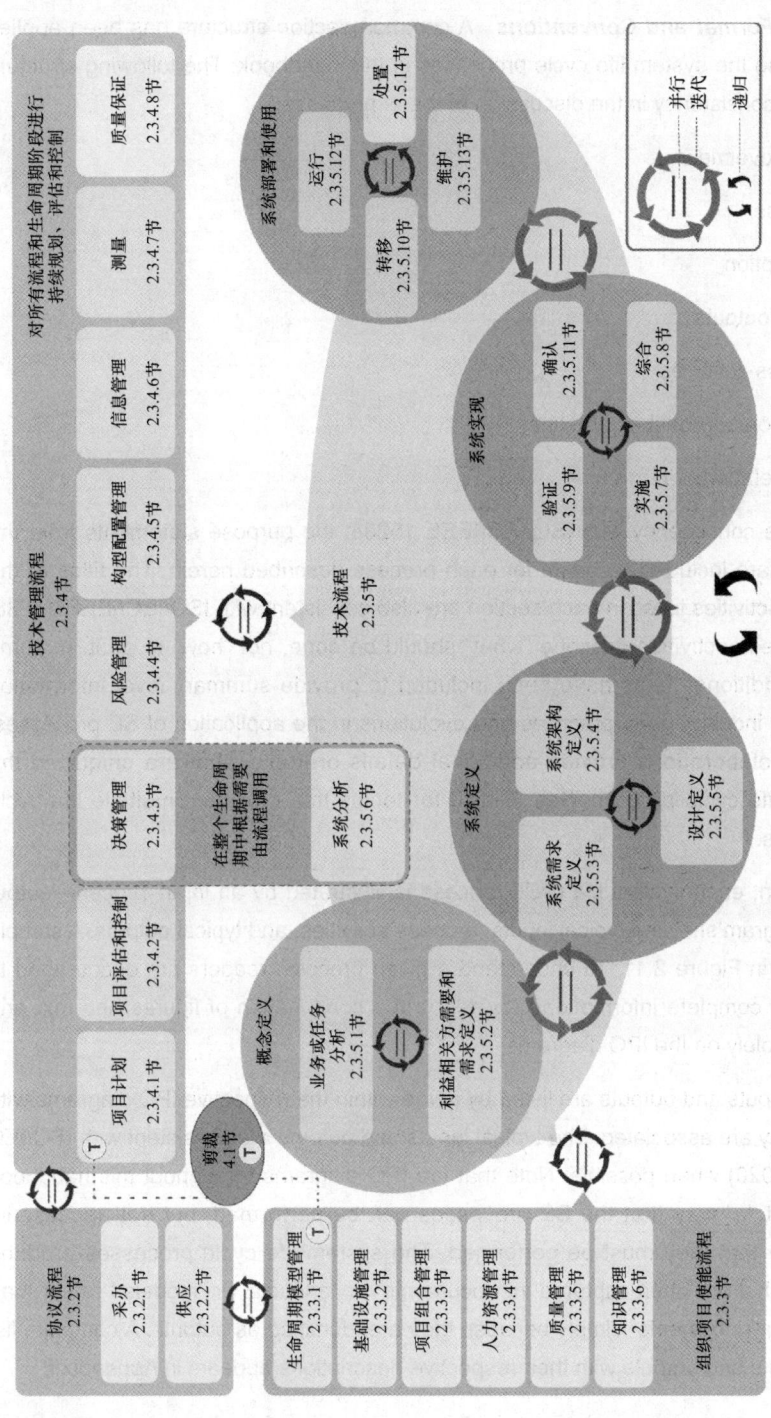

图 2.10 依据 ISO/IEC/IEEE 15288 的系统生命周期流程。INCOSE SEH 原始图由 Roedler 和 Walden 创建。根据 INCOSE 通知页使用。版权所有。

113

SYSTEM LIFE CYCLE CONCEPTS, MODELS, AND PROCESSES

2.3.1.1 Format and Conventions A common section structure has been applied to describe the system life cycle processes in this handbook. The following structure provides consistency in the discussion of these processes:

Process overview

  Purpose

  Description

  Inputs/outputs

  Process activities

  Common approaches and tips

Process elaboration

To ensure consistency with ISO/IEC/IEEE 15288, the purpose statements from the standard are included verbatim for each process described herein. The titles of the process activities listed in each section are also consistent with ISO/IEC/IEEE 15288. The process activities describe "what" should be done, not "how" to do it. In some cases, additional items have been included to provide summary-level information regarding industry good practices and evolutions in the application of SE processes. Process elaborations provide additional details on topics that are unique to the specific life cycle process. See Part III for topics that cross-cut multiple life cycle processes.

In addition, each system life cycle process is illustrated by an input–process–output (IPO) diagram showing typical inputs, process activities, and typical outputs. A sample is shown in Figure 2.11. To understand a given process, readers are encouraged to study the complete information provided in the combination of figures and text and not rely solely on the IPO diagrams.

Typical inputs and outputs are listed by name within the respective IPO diagrams with which they are associated. The typical inputs and outputs are consistent with ISO/IEC 33060 (2020) when possible. Note that the IPO diagrams throughout this handbook represent "a" way that the SE processes can be performed, but not necessarily "the" way that they must be performed. The system life cycle processes produce "results" that are often captured in "documents" or "artifacts" or "models," rather than producing "documents" simply because they are identified as outputs. A complete list of all inputs and outputs with their respective descriptions appears in Appendix E.

系统生命周期概念、模型和流程

2.3.1.1 格式和约定 本手册采用通用章节结构来描述系统生命周期流程。以下结构为这些流程的讨论提供了一致性：

流程概述

  目的

  描述

  输入/输出

  流程活动

  常用方法和提示

流程详细阐述

为确保与 ISO/IEC/IEEE 15288 的一致性，本标准中目的陈述逐字包含在本文所述的每个流程中。各节中列出的流程活动标题也与 ISO/IEC/IEEE 15288 一致。流程活动描述了应该做什么，而不是如何做。在某些情况下，还包括了其他内容，以提供有关系统工程流程应用中的行业优秀实践和发展的汇总信息。流程详细阐述提供了特定生命周期流程特有主题的其他详细信息。有关贯穿多个生命周期流程的主题，请参见三部分。

此外，每个系统生命周期流程都通过输入—流程—输出（IPO）图进行说明，该图展示了典型的输入、流程活动和典型的输出（示例见图 2.11）。为了理解一个给定的流程，鼓励读者研究以图和文本相结合的方式提供的完整信息，而不仅仅依赖 IPO 图。

典型的输入和输出在与之相关的各个 IPO 图表中按名称列出。在可能的时候典型的输入和输出符合 ISO/IEC 33060（2020）。请注意，本手册中的 IPO 图代表了系统工程流程可以执行的"一种"方式，但不一定是必须执行的"那种"方式。系统生命周期流程产生的"结果"通常被捕获在"文档"或"制品"或"模型"中，而不仅仅因为它们被标识为输出而记录在"文档"中。附录 E 中列出了所有输入和输出的完整列表及其各自的描述。

SYSTEM LIFE CYCLE CONCEPTS, MODELS, AND PROCESSES

The controls and enablers shown in Figure 2.11 govern all processes described herein and, as such, are not repeated on the subsequent IPO diagrams. Typically, IPO diagrams do not include controls and enablers, but since they are not repeated in the IPO diagrams throughout the rest of the handbook, we have chosen to label them IPO diagrams. The enablers work together with the inputs to be transformed by the process into the outputs under the direction of the controls. A complete list of all controls and enablers with their respective descriptions appears in Appendix E.

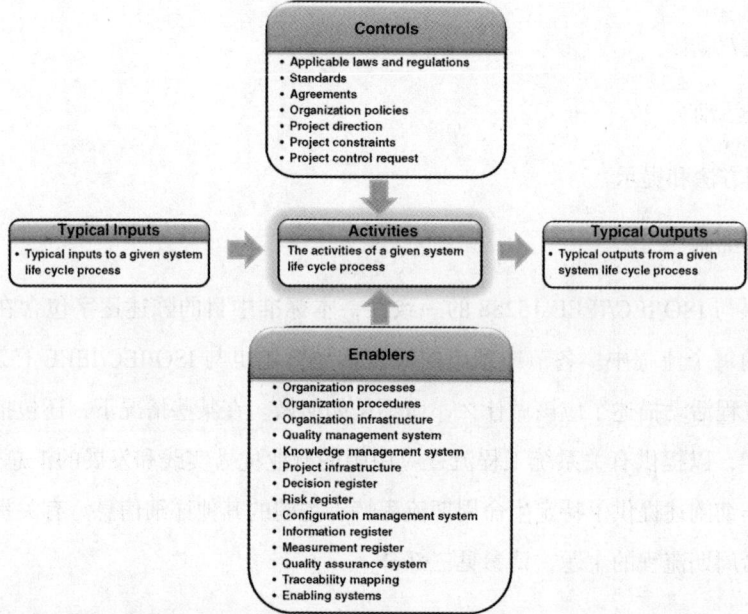

FIGURE 2.11 Sample IPO diagram for SE processes. INCOSE SEH original figure created by Walden, Shortell, and Yip. Usage per the INCOSE Notices page. All other rights reserved.

2.3.1.2 Concurrency, Iteration, and Recursion

Too often, the system life cycle processes are viewed as being applied in a sequential, linear manner at a single level of the system hierarchy. However, valuable information and insight need to be exchanged between the processes in order to ensure a good system definition that effectively and efficiently meets the stakeholder needs and requirements. The application of concurrency, iteration, and recursion to the system life cycle processes helps to ensure communication that accounts for ongoing learning and decisions. This facilitates the incorporation of learning from further analysis and process application as the technical solution evolves. Figure 2.12 shows an illustration of the concurrent, iterative, and recursive nature of the system life cycle processes.

图 2.11 所示的控制项和使能项控制了本文所述的所有流程，因此，在后续的 IPO 图中不会重复。通常，IPO 图不包括控制项和使能项，但由于在本手册其余部分的 IPO 图中没有重复这些控制项和使能项，因此我们选择将它们标记为 IPO 图。在控制项的指导下，使能项与流程输入一起将流程转化为输出。附录 E 中列出了所有控制项和使能项的完整列表及其各自的描述。

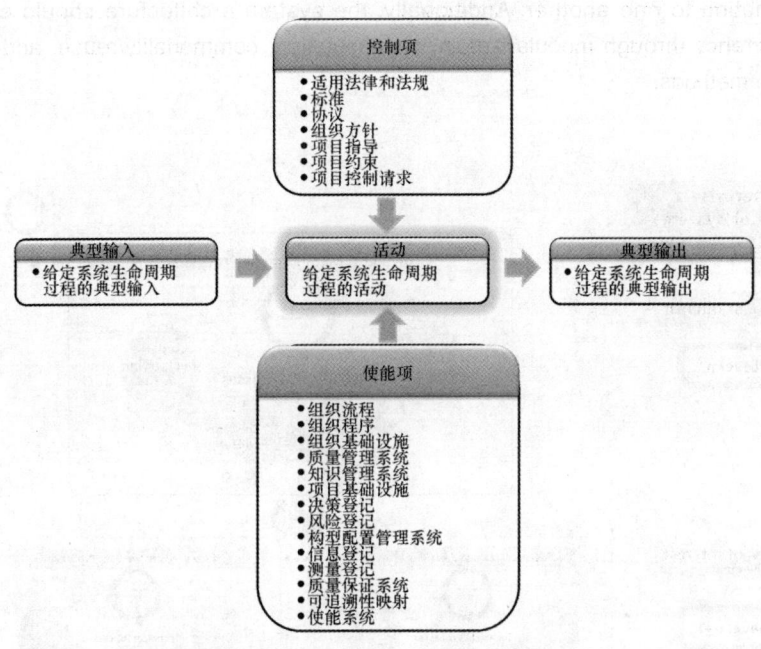

图 2.11 系统工程流程的 IPO 图。INCOSE SEH 原始图由 Walden、Shortell 和 Yip 创建。按照 INCOSE 通知页使用。版权所有。

2.3.1.2 并行、迭代和递归 通常，系统生命周期流程被视为在系统层次结构的单个层级上以连续、线性的方式应用。然而，需要在流程之间交换有价值的信息和见解，以确保良好的系统定义能够有效地满足利益相关方的需要和需求。将并行、迭代和递归应用到系统生命周期流程中，有助于确保沟通，从而考虑持续的学习和决策。随着技术解决方案的发展，这有助于从进一步的分析和流程应用中学习。图 2.12 展示了系统生命周期流程的并行、迭代和递归特征。

SYSTEM LIFE CYCLE CONCEPTS, MODELS, AND PROCESSES

Concurrency (indicated by the parallel lines in the figure) is the parallel application of two or more processes at a given level in the system hierarchy. Concurrent work is likely to happen on any project and the system life cycle processes can likewise be performed in a concurrent manner. It is not necessary for processes to be performed serially, especially when one process is not dependent on another for information or results. For example, the Risk Management process and Measurement process usually are performed in a continual and concurrent manner. This is illustrated in Figure 2.34, in which both of these processes occur concurrently, yet provide information to one another. Additionally, the system architecture should enable concurrency through modularization, encapsulation, commonality/reuse, and other design methods.

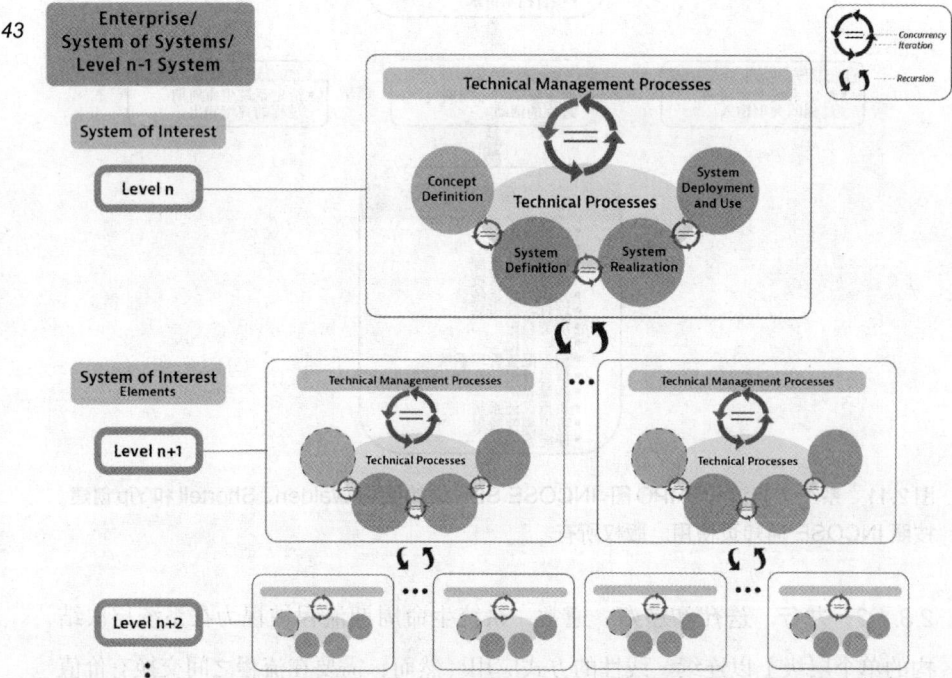

FIGURE 2.12 Concurrency, iteration, and recursion. INCOSE SEH original figure created by Roedler and Walden. Usage per the INCOSE Notices page. All other rights reserved.

系统生命周期概念、模型和流程

并行（由图中的平行线表示）是系统层次结构中给定层级上两个或多个流程的并行应用。任何项目都可能发生并行工作，系统生命周期流程也可以并行执行。没有必要连续执行流程，尤其是当一个流程在信息或结果方面不依赖于另一个流程时。例如，风险管理流程和测量流程通常以连续和并行的方式执行。如图2.34所示，其中这两个流程同时发生，但相互提供信息。此外，系统架构应通过模块化、封装、通用性／重用和其他设计方法实现并行。

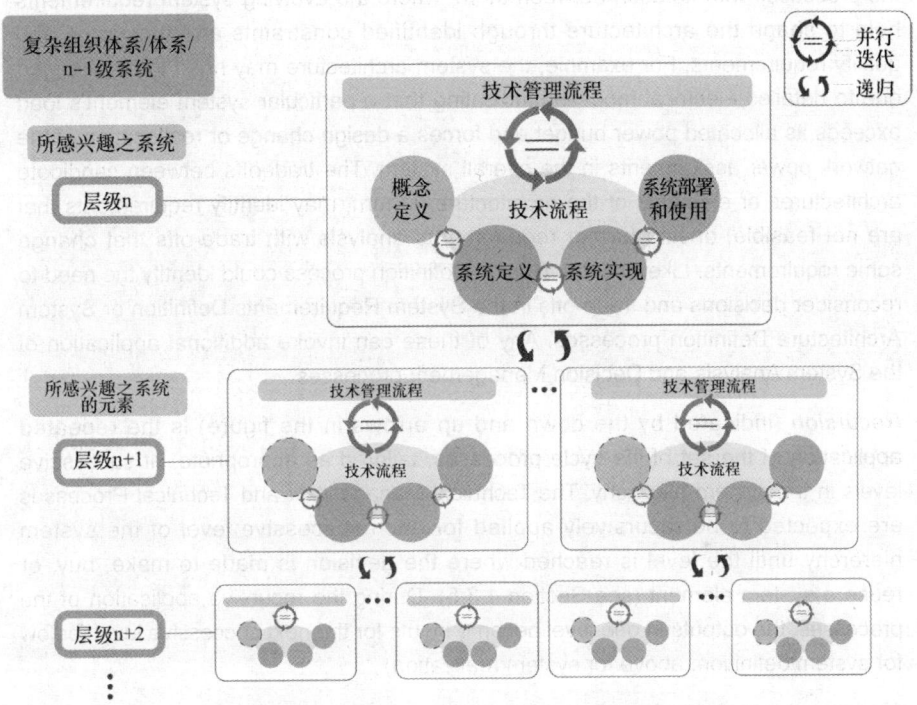

图 2.12　并行、迭代和递归。INCOSE SEH 原始图由 Roedler 和 Walden 创建。按照 INCOSE 通知页使用。版权所有。

SYSTEM LIFE CYCLE CONCEPTS, MODELS, AND PROCESSES

Iteration (indicated by the circular arrows in the figure) is the repeated application of and interaction between two or more processes at a given level in the system hierarchy. Iteration is needed to accommodate stakeholder decisions and evolving understanding, account for architectural decisions or constraints, and resolve trade-offs for affordability, adaptability, feasibility, resilience, etc. There can be iteration between any of the processes. For example, there is often iteration between System Requirements Definition and System Architecture Definition processes. The system architecture will reflect these design iterations through identification of functions, their allocation to system elements, assignment to logical and physical interfaces, and verification as intended in the design. In this case, there is a concurrent application of the processes with iteration between them, where the evolving system requirements help to shape the architecture through identified constraints and functional and quality requirements. For example, the system architecture may need to be changed due to detailed electrical modeling indicating that a particular system element's load exceeds its allocated power budget and forces a design change or reallocation of the network power assignments in the overall system. The tradeoffs between candidate architectures or elements of the architecture, in turn, may identify requirements that are not feasible, driving further requirements analysis with trade-offs that change some requirements. Likewise, the Design Definition process could identify the need to reconsider decisions and trade-offs in the System Requirements Definition or System Architecture Definition processes. Any of these can invoke additional application of the System Analysis and Decision Management processes.

Recursion (indicated by the down and up arrows in the figure) is the repeated application of the set of life cycle processes, tailored as appropriate, at successive levels in the system hierarchy. The Technical Management and Technical Processes are expected to be recursively applied for each successive level of the system hierarchy until the level is reached where the decision is made to make, buy, or reuse a system element (see Section 1.3.5). During the recursive application of the processes, the outputs at one level become inputs for the next successive level (below for system definition, above for system realization).

Horizontal integration ensures completeness before diving deeper and *vertical integration* ensures consistency between levels in this concurrent, iterative, and recursive environment (see Section 2.3.5.8). For example, one may have to define functions, their inputs and outputs, their associated performance and conditions of operations *before* writing the associated requirement. Then one can define the related verification (method, conditions, criteria), from which one can postulate the next-lower-level architecture to assess feasibility and perform the related function, performance, or requirements decomposition and allocation. However, teams may need to go down multiples levels to validate that the functions or elements at the lower levels are going to be suitable solutions for the SoI and its stakeholders.

系统生命周期概念、模型和流程

迭代（由图中的圆形箭头表示）是在系统层次结构中的给定层级上重复应用两个或多个流程以及它们之间的交互。需要迭代来适应利益相关方的决策和不断演进的洞察，考虑架构决策或约束，并解决可承受性、适应性、可行性、韧性等方面的权衡。任何流程之间都可以进行迭代。例如，系统需求定义和系统架构定义流程之间经常存在迭代。系统架构将通过功能识别、功能分配给系统元素、逻辑和物理接口分配以及设计中预期的验证来反映这些设计迭代。在这种情况下，存在流程的并行应用，流程之间进行迭代，不断演进的系统需求通过确定的约束以及功能和质量需求帮助形成架构。例如，由于详细的电气建模表明特定系统元素的负载超过其分配的功率预算，并迫使整个系统中的网络功率分配进行设计更改或重新分配，因此可能需要更改系统架构。候选系统架构或系统架构元素之间的权衡反过来可能会确定不可行的需求，从而推动进一步的需求分析，并通过权衡改变某些需求。同样，设计定义流程可以确定是否需要重新考虑系统需求定义或系统架构定义流程中的决策和权衡。其中任何一个都可以调用系统分析和决策管理流程。

递归（由图中的向下和向上箭头表示）是在系统层次结构的连续层级上重复应用生命周期流程集，并根据需要进行定制。技术管理和技术流程预计将递归地应用于系统层次结构的每个连续层级，直至决定制造、购买或重用系统元素的层级（见 1.3.5 节）。在流程的递归应用中，一个层级的输出将成为下一个连续层级的输入（向下为系统定义，向上为系统实现）。

横向综合 在深入细节之前确保完整性，而纵向综合确保了并行、迭代和递归环境中各个层级之间的一致性（见 2.3.5.8 节）。例如，在编写相关需求之前，可能必须定义功能、其输入和输出、其相关性能和运行条件。然后可以定义相关的验证（方法、条件、准则），从中可以假设下一个较低层级的架构，以评估可行性，并执行相关的功能、性能或需求的分解和分配。然而，团队可能需要深入到多个层级，以验证较低层级的功能或元素是否适合 SoI 及其利益相关方。

SYSTEM LIFE CYCLE CONCEPTS, MODELS, AND PROCESSES

2.3.2 Agreement Processes

The initiation of a project begins with the identification of a problem or opportunity to be addressed, which results in the development of needs to be satisfied. Once a need is identified and resources are committed to establish a project, it is possible to define the terms and conditions of an acquisition and supply relationship through the Agreement Processes, which are defined in ISO/IEC/IEEE 15288 as follows:

[5.7.2] [Agreement] Processes define the activities necessary to establish an agreement between two organizations.

The Agreement Processes in this handbook and in ISO/IEC/IEEE 15288 are focused on the acquisition and supply of systems, system elements, products, or services, although agreements could be established for other objectives. With respect to the acquisition and supply relationship, the acquirer and supplier could be two independent organizations (i.e., no common parent organization or enterprise) or two organizations from the same parent organization or enterprise.

The Agreement Processes are utilized under many conditions, including when:

- an organization cannot satisfy a defined need itself,
- a supplier can satisfy a defined need in a more economical or timely manner,
- a higher authority has directed the use of a specific supplier, and
- an organization needs materials or specialized services.

An overall objective of Agreement Processes is to identify the interfaces between the acquirer and supplier(s) and establish the terms and conditions of these relationships, including identifying the inputs required and the outputs that will be provided.

Agreement negotiations are handled in various ways depending on the specific organizations and the formality of the agreement. In a formal agreement, there is usually a contract negotiation activity to refine the contract terms and conditions. Note also that the Agreement Processes can be used for coordinating within an organization between different business units or functions. In this case, the agreement will usually be more informal, not requiring a formal or specific contract.

An important contribution of ISO/IEC/IEEE 15288 is the recognition that SE practitioners are relevant contributors to the Agreement Processes (Arnold and Lawson, 2003). The SE practitioner is usually in a supporting role to the project management practitioner during negotiations and is responsible for impact assessments for changes, trade studies on alternatives, risk assessments, and other technical input needed for decisions.

2.3.2 协议流程

项目的启动首先要确定需要解决的问题或机会，这将引出应满足的需要的开发。一旦确定需要并投入资源建立项目，就可以通过协议流程定义采办和供应关系的条款和条件，ISO/IEC/IEEE 15288 中定义如下：

[5.7.2][协议] 流程定义了在两个组织之间建立协议所需的活动。

本手册和 ISO/IEC/IEEE 15288 中的协议流程侧重于系统、系统元素、产品或服务的采办和供应，也可以为其他目标制定协议。就采办和供应关系而言，采办方和供应商可以是两个独立的组织（即没有共同的上级组织或复杂组织体系），也可以是来自同一上级组织或复杂组织体系的两个组织。

协议流程可在多种情况下使用，包括：

- 组织本身无法满足定义的需要；
- 供应商可以更经济或及时地满足定义的需要；
- 上级主管部门已指示使用特定供应商；
- 组织需要材料或专门服务。

协议流程的总体目标是确定采办方和供应商之间的接口，并确定这些关系的条款和条件，包括确定所需的输入和将提供的输出。

根据具体组织和协议的形式，协议谈判可以以各种方式进行。在正式协议中，通常有合同谈判活动来完善合同条款和条件。还请注意，协议流程可用于组织内不同业务部门或职能部门之间的协调。在这种情况下，协议通常是非正式的，不需要正式或具体的合同。

ISO/IEC/IEEE 15288 的一个重要贡献是认识到系统工程实践者是协议流程的相关贡献者（Arnold 和 Lawson，2003）。系统工程实践者通常在谈判期间为项目管理实践者提供支持，并负责变更的影响评估、备选方案的权衡研究、风险评估以及决策所需的其他技术输入。

45 Acceptance criteria are critical elements to each party because they protect both sides of the business relationship—the acquirer from being coerced into accepting a product with poor quality and the supplier from the unpredictable actions of an indecisive acquirer. It is important to note that the acceptance criteria are negotiated during the Agreement Processes. During negotiations, it is also critical that both parties are able to track progress toward an agreement. Identifying where further work toward achieving consensus in the documents and clauses is vital.

Two Agreement Processes are identified by ISO/IEC/IEEE 15288: the Acquisition process and the Supply process. These processes, subject of Sections 2.3.2.1 and 2.3.2.2, respectively, are two sides of the same coin. They conduct the essential business of the organization related to the SoI. They establish the relationships between organizations relevant to the acquisition and supply of products and services, regardless of whether the agreement is formal (as in a contract) or informal. Each process establishes the context and constraints of the agreement under which the other system life cycle processes belonging to the project scope are performed. Note that an organization can be both a supplier and acquirer for a given system. For example, an organization may be contracted to supply a system to an end customer. However, that organization may choose to acquire some of the system elements, materials, or services for developing or producing the system. So, that organization is the supplier to the end customer of the system and is the acquirer to those organizations providing it system elements, materials, or services.

Changes may happen during the execution of an agreement including acquirer change requests, deviations and waivers from the supply chain, or changes in the context of the project that were foreseen in risk analysis or not. Upon decision of the parties, this may lead to modifications to the initial state of the agreement. For that purpose, a statement of compliance may be initiated and updated all along the project describing the agreed changes and can include requirements impacted by a modification, the reference of modification, compliance verification by the supplier, and compliance validation by the acquirer.

2.3.2.1 Acquisition Process

Overview

Purpose As stated in ISO/IEC/IEEE 15288,

[6.1.1.1] The purpose of the Acquisition process is to obtain a product or service in accordance with the acquirer's requirements.

验收准则对每一方来说都是至关重要的因素，因为它们保护了业务关系的双方——采办方不受被强迫接受劣质产品、供应商不受优柔寡断的采办方不可预测的行为的影响。需要注意的是，验收准则是在协议流程中商定的。在谈判过程中，双方能够跟踪达成协议的进展也至关重要。确定在文档和条款中达成共识的进一步工作至关重要。

ISO/IEC/IEEE 15288 确定了两个协议流程：采办流程和供应流程，它们分别是 2.3.2.1 节和 2.3.2.2 节的主题，采办流程和供应流程就像同一枚硬币的两面。它们用于建立与 SoI 相关的组织的基本业务，建立与产品和服务的获取和供应相关的组织之间的关系，无论协议是正式的（如合同）还是非正式的。每个流程都建立协议的背景环境和约束条件，并根据该协议执行属于项目范围的其他系统生命周期流程。请注意，组织可以既是给定系统的供应商，也是采办方。例如，组织可以签订合同向最终客户提供系统。同时，该组织可以选择采办一些系统元素、材料或服务，以开发或生产该系统。因此，该组织是系统最终客户的供应商，也是提供系统元素、材料或服务的组织的采办方。

协议执行中可能会发生变更，包括采办方变更请求、供应链偏差和放弃，或风险分析中预见或未预见的项目背景下的变更。经双方决定，这可能导致对协议初始状态的变更。为此，可在整个项目流程中启动和更新合规声明，描述商定的变更，并在需要时包括受变更影响的需求、变更参考、供应商的符合性验证以及采办方的符合性验证。

2.3.2.1 采办流程

概述

目的　如 ISO/IEC/IEEE 15288 所述：

[6.1.1.1] 采办流程的目的是按照采办方的要求获得产品或服务。

SYSTEM LIFE CYCLE CONCEPTS, MODELS, AND PROCESSES

The Acquisition process is invoked to establish an agreement between two organizations under which one party acquires products and/or services from the other. The acquirer experiences a need for an operational system, for services in support of an operational system, for elements of a system being developed by a project, or for services in support of project activities.

Description This section is written from the perspective of the acquirer organization. An acquiring organization applies due diligence in the selection of a supplier to avoid costly failures and impacts to the organization's budgets and schedules and other issues. Therefore, the role of the acquirer demands familiarity with the Technical, Technical Management, and Organizational Project-Enabling Processes, as it is through them that the supplier will execute the agreement.

Inputs/Outputs Inputs and outputs for the Acquisition process are listed in Figure 2.13. Descriptions of each input

and output are provided in Appendix E.

Process Activities The Acquisition process includes the following activities:

• *Prepare for the acquisition*.

–Develop and maintain acquisition policies, plans, and procedures to meet the organization strategies, goals, and objectives as well as the needs of the project management and SE organizations.

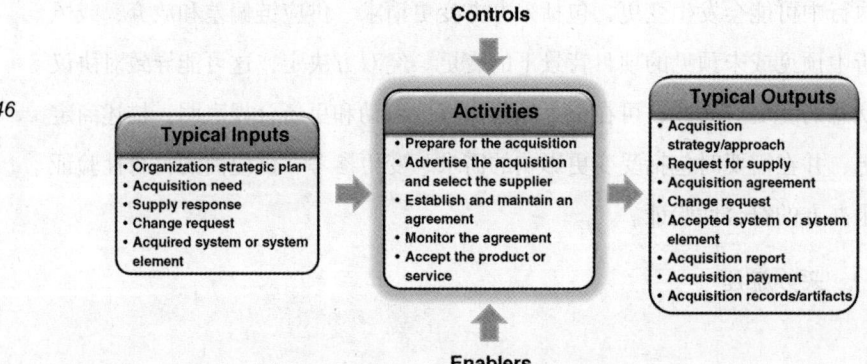

FIGURE 2.13 IPO diagram for the Acquisition process. INCOSE SEH original figure created by Shortell, Walden, and Yip. Usage per the INCOSE Notices page. All other rights reserved.

系统生命周期概念、模型和流程

采办流程用于在两个组织之间建立协议，根据该协议，一方从另一方采办产品和/或服务。采办方需要一个运行的系统、支持运行系统的服务、项目正在开发的系统元素或支持项目活动的服务。

描述 本节从采办方的角度编写。采办组织在选择供应商时应尽职尽责，以避免昂贵的失败和对组织预算与时间表的影响以及其他问题。因此，采办方的角色要求熟悉技术、技术管理和组织的项目使能流程，因为供应商将通过这些流程执行协议。

输入/输出 图 2.13 列出了采办流程的输入和输出。附录 E 中提供了每个输入和输出的描述。

流程活动 采办流程包括以下活动：

- *准备采办。*

  - 制定和维护采办政策、计划和程序，以满足组织战略、目的和目标以及项目管理和系统工程组织的需要。

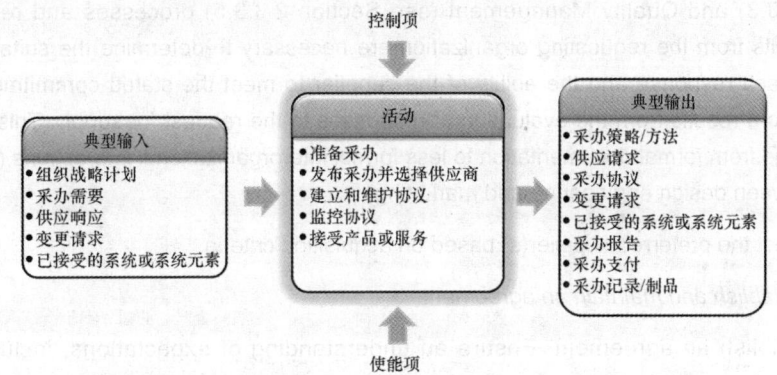

图 2.13 采办流程的 IPO 图。INCOSE SEH 原始图由 Walden、Shortell 和 Yip 创建。按照 INCOSE 通知页使用。版权所有。

– Collect needs in a request for supply—such as a Request for Proposal (RFP) or Request for Quotation (RFQ) or some other mechanism—to obtain the supply of the service and/or product. Through the use of the Technical Processes, the acquiring organization produces a set of requirements and models that will form the basis for the technical information of the agreement.

– Identify a list of potential suppliers—suppliers may be internal or external to the acquirer organization.

- *Advertise the acquisition and select the supplier.*

– Distribute the request for supply and select appropriate suppliers—using selection criteria, rank suppliers by their suitability to meet the overall need and establish supplier preferences and corresponding justifications. Viable suppliers should be willing to conduct ethical negotiations, able to meet obligations, and willing to maintain open communications throughout the Acquisition process. Note that the approach may be less formal when a function within the organization is a candidate for the supply need.

– Evaluate supplier responses to the request for supply—ensure the offered product and/or service can meet acquirer needs and complies with industry and other standards. Assessments from the Project Portfolio Management (see Section 2.3.3.3) and Quality Management (see Section 2.3.3.5) processes and review results from the requesting organization are necessary to determine the suitability of each response and the ability of the supplier to meet the stated commitments. Record results from the evaluation of responses to the request for supply. This can range from formal documentation to less formal interorganizational interactions (e.g., between design engineering and marketing).

– Select the preferred supplier(s) based on acquisition criteria.

- *Establish and maintain an agreement.*

– Establish an agreement. Ensure an understanding of expectations, including acceptance criteria.

– This agreement ranges in formality from a written contract to a verbal agreement. Appropriate to the level of formality, the agreement establishes requirements, development and delivery milestones, verification, validation and acceptance conditions, process requirements (e.g., configuration management, risk management, measurements), exception-handling procedures, agreement change management procedures, payment schedules, and handling of data rights and intellectual property so that both parties understand the basis for executing the agreement. For a written contract, this occurs when the contract is signed.

- 收集供应申请中的需要,如邀标书(RFP)或报价申请书(RFQ)或其他机制,以获得服务和/或产品的供应。通过使用技术流程,采办组织会产生一组需求和模型,这些需求和模型将构成协议技术信息的基础。

- 识别潜在供应商的名单——可能是采办方内部或外部的供应商。

- **发布采办需求并选择供应商**。

- 发布供应请求,并使用选择准则选择适当的供应商,根据供应商是否适合满足总体需求对其进行排名,并确定供应商偏好和相应的理由。可行的供应商应愿意进行合规谈判,能够履行义务,并愿意在整个采办流程中保持公开沟通。请注意,当组织内的某个职能部门是供应需求的候选人时,方法可以不太正式。

- 评估供应商对供应请求的响应,确保所提供的产品和/或服务能够满足采办方的需求,并符合行业和其他标准。项目组合管理(见 2.3.3.3 节)和质量管理(见 2.3.3.5 节)流程的评估以及请求供应组织的评审结果对于确定每个响应的适用性以及供应商履行所述承诺的能力是必要的。记录对供应请求响应的评估结果。这既包括正式的文档记录,也包括不太正式的组织间互动(如设计工程与市场营销之间的互动)。

- 根据采办准则选择首选供应商。

- **建立和维护协议**。

- 达成协议。确保理解预期,包括验收准则。

- 协议包括从正式书面合同到口头协议等。根据正式程度,协议确定了需求、开发和交付的里程碑、验证、确认和验收条件、流程要求(例如构型配置管理、风险管理、测量)、异常处理程序、协议变更管理程序、付款时间表以及数据权和知识产权的处理,以便双方了解执行协议的基础。对于书面合同,这发生在合同签订时。

SYSTEM LIFE CYCLE CONCEPTS, MODELS, AND PROCESSES

47 –Identify the necessary changes to the agreement and evaluate the related impacts on the agreement.

–Update the agreement with the supplier as necessary.

- *Monitor the agreement.*

–Manage Acquisition process activities, including decision making for agreements, relationship building and maintenance, interaction with organization management, responsibility for the development of plans and schedules, and final approval authority for deliveries accepted from the supplier.

–Maintain communications with supplier, stakeholders, and other organizations regarding the project.

–Status progress against the agreed-to schedule to identify risks and issues, to measure progress toward mitigation of risks and adequacy of progress toward delivery and cost and schedule performance, and to determine potential undesirable outcomes for the organization. The Project Assessment and Control process (see Section 2.3.4.2) provides necessary evaluation information regarding cost, schedule, and performance.

–Amend agreements when impacts on schedule, budget, or performance are identified.

- *Accept the product or service.*

–Accept delivery of products and services—in accordance with all agreements and relevant laws and regulations.

–Render payment—or other agreed consideration in accordance with agreed payment schedules.

–Accept responsibility in accordance with all agreements and relevant laws and regulations.

–When an Acquisition process cycle concludes, a final review of performance is conducted to extract lessons learned for continued process performance.

–Retire the agreement.

Note: The project is closed through the Portfolio Management process (see Section 2.3.3.3), which manages the full set of projects of the organization.

\- 确定协议的必要变更，并评估对协议的相关影响。

\- 必要时更新与供应商的协议。

- *监控协议。*

\- 管理采办流程活动，包括协议决策、关系建立和维护、与组织管理层的互动、制订计划和时间表的职责，以及接受供应商交付的最终批准权限。

\- 就项目与供应商、利益相关方和其他组织保持沟通。

\- 根据商定的进度计划确定进度，以识别风险和问题，衡量风险缓解进度以及交付进度、成本和进度绩效的充分性，并确定组织潜在的不良结果。项目评估和控制流程（见2.3.4.2节）提供了有关成本、进度和绩效的必要评估信息。

\- 确定对进度、预算或绩效的影响后，修订协议。

- *接受产品或服务。*

\- 根据所有协议和相关法律法规接受产品和服务的交付。

\- 根据约定的付款时间表或其他商定的对价支付款项。

\- 根据所有协议和相关法律法规承担职责。

\- 当采办流程周期结束时，将对绩效进行最终评审，以吸取经验教训，从而继续保持流程绩效。

\- 终止协议。

注：项目通过项目组合管理流程（见2.3.3.3节）结束，该流程管理组织的项目全集。

SYSTEM LIFE CYCLE CONCEPTS, MODELS, AND PROCESSES

Common approaches and tips:

- Establish acquisition guidance and procedures that inform acquisition planning, including recommended milestones, standards, assessment criteria, and decision gates. Include approaches for identifying, evaluating, choosing, negotiating, managing, and terminating suppliers.

- Establish a technical point of responsibility within the organization for monitoring and controlling individual agreements. This person maintains communication with the supplier and is part of the decision-making team to assess technical development and progress in the execution of the agreement.

Note: There can be multiple points of responsibility for an agreement that focus on technical, programmatic, marketing, etc.

- Define and track measures that indicate progress on agreements. Avoid measures that are not focused on the true information needs. Leading indicators are preferable (see Section 2.3.4.7).

- Include technical representation in the selection of the suppliers to critically assess the capability of the supplier to perform the required task.

- Past performance of the supplier is highly important, but changes to key supplier personnel should be identified and evaluated to understand any impact with respect to the current request for supply.

- Communicate clearly with the supplier about priorities and avoid conflicting statements or making frequent changes in the statement of need that introduce risk into the process.

- Maintain traceability between the supplier's responses to the acquirer's solicitation. This can reduce the risk of contract modifications, cancellations, or follow-on contracts to fix the product or service.

- Smart contracts can be used to establish and maintain an agreement. A smart contract is a transaction protocol intended to execute automatically and control or document legally relevant events and actions according to the terms of a contract or an agreement (Tapscott and Tapscott, 2018). The objectives of smart contracts are the reduction of need in trusted intermediaries, arbitrations and enforcement costs, fraud losses, and the reduction of malicious and accidental exceptions (Fries and Paal, 2019).

常用方法和提示：

- 制定采办指南和程序，为采办计划提供信息，包括建议的里程碑、标准、评估准则和决策门。包括识别、评估、选择、谈判、管理和终止供应商的实施方法。

- 在组织内设立一个技术的职责点，以监测和控制各个协议。该人员与供应商保持沟通，是决策团队的一员，负责评估技术开发和协议执行进度。

注：协议可以有多个职责点，重点是技术、计划、市场营销等。

- 定义和跟踪协议进展情况的测度。避免采取不关注真实信息需求的测度。优先采用领先测度指标（见 2.3.4.7 节）。

- 在选择供应商时包括技术代表，以严格评估供应商执行所需任务的能力。

- 供应商过去的表现非常重要，但应对关键供应商人员的变化进行识别和评估，以了解对当前供应请求的任何影响。

- 与供应商就优先事项进行明确沟通，避免相互冲突的陈述或频繁更改需求陈述，从而给流程带来风险。

- 保持供应商对采办方招标响应之间的可追溯性。这可以降低合同改进、取消或修复产品或服务的后续合同的风险。

- 智能合约可用于建立和维护协议。智能合约是一种交易协议，旨在根据合同或协议的条款自动执行并控制或记录法律相关的事件和行动（Tapscott 和 Tapscott，2018）。智能合约的目标是减少需要信任的中介机构、仲裁和执行成本、欺诈损失，以及减少恶意和意外情况（Fries 和 Paal，2019）。

SYSTEM LIFE CYCLE CONCEPTS, MODELS, AND PROCESSES

Elaboration

The Project Manager's role is to define, execute, and manage the acquisition. This is focused on the project needs to deliver the system, system elements, products, or services that meet the end user requirements and achieve the acquisition milestones. This is done in collaboration with the SE practitioners and the selected contractor to ensure the technical expectations and key performance parameters are achieved. The team needs to define plans and methods collectively, and refine them as more is learned about the nature and challenges inherent in the system or capability being built and its intended operating environment. For more information on PM-SE integration, see 5.3.3.

When the acquisition involves systems or system elements where technology or a system capability is not mature enough, it is necessary to account for uncertainty and the need for additional risk management actions in the planning. his includes allowing additional margin in the development/production timeframe, such as ample lead time in anticipation of inherent challenges, especially when technology maturation is required. These challenges may also include limited availability of adequate resources for the supplier (skilled labor and/or technologies), a need for customization of supplier products or equipment, poor or early understanding of interface requirements, integration challenges, and required verification and/or validation of the development. If there is no flexibility in the delivery date, then trade-offs may be needed to provide the system capabilities in an incremental manner.

Technical supplier management is about ensuring the supplier meets the allocated project requirements and that the supplier is effectively managed. This is usually achieved through the Statement of Work (SOW) and a set of requirements. The SOW is a mechanism to ensure progress is being made and describes the necessary work, quality, standards, designs, models, evidence, reviews, timescales, and meetings, etc. that the supplier is expected to provide contingent on the contract. To prove the system/system element functional, performance, and operational requirements are met, the supplier will also need to provide compliance matrices and verification and validation evidence.

2.3.2.2 Supply Process

Overview

Purpose As stated in ISO/IEC/IEEE 15288,

[6.1.2.1] The purpose of the Supply process is to provide an acquirer with a product or service that meets agreed requirements.

详细阐述

项目经理的职责是定义、执行和管理采办。重点是项目需要交付满足最终用户需要并实现采办里程碑的系统、系统元素、产品或服务。这是与系统工程实践者和选定的承包商合作完成的，以确保达到技术期望和关键性能参数。团队需要共同定义计划和方法，并随着对所构建的系统或能力及其预期运行环境中固有的性质和挑战的了解不断加深，对其进行细化。有关项目管理—系统工程集成的更多信息，请参阅 5.3.3 节。

当采办涉及技术或系统能力不够成熟的系统或系统元素时，有必要在计划中考虑不确定性和额外风险管理行动的需要。这包括在开发/生产时间段内留出更多余地，例如预留充足的准备时间，以应对固有的挑战，特别是在需要技术成熟的情况下。这些挑战还可能包括供应商可用的充足资源（熟练劳动力和/或技术）有限、需要定制供应商的产品或设备、对接口要求理解不深或理解过早、综合挑战以及开发所需的验证和/或确认。如果交付日期没有灵活性，则可能需要权衡以增量方式提供系统功能。

技术供应商管理是指确保供应商满足分配的项目要求，并对供应商进行有效管理。这通常通过工作说明书（SOW）和一组需求来实现。SOW 是一种确保进度的机制，描述了供应商根据合同要求提供的必要工作、质量、标准、设计、模型、证据、评审、时间表和会议等。为证明系统/系统元素功能、性能和运行需求得到满足，供应商还需要提供符合性矩阵以及验证和确认证据。

2.3.2.2 供应流程

概述

目的　如 ISO/IEC/IEEE 15288 所述：

[6.1.2.1] 供应流程的目的是向采办方提供符合约定需求的产品或服务。

SYSTEM LIFE CYCLE CONCEPTS, MODELS, AND PROCESSES

The Supply process is invoked to establish an agreement between two organizations under which one party supplies products or services to the other. Within the supplier organization, a project is conducted according to the recommendations of this handbook with the objective of providing a product or service to the acquirer that meets the agreed requirements. In the case of a mass-produced commercial product or service, a marketing, or similar, function may represent the acquirer and establish stakeholder expectations.

Description This section is written from the perspective of the supplier organization. The Supply process is highly dependent upon the Technical, Technical Management, and Organizational Project-Enabling Processes as it is through them that the work of executing the agreement is accomplished. This means that the Supply process is the larger context in which the other processes are applied under the agreement.

Inputs/Outputs Inputs and outputs for the Supply process are listed in Figure 2.14. Descriptions of each input and output are provided in Appendix E.

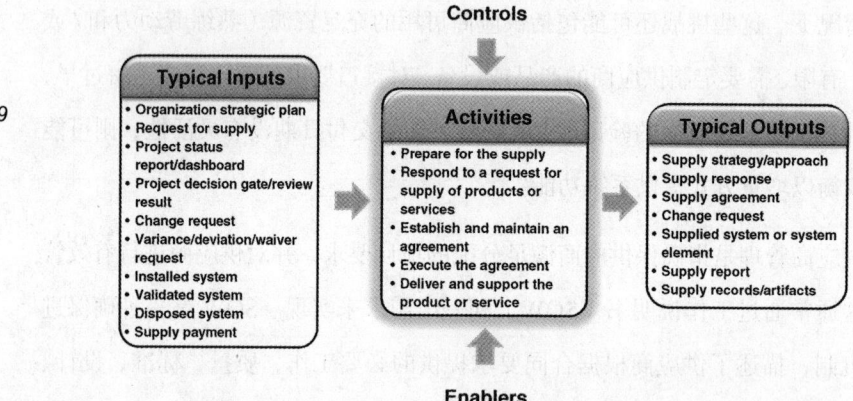

FIGURE 2.14 IPO diagram for the Supply process. INCOSE SEH original figure created by Shortell, Walden, and Yip. Usage per the INCOSE Notices page. All other rights reserved.

Process Activities The Supply process includes the following activities:

• *Prepare for the supply.*

–Develop and maintain strategic plans, policies, and procedures to meet the needs of potential acquirer organi zations, as well as internal organization goals and objectives including the needs of the project management and technical SE organizations.

系统生命周期概念、模型和流程

供应流程用于在两个组织之间建立协议，根据该协议，一方向另一方提供产品或服务。在供应商组织内，根据本手册的建议开展项目，目的是向采办方提供符合约定需求的产品或服务。在大规模生产的商业产品或服务的情况下，市场营销或类似职能可以代表采办方并建立利益相关方的期望。

描述 本节从供应商组织的角度编写。供应流程高度依赖于技术、技术管理和组织项目使能流程，因为执行协议的工作是通过这些流程完成的。这意味着供应流程是根据协议应用其他流程的更大背景。

输入/输出 图 2.14 列出了供应流程的输入和输出。附录 E 中提供了每个输入和输出的描述。

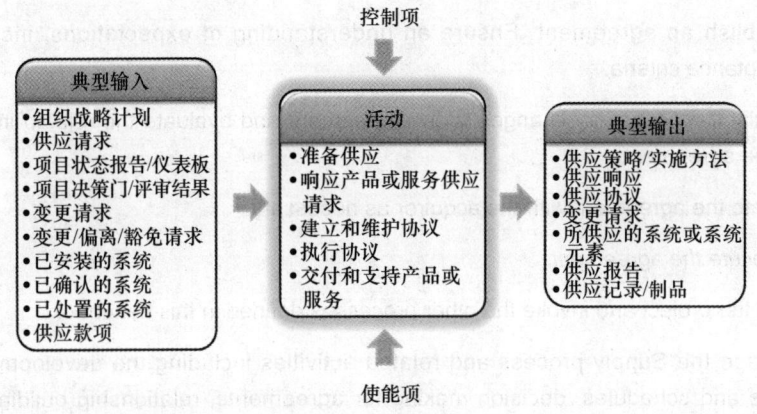

图 2.14 供应流程的 IPO 图。INCOSE SEH 原始图由 Walden、Shortell 和 Yip 创建。按照 INCOSE 通知页使用。版权所有。

流程活动 供应流程包括以下活动：

- *准备供应。*
  - 制订和维护战略计划、政策和程序，以满足潜在采办方组织的需要，以及内部组织目的和目标，包括项目管理和系统工程技术组织的需要。

SYSTEM LIFE CYCLE CONCEPTS, MODELS, AND PROCESSES

– Identify opportunities.

- *Respond to a request for supply of products or services.*

– Select appropriate acquirers willing to conduct ethical negotiations, able to meet financial obligations, and willing to maintain open communications throughout the Supply process.

– Evaluate the acquirer requests and propose a product or service that meets acquirer needs and complies with industry and other standards. Assessments from the Portfolio Management, Human Resource Management, Quality Management, and Business or Mission Analysis processes are necessary to determine the suitability of this response and the ability of the organization to meet these commitments.

- *Establish and maintain an agreement.*

– Establish an agreement. Ensure an understanding of expectations, including acceptance criteria.

– Identify the necessary changes to the agreement and evaluate the related impacts on the agreement.

– Update the agreement with the acquirer as necessary.

- *Execute the agreement.*

– Start the project and invoke the other processes defined in this handbook.

– Manage the Supply process and related activities including the development of plans and schedules, decision making for agreements, relationship building and maintenance, interaction with organization management, and final approval authority for deliveries made to acquirer.

– Maintain communications with acquirers, suppliers, stakeholders, and other organizations regarding the agreement.

– Carefully evaluate the terms of the agreement to identify risks and issues, progress toward mitigation of risks, and adequacy of progress toward delivery. Also evaluate cost and schedule performance and determine potential undesirable outcomes for the organization.

- *Deliver and support the product or service.*

– After acceptance and transfer of the final products and/or services, the acquirer will provide payment or other consideration in accordance with all agreements, schedules, and relevant laws and regulations. A support agreement is often ongoing after the transfer of products and/or services.

- 识别机会。

- **响应产品或服务供应请求。**

- 选择愿意进行合规谈判、能够履行财务义务并愿意在整个供应流程中保持公开沟通的适当采办方。

- 评估采办方的请求，并提出满足采办方需要并符合行业和其他标准的产品或服务。项目组合管理、人力资源管理、质量管理和业务或任务分析流程的评估对于确定该响应的适用性以及组织履行这些承诺的能力是必要的。

- **建立和维护协议。**

- 达成协议。确保理解预期，包括验收准则。

- 确定协议的必要变更，并评估对协议的相关影响。

- 必要时更新与采办方的协议。

- **执行协议。**

- 启动项目并调用本手册中定义的其他流程。

- 管理供应流程和相关活动，包括制订计划和时间表、协议决策制定、建立和维护关系、与组织管理层的互动以及向采办方交付货物的最终审批权。

- 与采办方、供应商、利益相关方和其他组织就该协议保持沟通。

- 仔细评估协议条款，以确定风险和问题、风险缓解进展以及交付进度的充分性。还要评估成本和进度绩效，并确定组织潜在的不良结果。

- **交付和支持产品或服务。**

- 在最终产品和/或服务验收和移交后，采办方将根据所有协议、时间表和相关法律法规提供付款或其他报酬。在产品和/或服务转让后，通常会签订支持协议。

SYSTEM LIFE CYCLE CONCEPTS, MODELS, AND PROCESSES

–When a Supply process cycle concludes, a final review of performance is conducted to extract lessons learned for continued process performance.

–Retire the agreement.

Note: The agreement is closed through the Portfolio Management process (see Section 2.3.3.3), which manages the full set of systems and projects of the organization. When the project is closed, action is taken to close the agreement.

Common approaches and tips:

- Relationship building and trust between the parties is a nonquantifiable quality that, while not a substitute for good processes, makes human interactions agreeable.

- Develop technology white papers or similar artifacts to demonstrate and describe to the (potential) acquirer the range of capabilities in areas of interest. Use traditional marketing approaches to encourage acquisition of massproduced products.

- When expertise is not available within the organization (legal and other governmental regulations, laws, etc.), retain subject matter experts to provide information and specify requirements related to agreements.

- Invest sufficient time and effort into understanding acquirer needs before the agreement. This can improve the estimations for cost and schedule and positively affect agreement execution. Evaluate any technical specifications for the product or service for clarity, completeness, and consistency.

- Involve personnel who will be responsible for agreement execution to participate in the evaluation of and response to the acquirer's request. This reduces the start-up time once the project is initiated, which in turn is one way to recapture the cost of writing the response.

- Make a critical assessment of the ability of the organization to execute the agreement; otherwise, the high risk of failure and its associated costs, delivery delays, and increased resource commitment needs will reflect negatively on the reputation of the entire organization.

Elaboration

Agreements fall into a large range, from formal to very informal based on verbal understanding (e.g., from a written contract to a verbal agreement). Agreements may call for a fixed price, cost plus fixed fee, incentives for early delivery, penalties for late deliveries, and other financial motivators. Appropriate to the level of formality, the agreement establishes requirements, development and delivery milestones, verification, validation and acceptance conditions, process requirements (e.g., configuration management, risk management, measurements), exception-handling procedures, agreement change management procedures, payment schedules, and handling of data rights and intellectual property so that both parties understand the basis for executing the agreement. For a written contract, this occurs when the contract is signed.

- 当供应流程周期结束时，将对绩效进行最终评审，以吸取经验教训，从而保证后续流程绩效。

- 终止协议。

注：协议通过项目组合管理流程结束（参见 2.3.3.3 节），该流程管理组织的全部系统和项目集合。项目结束后，将采取行动结束协议。

常用方法和提示：

- 双方之间的关系建设和信任是一种无法量化的属性，虽然不能替代良好的流程，但却能使人与人之间的互动变得愉快。
- 开发技术白皮书或类似制品，向（潜在）采办方展示和描述其所感兴趣领域的能力范围。使用传统营销方法鼓励购买批量生产的产品。
- 当组织内没有专业知识（司法和其他政府法规、法律等）时，聘请主题专家提供信息并指明与协议相关的要求。
- 在签订协议之前，投入足够的时间和精力了解采办方的需求。这可以改进对成本和进度的估计，并对协议执行产生积极影响。评估产品或服务的任何技术规范是否清晰、完整和一致。
- 让负责协议执行的人员参与评估和响应采办方的请求。这将减少项目发起后的启动时间，反过来又是降低编写响应的成本的一种方法。
- 对组织执行协议的能力进行关键评估；否则，失败的高风险及其相关成本、交付延迟和增加的资源投入需求将对整个组织的声誉产生负面影响。

详细阐述

协议的范围很广，从正式协议到基于口头理解的非正式协议等（例如，从书面合同到口头协议）。协议可能要求固定价格、成本加固定费用、提前交付奖励、延迟交付惩罚以及其他财务激励因素。根据正式程度，协议还会确定需求、开发和交付的里程碑、验证、确认和验收条件、流程需求（例如构型配置管理、风险管理、测量）、异常处理程序、协议变更管理程序、付款时间表以及数据权和知识产权的处理，以便双方了解执行该协议的基础。对于书面合同，这发生在合同签订时。

2.3.3 Organizational Project-Enabling Processes

The Organizational Project-Enabling Processes are defined in ISO/IEC/IEEE 15288 as follows:

[5.7.3] The Organizational Project-Enabling Processes are concerned with providing the resources needed to enable the project to meet the needs and expectations of the organization's stakeholders. The Organizational Project-Enabling Processes are typically concerned at a strategic level with the management and improvement of the organization's undertaking, with the provision and deployment of resources and assets, and with its management of risks in competitive or uncertain situations.… The Organizational Project-Enabling Processes establish the environment in which projects are conducted.

This section focuses on the capabilities of an organization relevant to enabling the system life cycle; they are not intended to address general business management objectives, although sometimes the two overlap. Six Organizational Project-Enabling Processes are identified by ISO/IEC/IEEE 15288. They are Life Cycle Model Management, Infrastructure Management, Portfolio Management, Human Resource Management, Quality Management, and Knowledge Management. As defined in ISO/IEC/IEEE 15288 and this handbook, these processes provide the resources and organizational support to enable the projects that are focused on the system life cycle. The organization will tailor these processes and their interfaces to meet specific strategic and tactical objectives in support of the organization's projects (see Section 4.1).

2.3.3.1 Life Cycle Model Management Process

Overview

Purpose As stated in ISO/IEC/IEEE 15288,

[6.2.1.1] The purpose of the Life Cycle Model Management process is to define, maintain, and help ensure availability of policies, life cycle processes, life cycle models, and procedures for use by the organization with respect to the scope of ISO/ IEC/IEEE 15288.

Description This process (i) establishes and maintains a set of policies and procedures at the organization level that support the organization's ability to acquire and supply products and services and (ii) provides integrated system life cycle models necessary to meet the organization's strategic plans, policies, goals, and objectives for all projects and all system life cycle stages. The processes are defined, adapted, and maintained to support the requirements of the organization, SE organizational units, individual projects, and personnel. The Life Cycle Model Management process is supplemented by recommended methods and tools. The resulting guidelines in the form of organization policies and procedures are still subject to tailoring by projects (see Section 4.1).

2.3.3 组织项目使能流程

ISO/IEC/IEEE 15288 中对组织项目使能流程的定义如下：

[5.7.3] 组织项目使能流程涉及提供必要的资源，使项目能够满足组织利益相关方的需要和期望。组织项目使能流程通常在战略层面上涉及组织事业的管理和改进，资源和资产的提供和部署，以及竞争或不确定情况下的风险管理等。组织项目使能流程建立了项目执行的环境。

本节重点介绍与使能系统生命周期相关的组织能力；它们并不旨在处理一般业务管理目标，尽管有时两者重叠。ISO/IEC/IEEE 15288 确定了六个组织项目使能流程，它们是生命周期模型管理、基础设施管理、项目群管理、人力资源管理、质量管理和知识管理。如 ISO/IEC/IEEE 15288 和本手册所定义，这些流程提供了资源和组织支持，以支持专注于系统生命周期的项目。组织将调整这些流程及其接口，以满足支持组织项目的特定战略和战术目标（见 4.1 节）。

2.3.3.1 生命周期模型管理流程

概述

目的 如 ISO/IEC/IEEE 15288 所述：

[6.2.1.1] 生命周期模型管理流程的目的是定义、维护并帮助确保政策、生命周期流程、生命周期模型和程序的可用性，以供组织在 ISO/IEC/IEEE 15288 范围内使用。

描述 该流程（i）在组织层面建立和维护一套政策和程序，以支持组织获取和提供产品和服务的能力，并（ii）提供必要的综合系统生命周期模型，以满足组织所有项目和系统生命周期各阶段的战略计划、政策、目的和目标。定义、调整和维护流程，以支持组织、系统工程组织单元、单个项目和人员的需求。生命周期模型管理流程由推荐的方法和工具进行补充。由此产生的组织政策和程序形式的指南仍需根据项目进行剪裁（见 4.1 节）。

SYSTEM LIFE CYCLE CONCEPTS, MODELS, AND PROCESSES

Inputs/Outputs Inputs and outputs for the Life Cycle Model Management process are listed in Figure 2.15. Descriptions of each input and output are provided in Appendix E.

Process Activities The Life Cycle Model Management process includes the following activities:

- *Establish the life cycle process.*

–Establish policies and procedures for managing and deploying life cycle processes.

–Establish the life cycle processes with process performance metrics to assess effectiveness and efficiency.

–Define roles, responsibilities, accountabilities, and authorities to enable the implementation of the life cycle processes.

–Establish entrance and exit criteria for decision gates.

–Define an appropriate set of life cycle models that are comprised of stages.

–Establish tailoring guidance for projects

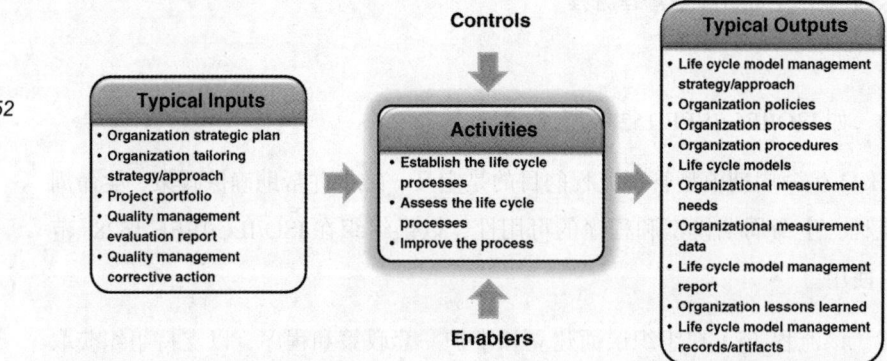

FIGURE 2.15 IPO diagram for Life Cycle Model Management process. INCOSE SEH original figure created by Shortell, Walden, and Yip. Usage per the INCOSE Notices page. All other rights reserved.

- *Assess the life cycle process.*

–Use assessments and reviews of the life cycle models' performance to confirm the adequacy and effectiveness of the Life Cycle Model Management process.

系统生命周期概念、模型和流程

输入 / 输出 生命周期模型管理流程的输入和输出如图 2.15 所示。附录 E 中提供了每个输入和输出的描述。

流程活动 生命周期模型管理流程包括以下活动：

- *建立生命周期流程。*

- 制定管理和部署生命周期流程的政策和程序。

- 建立生命周期流程的流程绩效指标，以评估有效性和效率。

- 定义角色、职责、责任和权限，以实现生命周期流程的实施。

- 建立决策门的进入和退出准则。

- 定义由阶段组成的一组适当的生命周期模型。

- 为项目制定剪裁指导。

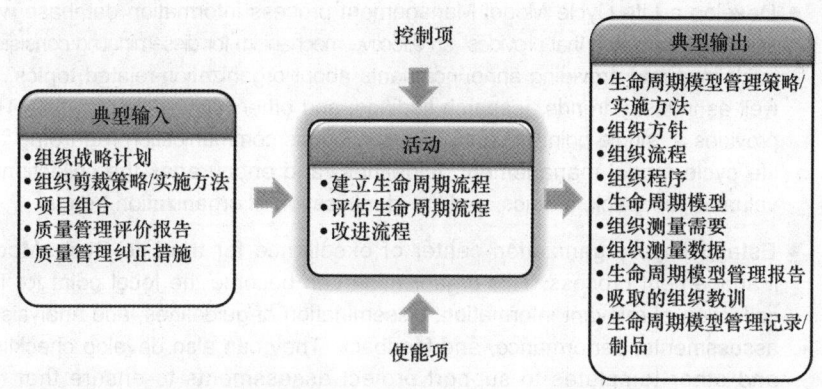

图 2.15　生命周期模型管理流程的 IPO 图。INCOSE SEH 原始图由 Walden、Shortell 和 Yip 创建。按照 INCOSE 通知页使用。版权所有。

- *评估生命周期流程。*

- 通过对生命周期模型绩效的评估和评审来确认生命周期模型管理流程的充分性和有效性。

SYSTEM LIFE CYCLE CONCEPTS, MODELS, AND PROCESSES

–Identify opportunities to improve the organization life cycle model management guidelines on a continuing basis based on individual project assessments, individual feedback, metrics, and changes in the organization strategic plan.

- *Improve the process.*

–Prioritize and implement the identified improvement opportunities.

–Communicate with all relevant organizations regarding the creation of and changes in the life cycle model management guideline.

NOTE: ISO/IEC/IEEE 15288 provides more details for the Life Cycle Model Management process that are aligned with the activities listed above.

Common approaches and tips:

- Base the policies and procedures on an organization-level strategic and business area plan that provides a comprehensive understanding of the organization's goals, objectives, stakeholders, competitors, future business, and technology trends.

- Ensure that policy and procedure compliance review is included as part of the business decision gate criteria.

- Develop a Life Cycle Model Management process information database with essential information that provides an effective mechanism for disseminating consistent guidelines and providing announcements about organization-related topics, as well as industry trends, research findings, and other relevant information. This provides a single point of contact for continuous communication regarding the life cycle model management guidelines and encourages the collection of valuable feedback, metrics, and the identification of organization trends.

- Establish an organization center of excellence for the Life Cycle Model Management process. This organization can become the focal point for the collection of relevant information, dissemination of guidelines, and analysis of assessments, performance, and feedback. They can also develop checklists and other templates to support project assessments to ensure that the predefined measures and criteria are used for evaluation.

- Manage the network of external relationships by assigning personnel to identify standards, industry and academia research, and other sources of organization management information and concepts needed by the organization. The network of relationships includes government, industry, and academia. Each of these external interfaces provides unique and essential information for the organization to succeed in business and meet the continued need and demand for improved and effective systems and products for its stakeholders. It is up to the Life Cycle Model Management process to fully define and utilize these external entities and interfaces (i.e., their value, importance, and capabilities that are required by the organization):

- 根据单个项目评估、单独反馈、指标和组织战略计划的变化，确定持续改进组织生命周期模型管理指南的机会。

- 改进流程。

- 优先考虑并实施已确定的改进机会。

- 就生命周期模型管理指南的创建和更改与所有相关组织进行沟通。

注：*ISO/IEC/IEEE 15288* 提供了与上述活动一致的生命周期模型管理流程的更多细节。

常用方法和提示：

- 以组织级战略和业务域计划为基础制定政策和程序，全面了解组织的目的、目标、利益相关方、竞争对手、未来业务和技术趋势。

- 确保将政策和程序合规性评审作为业务决策门准则的一部分。

- 开发一个生命周期模型管理流程信息数据库，其中包含基本信息，通过该数据库提供一种有效的机制，用于传播一致的指导方针，并提供有关组织相关主题的公告，以及行业趋势、研究结果和其他相关信息。这为有关生命周期模型管理指南的持续沟通提供了一个单一的联系点，并鼓励收集有价值的反馈、指标和识别组织趋势。

- 为生命周期模型管理流程建立一个卓越中心组织。该组织可以成为收集相关信息、传播指导方针、分析评估、绩效和反馈的协调中心。他们还可以制定清单和其他模板来支持项目评估，以确保预定义的措施和准则被用于评估。

- 指派人员来确定标准、行业和学术研究以及组织所需的组织管理信息和概念的其他来源，管理外部关系网络。关系网络包括政府、行业和学术界。每一个外部接口都为组织在业务上取得成功并满足其利益相关方对改进和有效的系统和产品的持续需求提供了独特和重要的信息。完全定义和使用这些外部实体和接口（例如，其价值、重要性和组织所需的能力）取决于生命周期模型管理流程：

SYSTEM LIFE CYCLE CONCEPTS, MODELS, AND PROCESSES

–Legislative, regulatory, and other government requirements

–Industry SE and management-related standards, training, and capability maturity models

–Academic education, research results, future concepts and perspectives, and requests for financial support

- Establish an organization communication plan for the policies and procedures. Most of the processes in this handbook include dissemination activities. An effective set of communication methods is needed to ensure that all stakeholders are well informed.

- Include stakeholders, such as engineering and project management organizations, as participants in developing the life cycle model management guidelines. This increases their commitment to the recommendations and incorporates a valuable source of organizational experience.

- Develop alternative life cycle models based on the type, scope, complexity, and risk of a project. This decreases the need for tailoring by engineering and project organizations.

Elaboration

Value Proposition for Organizational Processes. The value propositions to be achieved by instituting organizationwide processes for use by projects are as follows:

- Provide repeatable/predictable performance across the projects in the organization (this helps the organization in planning and estimating future projects and in demonstrating reliability to stakeholders)

- Leverage practices that have been proven successful by certain projects and instill those in other projects across the organization (where applicable)

- Enable process improvement across the organization

- mprove ability to efficiently transfer staff across projects as roles are defined and performed consistently

- Enable leveraging lessons that are learned from one project for future projects to improve performance and avoid issues

- Improve startup of new projects (less reinventing the wheel)

In addition, the standardization across projects may enable cost savings through economies of scale for support activities (tool support, process documentation, etc.).

- 立法、监管和其他政府要求
- 行业的系统工程和管理相关标准、培训和能力成熟度模型
- 学术教育、研究成果、未来概念和观点，以及财务支持请求

- 为政策和程序制订组织沟通计划。本手册中的大多数流程都包括信息传播活动。需要一套有效的沟通方法，以确保所有利益相关方都得到充分的信息。
- 纳入利益相关方，如工程和项目管理组织，作为制定生命周期模型管理指南的参与者。这可以增加他们对建议的承诺，并融入宝贵的组织经验。
- 根据项目的类型、范围、复杂性和风险，开发替代生命周期模型。这可以减少工程和项目组织对剪裁的需求。

详细阐述

组织级流程的价值。通过建立供项目使用的组织级流程来实现的价值如下：

- 在组织内的所有项目中提供可重复/可预测的绩效（这有助于组织计划和评估未来项目，并向利益相关方展示可靠性）
- 利用已被某些项目证明成功的做法，并将这些做法用到整个组织的其他项目中（如适用）
- 在整个组织内实现流程改进
- 通过角色的定义和一致执行，提高跨项目高效调动员工的能力
- 能够将从一个项目中学到的经验教训用于未来的项目，以提高绩效并避免问题
- 促进新项目的启动（减少重复投资）

此外，跨项目的标准化可以通过支持活动（工具支持、流程文档等）的规模经济性而节约成本。

SYSTEM LIFE CYCLE CONCEPTS, MODELS, AND PROCESSES

Benchmarking. SE benchmarking involves comparing an organization's system life cycle processes and practices to those of other entities that are considered as good performers, internally or externally, or comparing to industry standards or good practices. SE benchmarking results and comparisons can be used to generate ideas for driving process improvement to maximize efficiency and effectiveness.

Standard SE Processes. An organization engaged in SE provides the requirements for establishing, maintaining, and improving the standard SE processes and the policies, practices, and supporting functional processes necessary to meet the needs throughout the organization. Further, it defines the process for tailoring the standard SE processes for use on projects addressing the specific needs of the project and for making improvements to the project-tailored SE processes.

Analysis of Process Performance. A high-performing organization also reviews the process (as well as work products), conducts assessments and audits (e.g., assessments based on CMMI (2018), ISO/IEC 33060 (2020), and ISO 9000 (2015) audits), retains corporate memory through the understanding of lessons learned, and establishes how benchmarked processes and practices of related organizations can affect the organization. Successful organizations should analyze their process performance, its effectiveness and compliance to organizational and higher directed standards, and the associated benefits and costs and then develop targeted improvements.

The basic requirements for standard and project-tailored SE process control, based on CMMI (2018), ISO/IEC 33060 (2020), or other resources, are as follows:

- Process responsibilities for projects:

–Identify SE processes.

–Document the implementation and maintenance of SE processes.

–Use a defined set of standard methods and techniques to support the SE processes.

–Apply accepted tailoring guidelines to the standard SE processes to meet project-specific needs.

- Good process definition includes:

–Inputs and outputs

–Entrance and exit criteria

- Process responsibilities for organizations and projects:

–Assess strengths and weaknesses in the SE processes.

–Compare the SE processes to benchmark processes used by other organizations.

对标。系统工程对标涉及将一个组织的系统生命周期流程和实践与内部或外部被认为表现良好的其他实体的流程和实践进行对比，或与行业标准或优秀实践进行对比。系统工程对标结果和对比可用于产生推动流程改进的想法，以最大限度地提高效率和有效性。

标准系统工程流程。从事系统工程的组织需要建立、维护和改进标准系统工程流程以及政策、实践，支持必要的功能性流程，以满足整个组织的需要。此外，它还定义了定制标准系统工程流程的流程，以用于满足项目的特定需求，并对项目定制的系统工程流程进行改进。

流程绩效分析。高绩效组织还对流程（以及工作产品）进行评审，开展评估和审核［例如，基于 CMMI（2018）、ISO/IEC 33060（2020）和 ISO 9000（2015）审核的评估］，通过了解经验教训保留公司记忆，并明确相关组织的基准流程和实践如何影响组织。成功的组织应分析其流程绩效、其有效性和对组织和更高指导标准的遵从性，以及相关的收益和成本，然后制定有针对性的改进。

基于 CMMI（2018）、ISO/IEC 33060（2020）或其他资源，标准的和项目定制的系统工程流程控制的基本要求如下：

- 项目流程职责：

- 识别系统工程流程。

- 记录系统工程流程的实施和维护。

- 使用一套定义的标准方法和技术来支持系统工程流程。

- 将公认的剪裁指南应用于标准系统工程流程，以满足项目的特定需求。

- 良好的流程定义包括：

- 输入和输出。

- 进入和退出准则。

- 组织和项目的流程职责：

- 评估系统工程流程中的优势和劣势。

SYSTEM LIFE CYCLE CONCEPTS, MODELS, AND PROCESSES

–Institute SE process reviews and audits of the SE processes.

–Institute a means to capture and act on lessons learned from SE process implementation on projects.

–Institute a means to analyze potential changes for improvement to the SE processes.

–Institute measures that provide insight into the performance and effectiveness of the SE processes.

–Analyze the process measures and other information to determine the effectiveness of the SE processes.

Although it should be encouraged to identify and capture lessons learned throughout the performance of every project, the SE organization must plan and follow through to collect lessons learned at predefined milestones in the system life cycle. The SE organization should periodically review lessons learned together with the measures and other information to analyze and improve SE processes and practices. The results need to be communicated and incorporated into training. It should also establish good practices and capture them in an easy-to-retrieve form.

For more information on process definition, assessment, and improvement, see the resources in the bibliography, including the CMMI and ISO/IEC TS 33060.

2.3.3.2 *Infrastructure Management Process*

Overview

Purpose As stated in ISO/IEC/IEEE 15288,

[6.2.2.1] The purpose of the Infrastructure Management process is to provide the infrastructure and services to projects to support organization and project objectives throughout the life cycle.

Description The work of the organization is accomplished through projects, which are conducted within the context of the infrastructure environment. This infrastructure needs to be defined and understood within the organization and the project to ensure alignment of the working units and achievement of overall organization strategic objectives. This process exists to establish, communicate, and continuously improve the system life cycle process environment.

- 将系统工程流程与其他组织使用的标杆流程进行对比。

- 确立系统工程流程评审和审核。

- 确立一种方法，以获取从项目系统工程流程实施中获得的经验教训并采取行动。

- 确立一种分析潜在变化的方法，以改进系统工程流程。

- 制定措施，深入了解系统工程流程的绩效和有效性。

- 分析流程测度和其他信息，以确定系统工程流程的有效性。

虽然应鼓励在每个项目的整个执行过程中发现和总结经验教训，但系统工程组织必须制订计划并贯彻执行，在系统生命周期的预定里程碑节点收集经验教训。组织应定期评审经验教训以及措施和其他信息，以分析和改进系统工程流程和实践。需要就结果进行沟通并纳入培训。它还应该建立优秀实践，并以易于检索的形式获取它们。

有关流程定义、评估和改进的更多信息，请参阅参考书目中的资源，包括CMMI 和 ISO/IEC TS 33060。

2.3.3.2 基础设施管理流程

概述

目的　如 ISO/IEC/IEEE 15288 所述：

[6.2.2.1] 基础设施管理流程的目的是为项目提供基础设施和服务，以支持整个生命周期内的组织和项目目标。

描述　组织的工作是通过项目完成的，这些项目是在基础设施环境的背景下进行的。需要在组织和项目内部定义和理解该基础设施，以确保工作单元的一致性和组织总体战略目标的实现。该流程旨在建立、沟通和持续改进系统生命周期流程环境。

SYSTEM LIFE CYCLE CONCEPTS, MODELS, AND PROCESSES

55   Infrastructure Management is an organizational project-enabling process and foundational to all SE process management and improvement. Effective infrastructure management is imperative to an organization's ability to change and for that change to be positive, durable, and impactful. Each element of infrastructure is a SoI and both Technical Management and Technical Processes, as stated in ISO/IEC/IEEE 15288 apply to the establishment and maintenance of the infrastructure. Additionally, the Infrastructure Management process includes the physical, political, and process improvement infrastructures.

Inputs/Outputs Inputs and outputs for the Infrastructure Management process are listed in Figure 2.16. Descriptions of each input and output are provided in Appendix E.

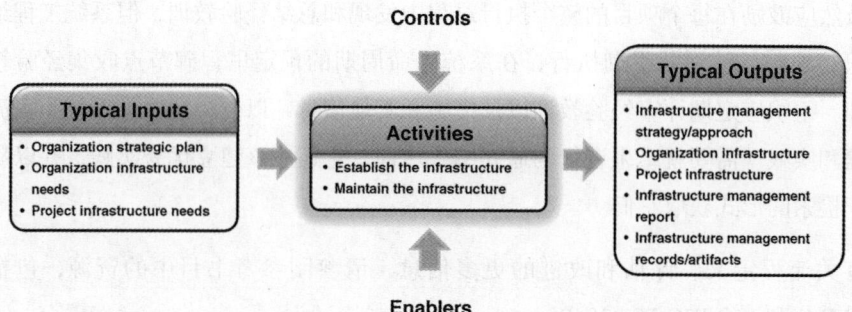

FIGURE 2.16   IPO diagram for Infrastructure Management process. INCOSE SEH original figure created by Shortell, Walden, and Yip. Usage per the INCOSE Notices page. All other rights reserved.

Process Activities The Infrastructure Management process includes the following activities:

- *Establish the infrastructure.*

–Define infrastructure requirements.

–Define infrastructure elements (e.g., facilities, tools, hardware, software, services, and standards).

–Define, gather, and negotiate infrastructure resource needs with the organization and projects.

–Identify, obtain, and provide the infrastructure resources and services to ensure organization goals and objectives are met.

基础设施管理是一个组织项目使能流程，是所有系统工程流程管理和改进的基础。有效的基础设施管理对于组织的变革能力以及变革的积极性、持久性和影响力至关重要。基础设施的每个元素都是 SoI，ISO/IEC/IEEE 15288 中所述的技术管理流程和技术流程均适用于基础设施的建立和维护。此外，基础设施管理流程还包括物理的、政治的和流程改进的基础设施。

输入 / 输出　图 2.16 列出了基础设施管理流程的输入和输出。附录 E 中提供了每个输入和输出的描述。

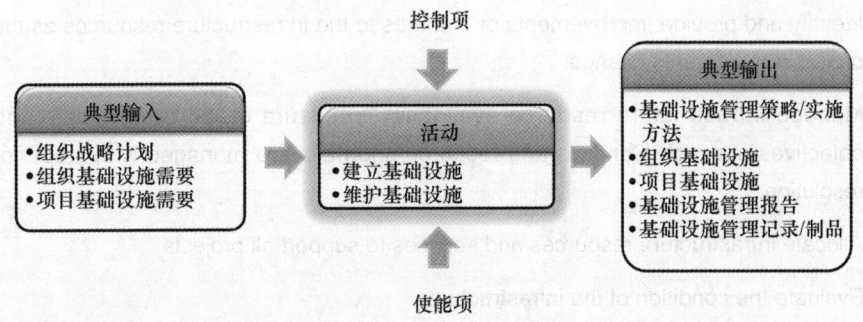

图 2.16　基础设施管理流程的 IPO 图。INCOSE SEH 原始图由 Walden、Shortell 和 Yip 创建。按照 INCOSE 通知页使用。版权所有。

流程活动　基础设施管理流程包括以下活动：

- *建立基础设施*。

- 定义基础设施需求。

- 定义基础设施元素（例如，设施、工具、硬件、软件、服务和标准）。

- 定义、收集并与组织和项目协商基础设施资源需求。

- 识别、获取并提供基础设施资源和服务，以确保实现组织目标。

SYSTEM LIFE CYCLE CONCEPTS, MODELS, AND PROCESSES

–Control the infrastructure elements, resources, and services.

–Conduct inventory management to include enumeration, lists, storage to establish ownership, accessibility, and expectations.

–Manage resource and service conflicts and shortfalls with steps for resolution.

–Conduct infrastructure management inventories including identification, status, type, location, access, and condition.

- *Maintain the infrastructure.*

–Continue to assess whether the project infrastructure needs are met.

–Identify and provide improvements or changes to the infrastructure resources as the project requirements change.

–Manage infrastructure resource availability to ensure organization goals and objectives are met. Conflicts and resource shortfalls are managed with steps for resolution.

–Allocate infrastructure resources and services to support all projects.

–Evaluate the condition of the infrastructure.

–Perform cost analysis toward the cost of infrastructure management.

–Control multi-project infrastructure resource management communications to effectively allocate resources throughout the organization; and identify potential future or existing conflict issues and problems with recommendations for resolution.

–Provide change control for the infrastructure management.

–Conduct risk analysis regarding infrastructure management.

–Evaluate infrastructure management alternatives through analysis of alternatives. This evaluation and analysis compliments risk management and cost reduction activities.

Common approaches and tips:

- Qualified resources may be leased (insourced or outsourced) or licensed in accordance with the investment strategy.
- Establish an organization infrastructure architecture. Integrating the infrastructure of the organization can make the execution of routine business activities more efficient.

- 控制基础设施元素、资源和服务。

- 进行库存管理，包括枚举、列表、存储，以确定所有权、可访问性和期望。

- 管理资源和服务方面的资源冲突和不足，并制定解决步骤。

- 建立基础设施管理库存，包括标识、状态、类型、位置、访问和条件。

- **维护基础设施**。

- 持续评估项目基础设施需求是否得到满足。

- 随着项目需求的变化，确定并提供基础设施资源的改进或变更。

- 管理基础设施资源可用性，以确保实现组织目的和目标。资源冲突和短缺通过制定解决步骤进行管理。

- 分配基础设施资源和服务以支持所有项目。

- 评估基础设施的状况。

- 对基础设施管理的成本进行分析。

- 控制多项目基础设施资源管理的沟通，在整个组织内有效分配资源；确定潜在的未来或现有资源冲突问题，并提出解决建议。

- 为基础设施管理提供变更控制。

- 进行有关基础设施管理的风险分析。

- 通过分析备选方案，评估基础设施管理备选方案。这种评估和分析有助于风险管理和降低活动的成本。

常用方法和提示：

- 可根据投资战略选择租赁（内包或外包）或许可使用合格资源。

- 建立组织基础设施架构。整合组织的基础设施可以使日常业务活动的执行更加高效。

SYSTEM LIFE CYCLE CONCEPTS, MODELS, AND PROCESSES

- Establish a resource management information system with enabling support systems and services to maintain, track, allocate, and improve the resources for present and future organization needs. Computer-based equipment tracking, facilities allocation, and other systems are recommended for organizations with over 50 people.

- Attend to physical factors, including facilities and human factors, such as ambient noise level and computer access to specific tools and applications.

- Begin planning in early life cycle stages of all system development efforts to address utilization and support resource requirements for system transition, facilities, infrastructure, information/data storage, and management. Enabling resources should also be identified and integrated into the organization's infrastructure.

- Engage project management, risk management, and business management processes to fully integrate Infrastructure Management processes to ensure organizational adoption.

Elaboration

Infrastructure Management Concepts. Projects all need resources to meet their objectives. Project planners determine the resources needed by the project and attempt to anticipate both current and future needs. The Infrastructure Management process provides the mechanisms whereby the organization infrastructure is made aware of project needs and the resources are scheduled to be in place when requested. While this can be simply stated, it is less simply executed. Conflicts must be negotiated and resolved, equipment must be obtained and sometimes repaired, buildings need to be refurbished, and information technology services are in a state of constant change. The infrastructure management organization collects the needs, negotiates to remove conflicts, and is responsible for providing the enabling organization infrastructure without which nothing else can be accomplished. Since resources are not free, their costs are also factored into investment decisions. Financial resources are addressed under the Portfolio Management process (see Section 2.3.3.3), but all other resources, except for human resources which are addressed under the Human Resource Management process (see Section 2.3.3.4), are addressed under this process.

Infrastructure management is complicated by the number of sources for requests, the need to balance the skills of the labor pool against the other infrastructure elements (e.g., computer-based tools), the need to maintain a balance between the budgets of individual projects and the cost of resources, the need to keep apprised of new or modified policies and procedures that might influence the skills inventory, and myriad unknowns.

系统生命周期概念、模型和流程

- 建立资源管理信息系统，使支持系统和服务能够维护、跟踪、分配和改进资源，以满足组织当前和未来的需要。建议 50 人以上的组织使用基于计算机的设备跟踪、设施分配和其他系统。

- 关注物理因素，包括设施和人的因素，如环境噪音水平和计算机对特定工具和应用程序的访问。

- 在所有系统开发工作的生命周期早期阶段开始计划，以处理系统转移、设施、基础设施、信息／数据存储和管理的使用率以及对支持资源的需求。还应确定使能资源，并将其纳入本组织的基础设施。

- 使项目管理、风险管理和业务管理流程充分整合基础设施管理流程，以确保组织采用这些流程。

详细阐述

基础设施管理概念。所有项目都需要资源来实现其目标。项目计划师确定项目所需的资源，并尝试预测当前和未来的需求。基础设施管理流程提供了一种机制，使组织基础设施了解项目需求，并在需要时安排资源到位。虽然这可以简单地说明，但执行起来却不那么简单。资源冲突必须通过协商解决，必须确保获得设备，有时还必须进行维修，建筑物需要翻修，信息技术服务处于不断变化的状态。基础设施管理组织收集需求，进行协商以消除冲突，并负责提供支持组织的基础设施，没有基础设施，其他任何事情都无法完成。由于资源不是免费的，因此在投资决策时也会考虑资源的成本。财务资源在项目组合管理流程（见 2.3.3.3 节）中处理，但除人力资源管理流程（见 2.3.3.4 节）处理的人力资源外，所有其他资源都在本流程下处理。

基础设施管理因请求来源的数量而变得复杂，需要平衡劳动力队伍的技能与其他基础设施元素（例如，基于计算机的工具），需要在单个项目的预算和资源成本之间保持平衡，需要随时了解可能影响技能库的新的或改进的政策和程序，以及无数未知因素。

Resources are allocated based on requests. Infrastructure management collects the needs of all the projects in the active portfolio and schedules or acquires nonhuman assets, as needed. Additionally, the infrastructure management process maintains and manages the facilities, hardware, and support tools required by the portfolio of organization projects. Infrastructure management is the efficient and effective deployment of an organization's resources when and where they are needed. Such resources may include inventory, production resources, or information technology. The goal is to provide materials and services to a project when they are needed to keep the project on target and on budget. A balance should be found between efficiency and robustness. Infrastructure management relies heavily on forecasts into the future of the demand and supply of various resources.

The organization environment and subsequent investment decisions are built on the existing organization infrastructure, including facilities, equipment, personnel, and knowledge. Efficient use of these resources is achieved by exploiting opportunities to share enabling systems or to use a common system element on more than one project. These opportunities are enabled by good communications within the organization. Integration and interoperability of supporting systems, such as financial, human resources (see Section 2.3.3.4), and training, is critically important to executing organization strategic objectives. Feedback from active projects is used to refine and continuously improve the infrastructure.

Further, trends in the market may suggest changes in the supporting environment. Assessment of the availability and suitability of the organization infrastructure and associated resources provides feedback for improvement and reward mechanisms. All organization processes require mandatory compliance with government and corporate laws and regulations. Decision making is governed by the organization strategic plan.

Infrastructure Management Process Maturity. The Infrastructure Management process primarily focuses on the establishment and deployment of infrastructure rather than the construction or actual use of the infrastructure. Since the quality of a product is related to the structure and use of the infrastructure employed, the maturity and quality of the process employed toward management of the infrastructure can help provide higher quality process inputs, outputs, and outcomes.

2.3.3.3 Portfolio Management Process

Overview

Purpose As stated in ISO/IEC/IEEE 15288,

[6.2.3.1] The purpose of the Portfolio Management process is to initiate and sustain necessary, sufficient, and suitable projects to meet the strategic objectives of the organization.

根据请求分配资源。基础设施管理需要收集项目群中所有进行中的项目需求，并根据需要安排或采办非人力资产。此外，基础设施管理流程维护和管理组织项目组合所需的设施、硬件和支持工具。基础设施管理是在需要的时候和地点高效地部署组织的资源。这些资源可能包括库存、生产资源或信息技术。目的是在需要时为项目提供材料和服务，以保持项目符合目标和预算。应在效率和稳健性之间找到平衡。基础设施管理在很大程度上依赖于对各种资源的未来需求和供应的预测。

组织环境和后续投资决策建立在现有组织基础设施的基础上，包括设施、设备、人员和知识。这些资源的有效利用是通过利用共享使能系统或在多个项目中使用一个共同系统元素的机会来实现的。这些机会是通过组织内部的良好沟通实现的。财务、人力资源（见 2.3.3.4 节）和培训等支持系统的综合和互操作性对于执行组织战略目标至关重要。活跃项目的反馈意见被用来完善和不断改进基础设施。

此外，市场趋势可能表明支持环境发生了变化。对组织基础设施和相关资源的可用性和适用性进行评估，为改进和奖励机制提供反馈。所有组织流程都要求强制遵守政府和公司法律法规。决策由组织战略计划管理。

基础设施管理流程成熟度。基础设施管理流程主要关注基础设施的建立和部署，而不是基础设施的建设或实际使用。由于产品的质量与所使用的基础设施的结构和使用有关，因此用于基础设施管理的流程的成熟度和质量可以帮助提供更高质量的流程输入、输出和结果。

2.3.3.3 项目组合管理流程

概述

目的　如 ISO/IEC/IEEE 15288 所述：

[6.2.3.1] 项目组合管理流程的目的是启动和维持必要、充分和适当的项目，以实现组织的战略目标。

SYSTEM LIFE CYCLE CONCEPTS, MODELS, AND PROCESSES

Portfolio management also provides organizational output regarding the set of projects, systems, and technical investments of the organization to external stakeholders, such as parent organizations, investors/funding sources, and governance bodies.

Description Projects create the products or services that meet the objectives and generate revenue for an organization. Thus, the conduct of successful projects requires an adequate allocation of funding and resources and the authority to deploy them to meet project objectives. Most business entities manage the commitment of financial resources using well-defined and closely monitored processes.

The Portfolio Management process also performs ongoing evaluation of the projects and systems in its portfolio. Based on periodic assessments, projects are determined to justify continued investment if they have the following characteristics:

- Contribute to the organization strategy
- Progress toward achieving established goals
- Comply with project directives from the organization
- Are conducted according to an approved plan
- Provide a service or product that is still needed and providing acceptable investment returns

Otherwise, projects may be redirected or, in extreme instances, terminated.

Inputs/Outputs Inputs and outputs for the Portfolio Management process are listed in Figure 2.17. Descriptions of each input and output are provided in Appendix E.

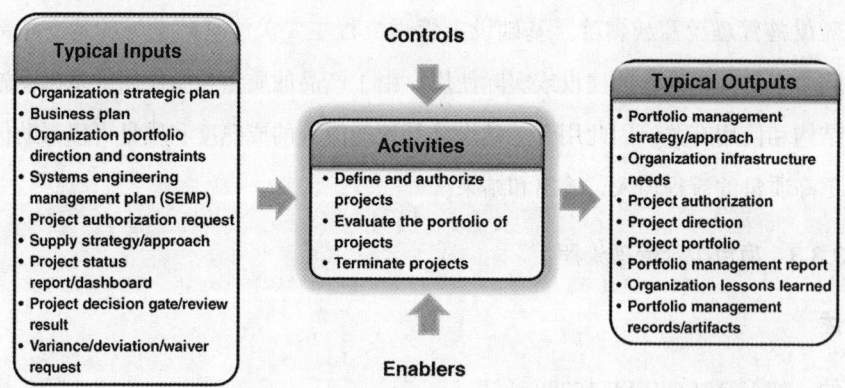

FIGURE 2.17   IPO diagram for Portfolio Management process. INCOSE SEH original figure created by Shortell, Walden, and Yip. Usage per the INCOSE Notices page. All other rights reserved.

系统生命周期概念、模型和流程

项目组合管理还向外部利益相关方（如上级组织、投资者/资金来源和治理机构）提供关于组织的项目组合、系统和技术投资的组织级输出结果。

描述 项目创造满足目标并为组织带来收入的产品或服务。因此，成功项目的实施需要充分分配资金和资源，并有权部署这些资金和资源以实现项目目标。大多数业务实体都使用定义明确且受到密切监控的流程来管理财务资源的投入。

项目组合管理流程还对其项目组合中的项目和系统进行持续评估。根据定期评估，如果项目具有以下特征，则确定其有理由继续投资：

- 为组织战略做出贡献
- 向实现既定目的的方向发展
- 遵守组织的项目指令
- 根据批准的计划进行
- 提供仍然需要的服务或产品，并带来可接受的投资回报

否则，项目可能会被重定向，或在极端情况下被终止。

输入/输出 项目组合管理流程的输入和输出如图 2.17 所示。附录 E 中提供了每个输入和输出的描述。

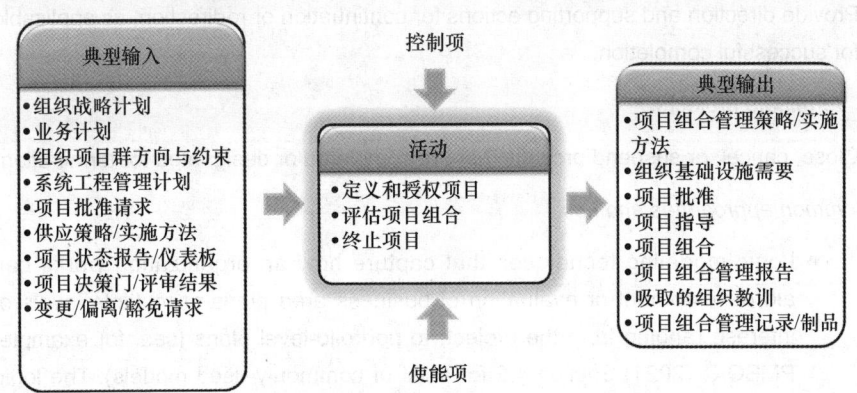

图 2.17 项目组合管理流程的 IPO 图。INCOSE SEH 原始图由 Walden、Shortell 和 Yip 创建。按照 INCOSE 通知页使用。版权所有。

SYSTEM LIFE CYCLE CONCEPTS, MODELS, AND PROCESSES

Process Activities The Portfolio Management process includes the following activities:

- *Define and authorize projects.*

–Obtain business area plans and organization strategic plans—use the strategic objectives to identify candidate projects to fulfill them.

–Identify, assess, prioritize, and select investment opportunities consistent with the organization strategic plan.

–Establish project scope, define project management accountabilities and authorities, and identify expected project outcomes.

–Establish the domain area of the product line defined by its main features and their suitable variability.

–Allocate adequate funding and other resources to selected projects.

–Identify interfaces and opportunities for multi-project synergies.

–Specify the project governance process including organizational status reporting and reviews.

–Authorize project execution.

- *Evaluate the portfolio of projects.*

–Evaluate ongoing projects to provide rationale for continuation, redirection, or termination.

–Provide direction and supporting actions for continuation or redirection, as applicable for successful completion.

- *Terminate projects.*

–Close, cancel, or suspend projects that are completed or designated for termination.

Common approaches and tips:

- Logic modeling techniques that capture how an organization works can aid development or evaluation of business area plans at multiple levels of interest, ranging from the project- to portfolio-level plans (see, for example, PMBOK® (2021) Section 4.2 for a list of commonly used models). The logic models typically describe the fundamental theory/assumptions, planned work (resources, inputs and activities) linked with intended results (outputs, outcomes, and impact).

流程活动　项目组合管理流程包括以下活动：

- *定义和授权项目。*

- 获取业务域计划和组织战略计划——使用战略目标来确定实现这些目标的候选项目。

- 识别、评估、优先级排序和选择符合组织战略计划的投资机会。

- 确定项目范围，定义项目管理职责和权限，并确定预期的项目结果。

- 根据产品线的主要特征及其适当的可变性确定产品线的领域。

- 为选定的项目分配充足的资金和其他资源。

- 确定多项目协同的接口和机会。

- 指定项目治理流程，包括组织状态报告和评审。

- 授权项目执行。

- *评估项目组合。*

- 评估正在进行的项目，以提供继续、重定向或终止的理由。

- 为继续或重定向提供指导和支持措施，如适用，成功完成项目。

- *终止项目。*

- 关闭、取消或暂停已完成或指定终止的项目。

常用方法和提示：

- 捕获组织工作方式的逻辑建模技术可以帮助开发或评估多个感兴趣层级的业务域计划，从项目到项目组合层级的计划［例如，参考 PMBOK®（2021）4.2 节中常用模型的列表］。逻辑模型通常描述与预期结果（输出、结果和影响）相关的基本理论/假设、计划工作（资源、输入和活动）。

SYSTEM LIFE CYCLE CONCEPTS, MODELS, AND PROCESSES

- When investment opportunities present themselves, prioritize them based on measurable criteria such that projects can be objectively evaluated against a threshold of acceptable performance. This assessment is done in the context of the business area planning to focus resources to best meet present and future objectives.

- Expected project outcomes should be based on clearly defined, measurable criteria to ensure that an objective assessment of progress can be determined. Specify the investment information that will be assessed for each milestone. Initiation should be a formal milestone that does not occur until all resources are in place as identified in the project plan.

- Establish organizational coordination mechanisms to manage the synergies between active projects in the organization portfolio. Complex and large organization architectures require the management and coordination of multiple interfaces and make additional demands on investment decisions. These interactions occur within and between the projects.

- Use a product line engineering approach (see Section 4.2.4) when stakeholders need the same or similar systems (e.g., common features), with some customizations (e.g., variants). The goal is to manage a product line as one product definition with planned variants as opposed to multiple separate products managed individually, thereby streamlining and simplifying the management effort.

- Include risk assessments (see Section 2.3.4.4) in the evaluation of ongoing projects. Projects that contain risks that may pose a challenge in the future might require redirection. Cancel or suspend projects whose disadvantages or risks to the organization outweigh the investment.

- Include opportunity assessments (see Section 2.3.4.4) in the evaluation of ongoing projects. Addressing project challenges may represent a positive investment opportunity for the organization. Avoid pursuing opportunities that are inconsistent with the capabilities of the organization and its strategic goals and objectives or contain unacceptably high technical risk, resource demands, or uncertainty.

- Allocate resources based on the requirements of the projects; otherwise, the risk of cost and schedule overruns may have a negative impact on quality and performance of the project.

- Establish effective governance processes that directly support investment decision making and communications with project management.

- 当投资机会出现时，根据可衡量的准则对其进行优先级排序，以便根据可接受的绩效阈值对项目进行客观评估。该评估应在业务领域计划的背景下进行，目的是集中资源，以最好地满足当前和未来的目标。

- 预期的项目成果应基于明确定义的、可衡量的准则，以确保能够确定对进展的客观评估。明确将针对每个里程碑评估所需的投资信息。项目启动应该是一个正式的里程碑，在项目计划中确定的所有资源到位之前不应发生。

- 建立组织协调机制，以管理组织项目组合中活跃项目之间的协同效应。复杂和大型的组织架构需要管理和协调多个接口，并对投资决策提出额外的要求。这些交互作用发生在项目内部和项目之间。

- 当利益相关方需要相同或类似的系统（例如，通用功能）以及一些定制化（例如，差异）时，使用产品线工程方法（见 4.2.4 节）。目标是将一个产品线作为一个产品定义进行管理，其中包含计划的差异，从而简化管理工作，而不是单独管理多个独立的产品。

- 对进行中的项目评估应包括风险评估（见 2.3.4.4 节）。包含可能在未来构成挑战的风险时，可能需要重新定向。取消或暂停对组织不利或风险大于投资的项目。

- 对进行中的项目评估应包括机会评估（见 2.3.4.4 节）。应对项目挑战可能是本组织的一个积极投资机会。避免寻求与组织能力及其战略目标和目的不一致的机会，或包含不可接受的高技术风险、资源需求或不确定性的机会。

- 根据项目要求配置资源；否则，成本和进度超支的风险可能会对项目的质量和绩效产生负面影响。

- 建立直接支持投资决策和与项目管理沟通的有效治理流程。

SYSTEM LIFE CYCLE CONCEPTS, MODELS, AND PROCESSES

Elaboration

Define the Business Cases and Assess Against Business Area Plans. Portfolio management tries to maximize the benefit obtained by the organization from the use of financial assets and other resources within the organization. Thus, business cases for potential projects are evaluated for cost-benefit and the business need before a project is approved for the proposed SoI. Each decision gate reviews the business case as the project matures. The result is reverification or perhaps restatement of the business case.

The business case may be validated in a variety of ways. For large projects, sophisticated engineering models, or even prototypes of key system elements, help prove that the objectives of the business case can be met, and that the system will work as envisioned prior to committing large amounts of resources to full-scale engineering and manufacturing development. For smaller projects, when the total investment is modest, proof-of-concept models may be constructed during the concept stage to prove the validity of business case assumptions.

Investment opportunities are not all equal, and organizations are limited in the number of projects that can be conducted concurrently. Further, some investments are not well aligned with the overall strategic plan of the organization. For these reasons, opportunities are evaluated against the portfolio of existing agreements and ongoing projects, taking into consideration the attainability of the stakeholders' requirements.

Project Management and SE considerations. Portfolios may have multiple projects. As previously stated, projects are added to the portfolio after the candidate project can show that it is both feasible and meets organizational business needs. In many organizations projects with defined scope are organized in programs focused on a set of objectives that are part of the organization's strategic plan. As stated in the PMI (2017), the focus of portfolio management is "doing the right work" as opposed to program or project management which is more concerned with "doing work right."

The disciplines of project management and SE have overlapping responsibilities regarding portfolio management. To save time, share knowledge, facilitate the accomplishment of shared objectives, and achieve success, a strong partnership should exist between each of these disciplines (see Section 5.3.3).

At the portfolio level, the scope is extensive with consideration external to the organization and internal across the organization's enterprise. At the other end of the spectrum, the focus is internal to the project with consideration for the context of the product/service/result. An example of this is to look at the range in scope in requirements development, as shown in Figure 2.18.

详细阐述

定义业务用例并根据业务领域计划进行评估。项目组合管理试图最大限度地提高组织从使用组织内的金融资产和其他资源中获得的收益。因此，在批准拟议的 SoI 项目之前，对潜在项目的业务用例进行成本效益和业务需求评估。随着项目的成熟，每个决策门都会评审业务用例。其结果是重新确认或重述业务用例。

业务用例可以通过多种方式进行验证。对于大型项目，复杂的工程模型，甚至关键系统元素的原型，有助于证明业务用例的目标能够得到满足，并且在投入大量资源进行全面工程和制造开发之前，系统将按照预期工作。对于较小的项目，当总投资不大时，可在概念阶段构建概念验证模型，以证明业务用例假设的有效性。

投资机会并不都是平等的，组织可以同时进行的项目数量有限。此外，一些投资与本组织的总体战略计划不太一致。出于这些原因，根据现有协议和正在进行的项目组合评估机会，同时考虑利益相关方需求的可实现性。

项目管理和系统工程注意事项。项目组合可能有多个项目。如前所述，在候选项目能够证明其既可行又满足组织业务需求之后，项目被添加到项目组合中。在许多组织中，具有确定范围的项目都是在项目集中组织的，项目集的重点是实现作为组织战略计划一部分的一组目标。正如 PMI（2017）所述，项目组合管理的重点是"做正确的事"，而不像项目集或项目管理一样更关注"正确地做事"。

项目管理和系统工程学科在项目组合管理方面有重叠的职责。为了节省时间、共享知识、促进实现共同目标并取得成功，这些学科之间应建立强有力的伙伴关系（见 5.3.3 节）。

在项目组合层级，范围是广泛的，考虑到组织外部和复杂组织体系内部。重点是项目内部，并考虑产品/服务/结果的背景环境。典型例子可以查看需求开发的范围，如图 2.18 所示。

SYSTEM LIFE CYCLE CONCEPTS, MODELS, AND PROCESSES

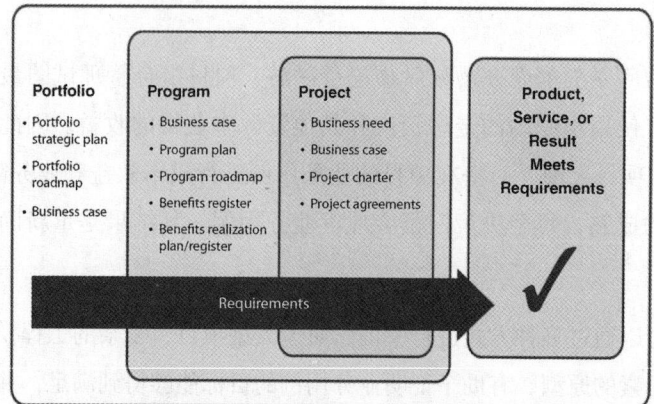

FIGURE 2.18 Requirements across the portfolio, program, and project domains. From PMI (2016). Used with permission. All other rights reserved.

At the portfolio level, the portfolio's strategic plan and roadmap address business and mission needs and provides direction and organizational focus, and plans/actions to realize the direction. Requirements often start at the concept or portfolio level as a high-level view associated with investment or business opportunities.

2.3.3.4 Human Resource Management Process

Overview

Purpose As stated in ISO/IEC/IEEE 15288,

[6.2.4.1] The purpose of the Human Resource Management process is to provide the organization with necessary human resources and to maintain their competencies, consistent with strategic needs.

Description Projects all need resources to meet their objectives. This process deals with human resources. Nonhuman resources, including tools, databases, communication systems, financial systems, and information technology, are addressed using the Infrastructure Management process (see Section 2.3.3.2).

Project planners determine the resources needed for the project by anticipating both current and future needs. The Human Resource Management process provides the mechanisms whereby the organization management is made aware of project needs and personnel are scheduled to be in place when requested. While this can be simply stated, it is less simply executed. Conflicts must be resolved, personnel must be trained, and employees are entitled to vacations and time away from the job.

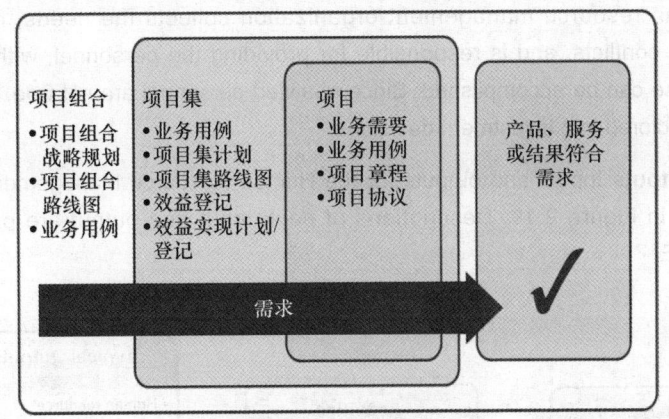

图 2.18 跨项目组合、项目集和项目领域的需求。源自 PMI（2016）。经许可后使用。版权所有。

在项目组合层面，项目组合的战略计划和路线图解决了业务和任务需要，并提供了方向和组织重点，以及实现方向的计划/行动。需求通常从概念或项目组合层级开始，作为与投资或业务机会相关的高级视图。

2.3.3.4 人力资源管理流程

概述

目的　如 ISO/IEC/IEEE 15288 所述：

[6.2.4.1] 人力资源管理流程的目的是为组织提供必要的人力资源，并根据战略需要保持其胜任力。

描述　项目都需要资源来实现其目标。这一流程涉及人力资源。非人力资源，包括工具、数据库、通信系统、财务系统和信息技术，使用基础设施管理流程进行处理（见 2.3.3.2 节）。

项目计划人员通过预测当前和未来的需求来确定项目所需的资源。人力资源管理流程提供了一种机制，使组织管理层了解项目需要，并及时安排人员到位。虽然这说起来简单，但执行起来却不简单。人力资源冲突必须得到解决，人员必须接受培训，员工有权休假和请假。

SYSTEM LIFE CYCLE CONCEPTS, MODELS, AND PROCESSES

The human resource management organization collects the needs, negotiates to remove conflicts, and is responsible for providing the personnel, without which nothing else can be accomplished. Since qualified personnel are not free, their costs are also factored into investment decisions.

Inputs/Outputs Inputs and outputs for the Human Resource Management process are listed in Figure 2.19. Descriptions of each input and output are provided in Appendix E.

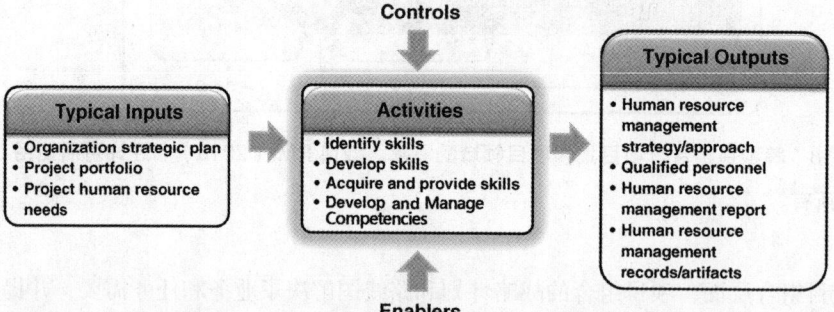

FIGURE 2.19 IPO diagram for Human Resource Management process. INCOSE SEH original figure created by Shortell, Walden, and Yip. Usage per the INCOSE Notices page. All other rights reserved.

Processes Activities The Human Resource Management process includes the following activities:

- *Identify skills.*

–Identify and record skills of existing personnel to establish a "skills inventory."

–Review current and anticipated projects to determine and record the skill needs across the portfolio of projects. The INCOSE Systems Engineering Competency Framework (SECF) (2018) and Systems Engineering Competency Assessment Guide (SECAG) (2023) can be used as resources to identify SE skills.

–Evaluate skill needs against available personnel with the prerequisite skills to determine if training, hiring, or other skill acquisition activities are indicated.

- *Develop skills.*

–Establish a strategy/approach for skills development.

–Plan for the skill development per the strategy.

人力资源管理组织负责收集需求，通过协商消除冲突，并负责提供人员，否则无法完成任何其他项目工作。由于合格人员不是免费的，他们的成本也需要纳入投资决策。

输入／输出　人力资源管理流程的输入和输出如图 2.19 所示。附录 E 中提供了每个输入和输出的描述。

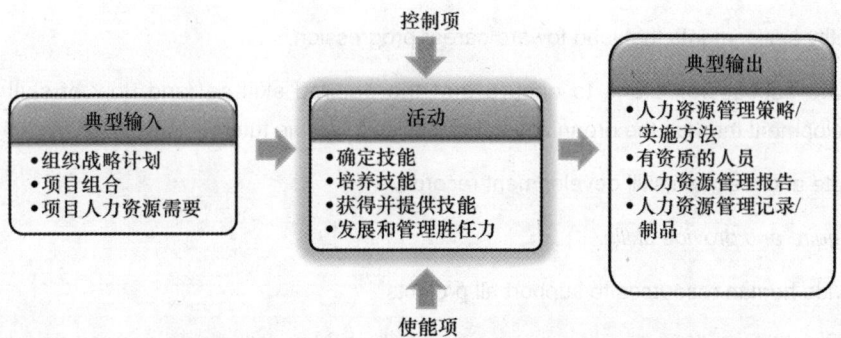

图 2.19　人力资源管理流程的 IPO 图。INCOSE SEH 原始图由 Walden、Shortell 和 Yip 创建。按照 INCOSE 通知页使用。版权所有。

流程活动　人力资源管理流程包括以下活动：

- *确定技能*。

- 识别并记录现有人员的技能，以建立"技能清单"。

- 评审当前和预期的项目，以确定和记录整个项目群的技能需求。INCOSE 系统工程胜任力框架（SECF）（2018）和系统工程胜任力评估指南（SECAG）（2023）可作为识别系统工程技能的资源。

- 根据具备必要技能的现有人员评估技能需求，以确定是否需要开展培训、招聘或其他技能学习活动。

- *培养技能*。

- 制定技能发展策略／方法。

- 根据策略制订技能培养计划。

SYSTEM LIFE CYCLE CONCEPTS, MODELS, AND PROCESSES

–Obtain (or develop) and deliver training, education, and mentoring to close identified gaps of project personnel.

–Identify skills, abilities, and behaviors needed for competencies. The INCOSE Systems Engineering Assessment Guide is a recommended resource for this. Identify training and development resources to match desired skills, abilities, and behaviors development. The INCOSE Professional Development Portal can help identify potential resources.

–Identify assignments that lead toward career progression.

–Create succession plans to ensure that the desired skill set and flow of skill development through the organization is sustained into the future.

–Create and maintain skill development records.

- *Acquire and provide skills.*

–Provide human resources to support all projects.

–Train or hire qualified personnel when gaps indicate that skill needs cannot be met with existing personnel.

–Maintain and manage a skilled personnel pool to staff ongoing projects.

–Assign personnel to projects based on personnel development and project needs.

–Create and maintain staff assignment records.

–Motivate personnel by providing career development and reward programs.

–Resolve personnel conflicts between or within projects.

–Maintain communication across projects to effectively allocate human resources throughout the organization and identify potential future or existing conflicts and problems with recommendations for resolution.

–Schedule other related assets or, if necessary, acquire them.

- *Develop and Manage Competencies.*

– Create and maintain job role definitions related to competencies required.

– Identify organization competency gaps.

– Align organization competencies with strategic objectives.

– Maintain organization-level competency definitions and frameworks.

- 获得（或发展）并提供培训、教育和指导，以弥补现有项目人员的差距。

- 确定胜任力所需的技能、能力和行为。INCOSE 系统工程评估指南为这方面提供了参考资源。识别培训和开发资源，以匹配所需的技能、能力和行为。INCOSE 专业开发门户可帮助识别潜在资源。

- 确定有助于职业发展的任务。

- 制订继任计划，确保所需的技能集合和技能开发工作流在未来得以持续。

- 创建和维护技能开发记录。

- **获得并提供技能。**

- 提供人力资源支持所有项目。

- 当现有人员无法满足技能需求时，培训或雇用合格人员。

- 维护和管理一个技术人员库，为正在进行的项目配备人员。

- 根据人员发展和项目需求为项目分配人员。

- 创建和维护员工派遣记录。

- 通过提供职业发展和奖励计划来激励员工。

- 解决项目之间或项目内部的人员冲突。

- 保持项目间的沟通，在整个组织内有效分配人力资源，并确定潜在的未来或现有冲突和问题，并提出解决建议。

- 安排其他相关资产，或在必要时采办这些资产。

- **发展和管理胜任力。**

- 创建和维护与所需胜任力相关的工作角色定义。

- 识别组织胜任力差距。

- 使组织胜任力与战略目标保持一致。

- 维护组织级的胜任力定义和框架。

SYSTEM LIFE CYCLE CONCEPTS, MODELS, AND PROCESSES

Common approaches and tips:

- The availability and suitability of personnel is one of the critical project assessments and provides feedback for improvement and reward mechanisms.

- Consider using an IPDT environment as a means to reduce the frequency of project rotation, recognize progress and accomplishments and reward success, and establish apprentice and mentoring programs for newly hired employees and students.

- Maintain both a listing of skill needs and the paths to obtain the necessary expertise, including a pipeline of candidates, training provisions, consultants, temporary outsourcing, reassignments, etc.

- Personnel are allocated based on requests and conflicts are negotiated. The goal is to provide personnel to a project when they are needed to keep the project on target and on budget.

- Try to avoid the overcommitment of project personnel, especially people with specialized skills.

- Skills inventory and career development plans are important documentation that can be validated by engineering and project management. The INCOSE SECF and SECAG are comprehensive resources of skills that can be used to develop career development plans.

- Maintain an organization career development program that is not sidetracked by project demands. Develop a policy that all personnel receive training or educational benefits on a regular cycle. This includes both undergraduate and graduate studies, in-house training courses, certifications, tutorials, workshops, and conferences.

- Remember to provide training on organization policies and procedures and system life cycle processes.

- Establish a resource management information infrastructure with enabling support systems and services to maintain, track, allocate, and improve the resources for present and future organization needs.

- Use the slack time in the beginning of a project to provide training to ensure necessary skills.

- Career development plans should be managed and aligned to the objectives of both the employee and the organization. Career development plans should be reviewed, tracked, and refined to provide a mechanism to help manage the employee's career within the organization.

常用方法和提示：

- 人员的可用性和适用性是关键项目评估之一，并可以为改进和奖励机制提供反馈。

- 考虑使用 IPDT 环境作为一种手段，以减少项目轮换的频率，认可进步和成就，奖励成功，并为新雇用的员工和学生建立学徒和指导计划。

- 维护技能需求清单和获得必要专业知识的途径，包括候选人渠道、培训规定、顾问、临时外包、调任等。

- 根据项目需要分配人员，并协调冲突。目标是在需要人员时为项目提供人员，以确保项目符合目标和预算。

- 尽量避免对项目人员，尤其是具有专业技能的人员的过度承诺。

- 技能清单和职业发展计划是可用于工程和项目管理验证的重要文档。INCOSE SECF 和 SECAG 是可用于制订职业发展计划的综合技能资源。

- 维护一个不受项目需求影响的组织职业发展计划。制定所有人员定期接受培训或教育福利的政策。这包括本科生和研究生学习、内部培训课程、认证、辅导、研讨会和会议。

- 记住提供有关组织政策和程序以及系统生命周期流程的培训。

- 建立资源管理信息基础设施，支持系统和服务维护、跟踪、分配和改进资源，以满足组织当前和未来的需要。

- 利用好项目开始时的空闲时间提供培训，以确保必要的技能。

- 职业发展计划应根据员工和组织的目标进行管理和调整。应评审、跟踪和完善职业发展计划，以提供一种机制，帮助管理员工在组织内的职业生涯。

SYSTEM LIFE CYCLE CONCEPTS, MODELS, AND PROCESSES

Elaboration

Human Resource Management Concepts. The Human Resource Management process maintains and manages the people required by the portfolio of organization projects. Human resource management is the efficient and effective deployment of qualified personnel when and where they are needed. A balance should be found between efficiency and robustness. Human resource management relies heavily on forecasts into the future of the demand and supply of various resources.

The primary objective of this process is to provide a pool of qualified personnel to the organization. This is complicated by the number of sources for requests, the need to balance the skills of the labor pool against the other infrastructure elements (e.g., computer-based tools), the need to maintain a balance between the budgets of individual projects and the cost of resources, the need to keep apprised of new or modified policies and procedures that might influence the skills inventory, and myriad unknowns.

Project managers face their resource challenges competing for scarce talent in the larger organization pool. They must balance access to the experts they need for special studies with stability in the project team with its tacit knowledge and project memory. Today's projects depend on teamwork and optimally multidisciplinary teams. Such teams are able to resolve project issues quickly through direct communication between team members. Such intrateam communication shortens the decision-making cycle and is more likely to result in improved decisions because the multidisciplinary perspectives are captured early in the process.

2.3.3.5 Quality Management Process

Overview

Purpose As stated in ISO/IEC/IEEE 15288,

[6.2.5.1] The purpose of the Quality Management process is to assure that products, services, and implementations of the Quality Management process meet organizational and project quality objectives and achieve customer satisfaction.

Description The overarching process for achieving quality goals is the Quality Management (QM) process and its supporting methods, values, and subprocesses. Properly communicated, through policy and procedure, it makes visible the goals of the organization to achieve customer satisfaction. These goals, when supported by measurable activities, provide feedback for maintaining consistency in work processes and delivering quality outcomes. Since primary drivers in any project are time, cost, and quality, inclusion of a comprehensive QM process and its subprocesses is essential to every organization and must be sustained by a work culture that is disciplined in the proper execution of QM foundational principles and values. System life cycle processes are concerned with quality issues, and this is sufficient justification for spending the time, money, and energy into establishing QM fundamentals in an organization, its processes, and its people.

系统生命周期概念、模型和流程

详细阐述

*人力资源管理概念。*人力资源管理流程维护和管理项目组合所需的人员。人力资源管理是在需要合格人员的时间和地点高效、有效地部署他们。应平衡效率和稳健性。人力资源管理在很大程度上依赖于对各种资源的未来需求和供应的预测。

该流程的主要目标是为组织提供一个合格人员库。由于需求来源的数量、平衡人员库技能与其他基础设施元素（例如，基于计算机的工具）的需要、保持各个项目预算与资源成本之间平衡的需要、随时了解可能影响技能库的新的或改进的政策和程序的需要，以及无数未知因素，这一点变得更加复杂。

在更大的组织人才库中争夺稀缺人才，是项目经理面临的资源挑战。他们必须平衡获得特殊研究所需专家的机会与项目团队的稳定性、隐性知识和项目记忆的延续性。当前，项目依赖于团队合作和最佳的多学科团队。这样的团队能够通过团队成员之间的直接沟通快速解决项目问题。这样的团队内部沟通可以缩短决策周期，更有可能带来决策的改进，因为这样可以让多学科视角在流程的早期被捕捉到。

2.3.3.5 *质量管理流程*

概述

目的 如 ISO/IEC/IEEE 15288 所述：

[6.2.5.1] 质量管理流程的目的是确保产品、服务和质量管理流程的实施符合组织和项目质量目标，并实现客户满意。

描述 实现质量目标的首要流程是质量管理（QM）流程及其支持方法、价值和子流程。通过政策和程序确保适当沟通，使组织实现客户满意度的目标是清晰可见的。当这些目标被可衡量的活动实现时，则可为保持工作流程的一致性和交付高质量的成果提供反馈。由于任何项目中的主要驱动因素都是时间、成本和质量，因此包含全面的质量管理流程及其子流程对每个组织都是至关重要的，并且必须通过在正确执行 QM 基本原则和价值方面的工作文化来确保。系统生命周期流程需要考虑质量方面的问题，因此花时间、金钱和精力在组织、流程和人员中建立质量管理基础是充分必要的。

SYSTEM LIFE CYCLE CONCEPTS, MODELS, AND PROCESSES

The QM process for SE ensures that all SE processes are deployed consistently by capable staff that can then produce systems designs that fulfill the stakeholder's requirements and lead to development and build processes that are aligned to produce high levels of performance throughout the organization.

Inputs/Outputs Inputs and outputs for the Quality Management process are listed in Figure 2.20. Descriptions of each input and output are provided in Appendix E.

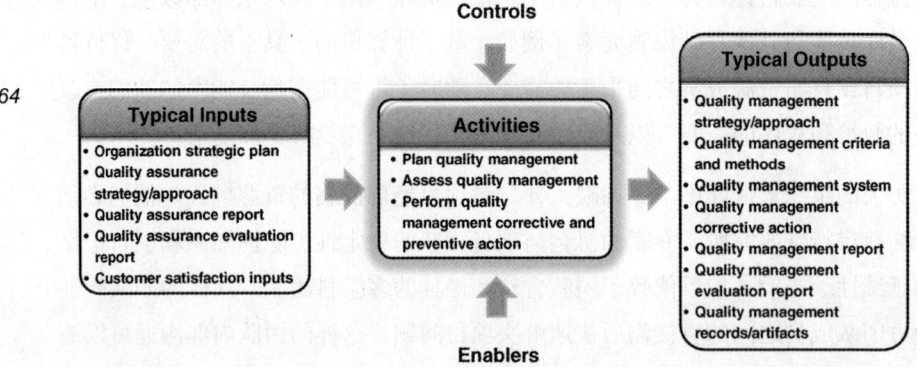

FIGURE 2.20 IPO diagram for the Quality Management process. INCOSE SEH original figure created by Shortell, Walden, and Yip. Usage per the INCOSE Notices page. All other rights reserved.

Process Activities The Quality Management process includes the following activities:

- *Plan quality management.*

–Identify, assess, and prioritize quality guidelines consistent with the organization strategic plan. Establish QM guidelines-policies, standards, and procedures.

–Establish organization and project QM goals and objectives, including QM Culture emphasis.

–Establish organization and project QM responsibilities and authorities.

- *Assess quality management.*

–Evaluate project assessments.

–Assess customer satisfaction against compliance with requirements and objectives.

–Continuously improve the QM guidelines.

系统工程的质量管理流程确保所有系统工程流程由有能力的员工一致部署，然后他们可以创造满足利益相关方需求的系统设计，并引导系统开发和构建流程，以在整个组织内产生高水平的绩效。

输入/输出　图 2.20 列出了质量管理流程的输入和输出。附录 E 中提供了每个输入和输出的描述。

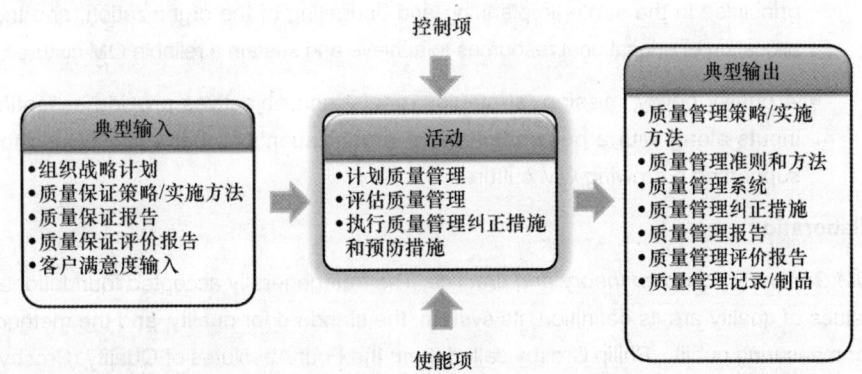

图 2.20　质量管理流程的 IPO 图。INCOSE SEH 原始图由 Walden、Shortell 和 Yip 创建。按照 INCOSE 通知页使用。版权所有。

流程活动　质量管理流程包括以下活动：

- *计划质量管理*。

- 确定、评估并优先考虑与组织战略计划一致的质量指导方针。建立质量管理方针、政策、标准和程序。

- 建立组织和项目质量管理目标，包括质量管理文化重点。

- 建立组织和项目质量管理职责和权限。

- *评估质量管理*。

- 对项目评估进行评价。

- 根据要求和目标的符合性评估客户满意度。

- 持续改进质量管理指南。

SYSTEM LIFE CYCLE CONCEPTS, MODELS, AND PROCESSES

- *Perform quality management corrective action and preventive action.*

–Recommend appropriate action, when indicated.

–Maintain open communications within the organization and with stakeholders.

Common approaches and tips:

- Management's commitment to quality is reflected in the integration of QM principles in the strategic planning and budgeting of the organization, and the allocation of educational resources to achieve and sustain a reliable QM culture.

- A quality policy, mission, strategies, goals, and objectives provide essential inputs along with a description of an organization's fundamental values for supporting a growing QM culture.

Elaboration

QM Generally accepted theory and practice. The four generally accepted foundational values of quality are its definition, its system, the standard for quality, and the method for measuring quality. Philip Crosby called them the Four Absolutes of Quality (Crosby, 1979).

1. *The definition of quality is meeting the stakeholder's requirements, needs and expectations.* Organizations (and individuals) are both producers and users of systems. One organization or person (acting as an acquirer) can task another (acting as a supplier) for products or services. This transaction is achieved using agreements that promise to fulfil the stakeholder's requirements in exchange for something of value, usually money. Quality pioneer W. Edwards Deming stressed that meeting stakeholder needs represents the defining criterion for quality and that all members of an organization need to participate actively in "constant and continuous" quality improvement (Deming, 1986).

2. *The system of quality is prevention.* One of the two QM prevention methods is Quality Assurance (QA). QA can be described as "putting good things into our processes" so that they perform as designed and conform to our stakeholder's requirements. QA was born in the aerospace industry and was originally referred to as "reliability engineering." It is generally associated with activities such as failure testing and pre-inspecting batches of materials and system elements that are then certified for use, thus preventing errors and defects from occurring by building-in quality. The QA methodology also includes infusing processes with reliable human resources and appropriate policies, procedures, and training (SEH Section 2.3.4.8). Quality Control (QC) is the

- 执行质量管理纠正措施和预防措施。

- 如有指示，建议采取适当措施。

- 在组织内部以及与利益相关方保持公开沟通。

常用方法和提示：

- 管理层对质量的承诺体现在将质量管理原则纳入组织的战略计划和预算中，以及分配教育资源以实现和维持可靠的质量管理文化。

- 质量方针、使命、战略、目标和目的提供了重要的输入，以及对组织基本价值的描述，以支持不断增长的质量管理文化。

详细阐述

QM 的公认理论和实践。质量的四个公认的基本价值是其定义、质量系统、质量标准和质量测量方法。Philip Crosby 称之为质量的四个绝对（Crosby，1979）。

1. *质量的定义是满足利益相关方的需求、需要和期望*。组织（和个人）既是系统的生产者，也是系统的用户。一个组织或个人（作为采办方）可以委托另一个组织或个人（作为供应商）提供产品或服务。该交易是通过协议实现的，协议承诺满足利益相关方的需求，以换取有价值的东西，通常是金钱。质量先锋 W.Edwards Deming 强调，满足利益相关方的需要是质量的定义标准，组织的所有成员都需要积极参与"持续不断"的质量改进（Deming，1986）。

2. *质量系统是预防*。质量管理的两种预防方法之一是质量保证（QA）。质量保证可以描述为"将好的东西放入我们的流程"，以便它们按照设计执行，并符合利益相关方的需求。质量保证诞生于航空航天行业，最初被称为"可靠性工程"。它通常与故障测试和预检查批次材料和系统元素等活动相关，这些材料和系统元素随后经过使用认证，从而防止因质量改进而发生错误和缺陷。质量保证方法还包括为流程注入可靠的人力资源和适当的政策、程序和培训（SEH 的 2.3.4.8 节）。质量

QM method for "taking bad things out of our processes after they occur" to prevent the defects that are discovered from reaching our stakeholders. QC includes checking, monitoring, and inspecting for defects and the removal, replacement, or rework of defective outcomes. One method of monitoring and statistically evaluating the stability and potential defect rates of processes is Statistical Process Control (SPC). Many manufacturing and high-volume service organizations use SPC to help achieve quality. Traditional SPC techniques include real-time, random sampling to test a fraction of the output for variances within critical tolerances (Juran, 1974).

3. *The standard for Quality is Zero Defects (ZD).* It is important to make a distinction between the tracking of defects from feedback loops to improve our processes and progress toward a ZD count, and the more fundamental human term which is the Zero Defects Attitude (ZDA) (Kennedy, 2005). A ZDA is not about achieving perfection; it is a commitment to make each stakeholder's experience as close to what was promised as possible. No one can achieve perfection, nor attain and sustain ZD, so we cannot expect perfection from any of our staff or processes. Like the "pride of workmanship," people with a ZDA have a "heart attitude" that desires to prevent all defects and to reach the highest level of personal performance and customer satisfaction. People with a ZDA want to keep their promises to everyone and make things right when we fail. A ZDA, coupled with appropriate metrics and plans to progress toward ZD, will result in continuous and incremental improvement.

4. *The method for measuring quality is the price of non-conformance* (Crosby, 1979). It is a calculation of the expenses incurred by defects and their related rework, replacement, warranties, customer service, etc. The American Society for Quality calls it the "cost of poor quality." It is an essential factor in calculating the actual "cost of quality" which is determined by comparing the "price of non-conformance (or doing things wrong)" that includes expense caused by re-work, defects, and warranties, with the "price of conformance (or doing things right)" which is a calculation of the expenses related to improving processes and applying preventive methods. The cost of quality includes a calculation of quantitative and qualitative parameters that are measured in both financial and human values. When the cost of doing things right is equal to or less than the price of non-conformance then, as Crosby said, "Quality is Free."

控制（QC）是一种质量管理方法，用于"在流程发生后将不好的事情从流程中去除"，以防止发现的缺陷影响到我们的利益相关方。质量控制包括检查、监控和检查缺陷，以及移除、更换或返工缺陷结果。监控和统计评估流程稳定性和潜在缺陷率的一种方法是统计过程控制（SPC）。许多制造业和大批量服务组织使用统计过程控制来帮助实现质量。传统的统计过程控制技术包括实时随机抽样，以测试部分输出是否在临界公差范围内（Juran，1974）。

3. *质量标准为零缺陷（ZD）*。重要的是要区分从反馈回路跟踪缺陷以改进我们的流程和零缺陷计数的进展，以及更基本的术语，即零缺陷态度（ZDA）（Kennedy，2005）。零缺陷态度不是为了达到完美；它承诺让每个利益相关方的体验尽可能接近承诺。没有人能够做到完美，也没有人能够做到并保持零缺陷，因此我们不能期望任何员工或流程都能做到完美。像"以工艺为荣"一样，拥有零缺陷态度的人也有一种"用心的态度"，希望防止所有缺陷，并达到个人表现和客户满意度的最高水平。有零缺陷态度的人希望遵守他们对每个人的承诺，并在失败时纠正错误。零缺陷态度，加上适当的指标和向零缺陷迈进的计划，将带来持续和增量的改进。

4. *衡量质量的方法是不合格的代价（Crosby，1979）*。这是对缺陷及其相关返工、更换、保修、客户服务等产生的费用的计算。美国质量协会称之为"劣质成本"。它是计算实际"质量成本"的一个重要因素，通过比较"不合格（或做错）的价格"（包括返工、缺陷和保修引起的费用）与"合格（或做对）的价格"（与改进流程和应用预防方法相关的费用）来确定。质量成本包括计算以财务和人力价值衡量的定量和定性参数。当正确做事的成本等于或小于不合规的代价时，正如克罗斯比所说，"质量是免费的"。

SYSTEM LIFE CYCLE CONCEPTS, MODELS, AND PROCESSES

QM Culture. SE practitioners need to have sufficient process knowledge and a QM knowledge base to be able to evaluate prevention options and make continuous, incremental improvements. When engineering disciplines are supported by planning and budgeting skills that resonate with the organization, we can achieve Process Quality with effective, efficient, and profitable outcomes, low defect rates, and delighted stakeholders. Deming, in his "14 Points" emphasized the need to "create constancy of purpose for improving products and services" and that it should be supported by "a vigorous program of education and self-improvement for everyone" (Deming, 1986). A high-performing work culture is measured by identifiable attributes or values within an organization's leadership style and workforce that directly influence the reliability of outputs. Kennedy (2005) leverages Deming's mandate and the work of Crosby by defining the Eight Attributes of a Quality Management Culture that are described in Table 2.3. Figure 2.21 shows a QM culture resulting from QM values and skills integration.

TABLE 2.3 Eight Attributes of a Quality Management Culture

1. Zero Defects Attitude: A measure of our commitment to keep our promises and to initiate systems with the goal of preventing defects from reaching our customers.
2. Vocational Certainty: A measure of our faithfulness to our career agenda. A QM culture is disciplined about developing their skills and talents and acquiring earned confidence.
3. Process Quality: A measure of our mastery of planning and budgeting disciplines and how effectively we apply them to create viable work processes.
4. Administrative Consistency: A measure of our attention to details. QM cultures carefully listen to their customer to identify and conform to their requirements and assure customer satisfaction.
5. Executive Credibility: A measure of our sincerity and skill with people. Sincerity comes naturally from the heart, but skills can be sharpened and improved to gain reliable influence.
6. Personal Authenticity: A measure of our resolve to be consistent with our customers and coworkers. Authentic QM cultures work diligently to make exceptional service feel normal.
7. Ethical Dependability: A measure of our trustworthiness in practical matters. QM cultures are what we turn to when we want things to work right, run on time, and be there when needed.
8. Create a Keeping the Promise Culture: A measure of the mutual respect, accountability, and professionalism in a work culture. These are the practiced values of effective QM cultures.

From Kennedy (2005). Used with permission. All other rights reserved.

2.3.3.6 Knowledge Management Process

Overview

Purpose As stated in ISO/IEC/IEEE 15288,

[6.2.6.1] The purpose of the Knowledge Management process is to create the capability and assets that enable the organization to exploit opportunities to re-apply existing knowledge.

质量管理文化。系统工程实践者需要有足够的流程知识和质量管理知识库，以便能够评估预防选项并进行持续、渐进的改进。当工程学科得到计划和预算技能的支持时，我们可以实现流程质量，获得有效、高效和盈利的结果，低缺陷率和满意的利益相关方。Deming 在其"14 点"中强调，需要"为改进产品和服务创造始终如一的目标"，并应得到"为每个人提供强有力的教育和自我完善计划"的支持（Deming，1986）。高效的工作文化是通过组织领导风格和员工队伍中可识别的属性或价值来衡量的，这些属性或价值直接影响产出的可靠性。Kennedy（2005）通过定义表 2.3 中所述的质量管理文化的八个特征，利用了 Deming 的授权和 Crosby 的工作。图 2.21 展示了由质量管理价值和技能整合形成的质量管理文化。

表 2.3　质量管理文化的八个特征

1. 零缺陷态度：衡量我们是否承诺信守诺言，并启动以防止缺陷影响客户为目标的系统。
2. 职业确定性：衡量我们是否忠实于我们的职业生涯日程。质量管理文化对发展他们的技能和才能以及获得自信是有严格要求的。
3. 流程质量：衡量我们对规划和预算专业的掌握程度，以及我们如何有效地运用这些专业来创建可行的工作流程。
4. 行政管理一致性：衡量我们对细节的关注程度。质量管理文化认真倾听客户的意见，确定并满足客户的需求，确保客户满意。
5. 执行信誉：衡量我们待人接物的诚意和技巧。真诚是发自内心的自然流露，而技巧则可以通过磨炼和提高来获得可靠的影响力。
6. 个体真实性：衡量我们与客户和同事保持一致的决心。真正的质量管理文化努力让卓越服务成为常态。
7. 道德可信赖性：衡量我们在实际事务中是否值得信赖。当我们希望事情运转正常、按时完成并在需要时出现时，我们就会求助于质量管理文化。
8. 创建"信守承诺"文化：衡量工作文化中的相互尊重、问责和专业精神。这些都是有效的质量管理文化的实践价值观。

源自 Kennedy（2005）。经许可后使用。版权所有。

2.3.3.6　知识管理流程

概述

目的　　如 ISO/IEC/IEEE 15288 所述：

[6.2.6.1] 知识管理流程的目的是创造能力和资产，使组织能够抓住机会重新应用现有知识。

SYSTEM LIFE CYCLE CONCEPTS, MODELS, AND PROCESSES

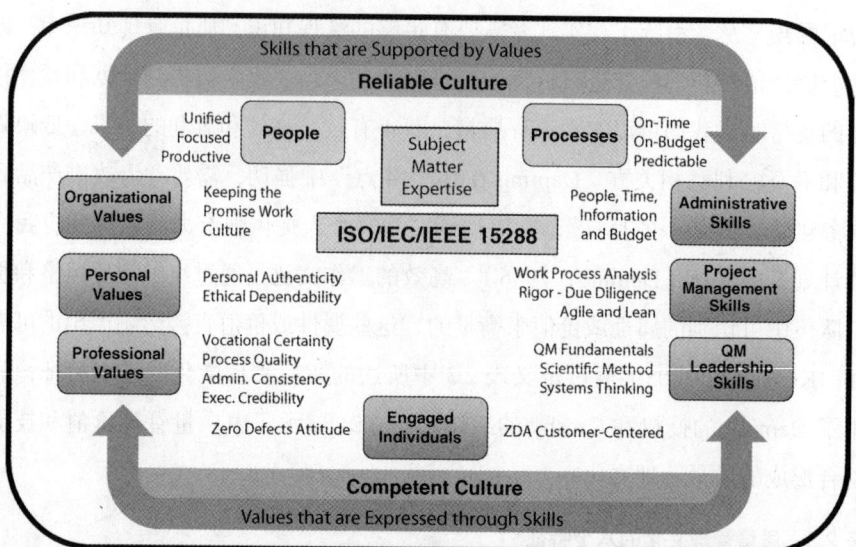

FIGURE 2.21 QM Values and Skills Integration. From Kennedy (2005). Used with permission. All other rights reserved.

Description Knowledge Management (KM) includes the identification, capture, creation, representation, dissemination, and exchange of knowledge across targeted groups of stakeholders. It draws from the insights and experiences of individuals and/or organizational groups or projects. The knowledge includes both explicit knowledge (conscious realization of the knowledge, often captured in artifacts and able to be communicated) and tacit knowledge (internalized in an individual or team without conscious realization) and can come from either individuals (through experience) or organizations (through processes, practices, and lessons learned) (Alavi and Leidner, 1999) (Roedler, 2010).

Within an organization, explicit knowledge is usually captured in its training, processes, practices, methods, policies, and procedures. In contrast, tacit knowledge is embodied in the individuals or teams of the organization and requires specialized techniques to identify and capture the knowledge, if it is to be passed along within the organization.

KM efforts typically focus on organizational objectives such as improved performance, competitive advantage, innovation, the sharing of good practices or lessons learned, avoidance of relearning practices, integration, and continuous improvement of the organization (Gupta and Sharma, 2004). KM captures knowledge that would otherwise be lost. So, it is generally advantageous for an organization to adopt a KM approach that includes building the framework, assets, and infrastructure to support the KM.

系统生命周期概念、模型和流程

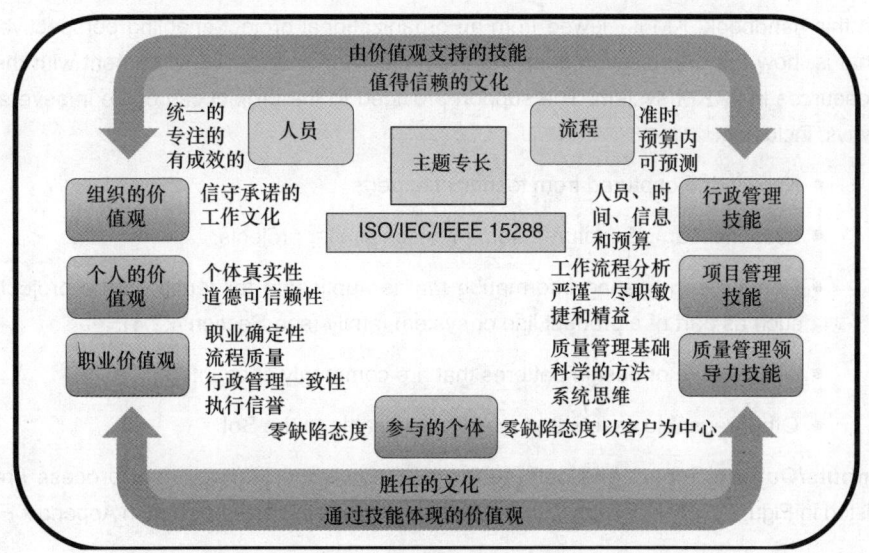

图 2.21　质量管理价值观和技能的综合。源自 Kennedy（2005）。经许可后使用。版权所有。

描述　知识管理（KM）包括在目标利益相关方群体之间识别、获取、创建、表示、传播和交流知识。它借鉴了个人和／或组织团体或项目的见解和经验。知识既包括显性知识（有意识地实现知识，通常从制品中获取，并能够交流），也包括隐性知识（在个人或团队中不自觉地内化），可以来自个人（通过经验）或组织（通过流程、实践和经验教训）（Alaviand Leidner，1999）（Roedler，2010）。

在一个组织内，显性知识通常在其培训、流程、实践、方法、政策和程序中获得。相反，隐性知识体现在组织的个人或团队中，如果要在组织内传递，则需要专门的技术来识别和获取知识。

知识管理工作通常侧重于组织目标，如提高绩效、竞争优势、创新、分享良好做法或经验教训、避免重新学习实践、整合和持续改进组织（Gupta 和 Sharma，2004）。知识管理可以获取不收集即丢失的知识。因此，组织采用知识管理方法通常是有利的，该方法包括构建框架、资产和基础设施来支持知识管理。

SYSTEM LIFE CYCLE CONCEPTS, MODELS, AND PROCESSES

In this handbook, KM is viewed from an organizational project-enabling perspective, that is, how the organization supports the project (or program) environment with the resources in its KM system. The support provided to the project can come in several ways, including:

- Knowledge captured from technical experts.
- Lessons learned captured from previous similar projects.
- Domain engineering information that is applicable for reuse on the project, such as part of a product line or system family (see Section 4.2.4).
- Architecture or design patterns that are commonly encountered.
- Other reusable assets that may be applicable to the SoI.

Inputs/Outputs Inputs and outputs for the Knowledge Management process are listed in Figure 2.22. Descriptions of each input and output are provided in Appendix E.

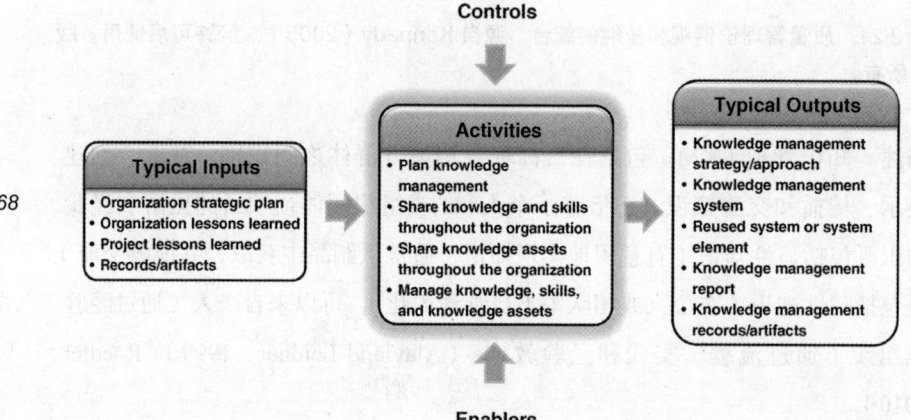

FIGURE 2.22 IPO diagram for Knowledge Management process. INCOSE original figure created by Shortell, Walden, and Yip. Usage per the INCOSE Notices page. All other rights reserved.

Process Activities The knowledge management process includes the following activities:

- *Plan knowledge management.*

系统生命周期概念、模型和流程

在本手册中,知识管理是从组织项目使能的角度来看的,即组织如何使用知识管理系统中的资源支持项目(或程序)环境。为项目提供支持可以有几种方式,包括:

- 从技术专家那里获取的知识。
- 从以往类似项目中获得的经验教训。
- 适用于项目复用的领域工程信息,例如产品线或系统族的一部分(见4.2.4节)。
- 常见的架构或设计模式。
- 可能适用于 SoI 的其他可复用资产。

输入/输出　知识管理流程的输入和输出如图 2.22 所示。附录 E 中提供了每个输入和输出的描述。

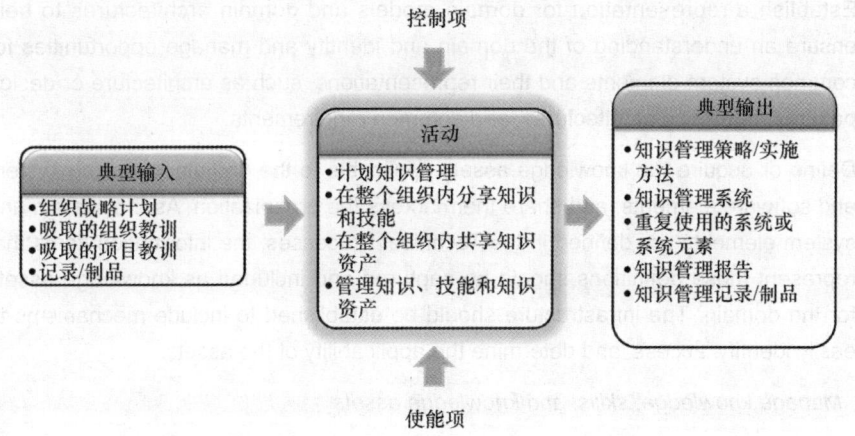

图 2.22　知识管理流程的 IPO 图。INCOSE SEH 原始图由 Walden、Shortell 和 Yip 创建。按照 INCOSE 通知页使用。版权所有。

流程活动　知识管理流程包括以下活动:

- *计划知识管理。*

SYSTEM LIFE CYCLE CONCEPTS, MODELS, AND PROCESSES

–Establish a KM strategy that defines the approach and priorities for how the organization and projects within the organization will interact to ensure the right level of knowledge is captured to provide useful knowledge assets.

–Establish the scope of the KM strategy—the organization and projects need to identify the specific knowledge information to capture and manage. Considerations include the importance and cost effectiveness of capturing the knowledge. If there is no identified project that will benefit from the knowledge asset, then it probably should not be considered.

- *Share knowledge and skills throughout the organization.*

–Capture, maintain, and share knowledge and skills per the strategy. The infrastructure should be established to include mechanisms to easily identify, access, and determine the applicability of the knowledge and skills.

- *Share knowledge assets throughout the organization.*

–Establish a taxonomy for the reapplication of knowledge.

–Establish a representation for domain models and domain architectures to help ensure an understanding of the domain and identify and manage opportunities for common system elements and their representations, such as architecture or design patterns, reference architectures, and common requirements.

–Define or acquire the knowledge assets applicable to the domain, including system and software elements, and share them across the organization. As the system and system elements are defined in the Technical Processes, the information items that represent those definitions should be captured and included as knowledge assets for the domain. The infrastructure should be established to include mechanisms to easily identify, access, and determine the applicability of the assets.

- *Manage knowledge, skills, and knowledge assets.*

–As the domain, family of systems, or product line changes, ensure the associated knowledge assets are revised or replaced to reflect the latest information. In addition, the associated domain models and architectures also may need to be revised.

–Assess and track where the knowledge assets are being used. This can help understand the utility of specific assets, as well as determine whether they are being applied where they are applicable.

–Determine whether the knowledge assets reflect current technology and continue to evolve.

- 制定知识管理战略，定义组织和组织内项目如何交互知识的方法和优先级，以确保获得正确的知识水平，从而提供有用的知识资产。

- 确定知识管理战略的范围，组织和项目需要确定要捕获和管理的特定知识信息。考虑因素包括获取知识的重要性和成本效益。如果没有确定的项目将从知识资产中受益，那么可能不应该考虑它。

- *在整个组织内分享知识和技能。*

- 根据战略获取、维护和共享知识和技能。应建立基础设施，以包括易于识别、获取和确定知识和技能适用性的机制。

- *在整个组织内共享知识资产。*

- 建立知识应用的分类法。

- 建立领域模型和领域架构的表示，以帮助确保对领域的理解，并识别和管理公共系统元素及其表示的机会，如架构或设计模式、参考架构和通用需求。

- 定义或获取适用于该领域的知识资产，包括系统和软件元素，并在整个组织内共享它们。由于系统和系统元素在技术流程中定义，代表这些定义的信息项应被捕获并作为领域的知识资产包含在内。应建立基础设施，以包括易于识别、访问和确定资产适用性的机制。

- *管理知识、技能和知识资产。*

- 随着领域、系统族或产品线的变化，确保相关知识资产得到修订或更新，以反映最新信息。此外，还可能需要改进相关的领域模型和架构。

- 评估和跟踪知识资产的使用位置。这有助于了解特定资产的效用，并确定它们是否在适用的地方得到应用。

- 确定知识资产是否反映当前技术并继续发展。

SYSTEM LIFE CYCLE CONCEPTS, MODELS, AND PROCESSES

Common approaches and tips:

- The planning for KM may include:

–Plans for obtaining and maintaining knowledge assets for their useful life.

–Characterization of the types of assets to be collected and maintained along with a scheme to classify them.

–Criteria for accepting, qualifying, and retiring knowledge assets.

–Procedures for controlling changes to the knowledge assets.

–A mechanism for knowledge asset storage and retrieval.

- In developing an understanding of the domain, it is important to identify and manage both the commonalities (such as features, capabilities, or functions) and the differences or variations of the system elements (including where a common system element has variations in parameters depending on the system instance). The domain representations should include:

–Definition of the boundaries.

–Relationships of the domains to other domains.

–Domain models that incorporate the commonalities and differences allowing for sensitivity analysis.

–An architecture for a system family or product line within the domain, including their commonalities and variations (see Section 4.2.4).

Elaboration

General KM Implementation. KM focuses on capturing the organizational, project, and individual knowledge for use throughout the organization in the future. It is important to capture end-of-project lessons learned prior to the project personnel moving on to new assignment. However, an effective Knowledge Management process has the knowledge capture mechanisms in place to capture the relevant information throughout the life of the project, rather than trying to piece it together at the end.

KM for Product Lines and Reuse. KM also includes identification of systems that are part of a product line or system family (see Section 4.2.4) and system elements that are designed for reuse. For the first instance of these systems and system elements, the KM system needs to capture the domain engineering artifacts in a way to facilitate their use in the future. For subsequent instances, the KM system needs to provide the domain engineering information and capture any variations, updates of technology, and lessons learned. Issues important to the organization include:

常用方法和提示：

- 知识管理计划可能包括：

- 获取知识资产并在其使用寿命内对其进行维护的计划。

- 待收集和维护资产类型的特征描述以及分类方案。

- 接受、鉴定和处置知识资产的标准。

- 控制知识资产变更的程序。

- 知识资产存储和检索机制。

- 在发展对领域的理解时，重要的是识别和管理系统元素的共性（如特征、能力或功能）和差异或变化（包括公共系统元素的参数变化取决于系统实例）。

  领域表示应包括：

- 边界的定义。

- 领域与其他领域的关系。

- 包含共性和差异的领域模型，允许进行敏感性分析。

- 领域内系统族或产品线的架构，包括其共性和变化（见 4.2.4 节）。

详细阐述

一般知识管理实施。 知识管理侧重于获取组织、项目和个人知识，以供将来在整个组织中使用。重要的是，在项目人员开始新任务之前，获取项目结束时的经验教训。然而，一个有效的知识管理流程应该有适当的知识捕获机制，以在项目的整个生命周期中捕获相关信息，而不是试图在最后将其拼凑在一起。

知识管理用于产品线和重用。 知识管理还包括识别属于产品线或系统族（见 4.2.4 节）一部分的系统和设计用于重用的系统元素。对于这些系统和系统元素的第一个实例，知识管理系统需要捕获领域工程制品，以便于将来使用。对于后续实例，知识管理系统需要提供领域工程信息，并捕获任何变化、技术更新和经验教训。对组织重要的问题包括：

SYSTEM LIFE CYCLE CONCEPTS, MODELS, AND PROCESSES

- Definition and planning of KM activities for domain engineering and asset preservation, including tasks dedicated to domain engineering of product lines or system families and to the preservation of reusable assets.

- Integration of architecture management into the KM system including frameworks, architecture reuse, architecture reference models, architecture patterns, platform-based engineering, and product line architecture.

- Characterization of the types of assets to be collected and maintained including an effective means for users to find the applicable assets.

- Determination of the quality and validity of the assets.

Potential Reuse Issues. There are serious traps in reuse, especially with respect to commercial off-the-shelf (COTS) (see Section 4.3.3) and non-developmental item (NDI) elements:

- Do the new system or system element requirements and operational characteristics closely match the prior one? Trap: the prior solution was intended for a different use, environment, or performance level, or it was only a prototype.

- How did the prior system or system element perform? Trap: it worked perfectly, but the new application is outside the qualified range (e.g., using a standard car for a high-speed track race).

- Is the new system or system element going to operate in the same environment as the prior one? Trap: it is not certain, but there is no time to study it. One NASA Mars probe was lost because the development team used a radiator design exactly as was used on a successful satellite in Earth orbit. When the Mars mission failed, the team then realized that Earth orbiting environment, while in space, is different from a deep space mission.

- Is the system/system element definition defined and understood (i.e., requirements, constraints, operating scenarios, etc.)? Trap: too often, the development team assumes that if a reuse solution will be applied (especially 70 System Life Cycle Concepts, Models, and Processes for COTS), there is no need for well-defined system definition. The issues may not show up until systems integration, causing major cost and schedule perturbations.

- Is the solution likely to have emergent requirements/behaviors where the reuse is being considered? Trap: a solution that worked in the past was used without consideration for the evolution of the solution. If COTS is used, there may be no way to adapt or modify it for emergent requirements.

系统生命周期概念、模型和流程

- 定义和计划领域工程和资产保护的知识管理活动,包括专门用于产品线或系统族领域工程和可复用资产保护的任务。
- 将架构管理集成到知识管理系统中,包括框架、架构复用、架构参考模型、架构模式、基于平台的工程和产品线架构。
- 要收集和维护的资产类型的特征,包括用户寻找适用资产的有效手段。
- 确定资产的质量和有效性。

潜在的复用问题。复用中存在严重陷阱,尤其是关于商用货架产品(COTS)(见 4.3.3 节)和非开发项目(NDI)元素:

- 新系统或系统元素要求和运行特性是否与之前的要求或元素要求和运行特性完全匹配?陷阱:之前的解决方案旨在用于不同的用途、环境或性能层级,或者它只是一个原型。
- 先前的系统或系统元素是如何执行的?陷阱:它工作得很好,但新应用超出了合格范围(例如,在高速赛道比赛中使用标准车)。
- 新系统或系统元素是否将在与先前系统或系统元素相同的环境中运行?陷阱:不确定,但没有时间研究。NASA 的一个火星探测器丢失了,因为开发团队使用的散热器设计与在地球轨道上成功的卫星上使用的散热器设计一模一样。当火星任务失败时,研究小组才意识到,在太空中的地球轨道环境不同于深空任务。
- 是否定义并理解系统/系统元素定义(即需求、约束、运行场景等)?陷阱:开发团队常常认为,如果要应用复用解决方案(尤其是 COTS),就不需要进行良好的系统定义。在系统集成之前,这些问题可能无法被发现,从而造成重大的成本和进度影响。
- 在考虑复用的情况下,解决方案是否可能有紧急需求/行为?陷阱:过去使用的解决方案没有考虑解决方案的演进。如果使用 COTS,可能无法根据紧急需求对其进行调整或改进。

SYSTEM LIFE CYCLE CONCEPTS, MODELS, AND PROCESSES

A properly functioning KM system paired with well-defined processes and engineering discipline can help avoid these problems.

2.3.4 Technical Management Processes

The engineering of new or existing systems is managed by the conduct of projects. For this reason, it is important to understand the contribution of SE to the management of the project. This contribution is provided through the Technical Management Processes, which ensure the successful management of the SE effort within the project.

The Technical Management Processes are defined in ISO/IEC/IEEE 15288 as follows:

[5.7.4] The Technical Management Processes are concerned with managing the resources and assets allocated by organization management and with applying them to fulfill the agreements into which the organization or organizations enter. The Technical Management Processes relate to the technical effort of projects, in particular to planning in terms of cost, time scales and achievements, to the checking of actions to help ensure that they comply with plans and performance criteria, and to the identification and selection of corrective actions that recover shortfalls in progress and achievement. They are used to establish and perform technical plans for the project, manage information across the technical team, assess technical progress against the plans for the system products or services, control technical tasks through to completion, and to aid in the decisionmaking process.

Technical management, which is the application of technical and administrative resources to plan, organize and control engineering functions, consists of the following eight processes: Project Planning, Project Assessment and Control, Decision Management, Risk Management, Configuration Management, Information Management, Measurement, and Quality Assurance. The Technical Management Processes are used consistently throughout the system life cycle so that system-specific Technical Processes can be conducted effectively. They work with the project management processes to establish and perform technical plans, manage information across the technical teams, assess technical progress against the plans, control technical tasks and risks through to completion, and aid in the decision-making process.

SE practitioners continually interact with project management practitioners. Both contribute to the project with unique professional competences. A life cycle from the project management practitioner's point of view (project start–project end) is defined differently than from the SE practitioner's point of view (system concept to system retirement). But there is a "shared space" where both must collaborate to drive the team's performance and success (Langley, et al., 2011). See Section 5.3.3 for treatment of the integration between SE and project management.

一个功能正常的知识管理系统，再加上定义良好的流程和工程准则，可以帮助避免这些问题。

2.3.4 技术管理流程

新系统或现有系统的工程活动通过项目进行管理。因此，了解系统工程对项目管理的贡献很重要。该贡献通过技术管理流程提供，确保项目内的系统工程工作得到成功管理。

ISO/IEC/IEEE 15288 中对技术管理流程的定义如下：

[5.7.4] 技术管理流程涉及管理组织管理层分配的资源和资产，并将其用于履行组织签订的协议。技术管理流程涉及项目的技术工作，特别是在成本、时间和成果方面的计划，检查行动以帮助确保其符合计划和绩效准则，以及识别和选择纠正行动以弥补进度和成果中的不足。它们用于制订和执行项目的技术计划，管理整个技术团队的信息，根据系统产品或服务的计划评估技术进展，控制技术任务直至完成，并辅助决策流程。

技术管理是应用技术和行政资源来计划、组织和控制工程职能，包括以下八个流程：项目计划、项目评估和控制、决策管理、风险管理、构型配置管理、信息管理、测量和质量保证。在整个系统生命周期中一致地使用技术管理流程，以便有效开展针对特定系统的技术流程。他们与项目管理流程合作，以制订和执行技术计划，管理技术团队的信息，根据计划评估技术进度，控制技术任务和风险直至完成，并协助决策流程。

系统工程实践者不断与项目管理实践者互动。两者都以独特的专业能力为项目做出贡献。从项目管理实践者的角度（项目开始–项目结束）定义的生命周期与从系统工程实践者的角度（系统概念到系统退役）定义的生命周期不同。但有一个"共享空间"，双方必须合作以推动团队的绩效和成功（Langley 等，2011）。有关系统工程与项目管理之间综合的处理，请参见 5.3.3 节。

SYSTEM LIFE CYCLE CONCEPTS, MODELS, AND PROCESSES

2.3.4.1 Project Planning Process

Overview

Purpose As stated in ISO/IEC/IEEE 15288,

[6.3.1.1] The purpose of the Project Planning process is to produce and coordinate effective and workable plans.

Description Project planning starts with the identification of a new potential project and continues after the authorization and activation of the project until its termination. The Project Planning process is performed in the context of the organization, and in compliance with the Life Cycle Model Management process (see Section 2.3.3.1) that identifies and establishes relevant policies and procedures applicable to all projects owned by the organization.

The Project Planning process identifies the project objectives, technical activities, interdependencies, resource requirements, risks and opportunities, and management approach for the technical effort. The planning includes the estimates of needed resources and budgets and the determination of the need for project enablers, including specialized equipment, facilities, and specialists during the project to improve efficiency and effectiveness and decrease cost overruns. This requires coordination across the set of processes to develop a set of consistent planning for all activities. For example, different disciplines work together in the performance of the System Requirements Definition, System Architecture Definition, and Design Definition processes to evaluate the parameters such as producibility, testability, operability, maintainability, and sustainability against product performance. Project tasking may be concurrent to achieve the best results.

Project planning establishes the direction necessary to enable execution of the project and the assessment and control of the project progress. It identifies the details of the work and the right set of personnel, skills, infrastructure, and facilities with a schedule for needed resources from within and outside the organization.

Inputs/Outputs Inputs and outputs for the Project Planning process are listed in Figure 2.23. Descriptions of each input and output are provided in Appendix E.

Process Activities The Project Planning process includes the following activities:

- *Define the project.*

–Analyze the project supply response and related agreements to define the project objectives, assumptions, constraints, and scope.

–Identify or establish tailoring of organization procedures and practices to carry out planned effort (see Section 4.1).

2.3.4.1 项目计划流程

概述

目的 如 ISO/IEC/IEEE 15288 所述：

[6.3.1.1] 项目计划流程的目的是制订和协调有效可行的计划。

描述 项目计划从确定新的潜在项目开始，并在项目授权和激活后持续到项目终止。项目计划流程在组织的背景下进行，并符合生命周期模型管理流程（见 2.3.3.1 节），该流程确定并建立适用于组织所有项目的相关政策和程序。

项目计划流程确定了项目目标、技术活动、相互依赖性、资源需求、风险和机遇以及技术工作的管理方法。该计划包括对所需资源和预算的估计，以及确定项目实施者的需求，包括项目期间的专用设备、设施和专家，以提高效率和效益，减少成本超支。这就需要对所有流程进行协调，为所有活动制订一套一致的计划。例如，在进行系统需求定义、系统架构定义和设计定义过程中，不同学科合作评估产品性能的可生产性、可测试性、可操作性、可维护性和可持续性等参数。项目任务可以同时进行，以获得最佳结果。

项目计划确立了执行项目以及评估和控制项目进展所需的方向。它确定了工作的细节以及适当的人员、技能、基础设施和设备，并制定了所需的组织内外资源的时间表。

输入 / 输出 项目计划流程的输入和输出如图 2.23 所示。附录 E 中提供了每个输入和输出的描述。

流程活动 项目计划流程包括以下活动：

- *定义项目。*

- 分析项目供应响应和相关协议，以定义项目目标、假设、约束和范围。

- 确定或建立组织程序和实践的剪裁，以开展计划的工作（见 4.1 节）。

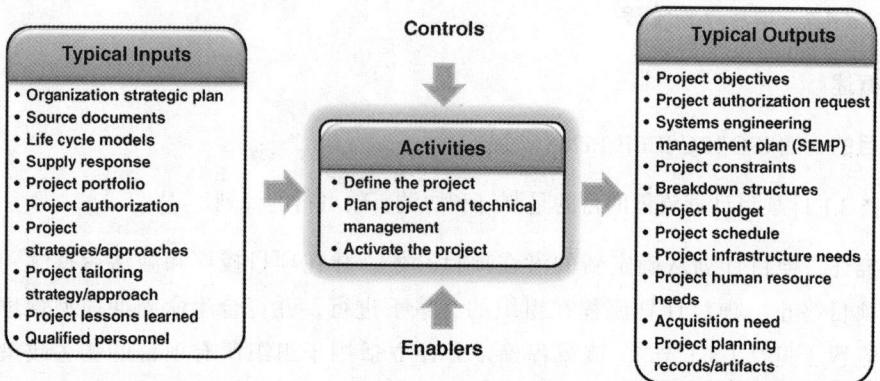

FIGURE 2.23 IPO diagram for Project Planning process. INCOSE SEH original figure created by Shortell, Walden, and Yip. Usage per the INCOSE Notices page. All other rights reserved.

–Develop or select Breakdown Structures based on the evolving system architecture (see paragraph on Breakdown Structures hereafter) and the constraints on the resources.

–Define and maintain a life cycle model that could be tailored from the defined life cycle models of the organization. This includes the identification of major milestones, decision gates, and project reviews.

- *Plan project and technical management.*

–Establish the roles and responsibilities for project authority.

–Define top-level work packages for each activity identified. Each work package should be tied to required resources including procurement strategies.

–Develop a project schedule (e.g., an integrated project schedule, a SE Master Schedule (SEMS)) based on objectives and work estimates.

–Determine the infrastructure and services needed for the project.

–Estimate the costs and establish a project budget.

–Plan the acquisition of materials, goods, and enabling systems.

–Generate and communicate a Systems Engineering Management Plan (SEMP), also called a Systems Engineering Plan (SEP), for project and technical management/ execution, including the technical reviews and audits (see Section 2.1.4).

系统生命周期概念、模型和流程

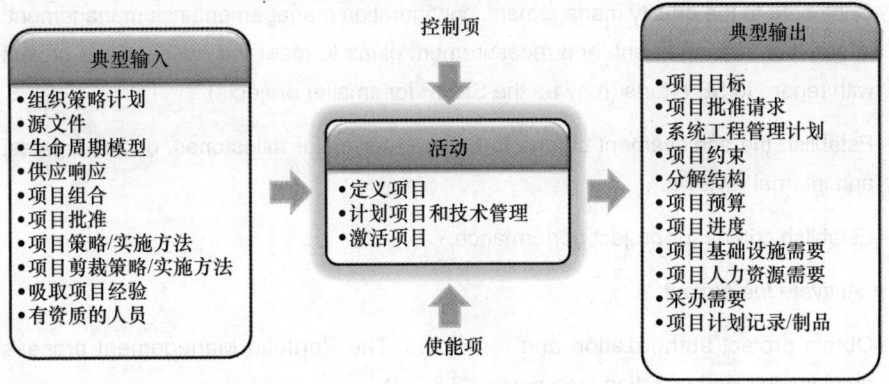

图 2.23 项目计划流程的 IPO 图。INCOSE SEH 原始图由 Walden、Shortell 和 Yip 创建。按照 INCOSE 通知页使用。版权所有。

- 基于演进的系统架构（见下文关于分解结构的段落）和资源约束，开发或选择分解结构。

- 定义和维护生命周期模型，该模型可以根据组织已定义的生命周期模型进行定制。这包括确定主要里程碑、决策门和项目评审。

● *计划项目和技术管理。*

- 确定项目授权角色和职责。

- 为确定的每个活动定义顶层工作包。每个工作包应与包括采办策略在内的所需资源相关联。

- 根据目标和工作评估制定项目进度表［例如，综合项目进度表、系统工程主进度表（SEMS）］。

- 确定项目所需的基础设施和服务。

- 估算成本并制定项目预算。

- 计划材料、货物和使能系统的采办。

- 为项目和技术管理／执行制定并沟通系统工程管理计划（SEMP），也称为系统工程计划（SEP），包括技术评审和审核（见 2.1.4 节）。

203

SYSTEM LIFE CYCLE CONCEPTS, MODELS, AND PROCESSES

–Contribute to the quality management, configuration management, risk management, information management, and measurement plans to meet the needs of the project with regard to SE efforts (may be the SEMP for smaller projects).

–Establish the achievement criteria to be used for major milestones, decision gates, and internal reviews.

–Establish criteria for project performance.

- *Activate the project.*

–Obtain project authorization and resources. The Portfolio Management process provides this authorization (see section 2.3.3.3).

–Obtain authorization for the necessary project resources.

–Commence execution of the project plans.

Common approaches and tips:

- The SEMP (or equivalent technical planning) is an important outcome that identifies activities, key events, work packages, and resources. It references other planning artifacts that are tailored for use on the project.

- The standard ISO/IEC/IEEE 24748–4 on Systems Engineering Planning is a reference to aid in writing a SEMP.

- Plans for developing software are often captured in a Software Development Plan. (See ISO/IEC/IEEE 24748–5.)

- The creation of the Work Breakdown Structure (WBS) and other breakdown structures (e.g., Function Tree/Functional Breakdown Structure (FBS), Product Tree/Product Breakdown Structure (PBS), Organizational Breakdown Structure (OBS), Cost Breakdown Structure (CBS)) is an activity where SE and Project Management intersect (Forsberg, et al., 2005). (See paragraph on Breakdown Structures hereafter and Section 5.3.3.)

- Taking shortcuts in the planning process reduces the effectiveness of other Technical Management Processes.

- Agile project management methods also include planning—the cycles may be shorter and more frequent, but planning is an essential process. Agile planning process is not related to the entire project but addressing only the next already known iterations while applying learning from the previous iterations.

- 参与质量管理、构型配置管理、风险管理、信息管理和测量方案，以满足项目对系统工程工作的需要（可能是小型项目的系统工程管理计划）。

- 建立用于重大里程碑、决策门和内部评审的成果准则。

- 制定项目绩效准则。

- *激活项目。*

- 获得项目授权和资源。项目群管理流程提供了这种授权（参见 2.3.3.3 节）。

- 获得必要项目资源的授权。

- 开始执行项目计划。

常用方法和提示：

- 系统工程管理计划（或等同的技术计划）是一项确定活动、关键事件、工作包和资源的重要产出物。它参考了为项目量身定制的其他计划制品。

- 关于系统工程计划的标准 ISO/IEC/IEEE 24748-4 是帮助编写系统工程管理计划的参考。

- 用于开发软件的计划通常包含在软件开发计划中。（见 ISO/IEC/IEEE 24748–5）

- 创建工作分解结构（WBS）和其他分解结构 [例如，功能树/功能分解结构（FBS）、产品树/产品分解结构（PBS）、组织分解结构（OBS）、成本分解结构（CBS）] 是系统工程和项目管理交叉的一项活动（Forsberg 等，2005）。（见下文关于分解结构的段落和 5.3.3 节）

- 在计划流程中走捷径会降低其他技术管理流程的效率。

- 敏捷项目管理方法也包括计划——周期可能更短、更频繁，但计划是一个必不可少的过程。敏捷计划过程与整个项目无关，只涉及下一个已知的迭代，同时应用从之前的迭代中学到的知识。

SYSTEM LIFE CYCLE CONCEPTS, MODELS, AND PROCESSES

- Defining project objectives, value, and the criteria for success are critical to guide project decision making. The project value should be expressed in technical performance measures (TPMs) (Roedler and Jones, 2006) (see Section 2.3.4.7).

- Incorporate risk assessment early in the planning process to identify areas that need special attention or contingencies (see Section 2.3.4.4). Always attend to the technical risks (PMI, 2013).

- If a Project Management Plan (PMP) already exists or is in preparation (in accordance with practices as defined by the Project Management Body of Knowledge (PMBOK®) (2021) from the Project Management Institute (PMI), for example), then it is important to coordinate in order to have a global consistency between these artifacts. The SEMP should reference, or provide a link to, the PMP for direction on how the SEMP will be updated and controlled on the project.

Elaboration

Project Planning Concepts. Project planning estimates the project budget and schedule against which project progress will be assessed and controlled. SE practitioners and PM practitioners must collaborate in project planning. SE practitioners perform technical management activities consistent with project objectives (see Section 5.3.3). Technical management activities include planning, scheduling, reviewing, and auditing the SE process as defined in the SEMP. Systems Engineering Management Plan (SEMP). The SEMP is the key technical management plan that integrates the SE effort. It defines how the total set of engineering processes will be organized, structured, and conducted and how it will be controlled to provide a product that satisfies stakeholder requirements. The SEMP typically includes the following content (a complete outline can be found in ISO/IEC/IEEE 24748–4 (2016), which is aligned with ISO/IEC/IEEE 15288 and this handbook):

- organization of how SE interfaces with the other parts of the organization
- responsibilities and authority of the key engineering roles
- clear system boundaries and scope of the system
- key, technical objectives, assumptions, and constraints (or link to them)
- infrastructure support and resource management (i.e., facilities, tools, IT, personnel)

- 确定项目目标、价值和成功准则对于指导项目决策至关重要。项目价值应以技术性能测度（TPM）表示（Roedler 和 Jones，2006）（见 2.3.4.7 节）。

- 在计划流程的早期进行风险评估，以确定需要特别关注或紧急的领域（见 2.3.4.4 节）。始终关注技术风险（PMI，2013）。

- 如果项目管理计划（PMP）已经存在或正在编制中［例如，根据项目管理协会（PMI）项目管理知识体系（PMBOK®）（2021）定义的实践］，则必须进行协调，以便在这些制品之间保持全局一致性。系统工程管理计划应参考项目管理计划或提供与项目管理计划的链接，以指导如何更新和控制项目的系统工程管理计划。

详细阐述

项目计划概念。项目计划评估项目预算和进度，并据此评估和控制项目进度。系统工程实践者和项目管理实践者必须在项目计划中进行合作。系统工程实践者执行与项目目标一致的技术管理活动（见 5.3.3 节）。技术管理活动包括系统工程管理计划中定义的系统工程流程的计划、安排、评审和审核。系统工程管理计划（SEMP）。系统工程管理计划是整合系统工程工作的关键技术管理计划。它定义了如何组织、构建和实施整套工程流程，以及如何控制这些流程以提供满足利益相关方需求的产品。系统工程管理计划通常包括以下内容［完整大纲见 ISO/IEC/IEEE 24748-4（2016），与 ISO/IEC/IEEE 15288 和本手册保持一致］：

- 系统工程与组织其他部分交互的组织方式

- 关键工程角色的职责和权限

- 明确系统边界和系统范围

- 关键、技术目标、假设和约束条件（或与之关联）

- 基础设施支持和资源管理（即设施、工具、IT、人员）

SYSTEM LIFE CYCLE CONCEPTS, MODELS, AND PROCESSES

- technical schedule, including key milestones, decision gates, and associated criteria
- definition of the SE processes, including interaction with other engineering and project processes
- approach and methods for planning and executing the Technical Processes (see Section 2.3.5)
- approach and methods for planning and executing the Technical Management Processes (see Section 2.3.4)
- approach and methods for planning and executing applicable quality characteristic (QC) approaches (see Section 3.1)
- major technical deliverables of the project

A SEMP should be prepared early in the project, submitted to the customer (or to management for in-house projects), and used in technical management for the concept and development stages of the project. The format of the SEMP can be tailored to fit project, customer, or company standards. In addition to being a stand-alone artifact, the SEMP can be a part of an integrated project plan, be a distributed set of plans, or be in a format other than a document (e.g., it may be composed of different models, management tools, or other artifacts).

The SEMS is an essential part of the SEMP and a tool for project control because it identifies the critical path of technical activities in the project. The schedule of tasks and dependencies helps prioritize the effort and justify requests for personnel and resources needed throughout the development life cycle.

Breakdown Structures. The purpose of the breakdown structures is to hierarchically decompose constructs in manageable and understandable elements. In projects, breakdown structures provide:

- a framework for ensuring that all requirements, functions, and products of the system design are identified and arranged in a logical relationship that can be traced to, and satisfy, the business and stakeholder needs;
- an identification of all activities and resources needed to the product;
- a cost relationship to the activities being performed;
- an organizational context for the project to perform the activities needed to the product;

- 技术进度表，包括关键里程碑、决策门和相关准则

- 系统工程流程的定义，包括与其他工程和项目流程的交互

- 计划和执行技术流程的实施途径和方法（见 2.3.5 节）

- 计划和执行技术管理流程的实施途径和方法（见 2.3.4 节）

- 计划和执行适用质量特性（QC）的实施途径和方法（见 3.1 节）

- 项目的主要技术交付物

系统工程管理计划应在项目早期编制，提交给客户（或内部项目的管理层），并用于项目概念和开发阶段的技术管理。系统工程管理计划的格式可以根据项目、客户或公司标准进行定制。除了作为一个独立的制品之外，系统工程管理计划还可以是综合项目计划的一部分，可以是一组分布式的计划，也可以是文档以外的格式（例如，它可以由不同的模型、管理工具或其他制品组成）。

系统工程主进度表是系统工程管理计划的重要组成部分，也是项目控制的工具，因为它确定了项目中技术活动的关键路径。任务和依赖关系的时间表有助于确定工作的优先级，并证明在整个开发生命周期中对所需人员和资源的请求是合理的。

分解结构。 分解结构的目的是将结构按层级分解为易于管理和理解的元素。在项目中，分解结构提供：

- 一个框架，用于确保系统设计的所有需求、功能和产品都得到识别，并以逻辑关系进行安排，这种逻辑关系可追溯并满足业务和利益相关方的需要；

- 确定产品所需的所有活动和资源；

- 与所开展的活动的成本关系；

- 为项目提供组织环境，以执行产品所需的活动；

- an identification, by name, within the organization of the responsible person for performing each activity;

- a basis for configuration control once a particular project breakdown structure is baselined, and a basis for effective management of changes;

- a framework to help identify risks and subsequent risk management;

- a basis for financial control and interface responsibilities resulting from business agreements.

The SE practice is to derive system functions from requirements and then allocate these functions into products or services, usually through the development of a functional and physical architecture (see Section 2.3.5.4). Functions and products are organized in breakdown structures that have the organizational framework of a tree, such as Function Tree and Product Tree. The Function Tree also, called Functional Breakdown Structure (FBS), is a breakdown of the functions of the required SoI into successively lower levels of its functional architecture. The Function Tree includes the technical characteristics of each function. The Product Tree, also called Product Breakdown Structure (PBS), is a breakdown of the SoI into successively lower-level details of its physical architecture (see Section 1.3.5).

The work to be carried out to reach the project objectives can be organized in a breakdown structure, as a hierarchical tree, where the lower-level activities provide more details. This is the Work Breakdown Structure (WBS), which is based on the FBS in the initial stages of system maturity (e.g., feasibility, conceptual design) and the PBS in the later stages.

The WBS includes all activities needed to develop the product. Each branch of the WBS is used to define a work package (WP). Each WP describes the work to be performed, related input and output, who is doing the work, the related interfaces with other WPs, the related cost and deliverables and the key dates and milestones. The WBS serves as a reference for the identification of cost elements arranged into a Cost Breakdown Structure (CBS). Along with the overall management organization, the WBS is also used to determine who does what. This is represented in an Organizational Breakdown Structure (OBS), which is a hierarchical tree of the organizational elements. Figure 2.24 illustrates these different project breakdown structures with their relationships. See Section 5.3.3 for the relationship between PM and SE.

- 组织内负责执行各项活动的负责人的姓名标识;

- 在特定项目分解结构确定后,为构型配置控制提供依据,并为有效管理变更提供依据;

- 有助于识别风险和后续风险管理的框架;

- 业务协议产生的财务控制和接口职责的基础。

系统工程实践是从需求中派生系统功能,然后将这些功能分配到产品或服务中,这通常是通过开发功能和物理架构实现的(见2.3.5.4节)。功能和产品在具有树形组织框架的分解结构中进行组织,如功能树和产品树。功能树,也称为功能分解结构(FBS),是将所感兴趣的系统的功能按其功能架构逐级分解的结构。功能树包括每个功能的技术特征。产品树,也称为产品分解结构(PBS),是将所感兴趣的系统按其物理架构逐级分解的结构(见1.3.5节)。

为实现项目目标而进行的工作可以组织成一个分解结构,作为一个层级树,其中较低层级的活动提供了更多的细节。这就是工作分解结构(WBS),在系统成熟的初期阶段(例如,可行性研究、概念设计)以功能分解结构(FBS)为基础,而在后期阶段则以产品分解结构(PBS)为基础。

工作分解结构包括开发产品所需的所有活动。工作分解结构的每个分支用于定义工作包(WP)。每个工作包都描述了要执行的工作、相关的输入和输出、工作负责人、与其他工作包的相关接口、相关成本和交付物以及关键日期和里程碑。工作分解结构可作为识别成本分解结构(CBS)中成本元素的参考。除整体的管理组织外,WBS还用于确定谁做什么。这在组织分解结构(OBS)中表示,OBS是组织元素的层级树。图2.24说明了这些不同的项目分解结构及其关系。项目管理和系统工程之间的关系见5.3.3节。

SYSTEM LIFE CYCLE CONCEPTS, MODELS, AND PROCESSES

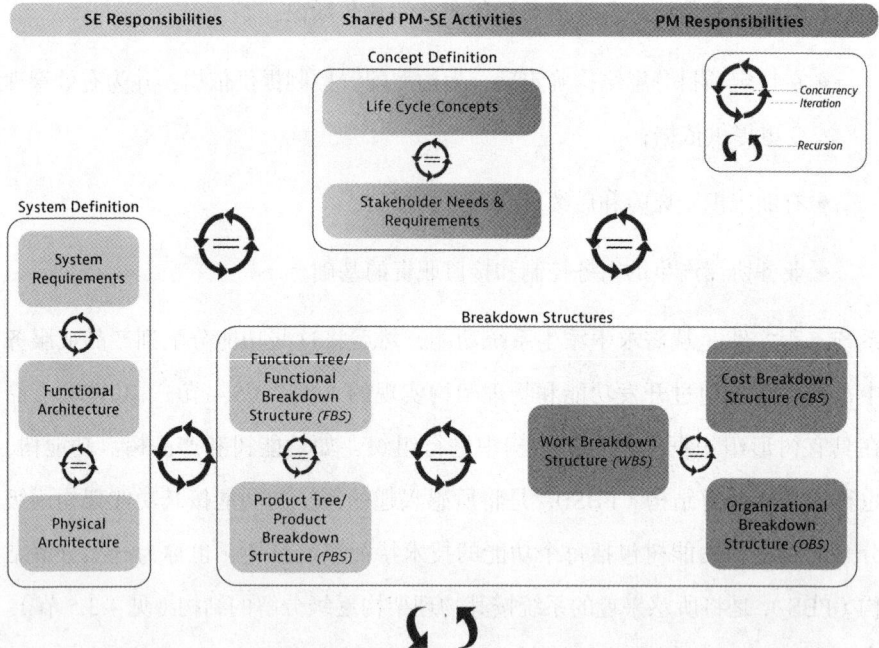

FIGURE 2.24 The breakdown structures. INCOSE SEH original figure created by Roussel and Dazzi on behalf of the INCOSE PM-SE Integration Working Group. Usage per the INCOSE Notices page. All other rights reserved.

2.3.4.2 Project Assessment and Control Process

Overview

Purpose As stated in ISO/IEC/IEEE 15288,

[6.3.2.1] The purpose of the Project Assessment and Control process is to assess if the plans are aligned and feasible; determine the status of the project, technical and process performance; and direct execution to help ensure that the performance is according to plans and schedules, within projected budgets, to satisfy technical objectives.

Assessments are scheduled periodically and for all milestones and decision gates. The intention is to maintain good communications within the project team and with the stakeholders, especially when deviations are encountered. The Project Assessment and Control process uses these assessments to direct the efforts of the project, including redirecting the project when the project does not reflect the anticipated maturity.

系统生命周期概念、模型和流程

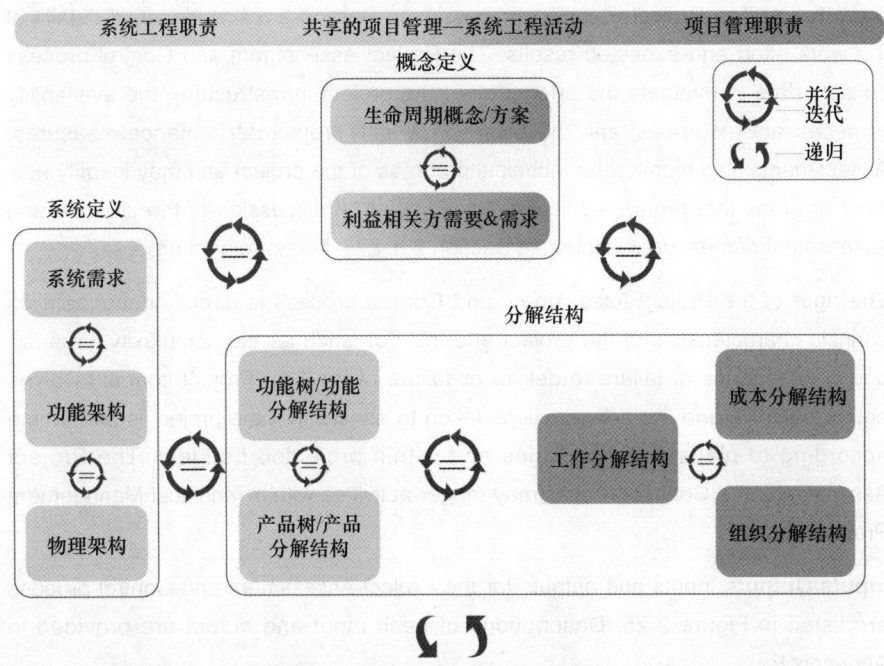

图 2.24 分解结构。INCOSE SEH 原始图由 Roussel 和 Dazzi 代表 INCOSE 项目管理—系统工程综合工作组创建。按照 INCOSE 通知页使用。版权所有。

2.3.4.2 项目评估和控制流程

概述

目的　如 ISO/IEC/IEEE 15288 所述：

[6.3.2.1] 项目评估和控制流程的目的是评估计划是否一致并可行；确定项目、技术和流程绩效的状况；指导执行工作，以帮助确保绩效符合计划和时间，不超出预计的预算，并满足技术目标。

定期对所有里程碑和决策门进行评估。目的是在项目团队内部以及与利益相关方保持良好的沟通，尤其是在遇到偏差时。项目评估和控制流程使用这些评估来指导项目的工作，包括在项目未反映预期成熟度时对项目重新定向。

SYSTEM LIFE CYCLE CONCEPTS, MODELS, AND PROCESSES

Description The Project Planning process (see Section 2.3.4.1) identified details of the work effort and expected results. The Project Assessment and Control process collects data to evaluate the adequacy of the project infrastructure, the availability of necessary resources, and the compliance with project performance measures. Assessments also monitor the technical progress of the project and may identify new risks or areas that require additional investigation. A discussion of the creation and assessment of measures is found in Section 2.3.4.7—Measurement process.

The rigor of the Project Assessment and Control process is directly dependent on intrinsic characteristics of the project and the SoI, such as the complexity, urgency, and consequence of failure to deliver or failure of the SoI. Project control involves both preventive and corrective actions taken to ensure that the project is performing according to plans and schedules and within projected budgets. The Project Assessment and Control process may trigger activities within Technical Management Processes.

Inputs/Outputs Inputs and outputs for the Project Assessment and Control process are listed in Figure 2.25. Descriptions of each input and output are provided in Appendix E.

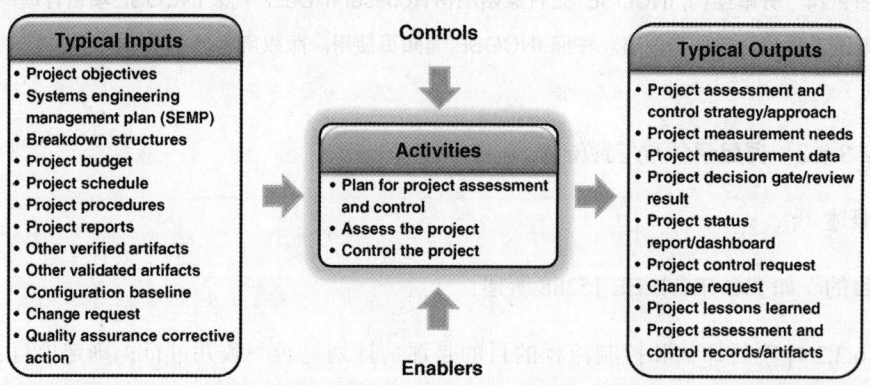

FIGURE 2.25 IPO diagram for Project Assessment and Control process. INCOSE SEH original figure created by Shortell, Walden, and Yip. Usage per the INCOSE Notices page. All other rights reserved.

Process Activities The Project Assessment and Control process includes the following activities:

- *Plan for project assessment and control.*

系统生命周期概念、模型和流程

描述　项目计划流程（见 2.3.4.1 节）确定了工作和预期结果的详细信息。项目评估和控制流程收集数据，以评估项目基础设施的充分性、必要资源的可用性以及是否符合项目绩效测度。评估还监测项目的技术进展，并确定可能需要额外调查的新风险或领域。2.3.4.7 节测量流程中讨论了测度的创建和评估。

项目评估和控制流程的严格程度直接取决于项目和 SoI 的固有特征，如未能交付或 SoI 失败的复杂性、紧迫性和后果。项目控制包括采取预防和纠正措施，以确保项目按照计划和时间并在预计预算内执行。项目评估和控制流程可能触发技术管理流程中的活动。

输入/输出　项目评估和控制流程的输入和输出如图 2.25 所示。附录 E 中提供了每个输入和输出的描述。

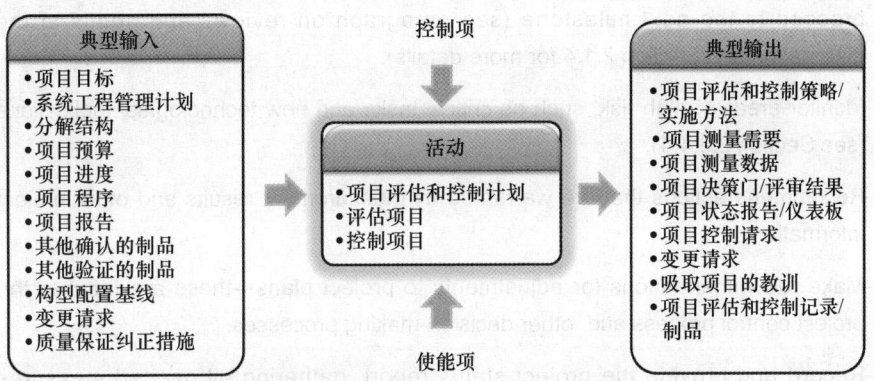

图 2.25　项目评估和控制流程的 IPO 图。INCOSE SEH 原始图由 Walden、Shortell 和 Yip 创建。按照 INCOSE 通知页使用。版权所有。

流程活动　项目评估和控制流程包括以下活动：

- *项目评估和控制计划。*

SYSTEM LIFE CYCLE CONCEPTS, MODELS, AND PROCESSES

—Develop a strategy/approach for assessment and control for the project.

- *Assess the project.*

—Determine whether project objectives and plans are aligned with the project context.

—Determine cost, schedule, and performance variances for the project and technical effort through assessment of status versus plans.

—Evaluate the effectiveness and efficiency of the performance of project activities.

—Determine if the project roles, responsibilities, accountabilities, and authorities are adequate.

—Assess the adequacy and the availability of the project infrastructure and resources.

—Using project measures and milestone status, assess the progress of the project.

—Conduct required reviews, audits, and inspections to determine readiness to proceed to the next milestone (see paragraph on reviews and audits in the elaboration and Section 2.1.4 for more details).

—Monitor areas of high risk, such as critical tasks and new technologies/applications (see Section 2.3.4.4).

—Recommend actions that are warranted by measurement results and other project information.

—Make recommendations for adjustments to project plans—these are input to the project control process and other decision-making processes.

—Record and provide the project status report, gathering all needed measures on technical progress aspects (e.g., performance, requirements compliance, verification and validation progress) and technical management aspects (e.g., schedule, cost, risk, configuration status).

—Communicate status in the project status report as designated in agreements, policies, and procedures.

- *Control the project.*

—Initiate preventive actions when assessments indicate a trend toward deviation.

—Initiate problem resolution when assessments indicate nonconformance with performance success criteria.

—Initiate corrective actions when assessments indicate deviation from approved plans.

- 制定项目评估和控制的策略／实施方法。

- *评估项目。*

- 确定项目目标和计划是否与项目背景一致。

- 通过评估状态与计划，确定项目和技术工作的成本、进度和绩效差异。

- 评估项目活动绩效的有效性和效率。

- 确定项目角色、职责、问责和权限是否充分。

- 评估项目基础设施和资源的充分性和可用性。

- 使用项目措施和里程碑状态，评估项目进度。

- 进行所需的评审、审核和检查，以确定进入下一个里程碑的就绪程度（更多详细信息，请参见详细说明中有关评审和审核的段落和 2.1.4 节）。

- 监控高风险领域，如关键任务和新技术／应用（见 2.3.4.4 节）。

- 根据测量结果和其他项目信息提出行动建议。

- 对项目计划提出调整建议，这些建议是项目控制流程和其他决策流程的输入。

- 记录并提供项目状态报告，收集技术进展方面（如性能、需求符合性、验证和确认进度）和技术管理方面（如进度、成本、风险、构型配置状态）的所有必要措施。

- 按照协议、政策和程序的规定，在项目情况报告中沟通项目情况。

- *控制项目。*

- 当评估显示偏差趋势时，启动预防措施。

- 当评估显示不符合绩效成功准则时，启动问题解决方案。

- 当评估显示偏离批准的计划时，启动纠正措施。

SYSTEM LIFE CYCLE CONCEPTS, MODELS, AND PROCESSES

–Update project planning as needed based on the project control or corrective actions.

–Implement change actions to reflect contractual changes to cost, time, or quality. This is usually due to the impact of acquirer or supplier request.

–Authorize the project to proceed when assessments support a decision gate or milestone event.

77 *Common approaches and tips:*

- One way to remain updated on project status is to conduct regular team meetings. Short stand-up meetings on a daily or weekly schedule are effective for smaller groups.

- Prevailing wisdom suggests that "what gets measured gets done," but projects should avoid the collection of measures that are not used in decision making.

- Good practices show that status should be concise and visual (e.g., usage of Red/Yellow/Green "traffic lights") in order to quickly and easily identify the critical issues on which urgent actions for recovery are required. Another useful tool is a project dashboard that provides a timely and easy summary of status.

- A template for the project status report is a good practice. This template may be included in the SEMP (or PMP).

- Methods and techniques for Project Assessment and Control should be formally described in the SEMP (or PMP) and agreed with the project team.

- The Project Management Institute (PMI) provides industry-wide guidelines for project assessment, including Earned Value Management techniques.

- Project teams need to identify critical areas and control them through measurement, risk management, analysis, configuration management, and information management.

- The Project Assessment and Control process requires close cooperation between the PM practitioner and SE practitioner, with PM being accountable for the overall results of the project and SE being accountable for the achievement of the technical activities.

- The typical common responsibilities between PM and SE practitioners are risk management, external supplier relations, quality management and life cycle planning.

系统生命周期概念、模型和流程

- 基于项目控制或纠正措施，根据需要更新项目计划。
- 实施变更措施以反映合同对成本、时间或质量的变更。这通常是由于采办方或供应商请求的影响。
- 当评估结果支持决策门或里程碑事件时，授权项目继续进行。

常用方法和提示：

- 保持项目状态更新的一种方法是定期召开团队会议。每日或每周安排的简短站立会议对较小的小组有效。
- 普遍认为"有测量就有结果"，但项目应避免收集不用于决策的测度。
- 良好实践表明，状态应简洁、直观（例如，使用红/黄/绿"交通灯"），以便快速、轻松地确定需要采取紧急恢复行动的关键问题。另一个有用的工具是项目仪表板，它可以提供及时而简单的状态摘要。
- 项目状态报告模板是一种良好的工具。该模板可能包含在系统工程管理计划（或项目管理计划）中。
- 项目评估和控制的方法和技术应在系统工程管理计划（或项目管理计划）中正式描述，并与项目团队达成一致。
- 项目管理协会（PMI）为项目评估提供全行业指导，包括挣值管理技术。
- 项目团队需要识别关键领域，并通过测度、风险管理、分析、构型配置管理和信息管理对其进行控制。
- 项目评估和控制流程需要项目管理实践者和系统工程实践者之间的密切合作，项目管理负责项目的总体结果，系统工程负责技术活动的完成。
- 项目管理和系统工程实践者之间的典型共同职责是风险管理、外部供应商关系、质量管理和生命周期计划。

SYSTEM LIFE CYCLE CONCEPTS, MODELS, AND PROCESSES

- An effective feedback control process is an essential element to enable the improvement of project performance.

- Incremental and evolutionary models typically schedule frequent assessments and make project control adjustments on tighter feedback cycles than sequential development models (see Section 2.2).

- Tailoring of organization processes and procedures (see Section 4.1) should not jeopardize any certifications. Processes must be established with effective reviews, assessments, audits, and improvements.

- Standard ISO/IEC 24748–8 / IEEE 15288.2 (2014) is a useful reference on how to define and manage technical reviews and establish requirements for the related milestones.

Elaboration

Integration of Technical Management Artifacts. Each of the Technical Management Processes provides essential insight into the health and progress of the project through the life cycle with respect to the specific focus of the particular process. However, it is important to look at the results of these processes in an integrated view, especially since there are relationships between these processes and their artifacts. For example, the results of the Measurement process provide useful insights into risks, technical reviews and audits, and quality assurance, as well as many other things. Similarly, other processes may identify new information needs for which new measures should be initiated. Mechanisms should be put in place to provide an integrated view of the results or artifacts in a way that the decision makers can interpret quickly and see trends and trigger points to aid decisions. Two such mechanisms are the project status report and the project dashboard. Both organize and provide a summary of similar information about the project; the status report usually presents the information in report form and the dashboard is usually a digital representation that uses gauges, graphs, indicators, or other visual representations of the information. In both mechanisms relationships are shown and trends or areas needing attention are highlighted.

Technical Reviews and Audits. Technical reviews and audits are a foundational element of an effective SE approach and form the backbone of robust technical assessment. Technical reviews and audits provide a venue for baselining stakeholder and system requirements, evaluating the system's technical maturity, and identifying and assessing risks to system performance, cost, and schedule. In order for a project's technical management to have a balanced information basis on which to base any required project control actions, each technical review or audit should be conducted from an integrated project viewpoint, including technical status and progress, cost and schedule status, and impacts and risk assessment, to help ensure that technical review decisions do not create unrecognized and unacceptable future project impacts. See Section 2.1.4 Technical Reviews and Audits and ISO/IEC 24748–8 / IEEE 15288.2 (2014) for more information.

- 有效的反馈控制流程是提高项目绩效的基本元素。

- 增量和演进模型通常安排频繁的评估，并以比顺序开发模型更紧密的反馈周期进行项目控制调整（见 2.2 节）。

- 组织流程和程序的剪裁（见 4.1 节）不应危及任何认证。必须通过有效的评审、评估、审核和改进来建立流程。

- 标准 ISO/IEC 24748–8/IEEE 15288.2（2014）是关于如何定义和管理技术评审以及制定相关里程碑要求的有用参考。

详细阐述

技术管理制品的综合。每个技术管理流程都会根据特定流程的具体重点，对项目在整个生命周期内的健康状况和进展情况提供重要的洞察。然而，在综合视图中查看这些流程的结果很重要，特别是因为这些流程及其制品之间存在关系。例如，测量流程的结果提供了对风险、技术评审和审核、质量保证以及许多其他事情的有用见解。同样，其他流程可能会确定新的信息需求，应针对这些需求启动新的措施。应建立机制，以提供结果或制品的综合视图，使决策者能够快速解释并看到趋势和触发点，以帮助决策。这样的两种机制是项目状态报告和项目仪表板。组织并提供项目类似信息的汇总；状态报告通常以报告形式展示信息，仪表板通常是一种数字表示，它使用仪表、图形、指示器或其他视觉方式表达信息。在这两种机制中都展示了关系，并强调了需要注意的趋势或领域。

技术评审和审核。技术评审和审核是有效的系统工程方法的基本元素，也是稳健技术评估的支柱。技术评审和审核为确定利益相关方和系统需求的基线、评估系统的技术成熟度以及识别和评估系统性能、成本和进度的风险提供了一个平台。为了使项目的技术管理有一个平衡的信息基础，据此采取任何所需的项目控制行动，每次技术评审或审核都应从综合项目的角度进行，包括技术状态和进展、成本和进度状态以及影响和风险评估，以确保技术评审决定不会对未来项目产生无法识别和不可接受的影响。更多信息，请参见 2.1.4 节技术评审和审核以及 ISO/IEC 24748–8/IEEE 15288.2（2014）。

SYSTEM LIFE CYCLE CONCEPTS, MODELS, AND PROCESSES

2.3.4.3 Decision Management Process

Overview

Purpose As defined by ISO/IEC/IEEE 15288,

[6.3.3.1] The purpose of the Decision Management process is to provide a structured, analytical framework for objectively identifying, characterizing and evaluating a set of alternatives for a decision at any point in the life cycle and select the most beneficial course of action.

Table 2.4 provides a partial list of decision situations (opportunities) that are commonly encountered throughout a system's life cycle. Buede and Miller (2009) provide a much larger list.

TABLE 2.4 Partial list of decision situations (opportunities) throughout the life cycle

Life cycle stage	Decision situation (opportunity)
Concept	Assess technology opportunity/initial business case
	Craft a technology development strategy
	Inform, generate, and refine a capability artifact
	Conduct analysis of alternatives
	Supporting program initiation decision
	Select system architecture
Development	Select system element
	Select lower-level elements
	Select verification and validation methods
	Perform make-or-buy decision
Production	Select production process and location
Utilization, support	Select maintenance approach
Retirement Select	disposal approach

INCOSE SEH original table created by Parnell, Kenley, and Roedler. Usage per the INCOSE Notices page. All other rights reserved.

Decision management as a critical SE activity. Consider the number of decisions involved in identifying a business/mission need, crafting a technology development strategy, defining the stakeholder and system requirements, selecting a system architecture, converging on a detailed design, developing verification and validation plans, determining makeor-buy decisions, creating production ramp-up plans, crafting maintenance and logistics plans, and selecting disposal approaches. New product developments entail an array of interrelated decisions throughout the system life cycle.

2.3.4.3 决策管理流程

概述

目的　如 ISO/IEC/IEEE 15288 所述：

[6.3.3.1] 决策管理流程的目的是提供一个结构化的分析框架，以便在生命周期的任意时刻客观地识别、描述和评估决策的备选方案集合，并选择最有利的行动方案。

表 2.4 提供了整个系统生命周期中常见的决策情况（机会）的部分列表。Buede 和 Miller（2009）提供了一个范围更大的列表。

表 2.4　系统生命周期中常见的决策情况（机会）的部分列表

生命周期阶段	决策情形（机会）
概念	评估技术机会 / 初始业务用例
	拟定技术发展战略
	提供信息、生成并完善能力制品
	对替代方案进行分析
	支持计划启动决策
开发	选择系统架构
	选择系统元素
	选择下级元素
	选择验证和确认方法
	开展制造或购买决策
生产	选择生产流程和地点
使用，支持	选择维护实施方法
退役	选择处置实施方法

INCOSE SEH 原始图由 Parnell、Kenley 和 Roedler 创建。按照 INCOSE 通知页使用。版权所有。

决策管理是一项关键的系统工程活动。考虑确定业务 / 任务需要、制定技术开发战略、定义利益相关方和系统需求、选择系统架构、融合详细设计、制订验证和确认计划、确定自制 – 外购决策、建立产能爬坡计划、制订维护和后勤计划以及选择处置方法所涉及的决策。新产品开发需要在整个系统生命周期中做出一系列相互关联的决策。

SYSTEM LIFE CYCLE CONCEPTS, MODELS, AND PROCESSES

Description The Decision Management process transforms a broadly stated decision situation into a recommended course of action and associated implementation plan. The process requires a decision maker with full responsibility, authority, and accountability for the decision, a decision analyst with a suite of decision tools, subject matter experts with performance models, and a representative set of end users and other stakeholders (Parnell, et al., 2013). The decision process is executed within the policy and guidelines established by the system sponsor. A well-structured decision process will capture and communicate the impact that different value judgments have on the overall decisions and facilitate the search for alternatives that remain attractive across a wide range of value schemes.

Inputs/Outputs Inputs and outputs for the Decision Management process are listed in Figure 2.26. Descriptions of each input and output are provided in Appendix E.

Process Activities The Decision Management process includes the following activities:

- Prepare for decisions.

–Develop the decision management strategy/approach for system or project decisions.

–Establish and challenge the decision statement and clarify the decision to be made.

–Determine the analyses methods, other processes, and tools required to support decision activities. (Note that the System Analysis process (see Section 2.3.5.6) is often applied to perform analyses to provide input for the decisions.)

–Provide resources to implement the strategy.

- *Analyze the decision information.*

–Frame, tailor, and structure each decision.

–Develop objectives and measures.

–Generate creative alternatives.

–Assess alternatives via deterministic analysis.

–Synthesize results.

–Identify uncertainties and conduct probabilistic analysis.

–Assess impact of the uncertainties.

–Improve alternatives.

描述　决策管理流程将广泛陈述的决策情况转化为建议的行动方案和相关的实施计划。该流程需要一个对决策负全部责任、有权威和有职责的决策者，一个拥有一套决策工具的决策分析师，一个拥有绩效模型的主题专家，以及一组具有代表性的最终用户和其他利益相关方（Parnell 等，2013）。决策流程在系统发起人制定的政策和指导方针范围内执行。结构良好的决策流程将捕获并传达不同价值判断对总体决策的影响，这有助于在广泛的价值方案中寻找具有吸引力的备选方案。

输入 / 输出　决策管理流程的输入和输出如图 2.26 所示。附录 E 中提供了每个输入和输出的描述。

流程活动　决策管理流程包括以下活动：

- *准备决策。*

- 为系统或项目决策制定决策管理策略 / 实施方法。

- 制定并质疑决策声明，并澄清将要做出的决策。

- 确定支持决策活动所需的分析方法、其他流程和工具。[请注意，系统分析流程（见 2.3.5.6 节）通常用于执行分析，为决策提供输入。]

- 为实施战略提供资源。

- *分析决策信息。*

- 框定、剪裁和组织每个决策。

- 制定目标和措施。

- 生成创造性的备选方案。

- 通过确定性分析评估备选方案。

- 综合结果。

- 识别不确定性并进行概率分析。

- 评估不确定性的影响。

- 改进替代方案。

SYSTEM LIFE CYCLE CONCEPTS, MODELS, AND PROCESSES

–Communicate trade-offs.

–Present recommendation and implement action plan.

• *Make and manage decisions.*

–Record the decision with relevant data, models, and supporting documentation (i.e., the decision authority, source, and rationale).

–Describe analyses methods, other processes, and tools actually used to support decision activities.

–Communicate new directions from the decision.

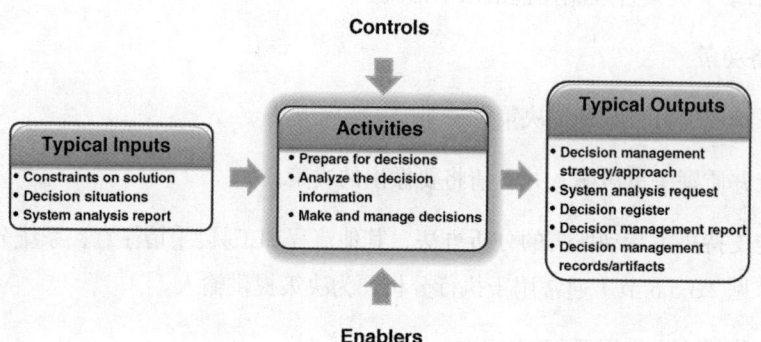

FIGURE 2.26 IPO diagram for the Decision Management process. INCOSE SEH original figure created by Walden, Shortell, and Yip. Usage per the INCOSE Notices page. All other rights reserved.

Common approaches and tips:

- Since there are many decisions across the spectrum of project management, system definition, and life cycle activities, the Decision Management process is applied in conjunction with most of the Technical Management and Technical Processes.

- It is important to verify and validate the data and assumptions used in the decision analyses, since the validity of the analysis results depends on the use of valid data and assumptions, and the application of appropriate analytic methods.

系统生命周期概念、模型和流程

- 沟通权衡。

- 提出建议并实施行动计划。

- *制定和管理决策*。

- 使用相关数据、模型和支持文件（即决策机构、来源和理由）记录决策。

- 描述实际用于支持决策活动的分析方法、其他流程和工具。

- 沟通决策的新方向。

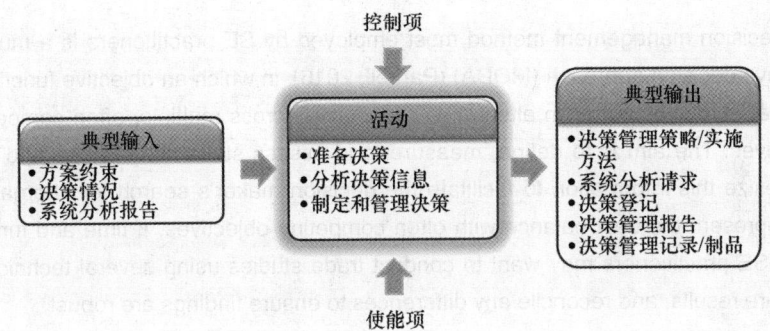

图 2.26 决策管理流程的 IPO 图。INCOSE SEH 原始图由 Walden、Shortell 和 Yip 创建。按照 INCOSE 通知页使用。版权所有。

常用方法和提示：

- 由于在项目管理、系统定义和生命周期活动范围内有许多决策，因此决策管理流程与大多数技术管理和技术流程结合使用。

- 验证和确认决策分析中使用的数据和假设非常重要，因为分析结果的有效性取决于有效数据和假设的使用以及适当分析方法的应用。

SYSTEM LIFE CYCLE CONCEPTS, MODELS, AND PROCESSES

Elaboration

SE practitioners face many decision situations throughout the life cycle of a project. They must choose the analytical approach that best fits the frame and structure of each decision problem. For instance, when there are "clear, important, and discrete events that stand between the implementation of the alternatives and the eventual consequences" (Edwards, et al., 2007), a decision tree is often a well-suited analytical approach, especially when the decision structure has only a few decision nodes and chance nodes. As the number of decision nodes and chance nodes grows, the decision tree quickly becomes unwieldy and loses some of its communicative power. Furthermore, decision trees require end node consequences be expressed in terms of a single number.

The decision management method most employed by SE practitioners is a multiple objective decision approach (MODA) (Parnell, 2016), in which an objective function is formulated to synthesize an alternative's response across multiple, often competing, objectives. The aim is to define, measure, and assess stakeholder value and then synthesize this information to facilitate the decision maker's search for alternatives that represent the best balance with often competing objectives. If time and funding allow, SE practitioners may want to conduct trade studies using several techniques, compare results, and reconcile any differences to ensure findings are robust.

The following are a summary of decision management good practices.

Framing, Tailoring, and Structuring Decisions. Capturing a description of the system baseline, as well as the concept of operations with some indication of system boundaries and anticipated interfaces, helps ensure the understanding of the decision context. This includes such details as the time frame allotted for the decisions, an explicit list of stakeholders, a discussion regarding available resources, and expectations regarding the type of action to be taken as a result of the decision at hand. It may also include decisions anticipated in the future (Edwards, et al., 2007).

Developing Objectives and Measures. Defining the decision to be made may require balancing a large number of ambiguous and potentially conflicting stakeholder need statements, engaging in uncomfortable discussions regarding the relative priority of each requirement, and establishing walkaway points and stretch goals. Per Keeney (2002):

"Most important decisions involve multiple objectives, and usually with multiple-objective decisions, you cannot have it all. You will have to accept less achievement in terms of some objectives to achieve more on other objectives. But how much less would you accept to achieve how much more?"

系统生命周期概念、模型和流程

详细阐述

系统工程实践者在项目的整个生命周期中面临许多决策情况。他们必须选择最适合每个决策问题框架和结构的分析方法。例如，当"在备选方案的实施和最终结果之间存在明确、重要和离散的事件"（Edwards 等，2007）时，决策树通常是一种非常合适的分析方法，尤其是当决策结构只有少数决策节点和机会节点时。随着决策节点和机会节点数量的增加，决策树很快变得笨拙，失去了一些沟通能力。此外，决策树要求端节点结果用单个数字表示。

系统工程实践者最常用的决策管理方法是多目标决策方法（MODA）（Parnell，2016），其中制定一个目标函数，以综合备选方案对多个往往相互竞争的目标的响应。其目的是定义、衡量和评估利益相关方的价值，然后综合这些信息，以促进决策者寻找替代方案，实现往往相互竞争的目标之间的最佳平衡。如果时间和资金允许，系统工程实践者可能希望使用多种技术进行权衡研究，比较结果，并协调任何差异，以确保结果可靠。

以下是决策管理良好实践的总结。

框定、剪裁和结构化决策。获取系统基线的描述及运行意图，以及一些系统边界和预期接口的指示，有助于确保理解决策背景环境。这包括分配给决策的时间框架、明确的利益相关方列表、关于可用资源的讨论，以及对手边决策后所采取的行动类型的预期等细节。它还可能包括未来预期的决策（Edwards 等，2007）。

制定目标和衡量准则。定义要做出的决策可能需要平衡大量模糊且潜在冲突的利益相关方需求声明，进行关于各需求相对优先级的不愉快讨论，并设立可接受的底线和挑战性目标。根据 Keeney（2002）：

"最重要的决策涉及多个目标，通常在多目标决策中，你不能什么都要。你将不得不在某些目标上接受较少的成果，以在其他目标上取得较多的成果。但你愿意接受多少较少的成果，以换取多少较多的成果呢？"

SYSTEM LIFE CYCLE CONCEPTS, MODELS, AND PROCESSES

Use the information obtained from the Business or Mission Analysis, Stakeholder Needs and Requirements Definition, System Requirements Definition, System Architecture Definition, and Design Definition processes to develop objectives and measures for MODA models that use fundamental objectives (why, what, where, and when), but not means objectives (how). For each fundamental objective, a measure must be established so that alternatives that more fully satisfy the objective receive a better score on the measure than those alternatives that satisfy the objective to a lesser degree. These measures (also known as measures of effectiveness (MOEs), key performance parameters (KPPs), measures of performance (MOPs), technical performance measures (TPMs), critical performance measures, attributes, criterion, or metrics) must be unambiguous, comprehensive, direct, operational, and understandable (Keeney and Gregory, 2005) (Roedler and Jones, 2005) (see Section 2.3.4.7).

Generating Creative Alternatives. For many trade studies, the alternatives will be systems composed of many interrelated system elements. It is important to establish a meaningful product structure for the SoI and to apply this product structure consistently throughout the decision analysis. The product structure should be a useful decomposition of the elements of the SoI that explores the trade space. Each alternative is composed of specific design choices for each element. The ability to communicate the differentiating design features of the alternatives is essential. An alternative to a finite number of alternatives is Set-Based Design (SBD). SBD has been shown to effectively and efficiently explore the trade space (Specking, et al., 2018).

Assessing Alternatives via Deterministic Analysis. The decision team should engage subject matter experts by creating models using operational and test data along with the defined objectives, measures, and alternatives to assess performance and using structured scoring sheets. Each score sheet contains a summary description of the alternative and the scoring criteria. Ideally, the models and simulations should be integrated with the performance, value, and cost models so a design change impacts all models.

Synthesizing Results. Using the data summarized in the objective measure consequence table, explore, understand, aggregate the data, and display results in a way that facilitates stakeholder understanding.

Identifying Uncertainty and Conducting Probabilistic Analysis. It is important to identify potential uncertainty surrounding the assessed score and variables that could impact one or more scores (see Section 1.4.1). One example of uncertainty is that system concepts are described as a collection of system element design choices, but knowledge of the system element performance during system design is often incomplete. Subject matter experts can often assess an upper, nominal, and lower bound score by making three separate assessments: (i) assuming a low performance, (ii) assuming moderate performance, and (iii) assuming high performance.

使用从业务或任务分析、利益相关方需要和需求定义、系统需求定义、系统架构定义和设计定义流程中获得的信息，制定用于 MODA 模型的目标和衡量准则。MODA 模型应使用基本目标（为何、何物、何地、何时），而非手段目标（如何）。对于每一个基本目标，都必须制定一个衡量标准，以便使更充分地满足该目标的备选方案在衡量准则上获得的分数要高于满足该目标程度较低的备选方案。这些测度［也称为有效性测度（MOEs）、关键性能参数（KPP）、性能测度（MOPs）、技术性能测度（TPM）、关键性能测度、属性、准则或度量］必须明确、全面、直接、可操作且可理解（Keeney 和 Gregory，2005）（Roedler 和 Jones，2005）（见 2.3.4.7 节）。

生成创造性的备选方案。对于许多权衡研究，备选方案将是由许多相互关联的系统元素组成的系统。为 SoI 建立一个有意义的产品结构，并在整个决策分析流程中始终应用该产品结构，这一点很重要。产品结构应该是探索权衡空间的 SoI 元素的有用分解。每个备选方案由每个元素的特定设计选择组成。沟通备选方案不同设计特征的能力至关重要。有限数量备选方案的替代方案是基于集合的设计（SBD）。SBD 已被证明能够有效地探索权衡空间（Specking 等，2018）。

通过确定性分析评估备选方案。决策团队应通过使用运行和测试数据以及定义的目标、测度和备选方案创建模型，以评估绩效，并使用结构化计分表，使得主题专家有效参与。每个评分表包含备选方案和评分标准的摘要说明。理想情况下，模型和仿真应与性能、价值和成本模型综合，以便设计更改可以影响所有模型。

综合结果。使用目标衡量结果表中总结的数据，探索、理解、聚合数据，并以便于利益相关方理解的方式展示结果。

识别不确定性并进行概率分析。确定评估分数和可能影响一个或多个分数的变量周围的潜在不确定性非常重要（见 1.4.1 节）。不确定性的一个例子是，系统概念被描述为系统元素设计选择的集合，但在系统设计期间，对系统元素性能的了解往往不完整。主题专家通常可以通过三个单独的评估来评估分数的上限、额定和下限：(i) 假设低绩效，(ii) 假设中等绩效，以及 (iii) 假设高绩效。

Accessing Impact of Uncertainty. Decision analysis uses many forms of sensitivity analysis including line diagrams, tornado diagrams, waterfall diagrams, and several uncertainty analyses, including Monte Carlo simulation, decision trees, and influence diagrams (Parnell, et al., 2013). Monte Carlo simulations are used to identify the relative impact of each source of uncertainty on the performance, value, and cost of each alterative. Risks should be identified when significant uncertainty is present.

Improving Alternatives. One could be tempted to end the decision analysis here, highlight the alternative that has the highest total value, and claim success. Such a premature ending would not be considered good practice. Good practice includes further analysis to mine the data generated for the first set of alternatives to reveal opportunities to modify some system element design choices to identify untapped value and reduce risk.

Communicating Trade-Offs. The decision team should identify key observations regarding what stakeholders seem to want and what they may be willing to give up to achieve it. The decision team highlights the design decisions that are least significant and/or most influential and provide the best stakeholder value. In addition, the important uncertainties and risks should also be identified. Observations regarding combinatorial effects of various design decisions are also important products of this process step. Finally, competing objectives that are driving the trade-offs should be highlighted as well.

Presenting Recommendations and Implementing the Action Plan. It is helpful to clearly describe the recommendation as an actionable task list to increase the likelihood of the decision analysis leading to some form of action showing tangible value. Decisions should be documented using digital engineering artifacts. Reports that include the analysis, decisions, and rationale are important for historical traceability and future decisions.

2.3.4.4 *Risk Management Process*

Overview

Purpose As stated in ISO/IEC/IEEE 15288,

[6.3.4.1] The purpose of the Risk Management process is to identify, analyze, treat and monitor the risks continually.

Description Risk Management is a disciplined approach to dealing with the uncertainty that is present throughout the entire system life cycle (see Section 1.4.1). Opportunity management may be performed in conjunction with or as part of risk management. A primary objective of risk management is to identify and manage uncertainties that threaten or reduce the value provided by a business enterprise or organization. A primary objective of opportunity management is to identify and manage uncertainties that enhance or increase the value provided by a business enterprise or organization. Since risk cannot be reduced to zero, another objective is to achieve a proper balance between risk and opportunity.

评估不确定性的影响。决策分析使用多种形式的敏感性分析，包括折线图、龙卷风图、瀑布图和几种不确定性分析，包括蒙特卡罗仿真、决策树和影响图（Parnell 等，2013）。蒙特卡罗仿真用于确定每个不确定性来源对每个备选方案的性能、价值和成本的相对影响。当存在重大不确定性时，应识别风险。

改进替代方案。人们可能会在这里结束决策分析，突出展示具有最高总价值的备选方案，并声称成功。这种过早的结束不被视为良好实践。良好实践包括进一步分析，以挖掘为第一组备选方案生成的数据，揭示修改某些系统元素设计选择的机会，以确定未开发的价值并降低风险。

沟通权衡。决策团队应确定关于利益相关方似乎想要什么以及他们可能愿意放弃什么来实现它的关键观察结果。决策团队强调最不重要和/或最具影响力的设计决策，并提供最佳利益相关方价值。此外，还应确定重要的不确定性和风险。关于各种设计决策的组合效应的观察也是该流程步骤的重要产物。最后，还应强调推动权衡的相互竞争的目标。

提出建议和执行行动计划。将建议明确描述为可执行的任务列表有助于提高决策分析促成某种形式的行动以展示出实际价值的可能性。应使用数字工程制品记录决策。包含分析、决策和基本原理的报告对于历史追溯和未来决策非常重要。

2.3.4.4 风险管理流程

概述

目的　如 ISO/IEC/IEEE 15288 所述：

[6.3.4.1] 风险管理流程的目的是持续识别、分析、处理和监控风险。

描述　风险管理是处理整个系统生命周期中存在的不确定性的一种规范方法（见 1.4.1 节）。机会管理可能与风险管理一起执行，或作为风险管理的一部分执行。风险管理的主要目标是识别和管理威胁或降低复杂组织体系或组织提供的价值的不确定性。机会管理的一个主要目标是识别和管理不确定因素，以提高或增加商业企业或组织提供的价值。由于风险不能降至零，另一个目标是在风险和机遇之间实现适当的平衡。

SYSTEM LIFE CYCLE CONCEPTS, MODELS, AND PROCESSES

82 Risk management, as it relates to SE, is defined in ISO/IEC/IEEE 15288 and elaborated upon in ISO/IEC/IEEE 16085 (2021). As stated in ISO/IEC/IEEE 16085,

[6.1] The Risk Management process is a continual process for systematically addressing risk throughout the life cycle of a system, product, or service. It can be applied to risks related to the acquisition, development, maintenance, or operation of a system.

When using this process for opportunity management, the above statement, with the term "opportunity" substituted for the term "risk," is also true.

Inputs/Outputs Inputs and outputs for the Risk Management process are listed in Figure 2.27. Descriptions of each input and output are provided in Appendix E.

Process Activities The Risk Management process includes the following activities:

- *Plan risk management.*

–Develop the risk management strategy/approach.

–Capture the Risk Management process context, including risk categories.

- *Maintain the risk profile.*

–Capture the thresholds and conditions of the risks.

–Establish and maintain a risk profile to include context of the risk and its likelihood of occurrence, severity of consequences, risk thresholds, and priority and the risk action requests along with the status of their treatment.

–Ensure updates of the risk profile are available to relevant stakeholders.

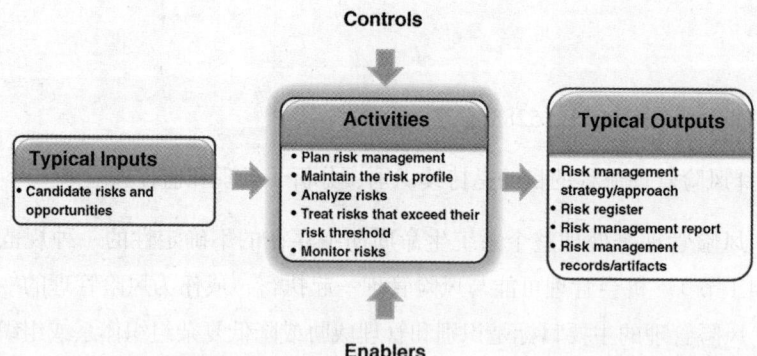

FIGURE 2.27 IPO diagram for Risk Management process. INCOSE SEH original figure created by Shortell, Walden, and Yip. Usage per the INCOSE Notices page. All other rights reserved.

与系统工程相关的风险管理在 ISO/IEC/IEEE 15288 中定义,并在 ISO/IEC/IEEE 16085(2021)中详细阐述。如 ISO/IEC/IEEE 16085 所述,

[6.1] 风险管理流程是一个持续的流程,用于在系统、产品或服务的整个生命周期内系统地解决风险。它可以应用于与系统的获取、开发、维护或运行相关的风险。

在将此流程用于机会管理时,上述用"机会"代替"风险"的说法也是正确的。

输入 / 输出 风险管理流程的输入和输出如图 2.27 所示。附录 E 中提供了每个输入和输出的描述。

流程活动 风险管理流程包括以下活动:

- 计划风险管理。
- 制定风险管理策略 / 实施方法。
- 捕获风险管理流程背景,包括风险类。
- 维护风险状况。
- 捕获风险的阈值和条件。
- 建立并维护风险概况,包括风险的背景及其发生的可能性、后果的严重性、风险阈值和优先级、风险行动请求及其处理状态。
- 确保相关的利益相关方可获得风险概况的更新。

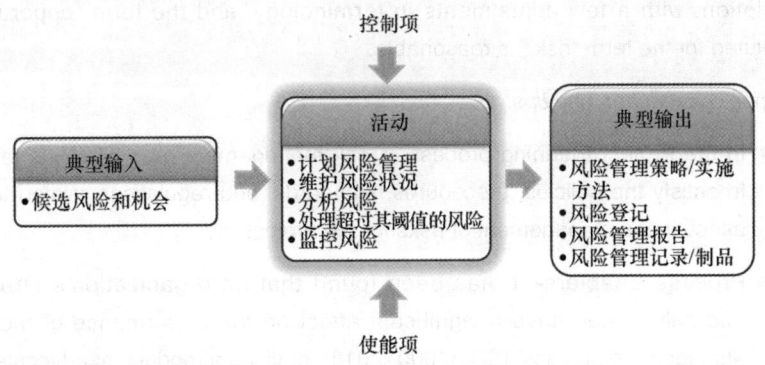

图 2.27 风险管理流程的 IPO 图。INCOSE SEH 原始图由 Walden、Shortell 和 Yip 创建。按照 INCOSE 通知页使用。版权所有。

SYSTEM LIFE CYCLE CONCEPTS, MODELS, AND PROCESSES

83
- *Analyze risks.*

   –Identify risks consistent with the risk management strategy/approach.

   –For each risk, estimate its likelihood and consequence of occurrence.

   –For each risk, use the risk thresholds to evaluate the risk for potential treatment.

   –For risks that exceed the threshold, capture recommended treatment strategies and measures.

- *Treat risks that exceed their risk threshold.*

   –Identify a set of feasible alternatives for the treatment of risks.

   –Establish measures to provide insight into the risk treatment effectiveness.

   –Execute the treatments for the risks.

   –When management action is needed for risk treatments, ensure effective coordination.

- *Monitor risks.*

   –Maintain the record of risk items and how they were treated.

   –Monitor high priority risks.

   –Monitor risks and the risk management context to capture changes and update priorities and actions.

   –Throughout the life cycle, monitor for new risks and sources of risk.

When using this process for opportunity management, the above process activity description, with a few adjustments in terminology, and the term "opportunity" substituted for the term "risk," is reasonable.

Common approaches and tips:

- In the Project Planning process, a risk management plan (RMP) is tailored to satisfy the policies, procedures, standards, and regulations related to and affecting the management of risks for the project.

- Process Enablers—It has been found that an organization's structure and culture can have a significant effect on the performance of the Risk Management process. ISO 31000 (2018), outlines a model that advocates the establishment of principles for managing risk and a framework for managing risk that work in concert with the process for managing risk.

- **分析风险。**

- 识别与风险管理策略/实施方法一致的风险。

- 对于每种风险，估计其发生的可能性和后果。

- 对于每种风险，使用风险阈值来评估潜在的处理风险。

- 对于超过阈值的风险，获取建议的处理策略和措施。

- **处理超过其阈值的风险。**

- 确定一套可行的风险处理方案。

- 制定措施，深入了解风险处理的有效性。

- 执行风险处理措施。

- 当风险处理需要管理措施时，确保有效协调。

- **监控风险。**

- 保存风险项目的记录及其处理方式。

- 监控高优先级风险。

- 监控风险和风险管理背景，以捕获变化并更新优先级和行动。

- 在整个生命周期中，监控新风险和风险源。

在将此流程用于机会管理时，上述流程活动的描述（在术语上做了一些调整）以及用"机会"代替"风险"是合理的。

常用方法和提示：

- 在项目计划流程中，风险管理计划是为满足与项目风险管理有关和影响项目风险管理的政策、程序、标准和规定而定制的。

- 流程使能项：组织的结构和文化可以对风险管理流程的绩效产生重大影响。ISO 31000（2018）概述了一个模型，该模型提倡建立风险管理原则和风险管理框架，该框架与风险管理流程一致。

SYSTEM LIFE CYCLE CONCEPTS, MODELS, AND PROCESSES

- Typical strategies for coping with risk include transference, avoidance, acceptance, or taking action to reduce the potential negative effects of the situation.

- Most Risk Management processes include a prioritization scheme whereby risks with the greatest potential negative consequence and the highest likelihood are treated before those deemed to have lower potential negative consequences and lower likelihood. The objective of risk management is to balance the allocation of resources such that a minimum amount of resources achieves the greatest risk mitigation (or opportunity realization) benefits.

- Communication errors and misunderstandings can be prevented by defining and communicating the risk terminology to be used by the project and including with the project's risk management plan (RMP).

- Experience has shown that terms such as "positive risk" and concept models that define opportunity as a subset of risks serve only to confuse. Take care to define the terminology and concepts to be used by the project team and provide training to reinforce a common understanding.

- Practices used for writing good requirements help with risk statements. For example, one good practice for identifying and clarifying risks is to use an "if <situation>, then <consequence>, for <stakeholder >" pattern. This pattern helps to determine the validity of a risk and assess its magnitude or importance.

- Risk management is most successful when risk-based thinking is embraced and integrated into the culture. All personnel are responsible for identifying risks early and continuously throughout the project life cycle.

- Negative feedback toward personnel who identify a potential problem will discourage the full cooperation of engaged stakeholders and could result in failure to identify and address serious risk-laden situations. Conduct a transparent Risk Management process to encourage all stakeholders to assist in risk mitigation efforts.

- Some situations can be difficult to categorize in terms of probability and consequences; involve all relevant stakeholders in this evaluation to capture the maximum variety in viewpoints.

- Risk measurement is not an exact science. Variation in stakeholder perspectives, perceptions, and tolerance levels, along with high uncertainty in available data, can make reliance on quantitative measures of risk insufficient. For example, some low-likelihood/high-severity risks might require treatment and monitoring regardless of the estimated likelihood of occurrence (Taleb, 2018) (Siegel, 2019).

- 应对风险的典型策略包括转移、规避、接受或采取行动以减少潜在的负面影响。

- 大多数风险管理流程都包括一个优先级排序计划，根据该计划，在处理那些被认为潜在负面后果较小、可能性较低的风险之前，先处理潜在负面后果最大、可能性最高的风险。风险管理的目标是平衡资源的分配，以使用最低数量的资源实现最大的风险缓解（或机会实现）效益。

- 通过定义和沟通项目使用的风险术语，包括项目风险管理计划（RMP），可以防止沟通错误和误解。

- 经验表明，"积极风险"等术语和将机会定义为风险子集的概念模型只会让人混淆。注意定义项目团队要使用的术语和概念，并提供培训以加强共识。

- 用于编写良好需求的实践有助于风险陈述。例如，识别和澄清风险的一个良好实践是使用"对于＜利益相关方＞，如果＜情况＞，那么＜结果＞"模式。这种模式有助于确定风险的有效性并评估其大小或重要性。

- 当基于风险的思维被接受并融入文化时，风险管理最为成功。所有人员负责在整个项目生命周期内尽早、持续地识别风险。

- 对发现潜在问题的人员的负面反馈将阻碍利益相关方的充分合作，并可能导致无法识别和解决严重的风险情况。实施透明的风险管理流程，鼓励所有利益相关方协助风险缓解工作。

- 某些情况可能难以按概率和后果进行分类；让所有涉及的利益相关方参与评估，以获取最大的视角多样性。

- 风险测量不是一门精确的科学。利益相关方视角、认知和容忍水平的变化，以及可用数据的高度不确定性，可能会导致对风险量化测度的依赖不足。例如，无论估计发生的可能性如何，一些低可能性／高严重性风险可能需要处置和监测（Taleb, 2018）（Siegel, 2019）。

SYSTEM LIFE CYCLE CONCEPTS, MODELS, AND PROCESSES

- External risks are often neglected in project management. External risks are risks caused by or originating from the surrounding environment of the project (Fossnes, 2005). Project participants often have no control or influence over external risk factors, but they can learn to observe the external environment and eventually take proactive steps to minimize the impact of external risks on the project. The typical issues are time-dependent processes, rigid sequence of activities, one dominant path for success, and little slack.

Elaboration

Definitions of Risk. Few terms used in engineering have as many different published definitions as the term "risk." In practice, risk terminology and concepts vary considerably across industries; however, most published definitions of risk align with one of two concept models. Below are two prominent definitions of risk that capture the essence of both concepts:

- The effect of uncertainty on objectives [see ISO/IEC/IEEE 15288, ISO Guide 73, ISO/IEC/IEEE 16085, ISO/IEC 31000, ISO 27000]

- The combination of the probability of occurrence of harm and the severity of that harm [see ISO Guide 51, ISO 22367, ISO 14971]

Both definitions may be used in an SE project. The first definition includes the concept that effects may be negative or positive. In this respect the first definition accommodates use of the second definition. In SE it is common to use the term "risk" when referring to scenarios with a negative effect, and the term "opportunity" when referring to scenarios with a positive effect. The second definition (which accommodates only negative effects) is commonly used in safety engineering, and its use may be required in order to demonstrate compliance to risk management standards and regulations applicable to products and systems that impact public health, safety, and security. For example, in the medical industry (see Section 4.4.2), particularly for medical devices, risk management is often centered on product (patient and user) safety risk (referred to as system safety in this handbook, see Section 3.1.11).

Evolving Risk and Opportunity Management Concepts. According to Conrow (2003), "Traditionally, risk has been defined as the likelihood of an event occurring coupled with a negative consequence of the event occurring. In other words, a risk is a potential problem—something to be avoided if possible, or its likelihood and/or consequences reduced if not." As a corollary to risk, Conrow (2003) defines opportunity as "the potential for the realization of wanted, positive consequences of an event." The idea of considering opportunities and positive outcomes (in addition to negative outcomes) as an integral part of a Risk Management process has gained favor with some experts and practitioners. New risk and risk management concepts intended to support this broadened scope for risk management are evolving.

- 项目管理中经常忽视外部风险。外部风险是由项目周围环境引起或源自项目周围环境的风险（Fossnes，2005）。项目参与者通常无法控制或影响外部风险因素，但他们可以学会观察外部环境，并最终采取主动措施，将外部风险对项目的影响降至最低。典型的问题是流程依赖于时间、活动顺序呆板、成功的主要途径只有一条、几乎没有余量。

详细阐述

*风险的定义。*工程中使用的术语很少能像"风险"一词那样有如此多不同的公开定义。在实践中，风险术语和概念因行业而异；然而，大多数已发布的风险定义与两个概念模型中的一个一致。以下是两个主要的风险定义，它们抓住了这两个概念的本质：

- 不确定性对目标的影响 [见 ISO/IEC/IEEE 15288、ISO 指南 73、ISO/IEC/IEEE 16085、ISO/IEC 31000、ISO 27000]

- 伤害发生的概率和伤害严重程度的组合 [见 ISO 指南 51、ISO 22367、ISO 14971]

这两种定义都可以在系统工程项目中使用。第一个定义包含影响可能是消极的或积极的这一概念。在这方面，第一个定义适用于第二个定义的使用。在系统工程中，当提及具有负面影响的情景时，通常使用术语"风险"，当提及具有正面影响的情景时，通常使用术语"机会"。第二个定义（只考虑负面影响）通常用于安全工程，可能需要使用这种定义来证明符合风险管理标准和适用于影响公共健康、安全和安保的产品和系统的法规。例如，在医疗行业（见 4.4.2 节），尤其是对于医疗设备，风险管理通常以产品（患者和用户）安全风险为中心（本手册中称为系统安全，见 3.1.11 节）。

*不断发展的风险和机会管理概念。*根据 Conrow（2003），"传统上，风险被定义为事件发生的可能性以及事件发生的负面后果。换言之，风险是一个潜在的问题，如果可能的话可以避免，或者如果不可能的话可以减少其可能性和/或后果"。作为风险的必然结果，Conrow（2003）将机会定义为"实现事件想要的积极后果的可能性"。将机会和积极结果（包括消极结果）作为风险管理流程的一个组成部分的想法受到了一些专家和实践者的青睐。旨在支持这一扩大的风险管理范围的新风险和风险管理概念正在演进。

SYSTEM LIFE CYCLE CONCEPTS, MODELS, AND PROCESSES

The measurement of risk has two components (see Figure 2.28):

- The likelihood that an event will occur
- The undesirable consequence of the event if it does occur

The generic consequence/likelihood matrix in Figure 2.28 is a way to display risks according to their consequence (illustrated with the generic a-e, high-to-low, consequence rating scale), and their likelihood (illustrated with the generic 1-5, low-to-high, likelihood rating scale), and to combine these characteristics to display a rating for risk level (illustrated with the generic Roman numeral I-V, high-to-low, risk significance scale). The combination of low likelihood and low undesirable consequences gives low risk, while high risk is produced by high likelihood and highly undesirable consequences. Risk prioritization and decision rules (such as the level of management attention or the urgency of response) can be linked to the matrix cells. Note that this generic matrix is conceptual and cannot be applied without careful customization to address the specific project. Detailed guidance and examples for designing rating scales and matrices suitable for use on specific projects, products and systems are provided in IEC 31010 (2019).

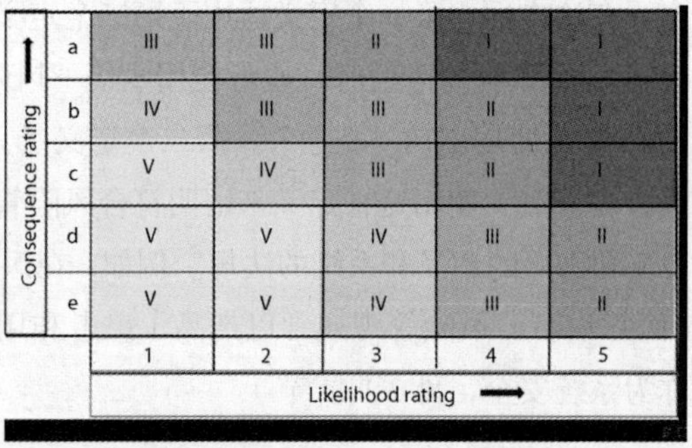

Consequence rating					
a	III	III	II	I	I
b	IV	III	III	II	I
c	V	IV	III	II	I
d	V	V	IV	III	II
e	V	V	IV	III	II
	1	2	3	4	5
	Likelihood rating →				

FIGURE 2.28 Level of risk depends upon both likelihood and consequence. From ISO/IEC 31010 (2019). Used with permission. All other rights reserved.

A positive consequence scale may be used in the matrix shown in Figure 2.28, thereby changing the outcome adjective from undesirable to desirable, and the cells in the matrix from risks to opportunities. Note that the foundational concept and structure of the matrix diagram remains the same.

风险测度有两个组成部分（见图 2.28）：

- 事件发生的可能性
- 事件发生时的不良后果

图 2.28 中的通用后果/可能性矩阵是根据其后果（一般用 a-e，从高到低，后果评级量表说明）和可能性（一般用 1-5，从低到高，可能性评级量表说明）展示风险的一种方法，并结合这些特征展示风险等级评级（一般用罗马数字 I-V，从高到低，风险重要性等级表说明）。低可能性和低不良后果的组合产生低风险，而高风险是由高可能性和高不良后果产生的。风险优先级和决策规则（如管理层的关注程度或响应的紧迫性）可以与矩阵单元相关联。请注意，此通用矩阵是概念性的，如果不仔细定制以解决特定项目，则无法应用此通用矩阵。IEC 31010（2019）提供了设计适用于特定项目、产品和系统的评级表和矩阵的详细指南和示例。

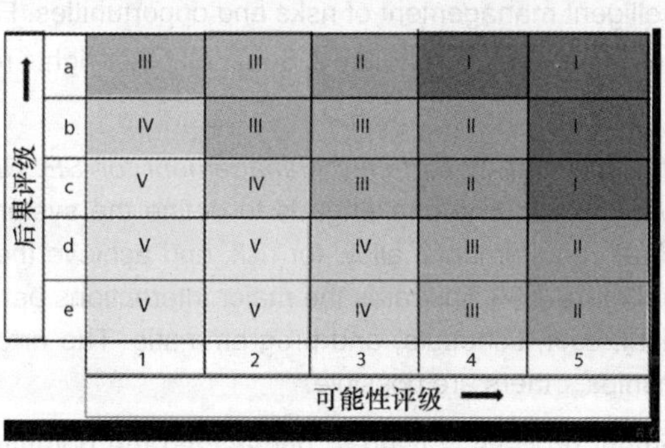

后果评级					
a	III	III	II	I	I
b	IV	III	III	II	I
c	V	IV	III	II	II
d	V	V	IV	III	II
e	V	V	IV	III	II
	1	2	3	4	5
			可能性评级		

图 2.28 取决于可能性和后果的风险等级。源自 ISO/IEC 31010（2019）。经许可后使用。版权所有。

在图 2.28 所示的矩阵中，可以使用积极后果量表，从而将结果形容词从"不可取"改为"可取"，并将矩阵中的单元格从风险改为机会。请注意，矩阵图的基本概念和结构保持不变。

SYSTEM LIFE CYCLE CONCEPTS, MODELS, AND PROCESSES

SE and project management are all about pursuing an opportunity to solve a problem or fulfill a need. Opportunities enable creativity in resolving concepts, architectures, designs, and strategic and tactical approaches, as well as the many administrative issues within the project. It is the selection and pursuit of these strategic and tactical opportunities that determine just how successful the project and system will be. Of course, opportunities usually carry risks, and each opportunity will have its own set of risks that must be intelligently judged and properly managed to achieve the full value (Forsberg, et al., 2005). These are the risks that must be managed to enhance the opportunity value and the overall value of the project (see Figure 2.29). Opportunity management and risk management are therefore essential to—and performed concurrently with—the planning process but require the application of separate and unique techniques that justify this distinct technical management element.

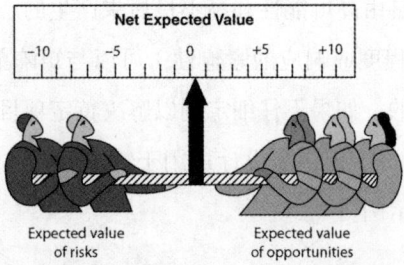

FIGURE 2.29   Intelligent management of risks and opportunities. From Forsberg, et al. (2005) with permission from John Wiley & Sons. All other rights reserved.

Balancing Project, Risk, and Opportunity Management for SE. No realistic project can be planned without risk. The challenge is to define the system and the project that best meet overall requirements, allow for risk, and achieve the highest chances of project success. Figure 2.30 illustrates the major interactions between the four risk categories: technical, cost, schedule, and programmatic. The arrow labels indicate typical risk relationships, others are possible.

The Risk Management process is used to understand the potential cost, schedule, and performance (i.e., technical) risks associated with a system, and then take a (proactive) structured approach to anticipate negative outcomes and respond to them before they occur. With respect to opportunities, this process is used to understand the potential cost, schedule, and performance (i.e., technical) improvement opportunities associated with a system, and then take a (proactive) structured approach to defining potential positive outcomes and responding to them by adopting the best candidate improvements before the "window of opportunity" is missed. Care is taken to consider new and increased risk created as a result of pursuing a new opportunity. This practice can help identify unintended negative consequences that might be introduced by the proposed change.

系统生命周期概念、模型和流程

系统工程和项目管理都是为了寻找机会来解决问题或满足需求。机会使我们能够创造性地解决概念、架构、设计、战略和战术方法,以及项目中的许多管理问题。正是对这些战略和战术机遇的选择和追求,决定了项目和系统的成功程度。当然,机遇通常会带来风险,每个机遇都有自己的风险,必须明智地判断和妥善管理,以实现全部价值(Forsberg 等,2005)。这些是必须加以管理的风险,以提高项目的机会价值和总体价值(见图 2.29)。因此,机会管理和风险管理对于计划流程至关重要,并与计划流程同时进行,但需要应用单独和独特的技术来证明这一独特的技术管理元素的合理性。

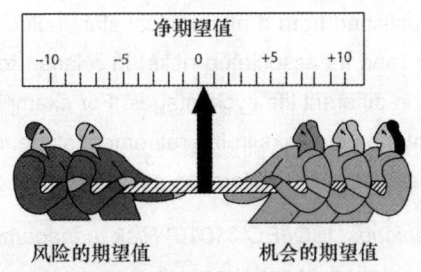

图 2.29 风险和机会的智能管理。源自 Forsberg 等(2005),经 John Wiley & Sons 许可。版权所有。

平衡系统工程的项目、风险和机会管理。任何现实的项目都不能没有风险地进行计划。面临的挑战是如何定义最能满足总体需求、考虑风险并实现项目成功最大机会的系统和项目。图 2.30 说明了四个风险类之间的主要相互作用:技术、成本、进度和计划。箭头标签表示典型的风险关系,其他的也可能存在。

风险管理流程用于了解与系统相关的潜在成本、进度和性能(即技术)风险,然后采取(主动)结构化方法预测负面结果,并在其发生之前做出响应。关于机会,此流程用于了解与系统相关的潜在成本、进度和性能(即技术)改进机会,然后采取(主动)结构化方法来定义潜在的积极结果,并在错过"机会窗"之前通过采用最佳备选改进来应对这些结果。注意考虑因寻求新机会而产生的新的和增加的风险。这种做法有助于识别提出变更可能带来的意外负面后果。

SYSTEM LIFE CYCLE CONCEPTS, MODELS, AND PROCESSES

Integrating Risk Management. Per ISO/IEC 31000, "integrating risk management with all organizational processes improves the performance of risk management while gaining efficiencies." Section 7 of ISO/IEC/IEEE 16085 "Risk management in life cycle processes" provides a methodical approach for the integration of risk management and "riskbased thinking" into all SE life cycle processes. Organizations typically manage risks and opportunities of many types, across and throughout the organization. Risks and opportunities associated with system development should be managed in a manner consistent with the organization's overall risk and opportunity management strategies.

86 *Risk Management and the System Life Cycle.* Once the scope and context of a system have been established from a hierarchical standpoint, it is possible to define and model the system (and its associated risks) in relation to its life cycle, i.e., the differences in the risks in different life cycle stages. For example, risks in the concept stage are quite different than the risks in the retirement stage. It is often necessary to consider risks in other stages while performing activities in the current stage.

Risk Assessment Techniques. ISO/IEC 31010, *Risk management—Risk assessment techniques,* provides detailed descriptions and application guidance for over 30 assessment techniques ranging from brainstorming and checklists to Failure Mode and Effects Analysis (FMEA), Fault Tree Analysis (FTA), Monte Carlo simulation, and Bayesian statistics and Bayes nets. Although a comparable set of (published) techniques for opportunity management is not available, it is notable that ISO/IEC 31010 is not without mention of opportunity, and contains the Strength, Weakness, Opportunity, and Threat (SWOT) Analysis technique. In addition, many of the techniques in ISO/IEC 31010 can be used to assess positive outcomes as well as negative outcomes. For example, FTA can be used to perform Success Tree Analysis, and techniques such as brainstorming, checklists, Monte Carlo simulation, and Bayesian statistical analysis are broadly used for most any purpose, including the assessment of opportunities. A variant of SWOT analysis that is not mentioned in ISO/IEC 31010 is Threats, Opportunities, Weaknesses, and Strengths (TOWS), which puts the emphasis on the external environment (threats and opportunities) rather than on the internal environment (strengths and weaknesses).including the assessment of opportunities. A variant of SWOT analysis that is not mentioned in ISO/IEC 31010 is Threats, Opportunities, Weaknesses, and Strengths (TOWS), which puts the emphasis on the external environment (threats and opportunities) rather than on the internal environment (strengths and weaknesses).

综合风险管理。根据 ISO/IEC 31000,"将风险管理与所有组织流程相结合,可以提高风险管理的绩效,同时提高效率"。ISO/IEC/IEEE 16085"生命周期流程中的风险管理"第 7 节提供了将风险管理和"基于风险的思维"综合到所有系统工程生命周期流程中的方法。组织通常在整个组织中管理多种类型的风险和机遇。与系统开发相关的风险和机遇应以与组织的总体风险和机遇管理战略一致的方式进行管理。

风险管理和系统生命周期。一旦从分层的角度确定了系统的范围和背景,就可以根据其生命周期定义系统并对系统(及其相关风险)进行建模,即不同生命周期阶段的风险差异。例如,概念阶段的风险与退役阶段的风险大不相同。在当前阶段执行活动时,通常需要考虑其他阶段的风险。

风险评估技术。ISO/IEC 31010,风险管理—风险评估技术为 30 多种评估技术提供了详细的描述和应用指南,包括头脑风暴和检查表、故障模式和影响分析(FMEA)、故障树分析(FTA)、蒙特卡洛仿真、贝叶斯统计和贝叶斯网络。虽然没有一套可比较的(已发布的)机会管理技术,但值得注意的是,ISO/IEC 31010 并非没有提到机会,它包含优势、劣势、机会和威胁(SWOT)分析技术。此外,ISO/IEC 31010 中的许多技术可用于评估积极结果和消极结果。例如,FTA 可用于执行成功树分析,头脑风暴、检查表、蒙特卡洛仿真和贝叶斯统计分析等技术广泛用于任何目的,包括机会评估。ISO/IEC 31010 中未提及的 SWOT 分析的一个变体是威胁、机会、劣势和优势(TOWS)分析,它强调外部环境(威胁和机会),而不是内部环境(优势和劣势)。

SYSTEM LIFE CYCLE CONCEPTS, MODELS, AND PROCESSES

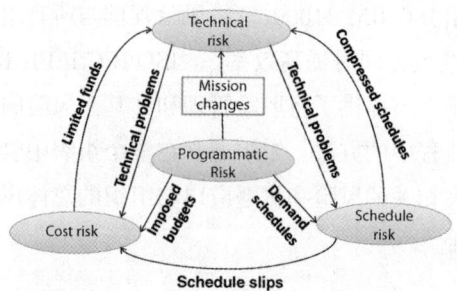

FIGURE 2.30 Typical relationship among the risk categories. INCOSE SEH original figure from INCOSE SEH v1 Figure 4.5-7. Usage per the INCOSE Notices page. All other rights reserved.

Risk Treatment Approaches. Risk treatment approaches (also referred to as risk handling approaches) are often established for the moderate- and high-risk items identified in the risk analysis effort. These activities are formalized in the RMP. There are four basic approaches to treat risks:

1. *Acceptance:* Accept the risk and do no more.
2. *Avoidance:* Avoid the risk through change of requirements or redesign.
3. *Control (or Mitigation):* Taking actions to reduce the risk by expending budget and/or other resources to reduce likelihood and/or consequence over time.
4. *Transference:* Transfer the risk by agreement with another party that it is in their scope to treat. Look for a partner that has experience in the dedicated risk area.

The following are some of the steps that can be taken to avoid or control unnecessary risks:

- *Requirements scrubbing*—Requirements that significantly complicate the system can be scrutinized to ensure that they deliver value equivalent to their investment. Find alternative solutions that deliver the same or comparable capability.

- *Selection of most promising options*—In most situations, several options are available. A trade study can include project risk as a criterion when selecting the most promising alternative.

- *Staffing and team building*—Projects accomplish work through people. Attention to training, teamwork, and employee morale can help avoid risks introduced by human errors.

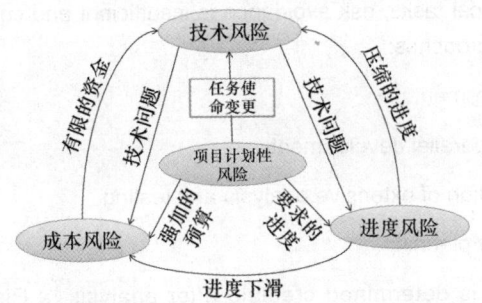

图 2.30 风险类别之间的典型关系。INCOSE SEH 原始图源自 INCOSE SEH v1 图 4.5-7。按照 INCOSE 通知页使用。版权所有。

风险处理方法。风险处理方法（也称为风险处置方法）通常针对风险分析工作中确定的中等风险和高风险项目制定。这些活动在风险管理计划中正式化。有四种处理风险的基本方法：

1. *接受*：接受风险，不采取更多行动。

2. *规避*：通过需求变更或重新设计来规避风险。

3. *控制（或缓解）*：通过使用预算和/或其他资源来降低风险发生的可能性和/或后果。

4. *转移*：通过与另一方达成协议，转移属于其处理范围的风险。寻找在专门风险领域有经验的合作伙伴。

以下是一些可以避免或控制不必要风险的步骤：

- 可以仔细检查使系统严重复杂化的需求，以确保它们提供的价值与投资相当。寻找提供相同或可比功能的替代解决方案。

- 选择最有希望的选项——在大多数情况下，有几种选项可用。权衡研究可以将项目风险作为选择最有希望的替代方案的准则。

- 人员配备和团队建设——项目通过人员完成工作。关注培训、团队合作和员工士气有助于避免人为错误带来的风险。

SYSTEM LIFE CYCLE CONCEPTS, MODELS, AND PROCESSES

For high-risk technical tasks, risk avoidance is insufficient and can be supplemented by the following approaches:

- Early procurement
- Initiation of parallel developments
- Implementation of extensive analysis and testing
- Contingency planning

For each risk that is determined credible after analysis, a Risk Treatment Plan should be created that identifies the risk treatment strategy, the trigger points for action, and any other information to ensuring the treatment is effectively executed. The Risk Treatment Plan can be part of the risk record on the risk profile. For risks that have significant consequences, a contingency plan should be created in case the risk treatment is not successful. It should include the triggers for enacting a contingency plan.

Risk Monitoring. Project management uses measures to simplify and illuminate the Risk Management process (see Figure 2.34). Measures can help identify new risks, as well as provide insight into the effectiveness of the risk treatments.

Each risk category has certain indicators that may be used to monitor project status for signs of risk. Tracking the progress of key system technical parameters can be used as an indicator of technical risk. The typical format in tracking technical performance is a graph of a planned value of a key parameter plotted against calendar time. A second contour showing the actual value achieved is included in the same graph for comparative purposes. Cost and schedule risk are monitored using the products of the cost/schedule control system or some equivalent technique. Normally, cost and schedule variances are used along with a comparison of tasks planned to tasks accomplished.

2.3.4.5 Configuration Management Process

Overview

Purpose As stated in ISO/IEC/IEEE 15288,

[6.3.5.1] The purpose of the Configuration Management (CM) process is to manage system and system element configura tions over their life cycle.

CM establishes and maintains consistency, integrity, traceability, and control of a product's configuration. CM provides enduring truth, trust and traceability across the full life cycle of the product. Appropriate CM across the enterprise and its supply chain, provides efficient, effective, lean, resilient, financially responsible, mature, need realization and sustainment through quantified knowledge and insight. Inadequate CM increases risk to the product— see the example in Section 6.1 about the case of the Therac-25.

对于高风险的技术任务，风险规避是不够的，可以通过以下方法进行补充：

- 早期采办
- 启动并行开发
- 实施广泛的分析和测试
- 应急计划

对于分析后确定可信的每个风险，应制订风险处理计划，确定风险处理策略、行动触发点以及确保有效执行处理的任何其他信息。风险处理计划可以是风险剖面中风险记录的一部分。对于具有重大后果的风险，应制订应急计划，以防止风险处理不成功。它应包括制订应急计划的触发因素。

风险监控。项目管理使用各种措施来简化和说明风险管理流程（见图 2.34）。措施可以帮助识别新风险，以及深入了解风险处理的有效性。

每个风险类都有某些指标，可用于监控项目状态，以发现风险迹象。跟踪关键系统技术参数的进展情况可作为技术风险的一个指标。跟踪技术性能的典型格式是关键参数的计划值与日历时间的对比图。同一图表中还包括第二条等值线，显示实际达到的值，以便进行比较。使用成本／进度控制系统的产品或一些同等技术来监测成本和进度风险。通常情况下，成本和进度差异与计划任务和已完成任务的比较一起使用。

2.3.4.5 构型配置管理流程

概述

目的 如 ISO/IEC/IEEE 15288 所述：

[6.3.5.1] 构型配置管理（CM）流程的目的是在其生命周期内管理系统和系统元素构型配置。

构型配置管理建立并维护产品构型配置的一致性、完整性、可追溯性和控制。构型配置管理在产品的整个生命周期中提供持久的真实性、信任和可追溯性。在整个复杂组织体系及其供应链中进行适当的构型配置管理，通过量化的知识和洞察力，提供高效、有效、精益、韧性、财务负责、成熟，需要实现和维持。构型配置管理不足会增加产品风险，参见 6.1 节关于 Therac-25 的案例。

SYSTEM LIFE CYCLE CONCEPTS, MODELS, AND PROCESSES

Description Configuration Management (CM) is a Technical Management Process applying appropriate processes, resources, and controls, to establish and maintain consistency between product configuration information, and the product (SAE-EIA 649C).

Evolving system requirements, technology and the operating environment are a reality that must be addressed over the life of a system development effort and throughout the utilization and support stages. Furthermore, CM extended to the enterprise level supports the internal goals needed to achieve an efficient, effective, lean, and resilient enterprise.

Configuration management helps ensure:

- that product functional, performance, and physical characteristics are properly identified, documented, controlled, validated, and verified to establish product integrity;
- that changes to these product characteristics are properly identified, reviewed, approved, documented, and implemented;
- that the products produced against a given set of data are known, verified and validated.

Inputs/Outputs The functional model for the Configuration Management process is listed in Figure 2.31. Descriptions of each input and output are provided in Appendix E.

Process Activities The Configuration Management process includes the following activities:

- *Prepare for configuration management.*

–Similar to other SE processes, configuration management needs to be planned as early as possible in the product life cycle. The result of CM planning could be a standalone configuration management strategy, could be incorporated in the SEMP, or could be part of the digital implementation of these principles throughout the development platform (e.g., in software development where we have an integrated platform).

–Planning and managing configuration management is accomplished in conjunction with and integrated through other SE activities and should include the following:

1) Identify the context and environment of the system that we want to apply this to

2) Applying adequate configuration management resources and assigning responsibility

描述 构型配置管理（CM）是一种技术管理流程，应用适当的流程、资源和控制，以建立和维护产品构型配置信息与产品之间的一致性（SAE-EIA 649C）。

不断变化的系统需求、技术和运行环境是现实情况，必须在系统开发工作的整个生命周期以及整个使用和支持阶段加以解决。此外，扩展到复杂组织体系级的构型配置管理支持实现高效、有效、精益和韧性复杂组织体系所需的内部目标。

构型配置管理有助于确保：

- 正确识别、记录、控制、验证和确认产品功能、性能和物理特性，以建立产品完整性；
- 正确识别、评审、批准、记录和实施这些产品特性的变更；
- 产品根据已知、得到验证和确认的给定数据集生产。

输入/输出 构型配置管理流程的输入和输出如图 2.31 所示。附录 E 中提供了每个输入和输出的描述。

流程活动 构型配置管理流程包括以下活动：

- *准备构型配置管理。*

- 与其他系统工程流程类似，构型配置管理需要在产品生命周期中尽早计划。配置管理计划的结果可以是一个独立的配置管理策略，也可以纳入 SEMP，还可以是在整个开发平台中以数字化方式实施这些原则的一部分（例如，在软件开发中我们有一个综合平台）。

- 计划和管理构型配置管理与其他系统工程活动一起完成，并通过其他系统工程活动进行整合，应包括以下内容：

1）确定我们要应用的系统的背景和环境

2）应用足够的构型配置管理资源并分配职责

3) Establishing performance and status measurements

4) Establish, implement and maintain procedures

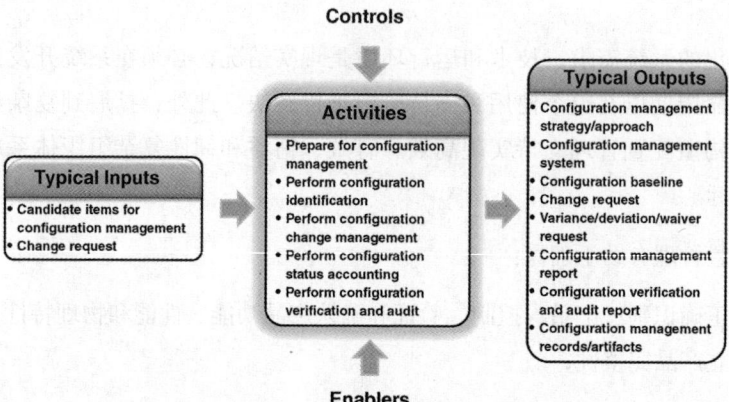

FIGURE 2.31   IPO diagram for Configuration Management process. INCOSE SEH original figure created by Shortell, Walden, and Yip. Usage per the INCOSE Notices page. All other rights reserved.

5) Configuration management training

6) Assessing compliance and effectiveness

7) Supplier configuration management

8) Product configuration information processes establishment (inc. collection and processing, controlling status, providing inter-operability and exchange, long-term preservation)

9) Planning for configuration identification, configuration change management, configuration status accounting, configuration verification, and audit.

- *Perform configuration identification.*

–Identify the items or elements of a system and associated data which should be under configuration management.

–Establish unique identifiers for the items and data under configuration management.

–Structure the items and information under configuration management.

–Validate and release items and information under configuration management.

3）建立性能和状态测度

4）建立、实施和维护程序

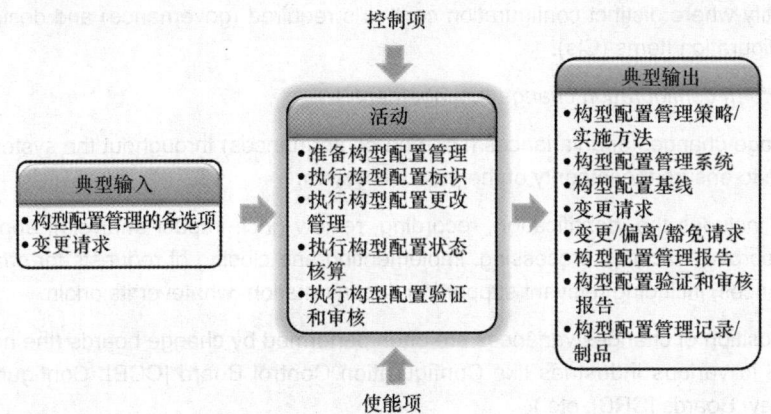

图 2.31 构型配置管理流程的 IPO 图。INCOSE SEH 原始图由 Walden、Shortell 和 Yip 创建。按照 INCOSE 通知页使用。版权所有。

5）构型配置管理培训

6）评估合规性和有效性

7）供应商构型配置管理

8）产品构型配置信息流程建立（包括收集和处理、控制状态、提供互操作性和交换、长期保存）

9）计划构型配置标识、构型配置更改管理、构型配置状态记账、构型配置验证和审核。

- **执行构型配置标识。**

- 确定应在构型配置管理下的系统项目或元素以及相关数据。

- 为构型配置管理下的项目和数据建立唯一标识符。

- 构建构型配置管理下的项目和信息。

- 验证和发布构型配置管理下的项目和信息。

SYSTEM LIFE CYCLE CONCEPTS, MODELS, AND PROCESSES

– Establish and identify baselines at appropriate points throughout the life cycle. Baselines may coincide with a project milestone or decision gate as shown in Figure 2.4.

– Manage interfaces and the constraints they impose.

– Identify where distinct configuration control is required (governance) and designate Configuration Items (CIs).

- *Perform configuration change management.*

– Manage changes and variances (i.e., non-conformances) throughout the system life cycle to ensure the integrity of the product/system.

– This includes the identification, recording, review (incl. impact analysis), approve/ disapprove, tracking, processing, implementing and closing of requests for change/ variances, including relevant supporting documentation, whatever its origin.

– Disposition of changes/variances are often performed by change boards (the names used in various industries like Configuration Control Board [CCB], Configuration Review Boards [CRB], etc.).

– An important practice for the change/variance process is to track and manage implementation activities and close the loop ensuring that both the product and its associated information have been evolved to the current approved configuration.

- *Perform configuration status accounting.*

– Communicate and maintain the status of controlled events, items, and data, as well as performance of CM processes across the life cycle of the product/system to the appropriate stakeholders.

– Measures and means of measuring performance are established by the Project Assessment and Control process and the configuration status accounting supports these metrics and performance assessments (e.g., Performing reconciliation of the As-Designed data with the As-Built data).

- *Perform configuration verification and audit.*

– Perform verification of CM processes, in conjunction with the Verification and Quality Assurance processes. Verification includes: review of CM processes; verifying to ascertain that the system has achieved specified requirements and the design of the system is accurately and completely documented in configuration information; verify physical, functional, and interface requirements defined in the approved product definition information, are achieved by the product; verify approved changes to its configuration. Auditing supports the verification process by validating traceability and status between the product to its design, product design to its requirements, and the implementation of changes. Auditing at events like a functional configuration audit (FCA) or a physical configuration audit (PCA), is often accomplished at the end of the development effort and/or testing.

- 在整个生命周期的适当点建立和确定基线。基线可能与项目里程碑或决策门重合，如图 2.4 所示。

- 管理接口及其施加的约束。

• *执行构型配置更改管理。*

- 在整个系统生命周期内管理变更和差异（即不符合项），以确保产品/系统的完整性。

- 这包括识别、记录、评审（包括影响分析）、批准/不批准、跟踪、处理、实施和关闭变更/差异请求，包括相关支持文件，无论其来源如何。

- 变更/差异的处理通常由变更委员会执行（各行业中使用的名称，如构型配置控制委员会 [CCB]、构型配置评审委员会 [CRB] 等）。

- 变更/差异流程的一个重要实践是跟踪和管理实施活动，并实现闭环，确保产品及其相关信息已演进为当前批准的构型配置。

• *执行构型配置状态核算。*

- 同相关利益相关方沟通和维护受控事件、项目和数据的状态，以及产品/系统生命周期内构型配置管理流程的绩效。

- 通过项目评估和控制流程确定衡量性能的措施和方法，构型配置状态核算支持这些指标和性能评估（例如，将设计数据与竣工数据进行核对）。

• *执行构型配置验证和审核。*

- 结合验证和质量保证流程，对构型配置管理流程进行验证。验证包括：评审构型配置管理流程；验证以确定系统已达到规定的要求，并且系统的设计被准确地、完整地记录在构型配置信息中；验证已批准的产品定义信息中定义的物理、功能和接口要求是否已由产品实现；验证已批准的构型配置更改。审核通过验证产品与其设计、产品设计与其需求以及变更实施之间的可追溯性和状态来支持验证流程。功能构型配置审核（FCA）或物理构型配置审核（PCA）等活动中的审核通常在开发工作和/或测试结束时完成。

SYSTEM LIFE CYCLE CONCEPTS, MODELS, AND PROCESSES

–Furthermore, the acquirer may have the requirement or wish to perform surveillance and, where necessary, audits to ensure the correct application of CM processes in their supply chain.

Common approaches and tips:

- Begin the Configuration Management process at the beginning of the system life cycle and continue through until retirement of the system. Tailoring of the configuration management approach is key for its successful applications across various domains; this includes an appropriate understanding of the information and processes that need to be in place to fulfill all CM requirements.

Elaboration

Additional guidance regarding configuration management can be found in the current versions of SAE-EIA 649C, ISO 10007, and IEEE 828. Application domain-specific practices, such as SAE ARP 4754A, GEIA HB 649, MIL HDBK 61 B, NIST 800–53, NIST 800–128 provide additional application details.

Configuration management must account for horizontal and vertical integration (see Section 2.3.5.8), in addition to other factors that can affect the system definition over time. Change is a fundamental characteristic of every large-scale system during its life cycle; baselines are set, design fidelity and completeness are improved, and problems are resolved as analyses are performed, impacts are assessed, and trade studies result in decisions that change the system definition. This constancy of change as the design matures makes it imperative to understand the impact of change across all interacting elements and to ensure the complete incorporation of change decisions. Consequently, configuration management, including change management, coordinates maturation of the system.

In Model-Based Systems Engineering (MBSE), CM is required to assure and ensure that the product/system and its product configuration information (i.e., the configuration) are appropriately captured, organized, managed, and communicated for the benefit of the model's stakeholders and participants (see Section 4.2.1).

The corresponding testing and deployment provisions need to be considered in terms of checks against validation rules, interface compatibility, flow time alignment, technical performance measure evaluation, physical clashing, and other domain-specific characteristics.

- 此外，采办方可能有要求或希望进行监督，并在必要时进行审核，以确保在其供应链中正确应用构型配置管理流程。

常用方法和提示：

- 在系统生命周期开始时就启动构型配置管理流程，并一直持续到系统退役。构型配置管理方法的定制是其跨多个领域成功应用的关键；这包括适当理解满足所有构型配置管理需求所需的信息和流程。

详细阐述

SAE-EIA 649C、ISO 10007 和 IEEE 828 的当前版本中提供了有关构型配置管理的其他指南。应用领域特定实践，如 SAE ARP 4754A、GEIA HB 649、MIL HDBK 61 B、NIST 800–53、NIST 800–128 提供了其他应用细节。

构型配置管理必须考虑横向和纵向综合（见 2.3.5.8 节），以及随时间推移可能影响系统定义的其他因素。变化是每个大型系统在其生命周期中的基本特征；设定基线，提高设计逼真度和完整性，并在进行分析、评估影响和权衡研究时解决问题，从而做出改变系统定义的决策。随着设计的成熟，这种变化的持续性使我们有必要了解变化对所有相互作用的元素的影响，并确保将变化决策完全纳入其中。因此，构型配置管理（包括变更管理）可以协调系统的成熟。

在基于模型的系统工程（MBSE）中，构型配置管理需要保证并确保产品 / 系统及其产品构型配置信息（即构型配置）被适当捕获、组织、管理和沟通，从而使模型的利益相关方和参与者受益（见 4.2.1 节）。

相应的测试和部署规定需要根据验证规则、接口兼容性、流程时间对准、技术性能评估、物理冲突和其他特定领域的特点进行检查。

SYSTEM LIFE CYCLE CONCEPTS, MODELS, AND PROCESSES

Moreover, although cyber security is traditionally thought of as a software engineering problem, it needs to be taken into account in a wider system's engineering thought process. Hardware components on which the software is deployed as well as system interfaces can be just as susceptible to cyber-attacks as software itself. That is why proper configuration management needs to also include continuous auditing of potential cyber vulnerabilities. CM processes that originated in agile software engineering (SWE), are now widely used in other Engineering disciplines, including MBSE where the most challenging aspect is the constant need to maintain the relationships between the appropriate configurations of each domain while ensuring accountability and consistency. Several well-established CM practices

in agile SWE help with addressing those pain points:

- revisions are managed as a stream of commits;
- baselines are established by tagging specific commits;
- concurrent changes are managed through branching and merging;
- testing, evaluation and/or deployment are automated through a Continuous Integration and Continuous Delivery (CI/CD) process;
- security is ensured through the DevSecOps life cycle by integrating security tools into DevOps (see Figure 2.8).

The digital thread establishes communication paths between the individually configured domains. It is also responsible for correctly tying together the appropriate configurations in each domain and to form a consistent configuration for a specific system/product and their elements. More details on traceability can be found in Section 3.2.3.

2.3.4.6 Information Management Process

Overview

Purpose As stated in ISO/IEC/IEEE 15288,

[6.3.6.1] The purpose of the Information Management process is to generate, obtain, confirm, transform, retain, retrieve, disseminate, and dispose of information to designated stakeholders.

Information management plans, executes, and controls the provision of information to designated stakeholders that is unambiguous, complete, verifiable, consistent, traceable, and presentable. Information includes technical, project, organizational, integration, contractual, agreement, and user information. Information is often derived from data artifacts of the organization, system, process, or project.

此外，尽管网络安全传统上被认为是一个软件工程问题，但它需要在更广泛的系统工程思维流程中加以考虑。部署软件的硬件组件以及系统接口可能与软件本身一样容易受到网络攻击。这就是为什么适当的构型配置管理还需要包括对潜在网络漏洞的持续审核。起源于敏捷软件工程（SWE）的构型配置管理流程现在广泛应用于其他工程学科，包括 MBSE，其中最具挑战性的方面是需要不断维护每个领域的适当构型配置之间的关系，同时确保职责和一致性。敏捷 SWE 中一些成熟的构型配置管理实践有助于解决这些痛点：

- 修订被作为一系列承诺进行管理；
- 通过标记特定的承诺来建立基线；
- 通过分支和合并管理并行变更；
- 测试、评估和/或部署通过持续综合/持续交付（CI/CD）流程实现自动化；
- 通过将安全工具综合到 DevSecOps 中，确保整个 DevSecOps 生命周期的安全性（见图 2.8）。

数字线索在单独的构型配置域之间建立通信路径。它还负责将每个域中的适当构型配置正确地结合在一起，并为特定系统/产品及其元素形成一致的构型配置。有关可追溯性的更多详细信息，请参见 3.2.3 节。

2.3.4.6 信息管理流程

概述

目的　如 ISO/IEC/IEEE 15288 所述：

[6.3.6.1] 信息管理流程的目的是生成、获取、确认、转换、保留、检索、沟通和处置指定利益相关方的信息。

信息管理计划、执行和控制向指定利益相关方提供的信息，这些信息是明确、完整、可验证、一致、可跟踪和可呈现的。信息包括技术的、项目、组织的、综合的、合同、协议和用户信息。信息通常来自组织、系统、流程或项目的数据制品。

SYSTEM LIFE CYCLE CONCEPTS, MODELS, AND PROCESSES

Information management needs to provide relevant, timely, complete, valid, and, if required, protected information to designated parties during and, as appropriate, after the product/system life cycle. It manages all defined information, including technical, project, organizational, integration, contractual, agreement, and user information.

Information management ensures that data is properly defined, stored, structured, maintained, secured, exchanged and accessible to those who need it, thereby establishing/maintaining integrity of relevant system life cycle artifacts.

Description Information exists in many forms, and different types of information have different values within an organization. Information assets, whether tangible or intangible, have become so widespread in contemporary organizations that they are indispensable. Information Security has become a fundamental requirement for every industry to work within digital environments with confidence. The following are important terms in information management:

- Information is what an organization has compiled or its employees know. It can be stored and communicated, and it may include classified or unclassified, export restrictive, proprietary, and/or protected (e.g., by copyright, trademark, or patent) and unprotected (e.g., business intelligence) intellectual property. Specific domain classification may apply as well (e.g., further classifications, like Controlled Unclassified Information (CUI) protections in the US defense domain).

- Information assets are intangible information and any tangible form of its representation, including drawings, models of all flavors (systems, software, design, simulation, manufacturing, etc.), specifications, memos, email, computer files, and databases.

- Information security generally refers to the protection, confidentiality, integrity, and availability of the information assets (ISO 17799, 2005).

- Information security management includes the controls used to achieve information security and is accomplished by implementing a suitable set of formalized controls, which could be policies, practices, procedures, organizational structures, and software.

- Information Security Management System is the life cycle approach to implementing, maintaining, and improving the interrelated set of policies, controls, and procedures that ensure the security of an organization's information assets in a manner appropriate for its strategic objectives.

信息管理需要在产品/系统生命周期期间和之后（视情况而定），向指定方提供相关、及时、完整、有效且受保护的信息。它管理所有定义的信息，包括技术、项目、组织、综合、合同、协议和用户信息。

信息管理确保数据得到正确定义、存储、结构化、维护、保护、交换并可供需要的人访问，从而建立/维护相关系统生命周期制品的完整性。

描述 信息以多种形式存在，不同类型的信息在组织中具有不同的价值。信息资产，无论是有形的还是无形的，在当代组织中已经变得如此广泛，以至于它们是不可或缺的。信息安全已成为每个行业在数字环境中自信工作的基本要求。以下是信息管理中的重要术语：

- 信息是一个组织编制的或其员工知道的信息。它可以存储和沟通，可能包括机密或非机密、出口限制、专有和/或受保护（例如版权、商标或专利）和未受保护（例如商业智能）的知识产权。具体的领域分类也可能适用［例如，进一步的分类，如美国国防领域中的受控非保密信息（CUI）保护］。

- 信息资产是无形信息及其任何有形表现形式，包括图纸、各种样式的模型（系统、软件、设计、仿真、制造等）、规范、备忘录、电子邮件、计算机文件和数据库。

- 信息安全通常指信息资产的保护、机密性、完整性和可用性（ISO 17799, 2005）。

- 信息安全管理包括用于实现信息安全的控制，通过实施一系列适当的正式控制来实现，这些控制可以是政策、实践、程序、组织结构和软件。

- 信息安全管理系统是一种生命周期方法，用于实施、维护和改进一套相互关联的政策、控制和程序，以确保组织的信息资产安全，并使其适合组织的战略目标。

SYSTEM LIFE CYCLE CONCEPTS, MODELS, AND PROCESSES

Information management must be associated very closely with configuration management to ensure the integrity, initial release and change control of the information and data. Information management provides the basis for the management of and access to information throughout the system life cycle from ideation through disposal. Designated information may include organizational, project, integration, contractual, agreement, technical, and user information. The mechanisms for maintaining historical knowledge in the prior processes—decision making, risk, and configuration management—are under the responsibility of configuration management working in concert with information management. Figure 2.32 is the IPO diagram for the Information Management process.

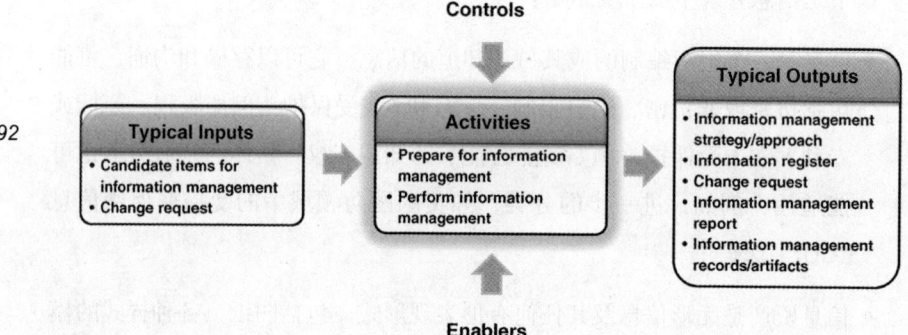

FIGURE 2.32 IPO diagram for Information Management process. INCOSE SEH original figure created by Shortell, Walden, and Yip. Usage per the INCOSE Notices page. All other rights reserved.

Knowledge management is also closely linked to information management. One of the motivations for putting knowledge management in place is for "Information sharing across the organization" thus information management is key for knowledge management. Whereas "Share knowledge and skills throughout the organization" as one of the process-activities for knowledge management draws an identifiable relationship between the information management and Knowledge Management processes via the feedback loop created with inputs and outputs between the processes if mapped out.

Inputs/Outputs Inputs and outputs for the Information Management process are listed in Figure 2.32. Descriptions of each input and output are provided in Appendix E.

系统生命周期概念、模型和流程

信息管理必须与构型配置管理密切相关，以确保信息和数据的完整性、首次发布和更改控制。信息管理为从构思到处置的整个系统生命周期中的信息管理和访问提供了基础。指定的信息可能包括组织、项目、综合、合同、协议、技术和用户信息。在先前流程决策、风险和构型配置管理中维护历史知识的机制由构型配置管理负责，与信息管理协同工作。图 2.32 是信息管理流程的 IPO 图。

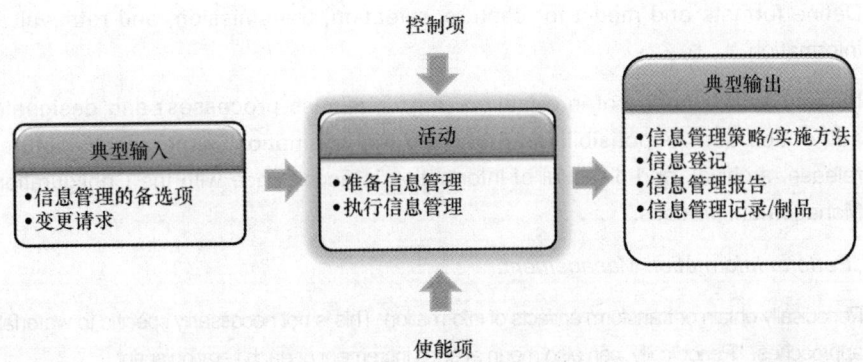

图 2.32 信息管理流程的 IPO 图。INCOSE SEH 原始图由 Walden、Shortell 和 Yip 创建。按照 INCOSE 通知页使用。版权所有。

知识管理也与信息管理密切相关。实施知识管理的动机之一是"整个组织的信息共享"，因此信息管理是知识管理的关键。而"在整个组织内共享知识和技能"作为知识管理的流程活动之一，通过流程之间的输入和输出所形成的反馈回路，在信息管理和知识管理流程之间建立了可识别的关系。

输入/输出 信息管理流程的输入和输出如图 2.32 所示。附录 E 中提供了每个输入和输出的描述。

SYSTEM LIFE CYCLE CONCEPTS, MODELS, AND PROCESSES

Process Activities   The Information Management process includes the following activities:

- *Prepare for Information Management.*

–Support establishing and maintaining a system data dictionary—see project planning outputs.

–Define system-relevant information, revisioning scheme, storage requirements, access privileges, and the duration of maintenance.

–Define formats and media for capture, retention, transmission, and retrieval of information.

–Identify valid sources of information (e.g., business processes) and designate authorities and responsibilities regarding the origination, generation, capture, release, archival, and disposal of information in accordance with the Configuration Management process.

- *Perform Information Management.*

–Periodically obtain or transform artifacts of information. This is not necessarily specific to waterfall approaches. "Periodically" can also mean at each increment or each iteration/sprint.

–Maintain information according to integrity, security, and privacy requirements.

–Retrieve and distribute information in an appropriate form to designated parties, as required by agreed schedules, definitions, or defined circumstances.

–Archive designated information for compliance with legal, audit, knowledge retention, and project closure requirements.

–Dispose of unwanted, invalid, or unverifiable information according to organizational policy, security, privacy, and legal requirements applicable to the data.

Common approaches and tips:

- Identify information-rich artifacts and store them for later use even if the information is informal, such as a design engineer's notebook (in any media or format).

- Identify the information set at the start of a project if you are going to follow a digital engineering approach.

- In the Project Planning process (see Section 2.3.4.1), an information management plan is tailored to satisfy the individual project procedures for information management. An information management plan identifies the systemrelevant information to be collected, retained, controlled, secured, and disseminated, with a schedule for disposal.

流程活动 信息管理流程包括以下活动：

- *准备信息管理。*

- 支持建立和维护系统数据字典，参见项目计划输出。

- 定义系统相关信息、修订方案、存储要求、访问权限和维护期限。

- 定义用于捕获、保留、传输和检索信息的格式和媒介。

- 根据构型配置管理流程，识别有效的信息源（如业务流程），并指定有关信息的来源、生成、捕获、发布、存档和处置的权限和职责。

- *执行信息管理。*

- 定期获取或转换信息制品。这并不一定特定是瀑布式方法。"周期性"也可以指每次增量或每次迭代/冲刺。

- 根据完整性、安全性和隐私要求维护信息。

- 按照约定的时间、定义或规定的情况，以适当的形式检索信息并将其分发给指定方。

- 归档指定信息，以符合法律、审核、知识保留和项目关闭要求。

- 根据适用于数据的组织政策、安全、隐私和法律要求，处置不需要的、无效的或无法验证的信息。

常用方法和提示：

- 识别信息丰富的制品，并将其存储起来以备日后使用，即使这些信息是非正式的，例如设计工程师的笔记本（任何媒介或格式）。

- 如果您打算采用数字工程方法，请在项目开始时确定信息集。

- 在项目计划流程中（见 2.3.4.1 节），信息管理计划是为满足信息管理的各个项目程序而定制的。信息管理计划确定了要收集、保留、控制、保护和沟通的系统相关信息，并制订了处置计划。

SYSTEM LIFE CYCLE CONCEPTS, MODELS, AND PROCESSES

Elaboration

The initial planning efforts for information management are defined in the information management plan (and should align with the Configuration Management Plan), which establishes the scope of information that is maintained; identifies the resources and personnel skill level required against the defined tasks to be performed; defines the rights, obligations, and commitments of parties for generation, management, and access; and identifies information management tools and processes, as well as methodologies, standards, and procedures that will be used on the project and managed by appropriate configuration management.

Effective information management provides readily accessible information and management means to authorized project and organization personnel. Database management, security, and revision of data, sharing data across multiple platforms and organizations are facilitated by information management. With all emphasis on knowledge management, organizational learning, and information as competitive advantage, these activities are gaining increased attention.

2.3.4.7 Measurement Process

Overview

Purpose As stated in ISO/IEC/IEEE 15288 (and ISO/IEC/IEEE 15939),

[6.3.7.1] The purpose of the Measurement process is to collect, analyze, and report objective data and information to support effective management and address information needs about the products, services, and processes.

Description The Measurement process defines the types of information needed to support project and technical management decisions and implement actions to manage and improve performance. The key SE measurement objective is to assess the SE processes and work products with respect to project and organization needs, including timeliness, meeting performance requirements and quality characteristics, product conformance to standards, effective use of resources, and continuous process improvement in reducing cost and cycle time.

The *Practical Software and Systems Measurement (PSM) Guide* (2003), Section 1.1, states:

Measurement provides objective information to help the project manager.

Specific measures are based on information needs and how that information will be used to make decisions and take action. Measurement thus exists as part of an integrated set of management processes and includes not just the project manager, but also SE practitioners, analysts, quality management/assurance, and nearly all other technical and management functions/roles. The decisions to be made drive the information needs and the information needs drive the data to be collected, analyzed, and reported. As a result, numerous benefits are realized from effective measurement (see Table 2.5).

详细阐述

信息管理计划中定义了信息管理的初始计划工作（并应与构型配置管理计划保持一致），该计划确定了所维护的信息范围；确定要执行的既定任务所需的资源和人员技能水平；定义各方在产生、管理和访问方面的权利、义务和承诺；并确定信息管理工具和流程，以及将在项目中使用并由适当的构型配置管理人员管理的方法、标准和程序。

有效的信息管理为授权的项目和组织人员提供易于访问的信息和管理手段。信息管理促进了数据库管理、安全和数据修订，以及跨多个平台和组织共享数据。随着对知识管理、组织学习和信息作为竞争优势的重视，这些活动越来越受到重视。

2.3.4.7 测量流程

概述

目的　如 ISO/IEC/IEEE 15288（和 ISO/IEC/IEEE 15939）所述：

[6.3.7.1] 测量流程的目的是收集、分析和报告客观数据和信息，以支持有效管理并满足有关产品、服务和流程的信息需求。

描述　测量流程定义了支持项目和技术管理决策以及实施管理和改进绩效的行动所需的信息类型。关键系统工程测量目标是评估系统工程流程和工作产品与项目和组织需求的关系，包括及时性、满足性能要求和质量特性、产品符合标准、有效使用资源以及持续改进流程以降低成本和周期。

《实用软件和系统测量（PSM）指南》（2003）第 1.1 节规定：

测量提供客观信息，以帮助项目经理。

具体测量基于信息需求以及如何使用这些信息做出决策和采取行动。因此，测量是一套综合的管理流程的一部分，不仅包括项目经理，还包括系统工程实践者、分析人员、质量管理/保证，以及几乎所有其他技术和管理职能/角色。要做出的决策驱动着信息需求，而信息需求驱动着收集、分析和报告数据。因此，有效的测量带来了许多好处（见表2.5）。

SYSTEM LIFE CYCLE CONCEPTS, MODELS, AND PROCESSES

TABLE 2.5 Measurement benefits

Benefit to Project Manager/Technical Lead
Communicate effectively throughout the project organization
Identify and correct problems early
Support making key trade-offs
Track specific project objectives
Defend and justify decisions
Enable continuous process improvement

From PSM (2003). Used with permission. All other rights reserved.

Successful measurement communicates meaningful information to the decision makers. The presentation of the information must be relevant and unambiguous to those using it, ensuring the intended interpretation.

Inputs/Outputs Typical inputs and outputs for the Measurement process are listed in Figure 2.33. Descriptions of each input and output are provided in Appendix E.

Process Activities The Measurement process includes the following activities:

- Prepare for measurement.

–Identify the measurement stakeholders and their measurement information needs and develop a strategy to meet them.

–Identify and select relevant prioritized measures that aid with the management and technical performance of the project.

–Define the base measures, derived measures, indicators, data collection, measurement frequency, measurement repository, reporting method and frequency, trigger points or thresholds, and review authority.

- *Perform measurement.*

–Gather, process, store, verify, and analyze the data to obtain measurement results (information products).

–Record and review the measurement information products with the measurement stakeholders and recommend action, as warranted by the results.

Common approaches and tips:

- Measurement for measurement sake is a waste of time and effort. Collecting data without an information need and an intended use is not effective use of limited resources.

表 2.5 测量的益处

对项目经理 / 技术负责人的益处
在整个项目组织中进行有效沟通
及早发现和纠正问题
支持做出关键权衡
跟踪具体的项目目标
为决策辩护并说明理由
使能流程的持续改进

源自 PSM（2003）。经许可后使用。版权所有。

成功的测量将有意义的信息告知决策者。信息的呈现必须与使用信息的人相关且明确，以确保达到预期的解释效果。

输入 / 输出 测量流程的典型输入和输出如图 2.33 所示。附录 E 中提供了每个输入和输出的描述。

流程活动 测量流程包括以下活动：

- 准备测量。

- 确定测量利益相关方及其测量信息需求，并制定满足这些需求的战略。

- 确定并选择有助于项目管理和技术绩效的相关优先措施。

- 定义基本测量、派生测量、指标、数据收集、测量频率、测量存储库、报告方法和频率、触发点或阈值以及评审权限。

- 实施测量。

- 收集、处理、存储、验证和分析数据，以获得测量结果（信息产品）。

- 与测量利益相关方一起记录和评审测量信息产品，并根据结果提出行动建议。

常用方法和提示：

- 为了测量而测量是浪费时间和精力。在没有信息需求和预期用途的情况下收集数据并不能有效使用有限的资源。

SYSTEM LIFE CYCLE CONCEPTS, MODELS, AND PROCESSES

- Each measure should be regularly reviewed by the measurement stakeholders. The frequency of review is determined by a number of factors, including frequency of data availability/change, level of risk, maturity of the organization, and cycle times.

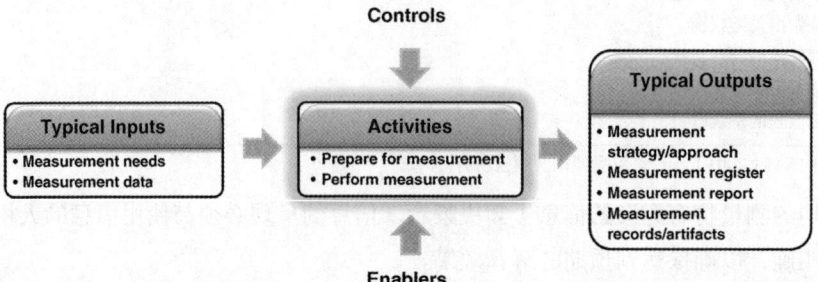

FIGURE 2.33   IPO diagram for Measurement process. INCOSE SEH original figure created by Shortell, Walden, and Yip. Usage per the INCOSE Notices page. All other rights reserved.

- Some agreements identify measures of effectiveness (MOEs) that must be met. The derived measures of performance (MOPs) and Technical Performance Measures (TPMs) that provide the necessary insight into meeting the MOEs are default measures to be included within the measurement plan. Other measures to consider should provide insight into technical and programmatic execution of the project (Roedler and Jones, 2005).

- The best measures are repeatable, can be implemented with automated data collection or require minimal effort for data collection, are straightforward to understand, and are presented in a consistent format on a regular basis (with trend data and, where applicable, projections).

- Many methods are available to present the data to the measurement stakeholders. Line graphs, control charts, and Red/Yellow/Green "traffic lights" are some of the more frequently used. Tools are available to help with measurement.

- If a need for corrective action is perceived, further investigation into the measures may be necessary to identify the root cause of the issue to ensure that corrective actions address the cause instead of a symptom.

- Measurement by itself does not control or improve process performance, project success, or product quality. Measurement results must be provided to decision makers in a manner that provides the needed insight for the right decisions to be made. Action must be taken, to realize any benefit.

- 测量的利益相关方应定期评审每项测量。评审的频率由许多因素决定，包括数据可用性/更改的频率、风险层级、组织的成熟度和周期时间。

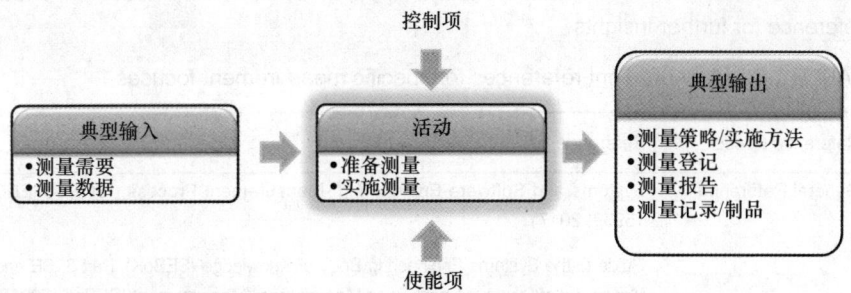

图 2.33　测量流程的 IPO 图。INCOSE SEH 原始图由 Walden、Shortell 和 Yip 创建。按照 INCOSE 通知页使用。版权所有。

- 一些协议确定了必须满足的有效性测量（MOEs）。性能测量（MOPs）和技术性能测度（TPM）为满足有效性测量提供了必要的洞察力，是测量计划中应包含的默认指标。需要考虑的其他测量应能深入了解项目的技术和计划执行情况（Roedler 和 Jones，2005）。

- 最佳测量是可重复的，可以通过自动数据收集来实施，或只需最少的数据收集工作，易于理解，并且定期以一致的格式呈现[包括趋势数据和预测（如适用）]。

- 有许多方法可用于向测量利益相关方提供数据。线形图、控制图和红/黄/绿"交通灯"是比较常用的方法。可以使用工具来帮助测量。

- 如果认为有必要采取纠正措施，可能有必要对测量进行进一步调查，以确定问题的根本原因，确保纠正措施针对的是问题的原因而不是症状。

- 测量本身不能控制或改善流程绩效、项目成功或产品质量。测量结果必须以提供正确决策所需洞察力的方式提供给决策者。必须采取行动，才能实现任何益处。

SYSTEM LIFE CYCLE CONCEPTS, MODELS, AND PROCESSES

Elaboration

Measurement Concepts. Measurement concepts have been expanded upon in the previous works shown in Table 2.6 that the SE measurement practitioner should reference for further insights.

TABLE 2.6 Measurement references for specific measurement focuses

Reference Focus	Reference
General Reference	Systems and Software Engineering -Measurement Process (ISO/IEC/IEEE 15939, 2017)
	Guide to the Systems Engineering Body of Knowledge (SEBoK), Part 3: SE and Management/Systems Engineering Management/Measurement (SEBoK, 2023)
	Practical Software and Systems Measurement (PSM) Guide V4.0c, (PSM, 2003)
	Capability Maturity Model Integration (CMMI®) for Development V2.0, Measurement and Quantitative Management Process Areas (CMMI, 2018)
Guidance for New Practitioners	INCOSE Systems Engineering Measurement Primer, Version 2.0 (INCOSE Measurement Primer, 2010)
Technical Measurement /Performance	Technical Measurement Guide (Roedler and Jones, 2005)
System Development	System Development Performance Measurement Report (NDIA, et al., 2011)
Project Management	Project Manager's Guide to Systems Engineering Measurement for Project Success (INCOSE PMGtSEMfPS, 2015)
Continuous Iterative Development	Continuous Iterative Development Measurement Framework (PSM, et al., 2021)
Digital Engineering	Practical Software and Systems Measurement (PSM) Digital Engineering Measurement Framework (INCOSE, et al., 2022)
Leading Indicators	Systems Engineering Leading Indicators Guide, Version 2.0 (Roedler, et al., 2010)

General Reference Systems and Software Engineering -Measurement Process (ISO/IEC/IEEE 15939, 2017)

Measurement Approach. As discussed in the INCOSE Measurement Primer (2010), measurement may be thought of as a feedback control system. Value is obtained from measurement when the data analysis provides insight for assessment or action by decision makers (e.g., action is taken due to a variance from a target value or the need to improve current performance to a more desirable level). Comparing the target value and the allowable difference between the target and actual values enables decisions based upon evaluation of risk to the project or product performance meeting their required goals.

详细阐述

测量概念。在表 2.6 所示的先前工作中，已对测量概念进行了扩展，系统工程测量实践者应参考这些概念以获得进一步的见解。

表 2.6 特定测量关注点的测量参考

参考的关注点	参考
一般性参考	系统和软件工程—测量流程（ISO/IEC/IEEE 15939, 2017） 系统工程知识体指南（SEBoK），第 3 部分：系统工程和管理 / 系统工程管理 / 测量（SEBoK, 2023） 实用软件和系统测量（PSM）指南 V4.0c，（PSM，2003） 研发能力成熟度模型综合（CMMI®）V2.0，测量和量化管理流程领域（CMMI，2018）
新实践者指南	NCOSE 系统工程测量入门，2.0 版（INCOSE 测量入门，2010）
技术测量 / 性能	技术测量指南（Roedler 和 Jones，2005）
系统开发	系统开发绩效测量报告（NDIA 等，2011）
项目管理	项目经理的项目成功系统工程测量指南（INCOSE PMGtSEMfPS，2015）
持续迭代开发	持续迭代开发测量框架（PSM 等，2021）
数字工程	实用软件和系统测量（PSM）数字工程测量框架（INCOSE 等，2022）
领先指标	系统工程领先指标指南，2.0 版（Roedler 等，2010）

INCOSE SEH 原始图由 Roedler 创建。按照 INCOSE 通知页使用。版权所有。

测量方法。如《INCOSE 测量入门指南》（2010）所述，测量可被视为反馈控制系统。当数据分析为决策者的评估或行动提供洞察时（例如，由于偏离目标值或需要将当前绩效提高到更理想的水平而采取的行动），则从测量中获得价值。通过比较目标值和目标值与实际值之间的允许差异，可以根据对项目或产品性能的风险评估做出决策，以达到其要求的目标。

Relationship of Measurement to Risk Management and Decision Management. The measures for a project are driven by the information needs of the project and its decision makers. One source of the information needs are the objectives of the project, which can be related to resources, technical performance of the system, product or process quality, or other aspects of the project that are considered essential. Another key source of information needs are the key risks of the project. As shown in Figure 2.34, the Risk Management process identifies risks that need to be monitored, thus creating information needs that drive new measures. The Measurement process helps characterize and quantify the risks. In turn, the results of the measurement analysis may uncover new risks that need to be considered by the Risk Management process. The results of both risk management and measurement provide essential insight to decision makers that is essential to the Decision Management process. Measurement also provides insight to all other processes, especially Project Planning, Project Assessment and Control, Quality Assurance, Life Cycle Model Management, and the Technical Processes.

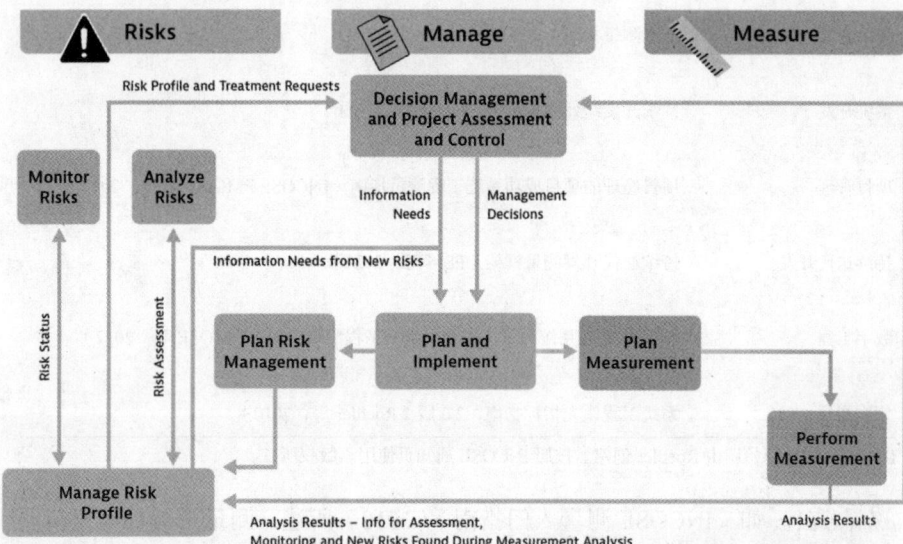

FIGURE 2.34 Integration of Measurement, Risk Management, and Decision Management processes. INCOSE SEH original figure created by Roedler. Usage per the INCOSE Notices page. All other rights reserved.

系统生命周期概念、模型和流程

测量与风险管理和决策管理的关系。项目的措施是由项目及其决策者的信息需求驱动的。信息需求的一个来源是项目的目标，它可能与资源、系统的技术性能、产品或流程质量或项目的其他方面有关，这些方面被认为是必不可少的。信息需求的另一个关键来源是项目的关键风险。如图 2.34 所示，风险管理流程确定了需要监控的风险，从而产生了推动新措施的信息需求。测量流程有助于描述和量化风险。反过来，测量分析的结果可能会发现风险管理流程需要考虑的新风险。风险管理和衡量的结果为决策者提供了对决策管理流程至关重要的重要见解。测量还提供了对所有其他流程的深入了解，尤其是项目计划、项目评估和控制、质量保证、生命周期模型管理和技术流程。

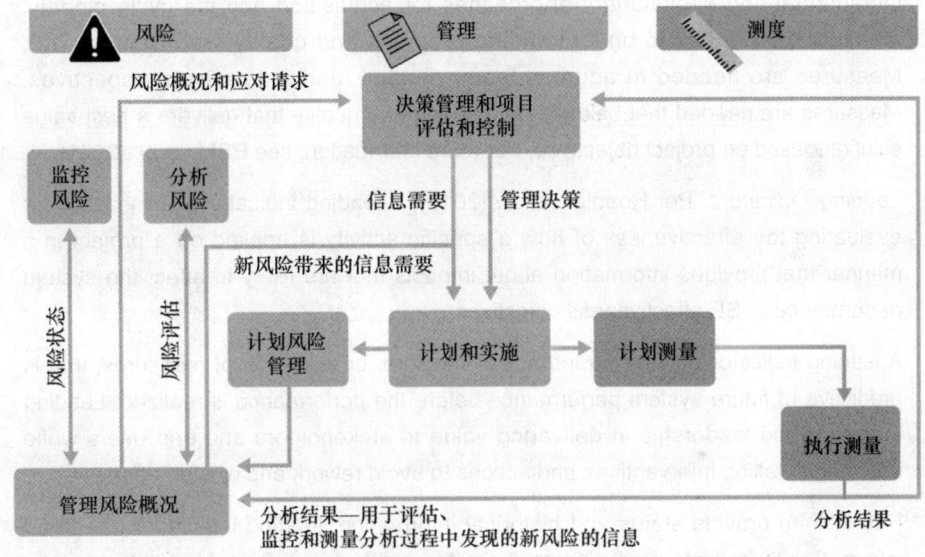

图 2.34　测量、风险管理和决策管理流程的综合。INCOSE SEH 原始图由 Roedler 创建。按照 INCOSE 通知页使用。版权所有。

Digital Engineering (DE) Measurement. DE has three interrelated concerns: the transformation of engineering activities to a fully digital infrastructure, artifacts, and processes; the use of authoritative sources of truth (ASOTs) to improve the efficiency and productivity of engineering practice; and the use of MBSE practice to fully integrate system data and models with engineering, project management, and other domains and disciplines. Measurement in DE focuses on the implementation of DE transformations on projects and in enterprises, including the realization of measurable benefits in performance, effectiveness, and product quality relative to traditional engineering methods. DE measures can also serve as useful leading indicators for other product related measures. For more information, see INCOSE, et al. (2022) and Section 5.4.

Continuous Iterative Development. As organizations and projects move toward incremental and evolutionary approaches for acquisition and life cycle models, measurement is key to understanding progress and quality (see Section 2.2). Measures are needed to address team, product, and enterprise perspectives. Measures are needed that balance both speed and quality that delivers a best value solution based on project objectives. For more information, see PSM, et al. (2021).

Leading Indicators. Per Roedler, et al. (2010), a leading indicator is a measure for evaluating the effectiveness of how a specific activity is applied on a project in a manner that provides information about impacts that are likely to affect the system performance or SE effectiveness objectives.

A leading indicator may be an individual measure, or collection of measures, that is predictive of future system performance before the performance is realized. Leading indicators aid leadership in delivering value to stakeholders and end users while assisting in taking interventions and actions to avoid rework and wasted effort.

Rather than provide status and historical information, leading indicators use trend information to facilitate predictive analysis (forward looking). By analyzing the trends, quantitative relationships of key factors can be developed with known correlations and predictions can be forecast on the outcomes of certain activities. Trends are analyzed for insight into both the entity being measured and potential impacts to other entities. This enables proactive decisions and actions (preventive and corrective).

For a more detailed treatment of this topic, including measurement examples, refer to Roedler, et al. (2010). In addition, NDIA, et al. (2011) provides specific leading indicators developed from the previously referenced guide for the defense and aerospace domains. However, most of the indicators have a broader application.

Product-Oriented Measures. As shown in Roedler and Jones (2005), product measures can be thought of as an interdependent hierarchy (see Figure 2.35).

数字工程（DE）测量。数字工程有三个相互关联的问题：将工程活动转换为完全数字化的基础设施、制品和流程；使用权威真相源（ASOT）提高工程实践的效率和生产力；以及使用 MBSE 实践将系统数据和模型与工程、项目管理和其他领域和学科充分综合。数字工程中的测度侧重于在项目和复杂组织体系中实施数字工程转换，包括相对于传统工程方法在性能、有效性和产品质量方面实现可衡量的效益。数字工程测量还可以作为其他产品相关指标的有用的领先指标。有关更多信息，请参见 INCOSE 等（2022）和 5.4 节。

持续迭代开发。随着组织和项目朝着采办和生命周期模型的增量和演进方法发展，测量是理解进度和质量的关键（见 2.2 节）。需要测量来解决团队、产品和复杂组织体系的问题。需要平衡速度和质量的措施，以提供基于项目目标的最佳价值解决方案。有关更多信息，请参见 PSM 等（2021）。

领先指标。根据 Roedler 等（2010），领先指标是一种测度，用于评估特定活动在项目中的应用效果，提供可能影响系统性能或系统工程效果目标的信息。

领先指标可以是单个测量或测量集合，在实现性能之前预测未来系统性能。领先指标有助于领导层向利益相关方和最终用户提供价值，同时协助采取干预措施和行动，避免返工和浪费精力。

领先指标不提供状态和历史信息，而是使用趋势信息促进预测分析（前瞻性）。通过分析趋势，可以使用已知的相关性建立关键因素的定量关系，并可以预测某些活动的结果。对趋势进行分析，以深入了解被测量的实体以及对其他实体的潜在影响。这可以实现主动决策和行动（预防性和纠正性）。

有关此主题的更详细说明，包括测量示例，请参阅 Roedler 等（2010）。此外，NDIA 等（2011）提供了根据先前参考的国防和航空航天领域指南制定的具体领先指标。然而，大多数指标的应用范围更广。

面向产品的测量。如 Roedler 和 Jones（2005）所示，产品测量可以被视为一个相互依赖的层级结构（见图 2.35）。

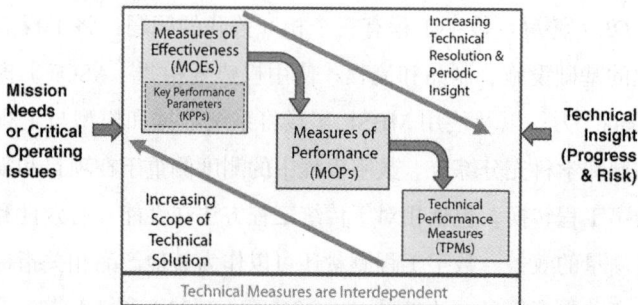

FIGURE 2.35 Relationship of product - oriented measures. From Roedler and Jones (2005). Usage per the INCOSE Notices page. All other rights reserved.

Measures of Effectiveness (MOEs), which are stated from the acquirer (customer/user) viewpoint, are the acquirer's key indicators of achieving the mission needs for performance, suitability, and affordability across the life cycle. Although they are independent of any particular solution, MOEs are the overall operational success criteria (mission performance, safety, operability, operational availability, etc.) to be used by the acquirer for the delivered system, services, and/or processes.

Key Performance Parameters (KPPs) are used in some domains to indicate the minimum number of performance parameters needed to characterize the major drivers of operational performance, supportability, and interoperability. Each KPP has a threshold and objective value. The acquirer defines the KPPs at the time the operational concepts and requirements are defined.

Measures of Performance (MOPs) measure attributes considered as important to ensure that the system has the capability to achieve operational objectives. MOPs are used to assess whether the system meets design or performance requirements that are necessary to satisfy the MOEs. MOPs should be derived from or provide insight for MOEs or other user needs.

Technical Performance Measures (TPMs) are used to assess design progress, show compliance to performance requirements, and track technical risks. They provide visibility into the status of important project technical parameters to enable effective management, thus enhancing the likelihood of achieving the technical objectives of the project. TPMs are derived from, or provide insight for, the MOPs and focus on the critical technical parameters of specific architectural elements of the system as it is designed and implemented. Selection of TPMs should be limited to critical technical thresholds or parameters that, if not met, put the project at cost, schedule, or performance risk. The TPMs are not a full listing of the requirements of the system or system element. The SEMP should define the approach to TPMs (Roedler and Jones, 2005).

系统生命周期概念、模型和流程

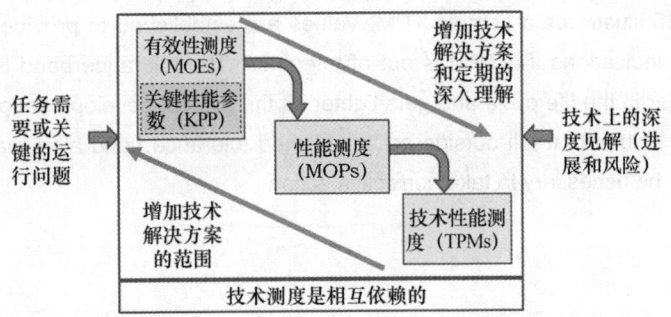

图 2.35　以产品为导向的测度间的关系。源自 Roedler 和 Jones（2005）。按照 INCOSE 通知页使用。版权所有。

有效性测度（MOEs），是从采办方（客户/用户）的角度来看，采办方在整个生命周期内实现绩效、适用性和可承受性等任务需要的关键指标。尽管 MOE 独立于任何特定解决方案，但 MOEs 是采办方用于交付系统、服务和/或流程的总体运行成功准则（任务绩效、安全性、可运行性、运行可用性等）。

关键性能参数（KPP） 在某些领域中，用于表征运行性能、可保障性和互操作性的主要驱动因素所需的最低性能参数数量。每个 KPP 都有一个阈值和目标值。采办方在定义运行概念和要求时定义 KPP。

性能测度（MOPs） 衡量被视为重要的属性，以确保系统有能力实现运行目标。MOPs 用于评估系统是否满足 MOEs 所需的设计或性能要求。MOPs 应来源于或提供 MOEs 或其他用户需求的见解。

技术性能测度（TPMs） 用于评估设计进度、展示性能要求的符合性以及跟踪技术风险。它们提供了重要项目技术参数状态的可见性，以实现有效管理，从而提高了达到项目技术目标的可能性。TPMs 源自 MOPs，或为 MOPs 提供见解，并在设计和实施时关注系统特定架构元素的关键技术参数。TPMs 的选择应限于关键技术阈值或参数，如果不满足这些阈值或参数，将使项目面临成本、进度或绩效风险。TPMs 不是系统或系统元素要求的完整列表。SEMP 应定义技术性能测度的方法（Roedler 和 Jones, 2005）。

SYSTEM LIFE CYCLE CONCEPTS, MODELS, AND PROCESSES

Figure 2.36 illustrates a sample TPM. Values are established to provide limits that give early indications if a TPM is out of tolerance. The tolerance band is generally wider earlier in the life cycle and gets tighter as the system development progresses. Measured values that fall outside an established tolerance band alert management that it may be necessary to take corrective action.

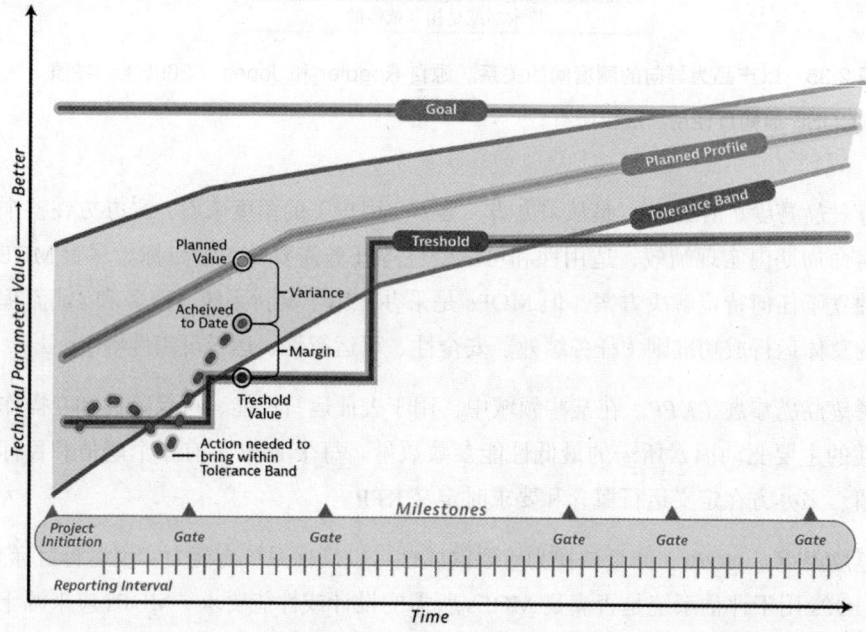

FIGURE 2.36 TPM monitoring. INCOSE SEH original figure created by Roedler and Walden. Usage per the INCOSE Notices page. All other rights reserved.

The progress of some TPMs relies on maturing a particular technology. Thus, it may be necessary to have a technology plan and technology readiness level (TRL) assessment as part of the input associated with a TPM.

2.3.4.8 Quality Assurance Process

Overview

Purpose As stated in ISO/IEC/IEEE 15288,

[6.3.8.1] The purpose of the Quality Assurance process is to help ensure the effective application of the organization's Quality Management process to the project.

图 2.36 展示了 TPM 示例。如果 TPM 超出公差范围，则确定的值可提供早期指示的限值。公差带通常在生命周期的早期更宽，并且随着系统开发的进展而变得更窄。超出既定公差带的测度值提醒管理层可能需要采取纠正措施。

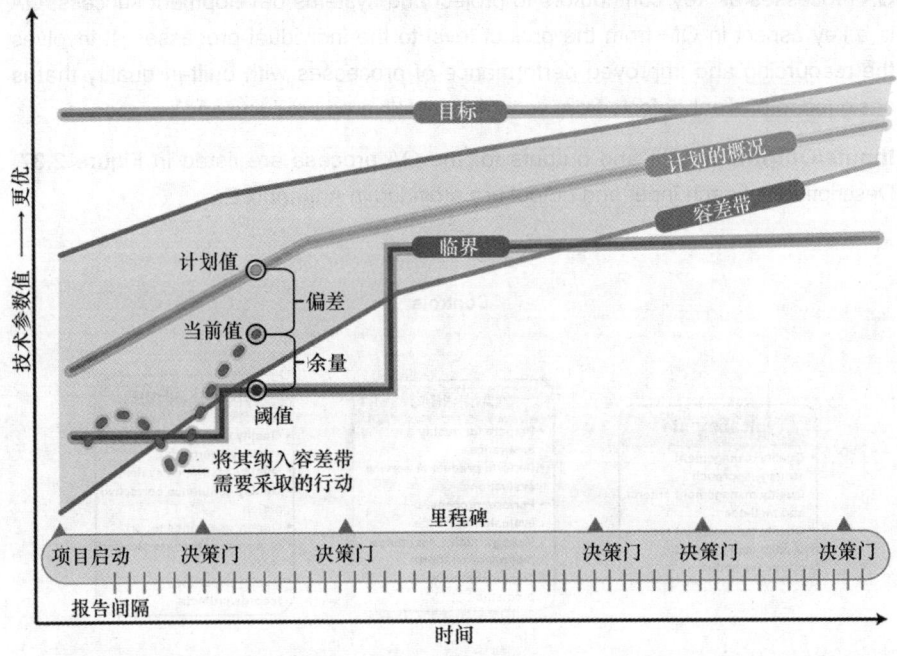

图 2.36 技术性能测度监控。INCOSE SEH 原始图由 Roedler 和 Walden 创建。按照 INCOSE 通知页使用。版权所有。

某些 TPM 的进步依赖于特定技术的成熟。因此，可能有必要将技术计划和技术准备水平（TRL）评估作为 TPM 相关输入的一部分。

2.3.4.8 质量保证流程

概述

目的　如 ISO/IEC/IEEE 15288 所述：

[6.3.8.1] 质量保证流程的目的是帮助确保组织的质量管理流程有效应用于项目。

SYSTEM LIFE CYCLE CONCEPTS, MODELS, AND PROCESSES

Description Quality Assurance (QA) is broadly defined as the set of activities throughout the entire project life cycle necessary to provide adequate confidence that a product or service conforms to stakeholder requirements or that a process adheres to established methodology (ASQ, 2007). SE practitioners adopt and use QA processes as key contributors to project and systems development success. QA is a key aspect in QM from the project level to the individual processes. It involves the resourcing and improved performance of processes with built-in quality that is designed to prevent defects from occurring in delivered products and services.

Inputs/Outputs Inputs and outputs for the QA process are listed in Figure 2.37. Descriptions of each input and output are provided in Appendix E.

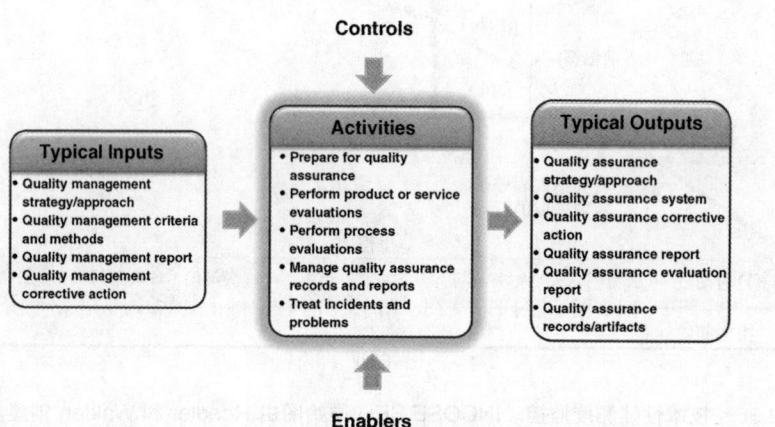

FIGURE 2.37 IPO diagram for the Quality Assurance process. INCOSE SEH original figure created by Shortell, Walden, and Yip. Usage per the INCOSE Notices page. All other rights reserved.

Process Activities The Quality Assurance process includes the following activities:

- *Prepare for quality assurance.*

–Establish and maintain the QA strategy (often captured in a QA plan).

–Establish and maintain QA guidelines, policies, standards, and procedures.

–Define responsibilities and authorities.

- *Perform product or service evaluations.*

系统生命周期概念、模型和流程

描述 质量保证（QA）被广泛定义为在整个项目生命周期内，为产品或服务符合利益相关方要求或流程符合既定方法提供足够信心所必需的一组活动（ASQ，2007）。系统工程实践者采用并使用质量保证流程是项目和系统开发成功的关键因素。从项目层面到各个流程，质量保证是质量管理的一个关键方面，涉及为具有内在质量的流程提供资源并提高其绩效，旨在防止交付的产品和服务中出现缺陷。

输入/输出 质量保证流程的输入和输出如图2.37所示。附录E中提供了每个输入和输出的描述。

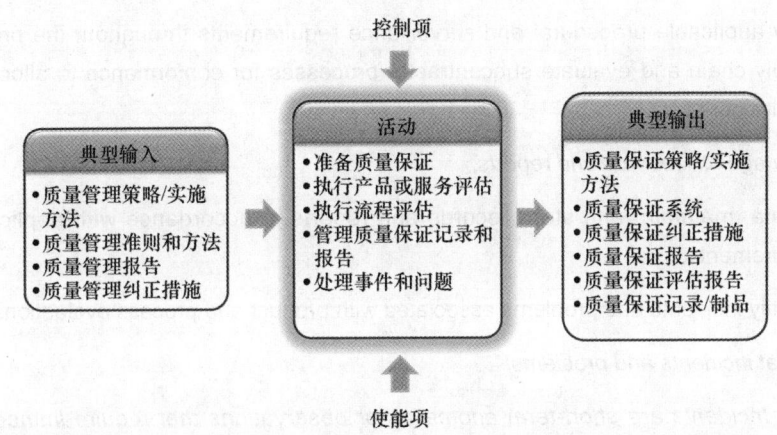

图2.37 质量保证流程的IPO图。INCOSE SEH原始图由Walden、Shortell和Yip创建。按照INCOSE通知页使用。版权所有。

流程活动 质量保证流程包括以下活动：

● *准备质量保证。*

- 建立和维护质量保证策略（通常在质量保证计划中捕获）。

- 建立和维护质量保证指导方针、政策、标准和程序。

- 定义职责和权限。

● *执行产品或服务评估。*

SYSTEM LIFE CYCLE CONCEPTS, MODELS, AND PROCESSES

–Perform the evaluations at appropriate times in the life cycle as defined by the QA plan, ensuring V&V of the outputs of the life cycle processes. Ensure that QA perspectives are appropriately represented during design, development, verification, validation, and production activities.

–Evaluate product verification results as evidence of QA effectiveness.

- *Perform process evaluations.*

–Implement prescribed surveillance on processes to provide an independent evaluation of whether the developing organization is in compliance with established procedures.

–Evaluate enabling tools and environments for conformance and effectiveness.

–Flow applicable procedural and surveillance requirements throughout the project supply chain and evaluate subcontractor processes for conformance to allocated requirements.

- *Manage QA records and reports.*

–Create, maintain, and store records and reports in accordance with applicable requirements.

–Identify incidents and problems associated with product and process evaluations.

- *Treat incidents and problems.*

Note: Incidents are short-term anomalies or observations that require immediate attention, and problems are confirmed nonconformities that would cause the project to fail to meet requirements.

–Document, classify, report, and analyze all anomalies.

–Perform root cause analysis and note trends.

–Recommend appropriate actions to resolve anomalies and errors, when indicated.

–Track all incidents and problems to closure.

Common approaches and tips:

- Management's commitment to QA is reflected in the integration of QM principles in the strategic planning and budgeting of the organization, and the allocation of educational resources to achieve and sustain a reliable QM culture (see Section 2.3.3.5).

系统生命周期概念、模型和流程

- 在质量保证计划规定的生命周期的适当时间进行评估，确保对生命周期流程的输出进行验证和确认。确保质量保证观点在设计、开发、验证、确认和生产活动中得到适当体现。

- 评估产品验证结果，作为质量保证有效性的证据。

• *执行流程评估。*

- 对流程实施规定的监督，以对发展中组织是否符合既定程序进行独立评估。

- 评估实现一致性和有效性的工具和环境。

- 在整个项目供应链中传递适用的程序和监督要求，并评估分包商流程是否符合分配的要求。

• *管理质量保证记录和报告。*

- 根据适用要求创建、维护和存储记录和报告。

- 识别与产品和流程评估相关的事件和问题。

• *处理事件和问题。*

注：事件是需要立即关注的短期异常或观察结果，问题是已确认的不符合项，会导致项目无法满足要求。

- 记录、分类、报告和分析所有异常。

- 进行根因分析并记录趋势。

- 如有指示，建议采取适当措施解决异常和错误。

- 跟踪所有事件和问题直至结束。

常用方法和提示：

- 管理层对质量保证的承诺体现在将质量管理原则纳入组织的战略计划和预算中，以及分配教育资源以实现和维持可靠的质量管理文化（见 2.3.3.5 节）。

- A quality policy, mission, strategies, goals, and objectives provide essential inputs along with a description of an organization's fundamental values for quality assurance and the support of a growing QM culture.

Elaboration

QA Generally accepted theory and practice. QA is one of the two Quality Management (QM) defect prevention methods. The second is Quality Control which is described and contrasted in Section 2.3.3.5. QA can be described as "putting good things into our processes" so that they perform as designed and conform to our stakeholder's requirements. Like QM, QA was born in the aerospace industry and was originally referred to as "reliability engineering." It is generally associated with activities such as failure testing and pre-inspecting batches of materials and system elements that are then certified for use, thus preventing errors and defects from occurring by building-in quality. QA also includes infusing processes with reliable human resources and the appropriate policies, procedures, and training. W. Edwards Deming noted that "Quality comes not from inspection, but from improvement of the production process" (Deming, 1986).

QA Culture. "Ultimately, it is the people in an organization who can create a work culture in which quality is promoted and value is delivered to stakeholders" (Kennedy, 2005). An effective QA methodology defines competent, well-prepared humans as the major asset within processes that are then supported by the appropriate corporate environment, resources, and technologies to improve outcomes. It supports a high-performing work culture that diligently defines and fulfills stakeholder requirements with a Zero Defects Attitude (ZDA) (see Section 2.3.3.5) and is focused on continuous improvement. Philip Crosby noted that "Quality is the result of a carefully crafted cultural environment. It has to be the fabric of the organization, not part of the fabric" (Crosby, 1979).

The fabric of a QA-strengthened work culture is defined by fundamental skills and supporting values that create a sense of ownership by all participants. Workers who identify with an organization's core values have a stronger sense of psychological ownership and higher job satisfaction. At its core, psychological ownership is about an employee's possession and stewardship of an organization's core values and the pride they have about their enterprise/mission (Journal of Organizational Behavior, 2004). The workforce must have skills and experience that are directly related to the output objectives, and when skills are supported by shared values it creates a reliable work culture. (See Section 2.3.3.5.) This strengthening of the work culture leads to greater employee engagement and naturally results in products and services with higher quality, along with other benefits to both the workforce and the corporation (Gallup, 2017, 2020).

- 质量政策、使命、战略、目标和目的提供了重要的输入，以及对组织质量保证基本价值观的描述，还有对不断发展的质量管理文化的支持。

详细阐述

质量保证公认的理论和实践。质量保证是两种质量管理（QM）缺陷预防方法之一。第二种是 2.3.3.5 节中描述和对比的质量控制。质量保证可以被描述为"将好的东西放入我们的流程"，以便它们按照设计执行，并符合利益相关方的要求。与质量管理一样，质量保证诞生于航空航天行业，最初被称为"可靠性工程"。它通常与故障测试和预检查批次材料和系统元素等活动相关，这些材料和系统元素经认证后方可使用，从而通过内建质量来防止错误和缺陷的发生。质量保证还包括为流程注入可靠的人力资源以及适当的政策、程序和培训。W. Edwards Deming 指出，"质量不是来自检验，而是来自生产流程的改进"（Deming，1986）。

质量保证文化。"归根结底，质量保证是组织中的人能够创造的一种工作文化，在这种文化中，质量得到提升，价值传递给利益相关方"（Kennedy，2005）。有效的质量保证方法将有能力、准备充分的人员定义为流程中的主要资产，然后由适当的公司环境、资源和技术支持，以改善结果。它支持高绩效的工作文化，以零缺陷态度（ZDA）（见 2.3.3.5 节）勤勉地定义和满足利益相关方的要求，并专注于持续改进。Philip Crosby 指出，"质量是精心打造的文化环境的结果。它必须是组织的结构，而不是结构的一部分"（Crosby，1979）。

质量保证强化的工作文化的结构由基本技能和支持价值观来定义，这些技能和价值观创造了所有参与者的主人翁意识。认同组织核心价值观的员工具有更强的心理主人翁意识和更高的工作满意度。主人翁意识的核心是员工对组织核心价值观的拥有和管理，以及他们对复杂组织体系/使命的自豪感（Journal of Organizational Behavior，2004）。员工必须具备与产出目标直接相关的技能和经验，当技能得到共享价值观的支持时，它会创造一种可靠的工作文化。（见 2.3.3.5 节）这种工作文化的加强会提高员工的参与度，自然会带来更高质量的产品和服务，以及对员工和公司的其他好处（Gallup，2017，2020）。

SYSTEM LIFE CYCLE CONCEPTS, MODELS, AND PROCESSES

QM is an educational technology with systems, methods and language that help us reach our business goals and QA performs an essential resourcing, educational and process improvement role in ensuring that all elements of an organization execute its activities in accordance with its plans, and procedures as a means of building quality into products or services. While QA is focused on improving processes to prevent errors from occurring, QC provides an essential feedback loop to QA by providing defect rates and identifying their source in processes. By applying Work Process Analysis (WPA) to the defect data, QA can define and initiate input and process improvements to produce lean outcomes.

101 As the complexity of a project increases, the challenges to effectiveness and risk management also increase. These factors further emphasize the need for a coordinated QM culture with the proper balance of QC and QA along with the skills, experience, and values that align with the requirements of the project. Kennedy calls this properly configured alignment "Vocational Certainty," and that a high-performing work culture is measured by identifiable professional and personal attributes or values within an organization's workforce (Kennedy, 2005). Professional values for an effective QA educational initiative must build upon personal vocational certainty, and on administrative consistency that extends our attention to process details beyond the initial documentation of requirements and progress reports. We must continue to interact with and challenge the stakeholders to mature their requirements so that stakeholder satisfaction can be assured.

2.3.5 Technical Processes

The ISO/IEC/IEEE 15288 includes 14 Technical Processes that are invoked concurrently, iteratively, and recursively throughout the system life cycle in conjunction with supporting agreement and technical management process activities. The Technical Processes are defined in ISO/IEC/IEEE 15288 as follows:

[5.7.5] The Technical Processes are used to define the requirements for a system, to transform the requirements into an effective product, to permit consistent reproduction of the product where necessary, to use the product, to provide the required services, to sustain the provision of those services and to dispose of the product when it is retired from service.

质量管理是一种教育技术，其系统、方法和语言有助于我们达到业务目标，质量保证在确保组织的所有元素按照其计划和程序执行其活动方面发挥着重要的资源、教育和流程改进作用，以此作为将质量构建到产品或服务中的手段。虽然质量保证专注于改进流程以防止错误发生，但质量控制通过提供缺陷率并确定其在流程中的来源，为质量保证提供了一个重要的反馈回路。通过对缺陷数据应用工作流程分析（WPA），质量保证可以定义并启动输入和流程改进，以产生精益结果。

随着项目复杂性的增加，对有效性和风险管理的挑战也在增加。这些因素进一步强调了协调质量管理文化的必要性，质量控制和质量保证以及符合项目要求的技能、经验和价值观的适当平衡。Kennedy将这种合理配置的一致性称为"职业确定性"，并认为高绩效的工作文化是通过组织的员工队伍中可识别的专业和个人属性或价值观来衡量的（Kennedy, 2005）。有效质量保证教育计划的专业价值观必须建立在个人职业确定性和管理一致性的基础上，这种一致性将我们的注意力扩展到需求和进度报告的初始文档之外的流程细节。我们必须继续与利益相关方互动并向其提出挑战，使其需求更加成熟，从而确保利益相关方的满意度。

2.3.5 技术流程

ISO/IEC/IEEE 15288 包括 14 个技术流程，这些流程在整个系统生命周期内与支持协议流程和技术管理流程的活动被并行、迭代和递归地调用。ISO/IEC/IEEE 15288 中对技术流程的定义如下：

[5.7.5] 技术流程用于定义系统的需求，将需求转化为有效的产品，允许在必要时一致地复制产品、使用产品、提供所需的服务、维持这些服务的提供，以及在产品退役时处置产品。

SYSTEM LIFE CYCLE CONCEPTS, MODELS, AND PROCESSES

Technical Processes enable SE practitioners to coordinate the interactions between engineering specialists, other engineering disciplines, acquirers, operators, manufacturing/production and other system stakeholders. They also address conformance with the expectations and legislated requirements of society. These processes lead to the creation of a necessary and sufficient set of needs and requirements as well as resulting system solutions that address the needed capabilities within the bounds of performance, environment, external interfaces, ethical norms, societal expectations, regulations, and design constraints. Without the Technical Processes, the risk of project failure would be unacceptably high. Figure 2.38 provides a graphical representation of the Technical Processes in context.

As shown in Figure 2.38, at the beginning of the system life cycle are stakeholder real-world expectations for a SoI. The SoI could be the integrated system, a set of system elements, or a system element within the system architecture.

For each SoI, through a series of transformational actions across the life cycle, the technical processes transform input artifacts into output artifacts that are inputs into other technical processes, which in-turn transform those artifacts into additional artifacts. This series of transformations results in an SoI that addresses the capabilities needed by the stakeholders.

It is important to understand several key points for Figure 2.38.

1. While the figure depicts the series of transformations in a linear fashion, in practice the Technical Processes are intended to be practiced concurrently, iteratively, and recursively as the project team moves down the layers of the system architecture. As such, the figure applies to each system element within the system architecture.

2. The Integration process is applied from the beginning of the project, managing the integrated system as the project team traverses the system architecture. In doing so, the project team is continuously addressing interactions of the parts that make up the integrated system as well as interactions with the macro system of which it is a part. In addition, the project team is assessing the behavior of the system as a function of these interactions and looking for emerging properties—both good and bad—which is a key activity involved in Interface Management (see Section 3.2.4).

3. Following each transformation, the output artifacts are verified against the system requirements via the Verification process to ensure the output artifacts' transformation was "right" as defined by their requirements.

技术流程使系统工程实践者能够协调工程专家、其他工程学科、采办方、运行方、制造／生产和其他系统利益相关方之间的互动。它们还涉及是否符合社会的期望和立法要求。通过这些流程，可以制定出一套必要且充分的需要和需求，以及由此产生的系统解决方案，在性能、环境、外部接口、道德规范、社会期望、法规和设计限制的范围内满足所需的能力。如果没有技术流程，项目失败的风险将高得令人无法接受。图 2.38 提供了背景环境中技术流程的图示。

如图 2.38 所示，在系统生命周期之初是利益相关方对 SoI 的真实期望。SoI 可以是综合的系统、一组系统元素或系统架构内的系统元素。

对于每个 SoI，通过整个生命周期中的一系列转换行动，技术流程将输入制品转换为输出制品，输出制品是其他技术流程的输入，而其他技术流程又将这些制品转换为其他制品。这一系列的转换产生了一个 SoI，它解决了利益相关方所需的能力。

了解图 2.38 的几个关键点很重要。

1. 虽然该图以线性方式描述了一系列转换，但在实践中，随着项目团队沿系统架构的各个层级向下移动，技术流程应并行、迭代和递归地实施。因此，该图适用于系统架构中的每个系统元素。

2. 综合流程从项目开始就应被应用，在项目团队遍历系统架构时管理综合的系统。通过这样做，项目团队不断处理组成综合系统的各部分之间的相互作用，以及与其宏观系统之间的相互作用。此外，项目团队还在评估作为这些交互功能的系统行为，并寻找涌现的属性（好的和坏的），这是接口管理涉及的一项关键活动（见 3.2.4 节）。

3. 在每次转换之后，通过验证流程根据系统需求验证输出制品，以确保输出制品的转换是需求所定义的"正确的"。

SYSTEM LIFE CYCLE CONCEPTS, MODELS, AND PROCESSES

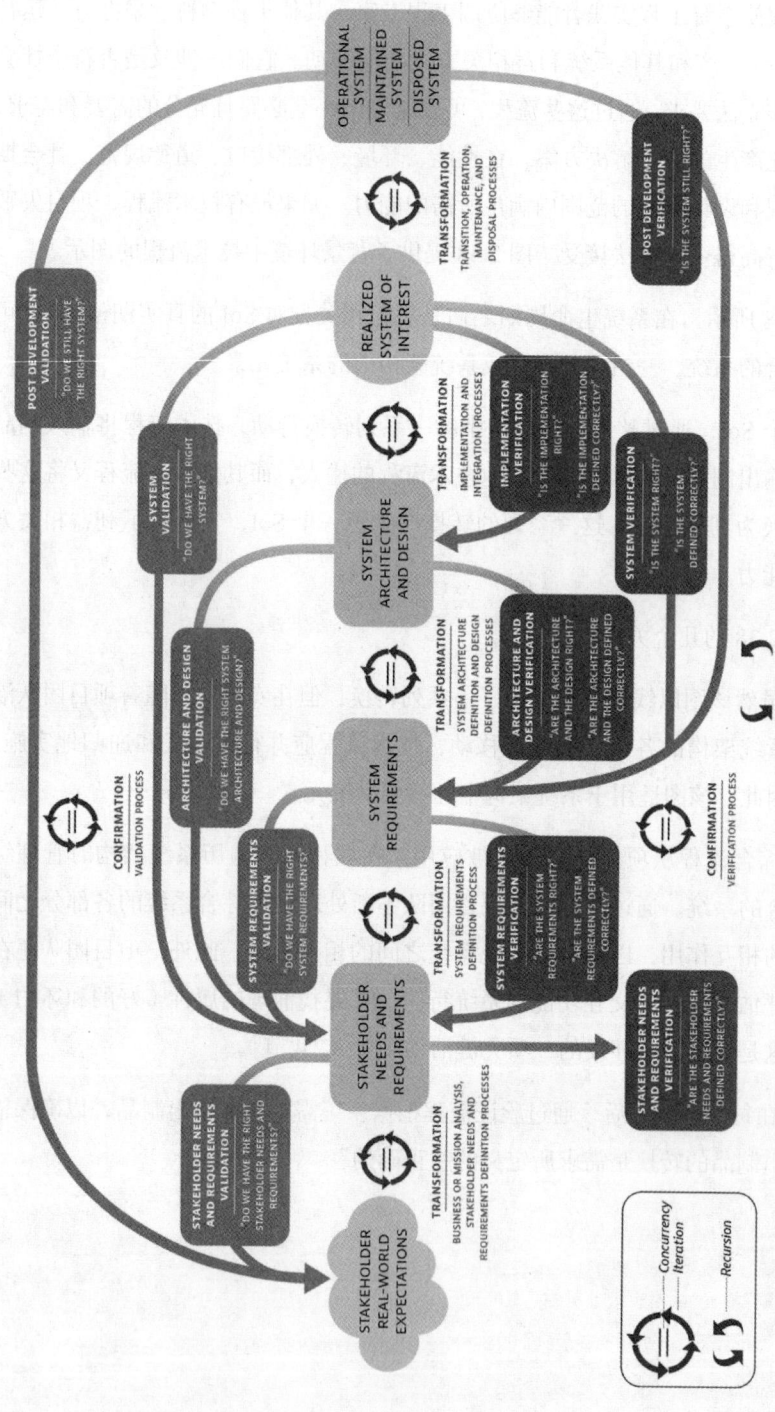

FIGURE 2.38 Technical Processes in context. INCOSE SEH original figure created by Roedler, Walden, and Wheatcraft derived from INCOSE NRM (2022). Usage per the INCOSE Notices page. All other rights reserved.

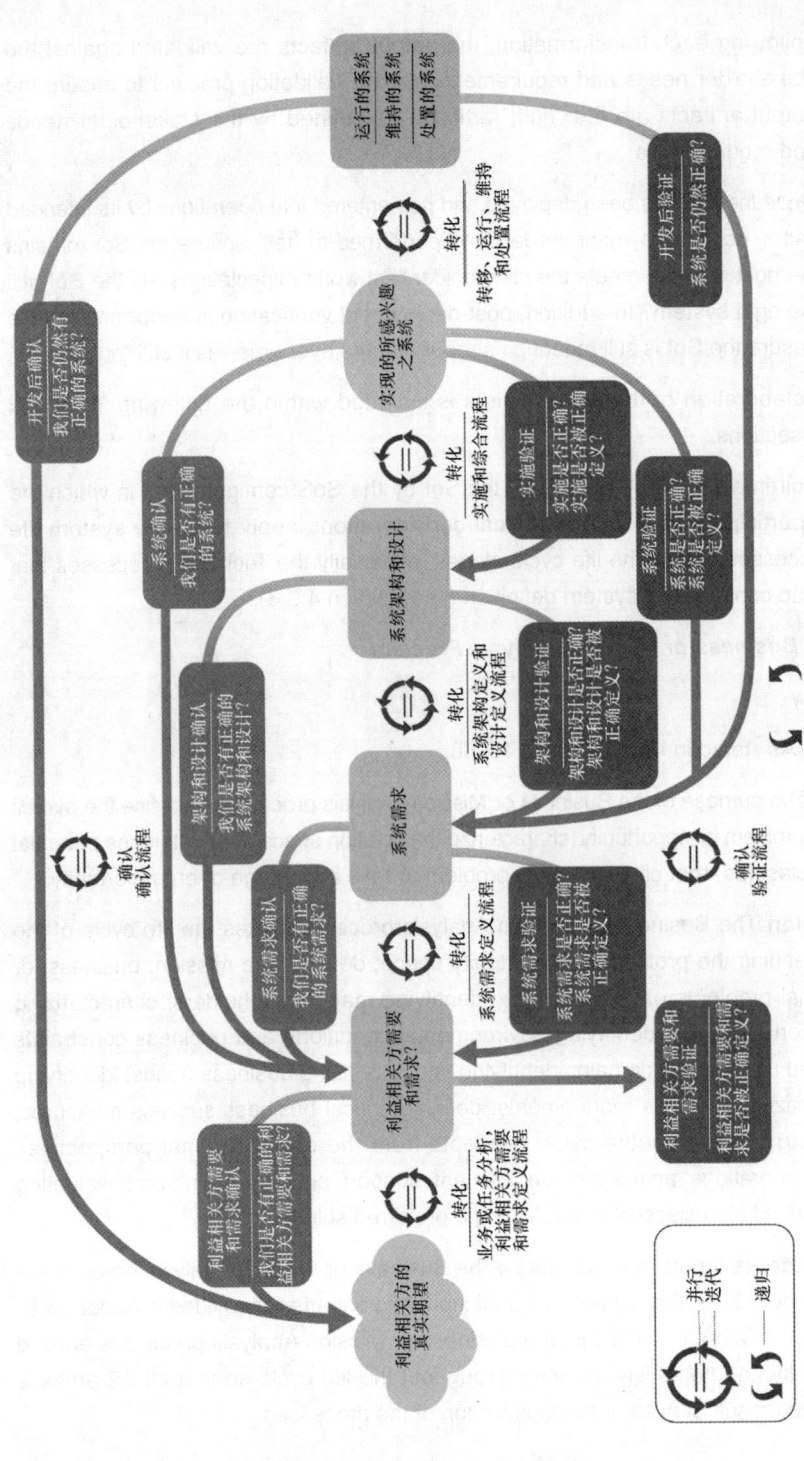

图 2.38 背景环境中的技术流程。INCOSE SEH 原始图由 Roedler、Walden 和 Wheatcraft 从 INCOSE NRM（2022）创建。按照 INCOSE 通知页使用。版权所有。

4. Following each transformation, the output artifacts are validated against the stakeholder needs and requirements via the Validation process to ensure the output artifacts are the "right" artifacts as defined by the stakeholder needs and requirements.

5. Once the SoI has been deployed and has entered into operations by its intended users, post-deployment validation is performed to help ensure the SoI remains the right SoI that meets the stakeholder real-world expectations—is the SoI still the right system? In addition, post-deployment verification is performed to help ensure the SoI is still meeting its requirements over time—is it still "right"?

Further elaboration of these key points is included within the following Technical Process sections.

New requirements can be placed on the SoI by the SoS configurations in which the SoI will participate. The SoS technical considerations apply to all the system life cycle processes across the life cycle stages, especially the Technical Processes that provide the concept and system definition (see Section 4.3.6).

2.3.5.1 Business or Mission Analysis Process

Overview

Purpose As stated in ISO/IEC/IEEE 15288,

[6.4.1.1] The purpose of the Business or Mission Analysis process is to define the overall strategic problem or opportunity, characterize the solution space, and determine potential solution class(es) that can address a problem or take advantage of an opportunity.

Description The Business or Mission Analysis process initiates the life cycle of the SoI by defining the problem or opportunity space; defining the mission, business, or operational problems or opportunities; identifying major stakeholders; characterizing the solution space by identifying environmental conditions and business constraints that bound the solution domain; identifying and prioritizing business needs; identifying and prioritizing business requirements, defining critical business success measures; developing preliminary life cycle concepts from the organizational perspectives including operations, acquisition, deployment, support, and retirement; and evaluating alternative solution classes and selecting a preferred solution class.

Inputs/Outputs Inputs and outputs for the Business or Mission Analysis process are listed in Figure 2.39. Descriptions of each input and output are provided in Appendix E. Note that, as with all processes, the Business or Mission Analysis process is applied concurrently and iteratively evolving throughout the life cycle so that all SE artifacts mature as a result of the iterative application of the processes.

4. 在每次转换之后，通过确认流程根据利益相关方的需要和需求确认输出制品，以确保输出制品是利益相关方需要和需求所定义的"正确"制品。

5. 一旦 SoI 被部署并由其预期用户投入运行，将执行部署后确认，以帮助确保 SoI 仍然是符合利益相关方在现实世界中所期望的正确的 SoI——SoI 仍然是正确的系统吗？此外，执行部署后的确认，以帮助确保 SoI 随着时间的推移仍能满足其要求——它是否仍然"正确"？

以下技术流程部分将进一步阐述这些要点。

SoI 将参与的体系构型配置可对 SoI 提出新的需求。体系技术考虑因素适用于整个生命周期阶段的所有系统生命周期流程，尤其是提供概念和系统定义的技术流程（见 4.3.6 节）。

2.3.5.1 业务或任务分析流程

概述

目的　如 ISO/IEC/IEEE 15288 所述：

[6.4.1.1] 业务或任务分析流程的目的是定义总体战略问题或机遇，描述解决方案空间，并确定可以解决问题或利用机遇的潜在解决方案类。

描述　业务或任务分析流程通过定义问题或机会空间，启动 SoI 的生命周期；确定任务、业务或运行问题或机会；确定主要利益相关方；通过识别约束解决方案域的环境条件和业务约束来描述解决方案空间；确定业务需要并确定其优先级；确定业务需求并确定其优先级，定义关键业务成功测度；从组织的角度制定初步的生命周期概念，包括运行、采办、部署、支持和退役；以及评估备选解决方案类并选择首选的解决方案类。

输入/输出　业务或任务分析流程的输入和输出如图 2.39 所示。附录 E 中提供了对每个输入和输出的描述。请注意，与所有流程一样，业务或任务分析流程在整个生命周期中是并行和迭代演进的，因此所有系统工程制品都会随着流程的迭代应用而成熟。

SYSTEM LIFE CYCLE CONCEPTS, MODELS, AND PROCESSES

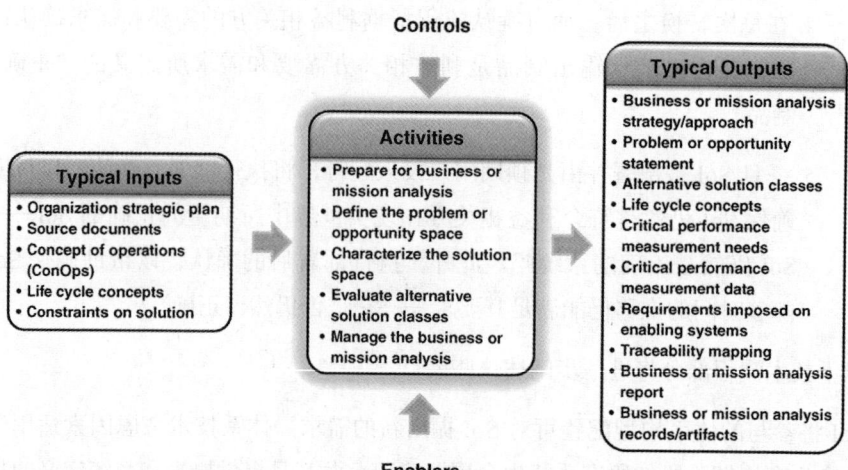

FIGURE 2.39 IPO diagram for Business or Mission Analysis process. INCOSE SEH original figure created by Shortell, Walden, and Yip. Usage per the INCOSE Notices page. All other rights reserved.

Process Activities The Business or Mission Analysis process includes the following activities:

- *Prepare for business or mission analysis.*

–Identify potential problems and opportunities resulting from changes in the organization's strategy and Concept of Operations, while considering desired organization mission(s), goals, objectives, and other organizational business needs and business requirements. This may involve the development of concepts for a new solution but may also involve identifying gaps or deficiencies in existing capabilities, systems, products, or services and concepts for addressing those gaps or deficiencies.

–Establish the strategy/approach for business or mission analysis. This involves the organizational approach(es) to defining the problem space, the characterization of the solution space, and the identification of an appropriate alternative solution classes.

–Plan for the necessary enabling systems or services needed through the life cycle for business or mission analysis. This includes interfaces to organizational enabling systems or services such as business, acquisition, operations, production, project management, and SE tools and applications, financial systems, information technology, databases, security controls, and other data and information repositories.

系统生命周期概念、模型和流程

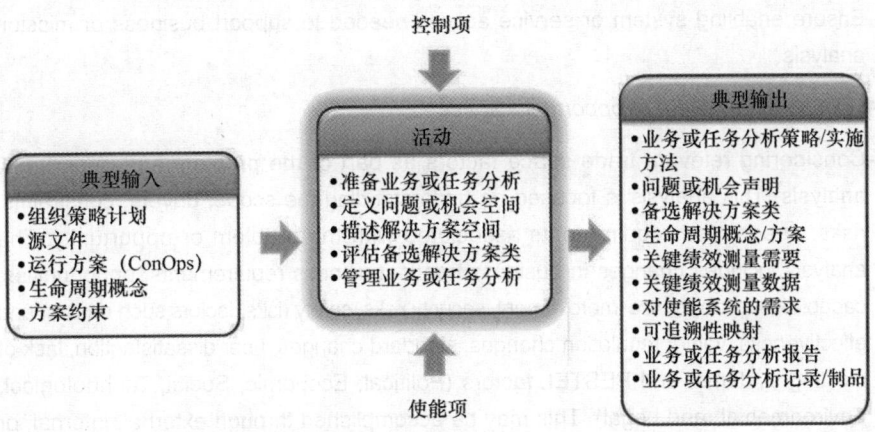

图 2.39　业务或任务分析流程的 IPO 图。INCOSE SEH 原始图由 Walden、Shortell 和 Yip 创建。按照 INCOSE 通知页使用。版权所有。

流程活动　业务或任务分析流程包括以下活动：

- *准备业务或任务分析。*

  - 识别组织战略和运行意图变化带来的潜在问题和机遇，同时考虑预期的组织使命、目的、目标和其他组织业务需要和需求。这可能涉及开发新解决方案的概念，但也可能涉及确定现有能力、系统、产品或服务的差距或不足，以及解决这些差距或不足的概念。

  - 制定业务或任务分析的战略/实施方法。这涉及定义问题空间的组织方法、解决方案空间的特征化以及确定适当的替代解决方案类。

  - 为业务或任务分析的整个生命周期所需的必要使能系统或服务制订计划。这包括与组织使能系统或服务的接口，如业务、采办、运行、生产、项目管理、系统工程工具和应用程序、金融系统、信息技术、数据库、安全控制以及其他数据和信息存储库。

SYSTEM LIFE CYCLE CONCEPTS, MODELS, AND PROCESSES

   —Ensure enabling system or service access needed to support business or mission analysis.

104 • *Define the problem or opportunity space.*

   —Considering relevant trade-space factors as part of the problem and opportunity analysis. This analysis is focused on understanding the scope, drivers, constraints, risks, needs, and requirements associated with the problem or opportunity. The analysis includes changes in business needs, business requirements, opportunities, capabilities, performance improvement, security risks, safety risks, factors such as cost and effectiveness, value, regulation changes, standard changes, user dissatisfaction, lack of existing systems, and PESTEL factors (Political, Economic, Social, Technological, Environmental, and Legal). This may be accomplished through external, internal, or SWOT (Strengths, Weaknesses, Opportunities, and Threats) analysis.

   —Define the problem or opportunity, mission, goals, objectives, and associated business needs and requirements to be addressed by a solution class. This definition is solution-class independent, since the solution could be an operational change, a change to an existing system or service, or a new system.

   —Prioritize the problem or opportunity, mission, goals, objectives, needs, and requirements against other business needs and business requirements.

   —Define critical business success measures. The business must define how it will know that the solution provided will meet its needs. Validation criteria establish critical and desired system performance—thresholds and objectives for system performance parameters that are critical for system success and those that are desired but may be subject to compromise to meet the critical parameters.

   —Obtain agreement on the problem or opportunity, mission, goals, objectives, business needs, business requirements, and success measures.

105 • *Characterize the solution space.*

   —Define preliminary life cycle concepts for acquisition, development, deployment, operations, support, and retirement of the solution. Business stakeholders identify the stakeholders (individuals or groups) who are to be involved in any of the life cycle concepts. The life cycle concepts define what the system needs to do and how well from the business stakeholder's perspective of the intended use in the intended operational environment, when operated by the intended users in the context of all its life cycle activities, the required interactions with external systems, drivers and constraints, security, risks, business needs, and business requirements at the strategic level.

- 确保能够访问支持业务或任务分析所需的系统或服务。

• *定义问题或机会空间。*

- 将相关权衡空间因素作为问题和机会分析的一部分。该分析侧重于了解与问题或机会相关的范围、驱动因素、约束、风险、需要和需求。该分析包括业务需要、业务需求、机会、能力、绩效提升、安保风险、安全风险、成本和效益、价值、法规变化、标准变化、用户不满意、缺少现有系统以及 PESTEL 因素（政治、经济、社会、技术、环境和法律）的变化。这可以通过外部、内部或 SWOT（优势、劣势、机会和威胁）分析来实现。

- 定义解决方案类要解决的问题或机会、任务、目的、目标以及相关的业务需要和需求。此定义与解决方案类无关，因为解决方案可以是运行更改、对现有系统或服务的更改或新系统。

- 将问题或机会、任务、目的、目标、需要和需求与其他业务需要和业务需求进行优先级排序。

- 定义关键业务成功测度。业务部门必须定义如何知道所提供的解决方案将满足其需要。确认准则建立了系统的关键性能和期望性能——对系统成功至关重要的系统性能参数的阈值和目标，以及所期望的性能参数，但为了满足关键参数的要求，可能会有所妥协。

- 就问题或机会、任务、目的、目标、业务需要、业务需求和成功测度达成一致。

• *描述解决方案空间。*

- 定义解决方案的获取、开发、部署、运行、支持和退役的初步生命周期概念。业务利益相关方确定任何将参与生命周期概念的利益相关方（个人或团体）。生命周期概念定义了当预期用户在其所有生命周期活动、与外部系统的所需交互、驱动因素和约束、安全、风险、业务需求和战略层面的业务需求中进行操作时，从业务利益相关方的角度来看，系统需要做什么以及在预期运行环境中的预期用途。

SYSTEM LIFE CYCLE CONCEPTS, MODELS, AND PROCESSES

–Establish a set of alternative classes spanning the potential solution space.

- Evaluate alternative solution classes that span the potential solution space.

–Evaluate the set of alternative solution concepts and select the preferred solution concepts against the organization's business needs, business requirements, and critical business success measures. Appropriate modeling, simulation, and analytical analysis will help determine the feasibility, value, and appropriateness of the alternative solution classes.

–Select the preferred solution class(es) and ensure each has been validated in the context of the proposed strategic level life cycle concepts. Feedback on feasibility, value, market factors, and alternatives is also provided for use in completing the definition of the organization's level life cycle concepts.

–Provide feedback to organization level life cycle concepts in terms of the selected solution class(es).

–Obtain agreement on the problem or opportunity statement, mission, goals, objectives, critical business success measures, life cycle concepts, business needs, and business requirements.

- *Manage the Business or Mission Analysis*:

–As key decisions are made, record the decision along with supporting information and rationale.

–Establish and sustain traceability (analysis, rationale, and alternative solution classes).

–Give CM the information items, work products, or other artifacts needed for baselines.

Common approaches and tips:

- Identify the enabling systems and materials needed for transition early in the life cycle to allow for the necessary

lead time to obtain or access them.

Elaboration

Identify Major Stakeholders. Although the identification of stakeholders is undertaken at each stage of system development, during the Business or Mission Analysis process, business managers are responsible for nominating key stakeholders and are often responsible for establishing a stakeholder register and means of exchanging information. It is fundamentally a business management function to ensure stakeholders are available and able to contribute to the system development activities for the SoI—stakeholders are often occupied in other business operations activities and must be authorized in terms of both budget and time to expend the needed effort and resources on other than their current operational tasks.

- 建立一组跨潜在解决方案空间的备选解决方案类。

• 评估跨越潜在解决方案空间的备选解决方案类。

- 评估备选解决方案概念集,并根据组织的业务需要、业务需求和关键业务成功测度选择首选解决方案概念。适当的建模、仿真和分析将有助于确定备选解决方案类的可行性、价值和适合性。

- 选择首选解决方案类,并确保各类都已在提出的战略级生命周期概念的背景环境中得到确认。提供关于可行性、价值、市场因素和备选方案的反馈,用于完成组织级生命周期概念的定义。

- 根据选定的解决方案类向组织级生命周期概念提供反馈。

- 就问题或机会陈述、任务、目的、目标、关键业务成功测度、生命周期概念、业务需要和业务需求达成一致。

• 管理业务或任务分析。

- 在做出关键决策时,记录决策以及支持信息和理由。

- 建立并保持可追溯性(分析、基本原理和备选解决方案类)。

- 为构型配置管理提供基线所需的信息项、工作产品或其他制品。

常用方法和提示:

• 在生命周期的早期阶段确定转移所需的使能系统和材料,以便有必要的提前期来获取或使用它们。

详细阐述

*确定主要利益相关方。*尽管在系统开发的每个阶段都会识别利益相关方,但在业务或任务分析流程中,业务经理负责提名关键利益相关方,并通常负责建立利益相关方清单和信息交换手段。从根本上说,这是一项业务管理职能,以确保利益相关方能够为系统开发活动做出贡献,因为 SoI 利益相关方通常参与其他业务运行活动,并且必须在预算和时间方面获得授权,以便在其当前运行任务以外的其他任务上花费所需的努力和资源。

SYSTEM LIFE CYCLE CONCEPTS, MODELS, AND PROCESSES

Identify Business Needs and Requirements. For each problem or opportunity, it is important to identify the business needs and business requirements associated with needed capabilities, functionality, performance, and security as well as risk and compliance with standards and regulations. Business needs exist at several levels of abstraction, consist of identification of "what is needed" by the business to address the problem or opportunity, and can be communicated in several forms, such as the mission statement, goals, objectives, critical success measures, use cases, user stories, and individual need statements. The business requirements communicate what the business requires of the solution to address their needs without stating a specific solution. The life cycle concepts are developed in response to the business needs and business requirements. Together, the business needs, business requirements, and critical business success measures communicate what is "necessary for acceptance" at the business level.

Life Cycle Concepts. Life cycle concepts address not only the concepts for the SoI during operations by the intended users in the operational environment, but also includes the concepts required to address the business needs, business requirements, critical business success measures, and higher-level stakeholder needs and stakeholder-owned system requirements across the system life cycle. Preliminary life cycle concepts are established and assured through the Business or Mission Analysis process to the extent needed to define the problem or opportunity space and characterize the solution space. Principal life cycle concepts include:

Concept of operations (ConOps)—Describes the way the organization will operate to achieve its missions, goals, and objectives. The ConOps captures how the system will potentially impact the acquiring and other organizations. "The ConOps describes the organization's assumptions or intent in regard to an overall operation or series of operations of the business with using the system to be developed, existing systems and possible future systems. The ConOps serves as a basis for the organization to direct the overall characteristics of the future business and systems, for the project to understand its background, and for [its] users ... to implement the stakeholder requirements elicitation" (ISO/IEC/IEEE 29148, 2018) Ideally, the enterprise level ConOps should be an input to the Business or Mission Analysis process, but if it does not exist, it may need to be jointly developed and maintained. The ConOps also describes the higher-level system in which the SoI must operate.

确定业务需要和需求。对于每个问题或机会，重要的是确定与所需的能力、功能、性能和安全性相关的业务需要和业务需求，以及风险和对标准和法规的遵从性。业务需求存在于多个抽象层级，包括确定业务为解决问题或机遇而"需要什么"，并可以多种形式传达，如任务说明、目的、目标、关键成功测度、用例、用户故事和个人需要说明。业务需求沟通了业务对解决方案的要求，以满足其需求，而无须说明具体的解决方案。生命周期概念是根据业务需要和业务需求开发的。业务需要、业务需求和关键业务成功测度共同沟通了业务层级的"接受必要条件"。

生命周期概念。生命周期概念不仅涉及预期用户在运行环境中操作 SoI 期间的概念，还包括在整个系统生命周期中用于解决业务需要、业务需求、关键业务成功测度以及更高层级的利益相关方需要和利益相关方所拥有的系统需求的概念。通过业务或任务分析流程，在定义问题或机会空间以及描述解决方案空间所需的范围内，建立并确保初步生命周期概念。主要生命周期概念包括：

运行意图（ConOps）——描述组织实现其任务、目标和目的的运行方式。ConOps 捕获系统将如何潜在地影响采办和其他组织。"ConOps 描述了组织对使用待开发系统、现有系统和可能的未来系统的整体运行或一系列业务运行的假设或意图。ConOps 是组织指导未来业务和系统总体特征的基础，是项目了解其背景的基础，也是 [其] 用户……实现利益相关方需求获取的基础"（ISO/IEC/IEEE 29148，2018）。理想情况下，复杂组织体系级 ConOps 应作为业务或任务分析流程的输入，但如果不存在，则可能需要联合开发和维护。ConOps 还描述了 SoI 必须运行其中的更高层级系统。

SYSTEM LIFE CYCLE CONCEPTS, MODELS, AND PROCESSES

Operational concept (OpsCon)—Describes the way the system will be used during operations, for what purpose, in its operational environment by its intended users and does not enable unintended users to negatively impact the intended use of the system nor allow unintended users from using the system in unintended ways. Also addressed are the needed capabilities, functionality, performance, quality, safety, security, compliance with standards and regulations, interactions with external systems, and operational risks. An OpsCon provides a user-oriented perspective that describes system characteristics of the to-be-delivered system. The OpsCon is used to communicate overall quantitative and qualitative system characteristics to the acquirer, user, supplier and other organizational elements.

Acquisition concept—For solutions that will be procured from a supplier, the acquisition concept describes the way the system will be acquired including aspects such as stakeholder engagement, needs definition, requirements definition, design, production, verification, validation, and contract deliverables. The supplier enterprise(s) may need to develop more detailed concepts for production, assembly, verification, validation, transport of system, and/or system elements. For solutions that will be provided internal to the organization, the acquisition concept will include a production concept that describes the way the system will be developed and produced including aspects such as stakeholder engagement, needs definition, requirements definition, design, production, integration, verification, and validation.

Deployment concept—Describes the way the system will be delivered, integrated into its operational environment, and introduced into operations, including deployment considerations when the system will be integrated with other systems that are in operation and/or replace any systems in operation.

Support concept—Describes the logistics, desired support infrastructure and staffing considerations for supporting the system after it is deployed. A support concept would address operating support, engineering support, maintenance support, supply support, training support, and post-deployment verification and validation.

Retirement concept—Describes the way the system will be removed from operation and retired, including the disposal of any hazardous materials used in or resulting from the process and any legal obligations—for example, regarding IP rights protection, any external financial/ownership interests, sustainability, environmental impacts, and security concerns.

These preliminary life cycle concepts are defined first at the organizational level, to the extent required at that level, for the identified solution classes that address the problem or opportunity. The preliminary life cycle concepts are then elaborated and refined through the Stakeholder Needs and Requirements Definition process (Section 2.3.5.2). Through iteration, the life cycle concepts are refined throughout the life cycle as required as a result of feedback obtained through the conduct of the rest of the Technical Processes.

运行概念（OpsCon）——描述预期用户在系统运行环境中使用系统的方式、用途，不允许非预期用户对系统的预期用途产生负面影响，也不允许非预期用户以非预期方式使用系统。还讨论了所需的能力、功能、性能、质量、安全、安保、遵守标准和法规、与外部系统的交互以及运行风险。OpsCon 提供了一个面向用户的视角，描述了待交付系统的系统特性。OpsCon 用于向采办方、用户、供应商和其他组织元素沟通总体的系统定量和定性特征。

采办概念——对于将从供应商处采办的解决方案，采办概念描述了系统的采办方式，包括利益相关方参与、需要定义、需求定义、设计、生产、验证、确认和合同交付物等方面。供应商复杂组织体系可能需要为系统和 / 或系统元素的生产、组装、验证、确认、运输制定更详细的概念。对于将在组织内部提供的解决方案，采办概念将包括一个生产概念，描述系统开发和生产的方式，包括利益相关方参与、需要定义、需求定义、设计、生产、综合、验证和确认等方面。

部署概念——描述系统的交付方式、与运行环境的综合方式以及引入运行的方式，包括系统与其他运行中的系统综合和 / 或替代任何运行中系统的部署考虑因素。

支持概念——描述部署系统后支持该系统所需的后勤、所需的支持基础设施和人员配备的注意事项。支持概念将涉及运行支持、工程支持、维护支持、供应支持、培训支持以及部署后验证和确认。

退役概念——描述了系统从运行中移除和退役的方式，包括处置流程中使用或产生的任何有害物质，以及任何法律义务，例如知识产权保护、任何外部财务 / 所有权利益、可持续性、环境影响和安保问题。

这些初步的生命周期概念首先在组织层级上定义，在该层级所需的范围内，用于确定解决问题或机会的解决方案类。然后，通过利益相关方需要和需求定义流程（见 2.3.5.2 节）对初步生命周期概念进行详细阐述和细化。通过迭代，在整个生命周期中，生命周期概念会根据在其他技术流程中获得的反馈意见进行必要的改进。

SYSTEM LIFE CYCLE CONCEPTS, MODELS, AND PROCESSES

Uncertainties and risk. There will be uncertainties (see Section 1.4.1) in the preliminary life cycle concepts. Uncertainties can be related to differing stakeholder perspectives, business factors, market, management, technical performance, schedule, development and production costs, operations and support costs, security, and sustainability. These uncertainties are a source of risk. Each of these uncertainties need to be addressed using the Risk Management process (Section 2.3.4.4) in conjunction with the rest of the Technical Processes, especially the Stakeholder Needs and Requirements Definition process (Section 2.3.5.2), the System Requirements Definition process (Section 2.3.5.3), and the System Architecture Definition process (Section 2.3.5.4).

2.3.5.2 *Stakeholder Needs and Requirements Definition Process*

Overview

Purpose As stated in ISO/IEC/IEEE 15288,

[6.4.2.1] The purpose of the Stakeholder Needs and Requirements Definition process is to define the stakeholder needs and requirements for a system that can provide the capabilities needed by users and other stakeholders in a defined environment.

Description Successful projects depend on meeting the stakeholder real-world expectations as communicated by the needs and requirements of the stakeholders throughout the system life cycle. A stakeholder is any entity (individual or organization) with a legitimate interest in the system. Stakeholders exist at each of the levels of an organization and system architecture. The focus of the Stakeholder Needs and Requirements Definition process is on elaboration of the preliminary the life cycle concepts, on the stakeholder needs transformed from those concepts, and on the stakeholder requirements transformed from those needs. The activities during the process are constrained and driven by the preliminary life cycle concepts, business needs, business requirements, and critical business success measures developed during the Business or Mission Analysis process (see Section 2.3.5.1).

In addition to identifying the stakeholders, this process elicits the operational use cases, scenarios, and life cycle concepts from stakeholders, identifies drivers and constraints, determines interactions with the operational and enabling systems, determines interactions with users and operators, characterizes the operational environment, and assesses risks associated with the development of a new or changed capability or new opportunities addressed by a solution class. The life cycle concepts are analyzed, matured, and transformed into a set of stakeholder needs. These needs are analyzed and transformed into a set of stakeholder requirements for the SoI. These stakeholder requirements communicate what the stakeholders expect from the SoI that will result in their needs being met using their terminology.

不确定性和风险。初步生命周期概念中存在不确定性（见 1.4.1 节）。不确定性可能与不同的利益相关方角度、业务因素、市场、管理、技术性能、进度、开发和生产成本、运行和支持成本、安全性和可持续性有关。这些不确定性是风险的来源。需要使用风险管理流程（见 2.3.4.4 节）和其他技术流程，尤其是利益相关方需要和需求定义流程（见 2.3.5.2 节）、系统需求定义流程（见 2.3.5.3 节）和系统架构定义流程（见 2.3.5.4 节）来解决这些不确定性。

2.3.5.2 利益相关方需要和需求定义流程

概述

目的 如 ISO/IEC/IEEE 15288 所述：

[6.4.2.1] 利益相关方需要和需求定义流程的目的是定义利益相关方对系统的需要和需求，该系统可以在定义的环境中提供用户和其他利益相关方所需的能力。

描述 成功的项目取决于能否满足利益相关方在整个系统生命周期中的需要和需求所传达的对现实世界的期望。利益相关方是指在系统中拥有合法权益的任何实体（个人或组织）。利益相关方存在于组织和系统架构的每个层级。利益相关方需要和需求定义流程的重点是生命周期概念的初步阐述、从这些概念转化的利益相关方需要以及从这些需要转化的利益相关方需求。该流程中的活动受到在业务或任务分析流程中制定的初步生命周期概念、业务需要、业务需求和关键业务成功测度的约束和驱动（见 2.3.5.1 节）。

除了确定利益相关方外，该流程还从利益相关方那里启发运行用例、场景和生命周期概念，确定驱动因素和约束，确定与运行和使能系统的交互，确定与用户和操作员的交互，描述运行环境的特征，并评估与开发新的或更改的能力或解决方案类所解决的新机会相关的风险。对生命周期概念进行分析，使其成熟并转化为一组利益相关方需要。分析这些需要并将其转化为 SoI 的一组利益相关方需求。这些利益相关方需求沟通利益相关方对 SoI 的期望，从而使用他们的术语满足他们的需求。

SYSTEM LIFE CYCLE CONCEPTS, MODELS, AND PROCESSES

The stakeholder requirements drive and constrain the solution space by addressing stakeholder expectations for the SoI, characterizing the operational environment, and identifying external interface boundaries between the SoI and external systems across which there is an interaction. Traceability between the life cycle concepts, stakeholder needs, and stakeholder requirements is established as part of this process.

Stakeholder requirements govern the SoI's development and are an essential factor in further defining or clarifying the scope of the development project and elaborating on what is "necessary for acceptance." If an organization is acquiring the system, this process provides the basis for the technical description of the deliverables in an agreement—typically in the form of a set of system requirements for a SoI and defined interfaces at the SoI boundaries.

Inputs/Outputs Inputs and outputs for the Stakeholder Needs and Requirements Definition process are shown in Figure 2.40. Descriptions of each input and output are provided in Appendix E.

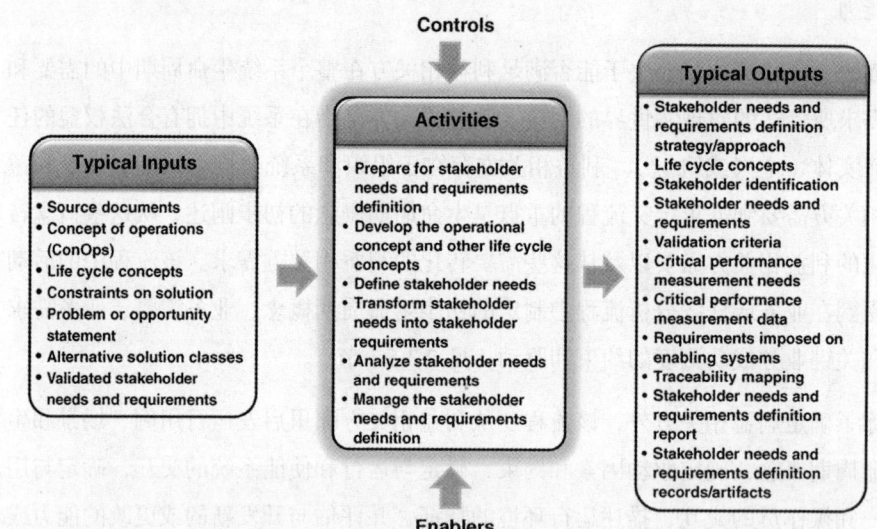

FIGURE 2.40 IPO diagram for Stakeholder Needs and Requirements Definition process. INCOSE SEH original figure created by Shortell, Walden, and Yip. Usage per the INCOSE Notices page. All other rights reserved.

Process Activities The Stakeholder Needs and Requirements Definition process includes the following activities:

利益相关方需求通过满足利益相关方对 SoI 的期望、描述运行环境以及确定 SoI 与存在交互的外部系统之间的外部接口边界来驱动和约束解决方案空间。生命周期概念、利益相关方需要和利益相关方需求之间的可追溯性是该流程的一部分。

利益相关方需求管理着 SoI 的开发，是进一步定义或澄清开发项目范围以及详细说明"验收所需"内容的关键因素。如果组织正在采办系统，该流程为协议中可交付成果的技术描述提供了基础，通常形式是 SoI 的一组系统需求和 SoI 边界处定义的接口。

输入/输出 利益相关方需要和需求定义流程的输入和输出如图 2.40 所示。附录 E 中提供了每个输入和输出的描述。

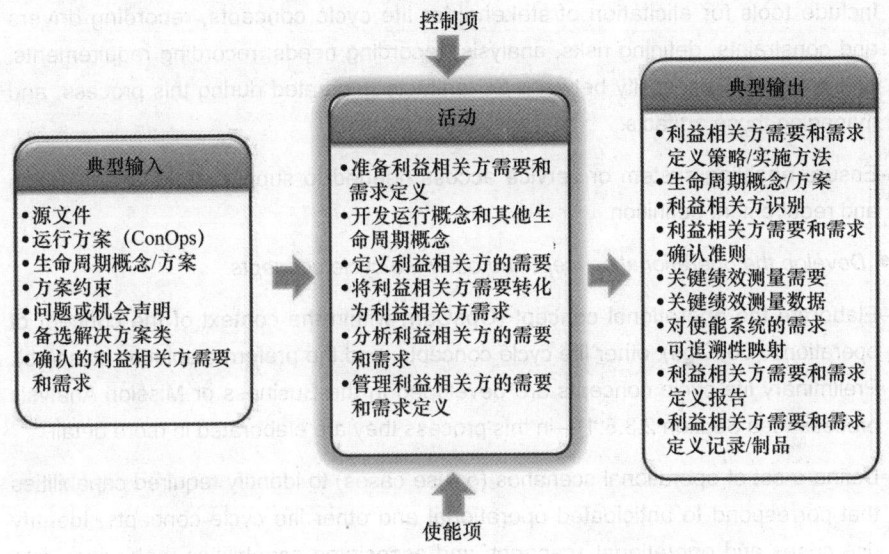

图 2.40 利益相关方需要和需求定义流程的 IPO 图。INCOSE SEH 原始图由 Walden、Shortell 和 Yip 创建。按照 INCOSE 通知页使用。版权所有。

流程活动 利益相关方需要和需求定义流程包括以下活动：

SYSTEM LIFE CYCLE CONCEPTS, MODELS, AND PROCESSES

- *Prepare for stakeholder needs and requirements definition.*

–Identify the stakeholders with an interest in the solution. Resolve differing interests. These stakeholders or classes of stakeholders will help identify constraints and define operational-level life cycle concepts, transform those concepts into operational-level stakeholder needs, which are then transformed into operational-level stakeholder requirements.

–Establish the strategy/approach for stakeholder needs and requirements definition. Understand the role and perspective of each stakeholder and identify any potential conflicts with other stakeholders to develop a stakeholder management plan and a strategy for defining life cycle concepts, stakeholder needs, and stakeholder requirements.

–Plan for the necessary enabling systems or services needed through the life cycle for stakeholder needs and requirements definition. Enabling systems may include tools for elicitation of stakeholder life cycle concepts, recording drivers and constraints, defining risks, analysis, recording needs, recording requirements, and providing traceability between SE artifacts generated during this process, and managing those artifacts.

–Ensure enabling system or service access needed to support stakeholder needs and requirement definition.

- *Develop the operational concept and other life cycle concepts.*

–Elaborate the operational concept (OpsCon) within the context of the concept of operations (ConOps), other life cycle concepts, and the preferred solution class(es). Preliminary life cycle concepts are developed in the Business or Mission Analysis process (see Section 2.3.5.1)—in this process they are elaborated in more detail.

–Define a set of operational scenarios (or use cases) to identify required capabilities that correspond to anticipated operational and other life cycle concepts. Identify use cases and operational scenarios and associated capabilities, behaviors, and responses of the system or solution and environments across the SoI life cycle (concept, development, production, utilization, support, and retirement). The use cases and operational scenarios provide the information from the stakeholders needed to define the life cycle concepts; the range of intended uses of the system; the intended operational environment and the system's impact on the environment; intended users, and interfacing systems, platforms, or products.

–Capture the characterization of the SoI's intended operational environment and users.

- *准备利益相关方需要和需求定义。*

- 确定对解决方案感兴趣的利益相关方。解决利益分歧。这些利益相关方或利益相关方类将有助于识别约束并定义运行级生命周期概念，将这些概念转化为运行级利益相关方需要，然后转化为运行级利益相关方需求。

- 建立利益相关方需要和需求定义的战略/实施方法。了解每个利益相关方的角色和观点，识别与其他利益相关方的任何潜在冲突，以制定利益相关方管理计划和战略，定义生命周期概念、利益相关方需要和利益相关方需求。

- 针对利益相关方需要和需求定义，计划整个生命周期所需的必要使能系统或服务。使能系统可能包括用于启发利益相关方生命周期概念、记录驱动因素和约束、定义风险、分析、记录需要、记录需求、提供此流程中生成的系统工程制品之间的可追溯性以及管理这些制品的工具。

- 确保可获得支持利益相关方需要和需求定义所需的系统或服务。

- *开发运行概念和其他生命周期概念。*

- 在运行意图（ConOps）、其他生命周期概念和首选解决方案类的背景下详细阐述运行概念（OpsCon）。初步生命周期概念是在业务或任务分析流程中制定的（见 2.3.5.1 节）在此流程中，将对其进行更详细的阐述。

- 定义一组运行场景（或用例），以确定与预期运行和其他生命周期概念相对应的所需能力。确定整个 SoI 生命周期（概念、开发、生产、使用、支持和退役）中系统或解决方案和环境的用例和运行场景以及相关功能、行为和响应。用例和运行场景提供了定义生命周期概念所需的利益相关方的信息；系统的预期用途范围；预期运行环境和系统对环境的影响；预期用户和接口系统、平台或产品。

- 捕获 SoI 预期运行环境和用户的特征。

– Considering usability, identify user interactions. Capture factors (e.g., skills) that can affect the interactions.

– Identify external interface boundaries across which the SoI interacts.

– Considering the stakeholder and technical objectives and limitations, identify constraints on the solution.

– Identify risks associated with management, development, operations, and disposal, including misuse and loss scenarios (see Sections 3.1.12 and 3.1.13).

- *Define stakeholder needs.*

– Identify stakeholder needs that reflect the intended life cycle concepts and associated constraints (see the INCOSE NRM [2022] and INCOSE GtNR [2022] for more details). Specify quality, health, safety, security, environment, compliance, and other stakeholder needs and functions that relate to critical qualities.

– In conjunction with the Decision Management process, prioritize and select the essential needs. The System Analysis process (see Section 2.3.5.6) is used to analyze the life cycle concepts, resolve conflicts, and access feasibility of those concepts. Needs are assessed and priorities are assigned in terms of critically, value, completeness, correctness, consistency, security and feasibility.

– As the stakeholder needs are selected, record the needs with their sources and rationale. Transform the life cycle concepts and other sources into a homogeneous, agreed-to integrated set of stakeholder needs. Establish traces from the needs to their sources. Although the stakeholder needs are not required to be as stated as rigorously as requirements, it is useful to follow the same rules as for quality requirements (see Section 2.3.5.3 and the INCOSE GtWR [2023] for more details) since better-formed needs and sets of needs will result in less ambiguity in the transformation of the needs into requirements. For each stakeholder need, define attributes such as source, rationale, priority, and criticality.

- *Transform stakeholder needs into stakeholder requirements.*

– Transform the needs into stakeholder requirements. Define a set of stakeholder requirements consistent with the stakeholder needs.

– Identify any additional stakeholder requirements. Define stakeholder requirements that relate to safety, security, sustainability, human systems integration, etc. (see Section 3.1). Define stakeholder requirements that relate to high priority and critical functionality, performance, the operational environment, interactions with users, interactions with external interfacing and enabling systems, and compliance with standards and regulations. Ensure the stakeholder requirements are consistent with the life cycle concepts, needs, scenarios, interactions, constraints, operational risks, and SoI considerations.

- 考虑可用性，确定用户交互。捕获可能影响互动的因素（如技能）。
- 确定 SoI 相互作用的外部接口边界。
- 考虑利益相关方、技术目标和限制，确定解决方案的限制因素。
- 识别与管理、开发、运行和处置相关的风险，包括误用和损失场景（见 3.1.12 节和 3.1.13 节）。

- **定义利益相关方的需要。**

- 确定反映预期生命周期概念和相关约束的利益相关方需要（有关更多详细信息，请参阅 INCOSE NRM [2022] 和 INCOSE GtNR [2022]）。指定与关键质量相关的质量、健康、安全、安保、环境、合规性和其他利益相关方需要和功能。
- 结合决策管理流程，优先考虑并选择基本需要。系统分析流程（见 2.3.5.6 节）用于分析生命周期概念，解决冲突，并获取这些概念的可行性。评估需要，并根据关键性、价值、完整性、正确性、一致性、安全性和可行性分配优先级。
- 在选择利益相关方需要时，记录需要及其来源和理由。将生命周期概念和其他来源转化为一组同质的、一致同意的综合的利益相关方需要。建立从需要到来源的追溯。尽管利益相关方的需要无须像需求那样严格地表述，但遵循与质量要求相同的规则（更多详情请参见 2.3.5.3 节和 INCOSE GtWR [2023] 的规定）是有用的，因为更好的需要和需求集将减少需要转化为需求的模糊性。针对每个利益相关方的需要，定义诸如来源、基本原理、优先级和关键性等属性。

- **将利益相关方需要转化为利益相关方需求。**

- 将需要转化为利益相关方需求。定义一组与利益相关方需要一致的利益相关方需求。
- 确定任何其他利益相关方需求。定义与安全、安保、可持续性、人与系统综合等相关的利益相关方需求（见 3.1 节）。定义与高优先级和关键功能、性能、运行环境、与用户的交互、与外部接口和使能系统的交互以及与标准和法规的合规性相关的利益相关方需求。确保利益相关方需求与生命周期概念、需要、场景、交互、约束、运行风险和 SoI 考虑因素一致。

SYSTEM LIFE CYCLE CONCEPTS, MODELS, AND PROCESSES

–Ensure high quality stakeholder requirements. Each stakeholder requirement should follow the rules for quality requirements and possesses characteristics such as necessary, singular, correct, unambiguous, feasible, appropriate to level, complete, conforming, and can be validated (see Section 2.3.5.3 and the INCOSE GtWR [2023] for more details). For each stakeholder requirement, define attributes such as source, rationale, priority, and criticality.

- *Analyze stakeholder needs and requirements.*

–Analyze the complete sets of stakeholder needs and stakeholder requirements. Analyze the sets of stakeholder needs and stakeholder requirements to ensure they are correct, complete, consistent, comprehensible, appropriate to level, and feasible (see Section 2.3.5.3 and the INCOSE GtWR [2023] for more details).

–Enable technical achievement monitoring through the definition of critical performance measures and quality characteristics.

–Define system validation criteria for each stakeholder need and requirement, the validation strategy, validation method, and responsible organization for providing evidence the stakeholder needs and requirements have been met.

–Review the analyzed stakeholder requirements with the applicable stakeholders to validate that their needs and expectations have been adequately captured and expressed.

–Resolve stakeholder needs and requirements issues. Negotiate changes, amendments, and modifications to resolve inconsistencies, conflicts, and unrealizable or impractical stakeholder needs and requirements.

- *Manage the stakeholder needs and requirements definition.*

–Obtain explicit agreement on the stakeholder needs and requirements.

–Establish and sustain traceability (stakeholder needs and requirements).

–Give CM the information items, work products, or other artifacts needed for baselines.

–Manage changes to the stakeholder needs and stakeholder requirements, as needed.

Common approaches and tips:

- Identify the enabling systems and materials needed for transition early in the life cycle to allow for the necessary lead time to obtain or access them.

- 确保高质量的利益相关方需求。各利益相关方的需求应遵循质量要求的规则，并具有必要性、唯一性、正确性、明确性、可行性、层级适用、完整性、符合性和可确认性等特征（更多详细信息，请参阅 2.3.5.3 节和 INCOSE GtWR［2023］）。对于每个利益相关方需求，定义诸如来源、基本原理、优先级和关键性等属性。

- *分析利益相关方的需要和需求。*

- 分析利益相关方的全部需要和需求。分析利益相关方需要和利益相关方需求集，以确保其正确、完整、一致、可理解、层级适用和可行（更多详细信息，请参阅 2.3.5.3 节和 INCOSE GtWR［2023］）。

- 通过定义关键绩效指标和质量特性，实现技术成果监控。

- 定义每个利益相关方需要和需求的系统确认准则、确认策略、确认方法和负责的组织，以提供利益相关方需要和需求已得到满足的证据。

- 与适用的利益相关方一起评审所分析的利益相关方需求，以确认其需要和期望已被充分捕获和表达。

- 解决利益相关方的需要和需求问题。协商变更、修订和修改，以解决不一致、冲突以及无法实现或不切实际的利益相关方需要和需求。

- *管理利益相关方的需要和需求定义。*

- 就利益相关方的需要和需求达成明确协议。

- 建立并保持可追溯性（利益相关方的需要和需求）。

- 为构型配置管理提供基线所需的信息项、工作产品或其他制品。

- 根据需要管理利益相关方需要和利益相关方需求的变更。

常用方法和提示：

- 在生命周期的早期阶段确定转移所需的使能系统和材料，以便有必要的提前期来获取或使用它们。

SYSTEM LIFE CYCLE CONCEPTS, MODELS, AND PROCESSES

Elaboration

This section elaborates and provides "how-to" information on the Stakeholder Needs and Requirements Definition process. Further guidance on elicitation, life cycle concepts, needs and requirements definition can be found in ISO/IEC/IEEE 29148 (2018), the INCOSE GtWR (2023), the INCOSE GtNR (2022), and the INCOSE NRM (2022).

Verified and validated stakeholder needs and stakeholder requirements are drivers and constraints for the majority of the system life cycle Technical Processes. Depending on the system development model, life cycle concepts definition, and maturation, the stakeholder needs and stakeholder requirements capture should be conducted at the beginning of the development cycle and assessed as a continuous, concurrent, and iterative activity as the project team moves recursively through the system architecture and across all life cycle activities. The reason for eliciting and analyzing the life cycle concepts, stakeholder needs, and stakeholder requirements is to understand the expectations of stakeholders well enough to support the System Requirements Definition processes.

Identify Stakeholders. One of the biggest challenges in system development is the identification of the set of stakeholders from whom life cycle concepts, needs, and requirements are elicited. When identifying stakeholders, take into account those who may be affected by, are able to influence, or will support the life cycle stages of the SoI, Typically, stakeholders include customers, users, operators, maintainers, procurement, organization decision makers, approving authorities, regulatory bodies, developing organizations, verifiers, validators, support organizations, and society at large (within the context of the business and proposed solution). This can include the stakeholders of external systems (e.g., interoperating, interfacing, other constituent systems in a system of systems) and enabling systems, as these will usually impose constraints that need to be identified and considered in the SoI or could have impacts on those systems or the environment. In sustainable development, this includes identifying representation for future generations. When direct contact is not possible, agents are identified, such as marketing or user groups to represent the concerns of classes of stakeholders such as consumers or future generations. There also may be stakeholders who oppose the system. These detractors of the system are first considered in establishing consensus needs. Beyond this, they are addressed through the Risk Management process, the threat analysis of the system, or the system requirements for security, adaptability, agility, or resilience.

系统生命周期概念、模型和流程

详细阐述

本节阐述并提供了利益相关方需要和需求定义流程的"如何做"的信息。ISO/IEC/IEEE 29148（2018）、INCOSE GtWR（2023）、INCOSE GtNR（2022）和 INCOSE NRM（2022）中提供了关于启发、生命周期概念、需要和需求定义的进一步指导。

经验证和确认的利益相关方需要和利益相关方需求是大多数系统生命周期技术流程的驱动因素和约束因素。当项目团队在系统架构和所有生命周期活动中递归移动时，根据系统开发模型，生命周期概念定义和成熟度，利益相关方需要和利益相关方需求的捕获应在开发周期开始时进行，并作为连续、并行和迭代活动进行评估。启发和分析生命周期概念、利益相关方需要和利益相关方需求的原因是为了充分理解利益相关方的期望，以支持系统需求定义流程。

确定利益相关方。系统开发中最大的挑战之一是确定利益相关方集合，从他们那里获取生命周期概念、需要和要求。在确定利益相关方时，考虑那些可能受 SoI 影响、能够影响或将支持 SoI 生命周期阶段的实体，通常，利益相关方包括客户、用户、操作人员、维护者、采办方、组织决策者、审批机构、监管机构、开发组织、验证者、确认者、支持组织和整个社会（在业务和提出解决方案的背景下）。这可能包括外部系统（例如，互操作、接口、体系中的其他成员系统）和使能系统的利益相关方，因为这些通常会施加需要在 SoI 中确定和考虑的约束，或者可能会对这些系统或环境产生影响。在可持续发展方面，这包括为后代明确代表。当无法直接联系时，确定代理人，如营销或用户组，以代表消费者或后代等利益相关方的关注。也可能有反对该制度的利益相关方。在建立共识需求时，首先考虑这些制度的批评者。除此之外，还通过风险管理流程、系统威胁分析或系统安保、适应性、敏捷性或韧性需求来解决这些问题。

SYSTEM LIFE CYCLE CONCEPTS, MODELS, AND PROCESSES

Elicit or Derive Stakeholder Needs and Stakeholder Requirements. Determining stakeholder needs and requirements requires the integration of a number of disparate views, which may not necessarily be harmonious. It is important to have a "reconcile" path in the establishment of stakeholder needs and stakeholder requirements, since the stakeholder expectations and the life cycle concepts may be in conflict, incomplete, ambiguous, infeasible, or unable to be satisfied collectively within project constraints. This circumstance illustrates an aspect of "horizontal integration" (see Section 2.3.5.8), recognizing that there will often be prioritization of competing concerns, or even outright rejection of some stakeholder concerns because of inconsistencies with other stakeholders' needs and requirements or a lack of feasibility.

As the SE processes are applied, a common paradigm for examining and prioritizing available information and determining the value of added information should be created. Each of the stakeholder's views of the needed systems can be translated to a common system description that is understood by all participants, and all decision-making activities recorded for future examination. The stakeholder views will be influenced by cognitive biases (see Section 1.4.2) based on their specific role, education, work experiences, culture, etc. Stakeholder views are framed in the context of these biases. It is important for the project team to understand this during elicitation to better understand the perspective of each stakeholder.

SE practitioners support project management in defining what must be done and gathering the information, personnel, and analysis tools to elaborate the life cycle concepts, needs, and requirements. This includes eliciting or deriving stakeholder needs, stakeholder requirements, system/project constraints (e.g., cost and schedule constraints, technology limitations, applicable specifications, and requirements), "drivers" (e.g., capabilities of the competition, external threats, and critical environments), and risks.

The output of the Stakeholder Needs and Requirements Definition process should be sufficient definition of the life cycle concepts, stakeholder needs, and stakeholder requirements to gain authorization and continuing funding for through the Portfolio Management process (see Section 2.3.3.3). The output should also provide necessary technical definition to the Acquisition process (see Section 2.3.2.1) to generate a request for supply if the system is to be acquired through an acquisition or to gain authorization to develop and market the system if the SoI is to be developed within the organization.

系统生命周期概念、模型和流程

启发或派生利益相关方需要和利益相关方需求。确定利益相关方的需要和需求应综合许多不同的、未必和谐的观点。在确定利益相关方需要和利益相关方需求时，必须有一条"协调"的路径，因为利益相关方的期望和生命周期概念可能存在冲突、不完整、不明确、不可行或无法在项目约束范围内集体满足。这种情况说明了"横向综合"的一个方面（见 2.3.5.8 节），认识到由于与其他利益相关方的需要和需求不一致或缺乏可行性，往往会优先考虑相互竞争的问题，甚至会彻底拒绝一些利益相关方的关切。

在应用系统工程流程时，应创建一个通用范式，用于可用信息的检查和优先排序，并确定附加信息的价值。每个利益相关方对所需系统的视图都可以转化为所有参与者都能理解的通用系统描述，并记录所有决策活动以备将来检查。利益相关方的观点将受到基于其特定角色、教育、工作经验、文化等的认知偏差的影响（见 1.4.2 节）。利益相关方的观点是在这些偏差的背景下形成的。项目团队在启发流程中理解这一点很重要，以便更好地理解每个利益相关方的观点。

系统工程实践者支持项目管理，定义必须做什么，收集信息、人员和分析工具，以阐述生命周期概念、需要和需求。这包括启发或派生利益相关方需要、利益相关方需求、系统／项目约束（例如成本和进度约束、技术限制、适用规范和要求）、"驱动因素"（例如竞争能力、外部威胁和关键环境）和风险。

利益相关方需要和需求定义流程的输出应充分定义生命周期概念、利益相关方需要和利益相关方需求，以通过项目群管理流程获得授权和持续资金（见 2.3.3.3 节）。该输出还应为采办流程提供必要的技术定义（见 2.3.2.1 节），以便在通过采办获得系统时生成供应请求，或在组织内开发 SoI 时获得开发和销售系统的授权。

SYSTEM LIFE CYCLE CONCEPTS, MODELS, AND PROCESSES

Since stakeholder needs and requirements come from multiple sources, eliciting and capturing them constitutes a significant effort on the part of the project. The life cycle concepts help the project team understand the context within which the needs and requirements are captured and defined. Modeling, analysis, and simulation tools can also be used to evaluate candidate solutions and select a desired solution (see Section 3.2.1).

It is essential to establish a database of the data and information which represents the artifacts generated during this process. The database also includes traces between the stakeholder needs, stakeholder requirements, and system requirements. They serve as a foundation for later refinement and/or revision by subsequent activities across the life cycle. Tools for capturing and managing requirements can be used.

Refine Life Cycle Concepts. Stakeholder needs and requirements result from obtaining an understanding of stakeholder expectations through the definition, analysis, and maturation of in a series of life cycle concepts (e.g., acquisition concept, deployment concept, operations concept, support concept, and retirement concept). Development of preliminary life cycle concepts were introduced in the Business or Mission Analysis process (see Section 2.3.5.1). These life cycle concepts need to be refined as part of the Stakeholder Needs and Requirements Definition process.

The primary objective of the development of life cycle concepts is to ensure that stakeholder needs and requirements are clearly understood and the rationale for each is incorporated into the decision mechanism for later transformation into the system requirements. Interviews with manufacturing/coding stakeholders, operators, maintainers, and disposers of current/similar systems, potential users, owners of interoperating, interfacing, and enabling systems (see Section 1.3.3), and site visits provide valuable stakeholder input toward establishing life cycle concepts. Other objectives are as follows:

- To provide traceability between stakeholder needs and stakeholder requirements and their source.

- To establish a holistic understanding of the capabilities needed to address the problem or opportunity in terms of people, process, and products.

- To establish a basis for needs and requirements to support the system over its life, such as personnel requirements, enabling systems, and support requirements.

- To establish a basis for design, system verification, and system validation planning across the life cycle and resulting artifacts and requirements for enabling systems needed as part of the validation and verification activities.

由于利益相关方的需要和需求来自多个来源，因此获取和捕获它们是项目的一项重要工作。生命周期概念有助于项目团队理解捕获和定义需要和需求的背景环境。建模、分析和仿真工具也可用于评估备选解决方案并选择所需的解决方案（见 3.2.1 节）。

必须建立一个数据和信息的数据库，该数据库表示在该流程中生成的制品。数据库还包括利益相关方需要、利益相关方需求和系统需求之间的追溯。它们为以后在整个生命周期中通过后续活动进行细化和／或修订奠定了基础。可以使用用于捕获和管理需求的工具。

完善生命周期概念。利益相关方的需要和需求是通过定义、分析和完善一系列生命周期概念（如采办概念、部署概念、运行概念、支持概念和退役概念）来理解利益相关方期望的结果。在业务或任务分析流程中引入初步生命周期概念的开发（见 2.3.5.1 节）。这些生命周期概念应作为利益相关方需要和需求定义流程的一部分加以完善。开发生命周期概念的主要目标是确保清楚地理解利益相关方的需要和需求，并将每个需要和需求的基本原理纳入决策机制，以便后续转换为系统需求。与当前／类似系统的制造／编码的利益相关方、操作人员、维护者和处置者、潜在用户、互操作系统、接口系统和使能系统的所有者（见 1.3.3 节）的访谈和现场访问为建立生命周期概念提供了有价值的利益相关方输入。其他目标如下：

- 提供利益相关方需要和利益相关方需求及其来源之间的可追溯性。
- 全面了解解决人员、流程和产品方面的问题或机遇所需的能力。
- 为在系统生命周期内支持系统的需要和需求建立基础，如人员需求、使能系统和支持需求。
- 为整个生命周期中的设计、系统验证和系统确认的计划，以及作为验证和确认活动一部分所需的使能系统所产生的制品和需求建立基础。

- To assess interactions of the SoI with users and its operating environment including interactions across interface boundaries with external and enabling systems.
- To provide the basis for analysis of system performance, behavior under (over)-load, and mission-effectiveness calculations.
- To validate needs and requirements at all levels and to discover implicit requirements overlooked from other sources.

112 The life cycle concepts are used to define an integrated set of stakeholder needs which are transformed into the set of stakeholder requirements.

Uncertainties and Risk. During the development of the preliminary life cycle concepts as part of the Business or Mission Analysis process (see Section 2.3.4.3), there may have been uncertainties (see Section 1.4.1) from several perspectives including business, market, management, technical performance, schedule, development and production costs, operations and support costs, security, and sustainability. These uncertainties are a source of risk. Each of these uncertainties must be addressed during the Stakeholder Needs and Requirements Definition process and further elaborated during the Systems Requirements Definition Process (see Section 2.3.4.3).

Record and manage the life cycle concepts, needs, and requirements. The life cycle concepts, stakeholder needs, and stakeholder requirements should be recorded and managed within the project database in a form that allows traceability between the life cycle concepts and the resulting stakeholder needs and requirements (see the INCOSE GtNR [2022] and the INCOSE NRM [2022] for more details).

2.3.5.3 System Requirements Definition Process

Overview

Purpose As stated in ISO/IEC/IEEE 15288,

[6.4.3.1] The purpose of the System Requirements Definition process is to transform the stakeholder, user-oriented view of desired capabilities into a technical view of a solution that *meets the operational needs of the user*.

Description System requirements are the foundation of system definition and form the basis for the System Architecture Definition, Design Definition, Integration, and Verification processes. Each requirement carries a cost, so the system requirements should be the minimum set necessary and sufficient to realize the intent of the stakeholder needs and requirements. Typically, the later in the project that changes are introduced to the system requirements, the greater the impact is to cost and schedule. Where there is more uncertainty in the requirements, the uncertainty should be managed until the requirements mature.

- 评估 SoI 与用户及其运行环境的交互，包括与外部系统和使能系统的跨接口边界的交互。

- 为分析系统性能、过载情况下的行为和任务效能计算提供依据。

- 确认各个层面的需要和需求，并发现从其他来源忽略的隐含需求。

生命周期概念用于定义一组综合的利益相关方需要，并将其转化为利益相关方需求集。

不确定性和风险。在作为业务或任务分析流程一部分的初步生命周期概念开发中（见 2.3.4.3 节），可能存在来自多个角度的不确定性（见 1.4.1 节），包括业务、市场、管理、技术性能、进度、开发和生产成本、运行和支持成本、安保性和可持续性。这些不确定性是风险的来源。所有这些不确定性都必须在利益相关方需要和需求定义流程中解决，并在系统需求定义流程中进一步阐述（见 2.3.4.3 节）。

记录和管理生命周期概念、需要和需求。生命周期概念、利益相关方需要和利益相关方需求应在项目数据库中进行记录和管理，其形式应允许在生命周期概念和由此产生的利益相关方需要和需求之间进行追溯（更多详细信息，请参见 INCOSE GtNR[2022] 和 INCOSE NRM[2022]）。

2.3.5.3 系统需求定义流程

概述

目的 如 ISO/IEC/IEEE 15288 所述：

[6.4.3.1] 系统需求定义流程的目的是将面向利益相关方和用户期望能力的视图转换为满足用户运行需求的解决方案的技术视图。

描述 系统需求是系统定义的基础，是系统架构定义、设计定义、综合和验证流程的基础。每个需求都有成本，因此系统需求应该是实现利益相关方需要和需求意图所必需和完备的最小集合。通常，项目中对系统需求进行更改的时间越晚，对成本和进度的影响就越大。如果需求中存在更多的不确定性，则应管理不确定性，直至需求成熟。

SYSTEM LIFE CYCLE CONCEPTS, MODELS, AND PROCESSES

The System Requirements Definition process generates system requirements from a technical perspective using the stakeholder needs and requirements that reflect the stakeholders' perspectives. As such, the stakeholder needs and requirements drive and constrain the SoI being developed. The quality of the resulting system requirements is dependent on the quality of the agreed-to stakeholder needs and requirements.

System requirements definition is concurrent, iterative, and recursive. Thus, the System Requirements Definition process is done concurrently and iteratively with the other Technical Processes, particularly the Stakeholder Needs and Requirements Definition and the System Architecture Definition processes. With each iteration, more detailed information is discovered and defined based on the analysis and maturation of the life cycle concepts and the system solution. In addition, the System Requirements Definition processes is recursively applied to define the requirements for each lower-level system element within the SoI architecture. The allocation of the system requirements is performed concurrently with the System Architecture Definition process. Lower-level system elements are defined via the System Architecture Definition process, and then the SoI level requirements are allocated to the system elements at the next level. For each lower-level system element, the Stakeholder Needs and Requirements Definition and System Requirements Definition processes are repeated recursively until all system elements have their system requirements defined. The outputs of System Requirements Definition process must be traceable and consistent with the life cycle concepts and stakeholder needs and stakeholder requirements, without introducing unnecessary implementation biases. The System Requirements Definition process adds the verification criteria to each system requirement as it is derived.

Inputs/Outputs Inputs and outputs for the System Requirements Definition process are listed in the IPO diagram in Figure 2.41. Descriptions of each input and output are provided in Appendix E.

Process Activities The System Requirements Definition process includes the following activities:

- *Prepare for system requirements definition.*

–Establish the strategy/approach for system requirements definition.

–Plan for the necessary enabling systems or services needed through the life cycle for system requirements definition. Enabling systems include tools for elicitation of requirements, life cycle concepts, recording drivers and constraints, defining risks, analysis, recording system needs, recording system requirements, and providing traceability.

系统需求定义流程使用反映利益相关方观点的利益相关方需要和需求,从技术视角生成系统需求。因此,利益相关方的需要和需求驱动并约束正在开发的 SoI。产生的系统需求的质量取决于商定的利益相关方需要和需求的质量。

系统需求的定义是并行的、迭代的和递归的。因此,系统需求定义流程与其他技术流程(尤其是利益相关方需要和需求定义以及系统架构定义流程)同时迭代完成。在每次迭代中,会根据生命周期概念和系统解决方案的分析和成熟度发现和定义更详细的信息。此外,系统需求定义流程被递归地应用于定义 SoI 架构中每个较低层级系统元素的需求。系统需求的分配与系统架构定义流程同时执行。通过系统架构定义流程定义较低层级的系统元素,然后在下一层级将 SoI 级需求分配给系统元素。对于每个较低层级的系统元素,利益相关方需要和需求定义以及系统需求定义流程将递归重复,直到所有系统元素都定义了其系统需求。系统需求定义流程的输出必须具有可追溯性,并与生命周期概念、利益相关方需要和利益相关方需求保持一致,而不会引入不必要的实施偏差。系统需求定义流程将验证准则添加到导出的每个系统需求中。

输入/输出　图 2.41 中的 IPO 图列出了系统需求定义流程的输入和输出。附录 E 中提供了每个输入和输出的描述。

流程活动　系统需求定义流程包括以下活动:

- 准备系统需求定义。

- 建立系统需求定义的策略/实施方法。

- 为系统需求定义的整个生命周期所需的必要使能系统或服务制订计划。使能系统包括用于需求获取、生命周期概念、记录驱动因素和约束、定义风险、分析、记录系统需要、记录系统需求和提供可追溯性的工具。

SYSTEM LIFE CYCLE CONCEPTS, MODELS, AND PROCESSES

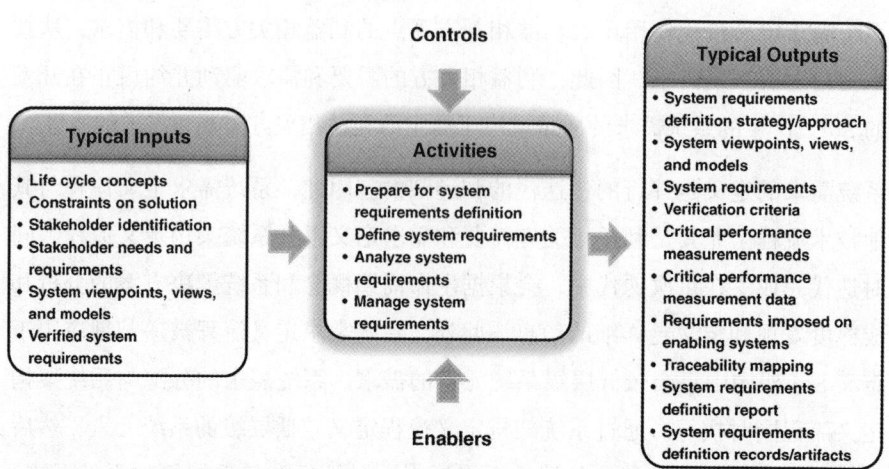

FIGURE 2.41   IPO diagram for System Requirements Definition process. INCOSE SEH original figure created by Shortell, Walden, and Yip. Usage per the INCOSE Notices page. All other rights reserved.

–Ensure enabling system or service access needed to support system requirements definition.

- *Define system requirements.*

–Define the functional boundary of the system in terms of the behavior and properties to be provided.

–Identify the life cycle concepts and stakeholder requirements from which the system requirements will be transformed and then define each function and associated performance.

–Define each expected system function, including the associated performance. Include both primary functions and enabling functions.

–Define necessary constraints. These include higher-level requirements allocated to the SoI, operational conditions, and interactions with external systems. Define interactions with users, operators, maintainers, and disposers.

–Identify system requirements that relate to risks, criticality of the system, critical quality characteristics, and compliance with standards and regulations.

–Define verification success criteria for each system requirement, the verification strategy, verification method, and responsible organization for providing proof the system requirements have been met (see Section 2.3.5.9).

–Capture the system requirements and their attributes.

系统生命周期概念、模型和流程

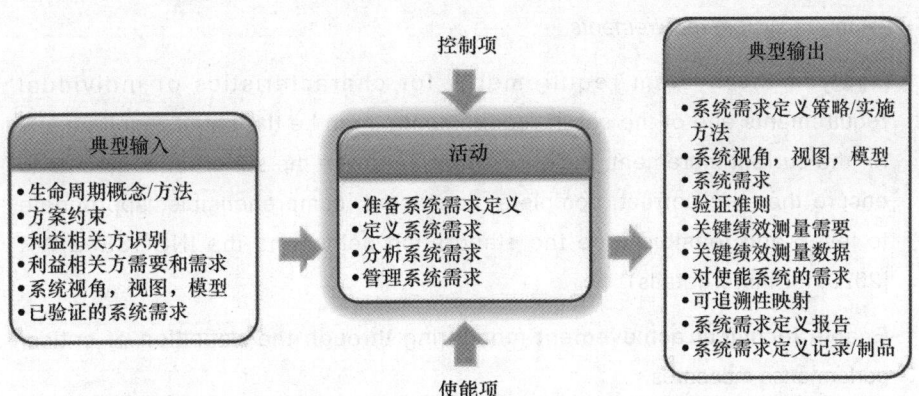

图 2.41 系统需求定义流程的 IPO 图。INCOSE SEH 原始图由 Shortell、Walden 和 Yip 创建。按照 INCOSE 通知页使用。版权所有。

- 确保可获得支持系统需求定义所需的系统或服务。

• *定义系统需求*。

- 根据要提供的行为和属性定义系统的功能边界。

- 确定生命周期概念和利益相关方需求，从中转换系统需求，然后定义每个功能和相关性能。

- 定义每个预期的系统功能，包括相关的性能，以及主要功能和使能功能。

- 定义必要的约束。这些包括分配给 SoI 的更高层级需求、运行条件以及与外部系统的交互。定义与用户、操作人员、维护人员和处置人员的交互。

- 识别与风险、系统的关键性、关键质量特性以及标准和法规遵从性相关的系统需求。

- 定义每个系统需求的验证成功准则、验证策略、验证方法和负责组织，以证明系统需求已得到满足（见 2.3.5.9 节）。

- 捕获系统需求及其属性。

SYSTEM LIFE CYCLE CONCEPTS, MODELS, AND PROCESSES

- *Analyze system requirements.*

–Analyze the system requirements for characteristics of individual requirements and of the set of requirements (can be the set of requirements for the current increment, build, or sprint). Analyze the set of requirements to ensure they are correct, complete, consistent, comprehensible, appropriate to level, and feasible (see the elaboration below and the INCOSE GtWR [2023] for more details).

–Enable technical achievement monitoring through the definition of critical performance measures.

–Review the analyzed requirements with the applicable stakeholders.

–Perform issue resolution for the system requirements. Negotiate changes, amendments, and modifications to resolve inconsistencies, conflicts, and unrealizable or impractical requirements.

- *Manage system requirements.*

–Confirm agreement that the system requirements meet the stakeholder needs and requirements.

–Capture key system requirements decisions, rationale, alternatives, and enablers.

–Establish and sustain traceability (system requirements).

–Manage system requirements change.

–Give CM the information items, work products, or other artifacts needed for baselines.

Common approaches and tips:

- Identify the enabling systems and materials needed for transition early in the life cycle to allow for the necessary lead time to obtain or access them.

Elaboration

This section elaborates and provides "how-to" information on the System Requirements Definition process. Additional guidance on needs and requirements definition can be found in ISO/IEC/IEEE 29148 (2018), the INCOSE GtWR (2023), the INCOSE GtNR (2022) and the INCOSE NRM (2022).

- 分析系统需求。

  - 分析系统需求的各个需求和需求集的特征（可以是当前的增量、构建或一次迭代的需求集）。分析一组需求，以确保其正确、完整、一致、可理解、适当且可行（有关更多详细信息，请参阅下面的详细说明和 INCOSE GtWR[2023]）。

  - 通过定义关键绩效指标，实现技术成果监控。

  - 与适合的利益相关方一起评审分析后的需求。

  - 解决系统需求存在的问题。协商变更、修订和修改，以解决不一致、冲突以及无法实现或不切实际的需求。

- 管理系统需求。

  - 确认系统需求满足利益相关方需要和需求的协议。

  - 捕获关键系统需求决策、基本原理、备选方案和使能项。

  - 建立并保持可追溯性（系统需求）。

  - 管理系统需求变更。

  - 为构型配置管理提供基线所需的信息项、工作产品或其他制品。

常用方法和提示：

- 在生命周期的早期阶段确定转移所需的使能系统和材料，以便有必要的提前期来获取或使用它们。

详细阐述

本节阐述并提供了有关系统需求定义流程的"如何做"的信息。有关需要和需求定义的其他指南，请参见 ISO/IEC/IEEE 29148（2018）、INCOSE GtWR（2023）、INCOSE GtNR（2022）和 INCOSE NRM（2022）。

SYSTEM LIFE CYCLE CONCEPTS, MODELS, AND PROCESSES

Stakeholder Requirements versus System Requirements. The set of stakeholder requirements are SoI requirements written from the stakeholders' perspectives to represent what they require of the SoI in order to meet their needs. The set of system requirements represent the technical perspective of what the SoI must meet during the System Architecture Definition and Design Definition processes that will result in a system that meets the stakeholder needs and stakeholder requirements. Another key distinction is that the focus of the stakeholder requirements is often on high-priority and critical functions, performance, quality, compliance, etc., while the system requirements are more encompassing and detailed including enabling functions, performance, quality, compliance, etc. that will result in the stakeholder requirements to be implemented.

In some cases, the stakeholder requirements can be copied directly into the set of system requirements "as is" and additional requirements added as needed. For smaller, internal projects, the set of stakeholder requirements could be used as the set of system requirements, depending on how much analysis went into the definition of the set of stakeholder requirements such that their implementation will result in the stakeholder needs to be met.

When a set of stakeholder requirements is provided to a supplier by an acquirer, the supplier uses these as inputs to their SE processes to develop the set of system requirements. When defining the system requirements, rather than treating the supplied stakeholder requirements as the only source of requirements, the supplier has an obligation to do an assessment for derived system requirements and as well as requirements from other "non-acquirer" stakeholders. For example, the supplier's production team needs the product to be manufacturable, their test team needs the product to be testable, the supplier and public need the product to be safe and secure from a cybersecurity perspective, the users and operators need the product to be easy and safe to interface with from a human perspective, and the organization has regulatory compliance considerations. For products to be developed by an outside supplier, the supplier's company may need the product to conform to a strategic development effort aligning with other products produced, internal standards, and technology maturation. The acquirer may not have included all of these considerations when developing their set of requirements. If the supplier blindly follows only the acquirer supplied requirements specified in their contract, they are likely to generate a SoI that may not work in the integrated system or operational environment, resulting in a system that fails system validation.

*利益相关方需求与系统需求。*利益相关方需求集是从利益相关方的角度编写的 SoI 需求，代表他们对 SoI 的需求，以满足他们的需要。系统需求集代表了 SoI 在系统架构定义和设计定义流程中必须满足的技术观点，这将导致系统满足利益相关方需要和利益相关方需求。另一个关键区别是，利益相关方需求的重点通常是高优先级和关键功能、性能、质量、合规性等，而系统需求则更为全面和详细，包括使能功能、性能、质量、合规性等，从而满足利益相关方需求。

在某些情况下，利益相关方需求可以"按原样"直接复制到一组系统需求中，并根据需要添加其他需求。对于较小的内部项目，利益相关方需求集可以用作系统需求集，这取决于对利益相关方需求集的定义进行了多少分析，以使其实现能够满足利益相关方的需要。

当采办方向供应商提供一组利益相关方需求时，供应商将其作为系统工程流程的输入，以开发一组系统需求。在定义系统需求时，供应商有义务对派生系统需求以及其他"非采办方"利益相关方的需求进行评估，而不是将所提供的利益相关方需求视为需求的唯一来源。例如，供应商的生产团队需要可制造的产品，他们的测试团队需要可测试的产品，供应商和公众需要从网络安保的角度看来安全可靠的产品，用户和操作员需要从人的角度看来易于与安全的产品交互，组织需要考虑法规遵从性。对于由外部供应商开发的产品，供应商的公司可能需要该产品符合与所生产的其他产品、内部标准和技术成熟度相一致的战略开发工作。采办方在制定其需求集时可能没有考虑到所有因素。如果供应商盲目地仅遵循其合同中规定的采办方提供的要求，则他们可能会生成一个 SoI，该 SoI 可能无法在综合的系统或运行环境中工作，从而导致系统无法通过系统确认。

SYSTEM LIFE CYCLE CONCEPTS, MODELS, AND PROCESSES

Plan for system requirements definition. The System Requirements Definition process should begin with a review of the problem, threat, or opportunity for which the SoI is to address, and the mission, goals, objectives and critical success measures defined by the Business or Mission Analysis process (see Section 2.3.5.1) and the set of stakeholder needs, stakeholder requirements, and life cycle concepts defined by the Stakeholder Needs and Requirement Definition process (see Section 2.3.5.2). For contracted development efforts, mission, goals, objectives, and critical success measures can come from both the acquirer and supplier organizations. Before the System Requirements Definition process, the project team will need to define the strategy to be used to transform the stakeholder needs and stakeholder requirements, define drivers and constraints, assess risks, define, analyze, and mature life cycle concepts, and derive an integrated set of system requirements resulting from these activities. Requirements Definition. The integrated set of stakeholder requirements is transformed into system requirements to address what the system must do to meet those needs. The transformation process involves additional analysis and further elaboration of the models developed during life cycle concept analysis and maturation. The system requirements must address function, fit, form, quality, and compliance with stakeholder and business needs. System requirements must also address interactions with external systems, users, operators, maintainers, disposers, and the operational environment. SE practitioners collaborate with the stakeholders of the external systems to define each of the interactions and record an agreement of those definitions in some configuration managed form, as well as any constraints or interface requirements (see Section 3.2.4).

Definition of the system requirements is a complex process that includes function and performance analysis; trade studies; constraint evaluation; inclusion of (or reference to) specific requirements from relevant standards and regulations; risk assessment; technology assessment; detailed characterization of the operational environment; detailed assessment of the interactions of the parts that make up the SoI, detailed assessment of the interactions between the SoI and users, operators, maintains, disposers, and external systems; and cost–benefit analysis. System requirements cannot be established without determining their impact (achievability) on lower-level system elements, especially in terms of cost, schedule, and technology. Therefore, system requirements definition is a concurrent, iterative, and recursive balancing process that works both "top-down" (called allocation, derivation, and flow-down) and "bottom-up" (called compliance analysis and flow-up).

系统需求定义计划。系统需求定义流程应首先评审 SoI 要解决的问题、威胁或机遇，以及业务或任务分析流程（见 2.3.5.1 节）定义的任务、目的、目标和关键成功测度，以及利益相关方需要和需求定义流程（见 2.3.5.2 节）定义的利益相关方需要、利益相关方需求和生命周期概念集。对于合同开发工作，任务、目的、目标和关键成功测度可以来自采办方和供应商组织。在系统需求定义流程之前，项目团队需要定义用于转换利益相关方需要和利益相关方需求、定义驱动因素和约束、评估风险、定义、分析和使生命周期概念成熟的策略，并从这些活动中得出一组完整的系统需求。需求定义。利益相关方需求的综合集合被转换为系统需求，以解决系统必须做什么来满足这些需求。转换流程包括对生命周期概念分析和成熟流程中开发的模型进行额外分析和进一步细化。系统需求必须解决功能、适合性、形式、质量以及与利益相关方和业务需求的符合性。系统需求还必须解决与外部系统、用户、操作人员、维护人员、处置人员和运行环境的交互。系统工程实践者与外部系统的利益相关方合作，定义每个交互，并以某种构型配置管理形式记录这些定义的一致性，以及任何约束或接口要求（见 3.2.4 节）。

系统需求的定义是一个复杂的流程，包括功能和性能分析；权衡研究；约束评估；包括（或参考）相关标准和法规中的具体要求；风险评估；技术评估；运行环境的详细描述；详细评估组成 SoI 的部件之间的相互作用，详细评估 SoI 与用户、操作人员、维护人员、处置人员和外部系统之间的相互作用；成本效益分析。如果不确定系统需求对下级系统元素的影响（可实现性），尤其是在成本、进度和技术方面，就无法确定系统需求。因此，系统需求定义是一个并行、迭代和递归的平衡流程，它既可以"自顶向下"（称为分配、派生和向下流动）也可以"自下而上"（称为遵从性分析和向上流动）。

SYSTEM LIFE CYCLE CONCEPTS, MODELS, AND PROCESSES

The system requirements are inputs to the System Architecture Definition and Design Definition processes, in some domains these requirements are referred to as "design-to" or "design input" requirements. When the requirements are defined, it is important that they are expressed at a level of abstraction that is appropriate to the SoI and systems hierarchy level to which they apply. Although it is good practice to avoid implementation when defining the system requirements, it is not always possible.

In defining system requirements, care should be exercised to ensure each requirement statement is appropriately crafted. The characteristics shown in Table 2.7 should be considered for each individual requirement statement (INCOSE GtWR, 2023). In addition to the characteristics of individual requirement statements, the characteristics shown in Table 2.8 should be considered for requirement sets (INCOSE GtWR, 2023).

TABLE 2.7 Requirement statement characteristics

Requirement Statement Characteristic	Definition
Necessary	The requirement statement defines a capability, characteristic, constraint, or quality factor needed to satisfy a life cycle concept, need, source, or parent requirement.
Appropriate	The specific intent and amount of detail of the requirement statement is appropriate to the level (e.g., the level of abstraction, organization, or system architecture) of the entity to which it refers.
Unambiguous	The requirement statement is stated such that the intent is clear and the requirement can be interpreted in only one way by all the intended stakeholders.
Complete	The requirement statement sufficiently describes the necessary capability, characteristic, constraint, conditions, or quality factor to meet the need, source, or higher-level requirement from which it was transformed.
Singular	The requirement statement states a single capability, characteristic, constraint, or quality factor.
Feasible	The requirement statement can be realized within entity constraints (e.g., cost, schedule, technical, legal, ethical, safety) with acceptable risk.
Verifiable	The requirement statement is structured and worded such that its realization can be verified to the approving authority's satisfaction.
Correct	The requirement statement is an accurate representation of the need, source, or higher-level requirement from which it was transformed.
Conforming	The requirement statement conforms to an approved standard pattern and style guide or standard for writing and managing requirements.

From INCOSE GtWR (2023). Usage per the INCOSE Notices page. All other rights reserved.

系统需求是系统架构定义和设计定义流程的输入，在某些领域，这些需求被称为"设计目标"或"设计输入"需求。定义需求时，重要的是要在一个抽象层级上表达需求，该抽象层级适合它们所应用的 SoI 和系统层级结构。虽然在定义系统需求时避免实现是一种很好的做法，但并不总是可行的。

在定义系统需求时，应注意确保每个需求语句都经过适当的编制。对于每个单独的需求声明，应考虑表 2.7 中所示的特征（INCOSE GtWR，2023）。除了个别需求陈述的特征外，还应考虑表 2.8 中所示的需求集特征（INCOSE GtWR，2023）。

表 2.7　需求声明特征

需求声明特征	定义
必要性	需求声明定义了满足生命周期概念、需要、来源或父级需求所需的能力、特性、约束或质量要素。
适宜性	需求声明的具体意图和详细程度要与所涉及实体的层级（如抽象层级、组织或系统架构）相适应。
无歧义性	需求声明的意图要明确，所有利益相关方只能以一种方式解释需求。
完备性	需求声明要充分描述必要的能力、特性、约束、条件或质量因素，以满足需要、来源或更高层级的需求。
单一性	需求声明阐述了单一的能力、特性、约束或质量因素。
可行性	需求声明可在实体约束（如成本、进度、技术、法律、道德、安全）范围内以可接受的风险实现。
可验证性	需求声明的结构和措辞应能使审批机构满意地核实其实现情况。
正确性	需求声明是对需要、来源或更高层级需求的准确表述，需求声明是由这些需求转化而来的。
符合性	需求声明符合经批准的标准模式和风格指南或需求编写和管理标准。

源自 INCOSE GtWR（2023）。按照 INCOSE 通知页使用。版权所有。

SYSTEM LIFE CYCLE CONCEPTS, MODELS, AND PROCESSES

System requirement statements may have a number of attributes attached to them (either as fields in a database or through relationships with other artifacts) shown in Table 2.9. *The attributes annotated with an asterisk ("*") represent a proposed minimum set.* See the INCOSE NRM (2022) for the definition and description of these attributes.

Allocation, derivation, and flow-down. The next level of the system hierarchy is defined in conjunction with the System Architecture Definition and Design Definition processes. System requirements are allocated to the system elements at the next level of the system hierarchy. Once the allocation has been determined, the system requirements are derived (assigned) for the next system elements at the level of system hierarchy such that the intent of the allocated parent requirement is met.

TABLE 2.8 Requirement set characteristics

Requirement Set Characteristic	Definition
Complete	The requirement set for a given SoI should stand alone such that it sufficiently describes the necessary capabilities, characteristics, functionality, performance, drivers, constraints, conditions, interactions, standards, regulations, and/or quality characteristics without requiring other sets of requirements at the appropriate level of abstraction.
Consistent	The requirement set contains individual requirements that are unique, do not conflict with or overlap with others in the set, and the units and measurement systems they use are homogeneous. The language used within the sets is consistent (i.e., the same words are used throughout the set to mean the same thing). All terms used within the requirement statements are consistent with the architectural model, project glossary, and project data dictionary.
Feasible	The requirement set can be realized within entity constraints (e.g., cost, schedule, technical) with acceptable risk.
Comprehensible	The requirement set is written such that it is clear as to what is expected of the entity and its relation to the macro system of which it is a part.
Able to be validated	The requirement set will lead to the achievement of the set of needs and higher-level requirements within the constraints (such as cost, schedule, technical, and regulatory compliance) with acceptable risk.
Correct	The requirement set is an accurate representation of the needs, sources, or higher-level requirements from which it was transformed.

From INCOSE GtWR (2023). Usage per the INCOSE Notices page. All other rights reserved.

如表 2.9 所示，系统需求语句可能具有许多附加属性（作为数据库中的字段或通过与其他制品的关系）。*带星号（"*"）的属性表示建议的最小集*。有关这些属性的定义和描述，请参见 INCOSE NRM（2022）。

分配、派生和向下流动。系统层级结构的下一级是结合系统架构定义和设计定义流程的。系统需求在系统层级结构的下一级分配给系统元素。一旦确定了分配，就会在系统层级结构中为下一个系统元素推导（分配）系统需求，以满足所分配的父级需求的意图。

表 2.8 需求集特征

需求集特征	定义
完备性	特定 SoI 的需求集应该是独立的，它能充分描述必要的能力、特性、功能、性能、驱动因素、约束、条件、交互、标准、法规和/或质量特征，而不需要其他适当抽象程度的需求集。
一致性	需求集所包含的单个需求是独一无二的，不会与需求集中的其他需求冲突或重叠，而且它们所使用的单位和测量系统是相同的。需求集中使用的语言是一致的（即整个需求集中使用相同的词语表示相同的意思）。需求声明中使用的所有术语与架构模型、项目术语表和项目数据字典一致。
可行性	需求集可在实体约束（例如成本、进度、技术）范围内实现，且风险可接受。
可理解性	在编写需求集时，要明确对实体的期望以及实体与宏观系统的关系。
可被确认性	需求集将在可接受的风险范围内（例如成本、进度、技术和法规遵从性），满足一系列需求和更高层级的需求。
正确性	需求集是需要、来源或更高层级需求的准确表述，它是由需要、来源或更高层级需求转化而来的。

源自 INCOSE GtWR（2023）。按照 INCOSE 通知页使用。版权所有。

117 TABLE 2.9 Requirement attributes

Attributes to Help Define Needs and Requirement and Their Intent	A21—Change Control Board
	A22—Change Proposed
	A23—Version Number
A1—Rationale*	A24—Approval Date
A2—Trace to Parent*	A25—Date of Last Change
A3—Trace to Source*	A26—Stability/Volatility
A4—States and Modes	A27—Responsible Person
A5—Allocation/Budgeting*	A28—Need or Requirement Verification Status*
Attributes Associated with System Verification and System Validation	A29—Need or Requirement Validation Status*
	A30—Status of the Need or Requirement
A6—System Verification or System Validation Success Criteria*	A31—Status (of Implementation)
	A32—Trace to Interface Definition
A7—System Verification or System Validation Strategy*	A33—Trace to Dependent Peer Requirements*
	A34—Priority*
A8—System Verification or System Validation Method*	A35—Criticality or Essentiality*
	A36—Risk (of Implementation)*
A9—System Verification or System Validation Responsible Organization*	A37—Risk (Mitigation)*
	A38—Key Driving Need or Requirement
A10—System Verification or System Validation Level	A39—Additional Comments
	A40—Type/Category
A11—System Verification or System Validation Phase	**Attributes to Show Applicability and Enable Reuse**
	A41—Applicability
A12—Condition of Use	A42—Region
A13—System Verification or System Validation Results	A43—Country
	A44—State/Province
A14—System Verification or System Validation Status	A45—Market Segment
	A46—Business Unit
Attributes to Help Manage the Requirements	**Attributes to Aid in Product Line Management**
A15—Unique Identifier*	A47—Product Line
A16—Unique Name	A48—Product Line Common Needs and Requirements
A17—Originator/Author*	A49—Product Line Variant Needs and Requirements
A18—Date Requirement Entered	
A19—Owner*	
A20—Stakeholders	

From INCOSE NRM (2022). Usage per the INCOSE Notices page. All other rights reserved.

The System Requirements Definition process is repeated recursively for each level of the system hierarchy until the system elements are to the level of detail needed to be realized via a make (e.g., build, code), buy, or reuse decision. The resulting sets of system requirements for the system elements represent the allocated baseline of the SoI.

表 2.9 需求属性

帮助定义需要和需求及其意图的属性

A1—理由 *

A2—追溯到父级 *

A3—追溯到来源 *

A4—状态和模式

A5—分配 / 预算 *

与系统验证和系统确认有关的属性

A6—系统验证或系统确认成功准则 *

A7—系统验证或系统确认策略 *

A8—系统验证或系统确认方法 *

A9—系统验证或系统确认负责组织 *

A10—系统验证或确认层级

A11—系统验证或确认阶段

A12—使用条件

A13—系统验证或确认结果

A14—系统验证或确认状态

帮助管理需求的属性

A15—唯一标识符 *

A16—唯一名字

A17—发起人 / 作者 *

A18—输入要求的日期

A19—所有者 *

A20—利益相关方

A21—变更控制委员会

A22—变更建议

A23—版本号

A24—批准日期

A25—最后变更日期

A26—稳定性 / 易变性

A27—负责人

A28—需要或需求验证状态 *

A29—需要或需求确认状态 *

A30—需要或需求的现状

A31—实施的状态

A32—追溯到接口定义

A33—追溯到依赖的同级需求

A34—优先级

A35—关键性或本质 *

A36—实施的风险 *

A37—风险（缓解）*

A38—关键驱动需要或需求

A39—附加备注

A40—类型 / 类别

显示适用性和实现重复使用的属性

A41—适用性

A42—地区

A43—国家

A44—州 / 省

A45—市场细分

A46—业务单元

辅助产品线管理的属性

A47—产品线

A48—产品线通用需要和需求

A49—产品线差异需要和需求

源自 INCOSE NRM（2022）。按照 INCOSE 通知页使用。版权所有。

系统需求定义流程针对系统层级结构的每一层递归重复，直到系统元素达到需要通过制造（例如构建、代码）、购买或复用决策实现的详细层级。系统元素的最终系统需求集表示 SoI 的分配基线。

SYSTEM LIFE CYCLE CONCEPTS, MODELS, AND PROCESSES

Requirements Management. According to ISO/IEC/IEEE 29148, requirements management encompasses those tasks that record and maintain the evolving requirements and associated context and historical information from the requirements engineering activities. Effective requirements management occurs within the context of an organization's project and Technical Processes. Requirements management also establishes procedures for defining, controlling, and publishing the baseline requirements for all levels of the SoI. The resulting sets of requirements are provided to the Configuration Management process (see Section 2.3.4.5) process for baselining at the appropriate time. The Configuration Management process is used to establish and maintain configuration items and baselines. Requirements management also ensures traceability is established between requirements and other artifacts (see Section 3.2.3), that appropriate requirements reviews occur, and requirements measures are established and used. See also the INCOSE GtNR (2022) and the INCOSE NRM (2022) for further elaboration concerning requirements management.

2.3.5.4 System Architecture Definition Process

Overview

Purpose As stated in ISO/IEC/IEEE 15288:

[6.4.4.1] The purpose of the System Architecture Definition process is to generate system architecture alternatives, select one or more alternative(s) that address stakeholder concerns and system requirements, and express this in consistent views and models.

System Architecture Definition process transforms related architectures (e.g., strategic, enterprise, reference, and SoS architectures), organizational and project policies and directives, life cycle concepts and constraints, stakeholder concerns and requirements, and system requirements and constraints into the fundamental concepts and properties of the system and the governing principles for evolution of the system and its related life cycle processes. This process results in a system architecture description for use by the project, its organization, other organizations, and various stakeholders. The Project Management Plan (PMP) and Systems Engineering Management Plan (SEMP) in some cases will provide management directives on how to perform this process, but usually the programmatic view and other related views developed by the System Architecture Definition activities will guide the PMP and the SEMP. The architecture governance activities at the organization level will provide additional direction for the System Architecture Definition process through its issuance of architecture governance directives. Since the directives and stakeholder requirements can evolve throughout the system life cycle, the system architecture description should be treated as a living artifact reflecting both the changing expectations and the evolution of our understanding of what the system solution should be.

需求管理。根据 ISO/IEC/IEEE 29148，需求管理包括记录和维护不断发展的需求以及来自需求工程活动的相关背景环境和历史信息的任务。有效的需求管理发生在组织的项目和技术流程中。需求管理还建立了定义、控制和发布各级 SoI 基线需求的程序。所产生的需求集将在适当的时候提供给构型配置管理流程（见 2.3.4.5 节）以进行基线化。构型配置管理流程用于建立和维护构型配置项和基线。需求管理还确保在需求和其他制品之间建立可追溯性（见 3.2.3 节），进行适当的需求评审，并建立和使用需求测度。有关需求管理的进一步阐述，请参见 INCOSE GtNR（2022）和 INCOSE NRM（2022）。

2.3.5.4 系统架构定义流程

概述

目的 如 ISO/IEC/IEEE 15288 所述：

[6.4.4.1] 系统架构定义流程的目的是生成系统架构备选方案，选择一个或多个回应利益相关方关切和系统需求的备选方案，并以一致的视图和模型进行表达。

系统架构定义流程将相关架构（例如，战略架构、复杂组织体系架构、参考架构和体系架构）、组织和项目政策和指令、生命周期概念和约束、利益相关方关切和需求以及系统需求和约束转化为系统的基本概念和属性以及系统及其相关生命周期流程演进的治理原则。该流程产生了一个系统架构描述，供项目、系统的组织、其他组织和各利益相关方使用。在某些情况下，项目管理计划（PMP）和系统工程管理计划（SEMP）将提供有关如何执行此流程的管理指令，但通常系统架构定义活动开发的程序视图和其他相关视图将指导 PMP 和 SEMP。组织层面的架构治理活动将通过发布架构治理指令为系统架构定义流程提供额外的指导。由于指令和利益相关方需求可以在整个系统生命周期中演进，因此系统架构描述应该被视为一个有生命力的制品，反映不断变化的期望和我们对系统解决方案应该是什么的理解的演进。

SYSTEM LIFE CYCLE CONCEPTS, MODELS, AND PROCESSES

Development practices for architecture are specified by ISO 15704 for enterprises and the ISO/IEC/IEEE 42000 series of standards in software, systems, and enterprise fields of application. ISO 15704 specifies terms, concepts, and principles considered necessary to address stakeholder concerns, carry out enterprise creation programs and any incremental change projects required by the enterprise throughout its whole life. ISO/IEC/IEEE 42000 series of standards establishes processes, key principles, and concepts for conceptualization, evaluation, and description of architectures.

Description The System Architecture Definition process provides information and data useful and necessary for identifying and characterizing the fundamental concepts and properties of the system and its elements. These concepts and properties can be fundamentally human-centric, with individual, social, organizational, and political aspects, in human activity systems considering technical elements as enablement assets. The architecture information and data will be implementable through system and system element designs, which satisfy as far as possible the problem or opportunity expressed by models and views for a set of stakeholder and system requirements (traceable to business/mission requirements, as applicable) and life cycle concepts (e.g., Operational, Acquisition, Deployment, Support, and Retirement). During a stage in the system life cycle, the relevant enabling systems and the SoI are considered together as a solution but are distinguished from each other in the overall solution conceptualization.

System architecture definition focuses on achieving associated missions and characterizing the operational concepts of the system and performing market analysis to ensure viability of the SoI. It utilizes architectural principles and concepts to define the high-level structure of a system and its elements, and the intended properties and characteristics of the SoI. It highlights and supports trade-offs for the other System Definition processes. and possibly Portfolio Management and Project Planning. It incorporates incremental insights obtained about the emergent properties and behaviors of the SoI while achieving a balance for suitability, viability, effectiveness, and affordability. This process is iterative and requires participation of architects, SE practitioners, and specialists in relevant domains, subject matter experts and other stakeholders. The process continues recursively through the levels of the system and its system elements, with consistent feedback to ensure the system design continues to satisfy stakeholder needs and system requirements.

Inputs/Outputs Inputs and outputs for the System Architecture Definition process are listed in Figure 2.42. Descriptions of each input and output are provided in Appendix E.

ISO 15704（适用于复杂组织体系）和 ISO/IEC/IEEE 42000（软件、系统和复杂组织体系应用领域）系列标准规定了架构的开发实践。ISO 15704 规定了解决利益相关方关切、执行复杂组织体系创建计划和复杂组织体系在其整个生命周期中所需的任何增量变更项目所需的术语、概念和原则。ISO/IEC/IEEE 42000 系列标准确立了架构概念化、评估和描述的流程、关键原则和概念。

描述 系统架构定义流程提供了识别和表征系统及其元素的基本概念和属性所需的有用信息和数据。在人类活动系统中，这些概念和属性可以从根本上以人为中心，包括个人、社会、组织和政治方面，将技术元素视为使能资产。架构信息和数据将可通过系统和系统元素设计来实现，这些设计将尽可能满足由模型和视图所表达的关于一组利益相关方和系统需求（可追溯到业务/任务需求，如适用）以及生命周期概念（如运行、采办、部署、支持和退役）的问题或机会。在系统生命周期的某个阶段，相关的使能系统和 SoI 一起被视为一个解决方案，但在整体解决方案概念化中加以区分。

系统架构定义聚焦于完成相关任务，表征系统的运行概念，并进行市场分析以确保 SoI 的可行性。它利用架构原则和概念来定义系统的高层结构及其元素，以及 SoI 的预期属性和特征。它强调并支持其他系统定义流程的权衡，以及项目组合和项目计划。它结合了从 SoI 的涌现特性和行为中获得的增量见解，同时实现了适用性、可行性、有效性和可承受性的平衡。这个流程是迭代的，需要架构师、系统工程从业人员、相关领域的专家、主题专家和其他利益相关方的参与。该流程在系统及其系统元素的各个层级上不断循环，并以一致的反馈确保系统设计持续满足利益相关方需要和系统需求。

输入/输出 系统架构定义流程的输入和输出如图 2.42 所示。附录 E 中提供了每个输入和输出的描述。

SYSTEM LIFE CYCLE CONCEPTS, MODELS, AND PROCESSES

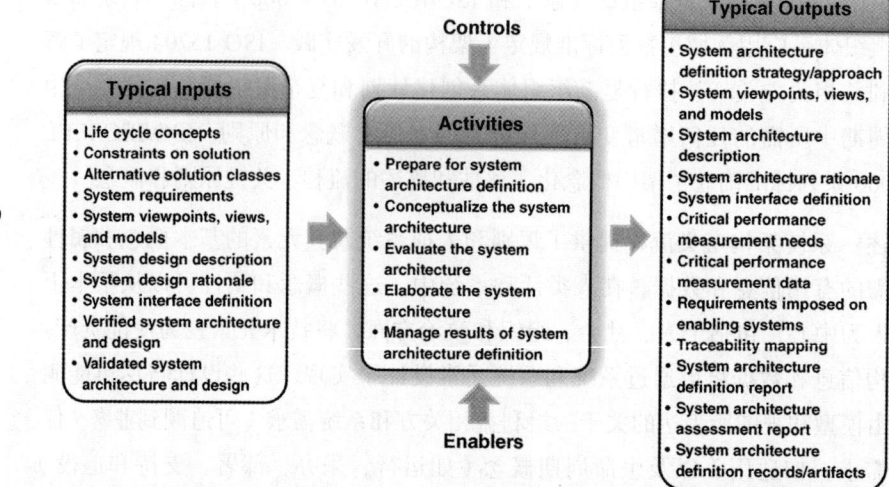

FIGURE 2.42 IPO diagram for System Architecture Definition process. INCOSE SEH original figure created by Shortell, Walden, and Yip. Usage per the INCOSE Notices page. All other rights reserved.

Process Activities The System Architecture Definition process includes the following activities:

Prepare for system architecture definition.

- Identify and analyze relevant market, industry, stakeholder, organizational, business, operations, mission, legal, and other information and related perspectives that will guide the development of the system architecture.

- Identify key milestones and decisions to be informed by the system architecture effort. In particular, identify those key architecture artifacts and resources that guide the system architecture development.

- In conjunction with the System Requirements Definition process, determine the system context (i.e., how the SoI fits into the external environment) and system boundary are refined, that reflect operational scenarios and expected system behaviors. This task includes identification of expected interactions of the SoI with system elements, or other systems or entities.

- Establish the approach for architecting. This includes an architecture roadmap and strategy, methods, frameworks (see Section 3.2.5), patterns (see Section 3.2.6), modeling techniques, tools, and the need for any enabling systems (see Section 1.3.3), products, or services. The approach should also include the process requirements (e.g., measurement approach and methods), evaluation (e.g., reviews and criteria), and necessary coordination.

系统生命周期概念、模型和流程

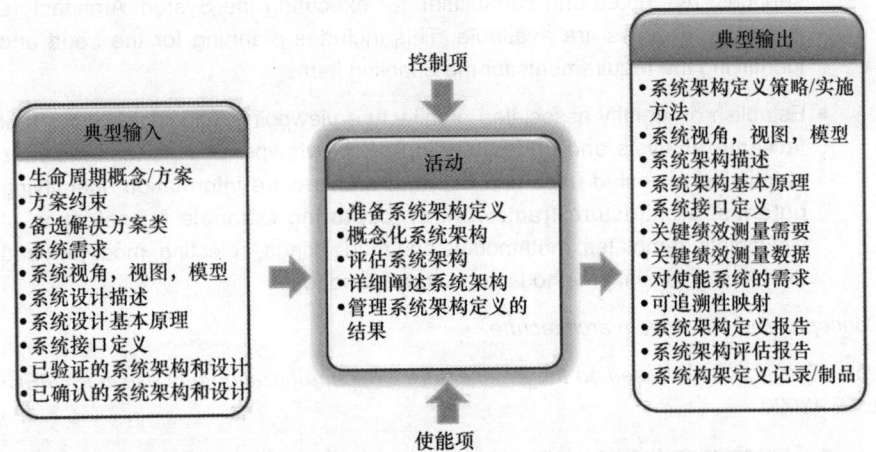

图 2.42 系统架构定义流程的 IPO 图。INCOSE SEH 原始图由 Shortell、Walden 和 Yip 创建。按照 INCOSE 通知页使用。版权所有。

流程活动 系统架构定义流程包括以下活动：

准备系统架构定义。

- 识别和分析相关的市场、行业、利益相关方、组织、业务、运行、使命、法律和其他信息以及将指导系统架构开发的相关角度。

- 确定系统架构工作的关键里程碑和决策。特别要确定那些指导系统架构开发的关键架构制品和资源。

- 结合系统需求定义流程，确定系统背景环境（即 SoI 如何适应外部环境）和系统边界，以反映运行场景和预期系统行为。该任务包括识别 SoI 与系统元素或其他系统或实体的预期交互。

- 建立架构实施方法。这包括架构路线图和战略、方法、框架（见 3.2.5 节）、模式（见 3.2.6 节）、建模技术、工具以及对任何使能系统（见 1.3.3 节）、产品或服务的需求。该实施方法还应包括流程要求（例如，测量实施方法和方法）、评估（例如，评审和准则）以及必要的协调。

- Ensure the enabling items (registry, repository, library, competencies), services, resources and capabilities for executing the System Architecture Definition process are available. This includes planning for the need and identifying the requirements for the enabling items.
- Establish or identify associated architecture viewpoints and model kinds that facilitate analysis and understanding of the viewpoint. This task includes identifying expected uses and users of architecture information, identifying potential architecture framework(s), capturing rationale for selection of viewpoints, templates, metamodels and model kinds, selecting, modifying and developing relevant methods, techniques, and tools.

Conceptualize the system architecture.

Note: This activity is based on the Architecture Conceptualization process in ISO/IEC/IEEE 42020

- Characterize the problem space in conjunction with the BMA process and document it. The report focuses on architecture considerations that span one or more system life cycle stages
- In conjunction with the SNRD process, the system context and system boundary are refined, including identification of expected interactions of the SoI with system elements, or other systems or entities. This task includes determination of boundary conditions, quality measures, situation contexts, assumptions, degrees of freedom, constraints, conditions, and challenges.
- Define architecture objectives and critical success criteria that will be used to assess the extent to which the problems and opportunities will be addressed.
- Based on existing or previous solutions, and problem mitigation strategies, address the highest priority requirements and architecture considerations to synthesize a set of potential solutions. This task includes scanning for relevant technologies, problem patterns, solution patterns, naturally occurring solutions, enhancements to existing systems, heuristics, tactics, and discussion with experts.
- For each potential solution, identify strengths, weaknesses, gaps or shortfalls, required trade-offs, consequences, obligations, assumptions, critical success factors affecting critical success criteria and key performance indicators. Devise structural, behavioral, organizational and architectural entities (functions, input/output flows and flow items, states and modes, functional and physical interfaces, nodes and links, computational and communication resources, etc.) to formulate candidate architecture(s). Based on the set of candidate architecture(s), select the best architecture(s) for downstream use by using the Decision Management and Risk Management process. This task includes identifying and characterizing tradeoffs, defining context and scope, determining and mitigating risks, and identifying issues and areas for improvement.

- 确保执行系统架构定义流程的使能项（注册表、存储库、库、用任力）、服务、资源和能力可用。这包括对需求进行计划，并识别使能项的需求。
- 建立或识别相关架构视角和模型类型，以便于分析和理解视角。该任务包括确定架构信息的预期用途和用户，确定潜在的架构框架，获取选择视角、模板、元模型和模型类型的基本原理，选择、修改和开发相关的方法、技术和工具。

概念化系统架构。

注：*本活动基于 ISO/IEC/IEEE 42020 中的架构概念化流程。*

- 结合 BMA 流程描述问题空间，并对其进行记录。该报告侧重于跨越一个或多个系统生命周期阶段的架构考虑因素。
- 结合 SNRD 流程，细化系统背景环境和系统边界，包括识别 SoI 与系统元素或其他系统或实体的预期交互。这项任务包括确定边界条件、质量测度、情境背景、假设、自由度、约束、条件和挑战。
- 定义架构目标和关键成功准则，用于评估问题和机遇的应对程度。
- 基于现有或以前的解决方案以及问题缓解策略，解决优先级最高的需求和架构考虑，以综合一组潜在的解决方案。此项任务包括扫描相关技术、问题模式、解决方案模式、自然出现的解决方案、现有系统的增强、启发式方法、战术，以及与专家的讨论。
- 针对每个潜在解决方案，识别优势、劣势、差距或不足、所需的权衡、后果、义务、假设、影响关键成功准则的关键成功因素和关键绩效指标。设计结构、行为、组织和架构实体（功能、输入/输出流和流动项、状态和模式、功能和物理接口、节点和链接、计算和通信资源等），以制定备选架构。根据备选架构集，通过使用决策管理和风险管理流程，为下游使用选择最佳架构。这项任务包括识别和特征化权衡、定义背景和范围、确定和减轻风险，以及识别需要改进的问题和领域。

- Select, adapt, or develop views and models of the best architecture(s), by capturing concepts, properties, decisions, processes, activities, tasks, characteristics, guidelines, and principles and utilizing architecture viewpoints to develop architecture descriptions. This task includes determining the scope, breadth and depth, use and users of each view and model, and expressing them in the specified form with sufficient level of detail.

Evaluate the system architecture.

Note: This activity is based on the Architecture Evaluation process in ISO/IEC/IEEE 42020.

- Determine evaluation objectives and criteria for value assessment and architecture analysis by identifying relevant mandates and imperatives, stakeholders and their concerns, policies and standards, value, and quality characteristics.

- Determine evaluation methods and integrate them with evaluation objectives and criteria.

- Collect and review evaluation related information including views and models, architecture concepts, properties, metrics and measures, sources of information, accuracy, errors, degrees of uncertainty, and qualification of correctness, completeness, and consistency of gathered information.

- Analyze, assess, and characterize architecture(s), by using evaluation methods and criteria, and applying the System Analysis and Measurement processes to produce architecture assessments. Architecture alternatives that are similar to each other or fail to meet identified mandates are eliminated and costs, risks, and opportunities are identified and characterized for appropriate actions.

- Formulate, capture, validate, and communicate the findings and recommendations, including implications, to relevant decision makers and stakeholders. The combined overall evaluation can be used to select a preferred system architecture solution.

Elaborate the system architecture.

Note: This activity is based on the Architecture Elaboration process in ISO/IEC/IEEE 42020.

- Based on the identified viewpoints, develop architecture models and views that adequately address stakeholder concerns, while, if applicable, conforming to selected architecture frameworks.

- Perform preliminary interface definition for interfaces with the level of detail necessary for understanding the architecture for decision making and risk management. The definition includes the internal interfaces between the system elements and the external interfaces with entities outside the system boundary.

- 通过捕获概念、属性、决策、流程、活动、任务、特征、指南和原则，并利用架构视角来开发架构描述，选择、调整或开发最佳架构的视图和模型。此项任务包括确定每个视图和模型的范围、广度和深度、用途和用户，并以指定的形式和足够的详细程度表达它们。

评估系统架构。

注：本活动基于ISO/IEC/IEEE 42020中的架构评估流程。

- 通过识别相关的任务和要求、利益相关方及其关切、政策和标准、价值和质量特性，确定价值评估和架构分析的评估目标和准则。
- 确定评估方法，并将其与评估目标和准则相结合。
- 收集和评审与评估相关的信息，包括视图和模型、架构概念、属性、指标和测度、信息来源、准确性、错误、不确定性程度，以及所收集信息的正确性、完整性和一致性鉴定。
- 通过使用评估方法和准则，并应用系统分析和测量流程对架构进行分析、评估和描述。消除彼此相似或无法满足已确定任务的架构备选方案，并识别和表征适当行动的成本、风险和机会。
- 制定、获取、验证并向相关决策者和利益相关方沟通调查结果和建议，包括影响。组合的总体评估可用于选择首选的系统架构解决方案。

详细阐述系统架构。

注：本活动基于ISO/IEC/IEEE 42020中的架构详细阐述流程。

- 根据确定的视角，开发架构模型和视图，以充分解决利益相关方的问题，同时，如果适用，遵循选定的架构框架。
- 对接口进行初步的接口定义，并提供了解架构所需的详细程度，以便进行决策和风险管理。定义包括系统元素之间的内部接口以及与系统边界外实体的外部接口。

- Analyze the architecture models and views for consistency and resolve any issues identified. ISO/IEC/IEEE 42010 correspondence rules from frameworks can aid in this analysis. This task includes relating architectural entities to elements of views and models, mapping related entities to relevant architecture and system concepts, properties, and principles, and assessing whether architecture views are consistent with corresponding viewpoints.

- In conjunction with the Verification and Validation processes (see Sections 2.3.5.9 and 2.3.5.11), verify and validate the models by execution or simulation, if modeling techniques and tools permit, and with traceability matrix of operational concepts. Where possible, use design tools to check their feasibility and validity. As needed, implement partial mock-ups or prototypes, or use executable architecture prototypes or simulators.

- Utilizing models and views, develop architecture descriptions by composing those views and models that adequately cover the uses and users of the architecture descriptions. Assess the architecture description against the intent of the architecture, as well as its suitability, correctness, completeness, and consistency.

Manage results of system architecture definition.

- Capture, maintain, and manage the rationale for selections among alternatives and decisions about the architecture, architecture framework(s), viewpoints, model kinds, views, and models. This task includes managing information for decisions, risks, constraints and assumptions and possible governance of upper-level architectures.

- Establish the means for the implementation of the directives of the governance of the architecture, including the roles, responsibilities, authorities, and other control functions. Monitor and assess whether governance directives and guidance are being followed.

- Establish a means for management of the architecture, including plans, measures, schedules, milestones, and other functional outcomes. Monitor and control the implementation of management instructions, provision of status reports, and corrective actions.

- Manage the maintenance and evolution of the architecture, including the architectural entities, their characteristics, and principles. Allocation and traceability matrices are useful to analyze impacts on the architecture.

- Manage the architecting effectiveness, including work performance tracking, reviewing, regulating the progress, dealing with management issues, dealing with resource allocation issues, dealing with methods and tools availability, and coordinating review of the architecture to achieve stakeholder agreement.

- 分析架构模型和视图的一致性，并解决发现的任何问题。框架中的 ISO/IEC/IEEE 42010 对应规则可以帮助进行此分析。此任务包括将架构实体与视图和模型的元素相关联，将相关实体映射到相关的架构和系统概念、属性和原则，以及评估架构视图是否与相应的视角一致。

- 结合验证和确认流程（见 2.3.5.9 节和 2.3.5.11 节），在建模技术和工具允许的情况下，通过运行或仿真以及使用运行意图的可追溯矩阵，验证和确认模型。在可能的情况下，使用设计工具检查其可行性和有效性。根据需要，实现部分实体模型或原型，或使用可执行的架构原型或仿真器。

- 利用模型和视图，通过组合那些充分覆盖架构描述的用途和用户的视图和模型来开发架构描述。对照架构的意图评估架构描述，以及其适用性、正确性、完整性和一致性。

管理系统架构定义的结果。

- 捕捉、维护和管理备选方案的选择理由，以及有关架构、架构框架、视角、模型种类、视图和模型的决策。此项任务包括管理决策、风险、约束和假设的信息，以及可能的上层架构治理。

- 制定实施架构治理指令的方法，包括角色、职责、权限和其他控制功能。监控和评定治理指令和指导是否被遵守。

- 建立架构管理方法，包括计划、措施、时间、里程碑和其他职能结果。监督和控制管理指示的实施、状态报告的提供和纠正措施。

- 管理架构的维护和演进，包括架构实体、其特征和原则。分配和跟踪矩阵有助于分析对架构的影响。

- 管理架构有效性，包括工作绩效跟踪、评审、管理进度、处理管理问题、处理资源分配问题、处理方法和工具可用性，以及协调架构评审，以达成利益相关方协议。

SYSTEM LIFE CYCLE CONCEPTS, MODELS, AND PROCESSES

- Maintain bi-directional traceability of the system architecture including traceability between the architectural entities to the requirements, interface definitions, analysis results, related architectures, and stakeholder concerns.

- Manage the maintenance, evolution, and use of the architecture descriptions, including the architecture viewpoints, views, and models.

Common approaches and tips:

- Define the problem and the solution spaces with regard to the identified stakeholders

- Define the main principles governing the whole life cycle processes of a SoI, in the scope of the solution space.

- Identify the enabling systems and materials needed for transition early in the life cycle to allow for the necessary lead time to obtain or access them.

- Ensure that conflicting interests (e.g., performance vs. quality characteristics, distributed control vs. central control, new technologies vs. COTS) have been properly addressed.

- Use the Risk Management process to help ensure that the inherent risks associated with the use of new technologies are adequately assessed.

Elaboration

Architecture Processes ISO/IEC/IEEE 42020 (2019) provides a generic process reference model for architecture processes for enterprise, system, and software levels. The concept of architecture as considered in this standard is applicable for different kinds of entities being architected. It specifies 6 architecture processes for use by organizations and projects. As shown in Figure 2.43, the core architecture processes as outlined in the standard are: Architecture Conceptualization, Architecture Evaluation, and Architecture Elaboration. The Architecture Conceptualization process characterizes the problem space and determines suitable solutions that address stakeholder concerns, achieve architecture objectives, and meet relevant requirements. The Architecture Evaluation process determines the extent to which one or more architectures meet their objectives, address stakeholder concerns, and meet relevant requirements. The Architecture Elaboration process describes or documents an architecture in a sufficiently complete and correct manner for the intended uses of the architecture.

- 维持系统架构的双向可追溯性,包括架构实体与需求、接口定义、分析结果、相关架构和利益相关方关切之间的可追溯性。

- 管理架构描述的维护、演进和使用,包括架构视角、视图和模型。

常用方法和提示:

- 针对识别的利益相关方定义问题和解决方案空间。

- 在解决方案空间的范围内,定义控制 SoI 整个生命周期流程的主要原则。

- 在生命周期的早期阶段确定转移所需的使能系统和材料,以便有必要的提前期来获取或使用它们。

- 确保利益冲突(例如,性能与质量特性、分布式控制与中央控制、新技术与 COTS)已得到妥善解决。

- 利用风险管理流程,帮助确保与使用新技术相关的固有风险得到充分评估。

详细阐述

架构流程 ISO/IEC/IEEE 42020(2019)为复杂组织体系、系统和软件层级的架构流程提供了通用流程参考模型。本标准中考虑的架构概念适用于正在构建的不同类型的实体。它指定了 6 个供组织和项目使用的架构流程。如图 2.43 所示,标准中概述的核心架构流程是:架构概念化、架构评估和架构详细阐述。架构概念化流程描述了问题空间的特征,并确定了解决利益相关方问题、实现架构目标和满足相关需求的合适解决方案。架构评估流程确定一个或多个架构满足其目标、解决利益相关方关切和满足相关需求的程度。架构详细阐述流程以足够完整和正确的方式描述或记录架构,以实现架构的预期用途。

SYSTEM LIFE CYCLE CONCEPTS, MODELS, AND PROCESSES

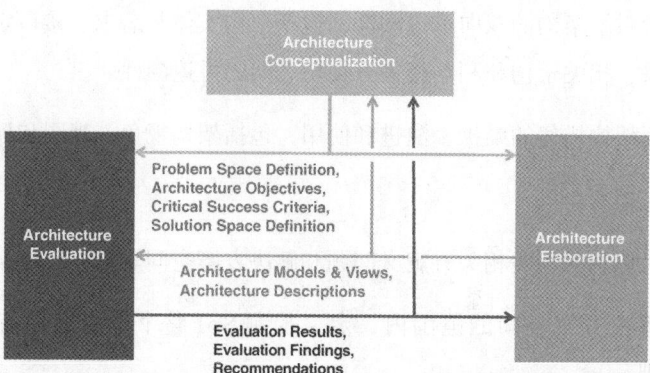

FIGURE 2.43 Core architecture processes. From ISO/IEC/IEEE 42020 (2019). Used with permission. All other rights reserved.

System Architecture The notion of a system is abstract, but it is a practical means to create, design, or redesign products, services, or enterprises. The SoI and the enabling systems that are necessary for development, utilization and support should be considered together in a solution to address a problem or an opportunity. Note that there may be several potential solutions to address the same problem or opportunity. System is represented with sets of interrelated entities—including human in socio-technical systems—achieving one or more stated purposes. These system entities may possess characteristics such as dimensions, environmental resilience, availability, robustness, learnability, execution efficiency, openness, modularity, scalability, and mission effectiveness.

123   *Architecture Description* ISO/IEC/IEEE 42010 specifies the normative features of architecture frameworks, architecture description languages, and viewpoints and views as they pertain to architecture description. An architecture description expresses the architecture of a system and is composed of architecture views. A view is an information part comprising portion of an architecture description. It is composed of view components which are derived from models and non-model sources of information. A viewpoint is the set of conventions for the creation, interpretation and use of views to frame one or more concerns of stakeholders and specifies the ways in which the view components should be generated and used. An architecture framework contains standardized viewpoints, view templates, metamodels, model templates, etc. that aid in development of architecture views. An architecture description language contains syntax and semantics intended for describing the architecture and provides a way to create and understand view components.

系统生命周期概念、模型和流程

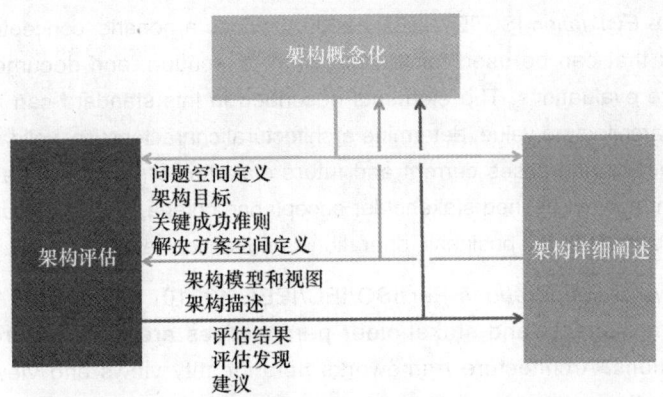

图 2.43　核心架构流程。源自 ISO/IEC/IEEE 42020（2019）。经许可后使用。版权所有。

系统架构　系统的概念是抽象的，但它是创建、设计或重新设计产品、服务或复杂组织体系的实用手段。在应对问题或机会的方案中，应同时考虑 SoI 和开发、利用和支持所需的使能系统。请注意，可能有几种潜在的解决方案来应对相同的问题或机会。系统用一组相互关联的实体来表示，包括社会技术系统中的人员，以达到一个或多个所述目的。这些系统实体可能具有维度、环境韧性、可用性、鲁棒性、可学习性、执行效率、开放性、模块化、可扩展性和任务有效性等特征。

架构描述　ISO/IEC/IEEE 42010 规定了架构框架、架构描述语言以及与架构描述相关的视角和视图的规范性特征。架构描述表示系统的架构，由架构视图组成。视图是包含部分架构描述的信息部分。它由从模型和非模型信息源派生的视图组件组成。视角是用于创建、解释和使用视图的一组约定，用于构建利益相关方的一个或多个关切，并指定生成和使用视图组件的方式。架构框架包含标准化的视角、视图模板、元模型、模型模板等，有助于开发架构视图。架构描述语言包含用于描述架构的语法和语义，并提供了创建和理解视图组件的方法。

Architecture Evaluation ISO/IEC/IEEE 42030 provides a generic, conceptual guiding framework that can be used for the planning, execution, and documentation of architecture evaluations. The elements described in this standard can be used to determine architecture value, determine architectural characteristics, validate whether the architecture addresses current and future stakeholder needs with architecture assessment against defined stakeholder acceptance criteria, and also provide inputs to decisions made at the business, operational and tactical levels.

Architecture Considerations Per ISO/IEC/IEEE 42010, Stakeholder concerns, architecture aspects and stakeholder perspectives are kinds of architecture considerations. Architecture frameworks help identify views and viewpoints to characterize the architectures with regard to these considerations.

Kinds of Architecture Entities Architecture is increasingly applied to systems and other entities that are not traditionally considered to be systems, such as enterprises, services, business functions, mission areas, product lines, families of systems, and software items. Corresponding to each of these entities, different kinds of architecture can be considered according to their purpose, domains of application, and roles within entity and architecture life cycles.

System Architecture vs System Design The System Architecture Definition process focuses on the essential concepts, properties' structure, behaviors, and features that apply to the system solution. It helps gain insights into the relation between the requirements for the system and the emergent properties and behaviors of the system that arise from the interactions and relations between the system elements. The Design Definition process focusses on developing an overall system design that is ultimately sufficiently detailed to allow its realization. An effective architecture is as design-agnostic as possible to allow for maximum flexibility in the design trade space. The Design Definition process provides feedback to the System Architecture Definition process to consolidate or confirm the allocation, partitioning, and alignment of architectural entities to system elements that comprise the system.

Architecting Styles Per (Evans, 2014), Architecting Styles provide a set of proven approaches for those who create, commission, use, and evaluate architecture products. These can help key decision makers to be better informed on the use and limitations of the architecture thereby ensuring that the different architecting activities consistently deliver value. These styles help to understand the architecting approach; architecture objectives; architectural entities; how value is created to make effective architecture-related decisions. The styles are driven by the purpose, culture, or reason for the architecture and reflect currently observed good practices. The four styles of architecting are: authoritative, directive, coordinative, and supportive.

系统生命周期概念、模型和流程

架构评估　ISO/IEC/IEEE 42030 提供了一个通用的概念性指导框架，可用于计划、执行和记录架构评估。该标准中描述的元素可用于确定架构价值、确定架构特征、验证架构是否满足当前和未来利益相关方的需求、根据定义的利益相关方验收准则进行架构评估，以及为业务、运行和战术层面的决策提供输入。

架构注意事项　根据 ISO/IEC/IEEE 42010，利益相关方关切、架构方面和利益相关方视角是各种架构考虑因素。架构框架有助于识别视图和视角，以根据这些考虑来描述架构。

架构实体的种类　架构越来越多地应用于传统上不被视为系统的系统和其他实体，如复杂组织体系、服务、业务功能、任务领域、产品线、系统族和软件项。与这些实体相对应，可以根据其目的、应用领域以及在实体和架构生命周期中的作用，考虑不同类型的架构。

系统架构与系统设计　系统架构定义过程重点在适用于系统解决方案的基本概念、属性结构、行为和特征。它有助于深入了解对系统的要求与由系统元素之间的相互作用和关系所产生的系统涌现属性和行为之间的关系。设计定义流程的重点是开发一个整体系统设计，该设计最终要足够详细，以便能够实现。一个有效的架构应尽可能与设计无关，以便在设计权衡空间中实现最大的灵活性。设计定义流程为系统架构定义流程提供反馈，以综合或确认架构实体与组成系统的系统元素之间的分配、分区和对准。

架构开发样式　根据（Evans，2014），架构开发样式为创建、委托、使用和评估架构产品的人提供了一套行之有效的方法。这些可以帮助关键决策者更好地了解架构的使用和限制，从而确保不同的架构活动始终提供价值。这些样式有助于理解架构方法；架构目标；架构实体；如何创造价值以做出有效的架构相关决策。这些样式是由架构的目的、文化或原因驱动的，反映了当前观察到的良好实践。四种架构开发样式是：权威性、指导性、协调性和支持性。

Architecture Styles Per (Garlan, et al., 1994, 1996), an architecture style is a set of design elements or principles or properties or a generic pattern that provides guidance for the System Architecture Definition process. The set helps in identification and classification of architectures. Architecture styles can be understood as language, system of types and as theory. Architecture styles can be defined by architecture views, architectural elements and their relationships, architecture viewpoints, layouts, connections, interfaces, interaction mechanisms, communication factors, and applicable constraints.

Architecture Patterns Per (Bass, et al., 2012), an architecture pattern is a reusable, configurable architectural entity comprising a minimal set of elements that is complete under certain aspects and exhibits rules for instantiation that is applicable for different situations. It solves and delineates certain elements of the system architecture and can be used in many system architecture efforts. It has a fundamental structure of predefined elements and relationships, principles, rules and guidelines. Architecture patterns promote communication, streamline documentation, support high levels of reuse, improve architect's efficiency and productivity, and provide a starting point for additional ideas.

124 *Value and Quality* While the Systems Architecture Definition process creates a framework for addressing stakeholder concerns and requirements; the goal is to deliver value to all stakeholders, which might correlate to quality factors deemed important. It is essential that value is created over the life of the system so that the system remains satisfactorily in use. The perception of what is of value to stakeholder changes over time, and hence it is necessary to account for the different times at which value is being presented or reported. This requires that sources of stakeholder value are determined, system capabilities are defined to produce or influence value, and vulnerabilities that cause value degradation are identified. Per Kumar (2020), value-based approaches helps one to learn and understand the stakeholder's value system, their principles of behavior, expectations, ideals and belief systems, motivation, and the boundaries within which the stakeholder can be engaged.

Notion of Interface The notion of interface is one of the key items to consider when defining the architecture of a system. The term "interface" comes from Latin words "inter" and "facere" and means "to *do* something *between* things." Therefore, the fundamental aspects of an interface are functional and defined as inputs and outputs of functions. Interoperability is a stakeholder need and requirement, ensuring interfaces use open, well maintained and enduring standards is key to reduce future integration challenges.

架构样式 根据（Garlan 等，1994、1996），架构样式是一组设计元素或原则或属性，或为系统架构定义流程提供指导的通用模式。该集合有助于识别和分类架构。架构的样式可以理解为语言、系统类型和理论。架构样式可以通过架构视图、架构元素及其关系、架构视角、布局、连接、接口、交互机制、通信因素和适用约束来定义。

架构模式 根据（Bass 等，2012），架构模式是一种可重用、可构型配置的架构实体，包括在某些方面完整的最小元素集，并展示适用于不同情况的实例化规则。它解决并划定了系统架构的某些元素，可用于许多系统架构工作。它具有预定义元素和关系、原则、规则和指南的基本结构。架构模式促进交流，简化文档，支持高层级的复用，提高架构师的效率和生产力，并为其他想法提供起点。

价值和质量 系统架构定义流程创建了一个应对利益相关方关切和需求的框架；目标是为所有利益相关方提供价值，这可能与被认为是重要的质量因素相关。至关重要的是，在系统的整个生命周期内创造价值，以使系统保持令人满意的使用状态。利益相关方对价值的感知会随着时间的推移而变化，因此有必要考虑价值呈现或报告的不同时间。这要求确定利益相关方价值的来源，定义系统能力以产生或影响价值，并识别导致价值下降的弱点。根据 Kumar（2020），基于价值的方法有助于学习和理解利益相关方的价值体系、行为原则、期望、理想和信仰体系、动机以及利益相关方可以参与的边界。

接口概念 接口的概念是定义系统架构时要考虑的关键项目之一。"接口"一词来自拉丁语单词"inter"和"facere"，意思是"在事物之间做一些事情"。因此，接口的基本方面是功能性的，定义为功能的输入和输出。互操作性是利益相关方的需要和需求，确保接口使用开放的、维护良好的和持久的标准是减少未来综合挑战的关键。

SYSTEM LIFE CYCLE CONCEPTS, MODELS, AND PROCESSES

Horizontal and vertical integration System Architectures ensure that requirements allocated throughout the system's design process account for system elements and interfaces as the design matures. The architecture establishes the significant operational and system development interfaces, both internal and external, that must be maintained through development and upgrades. The overall System Architecture is composed of system elements, which are integrated to form the entire system. It is essential to maintain cognizance of the end-to-end system performance expectations when evaluating integration of the system elements, so that those elements continue to perform as needed. When a dynamic relationship exists between one element in the system and another, there is an interdependency. This may involve relationships that are functional or physical in nature, or both. Depending on how tightly coupled these system elements are, the net effect on the system will vary. For example, there is often an interdependency between safety functional hazard conditions and certain function and physical system elements defined in the system architecture.

2.3.5.5 Design Definition Process

Overview

Purpose As stated in ISO/IEC/IEEE 15288,

[6.4.5.1] The purpose of the Design Definition process is to provide sufficient detailed data and information about the system and its elements to realize the solution in accordance with the system requirements and architecture.

This process is driven by requirements that have been vetted through the architecture and more detailed analyses of feasibility.

Description The Design Definition process transforms architecture and requirements into a design of the system that can be realized. This process results in sufficiently detailed data and information about the system and its elements to enable implementation consistent with architectural entities defined in models and views of the system architecture, in conformance with applicable system requirements, and in alignment with design guidelines and standards adopted by the organization or project. Often these system elements are identified, and their fundamental concepts and properties are characterized, by the System Architecture Definition process. The design information and data will define the expected properties and characteristics allocated to each system element and enable transition toward their realization.

Inputs and Outputs Inputs and outputs for the Design Definition process are listed in Figure 2.44. Descriptions of each input and output are provided in Appendix E.

横向和纵向综合　系统架构可确保在整个系统设计过程中分配的需求随着设计的成熟而考虑到系统元素和接口。架构确定了重要的运行和系统开发接口，包括内部和外部接口，这些接口必须在开发和升级过程中加以维护。整个系统架构由系统元素组成，这些元素被综合以形成整个系统。在评估系统元素的综合时，必须保持对端到端系统性能期望的认知，以便这些元素继续根据需要执行。当系统中的一个元素与另一个元素之间存在动态关系时，就存在相互依赖关系。这可能涉及功能性或物理性的关系，或两者兼而有之。根据这些系统元素的紧密耦合程度，对系统的净影响将有所不同。例如，安全功能性危害条件与系统架构中定义的某些功能和物理系统元素之间通常存在相互依赖关系。

2.3.5.5　设计定义流程

概述

目的　如 ISO/IEC/IEEE 15288 所述：

[6.4.5.1] 设计定义流程的目的是提供有关系统及其元素的足够详细的数据和信息，以根据系统需求和架构实现解决方案。

这一流程由通过架构审查的需求和更详细的可行性分析驱动。

描述　设计定义流程将架构和需求转换为可实现的系统设计。该流程产生关于系统及其元素的足够详细的数据和信息，以使实施过程与系统架构的模型和视图中定义的架构实体保持一致，符合适用的系统需求，并与组织或项目采用的设计指南和标准保持一致。通常，通过系统架构定义流程来识别这些系统元素，并表征其基本概念和特性。设计信息和数据将定义分配给每个系统元素的预期属性和特征，并使其能够转移到实现这些属性和特征。

输入和输出　设计定义流程的输入和输出如图 2.44 所示。附录 E 中提供了每个输入和输出的描述。

SYSTEM LIFE CYCLE CONCEPTS, MODELS, AND PROCESSES

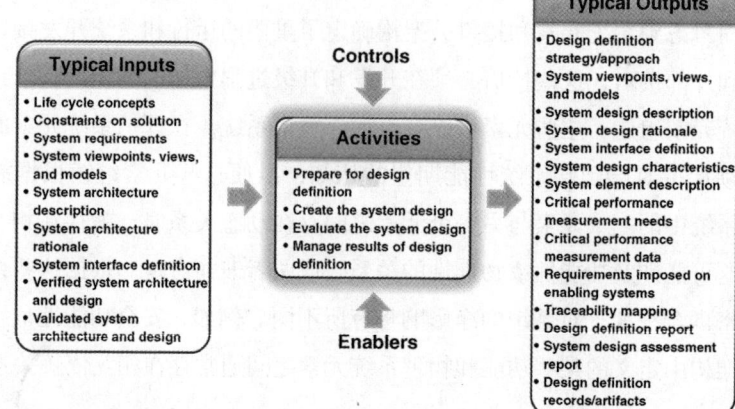

FIGURE 2.44 IPO diagram for Design Definition process. INCOSE SEH original figure created by Shortell, Walden, and Yip. Usage per the INCOSE Notices page. All other rights reserved.

Process Activities The Design Definition process includes the following activities:

Prepare for design definition.

- Determine design drivers for the system design and an appropriate design strategy and applicable approaches. Personnel (together with human factors), processes, products, and services intended to compose the system are among the many factors that will impact system design. Non-functional considerations and design constraints should be identified as these can also serve as design drivers.

- Determine the necessary technologies and the categories of system characteristics to be represented in the design. Capabilities, resources, and services should be identified as these can provide the necessary technologies. Quality models should be identified as these can categorize system characteristics.

- Examine the system architecture to determine the fundamental properties and concepts that apply to the system design, along with the principles that should govern the design and its evolution.

- Establish the approach for system design effort.

- Ensure the necessary system design-enabling elements, services, resources and capabilities are available.

- 确定成功综合所需的系统约束和目标，以便在系统需求、架构或设计中加以解决，例如可访问性、集成商的安全性、使能项所需的接口。

- 计划支持综合所需的必要使能系统或服务，如综合设施、培训系统或仿真器。

- 确保获得支持综合所需的使能系统或服务以及材料。

● *执行综合。*

- 综合系统元素构型配置，直到系统完成。

- 按计划管理接口可用性，并跟踪接口是否符合其要求。

- 解决任何一致性或可用性问题。

- 按照计划的顺序综合系统元素。

- 对不同综合层级的接口、选定功能和关键质量特性进行检查。

● *管理综合结果。*

- 捕获综合结果，包括发现的任何异常或其他问题。这包括由于综合策略、综合使能系统、综合执行、不正确的系统或元素定义导致的异常。

- 如果系统、其指定运行环境和任何使用阶段所需的使能系统之间的接口存在不一致，则偏差会导致纠正措施或需求变更。项目评估和控制流程（见2.3.4.2节）用于分析数据，以确定根本原因，指导纠正或改进措施，并记录经验教训。

- 保持被综合的系统元素和战略、计划和需求的双向可追溯性（见3.2.3节）。

- 为构型配置管理提供基线所需的信息项、工作产品或其他制品。构型配置管理流程（见2.3.4.5节）用于建立和维护基线。

常用方法和提示：

- 综合策略应考虑系统元素的可用性时间表，并考虑使用、操作、维护和维持系统的人员。它还应符合缺陷/故障隔离和诊断实践。

SYSTEM LIFE CYCLE CONCEPTS, MODELS, AND PROCESSES

- Development of integration enablers, such as tools and facilities, can take as long as the system itself and should be started early in the project.

- The Integration process of complex systems should use flexible approaches and techniques.

- Integrate aggregates in order to detect faults more easily. The use of the coupling matrix technique applies for all strategies and especially for the bottom-up integration strategy (see Section 3.2.4).

Elaboration

Integration occurs throughout the project from initial needs identification through utilization and support. The focus of integration evolves as the system evolves from concept definition to system definition to system realization to system deployment and use. As the system progresses, the emphasis of integration changes from its system definition, analysis, modeling, or prototypes to the deployed and operational system integrated into its intended environment, including interfacing systems. Integration should look proactively to mitigate risks and avoid integration issues, or discover them at the earliest point.

Concept of an "Aggregate." The integration of a system is based on the notion of an "aggregate." An aggregate is made up of several system elements and their physical and functional interfaces. Each aggregate is characterized by a configuration that specifies the system elements to be integrated and their configuration status. A set of verification actions is applied on each aggregate. To perform these verification actions, a verification configuration that includes the aggregate plus verification enabling systems is constituted. The verification enabling systems can be simulators (simulated system elements), emulators, stubs or caps, scaffolding, activators (launchers, drivers), harnesses, measuring devices, etc.

Integration Strategy and Approaches. The integration of evolving system elements is performed according to a predefined strategy. The strategy relies on the defined physical and functional architectures of the system and the organizational structure developing it. The detailed implementation of the strategy is described in an integration plan that defines the actions to be taken to mitigate integration risks and the configuration of expected aggregates of evolving system elements. It also defines the sequence these aggregates to carry out efficient verification actions and validation actions (e.g., inspections, analyses, demonstrations, or tests). The integration strategy is thus elaborated in coordination with the selected verification strategy and validation strategy (see Sections 2.3.5.9 and 2.3.5.11).

- 开发综合使能项（如工具和设施）所需时间与系统本身一样长，应在项目早期启动。
- 复杂系统的综合流程应使用灵活的方法和技术。
- 综合聚合体，以便更容易地检测故障。耦合矩阵技术的使用适用于所有策略，尤其是自下而上的综合策略（见 3.2.4 节）。

详细阐述

综合贯穿整个项目，从最初的需求识别到使用和支持。综合的重点随着系统从概念定义、系统定义、系统实现到系统部署和使用的发展而变化。随着系统的发展，综合的重点也从系统定义、分析、建模或原型转变为部署和运行的系统，并将其综合到预定的环境中，包括接口系统。综合工作应主动降低风险，避免综合问题，或尽早发现综合问题。

"聚合体"的概念。 系统的综合基于"聚合体"的概念。聚合体由多个系统元素及其物理和功能接口组成。每个聚合体都有一个构型配置，该构型配置指定了要综合的系统元素及其构型配置状态。对每个聚合体应用一组验证操作。为了执行这些验证操作，构建一个包含聚合体加验证使能系统的验证构型配置。验证使能系统可以是仿真器（仿真系统元素）、模拟器、桩或帽、脚手架、执行器（发射器、驱动器）、线束、测量装置等。

综合策略和实施方法。 演进中的系统元素的综合是根据预定义的策略执行的。该策略依赖于已定义的系统物理和功能架构以及开发该架构的组织结构。该策略的具体实施将在综合计划中加以说明，该计划确定了为降低综合风险而采取的行动，以及不断演进的系统元素的预期构型配置。它还定义了这些聚合体执行有效验证行动和确认行动（例如，检查、分析、演示或测试）的顺序。因此，综合策略是与选定的验证策略和确认策略协调制定的（见 2.3.5.9 节和 2.3.5.11 节）。

SYSTEM LIFE CYCLE CONCEPTS, MODELS, AND PROCESSES

Several possible integration approaches and techniques can be used to define an integration strategy. Any of these may be used individually or in combination. The selection of integration approaches and techniques depends on several factors, in particular the type of system element, delivery time, order of delivery of system elements, risks, constraints, etc. Each integration approach has strengths and weaknesses, which should be considered in the context of the SoI.

137 Integration of the SoI and enabling systems occurs during development as well as utilization and support. Early in the life cycle, integration is concerned with concepts, requirements, architecture, and design. Approaches include models, analysis, simulations, and prototypes. In later life cycle stages, integration focuses on changes during utilization and support.

There are multiple options for the combination of system elements or aggregation of completed system elements or aggregates. Some common integration techniques are:

- *Global (or Big Bang) integration*—The simplest approach for low-risk, complicated, or simple systems is integration of the entire SoI. While the process is simplified, any issues or interface problems are difficult to find and resolve.

- *Bottom-up integration*—A common approach follows the reverse order of decomposition from lowest system element through levels of the architecture to the final system. Problems can be found at lower levels and more easily isolated to specific system elements. System level issues may not be discovered until late in the process.

- *Top-down integration*—This is a common variation of incremental integration (see below) that starts with the system elements that most closely reflect overall system performance with peripheral elements simulated and integrated later. The purpose is to detect system level issues, particularly with external interfaces, early.

- *Incremental integration*—In a predefined order, one or a small number of system elements are added to an already integrated increment of system elements. It can also include a portion of the system being integrated into a predefined increment. This approach can be effective for incremental and evolutionary development (see Section 2.2). For agile development, the order can be defined by features.

- *Subset integration*—System elements are assembled by subsets, and then subsets are assembled together. Subsets can be defined by functional chains or threads to perform specific tasks.

可以使用几种可能的综合方法和技术来定义综合策略。其中任何一种都可以单独使用或组合使用。综合方法和技术的选择取决于多个因素，尤其是系统元素的类型、交付时间、系统元素的交付顺序、风险、约束等。每种综合方法都有优缺点，应在 SoI 的背景环境下加以考虑。

SoI 和使能系统的综合发生在开发、使用和支持流程中。在生命周期的早期，综合涉及概念、需求、架构和设计。实施方法包括模型、分析、仿真和原型。在生命周期的后期阶段，综合侧重于使用和支持期间的更改。

有多个选项可用于系统元素的组合或已完成的系统元素或聚合体的聚合。一些常见的综合技术包括：

- *全局（或大爆炸式）综合*——对于低风险、繁杂或简单系统的最简单方法是综合整个 SoI。虽然流程得到简化，但很难发现和解决任何重要问题或接口问题。

- *自下而上的综合*——一种常见的方法是按照从最低层级系统元素到架构各层级再到最终系统的相反顺序进行分解。问题可以在较低层级发现，也更容易与特定的系统元素隔离。系统级问题可能要到后期才能发现。

- *自上而下的综合*——这是增量综合（见下文）的常见变体，从最能反映系统整体性能的系统元素开始，随后仿真并综合外围元素。其目的是尽早检测系统级问题，尤其是外部接口问题。

- *增量综合*——按照预定义的顺序，将一个或少量系统元素添加到已综合的系统元素增量中。它还可以包括将系统的一部分综合到预定义增量中。这种方法对于增量和渐进式开发是有效的（参见 2.2 节）。对于敏捷开发，可以通过特性定义顺序。

- *子集综合*——系统元素由子集组装，然后将子集组装在一起。子集可以由功能链或线程定义以执行特定任务。

- *Criterion-driven integration*—The most critical system elements compared to the selected criterion are first integrated (e.g., dependability, complexity, technological innovation). The criteria are generally related to risks. This technique allows early integration and verification of intensively critical system elements.

- *Integration "with the stream"*—The delivered system elements are assembled as they become available.

- *Model-based integration*—The system elements are modeled physically or functionally and integrated in the model environment. Actual system elements can be inserted into the model environment as they developed.

Throughout the project, the integration strategy addresses management approaches to address risks such as communications issues. These include use of Integrated Product Teams (IPTs), Interface Control Working Groups (ICWGs), Systems Engineering Integration Teams (SEITs), or Technical Performance Measures (TPMs).

Horizontal & Vertical Integration. The Integration process needs to address the wide range of integration perspectives that apply across the life cycle. Horizontal integration typically refers to activities that are performed across elements that appear in a common hierarchy level of the system architecture. Structural aspects may be system elements that collectively constitute a system. Behavioral aspects include the sequence of discrete behaviors that together describe system functionality. Vertical integration typically refers to activities that are performed to help ensure that system elements at a given system hierarchy level are consistent with, and satisfy the expectations of, the system or higher-level system elements. The recursive nature of SE highlights how integration features span the levels of the system structure (see Section 2.3.1.2). As there is new information or learning on one level of the system structure, it is shared with both higher and lower levels. Other integration "directions" span additional viewpoints and stakeholder concerns, such as those relating to temporal or functional considerations, application of standards, satisfaction of regulatory expectations, or operational conditions and environments. Integration can also be viewed in relationship to the requirements concepts of horizontal traceability among parallel elements in the architecture and vertical traceability between system hierarchy levels (see Section 3.2.3).

2.3.5.9 Verification Process

Overview

Purpose As stated in ISO/IEC/IEEE 15288,

[6.4.9.1] The purpose of the Verification process is to provide objective evidence that a system, system element, or artifact fulfils its specified requirements and characteristics.

- *准则驱动的综合*——与选定标准相比，最关键的系统元素首先被综合（例如，可靠性、复杂性、技术创新）。准则通常与风险相关。这种技术允许早期综合和验证高度关键的系统元素。
- *"随流"综合*——交付的系统元素在可用时进行组装。
- *基于模型的综合*——系统元素在物理或功能上建模，并综合在模型环境中。实际系统元素可以在开发时插入模型环境中。

在整个项目中，综合策略回答了解决通信问题等风险的管理途径。这些包括使用综合产品团队（IPT）、接口控制工作组（ICWG）、系统工程综合团队（SEIT）或技术性能测度（TPM）。

横向和纵向综合。综合流程需要处理适用于整个生命周期的各种综合视角。横向综合通常是指在系统结构的共同层级中跨元素进行的活动。结构方面可以是共同构成系统的系统元素。行为方面包括共同描述系统功能的离散行为序列。纵向综合通常是指为帮助确保特定系统层级中的系统元素与系统或更高层系统元素保持一致并满足其期望而开展的活动。系统工程的递归性强调了综合功能如何跨越系统结构的各个层级（见 2.3.1.2 节）。当系统结构的某一层级出现新信息或新知识时，高一层级和低一层级都会共享。其他综合"方向"则涉及更多的视角和利益相关方的关切，如与时间或功能考虑、标准应用、满足监管期望或运行条件和环境有关的问题。综合还可以从架构中并行元素之间的横向可追溯性和系统层级之间的纵向可追溯性这两个需求概念的关系来看待（见 3.2.3 节）。

2.3.5.9 验证流程

概述

目的　如 ISO/IEC/IEEE 15288 所述：

[6.4.9.1] 验证流程的目的是提供客观证据，证明系统、系统元素或制品满足其规定的需求和特性。

SYSTEM LIFE CYCLE CONCEPTS, MODELS, AND PROCESSES

Description The Verification process can be applied to any engineering artifact, entity, or information item that has contributed to the definition and realization of the SoI (e.g., verification of stakeholder needs, stakeholder requirements, system requirements, models, simulations, the system architecture, design characteristics, verification procedures, or a realized system or system element). The Verification process provides objective evidence with an acceptable degree of confidence to confirm:

1. The artifact or entity has been made "right" according to its specified requirements and characteristics,

2. No anomaly (error/defect/fault) has been introduced at the time of any transformation of inputs into outputs.

3. The selected verification strategy, method, and procedures will yield appropriate evidence that if an anomaly were introduced, it would be detected.

As is often stated, verification is intended to ensure that "the artifact or entity has been built right," while validation is intended to ensure that "the right artifact or entity will be or was built."

Inputs/Outputs Inputs and outputs for the Verification process are listed in Figure 2.49. Descriptions of each input and output are provided in Appendix E.

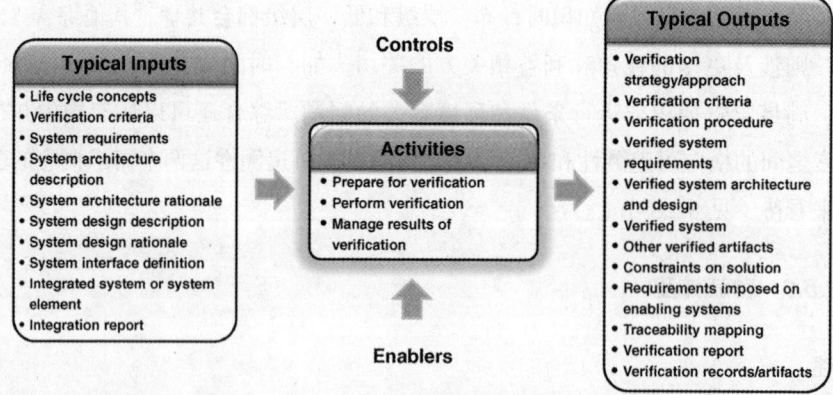

FIGURE 2.49 IPO diagram for Verification process. INCOSE SEH original figure created by Shortell, Walden, and Yip. Usage per the INCOSE Notices page. All other rights reserved.

系统生命周期概念、模型和流程

描述 验证流程可应用于任何有助于 SoI 定义和实现的工程制品、实体或信息项（例如，验证利益相关方需要、利益相关方需求、系统需求、模型、仿真、系统架构、设计特征、验证程序或已实现的系统或系统元素）。验证流程提供了具有可接受置信度的客观证据，以确认：

1. 该制品或实体已根据其规定的需求和特征被"正确"地实现，
2. 在将输入转换为输出时，未引入任何异常（错误/缺陷/故障）。
3. 选定的验证策略、方法和程序将提供适当的证据，证明如果出现异常，也会被发现。

正如通常所述，验证旨在确保"制品或实体已正确构建"，而确认旨在确保"正确的制品或实体将要或曾经被构建。"

输入/输出 验证流程的输入和输出如图 2.49 所示。附录 E 中提供了每个输入和输出的描述。

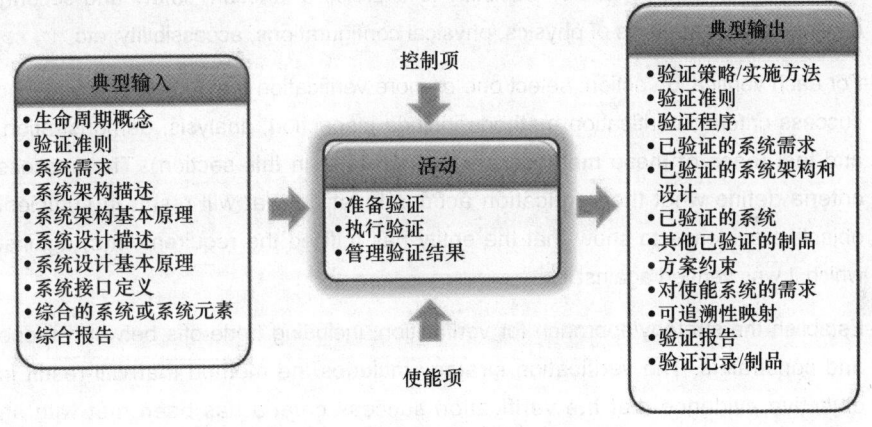

图 2.49 验证流程的 IPO 图。INCOSE SEH 原始图由 Shortell、Walden 和 Yip 创建。按照 INCOSE 通知页使用。版权所有。

SYSTEM LIFE CYCLE CONCEPTS, MODELS, AND PROCESSES

139 **Process Activities** The Verification process includes the following activities:

- *Prepare for verification.*

  –Define the scope (what will be verified) and the verification actions (strategy, method, and success criteria). Verification activities consume resources: time, labor, facilities, and funds. The scope of the organization's verification strategy/approach should be documented within the project's SEMP and system integration, verification, and validation plans.

  °Establish a list of entities to be verified, including stakeholder needs, stakeholder requirements, system requirements, system architecture, prototypes, models, simulations, the system design, design characteristics, the system elements within the SoI architecture, and the integrated SoI itself.

  °Identify the specified requirements against which each entity will be verified.

  –Consider and capture constraints that could impact the feasibility or effectiveness of verification actions. The constraints could impact the implementation of the verification actions and include contractual constraints, limitations due to regulatory requirements, cost, schedule, feasibility to exercise a function, safety and security considerations, the laws of physics, physical configurations, accessibility, etc.

  –For each verification action, select one or more verification methods and associated success criteria. Verification methods include inspection, analysis, demonstration, and test (each of these methods are defined later in this section). The success criteria define what the verification actions must do that will result in sufficient objective evidence to show that the entity has fulfilled the requirement(s) against which it was verified against.

  –Establish the strategy/approach for verification, including trade-offs between scope and constraints. The verification strategy includes the method that will result in objective evidence that the verification success criteria has been met with an acceptable degree of confidence.

  °Define verification activities. For each verification instance, define a specific verification action that will result in objective evidence needed to verify the SoI meets one or more requirements per the defined verification strategy.

  °Define verification procedure requirements for each verification action. The verification procedure requirements are requirements that will drive the formulation of steps and actions for a given verification procedure.

系统生命周期概念、模型和流程

流程活动 验证流程包括以下活动:

- *准备验证。*

- 定义范围(将要验证的内容)和验证行动(策略、方法和成功准则)。验证活动消耗资源:时间、人力、设施和资金。组织验证策略/实施方法的范围应记录在项目的 SEMP 和系统综合、验证和确认计划中。

  ° 建立待验证实体列表,包括利益相关方需要、利益相关方需求、系统需求、系统架构、原型、模型、仿真、系统设计、设计特征、SoI 架构内的系统元素以及综合的 SoI 本身。

  ° 识别验证每个实体所依据的具体需求。

- 考虑并捕获可能影响验证行动可行性或有效性的约束。这些限制可能会影响验证行动的实施,包括合同限制、监管要求造成的限制、成本、进度、执行功能的可行性、安全和安保考虑、物理定律、物理构型配置、可访问性等。

- 对于每个验证行动,选择一种或多种验证方法和相关成功准则。验证方法包括检查、分析、演示和测试(这些方法将在本节后面定义)。成功准则定义了验证行动必须执行的操作,这些操作将产生足够的客观证据,以表明该实体已满足验证所依据的需求。

- 制定验证策略/实施方法,包括范围和约束之间的权衡。验证策略包括产生客观证据的方法,证明验证成功准则已达到可接受的置信度。

  ° 定义验证活动。对于每个验证实例,定义一个特定的验证行动,该行动将产生所需的客观证据,以验证 SoI 是否符合定义的验证策略中的一个或多个需求。

  ° 定义每个验证行动的验证程序需求。验证程序需求是推动制定给定验证程序步骤和行动的需求。

SYSTEM LIFE CYCLE CONCEPTS, MODELS, AND PROCESSES

–Identify constraints and objectives from the verification strategy to be incorporated within the sets of system requirements, architecture, and design. These requirements are needed to support the defined strategy.

–Plan for the necessary enabling systems or services needed through the life cycle for verification. Enabling systems include organizational support, verification equipment, simulators, emulators, test beds, test automation tools, facilities, etc.

–Ensure enabling system or service access needed to support verification. This includes confirming everything required for the verification activities will be available, when needed and have passed their own verification and validation. The acquisition of the enablers can be done through several ways such as rental, procurement, development, reuse, and subcontracting.

- *Perform verification.*

–Define the procedures for the verification actions. A procedure can support one action or a set of actions.

–Execute the verification procedures for planned verification actions.

–Schedule the execution of verification procedures. Each scheduled verification event represents a commitment of personnel, time, resources, and equipment that would ideally show up on a project's schedule.

–Ensure readiness to conduct the verification procedures: availability and configuration status of the system/entity, the availability of the verification enablers, qualified personnel or operators, resources, etc.

- *Manage results of verification.*

–Record the verification results and any defects identified. Maintain the results in verification reports and records per organizational policy as well as contractual and regulatory requirements.

–Analyze the verification results against the verification success criteria to determine whether the entity being verified meets those criteria with an acceptable degree of confidence.

–Throughout verification, capture operational incidents and problems and track them until final resolution. Problem resolution and any subsequent changes will be handled through the Project Assessment and Control process (see Section 2.3.4.2) and the Configuration Management process (see Section 2.3.4.5). Any changes to the SoI definition (e.g., stakeholder needs, stakeholder requirements, system requirements, system architecture, system design, design characteristics, or interfaces) and associated engineering artifacts are performed within other Technical Processes.

- 识别验证策略中的约束和目标，将其纳入系统需求、架构和设计集合中。需要这些需求来支持定义的策略。

- 计划整个生命周期所需的必要使能系统或服务，以进行验证。使能系统包括组织支持、验证设备、仿真器、模拟器、测试台、测试自动化工具、设施等。

- 确保支持验证所需的系统或服务可用。这包括确认在需要时，验证活动所需的一切都将可用，并已通过自己的验证和确认。可以通过租赁、采办、开发、复用和分包等多种方式获取使能技术。

- 执行验证。

- 定义验证行动的程序。一个流程可以支持一个操作或一组操作。

- 执行计划验证行动的验证程序。

- 安排验证程序的执行。每个计划的验证事件代表了人员、时间、资源和设备的承诺，这些承诺将最理想地出现在项目的时间表上。

- 确保准备好执行验证程序：系统/实体的可用性和构型配置状态、验证使能项的可用性、合格人员或操作人员、资源等。

- 管理验证结果。

- 记录验证结果及发现的任何缺陷。根据组织政策以及合同和监管要求，将结果保存在验证报告和记录中。

- 根据验证成功准则分析验证结果，以确定被验证实体是否符合这些准则，并具有可接受的置信度。

- 在整个验证流程中，捕获运行事件和问题，并对其进行跟踪，直至最终解决。问题解决和任何后续变更将通过项目评估和控制流程（见 2.3.4.2 节）和构型配置管理流程（见 2.3.4.5 节）进行处理。对 SoI 定义（如利益相关方需要、利益相关方需求、系统需求、系统架构、系统设计、设计特征或接口）和相关工程制品的任何变更都将在其他技术流程中进行。

–Obtain agreement from the approval authority that the verification criteria have been met to their satisfaction. Combine the individual verification records into a verification approval package for the entity being verified and submit to the verification approval authority. The verification approval authority is the party authorized to determine whether sufficient evidence has been provided to show that the entity has passed verification with an acceptable degree of confidence.

–Establish and sustain traceability (verification). Establish and maintain bidirectional traceability of the verified entity and verification artifacts with the system architecture and design characteristics or requirements against which the entity is being verified.

–Give CM the information items, work products, or other artifacts needed for baselines. The Configuration Management process (see Section 2.3.4.5) is used to establish and maintain baselines. The Verification process identifies candidates for baseline and provides the items to the Configuration Management process.

Common approaches and tips:

- Identify the enabling systems and materials needed for verification early in the life cycle to allow for the necessary lead time to obtain or access them.
- Avoid conducting verification only late in the schedule or reducing the number of verification activities due to budget or schedule issues, since discrepancies and errors are more costly to correct later in the system life cycle.
- Review requirements as they are defined to ensure that the entities to which they apply can be verified against those requirements.

Elaboration

This section elaborates and provides "how-to" information on the Verification process. Additional guidance on verification can be found in the INCOSE NRM (2022) and INCOSE GtVV (2022).

Verification Planning. Planning for verification should begin when the system requirements are being defined. As the system requirements are defined, it is recommended to define the verification success criteria, method, and strategy and obtain acquirer and approval authority approval. Early planning helps drive cost and schedule estimates of the verification plan earlier in the project—maximizing the chance the full verification plan will be resourced.

- 获得审批机构的同意，即验证准则已达到其满意的程度。将各个验证记录合并到被验证实体的验证审批包中，并提交给验证批准机构。验证批准机构是指有权确定是否已提供足够证据证明该实体已经以可接受的置信度通过验证的一方。

- 建立并保持可追溯性（验证）。建立并维护已验证实体和验证制品的双向可追溯性，以及验证实体所依据的系统架构和设计特征或需求。

- 为构型配置管理提供基线所需的信息项、工作产品或其他制品。构型配置管理流程（见 2.3.4.5 节）用于建立和维护基线。验证流程确定基线的备选项，并将这些备选项提供给构型配置管理流程。

常用方法和提示：

- 在生命周期的早期阶段确定验证所需的使能系统和材料，以便有必要的提前期来获取或使用它们。
- 避免仅在计划的后期进行验证，或由于预算或计划问题减少验证活动的数量，因为在系统生命周期的后期纠正差异和错误的成本更高。
- 评审定义的需求，以确保其适用的实体可以根据这些需求进行验证。

详细阐述

本节详述并提供有关验证流程的"如何做"的信息。有关验证的其他指南，请参见 INCOSE NRM（2022）和 INCOSE GtVV（2022）。

验证计划。验证计划应在定义系统需求时开始。在定义系统需求时，建议定义验证成功准则、方法和策略，并获得采办方和审批机构的批准。早期计划有助于在项目早期对验证计划的成本和进度估计，从而最大限度地提高整个验证计划获得资源的机会。

SYSTEM LIFE CYCLE CONCEPTS, MODELS, AND PROCESSES

Reduction of Verification Activities and Risk. If verification activities must be reduced due to cost and schedule concerns or other constraints, this should be done using a risk-based approach. The SE practitioner is urged to resist the temptation to blindly reduce the number of, or the costliest, verification activities due to budget or schedule concerns. Gaps and misses are more costly and time consuming to correct later in the life cycle—especially when these gaps show up at the integrated SoI level from reduced system element verification. If additional resources become available that allow an opportunity to verify to additional depth, the project should do so to reduce risk and increase the degree of confidence.

Notion of a Verification Action. A verification action describes verification in terms of an entity, the reference item against which the entity will be verified (e.g., a requirement, design characteristic, or standard), the expected result (success criteria deduced from the reference item the entity is being verified against), the verification strategy and method to be used, and on which level of integration of the system (e.g., system, system element). The performance of a verification action onto the submitted entity provides an obtained result which is compared with the expected result as defined by the verification success criteria. The comparison enables the determination of the acceptable conformance of the entity to the reference item with some degree of confidence. Figure 2.50 illustrates several common verification actions.

Examples of verification actions include:

- *Verification of a stakeholder requirement (requirement verification)*—(1) Verify the stakeholder requirement statement correctly transforms the source or stakeholder need from which it was transformed or derived and (2) verify the stakeholder requirement satisfies the characteristics of good requirement statements (see Section 2.3.5.3).

- *Verification of a system requirement (requirement verification)*—(1) Verify the system requirement statement correctly transforms the source, stakeholder requirement, or parent from which it was transformed or derived and (2) verify the system requirement satisfies the characteristics of good requirement statements (see Section 2.3.5.3)

- *Verificati on of a model or simulation (model or simulation verification)*—(1) Verify that the model/simulation meets its requirements consistent with its intended purpose, (2) verify the model/simulation against syntactic and grammatical rules, characteristics, and standards defined for the type of model/simulation, and (3) verify the correct application of the appropriate patterns and heuristics used and the correct usage of modeling/simulation techniques or methods as defined by the organization's guidelines and requirements concerning model/simulation development and use.

减少验证活动和风险。如果由于成本和进度问题或其他限制必须减少验证活动，则应采用基于风险的方法。我们敦促系统工程实践者抵制诱惑，不要因为预算或进度问题而盲目减少验证活动的数量或成本最高的验证活动。在生命周期的后期，漏洞和失误的纠正成本更高、耗时更长，特别是当这些漏洞出现在综合的 SoI 层面时，系统元素验证的减少更是如此。如果有额外的资源可以进行更深入的验证，项目就应该这样做，以降低风险并提高可信度。

验证行动的概念。验证行动从实体、实体将被验证的参考项（例如，需求、设计特征或标准）、预期结果（从实体被验证的参考项推导出的成功准则）、将使用的验证策略和方法以及系统综合的层级（例如，系统、系统元素）等方面描述验证。对提交的实体执行验证操作将获得结果，该结果将与验证成功准则定义的预期结果进行比较。通过比较，可以确定实体对参考项目的可接受符合性，并具有一定的置信度。图 2.50 说明了几种常见的验证操作。

验证行动的示例包括：

- *利益相关方需求验证（需求验证）*——（1）验证利益相关方需求陈述是否正确地转换了来源或利益相关方需要，而该需求正是由来源或利益相关者需要转换或派生而来的；（2）验证利益相关方需求满足良好需求声明的特征（见 2.3.5.3 节）。

- *系统需求验证（需求验证）*——（1）验证系统需求声明是否正确转换了来源、利益相关方需求或父需求，以及（2）验证系统需求是否满足良好需求声明的特征（见 2.3.5.3 节）。

- *模型或仿真验证（对模型或仿真的验证）*——（1）验证模型/仿真符合其预期的需求，（2）根据为模型/仿真类型定义的句法和语法规则、特征和标准验证模型/仿真，以及（3）验证所使用的适当的模式和启发式方法的应用正确性，以及组织关于模型/仿真的开发和使用的指南和要求所定义的建模/仿真技术或方法的正确使用。

SYSTEM LIFE CYCLE CONCEPTS, MODELS, AND PROCESSES

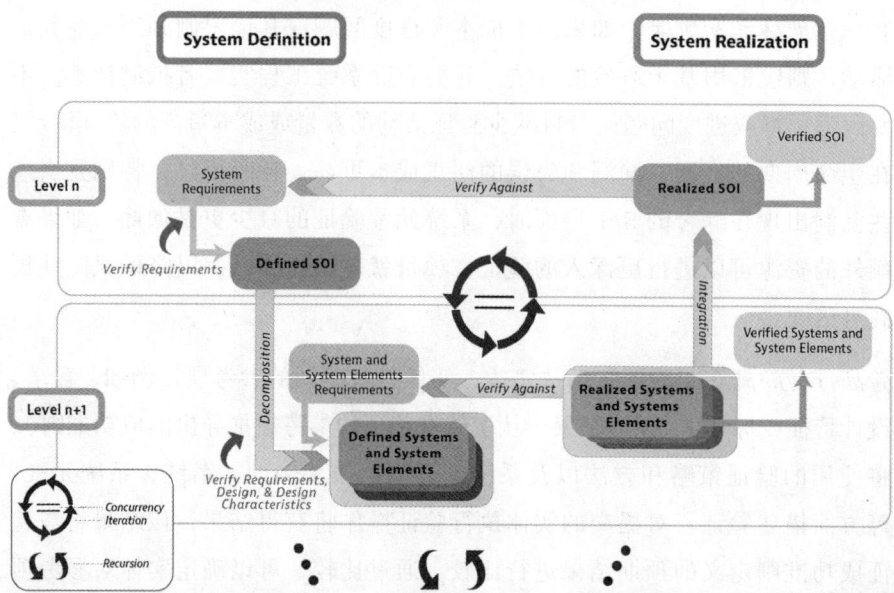

FIGURE 2.50 Verification per level. INCOSE SEH original figure created by Walden from Faisandier. Usage per the INCOSE Notices page. All other rights reserved.

142
- *Verification of the system architecture (architecture verification)*—(1) Verify that the SoI architecture, when realized by design, will result in a SoI that will pass system verification and (2) verify the correct application of the appropriate patterns and heuristics used and the correct usage of *architecture definition* techniques or methods as defined by the organization's guidelines and requirements concerning system architecture definition.

- *Verification of the system design (design verification)*—(1) Verify that the SoI design and associated design characteristics meets its system requirements and would result in a SoI that will pass system verification with an acceptable degree of confidence and (2) verify the correct usage of patterns, trade rules, or state of the art related to the concerned technology (e.g., software, mechanics, electronics, biology, chemistry) as defined by the organization's guidelines and requirements concerning system design.

- *Verification of a realized system (product, service, or enterprise) or system element (system verification)*—Verify the system or system element meets its system requirements and design characteristics with an acceptable degree of confidence.

Verification Methods. Basic verification methods are as follows (ISO/IEC/IEEE 29148, 2018):

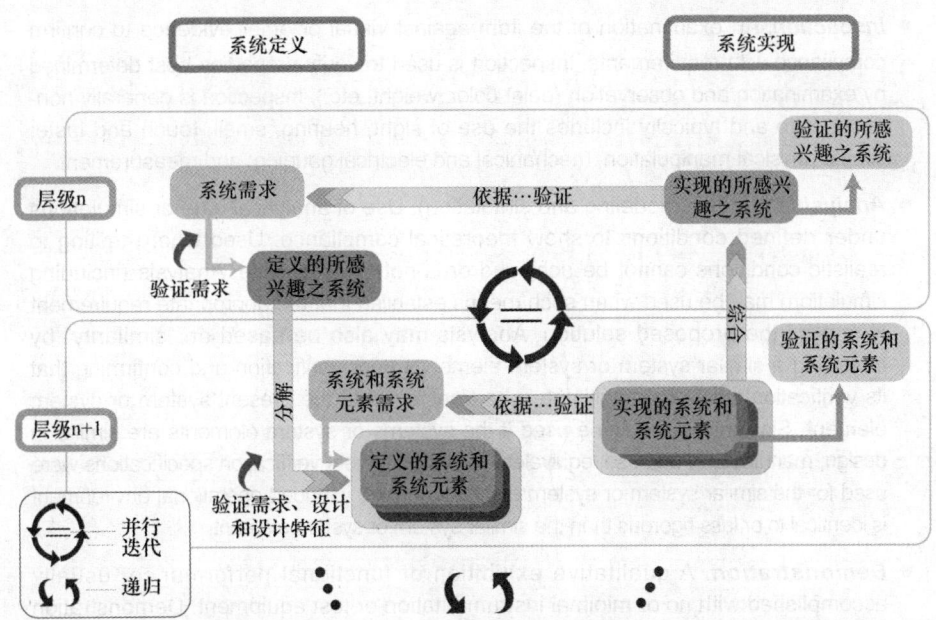

图 2.50 逐层验证。INCOSE SEH 原始图由 Walden 依据 Faisandier 创建。按照 INCOSE 通知页使用。版权所有。

- *系统架构验证（架构验证）*——（1）验证 SoI 架构在通过设计实现时，将产生一个能通过系统验证的 SoI；（2）验证所使用的适当的模式和启发式方法的应用正确性，以及组织关于系统架构定义的指南和要求所规定的架构定义技术或方法的正确使用。

- *系统设计验证（设计验证）*——（1）验证 SoI 设计和相关设计特征是否满足其系统需求，并将使 SoI 以可接受的置信度通过系统验证；（2）验证与相关技术（如软件、机械、电子、生物、化学）相关的模式、权衡规则或最新技术的正确使用，正如组织的系统设计指南和要求所定义的。

- *已实现系统（产品、服务或复杂组织体系）或系统元素（系统验证）的验证*——验证系统或系统元素满足其系统要求和设计特征，并具有可接受的置信度。

*验证方法。*基本验证方法如下（ISO/IEC/IEEE 29148，2018）：

SYSTEM LIFE CYCLE CONCEPTS, MODELS, AND PROCESSES

- *Inspection.* An examination of the item against visual or other evidence to confirm compliance with requirements. Inspection is used to verify properties best determined by examination and observation (paint color, weight, etc.). Inspection is generally non-destructive and typically includes the use of sight, hearing, smell, touch and taste; simple physical manipulation; mechanical and electrical gauging; and measurement.

- *Analysis* (including modeling and simulation). Use of analytical data or simulations under defined conditions to show theoretical compliance. Used where testing to realistic conditions cannot be achieved or is not cost-effective. Analysis (including simulation) may be used when such means establish that the appropriate requirement is met by the proposed solution. Analysis may also be based on "similarity" by reviewing a similar system or system element's prior verification and confirming that its verification status can legitimately be transferred to the present system or system element. Similarity can only be used if the systems or system elements are similar in design, manufacture, and use; equivalent or more stringent verification specifications were used for the similar system or system element; and the intended operational environment is identical to or less rigorous than the similar system or system element.

- *Demonstration.* A qualitative exhibition of functional performance, usually accomplished with no or minimal instrumentation or test equipment. Demonstration uses a set of test activities with system stimuli selected by the supplier to show that system or system element response to stimuli is suitable or to show that operators can perform their allocated functions when using the system. Often, observations are made and compared with predetermined responses.

- *Test.* An action by which the operability, supportability, or performance capability of an item is quantitatively verified when subjected to controlled conditions that are real or simulated. These verifications often use special equipment or instrumentation to obtain accurate quantitative data for analysis to determine verification.

Verification per Level. The SoI may have a number of hierarchical layers of system elements within its architecture. The planning of the verification is done recursively at each lower level as the definition of the system or a system element evolves. The execution of the verification actions occurs recursively for each layer as the elements are integrated as shown in Figure 2.50. For example, the stakeholder requirements are verified to ensure they meet their higher-level requirements, the system and system element requirements are verified to ensure they meet their higherlevel system requirements and the system architecture and design are verified to ensure they meet their system or system element requirements. Additionally, every layer of realized systems and system elements are verified to ensure they meet their system requirements before being integrated into the next higher level of the SoI architecture. Any issues or discrepancies must be corrected before a system element is integrated into the next higher level of the SoI. Having passed verification at a given level, that set of elements are integrated into the next higher-level system as defined in the Integration process (see Section 2.3.5.8). System integration, system verification, and system validation continues until the integrated SoI has passed system verification.

- *检查*。对照目视或其他证据对项目进行检查，以确认符合需求。检查用于验证通过检查和观察（油漆颜色、重量等）确定的最佳性能。检查通常是非破坏性的，通常包括视觉、听觉、嗅觉、触觉和味觉的使用；简单的物理操作；机械和电气计量和测量。

- *分析*（包括建模和仿真）。在规定条件下使用分析数据或仿真，以展示理论符合性。在无法达到实际条件或成本—有效性不高的情况下使用。当此类方法确定拟定解决方案满足适当要求时，可使用分析（包括仿真）。分析也可以基于"相似性"，通过评审类似系统或系统元素的先前验证，并确认其验证状态可以合法地转移到当前系统或系统元素。只有当系统或系统元素在设计、制造和使用上相似时，才能使用相似性；对类似系统或系统元素使用同等或更严格的验证规范；并且预期的操作环境与类似的系统或系统元素相同或不太严格。

- *演示*。功能性能的定性展示，通常在没有或很少使用仪器或测试设备的情况下完成。演示使用一组由供应商选择的系统刺激进行测试活动，以表明系统或系统元素对刺激的反应是合适的，或表明操作员在使用系统时可以执行其分配的功能。通常，会进行观察，并与预先确定的响应进行比较。

- *测试*。在真实或仿真的受控条件下，对项目的可操作性、可保障性或性能能力进行定量验证的行动。这些验证通常使用特殊设备或仪器来获得准确的定量数据，以便进行分析，以确定验证。

逐级验证。SoI 可能在其架构内具有多个系统元素的层级结构。随着系统或系统元素定义的发展，验证的计划在每个较低层级递归进行。如图 2.50 所示，当元素被综合时，每层的验证操作都会递归执行。例如，验证利益相关方需求以确保其满足更高层级的需求，验证系统和系统元素需求以确保其满足更高层级的系统需求，验证系统架构和设计以确保其满足其系统或系统元素需求。此外，在综合到下一个更高层级的 SoI 架构之前，对每一层已实现的系统和系统元素进行验证，以确保它们满足其系统需求。在将系统元素综合到 SoI 的下一个更高层级之前，必须纠正任何问题或差异。通过给定层级的验证后，该组元素将综合到综合流程中定义的下一个更高层级系统中（见 2.3.5.8 节）。系统综合、系统验证和系统确认将继续，直到综合的 SoI 通过系统验证。

143 *Early Verification and MBSE.* With the increased use of models and simulations as part of the design process, verification activities can be conducted earlier in the life cycle prior to implementation. Doing so will reduce the risk of issues and anomalies being discovered during system integration, system verification, and system validation activities with the actual physical hardware, mechanisms, and software and reduce the resulting expensive and time-consuming rework.

However, the SE practitioner is cautioned to resist substituting verification of the realized system with the verification results obtained using models and simulations, unless necessary. Doing so reduces the confidence level (as compared to verification against the actual realized system) and adds risk of the realized system failing system validation. As long as the realized system is not completely integrated and/or has not been validated to operate in the actual operational environment by the intended users, no result must be regarded as definitive until the acceptable degree of confidence is realized.

Managing the project's system verification program. In the progress of the project, it is important to know, at any time, the status of the verification activities, anomalies discovered, and noncompliances. This knowledge enables the project to better manage the budget and schedule as well as estimate the risks of noncompliance against the possibly of eliminating some of the planned verification actions to meet budget and schedule constraints.

2.3.5.10 Transition Process

Overview

Purpose As stated in ISO/IEC/IEEE 15288,

[6.4.10.1] The purpose of the Transition process is to establish a capability for a system to provide services specified by stakeholder requirements in the operational environment.

Description The Transition process installs a SoI into its operational and maintenance environment. This process makes the SoI an integral part of the acquiring organization systems, business processes, and capabilities so the organization starts to benefit from using and sustaining the system's services.

The Transition process coordinates with verification and validation performed in the target environment, with the activities of operation and maintenance of new systems and services, and with the disposal of systems, system elements, materials, and services no longer needed for operation.

早期验证和 MBSE。随着模型和仿真作为设计流程的一部分得到越来越多的使用，验证活动可以在实施之前的生命周期中更早地进行。这样做将减少使用实际物理硬件、机制和软件进行系统综合、系统验证和系统确认活动期间发现问题和异常的风险，并减少由此产生的昂贵和耗时的返工。

然而，除非必要，系统工程实践者应避免用模型和仿真获得的验证结果来代替对已实现系统的验证。这样做会降低可信度（与根据实际实现的系统的验证相比），并增加已实现系统未能通过系统验证的风险。只要实现的系统未完全综合和/或未经预期用户验证可在实际运行环境中运行，则在实现可接受的置信度之前，任何结果都不得视为确定的。

管理项目的系统验证计划。在项目进展流程中，随时了解验证活动的状态、发现的异常和不符合项非常重要。这些知识使项目能够更好地管理预算和进度，并根据为满足预算和进度限制而取消部分计划的验证行动的可能性来估计不合规的风险。

2.3.5.10 转移流程

概述

目的 如 ISO/IEC/IEEE 15288 所述：

[6.4.10.1] 转移流程的目的是为系统建立一种能力，以在运行环境中提供利益相关方需求规定的服务。

描述 转移流程将 SoI 安装到其运行和维护环境中。该流程使 SoI 成为采办方系统、业务流程和能力的一个组成部分，因此组织开始从使用和维护系统服务中受益。

转移流程与在目标环境中执行的验证和确认、新系统和服务的运行和维护活动以及运行不再需要的系统、系统元素、材料和服务的处置相协调。

SYSTEM LIFE CYCLE CONCEPTS, MODELS, AND PROCESSES

Transition may identify system requirements and design gaps. It may also drive changes, augmenting the initial stakeholder and system requirements.

Inputs/Outputs Inputs and outputs for the Transition process are listed in Figure 2.51. Descriptions of each input and output are provided in Appendix E.

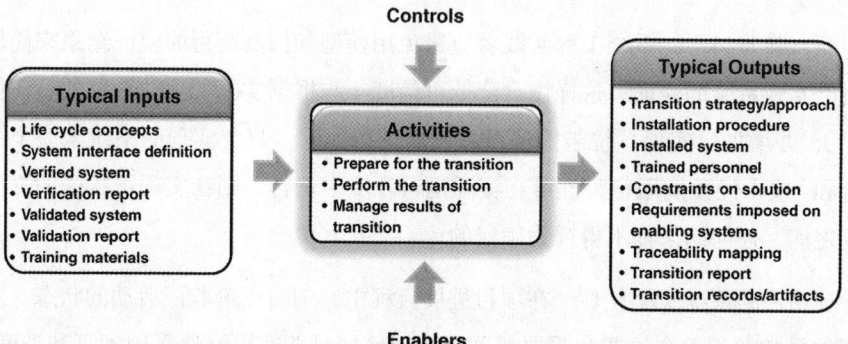

FIGURE 2.51 IPO diagram for Transition process. INCOSE SEH original figure created by Shortell, Walden, and Yip. Usage per the INCOSE Notices page. All other rights reserved.

Process Activities The Transition process includes the following activities:

- *Prepare for the Transition.*

–Analyze the intended environment for the system deployment, including the physical sites, information technology infrastructure, organizational structure, and processes of the receiving organization.

–Identify the changes to the existing environment to accommodate the system.

–Identify and obtain (e.g., procure, develop, reuse, rent, schedule, subcontract) the requisite enabling systems, controls, products, or services required for the transition, including the changes in the environment.

–Plan for coordinating the development of the SoI with the modifications of its intended environment.

–Determine the transition team structure, composition, and responsibilities for the transition activities.

–Plan for the system's transition, including allocating time and budget for all parts of the transition.

转移可能会识别系统需求和设计差距。它还可以推动变化，增加最初的利益相关方和系统需求。

输入 / 输出　转移流程的输入和输出如图 2.51 所示。附录 E 中提供了每个输入和输出的描述。

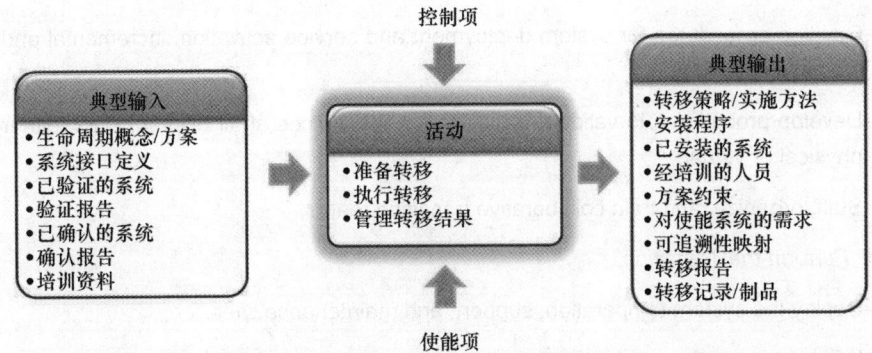

图 2.51　转移流程的 IPO 图。INCOSE SEH 原始图由 Shortell、Walden 和 Yip 创建。按照 INCOSE 通知页使用。版权所有。

流程活动　转移流程包括以下活动：

- *准备转移。*

- 分析系统部署的预期环境，包括接收组织的物理地点、信息技术基础设施、组织结构和流程。

- 识别现有环境的变化以适应系统。

- 识别并获取（例如，采办、开发、复用、租赁、计划、分包）转移所需的必要的使能系统、控制、产品或服务，包括环境变化。

- 制订计划，协调 SoI 的开发与预期环境的改造。

- 确定转移团队的结构、组成和转移活动的职责。

- 系统转移计划，包括为转移的各部分分配时间和预算。

–Plan for mitigation strategies if the transition if the system encounters difficulties. Ensure that stakeholders understand the process/risk of possible downtime of the system and even actions to restore the predecessor system (roll-back) and the "point-of-no-return."

–Plan the configuration management of the system's adaptation to the local operation and support context.

–Develop procedures for system deployment and service activation, incremental and staged if appropriate.

–Develop procedures to validate the system and services at all relevant sites, either physical or virtual.

–Staff, organize, and train collaborative transition teams.

- *Perform the Transition.*

–Deploy the system to operation, support, and maintenance sites.

–Invoke integration and verification processes to realize operable local system configurations.

–Establish systems, processes, and organizational capabilities for ongoing adaptation of the system to evolving context, including capabilities for integration with other systems, deployment to other sites, performance monitoring, and problem detection, investigation, and correction.

–Train the operation, maintenance, and other personnel. As applicable, perform complete review and hand-off of the operator, maintenance, and support manuals. Affirm that the personnel have the knowledge and skill levels necessary to operate, maintain, and support the system.

–Provide as-built information for configuration management.

–Activate/commission the system's services at each site. Ensure that the system delivers its intended services as expected, including collaboration with other systems and personnel.

–Receive final confirmation that the installed system can provide its required functions and be sustained. Assure that the system has been properly installed and verified and all issues and action items have been resolved. Assure that all agreements about developing and delivering a fully supportable system have been fully satisfied or adjudicated.

–Perform or support contractual acceptance of the system by the acquirer, followed by transfer of control, responsibility, ownership, and custody.

系统生命周期概念、模型和流程

- 如果系统在转移流程中遇到困难，应制定缓解策略。确保利益相关方了解系统可能宕机的流程/风险，甚至是恢复前置系统（回滚）和"不归点"的行动。

- 计划系统的构型配置管理，以适应本地操作和支持环境。

- 制定系统部署和服务激活程序，如适用，可增量和分阶段进行。

- 制定程序，以验证所有相关地点的系统和服务，无论是物理地点还是虚拟地点。

- 为协作转移团队配备人员、进行组织和培训。

• 执行转移。

- 将系统部署到运行、支持和维护地点。

- 调用综合和验证流程，以实现可运行的本地系统构型配置。

- 建立系统、流程和组织能力，使系统不断适应演进的环境，包括与其他系统综合、部署到其他地点、性能监控以及问题检测、调查和纠正的能力。

- 培训操作、维护和其他人员。如适用，对操作员、维护和支持手册进行全面评审和移交。确认人员具备操作、维护和支持系统所需的知识和技能水平。

- 为构型配置管理提供完工信息。

- 在每个地点激活/调试系统服务。确保系统按预期提供服务，包括与其他系统和人员的协作。

- 最终确认已安装的系统能够提供所需的功能并持续运行。确保系统已正确安装和验证，所有问题和行动项均已解决。确保所有关于开发和交付一个完全可支持系统的协议均已完全满足或裁决。

- 执行或支持采办方对系统的合同验收，然后转让控制权、职责、所有权和保管权。

SYSTEM LIFE CYCLE CONCEPTS, MODELS, AND PROCESSES

- *Manage results of Transition.*

–Capture incidents, problems, and anomalies. Investigate and document issues. Perform corrective actions as needed. Use the Quality Assurance process for managing incidents and problem resolution. If the transition is to multiple sites using a phased approach, ensure that any corrective actions are incorporated into the transition approach.

–Use the experience gained in the current transition instances for improving future instances.

–Maintain bidirectional traceability of the transitioned system elements, system services, and operational capabilities with the architecture, design, and system requirements. Initiate changes as needed.

Common approaches and tips:

- Identify the enabling systems and materials needed for transition early in the life cycle to allow for the necessary lead time to obtain or access them.

Elaboration

Transition Concepts. The Transition process is not limited to the SoI going into service as a part of the operating organization. Each system element undergoes transition during its integration into a larger element, and the element's transition must be formalized in the agreements between key stakeholders, such as prime contractors and its subcontractors.

The Transition process coordinates the system or system element deployment and activation with the modification of its environment. It pays particular attention to integrating the SoI and other systems in its environment. The Transition process should be fully integrated with an organizational change process led by the receiving organization, usually incremental and staged.

The Transition process comprises all activities required to establish the capability for a system to provide services for the benefit of the organization acquiring the system. The transition transfers the system from the development context ("system-in-the-lab") to the utilization context ("system-in-the field"). Successful transition typically marks the beginning of the SoI or system element's utilization stage.

Transition Considerations. The transition of new systems to a newly created organization (or a new element into a new system) differs from transitioning a new system or element into an existing organization or system. The former is sometimes referred to as "greenfield" or "clean sheet" transitioning, and the latter as "brownfield" or "legacy systems" (see Sections 4.3.1 and 4.3.2). The introduction of the new element disrupts the existing environment, so considerable effort must be invested to transition to the "new norm."

系统生命周期概念、模型和流程

- *管理转移结果。*

- 捕获事件、问题和异常。调查并记录问题。根据需要执行纠正措施。使用质量保证流程管理事件和解决问题。如果使用分阶段方法向多个现场转移，请确保将任何纠正措施纳入转移方法。

- 使用当前转移实例中获得的经验改进未来的实例。

- 根据架构、设计和系统需求，维护已转移系统元素、系统服务和运行能力的双向可追溯性。根据需要启动更改。

常用方法和提示：

- 在生命周期的早期阶段确定转移所需的使能系统和材料，以便有必要的提前期来获取或使用它们。

详细阐述

*转移的概念。*转移流程不限于 SoI 作为运行组织的一部分投入使用。每个系统元素在综合到更大元素的流程中都会经历转移，元素的转移必须在主要利益相关方（如主承包商及其分包商）之间的协议中正式确定。

转移流程通过修改其环境来协调系统或系统元素的部署和激活。它特别注意在其环境中综合 SoI 和其他系统。转移流程应与接收组织领导的组织变革流程充分整合，通常是渐进式和分阶段的。

转移流程包括建立系统能力所需的所有活动，以便为获取系统的组织提供服务。转移将系统从开发背景环境（"实验室中的系统"）转移到使用背景环境（"现场中的系统"）。成功的转移通常标志着 SoI 或系统元素使用阶段的开始。

*转移注意事项。*将新系统转移到新创建的组织（或将新元素转移到新系统）不同于将新系统或元素转移到现有组织或系统。前者有时被称为"绿地"或"空白的纸"转移，后者被称为"棕地"或"遗留系统"（见 4.3.1 和 4.3.2 节）。引入新元素会破坏现有环境，因此转移到"新规范"必须投入大量精力。

SYSTEM LIFE CYCLE CONCEPTS, MODELS, AND PROCESSES

A phase of provisional operation (also referred to as "burn-in") is sometimes included in the transition activities, allowing operations to get used to the new system before acceptance, resulting in concurrent and iterative application of the Transition and Operation processes. Burn-in involves activities taken to operate a system element in the operational or simulated environment to detect failures and improve reliability. Usually, the operation of the system is done at levels that would cover or exceed the range of expected environmental values (heat, vibration, power, etc.). The warranty period may delay the transfer of responsibility for the system maintenance, resulting in concurrency and iteration between the Transition and Maintenance Processes.

2.3.5.11 Validation Process

Overview

Purpose As stated in ISO/IEC/IEEE 15288,

[6.4.11.1] The purpose of the Validation process is to provide objective evidence that the system, when in use, fulfills its business or mission objectives and stakeholder needs and requirements, achieving its intended use in its intended operational environment.

Description The Validation process can be applied to any engineering artifact, entity, or information item that has contributed to the definition and realization of the SoI (e.g., validation of stakeholder needs, stakeholder requirements, system requirements, models, simulations, the system architecture, design characteristics, validation procedures, or a realized system or system element). The Validation process provides objective evidence with an acceptable degree of confidence to confirm:

1. The "right" artifact or entity has been made according to the stakeholder needs and stakeholder requirements.

2. Whether or not these artifacts, entities, or information items, will result in the right SoI, when realized, that can be validated to accomplish its intended use in its operational environment when operated by its intended users.

3. The system does not enable unintended users to negatively impact the intended use of the system or use the system in an unintended way.

As is often stated, validation is intended to ensure that "the right artifact or entity will be or was built," while verification is intended to ensure that "the artifact or entity has been built right."

转移活动中有时包括临时运行阶段（也称为"磨合"），允许在验收前开展运行以适应新系统，从而实现转移和运行流程的并行和迭代应用。磨合涉及在运行或仿真环境中运行系统元素的活动，以检测故障并提高可靠性。通常，系统的运行水平将覆盖或超过预期环境值的范围（热量、振动、功率等）。保修期可能会延迟系统维护职责的转移，导致转移和维护流程之间的并行和迭代。

2.3.5.11 确认流程

概述

目的 如 ISO/IEC/IEEE 15288 所述：

[6.4.11.1] 确认流程的目的是提供客观证据，证明系统在使用时满足其业务或任务目标以及利益相关方的需要和需求，在其预期的运行环境中实现其预期用途。

描述 确认流程可应用于任何有助于 SoI 定义和实现的工程制品、实体或信息项（例如，确认利益相关方需要、利益相关方需求、系统需求、模型、仿真、系统架构、设计特征、验证程序或已实现的系统或系统元素）。确认流程提供了具有可接受置信度的客观证据，以确认：

1. "正确的"制品或实体是根据利益相关方的需要和利益相关方的需求实现的。

2. 这些制品、实体或信息项在实现时是否会产生正确的 SoI，当由其预期用户运行时，可以确认这些 SoI 以在其运行环境中实现其预期用途。

3. 系统不会使非预期用户对系统的预期用途产生负面影响或以非预期方式使用系统。

正如通常所述，确认旨在确保"将要或曾经构建正确的制品或实体"，而验证旨在确保"制品或实体已经正确地构建"。

SYSTEM LIFE CYCLE CONCEPTS, MODELS, AND PROCESSES

Inputs/Outputs Inputs and outputs for the Validation process are listed in Figure 2.52. Descriptions of each input and output are provided in Appendix E.

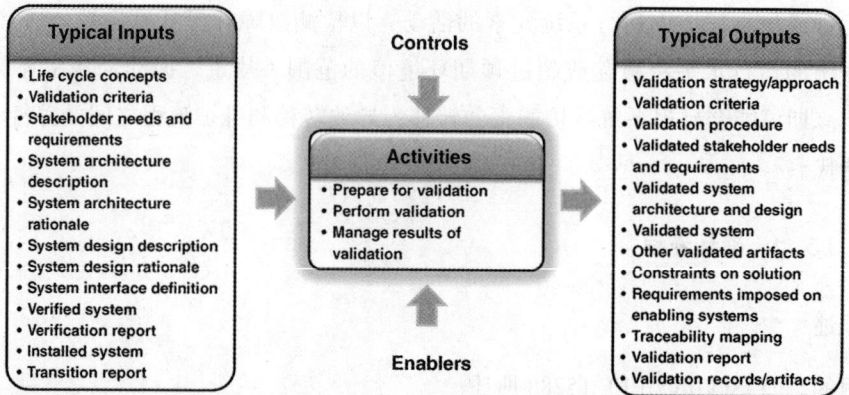

FIGURE 2.52   IPO diagram for Validation process. INCOSE SEH original figure created by Shortell, Walden, and Yip. Usage per the INCOSE Notices page. All other rights reserved.

147   **Process Activities** The Validation process includes the following activities:

- *Prepare for validation.*

–Define the scope (what will be validated) and the validation actions (strategy, method, and success criteria). Validation activities consume resources: time, labor, facilities, and funds. The scope of the organization's validation strategy/approach should be documented within the project's SEMP and system integration, verification, and validation plans.

°Establish a list of artifacts, entities, or information items to be validated.

°Identify the stakeholder needs and stakeholder requirements against which each entity will be validated.

–Consider and capture constraints that could impact the feasibility or effectiveness of validation actions. The constraints could impact the implementation of the validation actions and include contractual constraints, limitations due to regulatory requirements, cost, schedule, feasibility to exercise a function, safety and security considerations, the laws of physics, physical configurations, accessibility, etc.

SYSTEM LIFE CYCLE CONCEPTS, MODELS, AND PROCESSES

SYSTEM LIFE CYCLE CONCEPTS, MODELS, AND PROCESSES

系统生命周期概念、模型和流程

输入/输出 确认流程的输入和输出如图 2.52 所示。附录 E 中提供了每个输入和输出的描述。

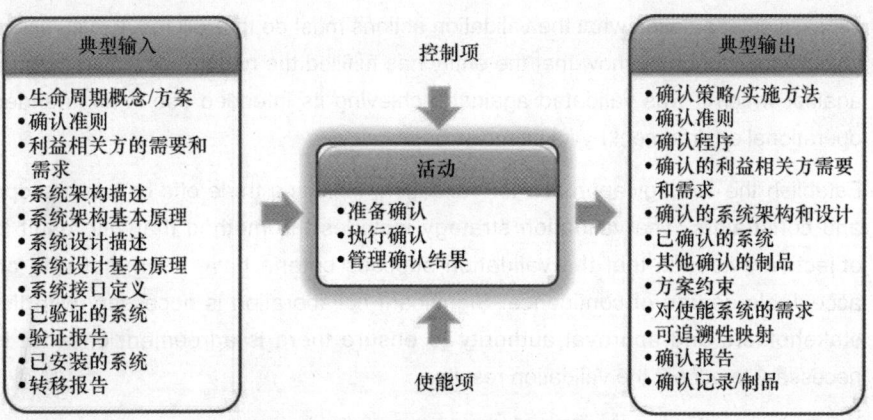

图 2.52 确认流程的 IPO 图。INCOSE SEH 原始图由 Shortell、Walden 和 Yip 创建。按照 INCOSE 通知页使用。版权所有。

流程活动 确认流程包括以下活动：

- *准备确认*。

- 定义范围（将要确认的内容）和确认行动（策略、方法和成功准则）。确认活动消耗的资源：时间、人力、设施和资金。组织确认策略/实施方法的范围应记录在项目的 SEMP 和系统综合、验证和确认计划中。

  ° 建立要确认的制品、实体或信息项的列表。

  ° 确定利益相关方的需要和利益相关方的需求，并根据这些对每个实体进行确认。

- 考虑并捕获可能影响确认行动可行性或有效性的约束。这些限制可能会影响确认行动的实施，包括合同限制、监管要求造成的限制、成本、进度、执行功能的可行性、安全和安保考虑、物理定律、物理构型配置、可访问性等。

SYSTEM LIFE CYCLE CONCEPTS, MODELS, AND PROCESSES

–For each validation action, select one or more validation methods and associated success criteria. Validation methods are similar to the methods defined for verification (inspection, analysis, demonstration, or test) (see Section 2.3.5.9). The success criteria define what the validation actions must do that will result in sufficient objective evidence to show that the entity has fulfilled the need(s) or requirement(s) against which it was validated against, achieving its intended use in its intended operational environment by its intended users.

–Establish the strategy/approach for validation, including trade-offs between scope and constraints. The validation strategy includes the method that will result in objective evidence that the validation success criteria have been met with an acceptable degree of confidence. Significant collaboration is necessary with the stakeholders and approval authority to ensure there is agreement on what is necessary to accept the validation results.

°Define validation activities. For each validation instance, define a specific validation action that will result in objective evidence needed to validate the SoI meets one or more stakeholder needs or stakeholder requirements per the defined validation strategy.

°Define validation procedure requirements for each validation action. The validation procedure requirements are requirements that will drive the formulation of steps and actions for a given validation procedure.

–Identify constraints and objectives from the validation strategy to be incorporated within the sets of stakeholder needs and requirements and the system requirements transformed from them.

–Plan for the necessary enabling systems or services needed through the life cycle for validation. Enabling systems include organizational support, validation equipment, simulators, emulators, test beds, test automation tools, facilities, etc.

–Ensure enabling system or service access needed to support validation. This includes confirming everything required for the validation activities will be available, when needed. The acquisition of the enablers can be done through several ways such as rental, procurement, development, reuse, and subcontracting.

- *Perform validation.*

–Define the procedures for the validation actions. A procedure can support one action or a set of actions.

–Execute the validation procedures for planned validation actions.

系统生命周期概念、模型和流程

- 对于每个确认操作，选择一个或多个确认方法和相关成功准则。确认方法类似于为验证（检验、分析、演示或测试）定义的方法（见 2.3.5.9 节）。成功准则定义了确认行动必须做什么，以产生足够的客观证据，证明实体已满足其确认所依据的需要或需求，并由其预期用户在其预期运行环境中实现其预期用途。

- 制定确认策略 / 实施方法，包括范围和约束之间的权衡。确认策略包括一种方法，该方法将产生客观证据，证明验证成功准则已达到可接受的置信度。必须与利益相关方和审批机构进行重要合作，以确保就接受确认结果所需的内容达成一致。

  ° 定义确认活动。对于每个确认实例，定义将产生的特定确认动作。根据确定的确认策略，确认 SoI 是否满足一个或多个利益相关方需要或利益相关方需求所需的客观证据。

  ° 定义每个确认动作的确认程序要求。确认程序需求是推动制定给定确认程序的步骤和动作的需求。

- 确定确认策略中的约束和目标，将其纳入利益相关方需要和需求集，以及由此转化的系统需求。

- 计划整个生命周期所需的必要使能系统或服务，以进行确认。使能系统包括组织支持、确认设备、仿真器、模拟器、测试台、测试自动化工具、设施等。

- 确保能够访问支持确认所需的系统或服务。这包括确保确认活动所需的一切都将在需要时提供。可以通过租赁、采办、开发、再利用和分包等多种方式获取使能工具。

- 执行确认。

- 定义确认动作的程序。一个流程可以支持一个运行或一组运行。

- 执行计划的确认动作的确认程序。

SYSTEM LIFE CYCLE CONCEPTS, MODELS, AND PROCESSES

°Schedule the execution of validation procedures. Each scheduled validation event represents a commitment of personnel, time, resources, and equipment that would ideally show up on a project's schedule. At the integrated SoI level, this should be done against the actual SoI in the operational environment or one as close to it as possible, by the intended users or equivalent surrogates.

°Ensure readiness to conduct the validation procedure: availability and configuration status of the system/entity, the availability of the validation enablers, qualified personnel or operators, resources, etc. At the integrated SoI level, since it often depends on customer and intended user involvement, this can be particularly important to plan out in advance to be sure the right individuals are present.

148
- *Manage results of validation.*

    –Record the validation results and any defects identified. Maintain the results in validation reports and records per organizational policy as well as contractual and regulatory requirements.

    °Analyze the validation results against the validation success criteria to determine whether the entity being validated meets those criteria with an acceptable degree of confidence.

    –Throughout validation, capture operational incidents and problems and track them until final resolution. Problem resolution and any subsequent changes will be handled through the Project Assessment and Control process (see Section 2.3.4.2) and the Configuration Management process (see Section 2.3.4.5). Any changes to the SoI definition (e.g., stakeholder needs, stakeholder requirements, system requirements, system architecture, system design, design characteristics, or interfaces) and associated engineering artifacts are performed within other Technical Processes.

    –Obtain agreement from the approval authority that the validation criteria have been met to their satisfaction. Combine the individual validation records into a validation approval package for the entity being validated and submit to the validation approval authority. The validation approval authority is the party authorized to deter mine whether sufficient evidence has been provided to show that the entity has passed validation with an acceptable degree of confidence.

    –At the integrated SoI level, validation may be performed with or by the acquirer as defined in the supplier agreement. However, at lower levels in the architecture, validation may be performed by the supplier without acquirer direct involvement.

○ 安排确认程序的执行。每个计划的确认事件都代表了人员、时间、资源和设备的承诺，这些承诺理想化地体现在项目的时间上。在综合的 SoI 层级上，应由预期用户或等效代理根据运行环境中的实际 SoI 或尽可能接近的 SoI 进行操作。

○ 确保做好执行确认程序的准备：系统/实体的可用性和构型配置状态、确认使能项、合格人员或操作人员、资源的可用性等。在综合的 SoI 层级，由于这通常取决于客户和预期用户的参与，因此提前计划以确保有合适的人员在场尤其重要。

• 管理确认结果。

- 记录确认结果和发现的任何缺陷。根据组织政策以及合同和监管要求，将结果保存在确认报告和记录中。

○ 根据确认成功准则分析确认结果，以确定被确认实体是否符合这些标准，并具有可接受的置信度。

- 在整个确认流程中，捕获运行事件和问题，并对其进行跟踪，直至最终解决。问题解决和任何后续变更将通过项目评估和控制流程（见 2.3.4.2 节）和构型配置管理流程（见 2.3.4.5 节）进行处理。对 SoI 定义（如利益相关方需要、利益相关方需求、系统需求、系统架构、系统设计、设计特征或接口）和相关工程制品的任何变更都将在其他技术流程中进行。

- 获得审批机构的同意，即确认准则已达到其满意的程度。将各个确认记录合并到被确认实体的确认审批包中，并提交给确认批准机构。确认批准机构是指有权确定是否已提供足够的证据证明该实体已经以可接受的置信度通过确认的一方。

- 在综合的 SoI 层面，可根据供应商协议的规定，与采办方或由采办方进行确认。然而，在架构的较低层级，确认可由供应商执行，而无须采办方直接参与。

–Establish and sustain traceability (validation). Establish and maintain bidirectional traceability of the validated entity and validation artifacts with the system architecture, system design, models, and the stakeholder needs and stakeholder requirements against which the entity is being validated.

–Give CM the information items, work products, or other artifacts needed for baselines. The Configuration Management process (see Section 2.3.4.5) is used to establish and maintain configuration items and baselines. The validation process identifies candidates for baseline, and then provides the items to the Configuration Management process.

Common approaches and tips:

- Identify the enabling systems and materials needed for validation early in the life cycle to allow for the necessary lead time to obtain or access them.
- Validation also reveals the effects the SoI may have on enabling, interfacing, and interoperating systems. Validation actions and analysis should include these system interactions in the scope.
- Involve the broadest range of stakeholders that is practical, including end users and operators,
- Validation should include actions that provide insight as early as possible, such as analysis, modeling, and simulation of anticipated operational characteristics and system behavior.
- Start to develop the validation planning as the OpsCon, operational scenarios, stakeholder needs, and stakeholder requirements are defined. Early consideration of the potential validation actions and methods helps to anticipate constraints, costs, and necessary enablers, as well as start the acquisition of those enablers.
- Validation actions during the Business or Mission Analysis process (see Section 2.3.5.1) include assessment of the OpsCon through operational scenarios that exercise all system operational modes and demonstrating systemlevel performance.

Elaboration

This section elaborates and provides "how-to" information on the Validation process. Additional guidance on validation can be found in the INCOSE NRM (2022) and INCOSE GtVV (2022).

系统生命周期概念、模型和流程

- 建立并保持可追溯性（确认）。建立并维护已确认实体和确认制品的双向可追溯性，包括系统架构、系统设计、模型、利益相关方需要和利益相关方需求，并根据这些确认实体。

- 为构型配置管理提供基线所需的信息项、工作产品或其他制品。构型配置管理流程（见 2.3.4.5 节）用于建立和维护构型配置项和基线。确认流程确定基线的备选项，然后将这些备选项提供给构型配置管理流程。

常用方法和提示：

- 在生命周期的早期阶段确定确认所需的使能系统和材料，以便有必要的提前期来获取或使用它们。
- 确认还揭示了 SoI 可能对使能、接口和互操作系统的影响。确认行动和分析应包括范围内的这些系统的交互。
- 让最广泛的实际利益相关方参与，包括最终用户和操作员。
- 确认应包括尽早提供洞察的行动，如对预期运行特性和系统行为的分析、建模和仿真。
- 在确定 OpsCon、运行场景、利益相关方需要和利益相关方需求时，开始制订确认计划。尽早考虑潜在的确认行动和方法有助于预测约束、成本和必要的使能因素，并开始获取这些使能因素。
- 业务或任务分析流程中的确认行动（见 2.3.5.1 节）包括通过演练所有系统运行模式和展示系统级性能的运行场景对 OpsCon 进行评估。

详细阐述

本节详细阐述并提供确认流程的"如何做"的信息。有关确认的其他指南，请参见 INCOSE NRM（2022）和 INCOSE GtVV（2022）。

149 *General Considerations.* The stakeholder needs and stakeholder requirements the SoI is being validated against are derived from the mission statement, goals, objectives, critical measures, constraints, risks, and set of life cycle concepts for the SoI defined by the organization or acquirer during the Stakeholder Needs and Requirements Definition and System Requirements Definition processes (see Sections 2.3.5.2 and 2.3.5.3). The life cycle concepts include scenarios and use cases that are performed in a specific operational environment by the intended users for not only operation, but during other life cycle stages including production, operation, support, and retirement. It is common for these scenarios and use cases to be exercised during the conduct of the validation procedures within the operational environment with the intended users. The common saying "test as you fly, fly as you test" applies. When using scenarios and use cases, in addition to nominal operations, it is important to also address off-nominal, alternate cases, misuse cases, and loss scenarios. A positive validation result obtained in a given environment by specific users can turn noncompliant if the environment or class of users change. These changes may not be immediately known by the developer; however, changing stakeholder needs and stakeholder requirements should be accommodated by the acquirer and developer's SE processes.

During validation, especially for walkthroughs and similar activities, it is highly recommended to involve intended users/operators. Validation will often involve going back directly to the users to have them perform an acceptance test under their own local operational conditions in the intended operational environment. When the system is validated at a supplier facility or organization, the acquirer will often want to conduct additional validation activities in their own facility, in the intended operational environment, and with the intended users. The stakeholders who were involved in defining the life cycle concepts and needs must be presented with the results of the validation activities to ensure their needs and requirements have been met.

Validation Planning. Planning for validation should begin when the stakeholder needs and stakeholder requirements are being defined. As they are defined, it is recommended to define the validation success criteria, method, and strategy and obtain acquirer and approval authority approval. Early planning helps drive cost and schedule estimates of the system validation plan earlier in the project—maximizing the chance the full system validation plan will be resourced.

Reduction of Validation Activities and Risk. If validation activities must be reduced due to cost and schedule concerns, this should be done using a risk-based approach. The SE practitioner is urged to resist the temptation to blindly reduce the number of, or the costliest, validation activities due to budget or schedule concerns. Gaps and misses are more costly and time consuming to correct later in the life cycle—especially when these gaps show up at final system acceptance by the acquirer or regulatory agency. If additional resources become available that allow an opportunity to validate lower-risk, non-critical stakeholder needs and stakeholder requirements, the project should do so to reduce risk and increase the degree of confidence.

一般注意事项。确认 SoI 所依据的利益相关方需要和利益相关方需求源自组织或采办方在利益相关方需要和需求定义流程和系统需求定义流程中定义的 SoI 任务声明、目标、关键措施、约束、风险和生命周期概念集（见 2.3.5.2 节和 2.3.5.3 节）。生命周期概念包括预期用户在特定运行环境中执行的场景和用例，这些场景和用例不仅用于运行，还用于其他生命周期阶段，包括生产、运行、支持和退役。这些情景和用例通常是在运行环境中与预期用户一起执行确认程序时演练。俗话说"边飞边试，边试边飞"。在使用场景和用例时，除了正常运行外，还必须解决非正常、备用用例、误用用例和损失场景。如果环境或用户类发生变化，特定用户在给定环境中获得的肯定确认结果可能会变得不符合要求。开发商可能不会立即知道这些变更；然而，不断变化的利益相关方需要和利益相关方需求应由采办方和开发商的系统工程流程来适应。

在确认期间，特别是对于演练和类似活动，强烈建议让预期用户／操作人员参与。确认通常涉及直接返回给用户，让他们在预期的运行环境中，在自己的本地运行条件下执行确认测试。当系统在供应商设施或组织进行确认时，采办方通常希望在其自己的设施、预期运行环境和预期用户中进行额外的确认活动。必须向参与定义生命周期概念和需要的利益相关方提供确认活动的结果，以确保其需要和需求得到满足。

确认计划。确认计划应在确定利益相关方需要和利益相关方需求时开始。根据定义，建议定义确认成功准则、方法和策略，并获得采办方和审批机构的批准。早期计划有助于在项目早期推动对系统确认计划的成本和进度的估计，最大限度地增加整个系统确认计划获得资源的机会。

减少确认活动和风险。如果由于成本和进度问题必须减少确认活动，则应采用基于风险的方法。我们敦促系统工程实践者抵制诱惑，不要因为预算或进度问题而盲目减少确认活动的数量或成本最高的确认活动。在生命周期的后期，漏洞和失误的纠正成本更高、耗时更长，尤其是当这些漏洞出现在采办方或监管机构最终确认系统时。如果有额外的资源可以确认风险较低、非关键的利益相关方需要和需求，项目就应该这样做，以降低风险并提高可信度。

SYSTEM LIFE CYCLE CONCEPTS, MODELS, AND PROCESSES

Notion of a Validation Action. Validation actions are similar to verification actions, and the reader is referred to the Verification process (see Section 2.3.5.9) for background. Figure 2.53 illustrates several common validation actions.

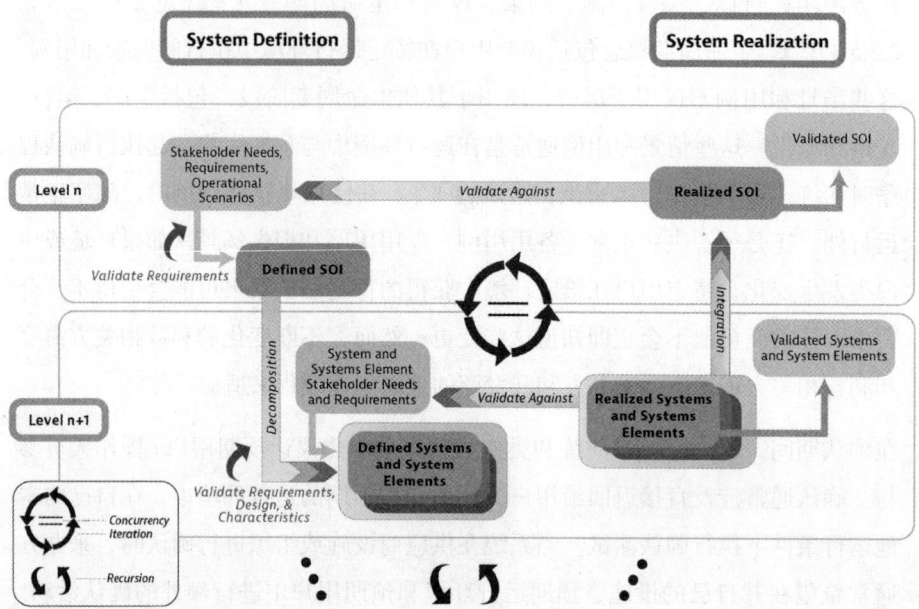

FIGURE 2.53 Validation per level. INCOSE SEH original figure created by Walden from Faisandier. Usage per the INCOSE Notices page. All other rights reserved.

Examples of validation actions include:

- *Validation of a stakeholder requirement (requirement validation)*—Validate that the stakeholder requirement is the right requirement and clearly and accurately communicates the need of the stakeholder, is in the stakeholder's language, and is actionable (i.e., can be transformed into one or more system requirements). For stakeholder requirements and sets of stakeholder requirements ask, "If a SoI were built to these requirements, would the SoI meet the needs from which these requirements were transformed?"

- *Validation of a system requirement (requirement validation)*—Validate that the system requirement is the right requirement and clearly and accurately communicates the need and requirement of the stakeholder, is expressed in technical terms, and is actionable (i.e., can be transformed into a system architecture and design). For system requirements and sets of system requirements ask, "If a SoI were built to the system architecture and design transformed from these requirements, would the SoI meet the intent of the requirements from which the architecture and design were transformed?"

438

系统生命周期概念、模型和流程

确认行动的概念。确认行动与验证行动类似，读者可参考验证流程（见 2.3.5.9 节）了解背景信息。图 2.53 说明了几种常见的确认行动。

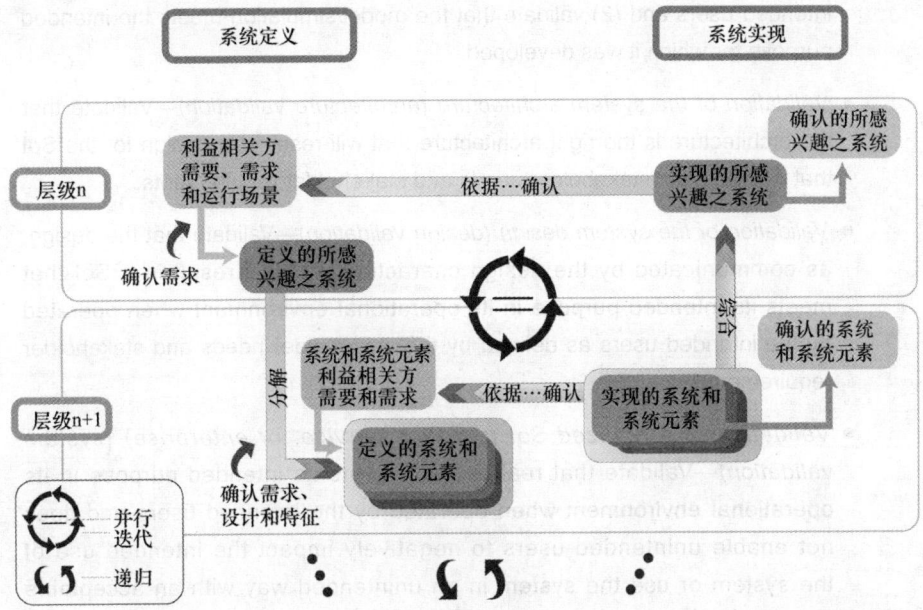

图 2.53 逐层确认。INCOSE SEH 原始图由 Walden 依据 Faisandier 创建。按照 INCOSE 通知页使用。版权所有。

确认行动的示例包括：

- *利益相关方需求确认（需求确认）*——确认利益相关方需求是正确的需求，清楚准确地沟通了利益相关方的需要，使用利益相关方的语言，并且是可操作的（即，可以转换为一个或多个系统需求）。对于利益相关方需求和利益相关方需求集，询问"如果按照这些需求建造 SoI，SoI 是否能满足由需求转化而来的需要？"

- *系统需求确认（需求确认）*——确认系统需求是正确的需求，清楚准确地沟通了利益相关方的需要和需求，以技术术语表达，是可操作的（即，是否可以转化为系统架构和设计）。对于系统需求和系统需求集，询问"如果 SoI 是根据这些需求转换的系统架构和设计构建的，SoI 是否符合架构和设计所转换的需求意图？"

SYSTEM LIFE CYCLE CONCEPTS, MODELS, AND PROCESSES

- *Validation of a model or simulation (model or simulation validation)*—(1) Validate that the model/simulation accurately reflects the intended behavior of the entity it represents in its operational environment when operated by the intended users and (2) validate that the model/simulation meets the intended purpose for which it was developed.

- *Validation of the system architecture (architecture validation)*—Validate that the architecture is the right architecture that will result in a design for the SoI that will meet the stakeholder needs and stakeholder requirements.

- *Validation of the system design (design validation)*—Validate that the design, as communicated by the design characteristics, will result in a SoI that meets its intended purpose in its operational environment when operated by the intended users as defined by the stakeholder needs and stakeholder requirements.

- *Validation of a realized SoI (product, service, or enterprise) (system validation)*—Validate that realized SoI meets its intended purpose in its operational environment when operated by the intended users and does not enable unintended users to negatively impact the intended use of the system or use the system in an unintended way with an acceptable degree of confidence as defined by the stakeholder needs and stakeholder requirements.

Validation Outcomes. Typical validation outcomes include:

- **Acceptance.** Acceptance is an activity conducted prior to transition to the acquirer such that the acquirer can decide if this transition is appropriate. A set of operational validation actions is often exercised, or a review of validation results performed by the supplier is systematically performed as part of acceptance.

- **Certification.** Certification is a written assurance that the system has been developed per a defined procedure and can perform its intended functions in accordance with identified legal or industrial standards (e.g., airworthiness standards for aircraft, information assurance). A host of information can be part of the certification package, including development reviews, verification results, and validation results. However, certification is typically performed by outside authorities, without direction as to how the needs are to be validated. For example, this method is used for electronics devices via Conformité Européenne (CE) certification in Europe and via Underwriters Laboratories (UL) certification in the United States and Canada.

- *模型或仿真确认（对模型或仿真的确认）*——（1）验证模型/仿真是否准确地反映了所代表的实体在其运行环境中由预期用户操作时的预期行为，以及（2）确认模型/仿真是否满足其开发的预期目的。

- *系统架构确认（架构确认）*——确认架构是否是正确的架构，从而为SoI设计出满足利益相关方需要和利益相关方需求的架构。

- *系统设计确认（设计确认）*——确认设计特性所传达的设计结果，即当利益相关方需要和利益相关方需求所定义的预期用户进行操作时，SoI能够在操作环境中满足其预期目的。

- *已实现SoI（产品、服务或复杂组织体系）的确认（系统确认）*——确认已实现的SoI在由预期用户操作时，在其运行环境中满足其预期目的，并且不会使非预期用户对系统的预期用途产生负面影响，或以非预期方式使用系统，并具有利益相关方需要和利益相关方需求定义的可接受置信度。

确认结果。典型的确认结果包括：

- **接受**。接受是指在向接收机构转移之前进行的活动，以便接收机构可以决定该转移是否合适。作为确认的一部分，通常会执行一组操作确认行动，或系统地评审供应商执行的确认结果。

- **认证**。认证是一种书面保证，证明系统已按照规定的程序开发，并可根据确定的法律或行业标准（如飞机适航标准、信息保证）执行其预期功能。大量信息可以是认证包的一部分，包括开发评审、验证结果和确认结果。然而，认证通常由外部机构执行，没有关于如何确认需求的指示。例如，该方法用于电子设备是通过欧洲的欧洲合格证（CE）认证以及美国和加拿大的保险商实验室（UL）认证。

SYSTEM LIFE CYCLE CONCEPTS, MODELS, AND PROCESSES

- **Readiness for Use.** As part of the analysis of the validation results, the project team and validation authority may need to make a readiness for use assessment. This may occur several times in the life cycle, including upon first article delivery, upon completion of production (if more than a single system is produced), following maintenance actions, or successful completion of field trials with a predefined user population. In the field, particularly after maintenance, it may be necessary to establish whether the system is ready for reintroduction to service.

- **Qualification.** System qualification requires that all verification and validation actions have been successfully performed, documented, and that the SoI is "qualified" for use as intended by the supplier organization. These verification and validation actions cover not only the SoI itself but also all the interfaces with its environment (e.g., for a space system, the validation of the interface between space segment and ground segment). The qualification process must demonstrate that the characteristics or properties of the realized system, including margins, meet the applicable system requirements and/or stakeholder requirements. The qualification is concluded by an acceptance review and/or an operational readiness review.

Validation per Level. The SoI may have a number of hierarchical layers of system elements within its architecture. The planning of the validation is done recursively for each level as the definition of the system or a system element evolves. The execution of the validation actions occurs recursively for each layer as the elements are integrated as shown in Figure 4.53. For example, the stakeholder needs and stakeholder requirements are validated against the stakeholder real world expectations to ensure they are the right stakeholder needs and stakeholder requirements, the systems requirements are validated against the stakeholder needs and requirements to ensure they are right system requirements, and the system architecture and design are validated against the stakeholder needs and requirements to ensure they are the right system architecture and design. Additionally, every layer of realized systems and system elements are validated to ensure they meet their stakeholder needs and stakeholder requirements in their operational environment before being integrated into the next higher level of the SoI architecture. Having passed system verification and system validation at a given level, that system element is integrated into the next higher-level system as defined in the Integration process (see Section 2.3.5.8). System integration, system verification, and system validation continue until the integrated SoI has passed system validation.

Early System Validation and MBSE. With the increased use of models and simulations as part of the design process, validation activities can be conducted earlier in the life cycle prior to implementation. Doing so will reduce the risk of issues and anomalies being discovered during system integration, system verification and system validation activities with the actual physical hardware, mechanisms, and software and reduce the resulting expensive and time-consuming rework.

- **使用准备就绪**。作为确认结果分析的一部分,项目团队和确认机构可能需要进行准备就绪评估。这可能在生命周期中发生多次,包括首件交付时、生产完成时(如果生产了多个系统)、维护行动后或使用预定义用户群成功完成现场试验时。在现场,尤其是维护后,可能需要确定系统是否准备好重新投入使用。

- **资质**。系统鉴定要求所有验证和确认行动均已成功执行并记录,且 SoI "合格" 可按供应商组织的预期使用。这些验证和确认行动不仅包括 SoI 本身,还包括其环境的所有接口(例如,对于空间系统,确认空间段和地面段之间的接口)。鉴定流程必须证明已实现系统的特征或特性(包括裕度)符合适用的系统需求和/或利益相关方需求。通过验收评审和/或运行准备状态评审,完成资格鉴定。

逐级确认。 SoI 可能在其架构内具有多个系统元素的层级结构。随着系统或系统元素定义的演进,确认的计划在每个较低层级递归进行。如图 4.53 所示,当元素被综合时,每层的确认操作都会递归执行。例如,确认利益相关方需求以确保其满足更高层级的需求,确认系统和系统元素需求以确保其满足更高层级的系统需求,确认系统架构和设计以确保其满足其系统或系统元素需求。此外,在综合到下一个更高层级的 SoI 架构之前,对每一层已实现的系统和系统元素进行确认,以确保它们满足其系统需求。在将系统元素综合到 SoI 的下一个更高层级之前,必须纠正任何问题或差异。通过给定层级的确认后,该组元素将综合到综合流程所定义的下一个更高层级的系统中(见 2.3.5.8 节)。系统综合、系统验证和系统确认将持续,直到综合的 SoI 通过系统确认。

早期系统确认和 MBSE。随着模型和仿真作为设计流程的一部分得到越来越多的使用,确认活动可以在实施之前的生命周期中更早地进行。这样做将减少在实际物理硬件、机制和软件的系统综合、系统验证和系统确认活动中发现问题和异常的风险,并减少由此产生的昂贵和耗时的返工。

SYSTEM LIFE CYCLE CONCEPTS, MODELS, AND PROCESSES

In addition, modeling and simulations early in the project allows not only expectation management but also early feedback from the acquirer and other stakeholders on the final system architecture and design before implementation. It will be much less expensive and time consuming to resolve issues before the realization of the actual physical hardware and software and before system integration, system verification, and system validation activities.

Because the behavior of a system is a function of the interaction of its elements, a major goal of systems validation is assessing the behavior of the integrated physical system and identifying emergent properties not specifically addressed in the stakeholder needs or stakeholder requirements nor identified during modeling and simulations. Emergent properties may be positive or negative. For example, cascading failures across multiple interface boundaries between the system elements that are part of the SoI's architecture. Relying on models and simulations of the SoI and operational environment may not uncover all the emerging properties and issues that occur in the physical realm. While validation using models and simulations allows a theoretical determination that the modeled system will meet its needs in the operational environment by the intended users once realized, the assessment of the actual system behavior (system validation) must be done, whenever possible, in the physical realm with the actual hardware and software integrated into the higher-level system which it is a part in the actual operational environment by the intended users.

There are cases when it may not be practical in terms of the intended use and actual operational environment to do all system validation activities. However, the SE practitioner is cautioned to not substitute validation of the realized system with the validation results obtained using models and simulations, unless absolutely necessary. Doing so adds risk to the project and reduces the confidence level (as compared to validation against the actual realized system in its actual operational environment when operated by the intended users) and adds risk of the realized system failing system validation when delivered to the acquirer or submitted to a regulatory agency. As long as the realized system is not completely integrated and/or has not been validated to operate in the actual operational environment by the intended users, no result must be regarded as definitive until the acceptable degree of confidence is realized.

Managing the project's validation program. In the progress of the project, it is important to know, at any time, the status of the validation activities, anomalies discovered, and noncompliances. This knowledge enables the project to better manage the budget and schedule as well as estimate the risks of noncompliance against the possibly of eliminating some of the planned validation actions to meet budget and schedule constraints.

此外，项目早期的建模和仿真不仅可以实现预期管理，还可以在实施前从采办方和其他利益相关方那里获得关于最终系统架构和设计的早期反馈。在实现实际物理硬件和软件之前，以及在系统综合、系统验证和系统确认活动之前，解决问题的成本和时间将大大降低。

由于系统的行为是其元素交互作用的函数，因此系统确认的主要目标是评估综合的物理系统的行为，并确定在利益相关方需要或利益相关方需求中未明确提及，也未在建模和仿真流程中确定的涌现属性。涌现属性可能为正或负。例如，作为 SoI 架构一部分的系统元素之间跨多个接口边界的连锁故障。依靠 SoI 和运行环境的模型和仿真可能无法揭示物理领域中出现的所有新特性和问题。

虽然使用模型和仿真进行确认可以从理论上确定一旦实现，模型系统将满足预期用户在运行环境中的需求，但必须尽可能在物理领域对实际系统行为（系统确认）进行评估，并将实际硬件和软件综合到更高层级的系统中，该系统是预期用户在实际运行环境中的一部分。

在某些情况下，就预期用途和实际运行环境而言，进行所有系统确认活动可能并不可行。然而，除非绝对必要，否则系统工程实践者应注意不要用使用模型和仿真获得的确认结果来替代对已实现系统的确认。这样做会增加项目风险，降低置信度（与预期用户在实际运行环境中对实际实现的系统进行确认相比），并增加已实现系统在交付给采办方或提交给监管机构时未通过系统确认的风险。只要实现的系统未完全综合和/或未经预期用户确认可在实际运行环境中运行，则在实现可接受的置信度之前，任何结果都不可视为确定的。

管理项目确认计划。在项目进展中，随时了解确认活动的状态、发现的异常和不合规情况非常重要。这一知识使项目能够更好地管理预算和进度，并根据消除一些计划确认行动以满足预算和进度限制的可能性，估计不符合的风险。

SYSTEM LIFE CYCLE CONCEPTS, MODELS, AND PROCESSES

2.3.5.12 Operation Process

Overview

Purpose As stated in ISO/IEC/IEEE 15288,

[6.4.12.1] The purpose of the Operation process is to use the system to deliver its services.

Description The Operation process focuses on delivering services provided by the system for the benefit of the operating organization. This process is often concurrent with the Maintenance process of sustaining the system's services. During Operation, the SoI functions as an integral part of the operating organization. The SoI contributes to the Business or Mission Analysis process by cooperating with human operators and diverse interfacing systems.

Operation may identify the system requirements and design gaps. It may also drive changes, augmenting the initial stakeholder and system requirements.

Inputs/Outputs Inputs and outputs for the operation process are listed in Figure 2.54. Descriptions of each input and output are provided in Appendix E.

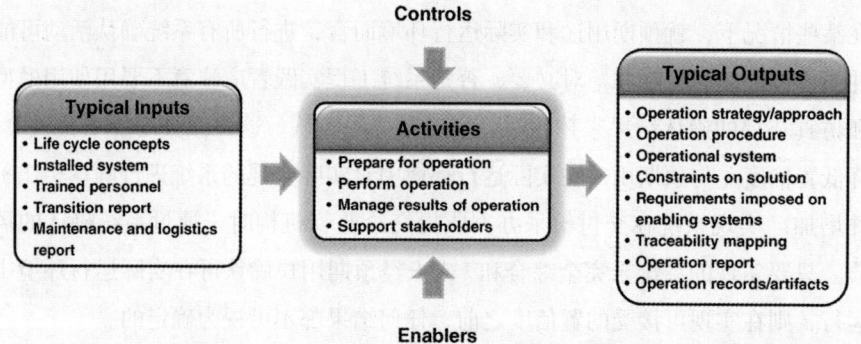

FIGURE 2.54 IPO diagram for Operation process. INCOSE SEH original figure created by Shortell, Walden, and Yip. Usage per the INCOSE Notices page. All other rights reserved.

Process Activities The Operation process includes the following activities:

- *Prepare for operation.*

2.3.5.12 运行流程

概述

目的 如 ISO/IEC/IEEE 15288 所述：

[6.4.12.1] 运行流程的目的是使用系统提供其服务。

描述 运行流程的重点是为运行组织的利益交付系统所提供的服务。该流程通常与维护系统服务的流程同时进行。在运行期间，SoI 作为运行组织的一个组成部分发挥作用。SoI 通过与操作人员和各种接口系统合作，为业务或任务分析流程做出贡献。

运行可识别系统需求和设计差距。它还可以推动变化，扩充最初的利益相关方和系统需求。

输入 / 输出 运行流程的输入和输出如图 2.54 所示。附录 E 中提供了每个输入和输出的描述。

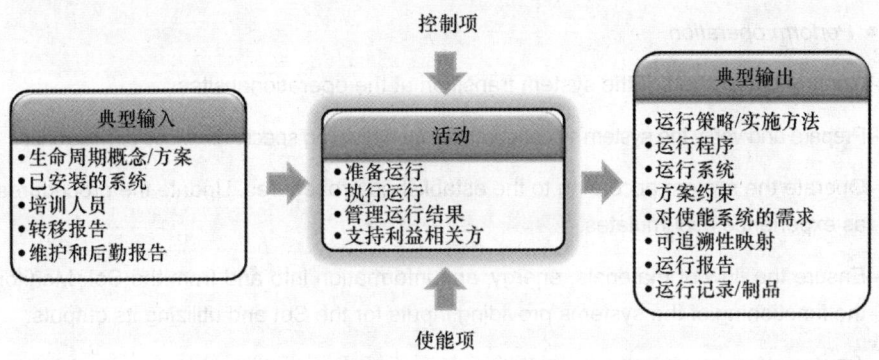

图 2.54 运行流程的 IPO 图。INCOSE SEH 原始图由 Shortell、Walden 和 Yip 创建。按照 INCOSE 通知页使用。版权所有。

流程活动 运行流程包括以下活动：

- *准备运行*。

SYSTEM LIFE CYCLE CONCEPTS, MODELS, AND PROCESSES

– Influence the Concept of Operations (ConOps) of the receiving organization, the Operational Concept (OpsCon) of the SoI, the stakeholder needs and requirements, and the system requirements impacting the operation of the SoI.

– Identify relevant regulations, legal requirements, environmental and ethical constraints.

– Define business rules related to modifications that sustain existing or enhanced services.

– Plan for operational capability build-up, including confirmation of site deployment schedules, personnel availability, training, and logistic support availability.

– Identify and obtain (procure, develop, reuse, rent, schedule, subcontract) the requisite enabling systems, controls, products, or services required for the operation.

– Verify that the SoI is accompanied by all relevant information products, such as documentation, manuals, and procedures. Identify gaps and initiate changes as necessary.

– Review the transition, validation, and maintenance strategies for compatibility with the OpsCon and their completeness concerning the expected operational capabilities.

- *Perform operation.*

– Confirm completion of the system transition at the operational sites.

– Prepare and verify the system's configurations for delivering specific services or missions.

– Operate the system according to the established procedures. Update the procedures as experience accumulates.

– Ensure the flow of materials, energy, and information into and from the SoI. Monitor the functioning of the systems providing inputs for the SoI and utilizing its outputs.

– Track system performance, including operational availability. Identify, investigate, and correct problems and anomalies.

– When abnormal operational conditions warrant, conduct planned contingency actions. Perform system contingency operations, if necessary.

- *Manage results of operation.*

– Capture incidents, problems, and anomalies. Investigate and document the issues. Perform corrective actions as needed. Use the Quality Assurance process for managing incidents and problem resolution.

- 影响接收组织的运行意图、SoI 的运行概念、利益相关方的需要和需求，以及影响 SoI 运行的系统需求。

- 确定相关法规、法律要求、环境和道德约束。

- 定义与维持现有或增强服务的改进相关的业务规则。

- 运行能力建设计划，包括确认现场部署时间、人员可用性、培训和后勤保障可用性。

- 识别并获得（采办、开发、复用、租赁、安排、分包）运行所需的必要使能系统、控制、产品或服务。

- 验证 SoI 是否附有所有相关信息产品，如文件、手册和程序。确定差距并在必要时发起更改。

- 评审转移、确认和维护策略是否与运行概念兼容，以及它们在预期运行能力方面的完整性。

- *执行运行*。

- 确认在运行地点完成系统转移。

- 准备并验证系统构型配置，以提供特定服务或任务。

- 按照既定程序运行系统。随着经验的积累，更新程序。

- 确保物质、能量和信息流入和流出 SoI。监控为 SoI 提供输入并使用其输出的系统的功能。

- 跟踪系统性能，包括运行可用性。识别、调查并纠正问题和异常。

- 当异常运行条件允许时，执行计划的应急行动。如有必要，执行系统应急操作。

- *管理运行结果*。

- 捕获事件、问题和异常。调查并记录问题。根据需要执行纠正措施。使用质量保证流程管理事件和问题解决。

SYSTEM LIFE CYCLE CONCEPTS, MODELS, AND PROCESSES

–Use the experience gained during the operation for improvement.

–Maintain bidirectional traceability of the system's assets, services, and operational capabilities with system architecture, design, and system requirements. Initiate changes as needed.

- *Support stakeholders*

–While the customer is responsible for the Operation process, the supplier should support the customer throughout the system life cycle leveraging the knowledge generated by the customer and the supplier.

Common approaches and tips:

- Identify the enabling systems, products, services, and materials needed for operation early in the life cycle to allow for the necessary lead time to obtain or access them.

Elaboration

Operation Concepts. Successful operation of the SoI as a part of the operating organization is the ultimate goal of SE. The stakeholders' needs and requirements regarding operation constitute a significant source of the system requirements and a significant input to the Validation and Transition processes.

During operation, the SoI interfaces with other systems in its environment (see Section 1.3.3). These systems are SoIs in their own right, and their life cycles must be coordinated with the life cycle of your SoI.

The operational environment may change and evolve while the system is being developed. Considerable effort must be invested in recognizing these changes and updating the life cycle concepts (especially ConOps and OpsCon) and all derived requirements.

2.3.5.13 Maintenance Process

Overview

Purpose As stated in ISO/IEC/IEEE 15288,

[6.4.13] The purpose of the Maintenance process is to sustain the capability of the system to provide a service.

Description The Maintenance process focuses on sustaining the system's ability to provide services for the operating organization's benefit. This process is often concurrent with the Operation process of delivering the system's services. Maintenance includes the activities to provide operations support, logistics, and material management to sustain satisfactory quality, performance, and availability of the system's services.

- 利用运行流程中获得的经验进行改进。

- 根据系统架构、设计和系统需求，维护系统资产、服务和运行能力的双向可追溯性。根据需要启动更改。

- 支持利益相关方。

- 虽然客户负责运行流程，但供应商应在整个系统生命周期内使用客户和供应商产生的知识为客户提供支持。

常用方法和提示：

- 在生命周期的早期阶段确定运行所需的使能系统和材料，以便有必要的提前期来获取或使用它们。

详细阐述

运行概念。 作为运行组织的一部分，SoI 的成功运行是系统工程的最终目标。利益相关方关于运行的需要和需求是系统需求的重要来源，也是确认和转移流程的重要输入。

在运行期间，SoI 与其环境中的其他系统具有接口关系（见 1.3.3 节）。这些系统本身也是 SoI，其生命周期必须与 SoI 的生命周期相协调。

在系统开发流程中，运行环境可能会发生变化和演进。在识别这些变化并且更新生命周期概念（尤其是 ConOps 和 OpsCon）以及所有派生需求方面，必须投入大量精力。

2.3.5.13 维护流程

概述

目的　如 ISO/IEC/IEEE 15288 所述：

[6.4.13] 维护流程的目的是维持系统提供服务的能力。

描述　维护流程的重点是维持系统为运行组织的利益提供服务的能力。此流程通常与交付系统服务的运行流程同时进行。维护包括提供运行支持、后勤和物资管理的活动，以维持系统服务的令人满意的质量、性能和可用性。

155 Maintenance may identify requirements and design gaps. It may also drive changes in the SoI, augmenting the initial stakeholder and system requirements.

Inputs/Outputs Inputs and outputs for the Maintenance process are listed in Figure 2.55. Descriptions of each input and output are provided in Appendix E.

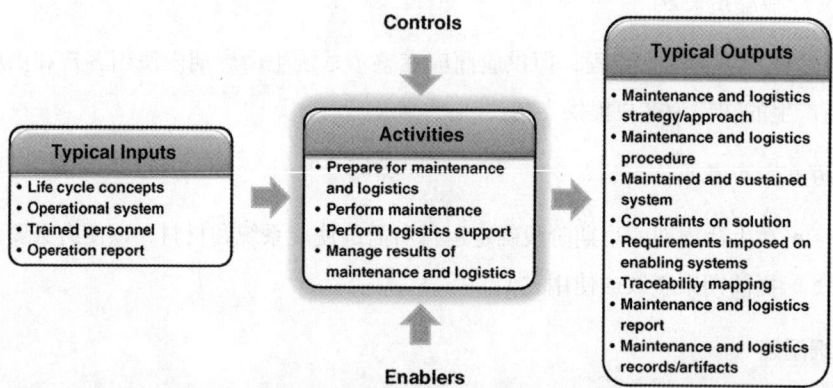

FIGURE 2.55   IPO diagram for Maintenance process. INCOSE SEH original figure created by Shortell, Walden, and Yip. Usage per the INCOSE Notices page. All other rights reserved.

Process Activities The Maintenance process includes the following activities:

- Prepare for maintenance and logistics.

–Define and maintain the maintenance and logistics strategies of the SoI and its elements and update the system requirements and attribute specifications impacting the maintenance and logistics support.

–Define business rules related to modifications that sustain existing or enhanced services.

–Identify relevant regulations, legal requirements, and ethical constraints and generate corresponding requirements.

–Plan for maintenance and logistics support capability build-up, including site deployment schedules, personnel availability, and training, including the logistic support availability.

–Establish appropriate warranty and licenses (e.g., software, legal) and the lines of communication to activate more support when needed.

系统生命周期概念、模型和流程

维护可以识别需求和设计差距。它还可能推动 SoI 的变化,扩充初始利益相关方需求和系统需求。

输入/输出　维护流程的输入和输出如图 2.55 所示。附录 E 中提供了每个输入和输出的描述。

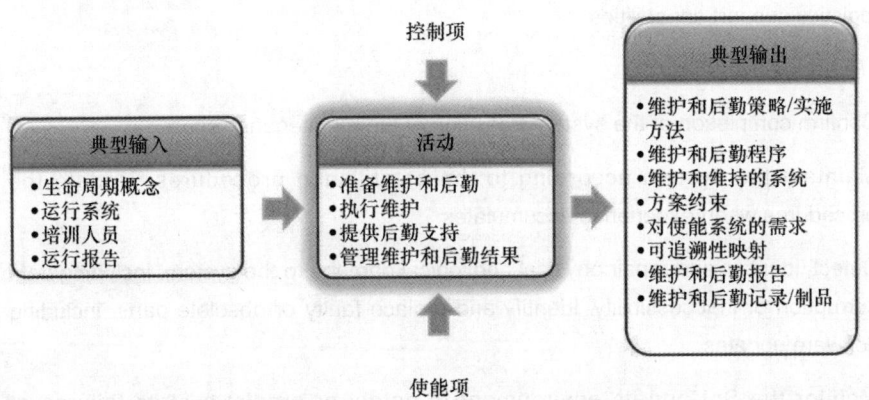

图 2.55　维护流程的 IPO 图。INCOSE SEH 原始图由 Shortell、Walden 和 Yip 创建。按照 INCOSE 通知页使用。版权所有。

流程活动　维护流程包括以下活动:

- *准备维护和后勤*。
- 定义和维持 SoI 及其元素的维护和后勤策略,更新影响维护和后勤保障的系统需求和属性规范。
- 定义与维护现有或增强服务的修改相关的业务规则。
- 确定相关法规、法律需求和道德约束,并生成相应的需求。
- 维护和后勤保障能力建设计划,包括现场部署时间、人员可用性和培训,包括后勤保障可用性。
- 建立适当的保修和许可证(如软件、法律)以及沟通渠道,以便在需要时激活更多支持。

SYSTEM LIFE CYCLE CONCEPTS, MODELS, AND PROCESSES

–Identify and obtain (procure, develop, reuse, rent, schedule, subcontract) the requisite enabling systems, controls, products, or services required for maintenance and logistics support.

–Review the transition, validation, and operation strategies for compatibility with the support concept and their completeness concerning the expected maintenance and logistics support capabilities.

- *Perform maintenance.*

–Confirm completion of the system transition at the maintenance sites.

–Maintain the system according to the established procedures. Update the procedures when experience accumulates.

–Detect, identify, and repair physical and logical damage to the system, including data corruption or inaccessibility. Identify and replace faulty or obsolete parts, including software updates.

–Monitor the SoI and its environment to detect or predict system failures or performance degradation, identifying and resolving operational problems minimizing operational interruptions.

–Prevent operation disruptions by scheduling repairs and replacements before failures occur, based on operations history or failure prediction.

–Ensure availability of materials and parts for replacement and repairs by production, acquisition, or repairs, including operations and maintenance of logistics processes and systems. Conduct logistics operations according to the established procedures. Update the procedures when experience accumulates.

–Track all maintenance repairs for analysis, which may lead to performance trends that can trigger warranty claims or new project needs.

- *Perform logistic support.*

–Conduct acquisition logistics actions.

–Conduct operational logistics actions.

- *Manage results of maintenance and logistics.*

–Capture incidents, problems, and anomalies. Investigate and document the issues. Perform corrective actions as needed. Use the Quality Assurance process for managing incidents and problem resolution.

- 识别并获得（采办、开发、复用、租赁、安排、分包）维护和后勤支持所需的必要的使能系统、控制、产品或服务。

- 评审转移、验证和运行策略是否与支持概念兼容，以及它们在预期维护和后勤支持能力方面的完整性。

- *执行维护。*

- 确认在维护现场完成系统转移。

- 按照既定程序维护系统。积累经验后更新程序。

- 检测、识别和修复系统的物理和逻辑损坏，包括数据损坏或无法访问。识别并更换故障或过时零件，包括软件更新。

- 监控 SoI 及其环境，以检测或预测系统故障或性能下降，识别和解决运行问题，最大限度地减少运行中断。

- 根据运行历史或故障预测，在故障发生之前安排维修和更换，以防止运行中断。

- 通过生产、采办或维修，包括后勤流程和系统的运行和维护，确保材料和零件的可用性，以进行更换和维修。按照既定程序进行后勤运作。积累经验后更新程序。

- 跟踪所有维护维修以进行分析，这可能导致性能趋势，从而引发保修索赔或新项目需求。

- *提供后勤支持。*

- 开展采办后勤行动。

- 开展运行后勤行动。

- *管理维护和后勤结果。*

- 捕获事件、问题和异常。调查并记录问题。根据需要执行纠正措施。使用质量保证流程管理事件和问题解决。

SYSTEM LIFE CYCLE CONCEPTS, MODELS, AND PROCESSES

–Use the experience gained while performing maintenance for improvement.

–Maintain bidirectional traceability of the maintenance and logistics assets, services, and capabilities with system architecture, design, and system requirements. Initiate changes as needed.

–Manage the configuration data items.

156 *Common approaches and tips*:

- Identify the enabling systems, products, services, and materials needed for maintenance and logistics support early in the life cycle to allow for the necessary lead time to obtain or access them.
- The maintenance of the SoI must be coordinated with the maintenance of other systems in its environment (the interoperating and enabling systems). The failure or malfunction of any system can trigger maintenance actions in other systems due to technical, organizational, economic, or political concerns.

Elaboration

The Maintenance process supports the operation of the SoI and its elements throughout its life cycle. The maintenance and logistics activities regarding the SoI must be integrated into the operating organization's existing support and logistics networks. This includes provisions for sustaining the skills and competencies of personnel performing operation and maintenance.

Different modes of maintenance should be considered:

- Corrective maintenance restores system services to normal operations (e.g., remove and replace hardware, reload software, apply a software patch).
- Preventive maintenance prevents failures and malfunctions by scheduling routine maintenance actions to sustain optimal system operational performance.
- Predictive maintenance is a more advanced preventive maintenance that utilizes data collected during the system operations to predict failures and malfunctions and schedule the maintenance actions in advance.
- System modification is a form of maintenance that extends the system's useful life by changing the system to sustain existing capabilities in the changing environment. Adding new capabilities (system upgrades) is sometimes considered part of the maintenance.

- 利用维护流程中获得的经验进行改进。

- 根据系统架构、设计和系统需求，维护维护和后勤资产、服务和能力的双向可追溯性。根据需要启动更改。

- 管理构型配置数据项。

常用方法和提示：

- 确定生命周期早期维护和后勤支持所需的使能系统、产品、服务和材料，以留出必要的提前期来获取或使用它们。

- SoI 的维护必须与其环境中其他系统（互操作和使能系统）的维护相协调。由于技术、组织、经济或政治方面的考虑，任何系统的故障或失灵都可能引发其他系统的维护行动。

详细阐述

维护流程支持 SoI 及其元素在其整个生命周期内的运行。有关 SoI 的维护和后勤活动必须综合到运行组织的现有支持和后勤网络中。这包括维持运行和维护人员技能和能力的规定。

应考虑不同的维护模式：

- 纠正性维护将系统服务恢复到正常运行状态（例如，移除和更换硬件、重新加载软件、应用软件补丁）。

- 预防性维护通过安排例行维护行动来预防故障和失灵，以保持最佳的系统运行性能。

- 预测性维护是一种更高级的预防性维护，使用系统运行期间收集的数据预测故障和故障，并提前安排维护行动。

- 系统修改是一种维护形式，通过改变系统来在不断变化的环境中维持现有能力，从而延长系统的使用生命。添加新功能（系统升级）有时被视为维护的一部分。

SYSTEM LIFE CYCLE CONCEPTS, MODELS, AND PROCESSES

2.3.5.14 Disposal Process

Overview

Purpose As stated in ISO/IEC/IEEE 15288,

[6.4.14.1] The purpose of the Disposal process is to end the existence of a system element or system for a specified intended use, appropriately handle replaced or retired elements, appropriately handle any waste products, and to properly attend to identified critical disposal needs.

The Disposal process is conducted in accordance with applicable guidance, policy, regulations, and statutes throughout the system life cycle.

Description The Disposal process generates requirements and constraints that must be balanced with defined stakeholders' needs and requirements and other design considerations. Further, environmental concerns drive the designer to consider reclaiming the materials or recycling them into new systems. Incremental disposal can be applied at any point in the life cycle (e.g., prototypes that are not to be reused or evolved, waste materials during manufacturing, parts that are replaced during maintenance). The Disposal process may also be used to manage the transition of system elements from a current SoI to a different system.

The Disposal process also includes any steps necessary to return the environment to an acceptable condition; handle all system elements and waste products in an environmentally sound manner in accordance with applicable legislation, organizational constraints, and stakeholder agreements; and document and retain records of disposal activities, as required for monitoring by external oversight or regulatory agencies.

Inputs/Outputs Inputs and outputs for the Disposal process are listed in Figure 2.56. Descriptions of each input and output are provided in Appendix E.

Process Activities The Disposal process includes the following activities:

- *Prepare for disposal.*

–Review the retirement concept (may be called a disposal concept), including any hazardous materials and other environmental impacts to be encountered during disposal.

–Plan for disposal, including the development of the strategy.

–Impose associated constraints on the system requirements.

系统生命周期概念、模型和流程

2.3.5.14 处置流程

概述

目的　如 ISO/IEC/IEEE 15288 所述：

[6.4.14.1] 处置流程的目的是为了终止特定预期用途的系统元素或系统的存在，适当处理更换或报废的元素，适当处理任何浪费产品，并适当满足确定的关键处置需求。

在整个系统生命周期内，按照适用的指导、政策、法规和章程执行处置流程。

描述　处置流程产生的要求和约束必须与定义的利益相关方的需要和需求以及其他设计考虑因素相平衡。此外，环境问题促使设计师考虑回收材料或将其回收到新系统中。可在生命周期的任何时候进行增量处置（例如，不可重复使用或进化的原型、制造流程中的废料、维护流程中更换的零件）。处置流程也可用于管理系统元素从当前 SoI 到不同系统的转移。

处置流程还包括将环境恢复到可接受状态所需的任何步骤；根据适用法律、组织约束和利益相关方协议，以环保方式处理所有系统元素和浪费；根据外部监督或监管机构的监控要求，记录和保留处置活动的记录。

输入 / 输出　处置流程的输入和输出如图 2.56 所示。附录 E 中提供了每个输入和输出的描述。

流程活动　处置流程包括以下活动：

- *准备处置*。

- 评审报废概念（可能称为处置概念），包括处置流程中遇到的任何危险材料和其他环境影响。

- 处置计划，包括制定战略。

- 对系统需求施加相关约束。

SYSTEM LIFE CYCLE CONCEPTS, MODELS, AND PROCESSES

–Ensure that the necessary enabling systems, products, or services required for disposal are available, when needed. The planning includes the identification of requirements and interfaces for the enablers. The acquisi tion of the enablers can be done through various ways such as rental, procurement, development, reuse, and subcontracting. An enabler may be a complete enabling system developed as a separate project from the project of the SoI.

–Identify elements that can be reused and that cannot be reused. Special methods may need to be implemented for hazardous materials.

–Specify containment facilities, storage locations, inspection criteria, and storage periods, if the system is to be stored.

- *Perform disposal.*

–Decommission the system or system elements to be disposed.

–Disassemble the elements for ease of handling. Include identification and processing of reusable elements.

–Extract all elements and waste materials that are no longer needed—this includes removing materials from storage sites, consigning the elements and waste products for destruction or permanent storage, and ensuring that the waste products or elements not intended for reuse cannot get back into the supply chain.

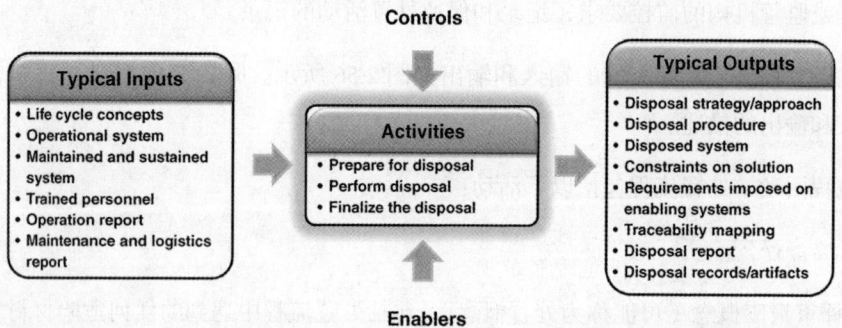

FIGURE 2.56   IPO diagram for Disposal process. INCOSE SEH original figure created by Shortell, Walden, and Yip. Usage per the INCOSE Notices page. All other rights reserved.

–Dispose of deactivated system elements per the disposal procedure.

–Ensure the disposal staff adheres to safety, security, privacy and environment regulations or policies and capture their tacit knowledge for future needs.

- 确保在需要时提供处置所需的必要使能系统、产品或服务。计划包括确定使能项的需求和接口。使能项的获取可以通过各种方式完成，如租赁、采办、开发、复用和分包。使能码可以是作为 SoI 项目的单独项目开发的完整使能系统。

- 识别可复用和不可复用的元素。危险品可能需要采用特殊方法。

- 如果要储存系统，则应明确防范设施、存放位置、检查标准和存放期限。

- *进行处置。*

- 使待处理的系统或系统元素退役。

- 拆卸元素以便于操作。包括可复用元素的标识和处理。

- 提取所有不再需要的元素和废料——这包括从存储场所移除材料，将元素和废料交付销毁或永久存储，并确保不打算复用的浪费或元素不能返回供应链。

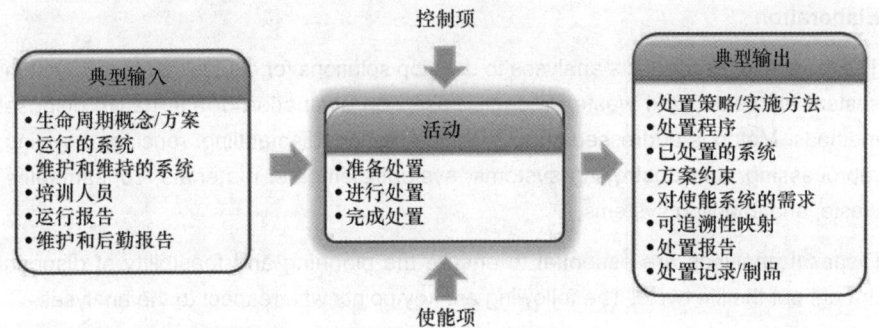

图 2.56　处置流程的 IPO 图。INCOSE SEH 原始图由 Shortell、Walden 和 Yip 创建。按照 INCOSE 通知页使用。版权所有。

- 按照处置程序处置停用的系统元素。

- 确保处置人员遵守安全、安保、隐私和环境法规或政策，并获取他们对未来需求的隐性知识。

SYSTEM LIFE CYCLE CONCEPTS, MODELS, AND PROCESSES

- *Finalize the disposal.*

–Confirm no adverse effects from the disposal activities and return the environment to its original state.

–Maintain documentation of all disposal activities and residual hazards.

Common approaches and tips:

- Consider donating an obsolete system—Many items, both systems and information, of cultural and historical value have been lost to posterity because museums and conservatories were not considered as an option during the retirement stage.

- Concepts such as zero footprint and zero emissions drive current trends toward corporate social responsibility that influence decision making regarding cleaner production and operational environments and eventual disposal of depleted materials and systems.

- Design the SoI to support the circular economy (see Section 3.1.10). Maintaining materials in closed loops maximizes material value without damaging ecosystems (McDonough, 2013).

Elaboration

The project team conducts analyses to develop solutions for disposition of the system, system elements, and waste products based on evaluation of alternative disposal methods. Methods addressed should include storing, dismantling, reusing, recycling, reprocessing, and destroying systems, system elements, materials, consumables, waste, and enabling systems,.

Disposal analyses are essential to ensure the planning and feasibility of disposal throughout the life cycle. The following are key points with respect to the analyses.

- Analyses include consideration of costs (including LCC), disposal sites, environmental impacts, health and safety issues, responsible agencies, handling and shipping, supporting items, and applicable international, national, and local regulations.

- Analyses support selection of system elements and materials that will be used in the system design and should be readdressed to consider design and project impacts from changing laws and regulations throughout the life cycle.

Disposal strategy and design considerations are updated throughout the system life cycle in response to changes in applicable laws, regulations, and policy.

The ISO 14000 (2015) series includes standards for environmental management systems and life cycle assessment.

- 完成处置。

- 确认处置活动没有不良影响,并将环境恢复到原始状态。

- 保存所有处置活动和残余危险的文件。

常用方法和提示:

- 考虑捐赠一个过时的系统——许多具有文化和历史价值的项目,包括系统和信息,都已被子孙后代丢失,因为博物馆和音乐学院在退役阶段没有被视为一种选择。

- 零足迹和零排放等概念推动了复杂组织体系社会职责的当前趋势,影响了有关清洁生产和运行环境的决策,以及最终处置耗尽的材料和系统。

- 设计 SoI 以支持循环经济(见 3.1.10 节)。将材料保持在闭环中可最大化材料价值,而不会破坏生态系统(McDonough,2013)。

详细阐述

项目团队进行分析,根据对替代处置方法的评估,制定系统、系统元素和浪费处置的解决方案。所述方法应包括存储、拆卸、复用、回收、再处理和销毁系统、系统元素、材料、耗材、浪费和使能系统。

处置分析对于确保整个生命周期内处置的计划和可行性至关重要。以下是有关分析的要点。

- 分析包括考虑成本(包括 LCC)、处置场、环境影响、健康和安全问题、职责机构、搬运和运输、支持项目以及适用的国际、国家和地方法规。

- 分析为选择系统设计中使用的系统元素和材料提供支持,应重新进行分析,以考虑在整个生命周期中不断变化的法律法规对设计和项目的影响。

处置策略和设计考虑事项在整个系统生命周期内更新,以响应适用法律、法规和政策的变化。

ISO 14000(2015)系列包括环境管理体系和生命周期评估标准。

LIFE CYCLE ANALYSES AND METHODS

3 LIFE CYCLE ANALYSES AND METHODS

3.1 QUALITY CHARACTERISTICS AND APPROACHES

3.1.1 Introduction to Quality Characteristics

159 ISO/IEC/IEEE 15288 (2023), Section 3.36 defines *Quality Characteristic (QC) as: inherent characteristic of a product, process, or system related to a requirement*. QCs are how the stakeholders will judge the quality of the system. Approaches exist that help ensure these characteristics are present in the SoI and its broader context or environment.

The objective of the following sections is to give enough information to a Systems Engineering (SE) practitioner to appreciate the significance of various QC approaches, even if they are not an expert in the subject. In previous editions of the handbook, the QC approaches were known as Specialty Engineering or the Engineering Specialties. These approaches are also known as Design for X (DFX) and Through-Life Considerations. The QCs are informally known as the -ilities since many, but not all, end in "ility" in the English language.

QC approaches, as used in this handbook, are life cycle perspectives that need to be considered to ensure the system is developed and its ecosystem cultivated so that QCs are present when the system is produced, utilized, supported, and ultimately retired. QC approaches often generate non-functional requirements. Some QC approaches, such as safety, security, and resilience may also generate functional requirements. These QC approaches are applied throughout the system's life cycle, as notionally shown in Figure 3.1. Consideration beyond the engineered system, including the system, SoS, or enterprise that it is a part of, and its interoperating and enabling systems, is also necessary.

The QC approaches in this section are covered in alphabetical order by name to avoid giving more weight to one over another. Table 3.1 summarizes the QC approaches included in the handbook. Not every QC approach will be applicable to every system or every application domain. It is recommended that subject matter experts are consulted and assigned as appropriate to conduct QC approaches. More information about the QC approaches can be found in references to external sources.

INCOSE Systems Engineering Handbook: A Guide for System Life Cycle Processes and Activities, Fifth Edition.

Edited by David D. Walden, Thomas M. Shortell, Garry J. Roedler, Bernardo A. Delicado, Odile Mornas, Yip Yew-Seng, and David Endler.

© 2023 John Wiley & Sons Ltd. Published 2023 by John Wiley & Sons Ltd.

3 生命周期分析和方法

3.1 质量特性和实施方法

3.1.1 质量特性介绍

ISO/IEC/IEEE 15288（2023）3.36 节将质量特性（QC）定义为：*与需求相关的产品、流程或系统的固有特性*。QC 是利益相关方将如何判断系统质量的方式。存在一些实施方法有助于确保这些特征在 SoI 及其更为广泛的背景或环境中得以呈现。

以下各节的目的在于为系统工程实践者提供充分的信息，从而了解各种质量特性实施方法的重要性，即使他们不是该主题的专家。在之前版本的手册中，将质量特性实施方法称为专业工程或工程专业。这些实施方法也称为 X 设计（DFX）和贯穿整个生命周期的考虑因素。非形式化地，将质量特性称为"- 性"（lities），因为许多质量特性（但不是全部）在英语中以"- 性"（"ilities"）结尾。

本手册中所使用的质量特性实施方法需考虑生命周期观点，以确保系统的开发和生态系统的培育，从而在系统生产、使用、支持和最终退役时体现质量特性。质量特性实施方法通常会产生诸多非功能需求。一些质量特性实施方法，如安全性、安保性和强韧性，也可能产生功能需求。这些质量特性实施方法应用于系统的整个生命周期，如图 3.1 所示。此外，还需考虑工程系统之外的因素，包括其所属的系统、体系或复杂组织体系，以及与其相关的互操作性和使能系统。

本节中的质量特性实施方法按照名称的首字母顺序分别进行介绍，避免有所偏重。表 3.1 总结本手册中包含的质量特性实施方法。并非每种质量特性实施方法都适用于每个系统或每个应用领域。建议咨询主题专家，并指派合适的专家开展质量特性实施方法。有关质量特性实施方法的更多信息，可参阅外部的资料来源。

LIFE CYCLE ANALYSES AND METHODS

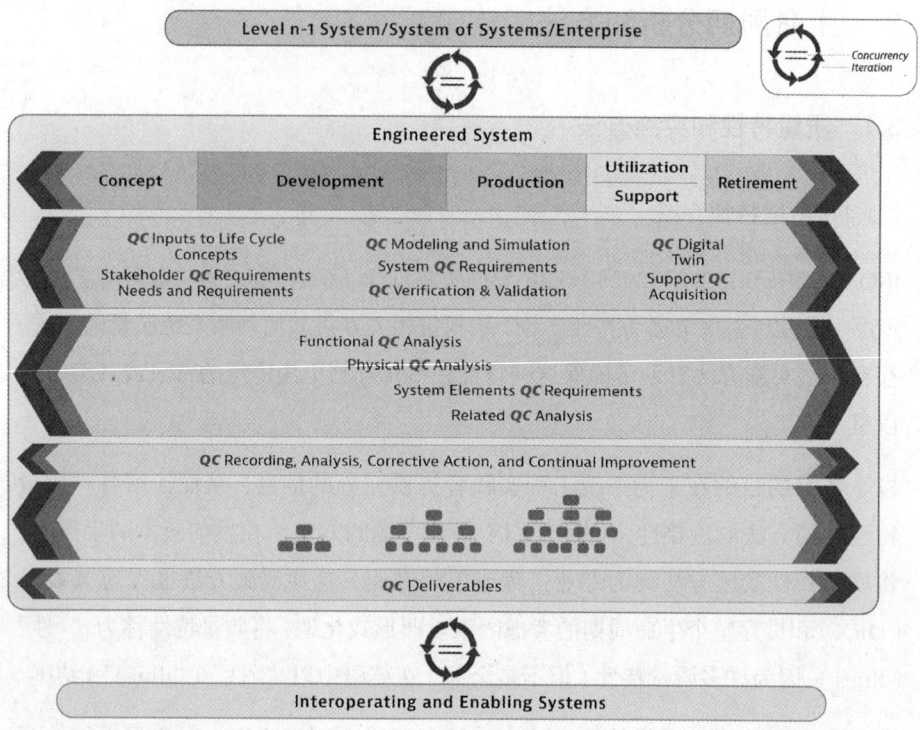

FIGURE 3.1 Quality characteristic approaches across the life cycle. INCOSE SEH original figure created by Taljaard, Kemp, and Walden. Usage per the INCOSE Notices page. All other rights reserved.

This handbook includes a set of QC approaches that are generally applicable in various applications and domains. However, the SE practitioner should ensure that any additional applicable QC approaches are also addressed.

3.1.2 Affordability Analysis

Definition Affordability Analysis is an approach that maximizes value, providing cost-effective capability over the entire life cycle.

INCOSE has defined system affordability as follows:

Affordability is the balance of system performance, cost, and schedule constraints over the system life while satisfying mission needs in concert with strategic investment and organizational needs.

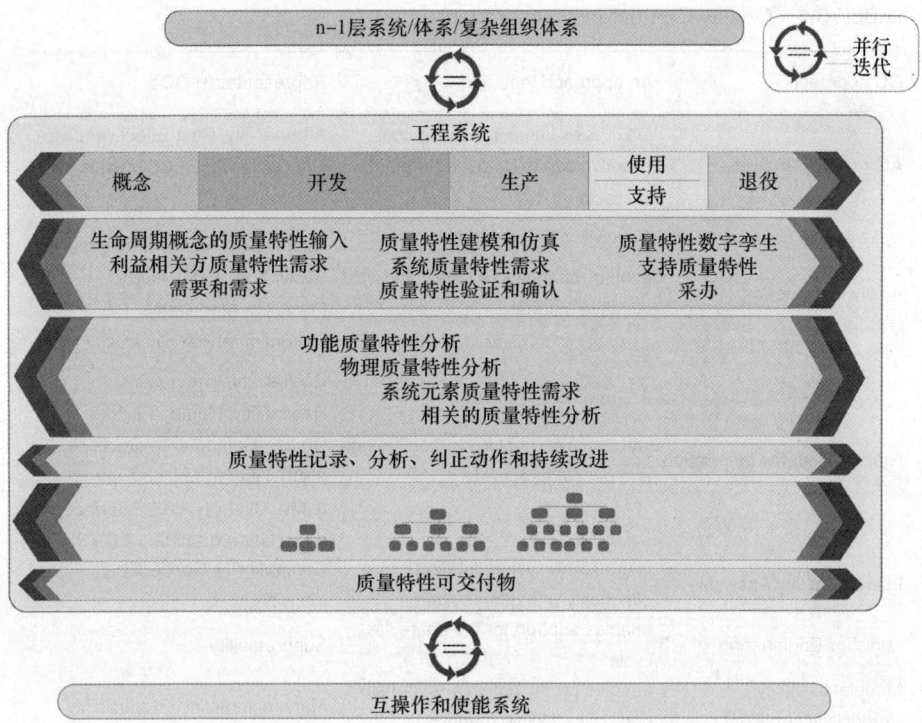

图 3.1 跨生命周期的质量特性实施方法。INCOSE SEH 原始图由 Taljaard、Kemp 和 Walden 创建。按照 INCOSE 通知页使用。版权所有。

本手册包括一套通常适用于各类应用和领域的质量特性实施方法，而系统工程实践者应确保任何其他适用的质量特性实施方法也能得以应用。

3.1.2 可承受性分析

定义 可承受性分析是一种保证价值最大化的实施方法，在整个生命周期内提供具有成本—有效性的能力。

INCOSE 对系统可承受性的定义如下：

可承受性是系统生命周期内在系统性能、成本和进度约束之间的平衡，同时满足与战略投资和组织要求一致的任务需要。

LIFE CYCLE ANALYSES AND METHODS

TABLE 3.1 Quality Characteristic approaches

QC approach	An approach that...	Representative QCs
Affordability Analysis	maximizes value, providing cost effective capability over the entire life cycle	Affordability, Cost-Effectiveness, Life Cycle Cost (LCC), Value Robustness
Agility Engineering	enables change in a timely and cost-effective manner	Adaptability, Agility, Changeability, Evolvability, Extensibility, Flexibility, Modularity, Reconfigurability, Scalability
Human Systems Integration	integrates technology, organizations, and people effectively	Desirability, Ergonomics, Habitability, Human Factors, Human-Computer Interaction (HCI), Human-Machine Interface (HMI), Usability, User Interface (UI). User eXperience (UX)
Interoperability Analysis	ensures the system interacts effectively with other systems	Compatibility, Connectivity, Interoperability
Logistics Engineering	enables support for the entire life cycle	Supportability
Manufacturability/ Producibility Analysis	enables production in a responsible and cost effective manner	Manufacturability, Producibility
Reliability, Availability, Maintainability Engineering	enables the system to perform without failure, to be operational when needed, and to be retained in or restored to a required functional state	Accessibility, Availability, Interchangeability, Maintainability, Reliability, Repairability, Testability
Resilience Engineering	provides required capability when facing adversity	Resilience, Robustness, Survivability
Sustainability Engineering	supports the circular economy over its life	Disposability, Environmental Impact, Sustainability
System Safety Engineering	reduces the likelihood of harm to people, assets, and the wider environment	Safety
System Security Engineering	identifies, protects from, detects, responds to, and recovers from anomalous and disruptive events, including those in a cyber contested environment	Cybersecurity, Information Assurance (IA), Physical Security, Trustworthiness

INCOSE SEH original table created by Walden and Yip. Usage per the INCOSE Notices page. All other rights reserved.

Key Concepts   As stated in Blanchard and Fabrycky (2011),

生命周期分析和方法

表 3.1 质量特性实施方法

质量特性实施方法	一种实施方法	代表性质量特性
可承受性分析	实现价值最大化，在整个生命周期内提供具有成本效益的能力	可承受性、成本—有效性、生命周期成本（LCC）、价值稳健性
敏捷工程	实现及时和具有成本—有效性的变更	适应性、敏捷性、可变性、可发展性、可扩展性、灵活性、模块性、可重构性、可扩展性
人与系统综合	有效整合技术、组织和人员	可欲性、人体工学、宜居性、人因、人机交互（HCI）、人机界面（HMI）、可用性、用户界面（UI）、用户体验（UX）
互操作性分析	确保系统与其他系统有效交互	兼容性、连接性和互操作性
后勤工程	实现对整个生命周期的支持	可支持性
可制造性/可生产性分析	以负责任和具有成本效益的方式实现生产	可制造性、可生产性
可靠性、可用性、可维护性工程	使系统能够在不发生故障的情况下运行，在需要时可运行，并保持或恢复到所需的功能状态	可访问性、可用性、可互换性、可维护性、可靠性、可维修性、可测试性
强韧性工程	提供面对逆境时所需的能力	强韧性、稳健性、生存性
可持续性工程	在其生命周期内支持循环经济	可处置性、环境影响、可持续性
系统安全性工程	降低对人员、资产和环境造成伤害的可能性	安全性
系统安保性工程	识别、防范、检测、应对和恢复异常和破坏性事件，包括网络竞争环境中的事件	网络安全、信息保障（IA）、实体安全、可信性

INCOSE SEH 原始表由 Walden 和 Yip 创建。按照 INCOSE 通知页使用。版权所有。

关键概念 正如 Blanchard 和 Fabrycky（2011）所述：

LIFE CYCLE ANALYSES AND METHODS

Many systems are planned, designed, produced, and operated with little initial concern for affordability and the total cost of the system over its intended lifecycle... The technical [aspects are] usually considered first, with the economic [aspects] deferred until later.

This section addresses economic and cost factors under the general topics of affordability and cost-effectiveness. The concept of life cycle cost (LCC) is also discussed. Improving design methods for affordability is critical for all application domains (Bobinis, et al., 2013; Tuttle and Bobinis, 2013). Case 4 (Design for Maintainability-Incubators) from Section 6.4 provides an illustration of its importance. A system is "affordable" if it can be developed to meet its requirements within cost and schedule constraints. The concept can seem straightforward. The difficulty arises when an attempt is made to specify and quantify the affordability of a system. This is significant when writing requirements or when comparing two solutions to conduct an affordability trade study. Affordability analysis is contextually sensitive, often leading to a misunderstanding and incompatible perspectives on what an "affordable system is."

Key affordability concepts include:

- Affordability context, system(s), and portfolios (of systems capabilities) need to be consistently defined and included in any understanding of what an affordable system is.
- An affordability process/framework needs to be established and documented.
- Accountability (system governance) for affordability needs to be assigned across the life cycle, which includes stakeholders from the various contextual domains.

Affordability costs include acquisition, operating, and support costs. It may be expanded to encompass additional elements required for the Life Cycle Cost (LCC) of a system, as an outcome of various contexts in which any system is embedded. In the SE domain, affordability as an attribute must be determined both inside the boundaries of the system of interest (SoI) and outside. The concept of affordability must encompass everything from a portfolio (e.g., family of automobiles) to an individual project (specific car model).

An affordability design model must be able to provide the ability to effectively manage and evolve systems over long life cycles. One of the major assumptions for measuring the affordability of competing systems is that given two systems, which produce similar output capabilities, it will be the *nonfunctional* attributes of those systems that differentiate system value to its stakeholders. As shown in Figure 3.2, the affordability model is concerned with operational attributes of systems that determine their value and effectiveness over time, typically expressed as the system's quality characteristics as they are called in this handbook. These attributes are properties of the system as a whole and as such represent the salient features of the system and are measures of the ability of the system to deliver the capabilities it was designed for over time.

许多系统在规划、设计、生产和运行时，最初很少考虑系统在其预期生命周期内的可承受性和总体成本……通常先考虑技术［方面］，然后再考虑经济［方面］。

本节在可承受性和成本—效益的一般主题下讨论经济和成本因素，还将讨论生命周期成本（LCC）的概念。对于所有的应用领域，可承受性设计方法的改进都是至关重要的（Bobinis 等，2013；Tuttle 和 Bobinis，2013）。6.4 节中的案例 4（可维护性保育箱的设计）说明了其重要性。

如果系统能够在成本和进度限制范围内满足其需求，那么它是"可承受的"。这个概念看似直观，但当试图规定和量化系统的可承受性时，就会遇到困难。这在编写需求或比较两种解决方案来进行可承受性权衡研究时非常重要。可承受性分析对背景环境敏感，通常会导致对"可承受系统"的误解和不兼容的观点。

关键的可承受性概念包括：

- 在理解什么是可承受系统中，需要一致地定义并包括可承受性的背景环境、系统和（系统能力的）组合。

- 需要建立并存档记录可承受性的流程/框架。

- 需要在整个生命周期中指派可承受性的职责（系统治理），包括来自不同背景环境领域的利益相关方。

可承受性的成本包括购置、运行和支持的成本。作为任何系统可能处于各种背景环境的结果，它还可能扩展到包含系统生命周期成本（LCC）所需的其他要素。在系统工程领域，可承受性作为一个属性，必须在所感兴趣之系统（SoI）边界内部和外部确定。可承受性的概念必须涵盖从项目组合（如汽车系列）到单个项目（特定车型）的所有内容。

可承受性设计模型必须能够提供在长期生命周期内有效管理和演进系统的能力。衡量竞争系统可承受性的一个主要假设是，给定产生类似输出能力的两个系统，这些系统的非功能属性将区分系统对于其利益相关方价值的不同。如图 3.2 所示，可承受性模型涉及系统的运行属性，由其决定着系统的价值和有效性，通常表示为本手册中所称的系统质量特性。这些属性是系统作为一个整体的属性，因此代表系统的显著特征，是衡量系统在一段时间内交付其设计功能的能力指标。

LIFE CYCLE ANALYSES AND METHODS

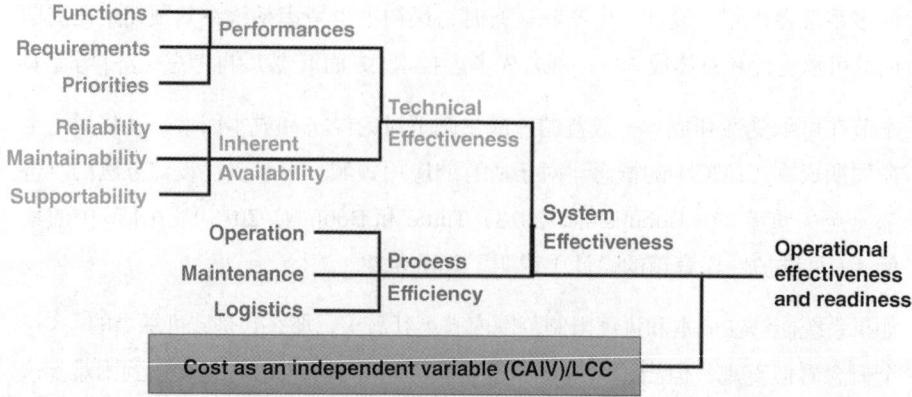

FIGURE 3.2 System operational effectiveness. From Bobinis et al. (2013). Used with permission. All other rights reserved.

Managing a system within an affordability trade space means that we are concerned with the actual performance of the fielded system, defined in one or more appropriate metrics, bounded by cost over time. The time dimension extends a specific "point analysis" (static) to a continuous life cycle perspective (dynamic). Quantifying a relationship between cost, performance, and time defines a functional space that can be graphed and analyzed mathematically. Then it becomes possible to examine how the output (e.g., performance, availability, capability) changes due to changes in the input (e.g., cost constraints, budget availability). This functional relationship between cost and outcome defines an affordability trade space to analyze the relationship between money spent and system performance and possibly determine the point of diminishing returns. This is illustrated in Figure 3.3. The capabilities and schedule have been fixed leaving either the cost or the performance to be the evaluation criteria, while the other becomes the constraint. This results in a relatively simple relationship between performance and cost. The maximum budget and the minimum performance are identified.

Below the maximum budget line in Figure 3.3 lie solutions that meet the definition of "conducting a project at a cost constrained by the maximum resources." The solutions to the right of the minimum performance line satisfy the threshold requirement. Thus, in the shaded rectangle lie the solutions to be considered since they meet the minimum performance and are less than the maximum budget. On the curve lay the solutions that are the "best value," in the sense that for a given cost the corresponding point on the curve is the maximum performance that can be achieved. *In actuality, the curve is rarely smooth or continuous and multiple curves need to be considered simultaneously.* Similarly, for a given performance, the corresponding point on the curve is the minimum cost for which that performance can be achieved. Selecting the decision criterion as cost will result in achieving the threshold performance. If the decision criterion is performance, all of the budget would be expended. Consequently, to specify affordability for a system

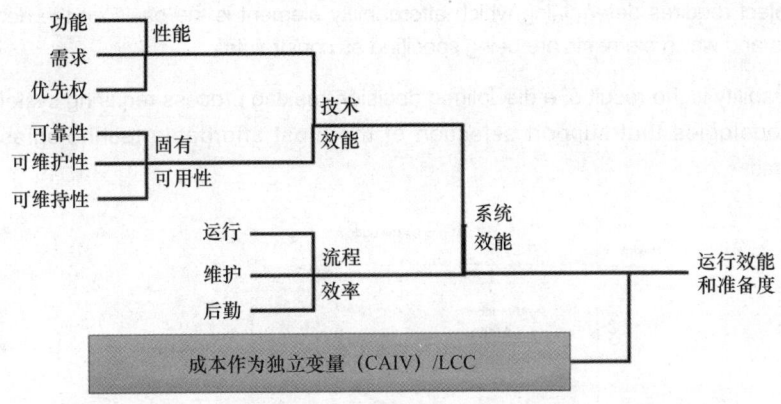

图 3.2 系统运行效能。源自 Bobinis 等（2013）。经许可后使用。版权所有。

在可承受性权衡空间内管理系统意味着，我们关注所部署系统的实际性能，以一个或多个适当的指标定义，并受到与时间相关的成本的限制。时间维度将特定的"点分析"（静态）扩展到连续的生命周期（动态）的视角。成本、性能和时间之间关系的量化定义了一个功能空间，可以使用图形表示并进行数学分析。然后，可以检查输出（例如，性能、可用性、能力）如何因输入（例如，成本约束、预算可用性）的变化而变化。这种成本与结果之间的函数关系定义了一个可承受性权衡空间，以分析支付的资金与系统性能之间的关系，并可能确定收益递减点。如图 3.3 所示。当能力和进度已固定时，将成本或性能作为评估准则，而另外一个成为约束条件。这使得性能和成本之间的关系相对简单，最高预算和最低性能得以确定。

图 3.3 中最大预算线以下的解决方案符合"以最大资源限制的成本开展项目"的定义。最低性能线右侧的解决方案满足阈值要求。因此，在阴影矩形中是所要考虑的解决方案，因其满足最低性能并且小于最大预算。位于曲线上的解决方案具有"最佳价值"，即对于给定成本，曲线上的对应点是可以实现的最大性能。实际上，曲线很少是平滑或连续的，需要同时考虑存在的多条曲线。同样，对于给定的性能，曲线上的对应点是可以实现该性能的最小成本。将成本作为决策准则将产生达到阈值性能的结果。如果将性能作为决策准则，则所有预算都将满足预期的花费。因此，规定系统或项目的可承受性，需要确定哪个可承受性要素作为决策准则基础，规定哪些要素作为约束条件。

LIFE CYCLE ANALYSES AND METHODS

or project requires determining which affordability element is the basis for the decision criteria and which elements are being specified as constraints.

Affordability is the result of a disciplined decision-making process requiring systematic methodologies that support selection of the most affordable technologies and systems.

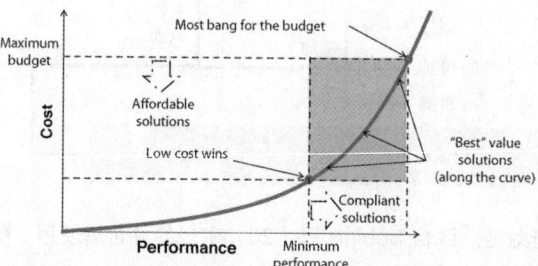

FIGURE 3.3   Cost versus performance. INCOSE SEH original figure created by Bobinis on behalf of the INCOSE Affordability Working Group. Usage per the INCOSE Notices page. All other rights reserved.

Elaboration

Cost-Effectiveness Analysis

Cost-effectiveness (CE) is a measure relating cost to system effectiveness. It is defined below with the achieved systems effectiveness as the numerator and cost as the denominator (Blanchard, 1967):

$$CE = SE / (IC + SC)$$

Where SE = System Effectiveness, IC = initial cost and SC = sustainment cost.

Reliability and maintainability are major factors in determining the cost effectiveness of a system since they impact sustainment costs.

System effectiveness is a term used in a broad context to reflect the technical characteristics of a system (e.g., performance, availability, supportability, dependability) such as examples mentioned in the preceding section. It may be expressed differently depending on the specific application. Sometimes a single-figure of merit is used to express system effectiveness and sometimes multiple figures-of-merit are employed (Blanchard and Fabrycky, 2011). The IC and SC can also be expressed in different ways depending on the application or system parameters under evaluation. It may include costs for concept, development, production, utilization, support, and retirement.

可承受性是一个严谨的决策流程的结果,需要系统的方法来支持选择最具可承受性的技术和系统。

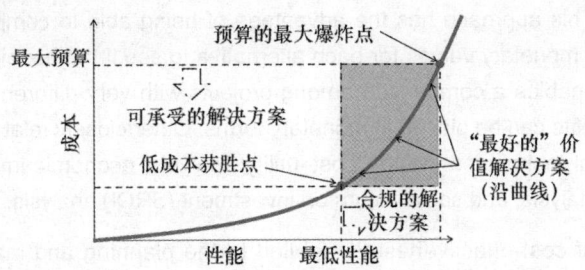

图 3.3 成本与性能的对比。INCOSE SEH 原始图由 Bobinis 代表 INCOSE 可承受性工作组创建。按照 INCOSE 通知页使用。版权所有。

详细阐述

成本—有效性分析

成本—有效性(CE)是一种将成本与系统有效性关联的衡量指标。其定义如下,以预期达成的系统有效性为分子,成本为分母(Blanchard, 1967):

$$CE = SE / (IC + SC)$$

其中:SE= 系统有效性,IC= 初始成本,SC= 维持成本。

在此,可靠性和维修性是决定系统成本有效性的主要因素,因为它们影响维持成本。

系统有效性是一个在广泛的背景环境中所使用的术语,反映系统的技术特征(例如,性能、可用性、可支持性、可信性),如前一节中提到的示例。根据具体应用,其表达方式可能有所不同。有时使用单个价值指标来表示系统的有效性,有时使用多个价值指标(Blanchard 和 Fabrycky, 2011)。IC 和 SC 也可以根据评估中的应用或系统参数以不同的方式表达。它可能包括概念、开发、生产、使用、支持和退役的成本。

LIFE CYCLE ANALYSES AND METHODS

Cost-Effectiveness Analysis (CEA) is distinct from cost–benefit analysis (CBA). The approach to measuring costs is similar for both techniques, but in contrast to CEA where the results are measured in performance terms, CBA uses monetary measures of outcomes. This approach has the advantage of being able to compare the costs and benefits in monetary values for each alternative to see if the benefits exceed the costs. It also enables a comparison among projects with very different goals if both costs and benefits can be placed in monetary terms. Other closely related, but slightly different, formal techniques include cost–utility analysis, economic impact analysis, fiscal impact analysis, and social return on investment (SROI) analysis.

The concept of cost-effectiveness is applied to the planning and management of many types of organized activity. It is widely used in many system aspects. Some examples are:

- Studies of the desirable performance characteristics of commercial aircraft to increase an airline's market share at lowest overall cost over its route structure (e.g., more passengers, better fuel consumption)

- Urban studies of the most cost-effective improvements to a city's transportation infrastructure (e.g., buses, trains, motorways, and mass transit routes and departure schedules)

- In health services, where it may be inappropriate to monetize health effect (e.g., years of life, premature births averted, sight years gained)

- In the acquisition of military hardware when competing designs are compared not only for purchase price but also for such factors as their operating radius, top speed, rate of fire, armor protection, and caliber and armor penetration of their guns

LCC Analysis

LCC refers to the total cost incurred by a system throughout its life. This "total" cost varies by circumstances, the stakeholders' points of view, and the system. For example, when purchasing an automobile, the major cost factors are the cost of acquisition, operation, maintenance, and disposal (or trade-in value). A more expensive car (acquisition cost) may have lower LCC because of lower operation and maintenance costs. But the car manufacturer has other costs such as development and production costs, including setting up the production line, to be considered. The SE Practitioner needs to look at costs from several aspects and be aware of the stakeholders' perspectives. LCC should not be equated to Total Cost of Ownership (TCO), Total Ownership Cost (TOC), or Whole Life Cost (WLC). These measures may only include costs once the system has been purchased or acquired.

成本—有效性分析（CEA）不同于成本—效益分析（CBA）。两种技术关于成本的计量方法相似，但与 CEA 以性能衡量结果不同，CBA 使用货币衡量结果。这种方法的优点是能够比较每种备选方案的成本和货币价值收益，以审视收益是否超过成本。如果成本和收益都可以用货币表示，那么它还可以在具有不同目标的项目之间进行比较。其他密切相关但略有不同的形式化技术包括成本—效用分析、经济影响分析、财务影响分析和社会投资回报（SROI）分析。

成本—有效性的概念适用于多类型组织活动的规划和管理，在许多系统方面得到广泛的应用。例如：

- 研究商用飞机的期望性能特征，在航线结构上以最低的总体成本而增加航空公司的市场份额（例如，更多的乘客，更少的燃油消耗）

- 研究城市交通基础设施最具成本—有效性的改进方向（如公共汽车、火车、高速公路、公共交通线路和发车时间安排）

- 在医疗服务中，可能不适合将健康效果货币化（例如，寿命、避免早产、增加的视力年数）

- 在采办军事硬件中，当比较相互竞争的设计方案时，不仅考虑购买价格，还要比较其作战半径、最高速度、射速、装甲防护以及火炮的口径和装甲穿透力等因素

LCC 分析

LCC 是指系统在其整个生命周期内发生的总体成本。该"总体"成本因所处环境、利益相关方的视角和系统而异。例如，在购买汽车时，主要的成本因素是购置、运行、维护和处置（或折价）的成本。由于运行和维护成本较低，更昂贵的汽车（购置成本）的 LCC 可能较低。但汽车制造商还需要考虑其他成本，如开发和生产成本，包括建立生产线。系统工程实践者需从多个方面考虑成本，并了解利益相关方的观点。LCC 不应等同于拥有总成本（TCO）、总拥有成本（TOC）或全生命周期成本（WLC）。这些指标可能只包括购买或采办系统后的成本。

LIFE CYCLE ANALYSES AND METHODS

LCC estimates are sometimes used to support internal project trade-off decisions and need only be accurate enough to support the relative trade-offs. The analyst should always attempt to prepare as accurate cost estimates as possible and assign risk to them. These estimates should be reviewed by upper management and potential stakeholders. Future costs, while unknown, can be predicted based on assumptions and risk assigned. All assumptions when doing LCC analysis should be documented.

LCC analysis can be used in affordability and system cost-effectiveness assessments. The LCC is not the definitive cost proposal for a project since LCC "estimates" (based on future assumptions) are often prepared early in a project's life cycle when there is insufficient detailed design information. Later, LCC estimates should be updated with actual costs from early project stages and will be more definitive and accurate due to hands-on experience with the system.

A major purpose of LCC studies is to help identify cost drivers and areas in which emphasis can be placed during the subsequent life cycle stages to obtain the best decisions. Accuracy in the estimates will improve as the system evolves and the data used in the calculation is less uncertain.

LCC analysis helps the project team understand the total cost impact of a decision, compare between project alternatives, and support trade studies for decisions made throughout the system life cycle. LCC normally includes the following costs, represented in Figure 3.4:

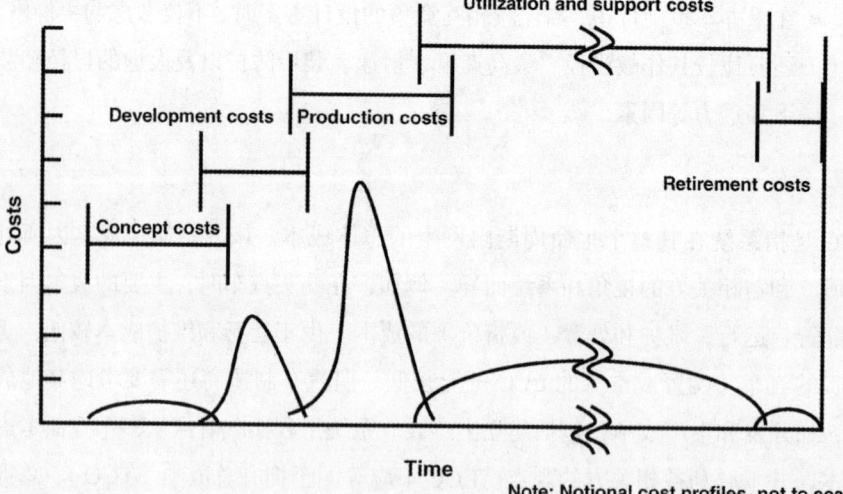

FIGURE 3.4 Life cycle cost elements. INCOSE SEH original figure from INCOSE SEH v2 Figure 4-83. Usage per the INCOSE Notices page. All other rights reserved.

LCC 估算有时用于支持内部项目的权衡决策，其准确性仅需足以支持相对的权衡。分析人员应始终尝试编制尽可能准确的成本估算，并将风险分配给它们。这些估计应由上级管理层和潜在利益相关方审核。未来成本虽然不可知，但可以根据假设和分配的风险进行预测。开展 LCC 分析时，应记录所有的假设。

LCC 分析可用于可承受性和系统成本—有效性估测。LCC 不是针对项目的最终成本，因为 LCC "估算"（基于未来假设）通常是在项目生命周期的早期编制的，当时并没有足够详细的设计信息。之后，LCC 估算值应根据项目早期阶段的实际成本予以更新，由于系统的实际运行经验，LCC 估算值将更加明确和准确。LCC 研究的一个主要目的是帮助确定成本动因和在后续生命周期阶段重点关注的方面，以获得最佳的决策。随着系统的演进和计算所用数据的不确定性降低，估算的准确性也会提高。

LCC 分析有助于项目团队了解决策中总成本的影响，比较项目备选方案，并支持在整个系统生命周期内对决策进行权衡研究。LCC 通常包括以下成本，如图 3.4 所示：

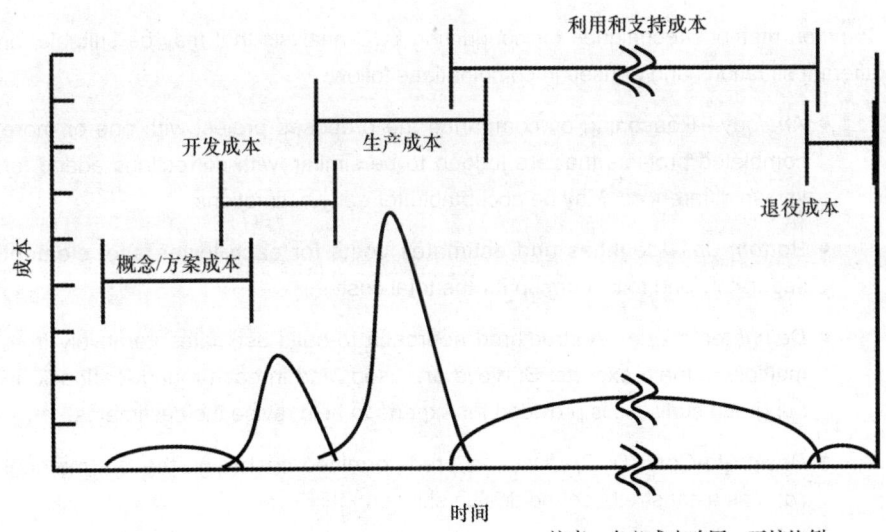

图 3.4　生命周期成本元素。源自 INCOSE SEH v2 图 4-83。按照 INCOSE 通知页使用。版权所有。

LIFE CYCLE ANALYSES AND METHODS

165
- *Concept costs*—Costs for the initial concept development efforts. These could be estimated based on average staffing and schedule spans and may include overhead, general and administrative (G&A) costs, and fees, as necessary.

- *Development costs*—Costs for the system development efforts. Similar to concept costs, these can be estimated based on average staffing and schedule spans and may include overhead, G&A costs, and fees, as necessary. Parametric cost models may also be used.

- *Production costs*—Usually driven by tooling and material costs for large-volume systems. Labor cost estimates are prepared by estimating the cost of the first production unit and then applying learning curve formula to determine the reduced costs of subsequent production units.

- *Utilization and support costs*—Typically based on future assumptions for ongoing operation and maintenance of the system, for example, fuel costs, personnel levels, and spare parts.

- *Retirement costs*—The costs for removing the system from operation and includes an estimate of trade-in or salvage costs. Could be positive or negative and should be mindful of the environmental impacts to dispose.

For global products, other sources of cost may include compliance costs (government regulations, import/export requirements, etc.) or other incidental costs of international business.

Common methods/techniques for conducting LCC analysis that may be suitable for different situations and/or used in combinations follow:

- *Analogy*—Reasoning by comparing the proposed project with one or more completed projects that are judged to be similar, with corrections added for known differences. May be acceptable for early estimations.

- *Bottom up*—Identifies and estimates costs for each lower-level element separately and rolls them up for the total cost.

- *Delphi technique*—A structured approach to build estimates iteratively from multiple domain experts. Surveys are used, and in each round feedback on the group statistics is provided for experts to help revise their estimates.

- *Design-to-Cost (DTC)*—Using a predetermined cost (e.g., the SoI material cost) as a constraint on the design solution.

- *Expert judgment*—Estimate performed by one or more experts using their experience and judgment. It can be used for comparison and sanity check against other methods.

- *概念成本*——初始概念开发工作的成本。这些费用可根据平均人员配置和进度跨度进行估算，可能包括间接费用、一般及行政管理（G & A）成本以及其他必要的费用。

- *开发成本*——系统开发工作的成本。与概念成本类似，这些成本可以根据平均人员配置和进度跨度进行估算，可能包括间接费用、一般及行政管理成本（如有必要），也可以使用参数化成本模型。

- *生产成本*——通常由庞大的系统加工设备和材料成本驱动。人工成本估算是通过估算第一次生产的单位成本，然后应用学习曲线公式确定后续降低的单位生产成本来编制的。

- *利用和支持成本*——通常基于系统持续运行和维护的未来假设，例如燃料成本、人员水平和备件。

- *退役成本*——将系统从运行中移除的成本，包括置换或抢救成本的估计。可以是正的，也可以是负的，并且应该注意待处置的环境影响。

对于全球化产品，其他成本来源可能包括合规成本（政府法规、进出口需求等）或国际业务的其他附带成本。

可能适合不同情况和/或组合使用的 LCC 分析常用方法/技术如下：

- *类比*——将提出项目与一个或多个判定为相似的、已完成的项目进行比较，并对已知差异进行更正。早期的估计也许可以接受。

- *自下而上*——分别识别和估计每个更低层级元素的成本，并将其汇总为总成本。

- *德尔菲技术*——一种从多个领域专家中反复迭代得出估计值的结构化方法。使用调查，并在每一轮中向专家提供关于分组统计数据的反馈，以帮助修订其估算。

- *面向成本的设计（DTC）*——使用预定成本（如 SoI 材料成本）作为设计解决方案的约束。

- *专家判断*——由一名或多名专家利用其经验和判断进行估算，可以用于与其他方法进行比较和正确性检查。

- *Parametric (algorithmic)*—Uses mathematical algorithms to compute cost estimates as a function of cost factors based on historical data. This technique is supported by public domain and commercial tools and models. Examples include the Constructive Systems Engineering Cost Model (COSYSMO) for SE effort and the Constructive Cost Model (COCOMO) for software engineering effort.
- *Parkinsonian technique*—Work estimates based on the available resources or schedules (Parkinson's Law states that work expands to fill the available volume).
- *Price to win*—Focuses on providing an estimate, and associated solution, at or below the price judged necessary to win the contract.
- *Taxonomy method*—Using a hierarchical structure or classification scheme as a basis of the estimates.
- *Top down*—Developing costs based on overall project characteristics at the top level of the architecture.

3.1.3 Agility Engineering

Definition Agility Engineering is an approach that enables change in a timely and cost-effective manner.

Key Concepts Agility is the ability to thrive and survive in uncertain, unpredictable operational environments; and manifests as effective response to situations presented by the environment (Dove and LaBarge, 2014). Effective response has four metrics:

- timely (fast enough to deliver value),
- affordable (at a cost that can be repeated as often as necessary),
- predictable (can be counted on to meet the need), and
- comprehensive (anything and everything within mission boundary).

Agile systems-engineering and agile-systems engineering are two different things (Haberfellner and de Weck, 2005) that share the word agile. In the first case the SoI is an engineering process (e.g., using an agile SE process). This is addressed in Section 4.2.2. In the second case, the SoI is what is produced by an engineering process (e.g., engineering an agile system). This is the subject of this section. Sustained agility is enabled by an architectural pattern and a set of design principles that are fundamental and common to both agile SE processes and engineered agile systems.

- *参数化（算法）估算*——使用数学算法进行成本估算，基于历史数据作为成本因子函数。这项技术得到了公共领域和商业工具及模型的支持。示例包括系统工程的构造性系统工程成本模型（COSYSMO）和软件工程工作的构造性成本模型（COCOMO）。
- *帕金森技术*——基于可用资源或时间安排的工作评估（帕金森定律指出，工作会不断扩展并填满可用的时间安排）。
- *价格取胜*——重点是提供估价和相关解决方案，价格不超过或低于赢得合同所需的判断价格。
- *分类法*——使用层级结构或分类方案作为估计的基础。
- *自上而下*——基于架构顶层的总体项目特征自上而下地开发成本。

3.1.3 敏捷工程

定义 敏捷工程（Agility Engineering）是一种能够以及时且具有成本—有效性的方式支持变化的实施方法。

关键概念 敏捷性是指在不确定、不可预测的运行环境中发展和生存的能力；表现为对环境状况的有效响应（Dove 和 LaBarge，2014）。有效响应具有四个指标：

- 及时的（足够快的交付价值）；
- 可承受的（低成本，通常可按需要重复）；
- 可预测的（可以期待需要被满足）；
- 全面的（任务边界内的一切事物）。

敏捷的系统工程和敏捷系统的工程是两个不同的事物（Haberfellner 和 de Weck，2005），它们共享敏捷这个词。在第一种情况下，SoI 是一个工程流程（例如，使用敏捷系统工程流程）。4.2.2 节对此予以说明。在第二种情况下，SoI 是由工程流程（例如，由工程开发的一个敏捷系统）产生的系统，这是本节的主题。持续的敏捷性是由一种架构模式和一组设计原则实现的，这些是敏捷的系统工程流程和工程化敏捷系统的基础和共同原则。

LIFE CYCLE ANALYSES AND METHODS

Elaboration

Agility Architectural Framework

The architecture that enables agility will be recognized in a simple sense as a drag-and-drop plug-and-play loosely coupled modularity, with some critical aspects not often called to mind with the general thoughts of a modular architecture. The architectural objective is to enable rapid and effective composability of processes and systems from available resources, appropriate for the needs at hand (Dove and LaBarge, 2014). Construction toys, like Lego or Meccano sets, are iconic architectural examples.

There are three critical elements in the architecture: a roster of drag-and-drop *encapsulated modules, a passive infrastructure* of minimal but sufficient rules and standards that enable and constrain plug-and-play operation, and an active infrastructure that designates specific responsibilities that sustain agile operational capability:

Encapsulated modules—Modules are self-contained encapsulated units complete with well-defined interfaces that conform to the plug-and-play passive infrastructure. They can be dragged and dropped into a system of response capability with relationship to other modules determined by the passive infrastructure. Modules are encapsulated so that their interfaces conform to the passive infrastructure, but their methods of functionality are not dependent on the functional methods of other modules except as the passive infrastructure dictates.

Passive infrastructure—The passive infrastructure provides drag-and-drop connectivity between modules. Its value is in isolating the encapsulated modules so that unexpected side effects are minimized and new operational functionality is rapid. Selecting passive infrastructure elements is a critical balance between requisite variety and parsimony—just enough in standards and rules to facilitate module connectivity but not so much to overly constrain innovative system configurations.

Active infrastructure—An agile system is not something designed and deployed in a fixed event and then left alone. Agility is most active as new system configurations are assembled in response to new requirements—something which may happen very frequently, even daily in some cases. In order for new configurations to be enabled when needed, five responsibilities are required:

- Module mix evolution—Who (or what process) is responsible for ensuring that new modules are added to the roster and existing modules are upgraded in time to satisfy response needs?

详细阐述

敏捷架构框架

从简单的意义上讲，支持敏捷性的架构将被认为是一种拖拽式、即插即用的松耦合模块化架构，在模块化架构的一般思想中，一些关键方面并不常被提及。架构目标是利用现有资源实现流程和系统的快速有效组合，以满足当前需要（Dove 和 LaBarge，2014）。构造玩具，如乐高或麦卡诺玩具，是标志性的架构范例。

架构中有三个关键元素：一个由可拖拽的封装模块组成的目录；一个由最少但充分的规则和标准组成的被动基础设施，以实现和约束即插即用的操作运行；以及一个指定特定职责以维持敏捷运行能力的主动基础设施：

封装模块——模块是自包含的封装单元，具有符合即插即用被动基础设施定义的良好接口。它们可以被拖拽到一个有响应能力的系统中，具有被动基础设施确定的与其他模块的关系。封装这些模块，以便其接口符合被动基础设施，但其功能方法不依赖于其他模块的功能方法，除非被动基础设施强制规定。

被动基础设施——被动基础设施提供模块之间的拖拽连接。它的价值在于隔离封装的模块，以便将非预期的副作用降至最低，并快速实现新的运行功能。在标准和规则中，选择被动基础设施元素的关键是在必要的多样性和经济性之间平衡，足以促进模块连接，但不会过度限制创新系统的构型配置。

主动基础设施——敏捷系统不是在固定事件中设计和部署，然后再单独使用的系统。敏捷性是最为主动积极的，因为新的系统构型配置是为了响应新的需求而组装的——这可能非常频繁，在某些情况下甚至每天都会发生。为了在需要时促成新的构型配置，需要五项职责：

- 模块组合演进——谁（或什么流程）负责确保将新模块添加到目录中，并及时升级现有模块以满足响应需要？

- Module readiness—Who (or what process) is responsible for ensuring that sufficient modules are ready for deployment at unpredictable times?
- Situational awareness—Who (or what process) is responsible for monitoring, evaluating, and anticipating the operational environment?
- System assembly—Who (or what process) assembles new system configurations when new situations require something different in capability?
- Infrastructure evolution—Who (or what process) is responsible for evolving the passive and active infrastructures as new rules and standards are anticipated and become appropriate?

167 Responsibilities for these five activities must be designated and embedded within the system to ensure that effective response capability is possible at unpredictable times

Agility Architectural Design Principles

Ten reusable, reconfigurable, scalable design principles are briefly itemized in this section:

Reusable principles are as follows:

- *Encapsulated modules*—Modules are distinct, separable, loosely coupled, independent units cooperating toward a shared common purpose.
- *Facilitated interfacing (plug compatibility)*—Modules share well-defined interaction and interface standards and are easily inserted or removed in system configurations.
- *Facilitated reuse*—Modules are reusable and replicable, with supporting facilitation for finding and employing appropriate modules.

Reconfigurable principles are as follows:

- *Peer–peer interaction*—Modules communicate directly on a peer-to-peer relationship; and parallel (rather than sequential) relationships are favored.
- *Distributed control and information*—Modules are directed by objective (rather than method); decisions are made at point of maximum knowledge, and information is associated locally and accessible globally.
- *Deferred commitment*—Requirements can change rapidly and continue to evolve. Work activity, response assembly, and response deployment that are deferred to the last responsible moment avoid costly wasted effort that may also preclude a subsequent effective response.

- 模块准备度——谁（或什么流程）负责确保在不可预测的时间准备好足够的模块以供部署？

- 态势感知——谁（或什么流程）负责监控、评估和预测运行环境？

- 系统组装——当新的情况需要不同的能力时，谁（或什么流程）组装新的系统构型配置？

- 基础设施演进——谁（或什么流程）负责根据新规则和新标准的预期和适应性来推动被动和主动基础设施的演进？

必须指定这五项活动的职责并将其嵌入系统中，以确保在不可预测的情况下能够实现有效的响应能力。

敏捷架构的设计原则

本节简要列举了十条可重用、可重构、可扩展的设计原则：

可重用原则如下：

- *封装的模块*——模块是不同的、可分离的、松耦合的、独立的单元，为实现共享的共同目标而协作。

- *简便的接口（接插的兼容性）*——模块间共享定义良好的交互和接口标准，并可在系统构型配置中轻易插入或移除。

- *方便的重用*——模块是可重用和可复制的，支持查询和部署合适的模块。

可重构原则如下：

- *对等交互*——模块直接通过对等关系进行通信；平行（而非顺序）关系更受青睐。

- *分布式控制和信息*——模块由目标（而非方法）引导；决策在知识最大化以及信息本地关联、全局可访问的情况下做出。

- *延后承诺*——需求可能会迅速变化并持续演进。工作活动以及对于组装和部署的响应要推迟到最后的职责时刻，从而避免可能导致的工作的浪费，这也会妨碍后续的有效响应。

- *Self-organization*—Module relationships are self-determined where possible, and module interaction is self-adjusting or self-negotiated.

Scalable principles are as follows:

- *Evolving infrastructure standards*—Passive infrastructure standardizes intermodular communication and interaction, defines module compatibility, and is evolved by designated responsibility for maintaining current and emerging relevance.
- *Redundancy and diversity*—Duplicate modules provide capacity right-sizing options and fail-soft tolerance, and diversity among similar modules employing different methods is exploitable.
- *Elastic capacity*—Modules may be combined in responsive assemblies to increase or decrease functional capacity within the current architecture.

Agility Metrics

Agility measures are enabled and constrained principally by architecture—in both the process and the product of development:

- *Time to respond*, measured in both the time to understand a response is necessary and the time to accomplish the response.
- *Cost to respond*, measured in both the cost of accomplishing the response and the cost incurred elsewhere as a result of the response.
- *Predictability of response*, measured before the fact in architectural preparedness for response and confirmed after the fact in repeatable accuracy of response time and cost estimates.
- *Scope of response*, measured before the fact in architectural preparedness for comprehensive response capability within mission and confirmed after the fact in repeatable evidence of broad response accommodation.

3.1.4 Human Systems Integration

Definition Human Systems Integration (HSI) is an approach that integrates technology, organizations, and people effectively.

HSI is an essential, transdisciplinary, sociotechnical, and management approach of SE used to ensure that the system's technical, organizational, and human elements are appropriately addressed across the whole system life cycle, service, or enterprise system. HSI considers systems in their operational context together with the necessary interactions between and among their human and technological elements to make them work in harmony and cost effectively, from concept to retirement.

- *自组织*——在可能的情况下模块关系是自决定的，模块交互是自调整或自协商的。

可扩展原则如下：

- *演进的基础设施标准*——被动基础设施制定模块之间通信和交互的标准，定义模块兼容性，并通过指定职责维护当前的和新出现的相关性而不断发展。
- *冗余和多样性*——副本模块提供合适规模选项和故障软容许度，可利用使用不同方法的相同模块之间的多样性。
- *弹性容量*——模块可组合成响应组件，以增加或减少当前架构的功能容量。

敏捷性指标

敏捷性测度在开发流程和开发产品中主要由架构来使能和约束。

- *响应时间*，以理解响应的必要时间以及完成响应的时间来衡量。
- *响应成本*，以完成响应的成本以及在其他方面做出响应所产生的成本来衡量。
- *响应的可预测性*，在架构响应准备度达到之前进行测量，以及在响应时间和成本估计的可重复准确度达到之后进行确认。
- *响应范围*，在任务中全面响应能力的架构准备度达到之前进行测量，并在广泛响应适应的可重复证据达到之后进行确认。

3.1.4 人与系统综合

定义 人与系统综合（HSI）是一种有效综合技术、组织和人员的实施方法。

HSI 是系统工程的一种基本的、跨学科的、社会技术的和管理的实施方法，用于确保在整个系统生命周期、服务或复杂组织体中适当地处理系统的技术、组织和人员元素。HSI 将考虑运行环境中的系统，以及系统的人员和技术元素之间的必要交互，以使其从概念到退役都能和谐且经济高效地工作。

LIFE CYCLE ANALYSES AND METHODS

Key Concepts

Human

The "human" in HSI includes all individuals and groups interacting within the SoI. Within HSI, these are typically referred to as "stakeholders." Stakeholders can include system acquirers, owners, users, operators, maintainers, trainers, support personnel, and the general public. While most people who interact within the SoI will be cooperative or have a vested interest in its performance, consideration may also need to be given to non-cooperative people or those with malign intent such as competitors, adversaries, criminals (physical and cyber), and those seeking to use the system outside of its design intent. Life, human, and social sciences have different representations of the human element and can all bring different perspectives to HSI activities.

Systems

HSI adopts a sociotechnical system perspective that considers a system as a representation of natural and artificial elements that are organizations of humans and machines (where machines include both hardware and software). Therefore, HSI considers that all systems include both humans and machines, and to optimize the system, all of these elements must be considered within SE activities.

Integration

HSI considers integration from two key viewpoints. The first is the effective integration of the human and technological elements in a system. The second is the efficient integration of the different perspectives of both human and machine elements within the system. An example of these different HSI perspectives can be seen in Figure 3.5. The specific perspectives relevant to a project will vary depending on the nature of the system and the organization's activities.

All systems involve or affect people and exist within a wider sociotechnical and organizational context. Therefore, HSI is an essential enabler to SE practice. The sociotechnical approach provided by HSI supports analysis, design, and evaluation activities in holistically understanding and effectively integrating the technological, organizational (including processes), and human elements of a system. As shown in Figure 3.5, HSI emerges from the overlapping of three main circles: (1) technology, organization, and people (the TOP Model) within an environment at the heart; (2) HSI perspectives; and (3) contributing disciplines associated with the operational domain shown in the periphery. It is particularly important that systems are designed to meet human capabilities, limitations, and goals.

生命周期分析和方法

关键概念

人

HSI 中的"人"包括在 SoI 中交互的所有个人和团体。在 HSI 中，通常将其称为"利益相关方"。利益相关方可以包括系统采办方、拥有方、使用方、运行方、维护方、培训方、支持方和公众。虽然在 SoI 内进行交互的大多数人都是合作的或对其性能有既得的利益，但也可能需要考虑非合作的人或具有恶意的人，如竞争者、对手、罪犯（物理的和赛博的）以及那些试图在超出其设计意图之外使用系统的人。生命科学、人文科学和社会科学对人的因素有不同的表示，都可以为 HSI 活动带来不同的视角。

系统

HSI 采用社会技术系统视角，将系统视为自然和人工元素的表示，这些元素是人和机器（其中机器包括硬件和软件）的组织。因此，HSI 认为所有系统都包括人和机器，为优化系统，必须在系统工程活动中考虑所有这些元素。

综合

HSI 从两个关键角度考虑综合。第一个是系统中人和技术元素的有效综合；第二个是系统中人和机器元素的不同视角的高效综合。图 3.5 表明这些不同 HSI 视角的示例。与某一项目相关的具体观点将根据系统的特质和组织活动而改变。

所有系统都涉及或影响着人，并存在于更为广泛的社会技术和组织背景中。因此，HSI 是系统工程实践的基本的使能项。HSI 提供的社会技术的实施方法支持分析、设计和评估活动，以全面理解和有效综合系统的技术的、组织的（包括流程）和人的元素。如图 3.5 所示，HSI 从三个主要圈的重叠部分中呈现出来：（1）核心环境中的技术、组织和人（顶层模型）；（2）HSI 观点；（3）在外围与运行领域相关的学科。尤其重要的是，系统的设计应满足人的能力、限制和目标。

LIFE CYCLE ANALYSES AND METHODS

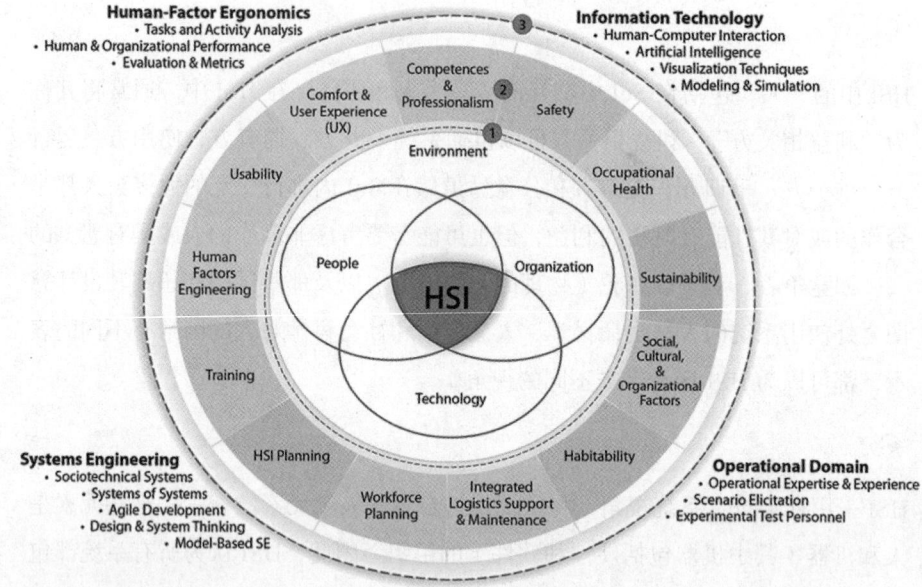

FIGURE 3.5 HSI technology, organization, people within an environment. INCOSE SEH original figure created by Boy. Usage per the INCOSE Notices page. All other rights reserved.

Elaboration

Purpose and Value of HSI

The purpose of HSI is to optimize total system performance and stakeholder satisfaction through the mutual integration of technology, organizations (including processes), people, and environment.

The benefits which can be realized by HSI vary from domain to domain, depending on their priorities and purpose (e.g., safety, cost, efficiency, performance, acceptability) and the nature of the system. They can be broken down into the following areas:

- *holistic optimization of system performance and efficiency*: participatory design, and human-in-the-loop (HITL) activities
- *improved safety*: hazard, risk, performance limitations and emergent properties analysis
- *reduced development costs*: consider the TOP Model

生命周期分析和方法

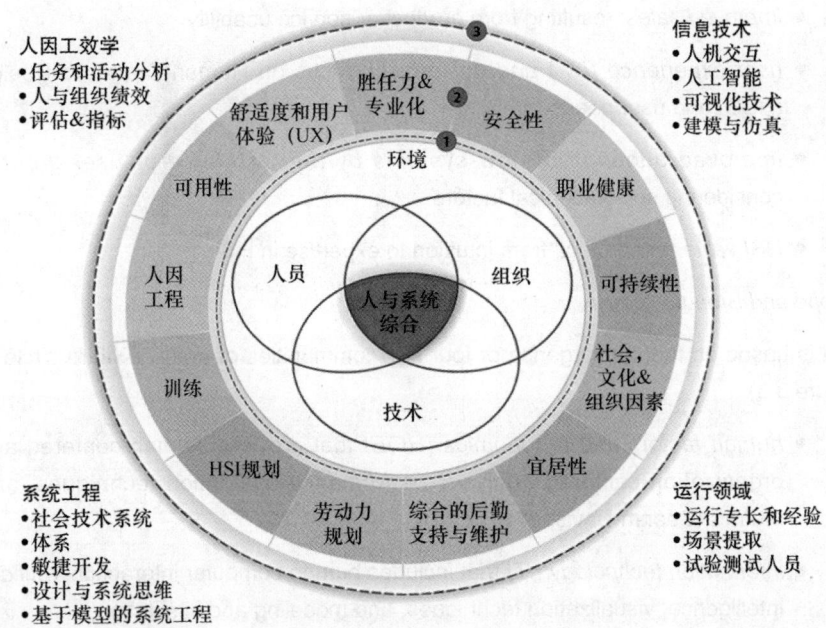

图 3.5 环境中的 HSI 技术、组织、人员。INCOSE SEH 原始图由 Boy 创建。按照 INCOSE 通知页使用。版权所有。

详细阐述

HSI 的目的和价值

HSI 的目的是通过技术、组织（包括流程）、人员和环境的相互综合，优化总体系统性能和利益相关方满意度。

HSI 可实现的益处因领域不同而不同，这取决于其优先级和目的（例如，安全性、成本、效率、性能、可接受性）以及系统的特质。可将它们分为以下几个方面：

- *系统性能和效率的整体优化*：参与式设计和人在回路（HITL）的活动；
- *提高安全性*：危险、风险、性能限制和涌现性分析；
- *降低开发成本*：考虑顶层模型；

493

- *reduced system LCC costs*: HSI from the beginning of the SE life cycle
- *improved sales*: resulting from product or service usability
- *user experience (UX) and desirability*: focus on Human-Centered Design (HCD) and user needs
- *improved adoption of new systems by the workforce or user groups*: considering sociotechnical factors
- *HSI value to a project*: from intuition to expertise in HSI

170 Scope and Breadth of HSI

HSI is based on the convergence of four key communities of practice (third circle in Figure 3.5):

- *human factors and ergonomics (HF/E)* that provides human-centered and organization-centered analysis, performance evaluation techniques, and metrics (Boehm-Davis, et al., 2015);
- *information technology (IT)* that includes human-computer interaction, artificial intelligence, visualization techniques, and modeling and simulation;
- *systems engineering* that includes socio-technical systems, systems of systems (see Section 4.3.6), agile development (see Section 4.2.2), design and system thinking (see Sections 3.2.7 and 1.5), and model-based SE (MBSE) (see Section 4.2.1); and
- *the operational domain* that includes operational expertise and experience, scenario elicitation, and experimental test personnel (see Section 4.4).

These communities enable support of HSI through HCD as a major process that involves development and use of domain ontology, prototypes and digital modeling, scenario-based design, modeling and HITL activities (simulations and physical tests), formative evaluations, agile design and development, as well as human performance and organizational metrics (e.g., maturity and flexibility) (Boy, 2013) (Boy, 2020). HCD validation both requires certification approval and contributes to certification rules evolution.

- *降低系统 LCC 成本*：从系统工程生命周期之初就开始考虑 HSI；

- *提高销售量*：源于产品或服务的可用性；

- *用户体验（UX）和可欲性*：关注以人为中心的设计（HCD）和用户需要；

- *改进工作者或用户群体对新系统的采用度*：在此考虑社会技术因素；

- *HSI 对项目的价值*：从直觉到 HSI 专业知识。

HSI 的范围和广度

HSI 基于四个关键实践群体的融合（图 3.5 中的第三圈）：

- *人因和人机工效学（HF/E）*，提供以人为中心和以组织为中心的分析、绩效评估技术和指标（Boehm Davis 等，2015）；

- *信息技术（IT）*，包括人—计算机交互、人工智能、可视化技术以及建模与仿真；

- *系统工程*，包括社会—技术系统、体系（见 4.3.6 节）、敏捷开发（见 4.2.2 节）、设计和系统思维（见 3.2.7 和 1.5 节）以及基于模型的系统工程（MBSE）（见 4.2.1 节）；

- *运行领域*，包括运行专业知识和经验、场景引导和实验测试人员（见 4.4 节）。

这些群体通过 HCD 支持 HSI，将其作为一个主要流程，其中涉及领域本体、原型和数字建模、基于场景的设计、建模和 HITL 活动（仿真和物理测试）、形成性评估、敏捷设计和开发以及人的表现和组织指标（如成熟度和灵活性）的开发与使用（Boy，2013）（Boy，2020）。HCD 验证既需要认证批准，也有助于认证规则的演进。

LIFE CYCLE ANALYSES AND METHODS

HSI considers systems complexity analysis as a baseline. It seeks simplification (where possible) and familiarity with complex systems (where necessary). HITL activities enable discovery and elicitation of complex systems' emergent behaviors, properties, functions, and structures, which are incrementally integrated into the SoI through its whole life cycle.HITL activities provide SE and HCD teams with improved understanding of the SoI early in the life cycle, contributing to design flexibility and better resource management. HSI is a foundational enabler for industrial endeavors, such as Industry 4.0, where digital engineering, enabling virtual HCD, requires increased physical and cognitive tangibility testing across the life cycle of a system (see Section 5.4). Case 5 (Artificial Intelligence in Systems Engineering - Autonomous Vehicles) from Section 6.5 illustrates the importance of all these aspects.

HSI can be considered as both an *enabling process*, associating HCD and SE during the life cycle of a system, and a *product* resulting from this process. HSI is the result of this HCD-based convergence, which requires optimizing the TOP Model. User eXperience (UX) and User Interface (UI) development are integral parts of the HSI process from the early stages and throughout the system life cycle. HSI processes are iterative and supported by two main types of assets, methods, and tools: expertise elicitation and creativity. The former enables effective elicitation from subject matter experts through knowledge and know-how, supporting design teams during system formative evaluations, agile development, and certification. The latter enables out-of-the-box projections that are validated using prototyping and HITL activities.

HSI Perspectives

HSI encompasses several important perspectives displayed in Figure 3.5 (second circle) and described in more detail in Table 3.2.

A wide variety of HSI methods, models, knowledge, and approaches can be used to support decisions made across the whole system life cycle. This can include support to requirements analysis, trade-studies, life cost benefit analysis, options or tender down select, risk management, safety case development, design decisions, acceptance testing, and workforce planning. Human-related trade studies are critical to determining holistic of operational concept (OpsCon) and thereby informing the design team in terms of effectivity, efficiency, suitability, usability, safety, and affordability. See the INCOSE HSI Primer (2023) for more detail.

HSI 将系统复杂性分析作为基线，寻求简化的（如有可能）和熟悉的（如有必要）复杂系统。HITL 活动能够发现和引出复杂系统的涌现行为、特性、功能和结构，并在 SoI 的整个生命周期中逐步将其综合到 SoI 中。HITL 活动使系统工程和以人为中心的设计（HCD）团队在生命周期早期更好地了解 SoI，有助于提高设计灵活性和更好的资源管理。HSI 是工业领域（如工业 4.0）的基础使能项，在此，覆盖系统整个生命周期，虚拟 HCD 使能的数字工程，需要增加物理和认知有形的测试（见 5.4 节）。6.5 节中的案例 5（系统工程中的人工智能—自动驾驶汽车）描述了所有这些方面的重要特征。

既可将 HSI 视为一个使能流程，在系统生命周期中将 HCD 和系统工程关联，也可以将其视为流程产生的结果。HSI 与 HCD 殊途同归，这需要优化 TOP 模型。从早期阶段到整个系统生命周期，用户体验（UX）和用户界面（UI）开发都是 HSI 流程的组成部分。HSI 流程是迭代的，由两类主要的资产、方法和工具支持：专业知识引导和创造性。前者能够通过知识和"如何做"从主题专家那里获得有效的启发，在系统的形成性评估、敏捷开发和认证中支持设计团队；后者支持使用原型和 HITL 活动确认的开箱即用的设想。

HSI 观点

HSI 包括图 3.5（第二个圈）中显示的几个重要的视角，表 3.2 中有更加详细的描述。

可以使用多样的 HSI 方法、模型、知识和方法来支持系统整个生命周期中的决策，可以包括需求分析、权衡研究、生命周期成本收益分析、选项或投标选择、风险用例管理、安全用例开发、设计决策、验收测试和劳动力规划的支持。与人相关的权衡研究对于确定整体运行概念（OpsCon）至关重要，从而为设计团队提供有效性、高效性、适用性、可用性、安全性和可承受性方面的信息。有关更多详细信息，参阅 INCOSE HSI 入门指南（2023）。

LIFE CYCLE ANALYSES AND METHODS

171 TABLE 3.2 HSI perspective descriptions

Human Factors Engineering (HFE) is the scientific discipline concerned with the understanding of interactions among humans and other elements of a system, and the profession that applies theory, principles, data, and other methods to design in order to optimize human well-being and overall system performance.
Social, Cultural, and Organizational Factors consider the organizational aspects of socio-technical systems and includes the organizations who will be using and supporting the operational system, as well as the organizations who are involved throughout the entire life cycle of the system.
HSI Planning addresses the implementation of HSI through the SE process to ensure the human element is effectively integrated with the system. HSI strategies and priorities need to be set up-front, can be formalized in the HSI Plan, and potentially adjusted during the life cycle, upon mission definition, and carried throughout the allocation of resources and project personnel.
Integrated Logistics Support (ILS) & Maintenance covers human performance during the whole life cycle of a system based on an ILS plan supported by an HSI plan. ILS includes training, operations, maintenance, potential redesign, and dismantling.
Workforce Planning addresses the number and type of personnel and the various occupational specialties required and potentially available to develop, train, operate, maintain, and support the system.
Competences and Professionalism consider the type of knowledge, skills, experience levels, and aptitudes (cognitive, physical, and sensory) required to operate, maintain, and support a critical system and the means to provide such people (through selection, recruitment, training, etc.).
Training encompasses designing to account for ease and reduction of operation time needed to provide training through trade studies evaluated to assess their impact on training, as well as the instructions and resources required to provide personnel with requisite competence, knowledge, skills, and attitudes to properly operate, maintain, and support systems.
Safety promotes system characteristics and procedures to minimize the risk of accidents or mishaps that cause death or injury to operators, maintainers, support personnel, or others who could come into intentional or unintentional contact with the system; threaten systems operations; or cause cascading failures in other systems. It includes survivability.
Occupational Health promotes system design features and procedures that serve to minimize physiological mental and social health hazards which might result in injury, acute or chronic illness, and disability; and to enhance job performance and wellbeing of personnel who operate, maintain, or support the system.
Sustainability covers the environmental considerations that can affect operations and particularly human performance and considers wider ranging concerns and long-term goals of how the humans within the system can affect the environment, society, and economy without compromising future generations' needs.
Habitability involves characteristics of system living and working conditions.
Usability involves objective evaluation methods to address aspects such as efficiency, conformity to human expectations, tolerance/resistance toward human errors, and learnability to improve the degree to which humans can reach their objectives when interacting with a system.
Comfort and UX are personal internal human aspects such as joy, guilt, opinions, and unconscious aspects which are to be considered, not only in regard to the primary users of the final product, but in regard to all humans involved in the systems engineering process.

INCOSE SEH original table created by Boy. Usage per the INCOSE Notices page. All other rights reserved.

生命周期分析和方法

表 3.2　HSI 观点描述

人因工程（*Human Factors Engineering, HFE*）是一门科学学科，研究如何理解人与系统中其他元素之间的相互作用，以及将理论、原理、数据和其他方法应用于设计以优化人类福祉和整体系统性能的专业。

*社会、文化和组织因素*考虑了社会技术系统的组织方面，包括将使用和支持运行系统的组织，以及参与系统整个生命周期的组织。

*HSI 规划*涉及通过 SE 流程实施 HSI，以确保人的因素与系统有效整合。HSI 策略和优先事项需要预先制定，可在 HSI 计划中正式确定，并可能在任务确定后的生命周期中进行调整，并贯穿于资源和项目人员分配的始终。

*综合后勤支持（ILS）*和维护涵盖系统整个生命周期内的人的表现，其依据是 ILS 计划由 HSI 计划提供支持。ILS 包括培训、操作、维护、潜在的重新设计和拆除。

*员工队伍规划*涉及开发、培训、运行、维护和支持系统所需和可能提供的人员数量和类型以及各种职业专业。

*胜任力和职业精神*考虑的是操作、维护和支持关键系统所需的知识、技能、经验水平和能力（认知、体能和感官），以及提供这些人员的手段（通过选拔、招聘、培训等）。

*培训*包括设计，以通过权衡研究评估其对培训的影响，从而考虑到提供培训所需的操作时间的简易性和减少，以及向人员提供正确操作、维护和支持系统所需的能力、知识、技能和态度所需的指示和资源。

*安全促进*系统特性和程序，以最大限度地降低事故或意外风险，这些事故或意外可能导致操作员、维护人员、支持人员或其他有意或无意接触系统的人员伤亡；威胁系统运行；或导致其他系统出现连锁故障。它包括生存能力。

*职业健康促进*系统的设计特征和程序，以最大限度地减少可能导致受伤、急性或慢性疾病和残疾的生理、心理和社会健康危害，并提高操作、维护或支持系统人员的工作绩效和福祉。

*可持续性*涵盖了可能影响运行，特别是人员绩效的环境因素，并考虑了更广泛的问题和长期目标，即系统内的人员如何在不损害后代需求的情况下影响环境、社会和经济。

*宜居性*涉及系统的生活和工作条件的特点。

*可用性*涉及客观评价方法，以解决效率、是否符合人类期望、对人类错误的容忍度/抵抗力以及可学习性等方面的问题，从而提高人在与系统交互时达到目标的程度。

*舒适度和用户体验*是人的内在方面，例如喜悦、内疚、意见和无意识等，不仅要考虑最终产品的主要用户，还要考虑参与系统工程流程的所有人。

INCOSE SEH 原始表由 Boy 创建。按照 INCOSE 通知页使用。版权所有。

LIFE CYCLE ANALYSES AND METHODS

3.1.5 Interoperability Analysis

Definition Interoperability Analysis is an approach that ensures the system interacts effectively with other systems. In the domains of data/information exchange and communications, there are four definitions of interoperability:

- The capability of systems to communicate with one another and to exchange and use information including content, format, and semantics (NIST SP 500-230, 1996).

- The ability of two or more systems or system elements to exchange data and use information (IEEE 610.12, 1990).

- The ability of two or more systems to exchange information and to mutually use the information that is exchanged (US Army, 1997).

- The condition achieved among communications-electronics systems or items of communications—electronics equipment when information or services can be exchanged directly and satisfactorily between them and/or their users (US DoD, 2021).

Key Concepts Interoperability reflects the ability of a system to work in conjunction with other system(s) to achieve an outcome. For example, a mobile phone can operate on different networks across the world, agricultural implements from different companies can work on each other's tractors, or a system provides an interface allowing remote control of its capabilities. Originally described in terms of computer/software systems, the concept of interoperability applies more widely, such as human interactions. A broad definition of interoperability also takes into account social, political, and organizational factors that impact system-to-system performance. Interoperability is a key enabler for a System of Systems (SoS), because it allows the elements of a large and complex system to work together as a single entity, toward a shared purpose (see Section 4.3.6).

Interoperability may be achieved in two principal ways, which can also be combined:

- Agreeing on one or more *published standards* as the definition of the interface. This exposure of interfaces complying with open interfaces is increasingly common in the consumer product area where "plug and play" is expected.

- Defining and implementing a *custom interface*. When a standard interface does not exist, or is not suitable, a custom interface can be defined as the agreed way in which two or more systems will connect, communicate, interact, or cooperate to achieve their shared purpose.

3.1.5 互操作性分析

定义 互操作性分析是一种确保系统与其他系统有效交互的实施方法。在数据/信息交换和通信领域，关于互操作性有四个定义：

- 系统相互通信以及交换和使用信息（包括内容、格式和语义）的能力（NIST SP 500-230，1996）。

- 两个或多个系统或系统元素交换数据和使用信息的能力（IEEE 610.12，1990）。

- 两个或多个系统交换信息和相互使用所交换信息的能力（美国陆军，1997）。

- 当信息或服务可以在通信电子系统或通信电子设备项和/或其使用方之间直接且圆满地交换时，通信电子系统或通信电子设备项之间达到的状态（美国国防部，2021）。

关键概念 互操作性反映系统与其他系统结合起来工作以达成结果的能力。例如，移动电话可以在世界各地的不同网络上运行，不同公司的农具产品可以在彼此的拖拉机上工作，或者系统提供一个接口，允许远程控制其功能。互操作性的概念最初是从计算机/软件系统的角度描述的，其应用范围更广，例如人员的交互。互操作性的广泛定义还考虑影响系统间性能的社会的、政治的和组织的因素。互操作性是体系（SoS）的关键使能因素，因其允许大型复杂系统的元素作为单个实体而协作，以达成共享的目的（见4.3.6节）。

互操作性可以通过两种主要方式实现，也可以结合使用：

- 同意使用一个或多个发布标准作为接口的定义。在要求"即插即用"的消费产品领域，符合开放式接口原则的接口越来越常见。

- 定制化接口的定义和实现。当标准接口不存在或不适用时，使用定制化接口定义，作为两个或多个系统连接、通信、交互或协作的商定方式，以达成共享目的。

LIFE CYCLE ANALYSES AND METHODS

Elaboration Interoperability will increase in importance as the world grows smaller due to expanding communications networks (e.g., the internet of things (IoT)), as nations continue to perceive the need to communicate seamlessly across international coalitions of commercial organizations or national defense forces, and as individuals increasingly expect that products and services will "work together."

The Øresund Bridge (see Section 6.2) demonstrates the interoperability challenges faced when just two nations collaborate on a project. For example, the meshing of regulations on health and safety, interfacing a left-handed (Sweden) and right-handed (Denmark) railway, and the resolution of two power supply systems for the railway. Hence careful choices were necessary for the standards selected for the bridge itself, and for its interfaces at the Swedish and Danish ends.

3.1.6 Logistics Engineering

Definition Logistics Engineering is an approach that enables support for the entire life cycle.

Key Concepts Logistics engineering, which may also be referred to as product support engineering, is the engineering discipline concerned with the identification, acquisition, procurement, and provisioning of all support resources required to sustain operation and maintenance of a system (Blanchard and Fabrycky, 2011). Logistics engineering is also concerned with engineering the inherent supportability of the design. Logistics should be addressed from a life cycle perspective and be considered in all stages and especially as an inherent part of system concept and development. Furthermore, logistics should be approached from a system perspective to include all activities associated with design for supportability, the acquisition and procurement of the elements of support, the supply and distribution of required support material, and the maintenance and support of systems throughout their planned period of utilization.

The scope of logistics engineering is thus

- to determine logistics support requirements,
- to design the system for supportability,
- to acquire or procure the support, and
- to provide cost-effective logistics support for a system during utilization and support stages.

详细阐述 随着通信网络（如物联网）的不断扩大，世界变得越来越小，各国持续认识到跨越国际商业组织联盟或国家防务力量的无缝通信的需要，以及个人日益期望产品和服务"协同工作"，互操作性将变得越来越重要。

Øresund 大桥（见 6.2 节）展示了仅两个国家在一个项目上合作时所面临的互操作性挑战。例如，健康和安全法规的网络化，左驾（瑞典）和右驾（丹麦）铁路的接口，以及铁路两个供电系统的解决方案。因此，有必要对桥梁本身以及瑞典和丹麦两端接口选择的标准进行谨慎的选择。

3.1.6 后勤工程

定义 后勤工程是一种能够为整个生命周期提供支持的实施方法。

关键概念 后勤工程，也称产品支持工程，是一门涉及识别、获取、采办和提供用以维持系统运行和维护所需的所有支持资源的工程学科（Blanchard 和 Fabrycky，2011）。后勤工程还要考虑工程设计的固有支持性能力。后勤应从生命周期的角度解决问题，并在所有阶段予以考虑，尤其是作为系统概念和开发的固有组成部分。此外，应从系统的角度来对待后勤问题，以包括与可支持性设计相关的所有活动、支持元素的获取和采办、所需支持材料的供应和分配，以及系统在整个规划的使用期内的维护和支持。

因此，后勤工程的范围是：

- 确定后勤保障需求；
- 面向支持性开展设计系统；
- 获取或采办所需的支持；
- 在使用和支持阶段为系统提供具有成本—有效性的后勤支持。

LIFE CYCLE ANALYSES AND METHODS

Logistics engineering has evolved into several related elements such as supply chain management (SCM) in the commercial sector and integrated logistics support (ILS) in the defense sector.

Elaboration

Support Elements

Support planning starts with the definition of the support (including maintenance) concept in the concept stage and continues through supportability analysis in the development stage, to the ultimate development of a support plan. The support concept describes the support environment in which the system will operate and which inherent supportability and support system elements are required for establishing the system operational capability.

The following elements of support are to be fully integrated with the system at the lowest possible LCC:

- *Product support integration and management*—Plan and manage cost and performance across the product support value chain, from concept to retirement.

- *Design interface*—Participate in the SE process to impact the design from inception throughout the life cycle. Facilitate supportability to maximize availability, effectiveness, and capability at the lowest LCC. Early application of the support concept drives the design inherent supportability objectives and trade-offs. It is an important mechanism for aligning design Reliability, Maintainability, and Supportability (RMS), maintenance planning, and establishment of support capabilities for the operational environment. It guides design modularity, reliability, maintainability, testability, and overall repair policies.

- *Sustained logistics engineering of the fielded system*—This effort spans those technical tasks (engineering investigations and analyses) to ensure continued dependable operation, including maintenance, for the life cycle. It characterizes the system and support capabilities' RMS performance as an input to dependable planning of operational use. It involves applying improved confidence level RMS characteristics data, gained from the operational experience, to enhance maintenance strategy and the support system, and to propose design RMS improvements.

- *Maintenance planning*—Identifying the system maintenance requirements, determining the maintenance strategy, and implementing the maintenance capabilities required to deliver the system operational capability. The support concept guides overall repair policies, such as "repair vs. replace" criteria.

后勤工程已演变为一些相关的方面，如商业领域的供应链管理（SCM）和防务领域的综合后勤支持（ILS）。

详细阐述

支撑元素

支持规划从概念阶段的支持（包括维护）概念定义开始，然后在开发阶段进行支持性分析，直至最终制订支持计划。支持概念描述系统运行的支持环境，以及建立系统运行能力所需的固有支持能力和支持系统元素。

以下支持元素将以尽可能低的生命周期成本与系统完全综合：

- *产品支持综合和管理*——从概念到退役，规划和管理整个产品支持价值链的成本和绩效。

- *设计接口*——参与系统工程流程，对整个生命周期的设计产生影响。提高支持能力，以最低的 LCC 最大限度地提高可用性、有效性和能力。支持概念的早期应用推动了设计固有的支持性目标和权衡。它是保持可靠性、维修性和支持性（RMS）设计对准、维护规划和建立运行环境支持能力的重要机制。它指导设计模块化、可靠性、可维护性、可测试性和总体维修策略。

- *现场系统的持续后勤工程*——这项工作涵盖一些技术任务（工程调查和分析），以确保在整个生命周期内持续可靠地运行，包括维护。它描述系统和支持能力的 RMS 性能，作为可靠的运行使用规划的输入，涉及应用从运行经验中获得的用于改进的可信 RMS 特性数据，以增强维护策略和支持系统，并提出设计 RMS 的改进。

- *维护规划*——识别系统维护需求，确定维护策略，并实施交付系统运行能力所需的维护能力。支持概念指导总体维修策略，如"维修与更换"准则。

LIFE CYCLE ANALYSES AND METHODS

- *Operation and maintenance personnel*—Identify, plan, and acquire personnel, with the training, experience, and skills required to operate, maintain, and support the system.

- *Training and training support*—Establish and maintain the required operator and maintainer skill levels across the system life cycle. Identify, develop, and acquire Training Aids, Devices, Simulators, and Simulations (TADSS) to maximize the effectiveness of the personnel to operate and sustain the system equipment.

- *Supply support*—determine requirements for supply, and acquire, catalog, receive, store, transfer, issue, and dispose of spares, repair parts, and supplies. This means having the right spares, repair parts, and all classes of supplies available, in the right quantities, at the right place, at the right time, at the right price.

- *Computer resources (hardware and software)*—Computers, associated software, networks, and interfaces necessary to enable long-term logistics engineering, maintenance management, system technical and associated support operations data management, and storage.

- *Technical data, reports, and documentation*—Represents recorded information of scientific or technical nature (e.g., equipment technical manuals, engineering drawings), engineering data, specifications, and standards.

- *Facilities and infrastructure*—This includes facilities (e.g., buildings, warehouses, hangars, waterways, associated facilities equipment) and infrastructure (e.g., IT services, fuel, water, electrical service, machine shops, dry docks, test ranges).

- *Packaging, handling, storage, and transportation (PHS&T)*—Ensure that all system equipment and support items are preserved, packaged, handled, and transported properly, including environmental considerations, equipment reservation for short and long storage, and transportability. Some items may require special environmentally controlled, shock-isolated containers for transport to and from storage, operational, and repair facilities via all modes of transportation (e.g., land, rail, sea, air, space).

- *Support equipment*—All equipment (mobile and fixed) required to sustain the operation and maintenance of a system, including, but not limited to, handling and maintenance equipment, trucks, air conditioners, generators, tools, metrology and calibration equipment, and manual and automatic test equipment.

- *操作和维护人员*——识别、规划和获取所需的运行、维护和支持系统的培训、经验和技能。

- *培训和培训支持*——建立并维持整个系统生命周期所需的操作人员和维护人员技能水平。识别、开发和获取培训辅助装置、设备、仿真器和仿真（TADSS），以最大限度地提高人员运行和维护系统设备的有效性。

- *供应支持*——确定用于供应、获取、编目、接收、存储、转移、发放和备件处置、维修零件和供应品的需求。这意味着以正确的数量、在正确的地点、在正确的时间、以正确的价格来提供正确的备件、维修零件和所有类别的供应。

- *计算机资源（硬件和软件）*——支持长期后勤工程、维护管理、系统技术和相关支持运行数据管理和存储所需的计算机、相关软件、网络和接口。

- *技术数据、报告和文档*——表示科学或技术特征的记录信息（如设备技术手册、工程图样）、工程数据、规范和标准。

- *设施和基础设施*——包括设施（如建筑物、仓库、机库、水道、相关设施设备）和基础设施（如IT服务、燃料、水、电气服务、机器车间、干船坞、测试场）。

- *包装、搬运、储存和运输（PHS&T）*——确保所有系统设备和支持项都得到妥善保存、包装、搬运和运输，包括环境因素、短期和长期储存的设备储备以及可运输性。有些物品可能需要特殊的环境控制、防震容器，以便通过各种运输方式（如陆运、铁路、海运、空运、航天）往返于存储、运行和维修设施之间。

- *支持设备*——维持系统运行和维护所需的所有设备（移动的和固定的），包括但不限于搬运和维护设备、卡车、空调、发电机、工具、计量和校准设备以及手动和自动测试设备。

LIFE CYCLE ANALYSES AND METHODS

Supportability Analysis

As shown in the Figure 3.1, supportability analysis addresses all elements of design supportability and of the support system required during all life cycle stages:

- *Functional failure analysis*—A Functional Breakdown Structure (FBS) is used as reference to perform functional FMECA (Failure Mode Effects and Criticality Analysis), FTA (Fault Tree Analysis) and/or RBD (Reliability Block Diagram) analysis. These analyses can be used to identify functional failure modes and to classify them according to criticality (e.g., severity of failure effects and probability of occurrence). The functional failure analysis can also provide valuable system design input (e.g., redundancy requirements). In describing functional failure compensation means, including compensation by support, the functional failure analysis provides early means of illustrating the system supportability interface and criticality of support.

- *Physical failure analysis*—A Product Breakdown Structure (PBS) is used as reference to perform hardware FMECA, FTA, and/or RBD analysis with the objective of optimizing the design and to identify all maintenance tasks for potential failure modes. An objective of logistic engineering is to minimize operational maintenance tasks and resource requirements. The FMECA (in assessing the design inherent reliability, protection, and testability versus reliance on preventive or corrective maintenance) allows in context trade-offs of the operational value of improving the design versus defaulting to reliance on operational maintenance. The FMECA findings are used to balance the level of repair allocation. Failure probability, criticality, detection means, the design modularity, and the complexity of failure restoration need to be in balance with the level of repair capabilities framed by the system support concept.

- *Task identification and optimization*—Corrective maintenance tasks are primarily identified using FMECA, while preventive maintenance tasks are identified using RCM (Reliability-Centered Maintenance). Trade-off studies may be required to achieve an optimized maintenance strategy. Associated support tasks, such as operational transportation, are identified from analysis of the operational concept and support workflows.

- *Detail task analysis*—Detail procedures for support tasks should be developed, and support resources identified and allocated to each task. The system Level of Repair Analysis (LORA), in conjunction with the support concept, may be used to determine the most appropriate location for executing these tasks.

支持性分析

如图 3.1 所示，支持性分析涉及生命周期所有阶段所需的设计支持性和支持系统的所有元素：

- *功能故障分析*——将功能分解结构（FBS）用作执行功能 FMECA（故障模式、影响与危害性分析）、FTA（故障树分析）和/或 RBD（可靠性块图）分析的参考。这些分析可用于识别功能故障模式，并根据重要性（例如，故障影响的严重程度和发生概率）对其进行分类。功能故障分析还可以提供具有价值的系统设计输入（例如冗余需求）。在描述功能故障补偿方法（包括支持补偿）时，功能故障分析提供了说明系统支持性接口和支持关键性的早期方式。

- *物理故障分析*——以产品分解结构（PBS）作为参考，执行硬件 FMECA、FTA 和/或 RBD 分析，目的是优化设计，并识别潜在故障模式的所有维护任务。后勤工程的目标是最大限度地减少运行维护的任务和资源需求。FMECA（在评估设计的固有可靠性、保护性和可测试性与对预防性或纠正性维护的依赖性时）可以在背景环境中权衡改进设计与默认依赖运行维护这二者的运行价值。FMECA 结果用于平衡维修分配水平。故障概率、关键性、检测方式、设计模块和故障恢复的复杂性需要与系统支持概念所确定的修复能力水平保持平衡。

- *任务识别和优化*——纠正性维护任务主要使用 FMECA 进行识别，而预防性维护任务则使用 RCM（以可靠性为中心的维护）进行识别。可能需要进行权衡研究，以实现优化的维护策略。通过对运行概念和支持工作流的分析，确定相关的支持任务，如作战运输。

- *详细任务分析*——应制定支持任务的详细程序，并确定支持资源及分配给各个任务。系统级维修分析（LORA）与支持概念可用于确定执行这些任务的最合适位置。

LIFE CYCLE ANALYSES AND METHODS

- *Support element specifications*—Support element specifications should be developed for all support deliverables. Depending on the system, specifications may be required for training aids, facilities, support equipment, publications, and packaging material. Establishment of support elements, such as facilities, may involve extended lead times requiring identification of requirements and initiation of acquisition from as early as the system concept stage. The support element requirements analysis is therefore iterated from the system concept stage to highlight long-lead time support element acquisition requirements.

- *Support deliverables, test, and evaluation*—All support deliverables should be acquired based on the individual specifications. The support deliverables should be tested and evaluated against support element specifications and the overall system requirements.

- *Support modeling and simulation*—Modeling and simulation are integral parts of supportability analysis that should be initiated during the early stages to frame and develop a compliant and optimized system design, maintenance strategy, and support system. Modeling and simulation during acquisition are progressed to become decision and planning optimization tools for the operational and support stages. The predictive modeling information during acquisition is progressively matured as experience is gained with the operational system and operational support capabilities (e.g., digital twin for operation and support).

- *Recording and corrective action*—Failure recording and corrective action during the utilization and support stages form the basis for continuous improvement. System operational value delivery metrics should be applied to continuously monitor the system to improve support where deficiencies are identified, and to highlight focus areas for operational enhancements to system inherent reliability, maintainability, and supportability.

3.1.7 Manufacturability/Producibility Analysis

Definition Manufacturability/Producibility Analysis is an approach that enables production in a responsible and cost-effective manner.

Key Concepts Production involves the repeated manufacture of the developed system. The capability to manufacture or produce a system or its elements is as essential as the ability to properly develop it. A system that cannot be effectively produced causes unnecessary costs and may lead to rework and project delays with associated cost overruns. For this reason, manufacturability/producibility analysis is an integral part of the SE process.

- *支持元素规范*——应为所有支持交付物开发支持元素规范。根据系统的不同，可能需要培训辅助装置、设施、支持设备、出版物和包装材料的规范。支持元素（如设施）的建立可能涉及较长的提前期，需要识别需求并从系统概念阶段就开始采办。因此，从系统概念阶段开始重复进行支持元素的需求分析，以突出长提前期的支持元素的采办需求。

- *支持交付物、测试和评估*——所有支持交付物都应根据各自的规范采办。支持交付物应根据支持元素规范和总体系统需求进行测试和评估。

- *支持建模与仿真*——建模与仿真是支持性分析的组成部分，应在早期阶段启动，以构建和开发符合的和优化的系统设计、维护策略和支持系统。采办期间的建模和仿真已发展成为运行和支持阶段的决策和规划优化工具。随着运行系统和运行支持能力（例如，运行和支持的数字孪生）方面经验的积累，采办期间的预测建模信息将逐步成熟。

- *记录和纠正行动*——使用和支持阶段的故障记录和纠正措施构成持续改进的基础。应采用系统运行价值交付指标来持续监控系统，以便在发现缺陷时改进支持，并突出重点领域，以增强系统固有的可靠性、可维护性和可支持性。

3.1.7 可制造性/可生产性分析

定义　可制造性/可生产性分析是一种以负责任和具有成本—有效性的方式支持生产的实施方法。

关键概念　生产包括重复制造开发的系统。制造或生产系统或其元素的能力与正确开发系统的能力一样重要。无法有效生产的系统会导致不必要的成本，并可能导致返工和项目延期，从而造成相关成本超支。因此，可制造性/可生产性分析是系统工程流程的一个组成部分。

LIFE CYCLE ANALYSES AND METHODS

Producibility considerations differ depending upon the type and number of systems being produced. For example, the manufacture of satellites (limited production runs), military tanks (medium production runs), and mobile phones (high production runs) would be vastly different. A unique aspect of infrastructure systems is that production typically takes place on-site, rather than in a factory (see Section 4.4.5). Multiple production cycles require the consideration of production maintenance and downtime.

One objective is to determine if existing production enabling systems are satisfactory (see Section 1.3.3), since this could be the lowest risk and most cost-effective approach. If not, the requirements for the production enabling systems and processes need to be determined, and the production enabling systems developed so they are ready when needed. A SE approach to manufacturing and production is necessary because the production enabling systems can sometimes cost more than the system being produced (Maier and Rechtin, 2009).

Elaboration Producibility analysis is a key task in developing cost-effective, quality products. Multidisciplinary teams work to simplify the design and stabilize the manufacturing process to reduce risks, manufacturing costs, lead times, and cycle times and to minimize strategic or critical material use. Producibility analysis draws upon the production and support life cycle concepts. Producibility requirements are identified in the Business or Mission Analysis and Stakeholder Needs and Requirements Definition processes (see Sections 2.3.5.1 and 2.3.5.2) and included in the project risk analysis, if necessary. Similarly, long-lead-time items, sole source items (where only one supplier for the required item is available), material limitations, special processes, and manufacturing constraints are evaluated. Design simplification also considers ready assembly and disassembly for ease of maintenance and preservation of material for recycling. When production requirements create a constraint on the system, they are communicated and documented. The selection of manufacturing methods and processes is included in early decisions. Manufacturing test considerations are captured and are taken into account in built-in test and automated test equipment.

IKEA® is often used as an example of supply chain excellence. IKEA has orchestrated a value creating chain that begins with motivating customers to perform the final stages of furniture assembly in exchange for lower prices and a fun shopping experience. They achieve this through designs that support low-cost production and transportability (e.g., the bookcase that comes in a flat package and goes home on the roof of a car).

可生产性考虑因素因所生产的系统类型和数量而不同。例如，卫星（有限批量生产）、军用坦克（中等批量生产）和移动电话（大批量生产）的制造将迥然不同。基础设施系统的一个独特方面是，生产通常在现场进行，而不是在工厂进行（见 4.4.5 节）。多个生产周期需要考虑生产维护和停机时间。

一个目标是确定现有的生产使能系统是否令人满意（见 1.3.3 节），因为这可能是风险最低、成本—有效性最高的实施方法。如果没有，则需要确定生产使能系统和流程的需求，并开发生产使能系统，以便在需要时做好准备。制造和生产的系统工程实施方法是必要的，因为生产使能系统有时可能比正在生产的系统成本更高（Maier 和 Rechtin，2009）。

详细阐述 可生产性分析是开发高成本—有效性、高质量的产品的关键任务。多学科团队致力于简化设计和稳定制造流程，以减少风险、制造成本、提前期和周期时间，并最大限度地减少战略或关键材料的使用。可生产性分析利用生产和支持的生命周期概念。可生产性需求在业务或任务分析以及利益相关方需要和需求定义流程中确定（见 2.3.5.1 节和 2.3.5.2 节），必要时包括在项目风险分析中。同样，对长周期项目、单一来源项目（所需项目仅有一个供应商）、材料限制、特殊工艺和制造限制进行评估。设计简化还考虑可随时组装和拆卸，以便于维护和保存材料以供回收。当生产需求对系统产生约束时，将对其进行沟通和记录。制造方法和工艺的选择包括在早期决策中。捕获制造测试考虑因素，并将其纳入内置测试和自动测试设备中。

宜家®通常被视为卓越供应链的典范。宜家精心策划了一条价值创造链，首先是激励顾客进行最后阶段的家具组装，以换取较低的价格和愉快的购物体验。他们通过支持低成本生产和可运输性的设计来达到这一目标（例如，书柜采用扁平包装，可放在车顶上载回家）。

LIFE CYCLE ANALYSES AND METHODS

3.1.8 Reliability, Availability, Maintainability Engineering

Definition Reliability, Availability, Maintainability Engineering is an approach that enables the system to perform without failure, to be operational when needed, and to be retained in or restored to a required functional state.

RAM (sometimes expressed as RMA) is a well-known acronym for Reliability, Availability, and Maintainability. These QCs are completely interrelated with each other and have a strong relationship with logistics and supportability.

Key Concepts From a SE perspective, RAM should not only be viewed as quality characteristics, but as nonfunctional requirements. RAM activities are often neglected during system development, resulting in a substantial increase in risk of project failure or stakeholder dissatisfaction. Since RAM often drives other system requirements, it is essential that these activities be selected, tailored, planned, and executed in an integrated manner with other SE processes. A practical way to achieve this is to develop detailed reliability and maintainability plans early in the system development process and to integrate these plans with the SE management plan (SEMP).

RAM, being important inputs to the system maintenance concept, support other SE processes in two ways. First, they should be used to influence both system and system support definitions (e.g., the system architecture depends on RAM requirements). Second, they should be used as part of system verification (e.g., system analysis or system test). Depending on the particular industry, availability is often seen as the most important of these three quality characteristics, especially from the viewpoint of a user or acquirer. Any availability loss can usually easily be translated to mission or production loss and increased costs.

Elaboration

Reliability

The IEEE Reliability Society defines:

Reliability is a design engineering discipline which applies scientific knowledge to assure a product will perform its intended function for the required duration within a given environment. This includes designing in the ability to maintain, test, and support the product throughout its total life cycle. Reliability is best described as product performance over time. This is accomplished concurrently with other design disciplines by contributing to the selection of the system architecture, materials, processes, and system elements—both software and hardware; followed by verifying the selections made by thorough analysis and test. "To be reliable, a system must be robust—it must avoid failure modes even in the presence of a broad range of conditions including harsh environments, changing oper- ational demands, and internal deterioration" (Clausing and Frey, 2005). An in-depth understanding of the inter- action between the system, the environment where it will be used, the operating conditions it will be subjected to, and potential failure modes and failure mechanisms is thus essential to design and manufacture reliable systems. Figure 3.6 shows the interaction between these aspects.

3.1.8 可靠性、可用性、可维护性工程

定义 可靠性、可用性和可维护性工程是一种能够使系统无故障运行,在需要时可运行、保持或恢复到所需功能状态的方法。

RAM(有时表示为 RMA)是可靠性、可用性和可维护性的著名的缩写。这些 QC 彼此完全相关,并与后勤和保障能力有着密切的关系。

关键概念 从系统工程的角度来看,不仅应该将 RAM 视为质量特性,而且应该将其视为非功能需求。在系统开发流程中经常忽视 RAM 活动,导致项目失败或利益相关方不满的风险大幅增加。由于 RAM 通常会驱动其他系统需求,因此必须以与其他系统工程流程综合的方式选择、定制、计划以及执行这些活动。实现这一方式的一种实用方法是在系统开发流程的早期制订详细的可靠性和可维护性计划,并将这些计划与系统工程管理计划(SEMP)综合。

RAM 是系统维护概念的重要输入,以两种方式支持其他系统工程流程。首先,它们应被用于影响系统和系统支持定义(例如,系统架构取决于 RAM 需求);其次,这两种方式应作为系统验证的一部分使用(例如,系统分析或系统测试)。

根据特定行业的不同,通常将可用性视为这三个质量特性中最重要的一个,尤其是从使用方或采办方的视角来看。任何可用性损失通常都很容易转化为任务或生产损失以及成本增加。

详细阐述

可靠性

IEEE 可靠性协会给出的定义:

可靠性是一门设计工程学科,其应用科学知识确保产品在给定环境中执行其预期功能,直到需求结束。这包括设计在其整个生命周期中维护、测试以及支持产品的能力。最好将可靠性描述为随时间变化的产品性能。通过选择系统架构、材料、流程以及系统元素(包括软件和硬件),与其他设计学科同时完成;然后通过彻底的分析和测试来验证所做的选择。"要可靠,系统必须具有鲁棒性,即使在各种条件下,包括恶劣环境、不断变化的运行要求以及内部退化等,也必须避免故障模式"(Clausing 和 Frey, 2005)。因此,深入理解系统之间的交互、使用环境、其所处的运行条件以及潜在的故障模式和故障机制,对于设计和制造可靠的系统至关重要。图 3.6 展示了这些方面之间的交互。

LIFE CYCLE ANALYSES AND METHODS

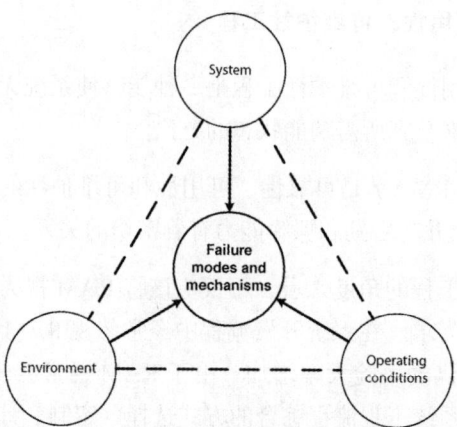

FIGURE 3.6 Interaction between system, environment, operating conditions, and failure modes and failure mechanisms. INCOSE SEH original figure created by Barnard. Usage per the INCOSE Notices page. All other rights reserved.

177 Reliability can be formally defined as "the ability of a system to perform as designed, without failure, in an operational environment, for a stated period of time" (Tortorella, 2015). Since "ability" is an abstract concept, many reliability metrics are available which can be used to measure and manage the reliability of a system during the development, utilization, and support stages (e.g., number of failures per time period, failure-free period, expected lifetime of nonrepairable parts, Mean Time Between Failure [MTBF]).

O'Connor and Kleyner (2012) state the objectives of reliability engineering, in the order of priority, are:

1. To apply engineering knowledge and specialist techniques to prevent or to reduce the likelihood or frequency of failures.
2. To identify and correct the causes of failures that do occur, despite the efforts to prevent them.
3. To determine ways of coping with failures that do occur, if their causes have not been corrected.
4. To apply methods for estimating the likely reliability of new designs and for analyzing reliability data.

The priority emphasis is important, since proactive prevention of failure is always more cost-effective than reactive correction of failure. Timely execution of appropriate reliability engineering activities is of utmost importance in achieving the required system reliability.

生命周期分析和方法

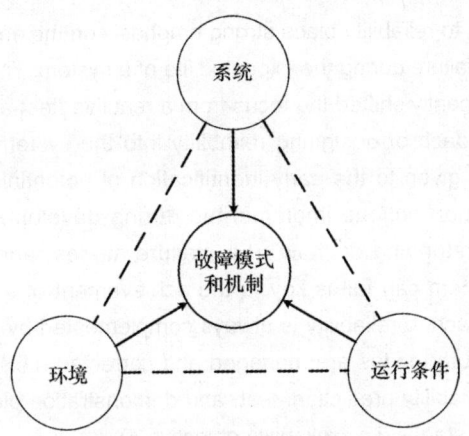

图 3.6 系统、环境、运行条件以及故障模式和故障机制之间的相互作用。INCOSE SEH 原始图由 Barnard 创建。按照 INCOSE 通知页使用。版权所有。

可靠性可以形式化地定义为"一个系统在规定的时间内,在运行环境中按设计运行而不发生故障的能力"(Tortorella,2015)。由于"能力"是一个抽象概念,因此有许多可靠性指标是可获得的,能够在开发、使用以及支持阶段用于衡量和管理系统的可靠性(例如,每个时间段的故障数、无故障周期、不可修复部件的预期生命、平均无故障时间 [MTBF])。

O'Connor 和 Kleyner(2012)指出,可靠性工程的目标按优先顺序为:

1. 应用工程知识和专业技术,从而防止或减少故障的可能性或频率。

2. 尽管做了大量的努力来预防,但确实发生了故障,识别导致故障的因素并予以纠正。

3. 在故障原因未得到纠正的情况下,确定应对故障的方法。

4. 应用估算新设计可能的可靠性和分析可靠性数据的方法。

重点优先很重要,因为积极主动预防故障总是比被动纠正故障更具成本效益。及时执行适当的可靠性工程活动对于实现所要求的系统可靠性至关重要。

LIFE CYCLE ANALYSES AND METHODS

Modern approaches to reliability place strong emphasis on the engineering processes required to prevent failure during the expected life of a system. The concept of "design for reliability" has recently shifted the focus from a reactive "test-analyze-fix" approach to a proactive approach of designing reliability into the system. This requires that design attention be given to the early identification of potential failure modes, with subsequent mitigation actions implemented during development (i.e., reliability objective 1). Understanding of "how" (i.e., failure modes) and "why" (i.e., failure mechanisms) a system can fail is key to the achievement of reliability. In practice, this proactive approach to reliability is always complemented by a reactive approach where observed failure modes are managed and corrected (i.e., reliability objectives 2 and 3). Finally, reliability prediction, test, and demonstration play an important role during development stages (i.e., reliability objective 4).

"Design for reliability" implies that reliability should receive adequate attention during requirements analysis. Reliability requirements may be specified either in qualitative or quantitative terms, depending on the specific industry. Care should be taken with quantitative requirements, since verification by test of reliability is often not practical (especially for high reliability requirements). Also, the misuse of some reliability metrics (e.g., MTBF) frequently results in "playing the numbers game" during system development, instead of focusing on the engineering effort necessary to achieve reliability (Barnard, 2008). For example, MTBF is often used as an indicator of "expected life" of an item, which is incorrect. It is therefore recommended that other reliability metrics be used for quantitative requirements (e.g., reliability (as success probability) at a specific time, or failure-free period).

Appropriate reliability engineering activities should be selected and tailored according to the objectives of the specific project. These activities should be captured in the reliability program plan. The plan should indicate which activities will be performed, the planned timing of the activities, the level of detail required for the activities, and the parties responsible for execution of the activities. ANSI/GEIA-STD-0009 Reliability Program Standard for Systems Design, Development, and Manufacturing which supports a system life cycle approach to reliability engineering, can be referenced for this purpose. This standard addresses not only hardware and software failures but also other common failure causes (e.g., manufacturing, operator error, operator maintenance, training, quality). "At the heart of the standard is a systematic 'design-reliability-in' process, which includes three elements:

- Progressive understanding of system-level operational and environmental loads and the resulting loads and stresses that occur throughout the structure of the system.

现代可靠性方法着重强调在系统预期生命周期内预防故障所需的工程流程。"可靠性设计"的概念最近从被动的"测试—分析—修复"方法聚焦到主动的系统可靠性设计方法。这要求设计关注早期的识别潜在故障模式，并在开发流程中实施后续缓解措施（即可靠性目标1）。理解系统"如何"（即故障模式）且"为什么"（即故障机制）系统会发生故障是实现可靠性的关键。在实践中，这种积极主动的可靠性方法总是由被动方法来补充的，在这种方法中，观察到的故障模式得到管理和纠正（即可靠性目标2和3）。最后，可靠性预测、测试以及演示在开发阶段（即可靠性目标4）发挥着重要作用。

"可靠性设计"意味着在需求分析时，可靠性应得到足够的重视。可靠性需求可能以定性或定量的方式规定，具体取决于特定行业。由于通过可靠性测试进行验证通常不可行（尤其是对于高可靠性需求），因此应谨慎对待定量的需求。此外，滥用一些可靠性指标（如MTBF），经常导致系统开发过程中"玩数字游戏"，而不是专注于实现可靠性所需的工程工作（Barnard，2008）。例如，MTBF通常用作项目"预期生命"的指标，这是不正确的。因此，建议将其他可靠性指标用于定量的需求（例如，特定时间或无故障期的可靠性，亦即成功的概率）。

应根据特定项目的目标选择定制适当的可靠性工程活动。这些活动应包含在可靠性计划中。该计划应说明将执行哪些活动、活动的计划时间安排、活动所需的详细程度以及负责执行活动的各方。为此，可参考 ANSI/GEIA-STD-0009 系统设计、开发和制造可靠性计划标准，该标准支持可靠性工程的系统生命周期方法。本标准不仅涉及硬件和软件故障，还涉及其他常见故障因素（如制造、操作人员错误、操作人员维护、培训、质量）。"该标准的核心是一个系统的'设计中的可靠性'流程，包括三个元素：

- 逐步了解系统级运行和环境负荷，以及由此产生的整个系统结构的负荷和压力。

LIFE CYCLE ANALYSES AND METHODS

- Progressive identification of the resulting failure modes and mechanisms.
- Aggressive mitigation of surfaced failure modes."

178 ANSI/GEIA-STD-0009 (2008) consists of the following objectives:

- Understand acquirer / user requirements and constraints.
- Design and redesign for reliability.
- Produce reliable systems / products.
- Monitor and assess user reliability.

The reliability program plan is often used to capture a forward-looking view on how to achieve reliability objectives. Complementary to the reliability program plan is the reliability case which provides a retrospective (and documented) view on achieved objectives during the system life cycle.

"Failure mode avoidance" approaches attempt to improve reliability of a system primarily early during development stages. It is performed by evaluating system functions, technology maturity, system architecture, redundancy, design options, etc., in terms of potential failure modes. The most significant improvements in system reliability can be achieved by avoiding physical failure modes in the first place and not by minor improvements after the system has been conceived, designed, and produced.

Reliability engineering activities can be divided into two groups: engineering analyses and tests and failure analyses. These activities are supported by various reliability management activities (e.g., design procedures, design checklists, design reviews, electronic part derating guidelines, preferred parts lists, preferred supplier lists).

Engineering analyses and tests refer to traditional design analyses and test methods performed during system development. Included in this group are Finite Element Analysis (FEA), Computational Fluid Dynamics (CFD), vibration and shock analysis, load-strength analysis, thermal analysis and measurement, electrical and mechanical stress analysis, wear-out life prediction, Accelerated Life Testing (ALT), and Highly Accelerated Life Testing (HALT).

Failure analyses refer to traditional reliability engineering analyses to improve understanding of cause-and-effect relationships. Included in this group are Failure Mode and Effects Analysis (FMEA), Fault Tree Analysis (FTA), Reliability Block Diagram (RBD) analysis, systems modeling, Monte Carlo simulation, failure data analysis, root cause analysis, and reliability growth analysis.

- 逐步识别产生的故障模式和机制。

- 积极缓解表面的故障模式。"

ANSI/GEIA-STD-0009（2008）包括以下目标：

- 理解采办方/使用方的需求和限制。

- 可靠性设计和再设计。

- 生产可靠的系统/产品。

- 监控和评估用户可靠性。

可靠性计划通常用于获取关于如何实现可靠性目标的前瞻性观点。可靠性用例是对可靠性项目计划的补充，它提供了系统生命周期内实现目标的具有回溯性要求（并记录）的视图。

"故障模式避免"方法主要是在开发阶段的早期尝试提高系统的可靠性。根据潜在故障模式，通过评估系统功能、技术成熟度、系统架构、冗余、设计选项等来执行。在系统可靠性方面，最显著的改进可以通过首先避免物理故障模式而实现，而不是在系统构思、设计和生产后进行微小的改进来实现。

可靠性工程活动可分为两组：工程分析和测试以及故障分析。这些活动由各种可靠性管理活动支持（例如，设计程序、设计检查表、设计评审、电子器件降低定额值指南、首选零件清单、首选供应商清单）。

工程分析和测试是指在系统开发流程中执行的传统设计分析和测试方法。这包括有限元分析（FEA）、计算流体力学（CFD）、振动和冲击分析、负载强度分析、热分析和测量、电气和机械应力分析、磨损生命预测、加速寿命试验（ALT）以及高加速寿命试验（HALT）。

故障分析是指传统的可靠性工程分析，目的是提高对因果关系的理解。这包括故障模式和影响分析（FMEA）、故障树分析（FTA）、可靠性块图（RBD）分析、系统建模、蒙特卡罗仿真、故障数据分析、根本原因分析以及可靠性增长分析。

LIFE CYCLE ANALYSES AND METHODS

Availability

As part of system effectiveness, availability requirements should be carefully derived from user needs and specified during system definition. These requirements play a key role in influencing a multitude of design decisions and availability should be monitored during the utilization and support stages. The simplest definition of availability is the ratio between uptime and total time of a system, usually expressed as a percentage. Since total time consists of uptime and downtime, availability is therefore dependent on the reliability (influencing uptime) and maintainability (influencing downtime) of the system. Furthermore, downtime is obviously highly dependent on the system support environment during the support stage (influencing delay times). Due to these direct relationships, availability is governed by reliability, maintainability, and various logistics engineering aspects. Since availability is a function of both reliability and maintainability (including logistics aspects), achievement of a required availability usually requires trade-offs between reliability and maintainability, and other requirements and constraints (e.g., performance, cost).

Availability can be formally defined as "the probability that a system, when used under stated conditions, will operate satisfactorily at any point in time as required" (Blanchard, 2004). It may be expressed and defined as inherent, achieved, or operational availability:

- *Inherent availability (A_i)* is based only on the inherent reliability and maintainability of the system. It assumes an ideal support environment (e.g., readily available tools, spares, maintenance personnel) and excludes preventive maintenance, logistics delay time, and administrative delay time.

- *Achieved availability (A_a)* is similar to inherent availability, except that preventive (i.e., scheduled) maintenance is included. It excludes logistics delay time and administrative delay time.

- *Operational availability (A_o)* assumes an actual operational environment and therefore also includes logistics delay time and administrative delay time.

Inherent availability thus focusses primarily on "design for reliability and maintainability" activities. Achieved availability takes a broader view to include preventive maintenance, and operational availability includes possible logistics and administrative delays.

A service-level agreement (SLA) between a service provider and an acquirer typically includes availability performance, usually measured for a certain period (e.g., one year) and is then translated into the maximum duration of downtime allowed for that period.

可用性

作为系统有效性的一部分，可用性需求应仔细地从用户需求中派生出来，并在系统定义中指定。这些需求在影响众多设计决策方面起着关键作用，应在使用和支持阶段监控可用性。可用性最简单的定义是系统正常运行时间与总时间之间的比率，通常以百分比表示。由于总时间包括正常运行时间和停机时间，因此可用性取决于系统的可靠性（影响正常运行时间）和可维护性（影响停机时间）。此外，在支持阶段，停机时间显然高度依赖于系统支持环境（影响延迟时间）。由于这些直接的关系，可用性受可靠性、可维护性和各种后勤工程方面的制约。由于可用性是可靠性和可维护性（包括后勤方面）的函数，因此实现所需的可用性通常需要在可靠性和可维护性以及其他要求和约束（如性能、成本）之间进行权衡。

可用性可以形式化地定义为"在规定条件下使用的系统在任何时间点按要求令人满意地运行的概率"（Blanchard，2004）。它可以表示且定义为固有的、可实现的或运行的可用性：

- *固有可用性*（A_i）仅基于系统的固有可靠性和可维护性。其假设有一个理想的支持环境（例如，现成的工具、备件、维护人员），不包括预防性维护、后勤延迟时间和管理延迟时间。

- 除了包括预防性（即计划）维护以外，*实现可用性*（A_a）与固有可用性相似。其不包括后勤延迟时间和行政延迟时间。

- *运行可用性*（A_o）假定实际的运行环境，因此也包括后勤延迟时间和管理延迟时间。

因此，固有可用性主要聚焦"可靠性和可维护性设计"活动；实现可用性从更广泛的视角考虑，包括预防性维护；而运行可用性包括可能的后勤和管理延迟。

服务提供商和采办方之间的服务水平协议（SLA）往往包括可用性性能，通常在特定时期（如一年）内进行衡量，然后转化为该时期允许的最长停机时间。

LIFE CYCLE ANALYSES AND METHODS

Maintainability

An objective in SE is to design and develop a system that can be maintained effectively, safely, in the least amount of time, in a cost-effective manner, and with a minimum expenditure of support resources without adversely affecting the mission of that system. Maintainability refers to all measures and activities implemented during the design, production, and use of a system that reduces the required maintenance (as measured in maintenance frequency, repair hours, tools, cost, skills, and facilities). Maintainability is thus the ability of a system to be maintained, whereas maintenance constitutes a series of actions to be taken to restore or retain a system in an effective operational state. Maintainability must be inherent or "built into" the design, while maintenance is the result of design. Maintainability can formally be defined as "the ability of a system to be repaired and restored to service when maintenance is conducted by personnel using specified skill levels and prescribed procedures and resources" (Tortorella, 2015). Case 4 (Design for Maintainability-Incubators) from Section 6.4 illustrates the importance of maintainability.

Maintenance can be broken down into the following groups:

- *Corrective maintenance*: unscheduled maintenance accomplished, as a result of failure, to restore a system to a specified level of performance.

- *Preventive maintenance*: scheduled maintenance accomplished to retain a system at a specified level of performance by providing systematic inspection and servicing or preventing impending failures through periodic item replacements.

- *Predictive maintenance*: scheduled maintenance based on the in-service condition of a system to estimate when maintenance should be performed.

- *System upgrades*: periodic maintenance to support system life extension and performance upgrades.

A maintainability engineering plan is often used to capture activities such as quantitative maintainability modeling and simulation, development of the system maintenance concept, level of repair analysis (LORA), diagnostic capabilities, identification of preventive maintenance activities, etc. It is thus closely related to logistics engineering (see Section 3.1.6). The maintainability engineering plan should consider various aspects such as interchangeability of parts, accessibility to parts for removal, and testability of equipment. Testability includes aspects such as built-in test (BIT) capability, diagnostic test equipment, and support software. Service providers such as telecommunication operators that serve the mass market may use OTA (Over-the-Air) technology to remotely provide maintenance (e.g., data transfer to update software or firmware). Like reliability, maintainability requirements should be derived from system availability requirements.

可维护性

系统工程的一个目标是设计和开发一个能够在最短时间内以成本效益高的方式进行有效、安全维护的系统，其支持资源的支出最小，并且不会对该系统的任务产生不利影响。可维护性是指在设计、生产和使用系统期间实施的所有措施和活动，从而减少所需求的维护（以维护频率、维修时间、工具、成本、技能以及设施衡量）。因此，可维护性是指系统维护的能力，而维护是指为恢复或保持系统处于有效运行状态而采取的一系列行动。可维护性必须是设计固有的或"内置的"，而维护是设计的结果。可维护性可以形式化地定义为"当人员使用规定的技能水平和规定的程序和资源进行维护时，系统维修和恢复使用的能力"（Tortorella，2015）。第 6.4 节中的案例 4（可维护性培养箱的设计）说明了可维护性的重要性。

维护可分为以下几组：

- *纠正性维护*：由于故障而完成的计划外维护，从而将系统恢复到指定的性能水平。

- *预防性维护*：通过提供系统检查和维修，或通过定期更换物品预防即将发生的故障，完成计划维护，从而使系统保持在规定的性能水平。

- *预测性维护*：基于系统在用状态的计划性维护，以估计何时应进行维护。

- *系统升级*：定期维护，以支持系统生命延长和性能升级。

维修性工程计划通常用于捕获活动，如定量维修性建模和仿真、系统维护概念的开发、维修水平分析（LORA）、诊断能力、防止性维护活动的识别等。因此，维修性工程计划与后勤工程密切相关（见 3.1.6 节）。维修性工程计划应考虑各个方面，如零件的互换性、拆卸零件的可及性以及设备的可测试性。可测试性包括内置测试（BIT）能力、诊断测试设备以及支持软件等方面。服务大众市场的电信操作员等服务提供商可以使用 OTA（Over-the-Air）技术远程提供维护（例如，用数据传输来更新软件或固件）。与可靠性一样，可维护性需求也应源自系统可用性需求。

LIFE CYCLE ANALYSES AND METHODS

Various maintainability metrics can be used to specify or measure maintainability. The most widely used metric, Mean Time to Repair (MTTR), measures the elapsed time to perform a certain maintenance activity. It typically includes time for activities such as failure detection/failure isolation (FD/FI), disassembly, active repair, reassembly, and finally system testing. It is important to note that MTTR refers to the mean time of the underlying probability distribution. Maintenance times tend to be lognormally distributed, especially for electronic systems without a built-in test capability and for many other electromechanical systems.

180 *Relationship with Other Engineering Disciplines*

As discussed in this section, RAM engineering is closely related to several other engineering disciplines. The primary objective of reliability engineering is prevention of failure. The primary objective of safety engineering is prevention and mitigation of harm under both normal and abnormal conditions (see Section 3.1.11). The primary objective of logistics engineering is the development of efficient logistics support (see Section 3.1.6). Furthermore, RAM is also related to engineering disciplines such as affordability (see Section 3.1.2), resilience engineering (see Section 3.1.9), and reusability of products in a product line (see Section 4.2.4). The life cycle cost (LCC) of a system is highly dependent on reliability and maintainability, which are considered major drivers in support resources and related in-service costs (see Section 3.1.2).

Many of these not only have "failure" as common theme, but they may also use similar activities, albeit from different viewpoints. For example, an FMEA may be applicable to reliability, safety, and logistics engineering. However, a reliability FMEA will be different to a safety or logistics FMEA, due to the different objectives. Common to all disciplines is the necessity of early implementation during the system life cycle.

More information on RAM can be found in ANSI/GEIA-STD-0009 (2008), Barnard (2008), Blanchard (2004), Clausing and Frey (2005), O'Connor and Kleyner (2012), and Tortorella (2015).

3.1.9 Resilience Engineering

Definition Resilience Engineering is an approach that provides required capability when facing adversity.

Resilience is a relatively new term in SE, appearing in the 2006 timeframe and becoming popularized around 2010. Resilience typically subsumes survivability. The recent application of "resilience" to engineered systems has led to a proliferation of alternative definitions. While the details of definitions will continue to be discussed and debated, there is general agreement that resilience of engineered systems is the ability to provide required capability when facing adversity.

可以使用各种可维护性指标来指定或测量可维护性。使用最广泛的指标是平均维修时间（MTTR），其衡量执行某项维护活动所花费的时间。其通常包括诸如故障检测/故障隔离（FD/FI）、拆卸、主动维修、重新组装以及最终系统测试等活动的时间。值得注意的是，MTTR 指的是潜在概率分布的平均时间。维护时间往往是对数正态分布的，尤其是对于没有内置测试能力的电子系统和许多其他机电系统。

与其他工程学科的关系

如本节所述，RAM 工程与其他几个工程学科密切相关。可靠性工程的主要目标是防止故障。安全工程的主要目标是在正常和异常条件下防止和减轻危害（见 3.1.11 节）。后勤工程的主要目标是开发高效的后勤保障（见 3.1.6 节）。此外，RAM 还与其他工程学科相关，如可承受性（见 3.1.2 节）、强韧性工程（见 3.1.9 节）以及产品线中产品的可重用性（见 4.2.4 节）。系统的生命周期成本（LCC）高度依赖于可靠性和可维护性，视其为支持资源和相关服务成本的主要驱动因素（见 3.1.2 节）。

其中许多人不仅将"故障"作为共同主题，而且可能会使用类似的活动，尽管观点不同。例如，FMEA 可能适用于可靠性、安全和后勤工程。然而，由于目标不同，可靠性 FMEA 将不同于安全或后勤 FMEA。所有学科的共同点是在系统生命周期中尽早实施的必要性。

有关 RAM 的更多信息，请参见 ANSI/GEIA-STD-0009（2008）、Barnard（2008）、Blanchard（2004）、Clausing 和 Frey（2005）、O'Connor 和 Kleyner（2012）以及 Tortorella（2015）。

3.1.9 强韧性工程

定义 强韧性工程是一种在面临逆境时提供所需能力的实施方法。

强韧性是系统工程中一个相对较新的术语，出现于 2006 年，并在 2010 年前后普及。强韧性通常包含生存能力。最近，"强韧性"在工程系统中的应用导致了备选定义的扩散。虽然定义的细节将继续讨论和辩论，但人们普遍认为，工程系统的强韧性是在面临逆境时提供所需能力的本领。

LIFE CYCLE ANALYSES AND METHODS

Key Concepts System development often focuses on system capability under nominal conditions. Resilience directs the SE focus to the system's ability to deliver capability when faced with adverse conditions. This perspective can be important to stakeholders but is sometimes overlooked. Resilience in the realm of SE involves identifying:

- the capabilities that are required of the system,
- the adverse conditions under which the system is required to deliver those capabilities, and
- the architecture and design that will ensure the system can provide the required capabilities.

It is important to emphasize that resilience focuses on providing the required capability—not necessarily with maintaining the architecture or composition of the system. While system continuity is one approach to achieving resilience, so is adaptability.

Elaboration

Scope of Resilience

The fundamental objectives of resilience are avoiding, withstanding, and recovering from adversity. In non-engineering contexts, resilience is often limited to the ability to recover after degradation. In the context of engineered systems, it is recommended that "avoiding" and "withstanding" adversity be considered in scope (Jackson and Ferris, 2016). Resilience, as does SE, applies to cyber-physical, organizational, and conceptual systems.

Scope of the Adversity

For the purpose of resilience, adversity is anything that might degrade the capability provided by a system. Achieving resilience requires consideration of all sources (e.g., environmental sources, human sources, system failure) and types of adversity (e.g., from adversarial, friendly, or neutral parties; adversities that are malicious or accidental; adversities that are expected or not). Adversities may be issues, risks, or unknown-unknowns. Adversities may arise from inside or outside the system. Adversity may be a single event or may take the form of complex causal chain of conditions and events that stress the system over multiple periods of time.

Taxonomy of Resilience Objectives

Resilience, and engineering its achievement, can be facilitated by considering a taxonomy of its objectives. A twolayer objectives-based taxonomy includes:

关键概念　系统开发通常聚焦标称条件下的系统能力。强韧性直接将系统工程聚焦于在面临不利条件时系统交付的本领。这一观点对利益相关方可能很重要，但有时会将其忽视。系统工程领域的强韧性包括识别：

- 系统需求的能力；
- 要求系统交付那些能力的不利条件；
- 确保系统能够提供所需能力的架构和设计。

重要的是强调强韧性聚焦于提供所需的能力，而不一定是维护架构或系统组合。虽然系统连续性是实现强韧性的一种实施方法，但适应性也是如此。

详细阐述

强韧性范围

强韧性的基本目标是避免、抵御和从逆境中恢复。在各种非工程环境中，强韧性通常仅限于退化后的恢复本领。在各个工程系统的背景下，建议在范围内考虑"避免"和"抵御"逆境（Jackson 和 Ferris，2016）。强韧性和系统工程一样，适用于赛博物理、组织以及概念系统。

逆境的范围

就强韧性而言，逆境是指任何可能降低系统所提供能力的因素。实现强韧性需要考虑所有来源（例如，环境来源、人为来源、系统故障）和逆境类型（例如，来自敌对、友好或中立方，恶意或意外的逆境，预期或非预期的逆境）。逆境可能是问题、风险或未知的未知因素。逆境可能来自系统内部或外部。逆境可能是单个事件，也可能是一连串复杂的条件和事件，在多个时间段对系统造成压力。

强韧性目标分类

通过考虑其目标的分类，可以促进强韧性及其工程目标达成。基于两层目标的分类法包括：

LIFE CYCLE ANALYSES AND METHODS

- First layer, the fundamental objectives of resilience and
- Second layer, the means objectives of resilience.

The layers relate by many-to-many relationships (Brtis, 2016) (Jackson and Ferris, 2013).

Taxonomy Layer 1: Resilience can be said to equate to achieving its three *fundamental objectives*. These are:

- **Avoid:** eliminate or reduce exposure to stress.
- **Withstand:** resist capability degradation when stressed.
- **Recover:** replenish lost capability after degradation.

Taxonomy Layer 2: These fundamental objectives can be achieved through the pursuit of *means objectives*. Means objectives are not values or ends in themselves. Their value resides in their ability to help achieve resilience and its three fundamental objectives. The means objectives include:

- **Adaptive Response:** reacting appropriately and dynamically to the specific situation to limit consequences and avoid degradation of system capability.
- **Agility:** ability of a system to adapt to deliver required capability in unpredictably evolving conditions.
- **Anticipation:** establishing awareness of the nature of potential adversities, their likely consequences, and appropriate responses, prior to the adversity stressing the system.
- **Constrain:** limit the propagation of damage within the system.
- **Continuity:** ensuring the endurance of the delivery of required capability, while and after being stressed.
- **Disaggregation:** dispersing missions, functions, or system elements across multiple systems or system elements.
- **Evolution:** restructuring the system to address changes to the adversity or needs over time.
- **Graceful Degradation:** ability of the system to transition to a state that has acceptable, potentially limited capabilities.
- **Integrity:** the quality of being complete and unaltered (ISO 13008 (2022)).
- **Prepare:** developing and maintaining courses of action that address predicted or anticipated adversity.

- 第一层，强韧性的基本目标；
- 第二层，强韧性的手段目标。

各层之间存在多对多关系（Brtis，2016）（Jackson 和 Ferris，2013）。

分类法第1层：强韧性可以说等同于达到其三个基本目标。分别是：

- **避免**：消除或减少暴露压力。
- **抵御**：承受压力时抵抗能力下降。
- **恢复**：在能力下降后补充失去的能力。

分类法第2层：这些基本目标可以通过追求手段目标来达到。意味着目标本身不是价值或目的。它们的价值在于帮助实现强韧性及其三个基本目标的能力。手段目标包括：

- **自适应响应**：对特定情况做出适当和动态的反应，从而限制后果，避免系统能力下降。
- **敏捷性**：在不可预测的条件下，系统适应交付所需能力的本领。
- **预测**：在逆境带给系统压力之前，建立对潜在逆境性质、其可能的后果和适当反应的认识。
- **约束**：限制系统内损坏的扩散。
- **连续性**：确保在承受压力的同时和之后持续交付所需的能力。
- **解聚性**：将任务、功能或系统元素分散在多个系统或系统元素之间。
- **演进性**：系统重组以应对逆境或需求随时间的变化。
- **正常降级**：系统过渡到具有可接受、潜在有限能力的状态的本领。
- **完整性**：完整和不变的质量［ISO 13008（2022）］。
- **准备度**：制定和维护应对预测或预期逆境的行动方案。

LIFE CYCLE ANALYSES AND METHODS

- **Prevent:** deterring or precluding the realization of adversity.
- **Re-architect:** modifying the system architecture for improved resilience.
- **Redeploy:** restructuring resources to provide capabilities after stress.
- **Robustness:** the ability of a structure to withstand adverse and unforeseen events or consequences of human errors without being damaged (damage insensitivity) (ISO 8930 (2021)).
- **Situational Awareness:** perception of elements in the environment, and a comprehension of their meaning, and could include a projection of the future status of perceived elements and the risk associated with that status (ISO 17757 (2019)).
- **Tolerance:** the ability of a material/structure to resist failure due to the presence of flaws for a specified period of unrepaired usage (damage tolerance) (ISO 21347 (2005)).
- **Transform:** changing aspects of system behavior.
- **Understand:** developing and maintaining useful representations of required system capabilities, how those capabilities are generated, the system environment, and the potential for degradation due to adversity.

The SEBOK section on resilience provides a more extensive taxonomy of design, architecture, and operational techniques for achieving resilience.

Key Activities, Methods, and Tools

While resilience must be considered throughout the SE life cycle, it is critical that resilience be considered in the early life cycle stages: those that lead to the development of resilience requirements. Once resilience requirements are established, they can, and should, be managed along with all other requirements in the trade space through the system life cycle. As shown in Table 3.3, Brtis and McEvilley (2019) identify specific considerations that need to be included in the early life cycle activities.

Content, Structure, and Development of Resilience Requirements

Brtis and McEvilley (2019) investigated the content and structure needed to specify resilience requirements. Resilience requirements often take the form of a resilience scenario. There can be many such scenario threads in the ConOps or OpsCon. The following information is often part of a resilience scenario:

- **抵抗性**：制止或阻止逆境的实现。
- **架构再设计**：修改系统架构以提高强韧性。
- **再部署**：重组资源，从而在受到压力后提供能力。
- **鲁棒性**：抵御不利和不可预见事件或人为错误后果而不受损的结构能力（损坏不敏感）[ISO 8930（2021）]。
- **态势感知**：感知环境中的元素，并理解其含义，包括预测感知元素的未来状态以及与该状态相关的风险[ISO 17757（2019）]。
- **容忍性**：材料/结构在规定的未修复使用时间内抵抗因缺陷而导致的故障的能力（损伤容忍性）[ISO 21347（2005）]。
- **转型**：改变系统行为的各个方面。
- **理解**：开发和维护所需系统能力的有用表述：那些能力是如何产生的、系统环境，以及由于逆境导致的功能下降的可能性。

关于强韧性的 SEBOK 部分提供了实现强韧性的更广泛的设计、架构和运行技术分类。

关键活动、方法和工具

虽然必须在整个系统工程生命周期中考虑强韧性，但在生命周期的早期阶段考虑强韧性至关重要：这些阶段会导致强韧性需求的发展。一旦建立了强韧性需求，就可以并且应该在整个系统生命周期中与权衡空间中的所有其他需求一起进行管理。如表 3.3 所示，Brtis 和 McEvilley（2019）确定了需要纳入早期生命周期活动的具体考虑因素。

强韧性需求的内容、结构和发展

Brtis 和 McEvilley（2019）调查了规定强韧性要求所需的内容和结构。强韧性需求通常采取强韧性场景的形式。ConOps 或 OpsCon 中可能有许多这样的场景线索。以下信息通常是强韧性场景的一部分：

LIFE CYCLE ANALYSES AND METHODS

TABLE 3.3   Resilience considerations

Business or Mission Analysis Process
- Defining the problem space includes identification of adversities and expectations for performance under those adversities.
- ConOps, OpsCon, and solution classes consider the ability to avoid, withstand, and recover from the adversities
- Evaluation of alterative solution classes consider the ability to deliver required capabilities under adversity

Stakeholder Needs and Requirements Definition Process
- The stakeholder set includes persons who understand potential adversities and stakeholder resilience needs.
- Identifying stakeholder needs identifies expectations for capability under adverse conditions, and degraded/alternate, but useful, modes of operation.
- Operational concept scenarios include resilience scenarios.
- Transforming stakeholder needs to stakeholder requirements includes stakeholder resilience requirements.
- Analysis of stakeholder requirements includes resilience scenarios in the adverse operational environment.

System Requirements Definition Process
- Resilience is considered in the identification of requirements.
- Achieving resilience and other adversity-driven considerations is addressed holistically.

System Architecture Definition Process
- Viewpoints selected support the representation of resilience.
- Resilience requirements significantly limit and guide the range of acceptable architectures. It is critical that resilience requirements are mature when used for architecture selection.
- Individuals developing candidate architectures are familiar with architectural techniques for achieving resilience.
- Achieving resilience and other adversity-driven considerations are addressed holistically.

Design Definition Process
- Individuals developing candidate designs are familiar with design techniques for achieving resilience.
- Achieving resilience and the other adversity-driven considerations are addressed holistically.

Risk Management Process
- Risk management is planned to handle risks and opportunities identified by resilience activities.

From Brtis and McEvilley (2019). Used with permission. All other rights reserved.

- Operational concept/scenario name
- System or system element of interest
- Capability(s) of interest their metric(s) and units
- Target value(s) (required amount) of the capability(s)

表 3.3　强韧性考虑因素

业务或任务分析流程

- 定义问题空间，包括识别逆境以及在这些逆境下对性能的期望。
- ConOps、OpsCon 和解决方案类，应考虑从逆境中避免、抵御和恢复的本领。
- 备选解决方案类的评估，应考虑在逆境中交付所需能力的本领。

利益相关方需要和需求定义流程

- 利益相关方集合，包括理解潜在逆境和利益相关方强韧性需要的人员。
- 确定利益相关方需要确定在不利条件下对能力的预期，以及降级 / 备选但有用的运行模式。
- 运行概念场景，包括强韧性场景。
- 将利益相关方需要转化为利益相关方需求，包括利益相关方强韧性需求。
- 利益相关方需求分析，包括不利运行环境中的强韧性场景。

系统需求定义流程

- 在确定需求时考虑强韧性。
- 实现强韧性和其他逆境驱动的考虑因素得到全面解决。

系统架构定义流程

- 选择的视角支持强韧性的表达。
- 强韧性需求极大地限制和指导可接受架构的范围。当用于架构选择时，强韧性需求必须成熟。
- 开发备选架构的人员应熟悉实现强韧性的架构技术。
- 全面处理了实现强韧性和其他逆境驱动因素。

设计定义流程

- 开发备选设计的人员应熟悉实现强韧性的设计技术。
- 全面处理了实现强韧性和其他逆境驱动因素。

风险管理流程

- 计划进行风险管理，以处理强韧性活动指定的风险和机遇。

来自 Brtis 和 McEvilley（2019）。经许可使用。版权所有。

- 运行概念 / 场景名称；
- 感兴趣的系统或系统元素；
- 感兴趣的能力及其指标和单位；
- 能力的目标值（需求数量）；

LIFE CYCLE ANALYSES AND METHODS

- System modes of operation during the scenario (e.g., operational, training, exercise, maintenance, update)
- System states expected during the scenario
- Adversity(s) being considered, their source, and type
- Potential stresses on the system, their metrics, units, and values (Note: Stresses are a type of adversity. They are proximate forces or influences, directly affecting the system that can cause degradation of the system's ability to deliver required capability.)
- Resilience related scenario constraints (e.g., cost, schedule, policies, regulations)
- Timeframe and sub-timeframes of interest
- Resilience metric(s), units, determination method(s), and resilience metric target(s) (e.g., expected availability of required capability, maximum allowed degradation, maximum length of degradation, total delivered capability). Note: There may be multiple resilience targets (e.g., threshold, objective, As Resilient as Practicable (ARAP)).

Importantly, many of these parameters may vary over the timeframe of the scenario. Figure 3.7 notionally shows the required capability, the stress on the system, and the delivered capability as they vary as a function of time. A single resilience scenario may involve multiple stresses, which may be involved at multiple times throughout the scenario.

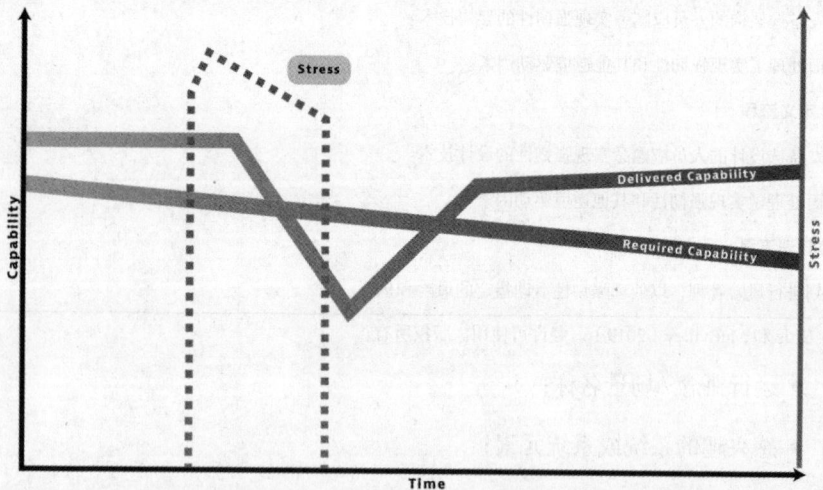

FIGURE 3.7 Timewise values of notional resilience scenario parameters. INCOSE SEH original figure created by Brtis and Cureton. Usage per the INCOSE Notices page. All other rights reserved.

生命周期分析和方法

- 场景中的系统运行模式（例如，运行、培训、演习、维护、更新）；
- 场景中预期的系统状态；
- 考虑的逆境、来源和类型；
- 系统、其指标、单位和价值上的潜在压力（注意：压力是一种逆境。是近因或影响，直接影响系统，可能导致系统交付所需能力的本领下降）；
- 强韧性相关场景约束（例如，成本、进度、政策、法规）；
- 感兴趣的时间框架和子时间框架；
- 强韧性指标、单位、确定方法以及强韧性指标目标（例如，需求能力的预期可用性、允许的最大退化、退化的最长时间、总交付能力）。注：可能有多个强韧性目标（例如，阈值、目标、可行的强韧性）。

重要的是，这些参数中的许多可能会在场景的时间框架内发生变化。图 3.7 从概念上显示了需求的能力、系统压力以及交付的能力，因为它们随时间而变化。一个单一的强韧性场景可能涉及多个压力，在整个场景中可能多次涉及这些压力。

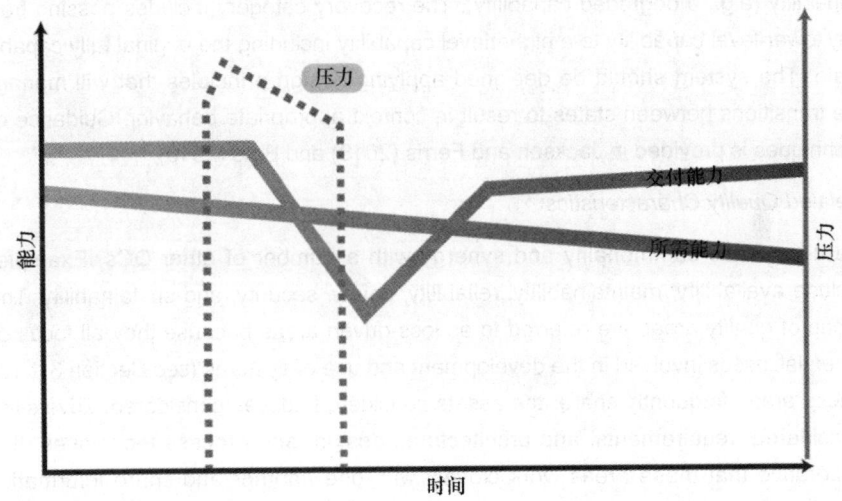

图 3.7 名义韧性场景参数的时间值。INCOSE SEH 原始图由 Brtis 和 Cureton 创建。按照 INCOSE 通知页使用。版权所有。

LIFE CYCLE ANALYSES AND METHODS

184   Requirement Patterns for Resilience

An example of a natural language pattern for representing this information would be:

`The<system, mode(t), state(t)>encountering<adversity(t), source, type>,which imposes<stress(t), metric, units, value(t)>thus affecting delivery of<capability(t), metric, units>during<scenario timeframe, start time, end time, units>and under <scenario constraints>,shall achieve<resilience target(t) (include excluded effects)>for<resilience metric, units, determination method>.`

Here, "(t)" is used to indicate that the item may vary as a function of time.

System State Considerations

When a system encounters an adversity, the system may pass through a number of states, from a fully capable state to a state minimally acceptable to the system stakeholders. Intermediate states include damaged or partially capable states. The transitions between these states fall into three categories. The robustness category defines the transitions for which the system maintains its level of capability. These transitions include maintaining fully capable or partially capable states. The tolerance category includes passing from any higher level of capability to a lower level of capability (e.g., a degraded capability). The recovery category includes passing from any lower-level capability to a higherlevel capability including the original fully capable state. The system should be designed applying design principles that will manage the transitions between states to result in context appropriate behavior. Guidance on techniques is provided in Jackson and Ferris (2013) and Brtis (2016).

Related Quality Characteristics

Resilience has commonality and synergy with a number of other QCs. Examples include availability, maintainability, reliability, safety, security, and sustainability. This group of quality areas are referred to as loss-driven areas because they all focus on potential losses involved in the development and use of systems (see Section 3.1.13). These areas frequently share: the assets considered, losses considered, adversities considered, requirements, and architectural, design, and process techniques. It is imperative that these areas work closely with one another and share information and decision-making in order to achieve a holistic approach that avoids unbalanced emphasis in any one area.

Further information and references on resilience (including the state-of-the-art) can be found in the resilience section of the SEBoK.

强韧性需求模式

表示此信息的自然语言模式示例如下：

这个 < 系统，模式（t），状态（t）> 遭遇 < 逆境（t），来源，类型 >，其中施加 < 应力（t）、指标、单位、值（t）>，从在 < 场景时间框架，开始时间，结束时间，单位 > 及以下 < 情景约束 > 影响 < 能力（t）的交付指标，单位 >，对于 < 强韧指标、单位、测定方法 > 应达到的 < 强韧性目标（t）（包括排除效应）>。

此处，"（t）"表示项目可能随时间而变化。

系统状态注意事项

当系统遭遇逆境时，系统可能会经历许多状态，从完全有能力的状态到系统利益相关方可接受的最低状态。中间状态包括损坏状态或部分可用状态。这些状态之间的转换分为三类。鲁棒性类别定义系统保持其能力水平的转换。这些转换包括保持完全可用或部分可用的状态。容忍性类别包括从任何较高水平的能力转移到较低水平的能力（例如，能力退化）。恢复性类别包括从任何较低水平的能力转移到较高水平的能力，包括原始的完全可用状态。应该应用设计原则设计系统，这些原则将管理状态之间的转换，从而在背景环境中产生适当的行为。Jackson 和 Ferris（2013）和 Brtis（2016）提供了技术指导。

相关质量特性

强韧性与许多其他 QC 具有共性和协同效应。示例包括可用性、可维护性、可靠性、安全性、安保性以及可持续性。这组质量领域被称为损失驱动领域，因其都聚焦于系统开发和使用中涉及的潜在损失（见 3.1.13 节）。这些领域经常共享：考虑的资产、考虑的损失、考虑的逆境、需求以及架构、设计和工艺技术。这些领域必须彼此密切合作，共享信息和决策，从而实现一种全面的实施方法，避免对任何一个领域的不平衡的重视。

有关强韧性（包括最先进的）的更多信息和参考可在 SEBoK 的强韧性部分找到。

LIFE CYCLE ANALYSES AND METHODS

3.1.10 Sustainability Engineering

Definition Sustainability Engineering is an approach that supports the circular economy over its life.

Key Concepts Design for sustainability is defined as the process that considers environmental and social aspects as key elements in product design to reduce the harmful impacts of the product throughout its life cycle (Sharma, et al., 2020). It entails environmentally conscious decisions that promote responsible disposability via product recycling and materials reuse as options for the preservation of scarce material resources. Sustainability and disposability are critical components toward the circular economy, which is based on a production and consumption model that involves sharing, reusing, repairing, and recycling existing products and materials as much as possible, expanding the life cycle of products, minimizing waste and pollution, and creating a closed-loop system (Geissdoerfer, et al., 2020). These goals are consistent with the 17 Sustainable Development Goals that were adopted by all UN Member States in 2015, as part of the 2030 Agenda for Sustainable Development (Haskins, 2021).

Elaboration

Role of Sustainability and Disposability in SE

Addressing sustainability effectively in context is highly complex, requiring the integration of multiple disciplines in balancing a wide range of interdependent issues (Pearce, et al., 2012). Sustainability is essential given the significant impacts that the SE processes, and the resulting systems, have had, and continue to have, on the environment. Achieving sustainability must include a holistic adoption of environmental stewardship in engineering activities (Alwi, et al., 2014) (Rosen, 2012).

The focus of environmental impact analysis is on potential harmful effects of a proposed system's development, production, utilization, support, and retirement stages. Concern extends over the full life cycle of the system, from the materials used and scrap waste from the production process, operation of the system, replacement parts, consumables and their packaging, to final disposal of the system.

Disposal analysis is a significant analysis area within environmental impact analysis. During System Architecture Definition and Design Definition (see Sections 2.3.5.4 and 2.3.5.5), one goal is to maximize the economic value of the residual system elements after useful life and minimize the amount of waste materials. Design for disassembly has become an important consideration in the design process so that the products are created in a way that minimizes destructive separation of system elements such that the material can be reused in future generations of products, remanufacturing, or recycling processes (Abuzied, et al., 2020). This may include designing for transformation (e.g., decomposition, biodegradation).

3.1.10 可持续性工程

定义 可持续性工程是一种在整个生命周期内支持循环经济的方法。

关键概念 可持续性设计是指将环境和社会因素视为产品设计中的关键因素，以减少产品在整个生命周期中的有害影响的流程（Sharma 等，2020）。这需要做出具有环保意识的决定，通过产品回收和材料再利用，促进负责任的处置，以此作为保护稀缺物质资源的选择方案。可持续性和可处置性是循环经济的关键组成部分，循环经济以生产和消费模式为基础，包括尽可能多地共享、再利用、修复以及回收现有产品和材料，扩大产品的生命周期，最大限度地减少废物和污染，以及创建闭环系统（Geissdoerfer 等，2020）。这些目标与联合国所有会员国 2015 年通过的 17 项可持续发展目标一致，这些目标是 2030 年可持续发展议程的一部分（Haskins，2021）。

详细阐述

可持续性和可处置性在系统工程中的作用

在环境中有效解决可持续性问题非常复杂，需要整合多个学科来平衡广泛的相互依赖的问题（Pearce 等，2012）。鉴于这些流程及其产生的系统已经并将继续对环境产生重大影响，可持续性至关重要。实现可持续性必须包括在工程活动中全面采用环境管理（Alwi 等，2014）（Rosen，2012）。

环境影响分析的焦点是所提出系统的开发、生产、使用、支持以及退役阶段的潜在有害影响。从生产流程中使用的材料和废料、系统运行、更换零件、耗材及其包装，到系统的最终处置，系统的整个生命周期都会受到关注。

处置性分析是环境影响分析中的一个重要分析领域。在系统架构定义和设计定义（见 2.3.5.4 节和 2.3.5.5 节）期间，一个目标是最大限度地提高使用寿命结束的剩余系统元素的经济价值，并最大限度地减少废料数量。拆卸设计已成为设计流程中的一个重要考虑因素，因此产品的制造方式应尽量减少系统元素的破坏性分离，以便材料可以在未来几代产品、再制造或回收流程中重复使用（Abuzied 等，2020）。这可能包括转化设计（例如分解、生物降解）。

LIFE CYCLE ANALYSES AND METHODS

Key Activities, Tools, and Methods of Sustainability and Disposability

The ISO 14000 (2015) series of environmental management standards are an excellent resource for methods to analyze and assess industrial operations and their impacts on the environment. Attention to environmental regulations should be addressed in the earliest activities of requirements analysis. The Øresund Bridge (see Section 6.2.) is an example of how early analysis of potential environmental impacts ensures that measures are taken in concept, development, and production to protect the environment with positive results. Two key elements of the success of this initiative were the continual monitoring of the environmental status and the integration of environmental concerns into the requirements of the two countries.

Another effort in the ISO community is the development of a standard for Environmental Product Declarations (EPD), based on carbon footprints, as an indicator of the global environmental impact of a product expressed in carbon emission equivalents (He, et al., 2018). EPD and labeling, such as the Nordic Swan and Blue Angel, offer consumers assistance in their purchasing decisions. Methods associated with life cycle assessment (LCA), life cycle impact assessment (LCIA), life cycle optimization (LCO), and life cycle management (LCM) are increasingly sophisticated and supported by software (Avraamidou, et al., 2020).

Related QCs

Achieving a circular closed-loop system relies on integrating additional quality characteristics. Useful life extensions rely on reliability and maintainability (see Section 3.1.8) alongside efficient logistical support (see Section 3.1.6) and products designed to be resilient (see Section 3.1.9). Recovery of valuable resources after useful life is highly dependent on decisions made when considering manufacturability (see Section 3.1.7).

More information on Sustainability/Disposability can be found in the Journal of Cleaner Production (2023), the Journal of Environmental Management (2023), Wood et al. (2023), ICE (2023), and MDPI (2023).

3.1.11 System Safety Engineering

Definition System safety engineering is an approach that reduces the likelihood of harm to people, assets, and the wider environment.

Key Concepts The goal of system safety engineering is to reduce and mitigate hazards of systems to an acceptable level of risk. Engineered systems have safety risks; they are not 100% safe. The definition of what is acceptably safe, safety regulations, processes, and culture vary across different industries and countries.

可持续性和可处置性的关键活动、工具和方法

ISO 14000（2015）系列环境管理标准是分析和评估工业运行及其对环境影响的方法的极好资源。在需求分析的早期活动中，应注意环境法规。Øresund 大桥（见 6.2 节）就是一个示例，说明对潜在环境影响的早期分析如何确保在概念、开发和生产过程中采取措施保护环境，并取得积极成果。该倡议成功的两个关键元素是持续监测环境状况，并将环境问题纳入两国的需求。

ISO 群体的另一项努力是制定基于碳足迹的产品环保声明（EPD）标准，作为以碳排放当量表示的产品对全球环境影响的指标（He 等，2018）。环保署和标签，如北欧天鹅和蓝天使，为消费者的购买决策提供帮助。与生命周期评估（LCA）、生命周期影响评估（LCIA）、生命周期优化（LCO）以及生命周期管理（LCM）相关的方法越来越复杂，并得到软件的支持（Avraamidou 等，2020）。

相关 QC

实现循环闭环系统依赖于综合其他质量特性。使用寿命的延长依赖于可靠性和可维护性（见 3.1.8 节），以及高效的后勤支持（见 3.1.6 节）和产品设计的强韧性（见 3.1.9 节）。使用寿命结束后宝贵资源的回收在很大程度上取决于考虑可制造性时做出的决策（见 3.1.7 节）。

有关可持续性／可处置性的更多信息，请参见《清洁生产杂志》（2023）、《环境管理杂志》（2023）、Wood 等（2023）、ICE（2023）和 MDPI（2023）。

3.1.11　系统安全工程

定义　系统安全工程是一种降低对人员、资产和更广泛环境造成伤害的可能性的实施方法。

关键概念　系统安全工程的目标是将系统的危险降低到可接受的风险层级。工程系统存在安全风险，不是 100% 安全。可接受安全、安全法规、流程以及文化的定义因行业和国家而异。

LIFE CYCLE ANALYSES AND METHODS

System safety engineering is not limited to ensuring that the engineered system is acceptably safe. It includes minimizing the risks to everyone involved in the production, utilization, support, and retirement of the system, as well as third parties who could also be affected by these activities. System safety engineering is about engineering the SoI, the wider socio-technical operational system, and the socio-technical (or even purely social) management system.

Safety is an emergent property of the engineered system in its real operational environment. How the system is used, maintained, and managed can have as big an impact on system safety as its inherent design. Understanding, and aligning, the mental models of designers, operators, and managers is critical.

Safety is managed by minimizing the hazards that can lead to an accident. This is either through reducing the likelihood the hazard will occur or minimizing the impact if it does. This is either through designing the hazard out, technical mitigations in the system, or procedural controls. This requires a mixture of suitably qualified people, effective processes, appropriate governance, and culture.

In-service systems need careful monitoring to ensure that design assumptions remain valid, no new hazards have been identified, and that operations/maintenance is as expected. Slow feedback loops and misaligned mental models can be particularly problematic, as issues can grow unseen for years before they appear with catastrophic impact.

Good systems safety engineering seeks to ensure operators do not misuse systems, leaders set the right tone and culture, and maintainers don't take shortcuts. System safety engineers and senior leaders are often accountable for predictable misuse of systems, failure to address poor behavior, and ineffective oversight of maintenance and operations.

Elaboration

Acceptably Safe

The safety regulations, processes, and culture vary across different industries and countries. What is acceptable in one industry and country may not be acceptable in another. There is a wide diversity in regulators, definitions, evidence, and perceived benefits that adds further complexity. Even the definition of what is "acceptably safe" varies. Typical perceptions of "acceptably safe" include:

- *"We have complied with the necessary [product] regulations."* This is generally accepted for simple, well understood, standardized system elements (e.g., electrical cable, bolts).

系统安全工程不限于确保所设计的系统具有可接受的安全性。其包括最大限度地降低系统生产、使用、支持和退役流程中涉及的每个人以及可能受这些活动影响的第三方的风险。系统安全工程是关于 SoI、更广泛的社会技术运行系统和社会技术（甚至纯粹的社会）管理系统的工程。

安全性是工程系统在其实际运行环境中的一项涌现特性。系统的使用、维护和管理方式对系统安全的影响不亚于其内在设计。理解并调整设计师、操作员和管理者的心智模型至关重要。

通过将可能导致事故的危险降至最低来管理安全。这可以通过降低危险发生的可能性，也可以通过减少影响来实现。这可以通过设计消除危险、系统中的技术缓解或程序控制来实现。这需要适当的合格人员、有效的流程、适当的治理以及文化的混合。

在役系统需要仔细监控，以确保设计假设仍然有效，没有发现新的危险，并且运行/维护符合预期。缓慢的反馈循环回路和错位的心智模型可能会造成特别严重的问题，因为问题可能在出现灾难性影响之前多年都被视而不见。

良好的系统安全工程旨在确保操作员不会误用系统、领导者设置正确的基调和文化、维护人员不走捷径。系统安全工程师和高级领导通常对可预测的系统误用、未能解决不良行为以及维护和运行监督不力负责。

详细阐述

可接受的安全

不同行业和国家的安全法规、流程和文化各不相同。在一个行业和国家可以接受的东西，在另一个行业和国家可能无法接受。监管机构、定义、证据以及所感知的利益的多样性进一步增加了复杂性。甚至"可接受的安全"的定义也各不相同。"可接受的安全"的典型概念包括：

- "我们遵守必要的*[产品]法规*。"这通常适用于简单、易于理解的标准化系统元素（如电缆、螺栓）。

LIFE CYCLE ANALYSES AND METHODS

- *"We have evaluated all identified hazards and have mitigated each to be 'as low as reasonably practicable' (ALARP)."* This would be the typical approach adopted for complicated, safety critical civilian systems (e.g., a railway signaling system, passenger aircraft).

- *"We have evaluated all the identified hazards of the system, and they are either ALARP, or the level of hazard of the new system is less than the alterative (of not having it)."* This would be the typical approach adopted for military, medical, or emergency response systems (e.g., artillery, pacemaker).

Eliminating all safety risk is not possible; therefore, no system can be described as 100% safe. There may be unknown hazards and hazards that cannot be eliminated but are determined to be acceptable given the perceived benefit. Similarly, assuming that the system must be safe because there haven't been any accidents yet, or reported, is equally incorrect. There may have been near misses (see below), the hazardous functionality/performance may not have been used, or the effect/damage has not yet been recognized.

Emergence, Accidents, and Hazards

Safety is an emergent property of a system. It is not the sum of system element level safety or reliability. Rather, it is impacted by interactions between system elements and affected by the environment in which it is used. Many factors affect the level of safety risk (e.g., who uses and maintains a system, how they do it, in what environment). Safety is not a static property as systems (and the surrounding ecosystems) are dynamic and evolve. The designers' expectations of risks often differ from the system under test and evaluation and from the system in operation (which continues evolves over time). The mental models of the humans interacting with the system and the related processes are also dynamic and subject to change.

Most accidents result from more than a single causal factor. When an unmitigated hazardous situation does occur but does not result in harm, it is referred to as a near miss. Near misses serve as critical feedback on the system safety level in operation. Safety culture often determines how near misses are treated and responded to. However:

- Accident investigations often reveal dependencies between hazards exist, despite earlier beliefs that causal factors were independent. A failure to recognize dependencies when applying statistical methods can result in flawed safety decisions.

- A hazardous situation can occur without a system element failure. This could be because of a design error, an implementation error, or a misalignment between mental models of designer and operators or maintainers.

- "我们已评估所有已识别的危害，并已将每个危害降低到'合理可行的最低水平'（ALARP）。"这将是复杂、安全的关键民用系统（如铁路信号系统、客机）采用的典型实施方法。

- "我们已经评估系统的所有已识别危险，要么是 ALARP，要么新系统的危险等级低于（没有新系统的）备选方案。"这将是军事、医疗或应急响应系统（如火炮、起搏器）采用的典型实施方法。

不可能消除所有安全风险；因此，任何系统都不能说是 100% 安全的。可能存在未知的危险和无法消除的危险，但考虑到可获得的益处，这些危险被确定为可接受的。同样，假设系统必须是安全的，因为还没有发生任何事故或报告，同样是不正确的。可能存在侥幸事件（见下文），可能未使用危险功能/性能，或尚未识别影响/损坏。

紧急情况、事故和危险

安全是系统的涌现性，不是系统元素级安全性或可靠性的总和。相反，其受到系统元素之间交互的影响，并受到使用环境的影响。许多因素会影响安全风险层级（例如，谁使用和维护系统，他们如何操作，在什么环境下）。安全不是静态的，因为系统（以及周围的生态系统）是动态的和不断发展的。设计师对风险的期望往往不同于测试和评估中的系统以及运行中的系统（随着时间的推移不断演进）。人类与系统和相关流程交互的心智模型也是动态的，并且会发生变化。

大多数事故都是由一个以上的原因造成的。当发生未缓解的危险情况但未造成伤害时，称为侥幸事件。侥幸事件是对系统运行安全水平的关键反馈。安全文化通常决定如何处理和应对侥幸事件。然而：

- 尽管早期认为因果因素是独立的，但事故调查往往揭示危险之间存在依赖关系。应用统计方法时未能识别依赖性可能会导致有缺陷的安全决策。

- 在没有系统元素故障的情况下，可能发生危险情况。这可能是由于设计错误、实现错误或设计者与操作员或维护者的心智模型之间的不一致造成的。

LIFE CYCLE ANALYSES AND METHODS

Regulators typically assess safety risk in terms of both:

- the *likelihood* of hazards occurring and leading to harm and
- the *severity* of the resulting harm.

Safety is managed by eliminating hazards where possible; and when not possible, by reducing risks to an acceptable level. When possible, design changes to eliminate potential hazards are the preferred options. The next preferred options are design mitigations to reduce the likelihood of hazards occurring. When designs changes or mitigations are not possible, other means are typically employed such as operational controls and limitations, maintenance inspections or activities, warnings via labeling, and training.

Hazards may result from a range of sources such as intrinsic, functional, socio-technical, or management/wider culture. Intrinsic hazards are typically caused by the material, or other design factors of the system elements used in the system. Functional hazards result from incorrect, unexpected, or undesirable functions or performance of the system. Socio-technical hazards result from interactions between the physical system and its operators and the wider environment. Finally, management/cultural hazards relate to the system and the wider management controls needed to realize and sustain the system.

Examples of safety hazards include:

- Interactions between system elements, the operating environment, and operators: A car on an icy road and an inexperienced driver is likely to result in an accident. Traction control, trained drivers, or not driving in icy conditions mitigates this hazard.

- Mistakes in system/system element requirements, design, manufacturing, or installation: A failure to specify the Maneuvering Characteristics Augmentation System (MCAS) system element as safety critical resulted in loss of two 737 Max aircraft (Cantwell, 2021).

- The system creates hazards in the wider SoI: Bull-bars / kangaroo bars reduce the risk of injury to a driver in vehicle to vehicle or vehicle to large animal collisions. However, they significantly increase the risks to pedestrians in vehicle to pedestrian collisions in urban areas (Desapriya, et al., 2012).

- The inherent material used in system elements: Asbestos or flammable substances present inherent hazards.

- Incorrect operation or maintenance: A failure to properly remove old wiring led to the Clapham junction rail accident (Hidden, 1989).

监管机构通常从以下两方面评估安全风险：

- 危险发生和导致伤害的*可能性*；
- 造成危害的*严重性*。

通过尽可能消除危险来管理安全；在不可能的情况下，将风险降低到可接受的层级。在可能的情况下，通过设计变更以消除潜在危险是首选方案。下一个首选方案是设计缓解措施，以降低危险发生的可能性。当无法进行设计变更或缓解时，通常会采用其他方法，如运行控制和限制、维护检查或活动、通过标签发出警告以及培训。

危险可能有一系列来源，如内在的、功能的、社会技术的或管理/更广泛的文化。固有危险通常由系统中使用的系统元素的材料或其他设计因素引起。功能危险源于系统的不正确、意外或不良功能或性能。社会技术危害源于物理系统及其操作员和更广泛环境之间的交互。最后，管理/文化危害与系统以及实现和维持系统所需的更广泛的管理控制有关。

安全危险的示例包括：

- 系统元素、运行环境和操作员之间的交互：结冰道路上的汽车和没有经验的驾驶员很可能导致事故。牵引力控制、训练有素的驾驶员或不在结冰条件下驾驶都可以缓解这种危险。

- 系统/系统元素需求、设计、制造或安装中的错误：未能将机动特性增强系统（MCAS）的系统元素指定为安全关键元素，导致两架 737 Max 飞机失事（Cantwell，2021）。

- 系统在更广泛的 SoI 中造成危害：牛栏/袋鼠栏可降低车辆对车辆或车辆对大型动物碰撞中驾驶员受伤的风险。然而，其显著增加了城市地区车辆与行人碰撞的危险性（Desapriya 等，2012）。

- 系统元素中使用的固有材料：石棉或易燃物质存在固有危险。

- 不正确的运行或维护：未能正确拆除旧接线导致 Clapham 连接轨事故（Hidden，1989）。

- Misaligned mental models between operators, maintainers, and designers: Prior to the Smiler accident, false alarms were a common occurrence. This led to operators believing all alarms were false positives. This resulted in alarms being overridden without investigation (Kemp and O'Neil, 2018).
- The activities undertaken to design, manufacture, test and maintain the system: The Piper-Alpha oil platform accident was caused by a failure to properly manage design changes, poor maintenance management, and poor contingency planning (Cullen, 1990).

Managing and Controlling Hazards

System safety engineering seeks to control hazards by:

- Understanding the system environment, wider SoI, proposed system, and how it will be used.
- Specifying the safety requirements for the system. System requirements flow from stakeholder needs and requirements and are derived into system element requirements (see Section 2.3.5.3). Maintaining traceability is key, as it may not be immediately obvious to a system element designer that a specific requirement is safety critical (see Section 3.2.3).
- Analyzing the potential safety hazards. There is a range of hazard analysis techniques looking at the system, and its functions, physical, process, and human interactions. An effective hazard analysis will use multiple techniques.
- Mitigating/controlling the known hazards, either by reducing the likelihood or severity of a hazard occurring. Approaches include removing the hazard entirely, designing-in passive or active controls to mitigate the hazard, or including operational or maintenance controls. A key element of including controls is ensuring effective feedback loops and recognizing the full control model beyond the engineered system (including the operating environment and management systems) (Leveson, 2011).
- Establishing a safety management system to ensure the system remains safe throughout its life cycle.

Establish an Appropriate Safety Management System

Each organization's safety management system needs to be tailored based on country, region, and industry/application considerations. Organizations need to understand the regulatory, operational, and physical environments that the systems they develop will be used. For example, the safety management system needed for a safety critical industry such as rail or aerospace would be inappropriate for consumer electronics.

- 操作员、维护人员和设计师之间的心智模型不一致：在 Smiler 事故之前，错误警报是常见的。这导致操作员认为所有报警都是误报，进而导致报警在未经调查的情况下被覆盖掉（Kemp 和 O'Neil，2018）。

- 为设计、制造、测试和维护系统而开展的活动：Piper Alpha 石油平台事故是由于未能正确管理设计变更、维护管理不善和应急计划不力造成的（Cullen，1990）。

管理和控制危险

系统安全工程旨在通过以下方式控制危险：

- 理解系统环境、更广泛的 SoI、提出的系统以及如何使用。

- 规定系统的安全需求。系统需求源于利益相关方的需要和需求，并派生到系统元素需求中（见 2.3.5.3 节）。保持可追溯性是关键，因为系统元素设计者可能不会立即意识到某个特定需求对安全至关重要（见 3.2.3 节）。

- 分析潜在的安全隐患。有一系列危害分析技术研究系统及其功能、物理、流程以及人员交互。有效的危险分析将使用多种技术。

- 通过降低危险发生的可能性或严重性，缓解/控制已知危险。方法包括完全消除危险，设计被动或主动控制以减轻危险，或包括运行或维护控制。纳入控制的一个关键元素是确保有效的反馈回路，并识别工程系统（包括运行环境和管理系统）之外的完整控制模型（Leveson，2011）。

- 建立安全管理体系，确保系统在整个生命周期内保持安全。

建立适当的安全管理体系

每个组织的安全管理体系都需要根据国家、地区和行业/应用考虑定制。组织需要理解他们开发的系统将要使用的管理、运行和物理环境。例如，铁路或航空航天等安全关键行业所需的安全管理系统不适用于消费电子产品。

The safety management system needs to: define the organizations approach to developing safe systems; manage the infrastructure, processes and information required to support system delivery; oversee the operations and maintenance of in-service systems; and ensure an effective safety culture.

The safety management system needs to be fully integrated into the wider organizations' business management systems. It needs to ensure that:

- Projects to deliver new systems are given clear safety objectives, measures, and targets.
- In-service systems are operated and maintained safely, with appropriate monitoring of changes to use, environment, and material state of the system.
- Incidents and near misses are reported without fear of retribution, and on-going monitoring and implementation of mitigation actions create an ongoing learning/improvement cycle (Dekker, 2014).

A key facet of the safety management system is the organization's safety and ethical culture, or "how we behave when no-one is looking" (see Section 5.1.4). Regular measurement of the safety is useful to track organization's safety culture (Hudson, 2001). Regular, frequent communications and stories of the behavior needed are necessary by senior and influential people to reinforce the safety culture (Kemp and O'Neil, 2018).

Establish and Run Projects with Safety at Their Core

Key issues to be aware of include:

- Ensuring that the tailoring of the SE approach is appropriate for the system under development.
- Ensuring that the safety engineering processes integrated as tightly as possible to the wider engineering and business processes, driving both operational efficiencies and reducing the risk of incorrect assumptions between the safety team and the wider project.
- Accepting the need to make assumptions, but recognizing that when the assumptions turn out to be incorrect and appropriate rework will be required (and accepting the cost and time impact of the rework).
- Ensuring the selection of an appropriate life cycle model. As Akroyd-Wallis (2018) notes, direct adoption of Agile software techniques to safety critical systems may be problematic. SE Practitioners should exercise caution when employing agile for safety critical systems.
- Terminating projects when they can no longer meet their safety objectives at a reasonable cost, timescales, or performance.

安全管理体系需要：定义组织制定安全体系的方法；管理支持系统交付所需的基础设施、流程和信息；监督运行中系统的运行和维护；确保有效的安全文化。

安全管理系统需要充分融入更广泛的组织业务管理系统。它必须确保：

- 交付新系统的项目有明确的安全目标、措施和指标。

- 在役系统安全运行和维护，并对系统的使用、环境和材料状态的变化进行适当监控。

- 报告事故和侥幸事件时不必担心遭到报复，持续监测和实施缓解措施创造一个持续的学习/改进周期（Dekker，2014）。

安全管理体系的一个关键方面是组织的安全和道德文化，或"无人注视时我们的行为"（见5.1.4节）。定期测量安全有助于跟踪组织的安全文化（Hudson，2001）。资深和有影响力的人有必要定期、频繁地交流和讲述所需的行为，以加强安全文化（Kemp 和 O'Neil，2018）。

以安全为核心建立和运行项目

需要注意的关键问题包括：

- 确保为正在开发的系统定制适合的系统工程方法。

- 确保安全工程流程尽可能紧密地综合到更广泛的工程和业务流程中，提高运行效率，降低安全团队和更广泛的项目之间出现错误假设的风险。

- 接受做出假设的必要性，但认识到当假设不正确时，需要进行适当的返工（并接受返工的成本和时间影响）。

- 确保选择适当的生命周期模型。正如 Akroyd Wallis（2018）所指出的，将敏捷软件技术直接应用于安全关键系统可能存在问题。系统工程实践者在将敏捷应用于安全关键系统时应谨慎行事。

- 当项目无法以合理的成本、时间或绩效满足其安全目标时，终止项目。

LIFE CYCLE ANALYSES AND METHODS

Embed Safety in the Core of the SE Process

Specific safety engineering considerations include:

- Ensuring Business or Mission Analysis (see Section 2.3.5.1) includes a high-level assessment of hazards and that analysis of alternatives includes their inherent safety potential

- Including a comprehensive hazard analysis during Stakeholder Needs and Requirements Definition (see Section 2.3.5.2) to identify potential hazards with the system being developed and the wider operational capability the SoI will be deployed into

- Ensuring that key safety functions and safety performance is captured during System Architecture Definition (see Section 2.3.5.4). A safety viewpoint will help ensure traceability from high level needs down to system element requirements.

- Where the system is to be part of a wider SoS, ensuring that system functions/performance necessary to mitigate SoS hazards are captured as safety requirements (see Section 4.3.6).

- Ensuring that verification and validation of safety requirements is sufficiently rigorous to meet the agreed levels of "acceptably safe."

- Ensuring that hazards that are managed by Operational or Maintenance (see Sections 2.3.5.12 and 2.3.5.13) activities are clearly embedded in relevant processes and are clearly communicated, precisely defined, and reasonable.

- Ensuring that the assumptions in the safety case remain valid through life. (Is the environment as expected? Have the operators (and their mental models) changed? Has the use of the system changed? Is maintenance being done as required and is the maintenance as effective as planned? Are there any new potential new hazards being seen? Is the frequency and severity of hazards as expected?)

Ensure the System Is Delivered Safely

System safety engineering needs to ensure that systems can be designed, built, and verified safely. The systems that manufacture, test, and maintain complicated and complex systems can be as hazardous as the SoI itself. The traditional split between product safety and occupational safety is becoming less clear as:

- Development becomes more agile.

- Organizations shift from product to service delivery.

将安全性嵌入系统工程流程的核心

具体的安全工程考虑因素包括：

- 确保业务或任务分析（见 2.3.5.1 节）中包括对危险的高层级的评估，并确保备选方案分析包括其固有的安全潜力。

- 在利益相关方需要和需求定义期间包括全面的危害分析（见 2.3.5.2 节），以识别正在开发的系统和将部署的 SoI 的更广泛运行能力的潜在危害。

- 确保在系统架构定义期间捕获关键安全功能和安全性能（见 2.3.5.4 节）。安全观点将有助于确保从高层级需要到系统元素需求的可追溯性。

- 当系统是更广泛 SoS 的一部分时，确保缓解 SoS 危害所需的系统功能/性能被捕获为安全需求（见 4.3.6 节）。

- 确保安全需求的验证和确认足够严格，以满足商定的"可接受安全"层级。

- 确保由运行或维护（见 2.3.5.12 和 2.3.5.13 节）活动管理的危险清楚地嵌入到相关流程中，并明确沟通、精确定义和使其合理。

- 确保安全用例中的假设在整个生命周期内保持有效。[环境是否如预期的那样？操作员（及其心智模型）是否发生了变化？系统的使用是否已更改？维护是否按要求进行，维护是否按计划有效？是否发现任何新的潜在新危险？危险的频率和严重程度是否与预期一致？]

确保系统安全交付

系统安全工程需要确保系统能够安全地设计、建造和验证。制造、测试和维护繁杂和复杂系统的系统可能与 SoI 本身一样危险。产品安全和职业安全之间的传统划分越来越不明确，因为：

- 开发变得更加敏捷。

- 组织从产品交付转向服务交付。

LIFE CYCLE ANALYSES AND METHODS

- Increased use of non-expert operators and maintainers.

Suitably Qualified and Experienced Personnel Drive Safety Performance

The effectiveness of safety management system is driven by the people who work within it. Good people may build safe systems despite poor processes and tools. Good processes and tools cannot make up for poorly qualified people.

Effective safety practitioners need to be numerate, critical thinkers, and system thinkers who understand the technologies being used, the environment the system will be deployed into, and the mental models of operators and maintainers. In addition, they need the influencing and persuasion skills to convince others of the right approach to take and the moral courage to "say no" when necessary (see Section 5.1.2).

Safety practitioners need to be in the room when key decisions are made. They need to lead the safety decision making, capturing key information in an audit trail. If they are involved too late, organizations can be left with systems that cannot be deployed. This happened to the UK Air Force when acquiring eight Chinook Mk3 helicopters (NAO, 2008).

For more illustrations on the importance of system safety, refer to Case 1 (Radiation Therapy - The Therac-25) from Section 6.1 and Case 5 (Artificial Intelligence in Systems Engineering – Autonomous Vehicles) from Section 6.5.

3.1.12 System Security Engineering

Definition System Security Engineering is an approach that identifies, protects from, detects, responds to, and recovers from anomalous and disruptive events, including those in a cyber contested environment.

Key Concepts System Security Engineering (SSE) is focused on ensuring a system can function under anomalous and disruptive events associated with misuse and malicious behavior. SSE involves a disciplined application of SE principles in analyzing security threats and vulnerabilities to the system and assessing and mitigating security risks to assets of the system during the life cycle. It blends technology, management principles and practices, and operational rules to ensure sufficient protections are available at all times.

Sources of potential anomalous and disruptive events (threats) are many and varied. They may emanate from external sources (e.g., theft, denial of service attacks, power interruptions) or may be caused by internal forces (e.g., user actions, supporting systems). A disruption may be unintentional (misuse) or intentional (malicious) in nature.

- 更多使用非专业操作人员和维护人员。

具备适当资质和经验的人员推动安全绩效

安全管理体系的有效性是由其内部的工作人员推动的。优秀的人员可以建立安全体系，尽管流程和工具较差。良好的流程和工具无法弥补资质较差的人员。

有效的安全实践者需要是数学家、批判性思考者和系统思考者，他们理解所使用的技术、系统将部署到的环境以及操作员和维护人员的心智模型。此外，他们需要影响力和说服技巧，从而说服他人采取正确的方法，并在必要时有道德上的勇气"说不"（见 5.1.2 节）。

在做出关键决策时，安全实践者必须在场。他们需要主导安全决策，在审核跟踪中捕获关键信息。如果他们参与得太晚，组织可能会留下无法部署的系统。英国空军在采购八架奇努克 Mk3 直升机时就遇到过这种情况（NAO，2008）。

有关系统安全重要性的更多说明，请参阅 6.1 节中的案例 1（放射治疗——Therac-25）和 6.5 节中的案例 5（系统工程中的人工智能——自动驾驶汽车）。

3.1.12　系统安保工程

定义　系统安保工程是一种针对异常和破坏性事件（包括赛博竞争环境中的事件）进行识别、保护、检测、响应以及恢复的实施方法。

关键概念　系统安保工程（SSE）聚焦确保系统能够在与误用和恶意行为相关的异常和破坏性事件下运行。系统安保工程涉及严谨地应用系统原则，分析系统的安全威胁和漏洞，评估和缓解生命周期内系统资产的安全风险。融合技术、管理原则和实践以及运行规则，以确保随时提供足够的保护。

潜在异常和破坏性事件（威胁）的来源多种多样。可能来自外部（如盗窃、拒绝服务攻击、电源中断），也可能由内部作用（如用户行为、支持系统）引起。中断可能是无意（误用）或故意（恶意）性质的。

LIFE CYCLE ANALYSES AND METHODS

Physical security protects a system from unauthorized access, misuse, or damage caused by physical actions and events such as theft, vandalism, and intrusion. Protecting physical facilities, equipment, resources, and personnel can involve the use of multiple layers of interdependent systems such as surveillance and intrusion detection systems, deterrent systems, security guards, protective barriers, locks, and access control. Hardware devices can employ antitampering features to detect unauthorized opening or altering of the packaging, either to ensure the content is authentic or to trigger actions to protect sensitive information in the devices.

As our world becomes increasingly digital, both hardware and software systems are increasingly at risk for disruption or damage caused by threats taking advantage of digital technologies. Integrating and implementing systems security using SSE approaches is the most efficient and effective way to ensure that security is addressed at each stage of the life cycle and becomes part of the overall SE solution instead of being done separately and isolated from other SE activities (NIST SP 800-160 Vol. 1, 2022 and NIST 800-160 Vol. 2, 2021). SSE provides the needed complementary engineering capability that extends the notion of trustworthiness to deliver trustworthy secure systems, which are less susceptible to the effects of modern adversity such as attacks orchestrated by an intelligent adversary (NIST SP 800-160 Vol. 1, 2022).

Cybersecurity generally refers to the confidentiality, integrity, and availability of information assets. Security management includes controls (e.g., policies, practices, procedures, organization structures, and software). Trustworthiness is a concept that includes privacy, reliability, resilience, safety, and security, therefore worthy of being trusted to fulfill whatever critical requirements may be needed for a particular system element, system, network, application, mission, business function, enterprise, or other entity (NIST 800-160 Vol. 2, 2021).

Elaboration SSE practitioners should have skills, expertise, and experience in multiple areas. Examples include security requirements, security architecture views, threat assessment, networking, security technologies, hardware and software security, security test and evaluation, vulnerability assessment, penetration testing, and supply chain security risk assessment. A major challenge in managing engineering projects is unclear security roles, responsibilities, and accountability. To assist in the security role development and understanding responsibilities, an SE/SSE roles and responsibilities framework can be used to break down tasks into a matrix format that enables the SE practitioner to understand the role contributions and identify the types of artifacts created by the execution of the SE life cycle processes. (Nejib, et al., 2017)

物理安全保护系统免受未经授权的访问、滥用或物理行为和事件（如盗窃、故意破坏和入侵）造成的损坏。保护物理设施、设备、资源和人员可能涉及使用多个层次相互依赖的系统，如监视和入侵检测系统、威慑系统、保安、防护屏障、安全锁以及访问控制。硬件设备可以使用防篡改功能来检测未经授权的打开或更改包装，从而确保内容真实，或触发保护设备中敏感信息的运行。

随着我们的世界变得越来越数字化，硬件和软件系统都面临着越来越多的因利用数字技术的威胁而造成中断或损坏的风险。使用系统工程方法综合和实施系统安保是确保在生命周期的每个阶段解决安全问题的最有效方法，并成为整个系统工程解决方案的一部分，而不是单独完成并与其他系统工程活动隔离（NIST SP 800-160 Vol.1，2022 和 NIST 800-160 Vol.2，2021）。系统安保工程提供了所需的补充工程能力，扩展可信的概念，从而提供可信的安全系统，这些系统不易受到现代灾难的影响，例如智能对手策划的攻击（NIST SP 800-160 第 1 卷，2022）。

赛博安保通常指信息资产的机密性、完整性和可用性。安保管理包括控制（例如，策略、实践、程序、组织结构和软件）。可信是一个包括隐私、可靠性、强韧性、安全性以及安保性的概念，因此值得信任，从而满足特定系统元素、系统、网络、应用程序、任务、业务功能、复杂组织体系或其他实体可能需要的任何关键需求（NIST 800-160 第 2 卷，2021）。

详细阐述　系统安保工程（SSE）实践者应具备多个领域的技能、专业知识和经验。示例包括安保需求、安保架构视图、威胁评估、网络、安保技术、硬件和软件安保、安保测试和评估、漏洞评估、渗透测试和供应链安全风险评估。管理工程项目的一个主要挑战是不清楚安保角色、职责和问责制度。为了帮助安保角色开发和理解职责，可以使用系统工程／系统安保工程角色和职责框架将任务分解为矩阵格式，使系统工程实践者能够理解角色贡献，并识别由执行系统工程生命周期流程创建的制品类型。（Nejib 等，2017）

LIFE CYCLE ANALYSES AND METHODS

Through NIST 800-160 Vol. 1 (2022) and Vol. 2 (2021), it has been determined that the best way to integrate cybersecurity into systems is through an SE process. NIST 800-160 Vol. 1 (2022) and Vol. 2 (2021) are based on ISO/IEC/IEEE 15288 (2023) and this handbook. They use the same terminology so that both SE and SSE practitioners can understand the key relationship that exists between the two disciplines. There is a direct correlation between SE and SSE, and SE practitioners need to understand and incorporate security components into each SE life cycle process. Table 3.4 shows an example of how the SSE technical processes in NIST SP 800-160 Vol. 1 (2022) can be reused and referenced by SE, SSE, and other disciplines practitioners. Specifically, Table 3.4 is an example of the Implementation process (see Section 2.3.5.7) breakout defined with extensions for SSE to include the purpose, outcomes, activities and tasks, inputs, and responsible and supporting roles. This same format was used to breakout each of the technical SSE processes in NIST 800-160 Vol. 1 Rev. 1 (2022) and the SE Technical Processes (see Section 2.3.5) to build an understanding of the relationships between the SE and SSE processes.

TABLE 3.4   Implementation process breakout

Implementation Process Breakout	
Purpose	• Realize the security aspects of the system element • Results in a system element that satisfies specified system security requirements, architecture, and design
Outcomes	• Security aspects of the implementation strategy are developed • Security aspects of implementation that constrain the requirements, architecture, or design are identified • Security system element • System elements securely packaged and stored • Enabling systems or services needed for security aspects of implementation • Traceability of security aspects of implemented system elements
Activities and Tasks	1. Prepare for the security aspects of implementation 2. Perform the security aspects of implementation 3. Manage results of the security aspects of implementation
Inputs	Security strategy, plan, traceability, requirements, design, architecture, secure system elements, assurance evidence, assurance results, and anomalies report
Responsible and Supporting Roles	Responsible: Systems Security Engineer (SSE) Supporting: Program Manager (PM), Chief Engineer (CE), Systems Engineer (SE), Systems Architect (SA), and Test Engineer (TE)

From NIST 800-160 Vol. 1 (2022). Used with permission. All other rights reserved.

通过 NIST 800-160 第 1 卷（2022）和第 2 卷（2021），已确定将赛博安保综合到系统中的最佳方式是通过系统工程流程。NIST 800-160 第 1 卷（2022）和第 2 卷（2021）基于 ISO/IEC/IEEE 15288（2023）和本手册。他们使用相同的术语，以便系统工程和系统安保工程实践者都能理解这两个学科之间存在的关键关系。系统工程和系统安保工程之间存在直接关联，系统工程实践者需要理解安保组件并将其纳入每个系统工程生命周期流程。表 3.4 展示了 NIST SP 800-160 第 1 卷（2022）中系统安保工程技术流程如何被系统工程、系统安保工程和其他学科实践者重用和引用的示例。具体而言，表 3.4 是实施流程（见 2.3.5.7 节）的一个示例，其中对系统安保工程进行扩展，包括目的、结果、活动和任务、输入以及职责和支持角色。使用相同的格式对 NIST 800-160 第 1 卷第 1 版（2022 年）和系统工程技术流程（见 2.3.5 节）中的每个系统安保工程技术流程进行详细分析，以了解系统工程和系统安保工程之间的关系。

表 3.4　实施流程分解讨论

实施流程分解讨论	
目的	• 实现系统要素的安保方面 • 产生满足指定系统安保需求、架构和设计的系统元素
结果	• 制定实施策略的安保方面 • 确定约束需求、架构或设计的实施的安保方面 • 安保系统元素 • 安全的包装和储存系统元素 • 实施安保方面所需的使能系统或服务 • 已实施系统要素安保方面的可追溯性
活动和任务	1. 为实施中的安保方面做准备 2. 执行实施中的安保方面的工作 3. 管理实施中的安保方面的结果
输入	安保策略、计划、可追溯性、需求、设计、架构、安全系统要素、保证证据、保证结果和异常报告
负责和支持角色	负责：系统安全工程师（SSE） 支持：项目经理（PM）、总工程师（CE）、系统工程师（SE）、系统架构师（SA）和测试工程师（TE）

源自 NIST 800-160 第 1 卷（2022）。经许可后使用。版权所有。

Case Study 3, Cybersecurity Considerations in Systems Engineering-The Stuxnet Attack on a Cyber Physical System (see Section 6.3) provides an example of the importance of system security.

3.1.13 Loss-Driven Systems Engineering

Loss-Driven Systems Engineering (LDSE) is the value adding unification of the QCs that address the potential losses associated with developing and using systems (Brtis, 2020). SE methodologies often focus on the delivery of desired capability. As a result, SE methodologies are largely capability-driven, and may not provide integrated attention to the potential losses associated with developing and using systems. Loss and loss-driven QCs are often considered in isolation—if at all. Examples of loss-driven QCs include resilience, safety, security, sustainability/disposability, and availability.

There is significant commonality and synergy among the loss-driven QCs, which needs to be leveraged. To do this, work on the loss-driven QCs should be collaborative on:

- the adversities considered,
- the weakness, defects, flaws, exposures, hazards, and vulnerabilities considered,
- the assets and losses considered, and
- the coping mechanism considered.

Further, SE practitioners should:

- elicit, analyze, and capture loss-driven requirements as an integrated part of the overall stakeholder and system requirements development,
- make architectural and design decisions holistically across the loss-driven QC areas, and
- integrate the management of risks associated with all loss-driven areas into the project's risk management activities.

3.2 SYSTEMS ENGINEERING ANALYSES AND METHODS

Part II of this handbook provided a set of SE life cycle processes used across the system life cycle. Each process contains a set of process activities and elaborations in the context of that specific life cycle process. This section provides insight into topics, techniques, and methods that cut across the SE life cycle processes, reflecting various aspects of the concurrent, iterative, and recursive nature of SE.

案例研究 3，系统工程中的网络安全考虑——对赛博物理系统的 Stuxnet 攻击（见 6.3 节），提供系统安保重要性的示例。

3.1.13 损失驱动的系统工程

损失驱动的系统工程（LDSE）是质量控制的增值统一方式，可解决与开发和使用系统相关的潜在损失的问题（Brtis，2020）。系统工程方法通常侧重于提供所需的能力。因此，系统工程方法在很大程度上是由能力驱动的，可能无法对与开发和使用系统相关的潜在损失提供综合的关注。通常单独考虑损失和损失驱动的质量特性（如有）。损失驱动的质量特性示例包括强韧性、安全性、安保性、可持续性/可处置性以及可用性。

损失驱动的质量特性之间存在着显著的共性和协同效应，需要加以利用。为此，损失驱动质量特性的工作应在以下方面进行协作：

- 考虑的灾难；
- 考虑的弱点、缺陷、瑕疵、暴露、危险以及脆弱性；
- 考虑的资产和损失；
- 考虑的应对机制。

此外，系统工程实践者应该：

- 作为总体利益相关方和系统需求开发的一个组成部分，引出、分析和捕获损失驱动的需求；
- 在损失驱动的质量控制领域全面做出架构和设计决策；
- 将与所有损失驱动领域相关的风险管理综合到项目的风险管理活动中。

3.2 系统工程分析和方法

本手册第二部分提供了一套贯穿整个系统生命周期的系统工程生命周期流程。每个流程都包含一组特定生命周期流程中的流程活动及详细说明。本节提供深入了解贯穿系统工程生命周期流程的主题、技术和方法，反映了系统工程并行、迭代和递归本质特征的各个方面。

LIFE CYCLE ANALYSES AND METHODS

3.2.1 Modeling, Analysis, and Simulation

Overview and Purpose The INCOSE Systems Engineering Vision 2035 (2022) predicts that "The future of systems engineering is model-based, leveraging next generation modeling, simulation, and visualization environments powered by the global digital transformation, to specify, analyze, design, and verify systems. High fidelity models, advanced visualization, and highly integrated, multidisciplinary simulations will allow SE Practitioners to evaluate and assess an order of magnitude more alternative designs more quickly and thoroughly than can be done on a single design today."

The essential artifact of modeling, analysis, and simulation (MA&S) is an explicit model, an idealized representation of one or more aspects of the as-is or to-be SoI. Systems Modeling and Simulation has been defined (NAFEMS and INCOSE, 2019) as the use of interdisciplinary functional, architectural, and behavioral models (with physical, mathematical, and logical representations) for all life stages.

The terms "modeling," "analysis," and "simulation" are sometimes used interchangeably. However, they clearly refer to distinct activities. *Modeling* is the conception, creation, and refinement of models. *Analysis* is the process of systematic, reproducible examination to gain insight. *Simulation* is the process of using a model to predict and study the behavior or performance of the SoI—for aspects represented in the model. Simulation is often performed to support a particular kind of analysis, but not all analysis is performed through simulation. In the classification of models presented below, two major types of models are distinguished: *physical models*, and *digital models*. The SE discipline primarily makes use of digital models, since they provide many benefits to the SE processes in a timely and affordable manner, in particular during the early life cycle stages. Other engineering disciplines make use of both physical and digital models throughout the product life cycle. Although sometimes the term "simulation" is used in conjunction with a physical model, in this section simulation always involves a digital model, and any examination involving a physical model is always a test.

For effective MA&S, digital models are often parameterized to enable analysis or simulation of multiple configurations or situations with one model. Each configuration is typically defined by grouping selected parameter values in an *experiment,* see also Minsky (1965). Alternatively, the terms "analysis case," "load case," or "verification case" are used, depending on the application domain or convention. An experiment specifies the purpose of the analysis or simulation as well as the combination of target scenario, environment, initial and boundary conditions, and any other user-defined parameters. Figure 3.8 shows a typical workflow.

3.2.1 建模、分析和仿真

概述和目的 INCOSE 系统工程愿景 2035（2022）预测，"系统工程的未来是基于模型的，利用由全球数字转型驱动的下一代的建模、仿真和可视化环境来定义、分析、设计和验证系统。高保真模型、高级可视化和高度综合的多学科仿真，将使系统工程实践者对比今天单一的设计方式会获得更快速、更彻底地评价和评估高出一个数量级的备选设计。"

建模、分析和仿真（MA&S）的基本制品是一个显性的模型，即当前或将来 SoI 的一个或多个方面的理想化的表示。将系统建模与仿真定义为（NAFEMS 和 INCOSE，2019）在生命周期的所有阶段使用跨学科的功能的、架构的和行为的模型（具有物理的、数学的和逻辑的表达形式）。

术语"建模"、"分析"和"仿真"有时可以互换使用。然而，它们明显指的是不同的活动。建模是模型的构思、创建和完善；分析是系统性的、可重复的检查流程，以获得洞察力；仿真是使用模型来预测和研究 SoI 在模型中所表示的各方面的行为或性能的流程，通常执行仿真以支持特定类型的分析，但并非所有分析都是通过仿真执行的。在下面介绍的模型分类中，区分了两种主要类型的模型：物理模型和数字模型。系统工程学科主要使用数字模型，因其以及时且可承受的方式为系统工程流程带来了多种益处，尤其是在早期生命周期阶段。其他工程学科在整个产品生命周期中使用物理模型和数字模型。虽然有时术语"仿真"与物理模型结合使用，但在本节中，仿真自始至终涉及数字模型，任何涉及物理模型的检查都是一种测试。

对于有效的 MA&S，数字模型通常被参数化，从而支持使用一个模型对多个构型配置或多个情景进行分析或仿真。每个构型配置通常由实验中分组选定的参数值来定义，另参见 Minsky（1965）。或者，根据应用领域或约定，使用术语"分析用例"、"负载用例"或"验证用例"。实验规定分析或仿真的目的，以及目标场景、环境、初始和边界条件以及任何其他用户定义的参数的组合。图 3.8 表明一个典型的工作流。

LIFE CYCLE ANALYSES AND METHODS

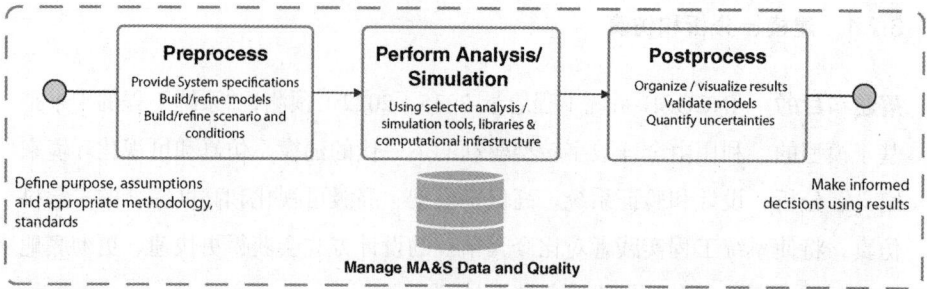

FIGURE 3.8 Schematic view of a generic MA&S process. INCOSE SEH original figure created by the NAFEMS-INCOSE Systems Modeling and Simulation Working Group (SMSWG)). Usage per the INCOSE Notices page. All other rights reserved.

193   MA&S links directly to the Core Competency "Systems Modeling and Analysis" in the INCOSE SE Competency Framework (INCOSE SECF, 2018). MA&S supports all Technical, Management and Integrating Competencies. Appropriate MA&S practices can clearly support SE professionals (individuals and teams) to perform better SE, more efficiently.

MA&S Related to Life Cycle Processes Creation and refinement of descriptive models in the Business or Mission Analysis process (see Section 2.3.5.1) and the Stakeholder Needs and Requirements Definition process (see Section 2.3.5.2) can be used to ensure that the business or mission proposition is understood correctly, the problem is understood correctly, is specified at the appropriate level of detail, and is fully shared with the stakeholders. MA&S can be used in the System Requirements Definition process (see Section 2.3.5.3) to flow-down the system requirements to system elements. This may include models that specify functional, interface, performance, and physical requirements, as well as other nonfunctional requirements (e.g., reliability, maintainability, safety, and security). In addition to bounding the system design parameters, MA&S can also be used to validate that the system requirements reflect stakeholder needs and requirements before proceeding with subsequent life cycle processes.

MA&S can be used in the System Architecture Definition process (see Section 2.3.5.4) concurrently with the Design Definition process (see Section 2.3.5.5) to synthesize and define alternative system concepts, compare and evaluate candidate options, and enable discovery of the best architecture and design, including the integration with other systems and unambiguously defining the system's capabilities and the value it is expected to deliver to its stakeholders (e.g., in the form of MOEs and MOPs). MA&S is often used extensively to realize an iterative model-based or model-driven design workflow.

图 3.8 通用 MA&S 流程示意图。INCOSE SEH 原始图由 NAFEMS-INCOSE 系统建模与仿真工作组（SMSWG）创建。按照 INCOSE 通知页使用。版权所有。

MA&S 与 INCOSE 系统工程资质框架（INCOSE SECF，2018）中的核心能力"系统建模与分析"直接相关。MA&S 支持所有技术的、管理的和综合的资质能力。适当的 MA&S 实践显然可以支持系统工程专业人员（个人和团队）以更高的效率更好地开展系统工程工作。

与生命周期流程相关的 MA&S　在业务或任务分析流程（见 2.3.5.1 节）以及利益相关方需要和需求定义流程（见 2.3.5.2 节）中创建和完善描述性模型，可用于确保正确地理解业务或任务主张，正确地理解问题，以适当的详细程度规定并与利益相关方充分共享。MA&S 可用于系统需求定义流程（见 2.3.5.3 节），以将系统需求向下传递至系统元素。这可能包括规定功能、接口、性能和物理需求以及其他非功能需求（如可靠性、可维护性、安全性和安保）的模型。除界定系统设计参数之外，MA&S 还可用于验证系统需求是否反映利益相关方的需要和需求，然后再继续后续的生命周期流程。

MA&S 可在系统架构定义流程（见 2.3.5.4 节）中与设计定义流程（见 2.3.5.5 节）并行使用，以综合和定义可选择备选系统概念，比较和评估备选选项，并发现最佳架构和设计，包括与其他系统的综合，明确定义系统的能力及其预期交付给利益相关方的价值（例如，以 MOE 和 MOP 的形式）。MA&S 通常广泛用于实现基于模型或模型驱动的迭代设计工作流。

LIFE CYCLE ANALYSES AND METHODS

In many application domains, it is much more cost—and schedule-effective to perform analysis and simulation with digital models than to prototype with physical models. Digital models also allow for full and continuous access to all model parameters and properties, which is often infeasible with physical models. MA&S lends itself to fast iterations between problem specification, architectural design, detailed design, and V&V, as well as between system elements at different levels of decomposition. Using MA&S in the System Analysis process (Section 2.3.5.6), related system analyses can be used to explore a trade space by modeling alternative system solutions, or even generate many candidate solutions, and assessing the impact of critical properties such as mass, speed, energy consumption, accuracy, reliability, and cost on the overall adequacy and performance.

MA&S can be used in the Implementation process (see Section 2.3.5.7) to support definition, understanding and prediction of behavior for various aspects of the enabling production (manufacturing) and supply chain processes for the envisaged SoI. Models that reflect the "as produced" state of the SoI can be used to develop production facilities (factory) and "digital twins." MA&S can be used in the Integration process (see Section 2.3.5.8) to support integration of the elements into a system, as well as in the Verification process (see Section 2.3.5.9) to support verification that the system satisfies its requirements. This often involves integrating lower-level hardware and software design models with system-level design models, thereby allowing verification that the system requirements are satisfied. Systems integration and verification may also include replacing selected hardware and design models with actual hardware and software products to incrementally verify that system requirements are satisfied: so-called hardware-in-the-loop and software-in-the-loop testing. In cases where testing is impossible or carries prohibitive cost, verification of the SoI can be done by analysis or simulation using high fidelity digital models. Models can be used to simulate relevant operational environments where actual environments are unattainable, too costly, or not reproducible. Simulation can use observed data as inputs for computation of critical parameters that are not directly observable.

In the Operation process (see Section 2.3.5.12), MA&S can support definition, understanding, and prediction of behavior for various aspects of the envisaged or actual operation of the SoI, to help train (future) users to interact with the system, and to develop training material. Models may form a basis for developing a simulator of the system with varying degrees of fidelity to represent user interaction in different usage scenarios. Models and simulators can also be used to perform dry runs to prepare for complex or risky operations with the real, deployed system. In the

在许多应用领域中，使用数字模型开展分析和仿真比使用物理模型开展原型开发更具成本和进度效益。数字模型还允许全面、连续地访问所有模型参数和特性，这在物理模型中通常是不可行的。MA&S 有助于在问题规范、架构设计、详细设计和验证与确认之间以及在不同分解层级的系统元素之间进行快速迭代。在系统分析流程中使用 MA&S（见 2.3.5.6 节），相关系统分析可用于探索权衡空间，通过对可选系统解决方案建模，甚至生成多个备选解决方案，并评估质量、速度、能耗、准确性、可靠性和成本等关键特性对于总体充分性和性能的影响。

MA&S 可用于实施流程（见 2.3.5.7 节），以支持所设想的 SoI 生产（制造）和供应链使能流程各个方面的定义、理解和预测的行为。反映 SoI 作为"生产"状态的模型可用于开发生产设施（工厂）和"数字孪生"。MA&S 可用于综合流程（见 2.3.5.8 节）中，以支持将元素综合到系统之中，也可用于验证流程（见 2.3.5.9 节），以支持验证系统是否满足其需求。这通常涉及将较低层级的硬件和软件设计模型与系统层级设计模型的综合，从而允许验证系统需求是否得到满足。系统综合和验证还可能包括用实际的硬件和软件产品替换选定的硬件和设计模型，以逐步验证是否满足系统需求——即所谓的硬件在环测试和软件在环测试。在无法进行测试或成本过高的情况下，可以通过使用高保真数字模型进行分析或仿真来验证 SoI。模型可用于仿真那些无法达到、成本过高或不可再现的相关实际运行，还可以使用观测数据作为输入，用于计算不可直接观测的关键参数。

在运行流程中（见 2.3.5.12 节），MA&S 可以支持所设想的或实际运行的 SoI 各个方面行为的定义、理解和预测，帮助培训（未来）用户与系统进行交互，并开发培训材料。模型可以作为开发具有不同逼真度的系统仿真器的基础，以表示不同使用场景中的用户交互方式。模型和仿真器也可用于执行演练，以便为实际部署系统的复杂性或具有风险性的运行做好准备。在维护流程中

LIFE CYCLE ANALYSES AND METHODS

Maintenance process (see Section 2.3.5.13), models that reflect the "as maintained" state of deployed systems can be used to develop "digital twins," possibly for individual deployed systems. Such models can be connected to data acquisition in the field and provide valuable insight and support for health monitoring and preventive maintenance. They can also be used to plan system upgrades and evolutions. MA&S in the Disposal process (see Section 2.3.5.14) can be used to predict and monitor system disposal. MA&S also enables model-based iterations between the development processes mentioned above, as depicted in Figure 3.9.

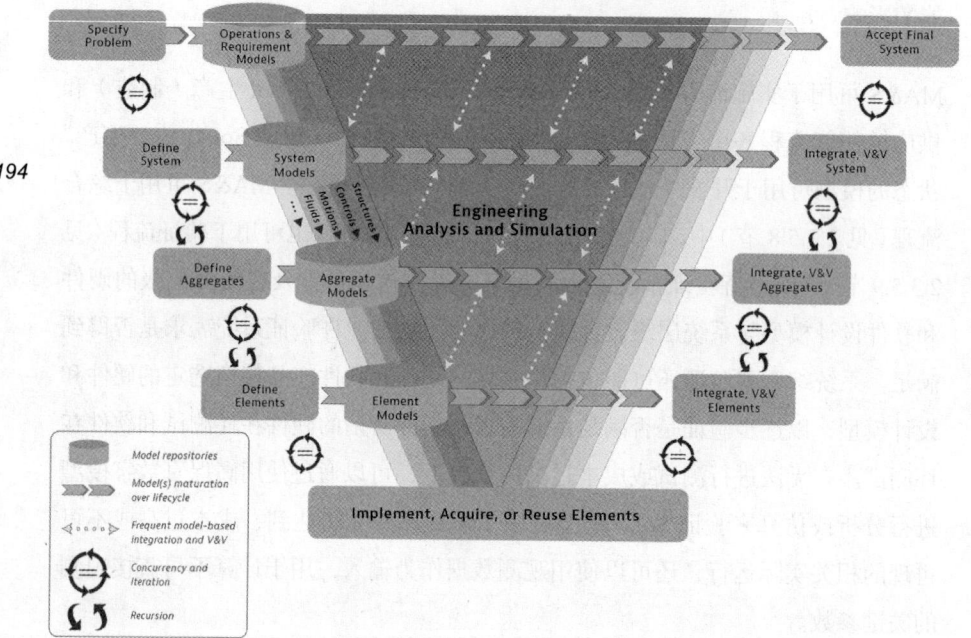

FIGURE 3.9 System development with early, iterative V&V and integration, via modeling, analysis, and simulation. Derived from NAFEMS and INCOSE (2019), based on NDIA, et al. (2011). Used with permission. All other rights reserved.

Cross-Cutting MA&S There are several cross-cutting uses of MA&S that are not tied to a particular life cycle process, including:

Characterizing an existing system—Existing systems may be poorly documented (in whole or in part). Modeling such a system can provide a concise way to capture its architecture and design. This model can then be used to facilitate maintenance of the system or its further evolution.

生命周期分析和方法

(见 2.3.5.13 节),可使用反映已部署系统"维护"状态的模型来开发"数字孪生",可能用于单个部署的系统。此类模型可以与现场的数据采集相连接,并为健康监测和预防性维护提供有价值的洞察和支持。它们还可用于规划系统升级和演进。处置流程中的 MA&S(见 2.3.5.14 节)可用于预测和监控系统处置。MA&S 还支持在上述开发流程之间基于模型的迭代,如图 3.9 所示。

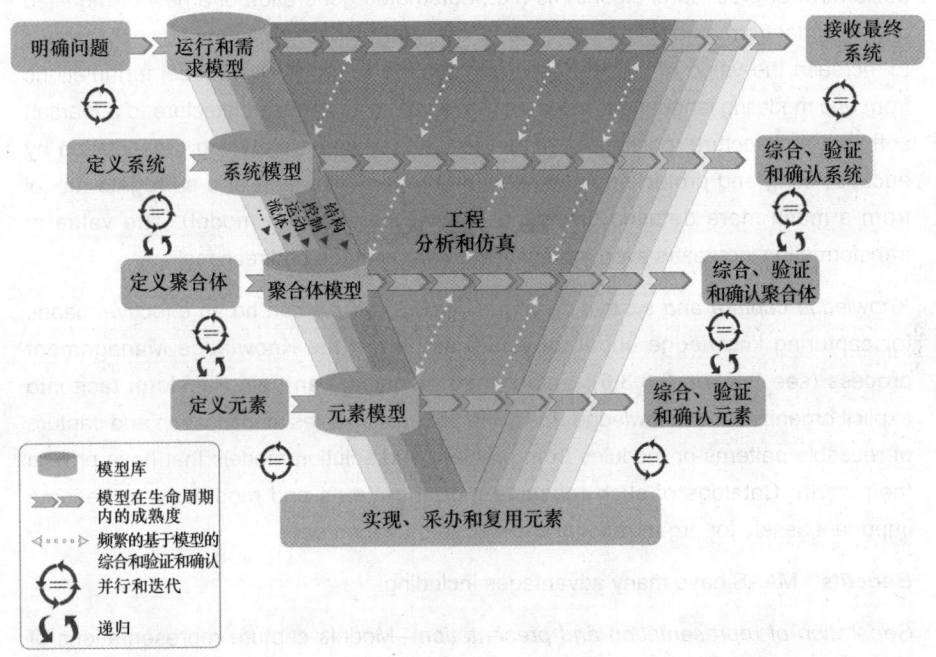

图 3.9 通过建模、分析和仿真,进行早期迭代 V&V 和综合的系统开发。源自 NAFEMS 和 INCOSE(2019),基于 NDIA 等(2011)。经许可后使用。版权所有。

跨领域/学科的 MA&S MA&S 具有多种与特定生命周期流程无关的跨领域/学科的用途,包括:

对现有系统特征化描述——现有系统可能缺乏文档(全部或部分)。对于这样一个系统的建模,可以提供一种简洁的方法来捕获其架构和设计。然后,该模型可用于促进系统的维护或进一步的演进。

LIFE CYCLE ANALYSES AND METHODS

Knowledge transfer within teams—MA&S enables the creation and maintenance of more precise, elaborate, and consistent specifications, including the rationale behind many requirements or design choices. Capturing specifications in rich models helps to mitigate the risk of loss of knowledge in case of team changes in long-duration projects.

Automated mapping and transformation—Digital models can be transformed by declarative or procedural algorithms (i.e., automated generation of a new or modified digital model from an existing one). Model transformations are a very powerful means to increase the value of model-based engineering (e.g., convert model formulations from one modeling language to another, move from a systems architecture to a (partial) software architecture, package a model for use outside the owning organization by encapsulating and protecting its intellectual property, creation of a surrogate model from a much more detailed discipline-specific engineering model). The value of transformation increases even more when it can be made bi-directional.

Knowledge capture and system design evolution—MA&S can be an effective means for capturing knowledge about a system as part of the Knowledge Management process (see Section 2.3.3.6). Established modeling can help transform tacit into explicit organizational knowledge. MA&S in projects enables identification and capture of reusable patterns or modules from problem and solution models that have proven their worth. Catalogs of such reusable model patterns and modules can become important assets for organizational knowledge management.

Benefits MA&S have many advantages including:

Separation of representation and presentation—Models capture representations of an SoI. MA&S tooling can then be used to maintain an "authoritative source of truth" and produce many different presentations, or views, of the model(s) that are correct-by-construction and enable effective communication with all engineering and non-engineering actors (humans and machines). The model-based approach can thus overcome the main problem of the documentcentric approach in which representation and presentation are often combined in single information containers, which leads to a lot of information duplication and therefore cumbersome maintenance and potential errors. This is one of the most important advantages of the model-centric over the traditional document-centric approach.

More explicit SE—SE Practitioners can use MA&S to systematically check their own thinking, assumptions, and decision making with quantitative analyses. They can capture rationales and decisions in an accessible, traceable, consistent way.

团队内知识转移——MA&S 支持创建和维护更加精确、详细和一致的规范，包括许多需求或设计选择背后的基本原理。通过丰富的模型捕获规范，有助于长期项目中出现团队变更时减少知识损失的风险。

自动映射和转换——数字模型可以通过声明性或程序性算法（即，从现有数字模型自动生成新的或修改的数字模型）进行转换。模型转换是增加基于模型的工程价值的一种非常强大的手段 [如，将模型公式从一种建模语言转换为另一种建模语言，从系统架构转换为软件架构（部分），通过封装和保护其知识产权将模型打包供所属组织之外使用，从更加详细的学科特定的工程模型中创建替身模型]。当转换可以双向进行时，变换的价值会增加更多。

知识获取与系统设计演进——作为知识管理流程的一部分，MA&S 是获取系统知识的有效手段（见 2.3.3.6 节）。所建立的模型有助于将隐性知识转化为显性的组织知识。项目的 MA&S 支持从经证明其价值的问题和解决方案模型中识别和捕获可重用的模式或模块。此类可重用模型模式和模块的编目可以成为组织知识管理的重要资产。

收益　建模分析与仿真有诸多优势，包括：

表征与展示的分离——模型捕获一个 SoI 的表征。然后，能够使用 MA&S 工具来维护"权威真相源"，并生成"构造即正确"模型的许多不同展示方式或视图，并且能够促进与所有工程和非工程参与者（人和机器）的有效沟通。因此，基于模型的方法可以克服以文档为中心的方法的主要问题，在以文档为中心的方法中，表征和展示通常组合在单一的信息容器中，这会导致大量信息的重复，从而导致烦琐的维护和潜在的错误。与传统的以文档为中心的方法相比，这是以模型为中心的方法最重要的优点之一。

更加显性的系统工程——系统工程实践者可以使用 MA&S，通过定量分析系统地检查自己的思维、假设和决策。他们可以以一种可访问、可追溯、一致的方式捕获基本原理和决策。

LIFE CYCLE ANALYSES AND METHODS

Better problem specification—The stakeholder needs and requirements can be refined and formalized as an integral and structured set of goals, assumptions, requirements, constraints, actors, typical usage scenarios, and critical capabilities, with full traceability between all model elements. Anticipated system behaviors and performances can be explored and vetted with the stakeholders before proceeding with the development of an actual solution and committing significant resources.

Rigorous, well-documented design—MA&S facilitates development of solutions in a more rigorous and consistent way which leads to higher quality specifications. Systematic design space exploration and structured trade-studies become possible. Interfaces can be defined rigorously. Simulation with digital models enables design experimentation and optimization that is impossible, not affordable, or not on time with physical models. Technical and business decision-making can also be integrated into the model repositories for future consultation.

Early V&V to reduce risk—Early validation and verification of solutions with respect to the problem specification can be performed. This enables stakeholders to be informed of the implications of their preferences, provides perspective for evaluating alternatives, and builds confidence in the solution as it develops. Systematic, regular checking of interfaces and actual interconnections is feasible. It also allows catching issues early in the life cycle, when mitigation is affordable and change of scope is still feasible. The ability to detect limitations and incompatibilities early in a project helps avoid cost and schedule overruns in later life cycle stages.

Multi-user collaboration—Use of modern MA&S tooling allows for multi-user and multi-discipline collaboration with integrated configuration and version control, including splitting work into distinct parallel branches and merging results back into a main branch, using well-established workflows. Once deployed, this workflow is much more sophisticated and effective than what could be achieved with a document-centric approach.

Better change impact assessment—Modeled specifications with traceability (see Section 3.2.3) and MA&S tooling allow for change impact assessments by highlighting the consequences of a considered change.

Improved mastering of complexity—The value of MA&S increases with the complexity of the SoI, be it functional or physical. MA&S is a means to master greater complexity by structuring, refining, evaluating, and sharing all information within integrated project teams. On-demand multiple views with dynamic filtering to a suitable level of detail are possible. Quick views to share and capture information for effective communication with other actors, such as non-engineering disciplines and stakeholders, become more feasible and affordable.

更好的问题规范——利益相关方的需要和需求可以细化并形式化为一组完整的和结构化的目标、假设、需求、约束、参与者、典型用例场景和关键功能，并在所有模型元素之间具有完全的可追溯性。在继续开发实际解决方案和投入大量资源之前，可以与利益相关方一起探索和评审预期的系统行为和性能。

严谨且记录翔实的设计——MA&S 以更加严谨和一致的方式促进解决方案的开发，从而实现更高质量的规范。系统的设计空间探索和结构化的权衡研究成为可能。接口可以严格定义。使用数字模型开展仿真可以实现物理模型可能做不到、无法承受或不能按时开展的设计实验和优化。还可以将技术和业务决策综合到模型存储库中，以便将来进行咨询。

早期验证和确认以降低风险——可以针对问题规范对解决方案进行早期的确认和验证。这使利益相关方能够了解其偏好的影响，为评估备选方案提供视角，并在解决方案开发流程中建立信心。系统化的、定期的检查接口和实际互连关系是可行的。它还允许在生命周期的早期发现问题，此时缓解措施是可以承受的，范围的改变也是可行的。在项目早期发现限制和不兼容的能力，有助于避免生命周期后期阶段的成本超支和进度延期。

多用户协作——使用现代 MA&S 工具，可以通过综合的构型配置和版本控制开展多用户和多学科的协同，包括使用完善的工作流将工作拆分为不同的并行分支，并将结果合并回主分支。当部署时，此工作流将比以文档为中心的方法更复杂、更有效。

更好的变更影响评估——具有可追溯性的建模规范（见 3.2.3 节）和 MA&S 工具的使用，允许通过强调所考虑变更的后果来开展变更影响评估。

改进对复杂性的掌握——MA&S 的价值随着 SoI 的复杂性而增加，无论是功能性的还是物理性的。MA&S 是一种通过在综合项目团队中构建、细化、评估和共享所有信息来掌握更大复杂性的方式。可以根据需要将多个视图动态过滤到适当的详细程度。快速查看以共享和捕获信息，以便与其他参与者（如非工程学科和利益相关方）进行有效沟通，使其变得更加可行和可承受。

Better team planning and handover—Development, deployment, and operational staff can more easily comprehend the design specifications, appreciate imposed limits from technology and management, and ensure an adequate degree of sustainability. Adequate, accurate, and timely MA&S helps an organization and its suppliers to plan and put in place the necessary and sufficient personnel, methods, tools, and infrastructure for system realization.

Enable efficient maintenance and traceability—Digital models (supported with appropriate tools) enable bookkeeping of SE artifacts as they evolve through the life cycle stages in a reliable, consistent, traceable, and timely manner, while also providing hyperlinked navigation.

Flexible and repeatable querying—A rigorous MA&S approach enables gaining insight into many different aspects by querying the models with pertinent questions (what-if, impact of change, etc.) and getting answers efficiently, in support of decision making. Queries can generate many different views from the modeled information that address concerns of selected stakeholders. Query formulations can also be persisted for reuse.

Classifying and Characterizing Models There are many different kinds of models to address different system aspects and different kinds of systems. Generally, a specific type of model focuses on some subset of the system characteristics, such as timing, process behavior, measures of performance, interfaces, and connections. It is useful to classify the types of models to assist in selecting the appropriate one. Figure 3.10 shows one possible (non-exhaustive) taxonomy as an example.

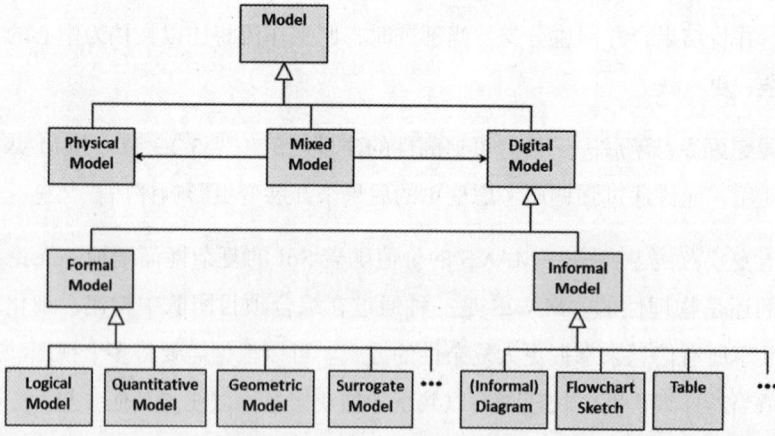

FIGURE 3.10 Illustrative model taxonomy (non-exhaustive). INCOSE SEH original figure created by the NAFEMS-INCOSE Systems Modeling and Simulation Working Group (SMSWG) derived from Friedenthal. Usage per the INCOSE Notices page. All other rights reserved.

更好的团队规划和移交——开发、部署和运行人员可以更容易地理解设计规范，理解技术和管理的限制，并确保充分的可持续性。充分、准确和及时的 MA&S 有助于组织及其供应商规划和落实系统实现所需的充足的人员、方法、工具和基础设施。

实现高效维护和可追溯性——数字模型（由合适的工具支持）能够可靠、一致、可跟踪和及时地记录系统工程制品在生命周期各个阶段的演进流程，同时还提供超链接导航。

灵活和可重复的查询——通过使用相关问题（假设、变更的影响等）查询模型并高效地得到答案，严谨的 MA&S 实施方法能够深入洞察许多不同的方面，以支持决策。查询可从建模信息中生成许多不同的视图，以解决所选利益相关方的问题。查询格式也可持久保存，以便重复使用。

模型分类和特征描述　　具有多种不同类型的模型处理不同的系统方面和不同类型系统的问题。通常，特定类型的模型聚焦于系统特性的一些子集，例如时间、流程行为、性能测度、接口以及连接。对模型类型进行分类有助于选择合适的模型。例如，图 3.10 表明一种可能的（非详尽的）分类法。

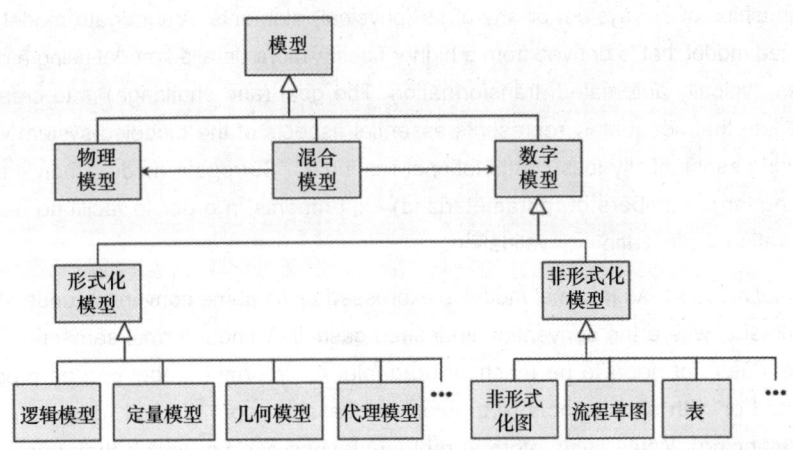

图 3.10　说明性模型分类（非详尽）。INCOSE SEH 原始图由 NAFEMS-INCOSE 系统建模与仿真工作组（SMSWG）创建。按照 INCOSE 通知页使用。版权所有。

LIFE CYCLE ANALYSES AND METHODS

Physical model—A physical model represents (aspects of) a system with real parts. Examples are a physical mockup, a scaled model airplane, a wind tunnel model, and a 3D-printed scale model from a digital model specification (the latter could be considered a physical view of a digital model). If simulation is performed with a physical model, it is typically called a test.

Digital model—Digital models can have many different expressions to represent (e.g., a system, entity, phenomenon, or process), each of which may vary in degrees of formalism. Therefore, the next level of classification is between informal and formal models.

Formal models—A formal model is expressed in a machine-readable language with explicitly defined semantics. The language may be textual and/or graphical, but with only one way of interpretation. Formal models can be further classified as logical, quantitative (i.e., mathematical), geometric, or surrogate models. A logical model, also referred to as a descriptive model or a conceptual model, represents logical relationships about the system such as whole–part relationships, interconnection relationships between elements, or precedence relationships between activities, to name a few. Logical models are often depicted using network graphs (with nodes and edges) or tables. A quantitative model represents quantitative relationships (e.g., mathematical equations) about the system or its elements that yield numerical results. A geometric model represents the geometry, geometric shapes, and spatial relationships of the system or any of its (physical) elements. A surrogate model is a reduced model that is derived from a higher fidelity, more detailed model using a data-driven, typically automated, transformation. The goal (and challenge) is to create a surrogate that adequately represents essential aspects of the modeled system while requiring substantially less computational resources. Surrogate models then enable running large numbers of (parameterized) experiments in order to facilitate design exploration, optimization, or validation.

Informal models—An informal model is expressed using some convention understood by humans, where the convention is defined casually without formal semantics. The model does not need to be machine-readable. An informal model can be created by hand or with simple tools (e.g., word-processing, spreadsheet, diagramming, mindmapping). While such informal representations can be useful, they often lack the rigor to be considered a type of model that is truly usable for MA&S for non-trivial systems. Informal model presentations may be used as views that are generated from or ingested into formal models in order to communicate with people not familiar with the notation.

物理模型——物理模型使用真实部件表示系统（方面）。例如物理模型、比例模型飞机、风洞模型以及源于数字模型规范的 3D 打印比例模型，可将后者视为数字模型的物理视图。如果使用物理模型进行仿真，通常称为测试。

数字模型——数字模型可用许多不同的表达方式来表示（例如，系统、实体、现象或流程），每个表达方式的形式化程度可能不同。因此，下一级的分类区分非形式化模型和形式化模型。

形式化模型——形式化模型使用具有明确定义语义的机器可读语言表示。语言可以是文本和/或图形，但仅有一种解释方式。形式化模型又可以进一步分为逻辑模型、定量模型（即数学模型）、几何模型或替身模型。逻辑模型，也称为描述性或概念模型，表示系统的逻辑关系，例如整体—部分关系、元素之间的互联关系或活动之间的优先关系等。逻辑模型通常使用网络图（包含节点和边）或表来描述。定量模型表示有关系统或其元素的定量关系（如数学方程），从而产生数值结果。几何模型表示系统或其任何（物理）元素的几何图形、几何形状和空间关系。代理模型是一种简化模型，使用数据驱动的、通常是自动的转换，从更高保真、更详细的模型派生而来。其目标（也是挑战）是创建一个代理，充分代表建模系统的基本方面，同时需要较少的计算资源。然后，代理模型可以运行大量（参数化）实验，以促进设计探索、优化或验证。

非形式化模型——非形式化模型使用人理解的某种约定表示，其中约定是随意定义的，没有形式化的语义。模型不需要是机器可读的。非形式化模型可以手动创建，也可以使用简单的工具（例如文字处理、电子表格、图表、思维导图）创建。虽然这种非形式化表示可能有用，但它们通常缺乏严谨性，不能被视为真正可用于有意义的系统的 MA&S 模型类型。非形式化模型表示可以用作从形式化模型生成或输入形式化模型的视图，以便与不熟悉符号的人员进行交流。

LIFE CYCLE ANALYSES AND METHODS

Mixed models—A mixed model is a combination of physical and digital models.

In addition to a selected type of model, any model can be further characterized for its intended purpose through the following three characteristics:

- The *model breadth* reflects what aspects of the SoI—and possibly its (actual or intended) environment(s)—are represented, and to what extent.

- The *model granularity* characterizes the amount of visible detail captured in the model, in terms of the represented depth of system decomposition as well as the represented level of details of individual system elements.

- The *model fidelity* indicates how accurately the model represents the real-world system. Where applicable, this includes the computational precision to be achieved and the discretization scheme to be used.

The type of model and the model characteristics must be balanced against project needs and resources. Another important aspect of modeling is to explicitly state the assumptions and limitations that almost inevitably apply to any model.

Model Interoperability Since the development of complex systems requires collaboration between all project members and disciplines, it is very important to have the ability to exchange and share models as well as analysis and simulation results across disciplines, projects, organizations, and life cycle stages. This is also referred to as *digital interchange*. In most projects and (extended) enterprises it is not possible to standardize on a single set of tools. The alternative is to develop and utilize open, tool-independent standards that enable information exchange and sharing. There is an increasing awareness and consensus between user communities and tool developers on the merit of international royalty-free standards. Standards can be categorized in terms of how MA&S is supported. The main categories are:

- Standardized data exchange file,

- Application programming interface (API),

- Modeling language, and

- Process.

Data exchange files are used for on-demand transfer of complete models or results. APIs usually support more finegrained data access and sharing, often implementing a service-oriented software architecture. Modeling languages can be graphical, textual or both, and are used to standardize the way of expressing a model. Process standards specify (aspects of) the MA&S processes. Most modeling languages do not prescribe a particular methodology to be followed. This

混合模型——混合模型是物理模型和数字模型的组合。

除了所选类型的模型外，任何模型都可通过以下三个特征进一步确定其预期目的：

- *模型广度*反映 SoI 及其（实际或预期）环境的哪些方面得到体现，以及体现的程度。

- *模型粒度*表征模型中捕获的可见细节的数量，即系统分解的表示深度以及单个系统元素的细节表示程度。

- *模型保真度*表示模型如何准确地反映真实世界的系统。在适用的情况下，这包括要达到的计算精度和所使用的离散化方案。

模型类型和模型特征必须与项目需要和资源相平衡。建模的另一个重要方面是明确说明几乎不可避免地适用于任何模型的假设和限制。

模型互操作性　由于复杂系统的开发需要所有项目成员和学科之间的协同，因此具有跨学科、项目、组织和生命周期阶段交换和共享模型以及分析和仿真结果的能力非常重要。这也称为数字交换。在大多数项目和（扩展的）复杂组织体系中，不可能在单个工具集上实现标准化。另一种选择是开发和利用开放的、工具独立的标准，以实现信息交换和共享。用户群体和工具开发人员对国际免版税标准的价值有了进一步的认识和共识。可以根据支持 MA&S 的方式对标准进行分类。主要类别包括：

- 标准化数据交换文件；

- 应用编程接口（API）；

- 建模语言；

- 流程。

数据交换文件用于按需传输完整的模型或结果。API 通常支持更细粒度的数据访问和共享，通常支持面向服务的软件架构的实施。建模语言可以是图形语言、文本语言或两者兼有，并用于标准化模型的表达。流程标准规定 MA&S 流程（及其各个方面）。大多数建模语言都没有规定需遵循的特定方法。这种

flexibility is a feature of a general-purpose modeling language that enables economies of scale for implementations which are in the interest of the SE community as a whole. However, in order to align how SE practitioners in a team, organization, or application domain approach MA&S, a methodology is needed. A methodology provides guidance and examples on how to organize MA&S over a typical system life cycle, how to structure model artifacts, as well as what stages and milestones to respect. A methodology can also capture proven modeling patterns and checklists, as well as good practices in general. For further details se Section 4.2.1 or consult the OMG MBSE Wiki (2023).

Tools For physical models, the tools are generally the same as those used for production of the final SoI, plus general or dedicated test facilities. For digital models, the tools are typically MA&S software applications running on general-purpose digital computers. For some computationally intensive applications, HPC (High Performance Computing) facilities may be needed. A MA&S software application may consist of one integrated tool or a set of tools that each implement part of the needed capabilities. The typical features of such tools are a graphical user interface with a hierarchical model structure browser, palettes of model constructs, a graphical and/or textual editor for creation and modification of the model, and multiple views for visualization, reporting, diagnostics, etc. The tool typically checks on-the-fly for adherence to the supported modeling formalism or language. If analysis or simulation support is included, there are also model execution views. For further details consult INCOSE SETDB (2021) or NAFEMS (2021).

Modeling Quality and Metrics The quality of a model should not be confused with the quality of the design that the model represents. A perfect model can represent a bad design. On the other hand, a low-quality model can in principle represent a good design, although that is not very useful.

A completed model or simulation can be considered a system or a product in its own right. Therefore, the general steps in the development and application of a model are closely aligned to the SE processes described within this handbook. MA&S needs to be planned and tracked, just like any other developmental effort. An essential good practice is to define clearly the purpose and intended life cycle of any (type of) model upfront. In particular, verification and validation of the MA&S methods, procedures, and infra-structure themselves are essential to ensure that the resulting models, analyses, and simulations possess the required quality and credibility that make them "fit for purpose" in an application domain or project. The required rigor of the approach depends on the criticality of the SoI. As an example, the US DoD Modeling and Simulation Enterprise has developed comprehensive guidance on Verification, Validation and Accreditation (VV&A, 2021).

灵活性是通用建模语言的一个特性，它可以为符合整个系统工程群体的利益的实现带来规模经济。然而，为了使团队、组织或应用领域中的系统工程实践者在处理 MA&S 问题时保持一致，需要一种方法论。方法论提供关于如何在典型的系统生命周期中组织 MA&S、如何构建模型制品以及需要遵守哪些阶段和里程碑的指导和示例。方法论还可以捕获经证明的建模模式和检查表，以及一般的良好实践。更多相关的详细信息，参阅 4.2.1 节或 OMG MBSE Wiki（2023）。

工具　对于物理模型，工具通常与用于生产最终 SoI 的工具相同，再加上通用或专用测试设施。对于数字模型，这些工具通常是在通用数字计算机上运行的 MA&S 软件应用。对于一些计算密集型的应用，可能需要高性能计算（HPC）设施。一个 MA&S 软件应用可能由一个综合工具或一组工具组成，每个工具实现所需功能的一部分。此类工具的典型特征是具有层级模型结构浏览器的图形用户界面、模型构造选项板、创建和修改模型的图形和/或文本编辑器以及用于可视化、报告、诊断等的多个视图。该工具通常会动态检查是否符合支持的建模形式或语言。如果包含分析或仿真支持，则还存在模型执行视图。有关更多详细信息，咨询 INCOSE SETDB（2021）或 NAFEMS（2021）。

建模质量和指标　模型的质量不应与模型所代表的设计质量相混淆。完美的模型可以表示糟糕的设计。另一方面，低质量的模型原则上可以表示一个好的设计，尽管这不是很有用。

可将一个完整的模型或仿真本身视为一个系统或一个产品。因此，模型开发和应用的一般步骤与本手册中描述的系统工程流程密切相关。与其他开发工作一样，需要规划和跟踪 MA&S。一个基本的良好实践是预先明确定义任何（类型）模型的目的和预期生命周期。尤其是，MA&S 方法、程序和基础设施本身的验证和确认对于确保生成的模型、分析和仿真具有所需的质量和可信度，使其"适配目标"应用领域或项目而言至关重要。该实施方法所需的严谨性取决于 SoI 的关键性。例如，美国国防部建模与仿真复杂组织体制定了关于验证、确认和认可的综合指南（VV&A，2021）。

LIFE CYCLE ANALYSES AND METHODS

A valuable feature of digital models is that they are amenable to many other kinds of computation than pure analysis or simulation. This enables the assertion of many modeling metrics such as:

- compliance with design or certification rules, including naming conventions, and associated model quality requirements,
- structural consistency of the system architecture,
- compliance of system element interconnections with interface specifications,
- coverage, consistency, and completeness of traceability, such as requirements satisfaction and verification, as well as function allocation,
- consistency and completeness of logical to physical architecture mapping and allocation,
- statistics that assist in monitoring and establishing specification maturity, uncertainty quantification, and resource planning,

MA&S Industrial Practice A big driver for the adoption of MA&S via all engineering disciplines is the trend that complex systems are becoming more and more software intensive. Analysis and simulation using digital models is much more economical and scalable than prototyping and testing with physical models, especially in the earlier stages of the life cycle. In the later stages, a mixed approach is often used. An example of the latter is an incremental hard-ware-in-the-loop approach in performing dynamic simulations. When it can be justified, verification through a purely digital model may be used.

199 Since a major responsibility of SE is to regard the system as a whole and coordinate between all disciplines in a multidisciplinary team, it follows that SE MA&S must interoperate at some level with the modeling and simulation of each of the other engineering disciplines in a team. As shown in Figure 3.11, the trend is to use an integrated system model to ensure information consistency between all engineering disciplines through a hub-and-spokes pattern, where a system model repository forms the hub.

A different way to look at multidisciplinary MA&S coordination is shown in the life cycle view presented in Figure 3.12. The information needed by two or more disciplines in a project team is shared via the integrated system model repository, which acts as the "authoritative source of truth." Within a project, there is then one authoritative repository. The one authoritative repository is a logical concept that may be implemented as a federation of distributed physical repositories. The figure schematically depicts several examples of synchronizations, milestones, and baselines (in a real project there will of course be many more). In addition, MA&S data management supporting versioning, branching, merging, and archiving needs to be implemented for each of the threads, as well as across all organizations in an extended enterprise.

数字模型的一个有价值的特点是，除了单纯的分析或仿真之外，它们还可以进行许多其他类型的计算。这支持建立许多建模指标，例如：

- 符合设计或认证规则，包括命名约定和相关模型质量需求；
- 系统架构的结构一致性；
- 系统元素互连符合接口规范；
- 可追溯性的覆盖范围、一致性和完整性，如需求的满足和验证，以及功能分配；
- 逻辑到物理架构映射和分配的一致性和完整性；
- 辅助监测和建立规范成熟度、不确定性量化和资源规划的统计数据。

建模分析与仿真行业实践 所有工程学科采用 MA&S 的一个重大驱动力是复杂系统软件密集程度越来越高。使用数字模型进行分析和仿真要比使用物理模型进行原型开发和测试更经济、更具可扩展性，尤其是在生命周期的早期阶段。在后期阶段，通常使用混合方法。后者的一个示例是执行动态仿真时的增量硬件在环的实施方法。在合理的情况下，可以使用纯数字模型进行验证。

由于系统工程的主要职责是将系统视为一个整体，并在多学科团队中协调所有学科，因此，系统工程 MA&S 必须在一定程度上与团队中其他每个工程学科的建模和仿真互操作。如图 3.11 所示，当前的趋势是使用综合系统模型，通过"枢纽—辐条"模式确保所有工程学科之间的信息一致性，系统模型库构成其中的枢纽。

图 3.12 所示的生命周期视图表明了看待多学科 MA&S 协同的不同方式。项目团队中两个或多个学科所需的信息通过综合的系统模型存储库共享，该存储库充当"权威真相源"。在一个项目中，就有一个权威存储库。权威存储库是一个逻辑概念，可以作为分布式物理存储库的联合体得以实施。该图示意性地描述同步、里程碑和基线的若干示例（在实际项目中，当然还有更多）。此外，需要为每个线索以及扩展的复杂组织体系中的所有组织实施支持版本控制、分支、合并和归档的 MA&S 数据管理。

LIFE CYCLE ANALYSES AND METHODS

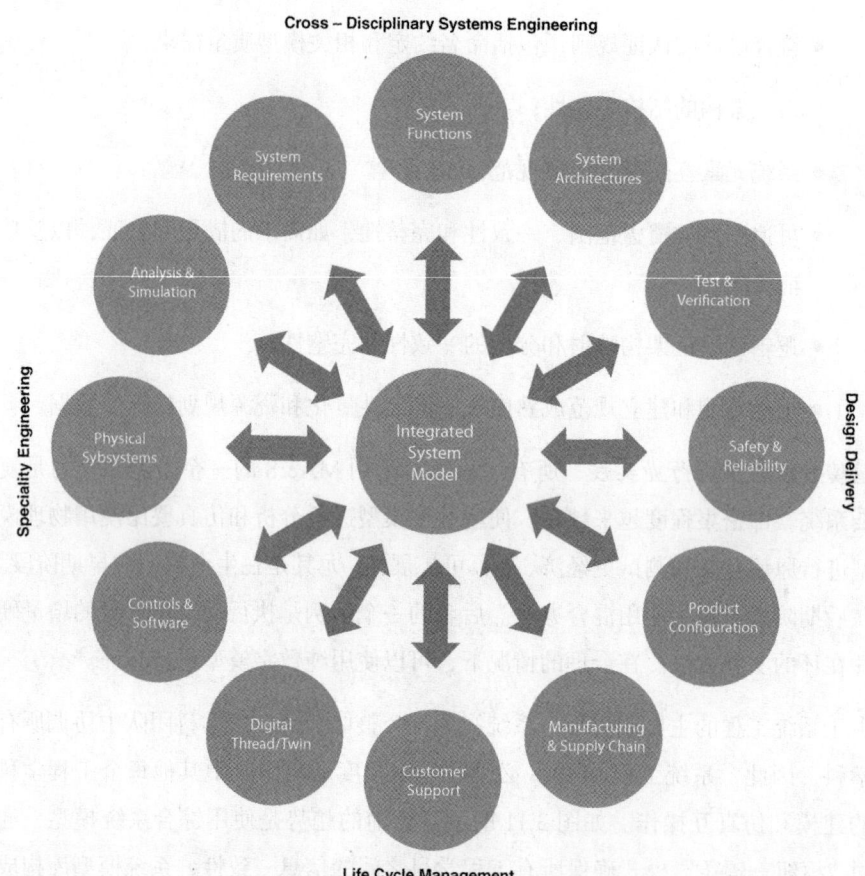

FIGURE 3.11 Model-based integration across multiple disciplines using a hub-and-spokes pattern. Derived from NAFEMS and INCOSE (2019). Used with permission. All other rights reserved.

200   When different organizations collaborate in an extended enterprise, the need may arise to protect intellectual property, which naturally includes the know-how captured in models. To enable such collaboration, often so-called *black box* (also known as opaque box) models are created and maintained, which hide or obfuscate intellectual property, while still providing a publicly accessible external interface for using them to perform simulations. In contrast, *white box* (also known as *transparent box*) *models* provide full visibility of their internals.

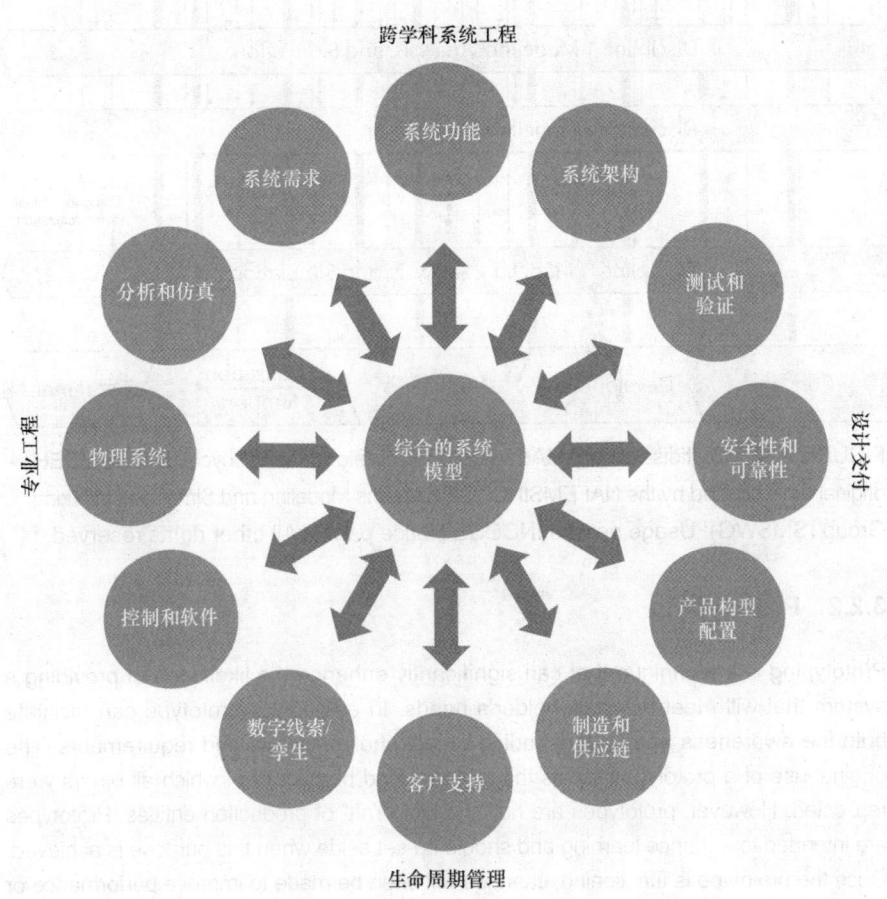

图 3.11 利用 "枢纽—辐条" 模式实现基于模型的跨学科综合。源自 NAFEMS 和 INCOSE（2019）。经许可后使用。版权所有。

当不同的组织在一个扩展的复杂组织体系中协同时，可能需要保护知识产权，这自然包括模型中捕获的专有技术。为了实现这种协同，通常会创建和维护所谓的黑盒（也称为不透明盒）模型，这些模型会隐藏或混淆知识产权，同时仍然提供了一个公开访问的外部接口，以便使用它们执行仿真。相比之下，白盒（也称为透明盒）模型提供其内部的完整可见性。

LIFE CYCLE ANALYSES AND METHODS

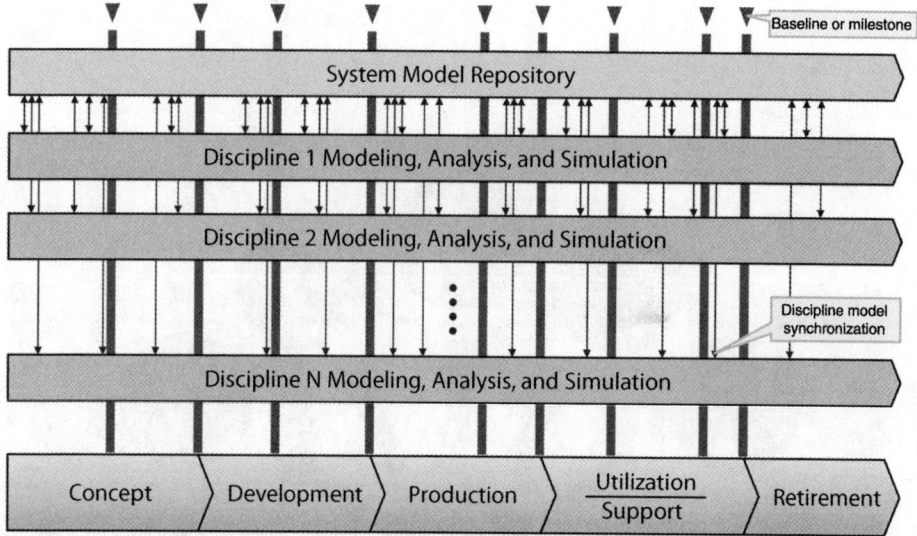

FIGURE 3.12   Multidisciplinary MA&S coordination along the life cycle. INCOSE SEH original table created by the NAFEMSINCOSE Systems Modeling and Simulation Working Group (SMSWG). Usage per the INCOSE Notice pages. All other rights reserved.

3.2.2   Prototyping

Prototyping is a technique that can significantly enhance the likelihood of providing a system that will meet the stakeholder's needs. In addition, a prototype can facilitate both the awareness and understanding of stakeholder needs and requirements. The original use of a prototype was as the first-of-a-kind product from which all others were replicated. However, prototypes are not "the first draft" of production entities. Prototypes are intended to enhance learning and should be set aside when this purpose is achieved. Once the prototype is functioning, changes will often be made to improve performance or reduce production costs. Thus, the production entity may exhibit different behavior. Two types of prototyping are commonly used: rapid and traditional.

Rapid prototyping is an easy and one of the fastest ways to get system performance data and evaluate alternate concepts (Noorani, 2008). A rapid prototype is a particular type of physical model or simulation quickly assembled from a menu of existing physical, graphical, or mathematical elements. Examples include tools such as laser lithography or computer simulation shells. 3-D printing, or additive manufacturing, has significantly enhanced the physical elements that can be prototyped (Gebhardt and Hotte, 2016). Rapid prototypes are frequently used to investigate form and fit, human–system interface, operations, or producibility considerations. They are widely used and are particularly useful; but except in rare cases, they are not traditional "prototypes."

生命周期分析和方法

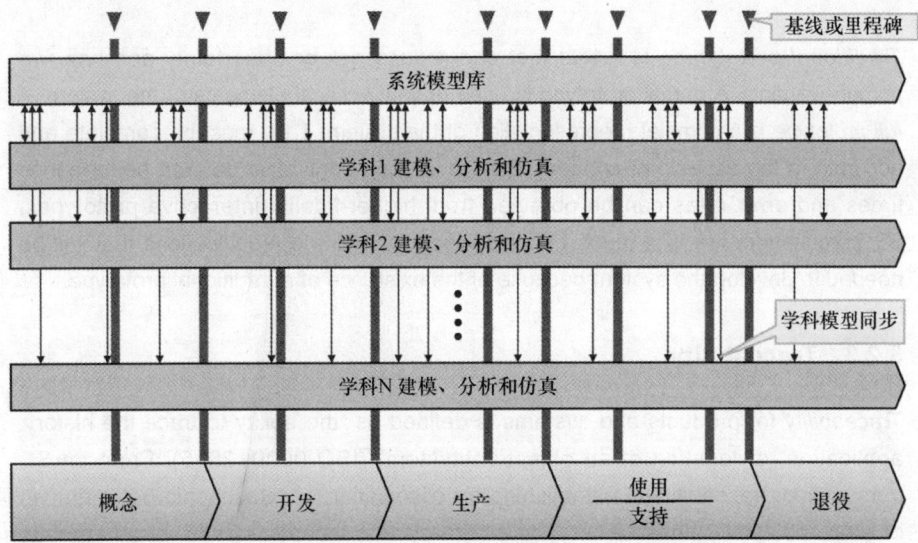

图 3.12 生命周期内的多学科 MA&S 协同。INCOSE SEH 原始图由 NAFEMS-INCOSE 系统建模与仿真工作组（SMSWG）创建。按照 INCOSE 通知页使用。版权所有。

3.2.2 原型开发

原型开发是一种能够显著提高提供满足利益相关方需求的系统的可能性的技术。此外，原型可以促进对利益相关方需要和需求的认识和理解。原型的最初用途是作为第一种产品，所有其他产品都是从中复制出来的。然而，原型并不是生产实体的"初稿"。原型旨在增强学习，当达到此目的时，应将其放在一边。一旦原型正常运行，通常会进行更改以提高性能或降低生产成本。因此，生产实体可能表现出不同的行为。通常使用两种类型的原型：快速原型和传统原型。

*快速原型开发*是获取系统性能数据和评估备选概念的简单且最快的方法之一（Noorani，2008）。快速原型是从现有物理、图形或数学元素菜单中快速组装的一种特定类型的物理模型或仿真。例如，激光光刻或计算机仿真 Shell 等工具。3D 打印或增材制造显著增强原型化的物理元素（Gebhardt 和 Hotte，2016）。快速原型通常用于研究形状和匹配性、人机界面、运行或可生产性的考虑因素。它们被广泛使用，而且特别有用；但除了少数情况外，快速原型不是传统的"原型"。

LIFE CYCLE ANALYSES AND METHODS

Traditional prototyping is a tool that can reduce risk or uncertainty and has two primary variants. A partial prototype is used to verify critical elements of the system. *A full prototype* is a complete representation of the system. They must be complete and accurate in the aspects of concern. Objective and quantitative data on performance times and error rates can be obtained from higher-fidelity interactive prototypes. SE practitioners are in a much better position to evaluate modifications that will be needed to develop the system because of the existence of a traditional prototype.

3.2.3 Traceability

Traceability for products and systems is defined as "the ability to trace the history, application, or location of an object/entity/item" (ISO 9000, 2015). From an SE perspective, traceability is establishing an association or relationship between two or more objects/entities/items such as life cycle concepts, needs, requirements, architectural definition artifacts (e.g., systems, system elements), design definition artifacts, verification artifacts, validation artifacts, information, models, and acquired or supplied systems or system elements.

Bidirectional traceability is the ability to trace an object/entity/item to another object/entity/item while automatically establishing a reverse link back to the initial object/entity/item. Thus, once a given object/entity/item has been linked to its source/destination, the source/destination is automatically linked to that object/entity/item. Bidirectional traceability is facilitated by SE tools which support the establishment of two-way links (bidirectional traceability) between objects/entities/items.

Vertical traceability is most often referred to in context of organization levels or architectural levels of the system or product under development. From a hierarchical architecture view (see Section 1.3.5), there are various system levels. The SoI level (Level n) has lower-level systems elements (Level n+1), some of which are further decomposed into lower-level system elements (Levels n+2, n+3, etc.) until the elements are defined to the level at which they can be made, bought, or reused. Entities at each level have objects/entities/items defined at various levels of abstraction. As the objects/entities/items are refined level-by-level, bidirectional traceability is established. Many times, these vertical traceability relations are referred to as "parent" and "child" relationships, depending upon the perspective (parent being the relationship to the higher level, child being the relationship to the lower level).

Horizontal traceability involves traceability across the elements of a given level of the architectural or system structure and across the life cycle. From a hierarchical architecture view, as relationships between objects/entities/items at the same level

*传统原型开发*是一种可以降低风险或不确定性的工具，有两个主要变体。部分原型用于验证系统的关键元素。完整的原型是系统的完整表示。必须在关注的方面完整准确。有关性能时间和错误率的客观和定量数据可以从高保真的交互式原型中获得。由于传统原型的存在，系统工程实践者能够更好地评估开发系统所需的修改。

3.2.3 可追溯性

可追溯性 产品和系统的可追溯性被定义为"追溯对象/实体/项的历史、应用或位置的能力"（ISO 9000，2015）。从系统工程的角度来看，可追溯性是在两个或多个对象/实体/项之间建立关联或关系，例如生命周期概念、需要、需求、架构定义制品（例如系统、系统元素）、设计定义制品、验证制品、确认制品、信息、模型以及获取或提供的系统或系统元素。

*双向可追溯性*能够将一个对象/实体/项跟踪到另一个对象/实体/项，同时自动建立返回初始对象/实体/项的反向链接。因此，一旦给定的对象/实体/项链接到其来源/目标，其来源/目标将自动链接到该对象/实体/项。系统工程工具支持在对象/实体/项之间建立双向链接（双向追溯），从而促进了双向追溯。

*垂直可追溯性*通常在开发中的系统或产品的组织层级或架构层级的背景环境中提及。从层级架构视图（见 1.3.5 节）来看，有各种系统层级。SoI 层级（层级 n）具有较低层级的系统元素（层级 n+1），其中一些元素进一步分解为较低层级的系统元素（层级 n+2、n+3 等），直到元素被定义为可以制造、购买或重用的层级。每个层级的实体都有在不同抽象层级定义的对象/实体/项。随着对象/实体/项逐级细化，建立了双向可追溯性。很多时候，这些垂直可追溯性关系被称为"父"与"子"关系，具体取决于视角（父是与更高层级的关系，子是与更低层级的关系）。

*水平可追溯性*涉及跨给定架构或系统结构层级的元素以及整个生命周期的可追溯性。从层级架构的角度来看，当同一层级（即 n 层级）的对象/实体/项之间的关系被识别时，就建立了双向可追溯性。很多时候，这些水平追溯关系被

LIFE CYCLE ANALYSES AND METHODS

(i.e., Level n) are identified, bidirectional traceability is established. Many times, these horizontal traceability relations are referred to as "peer" relationships. Horizontal traceability also links objects/entities/items generated in one life cycle stage or process to data, information, and artifacts generated in other life cycle stage or process, resulting in connecting these objects/entities/items across the life cycle. For example, from a life cycle stage perspective, concept objects/entities/items are traced to development; which are traced to production; which are traced to utilization and support; which are ultimately traced to retirement. From a life cycle process perspective, a stakeholder requirement can be traced to its system requirements; which can be traced to architecture and design artifacts; which can be traced to the realized product; which can be traced to the system verification and system validation artifacts.

Establishing traceability is a critical activity of the Technical Processes (see Section 2.3.5), especially Business or Mission Analysis; Stakeholder Needs and Requirements Definition; System Requirements Definition; System Architecture Definition; Design Definition; System Analysis; Verification; and Validation. Traceability is facilitated through the appropriate application of the Configuration Management (CM) process (see Section 2.3.4.5). The CM Identification activity enables the SE practitioner to "connect the dots" and understand the identity, location, relationships, pedigree, origin of data, materials and parts of the objects/entities/items. CM also enables the traceability of the history and location of the product after delivery. The management of products/systems, their system elements, and their configuration information requires unique identification so traceability of these items can be accurately determined. For traceability purposes the product/system identifier consists of a unique identifier which, once issued to a specific project/product/system, should never be reused.

Traceability is also a crucial component of the digital thread, enabling the connection between uniquely identified configurations of digital system models, digital twins, and physical assets (see Section 5.4). In an MBSE environment (see Section 4.2.1), the underlying system model enables a stakeholder requirement to be traced through the functional representations, to the physical product, thus enabling the identification of specific physical elements (and their specific configurations) that are impacted by a change in a given requirement. Vice versa, traceability enables the identification of the requirements that will need to be assessed when a given physical element is modified (e.g., due to a change of supplier or manufacturing process). Digitally enabled traceability methods help ensure the stakeholders get what they asked for. Digitally enabled traceability also supports the transparency of information.

More information on traceability can be found in INCOSE GtNR (2022) and the INCOSE NRM (2022).

称为"对等"关系。水平可追溯性还将一个生命周期阶段或流程中生成的对象/实体/项与其他生命周期阶段或流程中生成的数据、信息和制品联系起来，从而在整个生命周期中连接这些对象/实体/项。例如，从生命周期阶段的角度来看，概念对象/实体/项可追溯到开发阶段；追溯到生产；可追溯到使用和支持；最终追溯到退役。从生命周期流程的角度来看，利益相关方需求可以追溯到其系统需求；可以追溯到架构和设计制品；可追溯到已实现的产品；可以追溯到系统验证和系统确认制品。

建立可追溯性是技术流程的一项关键活动（见 2.3.5 节），尤其是业务或任务分析；利益相关方需要和需求定义；系统需求定义；系统架构定义；设计定义；系统分析；验证和确认。通过构型配置管理流程的适当应用，可促进可追溯性（见 2.3.4.5 节）。构型配置管理识别活动使系统工程实践者能够"连点成线"，并理解对象/实体/项的标识、位置、关系、谱系、数据来源、材料以及部件。构型配置管理还可以在交付后追溯产品的历史和位置。产品/系统、其系统元素及其构型配置信息的管理需要唯一标识，以便准确确定这些项目的可追溯性。出于可追溯性目的，产品/系统识别符由唯一识别符组成，该识别符一旦发布到特定项目/产品/系统，就不应重复使用。

可追溯性也是数字线索的一个重要组成部分，支持数字系统模型、数字孪生和物理资产的唯一识别构型配置之间的连接（见 5.4 节）。在 MBSE 环境中（见 4.2.1 节），基础系统模型使利益相关方需求能够通过功能表示追溯到物理产品，从而识别受给定需求变化影响的特定物理元素（及其特定构型配置）。反之亦然，可追溯性能够识别当给定的物理元素被修改时（例如，由于供应商或制造流程的变更）需要评估的需求。数字化的可追溯性方法有助于确保利益相关方得到他们想要的东西。数字可追溯性还支持信息的透明度。

有关可追溯性的更多信息，请参见 INCOSE GtNR（2022）和 INCOSE NRM（2022）。

LIFE CYCLE ANALYSES AND METHODS

3.2.4   Interface Management

The purpose of Interface Management is to facilitate and manage the identification, definition, design, and management of interfaces of the system across the system life cycle. It manages interface boundaries and interactions across those boundaries, the definition and agreement for each interaction, and interface requirements for all interactions identified by the various Technical Processes. Interface Management cuts across the Agreement, Technical Management, and Technical Processes. Because of its importance, the project team should focus on Interface Management as a distinct activity across all life cycle process activities.

Given that the behavior of a system is a function of the interaction of its elements and the interaction of the SoI and external systems, it is critical for the project team to identify and define each of the interactions between all system elements that make up the integrated system as well as interactions of the integrated system with external systems and users. Failing to do so will result in costly and time-consuming rework during system integration, system verification, and system validation. Because of the criticality of interfaces, the project team must define how they will manage interfaces in their project planning (e.g., SEMP). For more complex systems, projects often develop a separate Interface Management Plan. It is often useful to have the interfaces managed using an Interface Control Working Group. Additional elaboration concerning interface identification, interface definition, interface requirements, risk assessment, and managing interfaces across the life cycle is included in the INCOSE NRM (2022).

When interface management is applied as a distinct objective and focus of the SE processes, it will help highlight underlying critical issues much earlier in the project than would otherwise be revealed that could impact the project's budget, schedule, and system performance. Identifying interface boundaries and interactions across those boundaries early in the life cycle facilitates definition of the SoI's boundaries and clarifies the dependencies the SoI has on other systems and dependencies other systems have on the SoI (see Sections 1.3.1 and 1.3.3). Identifying interface boundaries and interactions across those boundaries also helps ensure compatibility between the SoI and those external systems in which it interacts. Of particular importance is the Human Machine Interface (HMI), as ultimately it is the interaction between users, operators, and maintainers that will result in acceptance of the SoI for its intended use by its intended users (see Section 3.1.4). Failure to identify all interface boundaries and interactions across those boundaries is a significant risk to the project, especially during system integration, system verification, system validation, operations, and maintenance. Because of this, it is extremely important the project defines life cycle concepts for how it will make sure the system will work safely and securely with all the external systems and personnel with which it must interact in the intended operational environment when operated by its intended users and is protected from outside threats across those interfaces.

3.2.4 接口管理

接口管理的目的是促进和管理整个系统生命周期内系统接口的识别、定义、设计以及管理。管理接口边界和跨越这些边界的交互，每个交互的定义和协议，以及各种技术流程确定的所有交互的接口需求。接口管理跨越协议、技术管理和技术流程。由于其重要性，项目团队应将接口管理作为贯穿所有生命周期流程活动的一项独特活动来关注。

鉴于系统的行为是其元素交互以及 SoI 和外部系统交互的功能，项目团队必须识别和定义构成综合系统的所有系统元素之间的交互以及综合系统与外部系统和用户之间的交互。如果不这样做，将导致在系统综合、系统验证和系统确认期间进行成本高昂且耗时的返工。由于接口的重要性，项目团队必须定义如何在项目规划（例如 SEMP）中管理接口。对于更复杂的系统，项目通常会制定单独的接口管理计划。使用接口控制工作组管理接口通常很有用。INCOSE NRM（2022）中包含有关接口识别、接口定义、接口需求、风险评估以及跨生命周期管理接口的其他详细说明。

把接口管理作为系统工程流程的一个独特目标和重点来实施，将有助于在项目早期突出潜在的关键问题，而不是在其他情况下揭示可能影响项目预算、进度和系统性能的问题。在生命周期的早期识别接口边界和跨越这些边界的交互有助于定义 SoI 的边界，并澄清 SoI 对其他系统的依赖性和其他系统对 SoI 的依赖性（见 1.3.1 和 1.3.3 节）。确定接口边界和跨越这些边界的交互也有助于确保 SoI 与其交互的外部系统之间的兼容性。人机界面（HMI）尤其重要，因为最终用户、操作员和维护人员之间的交互将导致 SoI 被其预期用户接受并用于其预期用途（见 3.1.4 节）。未能识别所有界面边界和跨越这些边界的交互对项目是一个重大风险，尤其是在系统综合、系统验证、系统确认、运行和维护期间。因此，项目定义生命周期概念非常重要，其将确保系统与所有外部系统和人员安全可靠地工作，当系统由预期用户操作时，必须在预期的运行环境中与这些系统和人员进行交互，并保护系统免受这些接口的外部威胁。

LIFE CYCLE ANALYSES AND METHODS

203 A key characteristic of today's increasingly complex, software-intensive systems is the number of internal interactions within systems and between a system and external systems. The increased number of interactions relates directly to the complexity of a system. It greatly increases the complexity of integration of the system elements that are part of the SoI, and integration of the realized SoI within the system it is part of. It also increases the complexity of assessing the behavior of the integrated system when operated as part of a larger system. Another key characteristic of modern software-intensive systems is the form of the interactions. In the past, when many of the systems were mostly mechanical/electrical, the interactions were more visible involving connectors, wires, pipes, mechanical parts, bolts, etc. In software-intensive systems, there can be multiple computer modules, each with software that communicates commands, messages, and data across one or more communication busses. For example, in modern automobiles there can be more than 150 computer modules connected to each other and multiple sensors and actuators.

Interface Management Related to Life Cycle Processes Major interface boundaries between the SoI and external systems are identified during preliminary life cycle concept definition activities within the Business or Mission Analysis process (see Section 2.3.5.1). Through the application of the Stakeholder Needs and Requirements Definition process (see Section 2.3.5.2) the life cycle concepts are further elaborated, interface boundaries between external systems are further refined to include all interface boundaries, and interactions across each of those boundaries are identified. Risks associated with each interface boundary and associated interactions are assessed as part of the Risk Management process (see Section 2.3.4.4). Using the System Requirements Definition process (see Section 2.3.5.3), the interactions are further refined and the characteristics of what is involved in each interaction are defined. Using this information, interface requirements are defined.

As the system architecture and system elements are defined, the System Architecture Definition process (see Section 2.3.5.4) concurrently with the System Requirements Definition process identify and define interface requirements for external systems, including enabling systems, which are also allocated to the applicable system elements. Internal interface boundaries and interactions across those boundaries are identified, and interface requirements defined for each of the interactions across the interface boundaries internal to the SoI (i.e., between system elements). The focus is on defining and agreeing on the characteristics of what is involved in the interactions, not on how those interactions are realized. The interface identification, definition, and requirements continue to evolve as the system requirements, architecture, design, and models evolve. These definitions are recorded in some form of interface control artifacts (e.g., Interface Control Document (ICD)) that are put under configuration control. For each interaction across an interface boundary, the identified interaction is input to the System Requirements Definition process to define the interface requirements.

当今日益复杂的软件密集型系统的一个关键特征是系统内部以及系统与外部系统之间的内部交互数量。交互次数的增加与系统的复杂性直接相关。这极大地增加了综合 SoI 系统元素的复杂性，以及在其所属系统内综合已实现的 SoI 的复杂性。当作为更大系统的一部分运行时，还增加了评估综合系统行为的复杂性。现代软件密集型系统的另一个关键特征是交互的形式。在过去，当许多系统主要是机械/电气系统时，交互更加明显，涉及连接器、电线、管道、机械部件、螺栓等。在软件密集型系统中，可以有多个计算机模块，每个模块都带有通过一条或多条通信总线执行命令、传递消息和数据通信的软件。例如，在现代汽车中，可以有 150 多个相互连接的计算机模块以及多个传感器和执行器。

与生命周期流程相关的接口管理　SoI 和外部系统之间的主要接口边界在业务或任务分析流程中的初步生命周期概念定义活动中确定（见 2.3.5.1 节）。通过应用利益相关方需要和需求定义流程（见 2.3.5.2 节），进一步阐述了生命周期概念，进一步细化外部系统之间的接口边界，以包括所有接口边界，并确定每个边界之间的交互。与每个接口边界和相关交互相关的风险都应作为风险管理流程的一部分进行评估（见 2.3.4.4 节）。使用系统需求定义流程（见 2.3.5.3 节），进一步细化交互，并定义每个交互中涉及的特征。使用此信息定义接口需求。

随着系统架构和系统元素的定义，系统架构定义流程（见 2.3.5.4 节）与系统需求定义流程同时识别和定义外部系统（包括使能系统）的接口需求，这些接口需求也分配给适用的系统元素。确定内部接口边界和这些边界之间的交互，并为 SoI 内部接口边界（即系统元素之间）的每个交互定义接口需求。重点是定义和商定交互中所涉及的特性，而不是如何实现这些交互。随着系统需求、架构、设计以及模型的发展，接口标识、定义和需求不断发展。这些定义记录在某种形式的接口控制制品（例如，接口控制文档——ICD）中，并置于构型配置控制之下。对于跨接口边界的每个交互，已识别的交互将输入到系统需求定义流程中，以定义接口需求。

How those interactions are realized is addressed by the Design Definition process (see Section 2.3.5.5). Definitions of interactions across interface boundaries are refined to include what each system element involved in the interaction looks like at the interface boundary and the media (e.g., a data bus, a wiring harness, a physical connection, Wi-Fi, Bluetooth) involved in the interaction is determined. Additional interface boundaries and interactions may need to be identified and defined that were not addressed by the System Architecture Definition and System Requirements Definition processes. The definition of these additional interfaces often drives additional iteration between these processes to capture the interface characteristics and requirements definition. Interactions across interface boundaries are primary considerations in both horizontal and vertical integration across the life cycle as part of the Integration Process (see Section 2.3.5.8).

A major issue concerning interface definition is that when a system element is contracted out to a supplier or the SoI interacts with other supplier-developed system elements. Often the contracts are issued prior to design and thus the design definitions of what the SoI and system elements look like at the interface boundary and the media involved in the interaction have not yet been defined. In addition, it is common for the suppliers to have little insight into the workings of other suppler-developed system elements with which they interact and how changes to those system elements could affect the interactions and performance of their system element (or changes to their system element could affect other system elements). In these cases, it is important that the acquirer clearly addresses how each supplier will support, participate in, and comply with the interface management activities during interface definition, design, system integration, system verification, and system validation in the agreements via the Agreement Processes (see Section 2.3.2).

Using the System Analysis process (see Section 2.3.5.6), the level and type of analysis needed to understand the trade space with respect to the interface requirements and definition is determined and performed. This can include mathematical analysis, modeling, simulation, experimentation, and other techniques. The analysis results are input to trade-offs made through the Decision Management process (see Section 2.3.4.3).

The Implementation process (see Section 2.3.5.7) is used to develop the system element interfaces and record evidence of meeting the interface requirements for an implemented system element.

The Integration process (see Section 2.3.5.8) considers the integration of the system and system element interfaces in the integration planning and integrates the implemented system elements together at the interface boundaries. Each system element is verified to have met their interface requirements using the Verification process (see Section 2.3.5.9).

如何实现这些交互由设计定义流程解决（见 2.3.5.5 节）。对跨接口边界的交互定义进行细化，以包括参与交互的每个系统元素在接口边界的外观，并确定交互中涉及的媒介（如数据总线、线束、物理连接、Wi-Fi、蓝牙）。可能需要识别和定义系统架构定义和系统需求定义流程中未涉及的其他接口边界和交互。这些额外接口的定义通常会驱动这些流程之间的额外迭代，从而捕获接口特征和需求定义。作为综合流程的一部分，跨接口边界的交互是贯穿整个生命周期的横向和纵向综合的主要考虑因素（见 2.3.5.8 节）。

关于接口定义的一个主要问题发生在当系统元素外包给供应商或 SoI 与其他供应商开发的系统元素交互时。合同通常在设计之前发布，因此 SoI 和系统元素在接口边界上的外观以及交互所涉及的媒介的设计定义尚未确定。此外，供应商通常对与其交互的其他供应商开发的系统元素的工作原理以及这些系统元素的更改如何影响其系统元素的交互和性能（或其系统元素的更改可能影响其他系统元素）知之甚少。在这些情况下，采办方必须明确说明各供应商将如何通过协议流程在协议中的接口定义、设计、系统综合、系统验证以及系统确认期间支持、参与和遵守接口管理活动（见 2.3.2 节）。

使用系统分析流程（见 2.3.5.6 节），确定并执行所需的分析层级和类型，以了解与接口需求和定义相关的权衡空间。这可以包括数学分析、建模、仿真、实验以及其他技术。分析结果是通过决策管理流程进行权衡的输入（见 2.3.4.3 节）。

实施流程（见 2.3.5.7 节）用于开发系统元素接口，并记录已实施系统元素满足接口需求的证据。

综合流程（见 2.3.5.8 节）考虑综合规划中系统和系统元素接口的综合，并在接口边界处将已实施的系统元素综合在一起。使用验证流程（见 2.3.5.9 节）验证每个系统元素是否满足其接口需求。

LIFE CYCLE ANALYSES AND METHODS

The system interfaces are validated using the Validation process (see Section 2.3.5.11) against the stakeholder needs and stakeholder requirements concerning interactions with systems or users external to the SoI in the operational environment. The Transition process (see Section 2.3.5.10) checks the installation and operational state of the interfaces in the operational environment.

Key activities that are part of interface management include facilitating cooperation and agreements with other stakeholders, defining roles and responsibilities, enabling open communication concerning issues, establishing timing for providing interface information, problem resolution, and agreeing on the interaction characteristics across interface boundaries early in the project. These functions are done through the Project Planning process (see Section 2.3.4.1). An important interface analysis activity is assessing and managing risks as part of the Risk Management process (see Section 2.3.4.4), avoiding potential impacts especially during system integration, system verification, system validation, operation, and maintenance. Other processes may also contribute to the management of the interfaces.

After establishing baselines for interface requirements, interface definitions, architecture, and design, the Configuration Management process (see Section 2.3.4.5) provides the ongoing management and control of the interface requirements and definitions, as well as any associated artifacts.

Recording Definitions of Interactions across Interface Boundaries In a document-centric practice of SE, definitions concerning interface boundaries, the interaction across those boundaries, and the media involved are commonly recorded in some type of interface definition artifact (e.g., Interface Control Document (ICD), Data Dictionary (DD), Interface Definition Document (IDD), Interface Agreement Document (IAD)) or within the project's integrated dataset from which the associated report may be generated. In a data-centric practice of SE, these are often captured in databases and models. A data-centric practice enables effective impact and change analysis, as well as helping ensure consistency of interface requirements and definitions across the architecture.

Interface Analysis In conjunction with the other Technical Processes, the System Analysis process (see Section 2.3.5.6) applies various analysis methods to identify interface boundaries, and interactions across those boundaries, to better understand how the SoI interacts with the other systems that make up the system of which it is a part and to help ensure there are no missing interface boundaries, definitions, and interface requirements. Some common diagrams, methods, and tools used for analysis include functional flow block diagrams (FFBD), data flow diagrams (DFD), context diagrams, boundary diagrams, external interface diagrams, input, process, output (IPO) diagrams, N^2 diagrams, and internal interface diagrams, Failure Modes and Effects Analysis (FMEA), System-Theoretic Process Analysis (STPA), language-based models (e.g., SysML diagrams), and simulations.

使用确认流程（见 2.3.5.11 节）验证系统接口，从而满足与运行环境中 SoI 外部系统或用户交互相关的利益相关方需要和利益相关方需求。转移流程（见 2.3.5.10 节）检查运行环境中接口的安装和运行状态。

作为接口管理一部分的关键活动包括促进与其他利益相关方的合作和协议，定义角色和职责，实现有关问题的公开沟通，确定提供接口信息的时间，解决问题，以及在项目早期就跨接口边界的交互特征达成一致。这些功能通过项目规划流程（见 2.3.4.1 节）完成。一项重要的接口分析活动是评估和管理风险，作为风险管理流程的一部分（见 2.3.4.4 节），避免潜在影响，尤其是在系统综合、系统验证、系统确认、运行以及维护期间。其他流程也可能有助于接口的管理。

在为接口需求、接口定义、架构和设计建立基线后，构型配置管理流程（见 2.3.4.5 节）提供对接口需求和定义以及任何相关制品的持续管理和控制。

记录跨接口边界的交互定义　在系统工程以文档为中心的实践中，有关接口边界的定义、这些边界之间的交互以及涉及的媒介通常记录在某种类型的接口定义制品［例如，接口控制文档（ICD）、数据字典（DD）、接口定义文档（IDD）、接口协议文档（IAD）］中，或者记录在项目的综合数据集中，从中可以生成相关报告。在以数据为中心的系统工程实践中，这些信息通常被捕获到数据库和模型中。以数据为中心的实践支持有效的影响和更改分析，并有助于确保整个架构中接口需求和定义的一致性。

接口分析　系统分析流程（见 2.3.5.6 节）与其他技术流程相结合，采用各种分析方法来确定接口边界和跨越这些边界的交互，以便更好地了解 SoI 如何与组成系统的其他系统交互，并帮助确保不遗漏接口边界、定义和接口需求。用于分析的一些常见图、方法和工具包括功能流程框图（FFBD）、数据流程图（DFD）、背景图、边界图、外部接口图、输入—流程—输出（IPO）图、N^2 图和内部接口图、故障模式和影响分析（FMEA）、系统论的流程分析（STPA）、基于语言的模型（如 SysML 图）和仿真。

LIFE CYCLE ANALYSES AND METHODS

A critical part of interface analysis includes an assessment of each interaction across an interface boundary in terms of maturity, stability, documentation, threats, and risks. The SoI is particularly vulnerable when interfacing with external systems over which they may have little or no control. Because of this, the SoI is vulnerable to undesirable effects at and across the interface boundaries. Therefore, identifying and managing risks associated with interface boundaries and interactions across those boundaries is key to exposing potential risks to the project across applicable life cycle stages. Many of the major issues discovered during system integration, system verification, and system validation involve interfaces.

An example analysis tool is the N^2 diagram shown in Figure 3.13, which enables a systematic approach to identifying interface boundaries and interactions across those boundaries. N^2 diagrams enable the SE practitioner to assess and identify interface boundaries and interactions across those boundaries in a structured, bidirectional, fixed framework. The N^2 diagrams can be used at several levels of abstraction of the SoI: a functional view and a physical view.

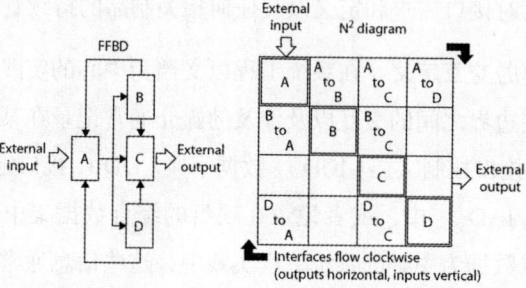

FIGURE 3.13 Sample N-squared diagram. INCOSE SEH original figure created by Krueger and Forsberg. Usage per the INCOSE Notices page. All other rights reserved.

An N^2 diagram is created using an N × N matrix. The system elements (functional or physical) are placed in squares forming a diagonal from upper left to lower right. The rest of the squares in the matrix represent potential interactions (interfaces) between the elements. In an N^2 diagram, interactions between elements flow in a clockwise direction. For example, the entity being passed from element A to element B, can be defined in the appropriate off-diagonal square. A blank square indicates there is no interaction between the respective elements. Sometimes, characteristics of the entity passing between elements may be included in the *off-diagonal* square where the interacting entity is identified. When all elements have been compared to all other elements, then the matrix is complete. If lowerlevel elements are identified in the process with corresponding lower-level interactions, then they can be successively described in expanded lower-level N^2 diagrams. The Design Structure Matrix (DSM)

接口分析的一个关键部分包括从成熟度、稳定性、文档、线索以及风险方面评估跨接口边界的每个交互。SoI 在与外部系统连接时尤其容易受到攻击，因为它们可能对这些系统几乎没有控制权。因此，SoI 容易受到接口边界处和跨界面边界的不良影响。因此，识别和管理与接口边界和跨越这些边界的交互作用相关的风险，是暴露项目在各个适用的生命周期阶段潜在风险的关键。在系统综合、系统验证和系统确认期间发现的许多主要问题都涉及接口。

图 3.13 中所示的 N^2 图是一个示例分析工具，支持一种系统方法来识别界面边界和这些边界之间的交互。N^2 图使系统工程实践者能够在结构化、双向、固定的框架中评估和识别接口边界和跨这些边界的交互。N^2 图可用于 SoI 的多个抽象层级：功能视图和物理视图。

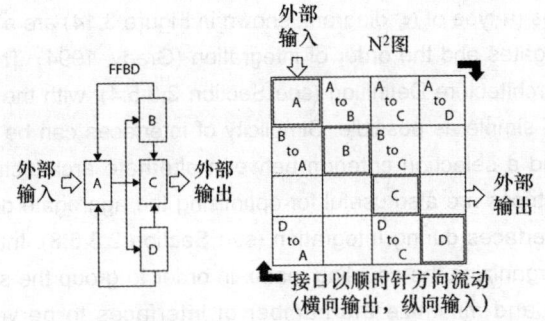

图 3.13 N^2 图示例。INCOSE SEH 原始图由 Krueger 和 Forsberg 创建。按照 INCOSE 通知页使用。版权所有。

使用 N×N 矩阵创建 N^2 图。系统元素（功能的或物理的）放置在从左上角到右下角形成的对角线正方形中。矩阵中其余的方块表示元素之间的潜在交互（界面）。在 N^2 图中，元素之间的交互以顺时针方向流动。例如，从元素 A 传递到元素 B 的实体可以在适当的非对角正方形中定义。空白方块表示各个元素之间没有交互。有时，元素之间传递的实体的特征可能包含在识别交互实体的非对角正方形中。将所有元素与所有其他元素进行比较后，矩阵就完成了。如果在流程中识别出具有相应低层级交互的低层级元素，则可以在扩展的低层级 N^2 图中对其进行连续描述。设计结构矩阵（DSM）在外观

LIFE CYCLE ANALYSES AND METHODS

is very similar in appearance and usage to the N^2 diagram, but a different input and output convention is typically used (inputs on the horizontal rows and outputs on the vertical columns) resulting in interactions between elements flowing in a counterclockwise direction (Eppinger and Browning, 2012). Figure D.1 illustrates an N^2 diagram for the interactions amongst the system life cycle processes.

One of the main functions of the N^2 diagram, besides the identification of interactions, is to pinpoint areas where conflicts may arise between elements so that systems integration later in the development cycle can proceed efficiently (Becker, et al., 2000) (DSMC, 1983) (Lano, 1977). Alternatively, or in addition, functional and physical diagrams can be used with N^2 diagrams to characterize the flow of information among system elements and between system elements and the external systems. As the system architecture is decomposed to lower levels, it is important to ensure the interface interaction definitions keep pace and that interactions are defined so that decompositions of lower levels are considered.

Coupling matrices (a type of N^2 diagram, shown in Figure 3.14) are a basic method to define the aggregates and the order of integration (Grady, 1994). They can be used during System Architecture Definition (see Section 2.3.5.4), with the goal of keeping the interfaces as simple as possible. Simplicity of interfaces can be a distinguishing characteristic and a selection criterion between alternate architectural candidates. The coupling matrices are also useful for optimizing the aggregate definition and the verification of interfaces during Integration (see Section 2.3.5.8). Integration can be optimized by reorganizing the coupling matrix in order to group the system elements into aggregates and minimize the number of interfaces to be verified between aggregates. When verifying the interactions between aggregates, the coupling matrix can be an aid for fault detection.

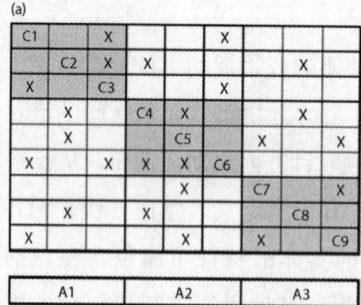

FIGURE 3.14 Sample coupling matrix showing: (a) Initial arrangement of aggregates; (b) final arrangement after reorganization. INCOSE SEH original figure created by Faisandier. Usage per the INCOSE Notices page. All other rights reserved.

和用途上与 N^2 图非常相似，但通常使用不同的输入和输出约定（水平行上的输入和垂直列上的输出），导致元素之间以逆时针方向流动的交互（Eppinger 和 Browning，2012）。图 D.1 展示了系统生命周期流程之间交互的 N^2 图。

除识别交互之外，N^2 图的主要功能之一是确定元素之间可能发生冲突的区域，以便在开发周期的后期能够有效地进行系统综合（Becker 等，2000）（DSMC，1983）（Lano，1977）。此外，功能图和物理图也可以与 N^2 图一起使用，以描述系统元素之间以及系统元素与外部系统之间的信息流。随着系统架构分解到较低层级，重要的是确保接口交互定义保持同步，并定义交互，以便考虑较低层级的分解。

耦合矩阵（N^2 图的一种，见图 3.14）是定义聚合以及综合顺序的基本方法（Grady，1994）。可在系统架构定义期间使用（参见 2.3.5.4 节），目的是尽可能保持接口的简单。接口的简单性可以是一个显著特征，也是备选架构之间的一个选择准则。耦合矩阵还可用于优化聚合定义和综合期间的接口验证（见 2.3.5.8 节）。可通过重组耦合矩阵来优化综合，以便将系统元素分组为聚合，并尽量减少聚合之间待验证的接口数量。在验证聚合之间的交互时，耦合矩阵可以帮助进行故障检测。

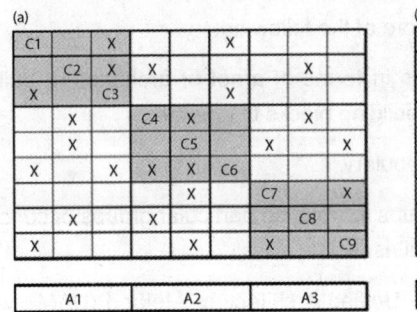

图 3.14　耦合矩阵示例显示：（a）聚合体的初始排列；（b）重组后的最终排列。INCOSE SEH 原始图由 Faisandier 创建。按照 INCOSE 通知页使用。版权所有。

3.2.5 Architecture Frameworks

An architecture description framework is defined in ISO/IEC/IEEE 42010 (2022) as:

A set of "conventions, principles and practices for the description of architectures established within a specific domain of application or community of stakeholders."

The term "description" is used in the definition to avoid confusion between architecture description frameworks and other frameworks (e.g., enterprise architecture framework, architecture evaluation framework). Other definitions for *architecture framework* (AF) can be found in the technical literature, for example The Open Group Architecture Framework (OMG TOGAF, 2023) defines AF as:

A foundational structure, or set of structures, which can be used for developing a broad range of different architectures.

Architecture frameworks are used in various domains to help ensure harmonization, consistency, and re-use. When a commonly agreed upon architecture framework is adhered to by all project teams involved, better aligned project artifacts typically result. This benefit will be particularly evident in distributed teams and within enterprises when architecture descriptions and architectural artefacts are reused across projects.

Most architecture frameworks are organized to provide one or more viewpoints to cover the target domains and their typical stakeholders' concerns (e.g., NATO AF (NAF), Unified AF (UAF), and Department of Defense AF (DoDAF)).

Some frameworks also provide one or more of the following:

- A method for describing systems in terms of a set of architecture building blocks, and for showing how the building blocks fit together.
- A set of tools and a common vocabulary.
- Multiple dimensions with coordinates for relating particular groups of concerns or solutions along the dimensional aspects.

Figure 3.15 provides an overview of the Unified Architecture Method (UAM), which provides dimensions for perspectives and aspects.

Others advocate that architecture frameworks should include a list of recommended standards, libraries of patterns, and compliant products that can be used to accelerate architecting. Finally, it is useful for architecture frameworks, or more broadly, architecting environments, to define activities and resources for architecture governance, in addition to the governance of skills and competencies in place, with regard to enterprise objectives.

3.2.5 架构框架

架构描述框架在 ISO/IEC/IEEE 42010（2022）中的定义是：

一组"用于描述在特定应用领域或利益相关方群体内建立的架构的约定、原则和实践"。

定义中使用术语"描述"，以避免架构描述框架与其他框架（例如，复杂组织体系架构框架、架构评估框架）之间的混淆。架构框架（AF）的其他定义可以在技术文献中找到，例如，开放组织架构框架（OMG TOGAF，2023）将 AF 定义为：

一种基础结构或结构集合，可用于开发广泛的不同架构。

架构框架用于各个领域，以帮助确保协调、一致性和重用。当所有相关的项目团队都遵守一个共同商定的架构框架时，通常会产生更好的、协调一致的项目制品。当跨项目重用架构描述和架构制品时，这一好处在分布式团队和复杂组织体系中尤其明显。

大多数架构框架都被组织为提供一个或多个视角，以涵盖目标领域及其典型的利益相关方关切 [例如，北约架构框架（NAF）、统一架构框架（UAF）和美国国防部架构框架（DoDAF）]。一些框架还提供以下一个或多个功能：

- 依据一组架构构建块描述系统的方法，以及表明构建块如何组合起来的方法。
- 一套工具和公共词汇表。
- 沿不同维度的方面将特定的关切或解决方案组与多个维度的坐标关联。

图 3.15 概述了统一架构方法（UAM），该方法提供视角和方面两个维度。

其他人则主张架构框架应包括一系列建议的标准、模式库和可用于加速架构设计的兼容产品。最后，对于架构框架或更广泛的架构环境来说，定义架构治理的活动和资源，以及针对复杂组织体系目标的现有技能和能力的治理，是非常有用的。

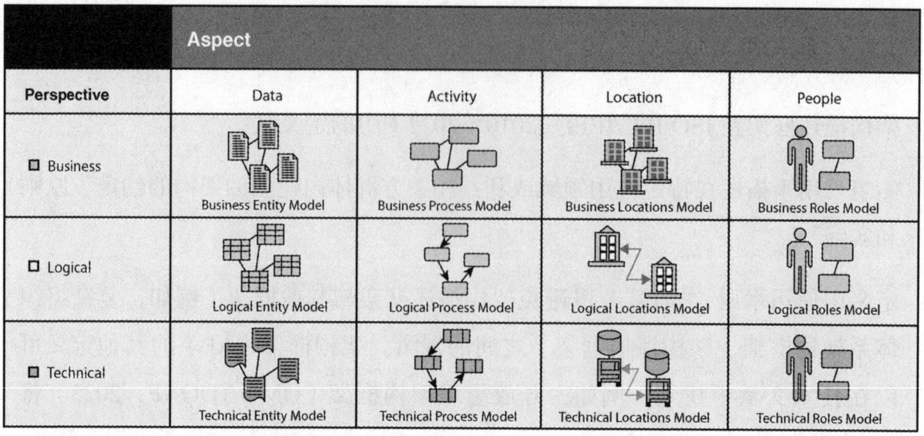

LIFE CYCLE ANALYSES AND METHODS

Perspective	Aspect			
	Data	Activity	Location	People
☐ Business	Business Entity Model	Business Process Model	Business Locations Model	Business Roles Model
☐ Logical	Logical Entity Model	Logical Process Model	Logical Locations Model	Logical Roles Model
☐ Technical	Technical Entity Model	Technical Process Model	Technical Locations Model	Technical Roles Model

FIGURE 3.15 Unified Architecture Method. From UAM (2022). Used with permission. All other rights reserved.

Framework Support to Architecture Activities Architecture activities are described in the System Architecture Definition process (see Section 2.3.5.4). This section explains how some of the major architecture frameworks can be used to perform the key architecture activities.

Architecture Enablement Frameworks like Pragmatic Enterprise AF (PEAF) (Pragmatic 365, 2023) and Generalized Enterprise Reference Architecture and Methodology (GERAM) (Bernus, 1999) can be used to establish and maintain a set of capabilities, services, and resources that support the architecture process. The enablement activities include:

- Analysis of context in the organization where the architecture activities can take place.
- Definition of the main principles and the overall organization where the processes, methods, roles, and technologies can be used for architecting.
- Implementation of these high-level principles with methodologies provided by frameworks like TOGAF for IT domain or NAF and DoDAF for defense domains. This implementation comprises development of a metamodel to capture the terminology and a collection of architecture development methods, standards library, architecture repository and registry, and architecture capability. Architecture capability includes skills and governance logic.
- Reference documents like Evans (2014) help assess the architecture context and environment with regard to the architecting styles of the enterprise programs and projects.

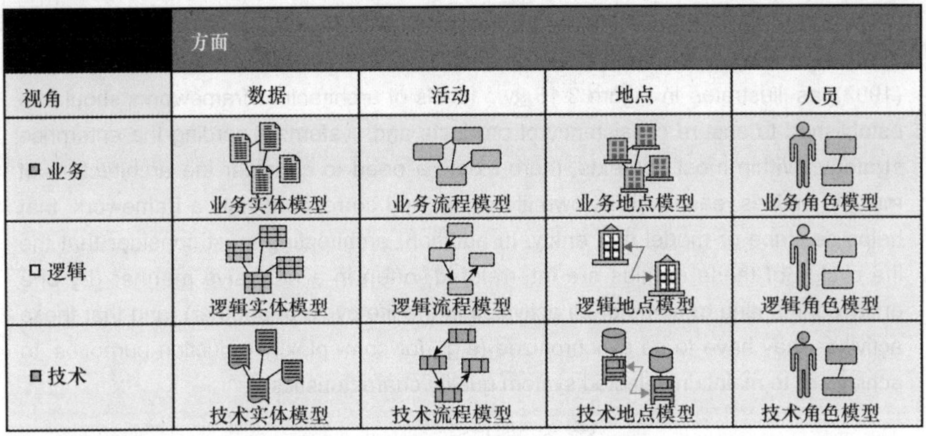

视角	方面			
	数据	活动	地点	人员
☐ 业务	业务实体模型	业务流程模型	业务地点模型	业务角色模型
☐ 逻辑	逻辑实体模型	逻辑流程模型	逻辑地点模型	逻辑角色模型
☐ 技术	技术实体模型	技术流程模型	技术地点模型	技术角色模型

图 3.15 统一架构方法。源自 UAM（2022）。经许可后使用。版权所有。

架构活动的框架支持 架构活动在系统架构定义流程中进行描述（见 2.3.5.4 节）。本节说明了一些主要架构框架可用于执行关键架构活动。

架构支持 实用复杂组织体系 AF（PEAF）（实用 365，2023）和通用复杂组织体系参考架构和方法（GERAM）（Bernus，1999）等框架可以用来建立和维护支持架构流程的能力、服务和资源的集合。支持活动包括：

- 分析组织中架构活动可能发生的环境。

- 定义主要原则和总体组织，其中的流程、方法、角色以及技术可用于架构设计。

- 通过面向 IT 领域的 TOGAF 或用于防务领域的 NAF 和 DoDAF 等框架提供的方法实施这些高层级原则。此实现包括开发一个元模型来捕获术语和架构开发方法、标准库、架构存储库和注册表以及架构能力的集合。架构能力包括技能和管控逻辑。

- Evans（2014）等参考文档有助于评估与复杂组织体系计划和项目架构风格相关的架构背景和环境。

LIFE CYCLE ANALYSES AND METHODS

Architecture Governance Related concepts are objective, goal, strategy, policy, directive, roadmap, life cycle stage, and statement of work. Per Sowa and Zachman (1992), as illustrated in Figure 3.16, two levels of architecture frameworks should be established to ensure consistency of products and systems regarding the enterprise strategy. Within most contexts, there exists a need to consider the architecture of multiple entities, each with its own life cycle, and correspondingly a framework, that helps describe or model that entity. In addition, architecting must consider that the life cycles of these entities are interrelated, often in a recursive manner (by one entity contributing to some or all activities in the life cycle of another), and that these activities may have to be synchronized (e.g., for com- plexity reduction purposes, to achieve or to maintain selected system quality characteristics).

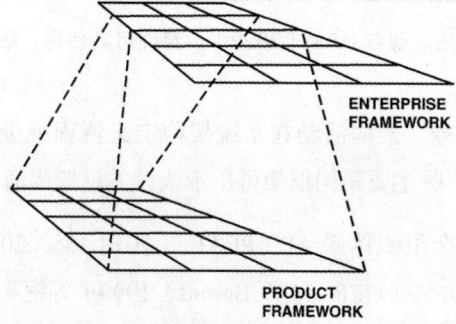

FIGURE 3.16 Enterprise and product frameworks. From Sowa and Zachman (1992). Used with permission. All other rights reserved.

Frameworks like NAF and TOGAF consider two levels of architecture governance:

- At *enterprise* level, in accordance with enterprise objectives, goals, strategy, roadmap, policies and directives.
- At *project* level, with regard to internal or external contracts of the projects of produced architecture(s) along the whole life cycle of the entity of interest related to the architecture(s).

Architecture Management Architecture management implements the governance directives in the frame of the project contract. Frameworks like NAF explain that the architecting effort should be defined in a management plan. This plan should also include the management of the work products throughout their whole life cycle. The management activities coordinate the architecting effort and report to the governance level with rationales about the application of the governance directives and the agreement.

架构治理 相关的概念包括目标、目的、策略、政策、指令、路线图、生命周期阶段以及工作说明书。根据 Sowa 和 Zachman（1992），如图 3.16 所示，应建立两个层级的架构框架，从而确保与复杂组织体系战略相关的产品和系统的一致性。在大多数情况下，需要考虑多个实体的架构，每个实体都有自己的生命周期，相应地，还需要一个框架来帮助描述或对该实体建模。此外，架构必须考虑到这些实体的生命周期是相互关联的，通常是以递归的方式（由一个实体参与另一个实体生命周期中的一些或所有活动），并且这些活动可能必须同步（例如，为了降低复杂性，为了实现或保持选定的系统质量特征）。

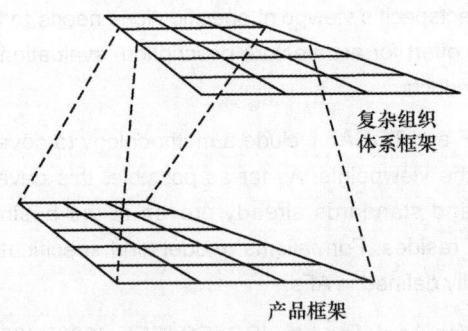

图 3.16 复杂组织体系和产品框架。源自 Sowa 和 Zachman（1992）。经许可后使用。版权所有。

NAF 和 TOGAF 等框架考虑了两个层级的架构管控：

- 在复杂组织体系层级，根据复杂组织体系目标、目的、战略、路线图、策略以及指令。

- 在项目层面，关于所产生架构项目的内部或外部合同，贯穿与架构相关的实体的整个生命周期。

架构管理 在项目合同的框架中实施管控指令。NAF 等框架解释，架构工作应该在管理计划中定义。该计划还应包括工作产品在其整个生命周期中的管理。管理活动协调架构设计工作，并向治理层报告治理指令和协议的应用理由。

Architecture Description Architecture Description, as defined by ISO/IEC/IEEE 42010 (2022), is accomplished with *Architecture Conceptualization and Architecture Elaboration*, as defined by ISO/IEC/IEEE 42020 (2019). These architecting activities are performed as planned by the management plan covering the architecture effort. Frameworks like Zachman explain how architecture viewpoints characterize the problem and represent the solution with regard to the stakeholders' concerns, possibly structured as architecture aspects and stakeholders' perspectives. These viewpoints can be defined in architecture frameworks or developed within the project for the benefit of the enterprise. ISO/IEC/IEEE 42010 defines views and viewpoints as they apply to the architecture description. Annex F of ISO/IEC/IEEE 42010 includes tables of requirements compliance for Architecture Description Frameworks. Development of projectspecific viewpoint specifications needs to be justified because they imply additional effort for architecture description, evaluation, management, and usage of the work products.

Frameworks like NAF and TOGAF include a methodology to develop the architecture views governed by the viewpoints. As far as possible, this development should be based on patterns and standards already proven in the business domain where the entity of interest resides. Formalisms, model kind specifications, and modeling languages are typically defined in AFs.

Architecture Evaluation As defined by ISO/IEC/IEEE 42030 (2019), the evaluation activities determine the extent to which one or more architectures meet their objectives, address stakeholder concerns, and meet relevant requirements. These activities are performed as planned by the management plan covering the architecture effort. Frameworks like Architecture Tradeoff Analysis Method (ATAM) (CMU/SEI, 2000) and Method Framework for Engineering System Architectures (MFESA) (Firesmith, et al. 2008) allow performing architecture evaluation in three steps:

- Definition of the objectives and evaluation criteria agreed by the stakeholders to cover their concerns.
- Definition or development of a method to cover the activities normally structured in analysis, assessment, and evaluation tasks.
- Analysis of the architecture concepts and properties, assessment of the value and utility for the stakeholders, and formulation of findings and recommendations in evaluation reports.

架构描述 按照 ISO/IEC/IEEE 42010（2022）的定义，架构描述通过架构概念化和架构详细阐述完成，如 ISO/IEC/IEEE 42020（2019）所定义。这些架构活动按照覆盖架构工作的管理计划执行。Zachman 等框架解释架构视角是如何描述问题的，并根据利益相关方的关切表示解决方案，可能被结构化为架构方面和利益相关方的视角。这些视角可以在架构框架中定义，也可以在项目中为复杂组织体系的利益而开发。ISO/IEC/IEEE 42010 定义适用于架构描述的视图和视角。ISO/IEC/IEEE 42010 的附录 F 包括架构描述框架的需求符合性表。需要证明项目特定视角规范的开发是合理的，因为这意味着在架构描述、评价、管理以及工作产品的使用方面需要付出额外的努力。

NAF 和 TOGAF 等框架包括一种方法论，用于开发由视角所规范的架构视图。这种开发应尽可能基于已在相关实体所在的业务领域中得到证明的模式和标准。形式化、模型种类规范和建模语言通常都是在 AF 中定义的。

架构评估 根据 ISO/IEC/IEEE 42030（2019）的定义，评估活动确定一个或多个架构满足其目标、解决利益相关方的关切以及满足相关需求的程度。这些活动按照覆盖架构工作的管理计划执行。架构权衡分析方法（ATAM）（CMU/SEI，2000）和工程系统架构的方法框架（MFESA）（Firesmith 等，2008）等框架允许分三步进行架构评估：

- 定义利益相关方商定的目标和评价准则，以涵盖其关注的问题。
- 定义或开发一种方法，以涵盖分析、评估和评价任务中通常结构化的活动。
- 分析架构概念和特性，评价利益相关方的价值和效用，并在评价报告中制定调查结果和建议。

LIFE CYCLE ANALYSES AND METHODS

3.2.6 Patterns

Introduction to Patterns The scientific disciplines, whether concerned with phenomena at a molecular, global, or astronomical scale, are based upon discovery and effective modeling of *patterns*. Patterns are recurrences—repeated regularities observed across time, space, or other dimensions. Patterns lie at the heart of physical sciences and the related engineering disciplines, as laws of nature whose mathematical representation and engineering exploitation have transformed the nature and possibilities of human life. In SE, recurring patterns are observable in engineered system requirements, solution architectures, stakeholder value, missions, fitness and trade spaces, parametric couplings, failure modes and risks, markets, system phenomena, principles, and the socio-technical systems of engineering and life cycle management. For example, there are patterns for requirements for refrigerators, patterns for design of coolant compressors, patterns for refrigerant failures, and patterns for maintaining refrigerators. Patterns are visible for products developed for commercial markets and systems engineered under defense contracts, as well as for the socio-technical systems that produce them, such as methodology patterns for eliciting and validating requirements. Whether the patterns are only implicitly and informally recognized and used, or explicit and formal, they can be found across the System of Innovation Pattern shown in Figure 1.6, where they are the basis of group learning. Explicitly modeled patterns help us surface and more efficiently share (learn, teach, practice) what earlier generations of SE practitioners treated as expertise and intuition only obtainable over decades of personal practice. As in the physical sciences, engineering patterns of all kinds are also subject to issues of credibility, validity, applicability, and trust as a basis for decision-making and action. Patterns are not "one size fits all", but instead have both fixed (recurring) and variable (parameterized) aspects, distilled by abstraction across individual instances. Depending on how they are recognized, represented, managed, and applied, patterns may be *informal or formal*.

Informal Patterns The most informally described patterns are those implicit in the expertise or judgement of individual practitioners and teams (as in tribal knowledge), when subject matter experts recognize new occurrences of past experiences. Examples are Jean's expertise in packaging systems, or Jose's expertise in risk assessment. Because of the high value of this experience and interest in making it available to others, historical efforts have been made to explicitly capture and record such patterns, even in informal form, so that they can be transmitted to others. SE *principles and heuristics*, often captured as informal prose, illustrate such explicit but informal patterns (see Sections 1.4.3 and 1.4.4). The informal but explicit prose representation of engineering patterns has created popular followings in civil and software engineering communities of practice (Alexander, et al., 1977)

3.2.6 模式

模式简介 科学学科，无论是涉及分子、地球还是天文尺度的现象，都是建立在对模式的发现和有效建模的基础之上。模式是重复出现的——在时间、空间或其他维度上观察到的重复规律。模式是物理科学和相关工程学科的核心，是自然法则，其数学表示和工程开发已改变人类生活的性质和可能性。在系统工程中，可在工程系统需求、解决方案架构、利益相关方价值、任务、适应性和权衡空间、参数耦合、故障模式和风险、市场、系统现象、原则以及工程和生命周期管理的社会技术系统中观察到重复出现的模式。例如，有冰箱需求模式、冷却液压缩机设计模式、制冷剂故障模式和冰箱维护模式。对于为商业市场开发的产品和根据防务合同设计的系统，以及生产这些产品的社会技术系统，模式是可见的，例如用于获取和验证需求的方法模式。无论这些模式是隐性和非形式化的认可和使用，还是显性和形式化的，都可以在图 1.6 所示的整个创新系统模式中找到，这是团组学习的基础。显性化建模的模式有助于我们发现并更有效分享（学习、教学、实践）前几代系统工程从业者认为只有通过数十年的个人实践才能获得的专业知识和直觉。正如在物理科学中一样，各种工程模式也受到可信度、有效性、适用性以及作为决策和行动基础的信任问题的影响。模式不是"一刀切"，而是具有固定（重复）和可变（参数化）两个方面，通过对各个实例的抽象来提炼。模式可以是非形式化的，也可以是形式化的，这取决于如何识别、表示、管理和应用这些模式。

非形式化模式 当主题专家认识到过去经验中出现的新情况时，最为非形式化的描述模式是个体实践者和团队的专业知识或判断中隐含的模式（如工作群组知识）。例如，Jean 在包装系统方面的专业知识，或 Jose 在风险评估方面的专业知识。由于这一经验的价值很高，而且有兴趣将其提供给他人，因此在历史上做出了努力，从而明确地捕捉和记录这种模式以便将其与他人沟通，即使是以非形式化的形式。系统工程原则和启发式方法通常被捕获为非形式化的文章，说明了这种明确但非形式化的模式（见 1.4.3 和 1.4.4 节）。工程模式的非形式化但明确的文章表示在民用工程和软件工程实践群体中创造了流行的追随者（Alexander 等，1977）（Gamma 等，1995）。这些模式通常包括问题的文章

LIFE CYCLE ANALYSES AND METHODS

(Gamma, et al., 1995). These patterns typically include a prose template description of a problem and an informal description of a design pattern suited to such a problem. Examples of these explicit, informal, but effective patterns include building structural patterns and city layout patterns (in civil architecture patterns), as well as sorting algorithms and graphic user interface designs (in software design patterns). SE practitioners and leaders should not underestimate the value of explicit informal patterns for transmitting knowledge.

Formal Patterns The sciences' transition from informal prose to formal models powered much of the Science, Technology, Engineering, and Math (STEM) revolution's transformative impact, where model-based representations of patterns are the heart of the related physical sciences. These models have also enabled several generations of powerful automation tools for design, simulation, and production across the engineering disciplines, and more recently this is also impacting SE.

The practice of SE has increased use of explicit formal system descriptive models as central to SE methods, described as Model-Based Systems Engineering (MBSE) (see Section 4.2.1). This also enables the shift to formal model-based representation of patterns and their application in SE, because patterns based in models can be readily transformed (including automated assistance) into configured models specific to an application or project. Likewise, such patterns can be used in automated conformance-checking of other models. Provided the credibility of the patterns for the uses intended is managed, this not only shortens time to a trustable specific model, it also helps shift the language and perspective of multiple systems practitioners and teams into common semantic frameworks specific to a domain or specialty, for improved compatibility and interoperability. For example, do designers of tractors and trailers have a common perspective on the interactions between these engineered products? Can their work be readily checked for consistency? These issues have major impacts on SE effectiveness and productivity.

Formal patterns, particularly when model-based, appear under different names and "flavors" across SE practice and this handbook. Among these are ontologies, Architectural Frameworks, schemas, and Product Line Engineering (PLE) datasets. For more on these, refer to INCOSE S*Patterns Primer (2022) and the other sections of this handbook. Formal patterns also include general and domain-specific system modeling languages.

The power of models in the STEM revolution was not simply that they reflected agreements across groups (as in standards), but also agreements with observed natural phenomena, reduced to simplest form in the patterns of physical laws. These phenomena-based patterns continue to provide the theoretical basis for the individual engineering disciplines, as well as for the foundations of SE (Schindel, 2016, 2020). The central question they address is:

模板描述和适合此类问题的设计模式的非形式化描述。这些明确、非形式化但有效的模式包括建筑结构模式和城市布局模式（在民用建筑模式中），以及排序算法和图形用户界面设计（在软件设计模式中）。系统工程实践者和领导者不应低估明确的非形式化模式在传播知识方面的价值。

形式化模式 科学从非形式化文章到形式化模型的转变，为科学、技术、工程和数学（STEM）革命的变革性影响提供了动力，其中基于模型的模式表达是相关物理科学的核心。这些模型还为跨工程学科的设计、仿真和生产提供了数代强大的自动化工具，最近这也对系统工程产生了影响。

系统工程实践增加对显性的形式化系统描述模型的使用，将其作为系统工程方法的核心，称为基于模型的系统工程（MBSE）（见 4.2.1 节）。这也使模式及其在系统工程中的应用转向形式化的基于模型的表示，因为基于模型的模式可以很容易地转换（包括自动辅助）为特定于应用程序或项目的构型配置模型。同样，这种模式可以用于其他模型的自动化一致性检查。只要能保证模式在预期用途上的可信度，这不仅能缩短建立可信任的特定模型的时间，还有助于将多个系统实践者和团队的语言和角度转变为特定于某个领域或专业的通用语义框架，从而改进兼容性和互操作性。例如，拖拉机和拖车的设计师是否对这些工程产品之间的交互有共同的角度？他们的工作是否可以随时检查一致性？这些问题对系统工程有效性和生产力有重大影响。

形式化模式，尤其是基于模型的模式，在系统工程实践和本手册中以不同的名称和"风格"出现。其中包括本体、架构框架、模式以及产品线工程（PLE）数据集。有关这些方面的更多信息，请参阅 INCOSE S* 模式入门指南（2022）和本手册的其他章节。形式化模式还包括通用的和领域特定的系统建模语言。

STEM 革命中模型的力量不仅在于其反映了不同群体之间的一致性（如标准），而且还反映了与观察到的自然现象的一致性，并简化为物理定律模式中的最简单形式。这些基于现象的模式继续为各个工程学科以及系统工程的提供理论基础（Schindel，2016，2020）。他们解决的中心问题是：为了工程和生命周期管

LIFE CYCLE ANALYSES AND METHODS

What is the *smallest* system model content necessary to represent a SoI, across its life cycle, for purposes of engineering and life cycle management (Schindel, 2011)? This question has practical implications, but is also rooted in the foundations of SE:

- The *practitioner* has an interest in keeping things as simple as possible, but not simpler. "Too large" a model implies the burden of more information than is needed, including redundancies which often include inconsistencies. "Too small" a model implies that information needed during the life cycle is missing.

- *Foundations of an engineering discipline* include representing recurring phenomena fundamental to its corresponding science. The smallest set of elements generating a discipline identifies its foundations (e.g., Newton's Laws generating Mechanics, Maxwells' Equations generating Electrical Science). A definition of a system's mathematical complexity is the size of its smallest generating representation (Li and Vitanyi, 2009).

The *Systematica Metamodel (S*Metamodel)* is a formal pattern describing a neutral (independent of specific modeling languages or tools) answer to the above "smallest model" question, mapped into contemporary model tooling and languages, such as SysML, simulations, or modeling frameworks. An *S*Model* is any model, expressed in any modeling language or tooling, that is mapped to the reference S*Metamodel. The S*Metamodel spans disciplines, tooling, and languages, and is rooted in the phenomena-based models of the physical sciences.

Modern word processing tools are powerful, but varying writer composition skills and practices allow authoring that may produce valuable literature or faulty descriptions and broken semantics. Similarly, observed methods of use of contemporary modeling languages and automated tools allow the generation of system models that are both too small (are missing important elements) and too large (contain undetected redundancies and contradictions) at the same time. Fortunately for formal models, the history of the physical sciences provides patterns about the nature of phenomena and their models, and these can guide the users of contemporary tools and languages to more effective models than bare languages and tools alone. Accordingly, the S*Metamodel provides that guidance in any language or tooling into which it is mapped. Three examples from the S*Metamodel are:

- *All behavior is interaction-based*: Physics has made it clear that there is no "naked" behavior in the absence of interactions, although system modelers sometimes create models that incorrectly assert otherwise. Interactions are the heart of system phenomena, emergence, SE, and S*Models. Failure to understand and represent interactions leads to well-known engineering problems such as overlooking the impact of "external" actor behavior on the performance of an in-service engineered system (Schindel, 2013, 2016).

理的目的，在 SoI 的整个生命周期中，表示 SoI 所需的最小系统模型内容是什么（Schindel，2011）？这个问题具有实际意义，也植根于系统工程的基础：

- 实践者有兴趣让事情尽可能简单，但不要简单。"太大"的模型意味着需要的信息太多，包括冗余，而冗余往往包括不一致。"太小的"模型意味着生命周期中所需信息的缺失。

- 工程学科的基础包括再现其相应科学的基本现象。生成学科的最小元素集合确定了学科的基础（例如，牛顿定律产生力学，麦克斯韦方程产生电气科学）。系统的数学复杂性的定义取决于其最小生成表示的规模（Li 和 Vitanyi，2009）。

Systematica 元模型（S* 元模型）是一种形式化模式，描述了对上述"最小模型"问题的中性（独立于特定建模语言或工具）答案，映射到当代模型工具和语言中，如 SysML、仿真或建模框架。S* 模型是以任何建模语言或工具表示的、映射到参考元模型的任何模型。S* 元模型跨越学科、工具和语言，并植根于物理科学中基于现象的模型。

现代文字处理工具功能强大，但不同的作家写作技巧和实践允许创作可能产生有价值的文献或错误的描述和不完整的语义。类似地，观察到的当代建模语言和自动化工具的使用方法，使得生成的系统模型既太小（缺少重要元素）又太大（包含未检测到的冗余和矛盾）。幸运的是，对于形式化模型而言，物理科学史提供了有关现象本质及其模型的模式，这些模式可以指导当代工具和语言的使用者建立比单纯的语言和工具更有效的模型。因此，S* 元模型在任何语言或工具中都能提供这种指导。S* 元模型的三个示例是：

- *所有行为都是基于交互的*：物理学已经清楚地表明，在没有交互的情况下，不存在"赤裸"的行为，尽管系统建模者有时会创建一些错误的模型。交互是系统现象、涌现、系统工程和元模型的核心。不能理解和表示交互会导致众所周知的工程问题，例如忽视"外部"参与者行为对在役工程系统性能的影响（Schindel，2013，2016）。

LIFE CYCLE ANALYSES AND METHODS

- *Requirement statements are transfer functions*: Models can help make it clear that requirement statements are not simply prose, but always represent input-output relationships parameterized by state variables. S*Models make this clear and enable improved auditing for problematic or overlooked requirements (Schindel, 2005).

- Stakeholder value trade space, failure effects in risk analysis, and configurability of product line families are all manifestations of the same variables: These are frequently treated as relatively independent specialties and dimensions, greatly over-complicating system representation and understanding, when that apparent dimensionality can be substantially reduced by S*Models (Schindel, 2010).

Other aspects of the S*Metamodel, and the S*Models generated from it, are described in Schindel (2011), INCOSE S*MBSE (2022), and INCOSE S*Patterns Primer (2022).

211 **S*Patterns** S*Patterns are reusable S*Models of families of systems, often domain-specific, configurable to represent multiple individual applications, market segments, or other configurations (Schindel, 2022a). There are also more generic S*Patterns, such as the S*Metamodel itself (INCOSE S*MBSE, 2022), the System Innovation Ecosystem Pattern introduced in Figure 1.6 (Schindel and Dove, 2016) (INCOSE Innovation Ecosystems, 2022), and the Model Characterization Pattern used to generate requirements and metadata for unified characterization of virtual models of all types (INCOSE S*MCP, 2019). Pattern-based MBSE using S*Patterns involves authoring of system patterns and their configuration to application and project-specific S*Model instances, as summarized by Figure 3.17. Part of the "minimality" of the S*Metamodel is its sufficiency for such representations, including configuration rules. Instructional examples of system pattern representations may be found in Schindel and Peterson (2013). System patterns have been used in automotive, heavy equipment, aerospace, medical device, diesel and gas turbine engines, advanced manufacturing, consumer product, cybersecurity, and other domains (Bradley, et al., 2010) (Cook and Schindel, 2015) (Schindel and Smith, 2002) (Schindel, 2012).

There is more to pattern-based methods than just representing the patterns. Historical descriptions of SE processes can appear to describe all the processes practitioners ought to perform in order to discover, validate, and utilize all the information the system life cycle requires. However, those descriptions have by volume had less to say on the question of "what about what we already know?" Such descriptions might be viewed as relying on practitioners to separately work out informal means of exploiting existing knowledge within what the process specifies. To address such questions, the System Innovation Ecosystem Pattern shown in Figure 1.6 describes the curation and mixing of information believed already credible with required new information extraction and validation. Schindel and Dove (2016), INCOSE S*Patterns

- *需求语句是传递函数*：模型有助于明确需求陈述不是简单的文章，而是始终表示由状态变量参数化的输入输出关系。S* 元模型明确这一点，并改进对有问题的或被忽视的需求的审核（Schindel，2005）。

- 利益相关方的价值权衡空间、风险分析中的故障影响和产品线系列的可配置性都是相同变量的表现形式：通常将这些变量视为相对独立的特殊性和维度，大大超过了系统表示和理解的复杂性，而元模型可以大幅降低这些明显的维度（Schindel，2010）。

关于 S* 元模型及其生成的 S* 模型的其他方面，请参阅 Schindel（2011）、INCOSE S*MBSE（2022）和 INCOSE S* 模式入门指南（2022）。

S 模式* S* 模式是可重复使用的系统族 S* 模型，通常特定于领域，可配置为表示多个单独的应用、细分领域或其他构型配置（Schindel，2022a）。还有更通用的 S* 模式，如 S* 元模型本身（INCOSE S*MBSE，2022），图 1.6 中引入的系统创新生态模式（Schindel 和 Dove，2016）（INCOSE Innovation Economics，2022），以及用于生成所有类型的虚拟模型统一特征的需求和元数据的模型特征模式（INCOSE S*MCP，2019）。如图 3.17 所示，使用 S* 模式的基于模式的 MBSE 包括编写系统模式并将其配置到应用和项目特定的 S* 模型实例中。S* 元模型的"最小性"部分在于对此类表示（包括配置规则）的充分性。系统模式表示的教学示例参见 Schindel 和 Peterson（2013）。系统模式已用于汽车、重型设备、航空航天、医疗设备、柴油和燃气涡轮发动机、先进制造、消费品、网络安全以及其他领域（Bradley 等，2010）（Cook 和 Schindel，2015）（Schindel 和 Smith，2002）（Schindel，2012）。

基于模式的方法不仅仅用于表示模式。对系统工程流程的历史性描述似乎表述实践者为发现、确认和利用系统生命周期所需的所有信息而需要执行的所有流程。然而，这些描述在"我们已经知道了什么？"这一问题上没有多少发言权。这种描述可能会被视为依赖于实践者在流程规定的范围内各自找出利用现有知识的非形式化手段。为了解决这些问题，图 1.6 所示的"系统创新生态模式"描述如何将被认为已经可信的信息与所需的新信息提取和确认进行整理和混合。Schindel 和 Dove（2016 年）、INCOSE S* 模式入门指

LIFE CYCLE ANALYSES AND METHODS

Primer (2022) and others describe multiple additional levels of detail decomposition of processes, information, ecosystem capabilities, and limitations. Those details show how life cycle processes of ISO/IEC/IEEE 15288 (2023) and this handbook are incorporated to manage group learning and controlled sharing, and especially pattern credibility and uncertainty, across multiple programs of an enterprise, supply chain, or industry group. The System Innovation Ecosystem Pattern is further concerned with the effective linkage between the processes of pattern learning, validation, and curation versus the execution processes of making use of the content of trusted patterns—often by different people, at different times, in different places or organizations.

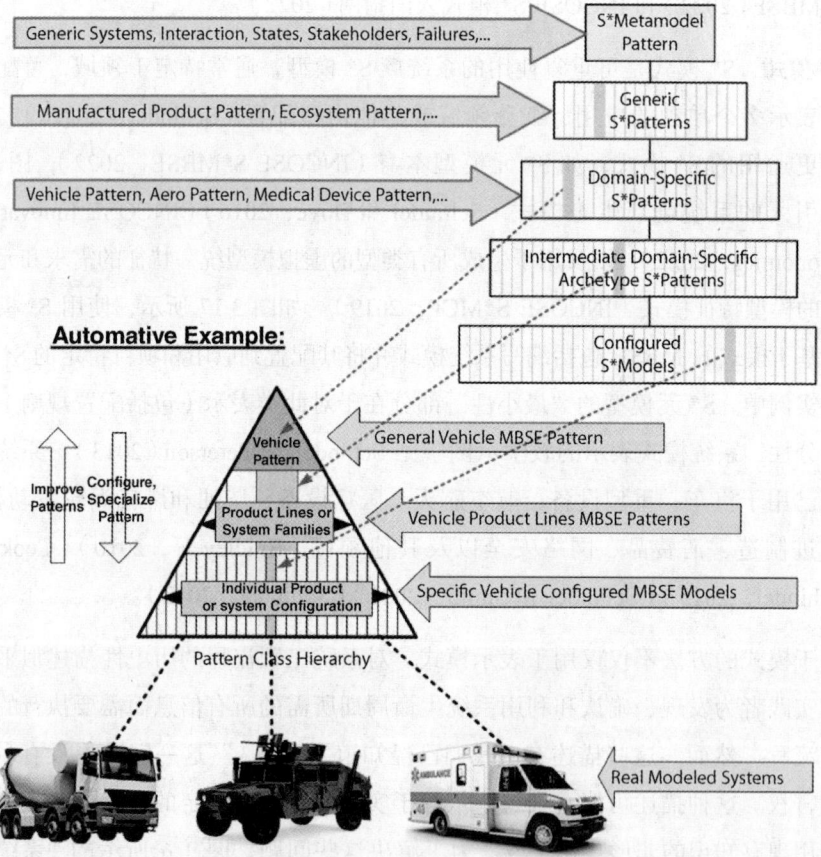

FIGURE 3.17 S*Pattern class hierarchy. From (Schindel and Peterson, 2013). Used with permission. All other rights reserved.

生命周期分析和方法

南（2022）和其他人描述流程、信息、生态系统能力和限制的多层级的详细分解。这些详细信息展示如何将 ISO/IEC/IEEE 15288（2023）和本手册的生命周期流程结合起来，以管理团队学习和受控共享，尤其是跨复杂组织体系、供应链或行业的多个项目的模式可信度和不确定性。系统创新生态系统模式进一步关注模式学习、确认和整理过程与使用可信模式内容的执行过程之间的有效联系，这些过程往往由不同的人在不同的时间、不同的地点或组织实施。

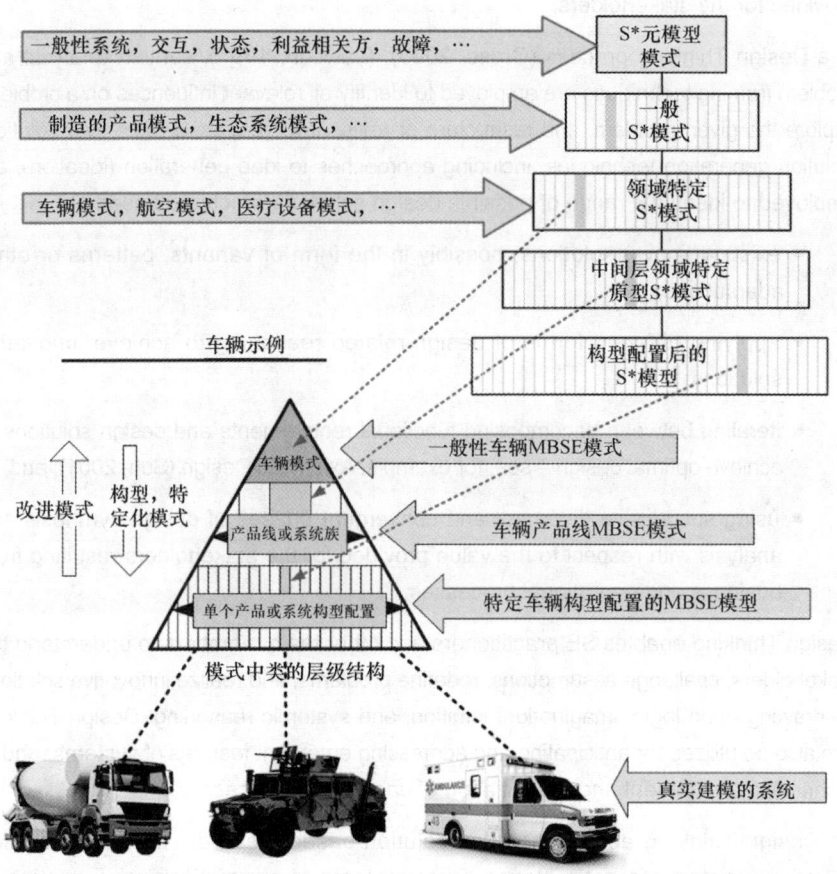

图 3.17　S*模式中类的层级结构。源自 Schindel 和 Peterson（2013）。经许可后使用。版权所有。

LIFE CYCLE ANALYSES AND METHODS

3.2.7 Design Thinking

Understanding and leveraging the technical, business, and social relationships to successfully design and manage engineered systems is still a challenge in SE practice. SE solutions to this challenge tend to focus on system components, human activities, machine functionality, and human-system integration . Solution design can take advantage of Design Thinking (Dorst, 2015) as a complementary approach to Systems Thinking (see Section 1.5). Design Thinking explores (1) the human needs, (2) the operational and business processes and reasoning by which design concepts are devised and realized, especially those which are creative in nature, together with (3) the systems being realized, (4) its specialization, and (5) their utilities and value provided for the stakeholders.

In a Design Thinking process (Cross, 2000), (Lawson, 1997), context analysis and problem framing techniques are employed to identify all relevant influences on a problem, explore the given problem, and restructure or revise it to suggest a route to a solution. Solution generation techniques, including approaches to idea generation (ideation), are employed to identify a range of possible design solutions which are based on:

- existing known solutions, possibly in the form of variants, patterns or other adaptations;
- applying different forms of design-related reasoning to achieve innovative solutions;
- iterating between decomposing functional requirements and design solutions to achieve optimal design – see, for example, Axiomatic Design (Suh, 2001); and,
- using successive divergent and convergent phases of design synthesis and analysis with respect to the value provided for the stakeholders resulting from business and operational processes.

Design Thinking enables SE practitioners and other team members to understand the stakeholders, challenge assumptions, redefine problems, and realize innovative solutions by drawing upon logic, imagination, intuition, and systemic reasoning. Design Thinking can also be utilized for anticipating and addressing emergent features of systems, and in technical management and organization of engineering processes.

As Design Thinking approaches use solution-based methods, they can be used in various system life cycle stages. Examples are to support business or mission analysis (see Section 2.3.5.1), to identify and validate stakeholder or system requirements (see Sections 2.3.5.2 and 2.3.5.3), or to define the system architecture or its design solution (see Sections 2.3.5.4 and 2.3.5.5).

3.2.7 设计思维

理解和利用技术、业务和社会关系来成功设计和管理工程系统，这在系统工程实践中仍然是一个挑战。针对这一挑战的系统工程解决方案往往侧重于系统组件、人员活动、机器功能和人与系统综合。解决方案设计可以利用设计思维（Dorst，2015）作为系统思维的补充方法（见 1.5 节）。设计思维探索（1）人的需要，（2）开发和实现设计概念的运行和业务流程及推理，特别是那些具有创造性的概念，（3）正在实现的系统，（4）其实例化，以及（5）其为利益相关方提供的效用和价值。

在设计思维流程中（Cross，2000）（Lawson，1997），背景环境分析和问题框定技术用来识别问题的所有相关影响，探索给定的问题，并对其进行重组或修改，以提出解决方案的途径。解决方案生成技术，包括想法生成（构思）方法，用于确定一系列可能的设计解决方案，这些解决方案基于：

- 现有的已知解决方案，可能以变体、模式或其他调整的形式存在。

- 应用不同形式的设计相关推理，以实现创新解决方案。

- 在分解功能需求和设计解决方案之间迭代，以实现最佳设计——例如，参见公理化设计（Suh，2001）。

- 针对业务和运行流程为利益相关方提供的价值，利用连续的发散和收敛阶段开展设计综合和分析。

设计思维使系统工程实践者和其他团队成员能够理解利益相关方、挑战假设、重新定义问题，并通过逻辑、想象力、直觉以及系统推理实现创新解决方案。设计思维还可用于预测和解决系统的涌现性，以及工程流程的技术管理和组织。

由于设计思维方法使用基于解决方案的方法，因此可将其用于不同的系统生命周期阶段。例如，支持业务或任务分析（见 2.3.5.1 节），识别和验证利益相关方或系统需求（见 2.3.5.2 节和 2.3.5.3 节），或定义系统架构或其设计解决方案（见 2.3.5.4 节和 2.3.5.5 节）。

LIFE CYCLE ANALYSES AND METHODS

3.2.8 Biomimicry

Definition *Natural systems* include living and nonliving systems—anything that is not human-made. Natural systems differ from engineered systems (see Section 1.1), which are the primary focus of this handbook.

"*Biomimicry* is a practice that learns from and mimics the strategies found in nature to solve human design challenges—and find hope" (Biomimicry Institute, 2022).

Purpose Nature inspired SE and biomimicry can improve processes, practices, and products through the understanding of how nature is structured, behaves, adapts, interacts, accomplishes functions, and recovers from disturbance. Applying natural systems thinking and engineering can improve system capability, efficiency, and performance, while benefiting operations, support, and the effects on external environments. Examples include optimized information processing and sensing, operation in extreme environments, innovative materials application, distributed architectures, understanding of how emergence arises, lowered environmental impact, and system resilience. Nature has strategies to improve performance in all these areas, including circular approaches to materials and energy. To utilize nature-inspired solutions, SE looks to a universal solution space and asks regularly, "Can nature help me solve this problem?" and, "How can nature help me improve my SoI, product, or process?"

FIGURE 3.18 Examples of natural systems applications and biomimicry. INCOSE SEH original figure created by McNamara and Anway derived from Studor (2016) and Hoeller, et al. (2016) using NASA images. Usage per the INCOSE Notices page. All other rights reserved.

3.2.8 仿生学

定义 自然系统包括生命系统和非生命系统——任何非人造的系统。自然系统不同于工程系统（见 1.1 节），这是本手册的主要重点。

"仿生是一种从自然界中学习和模仿策略的实践，从而解决人类设计挑战并寻找希望"（仿生研究所，2022）。

目的 通过了解自然界的结构、行为、适应、互动、功能以及从干扰中恢复的方式，受自然启发的系统工程和生物仿生学可以改进流程、实践和产品。应用自然的系统思维和工程学可以提高系统能力、效率和性能，同时有利于运行、支持以及施加对外部环境的影响。其中的示例包括优化的信息处理和传感、极端环境中的运行、创新材料应用、分布式架构、理解新现象是如何发生的、降低环境影响以及系统强韧性。大自然有各种策略来提高所有这些领域的性能，包括材料和能源的循环方法。为了利用自然启发的解决方案，系统工程着眼于一个通用的解决方案空间，并定期询问："自然能帮助我解决这个问题吗？"以及"自然如何帮助我改进 SoI、产品或流程？"

图 3.18 自然系统应用和仿生学示例。INCOSE SEH 原始图由 McNamara 和 Anway 创建，源自 Studor（2016）和 Hoeller 等（2016）使用的 NASA 图片。按照 INCOSE 通知页使用。版权所有。

LIFE CYCLE ANALYSES AND METHODS

Examples Examples of successful natural systems applications and biomimicry abound. Select examples are shown in Figure 3.18: Velcro® inspired by burdock (Velcro, 2023); an impeller inspired by the calla lily and nautilus shell (Pax Water Technologies, 2022); grippers inspired by the gecko (NASA JPL, 2013, 2014, 2015); and a sensor inspired by an insect's compound eye (Frost, et al, 2016).

Description Over time, natural systems have developed a very close fit to their surroundings and other systems. The result is that they exhibit optimized attributes that often exceed the performance of engineered systems. In addition, they often have positive impacts on the environment. The study of natural systems includes forms, structures, materials, behaviors, processes, regenerative strategies, and interactions. Studying natural systems will increase an SE practitioners' repertoire of solutions, architectural variations, and strategies. The SE practitioner on a project is ideally suited to explore opportunities for application of natural systems across all life cycle stages.

To develop natural systems solutions, the SE practitioner uses a systematic process that:

- Begins by being open to alternate solutions;
- Defines requirements in terms of abstract functions or goals, including specific relevant metrics whenever practical;
- In the early stages of solution exploration, uses the abstracted functions to search for and identify multiple natural systems that could satisfy the desired function and examines characteristics of each;
- Selects one or more candidate natural systems;
- Abstracts the strategy that accomplishes the function in nature;
- Explores architectural variations that translates the strategy and generates alternate system element alternatives;
- Transfers the strategy to the SoI;
- Evaluates system element performance at the system level; and
- Evaluates the environmental impact of the system production, operation, support, and retirement.

Partnering with and supporting natural systems scientists can be essential to a successful implementation. An SE team gains from the in-depth knowledge provided by a cross-disciplinary team.

For more information, see INCOSE NS Primer (2023).

示例 成功的自然系统应用和仿生的示例比比皆是。图 3.18 展示了部分示例：灵感来自牛蒡的 Velcro® 魔术贴（Velcro，2023）；叶轮灵感来自马蹄莲和鹦鹉螺（Pax Water Technologies，2022）；以壁虎为灵感的抓具（NASA JPL，2013，2014，2015）；以及一种受昆虫复眼启发的传感器（Frost 等，2016）。

说明 随着时间的推移，自然系统与周围环境以及其他系统形成非常紧密的配合。其结果是表现出的优化属性往往超过了工程系统的性能。此外，这常常对环境产生积极影响。对自然系统的研究包括形式、结构、材料、行为、流程、再生策略和交互。研究自然系统将增加系统工程实践者的解决方案、架构变化和策略储备。项目中的系统工程实践者非常适合探索自然系统在所有生命周期阶段的应用机会。

为了开发自然系统解决方案，系统工程实践者使用一个系统化的流程，该流程包括：

- 首先对备选解决方案持开放的态度；
- 用抽象的功能或目标来定义需求，在可行的情况下包括具体的相关指标；
- 在解决方案探索的早期阶段，使用抽象功能来搜索和识别能够满足所需功能的多个自然系统，并检查每个系统的特征；
- 选择一个或多个备选自然系统；
- 抽象自然界中实现功能的策略；
- 探索可转换策略并生成备选系统元素备选方案的架构变体；
- 将策略转移到 SoI；
- 在系统层评估系统元素的性能；
- 评估系统生产、运行、支持和退役的环境影响。

与自然系统科学家合作并为其提供支持，对成功实施至关重要。系统工程团队可以从跨学科团队提供的深度的知识中获益。

更多相关信息，参阅 INCOSE NS 入门指南（2023）。

4 TAILORING AND APPLICATION CONSIDERATIONS

215 This section provides considerations for the application of SE with respect to different methodologies, approaches, system types, product sectors, and application domains.

4.1 TAILORING CONSIDERATIONS

There are many standards and handbooks that address life cycle models and SE processes. However, in most cases, these cannot be directly applied to a given organization or project. There is usually a need to tailor them for the specific project, organization, environment, or other situational factors.

The principle behind tailoring is to adapt the processes to ensure that they meet the needs of an organization or a project while being scaled to the level of rigor that allows the system life cycle activities to be performed with an acceptable level of risk. In general, all system life cycle processes can be applied during all stages of the system life cycle, tailoring determines the process level that applies to each stage. Additionally, processes are applied iteratively, recursively, and concurrently as shown in Figure 2.10.

Tailoring scales the rigor of application to an appropriate level based on risk. Figure 4.1 is a notional graph for balancing formal process against the risk of cost and schedule overruns (Salter, 2003). Insufficient SE effort is generally accompanied by high risk of schedule and cost overruns. If too little rigor is applied, the risk of technical issues increases. However, as illustrated in Figure 4.1, too much formal process may also lead to increased cost. If too much rigor is applied or unnecessary process activities or tasks are performed, the risk of cost and schedule slips increases. Tailoring occurs dynamically over the system life cycle depending on risk and the situational environment. Therefore, it should be continually monitored and adjusted as needed.

This section describes the process of tailoring the system life cycle models and SE

INCOSE Systems Engineering Handbook: A Guide for System Life Cycle Processes and Activities, Fifth Edition.

Edited by David D. Walden, Thomas M. Shortell, Garry J. Roedler, Bernardo A. Delicado, Odile Mornas, Yip Yew-Seng, and David Endler.

© 2023 John Wiley & Sons Ltd. Published 2023 by John Wiley & Sons Ltd.

4 剪裁和应用的考虑因素

本节针对不同的方法论、实施方法、系统类型、产品行业和应用领域，提出了系统工程应用的考虑因素。

4.1 剪裁考虑因素

有许多标准和手册介绍了生命周期模型和系统工程流程。然而，在大多数情况下，这些标准和手册不能直接应用于给定的组织或项目。通常需要根据具体的项目、组织、环境或其他情景因素对其进行剪裁。

剪裁背后的原则是调整流程，以确保它们满足组织或项目的需求，同时达到一定的严格程度，使系统生命周期活动在可接受的风险水平下进行。一般来说，所有系统生命周期流程都可以应用于系统生命周期的所有阶段，剪裁决定了适用于每个阶段的流程等级。此外，流程以迭代、递归和并行方式应用，如图2.10所示。

剪裁根据风险将应用的严格程度调整到适当的水平。图4.1是平衡形式化的流程与成本和进度超支风险的概念图（Salter, 2003）。系统工程工作不足通常伴随着进度和成本超支的高风险。如果应用的严格程度太低，技术问题的风险就会增加。然而，如图4.1所示，过多的形式化流程也可能导致成本增加。如果过于严格或执行了不必要的流程活动或任务，则成本和进度变差的风险会增加。根据风险和情景环境，在系统生命周期内进行动态剪裁。因此，应根据需要对其进行持续监控和调整。

本节描述了系统生命周期模型和系统工程流程的剪裁流程，以满足组织和项目的需要。

TAILORING AND APPLICATION CONSIDERATIONS

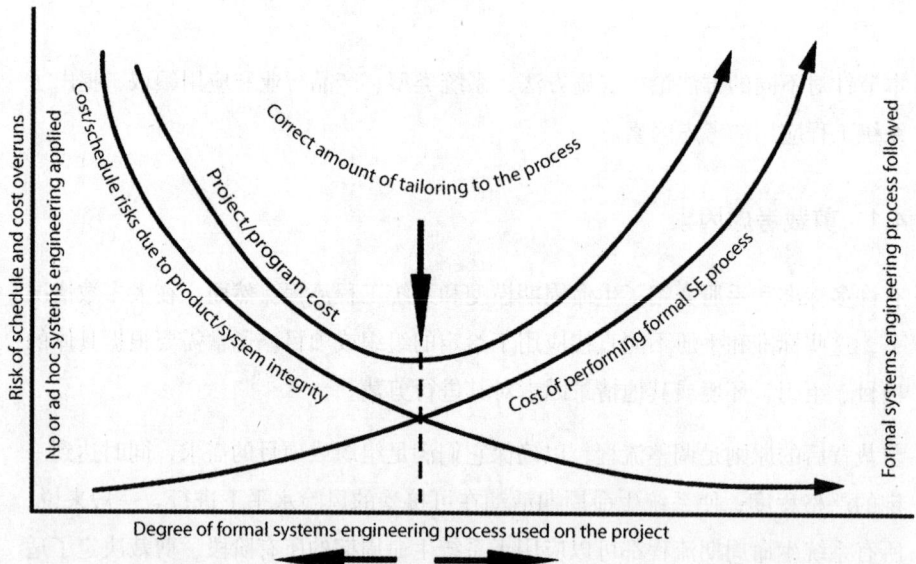

FIGURE 4.1 Tailoring requires balance between risk and process. INCOSE SEH original figure created by Krueger adapted from Salter (2003). Usage per the INCOSE Notices page. All other rights reserved.

216 Tailoring Process

Overview

Purpose As stated in ISO/IEC/IEEE 15288,

[A.2.1] The purpose of the Tailoring process is to adapt the processes of ISO/IEC/IEEE 15288 (and of this handbook) to satisfy particular circumstances or factors that:

a) Surround an organization that is employing ISO/IEC/IEEE 15288 in an agreement;

b) Influence a project that is required to meet an agreement in which ISO/IEC/IEEE 15288 is referenced;

c) Reflect the needs of an organization in order to supply products or services.

Description At the organization level, the tailoring process adapts external standards in the context of the organizational processes to meet the needs of the organization. At the project level, the tailoring process adapts organizational processes for the unique needs of the project.

剪裁和应用的考虑因素

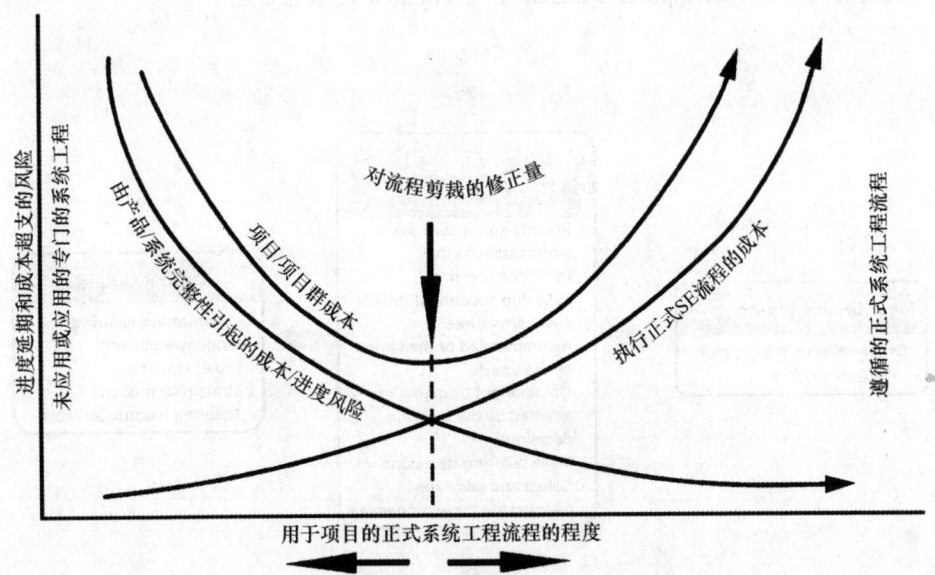

图 4.1 剪裁要求风险和流程之间的平衡。INCOSE SEH 原始图由 Michael Krueger 创建，借鉴于 Ken Salter。按照 INCOSE 通知页使用。版权所有。

剪裁流程

概述

目的　如 ISO/IEC/IEEE 15288 所述：

[A.2.1] 剪裁流程的目的是调整 ISO/IEC/IEEE 15288（以及本手册）的流程，以满足以下特定情况或因素：

a）围绕在协议中采用 ISO/IEC/IEEE 15288 的组织；

b）影响一个必须满足 ISO/IEC/IEEE 15288 协议要求的项目；

c）反映组织的需要，以便提供产品或服务。

描述　在组织层级，剪裁流程在组织流程的背景环境中调整外部标准，以满足组织的需要。在项目层级，剪裁流程根据项目的独特需要调整组织流程。

TAILORING AND APPLICATION CONSIDERATIONS

Inputs/Outputs Inputs and outputs for the Tailoring process are listed in Figure 4.2. Descriptions of each input and output are provided in Appendix E.

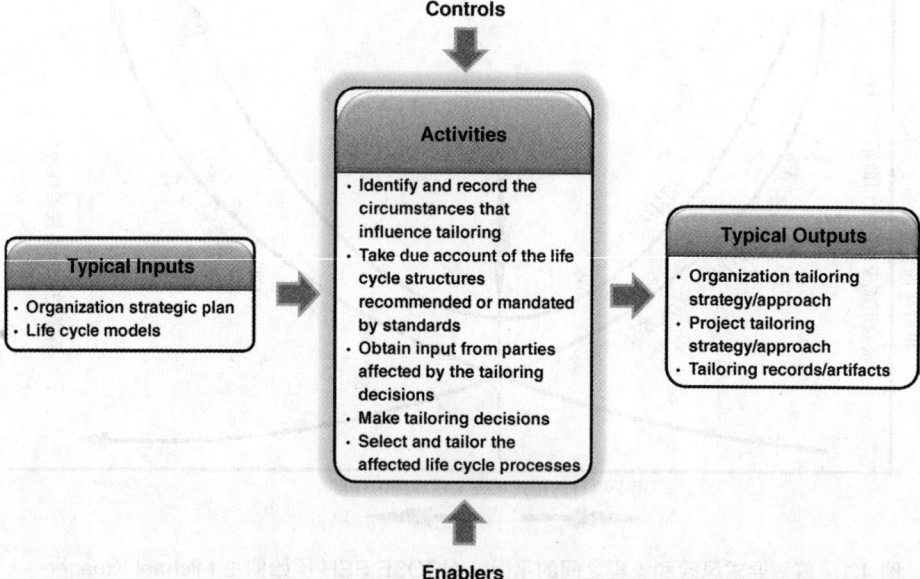

FIGURE 4.2 IPO diagram for Tailoring process. INCOSE SEH original figure created by Shortell, Walden, and Yip. Usage per the INCOSE Notices page. All other rights reserved.

Process Activities The Tailoring process includes the following activities:

- *Identify and record the circumstances that influence tailoring.*

–Identify the strategic, programmatic, and technical risks for the organization or project.

–Identify the level of novel concepts or the complexity of the system solution.

–Identify administrative effects (e.g., geographic distribution, organizational distribution, team size) that may impact tailoring.

–Record the relative importance of circumstances that influence tailoring.

–Identify tailoring criteria for each stage.

- *Take due account of the life cycle structures recommended or mandated by standards.*

–Identify relevant standards.

输入 / 输出 剪裁流程的输入和输出如图 4.2 所示。附录 E 中提供了每个输入和输出的描述。

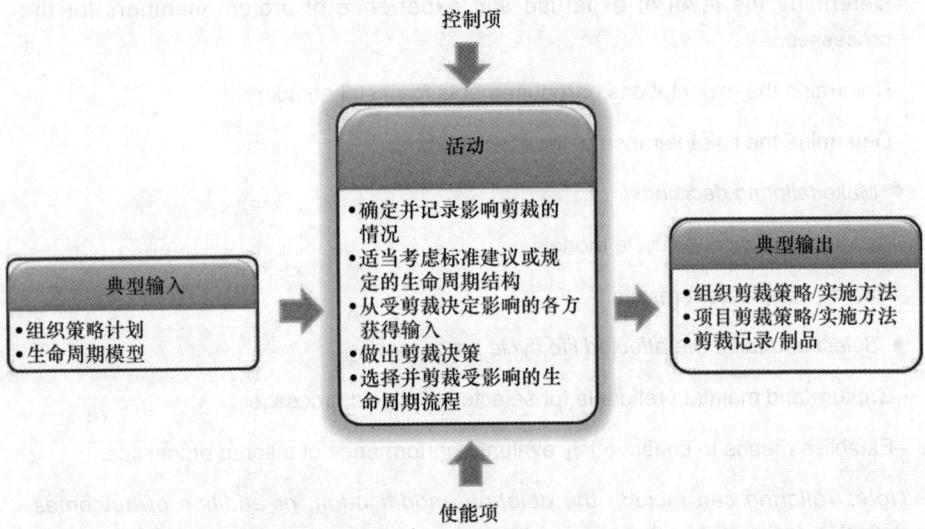

图 4.2 剪裁流程的 IPO 图。INCOSE SEH 原始图由 Shortell、Walden 和 Yip 创建。按照 INCOSE 通知页使用。版权所有。

流程活动 剪裁流程包括以下活动：

- *识别并记录影响剪裁的情况。*

- 识别组织或项目的战略、计划和技术风险。

- 确定新概念的层级或系统解决方案的复杂性。

- 识别可能会对剪裁产生影响的管理影响（例如，地理分布、组织分布、团队规模）。

- 记录影响剪裁的环境的相对重要性。

- 确定每个阶段的剪裁准则。

- *适当考虑标准建议或规定的生命周期结构。*

- 识别相关标准。

TAILORING AND APPLICATION CONSIDERATIONS

—Evaluate impact on tailoring and implementation across the life cycle.

- *Obtain input from parties affected by the tailoring decisions.*

—Determine the level of expertise and experience of project members for the processes.

—Determine the expectations or requirements from stakeholders.

—Determine the risk tolerance of the stakeholders.

- *Make tailoring decisions.*

—Assess candidate life cycle models.

—Record assessment results.

- *Select and tailor the affected life cycle processes.*

—Capture and maintain rationale for selected life cycle processes.

—Establish means to continuously evaluate performance of tailored processes.

Note: Tailoring can include the deletion, modification, or addition of outcomes, activities, tasks, typical inputs, or typical outputs.

218 *Common approaches and tips:*

- Base decisions on facts and obtain approval from an independent authority.
- Use the Decision Management process to assist in tailoring decisions.
- Constrain the tailoring based on agreements between organizations.
- Control the extent of tailoring based on issues of compliance to stakeholder, customer, and organization policies, objectives, and legal requirements.
- Have different organizations propose and approve the tailoring.
- Influence the extent of tailoring of the agreement process activities based on the methods of procurement or intellectual property.
- Remove extra activities as the level of trust builds between parties.
- Identify the assumptions and criteria for tailoring throughout the life cycle to optimize the use of formal processes.
- Document the rationale for tailoring decisions.

剪裁和应用的考虑因素

- 评估整个生命周期的剪裁和实施的影响。

- 从受剪裁决定影响的各方获得输入。

- 确定流程中项目成员的专业知识和经验的等级。

- 确定利益相关方的期望或需求。

- 确定利益相关方的风险承受能力。

- *做出剪裁决策。*

- 评估备选生命周期模型。

- 记录评估结果。

- *选择并剪裁受影响的生命周期流程。*

- 捕获并维护所选生命周期流程的基本原理。

- 建立持续评估剪裁流程绩效的方式。

注：剪裁可以包括结果、活动、任务、典型输入或典型输出的删除、修改或添加。

常用方法和提示：

- 基于事实做出决策，并获得独立权威机构的批准。

- 使用决策管理流程协助剪裁决策。

- 根据组织之间的协议约束剪裁。

- 根据利益相关方、客户和组织的政策、目标和法律需求的符合性事项，控制剪裁的程度。

- 让不同的组织提出并批准剪裁。

- 根据采办方法或知识产权影响协议流程活动的剪裁程度。

- 随着各方之间建立信任等级，移除额外活动。

- 识别在整个生命周期内进行剪裁的假设和准则，以优化形式化的流程使用。

- 记录剪裁决策的理由。

TAILORING AND APPLICATION CONSIDERATIONS

Elaboration

Organizational Tailoring Organizational tailoring applies specifically to the creating and maintaining organizational-level processes used by all projects. It is done in conjunction with the Life Cycle Model Management process (see Section 2.3.3.1). When contemplating if and how to incorporate a new or updated external standard into an organization, the following should be considered (Walden, 2007):

- Understand the organization;
- Understand the new standard;
- Adapt the standard to the organization (not vice versa);
- Institutionalize standards compliance at the "right" level;
- Allow for tailoring.

Project Tailoring Project tailoring applies specifically to the work executed through projects. It is done in conjunction with the Project Planning process (see Section 2.3.4.1). Factors that influence tailoring at the project level typically include, but are not limited to:

- Stakeholders and acquirers (e.g., number of stakeholders, quality of working relationships);
- Project budget, schedule, and requirements;
- Risk tolerance;
- Complexity and precedence of the system;
- The need for horizontal and vertical integration (see Section 2.3.5.8).

As mentioned in SE principle #12 (see Section 1.4.3), complex systems are engineered by complex organizations. Consequently, today's systems are more often jointly developed by many different organizations. Cooperation must transcend the boundaries of any one organization. Harmony between multiple organizations is often best maintained by agreeing to follow a set of consistent processes, methods, and tools.

Traps in Tailoring Common traps in the tailoring process include, but are not limited to, the following:

- Reuse of a tailored baseline from another system without repeating the tailoring process;
- Using all processes and activities "just to be safe";
- Assuming there is a single set of measures, risks, or other controls that apply to all projects without tailoring;

详细阐述

组织剪裁　组织剪裁特别适用于创建和维护所有项目都使用的组织级流程。它与生命周期管理流程（见 2.3.3.1 节）一起进行。当考虑是否以及如何将新的或更新的外部标准纳入组织时，应考虑以下事项（Walden, 2007）：

- 理解组织；
- 理解新标准；
- 使标准适应组织（反之则不然）；
- 在"正确"的层级将标准符合性制度化；
- 允许剪裁。

项目剪裁　项目剪裁特别适用于在项目中执行的工作。它与项目规划流程一起进行（见 2.3.4.1 节）。在项目层级影响剪裁的因素通常包括但不限于：

- 利益相关方和采办方（例如，利益相关方的数量、工作关系的质量）；
- 项目预算、进度和需求；
- 风险承受能力；
- 系统的复杂性和优先级；
- 横向和纵向综合的需要（见 2.3.5.8 节）。

正如系统工程原则 #12（见 1.4.3 节）所述，复杂系统由复杂组织设计。因此，今天的系统往往是由许多不同的组织联合开发的。合作必须超越任何一个组织的界限。多个组织之间和谐关系的维护通常最好是通过同意遵循一套一致的流程、方法和工具。

剪裁中的陷阱　剪裁流程中的常见陷阱包括但不限于以下内容：

- 重用另一个系统的剪裁基线，无须重复剪裁流程；
- 使用所有流程和活动"只是为了安全"；
- 假设存在一套适用于所有项目的测度、风险或其他控制措施，而无须剪裁；

TAILORING AND APPLICATION CONSIDERATIONS

- Using a pre-established tailored baseline;
- Failure to include relevant stakeholders.

219 *Tailoring for Very Small Enterprises* The ISO/IEC/IEEE 29110 series defines Very Small Enterprises (VSEs) as enterprises, organizations, departments, or projects with up to 25 people. In many cases, VSEs find it difficult to apply international standards to their business needs and to justify the application of standards to their business practices. Typical VSEs do not have a comprehensive infrastructure, and the limited personnel usually are performing multiple roles. This may also happen in a large organization when the task is to perform a small project with less than 25 people involved. In this case, it can be extremely challenging to downscale the organization's life cycle model that is designed for much larger projects.

The ISO/IEC/IEEE 29110 series defines guides for VSEs based on a set of VSE characteristics (e.g., business models, situational factors, risk levels). From that, four profiles were derived:

- *Entry* (less than 6 people or start-ups);
- *Basic* (single application by a single work team);
- *Intermediate* (more than one project in parallel with more than one work team); and
- *Advanced* (for VSEs that want to sustain and grow as an independent competitive system developer).

These profiles cover the needs of most VSEs. Each of the profiles defines subsets of international standards (e.g., ISO/IEC/IEEE 15288) relevant to the VSE's respective context. For critical projects, such as mission critical or safety critical, these profiles do not apply, since the criticality of the projects would dictate a much greater level of rigor and comprehensive SE.

4.2 SE METHODOLOGY/APPROACH CONSIDERATIONS

The system definition activities, especially the partitioning of the system, requires that integration is considered throughout the development stage of the life cycle. The integration considerations may also require refinement based on when and how the work is performed. The choice of SE methodology or approach, along with the chosen life cycle model, often affects the sequence of work, which can help determine the focus of resources to address the unique challenges of the project.

- 使用预先建立的剪裁的基线；
- 未能包括相关的利益相关方。

为极小的复杂组织体系剪裁 ISO/IEC/IEEE 29110 系列将极小型复杂组织体系（VSE）定义为最多 25 人的复杂组织体系、组织、行业或项目。在许多情况下，VSE 发现很难将国际标准应用于其业务需求，也很难证明将标准应用于其业务实践的合理性。典型的 VSE 没有全面的基础设施，有限的人员通常执行多个角色。当一个大型组织的任务是执行一个只有不到 25 人参与的小项目时，这种情况也可能发生。在这种情况下，降低为更大项目设计的组织生命周期模型的规模可能是极具挑战性的。

ISO/IEC/IEEE 29110 系列根据一组 VSE 特征（例如，业务模型、情景因素、风险水平）定义了 VSE 指南。由此，衍生出四个剖面：

- *进入*（少于 6 人或初创复杂组织体系）；
- *基础*（单个工作组的单个应用）；
- *中级*（多个项目与多个工作组并行）；
- *高级*（适用于希望作为独立的有竞争力的系统开发者而保持和发展的 VSE）。

这些剖面覆盖了大多数 VSE 的需求。每个剖面定义了与 VSE 各自背景环境相关的国际标准子集（如 ISO/IEC/IEEE 15288）。对于关键项目，如使命任务关键型或安全性关键型，这些剖面不适用，因为项目的关键度将要求更高层级的严格性和全面的系统工程。

4.2 系统工程方法论 / 实施方法考虑因素

系统定义的活动，特别是系统分区，要求在生命周期的整个开发阶段考虑综合。综合的考虑因素还可能需要根据何时以及如何执行工作进行细化。系统工程方法论或实施方法的选择，以及所选的生命周期模型，通常会影响工作顺序，可以帮助确定资源的关注点，从而解决项目中的特殊挑战。

TAILORING AND APPLICATION CONSIDERATIONS

This section introduces considerations for the following SE methodologies and approaches:

- Model-Based Systems Engineering (MBSE);
- Agile Systems Engineering;
- Lean Systems Engineering;
- Product Line Engineering (PLE).

Note that other types of SE methodologies and approaches exist.

4.2.1 Model-Based SE

This section provides an overview of the Model-Based Systems Engineering (MBSE) approach and includes a summary of its benefits relative to a more document-based approach. It also references a set of MBSE methodologies and provides a brief description of one representative methodology called the Object-Oriented Systems Engineering Method (OOSEM).

MBSE Overview The INCOSE Systems Engineering Vision 2020 (2007) defines MBSE as:

The formalized application of modeling to support system requirements, design, analysis, verification, and validation activities beginning in the [concept stage] and continuing throughout development and later life cycle [stages].

MBSE is often contrasted with a document-based approach to SE. In a document-based SE approach, there is often considerable information generated about the system that is contained in documents and other artifacts such as specifications, interface control documents, system description documents, trade studies, analysis reports, and verification plans, procedures, and reports. The information contained within these documents is often difficult to synchronize and maintain, and difficult to assess in terms of its quality (correctness, completeness, and consistency). Although many systems have been developed using a traditional document-based approach, a model-based approach is becoming essential to address the increasing complexity of systems and support approaches that can more effectively and efficiently adapt to requirements and design changes.

MBSE enhances the ability to capture, analyze, share, and manage the information associated with the specification of a product that can result in the benefits listed below. There is some quantitative data (Rogers and Mitchell, 2021) and considerable qualitative data (OMG MBSE Wiki, 2023, MBSE Events and Related Meetings) from industry papers and presentations that support the following benefits of MBSE:

本节介绍了以下系统工程方法论和实施方法的考虑因素：

- 基于模型的系统工程（MBSE）；
- 敏捷系统工程；
- 精益系统工程；
- 产品线工程（PLE）。

请注意，还存在其他类型的系统工程方法论和实施方法。

4.2.1 基于模型的系统工程

本节概述了基于模型的系统工程（MBSE）实施方法，并总结了相对于基于文档的实施方法的优势。本节参考了一组 MBSE 方法论，并简要介绍了一种具有代表性的方法论，即面向对象的系统工程方法（OOSEM）。

MBSE 概述 国际系统工程委员会系统工程愿景 2020（2007）将 MBSE 定义为：

通过建模的形式化应用，支持系统需求、设计、分析、验证和确认活动，从 [概念阶段] 开始，并在整个开发和随后的生命周期 [阶段] 中持续。

MBSE 通常与基于文档的系统工程实施方法形成对比。在基于文档的系统工程实施方法中，通常会生成大量关于系统的信息，这些信息包含在文档和其他制品中，如规范、接口控制文档、系统描述文档、权衡研究、分析报告和验证计划、程序和报告。这些文档中包含的信息通常很难同步和维护，也很难评估其质量（正确性、完整性和一致性）。虽然许多系统都是使用传统的基于文档的实施方法开发的，但基于模型的实施方法对于解决系统日益增加的复杂性，支持更有效和高效地适应需求和设计变更的实施方法变得至关重要。

MBSE 增强了捕获、分析、共享和管理与产品规格相关的信息的能力，可带来以下好处。行业论文和演讲中的一些定量数据（Rogers 和 Mitchell，2021）和大量定性数据（OMG MBSE Wiki，2023，MBSE 活动和相关会议），支持表明了 MBSE 的以下益处：

TAILORING AND APPLICATION CONSIDERATIONS

- *Improved communications* among the development stakeholders (e.g., the acquirer, project management, SE practitioners, hardware and software developers, testers, quality characteristic disciplines).

- *Increased ability to manage system complexity* by enabling the system to be viewed from multiple perspectives.

- *Improved product quality* by providing an unambiguous and precise model of the system that can be evaluated for consistency, correctness, and completeness.

- *Reduced cycle time* by enabling better control of the technical baseline, more rapid impact analysis, improved specification and design reuse, early insight for design decisions, and early discovery of potential defects.

- *Reduced risk by surfacing requirements and design issues early.*

- *Enhanced knowledge capture and reuse* of the information by capturing information in more standardized ways and reducing redundancy of information.

- *Improved ability to teach and learn SE fundamentals* by providing a clear and unambiguous representation of systems and system concepts.

MBSE Methodologies In an MBSE approach, much of the information that has been traditionally captured in informal diagrams, text, and tables is captured in a *descriptive system model* (see Section 3.2.1). This includes information about the system context, the requirements on the system and its elements, the system architecture including its structure and behavior, the critical parameters needed to specify the analysis of the system, and information about how the system is verified to satisfy its requirements. Modeling languages such as SysML™ (OMG SysML, 2021) are often used to capture this information in a standard way (see Section 3.2.1). The system descriptive model is augmented by other models, such as models to capture the system geometric configuration and various analytical models, to analyze the performance and other quality characteristics of the system. Each kind of model captures different kinds of information about the system. The different models must be managed as the design evolves to ensure a coherent representation of the overall system.

In an MBSE approach, the system descriptive model is a primary artifact of the SE process. MBSE formalizes the application of SE by creating the system descriptive model and integrating it with the other kinds of models. The kind of information and the level of detail of the information that is captured in models and maintained throughout the life cycle depends on the scope of the MBSE effort. An effective MBSE methodology supported by appropriate tools and a team with the requisite SE skills and knowledge are essential to fully realize the benefits of MBSE.

- 改善开发利益相关方之间的沟通（例如，采办方、项目管理人员、系统工程实践者、硬件和软件开发人员、测试人员、质量特性学科）。
- 通过允许从多个角度查看系统，提高了管理系统复杂性的能力。
- 通过提供一个无二义、精确的系统模型，以评估一致性、正确性和完整性，提高了产品质量。
- 通过更好地控制技术基线、更快速地进行影响分析、改进规范和设计重用、尽早洞察设计决策以及尽早发现潜在缺陷，缩短周期时间。
- 通过尽早提出需求和设计问题，降低了风险。
- 通过以更标准化的方式捕获信息并减少信息的冗余，增强了知识的获取和信息的重用。
- 通过提供系统和系统概念的清晰、无二义的表示，提高了讲授和学习系统工程基础知识的能力。

MBSE 方法论　在 MBSE 实施方法中，传统上在非正式图表、文本和表格中捕获的大部分信息都在描述性系统模型中得以捕获（见 3.2.1 节）。这包括关于系统背景环境的信息、系统及其元素的需求、系统架构（包括其结构和行为）、指定系统分析所需的关键参数，以及关于如何验证系统以满足其需求的信息。建模语言，如 SysML™（OMG SysML，2021）通常用于以标准的方式捕获这些信息（见 3.2.1 节）。系统描述模型由其他模型补充，例如用于捕获系统几何构型配置的模型和各种解析模型，以分析系统的性能和其他质量特性。每种模型都捕获关于系统的不同类型的信息。随着设计的发展，必须管理不同的模型，以确保整个系统的一致表示。

在 MBSE 实施方法中，系统描述模型是系统工程流程的主要制品。MBSE 通过创建系统描述模型并将其与其他类型的模型综合，将系统工程的应用形式化。在模型中捕获并在整个生命周期中维护的信息类型和信息的细节程度取决于 MBSE 工作的范围。一种有效的 MBSE 方法论，由适当的工具和具备必要的系统工程技能和知识的团队支持，对于充分实现 MBSE 的收益至关重要。

TAILORING AND APPLICATION CONSIDERATIONS

An *MBSE methodology* describes how MBSE is performed to capture the required information in the system descriptive model and related artifacts. Like any methodology, it must be tailored to the particular need of the organization and/or project (see Section 4.1). This includes defining the appropriate life cycle model, tailoring the activities and work products to align with the project scope and modeling objectives, and selecting the appropriate tools to create and manage the models and other relevant data. Estefan (2008) published a survey of candidate MBSE methodologies under the auspices of an INCOSE technical publication. Information on these methodologies is available on the Methodology and Metrics web page of the INCOSE MBSE Wiki (2022). These methodologies and others continue to evolve based on their application to real world projects. OOSEM is summarized below as a representative MBSE method.

OOSEM Summary OOSEM is an MBSE method intended to help architect systems that satisfy evolving mission and system requirements and can accommodate changes in technology and design. OOSEM is generally consistent with processes in this handbook. It can be adapted to different life cycle models to support the specification, analysis, design, and verification of systems. The method enables the flow-down of requirements from mission, to system, to system element levels, which are realized by applicable hardware, software, data, and other discipline-specific design methods.

OOSEM describes fundamental SE activities whose outputs are model-based artifacts. The modeling artifacts are captured in a system descriptive model using the Systems Modeling Language (SysML™) along with other analytical models. A process model for OOSEM can be downloaded from the INCOSE OOSEM Working Group website (2022).

The OOSEM supports a development process that includes the following subprocesses and activities:

- *Manage the system development*—activities include plan and control the technical effort, including planning, risk management, configuration management, and other project monitoring and control activities;

- *Specify and design the system*—activities include analyze stakeholder needs, specify the system requirements, develop the system architecture, and allocate the system requirements to system elements;

- *Develop the system elements*—activities include design the elements, implement the elements, and verify the elements satisfy the allocated requirements; and

- *Integrate and verify the system*—activities include integrate the system elements and verify that the integrated system elements satisfy the system requirements.

MBSE 方法论描述了如何执行 MBSE 以捕获系统描述模型和相关制品中所需的信息。与任何方法论一样，它必须根据组织和 / 或项目的特殊需要进行剪裁（见 4.1 节）。这包括定义适当的生命周期模型，剪裁活动和工作产品从而符合项目范围和建模目标，并选择适当的工具创造和管理模型和其他相关数据。Estefan（2008）在国际系统工程委员会技术出版物的赞助下发布了一份备选 MBSE 方法论调查报告。有关这些方法论的信息，可访问国际系统工程委员会 MBSE Wiki（2022）的方法论和指标网页了解。这些方法论和其他方法论在应用到实际项目的基础上继续发展。现将具有代表性的 MBSE 方法 OOSEM 概述如下。

OOSEM 总结 OOSEM 是一种 MBSE 方法，旨在帮助架构满足不断发展的使命任务和系统需求的系统，并且适应技术和设计的变化。OOSEM 通常与本手册中的流程一致。它可以适应不同的生命周期模型，以支持系统的规格、分析、设计和验证。该方法实现了需求从使命任务到系统再到系统元素的向下流动，这些需求通过适用的硬件、软件、数据和其他特定学科的设计方法实现。

OOSEM 描述了基本的系统工程活动，其输出是基于模型的制品。使用系统建模语言（SysML™）在系统描述模型中捕获建模制品以及其他解析模型。OOSEM的流程模型可从国际系统工程委员会OOSEM工作组网站（2022）下载。

OOSEM 支持开发流程，该流程包括以下子流程和活动：

- *管理系统开发*：活动包含计划和控制技术工作，包括规划、风险管理、配置管理和其他项目监控和控制活动；
- *明确系统规格并进行设计*：活动包含分析利益相关方需求，规定系统需求，开发系统架构，并将系统需求分配给系统元素；
- *开发系统元素*：活动包含设计元素、实施元素，并验证元素是否满足分配的需求；
- *综合和验证系统*：活动包含综合系统元素，并验证综合的系统元素是否满足系统需求。

TAILORING AND APPLICATION CONSIDERATIONS

This OOSEM process can be applied at each level of the system hierarchy to specify the requirements of the system and its elements. Applying the process recursively at successive levels of the hierarchy may involve multiple iterations throughout the development process. To be effective, the fundamental tenets of SE must be applied including the use of multi-disciplinary teams and a disciplined management process.

4.2.2 Agile Systems Engineering

The knowledge of requirements for an effective system often continues to change during the system life cycle. Common causes include insufficient initial knowledge, new knowledge revealed during development and utilization, and continual evolution in the targeted operational environment of the system. When evolution of the system's operational environment doesn't stop with initial deployment, a system's functional capabilities must evolve if it is to remain viable. Under these circumstances system engineering is virtually never ending, and retirement is generally an issue of safe and secure functional capability disposal rather than system decommissioning.

Agile Systems Engineering is a principle-based approach for designing, building, sustaining, and evolving systems when knowledge is uncertain, or environments are dynamic. Thus, Agile System Engineering is a what, not a how. As stated in Section 2.2, there are many life cycle models (e.g., Vee, Incremental Commitment Spiral Model (ICSM), DevSecOps (Development, Security, Operations)). Some of them are targeted on a single engineering domain (e.g., XP (Extreme Programming), Scrum, DevOps (Development, Operations), and various scaled approaches such as SAFe (Scaled Agile Framework) in the software engineering domain). Most of them have a strong focus on the development stage.

Agile Systems Engineering is best understood when contrasted to the sequential life cycle approach and in how the two relate to the system life cycle spectrum. Figure 4.3 shows extreme forms of these two life cycle approaches in terms of their activity stages and data flows. All life cycle approaches fall somewhere between the two ends of the spectrum, depending upon the process-encoded degree of attentiveness and responsiveness to dynamics in knowledge and environment. It is unlikely that either depicted extreme would be effective in actual practice.

An Agile Systems Engineering process is based on strategies for timely and continual knowledge development and affordable application of new knowledge in system development activity. Virtually all forms of Agile Systems Engineering employ incremental or evolutionary development in some way (see Sections 2.2.2 and 2.2.3) as a means to produce demonstrable and/or usable work in process that provokes feedback for real time learning and subsequent application.

该 OOSEM 流程可以应用于系统层级结构的每个层级，以规定系统及其元素的需求。在层级结构的连续层级递归地应用该流程，可能需要在整个开发过程中进行多次迭代。为使其有效，必须应用系统工程的基本原则，包括使用多学科团队和规范的管理流程。

4.2.2 敏捷系统工程

有效的系统需求知识通常在系统生命周期中持续变化。常见原因包含最初的知识不足，在开发和利用流程中发现的新知识，以及系统在目标运行环境中的持续演进。当系统运行环境的演进并不止步于最初的部署时，系统的功能能力就必须演进，从而保证系统可用。在这种情况下，系统工程实际上是永无止境的，退役通常是一个有关安全和安保功能能力的处置事项，而不是系统停止运行。

*敏捷系统工程*是一种基于原则的实施方法，用于在知识不确定或环境是动态的情况下设计、构建、维持和演进系统。因此，敏捷系统工程是"是什么"，而不是"如何做"。如 2.2 节所述，有许多生命周期模型 [如 Vee、增量承诺螺旋模型（ICSM）、DevSecOps（开发、安保性、运行）]。其中一些是针对单个工程领域的 [例如 XP（极限编程）、Scrum、DevOps（开发、运行）和各种大规模实施方法，例如软件工程领域中的 SAFe（大规模敏捷框架）]。其中大多数都非常重视开发阶段。

与顺序生命周期实施方法相比，敏捷系统工程最容易理解，也最容易理解二者与系统生命周期的关系。图 4.3 展示了这两种生命周期实施方法在活动阶段和数据流方面的极端形式。所有生命周期实施方法都介于这两个极端之间，取决于过程编码对知识和环境动态的关注和响应程度。所描述的这两个极端在实际实践中都不太可能有效。

敏捷系统工程流程基于在系统开发活动中及时、持续地开发知识和以可承受的代价应用新知识的策略。实际上，所有形式的敏捷系统工程都以某种方式（见 2.2.2 节和 2.2.3 节）采用增量或渐进式开发，作为在流程中产生可证明和/或可用工作的一种手段，以激发实时学习和后续应用的反馈。

TAILORING AND APPLICATION CONSIDERATIONS

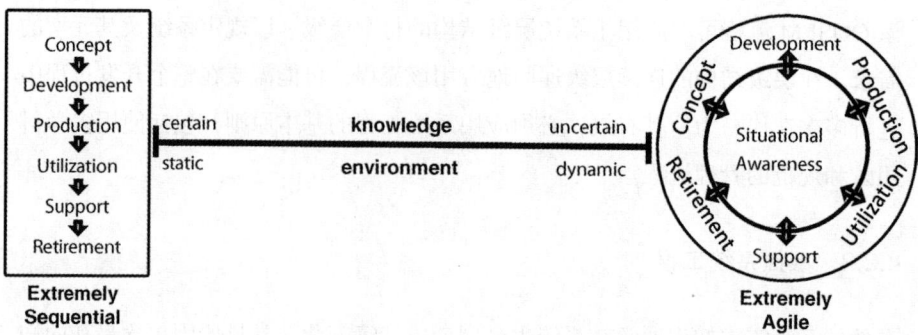

FIGURE 4.3 SE life cycle spectrum. From Dove (2022). Used with permission. All other rights reserved.

Software plays an increasingly major role in most systems today. Codified agile software development methodologies offer relevant approaches for rapid knowledge discovery and deployment in the software domain. Patterns from these software approaches can inform agile engineering approaches in other domains and in the encompassing domain of SE; but each domain has unique differences (e.g., external dependencies, fabrication techniques, development cycle time constraints, development support tools).

Agile Systems Engineering Life Cycle Model   The Agile Systems Engineering life cycle model is depicted on the far right of Figure 4.3 and with more detail in Figure 4.4. The six system life cycle stages run around the perimeter, with situational awareness featured in the center. The agile life cycle model can accommodate activities in any and all of the stages concurrently without progressive sequencing. Figure 4.4 depicts a life cycle model (Dove and Schindel, 2019), not to be confused with the Vee model (see Section 2.2.1) which depicts relationships among SE activities applicable in sequential, iterative, and evolutionary approaches.

223 Situational awareness has no entry or exit criteria, as it should, in principle, be a continuous activity. Entry criteria for all of the other stages begins with a decision to act upon specific triggering awareness, and may require process-prudent, or contract-required, engagement criteria for a stage or stages to be entered. An Agile Systems Engineering process is predicated upon real-time experimentation and learning in all stages, and as such, the entry criteria may be as simple as the decision to enter a stage for experimental knowledge development that may or may not produce artifacts for use in other stages. On the other hand, exit criteria for a stage that produces artifacts for use in other stages should have some fixed requirements for satisfactory stage completion, with recognition that the outcome of stage activity may simply be valuable learned knowledge that aborts the need for producing artifacts of use in other stages.

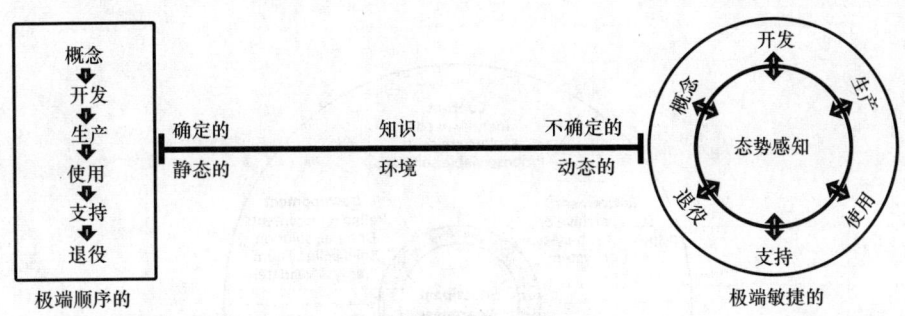

图 4.3　系统工程生命周期谱系。源自 Dove（2022）。经许可后使用。版权所有。

软件在当今大多数系统中扮演着越来越重要的角色。编纂的敏捷软件开发方法论为软件领域中的快速知识发现和部署提供了相关的实施方法。这些软件实施方法的模式可以为其他领域和涵盖系统工程领域的敏捷工程实施方法提供信息；但每个领域都有独特的差异（例如，外部依赖性、制造技术、开发周期时间限制、开发支持工具）。

敏捷系统工程生命周期模型　敏捷系统工程生命周期模型如图 4.3 最右侧所示，更多详情如图 4.4 所示。六个系统生命周期阶段以情景感知为中心围绕在其周围。敏捷生命周期模型可以同时容纳任何和所有阶段中的活动，而无须渐进式排序。图 4.4 描述了一个生命周期模型（Dove 和 Schindel，2019），不要与 V 模型混淆（见 2.2.1 节），V 模型描述了适用于顺序、迭代和进化方法的系统工程活动之间的关系。

情景感知没有进入或退出准则，因为它原则上应该是一种连续的活动。所有其他阶段的进入准则都始于对特定触发感知而采取行动的决定，并可能需要为进入一个或多个阶段而制定流程谨慎的或合同要求的进入准则。敏捷系统工程流程基于所有阶段的实时实验和学习，因此，进入准则可能与基于经验知识开发的进入某个阶段的决策一样简单，可能产生也可能不产生适用于其他阶段的制品。另一方面，一个阶段的退出准则如果要产生供其他阶段使用的制品，那么该阶段的退出准则就应该有一些固定需求，以使该阶段令人满意地完成。同时也要认识到，阶段活动的结果可能仅仅是有价值的习得知识，而不需要产生供其他阶段使用的制品。

TAILORING AND APPLICATION CONSIDERATIONS

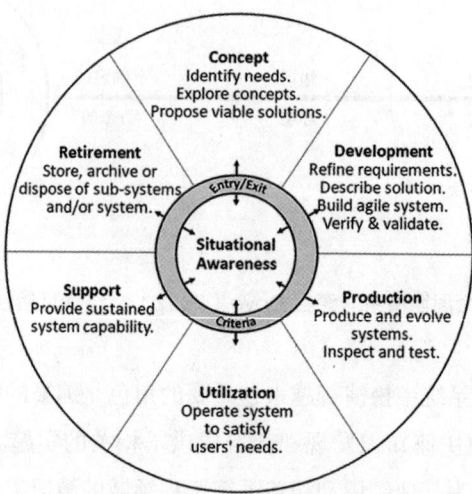

FIGURE 4.4 Agile SE life cycle model. From Dove and Schindel (2019). Used with permission. All other rights reserved.

The retirement stage deals with system elements and older system versions that are retired frequently, as the "current" system evolves. This has implications for safe and secure maintenance, disposal, and reversion processes.

Fleshing out a generic Agile SE Life Cycle Model for a specific project likely starts with default standard processes in each stage, tailored and augmented for specific agile SE differences. Adapting the generic model to a specific organization's process will tailor and augment the generic model as the organization's standard process evolves.

Agile Systems Engineering Life Cycle Operational Considerations As described in Section 1.3.4, Figure 1.6 depicts the life cycle operational "pattern" as three nested systems:

- **System 1 – The Engineered System** is the target system under development.
- **System 2 – The Life Cycle Project Management System** includes the basic SE development and maintenance processes, and their operational domains that produces System-1.

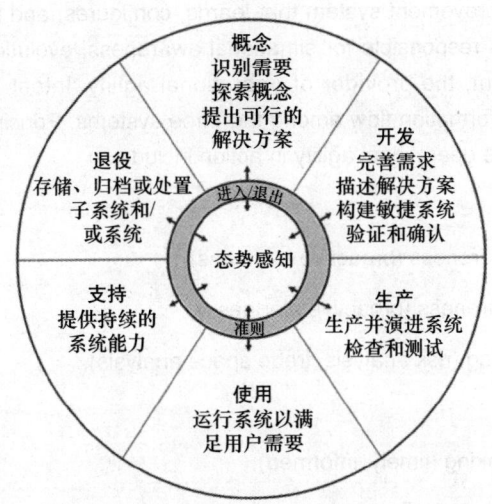

图 4.4　敏捷的系统工程生命周期模型。源自 Dove 和 Schindel（2019）。经许可后使用。版权所有。

退役阶段处理随着"当前"系统的演进而频繁退役的系统元素和较旧的系统版本。这对安全的、安保的维护、处置和恢复流程有影响。

为特定的项目充实一个通用的敏捷系统工程生命周期模型可能从每个阶段的默认标准流程开始，针对特定的敏捷系统工程差异进行剪裁和扩充。随着组织的标准流程的演进，将通用模型调整为特定组织的流程将对通用模型进行剪裁和扩充。

敏捷系统工程生命周期运行考虑因素　如第 1.3.4 节所述，图 1.6 将生命周期运行"模式"描述为三个嵌套系统：

- **系统 1**——工程系统是正在开发的目标系统。
- **系统 2**——生命周期项目管理系统包括基本的系统工程开发和维护流程，以及产生系统 1 的运行域。

TAILORING AND APPLICATION CONSIDERATIONS

- **System 3 – The Enterprise Process and Innovation System** is the process improvement system that learns, configures, and matures System-2. System 3 is responsible for situational awareness, evolution, and knowledge management, the provider of operational agility. Intent is continuous, not episodic, information flow among the three systems. Principles and strategies that facilitate operational agility in action include:

Sensing:

- External awareness (proactive alertness);
- Internal awareness (proactive alertness);
- Sense making (risk analysis, trade space analysis).

Responding:

- Decision making (timely, informed);
- Action making (invoke/configure process activity to address the situation);
- Action evaluation (verification and validation).

Evolving:

- Experimentation (variations on process ConOps);
- Evaluation (internal and external judgement);
- Memory (evolving culture, response capabilities, and process ConOps).

The architecture and structural principles that enable system agility are covered in Section 3.1.3.

224 **Agile Systems Engineering Examples** Agile system engineering methodologies are project-context dependent. What is common across methodologies are certain fundamental strategies that get tailored for a specific context. Four published examples illuminate this tailoring in four different contexts:

- As shown in Figure 2.9, Rockwell Collins employed a product line engineering (PLE) (see Section 4.2.4) approach for a large family of radio products composed of software, firmware, and electronic circuit boards with a continuous integration platform that accommodated asynchronous evolution of mixed-domain system element work in process (Dove, et al., 2017).

- **系统 3**——复杂组织体系流程和创新系统是学习、配置和成熟系统 2 的流程改进系统。系统 3 对情景感知、演进和知识管理负责,是运行敏捷性的提供者。意图是三个系统之间连续的,而不是片段的信息流动。促进行动中的运行敏捷性的原则和战略包括:

感知:

- 外部意识(主动警觉性);
- 内部意识(主动警觉性);
- 判断力(风险分析、权衡空间分析)。

响应:

- 做出决策(及时、知情);
- 行动制定(调用/配置流程活动来应对情况);
- 行动评估(验证和确认)。

演进:

- 实验(流程 ConOps 的变化);
- 评估(内部和外部判断);
- 记忆(演进的文化、响应能力和流程 ConOps)。

实现系统敏捷性的架构和结构原则见 3.1.3 节。

敏捷系统工程示例 敏捷系统工程方法论依赖于项目背景环境。方法论中常见的是某些基本策略,这些策略可以根据特定的背景环境进行剪裁。四个已发布的示例在四个不同的背景环境中说明了这种剪裁:

- 如图 2.9 所示,罗克韦尔柯林斯公司(Rockwell Collins)采用了产品线工程(PLE)(见 4.2.4 节)实施方法来开发由软件、固件和电子线路板组成的大型无线电产品系列,该系列具有连续综合平台,可适应流程中混合域系统元素工作的异步演进(Dove 等,2017)。

TAILORING AND APPLICATION CONSIDERATIONS

- The US Navy SpaWar delivered innovative off-road autonomous vehicle technology in continuous six-month development increments with parallel tracks of integration, test, and architecture evolution (Dove, et al., 2016).

- Northrop Grumman evolved user capabilities in six month increments for a software systems-of-systems singlepoint hub that provided access to 22 independent logistics data bases, with three successive generations under active life cycle control at all times (Dove and Schindel, 2017).

- Lockheed Martin evolved F16, F22, and F35 weapons capabilities with internally developed software and externally subcontracted hardware in roughly six month development increments in a tailored SAFe approach; featuring a continuous integration and demonstration platform with asynchronous evolution of system element simulations, low fidelity proxies, work in process, and completed system elements (Dove, et al., 2018).

4.2.3 Lean Systems Engineering

SE is regarded as an established, sound practice, but is not always delivered efficiently. US Government Accountability Office (GAO, 2008) and NASA (2007a) studies of space systems document major budget and schedule overruns. Similarly, studies by the MIT-based Lean Advancement Initiative (LAI) have identified a significant amount of waste in government projects, averaging 88% of charged time (LAI MIT, 2013; McManus, 2005; Oppenheim, 2004; Slack, 1998). Most projects are burdened with some form of waste: politicization, poor coordination, premature and unstable requirements, quality problems, and management frustration. This waste represents a vast productivity reserve in projects and major opportunities to improve project efficiency.

Lean system development and the broader methodology of lean thinking have their roots in the Toyota "just-in-time" philosophy, which aims at "producing quality products efficiently through the complete elimination of waste, inconsistencies, and unreasonable requirements on the production line" (Toyota, 2009). Lean SE is the application of lean thinking to SE and related aspects of organization and project management. SE is the discipline that enables flawless development and integration of complex technical systems. Lean thinking is a holistic paradigm that focuses on delivering maximum value to the customer and minimizing waste. A popular description of lean is "doing the right job right the first time." Lean thinking has been successfully applied in manufacturing, healthcare, administration, supply chain management, and product development, including engineering.

- 美国海军 SpaWar 以连续六个月的开发增量交付了创新的越野自动驾驶汽车技术，并平行跟踪综合、测试和架构演进（Dove 等，2016）。

- 诺斯罗普·格鲁曼公司（Northrop Grumman）以六个月为增量为一个软件体系的单点枢纽发展用户能力，该枢纽提供了对 22 个独立后勤数据库的访问，连续三代始终处于主动的生命周期控制下（Dove 和 Schindel，2017）。

- 洛克希德·马丁公司（Lockheed Martin）利用内部开发的软件和外部分包的硬件，通过剪裁的 SAFe 实施方法，以大约六个月的开发增量演进 F16、F22 和 F35 武器能力；该方法以连续综合和演示平台为特色，系统元素仿真、低逼真度代理、流程中的工作和已完成的系统元素均可异步演进（Dove 等，2018）。

4.2.3 精益系统工程

系统工程被视为一种确定的、良好的实践，但并不总是能有效实施。美国政府问责局（GAO，2008）和 NASA（2007a）对空间系统的研究记录了重大预算和进度超支。同样，麻省理工学院精益推进计划（LAI）的研究也发现，政府项目中存在大量浪费，平均浪费 88% 的承担时间（LAI-MIT，2013；McManus，2005；Oppenheim，2004；Slack，1998）。大多数项目都背负着某种形式的浪费：政治化、协调不善、过早和不稳定的需求、质量问题和管理挫折。这种浪费代表着项目中巨大的生产力储备和提高项目效率的主要机会。

*精益*系统开发和精益思想更广泛的方法论根植于丰田的"准时制"理念，该理念旨在"通过彻底消除生产线上的浪费、不一致和不合理的需求，高效地生产优质产品"（丰田，2009）。精益系统工程是精益思想在系统工程以及组织和项目管理相关方面的应用。系统工程是一门使复杂技术系统得以完美开发和综合的学科。精益思维是一种整体范式，专注于为客户提供最大价值和最小的浪费。精益的一个流行描述是"在一开始就做正确的工作"。精益思维已成功应用于制造业、医疗卫生、行政管理、供应链管理和产品开发，包括工程。

TAILORING AND APPLICATION CONSIDERATIONS

Lean SE is the area of synergy between lean thinking and SE, with the goal to deliver the best life-cycle value for technically complex systems with minimal waste. The early use of the term lean SE is sometimes met with concern that this might be a "repackaged faster, better, cheaper" initiative, leading to cuts in SE at a time when the profession is struggling to increase the level and quality of SE effort in projects. Lean SE does not take away anything from SE and it does not mean less SE. It means better SE with higher responsibility, authority, and accountability, leading to better, waste-free workflows with increased mission assurance.

Three concepts are fundamental to the understanding of lean: value, waste, and the process of creating value without waste (captured into lean principles).

Value The value proposition in engineering projects is often a multiyear, complex, and expensive acquisition process involving numerous stakeholders and resulting in hundreds or even thousands of requirements, which, notoriously, are rarely stable. In lean SE, value is defined simply as mission assurance (i.e., the delivery of a flawless complex system, with flawless technical performance, during the product or mission development life cycle) and satisfying the customer and all other stakeholders. This implies completion with minimal waste, minimal cost, and the shortest possible schedule.

Waste in Product Development Waste is "the work element that adds no value to the product or service in the eyes of the customer. Waste only adds cost and time" (Womack and Jones, 1996). The LAI classifies waste into seven categories (McManus, 2005). An eighth category, the waste of human potential, is increasingly added. These categories are defined and illustrated as follows.

- *Overprocessing*—Processing more than necessary to produce the desired output; excessive refinement, beyond what is needed for value.
- *Waiting*—Waiting for people, material or information, or people waiting for information or material; late delivery of material or information, or delivery too early—leading to eventual rework.
- *Unnecessary movement*—Moving people (or people moving) unnecessarily to access or process material or information; unnecessary motion in the conduct of the task; lack of direct access; manual intervention.
- *Overproduction*—Creating too much material or information; performing a task that nobody needs; information over-dissemination and pushing data.

精益系统工程是精益思想和系统工程之间的协同领域，其目标是以最少的浪费为技术复杂的系统提供最佳的生命周期价值。早期使用精益系统工程这一术语有时会引起担心，认为这可能是一种"重新包装的更快、更好、更便宜"的举措，导致在系统工程行业努力提高项目中系统工程工作的水平和质量时削减系统工程。精益系统工程并没有从系统工程上带走任何东西，也不意味着更少的系统工程。它意味着更好的系统工程，具有更高的责任、权威和职责，从而实现更好的无浪费工作流程，提高任务保证。

有三个概念是理解精益的基础：价值、浪费和无浪费的创造价值的流程（被纳入精益原则）。

价值 工程项目的价值主张往往是一个历时多年、复杂而昂贵的采办过程，涉及众多利益相关方，并产生成百上千个需求，而众所周知，这些需求很少是稳定的。在精益系统工程中，价值被简单定义为任务保证（即在产品或使命任务开发生命周期内，交付无缺陷的复杂系统，具有无缺陷的技术性能），并满足客户和所有其他利益相关方。这意味着以最少的浪费、最少的成本和最短的可能时间完成。

产品开发中的浪费 浪费指"在客户眼中没有为产品或服务增加任何价值的工作要素。浪费只会增加成本和时间"（Womack 和 Jones，1996）。LAI 将浪费分为七类（McManus，2005）。第八类，即人类潜力的浪费，日益增多。这些类别的定义和说明如下。

- *过度处理：* 为产生期望的输出而过度加工处理；过度细化，超出了价值所需的范围。

- *等待：* 等待人员、物料或信息，或等待信息或物料的人员；物料或信息延迟交付，或交付太早，最终导致返工。

- *不必要的移动：* 不必要地移动人员（或人员移动），以访问或处理物料或信息；执行任务时不必要的动作；缺乏直接访问；手动干预。

- *生产过剩：* 产生过多的物料或信息；执行无人需要的任务；信息过度沟通和推送数据。

TAILORING AND APPLICATION CONSIDERATIONS

- *Transportation*—Moving material or information unnecessarily; unnecessary hand-offs between people; incompatible communication—lost transportation through communication failures.

- *Inventory*—Maintaining more material or information than needed; too much "stuff" buildup; complicated retrieval of needed "stuff"; outdated, obsolete information.

- *Defects*—Errors or mistakes causing the effort to be redone to correct the problem.

- *Waste of human potential*—Not utilizing or even suppressing human enthusiasm, energy, creativity, and ability to solve problems and general willingness to perform excellent work.

Lean Principles and Lean Enablers for Systems Engineering Womack and Jones (1996) captured the *process of creating value without waste* into six *lean principles* described in (Oppenheim, 2011), as follows:

The *value principle* promotes a robust process of establishing the value of the system to the customer with crystal clarity early in the project. The process should be customer-centric, involving the customer frequently and aligning employees accordingly.

The *value stream principle* emphasizes detailed project planning and waste-preventing measures, solid preparation of the personnel and processes for subsequent efficient workflow, and healthy relationships between stakeholders (e.g., acquirer, contractor, suppliers, and employees); project frontloading; and use of leading indicators and quality measures. SE practitioners should prepare for and plan all end-to-end linked actions and processes necessary to realize streamlined value, after eliminating waste.

The *flow principle* promotes the uninterrupted flow of robust quality work and first-time-right products and processes, broad steady competence instead of hero behavior in crises, excellent communication and coordination, concurrency, frequent clarification of the requirements, and making project progress visible to all.

The *pull principle* is a powerful guard against the waste of rework and overproduction. It promotes pulling tasks and outputs based on internal and external customer needs (and rejecting others as waste), and better coordination between the pairs of employees handling any transaction before their work begins so that the result can be first-time right.

- *运输*：不必要地移动物料或信息；人员之间不必要的交接；通信不兼容，由于通信故障而造成传输损失。

- *库存*：维护超过需要的更多材料或信息；"东西"堆积过多；所需"材料"的复杂检索；过时的信息。

- *缺陷*：错误或过失，导致重新努力去纠正问题。

- *浪费人的潜力*：不利用甚至抑制人的热情、精力、创造力、解决问题的本领以及出色完成工作的普遍意愿。

系统工程的精益原则和精益使能技术　Womack 和 Jones（1996）将无浪费创造价值的流程归纳为（Oppenheim，2011）中描述的六项精益原则，如下所示：

价值原则提倡在项目初期就清晰地为客户确立系统价值的稳健流程。流程应以客户为中心，让客户经常参与，并相应地调整员工。

价值流原则强调详细的项目规划和防止浪费的措施，为后续高效的工作流做好充分的人员和流程准备，以及利益相关方（如采办方、承包商、供应商和员工）之间的健康关系；项目前置；并使用领先指标和质量测度。系统工程实践者应在消除浪费后，准备并规划所有端到端的关联行动和流程，以实现简化后的价值。

流程原则促进不间断地提供高质量的工作和一次正确的产品和流程，广泛而稳定的能力而非危机中的英雄行为，良好的沟通和协调、并行性、经常澄清需求，以及让所有人都能看到项目的进展。

拉动原则是防止返工和过度生产所造成的浪费的有力保障。它促进基于内部和外部客户的需要拉动任务和输出（并拒绝其他浪费），并在工作开始前，对员工之间任何事务的处理进行更好的协调，以便取得一次正确的结果。

TAILORING AND APPLICATION CONSIDERATIONS

The *perfection principle* promotes excellence in the SE and organization processes, utilization of the wealth of lessons learned from previous projects into the current project, the development of perfect collaboration policy across people and processes, and driving out waste through standardization and continuous improvement. Imperfections should be made visible in real time, and continuous improvement tools (Six Sigma) should be applied as soon as possible. It calls for a more important role of SE practitioners, with responsibility, accountability, and authority for the overall technical success of the project.

Finally, the *respect-for-people principle* promotes the enterprise culture of trust, openness, honesty, respect, empowerment, cooperation, teamwork, synergy, and good communication and coordination and enables people for excellence.

In 2011, a project undertaken jointly by PMI, INCOSE, and the LAI at MIT developed the Lean Enablers for Managing Engineering Programs (LEfMEP, 2012), adding lean enablers for project management and holistically integrating lean project management with lean SE. A major section of the book is devoted to a rigorous analysis of challenges in managing engineering projects. They are presented under the following 10 challenge themes:

1. Firefighting—reactive project execution;

2. Unstable, unclear, and incomplete requirements;

3. Insufficient alignment and coordination of the extended enterprise;

4. Processes that are locally optimized and not integrated for the entire enterprise;

5. Unclear roles, responsibilities, and accountability;

6. Mismanagement of project culture, team competency, and knowledge;

7. Insufficient project planning;

8. Improper metrics, metric systems, and key performance indicators;

9. Lack of proactive project risk management; and

10. Poor project acquisition and contracting practices.

4.2.4 Product Line Engineering (PLE)

Rarely does anyone build just one edition, just one flavor, just one point solution of anything. In many cases, SE is performed in the context of a product line—a family of similar systems with variations in features and functions. *Product Line Engineering* (PLE) addresses this mismatch by providing models, tools, and methods for holistic engineering of system families.

完善原则促进了系统工程和组织流程的卓越，将以往项目的丰富经验教训应用到当前项目中，在人员和流程之间开发完善的协作政策，并通过标准化和连续改进消除浪费。不完善之处应实时显现，并应尽快应用持续改进工具（六西格玛）。这要求系统工程实践者发挥更重要的作用，对项目的总体技术成功负有责任、承担职责和行使权力。

最后，尊重他人原则促进了信任、开放、诚实、尊重、授权、协作、团队合作、协同以及良好的沟通和协调的复杂组织体系文化，使人们能够追求卓越。

2011 年，由 PMI、国际系统工程委员会和麻省理工学院 LAI 联合开展的一个项目开发了管理工程项目的精益使能项（LEfMEP，2012），为项目管理添加了精益使能项，并将精益项目管理与精益系统工程进行了全面整合。本书的主要章节主要致力于对管理工程项目的挑战进行严格的分析。以下是 10 个挑战主题：

1. 救火——反应式的项目执行；
2. 不稳定、不明确、不完整的需求；
3. 扩展的复杂组织体系的对准和协调不足；
4. 对流程进行局部优化，未面向整个复杂组织体系进行综合；
5. 角色、职责、责任不明确；
6. 项目文化、团队资质能力和知识管理不善；
7. 项目规划不足；
8. 指标、指标体系和关键绩效指标不当；
9. 缺乏主动的项目风险管理；
10. 项目采办和分包实践不佳。

4.2.4　产品线工程（PLE）

很少有人只构建一个版本、一种风格和一个点的解决方案。在许多情况下，系统工程是在产品线的背景环境下进行的，这是一系列具有不同特征和功能的类似系统。产品线工程（PLE）通过为系统族的整体工程提供模型、工具和方法，解决了这种不匹配问题。

TAILORING AND APPLICATION CONSIDERATIONS

A note on terminology: Where the PLE field and standards refer to "product," "product line," and "product line engineering," the equivalent terms in SE are "system," "system family," and "system family engineering," respectively. These terms can be used interchangeably (Krueger, 2022).

Challenges with Early Generation System Family Engineering Approaches   When systems in a *system family* are engineered as individual point solutions, techniques such as *clone-and-own reuse or branch-and-merge* result in evergrowing duplicate and divergent engineering effort. Trying to manage the commonality and variability among these individually engineered systems in the family has traditionally relied on tribal knowledge and high bandwidth, errorprone interpersonal communication. Furthermore, when each engineering discipline adopts a different ad hoc technique for managing variations among the members of the system family, the result is error prone dissonance when trying to translate and communicate across the different life cycle disciplines.

This is a self-inflicted complexity, over and above the complexity inherent in the systems being engineered. It consumes engineering teams with low-value, trivial, replicative work that deprives them of time and energy that would be better spent on high-value innovative work that advances system and business objectives.

Feature-based Product Line Engineering   Feature-based PLE is the modern digital engineering industry good practice for PLE, as defined in the INCOSE PLE Primer (2019) and ISO/IEC 26580 (2021). Feature-based PLE offers significant improvements and benefits in effort, cost, time, scale, and quality by exploiting system similarity while formally managing variation.

Feature-based PLE is used to engineer a system family as a single holistic system rather than a multitude of individual systems. Engineering assets in each engineering discipline are consolidated to eliminate duplication and divergence. A single authoritative variation management model is applied consistently across all assets in all engineering disciplines to eliminate that source of dissonance across the life cycle and to enable organizations to make informed and deliberate cost-benefit decisions about the variations designed into their system family.

Key Elements of a Feature-based PLE Factory   Feature-based PLE uses a PLE Factory metaphor, as illustrated in Figure 4.5. See ISO/IEC 26580 (2021) for a full description.

- **Feature Catalogue**, as shown in the upper left, captures a formal model of the distinguishing characteristics about how the members of the system family differ from each other and provides a common language and single authoritative source of truth about variation throughout the engineering organization.

术语注记：当 PLE 领域和标准中涉及"产品"、"产品线"和"产品线工程"时，系统工程中的等效术语分别为"系统"、"系统族"和"系统族工程"。这些术语可以互换使用（Krueger，2022）。

早期系统族工程实施方法面临的挑战　　当系统族中的系统被设计为单个的点解决方案时，克隆和重复使用或分支和合并等技术会导致不断增加的重复和不同的工程工作。试图管理系统族中这些单独设计的系统之间的共性和异质性，传统上依赖于部落知识和高带宽、易出错的人际沟通。此外，当每个工程学科采用不同的特殊技术来管理系统族成员之间的变化，结果是在尝试跨不同生命周期学科进行翻译和交流时，容易出现差错和不和谐。

这是一种自我造成的复杂性，超越了正在开发的系统的固有复杂性。它通过低价值、琐碎、可复制的工作消耗工程团队的时间和精力，而这些时间和精力本可以更好地用于推进系统和业务目标的高价值创新工作。

基于特征的产品线工程　　基于特征的 PLE 是 PLE 在现代数字工程领域的良好实践，如国际系统工程委员会 PLE 入门指南（2019）和 ISO/IEC 26580（2021）中所定义。基于特征的 PLE 在对差异进行正式管理时，通过利用系统相似性，在工作量、成本、时间、规模和质量方面提供了显著的改进和收益。

基于特征的 PLE 用于将系统族设计为单个整体系统，而不是众多个体系统。每个工程专业的工程资产都进行了整合，以消除复制品和分歧。在所有工程学科的所有资产中，统一应用一个权威的差异管理模型，以消除整个生命周期中不一致的源头，并使组织能够就涉及其系统族中的变更做出明智和审慎的成本效益决策。

基于特征的 PLE 工厂的关键元素　　基于特征的 PLE 使用 PLE 工厂比喻，如图 4.5 所示。完整的描述见 ISO/IEC 26580（2021）。

- **如左上角所示**，特征目录捕获了关于系统族成员如何区分彼此的不同特征的形式化模型，并为整个工程组织提供了关于差异的通用语言和单一权威来源。

TAILORING AND APPLICATION CONSIDERATIONS

- **Bill-of-Features**, as shown in the upper right, specifies the features selected from the Feature Catalogue for each system in a system family portfolio.
- **Shared Asset Supersets**, as shown in the lower left, are the engineering artifacts that support the creation, design, implementation, deployment, and operation of systems in a system family. They contain *variation points*, which are pieces of content that can be included, omitted, generated, or transformed for a system instance, based on the features selected in a Bill-of-Features for that system.
- **PLE Factory Configurator**, shown in the center, is an automation that applies a Bill-of-Features for a system to each variation point in the Shared Asset Supersets, to determine each variation point's content for the system instance.
- **Product Asset Instances**, shown in the lower right, each contain only the shared asset content suited for that one system in the system family.

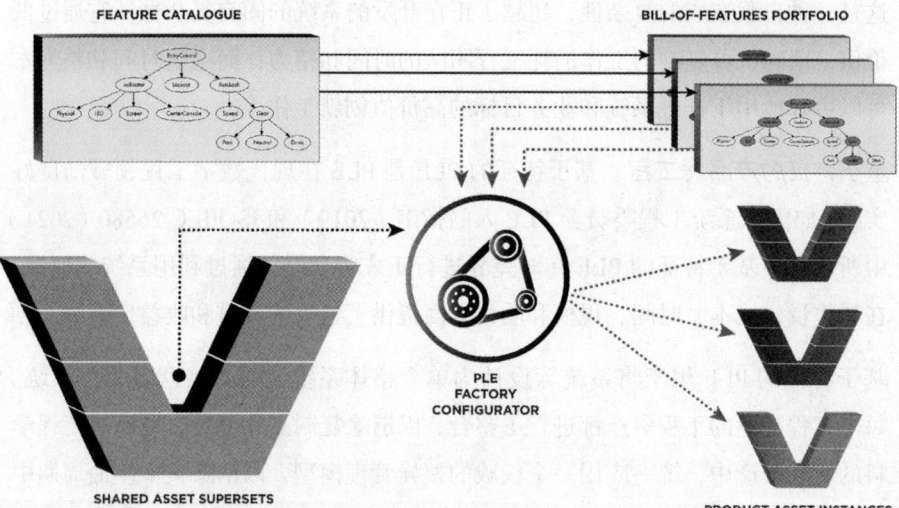

FIGURE 4.5 Feature-based PLE factory. From INCOSE PLE Primer (2019). Usage per the INCOSE Notices page. All other rights reserved.

228 With Feature-based PLE, engineers now work in the PLE Factory on the Shared Asset Supersets, the Feature Catalogue, and the Bills-of-Features rather than on the individual system instances. Once the PLE Factory is established, engineering assets for the individual systems are automatically instantiated rather than manually engineered. Feature-based PLE transforms the task of engineering a plethora of individual systems into the much more efficient task of producing a single system: The PLE Factory itself. This consolidation also means that change management and configuration management are performed on the single PLE Factory rather than separately on each of the system instances.

剪裁和应用的考虑因素

- **如右上角所示**，特征清单规定了从特征目录中为系统族组合中的每个系统选择的特征。
- **如左下角所示**，共享资产超集是支持系统族中系统的创造、设计、实施、部署和运行的工程制品。它们包含差异点，可以是系统实例中包含、省略、生成或转换的内容片段，基于在系统的特征清单中选择的特征。
- **居中展示的 PLE 工厂配置器**是一种自动化工具，它将系统的特征清单应用于共享资产超集中的每个差异点，以确定系统实例的每个差异点的内容。
- **右下角展示的产品**资产实例仅包含适合系统族中该系统的共享资产内容。

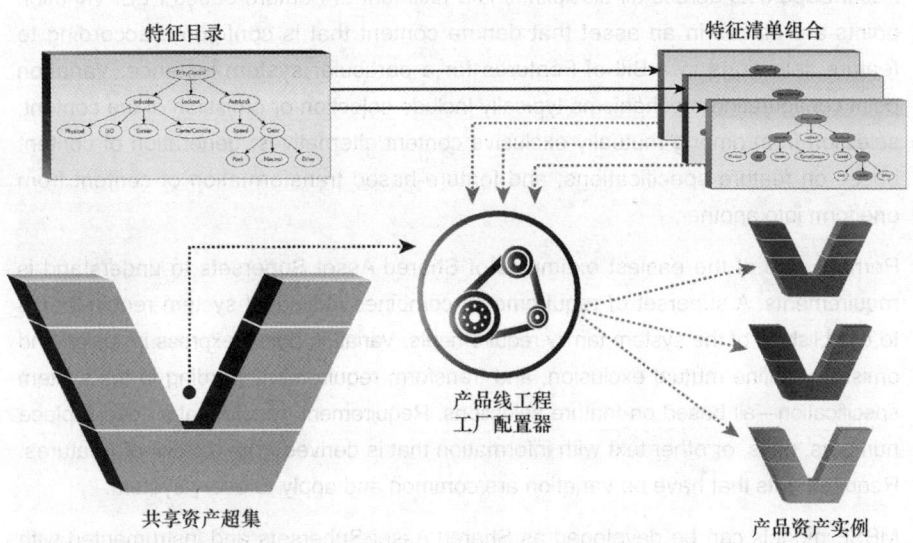

图 4.5 基于特征的产品线工程工厂。源自 INCOSE 产品线工程入门指南（2019）。按照 INCOSE 通知页使用。版权所有。

通过基于特征的 PLE，工程师现在在 PLE 工厂中处理共享的资产超集、特征目录和特征清单，而不是单个的系统实例。一旦 PLE 工厂建立，个体系统的工程资产将自动实例化，而不是手动工程化。基于特征的 PLE 将设计大量个体系统的任务转换为生产单个系统的更高效的任务：PLE 工厂本身。这种整合还意味着在单个 PLE 工厂上执行变更管理和配置管理，而不是在每个系统实例上单独执行。

TAILORING AND APPLICATION CONSIDERATIONS

Shared Asset Supersets and Variation Points To work in a PLE Factory, engineers must learn how to create and maintain Shared Asset Supersets, including variation points, for their discipline. For example, requirements engineers learn how to create requirements Shared Asset Supersets with variation points, test engineers learn how to create verification and validation Shared Asset Supersets with variation points, and software engineers learn how to create source code Shared Asset Supersets with variation points.

A Shared Asset Superset contains a single copy of all content used in any system—that is, there is no duplication of content. Content that appears in every system is said to be *common* content, while content that varies from system to system is encapsulated in a variation point. Consistent treatment of variation points in Shared Asset Supersets across all disciplines is a hallmark of Feature-based PLE. Variation points are places in an asset that denote content that is configured according to feature selections in a Bill-of-Features for a particular system instance. Variation point configuration mechanisms typically include selection or omission of the content; selection from among mutually exclusive content alternatives; generation of content based on feature specifications; and feature-based transformation of content from one form into another.

Perhaps one of the easiest examples of Shared Asset Supersets to understand is requirements. A superset of requirements combines individual system requirements to establish all of the system family requirements. Variation points express inclusion and omission, define mutual exclusion, and transform requirement wording in the system specification—all based on feature selections. Requirement transformation can replace numbers, units, or other text with information that is derived from the Bill-of-Features. Requirements that have no variation are common and apply to every system.

MBSE models can be developed as Shared Asset Supersets and instrumented with variation points. For example, system design or architecture models using SysML™ include variation points to specify optional, mutually exclusive, and varying structural elements such as blocks, ports, relationships, objects, classes, activities, states, transitions, usecases, packages, and others, as well as generation or transformation of values, attributes, and constraints associated with those elements.

Shared Asset Supersets for Electronic Design Automation, Mechanical Design Automation, and Computer-aided Design (CAD) for electronic, mechanical, mechatronic, and cyber-physical systems take the form of supersets of parts, properties, relationships, assemblies, system elements, circuit boards, wiring harnesses, and more. Variation points instrument optional, mutually exclusive, and varying content in these models.

共享资产超集和差异点 要在 PLE 工厂工作，工程师必须学习如何为他们的专业创造和维护共享的资产超集，包括差异点。例如，需求工程师学习如何使用差异点创造需求共享资产超集，测试工程师学习如何使用差异点创造验证和确认共享资产超集，软件工程师学习如何使用差异点创造源代码共享资产超集。

共享资产超集包含在任何系统中所使用的所有内容的单个副本，即内容不重复。在每个系统中都出现的内容被称为通用内容，而在不同系统中出现的内容则被封装在一个差异点中。在所有学科中对共享资产超集中的差异点进行一致处理是基于特征的 PLE 的一个标志。差异点是资产中的位置，表示根据特定系统实例的特征清单中的特征选择配置的内容。差异点配置机制通常包括选择或省略内容；从相互排斥的内容备选方案中进行选择；基于特征规范生成内容；以及基于特征将内容从一种形式转换到另一种形式。

共享资产超集最容易理解的例子之一可能是需求。需求的超集结合了个体系统需求，以建立所有系统族需求。差异点表示包含和省略，定义互斥，并转换系统规范中的需求措辞，所有这些都基于特征选择。需求转换可以用从特征清单中衍生出来的信息替换数字、单位或其他文本。没有差异的需求很常见，适用于每个系统。

MBSE 模型可以开发为共享资产超集，并且使用差异点作为工具。例如，使用 SysML™ 的系统设计或架构模型可包含差异点，用于规定可选的、互斥的和变化的结构元素，如块、端口、关系、对象、类、活动、状态、转换、用例、包和其他，以及与这些元素相关的值、属性和约束的生成或转换。

电子、机械、机电和赛博物理系统的电子设计自动化、机械设计自动化和计算机辅助设计（CAD）的共享资产超集采用零件、特性、关系、组件、系统元素、电路板、线束等超集的形式。在这些模型中，差异点工具是可选的、互斥的和可变内容。

TAILORING AND APPLICATION CONSIDERATIONS

In software systems, Shared Asset Supersets are constructed for source code, resources, and build scripts. Source code variation points can be defined in several ways, including blocks of code, optional or mutually exclusive source files, and macro substitutions.

Verification and validation Shared Asset Supersets for automated and manual test plans and test cases can be instrumented with variation points to identify and configure the tests for each system, based on feature selections. It is possible to streamline or even eliminate redundant testing of common capability across multiple systems in the system family.

A broad array of additional assets with digital representations can serve as Shared Asset Supersets in system families. These include system budgets or cost models, schedules and work plans, user manuals and installation guides, process documentation, marketing brochures, simulation models, system descriptions, digital twins, supply chain orders, manufacturing specs, contract proposals, and much more. Feature-based PLE can be applied to all SoI types defined in Section 4.3.

229 ***Organizational Change and Return-on-Investment with Feature-based Product Line Engineering*** For many organizations, Feature-based PLE represents a shift in engineering approach that requires organizational change, along with commitment from engineering and business leadership to make that change. The ROI to justify the organizational change is in most cases compelling, based on the elimination of low-value, mundane, replicative work, with doubling, tripling and larger improvements in engineering metrics such as: lowering engineering complexity; reducing overall engineering time, cost, and effort; increasing portfolio scalability; and improving system quality (Gregg, et al., 2015 and McNicholas, 2021). In consideration of this ROI, the question to leadership is, "What if your engineers could do their normal day's work before lunch; what would you have them do in the afternoon?" There are many answers to this question, all of them good.

4.3 SYSTEM TYPES CONSIDERATIONS

The concept of SoI was introduced in Section 1.3.1. The type of SoI has significant implications on SE. This section introduces SE considerations for the following types of SoIs:

- Greenfield/Clean Sheet Systems
- Brownfield/Legacy Systems

在软件系统中，为源代码、资源和构建脚本所构建的共享资产超集。源代码差异点可以通过多种方式定义，包括代码块、可选或互斥源文件以及宏替换。

自动和手动测试计划和测试用例的验证和确认共享资产超集可以插入差异点，以根据特征选择来识别和配置每个系统的测试。有可能简化甚至消除对系统族中多个系统的通用能力的冗余测试。

具有数字表示的大量附加资产可以作为系统族中的共享资产超集。这些包含系统预算或成本模型、时间表和工作计划、用户手册和安装指南、流程文档、营销手册、仿真模型、系统描述、数字孪生、供应链订单、制造规范、合同提案等。基于特征的 PLE 可以应用于 4.3 节中定义的所有 SoI 类型。

基于特征的产品线工程的组织变革和投资回报

对于许多组织来说，基于特征的 PLE 代表了工程方法的转变，需要组织变革，以及工程和业务领导层做出变革的承诺。在大多数情况下，证明组织变革合理性的投资回报率是令人信服的，其基础是消除低价值、单调、可复制的工作，并在工程指标上实现两倍、三倍和更大的改进，例如：降低工程复杂性；减少总体工程时间、成本和工作量；提高组合能力；以及提高系统质量（Gregg 等，2015 和 McNicholas，2021）。考虑到这种投资回报率，领导层面临的问题是"如果你的工程师可以在午餐前完成一天的正常工作，你会让他们在下午做什么？"这个问题有很多答案，都很好。

4.3　系统类型考虑因素

1.3.1 节介绍了 SoI 的概念。SoI 类型对系统工程有重要影响。本节介绍了以下 SoI 类型的系统工程考虑因素：

- 绿地 / 全新的系统

- 棕地 / 遗留的系统

TAILORING AND APPLICATION CONSIDERATIONS

- Commercial-off-the-Shelf (COTS)-Based Systems
- Software-Intensive Systems
- Cyber-Physical Systems (CPS)
- System of Systems (SoS)
- Internet of Things (IoT)/Big Data-Driven Systems
- Service Systems
- Enterprise Systems

Note that other types of SoIs exist.

4.3.1 Greenfield/Clean Sheet Systems

"Greenfield" and "brownfield" are terms used in real estate. Greenfield land is previously undeveloped space, such as a (green) farmer's field. Brownfield land has been previously developed, typically has existing structures and services in place, and may contain undesirable or hazardous materials (also known as waste) that must be remediated. Greenfield SE, also known as "clean sheet" or "blank slate" SE, involves systems that are new designs and have no, or limited, legacy systems constraints, other than system interfaces. Given the incremental and spiral development life cycle approaches of today, a greenfield system may evolve toward brownfield even before it is delivered, from the developer's perspective.

Traditionally, SE has been taught by considering systems from a greenfield perspective. One starts with a "clean or blank sheet of paper" and determines the set of stakeholders and their needs and requirements, translates them into system requirements, architects and designs a system solution, implements the system elements, and then integrates, verifies, and validates the system elements and the system solution. While this is an effective way to teach SE and to prepare practitioners with skills applicable to the entire system life cycle, few system development efforts are truly greenfield. Greenfield, therefore, is an almost theoretical situation that is rarely seen in practice. The remaining considerations provide different perspectives and implications beyond greenfield SE.

Sometimes, it can be quite traumatic for organizations that make brownfield updates to its legacy products over a long period of time to transition from brownfield development back to greenfield (Axehill, 2021). They may need to "relearn" how to do greenfield.

- 基于商用货架产品（COTS）的系统
- 软件密集型系统
- 赛博物理系统（CPS）
- 体系（SoS）
- 物联网 / 大数据驱动的系统
- 服务系统
- 复杂组织体系系统

请注意，存在其他类型的 SoI。

4.3.1 绿地 / 全新的系统

"绿地"和"棕地"是房地产中使用的术语。绿地是以前未开发的空间，例如（绿色的）农民的田地。棕地之前已经开发过，通常已有现存结构和服务设施，可能含有必须修复的不良或有害物质（也称为废物）。绿地系统工程，也称为"全新的"或"空白的"系统工程，涉及新设计的系统，除系统接口外，没有或只有有限的遗留系统约束。考虑到当今增量和螺旋式开发生命周期实施方法，从开发人员的角度来看，绿地系统甚至在交付之前就可能向棕地发展。

传统上，系统工程的教学是从绿地的角度来考虑系统的。一种是从一张"干净或空白的纸"开始，确定利益相关方及其需要和需求，将其转化为系统需求，构建和设计系统解决方案，实施系统元素，然后综合、验证和确认系统元素和系统解决方案。虽然这是讲授系统工程和让实践者具备适用于整个系统生命周期的技能的有效方法，但很少有系统的开发工作是真正的绿地。因此，绿地几乎是一种理论上的情况，在实践中很少见到。除绿地系统工程外，其余的考虑因素提供了不同的角度和影响。

有时，对于长期对其传统产品进行棕地更新的组织而言，从棕地开发过渡回绿地开发可能会带来相当大的创伤（Axehill，2021）。它们可能需要"重新学习"如何进行绿地建设。

TAILORING AND APPLICATION CONSIDERATIONS

4.3.2 Brownfield/Legacy Systems

As described in Section 4.3.1, brownfield (and greenfield) are terms used in real estate. Brownfield land has been previously developed, typically has existing structures and services in place, and may contain undesirable or hazardous materials (also known as waste) that must be remediated. Brownfield SE, also known as "legacy" SE, involves significant modifications, extensions, or replacement of an existing "as-is" system in an existing environment to an updated "to-be" system. Brownfield systems often contain waste (e.g., technical debt) that may need to be remediated (Seacord, et al., 2003) (Hopkins and Jenkins, 2008). "In-service" systems are another example of brownfield system (Kemp, 2010) (Van De Ven, et al., 2012). Brownfield systems typically have explicit continuity requirements, where the operation of the as-is system needs to continue, resulting in a deliberate transition to the updated system.

The nature of greenfield and brownfield systems drives different life cycle approaches that reflect different areas of emphasis. Table 4.1 lays out some of the key differences across a set of aspects important to SE (Walden, 2019) (Baley and Belcham, 2010). This impacts not only the system solution, but also the team that is put in place to develop the system. As with all development efforts, SE processes need to be tailored to fit the needs of a given project (see Section 4.1). SE in a brownfield environment augments the SE life cycle processes described in this handbook with site surveys and reconstruction activities to understand the as-is systems, identify gaps, and engineer the to-be system (Walden, 2019).

TABLE 4.1 Considerations of greenfield and brownfield development efforts

Aspect	Greenfield	Brownfield
Life Cycle Stage(s)(of Initial SoI)	Concept, Development	Utilization, Support
Focus	New or novel features	Maintenance or adding new features while retaining select legacy functionality
Maturity (of Initial SoI)	Low to Moderate	High for maintenance; Mix for existing system and environment, plus new development for upgrade or replacement
Architecture and Design Review	Reviewed and modified at multiple levels	Reviewed only when significant updates are made/performed
Verification	The entire SoI typically needs to verified	Only the updated and impacted parts of the system need to be verified (there may be regression testing for the unchanged parts)
Validation	The entire SoI typically needs to validated with the customer/user	The entire SoI (including changes) typically needs to validated with the customer/user to check for new emergent behavior

4.3.2 棕地/遗留的系统

如 4.3.1 节所述，棕地（和绿地）是房地产中使用的术语。棕地之前已经开发过，通常已有现存结构和服务设施，可能含有必须修复的不良或有害物质（也称为废物）。棕地系统工程也称为"遗留"系统工程，涉及对现有环境中的现有"现状"系统进行重大修改、扩展或更换，以更新"未来"系统。棕地系统通常包含可能需要补救的废物（如技术债务）（Seacord 等，2003）（Hopkins 和 Jenkins, 2008）。"在用"系统是棕地系统的另一个例子（Kemp, 2010）（Van De Ven 等，2012）。棕地系统通常有明确的连续性需求，即需要继续运行现有系统，从而有意识地过渡到更新系统。

绿地系统和棕地系统的性质决定了其不同的生命周期方法，反映了不同的关注重点。表 4.1 列出了对绿地和棕地系统工程一系列重要方面的一些关键差异（Walden, 2019）（Baley 和 Belcham, 2010）。这不仅会影响系统解决方案，还会影响为开发系统而部署的团队。与所有开发工作一样，系统工程流程需要根据给定项目的需要进行调整（见 4.1 节）。棕地环境中的系统工程通过现场调查和重建活动来增强本手册中描述的系统工程生命周期流程，以了解现状系统，确定差距，并设计未来系统（Walden, 2019）。

表 4.1 绿地和棕地开发工作的考虑因素

方面	绿地	棕地
生命周期阶段（初始 SoI）	概念、开发	使用、支持
关注	新的或新颖的特征	维护或添加新特征，同时保留选定的旧功能
（初始 SoI 的）成熟度	低至中等	维护费用高 针对现有系统和环境的组合，以及针对升级或更换的新开发
架构和设计评审	在多个层级评审和修改	仅在进行/执行重大更新时评审
验证	整个 SoI 通常需要验证	只需验证系统的更新和受影响的部分（可能会对未更改的部分进行回归测试）
确认	整个 SoI 通常需要与客户/用户确认	整个 SoL（包括更改）通常需要与客户/用户进行确认，以检查新涌现的行为

TAILORING AND APPLICATION CONSIDERATIONS

(Continued)

Aspect	Greenfield	Brownfield
Manufacturing/Production	May be in place if using the existing line, or is developed (or tailored) as development progresses	Mostly in place, reverse engineering of existing designs may be required if the original design can no longer be produced (e.g., due to as-is use of banned materials)
Maintenance and Logistics	Developed (or tailored) as development progresses	Mostly in place, but may need changes or upgrades depending on the replacement system elements
Practices and Processes	Developed (or tailored) as work progresses	Mostly in place, though not necessarily relevant to the new team
Team Composition	Newly formed group	Mix of old and new, bringing both historical biases and fresh ideas

From Walden (2019) derived from Baley and Belcham (2010). Used with permission. All other rights reserved.

4.3.3 Commercial-off-the-Shelf (COTS)-Based Systems

One of the key trade-off studies SE practitioners perform is the "make vs. buy" decision on system elements. "Make" represents custom-built solutions; "buy" represents outsourced development and commercial-off-the-shelf (COTS) solutions. Directed use also can result in COTS. Most systems have some COTS content. The following characteristics can be useful when deciding if a particular system or system element can be characterized as COTS (Oberndorf, et al., 2000) (Tyson, et al., 2003):

- Sold, leased, or licensed to the general public;
- Offered by a vendor trying to profit from it;
- Supported and evolved by the vendor, who retains the intellectual property rights;
- Vendor (not acquirer) controls the frequency of the product's maintenance and updates;
- Available in multiple, identical copies;
- Used without hardware or source code modification.

The promise of COTS is to save development time, reduce technical risk, reduce time-to-market, reduce cost-to-market, and take advantage of latest technology. However, often these promises are not realized. Considerations for COTS-based systems include (Long, 2000):

(续)

方面	绿地	棕地
制造/生产	如果使用现有线路,可能会就位,或随着开发进展而开发(或剪裁)	大部分已就位,如果无法再生产原创设计(例如使用了禁用的物料),则需要对已有设计进行逆向工程
维护和后勤	随着开发进展而开发(定制)	大部分已就位,但可能需要根据更换的系统元件进行更改或升级
实践和流程	随着工作进展而开发(或剪裁)	基本就位,但不一定与新团队相关
团队组成	新成立的小组	新旧交融,既有历史偏见,又有新鲜想法

由 Walden(2019)取自 Baley 和 Belcham(2010)。经许可后使用。版权所有。

4.3.3 基于商用货架产品(COTS)的系统

系统工程实践者进行的关键权衡研究之一是关于系统元素的"制造 vs. 购买"决策。"制造"代表定制的解决方案;"购买"代表外包开发和商用货架产品(COTS)解决方案。直接使用也会导致 COTS。大多数系统都有一些 COTS 构成。在决定是否可以将特定系统或系统元素描述为 COTS 时,以下特征非常有用(Oberndorf 等,2000)(Tyson 等,2003):

- 向公众出售、出租或发放许可证;
- 由试图从中获利的供应商提供;
- 由保留知识产权的供应商支持和发展;
- 供应商(非采办方)控制产品的维护和更新频率;
- 可提供多份相同的副本;
- 使用时无须修改硬件或源代码。

COTS 的承诺是节省开发时间,降低技术风险,缩短上市时间,降低上市成本,并利用最新技术。然而,这些承诺往往没有实现。基于 COTS 系统的考虑因素包括(Long,2000):

TAILORING AND APPLICATION CONSIDERATIONS

- COTS products not built to your specific requirements (including missing functionality, extra functionality, and unwanted behaviors).

- Unique, or different than expected, interfaces, including a vendor's use of proprietary data formats and/or communications protocols, may occur.

- Vendor claims and decisions may impact schedule.

- The details needed to understand how COTS products may impact the safe and secure operation of the SoI may not be readily available, including the trustworthiness of the vendor, the use of open-source software, and the use of third-party software of unknown origin.

- COTS product may be insufficiently documented.

- "Not Invented Here" (NIH) syndrome may deter engineers from using COTS.

- Delivery times may not be met.

- Special integration challenges may occur.

- COTS products are often not verified to your specific requirements and may lack verification data for the operating environment for the SoI.

- "Sole Source" suppliers result in more risk.

- Need to consider the entire life cycle cost (LCC) of maintenance and technology rolls/refresh due to COTS obsolescence and diminishing manufacturing sources and material shortages (DMSMS) (Note: IEC 62402 (2019) provides guidance for establishing a framework for obsolescence management process which is applicable through all stages of system life cycle).

There are differences in approaches to SE for COTS-based systems development. Some of the key COTS-based SE considerations are shown in Table 4.2. Effective use of COTS generally requires COTS evaluation starting during needs analysis. In some circumstances, an "internal sales pitch" for each viable candidate COTS-based system needs to be developed, highlighting which requirements are met, which are partially or not met, and what additional capabilities and cost advantages (now and potentially in the future) each possible system provides. For an organization which has only done "make" system development in the past, moving to a COTS-based development requires a different mind-set and different development skills, including the new role of COTS integrator. These skills are often different than those needed for non-COTS-based system development.

- COTS 产品不符合特定需求（包括功能缺失、额外功能和不需要的行为）。

- 可能出现独特或不同于预期的接口，包括供应商使用专有数据格式和/或通信协议。

- 供应商的主张和决策可能会影响进度。

- 了解 COTS 产品如何影响 SoI 的安全和安保运行所需的详细信息可能并不容易获得，包括供应商的可信度、开源软件的使用以及未知来源的第三方软件的使用。

- COTS 产品可能文档化不足。

- "未在此处发明"（NIH）综合征可能会阻止工程师使用 COTS。

- 交付时间可能无法满足。

- 可能会出现特殊的综合挑战。

- COTS 产品通常未按照特定需求进行验证，并且可能缺少 SoI 运行环境的验证数据。

- "唯一来源"供应商会带来更多风险。

- 需要考虑因 COTS 过时、制造资源减少及材料短缺（DMSMS）而导致的维护和技术滚动/更新的整个生命周期成本（LCC）[注：IEC 62402（2019）为建立适用于系统生命周期所有阶段的过时管理流程框架提供了指导]。

基于 COTS 的系统开发所采用的系统工程实施方法存在差异。表 4.2 展示了一些基于 COTS 的关键系统工程考虑因素。COTS 的有效使用通常需要在需要分析期间开始 COTS 评估。在某些情况下，需要为每个可行的基于 COTS 的候选系统开发一个"内部销售计划"，强调哪些需求得到了满足，哪些部分得到了满足或没有得到满足，以及每个可能的系统提供了哪些额外的能力和成本优势（现在的和将来的）。对于过去只进行"制造"系统开发的组织来说，转向基于 COTS 的开发需要不同的心态和不同的开发技能，包括 COTS 集成商的新角色。这些技能往往不同于非 COTS 系统开发所需的技能。

TAILORING AND APPLICATION CONSIDERATIONS

TABLE 4.2 Considerations for COTS-based development efforts

Aspect	Traditional Systems Engineering	COTS-Based Considerations
Focus	The SoI	The SoI as well as how potential COTS products in the marketplace could be assembled to meet most/all the needs
Stakeholder Needs and Requirements	Fairly explicit stakeholder requirements	Flexible and prioritized capabilities stated in broad terms
System Requirements and Functionality	Requirements and functionality are defined and allocated based on technical considerations	COTS capabilities and functionality form the basis for the system requirements allocation and evolution and COTS may introduce additional system-level constraints
System Element Requirements	Extra or missing system element requirements are typically bad	Need to strike a balance between what the system needs and what the market can provide, missing or extra COTS requirements may be a reality due to the marketplace and they may also necessitate extra COTS wrappers and glue
System Architecture and Design	Focus is on optimizing the SoI	Focus is on optimizing the set of COTS and custom components that make up the SoI
Integration, Verification, and Validation	Done with known (internal) system element owners	Can typically get an early version of the system up and operating dramatically sooner than with a "make" system, criteria more difficult to establish since COTS performance must satisfy the market requirements while balancing the needs of the system, execution and defect resolution more difficult due to external COTS element owners
Technical Management	Well understood set of processes	More challenging decision environment, additional risks are present for COTS, and potentially increased configuration and information management (CM and IM) activities
Agreements	Acquisition agreements are primarily outsourced development efforts	Acquisitions also include COTS items and must consider other aspects such as licensing, additional COTS vendor support, and obsolescence management
Quality Characteristics	Known with internal team support and data, but the full picture may not be obtainable until after system deployment	For proven COTS, can be determined up front, may have to rely on COTS vendors for some data, consideration of life cycle cost (LCC) is critical for COTS

INCOSE SEH original table created by Walden. Usage per the INCOSE Notices page. All other rights reserved.

表 4.2 基于商用货架产品的开发工作的考虑因素

方面	传统系统工程	基于商用货架产品的考虑因素
关注点	SoI 公司	SoI 以及如何组装市场上潜在的 COTS 产品以满足大多数/所有需求
利益相关方需要和需求	相当明确的利益相关方需求	概括地描述灵活且优先的能力
系统需求和功能	需求和功能是根据技术考虑因素定义和分配的	COTS 能力和功能构成了系统需求分配和演进的基础,COTS 可能会引入额外的系统级约束
系统元素需求	额外或缺失系统元素需求通常很差	需要在系统需要和市场能够提供的之间取得平衡,由于市场的原因,缺少或额外的 COTS 需求可能成为现实,并且可能需要额外的 COTS 包装和黏合剂
系统架构和设计	重点是优化 SoI	重点是优化组成 SoI 的 COTS 和定制组件集
综合、验证和确认	与已知(内部)系统元素所有者一起完成	通常可以启动并运行早期版本的系统与"制造"系统相比,准则更难以建立,因为 COTS 性能必须满足市场需求,同时平衡系统需求,由于外部 COTS 元素所有者,执行和缺陷解决更加困难
技术管理	易于理解的一组流程	决策环境更具挑战性,COTS 面临更多风险,配置和信息可能会增加管理(CM 和 IM)活动
协议	采办协议主要外包开发工作	采办还包括 COTS 项目,必须考虑其他方面,如许可、额外的 COTS 供应商支持和过时管理
质量特征	已知内部团队支持和数据,但可能要等到系统部署才能获得整体图像	对于经验证的 COTS,可以提前确定,可能必须依赖 COTS 供应商的某些数据,考虑生命周期成本(LCC)对 COTS 至关重要

INCOSE SEH 原始表格由 Walden 创建。按照 INCOSE 通知页使用。版权所有。

TAILORING AND APPLICATION CONSIDERATIONS

4.3.4 Software-Intensive Systems

ISO/IEC/IEEE 42010 (2022) defines a software-intensive system as:

Any system where software contributes essential influences to the design, construction, deployment, and evolution of the system as a whole.

Software, like physical entities, is encapsulated in system elements. Software elements often contribute to system functionality, behavior, quality characteristics, interfaces, and observable performance indicators for softwareintensive systems. Encapsulated software is sometimes custom-built and is sometimes obtained by using software elements from libraries. Reused software elements may be modified by tailoring them for intended use. Also, software elements may be licensed from software vendors. In most cases, licensed software packages cannot be modified. Software engineers sometimes encapsulate licensed software packages in software shells or wrappers that provide the interfaces needed to integrate the needed capabilities of the software into a system while masking unwanted capabilities.

Software is widely incorporated in systems and provides "essential influences" because software is a malleable entity composed of textual and iconic symbols that in many cases, but not always, can be constructed, modified, or procured sooner and at less expense than fabricating, modifying, or procuring physical elements that have equivalent capabilities. In some cases, but not always, software elements can provide capabilities that would be difficult to realize in hardware.

But in some cases, a physical element of equivalent capability may be preferred to a software element because software may not provide certifiable safety, security, or performance at the necessary levels of assurance. Making tradeoffs between physical elements and software elements is an essential aspect of developing and modifying software-intensive systems. Trade studies are best conducted when SE practitioners consult physical engineers and software engineers who are working collaboratively.

Interfaces provided by software in a software-intensive system can provide passive pass-through connections or, if desired, software included in an interface can actively coordination interactions among the connected elements. Software interfaces may be internal and/or external to a system. Internal software interfaces can provide connections that coordinate interactions among physical elements, among software elements, and between physical elements and software elements. External software interfaces can provide passive and active connections to entities in the physical environment, including humans and other sentient entities that are software-enabled, plus connections to the external interfaces of other physical-only, software-only, and software-intensive systems. A "software-only" system is a software application implemented on a stable computing platform. The computing platform includes hardware and software that support the software application. The platform is often implemented using commodity items.

4.3.4 软件密集型系统

ISO/IEC/IEEE 42010（2022）将软件密集型系统定义为：

软件对整个系统的设计、构建、部署和演进产生重要影响的任何系统。

软件与物理实体一样，都封装在系统元素中。软件元素通常有助于实现软件密集型系统的系统功能、行为、质量特性、接口和可观测的性能指标。封装的软件有时是定制的，有时是通过使用库中的软件元素获得的。重用的软件元素可以根据预期用途进行剪裁修改。此外，软件元素可以从软件供应商处获得许可。在大多数情况下，无法修改被授权的软件包。软件工程师有时会将授权软件包封装在软件外壳或包装器中，提供将软件所需能力综合到系统中所需的接口，同时屏蔽不需要的能力。

软件被广泛纳入系统并提供"重要影响"，因为软件是一个由文本和图标组成的可塑实体，在许多情况下（但并非总是），软件的构建、修改或采购比制造、修改或采购具有同等能力的物理元素更快，成本更低。在某些情况下，但并非总是如此，软件元素可以提供难以在硬件中实现的能力。

但在某些情况下，同等能力的物理元素可能优于软件元素，因为软件可能无法在必要的保证级别上提供可认证的安全、安保或性能。在物理元素和软件元素之间进行权衡是开发和修改软件密集型系统的一个重要方面。进行权衡研究的最佳方式，是系统工程实践者咨询合作开展工作的物理工程师和软件工程师。

软件密集型系统中软件提供的接口可以提供被动直通连接，或者，如果需要，接口中包含的软件可以主动协调连接元素之间的交互。软件接口可以是系统的内部和/或外部接口。内部软件接口可以提供连接，协调物理元素之间、软件元素之间以及物理元素和软件元素之间的交互。外部软件接口可以提供与物理环境中实体的被动和主动连接，包括人和其他软件使能的感知实体，以及与其他纯物理、纯软件和软件密集型系统的外部接口的连接。"纯软件"系统是在稳定的计算平台上实现的软件应用程序。计算平台包括支持软件应用程序的硬件和软件。该平台通常使用商品来实现。

TAILORING AND APPLICATION CONSIDERATIONS

Sometimes the essential influences of software are observable in a system's external interfaces, as in human-user interface displays, and sometimes not, as in the interfaces for direct interaction with an external system. In the latter case, the software is said to be embedded in the SoI because performance of the interface is not directly observable by a human, although the effects of interface performance may be observable. Software is also used to provide interfaces among the systems that constitute an SoS. Software can contribute to functionality, behavior, quality attributes, external interfaces, and performance indicators for a composite SoS.

Developing and modifying software-intensive systems presents challenges for SE practitioners when partitioning system requirements and elements of the architecture, allocating performance parameters to physical elements and to software elements, establishing and controlling physical-software interfaces, and facilitating integration of physical elements with software elements (Fairley, 2019). These challenges sometimes arise because the culture, terminology, processes, and practices of software engineering are unfamiliar to SE practitioners and conversely, the various aspects of SE may be unfamiliar to software engineers. Techniques for improving communication between SE practitioners and software engineers are presented in Section 5.3.1 and in Fairley (2019).

4.3.5 Cyber-Physical Systems (CPS)

CPS are the integration of physical and cyber (software) processes in which the software monitors and controls the physical processes and is, in turn, affected by them. CPS are enabled by sensors and feedback loops and their provenance has increased because of significant advances in sensor technology and affordability. Figure 4.6 illustrates the behavior of a CPS: sensors may be deployed in the system hardware and/or its environment. Sensor data is used by software algorithms to control the hardware in responses to changes in the environment and/or in the hardware itself. The algorithms control the dynamic behavior of the CPS to achieve one or more goals, which could include homeostasis (maintaining equilibrium). An example might be an automobile with sensors to detect obstacles (in the environment) and take evasive action if an obstacle is detected ahead (the actuators would be steering or braking). Other sensors may be deployed to monitor the health of the vehicle, for instance, wear of the brake pads may trigger an action to modify the driving or notify the owner of the need for maintenance. Digital twins are also an important concept in this regard that refers to a digital surrogate that is a dynamic physic-based description of physical assets (physical twin), processes, people, places, systems, and devices that can be used for various purposes. The digital representation provides both the elements and the dynamics of how an Internet of Things (IoT) device operates and lives throughout its life cycle (see Section 4.3.7).

有时，软件的重要影响可以在系统的外部界面（如人机界面显示）中观察到，有时则无法观察到，如与外部系统直接交互的界面。在后一种情况下，软件被称为嵌入到 SoI 中，因为接口的性能无法被人直接观察到，尽管接口性能的影响可能是可以观察到的。软件还用于在构成 SoS 的系统之间提供接口。软件可以为一个复合 SoS 的功能、行为、质量特性、外部接口和性能指标做出贡献。

开发和修改软件密集型系统对系统工程实践者提出了挑战，包括划分系统需求和架构元素，将性能参数分配给物理元素和软件元素，建立和控制物理—软件接口，以及促进物理元素与软件元素的综合（Fairley，2019）。这些挑战的出现有时是因为软件工程的文化、术语、流程和实践对于系统工程实践者来说并不熟悉，相反，软件工程师可能对系统工程的各个方面同样都不熟悉。5.3.1 节和 Fairley（2019）介绍了用于改善系统工程实践者和软件工程师之间沟通的技术。

4.3.5 赛博物理系统（CPS）

CPS 是物理过程和赛博（软件）过程的综合，其中软件监视和控制物理流程，并反过来受到物理流程的影响。CPS 由传感器和反馈回路实现，由于传感器的技术和可承受性的显著进步，CPS 的来源也随之增加。图 4.6 说明了 CPS 的行为：传感器可能部署在系统硬件和/或其环境中。软件算法使用传感器数据来控制硬件，以响应环境和/或硬件本身的变化。这些算法控制 CPS 的动态行为，以达到一个或多个目标，其中可能包括动态平衡（维持平衡）。例如，一辆装有传感器的汽车可以检测（环境中的）障碍物，并在前方检测到障碍物时采取规避措施（执行器将用于转向或制动）。可以部署其他传感器来监测车辆的健康状况，例如，刹车片的磨损可能会触发改变驾驶的操作或通知车主需要维护的操作。数字孪生也是这方面的一个重要概念，它指的是数字替身，是对可用于各种目的的物理资产（物理孪生）、流程、人员、地点、系统和设备的基于物理的动态描述。数字表示提供了物联网（IoT）设备在其整个生命周期中如何运行和存在的元素和动态（见 4.3.7 节）。

TAILORING AND APPLICATION CONSIDERATIONS

The CPS concept is closely aligned to Industry 4.0, an initiative to revolutionize industry through so-called smart systems (Kagermann, 2013). CPS always include both software and hardware and are almost always networked, in which case they are CyberPhysical Systems of Systems (CPSoS). If the individual CPS are networked using Internet Protocols, then they form part of an IoT, but they may interact through other mechanisms (e.g., mechanical, electromagnetic, thermal). The relationships between the concepts of SoS, CPS, and IoT are illustrated in Figure 4.7. The "Things" in IoT are constituent systems and they are always networked, and therefore, always an SoS.

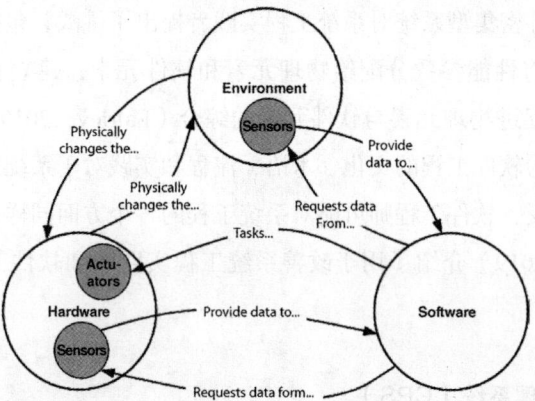

FIGURE 4.6 Schematic diagram of the operation of a Cyber-Physical System. INCOSE SEH original figure created by Henshaw. Usage per the INCOSE Notices page. All other rights reserved.

CPS are a feature of almost every industry and many aspects of society. They provide automated, and even autonomous, control of technologies ranging from robotic manufacture to SMART cities and from automated insulin delivery to control of critical infrastructure. They may form a contribution to business models that include physical systems and can even underpin a business concept by providing resilience or cost savings.

There are many implications of CPS for engineers. Two of the most significant are complexity and ethics. The increased level of complexity is due to both extensive networks and the problem of modeling the combination of physical dynamics with computational processes. Lee (2015) has pointed out that such models are nearly always nondeterministic due to the lack of temporal semantics in the cyber and physical modeling programs. This has significant implications for modeling and verification within the SE processes. The lack of determinism, together with questions concerning the transfer of decision making from humans to machines have ethical challenges that engineers must face in terms of definition and realization of CPS (European Parliament Research Service, 2016).

CPS 概念与工业 4.0 密切相关，这是一项通过所谓的智能系统实现工业革命的倡议（Kagermann，2013）。CPS 始终包括软件和硬件，并且几乎总是联网的，在这种情况下，它们是赛博物理体系（Cyber Physical Systems of Systems，CPSOS）。如果各个 CPS 使用互联网协议联网，则它们构成物联网的一部分，但它们可能通过其他机制（例如，机械、电磁、热）进行交互。SoS、CPS 和 IoT 概念之间的关系如图 4.7 所示。物联网中的"事物"是组成系统，它们总是联网的，因此总是一个 SoS。

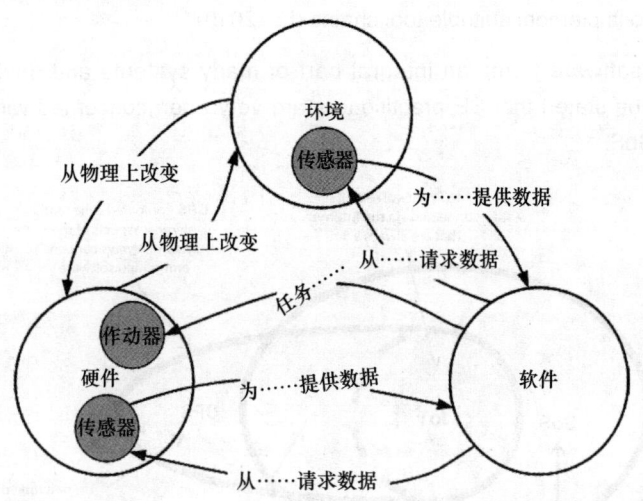

图 4.6　赛博物理系统运行示意图。INCOSE SEH 原始图由 Henshaw 创建。按照 INCOSE 通知页使用。版权所有。

CPS 几乎是每个行业和社会许多方面的特征。从机器人制造到智能城市，从自动胰岛素输送到关键基础设施的控制，他们提供自动化甚至自主的技术控制。它们可能对包括物理系统的业务模型做出贡献，甚至可以通过提供强韧性或节约成本来支撑业务概念。

CPS 对工程师有很多影响。其中最重要的两个因素是复杂性和道德。复杂性的增加是由于广泛的网络和物理动力学与计算流程相结合的建模问题。Lee（2015）指出，由于网络和物理建模程序中缺乏时间语义，此类模型几乎总是不确定的。这对 SE 流程中的建模和验证具有重要意义。缺乏确定性，以及有关决策权从人类转移到机器的问题，都是工程师在定义和实现 CPS 时必须面对的伦理挑战（欧洲议会研究服务，2016）。

TAILORING AND APPLICATION CONSIDERATIONS

The scope and dimensions of CPS is well-illustrated by the CPS Concept Map (Asare, et al., 2012), which essentially defines CPS as feedback systems that are applicable across a wide range of applications such as infrastructure, healthcare, manufacturing, military and many more. One might consider them relevant to any application in which the system is required to be dynamic and the control thereof is managed by software. The concept map also highlights the explicit need for security and safety considerations in design as well as the challenges of verification and validation in large complex systems. It points toward the need for improved modeling and, indeed, progress has been made in the use of MBSE for CPS development through a framework to implement suitable tool chains (Lu, 2019).

Given that software forms an integral part of many systems and devices, it can reasonably be stated that SE practitioners are very often concerned with CPS and usually CPSoS.

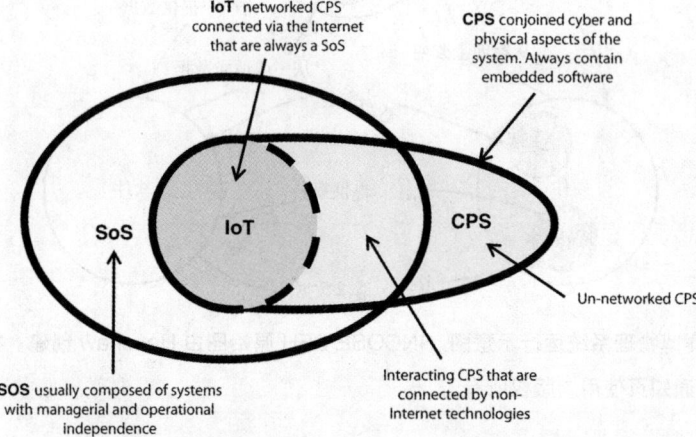

FIGURE 4.7 The relationship between Cyber-Physical Systems (CPS), Systems of Systems (SoSs), and an Internet of Things (IoT). From Henshaw (2016). Used with permission. All other rights reserved.

4.3.6 Systems of Systems (SoS)

ISO/IEEE/IEC 21839 (2019) defines a System of Systems (SoS) as:

A set of systems or system elements that interact to provide a unique capability that none of the constituent systems can accomplish on its own.

CPS 概念图（Asare 等，2012）很好地说明了 CPS 的范围和维度，该概念图将 CPS 定义为反馈系统，适用于基础设施、医疗卫生、制造业、军事等广泛的应用。人们可能会认为它们与任何应用程序相关，在这些应用程序中，系统被要求是动态的，并且其控制由软件管理。概念图还强调了设计中对安全和安保考虑的明确需要，以及大型复杂系统中验证和确认的挑战。它指出了改进建模的必要性，事实上，通过一个框架来实施适当的工具链，在使用 MBSE 进行 CPS 开发方面已经取得了进展（Lu，2019）。

考虑到软件是许多系统和设备不可分割的一部分，可以合理地说系统工程实践者经常关注的 CPS 通常是 CPSoS。

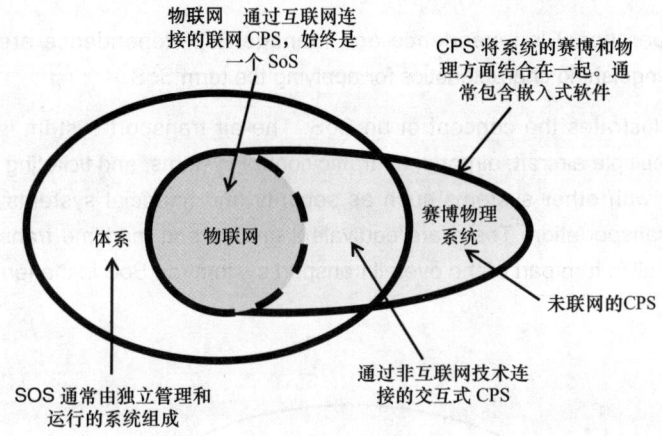

图 4.7 赛博物理系统、体系、物联网之间的关系。源自 Henshaw（2016）。经许可后使用。版权所有。

4.3.6 体系（SoS）

ISO/IEEE/IEC 21839（2019）将体系（SoS）定义为：

一组系统或系统元素，它们相互作用以提供任何成员系统都无法单独完成的独特能力。

TAILORING AND APPLICATION CONSIDERATIONS

Constituent systems can be part of one or more SoS. Each constituent system is a useful system by itself, having its own development, management goals, and resources, but interacts within the SoS to provide the unique capability of the SoS (ISO/IEEE/IEC 21839, 2019).

The following characteristics can be useful when deciding if a particular SoI can better be understood as an SoS (Maier, 1998):

- Operational independence of constituent systems;
- Managerial independence of constituent systems;
- Geographical distribution;
- Emergent behavior;
- Evolutionary development processes.

Of these, operational independence and managerial independence are the two principal distinguishing characteristics for applying the term SoS.

Figure 4.8 illustrates the concept of an SoS. The air transport system is an SoS comprising multiple aircraft, airports, air traffic control systems, and ticketing systems, which along with other systems such as security and financial systems facilitate passenger transportation. There are equivalent ground and maritime transportation SoS that are all in turn part of the overall transport system (an SoS in the terms of this description).

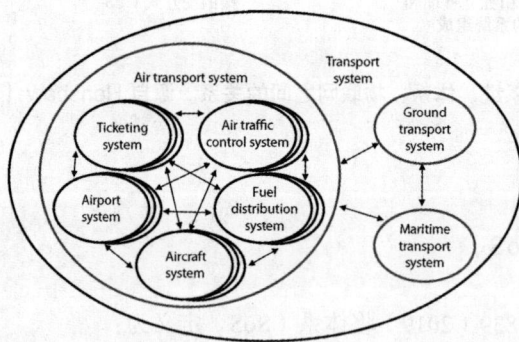

FIGURE 4.8 Example of the systems and systems of systems within a transport system of systems. From ISO/IEC/IEEE 21841 (2019). Used with permission. All other rights reserved.

成员系统 可以是一个或多个体系的一部分。每个成员系统本身都是一个有用的系统，有自己的开发、管理目标和资源，但在体系内相互作用，以提供体系的独特能力（ISO/IEEE/IEC 21839，2019）。

在决定是否可以更好地将特定 SoI 理解为体系时，以下特征非常有用（Maier，1998）：

- 成员系统的运行独立性；
- 成员系统的管理独立性；
- 地理分布；
- 涌现行为；
- 演进式开发流程。

其中，运行独立性和管理独立性是应用体系这一术语的两个主要区别特征。

图 4.8 说明了体系的概念。航空运输系统是一个体系，包括多架飞机、机场、空中交通管制系统和票务系统，与其他系统（如安保和金融系统）一起为旅客运输提供便利。有等效的地面和海上运输体系，它们依次是整个运输系统（此处指体系）的一部分。

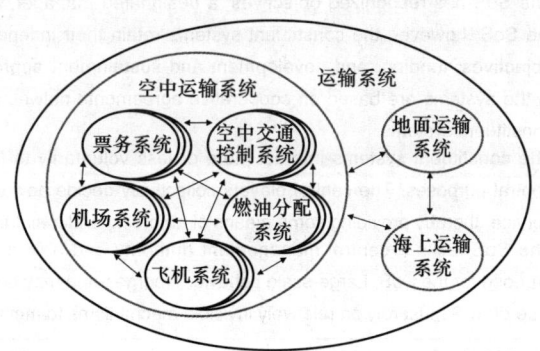

图 4.8 运输体系内的系统及体系的示例。源自 ISO/IEC/IEEE 21841（2019）。经许可后使用。版权所有。

TAILORING AND APPLICATION CONSIDERATIONS

There are three international standards that provide useful guidance on SoS:

- ISO/IEC/IEEE 21839 (2019)—"System of systems (SoS) considerations in life cycle stages of a system" focuses on the SE of an individual constituent system and identifies considerations to be addressed as the engineering of the systems progresses from concept through retirement.

- ISO/IEC/IEEE 21840 (2019)—"Guidelines for the utilization of ISO/IEC/IEEE 15288 in the context of system of systems (SoS)" provides guidance on the application of the processes to the special case of SoS, including considerations for how constituent systems relate within the SoS.

- ISO/IEC/IEEE 21841 (2019)—"Taxonomy of systems of systems" lays out a taxonomy of SoS types based on

ISO/IEC/IEEE 21840 (2019) guidance on application of ISO/IEC/IEEE 15288 (2023) life cycles processes (see Section 2.3) is based on the differences between systems and SoS and the impact on the SE processes as shown in Table 4.4.

TABLE 4.3 SoS types

Directed	The SoS is created and managed to fulfill specific purposes and the constituent systems are subordinated to the SoS. The constituent systems maintain an ability to operate independently; however, their normal operational mode is subordinated to the central managed purpose.
Acknowledged	The SoS has recognized objectives, a designated manager, and resources for the SoS; however, the constituent systems retain their independent ownership, objectives, funding, and development and sustainment approaches. Changes in the systems are based on cooperative agreements between the SoS and the constituent systems.
Collaborative	The constituent systems interact more or less voluntarily to fulfill agreed upon central purposes. The central players collectively decide how to provide or deny service, thereby providing some means of enforcing and maintaining standards.
Virtual	The SoS lacks a central management authority and a centrally agreed upon purpose for the SoS. Large-scale behavior emerges-and may be desirable-but this type of SoS must rely on relatively invisible mechanisms to maintain it.

From ISO/IEC/IEEE 21841 (2019) derived from SEBOK. Used with permission. All other rights reserved.

有三个国际标准可为体系提供有用的指导：

- ISO/IEC/IEEE 21839（2019）——"系统生命周期阶段的体系（SoS）考虑因素"侧重于单个成员系统的系统工程，并确定了在系统工程从概念到退役的流程中需要考虑的因素。

- ISO/IEC/IEEE 21840（2019）——"在体系（SoS）环境中使用 ISO/IEC/IEEE 15288 的指南"提供了将流程应用于 SoS 特殊情况的指南，包括考虑成员系统在体系中的关系。

- ISO/IEC/IEEE 21841（2019）——"体系（SoS）分类"根据权限关系列出了体系类型的分类，如表 4.3 所示。

ISO/IEC/IEEE 21840（2019）《ISO/IEC/IEEE 15288（2023）生命周期流程应用指南》（见 2.3 节）基于系统和体系之间的差异以及对系统工程流程的影响建立，如表 4.4 所示。

表 4.3　体系的类型

指挥的	通过创建和管理体系以达到特定目的，组成系统从属于体系。组成系统保持独立运行的能力；然而，它们的正常运行模式从属于中央管理目的
认可的	体系已识别目标，并且为体系指定管理者和资源；然而，组成系统保留其独立的所有权、目标、资金以及开发和维持实施方法。系统的变更基于体系和组成系统之间的合作协议
协同的	各组成系统或多或少自愿互动，以达到商定的中心目标。中心参与者共同决定如何提供或拒绝服务，从而提供一些实施和维护标准的手段
虚拟的	体系缺乏中央管理机构和中央商定的体系目的。大规模行为能够涌现，这可能是被期望的，但这种类型的体系必须依靠相对不可见的机制来维持

源自 ISO/IEC/IEEE 21841（2019），采用自 SEBOK。经许可后使用。版权所有。

TAILORING AND APPLICATION CONSIDERATIONS

TABLE 4.4   Impact of SoS considerations on the SE processes

SE Process	Implementation as Applied to SoS
Agreement Processes	Because there is often no top level SoS authority, effective agreements among the systems in the SoS are key to successful SoSE.
Organizational Project Enabling Processes	SoSE develops and maintains those processes which are critical for the SoS within the constraints of the system level processes.
Technical Management Processes	SoSE implements Technical Management Processes applied to the particular considerations of SoS engineering - planning, analyzing, organizing, and integrating the capabilities of a mix of existing and new systems into a system of systems capability while systems continue to be responsible for technical management of their systems.
Technical Processes	SoSE Technical Processes define the cross-cutting SoS capability, through SoS level business or mission analysis and stakeholder needs and requirements definition. SoS architecture and design frame the planning, organization, and integration of the constituent systems, constrained by system architectures. Development, integration, verification, transition, and validation are implemented by the systems. with SoSE monitoring and review. SoSE integration, verification, transition and validation applies when constituent systems are integrated into the SoS and performance is verified and validated.

From ISO/IEC/IEEE 21840 (2019) adapted from SEBOK. Used with permission. All other rights reserved.

Dahmann (2014) identified the following challenges that influence the engineering of an SoS:

- *SoS authorities*—In an SoS, each constituent system has its own local "owner" with its stakeholders, users, business processes, and development approach. As a result, the type of organizational structure assumed for most traditional SE under a single authority responsible for the entire system is absent from most SoS. In an SoS, SE relies on crosscutting analysis and on composition and integration of constituent systems, which in turn depend on an agreed common purpose and motivation for these systems to work together toward collective objectives that may or may not coincide with those of the individual constituent systems.

- *Leadership*—Recognizing that the lack of common authorities and funding poses challenges for SoS, a related issue is the challenge of leadership in the multiple organizational environments of an SoS. This question of leadership is experienced where a lack of structured control normally present in SE requires alternatives to provide coherence and direction, such as influence and incentives.

表 4.4　体系考虑因素对系统工程流程的影响

系统流程	应用于 SoS 的实施
协议流程	由于通常没有顶层体系权限，体系中各系统之间的有效协议是成功 SoSE 的关键
组织的项目使能流程	SoSE 在系统级流程的约束范围内开发和维护对 SoS 至关重要的流程
技术管理流程	SoSE 将技术管理流程应用到 SoSE 的特定考虑因素之中，包括将已有的和新的系统能力规划、分析、组织、综合为一个体系的能力，与此同时各系统依然对各自的技术管理负责
技术流程	SoSE 技术流程通过体系级的业务或任务分析以及利益相关方需要和需求定义，定义了贯穿各领域的体系能力。体系架构和设计框定了受系统架构约束的组成系统的规划、组织和综合。开发、综合、验证、转移和确认由系统实施，并通过 SoSE 监控和评审。当组成系统综合到体系中，并且通过了性能验证和确认，SoSE 就可以开展综合、验证、转移和确认

源自 ISO/IEC/IEEE 21840（2019）采用自 SEBOK。经许可后使用。版权所有。

Dahmann（2014）确定了影响体系工程的以下挑战：

- **体系权限**：在体系中，每个成员系统都有自己的本地"所有者"，以及其利益相关方、用户、业务流程和开发实施方法。因此，大多数体系都不存在大多数传统系统工程所假定的那种由单一机构负责整个系统的组织结构。在体系中，系统工程依赖于跨领域/学科的分析以及成员系统的组合和综合，而组合和综合又取决于协商的共同目的和动机，以使这些系统共同努力达到可能与单个成员系统的目标一致或不一致的集体目标。

- **领导力**：认识到缺乏共同权限和资金对体系构成的挑战，另一个相关问题是体系在多组织环境中的领导力挑战。在缺乏结构化控制的情况下，就会出现领导力问题，而结构化控制通常存在于系统工程中，这就需要其他方法来提供连贯性和方向性，如影响力和激励机制。

TAILORING AND APPLICATION CONSIDERATIONS

- *Constituent systems*—SoS are typically composed, at least in part, of in-service systems, which were often devel oped for other purposes and are now being leveraged to meet a new or different application with new objectives. This is the basis for a major issue facing the application of SE to SoS, that is, how to technically address issues that arise from the fact that the systems identified for the SoS may be limited in the degree to which they can support the SoS. These limitations may affect initial efforts at incorporating a system into an SoS, and systems' commitments to other users may mean that they may not be compatible with the SoS over time. Further, because the systems were developed and operate in different situations, there is a risk that there could be a mismatch in understanding the services or data provided by one system to the SoS if the particular system's context differs from that of the SoS.

- *Capabilities and requirements*—Traditionally (and ideally), the system engineering process begins with a clear, complete set of initial user requirements and provides a disciplined approach to develop and evolve a system to meet these and emerging requirements. Typically, SoS are composed of multiple independent systems with their own requirements, working toward broader capability objectives. In the best case, the SoS capability needs are met by the constituent systems as they meet their own local requirements. However, in many cases, the SoS needs may not be consistent with the requirements for the constituent systems. In these cases, SE of an SoS needs to identify alternative approaches to meeting those needs either through changes to the constituent systems or through the addition of other systems to the SoS. In effect, this is asking the systems to take on new requirements with the SoS acting as the "user."

- *Autonomy, interdependence, and emergence*—The independence of constituent systems in an SoS is the source of a number of technical issues when applying SE to an SoS. The fact that a constituent system may continue to change independently of the SoS, along with interdependencies between that constituent system and other constituent systems, adds to the complexity of the SoS and further challenges SE at the SoS level. These dynamics can lead to unanticipated effects at the SoS level leading to unexpected or unpredictable behavior in an SoS even if the behavior of the constituent systems is well understood.

- *Testing*—The fact that SoS are typically composed of constituent systems that are independent of the SoS poses challenges in conducting end-to-end SoS testing, as is typically done with systems. First, unless there is a clear understanding of the SoS-level expectations and measures of those expectations,

- *成员系统*：体系通常至少有一部分是由在役系统组成的，这些系统通常是为其他目的而开发的，现在被用来满足具有新目标的新的或不同的应用。这是系统工程应用于体系所面临的一个主要问题的基础，即如何从技术上解决为体系确定的系统在支持体系的程度上可能有限这一事实所产生的问题。这些限制可能会影响将系统纳入体系的初始工作，系统对其他用户的承诺可能意味着随着时间的推移，它们可能与体系不兼容。此外，由于系统是在不同的情况下开发和运行的，如果特定系统的背景环境与体系的背景环境不同，那么在理解一个系统向体系提供服务或数据时就可能存在不匹配的风险。

- *能力和需求*：传统上（理想情况下），系统工程流程从一组清晰的、完整的初始用户需求开始，提供一种严格的方法来开发和演进系统，以满足初始的和涌现的需求。通常，体系由多个具有各自需求的独立系统组成，致力于达到更广泛的能力目标。在最佳情况下，各成员系统满足其自身的局部需求，从而满足体系的能力需求。然而，在许多情况下，体系需求可能与成员系统的需求不一致。在这种情况下，体系的系统工程需要确定满足这些需求的替代实施方法，或通过改变成员系统，或通过在体系中增加其他系统。实际上，这就是要求系统以体系作为"用户"而承担新需求。

- *自主性、相互依赖性和涌现性*：在将系统工程应用于体系时，体系中各成员系统的独立性是许多技术问题的根源。成员系统可能会独立于体系而继续进行更改，加上该成员系统与其他成员系统之间的相互依赖关系，这增加了体系的复杂性，进一步挑战了体系层级的系统工程。即使对成员系统的行为有很好的了解，这些动态行为也会对体系层级产生意外影响，从而导致体系中出现意外或不可预测的行为。

- *测试性*：体系通常由独立于体系的成员系统组成，这一事实为进行端到端的体系测试（正如通常对系统进行的测试那样）带来了挑战。首先，除非对体系级的期望和这些期望的测度有明确的理解，否则很难评估其性能等级，以此为基础确定需要关注的领域，或确保用户了解体系服

TAILORING AND APPLICATION CONSIDERATIONS

it can be very difficult to assess the level of performance as the basis for determining areas that need attention or to ensure users of the capabilities and limitations of the SoS. Even when there is a clear understanding of SoS objectives and metrics, testing in a traditional sense can be difficult. Depending on the SoS context, there may not be funding or authority for SoS testing. Often, the development cycles of the constituent systems are tied to the needs of their owners and original ongoing user base. With multiple constituent systems subject to asynchronous development cycles, finding ways to conduct traditional end-to-end testing across the SoS can be difficult if not impossible. In addition, many SoS are large and diverse, making traditional full end-to-end testing with every change in a constituent system prohib itively costly. Often, the only way to get a good measure of SoS performance is from data collected from actual operations or through estimates based on modeling, simulation, and analysis. Nonetheless, the SoS SE team needs to enable continuity of operation and performance of the SoS despite these challenges.

- *SoS principles*—SoS is a an area where there has been limited attention given to ways to extend systems thinking to the issues particular to SoS. The community is beginning to identify and articulate the crosscutting principles that apply to SoS in general and to develop working examples of the application of these principles. There is a major learning curve for the average SE practitioner moving to an SoS environment and a problem with SoS knowledge transfer within or across organizations.

Beyond these general SE challenges, in today's environment, SoS pose particular issues from a security perspective. This is because constituent system interface relationships are rearranged and augmented asynchronously and often involve COTS elements from a wide variety of sources. Security vulnerabilities may arise as emergent phenomena from the overall SoS configuration even when individual constituent systems are sufficiently secure in isolation.

The SoS challenges cited in this section require SE approaches that combine both the systematic and procedural aspects described in this handbook with holistic, nonlinear, iterative methods. There is a growing set of approaches to applying SE to SoS (Cook and Unewisse, 2019). These include SoS life cycle engineering approaches such as the SoS Wave Model (Dahmann, et al., 2011) and the Designing for Adaptability and evolutioN in System of Systems Engineering (DANSE). These approaches address both functionality of constituents to create coherent aggregate SoS capability (Axelsson, 2020) as well as management of interfaces among constituents (Hoehne, 2020).

务的能力和局限性。即使对体系目标和测度有清晰的理解，传统意义上的测试也可能很困难。根据体系背景环境，可能没有用于体系测试的资金或权限。通常，成员系统的开发周期与其所有者和原有用户群的需求相关。由于多个成员系统受到异步开发周期的影响，找到跨体系进行传统端到端测试的方法可能很困难（如果不是不可能的话）。此外，许多体系都是规模庞大和多样化的，这使得传统的完整端到端测试以及成员系统中的每一次更改的成本都高得令人望而却步。通常，获得良好的体系性能测度的唯一方法是从实际运行中收集的数据，或通过基于建模、仿真和分析的估计。然而，尽管存在这些挑战，体系系统工程团队仍需要确保体系运行和性能的连续性。

- *体系原则*：体系是一个领域，在该领域中，人们对如何将系统思维扩展到体系特定问题的关注是有限的。系统工程群体开始识别和阐明适用于体系的跨领域/学科原则，并开发应用这些原则的工作示例。对于转入体系环境的一般系统工程实践者来说，存在一个明显的学习曲线，以及组织内部或跨组织的体系知识转移问题。

除了这些一般系统工程挑战之外，在当今的环境中，体系还从安保角度提出了特殊的问题。这是因为成员系统的接口关系是异步重新排列和扩充的，并且通常涉及各种来源的 COTS 元素。即使单个成员系统本身足够安全，安保漏洞也可能作为体系整体配置的涌现现象出现。

本节中提到的体系挑战要求系统工程方法将本手册中描述的系统性和程序性方面与整体、非线性、迭代方法相结合。将系统工程应用于体系的实施方法越来越多（Cook 和 UNEWISE，2019）。其中包括体系生命周期工程实施方法，如体系波浪模型（Dahmann 等，2011）和体系工程中的适应性和进化设计（DANSE）。这些实施方法既涉及成员的功能，以创建一致聚合的体系能力（Axelsson，2020），也涉及成员之间接口的管理（Hoehne，2020）。

TAILORING AND APPLICATION CONSIDERATIONS

4.3.7 Internet of Things (IoT)/Big Data-Driven Systems

SE is based on engineering requirements, engineering calculations, testing, modeling, and simulations—and all are based on data or data generation. SE practitioners often make decisions based on intuition, previous experience, or qualitative assessments. The 4th Industrial Revolution, with its proliferation of sensors of various types and big data analytics, creates an opportunity for SE, as a discipline, and for SE practitioners, as professionals and decisions makers, to be more data-driven. The following recommendations apply to modern SE tasks and decisions:

- Bring as much diverse data and as many diverse viewpoints to maximize the generation of information quality.
- Use data to develop a deeper understanding of the business context and the problem at hand.
- Develop an appreciation for the impact of variation, both in data and in the overall business.
- Deal with uncertainty, which means that SE also recognizes mistakes.
- Recognize the importance of high-quality data and invest in trusted sources and in making improvements.
- Conduct good experiments and research to supplement existing data and address new questions.
- Recognize the criteria used to make decisions and adapt under varying circumstances.
- Realize that making a decision is only the first step; SE practitioners must keep an open mind and revise decisions if new data suggests a better course of action.
- Work to bring new data and new data technologies into the organization.
- Learn from mistakes and help others to do so, by applying lessons-learned processes.
- As SE practitioners, strive to be a role model when it comes to data, working with leaders, peers, and subordinates to help them become data driven.

There are three general goals in analyzing data:

1. *Prediction*: To predict the response to future values of the input variables.
2. *Estimation*: To infer how response variables are associated with input variables.
3. *Explanation*: To understand the relative contribution of input variables to response values.

4.3.7 物联网／大数据驱动的系统

系统工程基于工程需求、工程计算、测试、建模和仿真，而所有这些都以数据或数据生成为基础。系统工程实践者通常根据直觉、以往经验或定性评估做出决策。随着各种类型的传感器和大数据分析的激增，第四次工业革命为作为一门学科的系统工程以及作为专业人员和决策者的系统工程实践者创造了更多的数据驱动的机会。以下建议适用于现代系统工程任务和决策：

- 提供尽可能多的不同数据和视角，以最大限度地提高信息质量。
- 使用数据加深对业务背景环境和当前问题的理解。
- 提升对数据和整体业务差异影响的认识。
- 处理不确定性，这意味着系统工程也能认识错误。
- 认识到高质量数据的重要性，投资可靠的来源并进行改进。
- 开展良好的实验和研究，以补充现有数据并解决新问题。
- 认识到用于做出决策的准则，并在不同情况下进行调整。
- 认识到做出决策只是第一步；如果新数据表明有更好的行动方案，系统工程实践者必须保持开放的心态并修改决策。
- 努力将新数据和新数据技术引入组织。
- 从错误中吸取经验教训，并帮助他人从错误中吸取经验教训。
- 作为系统工程实践者，在数据方面，努力成为一个榜样，与领导者、同行和下属合作，帮助他们成为数据驱动者。

分析数据有三个一般的目标：

1. *预测*：预测对输入变量未来值的响应。

2. *估计*：推断响应变量如何与输入变量相关联。

3. *解释*：了解输入变量对响应值的相对贡献。

TAILORING AND APPLICATION CONSIDERATIONS

Predictive modeling is the process of applying models and algorithms to data for the purpose of predicting new observations. In contrast, explanatory models aim to explain the causality and relationship between the independent variables and the dependent variables. Classical statistics focuses on modeling the stochastic system generating the data. Statistical learning, or computer age statistics, builds on big data and the modeling of the data itself. If the former aimed at properties of the model, the latter is looking at the properties of computational algorithms. SE practitioners need to be educated in data sciences to enable them to practice the above tools and methods as an integral part of SE.

Data analytics and IoT are wide-scope revolutions of digital surroundings. They create complex CPS that add new functionalities and capabilities to the existing physical environment. Designing an IoT system that has analytic capabilities involves "multi stack" layers, addressing SoS and network of networks.

SE practitioners should view a system as interconnected system elements performing the system functions. To meet this challenge, the SE practitioner who leads data-driven designs needs interdisciplinary knowledge of the main aspects of IoT: computing, sensors/actuators, software, network, analytics and data science.

4.3.8 Service Systems

OASIS (2012) defines a service as:

A mechanism to enable access to one or more capabilities, where the access is provided using a prescribed interface and is exercised consistently with constraints and policies as specified by the service description.

It involves application of specialized competences (knowledge and skills) through deeds, processes, and performances for the benefit of another entity or the entity itself in real world. The entity involved with the service can be technical, socio-technical, or strictly social.

For service systems, understanding the integration needs among loosely coupled systems and system elements, along with the information flows required for both governance and operations, administration, maintenance, and provisioning of the service, presents major challenges in the definition, design, and implementation of services (Domingue, et al., 2009; Maier, 1998). Cloutier, et al. (2009) presented the importance of Network-Centric Systems (NCS) for dynamically binding different system entities in engineered systems rapidly to realize adaptive SoSs that, in the case of service systems, are capable of knowledge emergence and real-time behavior emergence for service discovery and delivery.

预测建模是将模型和算法应用于数据以预测新观测值的流程。相反，解释模型旨在解释自变量和因变量之间的因果关系。经典统计学侧重于对生成数据的随机系统进行建模。统计学习，或计算机时代的统计，建立在大数据和数据本身建模的基础上。如果前者着眼于模型的特性，后者则着眼于计算算法的特性。系统工程实践者需要接受数据科学方面的教育，以使他们能够将上述工具和方法作为系统工程的一个组成部分进行实践。

数据分析和物联网是数字环境的大范围革命。它们创建复杂的 CPS，为现有物理环境添加新的功能和能力。设计具有分析能力的物联网系统涉及"多堆栈"层，解决体系和网络之网络问题。

系统工程实践者应将系统视为执行系统功能的互联系统元素。为了应对这一挑战，领导数据驱动设计的系统工程实践者需要具备物联网主要方面的跨学科知识：计算、传感器/执行器、软件、网络、分析和数据科学。

4.3.8 服务系统

OASIS（2012）将服务定义为：

一种允许访问一个或多个能力的机制，使用指定的接口提供访问，并按照服务描述中指定的约束和策略一致地执行访问。

它涉及通过行动、流程和表现来应用专业胜任力（知识和技能），以造福于现实世界中的另一个实体或实体本身。参与服务的实体可以是技术实体、社会—技术实体或严格的社会实体。

对于服务系统而言，了解松散耦合系统和系统元素之间的综合需求，以及治理和运行、管理、维护和提供服务所需的信息流，是服务定义、设计和实施过程中的重大挑战（Domingue 等，2009；Maier，1998）。Cloutier 等（2009）介绍了以网络为中心的系统（NCS）的重要性，该系统可在工程系统中快速动态地绑定不同的系统实体，以实现自适应体系，就服务系统而言，该系统能够为服务发现和交付提供知识涌现和实时行为涌现。

TAILORING AND APPLICATION CONSIDERATIONS

240   Figure 4.9 illustrates the conceptual framework of a service system. Typically, a service system is composed of service system entities that interact through processes defined by governance and management rules to create different types of outcomes in the context of stakeholders with the purpose of providing improved customer interaction and value cocreation.

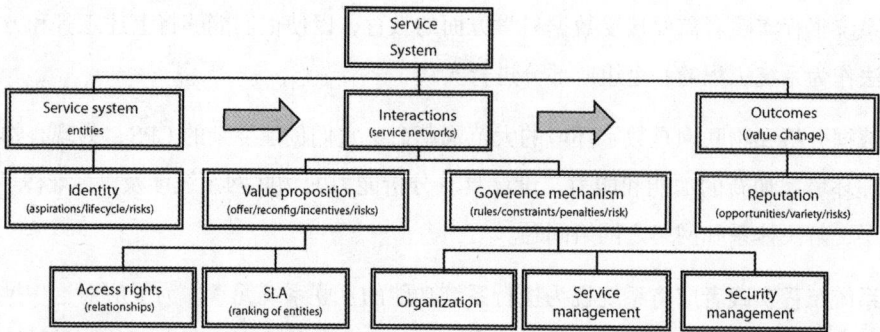

FIGURE 4.9   Service system conceptual framework. From Spohrer (2011). Used with permission. All other rights reserved.

Services not only involve the interaction between the service provider and the consumer to produce value, but have other intangible attributes like quality of service (e.g., ambulance service availability, response time to an emergency request). The demand for service may have loads dependent on time of day, day of week, season, or unexpected needs (e.g., natural disasters), and services are rendered at the time they are requested. Thus, the design and operations of service systems "is all about finding the appropriate balance between the resources devoted to the systems and the demands placed on the system, so that the quality of service to the customer is as good as possible" (Daskin, 2010).

In many cases, taking a service SE approach is imperative for the service-oriented, customer-centric, holistic view to select and combine service system entities to define and discover relationships among service system entities to plan, design, adapt, or self-adapt to cocreate value. Typically, five types of resources need to be considered: people; tangible products and environment infrastructure; organizations and institutions; protocols; and shared information and symbolic knowledge in the service delivery process. Major challenges include the dynamic nature of service systems evolving and adapting to constantly changing operations and/or business environments and the need to overcome silos of knowledge. Interoperability of service system entities through interface agreements must be at the forefront of the service SE design process for the harmonization of operations, administration, maintenance, and provisioning procedures of the individual service system entities (Pineda, 2010). In addition, service systems require open collaboration among all stakeholders, but recent research on mental models of multidisciplinary teams shows integration and collaboration into cohesive teams has proven to be a major challenge (Carpenter, et al., 2010).

图 4.9 说明了服务系统的概念框架。通常，服务系统由服务系统实体组成，这些实体通过治理和管理规则定义的流程进行交互，以在利益相关方的背景环境中创建不同类型的结果，目的是提供改进的客户交互和价值创造。

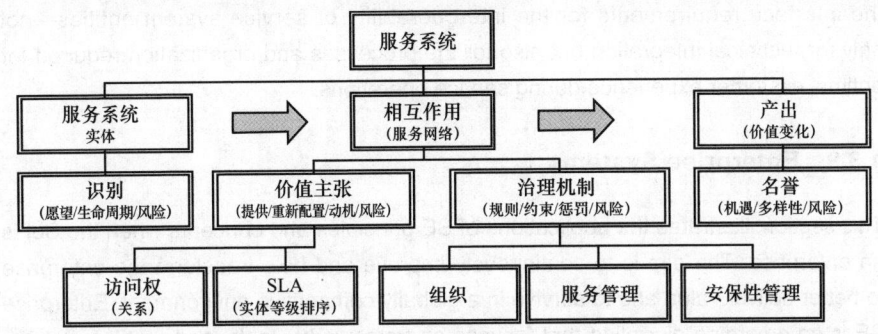

图 4.9 服务系统概念框架。源自 Spohrer（2011）。经许可后使用。版权所有。

服务不仅涉及服务提供者和消费者之间的互动以产生价值，还具有其他无形属性，如服务质量（例如，救护车服务可用性、对紧急请求的响应时间）。服务需求可能因时间、星期、季节或意外需求而变化（如自然灾害），并且服务是在请求时提供的。因此，服务系统的设计和运行"就是要在投入系统的资源和对系统提出的要求之间找到适当的平衡，从而尽可能提高为客户提供服务的质量"（Daskin，2010）。

在许多情况下，必须采用服务系统工程实施方法，以服务为导向，以客户为中心，从整体上选择和组合服务系统实体，以定义和发现服务系统实体之间的关系，从而进行规划、设计、调整或自我调整，共同创造价值。通常，需要考虑五种类型的资源：人；有形产品和环境基础设施；组织和机构；协议；以及在服务提供流程中共享信息和符号知识。主要的挑战包括服务系统的动态特性不断发展和适应不断变化的运行和/或业务环境，以及克服知识孤岛的需要。通过接口协议实现的服务系统实体的互操作性必须处于服务系统工程设计流程的最前沿，以协调各个服务系统实体的运行、管理、维护和供应程序（Pineda，2010）。此外，服务系统需要所有利益相关方之间的开放式协作，但最近对多学科团队心智模式的研究表明，整合与合作成为一个有凝聚力的团队是一项重大挑战（Carpenter 等，2010）。

TAILORING AND APPLICATION CONSIDERATIONS

In summary, in a service system environment, SE practitioners should bring a customer focus to promote service excellence and to facilitate service innovation through the use of emerging technologies to propose creation of new service systems and value cocreation. SE practitioners must play the role of an integrator, considering the interface requirements for the interoperability of service system entities—not only for technical integration but also for the processes and organization required for optimal customer experience during service operations.

4.3.9 Enterprise Systems

This section illustrates the applications of SE principles and concepts when the SoI is an enterprise. The aim is to continuously improve and help transform the enterprise to better deliver value and to survive in a globally competitive environment. Enterprise SE is an emerging discipline that focuses on frameworks, tools, and problem-solving approaches for dealing with the inherent complexities of the enterprise including exploitation of new opportunities that can facilitate achievement of enterprise goals. A good overall description of enterprise SE is provided in Rebovich and White (2011). For more detailed information on this topic, please see the Enterprise SE articles in Part 4 of SEBoK (2023).

Enterprise An enterprise consists of a purposeful combination (e.g., a network) of interdependent resources (e.g., people, processes, organizations, supporting technologies, and funding) that interact with each other to coordinate functions, share information, allocate funding, create workflows, and make decisions, and that interact with their environment(s) to achieve business and operational goals through a complex web of interactions distributed across geography and time (Rebovich and White, 2011).

An enterprise must do two things: (1) develop things within the enterprise to serve as either external offerings or as internal mechanisms to enable achievement of enterprise operations, and (2) transform the enterprise itself so that it can more effectively and efficiently perform its operations and survive in its competitive and constrained environment.

It is worth noting that an enterprise is not equivalent to an "organization." As shown in Figure 4.10, an enterprise has organizations that participate in it, but these organizations are not necessarily "part" of the enterprise. The organizations that participate in the enterprise will manage a variety of resources for the benefit of the enterprise, such as people, knowledge, and other assets such as processes, principles, policies, practices, culture, doctrine, theories, beliefs, facilities, land, and intellectual property. These organizational resources will consume or produce money, time, energy, and material when acting on behalf of the enterprise.

总之，在服务系统环境中，系统工程实践者应以客户为中心，促进卓越服务，并通过利用新兴技术促进服务创新，提出创建新服务系统和价值共创的建议。系统工程实践者必须扮演综合者的角色，考虑到服务系统实体互操作性的接口要求，不仅是技术综合，还包括服务运行期间最佳客户体验所需的流程和组织。

4.3.9 复杂组织体系系统

本节说明了当 SoI 是复杂组织体系时系统工程原则和概念的应用。目标是不断改进和帮助复杂组织体系转型，以更好地提供价值，并在全球竞争环境中生存。复杂组织体系系统工程是一门新兴学科，专注于应对复杂组织体系固有复杂性的框架、工具和问题解决的实施方法，包括利用新的机会来促进复杂组织体系目标的达成。Rebovich 和 White（2011）对复杂组织体系系统工程进行了全面的描述。有关此主题的更多详细信息，请参阅 SEBoK（2023）第 4 部分中的复杂组织体系系统工程的文章。

复杂组织体系 复杂组织体系由相互依赖的资源（如人员、流程、组织、支持技术和资金）的有目的的组合（如网络）组成，这些资源相互作用，以协调功能、共享信息、分配资金、创建工作流和做出决策，并通过跨地理和时间分布的复杂交互网络与环境交互，以达成业务和运行目标（Rebovich 和 White，2011）。

复杂组织体系必须做两件事：（1）在复杂组织体系内部开发事物，作为外部产品或内部机制，以实现复杂组织体系运行；（2）改造复杂组织体系自身，使其能够更有效、更高效地运行，并在竞争激烈和受到限制的环境中生存。

值得注意的是，复杂组织体系并不等同于"组织"。如图 4.10 所示，复杂组织体系有参与其中的组织，但这些组织不一定是复杂组织体系的"一部分"。参与复杂组织体系的组织将为复杂组织体系的利益管理各种资源，如人员、知识和其他资产，如流程、原则、政策、实践、文化、条令、理论、信仰、设施、土地和知识产权。当代表复杂组织体系行事时，这些组织资源将消耗或产生金钱、时间、精力和物料。

TAILORING AND APPLICATION CONSIDERATIONS

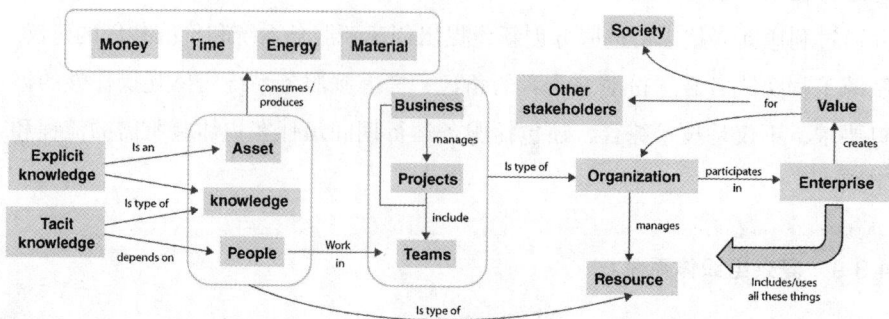

Notes:
1. All entities shown are decomposable, except people. For example, a business can have sub-businesses, a project can have subprojects, a resource can have sub-resources, an enterprise can have sub-enterprises.
2. All entities have other names. For example, a program can be a project comprising several subprojects (often called merely projects). Business can be an agency, team can be group, value can be utility, etc.
3. There is no attempt to be prescriptive in the names chosen for this diagram. The main goal of this is to show how this chapter uses these terms and how they are related to each other in a conceptual manner.

FIGURE 4.10   Organizations manage resources to create enterprise value. From SEBoK (2023). Used with permission. All other rights reserved.

Creating Value   As shown in Figure 4.10, an enterprise creates value for society, for other stakeholders, and for the organizations that participate in that enterprise. It also shows other key elements that contribute to the value creation process. There are many types of organizations to implement value-creating enterprises: businesses (companies), networks of companies, programs and projects, virtual organizations, etc. A typical business may participate in multiple enterprises through its portfolio of projects. A large SE project can be an enterprise in its own right (implemented as a virtual organization), with participation by many different businesses, and may be organized as a number of interrelated subprojects. In many cases, enterprises find themselves in a rapidly changing environment where stakeholder needs change over time. Therefore, an enterprise must constantly adapt its capabilities to meet the enterprise strategic goals and objectives.

Capabilities in the Enterprise   As shown in Figure 4.11, the enterprise acquires or develops systems or individual elements of a system. The enterprise can also create, supply, use, and operate systems or system elements. Since there could possibly be several organizations involved in this enterprise venture, each organization could be responsible for particular systems or perhaps for certain kinds of elements. Each organization brings their own organizational capability with them, and the unique combination of these organizations leads to the overall operational capability of the whole enterprise.

剪裁和应用的考虑因素

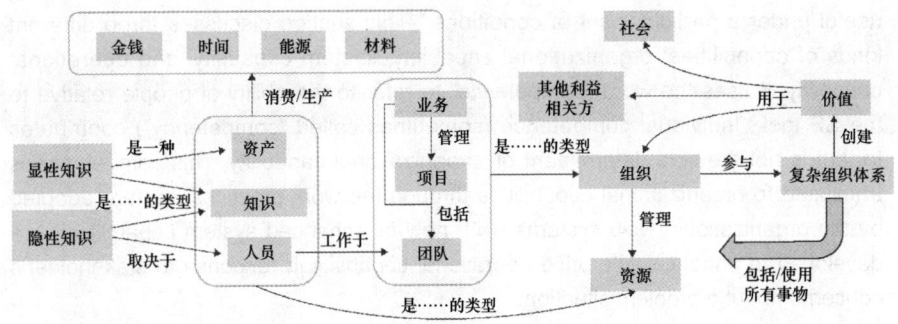

注：
1. 除人以外，所示的所有实体都是可分解的。例如，业务可以有子业务，项目可以有子项目，资源可以有子资源，复杂组织体系可以有子复杂组织体系。
2. 所有实体都有其他名称。例如，一个项目群可以是一个由多个子项目组成的项目（通常仅称为项目）。业务可以是机构，团队可以是团体，价值可以是效用等。
3. 本图所选用的名称并不具有规范性。其主要目的是说明本章如何使用这些术语，以及它们在概念上是如何相互关联的。

图 4.10 组织管理资源以创建复杂组织体系价值。源自 SEBoK（2023）。经 BKCASE 编辑委员会许可后使用。版权所有。

创造价值 如图 4.10 所示，复杂组织体系为社会、其他利益相关方以及参与该复杂组织体系的组织创造价值。它还显示了促进价值创造过程的其他关键因素。实施价值创造的复杂组织体系的组织有多种类型：业务（公司）、公司网络、项目群和项目、虚拟组织等。一个典型的复杂组织体系可以通过其项目组合参与多个复杂组织体系。大型系统工程项目本身可以是一个复杂组织体系（作为虚拟组织实施），由许多不同的复杂组织体系参与，并且可以作为许多相互关联的子项目进行组织。在许多情况下，复杂组织体系发现自己处于一个快速变化的环境中，利益相关方需要随着时间的推移而变化。因此，复杂组织体系必须不断调整其能力，以满足复杂组织体系的战略目的和目标。

复杂组织体系中的能力 如图 4.11 所示，复杂组织体系获取或开发系统或系统的单个元素。复杂组织体系还可以创建、提供、使用和运行系统或系统元素。由于可能会有多个组织参与这一复杂组织体系的风险投资，每个组织都可能负责特定的系统或某些类型的元素。每个组织都有自己的组织能力，这些组织的独特组合将带来整个复杂组织体系的整体运行能力。

TAILORING AND APPLICATION CONSIDERATIONS

The word "capability" is used in SE in the sense of "the ability to do something useful under a particular set of conditions." This section discusses three different kinds of capabilities: organizational capability, system capability, and operational capability. It uses the word "competence" to refer to the ability of people relative to the SE task. Individual competence (sometimes called "competency") contributes to, but is not the sole determinant of, organizational capability. This competence is translated to organizational capabilities through the work practices that are adopted by the organizations. New systems (with new or enhanced system capabilities) are developed to enhance enterprise operational capability in response to stakeholder's concerns about a problem situation.

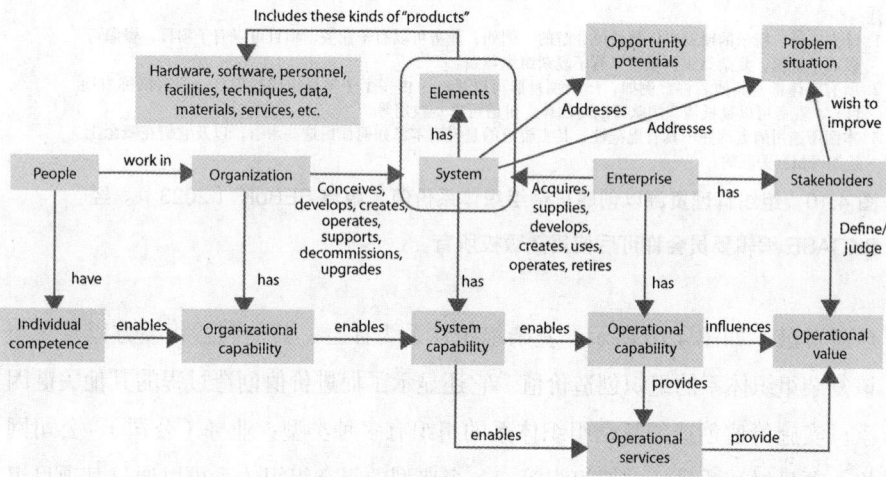

FIGURE 4.11 Individual competence leads to organizational, system, and operational capability. From SEBoK (2023). Used with permission. All other rights reserved.

As also shown in Figure 4.11, operational capabilities provide operational services that are enabled by system capabilities. These system capabilities are inherent in the system that is conceived, developed, created, and/or operated by an enterprise. Enterprise SE concentrates its efforts on maximizing operational value for various stakeholders, some of whom may be interested in the improvement of some problem situation.

Enterprise SE, however, addresses more than just solving problems; it also deals with the exploitation of opportunities for better ways to achieve the enterprise goals. These opportunities might involve lowering operating costs, increasing market share, decreasing deployment risk, reducing time to market, and any number of other enterprise goals. The importance of addressing opportunity potentials should not be underestimated in the execution of enterprise SE practices.

"能力"一词在系统工程中的含义是"在特定条件下做有用事情的本领"。本节讨论三种不同类型的能力：组织能力、系统能力和运行能力。"能力"一词被用来表示人们相对于系统工程任务的本领。个人胜任力（有时称为"资质能力"）有助于但不是组织能力的唯一决定因素。这种胜任力通过组织采用的工作实践转化为组织能力。开发新系统（具有新的或增强的系统能力）以增强复杂组织体系运行能力，以应对利益相关方对问题情况的关切。

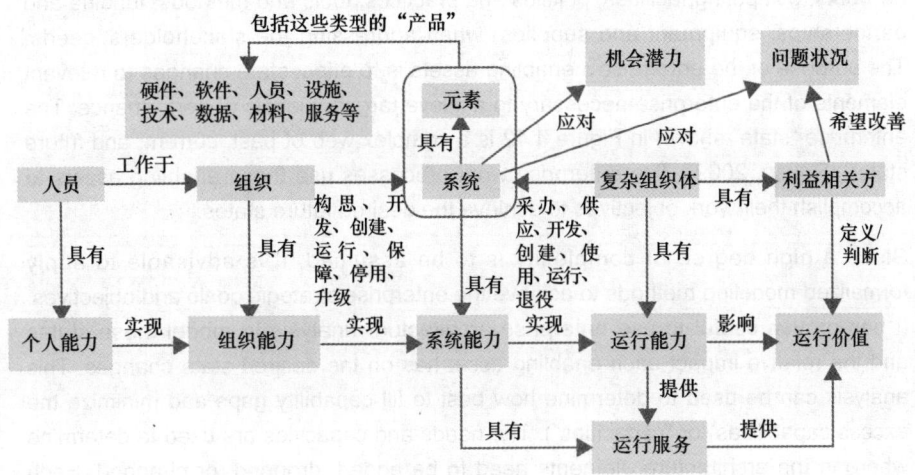

图 4.11 个人胜任力产生组织的、系统的以及运行的能力。源自 SEBoK（2023）。经 BKCASE 编辑委员会许可后使用。版权所有。

如图 4.11 所示，运行能力提供由系统能力支持的运行服务。这些系统能力是复杂组织体系构思、开发、创建和 / 或运行的系统所固有的。复杂组织体系系统工程致力于为各种利益相关方实现运行价值最大化，其中一些利益相关方可能对改善某些问题状况感兴趣。

然而，复杂组织体系系统工程不仅仅解决问题；它还涉及利用机会以更好的方式达到复杂组织体系目标。这些机会可能涉及降低运行成本、增加市场份额、降低部署风险、缩短上市时间以及任何其他复杂组织体系目标。在执行复杂组织体系系统工程实践时，不应低估处理机会潜力的重要性。

TAILORING AND APPLICATION CONSIDERATIONS

The operational capabilities of an enterprise will have a contribution to operational value (as perceived by the stakeholders). Notice that the organization or enterprise can deal with either the system as a whole or with only one (or a few) of its elements. These elements are not necessarily hard items, like hardware and software, but can also include "soft" items, like people, processes, principles, policies, practices, organizations, doctrines, theories, beliefs, and so on.

Enterprise Drivers and Outcomes An enterprise needs to consider its own needs that relate to enabling assets (e.g., personnel, facilities, communication networks, computing facilities, policies and practices, tools and methods, funding and partnerships, equipment and supplies) when addressing the stakeholders' needs. The purpose of the enterprise's enabling assets is to effect state changes to relevant elements of the enterprise necessary to achieve targeted levels of performance. The enterprise "state" shown in Figure 4.12 is a complex web of past, current, and future states (Rouse, 2009). The enterprise work processes use these enabling assets to accomplish their work objectives to achieve the desired future states.

Since a high degree of complexity is to be assumed, it is advisable to apply formalized modeling methods to achieve the enterprise strategic goals and objectives. It has proven useful to use enterprise architecture analysis to model these states and the relative impact each enabling asset has on the desired state changes. This analysis can be used to determine how best to fill capability gaps and minimize the excess capabilities (or "capacities"). The needs and capacities are used to determine where in the architecture elements need to be added, dropped, or changed. Each modification represents a potential benefit to various stakeholders, along with associated costs and risks for introducing that modification.

Enterprise Opportunities and Opportunity Assessments The potential modifications that are identified represent opportunities for improvement. Usually, these opportunities require the investment of time, money, facilities, personnel, and so on. There might also be opportunities for "divestment," which could involve selling of assets, reducing capacity, canceling projects, and so on. Each opportunity can be assessed on its own merits, but usually these opportunities have dependencies and interfaces with other opportunities, with the current activities and operations of the enterprise, and with the enterprise's partners. Therefore, the opportunities may need to be assessed as a "portfolio," or, at least, as sets of related opportunities. Typically, a business case assessment is required for each opportunity or set of opportunities. If the set of opportunities is large or has complicated relationships, it may be necessary to employ portfolio management techniques. The portfolio elements could be bids, projects, products, services, technologies, intellectual property, etc., or any combination of these items. Examples of an enterprise portfolio captured in an architecture modeling tool can be found in Martin (2005), Martin et al. (2004), and Martin (2003).

复杂组织体系的运行能力将对运行价值做出贡献（正如利益相关方所认为的那样）。请注意，组织或复杂组织体系可以将系统作为一个整体来处理，也可以仅处理其中一个（或几个）元素。这些元素不一定是硬件和软件等硬项目，但也可以包括"软"项目，如人员、流程、原则、政策、实践、组织、条令、理论、信仰等。

复杂组织体系驱动因素和产出 复杂组织体系在满足利益相关者的需要时，需要考虑自身与使能资产（例如，人员、设施、通信网络、计算设施、政策和实践、工具和方法、资金和伙伴关系、设备和用品）的有关需要。复杂组织体系使能资产的目的是对复杂组织体系的相关元素进行必要的状态变更，以达到目标绩效水平。图 4.12 所示的复杂组织体系"状态"是过去、现在和未来状态的复杂网络（Rouse，2009）。复杂组织体系工作流程利用这些使能资产来达到其工作目标，以实现所期望的未来状态。

由于假设了高度的复杂性，建议应用形式化建模方法来达到复杂组织体系战略目标。事实证明，使用复杂组织体系架构分析对这些状态以及每种使能资产对所需状态变化的相对影响进行建模非常有用。该分析可用于确定如何以最佳方式填补能力差距，并将过剩能力（或"容量"）降至最低。需要和容量用于确定需要在架构中的何处添加、删除或更改元素。每项修改都代表着对各利益相关方的潜在利益，以及引入该修改的相关成本和风险。

复杂组织体系机会和机会评估 识别的潜在修改代表了改进的机会。通常，这些机会需要投入时间、金钱、设施、人员等。也可能有"撤资"的机会，这可能涉及出售资产、降低产能、取消项目等。每个机会都可以根据自身的优点被评估，但通常这些机会与其他机会、复杂组织体系当前的活动和运行以及复杂组织体系的合作伙伴具有依赖关系和接口。因此，可能需要将这些机会评估为一个"项目组合"，或者至少是一组相关的机会。通常，需要对每个机会或机会的集合进行业务用例评估。如果机会的集合很大或关系复杂，则可能需要采用项目组合管理技术。项目组合元素可以是投标、项目、产品、服务、技术、知识产权等，也可以是这些项目的任何组合。Martin（2005）、Martin 等（2004）和 Martin（2003）提供了使用架构建模工具捕获复杂组织体系项目组合的示例。

TAILORING AND APPLICATION CONSIDERATIONS

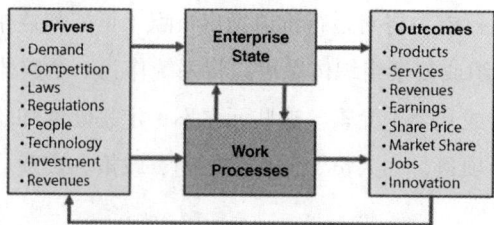

FIGURE 4.12 Enterprise state changes through work process activities. From Rouse (2009). Used with permission. All other rights reserved.

The results of the opportunity assessment can be compiled and laid out in an enterprise plan (sometimes conveyed as an enterprise ConOps) that considers all relevant factors, including system capabilities, organizational capabilities, funding constraints, legal commitments and obligations, partner arrangements, intellectual property ownership, personnel development and retention, and so on. The plan usually goes out to some long horizon, typically more than a decade, depending on the nature of the enterprise's business environment, technology volatility, market intensity, and so on. The enterprise plan needs to be in alignment with the enterprise's strategic goals and objectives and leadership priorities.

Practical Considerations When it comes to performing SE at the enterprise level, Rebovich and White (2011) provide several good practices:

- Set enterprise fitness as the key measure of system success. Leverage game theory and ecology, along with the practices of satisfying and governing the commons.

- Deal with uncertainty and conflict in the enterprise through adaptation: variety, selection, exploration, and experimentation.

- Leverage the practice of layered architectures with loose couplers and the theory of order and chaos in networks.

Enterprise governance involves shaping the political, operational, economic, and technical landscape. One should not try to control the enterprise like one would in a traditional SE effort at the project level.

4.4 APPLICATION OF SYSTEMS ENGINEERING FOR SPECIFIC PRODUCT SECTOR OR DOMAIN APPLICATION

This chapter presents how SE is applied in different product sectors or application domains. For each of these, unique and domain-specific terms, concepts, activities, methods, and practices are introduced.

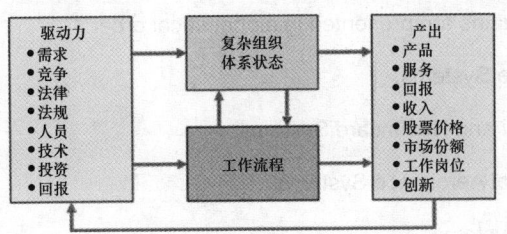

图 4.12 通过工作流程活动改变复杂组织体系状态。源自 Rouse（2009）。经许可后使用。版权所有。

机会评估的结果可以在复杂组织体系规划（有时沟通为复杂组织体系 ConOps）中进行汇编和阐述，该规划考虑了所有相关因素，包括系统能力、组织能力、资金约束、法律承诺和义务、合作伙伴安排、知识产权所有权、人员发展和留用等。该规划通常涉及一些长期的问题，通常超过十年，具体取决于复杂组织体系业务环境的性质、技术波动性、市场密度等。复杂组织体系规划需要与复杂组织体系的战略目标和领导力优先事项保持一致。

实际考虑因素　在复杂组织体系层执行系统工程时，Rebovich 和 White（2011）提供了几个良好实践：

- 将复杂组织体系的适应性设置为系统成功的关键测度。利用博弈论和生态学，以及满足和治理公共资源的实践。
- 通过适应：多样性、选择、探索和实验来处理复杂组织体系中的不确定性和冲突。
- 利用松散耦合器的分层架构实践以及网络中的有序和混沌理论。

复杂组织体系治理涉及塑造政治、运行、经济和技术领域。人们不应该像在项目层的传统系统工程工作中那样试图控制复杂组织体系。

4.4　系统工程在特定产品行业或领域的应用

本章展示了系统工程在不同产品行业或领域的应用。对于其中的每一个，都介绍了独特的和领域特定的术语、概念、活动、方法和实践。

TAILORING AND APPLICATION CONSIDERATIONS

The following domains are presented in alphabetical order:

- Automotive Systems;
- Biomedical and Healthcare Systems;
- Commercial Aerospace Systems;
- Defense Systems;
- Infrastructure Systems;
- Oil & Gas Systems;
- Power & Energy Systems;
- Space Systems;
- Telecommunication Systems;
- Transportation Systems.

Note that the application of SE is not limited to the product sectors and application domains listed above. SE is a generic discipline that can be applied in most situations and domains (with varying levels of value). However, the details of how the practice is applied will vary in different product sectors or application domains.

4.4.1 Automotive Systems

Overview of SE Applications within the Automotive Domain The automotive industry has a long history of engineering complicated and more and more complex consumer products, characterized by diverse product ranges, high production volumes, and a very competitive market. To make vehicles attractive, manufacturers have to balance efficiency for mass production with driving performance. Strong, well-orchestrated processes across the supply chain are key to meeting this challenge. Quality is highly dependent on good processes being followed rigorously, and economic performance relies on optimization. Electrification, connectivity, autonomy, and consumer choice are driving complexity, creating opportunities for SE to enter the mainstream in coming years. The INCOSE Automotive SE Vision 2025 document (2020) provides an excellent summary of the current and future trends in this domain. See Table 4.5 for a comparison of automotive with two other domains considering some of the characteristics that may affect SE approaches.

以下领域按字母顺序排列：

- 汽车系统；
- 生物医学和医疗卫生系统；
- 商用航空航天系统；
- 防务系统；
- 基础设施系统；
- 油气系统；
- 电力和能源系统；
- 空间系统；
- 电信系统；
- 运输系统。

请注意，系统工程的应用不限于上述产品行业和应用领域。系统工程是一门通用学科，可以应用于大多数的情况和领域（具有不同的价值水平）。然而，在不同的产品行业或应用领域，如何应用实践的细节将有所不同。

4.4.1 汽车系统

系统工程在汽车领域的应用概述　　汽车行业在制造繁杂且越来越复杂的消费品方面有着悠久的历史，其特点是产品范围多样，产量高，市场竞争激烈。为了使车辆具有吸引力，制造商必须在大规模生产的效率和驾驶性能之间取得平衡。整个供应链中强大、协调良好的流程是应对这一挑战的关键。质量在很大程度上取决于严格遵循良好的流程，而经济效益取决于优化。电气化、连通性、自主性和消费者的选择推动了复杂性的发展，为系统工程在未来几年成为主流创造了机会。INCOSE 汽车系统工程愿景 2025 文件（2020）对该领域的当前和未来趋势进行了极好的总结。考虑到可能影响系统工程实施方法的一些特征，汽车与其他两个领域的比较见表 4.5。

TAILORING AND APPLICATION CONSIDERATIONS

TABLE 4.5 Comparison of automotive, aerospace/defense, and consumer electronics domains

	Automotive	Aerospace/Defense	Consumer Electronics
Customer requirements	Assumed by manufacturer	Defined by customer	Assumed by manufacturer
Legislative environment	Certification/inspection of product design, auditing of development and production processes (e.g., ISO/TS 16949 (2009)/IATF 16949, ISO 26262 (2018), E-marking, conformity of production, many regulatory Inc) standards (UNR, FMRSS, etc.) applicable to the overall system and its elements. Process regulations/standards are a new development.	Certification (e.g., DO-178C from RTCA Inc) in process, tooling and product. Auditing of development and production processes	CE/UL/FCC marking, according to a small number of standards (typically <10 per product)
User skill level	Somewhat trained	Highly trained	Untrained
Complexity (PLE/component reuse)	High	Low	Medium
Complexity (sociodynamic)	High	High	Low
Product development cycle time	Medium (3-7 years)	Long (10+ years)	Short (1-2 years)
Delivery cadence	Annual	Decade	Annual
Product design life	Medium (10-20 years)	Long (30+ years)	Short (1-2 years)
Approach to maintenance	Repair	Repair	Replacement
Connectivity need	Medium (trend to high)	Low-medium (defined in stakeholder requirements)	Medium-high
Number of external integration interfaces	Medium (trend to high)	Medium (trend to high)	Medium
Safety/cybersecurity criticality	High	High	Medium-high
Typical industry operating margin	4%-6%	6%-8%	8%-10%
Annual production volume	10k-900k	100-100k	100k-100M

INCOSE SEH original table created by the INCOSE Automotive Working Group (AWG). Usage per the INCOSE Notices page. All other rights reserved.

表 4.5 汽车、航空航天 / 防务和消费者电子设备产品领域的比较

	汽车	航空航天 / 防务	消费者电子设备
客户需求	由制造商假定	由客户定义	由制造商假定
立法环境	产品设计认证 / 检查、开发和生产流程审核 [如 ISO/TS16949（2009）/IATF 16949, ISO 26262（2018），电子标记，生产一致性，许多监管公司] 标准（UNR、FMRSS 等）适用于整个系统及其元件。工艺规程 / 标准是一项新的发展	在流程、工具和产品中的认证（例如来自 RTCA 公司的 DO-178C）。开发和生产流程中的审核	根据少量标准（通常每种产品 <10 个），由 CE/UL/FCC 标记
用户技能水平	受过一定训练	训练有素的	未经培训
复杂性（产品线工程 / 组件复用）	高	低	中等
复杂性（社会动力学）	高	高	低
产品开发周期	中等（3~7 年）	长期（10 年以上）	短期（1~2 年）
交付节奏	年度	十年	年度
产品设计生命	中等（10~20 年）	长期（30 年以上）	短期（1~2 年）
维修的实施方法	修理	修理	更换
连接需要	中等（趋向高）	中低（在利益相关方需求中定义）	中—高
外部综合接口数量	中等（趋向高）	中等（趋向高）	中等
安全性 / 赛博安保关键性	高	高	中—高
典型的行业运营利润	4%~6%	6%~8%	8%~10%
年度产量	10k~900k	100~100k	100k~100M

INCOSE SEH 原始表由 INCOSE 汽车工作组创建。按照 INCOSE 通知页使用。版权所有。

TAILORING AND APPLICATION CONSIDERATIONS

Emergence of SE in the Automotive Domain Since General Motors vehicles first shared a common chassis in 1908, the automotive industry has employed extensive reuse in combination with variant management techniques to manage costs and keep delivery cycles short. Until the late 1960s, activities familiar to the SE domain centered on parts development, promoting reuse through standards and matrix organizations. Architects mainly addressed geometry until the on-board electronics and software revolution started in the 1970s. Standalone mechatronic and automated control systems appeared first, delivering applications such as engine control, anti-lock braking, and automatic heating and air conditioning. During the 1990s, vehicles acquired extensive networks of interconnected electronic control units. In the same period, many manufacturers invested heavily in engineering teams that focused on elicitation and refinement of stakeholder needs to address emergent properties such as safety, environmental impact, dynamic performance, and occupant comfort. This subset of activities (e.g., stakeholder requirements, electrical and electronic architecture) provided the ingredients for the emergence of SE in automotive.

Contemporary SE in the Automotive Domain Increasing complexity, driven by the parallel trends of electrification, on- and off-board networks, automation, and autonomy has led to growing interest in automotive SE since 2000. Electronics and software began to outstrip mechanical design as a means for manufacturers to provide distinctive products. As shown in Table 4.6, the automotive industry is very standards-driven and the last decade has seen many new developments. These standards address, in particular, architectural approaches, software elements, safety, and security processes. Practices have evolved in isolated pockets, leading to significant variation in how the discipline is interpreted and executed. Convergence of capabilities at different maturity levels, led by engineering executives with different worldviews and backgrounds, has led to the adoption of many different SE paradigms with varying enthusiasm. SE practitioners might draw the system boundary at the vehicle level, or be restricted to applying their techniques to individual features, system elements, or domains, sometimes focusing on electronics and software. Approaches differ too, with some being requirements-led, others architecture-centric. SE has entered the automotive domain in incremental steps, and continues to do so, due to the need to accommodate the special features and legacy of each company. Disruptive change is hard for established players because their business models have low margins, and rely on trusted, repeatable processes that leverage extensive reuse of system elements. Similarly, production needs efficient processes to continuously deliver high volumes of system elements and assemblies on a just-in-time basis, making interruptions to manufacturing difficult to tolerate.

汽车领域系统工程的涌现 自1908年通用汽车首次共享通用底盘以来，汽车行业采用了广泛的重用，并结合各种管理技术来管理成本和缩短交付周期。直到20世纪60年代末，系统工程领域熟悉的活动都集中在零件开发上，通过标准和矩阵化组织促进重用。在20世纪70年代车载电子和软件革命开始之前，架构师主要研究几何问题。独立的机电一体化和自动化控制系统的首先出现，提供了发动机控制、防抱死制动、自动加热和空调等应用。20世纪90年代，汽车上出现了大量相互连接的电子控制单元网络。在同一时期，许多制造商对工程团队进行了大量投资，这些团队专注于捕获和完善利益相关方的需要，以解决安全、环境影响、动态性能和乘员舒适性等涌现的特性。这部分活动（例如，利益相关方需求、电气和电子架构）为系统工程在汽车中的出现提供了要素。

汽车领域的当代系统工程 自2000年以来，在电气化、车载和非车载网络、自动化和自主化等并行趋势的推动下，汽车复杂性不断增加，导致人们对汽车系统工程的兴趣与日俱增。作为制造商提供独特产品的手段，电子和软件开始超越机械设计。如表4.6所示，汽车行业是非常标准化的行业，在过去十年中出现了许多新的发展。这些标准特别涉及架构实施方法、软件元素、安全和安保流程。实践在孤立的领域中不断发展，导致了该学科的解释和执行方式发生了重大变化。在具有不同世界观和背景的工程管理人员的领导下，不同成熟度水平的能力趋于一致，导致许多不同的系统工程范式以不同的热情被采用。可能会在车辆层级划定系统边界，或仅限于将其技术应用于单个特征、系统元素或领域，有时侧重于电子设备和软件。实施方法也有所不同，有些是以需求为导向的，有些是以架构为中心的。由于需要适应每家公司的特点和传统，系统工程已逐步进入汽车领域，并将持续发展。颠覆性变革对于成熟的参与者来说很难实现，因为他们的业务模型利润率很低，并且依赖于可靠的、可重复的流程，这些流程利用了系统元素的广泛重用。同样，生产也需要高效的流程，以持续、及时地交付大量系统元件和组件，因此很难容忍生产中断。

TAILORING AND APPLICATION CONSIDERATIONS

247   TABLE 4.6   Representative organizations and standards in the automotive industry

Organization/standard	Description
SAE International, formerly the Society of Automotive Engineers	One of the main organizations that coordinate the development of technical standards for the automotive industry. Currently, SAE International is a globally active professional association and standards organization for engineering professionals in various industries, whose principal emphasis is placed on transport industries such as automotive, aerospace, and commercial vehicles
Japan Society of Automotive Engineers (JSAE)	An organization that sets automotive standards in Japan, analogous to the SAE
Association for Standardization of Automation and Measuring	An incorporated association under German law whose members are primarily international car manufacturers, suppliers, and engineering service providers from the automotive industry. The ASAM standards define protocols, data models, file formats, and application programming interfaces (APIs) for the use in the development and testing of automotive electronic control units
AUTomotive Open System ARchitecture (AUTOSAR)	An open and standardized automotive software architecture, jointly developed by automobile manufacturers, suppliers, and tool developers. Some of its key goals include the standardization of basic system functions, scalability to different vehicle and platform variants, transferability throughout the network, integration from multiple suppliers, maintainability
The GENIVI Alliance	A nonprofit consortium whose goal is to establish a globally competitive, Linux-based operating system, middleware, and platform for the automotive in-vehicle infotainment (IVI) industry. GENIVI specifications cover the entire product life cycle and software updates and upgrades over the vehicle's lifetime
ISO/TS 16949 (2009)/IATF 16949	An international standard for particular requirements for the application of ISO 9001 quality management systems for automotive production and relevant service part organizations
IEC 62196 (2022)	An international standard for set of electrical connectors and charging modes for electric vehicles maintained by the International Electrotechnical Commission (IEC)
ISO 26262 (2018)	Road vehicles - Functional safety
ISO/SAE 21434 (2021)	Road vehicles - Cybersecurity engineering

INCOSE SEH original table created by the INCOSE Automotive Working Group (AWG). Usage per the INCOSE Notices page. All other rights reserved.

The explosion of electrical, electronic, and software systems is driving awareness that engineering based on assembling parts from suppliers without a systems approach is no longer enough. Full autonomy is on the horizon, and advanced driver assistance features like lane keeping and emergency braking are well established. Many new vehicles have highintegrity system elements linked to the outside world. Managing the complexity and cybersecurity risks this creates is a great challenge (see Section 6.5). Cultural and methodological changes are ongoing in industry incumbents. They

剪裁和应用的考虑因素

表 4.6 汽车产业的代表性组织和标准

组织 / 标准	描述
国际汽车工程师学会，前身为汽车工程师学会	汽车工业协调制定技术标准的主要组织之一。目前，SAE 国际是一个全球活跃的专业协会和标准组织，面向各个行业的工程专业人员，其主要负责人重点放在运输行业，如汽车、航空航天和商用车
日本汽车工程师学会	在日本制定汽车标准的组织，类似于 SAE
自动化和测量标准协会	根据德国法律成立的协会，其成员主要是国际汽车制造商、供应商和汽车行业的工程服务提供商。ASAM 标准定义协议、数据模型、文件格式和应用编程接口（API），用于开发和测试汽车电子控制单元
汽车开放系统架构	由汽车制造商、供应商和工具开发人员联合开发的开放式标准化汽车软件架构。其中一些关键目标包括基本系统功能的标准化，对不同车辆和平台变体的可扩展性，基于网络的可转移性，多个供应商的可综合性和可维护性
GENIVI 联盟	一个非营利财团，其目标是建立一个具有全球竞争力的基于 Linux 的汽车车载信息娱乐（IVI）行业的操作系统、中间件和平台。GENIVI 规范涵盖整个产品生命周期以及车辆生命周期内的软件更新和升级
ISO/TS 16949（2009）/IATF 16949	有关汽车生产和相关服务部件组织应用 ISO 9001 质量管理体系的特殊需求的国际标准
IEC 62196（2022）	国际电工委员会（IEC）制定的电动汽车电气连接器和充电模式的国际标准
ISO 26262（2018）	道路车辆功能安全性
ISO/SAE 21434（2021）	道路车辆赛博安保性工程

INCOSE SEH 原始表由 INCOSE 汽车工作组（AWG）创建。按照 INCOSE 通知页使用。版权所有。

电气、电子和软件系统的爆炸式增长促使人们认识到，仅靠从供应商那里组装零件而不采用系统实施方法进行工程设计已远远不够。完全自主即将实现，全自动驾驶即将实现，车道保持和紧急制动等先进的驾驶辅助功能也已成熟。许多新车都有与外界相连的高综合性系统元件。管理由此带来的复杂性和网络安全风险是一个巨大的挑战（见 6.5 节）。行业现有复杂组织体系的文化和方法

TAILORING AND APPLICATION CONSIDERATIONS

increasingly face competition from newcomers with backgrounds in software-intensive industries (see Section 4.3.4), who in turn must adapt their culture and scale their business models to the realities of high-volume automotive manufacturing.

New Eco-Systems Involving the Automotive Industry: The Example of "Mobility as a Service" In many urban areas, local governments implement policies to reduce the number of private cars and to foster the deployment of mobility services as a complement to public transport. The number of privately owned, individual cars has decreased dramatically in some big cities. For instance, in Paris, capitol of France, the percentage of cars as a mode of transportation has decreased from 46% in 2002, to only 13% in 2022. Vehicle manufacturers should not expect that this trend will change. Vehicles they used to sell are more and more being replaced by public transport, biking, and walking, as well as services still involving vehicles like car-sharing or ridesharing. All these service offers can be integrated into a larger service enabling them to combine and thus making on-demand mobility faster and easier. This is called Mobility as a Service (MaaS), with a lot of initiatives around the world triggered by the Sustainable Development Goals introduced in Section 3.1.10. However, MaaS is not a silver bullet nor standard yet. MaaS may be considered as the mission for an SoS involving mobility service operators, both public and private. They have to cooperate in order to offer a more attractive user experience and at the same time to make the conditions for local mobility more sustainable.

The Future of SE in the Automotive Domain Dealing with massively expanding complexity in an extremely challenging environment where standards and regulation trail fast-paced innovation is a challenge for this process-driven industry, but an opportunity for SE. As connectivity and autonomy become the norm, vehicles are built on highly configurable software platforms for providing mobility as a service. Development cycles that took five years are being compressed, where service updates that took a year will be expected in weeks. Delivering change like this means fundamental shifts in thinking are required across the board: from new business models, through service-centric architectures, to security-informed safety paradigms. SE is the means by which this can be achieved.

4.4.2 Biomedical and Healthcare Systems

Overview of SE Applications within the Biomedical and Healthcare Domain SE has become more important to the healthcare industry (SEBoK, 2023), especially as systems and processes get more complex and quality characteristics such as safety, security, reliability, and human systems integration become more challenging. SE offers numerous benefits to biomedical and healthcare systems including the following:

正在发生变化。它们越来越多地面临来自具有软件密集型产业背景的新进入者的竞争（见 4.3.4 节），而这些新进入者又必须根据大批量汽车制造的实际情况调整其文化和业务模式。

涉及汽车行业的新生态系统：以"出行即服务"为例　在许多城市地区，地方政府实施政策，减少私家车数量，并鼓励部署出行服务作为公共交通的补充。在一些大城市，私人拥有的汽车数量急剧减少。例如，在法国首都巴黎，汽车作为一种交通方式的比例从 2002 年的 46% 下降到 2022 年的 13%。汽车制造商不应期望这种趋势会改变。越来越多的公共交通、骑行和步行，以及汽车共享或共享骑车等仍涉及车辆的服务取代了他们过去销售的车辆。所有这些服务都可以综合到一个更大的服务中，使它们能够结合起来，从而使按需出行更快、更容易。这被称为出行即服务（MaaS），由 3.1.10 节中介绍的可持续发展目标引发了世界各地的许多倡议。然而，MaaS 还不是灵丹妙药或标准。MaaS 可被视为涉及公共和私人出行服务运营商的 SoS 任务。它们必须进行合作，以提供更具吸引力的用户体验，同时使当地出行条件更具可持续性。

汽车领域系统工程的未来　在一个极具挑战性的环境中，标准和法规与快节奏的创新并行不悖，如何应对大规模扩展的复杂性，对这个以流程为导向的行业来说是一个挑战，但对系统工程来说却是一个机遇。随着连通性和自主性成为常态，车辆构建在高度可配置的软件平台上，以提供出行即服务。耗时五年的开发周期正在被压缩，耗时一年的服务更新预计将在几周内完成。实现这样的变革意味着需要全面转变思维方式：从新的业务模型到以服务为中心的架构，再到安保性知悉的安全性范式。系统工程是达到这一目标的手段。

4.4.2　生物医学和医疗卫生系统

SE 在生物医学和医疗卫生领域的应用概述

SE 对医疗行业来说正变得越来越重要（SEBoK，2023），尤其是随着系统和流程变得越来越复杂，安全性、安保性、可靠性和人—系统综合等质量特性变得更具挑战性。SE 为生物医学和医疗卫生系统提供了许多益处，包括：

TAILORING AND APPLICATION CONSIDERATIONS

- Supports design and development of healthcare systems using well-defined processes and standards,
- Offers well-defined approaches to design and implement architectures for proper interfacing, networking and communications using open industry standards,
- Enables operators and enterprises to scale up without compromising quality of operations,
- Enables better insights and control of many production systems including quality assurance, inventory, and cost control, and
- Augments user experience of various stakeholders like doctors, and surgeons by system level integration of emerging digital platforms like augmented reality, virtual reality, and robotics.

In the medical industry, especially for medical devices, it is important to understand that "risk management" is generally centered around product (user safety) risk and (called system safety in this handbook—see Section 3.1.11) rather than project (technical or business) risk (called risk management in this handbook—see Section 2.3.4.4).

Unique Considerations for Healthcare Delivery SE applied to healthcare delivery differs significantly from conventional SE as applied in traditional fields such as defense, aerospace, and automotive. Most healthcare delivery projects involve improvement of an imperfect workflow or care process or the design of a limited scope new workflow or care process in a local clinic, hospital, laboratory, or in population health. If successful, solutions are shared with peer institutions in the same medical organization. As a result, most SE projects in healthcare delivery involve only a few stakeholders and a handful of requirements. Approaches leveraging lean SE have shown to be successful in many cases (Oppenheim, 2021) (see Section 4.2.3). Healthcare delivery operations have a critical need for the SE process to address pervasive healthcare problems such as care fragmentation (e.g., the systemic misalignment of incentives) or lack of coordination that spawn inefficient allocation of resources or harm to patients. Just as in medical device development, SE in healthcare delivery also strongly emphasizes patient safety. Methods such as the Systems Engineering Intervention for Patient Safety (SEIPS) (Carayon, 2006) focus on tailoring SE processes to the specific context of patient-centered medicine.

- 利用明确的流程和标准,支持医疗卫生系统的设计和开发;
- 提供明确的实施方法,利用开放式的行业标准设计和实施适当的接口、网络和通信架构;
- 使操作人员和复杂组织体系能够在不影响运行质量的情况下扩大规模;
- 能够更好地洞察和控制许多生产系统,包括质量保证、库存和成本控制;
- 通过对增强现实、虚拟现实和机器人等新兴数字平台进行系统级集成,增强医生和外科医生等各利益相关方的用户体验。

在医疗行业,尤其是医疗器械行业,"风险管理"通常以产品(用户安全性)风险(本手册中称为系统安全性,请参见 3.1.11 节)而不是项目(技术或业务)风险(本手册中称为风险管理,请参见 2.3.4.4 节)为中心,这一点很重要。

医疗卫生服务的独特考虑因素 应用于医疗服务的流程与应用于防务、航空航天和汽车等传统领域的传统流程有着显著的不同。大多数医疗服务项目涉及改进不完善的工作流程或护理流程,或在当地诊所、医院、实验室或人口健康中设计有限范围的新工作流程或护理流程。如果成功,则与同一医疗组织的同行机构共享解决方案。因此,医疗卫生服务中的大多数流程项目只涉及少数利益相关方和少量需求。利用精益流程的实施方法在许多情况下都是成功的(Oppenheim,2021)(见 4.2.3 节)。医疗卫生服务的运行亟须通过 SE 流程来解决普遍存在的医疗卫生问题,如医疗卫生分散(如激励机制的系统性错位)或缺乏协调,从而导致资源分配效率低下或对患者造成伤害。正如在医疗设备开发中一样,医疗服务中的流程也非常强调患者安全。患者安全性系统工程干预(SEIPS)(Carayon,2006)等方法侧重于根据以患者为中心的医疗的具体情况调整流程。

TAILORING AND APPLICATION CONSIDERATIONS

Unique Considerations for Medical Devices In contrast to healthcare delivery systems, some medical device and healthcare IT companies use a more traditional form of SE. However, some are heavily tailoring SE approaches to incrementally demonstrate the value of SE. Many devices must work in harsh environments, including inside the human body. Interoperability, interconnectivity, and transportability are increasingly critical for medical devices and SaMDs (Software as Medical Devices). During audits and submissions, regulators require device developers to follow standard quality system processes (e.g., ISO 13485). Standards such as ISO 14971 (application of risk management to medical devices), IEC 60601 (medical device safety), IEC 62304 (Medical Device software—Software life cycle processes), and IEC 62366 (application of usability engineering to medical devices) are driving medical device organizations to take a deeper look into system safety and the engineering practices behind it. Thus, SE practitioners are increasingly being brought on board to leverage their life cycle management skills and support validating that the final product does indeed meet the needs of its stakeholders. In addition to an emphasis on systems safety, the medical device sector is seeing an increasing need for several SE methodologies including, but not limited to, SoS management, stakeholder management, agile systems development, trade analysis, MBSE, and PLE.

Unique Activities, Methods, and Practices Healthcare Systems are often broad in context including a population of diverse patients, many healthcare professionals, many medical devices, many insurance companies, many delivery systems, regulators, and the government. One emphasis of SE practitioners in the biomedical and healthcare domain is patient safety risk, often more so than technical or business risks (see Section 6.1). Traceability is often a key factor in regulatory submissions and audits. Organizations that have strong SE practices are therefore in a better position to avoid pitfalls and to effectively defend their decisions if a regulatory audit does occur. In general, applicable standards do not need to be excessively tailored, although organizations with new or maturing practices may want to focus on lean implementations to obtain early and effective system adoption. Carefully balancing the trades between healthcare costs, better health outcomes for populations, and profits for shareholders is an ongoing challenge for Healthcare SE practitioners. On a larger scale, healthcare SE practitioners that can influence policy and incentives will become even more valuable to their organizations.

医疗设备的独特考虑因素 与医疗卫生服务系统相比，一些医疗设备和医疗卫生 IT 公司采用的是更为传统的系统工程形式。然而，一些公司正在大量定制系统工程实施方法，以逐步证明系统工程的价值。许多设备必须在恶劣环境中工作，包括人体内。互操作性、互连性和可移植性对于医疗设备和 SAMD（软件即医疗设备）越来越重要。在审核和提交流程中，监管机构要求设备开发商遵守标准质量系统流程（如 ISO 13485）。ISO 14971（医疗设备风险管理的应用）、IEC 60601（医疗设备安全）、IEC 62304（医疗设备软件生命周期流程）和 IEC 62366（医疗设备可用性工程的应用）等标准正在推动医疗设备组织更深入地研究系统安全性及其背后的工程实践。因此，系统工程实践者越来越多地参与进来，利用他们的生命周期管理技能和支持来验证最终产品确实满足了利益相关方的需求。除了强调系统安全性外，医疗器械行业对几种系统工程方法的需求也在不断增加，包括但不限于体系管理、利益相关方管理、敏捷系统开发、权衡分析、MBSE 和 PLE。

独特的活动、方法和实践 医疗卫生系统的范围通常很广，包括不同的患者群体、许多医疗卫生专业人员、许多医疗设备、许多保险公司、许多传送系统、监管机构和政府。生物医学和医疗卫生领域的系统工程实践者的一个重点是患者安全性风险，通常比技术或业务风险更重要（见 6.1 节）。可追溯性往往是监管提交和审计的关键因素。因此，拥有强大 SE 实践的组织能够更好地避免陷阱，并在监管审计发生时有效地捍卫其决策。一般来说，适用的标准不需要过度定制，尽管新的或正在成熟的组织可能希望将重点放在精益实施上，以尽早有效地采用系统。谨慎平衡医疗成本、改善人群健康状况和股东利润之间的关系，是医疗卫生系统工程实践者一直面临的挑战。在更大的范围内，能够影响政策和激励的医疗卫生系统工程实践者将对其组织更有价值。

TAILORING AND APPLICATION CONSIDERATIONS

4.4.3 Commercial Aerospace Systems

Overview of SE Applications within the Commercial Aerospace Domain SE is part of the strategies for the development of solutions and products in the commercial aerospace system domain. Commercial aerospace systems are complex, and their complexity continues to increase. The increased use of software makes it possible to implement more functions than before, which contributes to a further increase in complexity. At the same time, the expectation is raised that the increased use of software will make solutions and products available more quickly than the historic mechanical systems of the past. As shown in Figure 4.8, commercial aerospace systems are often part of larger SoSs. Future commercial aerospace systems will include autonomy, artificial intelligence, neural networks, novel propulsion, advanced human system integration (HSI), and cybersecurity.

Commercial aerospace systems use sequential as well as incremental and evolutionary life cycle models, including agile methods with smaller cycles. Thus, the processes in this handbook can be used to address and help organizations manage these new factors derived from complexity settings. The adoption of new technologies and perspectives emphasize some concepts such as the systemic approaches and use of SoS approaches to support organizations by putting them on the forefront of the market with competitive products, adapted to the new reality of increasing interoperability.

Unique Terms & Concepts The commercial aerospace organizations of many countries have specific policies, standards, and guidebooks to guide the application of SE in their organizational environment. For example, ARP 4754A (2010) describes the standard practices for verifying commercial aircraft requirements.

There are many other systems related to this domain. For example, in the aviation domain, there are systems that go far beyond the aircraft itself according to the interaction characteristic of system elements described on system concept definition. Examples include an air traffic control system.

New applications of commercial aerospace systems are being continually introduced. For example, some organizations specifically created to address the new aerospace segment of flying cars have started a great race in a totally different way. By using new methodologies and approaches, these systems are being developed by considering their integration in completely new context. The same is happening with unmanned and autonomous vehicles. These new applications require an understanding of the ecosystem of the new operational contexts, as well as the lifestyles of its users.

4.4.3 商用航空航天系统

商用航空航天领域的系统工程应用概述　　系统工程是商用航空航天系统领域解决方案和产品开发战略的一部分。商用航空航天系统非常复杂，其复杂性不断增加。随着软件使用的增加，可以实现比以前更多的功能，从而进一步提高了复杂性。与此同时，人们还期望与过去历史悠久的机械系统相比，越来越多地使用软件能更快地提供解决方案和产品。如图 4.8 所示，商用航空航天系统通常是大型体系的一部分。未来的商用航空航天系统将包括自主、人工智能、神经网络、新型推进系统、先进的人与系统综合（HSI）和网络安全。

商用航空航天系统使用顺序的、增量的和演进的生命周期模型，包括具有较小周期的敏捷方法。因此，本手册中的流程可用于解决和帮助组织管理这些源自复杂环境的新因素。新技术和新视角的采用强调了一些概念，如系统的实施方法和体系实施方法的使用，以支持组织通过具有竞争力的产品站在市场前沿，适应互操作性日益增强的新现实。

独特的术语和概念　　许多国家的商用航空航天组织都有具体的政策、标准和指南，以指导系统工程在其组织环境中的应用。例如，ARP 4754A（2010）描述了验证商用飞机需求的标准实践。

还有许多其他系统与此领域相关。例如，在航空领域，根据系统概念定义中描述的系统元素的交互特性，有一些系统远远超出了飞机本身。例如空中交通管制系统。

商用航空航天系统的新应用正在不断引入。例如，一些专门针对飞行汽车这一新的航空航天领域而成立的组织，以完全不同的方式开始了一场伟大的竞赛。通过使用新的方法论和实施方法，这些系统的开发考虑到了它们在全新环境下的综合。无人驾驶和自动驾驶车辆也是如此。这些新应用需要了解新运行背景环境的生态系统及其用户的生活方式。

TAILORING AND APPLICATION CONSIDERATIONS

Unique Activities, Methods, and Practices SE may help the realization of effective commercial aerospace systems through the following activities, methods, and practices:

- **Stakeholders.** Stakeholders vary greatly and can range from federal government services, to aircraft manufacturers, to passengers.
- **Design and construction practices.** Model-based design is generally used from construction model specifications, which enables and maintains traceability between requirements and models.
- **Interfaces.** Because commercial aerospace systems' system elements are developed in various parts of the world and brought to a single (or multiple) location for assembly, adherence to interface management principles is critical.
- **Risk management.** Risk management is essential, especially for the introduction of new technologies.
- **Safety.** Finally, it is important for SE management to assure that safety is not compromised by organizational factors, as described by Paté-Cornell (1990).

Examples of how SE helps is resolving unique domain challenges include:

For aircraft original equipment manufacturers (OEMs), SE:

- Helps in design and manufacturing of aircraft subsystems, assembly and integration testing using well-defined process, standards, and quality standards.
- Offers well-defined approaches to create designs or architectures, processes, and roadmaps for proper interfaces, instrumentation, and communications that enable better visibility of the static and dynamic operational data and status of the subsystems.
- Enables operators and enterprises to scale up without compromising quality of production using a well-defined SE framework, tools, and emerging technologies.
- Enables better insights and control of congestion and traffic control of many schedules like flights, passenger, luggage, and food.
- Augments user experience of various stakeholders by system level integration of emerging digital technologies like augmented reality and virtual reality for enriched cockpit and instruments.

独特的活动、方法和实践　系统工程可通过以下活动、方法和实践帮助实现有效的商用航空航天系统：

- **利益相关方**。利益相关方差异很大，范围从联邦政府部门、飞机制造商到乘客。
- **设计和构建实践**。基于模型的设计一般是从构造模型规范开始使用的，这样可以实现并保持需求与模型之间的可追溯性。
- **接口**。由于商用航空航天系统的系统元件是在世界各地开发的，并被带到一个（或多个）位置进行组装，因此遵守接口管理原则至关重要。
- **风险管理**。风险管理至关重要，尤其是在引进新技术时。
- **安全**。最后，正如 Paté-Cornell（1990）所述，系统工程管理必须确保安全性不受组织因素的影响。

系统工程帮助解决独特领域挑战的例子包括：

对于飞机原始设备制造商（OEMs），系统工程：

- 采用明确的流程、标准和质量标准，帮助设计和制造飞机子系统、组装和综合测试。
- 提供定义良好的实施方法，为适当的接口、仪器和通信创建设计或架构、流程和路线图，从而更好地查看静态和动态运行数据以及子系统的状态。
- 使用定义良好的系统工程框架、工具和新兴技术，使操作人员和复杂组织体系能够在不影响生产质量的情况下扩大规模。
- 能够更好地洞察和控制拥堵情况，以及航班、乘客、行李和食品等众多日程的交通管制。
- 通过系统级综合新兴数字技术（如增强现实技术和虚拟现实技术），为丰富的驾驶舱和仪器增强各种利益相关方的用户体验。

TAILORING AND APPLICATION CONSIDERATIONS

For airlines, SE:

- Helps in the support stage, to maintain the fleet.
- Helps balance performance and environmental impacts.
- Offers a set of procedures and activities to manage the services that consider human resources, information, and operation data.

Other Unique Considerations SE is increasingly being applied in commercial practice. Petersen and Sutcliffe (1992), for example, discuss the principles of SE as applied to aircraft development. Life cycle functions of the commercial aerospace industry gives SE its own unique characteristics.

4.4.4 Defense Systems

Overview of SE Applications within the Defense Domain While SE has been practiced in some form from antiquity, what has now become known as the modern definition of SE has its roots in defense systems of the twentieth century. It became recognized as a distinct activity in the late 1950s and early 1960s due to technological advances taking place that led to increasing levels of system complexity and systems integration challenges, and the need for SE further increased with the large-scale introduction of digital computers and software.

SE within defense evolved to address systemic approaches to issues such as the widespread adaptation of COTS technologies and the use of SoS approaches. It offers well-defined designs/architecture, processes and roadmaps for proper interfacing, networking, and communications. This enables better integrity and interoperability of real-time intelligence data across various devices, from various vendors, and platforms using open industry standards. Today, with increasing emphasis on networks and capabilities the defense organizations of many countries are recognizing the criticality of end-to-end SoS performance and increasing focus on integration to deliver these capabilities.

Unique Considerations Defense systems have numerous characteristics and consequently, a huge complexity, making SE essential for their development:

- They are complex technical systems with many stakeholders and compressed development timelines.
- The systems must be highly available and work in extreme conditions all over the world—from deserts to rain forests and to arctic outposts.

对于航空公司，系统工程：

- 在支持阶段帮助维护机队。

- 有助于平衡绩效和环境影响。

- 提供一套程序和活动，以管理考虑人力资源、信息和运行数据的服务。

其他独特考虑因素　系统工程越来越多地应用于商用实践中。例如，Petersen 和 Sutcliffe（1992）讨论了系统工程应用于飞机开发的原则。商用航空航天行业的生命周期功能使系统工程具有自身的独特性。

4.4.4 防务系统

防务领域 SE 应用概述　虽然系统工程从古代就开始以某种形式进行实践，但现在系统工程的现代定义源于 20 世纪的防务系统。在 20 世纪 50 年代末和 60 年代初，由于技术进步导致系统复杂性和系统综合挑战不断增加，对系统工程的需要随着数字计算机和软件的大规模引入而进一步增加，因此它被认为是一项独特的活动。

防务领域内的系统工程逐渐演进，以解决系统性问题，如 COTS 技术的广泛应用和体系实施方法的使用。它为适当的接口、网络和通信提供了定义良好的设计/架构、流程和路线图。这使得使用开放行业标准的各种设备、供应商和平台的实时智能数据能够具有更好的完整性和互操作性。如今，随着对网络和能力的日益重视，许多国家的防务组织正在认识到端到端体系性能的重要性，并越来越重视综合以提供这些能力。

独特的考虑因素

防务系统具有许多特征，因此具有巨大的复杂性，因此系统工程对其发展至关重要：

- 它们是复杂的技术系统，有许多利益相关方，并且开发时间紧迫。

- 系统必须高度可用，并在世界各地的极端条件下工作，从沙漠到雨林，再到北极前哨。

TAILORING AND APPLICATION CONSIDERATIONS

- There are long system life cycles, so logistics is of prime importance.

- There is typically a strong human interaction, so usability/human systems integration is critical for successful operations.

- There is at times a need for defense operators and enterprises to accelerate development and production (e.g., quick response in event of national emergency or increased threats) without compromising quality of operations using a well-defined SE framework, tools, and emerging technologies

Unique Activities, Methods, and Practices SE has a strong heritage in defense, and much of the SE processes in this handbook can be used as is in a straightforward manner, with normal project tailoring to address unique aspects of the project. It is important to note that as ISO/IEC/IEEE 15288 (2023) has evolved into a more domain- and countryneutral SE standard, so care must be taken to ensure that the defense focus is reasserted upon application. An example of specific implementation of ISO/IEC/IEEE 15288 when utilized for US Department of Defense projects is provided in IEEE 15288.1 (2014). This standard provides the basis for selection, negotiation, agreement, and performance of necessary SE activities and delivery of products. Additionally, the standard allows flexibility for both innovative implementation and tailoring of the specific SE processes to be used by system suppliers, either contractors or government system developers, integrators, maintainers, or sustainers. The defense organizations of many countries also have specific policies, standards, and guidebooks to guide the application of SE in their environment.

4.4.5 Infrastructure Systems

Overview of SE Applications within the Infrastructure Domain This section addresses physical capital projects infrastructure including public works, transport, complex buildings, and industrial facilities. Within the infrastructure domain, SE practices are more developed in the high-technology system elements that involve software development, control systems, system security, or system safety. Infrastructure projects tend to define the high-level design solution without requirements decomposition, allocation, or interface identification. Architectures, traceability, and relationships within the project are often implied rather than specified. Infrastructure owners can benefit by applying SE to provide systematic, formal, verifiable connections between the business needs and the final product.

- 系统生命周期长，因此后勤至关重要。
- 人与人之间通常有很强的互动性，因此可用性/人机与系统综合对于成功运行至关重要。
- 防务运营商和操作人员复杂组织体系有时需要使用定义明确的系统工程框架、工具和新兴技术，在不影响作战运行质量的情况下，加快开发和生产（例如，在国家紧急情况或威胁增加的情况下快速响应）。

独特的活动、方法和实践 系统工程在防务方面有着很强的传统，本手册中的许多系统工程流程可以直接使用，通过常规的项目剪裁来解决项目的独特方面。需要注意的是，随着 ISO/IEC/IEEE 15288（2023）已发展成为一个更具领域性和国家中立性的系统工程标准，因此必须小心的确保在应用时重新确定防务重点。IEEE 15288.1（2014）提供了美国国防部项目使用 ISO/IEC/IEEE 15288 的具体实施示例。本标准为必要的系统工程活动和产品交付的选择、谈判、协议和执行提供了依据。此外，该标准允许系统供应商、承包商或政府系统开发人员、综合商人员、维护人员或维持人员灵活地创新实施和定制特定系统工程流程。许多国家的防务组织也有具体的政策、标准和指南，以指导系统工程在其环境中的应用。

4.4.5 基础设施系统

基础设施领域的系统工程应用概述 本节介绍有形资本项目基础设施，包括公共工程、交通、综合建筑和工业设施。在基础设施领域内，系统工程实践在涉及软件开发、控制系统、系统安保或系统安全的高科技系统元素中得到了更大的发展。基础设施项目倾向于定义高层设计解决方案，而无须进行需求分解、分配或接口识别。项目中的架构、可追溯性和关系通常是隐含的，而不是指定的。基础设施所有者可以通过应用系统工程，在业务需求和最终产品之间建立系统的、形式化的、可验证的联系，从而从中获益。

TAILORING AND APPLICATION CONSIDERATIONS

Unique Terms and Concepts Infrastructure projects are distinguished from manufacturing and production, as they usually focus on unique, large physical systems where construction takes place on site rather than in a factory. These projects are adapted and integrated to existing environments, and are often characterized by loosely defined boundaries, evolving system architectures, multiphase implementation efforts which can exceed a few decades, and multiple-decade asset life cycles. As a result, stakeholders' expectations and design solutions evolve over an extended timeframe. Unlike other SE domains, most infrastructure projects cannot be standardized and do not involve a prototype.

Many of the processes described in this handbook can be used to manage infrastructure projects but in some cases with different terminology, as illustrated in Table 4.7. There are some areas where existing infrastructure practices could be adjusted slightly to better align with SE practices.

TABLE 4.7 Infrastructure and SE definition correlation

Systems Engineering Term	Infrastructure Term	Recommendation
Acquirer	Owner or Agency	
Acquisition	Contracting phase; Procurement	Share good practices and lessons learned to improve procurement documents to enable better owner control of the project.
Business requirements	Project need; Business case	Derives contractor requirements from the business requirements, hold requirement reviews and include in the contractors' scope.
Configuration control	Versioning	Configuration identification, change management, status accounting, configuration audit according to ISO 10007 (2017).
Decision gate	Milestone	Clearly define entry and exit criteria for decision gates
Life cycle	Project life cycle	Include how the infrastructure will deliver its intended function and long-term asset management. Add in contractor's scope expectations that will benefit the entire project life cycle.
Performance requirement	Often found in Technical Specifications	Allocate top-level system performance requirements to system elements, defining performance requirements. Best performed by the acquiring entity unless the procurement method is a PPP.
Requirements	Design Criteria; Scope of Work; or Specifications	Integrate full life cycle considerations into design criteria, including operations, maintenance, and disposal/replacement planning.

独特的术语和概念 基础设施项目不同于制造业和生产项目，因为它们通常侧重于独特的大型物理系统，施工在现场而不是在工厂进行。这些项目根据现有环境进行调整和综合，其特点通常是定义松散的边界、不断发展的系统架构、可能超过几十年的多阶段实施工作以及数十年的资产生命周期。因此，利益相关方的期望和设计解决方案会随着时间的延长而演进。与其他系统工程领域不同，大多数基础设施项目无法标准化，并且不涉及原型。

本手册中描述的许多流程可用于管理基础设施项目，但在某些情况下使用不同的术语，如表 4.7 所示。在某些领域，现有的基础设施实践可以稍作调整，以更好地与系统工程实践保持一致。

表 4.7 基础设施与系统工程定义的相关性

系统工程术语	基础设施术语	建议
采办方	所有者或代理	
采办	承包阶段；采办	分享良好做法和经验教训，以改进采办文件，使所有者能够更好地控制项目
业务需求	项目需要；商用用例	从业务需求中获取承包商需求，进行需求评审，并将其纳入承包商的范围
构型配置控制	版本控制	根据 ISO 10007（2017）进行配置标识、变更管理、状态审核、配置审核
决策门	里程碑	明确定义决策门的进入和退出准则
生命周期	项目生命周期	包括基础设施如何实现其预期功能和长期资产管理。加入将有利于整个项目生命周期的承包商范围期望
性能需求	常用于技术规格	将顶层系统性能需求分配给系统元素，定义性能需求。除非采办方法为 PPP，否则最好由采办实体执行
需求	设计准则；工作范围；规格	将全生命周期考虑纳入设计准则，包括运行、维护和处置/更换计划

TAILORING AND APPLICATION CONSIDERATIONS

(Continued)

Systems Engineering Term	Infrastructure Term	Recommendation
Supplier	Design Consultant; Contractor	Use requirements management to strengthen procurement language and enforce contract requirements during the project. Clearly define acceptance criteria and performance measures.
System architecture	Context diagram; Schematics; Process and Instrumentation Diagrams	Consider creating early in project life cycle to support requirement allocation and interface management. Use ICDs or N^2 diagrams to complement the system architecture.
Verification	Design Review; Quality Control (QC)/Quality Assurance (QA)	Provide sufficient schedule and budget for both QC and QA activities, including specific audit periods and "pens down" dates for each milestone. In the design phase, confirm the design meets requirements (QC), and procedures were followed (QA)
Validation	Construction Inspection; Quality Control (QC) / Quality Assurance (QA)	Include sufficient budget and authority for QA to ensure compliance. Ensure acceptance testing refers back to stakeholder needs and includes a focus on whether it meets its intended use.

INCOSE SEH original table created by Kouassi on behalf of the INCOSE Infrastructure Working Group members. Usage per the INCOSE Notices page. All other rights reserved.

Unique Activities, Methods, and Practices SE may help the realization of effective infrastructure systems through the following activities, methods, and practices:

- **Stakeholders.** Stakeholders can range from governmental legislators who control funding for the project, to local/regional agencies that add beautification needs, to landowners with adjacent property impacted by a proposed project. In all government-funded projects, segments of the public may also be a stakeholder group. The wide array of potential stakeholders makes requirements gathering, cost, and schedules volatile. Public and political pressure can cause premature initiation of projects, with incomplete project scope and ill-defined metrics.

- **Design and construction practices.** Within infrastructure, the engineering disciplines have well-established, traditional practices and are guided by independent industry codes and standards that are not shared between disciplines. Design requirements are generally dissociated from construction specifications, therefore limiting traceability between design and construction.

剪裁和应用的考虑因素

（续）

系统工程术语	基础设施术语	建议
供应方	设计顾问；承包商	在项目期间利用需求管理加强采办语言并强化承包需求。明确定义验收准则和性能度量
系统架构	背景环境图；示意图；流程和计装图	考虑在项目生命周期的早期创建，以支持需求分配和接口管理。使用 ICD 或 N^2 图补充系统架构
验证	设计评审；质量控制（QC）；质量保证（QA）	为 QC 和 QA 活动提供充足的时间表和预算，包括特定审核期和"关闭"每个里程碑的日期。在设计阶段，确认设计符合需求（QC），并遵循程序（QA）
确认	施工检查；质量控制（QC）/质量保证（QA）	包括足够的预算和 QA 权限，以确保符合性。确保验收测试参考利益相关方需要并关注其是否满足预期用途

INCOSE SEH 原始表由 Kouassi 代表 INCOSE 基础设施工作组成员创建。按照 INCOSE 通知页使用。版权所有。

独特的活动、方法和实践 系统工程可通过以下活动、方法和实践帮助实现有效的基础设施系统：

- **利益相关方**。利益相关方包括控制项目资金的政府立法者、提出市容美化需要的地方/地区机构，以及受拟建项目影响的相邻物业的土地所有者。在所有政府资助的项目中，公众群体也可能是利益相关方群体。广泛的潜在利益相关方使得需求收集、成本和进度不稳定。公众和政治压力可能导致项目过早启动，项目范围不完整，指标定义不明确。

- **设计和施工实践**。在基础设施领域，工程学科有着良好的传统实践，并以独立的行业规范和标准为指导，这些规范和标准在各学科之间并不共享。设计要求通常与施工规范分离，因此限制了设计和施工之间的可追溯性。

TAILORING AND APPLICATION CONSIDERATIONS

- **Interfaces.** Infrastructure projects have external, often uncontrollable interfaces that can impact the project. Interfaces can include existing built systems, natural systems, environmental, and other internal and external dynamics.

- **Risks.** The contractual framework and allocation of liability and commercial risk are major factors impacting procurement and contracting processes. SE practices may therefore help to manage risk associated with cost estimating, changing scope, system integration, and verification. They may also improve construction productivity, making infrastructure development more cost-effective.

Other Unique Considerations SE concepts are relatively newly applied in the infrastructure domain. As the application of SE grows within the infrastructure domain, an effort should be made to train engineering discipline specialists in SE concepts. Four key SE processes are useful to introduce SE on infrastructure projects: requirements management, interface management, verification, and validation. These processes can improve infrastructure project delivery, and total life cycle view that integrates design, construction, and asset management.

4.4.6 Oil and Gas Systems

Overview of SE Applications within the Oil and Gas Domain The emergence of SE within the Oil and Gas (O&G) domain is relatively new compared to other sectors of similar complexity. Most applications of SE have occurred within the past decade to varying levels of implementation. Due to fluctuation in oil prices, new systems with increasing complexity and efforts to reduce greenhouse gas emissions have motivated a risk-averse industry to adapt to, and in some cases drive, change. This has encouraged an entire culture known to resist change to challenge assumptions and traditional ways of working, especially working in a document-centric environment.

The greatest SE-related need has been in the system requirements definition and requirements management space. With a domain-wide focus on digitalization, the change in how requirements are defined and transmitted throughout the supply chain has benefited from an SE approach. The industry leaders have either switched, or are switching, to data-centric requirement sets. There has been collaboration between suppliers and acquirers to improve the quality and traceability of requirements and create metrics for measurement of progress. INCOSE and American Petroleum Institute (API) cooperated on some trials in 2017 and 2018 that explained the aims and elements of good requirement writing to a panel of experts involved in updating a standard. They then supported the engineers in the writing and recrafting of the content, resulting in higher quality requirements and clearly separating between instruction, information, and verification (IOGP, 2021).

- **接口**。基础设施项目具有外部的、通常无法控制的接口，这些接口可能会影响项目。接口可以包括现有的建筑系统、自然系统、环境以及其他内部和外部动态因素。

- **风险**。合同框架、职责分配和商用风险是影响采办和合同流程的主要因素。因此，系统工程实践可能有助于管理与成本估算、变更范围、系统综合和验证相关的风险。它们还可以提高施工生产率，使基础设施开发更具成本效益。

其他独特考虑因素 系统工程概念在基础设施领域的应用相对较新。随着系统工程在基础设施领域的应用不断增长，应努力在系统工程概念方面培训工程学科专家。四个关键的系统工程流程有助于在基础设施项目中引入系统工程：需求管理、接口管理、验证和确认。这些流程可以改进基础设施项目交付，以及综合设计、施工和资产管理的全生命周期视图。

4.4.6 油气系统

系统工程在油气领域的应用概述 与其他具有类似复杂性的行业相比，在油气领域出现的系统工程相对较新。系统工程在油气领域的大多数应用都发生在过去十年中，实现程度各不相同。由于油价波动、新系统日益复杂以及减少温室气体排放的努力，促使规避风险的行业适应变化，在某些情况下推动了变化。这鼓励了一种抵制变革的文化，以挑战假设和传统的工作方式，尤其是在以文档为中心的环境中工作。

与系统工程相关的最大需要是系统需求定义和需求管理空间。随着整个领域对数字化的重视，需求定义和需求在整个供应链中传输方式的变化得益于系统工程的实施方法。行业领导者已经或正在转向以数据为中心的需求集。供应商和采办方之间进行了协作，以提高需求的质量和可追溯性，并创建测量进度的指标。INCOSE 和美国石油协会（API）在 2017 年和 2018 年进行了一些试验，向参与标准更新的专家小组解释了良好需求书写的目的和元素。然后，他们支持工程师编写和重新编辑内容，从而提出更高质量的要求需求，并明确区分指导、信息和验证（IOGP，2021）。

TAILORING AND APPLICATION CONSIDERATIONS

Beyond requirements, additional SE practices are also being introduced in the O&G domain. For example, SE practitioners take advantage of requirement definition to develop system architectures and systematically define interfaces. By using requirement management tools, configuration management and change management of requirements can be implemented in projects. In other cases, systems thinking tools, such as context diagrams and functional trees, are used as a foundation for SE practices, such as functional modeling. Technical requirements are also leading to conversations and implementation of verification and validation strategies and realization. With the companies incorporating digital design data across disciplines and throughout the life cycle, the digitalization of requirements has led to the auto-creation of specifications and test plans.

254 *Unique Considerations for SE within Oil and Gas*   One of the challenges when considering SE in O&G is that it is difficult to evaluate the entire domain as one. The long and complicated supply chain includes diverse and segmented companies across the globe. And it is not solely crude oil or natural gas. With the current energy transition affecting all aspects of engineering, most O&G companies have been shifting focus from fossil-based systems to include renewable sources that are efficient solutions with net-zero emissions. Many oil and gas companies have targets of net-zero greenhouse gas emissions for operations by 2050.

Another challenge for the domain is that since SE has not been implemented as a holistic approach, there are pockets of SE maturity that do not always intersect. This is a result of most O&G companies following a well-established and practiced sequential (waterfall) stage gate process. Therefore, SE implementation is generally only implemented where a clear case for change is needed and demonstrated, or when all other approaches have been exhausted. To help with this, the INCOSE O&G working group developed a scalable presentation for various high-level conversations and presenting success case studies from participating O&G companies. One area where SE continues to gain traction and show value is in new product development projects. By introducing SE principles and methods early in the project, the project team can see the benefits of applying SE and embrace the changes to the traditional ways of working.

4.4.7   Power & Energy Systems

Overview of SE Applications within the Power and Energy Domain   During the first two decades of the twenty-first century, the global energy system has been subject to a complex set of requirements stemming from the Paris Agreement, the United Nations Sustainable Development Goals (see Section 3.1.10), reduction in greenhouse gas emissions, and other efforts to avoid degradation of our social foundations and ecological ceiling (Raworth, 2017).

除了需求之外，在油气领域还引入了其他系统工程实践。例如，系统工程实践者利用需求定义来开发系统架构并系统地定义接口。通过使用需求管理工具，可以在项目中实现需求的构型配置管理和变更管理。在其他情况下，系统思维工具（如背景环境图和功能树）被用作系统工程实践（如功能建模）的基础。技术需求也导致了验证和确认策略的对话和实施以及实现。随着公司将跨学科和整个生命周期的数字设计数据进行整合，需求的数字化带来了规范和测试计划的自动创建。

油气领域中系统工程的独特考虑因素　在油气领域考虑系统工程的挑战之一是很难将整个领域作为一个整体进行评估。这条漫长而复杂的供应链包括全球范围内各种各样的细分公司。而且不仅仅是原油或天然气。随着当前能源转型影响到工程的各个方面，大多数油气公司已经将重点从基于化石的系统转移到包括可再生能源，这些可再生能源是零排放的高效解决方案。许多石油和天然气公司的目标是到2050年实现运营过程中温室气体的净零排放。

该领域面临的另一个挑战是，由于系统工程并未作为一种整体方法来实施，因此系统工程的成熟度不一定总是相互交叉的。这是因为大多数石油和天然气公司都采用了成熟的顺序式（瀑布式）阶段门流程。因此，系统工程实施通常仅在需要和证明明确的变更用例时，或在用尽所有其他实施方法时实施。为此，INCOSE油气工作组开发了一个可扩展的演示文稿，用于各种高层对话，并介绍参与的油气公司的成功案例研究。在新产品开发项目中，系统工程不断受到重视并显示出价值。通过在项目早期引入系统工程原则和方法，项目团队可以看到应用系统工程的好处，并接受对传统工作方式的改变。

4.4.7　电力和能源系统

系统工程在电力和能源领域的应用概述　在21世纪的前20年，全球能源系统一直受到《巴黎协定》、联合国可持续发展目标（见3.1.10节）、减少温室气体排放以及避免社会基础和生态上限退化的其他努力所产生的一系列复杂要求的制约（Raworth，2017）。要为如此复杂的一组问题提供有效的解决方案，

TAILORING AND APPLICATION CONSIDERATIONS

To provide an effective solution for such a complex set of problems demands the realization, or modification, of many new systems, elements, and enabling systems supported by a holistic systems approach. The United Kingdom's (UK) Council for Science and Technology stated with respect to the UK's Net Zero ambitions that "by drawing on SE principles, a detailed and credible plan can provide the framework required to drive change, give reassurance to businesses, investors and consumers, and engage the whole of society in delivering this change" (CST, 2020).

At the heart of the sustainability transition is the convergence of business, technology, and socio-politics to guide innovation around what is viable, feasible, and desirable. This new intersection of disciplines can be enabled through SE. Yet many incumbent organizations and legacy approaches dominate the power and energy landscape, meaning a change in thinking or practice is resisted, or even directly opposed. As a result, the application of SE in power and energy remains largely immature in the first quarter of the twenty-first century compared to more established sectors such as defense, space, and transportation. A cultural shift toward shared knowledge management systems, portfolio management, and organization infrastructure is required to fully embrace and adopt SE.

Unique Terms and Concepts The language used in SE is made effective through SE heuristics or when translated to real-world examples in the power and energy context. For example, an SoS may be considered an abstract SE term, yet it perfectly describes the nature of distributed energy resources.

Unique Activities, Methods, and Practices SE may help the realization of effective power and energy systems through the following activities, methods, and practices:

- **Architecture and design.** Provides robust architecture, design, and development processes for higher integrity and interoperability across the supply chain infrastructure from upstream (e.g., solar plant, nuclear, wind farms), mid-stream (e.g., large-scale storage, energy vector processing, transmission and distribution networks) and downstream (e.g., retail outlets, local area networks, domestic microgeneration, private storage).
- **Risks.** Enables better identification and handling of risks associated with energy security and resilience.
- **Portfolio management.** Provides the platform for joined up roadmaps and communication channels which enables stakeholder acceptance, transition, and utilization of emerging paradigms such as smart grids, district heat networks, renewable technologies, demand side response, and electric vehicles.

就需要在整体系统实施方法的支持下，实现或修改许多新的系统、要素和使能系统。英国科学技术委员会就英国的净零排放目标表示，"通过借鉴系统工程原则，一个详细而可信的计划可以提供推动变革所需的框架，让企业、投资者和消费者放心，并让整个社会参与实现这一变革"（CST，2020）。

可持续性转型的核心是业务、技术和社会政治的融合，以指导围绕可行、可能和可取的创新。这种新的学科交叉可以通过系统工程来实现。然而，许多现有组织和遗留方法仍然主导着电力和能源领域，这意味着思维或实践的改变受到抵制，甚至直接遭到反对。因此，与防务、航天和交通等更成熟的领域相比，系统工程在电力和能源领域的应用在21世纪的前25年仍很不成熟。为了完全接受和采用系统工程，就必须在共享知识管理系统、项目群组合管理和组织基础设施方面进行文化转变。

独特的术语和概念　系统工程中使用的语言通过系统工程启发式方法或在电力和能源背景环境中翻译为现实世界的示例时才会变得有效。例如，体系可能被认为是一个抽象的系统工程术语，但它完美地描述了分布式能源的性质。

独特的活动、方法和实践　系统工程可通过以下活动、方法和实践帮助实现有效的电力和能源系统：

- **架构和设计**。提供稳健的架构、设计和开发流程，以提高上游（如太阳能发电厂、核能发电厂、风电场）、中游（如大规模存储、能源矢量处理、传输和配电网络）和下游（如零售店、局域网、国内微型发电、私人存储）供应链基础设施的完整性和互操作性。

- **风险**。能够更好地识别和处理与能源安保和强韧性相关的风险。

- **项目群组合管理**。为联合路线图和沟通渠道提供平台，使利益相关方能够接受、过渡和利用新兴范式，如智能电网、地区热网、可再生技术、需求侧响应和电动汽车。

TAILORING AND APPLICATION CONSIDERATIONS

- **Sustainability.** Enables better management of reductions in greenhouse gas emissions through robust technical and management processes with a whole life cycle perspective, open industry standards, quality management, and assurance.

Other Unique Considerations Power and energy systems are typically at the SoS level, so activities follow the key characteristics and challenges associated with an SoS. As an example, achieving the goal of energy security requires as much understanding of geo-politics as it does the evolution of cybersecurity as digitalization grows.

The application of SE needs to transcend geographic boundaries and domain silos. For example, consideration for how SE supports the implementation of the Clydebank declaration, which calls for the establishment of green shipping corridors for zero-emission maritime transport between shipping ports, presents an energy, transport, and logistics challenge on an international scale.

On a global scale, power and energy systems must remain persistently operational for billions of system users whilst maintaining a constant state of equilibrium with demand balanced by supply (augmented by flexibility solutions such as demand side response and storage). In addition, power and energy systems typically have a life cycle of 30-100 years or even into the thousands of years for end-of-life decommissioning and waste storage from nuclear fission facilities. These considerations form complexity multipliers for the sustainable energy transition.

Adapting the mental models and behaviors of system users will be crucial to effecting change. This demands elements of social sciences, systems science, and systems thinking to complement the rigor of SE processes. To support this, there is a need to provide feedback mechanisms to influence the micro-behavior of the human actors in the system in such a way as to maintain the macro-stability of the system (Sillitto, 2010) achieved through HSI (see Section 3.1.4). But SE cannot focus on change in human behaviors without consideration for market dynamics and political levers. SE can help provide the coherence and joined-up thinking necessary to make energy policy an enabling system for delivering the overarching goals of energy decarbonization, digitalization, decentralization, and democratization. We must also avoid the trap of pushing technology solutions that deliver undesirable user experience. Considerations range from consumer price point, to acoustic noise of technologies, to retrofit disruptions, to the availability of energy in remote or isolated communities. Our challenge, as future ancestors, will be to find ways to support growing energy demands whilst delivering a sustainable energy supply chain that is available and affordable to everyone on a global scale.

- **可持续性**：从全生命周期的角度出发，通过健全的技术和管理流程、开放的行业标准、质量管理和保证，更好地管理温室气体减排。

其他独特考虑因素 电力和能源系统通常处于体系层级，因此活动遵循与体系相关的关键特征和挑战。例如，要达到能源安全的目标，既需要了解地缘政治，也需要了解随着数字化发展的网络安全的演变。

系统工程的应用需要超越地理边界和领域壁垒。例如，考虑系统工程如何支持实施《克莱德班克宣言》，该宣言呼吁为航运港口之间的零排放海上运输建立绿色航运走廊，这在国际范围内对能源、运输和物流提出了挑战。

在全球范围内，电力和能源系统必须为数十亿系统用户保持持续运行，同时保持需求与供应平衡的恒定状态（通过需求侧响应和存储等灵活解决方案来增强）。此外，电力和能源系统的生命周期通常为 30~100 年，核裂变设施的报废和废物储存甚至长达数千年。这些因素构成了可持续能源转型的复杂性倍增。

适应系统用户的心智模型和行为对于实现更改至关重要。这需要社会科学、系统科学和系统思维等要素来补充系统工程流程的严密性。为此，有必要提供反馈机制，以影响系统中人类行为者参与者的微观行为，从而通过人与系统综合维持系统的宏观稳定性（Sillitto，2010）（见 3.1.4 节）。但是，系统工程不能只关注人类行为的改变，而不考虑市场动态和政治杠杆。系统工程可以帮助提供必要的一致和联合的思维，使能源政策成为实现能源去碳化、数字化、去中心化和民主化等总体目标的有利系统。我们还必须避免陷入推崇带来不良用户体验的技术解决方案的陷阱。考虑因素包括消费者价位、技术的声学噪音、改造的干扰，以及偏远或孤立社区的能源供应。作为未来的祖先，我们面临的挑战是找到支持日益增长的能源需求的方法，同时在全球范围内为每个人提供可负担得起的可持续能源供应链。

4.4.8 Space Systems

Overview of SE Applications within the Space Domain Space systems are systems that are designed to operate and perform tasks into and within the space environment. This may consist of: spacecraft (and their associated payloads and instruments); mission packages(s); ground stations; data links between spacecraft and ground, launch systems; and directly related supporting infrastructure. Due to the relatively high costs of deploying assets into earth orbit or beyond, space systems typically require high reliability with little maintenance other than software changes (note that designing for maintainability in space one of the many trade-offs that need to be considered during conceptual design). This makes it necessary for all system elements to work the first time or be compensated by operational workarounds; this can impact the risk posture of the system being developed.

The space domain has evolved into three main areas of interest, with some overlap:

- Civil,
- Commercial, and
- National Security Space.

Each of these areas have their own motivations that can influence the way they develop systems.

Unique Activities, Methods, and Practices Key emphases of SE in the space domain are integration, verification (including testing), and validation of highly reliable, well-characterized systems. Risk management is also key in determining when to incorporate new technologies and how to react to changing requirements through multiyear developments and programmatic challenges. SE provides coordination for multi-disciplinary engineering expertise that enables optimized designs.

Civil systems are typically acquired by government agencies, which typically focus on performance risk, determining when to incorporate new technologies, and how to react to changing requirements through multiyear developments and programmatic challenges. This lends itself to the use of the sequential approaches, such as the SE Vee model, or, in some cases, the waterfall model.

Commercial systems strive for profitability (cost and schedule) and are more amenable to using incremental and evolutionary approaches. This allows them to deploy systems faster, and rapidly gain experience that can improve later iterations of their product.

4.4.8 空间系统

空间领域系统工程应用概述 空间系统是设计用于在空间环境中运行和执行任务的系统。这可能包括：航天器（及其相关的有效载荷和仪器）；任务包；地面站；航天器与地面、发射系统之间的数据链路；以及直接相关的支持基础设施。由于将资产部署到地球轨道或更远的轨道的成本相对较高，空间系统通常需要高可靠性，除软件更改外，几乎不需要维护（请注意，在空间进行可维护性设计是概念设计期间需要考虑的众多权衡之一）。这就要求所有系统元素都必须在第一次运行时就能正常工作，否则就需要通过操作变通来弥补；这可能会影响正在开发的系统的风险态势。

空间领域已演进为三个主要的关注领域，但有一些重叠：

- 民用领域；
- 商用领域；
- 国家安全空间领域。

每个领域都有自己的动机，这些动机可以影响他们开发系统的方式。

独特的活动、方法和实践 系统工程在空间领域的关键重点是高度可靠、特性良好的系统的综合、验证（包括测试）和确认。风险管理也是决定何时采用新技术以及如何通过多年开发应对不断变化的需求和计划中的挑战的关键。系统工程为实现优化设计的多学科工程专业知识提供协调。

民用系统通常由政府机构购置，政府机构通常关注性能风险，确定何时采用新技术，以及如何通过多年开发应对不断变化的需求和计划中的挑战。这有助于使用顺序方法，例如系统工程 V 模型，或者在某些情况下是瀑布模型。

商用系统致力于盈利（成本和进度），并且更易于使用增量和进化的实施方法。这使他们能够更快地部署系统，并快速获得可以改进其产品后续迭代的经验。

TAILORING AND APPLICATION CONSIDERATIONS

National Security Space, much like Civil, may emphasize performance over cost and schedule, and have traditionally used the Vee and waterfall models for development. They typically are more tolerant of accepting risk from the injection of new technologies.

Unique Standards Overall, proper application of SE in the space domain helps in design and development of space elements for easier manufacturing and lowering maintenance cost using well-defined processes and standards. SE offers well-defined architecture and design processes and roadmaps for proper interfacing, networking, and communications that enable better integrity and interoperability of space systems and elements provided by various contractors, and across the supply chain using open industry standards.

Civil, commercial, and national security entities have their own drivers that determine how standards are created and adopted. Most space-faring nations and international consortiums have developed and adopted their own standards that are specific for space systems. Some examples include:

- In the United States, the Department of Defense has created Military (or "Mil") Standards that have been readily adopted by both Civil and Commercial primarily due to the need for high reliability and survivability in a hostile environment. NASA has also created a set of technical standards, as has the AIAA and other organizations.

- The European Cooperation for Space Standardization is an initiative established to develop a coherent, single set of user-friendly standards for use in all European space activities.

- The Euro-Asian Council for Standardization, Metrology and Certification, a regional standards organization operating under the auspices of the Commonwealth of Independent States, has developed GOST (Russian: OCT), a set of spacecraft certification standards that is commonly used by Russia.

- JAXA (Japan Aerospace Exploration Agency) has developed a library of standards known as JERG (JAXA Engineering Requirement, Guideline).

- International organizations such as ISO and IEEE have also been involved in the development of standards that enhance interoperability.

Other Unique Considerations An additional challenge in the space domain occurs when humans are integrated into the system. Typically, it includes the incorporation of design features and capabilities that accommodate human interaction with the system to enhance overall safety and mission success.

国家安全空间与民用领域非常相似，可能强调性能而不是成本和进度，并且传统上使用 V 和瀑布模型进行开发。他们通常更能容忍新技术注入带来的风险。

独特的标准　总的来说，在空间领域正确应用系统工程有助于设计和开发空间元素，以便使用定义良好的流程和标准简化制造并降低维护成本。系统工程为适当的接口、网络和通信提供了定义良好的架构和设计流程及路线图，使各种承包商提供的空间系统和元素具有更好的完整性和互操作性，并跨供应链使用开放的行业标准。

民用、商用和国家安保实体有自己的驱动因素，决定如何创建和采用标准。大多数航天国家和国际联盟都制定并采用了自己的空间系统专用标准。一些示例包括：

- 在美国，国防部制定了军事（或"Mil"）标准，这些标准很容易被民用领域和商用领域采用，主要是因为在敌对环境中需要高可靠性和生存能力。NASA 还制定了一套技术标准，AIAA 和其他组织也制定了一套技术标准。
- 欧洲空间标准化合作是一项倡议，旨在制定一套统一、方便用户的标准，供所有欧洲空间活动使用。
- 欧亚标准化、计量和认证理事会是在独立国家联合体主持下运作的一个区域标准组织，它制定了 GOST（俄语：OCT），这是一套俄罗斯常用的航天器认证标准。
- JAXA（日本航空航天局）开发了一个标准库，称为 JERG（JAXA 工程需求指南）。
- ISO 和 IEEE 等国际组织也参与了增强互操作性的标准的制定。

其他独特考虑因素　当人员被综合到系统中时，空间领域会出现另一个挑战。通常，它包括结合设计特征和能力，以适应人与系统的交互，从而提高总体安全性和任务成功率。该系统需要确保在有效利用人的能力和表现方面满足人的需要，将危害控制在对人类活动安全的水平上，并在实际可行的最大程

TAILORING AND APPLICATION CONSIDERATIONS

The system needs to ensure that the human needs are addressed in terms of effectively utilizing human capabilities and performance, hazards are controlled to a level considered safe for human operations, and provide, to the maximum extent practical, the capability to safely recover the crew from hazardous situations. At the time of this writing, only missions led by three nations (Russia, the United States, and China) have sent humans into space. Each country has developed their own set of standards:

- Rovcosmos for Russia, and
- Human Space Flight Requirements for Civil, typically governed by NASA, for the United States,
- CNSA for China.

Of the three, only the United States has begun to explore human commercial space flight, where such requirements are governed by the US Federal Aviation Administration (FAA).

4.4.9 Telecommunication Systems

Overview of SE Applications within the Telecommunication Domain Telecommunication systems are defined by having a route to transfer information across and to distinct endpoints that are used to share (send and/or receive) information. They differ from postal systems in that the information shared is in the form of electronic media (applications or services) rather than transporting packages or handwritten letters.

Telecommunication systems are enablers for other services. Almost all modern systems either make use of telecommunication technologies provided by other systems, or contain telecommunication technologies within them (e.g., digital signage and ticketing systems within public transport systems; battlespace communication systems used by the military; environmental monitoring systems such as those used to monitor/predict the weather or detect and provide advance warning of earthquakes and other environmental events). Lives and livelihoods depend on telecommunication systems.

Communication network complexity and the social cost of telecommunication failures will only increase (White and Tantsura, 2016). It is therefore opportune for telecommunication leaders and practitioners to advocate, apply, and extend the best telecommunication SE approaches to cope with this complexity and risk.

度上提供使机组人员从危险情况中安全恢复的能力。在撰写本文时，只有三个国家（俄罗斯、美国和中国）领导的使命任务将人类送入了太空。每个国家都制定了自己的一套标准：

- 俄罗斯的 Rovcosmos；
- 美国民用载人航天需求，通常由 NASA 管理；
- 中国的 CNSA。

在这三个国家中，只有美国开始探索人类商用太空飞行，这些要求由美国联邦航空管理局（FAA）管理。

4.4.9 电信系统

系统工程在电信领域的应用概述　　电信系统的定义是，有一条线路可以在用于共享（发送和/或接收）信息的不同端点之间传输信息。它们与邮政系统的不同之处在于，共享的信息是电子媒介（应用程序或服务）的形式，而不是运输的包裹或手写的信件。

电信系统是其他服务的使能项。几乎所有现代系统要么利用其他系统提供的电信技术，要么包含其中的电信技术（例如，公共交通系统中的数字标牌和售票系统；军方使用的作战空间通信系统；环境监测系统，如用于监测/预测天气或探测地震和其他环境事件并提供预警的系统）。人们的生活和生计依赖于电信系统。

通信网络的复杂性和电信故障的社会成本只会增加（White 和 Tantsura，2016）。因此，对于电信领导者和实践者来说，倡导、应用和推广最佳的电信系统工程 SE 方法以应对这种复杂性和风险是一个很好的时机。

TAILORING AND APPLICATION CONSIDERATIONS

Unique Terms and Concepts Telecommunication systems are built on a wide range of technologies: satellite communication, cellular networks, land mobile radio, microwave, radio, television, Wi-Fi, Bluetooth, and global positioning systems. They are increasingly software-intensive systems (Donovan and Prabhu, 2017). Telecommunications includes communication networks owned by carriers, internet service providers, government agencies, and other enterprises, as well as broadcast networks (e.g., radio, cable, television) and over-the-top service provider applications (e.g., messaging, video conferencing, social media applications) (Adkins, et al., 2020) (Birman, 2012). Some telecommunication systems, like the internet and the public switched telephone network, have no single owner; their design depends upon collaboration in international telecommunication standards bodies.

The telecommunication transport network may be dedicated for a specific purpose (service or application) or shared for multiple services or applications. Communication networks may be employed for emergency services, defense, transportation, health, financial, industrial supervisory control, and data acquisition purposes. Many of these are considered to be national critical infrastructure (Lewis, 2019).

Telecommunication systems typically have some of the following characteristics:

- Diverse geographical distribution;
- Multi-party ownership and management (network domains or applications);
- Multiple constituent systems with independent life cycles that continuously evolve over many decades;
- A small stable set of functions, allocated across system elements, to achieve the common purpose of enabling communication;
- Many nodes and types of nodes; and
- Strong interdependence between nodes (failures within one node may cause other nodes to become isolated unless the specific failure mode is anticipated and the network is designed to withstand the failure).

Unique Activities, Methods, and Practices Network specifications, architectures, and models have a small number of functions and node types at their core, but they must also support many function and node variants. Engineering planning and architecture must be flexible enough to accommodate change in parts of the network owned and operated by others. Design and verification activities depend on a thorough analysis of failure modes and interactions across the network. Scale and variation lead to significant configuration management challenges (Xu and Zhou, 2015). These characteristics affect engineering activities throughout the life cycle. Like other types of networks, communication networks can be represented by a network model that defines a grouping of nodes and links to help understand how resources flow from one node to another.

独特的术语和概念 电信系统建立在广泛的技术基础上：卫星通信、蜂窝网络、陆地移动无线电、微波、无线电、电视、Wi-Fi、蓝牙和全球定位系统。它们是软件密集型系统（Donovan 和 Prabhu，2017）。电信包括运营商、互联网服务提供商、政府机构和其他复杂组织体系拥有的通信网络，以及广播网络（如无线电、有线电视）和顶级服务提供商应用程序（如消息、视频会议、社交媒体应用程序）（Adkins 等，2020）（Birman，2012）。一些电信系统，如互联网和公共交换电话网，没有单一所有者；它们的设计依赖于国际电信标准机构的合作。

电信传输网络可以专用于特定目的（服务或应用），也可以为多种服务或应用所共享。通信网络可用于应急服务、国防、运输、卫生、金融、工业监控和数据采集等目的。其中许多被视为国家关键基础设施（Lewis，2019）。

电信系统通常具有以下一些特征：

- 地理分布多样；
- 多方所有权和管理（网络域或应用程序）；
- 具有独立生命周期的多个组成系统，几十年来不断发展；
- 一组小而稳定的功能，跨系统元素分配，以实现通信的共同目的；
- 许多节点和节点类型；
- 节点之间相互依赖性强（一个节点的故障可能会导致其他节点被孤立，除非特定的故障模式是可以预见的，而且网络的设计可以承受这种故障）。

独特的活动、方法和实践 网络规范、架构和模型的核心是少量功能和节点类型，但它们还必须支持许多功能和节点的变体。工程规划和架构必须足够灵活，以适应由他人拥有和运营的网络部分的变化。设计和验证活动取决于对整个网络的故障模式和交互的彻底分析。规模和变化导致了重大的构型配置管理挑战（Xu 和 Zhou，2015）。这些特性影响整个生命周期的工程活动。与其他类型的网络一样，通信网络可以由一个网络模型来表示，该模型定义了一组节点和链接，以帮助理解资源如何从一个节点流向另一个节点。

TAILORING AND APPLICATION CONSIDERATIONS

While some telecommunication systems in slowly changing environments can survive on implicit engineering practices, such approaches have been found to be ineffective and inefficient. They typically fall short when one or more of the following exist:

- New and/or complex stakeholder needs;
- New operating models;
- Significant safety or security risks;
- High complexity; or
- Constrained, high-cost operating environments.

Other Unique Considerations Many vendor services and technologies are mature and are slow to evolve. Telecommunication networks typically comprise COTS vendor equipment/applications using industry interface standards and semi-standardized architectures (see Section 4.3.3). This equipment is typically integrated together without the use of SE. The promise from COTS vendors is that their equipment is suitable for rapid configuration and integration, and implicitly can survive with simpler requirements/business analysis and engineering processes, including outsourced vendor standardized engineering. This can lead to situations where there are unexpected outcomes. Without an appropriate set of engineering disciplines, such as those based on SE, it is difficult to assess, let alone manage, the risks.

4.4.10 Transportation Systems

Overview of SE Applications within the Transportation Domain Ground transportation systems, such as highways, busses, people-movers, mass transit, and rail involve complex capital programs for fleet acquisition and/or building of related infrastructures and are invariably within a SoS on an operational level. The system life cycle for ground transportation assets is 25 to 100+ years and often involves public funding and a related fiducial public trust. During this life cycle, operational processes are continuously optimized and improved using block changes.

The ground transportation industry segment is an emerging SE practice area, largely consisting of transit authorities, railroad operators rolling stock manufacturing industries, and civil engineering construction firms. Globally, some geographic regions are progressing the deployment and acceptance of SE more rapidly. They have created effective SoS approaches that are in concert with emergent societal trends such as smart cities, an embedded safety culture, and a through life approach to service delivery. For example, in the UK, the Institution of Civil Engineers has made solid progress in moving toward

虽然在缓慢变化的环境中，一些电信系统可以通过隐性的工程实践存活下来，但这种实施方法被发现是无效和低效的。当存在以下一种或多种情况时，它们通常达不到要求：

- 新的和/或复杂的利益相关方需要；
- 新的运行模式；
- 重大安全或安保风险；
- 高复杂性；
- 受限的、高成本的运行环境。

其他独特考虑因素 许多供应商的服务和技术已经成熟，并且发展缓慢。电信网络通常包括使用行业接口标准和半标准化架构的 COTS 供应商设备/应用程序（见 4.3.3 节）。该设备通常在不使用系统工程的情况下被综合在一起。COTS 供应商的承诺是，他们的设备适合快速构型配置和综合，并且可以通过更简单的需求/业务分析和工程流程（包括外包供应商标准化工程）生存下来。这可能导致出现意外结果的情况。如果没有一套合适的工程学科，例如基于系统工程的学科，就很难评估风险，更不用说管理风险了。

4.4.10 运输系统

系统工程在运输领域的应用概述 地面运输系统，如公路、公共汽车、大众运输工具、公共交通和铁路，涉及复杂的车队采办和/或相关基础设施建设资本项目，在运行层面上始终处于体系范围内。地面运输资产的系统生命周期为 25 至 100 多年，通常涉及公共资金和相关的公共信托。在这一生命周期内，运营流程会不断优化，并通过分块变更加以改进。

地面运输行业是一个新兴的系统工程实践领域，主要由运输行业、铁路运营商、机车车辆制造行业和市政工程施工公司组成。在全球范围内，一些地理区域正在加快系统工程的部署和接受。他们创建了有效的体系实施方法，与智能城市、嵌入式安全文化和终身服务交付实施方法等新兴社会趋势一致。例如，在英国，市政工程师研究院（Institute of Civil Engineers）在市政工程

TAILORING AND APPLICATION CONSIDERATIONS

an SE approach within the civil engineering domain. Other regions are at the early stages of integrating SE into their ground transportation systems processes. These imbalances can be overcome in time through global collaboration.

Unique Considerations Additional mandates for the use of SE methods, skills, and competencies are generated from rapidly increasing system complexities in modern transportation systems, as evidenced by Intelligent Transportation System (ITS) concepts including regional, national, and local smart cities initiatives. Train control automation, bus scheduling, and ride-share coordination, coupled with autonomous vehicles, micro-grid hybrid traction power, passenger fare collection, and related trip planner smartphone apps provide emerging complexities within modern ground transportation capability. However, public transportation must improve as public needs change, new technologies are introduced, or as environmental concerns and quality-of-life concerns encourage greater use of public transit. Ground transportation services are typically "in-service" brownfield systems and must migrate to an updated version, while still maintaining service, so that assets may be cost effectively managed in the public's interest (see Section 4.3.2). Some transit assets in large cities run 24/7 service as a matter of public safety and demand, requiring careful planning. A "whole" organization approach is needed for success.

Unique Terms and Concepts The transportation domain uses the same terms as the infrastructure domain, see Table 4.7.

Unique Activities, Methods, and Practices Some examples of early initiatives on the application of SE are in the United Kingdom, the European Union, and, specifically, the Netherlands. In the UK, Network Rail established the Governance for Railway Investment Projects (GRIP) to help manage projects and to align them with SE processes. Leading EU train operating companies and the main rolling stock manufacturers seek to develop a common, open architecture such as EULYNX and the Reference Command and Control System Architecture to support and optimize trackside and rolling stock acquisitions and upgrades. In the Netherlands, SE is advocated by the network management institution, ProRail, as part of their project management approach for delivering rail infrastructure projects. ProRail created a SE Handbook for their project life cycle approach which is comparable to GRIP.

领域向系统工程实施方法迈进的方面取得了坚实的进展。其他地区正处于将系统工程融入其地面运输系统流程的早期阶段。这些不平衡可以通过全球合作及时克服。

独特的考虑因素　现代交通系统中快速增加的系统复杂性产生了使用系统工程的方法、技能和能力的额外要求，智能交通系统（ITS）概念（包括区域、国家和地方智能城市倡议）证明了这一点。列车控制自动化、公交调度和共享骑行协调，再加上自动驾驶车辆、微电网混合牵引电力、乘客收费和相关的出行规划智能手机应用程序，为现代地面运输能力带来了新的复杂性。然而，公共交通必须随着公众需求的变化、新技术的引入，或环境问题和生活质量问题鼓励更多人使用公共交通而得到改善。地面交通服务通常是"在用"棕地系统，必须迁移到更新版本，同时仍保持服务，以便为公众利益经济高效地管理资产（见 4.3.2 节）。大城市的一些公交资产出于公共安全和需求全天候运行，因此需要仔细规划。为了确保成功需要采用"整体"组织实施方法。

独特的术语和概念　运输领域使用与基础设施领域相同的术语，见表 4.7。

独特的活动、方法和实践　英国、欧盟，尤其是荷兰，都有早期的系统工程应用举措。在英国，英国国营铁路公司建立了铁路投资项目治理（GRIP），以帮助管理项目并使其与系统工程流程保持一致。欧盟领先的列车运营公司和主要机车车辆制造商寻求开发一种通用的开放式架构，如 Eulenx 和参考指挥和控制系统架构，以支持和优化轨道和机车车辆的采办和升级。在荷兰，网络管理机构 ProRail 倡导将系统工程作为其交付铁路基础设施项目的项目管理方法的一部分。ProRail 为其项目生命周期实施方法创建了一本系统工程手册，与 GRIP 相当。

5 SYSTEMS ENGINEERING IN PRACTICE

5.1 SYSTEMS ENGINEERING COMPETENCIES

The terms "competence" and "competency" are two distinct terms used to define the personal attributes of individual Systems Engineering (SE) practitioners. Competence is the ability to perform an activity or task. Competency is the set of skills required in the performance of a job. The competence reflects the total capacity of the individual, whereas a competency is a set of skills that the individual will be required to perform for a job. The sum of an individual's competencies will make up their competence. Those competencies are measured and assessed to provide an estimate or a picture of the overall competence of a SE practitioner.

The INCOSE Systems Engineering Competency Framework (SECF) (2018) provides a set of competencies that identify knowledge, skills, abilities, and behaviors important to effective SE that can be applied in any domain context. The INCOSE SECF spans a wide range of competencies organized into five themes: core, professional, technical, management, and integrating.

- The *core competencies* underpin engineering, as well as SE.
- The *professional competencies* are primarily based in behavior as a SE practitioner (see Section 5.1.2).
- The *management competencies* relate to performing tasks associated with controlling and managing SE activities.
- The *technical competencies* are associated with technical processes to accomplish SE.
- The *integrating competencies* recognize SE as an integrating discipline, considering activities from other specialists from project management, logistics, quality, and finance to create a coherent whole.

INCOSE Systems Engineering Handbook: A Guide for System Life Cycle Processes and Activities, Fifth Edition.
Edited by David D. Walden, Thomas M. Shortell, Garry J. Roedler, Bernardo A. Delicado, Odile Mornas, Yip Yew-Seng, and David Endler.
© 2023 John Wiley & Sons Ltd. Published 2023 by John Wiley & Sons Ltd.

5 实践中的系统工程

5.1 系统工程胜任力

术语"才能"和"胜任力"是两个不同的术语,用于定义各个系统工程实践者的个人属性。才能是指执行一项活动或任务的能力。胜任力是一项工作所需的一组技能。才能反映了个人的总体能力,而"胜任力"是个人为完成一项工作所需的一组技能。个人胜任力的总和将构成其才能。对这些胜任力进行测量和评估可以得到系统工程实践者总体才能的评估或写照。

INCOSE 系统工程胜任力框架(Systems Engineering Competency Framework,SECF)(2018)提供了一套胜任力,用于分辨出对于有效的系统工程而言重要的且可应用于任何领域背景的知识、技能、能力和行为。INCOSE SECF 涵盖了广泛的胜任力范围,并分为五个主题:核心、专业、技术、管理和综合。

- 核心胜任力是工程和系统工程的基础。
- 专业胜任力主要基于系统工程实践者的行为(见 5.1.2 节)。
- 管理胜任力及执行及控制和管理系统工程活动相关的任务有关。
- 技术胜任力与完成系统工程的技术流程相关。
- 综合胜任力将系统工程视为一门综合学科,考虑来自其他项目管理、后勤、质量和财务专家的活动,以创建一个连贯的整体。

The INCOSE Systems Engineering Competency Assessment Guide (SECAG) (2022) provides guidance on how to evaluate individuals for proficiency in the competencies and how to differentiate between proficiency at each of five levels defined within the INCOSE SECF. For each competency, the INCOSE SECAG provides a description, why it matters, and possible contributory evidence. Indicators of competence are provided along with examples of relevant knowledge, experience, and possible objective evidence of personal involvement in activities or professional behaviors applied.

Both the INCOSE SECF and INCOSE SECAG are comprehensive resources that are globally accepted and tailorable to the needs of the organization or individual. The INCOSE SECF and INCOSE SECAG are intended for use in hiring, assessing, training, and advancing SE practitioners; and may be used for other purposes as deemed appropriate.

Given the complexity and multidisciplinary nature of today's systems and system of systems, it is not possible for a single person to know everything about a system of interest (SoI). As shown in Figure 5.1 SE practitioners are often referred to as "T-shaped" in describing their professional expertise (Delicado, et al., 2018). SE practitioners must have both a depth of knowledge of a fundamental engineering discipline, while at the same time develop and maintain a breadth of knowledge about systems and the multiple disciplines involved.

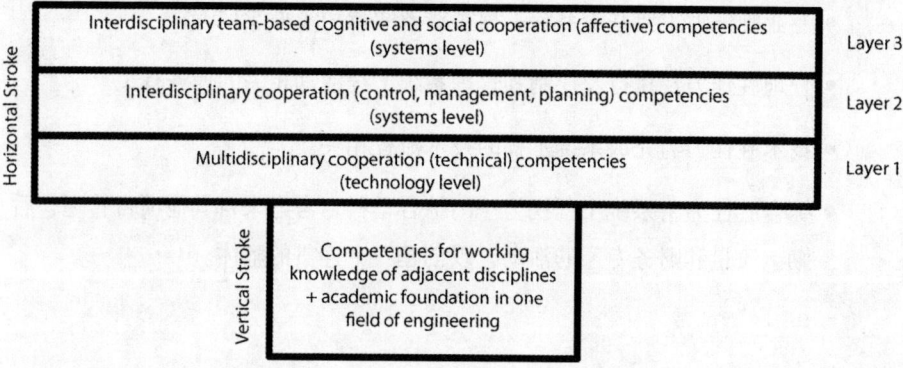

FIGURE 5.1   The "T-shaped" SE practitioner. From Delicado, et al. (2018). Used with permission. All other rights reserved.

5.1.1   Difference between Hard and Soft Skills

"The complexity of modern system designs, the severity of their constraints, and the need to succeed in a high tempo, highstakes environment where competitive advantage matters, demands the highest levels of technical excellence and integrity throughout the life cycle" (INCOSE SECF, 2018, Page 47). Interactions

《INCOSE 系统工程胜任力评估指南》（2022）提供了关于如何评估个人胜任力的熟练程度以及如何区分INCOSE SECF中定义的五个层级的熟练程度的指南。对于每一项胜任力，INCOSE SECAG 都提供了说明，阐明其重要的原因，以及其可能产生的贡献的根据。指南同时也提供了能力指标以及相关知识、经验以及个人参与活动或专业行为的可能客观证据的示例。

INCOSE SECF 和 INCOSE SECAG 都是全球公认的综合资源，可根据组织或个人的需要进行定制。INCOSE SECF 和 INCOSE SECAG 旨在用于招聘、评估、培训和提升系统工程实践者；并可用于其他适当用途。

鉴于当今系统和体系的复杂性和多学科性质，一个人不可能了解所感兴趣之系统（SoI）的一切。如图 5.1 所示，系统工程实践者在描述其专业知识时通常被形容为"T形"（Delicado 等，2018）。系统工程实践者必须具备基础工程学科的深度知识，并同时发展和保持有关系统和多学科知识的广度。

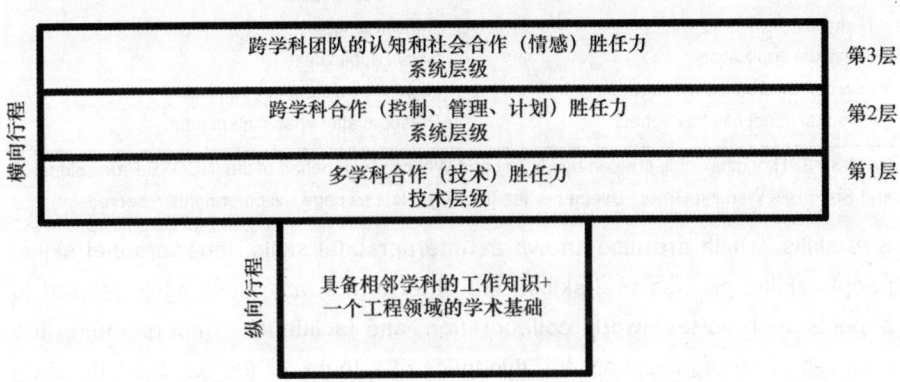

图 5.1 "T 形"系统工程从业人员。源自 Delicado 等（2018）。经许可后使用。版权所有。

5.1.1 硬技能和软技能的区别

"现代系统设计的复杂性、约束的严格性，以及在高节奏、高风险的环境中取得成功的需要（竞争优势至关重要），需要在整个生命周期内达到最高水平的技术卓越性和完整度"（INCOSE SECF，2018，第 47 页）。与利益相关方（包

with stakeholders, including customers, project managers, all types of engineers, operations, marketing, and various departments contribute to the overall success of a system and to the life cycle cost (LCC) to conceive, produce, utilize, support, and retire that system. SE practitioners and SE teams need both hard skills and soft skills to meet these challenges. Table 5.1 contrasts the differences between hard skills and soft skills. As examples in the hard skills category, consider typical engineering technical aspects like structural, hydrodynamic, reliability, or electrical analyses, because they require science, mathematics, and quantitative modeling in order to solve engineering-related problems. Examples of hard skills for SE practitioners include requirements analysis, architectural evaluation, and risk management. As examples in the soft skills category, consider influencing a peer, motivating a team, and resolving a conflict. They require emotional intelligence and appropriate behaviors to solve people-related problems.

TABLE 5.1 Differences between the hard skills and soft skills

Hard Skills	Soft Skills
• Concrete definitions	• Subjective definitions
• Measurable	• Difficult to measure
• Testable	• Difficult to test
• Individual application	• Social application
• Low self-awareness required	• High self-awareness required
• Personal affect has low impact	• Personal affect has high impact

INCOSE SEH original table created by McCoy and Whitcomb on behalf of the INCOSE Professional and Soft Skills Working Group. Usage per the INCOSE Notices page. All other rights reserved.

Soft skills, which are also known as interpersonal skills, intrapersonal skills, people skills, professional skills, and other terms, are those skills related to aspects such as teamwork, collaboration, and facilitation. Understanding the nuances of an organization, the dynamics of a team, or the experiences of an individual requires soft skills. It is not uncommon for an engineer to question the value of soft skills, and question how these skills apply to a specific engineering problem. However, soft skills often make the difference between a smooth application of SE and one riddled with challenges. Both the INCOSE SECF and INCOSE SECAG outline areas of professionalism and ethics that provide insights and information related to important soft skills for ensuring long-term sustainability for the life cycle of a system.

括客户、项目经理、所有类型的工程师、运营、市场营销和各个部门）的互动有助于系统的整体成功，并有助于降低系统构思、生产、使用、支撑和退役的生命周期成本（LCC）。系统工程实践者和系统工程团队同时需要硬技能和软技能来应对这些挑战。表 5.1 对比了硬技能和软技能之间的差异。作为硬技能的例子，可以考虑典型的工程技术方面，如结构、流体动力、可靠性或电气分析，因为它们需要科学、数学和定量建模来解决工程相关的问题。系统工程实践者的硬技能例子包括需求分析、架构评估和风险管理。软技能方面的例子包括影响同伴、激励团队和解决冲突。它们需要情商和适当的行为来解决与人相关的问题。

表 5.1 硬技能和软技能的差异

硬技能	软技能
• 具体定义	• 主观定义
• 可测量	• 难以测量
• 可测试	• 难以测试
• 个体应用	• 社会应用
• 自我意识要求低	• 自我意识要求高
• 个人情感影响较小	• 个人情感影响较大

INCOSE SEH 原始表由 McCoy 和 Whitcomb 代表 INCOSE 专业和软技能工作组创建。按照 INCOSE 通知页使用。版权所有。

软技能，也用人际交往技能、个人内在技能、人际交往能力、专业技能和其他术语表示，是指与团队合作、协作和促进等方面相关的技能。理解组织的细微差别、团队的动态或个人的经验需要软技能。工程师质疑软技能的价值，质疑这些技能如何应用于特定的工程问题的情况并不少见。然而，软技能往往会对系统工程在应用上是顺利还是充满难题产生影响。INCOSE SECF 和 INCOSE SECAG 都概述了专业和道德领域，提供了与重要的软技能相关的见解和信息，以确保系统生命周期的长期可持续性。

263 The field of engineering brings a unique perspective toward developing competencies in these hard and soft skills. Early in the career of an engineer, there is a strong emphasis toward competency in the hard skills, such as those related to engineering, math, physics, chemistry, industrial processes, and technical management. The INCOSE SECF outlines these skills in the areas of Technical Competencies, Management Competencies, and Core Competencies. As the career of an engineer develops, the emphasis moves toward a balance between hard and soft skills. For an SE practitioner, a higher demand is often placed on these soft skills due to interactions with stakeholders, team members, and senior managers. The INCOSE SECF outlines these skills in the Professional Competencies.

5.1.2 System Engineering Professional Competencies

Professionalism can be summarized as a personal commitment to professional standards of behavior, ethics, obligations to society, the profession, and the environment. SE practitioners are trusted to apply reasoning, judgment, and problem solving to reach unbiased, informed, and potentially significant decisions because of their specialized knowledge, skills, abilities, and behaviors. SE professionalism includes consideration of personal behaviors beyond using methods and tools. SE practitioners recognize the benefits of behaviors and outcomes related to professional competencies from ethics, professionalism, and technical leadership to communications, negotiation, team dynamics, facilitation, emotional intelligence, coaching, and mentoring. These Professional Competencies are documented in the INCOSE SECF (2018). The evaluation of an individual's Professional Competencies can be accomplished using the INCOSE SECAG (2023).

5.1.3 Technical Leadership

Leadership can be generally defined as: "The act (or art!) of enabling people to produce results or achieve outcomes they would not have on their own." Technical Leadership is leadership in situations that involve technology. As illustrated in Figure 5.2, Technical Leadership exists at the intersection of Technical Expertise and Leadership Skills.

Strong technical leadership is critical for the successful development, operation, sustainment, and evolution of engineered systems. To successfully lead technical teams and technical enterprises, technical leaders must possess all the leadership skills required of any effective leader. Technical leaders must also possess, and be recognized as possessing, significant technical expertise. A good technical leader must possess expertise in one or more technical areas and have some level of understanding across a wide range of disciplines to earn credibility for leading technical teams. They must also be aware of the limits of their own knowledge so they know when to seek the expertise of others.

工程领域为培养这些硬技能和软技能的胜任力带来了独特的视角。在工程师职业生涯的早期，非常重视硬技能方面的胜任力，例如与工程、数学、物理、化学、工业流程和技术管理相关的技能。INCOSE SECF 将这些技能概述在技术胜任力、管理胜任力和核心胜任力领域。随着工程师职业生涯的发展，胜任力的重点逐渐转向硬技能和软技能之间的平衡。对于系统工程实践者来说，与利益相关方、团队成员和高级管理人员的互动需要，对软技能提出了更高的要求。INCOSE SECF 将这些技能概述在专业胜任力领域中。

5.1.2 系统工程专业胜任力

职业精神可以概括为个人对行为、道德、社会义务、职业和环境等职业标准的承诺。系统工程实践者凭借其专业知识、技能、能力和行为，通过进行推理、判断和解决问题来做出公正的、可靠的和潜在重大的决策。系统工程职业精神包括对个人行为的考虑，而不仅仅是使用方法和工具。系统工程实践者认识到与专业能力相关的行为和成果所带来的益处，从道德、职业精神和技术领导力到沟通、谈判、团队动向、合作进步化、情商、辅导和指导。这些专业胜任力被收录在 INCOSE SECF（2018）中。可以使用 INCOSE SECAG（2023）对个人的专业胜任力进行评估。

5.1.3 技术领导力

领导力通常可以定义为："使人们产生自己无法产生的结果或取得他们自己无法取得的效果的行为（或艺术！）。"技术领导力是指在涉及技术的情况下的领导力。如图 5.2 所示，技术领导力存在于技术专长和领导技能的交叉点。

强大的技术领导力对于工程系统的成功开发、运行、维持和迭代至关重要。要成功领导技术团队和技术企业，技术领导者必须具备有效领导者所需的所有领导技能。技术领导者还必须拥有，并被公认为拥有重要的技术专长。一个好的技术领导者必须拥有一个或多个技术领域的专业知识，并对广泛的学科领域有一定程度的了解，才能为其领导技术团队赢得信誉。他们还必须意识到自己知识的局限性，以便知道何时向他人寻求专业知识。

SYSTEMS ENGINEERING IN PRACTICE

Why Is Technical Leadership Important for SE Practitioners? SE practitioners are responsible for the success of the system as a whole. They must understand the needs of a broad range of stakeholders and ensure those needs are met. They must work across traditional engineering disciplines to ensure the individual contributions of each integrate harmoniously to produce the desired outcome. Because they seldom have the positional authority to ensure these outcomes, they must lead through influence, leveraging their technical knowledge and their personal qualities to create an environment in which the individuals and teams accomplish the desired goals.

What Does It Take to Be a Good Technical Leader? The INCOSE Technical Leadership Institute (TLI) developed a model that identifies and describes six interrelated behaviors that technical leaders must master to successfully lead through influence. Each behavior is described in Technical Technical Leadership Table 5.2, and each includes a question technical leaders Expertise Leadership Skills should continually ask themselves as they seek to lead.

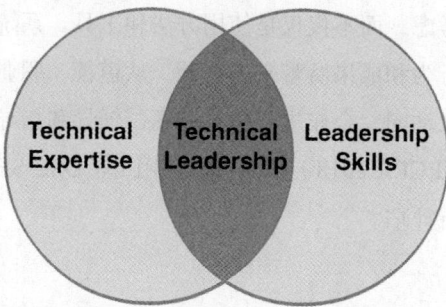

FIGURE 5.2 Technical leadership is the intersection of technical expertise and lead-ership skills. INCOSE SEH original figure created by Gelosh and Pennotti on behalf of the INCOSE Technical Leadership Institute. Usage per the INCOSE Notices page. All other rights reserved.

5.1.4 Ethics

There will always be pressure to cut corners to deliver projects faster or at lower costs, especially for a profession such as SE. As stated in the INCOSE Code of Ethics (2023), The practice of SE can result in significant social and environmental benefits, but only if unintended and undesired effects are considered and mitigated.

为什么技术领导力对系统工程实践者很重要？ 系统工程实践者对整个系统的成功负责。他们必须了解广泛的利益相关方的需要，并确保这些需要得到满足。他们必须跨传统工程学科开展工作，以确保每个学科的贡献能够和谐地综合起来，从而产生预期的结果。由于他们很少拥有确保取得这些成果的职权，他们必须通过影响力进行领导，利用自己的技术知识和个人素质来创造一种环境，使个人和团队都能达到预期目标。

成为一名优秀的技术领导者需要什么？ INCOSE 技术领导力学院（Technical Leadership Institute，TLI）开发了一个模型，该模型确定并描述了技术领导者必须掌握的六种相互关联的行为，以成功地通过影响力进行领导。表 5.2 描述了每一种行为，且每种行为都包含一个技术领导者在试图领导时应该不断问自己的问题。

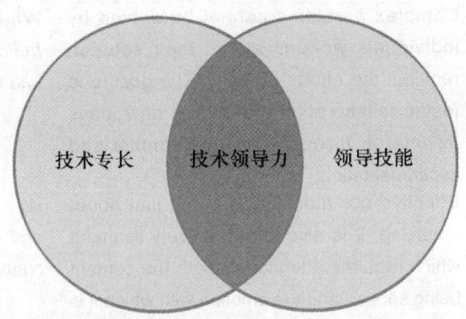

图 5.2　技术领导力是技术专长与领导技能的交集。INCOSE SEH 原始图由 Gelosh 和 Pennotti 代表 INCOSE 技术领导力学院创建。按照 INCOSE 通知页使用。版权所有。

5.1.4　道德

为了更快或以更低的成本交付项目，总是存在偷工减料的压力，对于系统工程这样的专业而言尤其如此。正如 INCOSE 道德规范（2023）所述，系统工程的实践可以带来显著的社会和环境效益，但只有在考虑并避免意外和不良影响的情况下才可以实现。

SYSTEMS ENGINEERING IN PRACTICE

TABLE 5.2 Technical leadership model

Technical Leadership Behavior	Description	Question for the Technical Leader
Holding the Vision	A vision is an aspirational statement that defines who we are and where we want to go. It provides an impelling purpose. It must be the start of a continual and ongoing conversation that SE practitioners are well positioned to support, reinforce, and encourage.	*What outcome are we striving to achieve and how am I advancing that vison?*
Thinking Strategically	Using Strategic Thinking, technical leaders formulate a hypothesis before acting, treat the action as an experiment to test their hypothesis, and, based on the results they observe, continue along the path they are on or formulate a new hypothesis and begin the testing anew.	*What patterns are emerging from my actions, and what are the implications for what I should do next?*
Fostering Collaboration	Complex problems cannot be solved by individuals working alone; their solution requires the efforts of many. The goal is to foster collaboration that allows new ideas to emerge through creative conflict and experimentation.	*What relationships am I building today for myself and for others?*
Communicating Effectively	Effective communication is not just about speaking, it is also about actively listening which requires attention to both the content being spoken and the emotion with which it is communicated.	*Who am I trying to influence and what is their greatest challenge?*
Enabling Others to Succeed	The technical leader's role is to influence, guide, encourage, and support those who can produce desired outcomes. The leader's success will derive from their success, and their acknowledgment that the leader contributed to it.	*What obstacles are preventing others from acting, and how can I help remove those obstacles?*
Demonstrating Emotional Intelligence	In order to lead others, technical leaders must continually seek feedback to decrease their blind spots and be willing to reveal things that help others know them better. While the former can make them uncomfortable and the latter make them more vulnerable, the payoff will be more than worth the effort.	*That am I afraid of admitting to others and how might disclosing it improve our relationship?*

INCOSE SEH original table created by Gelosh and Pennotti on behalf of the INCOSE Technical Leadership Institute. Usage per the INCOSE Notices page. All other rights reserved.

表 5.2 技术领导力模型

技术领导力行为	说明	向技术领导者提出的问题
保持愿景	愿景是一种雄心壮志的宣言，它定义了我们是什么角色以及我们想达成什么目标。它提供了一个强有力的目的。它必须是持续不断的对话的开始，且系统工程实践者支持、加强和鼓励它	我们想努力得到的结果是什么，以及我如何使愿景更进一步？
战略性思考	利用战略思维，技术领导者在行动之前制定一个假设，将行动视为一个实验来检验他们的假设，并根据他们观察到的结果，沿着他们所走的道路继续前进，或者制定一个新的假设，然后重新开始测试	我的行为产生了怎样的模式，它对我接下来要做的事有什么影响？
促进合作	复杂的问题不能由单独工作的个人来解决；解决这些问题需要许多人的努力。目标是促进合作，通过创造性冲突和实验产生新想法	我今天为我和他人建立了什么关系？
有效地沟通	有效的沟通不仅仅是说话，还包括积极倾听，倾听时需要同时注意所说的内容和交流的情感	我想要影响谁以及他们最大的挑战是什么？
使其他人能够成功	技术领导者的职责是影响、引导、鼓励和支持那些能够产生预期结果的人。领导者的成功将源于他们的成功，以及他们承认领导者为其做出了贡献	有哪些障碍在阻止其他人采取行动，以及我可以如何帮助消除这些障碍？
展现情商	为了领导他人，技术领导者必须不断寻求反馈以减少他们的盲点，并愿意透露信息，有助于他人更好地了解他们。虽然前者会让他们感到不舒服，后者会让他们更加脆弱，但付出的努力将是值得的	我是否担忧向其他人承认的内容，以及披露它能改善我们的关系吗？

INCOSE SEH 原始表由 Gelosh 和 Pennotti 代表 INCOSE 技术领导力学院创建。按照 INCOSE 通知页使用。版权所有。

SYSTEMS ENGINEERING IN PRACTICE

265   Part of the role of the SE practitioner as a leader and professional is knowing when unacceptable risks or trade-offs are being made, knowing how to influence key stakeholders, and having the courage to stand up for stakeholders, the community, and the profession when necessary. The INCOSE Code of Ethics contains sections on "Fundamental Principles," "Fundamental Duties to Society and Public Infrastructure," and "Rules of Practice" to help the SE practitioner in practical applications of ethics to their work and daily lives.

5.2 DIVERSITY, EQUITY, AND INCLUSION

The following definitions are taken from the Accreditation Board for Engineering & Technology (ABET) (2017) and provide a reference point for conversations and materials about diversity, equity, and inclusion.

- *Diversity* is the range of human differences, encompassing the characteristics that make one individual or group different from another.
- *Equity* is the fair treatment, access, opportunity and advancement for all people, achieved by intentional focus on their disparate needs, conditions, and abilities.
- *Inclusion* is the intentional, proactive, and continuing efforts and practices in which all members respect, support, and value others.
- INCOSE uses the compound term Diversity, Equity, and Inclusion (abbreviated to DEI) when referring to the broad subject matter.

Diversity encompasses a wide range of characteristics. Figure 5.3 shows a representative set of characteristics grouped into five areas: intrinsic, employment, environment, interaction, and family (Harding and Pickard, 2019).

DEI is vital to successful SE because of the wide range of contexts in which SE is applied and the consideration of multiple stakeholder viewpoints at the heart of the systems approach. SE practitioners play a pivotal role in integrating DEI concepts into the team's composition and approach and in the system design and development process through:

1. Ensuring that the SE team and its leadership is inclusive, welcomes a diverse range of talent, promotes cognitive diversity and diversity of ideas, and, where necessary, takes deliberate action to provide psychological safety and communication equity.

系统工程实践者作为领导者和专家的部分职责是了解何时会出现不可接受的风险或需要做出权衡，知道如何影响关键利益相关方，并勇敢地在必要时为利益相关方、群体和专业挺身而出。INCOSE 道德准则包含"基本原则""对社会和公共基础设施的基本义务"和"实践规则"等章节，以帮助系统工程实践者在工作和日常生活中应用实践。

5.2 多样性、公平性和包容性

以下定义摘自工程技术认证委员会（ABET）（2017），为关于多样性、公平性和包容性的对话和材料提供了参考。

- *多样性*是指人类差异的范围，包括使一个人或群体与另一个人或群体不同的特征。
- *公平性*是通过有意识地关注所有人的不同需要、条件和能力，实现所有人的公平待遇、准入、机会和进步。
- *包容性*是指所有成员都尊重、支持和重视他人的有意、主动和持续的努力和实践。
- INCOSE 在提及广泛的主题时，使用复合术语"多样性、公平性和包容性"（缩写为 DEI）。

多样性包含广泛的特征。图 5.3 展示了一组具有代表性的特征，分为五个方面：内在、就业、环境、互动和家庭（Harding 和 Pickard，2019）。

由于系统工程应用的背景非常广泛，并且系统方法的核心考虑了多个利益相关方的视角，因此 DEI 对于成功的 SE 来说至关重要。系统工程实践者在将 DEI 概念融入团队的组成和实施方法以及系统设计和开发过程中发挥着关键作用，主要通过以下方式：

1. 确保系统工程团队及其领导层具有包容性，欢迎多样化人才，促进认知多样性和思想多样性，并在必要时采取谨慎行动，提供心理安全感和平等的交流。

SYSTEMS ENGINEERING IN PRACTICE

2. Ensuring that the systems we realize are as accommodating as possible of the differences within the entire stakeholder community.

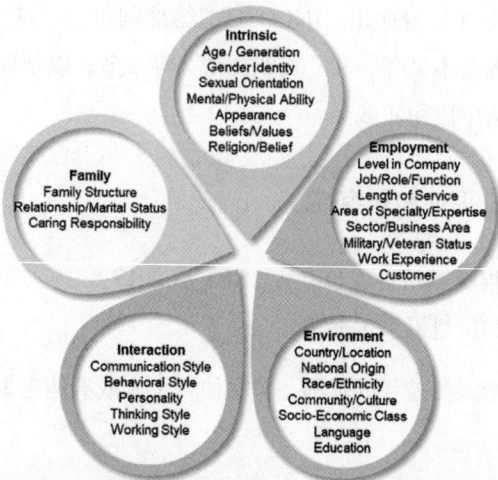

FIGURE 5.3 Categorized dimensions of diversity. From Harding and Pickard (2019) derived from SEBoK (2023). Used with permission. All other rights reserved.

Failure to address either of these aspects results in sub-optimal outcomes, whether in terms of missed solutions, lower productivity, or delivering a system that does not equitably meet the needs of the full range of the stakeholder community (i.e., essentially failing to meet the ultimate goal of delivering a total optimal system solution for all). Furthermore, in providing total optimal system solutions, one purpose of the system is to provide similar (equal) outcomes to each user. To accomplish this, the SE practitioner must understand the difference between equality and equity. Equality is providing each user exactly the same resources but may not result in similar (equal) outcomes. Equity, however, is proactively addressing disparities that exist between individual users (e.g., different situations, needs, requirements, life experiences, challenges) and changing the system so that each user can experience a similar outcome.

5.3 SYSTEMS ENGINEERING RELATIONSHIPS TO OTHER DISCIPLINES

SE practitioners routinely work within broad multidisciplinary teams. The following sections highlight SE practitioner interactions with some key related disciplines.

2. 确保我们实现的系统尽可能适应整个利益相关方群体内的差异。

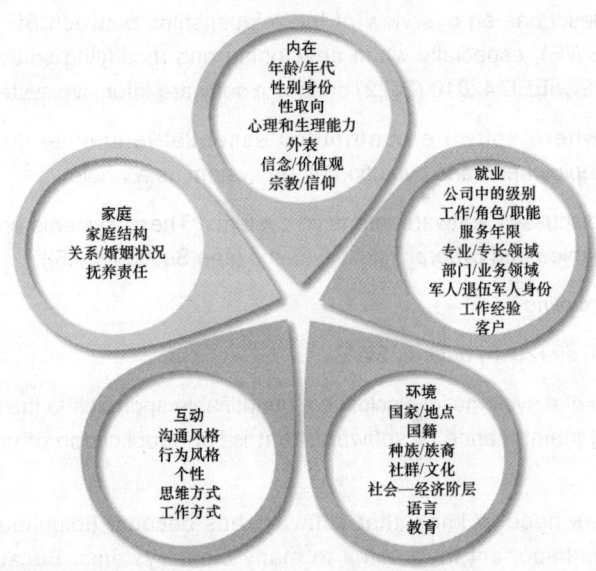

图 5.3 多样性的分类维度。源自 Harding 和 Pickard（2019），采用自 SEBoK（2023）。经许可后使用。版权所有。

未能解决这两个方面中的任何一个，都会导致次优结果，不论是遗漏解决方案、生产率降低，还是在提供无法公平满足所有利益相关方需要的系统方面都是如此（即，基本上未能达到为所有人提供总体最优系统解决方案的最终目标）。此外，在提供总体最优系统解决方案时，系统的其中一个目的是为每个用户提供类似（同等）的结果。要做到这一点，SE 实践者必须理解平等和公平之间的区别。平等是指为每个用户提供完全相同的资源，但可能不会产生类似（同等）的结果。然而，公平是指积极解决各个用户之间存在的差异（例如，不同的情况、需要、需求、生活经历、挑战），并改变系统，使每个用户都能体验到类似的结果。

5.3 系统工程与其他专业的关系

系统工程实践者通常在广泛的多学科团队中工作。以下章节重点介绍 SE 实践者与一些关键的相关学科的交集。

SYSTEMS ENGINEERING IN PRACTICE

5.3.1 SE and Software Engineering (SWE)

This section describes an overview of the relationships between SE and software engineering (SWE), especially when developing and modifying software-intensive systems. ISO/IEC/IEEE 42010 (2022) defines a software-intensive system as:

Any system where software contributes essential influences to the design, construction, deployment, and evolution of the system as a whole.

Section 4.3.4 discusses software-intensive systems. These systems are also known as software-enabled and cyberphysical systems (see Section 4.3.5).

What is this discipline?

ISO/IEC TR 19759 (2015) defines SWE as:

The application of a systematic, disciplined, quantifiable approach to the development, operation, and maintenance of software; that is, the application of engineering to software.

SE practitioners need to know that software has become ubiquitous in modern systems and is important in updates to many older systems. Because software elements are malleable, software can thus, in most cases, be tailored, adapted, and modified more readily than can physical elements, especially in the support stage of the system life cycle. Software elements, like physical elements, can be improved and replaced if the interfaces are preserved. Software often provides or facilitates provision of the following system attributes: functionality, behavior, quality characteristics (QCs), and system interfaces (both internal and external). Software embedded in software-intensive systems can also monitor system performance and provide observable performance indicators.

The differences between software elements and physical elements present significant challenges for SE practitioners when facilitating development and modification of software-intensive systems. Software elements are logical entities composed of textual and iconic symbols that are processed and interpreted by other software that is executed on computer hardware. A single mistyped symbol, including a single mistake in a logical expression, in large system that may include thousands or millions of symbols and logical expressions can result in failure of the entire system. The mistake may not be detected during system development or modification because even small software programs contain large numbers of logical branches and iteration loops that prevent exhaustive testing in reasonable amounts of time. Assuring the quality of a software-intensive system is thus challenging. Detailed concentration on the precise development of software elements and software interfaces may cause SWE practitioners to lose sight of the impacts of their software on larger system issues.

5.3.1 系统工程和软件工程（SWE）

本节概述系统工程和软件工程（SWE）之间的关系，尤其是在开发和修改软件密集型系统时。ISO/IEC/IEEE 42010（2022）将软件密集型系统定义为：

软件对整个系统的设计、构建、部署和演进产生重要影响的任何系统。

4.3.4 节讨论了软件密集型系统。这些系统也被称为软件使能的和赛博物理的系统（见 4.3.5 节）。

这门学科是什么？

ISO/IEC TR 19759（2015）将 SWE 定义为：

系统的、规范的、可量化的方法对软件的开发、操作和维护的应用；即工程在软件中的应用。

系统工程实践者需要知道，软件在现代系统中已变得无处不在，并且在许多旧系统的更新中非常重要。由于软件元素具有可塑性，因此在大多数情况下，软件比物理元素更容易定制、调整和修改，尤其是在系统生命周期的支持阶段。如果保留接口，软件元素可以像物理元素一样得到改进和替换。软件通常提供或促进提供以下系统属性：功能、行为、质量特性（QCs）和系统接口（内部和外部）。嵌入在软件密集型系统中的软件还可以监控系统性能，并提供可观察的性能指标。

在促进软件密集型系统的开发和修改时，软件元素和物理元素之间的差异给系统工程实践者带来了重大挑战。软件元素是由文本和图标符号组成的逻辑实体，由在计算机硬件上执行的其他软件处理和解释。在可能包含数千或数百万个符号和逻辑表达式的大型系统中，一个错误的符号（包括逻辑表达式中的一个错误）可能会导致整个系统出现故障。在系统开发或修改过程中可能无法发现错误，因为即使是小型软件程序也包含大量逻辑分支和迭代循环，无法在合理时间内进行穷举测试。因此，确保软件密集型系统的质量具有挑战性。过分专注于软件元素和软件界面的精确开发，可能会使软件工程师忽视软件对更大的系统问题的影响。

SYSTEMS ENGINEERING IN PRACTICE

267 *What is its relationship to SE?*

The relationship of SWE to SE is becoming increasingly important because software is a large and growing part of modern systems. The issues that arise for SE practitioners when developing or modifying software-intensive systems involve partitioning of requirements and architecture so that SWE practitioners (and hardware engineering (HWE) practitioners of various kinds) can design their elements and interfaces and pursue their development practices based on the differing natures of the mediums in which they work (Fairley, 2019). Well-defined and controlled interfaces, both provided and required, are essential so that separately developed elements can be efficiently integrated. Integration of software and hardware elements is typically accomplished in an incremental manner, as the elements become available. Defining and controlling interfaces is an ongoing challenge.

The primary benefit of coordinating SE and SWE during system development and modification is incorporation of software-provided capabilities in a manner that results in efficient and effective systems. SE practitioners can consult with SWE practitioners during system analysis and design to develop options and tradeoffs for configuring software and hardware elements and their interfaces. In addition, SWE practitioners can provide recommendations to SE practitioners for processes that can be used when developing and integrating software and hardware elements and when performing system verification, validation, and deployment (Fairley, 2019). Consultations and recommendations can ameliorate the software problems that sometimes result in late deliveries, insufficient system performance, and difficult system modifications.

How does it impact/is it impacted by SE?

SE practitioners who develop software-intensive systems are, as always, concerned with facilitating development of systems that are delivered in a timely manner, that satisfy performance parameters, and that can be modified efficiently and effectively. SE practitioners can better achieve these goals by taking advantage of the expertise of SWE practitioners, but they may fail to do so because they may not be familiar with the culture, terminology, and practices of SWE. SWE practitioners may not contribute their expertise because they are not consulted or if consulted may have insufficient knowledge of system level issues to provide recommendations. Involving knowledgeable SWE practitioners at the system level can improve communication. Cross-training, shadowing, mentoring, and collaborative workshops that include SE practitioners and SWE practitioners can result in synergetic relationships that will provide better communication and allow more effective and efficient development and modification of software-intensive systems.

它与系统工程的关系是什么？

SWE 与系统工程的关系变得越来越重要，因为软件在现代系统中所占的比重越来越大。系统工程实践者在开发或修改软件密集型系统时遇到的问题涉及需求和系统架构的划分，以便 SWE 实践者［以及各种硬件工程（HWE）实践者］可以设计其元素和接口，并根据其工作的媒介的不同性质进行开发实践（Fairley，2019）。定义明确和受控的接口（包括提供的接口和要求的接口）是必不可少的，这样才能有效地综合单独开发的元素。由于软件和硬件元素逐渐变为可用，它们的综合通常以增量方式完成。定义和控制接口是一个持续不断的挑战。

在系统开发和修改过程中，协调系统工程和软件工程的主要好处是，可以将软件提供的功能融入系统中，从而提高系统的效率和效能。在系统分析和设计过程中，系统工程实践者可与软件工程实践者进行协商，为配置软件和硬件元素及其接口提供选择和权衡。此外，SWE 实践者可以向系统工程实践者提供开发和综合软件和硬件元素以及执行系统验证、效果确认和部署时可使用的流程建议（Fairley，2019）。咨询和建议可以改善软件问题，这些问题有时会导致延迟交付、系统性能不足和系统修改困难。

它如何影响/受到系统工程的影响？

开发软件密集型系统的系统工程实践者一如既往地关注如何促进系统的开发，使其能够及时交付，满足性能参数的要求，并能有效和高效地进行修改。系统工程实践者可以通过利用 SWE 实践者的专业知识更好地达到这些目标，但他们可能无法做到这一点，因为他们可能不熟悉 SWE 的文化、术语和实际操作。软件工程实践者可能不会贡献自己的专业知识，因为他们没有被征求意见，或者即使被征求意见，也可能对系统级问题了解不足，无法提供建议。让知识渊博的 SWE 实践者参与系统层面可以改善沟通。让系统工程实践者和 SWE 实践者参加交叉培训、跟班学习、指导和协作研讨会可以产生协同关系，从而提供更好的沟通，并导致对软件密集型系统更加有效和高效的开发和修改。

SYSTEMS ENGINEERING IN PRACTICE

More information on SE for software-intensive systems can be found in The Guide to the System Engineering Body of Knowledge (SEBoK) in the Part 6 knowledge area titled "SE and Software Engineering."

5.3.2 SE and Hardware Engineering (HWE)

This section describes an overview of the relationships between SE and hardware engineering (HWE).

What is this discipline?

HWE includes the development and implementation of physical elements for systems, enabling systems, and support equipment for systems. HWE includes mechanical engineering (ME) for mechanical elements and electrical engineering (EE) for electrical and electronic elements.

What is its relationship to SE?

The SE team must assist the hardware team in establishing hardware requirements, physical interface requirements, and establishing and tracking key physical measures (e.g., size, weight, and power (SWaP) budgets) at every level of the system architecture. During the System Architecture Definition and Design Definition processes (see Section 2.3.5.4 and 2.3.5.5), requirements will be allocated and derived across many hardware elements. Initially, these allocations may be required to meet a set of requirements at the system level without a full understanding of the actual values at the element level. This is where a requirements budget can be utilized by the SE team to derive these critical hardware attributes across all the applicable hardware elements and design teams. These hardware design teams will consist of diverse HWE fields, with a focus on the hardware design. The hardware design teams will accept an initial budget allocation from the SE team based on a summary analysis of the system requirements and design. The SE team gives allocations based on the requirements and hardware design team inputs. The SE team will then track progress to those budgets, determine any impacts at the system level, and relay change requests as needed. Hardware considerations include SWaP, inertia, balance, frequency, phase, and others.

Interface management is an important consideration for SE and HWE. Interface decisions will have an impact on both the interconnectivity of the system and hardware selection. Utilizing open source or standard interfaces, if feasible, can reduce costs and development time. If unique or custom interfaces are necessary, they must be documented in the architecture before design, development, and testing can occur. This requires the SE team to balance interface decisions between capability and hardware standards.

有关软件密集型系统的系统工程的更多信息,可参阅《系统工程知识体指南》(SEBoK)第 6 部分"系统工程与软件工程"知识领域。

5.3.2 系统工程和硬件工程(HWE)

本节概述系统工程和硬件工程(HWE)之间的关系。

这门学科是什么?

硬件工程包括系统、使能系统和系统支持设备的物理元素开发和实施。硬件工程包括机械元素的机械工程(ME)和电气和电子元素的电气工程(EE)。

它与系统工程的关系是什么?

系统工程团队必须协助硬件团队确定硬件需求和物理接口需求,并在系统架构的每个层级分别建立和跟踪关键物理测度 [例如尺寸、重量和功率(SWaP)预算]。在系统架构定义和设计定义流程中(见 2.3.5.4 节和 2.3.5.5 节),需求的分配和派生将会跨多种硬件元素进行。最初,这些分配可能需要在不完全了解元素级实际值的情况下满足系统级的一组需求。系统工程团队可以利用需求预算在所有适用的硬件元素和设计团队中推导这些关键硬件属性。

这些硬件设计团队将会包含不同的硬件工程领域,并着重于硬件设计。硬件设计团队将接受一份系统工程团队的初始预算分配,其根据是对系统需求和设计的总结分析。系统工程团队根据需求和硬件设计团队的输入进行分配。然后,系统工程团队将跟踪这些预算的进展情况,确定系统层面产生的任何影响,并根据需要传递更改请求。硬件考虑因素包括 SWaP、惯性、平衡、频率、相位等。

接口管理是系统工程和 HWE 的重要考虑因素。接口决策将对系统的互连性和硬件选择均产生影响。如果可行,利用开源或标准接口可以减少成本和开发时间。如果需要唯一或自定义的接口,则必须在设计、开发和测试之前将其记录在系统架构中。这要求系统工程团队在能力和硬件标准之间平衡接口决策。

268 The application of SE to hardware differs from software-only applications in two primary ways: hardware solutions may exist that can meet all or part of a decomposed requirement and the hardware performance requirements generally must be built into the initial hardware deliverable rather than iterated into the design (with some exceptions). A make or buy decision is often performed at each level of the architecture based on the results of a market analysis and tradeoff study of existing solutions that will satisfy the requirements. If the result of the decision is to make, the architecture can be further decomposed or Implementation process initiated. However, if the result of the decision is to buy, then the architecture decomposition for that system element will end (see Section 1.3.5).

How does it impact/is it impacted by SE?

Hardware material selection is supported by existing application or domain-specific standards. On a smaller, less complicated systems, HWE may be able to select all materials without the need of a formal SE process. With the increasing complexity of large systems and SoSs, the role of SE in hardware material selection becomes paramount, especially in applications where human lives could be affected. For instance, when multiple hardware sources could have system elements with mechanical or electrical interactions, the role of SE is to document architecture and design decisions and provide timely input into the material selection process before costly errors are found in verification or production. Sometimes SE acts to balance the software and hardware requirements, because software requirements can influence the hardware requirements, and vice versa. For instance, having a high availability requirement can result in the need for redundant software systems deployed on redundant hardware systems, meaning that the weight and the power budgets are increasing. SE serves as the bridge between software and hardware.

5.3.3 SE and Project Management (PM)

This section describes an overview of the relationships between SE and project management (PM).

What is this discipline?

As defined by the Project Management Institute (PMI), PM is defined as:

The application of knowledge, skills, tools, and techniques to project activities to meet the project requirements. (PMI, 2022)

PM activities include initiating, planning, executing, monitoring, and closing projects. Within this handbook these are primarily distributed across the Technical Management Processes (see Section 2.3.4) for the SE portion of the responsibilities, but also include some activities in the Agreement Processes (see Section 2.3.2) and Organizational Project Enabling Processes (see Section 2.3.3). In the PMI Project Management Body

系统工程在硬件与纯软件上的应用主要有两处不同：能够满足全部或部分分解需求的硬件方案可能存在，硬件性能需求通常必须构建到初始硬件交付物中，而不是在设计中反复迭代（存在例外情况）。通常要根据市场分析结果和对满足需求的现有解决方案的权衡研究结果，在架构的每个层次做出"制造"或"购买"的决策。如果决策的结果是进行制造，则架构会被进一步分解或启动实施流程。然而，如果决策的结果是购买，那么该系统元素的架构分解将结束（见 1.3.5 节）。

它如何影响/受到系统工程的影响？

硬件材料的选择是由现有应用或特定领域标准支持的。在规模较小、不太繁杂的系统上，硬件工程可以选择所有材料，而无须正式的系统工程流程。随着大型系统和体系的日益复杂，系统工程在硬件材料选择中的作用变得至关重要，尤其是在可能影响人们生活的应用中。例如，当多个硬件源可能具有机械或电气相互作用的系统元素时，系统工程的作用是记录架构和设计决策，并在验证或生产中发现代价高昂的错误之前，及时向材料选择流程提供输入。有时系统工程会平衡软件和硬件需求，因为软件需求会影响硬件需求，反之亦然。例如，高可用性需求可能导致需要在冗余硬件系统上部署冗余软件系统，造成重量和功率预算增加。系统工程是软件和硬件之间的桥梁。

5.3.3 系统工程和项目管理（PM）

本节概述系统工程与项目管理（PM）之间的关系。

这门学科是什么？

根据项目管理协会（PMI）的定义，PM 的定义如下：

将知识、技能、工具和技术应用于项目活动，以满足项目需求（PMI，2022）。

项目管理活动包括启动、规划、执行、监控和结束项目。在本手册中，这些项目管理活动主要分布在技术管理流程（见 2.3.4 节）中以支撑系统工程的部分职责，但也包括协议流程（见 2.3.2 节）和组织的项目使能流程（见 2.3.3 节）

SYSTEMS ENGINEERING IN PRACTICE

of Knowledge (PMBoK) (2017), they are part of Project Integration Management, Project Scope Management, Project Schedule Management, Project Cost Management, Project Quality Management, Project Resource Management, Project Communications Management, Project Risk Management, Project Procurement Management, and Project Stakeholder Management. According to the PMBoK, a program is a set of related projects that are viewed as an entity that requires coordinated management.

What is its relationship to SE?

While SE and PM are distinct disciplines, extensive research has shown that effective integration between PM and SE improves project performance, achieving better results in schedule and budget performance, as well as stakeholder requirements satisfaction, when compared with projects with lesser integration. In 2011, INCOSE formed a strategic alliance with PMI and Massachusetts Institute of Technology (MIT) to research and advance the integration of the two disciplines, driven by the vision that better integration would lead to the delivery of better solutions for organizations and their stakeholders. One output of this alliance was *Integrating Program Management and SE* (Rebentisch, 2017), which defines this integration as "a reflection of the organization ability to combine project management and SE practices, tools and techniques, experience and knowledge in a collaborative and systematic approach in the face of challenges in order to be more effective in achieving common goals/objectives in complex project environments." A summary of the respective and shared responsibilities between PM and SE is shown in Figure 5.4. Cooperation between project managers and SE practitioners must exist within all these shared activities.

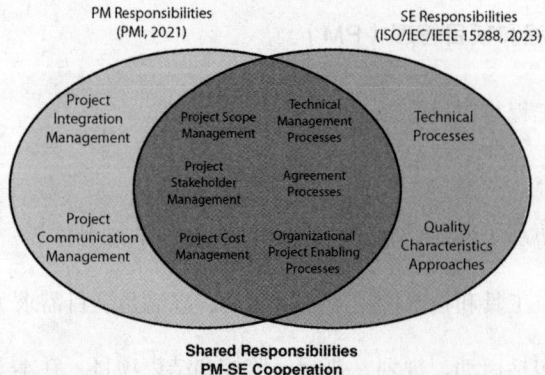

FIGURE 5.4 The intersection between PM and SE. INCOSE SEH original figure created by Roussel on behalf of the INCOSE PM-SE Integration Working Group. Usage per the INCOSE Notices page. All other rights reserved.

的一些活动。在PMI项目管理知识体（PMBoK）(2017)中，它们是项目综合管理、项目范围管理、项目进度管理、项目成本管理、项目质量管理、项目资源管理、项目沟通管理、项目风险管理、项目采办管理和项目利益相关方管理的一部分。根据PMBoK，项目组是一组相关的项目，被视为需要协调管理的实体。

它与系统工程的关系是什么？

虽然系统工程和PM是不同的学科，但有充分的研究表明，PM和系统工程之间的有效综合可以提高项目绩效，与综合程度较低的项目相比，在进度和预算绩效以及利益相关方需求满意度方面取得更好的结果。2011年，由更好的综合将为组织及其利益相关方交付更好的解决方案的愿景所驱动，INCOSE与PMI和麻省理工学院（MIT）结成战略联盟，研究和推进这两个学科的综合。该联盟的一项成果是将项目管理与系统工程进行综合（Rebentisch，2017年），该成果将这种综合定义为"反映了组织在面对挑战时，以协作和系统的方式将项目管理与系统工程实践、工具和技术、经验和知识相结合的能力，以便在复杂的项目环境中更有效地达到共同的目标/目的。"图5.4总结了PM和系统工程之间各自和共享的职责。项目经理和系统工程实践者之间的合作必须存在于所有这些共享活动中。

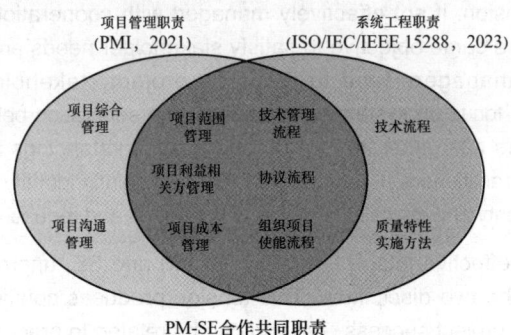

图5.4 项目管理和系统工程的交集。INCOSE SEH原始图由Roussel代表INCOSE项目管理—系统工程综合工作组创建。按照INCOSE通知页使用。版权所有。

How does it impact/is it impacted by SE?

A high degree of integration between PM and SE is characterized by collaborative decision making, a shared responsibility toward a common goal, having the project manager involved in technical aspects of the project, and having the SE practitioners involved in programmatic aspects of the project. An understanding of the differences, culture, background, and behavior of the two disciplines is also required. A team's ability to combine PM and SE practices, tools and techniques, experience, and knowledge in a collaborative and systematic approach enables addressing challenges in order to achieve common goals and objectives. Specifically, an integrated team achieves rapid and effective decision making, effective collaborative work, and effective information sharing (Rebentisch, 2017).

PM and SE overlap in the early stages of concept and development but tend to diverge in the later stages of development and production. For example, in the early life cycle stages the SE practitioner focuses on the technical details of the SoI, verification, and validation. The project manager focuses on the overall project performance and delivery of benefits, including high-level finance and budgetary requirements. PM and SE should cooperate on concurrent development of the breakdown structures (see Section 2.3.4.1), and in the management of them through the life cycle. If the different structures are managed separately by the respective teams without coordination, problems may arise in the project. As the project proceeds through the later life cycle stages, greater integration between PM and SE reduces unproductive tension, a cause of project delays, cost increases, and, sometimes, project failure (Rebentisch, 2017).

As stated in Rebentisch (2017), PM delivers the sustainable benefits of the overall project, while SE delivers the technical aspect of the project. These two roles overlap to integrate technical and programmatic aspects of the project and create potential for unproductive tension, if not effectively managed with cooperation. For example, PM and SE share the same objective to satisfy stakeholder needs and requirements. However, project managers tend to focus on project stakeholders, while SE practitioners tend to focus on system stakeholders. The separation between these two types of stakeholders can generate tension and misunderstandings between project managers and SE practitioners. It is important that they jointly identify all stakeholders and agree on the priority and criticality of stakeholder needs and requirements.

Where there is not effective integration between PM and SE, unproductive tension emerges between the two disciplines. This tension produces conflict and works at cross purposes with project success. Tension can be related to practices, techniques, as well as responsibilities. Misaligned measures can cause tension. Common measures are critical to ensuring that each party has the same concerns and information. The maturity level of each party is critical. An immature or inexperienced PM organization can render ineffective a mature, high-performing SE organization (and vice versa). When one or both disciplines perform inadequately, the entire effort is impaired.

它如何影响系统工程/受到系统工程的影响？

PM 和系统工程之间的高度综合以协作决策、为共同目标分担责任、项目经理参与项目的技术方面以及系统工程实践者参与项目的计划方面为特征。这需要了解这两个学科的差异、文化、背景和行为。团队能够以协作和系统的方式将 PM 和系统工程实践、工具和技术、经验和知识结合起来，从而能够应对挑战，以达到共同的目标和目的。具体而言，一个综合团队可以实现快速有效的决策、有效的协同工作和有效的信息共享（Rebentisch，2017）。

项目管理和系统工程在概念和开发的早期阶段有重叠，但在开发的后期和生产阶段有差异。例如，在生命周期的早期阶段，系统工程实践者关注 SoI、验证和确认的技术细节。项目经理关注项目的整体绩效和效益交付，包括高层级的财务和预算要求。项目管理和系统工程应合作同步开发分解结构（见 2.3.4.1 节），并在整个生命周期内对其进行管理。如果不同的分解结构由各自团队在没有协调的情况下单独管理，则项目可能会出现问题。随着项目进入生命周期的后期阶段，项目管理和系统工程之间的进一步综合可以减少无益的紧张关系，这是导致项目延期、成本增加，有时甚至是项目失败的原因之一（Rebentisch，2017）。

如 Rebentisch（2017）所述，项目管理交付整个项目的可持续效益，而系统工程交付项目的技术方面。这两个角色相互重叠，以综合项目的技术和计划方面，如果不进行有效地合作管理，则可能会造成潜在的无益的紧张关系。例如，项目管理和系统工程具有相同的目标，以满足利益相关方的需要和需求。然而，项目经理倾向于关注项目利益相关方，而系统工程实践者倾向于关注系统利益相关方。这两类利益相关方之间的分离可能会在项目经理和系统工程实践者之间产生矛盾和误解。重要的是，他们共同确定所有利益相关方，并就利益相关方需要和需求的优先级和关键性达成一致。

如果项目管理和系统工程之间没有有效的综合，这两个学科之间就会涌现无益的紧张关系。这种紧张关系会产生冲突，并对项目成功产生反作用。紧张关系可能与实践、技巧以及职责有关。未对齐的措施可能会导致紧张关系。共同措施对于确保各方拥有相同的关注点和信息至关重要。各方的成熟度水平都是至关重要的。不成熟或缺乏经验的项目管理组织可能会使成熟、高绩效的系统工程组织失效（反之亦然）。当一个或两个学科表现不佳时，整体效果就会被削弱。

5.3.4 SE and Industrial Engineering (IE)

This section describes an overview of the relationships between SE and industrial engineering (IE).

What is this discipline?

Bidanda (2022) defines Industrial Engineering as:

Optimizing the utilization of human resources, facilities, equipment, tools, technologies, information, and handling of materials to produce quality products and services safely and cost-effectively considering the needs of customers and employers.

The Institute of Industrial and Systems Engineers (IISE) Industrial and SE Body of Knowledge (ISEBoK) (2022) is composed of 14 knowledge areas. The knowledge areas include: Operations Research & Analysis, Economic Analysis, Facilities Engineering & Energy Management, Quality and Reliability Engineering, Ergonomics & Human Factors, Operations Engineering & Management, Supply Chain Management, Safety, Information Engineering, Design and Manufacturing Engineering, Product Design & Development, Systems Design & Engineering.

What is its relationship to SE?

IE is closely related to SE. The IISE states that "Industrial and SE is concerned with the design, improvement, and installation of integrated systems of people, materials, information, equipment and energy. It draws upon specialized knowledge and skill in the mathematical, physical, and social sciences together with the principles and methods of engineering analysis and design, to specify, predict, and evaluate the results to be obtained from such systems." As evidence of the close relationship of IE and SE, Figure 5.5 compares the ISEBoK (2022) with SE topics in this handbook. The numbered topics on the figure are the knowledge areas explicitly identified in the ISEBoK. The figure identifies the knowledge areas that are usually performed by SE practitioners, the ones usually performed by industrial engineers (IE), and the knowledge area descriptions that are used by both disciplines.

As an illustration of the relationships between IE and SE, four knowledge areas are discussed below.

Operations Research and Analysis—Operations Research (OR) includes a variety of techniques to quantify and improve the efficiency of systems and organizational processes using scientific mathematical models. The mathematical techniques include linear programming, transportation models, linear assignment models, network flows, dynamic programming, integer programming, nonlinear programming, metaheuristics, decision analysis, game theory, stochastic modeling, queuing systems, simulation, systems dynamics, and analytics. Industrial engineers use OR to understand, design, and improve the operation of industrial systems and processes. SE practitioners can perform OR analyses or use OR studies performed by others to make system decisions (see Section 5.3.5).

5.3.4 系统工程和工业工程（IE）

本节概述系统工程与工业工程（IE）之间的关系。

这门学科是什么？

Bidanda（2022）将工业工程定义为：

考虑客户和雇主的需要，优化人力资源、设施、设备、工具、技术、信息、物料搬运系统，以安全、经济高效地生产优质产品和服务。

工业与系统工程师协会（IISE）工业和系统工程知识体（ISEBoK）（2022）由14个知识领域组成。知识领域包括：运筹学与分析、经济分析、设施工程与能源管理、质量与可靠性工程、人因与工效学、运作工程学与管理、供应链管理、安全、信息工程、设计与制造工程、产品设计与开发、系统设计与工程。

它与系统工程的关系是什么？

工业工程与系统工程密切相关。IISE指出，"工业和系统工程与人、物料、信息、设备和能源综合系统的设计、改进和安装有关。它利用数学、物理和社会科学的专业知识和技能，以及工程分析和设计的原则和方法，用来指定、预测和评估从此类系统中获得的结果"。作为工业工程和系统工程密切相关的证据，图5.5将ISEBoK（2022）与本手册中的系统工程主题进行了比较。图中编号的主题是ISEBoK中明确确定的知识领域。图中标明了系统工程实践者通常从事的知识领域、工业工程师通常从事的知识领域，以及两个学科都使用的知识领域描述。

下面将讨论四个知识领域，以说明工业工程和系统工程之间的关系。

运筹学与分析——运筹学（OR）包括使用科学的数学模型量化和提高系统和组织流程效率的各种技术。数学技术包括线性规划、运输模型、线性分配模型、网络流量、动态规划、整数规划、非线性规划、元启发式算法、决策分析、博弈论、随机建模、排队系统、仿真、系统动力学和分析学。工业工程师使用运筹学来理解、设计和改进工业系统和流程的运行。系统工程实践者可以进行运筹学分析或使用他人进行的运筹学研究来做出系统决策（见5.3.5节）。

SYSTEMS ENGINEERING IN PRACTICE

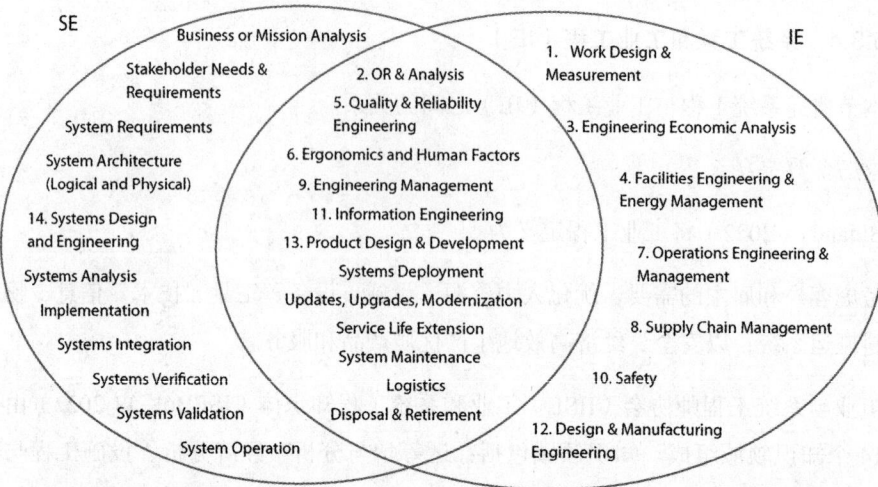

FIGURE 5.5 IE and SE relationships. From Parnell, et al. (2022). Used with permission. All other rights reserved.

Information engineering—Information engineering is a "methodology for developing an integrated information system based on the sharing of common data, with emphasis on decision support needs as well as transaction-processing (TP) requirements" (Gartner, 2022). Information engineering topics include: data types; information system concepts; information requirements; output design; data processing; database concepts; storage and processing; system analysis; system design; system evaluation; information management; and data analytics. Since information systems are a critical component of modern engineering systems, IE and SE practitioners work closely with information engineers.

Product Design and Development—As stated in ISEBoK (2022), "From an Industrial Engineering knowledge view, it is the processes and analysis employed supporting efficient decision-making during Product Design and Development." Product design and development topics include: design process; preliminary and detailed design; verification and testing; planning for manufacture; metrics for design and development; life cycle costing; and risk and opportunity management. SE practitioners may provide inputs to the product design and development process throughout the system life cycle.

System Design and Engineering—The ISEBoK (2022) lists the SEBoK (2022) as the reference for this section. The topics include the system life cycle concepts from mission engineering to operations.

How does it impact/is it impacted by SE?

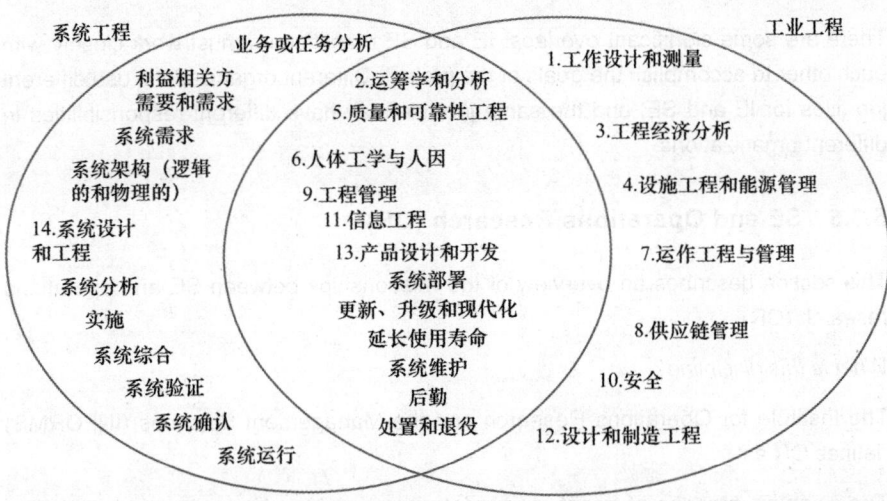

图 5.5　工业工程和系统工程的关系。源自 Parnell 等（2022）。经许可使用。版权所有。

信息工程——信息工程是一种"基于共享公共数据开发综合信息系统的方法论，强调决策支持需要和事务处理（TP）需求"（Gartner，2022）。信息工程主题包括：数据类型、信息系统概念、信息需求、输出设计、数据处理、数据库概念、储存和处理、系统分析、系统设计、系统评估、信息管理和数据分析。由于信息系统是现代工程系统的关键组成部分，IE 和 SE 实践者与信息工程师合作密切。

产品设计与开发——正如 ISEBoK（2022）所述，"从工业工程知识的角度来看，它是在产品设计和开发期间支持有效决策的流程和分析"。产品设计和开发主题包括：设计流程、初步和详细设计、验证和测试、制造计划、设计和开发指标、生命周期成本计算、风险和机会管理。SE 实践者可以在整个系统生命周期中为产品设计和开发流程提供输入。

系统设计与工程——ISEBoK（2022）列出了 SEBoK（2022）作为本节的参考。主题包括从任务工程到运行的系统生命周期概念。

它如何影响系统工程/受到系统工程的影响？

SYSTEMS ENGINEERING IN PRACTICE

There are some significant overlaps. IE and SE practitioners must work closely with each other to accomplish the goals of the project. Different organizations use different job titles for IE and SE, and the same job title may have different responsibilities in different organizations.

5.3.5 SE and Operations Research (OR)

This section describes an overview of the relationships between SE and operations research (OR).

What is this discipline?

The Institute for Operations Research and the Management Sciences (INFORMS) defines OR as:

The scientific process of transforming data into insights using advanced analytical methods to making better decisions. (INFORMS, 2022)

The name "operations research" originated from the recognition of the successful use of scientific and mathematical modeling techniques for military operations during World War II (Gass and Harris, 2001). For example, mathematical modeling assisted in developing strategies to employ bombers as well as arrange convoys against submarine attacks. OR is sometimes referred to as Management Science, particularly in business applications, as well as Operational Research in some countries (Quade and Boucher, 1968).

A branch of applied mathematics, OR includes wide range of approaches. Common to all is the establishment of a model to represent the system to support analysis for decision making. In some cases, the model may be solved directly, but other common approaches include optimization, simulation, and decision analysis.

Optimization is useful in determining the best combination of decision variables. Optimization models can be linear, integer, and nonlinear depending on the form of the objective function and constraints. Goal programming is useful when thresholds are established as an achievement target on multiple objectives. The approach avoids falling short of goals and incurring a penalty but permits a broader trade-off analysis.

Simulation is useful for assessing how well the system as a whole will perform its role in a given environment. Systems will typically be analyzed using stochastic discrete event simulations. These are often called Monte Carlo simulations, as random numbers are drawn to represent outcomes from distributions for the input uncertainties. These models are run multiple times and the output probabilities of occurrence are established by aggregating the simulation runs and using statistical tools for interpretation (Fishman, 1997).

二者有一些重要的重叠。工业工程和系统工程实践者必须密切合作，以达到项目目标。不同的组织对工业工程和系统工程使用不同的称谓，同一称谓在不同的组织中可能有不同的职责。

5.3.5 系统工程和运筹学（OR）

本节概述系统工程与运筹学（OR）之间的关系。

这门学科是什么？

运筹学与管理科学协会（INFORMS）将运筹学定义为：

利用先进的分析方法将数据转化为见解以做出更好的决策的科学流程。（INFORMS，2022）

运筹学的名称源于人们对第二次世界大战期间在军事行动中成功使用科学和数学建模技术的认识（Gass 和 Harris，2001）。例如，数学建模辅助制定使用轰炸机以及安排护卫舰对抗潜艇攻击的战略。运筹学有时被称为管理科学，特别是在商业应用中，在一些国家还被称为运作研究（Quade 和 Boucher，1968）。

运筹学是应用数学的一个分支，包含多种方法。共同点是建立一个模型来表示系统，以支持分析决策。在某些情况下，可以直接求解模型，而其他常用方法包括优化、仿真和决策分析。

优化有助于确定决策变量的最佳组合。根据目标函数和约束的形式，优化模型可以是线性、整数和非线性的。将阈值设定为多个目标的实现时，目标规划就非常有用。这种方法可以避免达不到目标而受到惩罚，同时还可以进行更广泛的权衡分析。

仿真有助于评估系统作为一个整体在给定环境中执行其角色的情况。系统通常使用随机离散事件仿真进行分析。通常被称为蒙特卡罗仿真，因为随机数被用来表示输入的不确定性分布结果。这些模型多次运行，通过联合仿真运行并使用统计工具进行解释，来建立事件的输出概率（Fishman，1997）。

Decision analysis uses a model of the decision makers' preferences and risk attitudes to analyze tradeoffs between alternatives and is often used for strategic decision making.

What is its relationship to SE?

OR techniques frequently support SE by assisting in understanding stakeholder needs and estimating how a proposed system will behave. Decision analysis is used to elicit stakeholder needs and preferences to construct a value model. The value model is used to understand value tradeoffs between different system or system element alternatives. The performance of the anticipated system alternatives may be represented through a simulation. This has been so successful that model-based SE (MBSE) has become an important area (see Section 4.2.1). Optimization may be applied to improve designs. For example, by minimizing a system element weight while providing required structural strength. Optimization may be used to minimize life cycle costs using inventory theory. Queueing theory may be used to understand system processing times. Forecasting may be used to project forward from historical data. Network flow analysis may be used to improve network capacity.

Blanchard and Fabrycky (2011) discuss the SE morphology for product (system) realization. They note the steps after design synthesis are (1) Estimation and Prediction, and (2) Design Evaluation. Estimation and Prediction often rely heavily on OR. For example, assessing the response times associated with different possible locations for a new firehouse or estimating spare parts requirements as part of a life cycle cost perspective.

Optimization may be applied in the development stage as well as in the production stage. Optimization may be applied at higher levels of the systems hierarchy. For example, a less costly design may support a larger number of employed systems for the same results.

Operations research techniques may be applied to historical and test data. Data analytics may be used to establish system performance as a mathematical function of inputs. Sensitivity analysis may be used to establish acceptable system inputs. Response surface methodology may be used to establish more abstract but tractable models. Forecasting methods may be applied to time series data.

Decision analysis provides the ability to understand decision quality and assess the value or utility delivered under certainty and uncertainty. Decision analysis provides not only the ability to select the best presented alternative but also supports insight in examination of hybrid alternatives, allowing searching for improved designs. It is also transparent and traceable, and so is fully defensible and allows representation of differing preferences of various stakeholders.

决策分析使用决策者偏好和风险态度的模型来分析备选方案之间的权衡，通常用于战略决策。

它与系统工程的关系是什么？

运筹学技术通常通过帮助理解利益相关方的需要和估计所提出系统的运行方式来支持系统工程。决策分析用于引出利益相关方的需要和偏好，以构建价值模型。价值模型用于理解不同系统或系统元素备选方案之间的价值权衡。预期系统备选方案的性能可以通过仿真来表达。这种方法非常成功，基于模型的系统工程（MBSE）已成为一个重要领域（见 4.2.1 节）。优化可用于改进设计。例如，在提供所需结构强度的同时，最小化系统元素的重量。利用库存理论，优化可用于最小化生命周期成本。排队论可以用来理解系统的处理时间。预测可用于根据历史数据进行前瞻性预测。网络流量分析可用于提高网络容量。

Blanchard 和 Fabrycky（2011）讨论了产品（系统）实现中的系统工程。他们指出，设计综合后的步骤是（1）估计和预测，以及（2）设计评估。估计和预测通常严重依赖运筹学。例如，评估新消防站不同可能位置的响应时间，或作为生命周期成本的一部分估算备件需求。

优化可应用于开发阶段和生产阶段。优化可应用于系统层级结构的更高层级。例如，成本较低的设计可能支持大量使用的系统，以获得相同的结果。

运筹学技术可应用于历史和测试数据。数据分析可用于将系统性能建立为输入的数学函数。敏感性分析可用于确定可接受的系统输入。响应曲面法可用于建立更抽象但易于处理的模型。预测方法可应用于时间序列数据。

决策分析提供了理解决策质量和评估在确定性和不确定性下交付的价值或效用的能力。决策分析不仅提供了选择最佳备选方案的能力，还支持对混合方案进行深入研究，从而可以搜索更好的设计。它也是透明和可追踪的，因此是完全合乎情理的，并允许代表不同利益相关方的不同偏好。

SYSTEMS ENGINEERING IN PRACTICE

How does it impact/is it impacted by SE?

OR and SE practitioners must work closely with each other to accomplish the goals of the project. SE practitioners can perform OR analyses or use OR studies performed by others to make system decisions.

5.4 DIGITAL ENGINEERING

Definitions

The US Defense Acquisition University Glossary (DAU, 2022) defines Digital Engineering as:

An integrated digital approach that uses authoritative sources of systems' data and models as a continuum across disciplines to support life cycle activities from concept through [retirement].

Digital Engineering is crosscutting: it includes all engineering disciplines using well-formed models to execute their processes and communicate a system's design. Digital Engineering emphasizes continuity of models and their use across the life cycle. Digital Engineering seeks to maximize the use of models and the computer and places emphasis on consistent and rigorous engineering, strong data management practices, and continuous improvement through technologic innovation. It requires a supporting infrastructure and environment and a capable workforce and culture that is committed to working in accordance with process, following methods, and using tool the organization supplies them.

Model-based SE (MBSE) (see Section 4.2.1) is one of core elements of Digital Engineering. In MBSE and Digital Engineering, a Digital System Model is a digital representation of a system. It integrates the authoritative MBSE and other Digital Engineering technical data and associated artifacts, defining all aspects of the system throughout the system life cycle. The Digital System Model is composed of a federated set of models that serve as an authoritative source of truth (ASOT) for the system's design.

Digital Engineering leverages MBSE and the Digital System Model to enable digital threads and digital twins. A *digital twin* is a digital surrogate of the system, incorporating models to emulate the actual system or some of its elements. The digital twin evolves through the life cycle with the mission and definition of the system. A *digital thread* is a set of interconnected, cross-discipline model data that seamlessly expedite the controlled interplay of digital artifacts to inform decision makers throughout a system's life cycle. Digital threads can be used to produce *digital artifacts* that are a combination of authoritative data, information, knowledge, and wisdom addressing stakeholders' unique perspective.

它如何影响系统工程 / 受到系统工程的影响？

OR 和 SE 实践者必须密切合作，以达到项目的目标。系统工程实践者可以进行运筹学分析或使用他人进行的运筹学研究来做出系统决策。

5.4 数字工程

定义

美国国防军需大学词汇表（DAU，2022）将数字工程定义为：

一种综合的数字方法，使用系统数据和模型的权威来源作为跨学科的连续统一体，支持从概念到 [退役] 的生命周期活动。

数字工程是交叉学科：它包括所有使用规范的模型来执行其流程并沟通系统设计的工程学科。数字工程强调模型的连续性及其在整个生命周期中的使用。数字工程寻求最大限度地利用模型和计算机，并强调一致和严格的工程、强大的数据管理实践以及通过技术创新的持续改进。它需要一个支持性的基础设施和环境，以及一套有能力的致力于按照流程、遵循方法和使用组织提供的工具开展工作的员工队伍和文化。

基于模型的系统工程（MBSE）（见 4.2.1 节）是数字工程的核心元素之一。在 MBSE 和数字工程中，数字系统模型是系统的数字表示。它综合了权威的 MBSE 和其他数字工程技术数据及相关制品，定义了整个系统生命周期中系统的所有方面。数字系统模型由一组联合模型组成，这些模型是系统设计的权威真相源（ASOT）。

数字工程利用 MBSE 和数字系统模型实现数字线索和数字孪生。数字孪生是系统的数字代理，结合模型来仿真实际系统或其某些元素。数字孪生随着系统的使命和定义在整个生命周期中不断发展。数字线索是一组相互关联的跨学科模型数据，可以无缝地促进数字制品的受控相互作用，从而在整个系统生命周期中为决策者提供依据。数字线索可用于制作*数字制品*，这些制品集权威数据、信息、知识和智慧于一体，可满足利益相关方的独特视角。

SYSTEMS ENGINEERING IN PRACTICE

Digital Engineering in Projects

Digital Engineering performed on projects needs to be based around the project and SoI requirements, as well as opportunities and risks that are identified from stakeholders including customers, users, organizational leadership, the infrastructure, decision makers, and project managers. It is important to pay special attention to Digital Engineering contributions and inputs when doing the technical planning across the life cycle.

As each life cycle stage is considered, it is critical to research and document opportunities for future project use, as well as for reuse of models, simulations, and data across the life cycle. For example, models and simulations developed during earlier life cycle stages may be reused for verification and training in later life cycle stages.

Digital Engineering for the Enterprise

Digital Engineering is an approach for projects, but is also important as an enterprise digital transformation initiative (see Section 5.5). To achieve maximum benefit both project and enterprise level concerns should be considered together. Enterprise level implementation efforts are necessary to position the engineering infrastructure and environment so that a project will be able to perform their engineering activities in a digital manner. Consistent use of the infrastructure and environment on a project, and across projects, will yield increasingly consistent engineering work products. Consistency across work products will lead to great gains in reuse and will enable greater speed through computer automation.

Digital Engineering Ecosystem

The Digital Engineering ecosystem can be vast, crossing engineering domain and organizational boundaries. The Digital Engineering ecosystem should be treated as an SoS and must be developed using SE good practices. The Digital Engineering ecosystem consists of the models, tools, processes, and people/roles that come together to develop the systems the organization cares about. The ecosystem can be broader than this, depending on the scope. For example, some organizations utilize their Digital Engineering ecosystems to support the operation of their systems. Others include cross-project libraries and methods in their Digital Engineering ecosystems, as well as interconnections with external Digital Engineering ecosystems across their supply chain.

项目中的数字工程

在项目中实施的数字工程需要基于项目和 SoI 需求，以及利益相关方（包括客户、用户、组织领导层、基础设施、决策者和项目经理）确定的机会和风险。在整个生命周期内进行技术规划时，必须特别注意数字工程的贡献和投入。

在考虑每个生命周期阶段时，研究和记录未来项目使用的机会以及整个生命周期中模型、仿真和数据的重用至关重要。例如，在早期生命周期阶段开发的模型和仿真可重复用于后期生命周期阶段的验证和培训。

复杂组织体系数字工程

数字工程是项目的一种实施方法，但在复杂组织体系数字转型中也很重要（见 5.5 节）。为了实现最大效益，应同时考虑项目和复杂组织体系层面的问题。复杂组织体系层面的实施工作对于工程基础设施和环境的定位十分必要，以便项目能够以数字化方式执行其工程活动。在一个项目上和跨项目上一致地使用基础设施和环境，将产生越来越一致的工程产品。跨工作产品的一致性将带来复用方面的巨大收益，并将通过计算机自动化实现速度的更快提升。

数字工程生态系统

数字工程生态系统可以是巨大的，可以跨越工程领域和组织边界。数字工程生态系统应视为体系，必须使用系统工程的良好实践进行开发。数字工程生态系统由模型、工具、流程和人员 / 角色组成，它们共同开发组织关心的系统。根据范围的不同，数字工程生态系统可以更加广泛。例如，一些组织利用其数字工程生态系统来支持其系统的运行。其他则包括数字工程生态系统中跨项目的库和方法，以及供应链与外部数字工程生态系统的互联。

Technological Innovation

Technological innovation is an important part of Digital Engineering. It is the catalyst that drives change into the engineering practice through strategic and planned implementation. It is an essential part of a continuous process improvement program that seeks out and injects technology into the systems that are used to develop the SoI. Technological innovation seeks to optimize the use of computer and information technologies to enhance the speed, agility, quality, and precision of all engineering activities that occur through the development life cycle.

5.5 SYSTEMS ENGINEERING TRANSFORMATION

In discussing SE transformation, there are three important transformations to be considered:

- Transforming from no SE to full use of SE,
- The internal SE from traditional to agile methodologies as appropriate, and
- The internal SE from document-based to model-based disciplines.

Considering the first, for an organization to begin implementing SE requires a cultural shift to understand the basics of the system life cycle and implement the life cycle processes described in this handbook in the organization's set of processes (see Section 2.3.3.1). When performing this type of transformation, organizations will need to prepare for the major cultural shift required for the team members to learn, understand, and perform SE tasks.

The second type of transformation for internal SE from traditional to agile methodologies also requires a cultural shift to understand the basics of agile SE (see Section 4.2.2) in the organization's set of processes. Agile SE requires tools and capabilities that may also cause the organization to need additional infrastructure and human talent. Every organization will need to determine the best way to integrate agile SE practices and methodologies, whether as a wholesale change or a gradual change for their SE processes. In practice, the main reasons why are required these two types of transformations are that the system life cycle is either being compressed during the concept and development stages and/or the life cycle is being shifted to the left with early concept task being anticipated with early involvement of SE.

The third transformation is SE's transformation to a model-based discipline supports transdisciplinary digital engineering through model-based activity, advancement, organizational change, and a broad model community engagement (Peterson, 2019). This transformation addresses:

技术创新

技术创新是数字工程的重要组成部分。它是通过战略和计划实施推动工程实践变革的催化剂。它是持续流程改进计划的重要组成部分，该计划旨在寻求新技术并将其注入用于开发 SoI 的系统中。技术创新旨在优化计算机和信息技术的使用，以提高整个开发生命周期中所有工程活动的速度、灵活性、质量和精确度。

5.5 系统工程转型

在讨论系统工程转型时，需要考虑三个重要的转型：

- 从无系统工程转变为充分利用系统工程；
- 内部系统工程适当地从传统方法转到敏捷方法；
- 内部系统工程从基于文档的学科转向基于模型的学科。

考虑到第一种情况，对于开始实施系统工程的组织来说，需要进行文化转变，以了解系统生命周期的基本知识，并在组织的流程中实施本手册中描述的生命周期流程（见 2.3.3.1 节）。当执行这种类型的转型时，组织需要为团队成员学习、理解和执行系统工程任务所需的重大文化转变做好准备。

内部系统工程从传统方法向敏捷方法的第二种转型同样也需要文化转变，以了解组织流程中敏捷系统工程的基础知识（见 4.2.2 节）。敏捷系统工程需要的工具和能力，也可能导致组织需要额外的基础设施和人才。每个组织都需要确定综合敏捷系统工程实践和方法论的最佳方式，无论是整体改变还是逐步改变其系统工程流程。在实践中，需要进行这两类转换的主要原因是，系统生命周期在概念和开发阶段被压缩，和/或生命周期被左移，早期概念任务在系统工程的早期参与下被预见。

第三种转型是系统工程向基于模型的学科的转型，通过基于模型的活动、发展、组织变革和广泛的模型群体的参与支持跨学科数字工程（Peterson, 2019）。此转型解决了以下问题：

SYSTEMS ENGINEERING IN PRACTICE

- Knowledge representation and immersive technologies,
- Product (System) modeling,
- Model-based SE (MBSE) approaches and methods,
- Virtual prototyping and virtual product integration at scale,
- Foundational theory, principles, and heuristics, and
- MBSE in support of Digital Engineering.

Knowledge representation and immersive virtual reality technologies (characterized by deep absorption or immersion) enable highly efficient and shared human understanding of systems in a virtual environment that spans the full life cycle. Systems modeling forms the product-centric backbone of the digital enterprise which incorporates a model-centric approach to integrate technical, programmatic, business, regulatory, and governance concerns (see Section 3.2.1). Model-based approaches and sophisticated model-based methods extend beyond product modeling to include systems of systems (SoSs) and enterprise-level modeling and analysis (see Section 4.2.1). Large scale virtual prototyping and virtual product integration based on integrated models enable significant time-to-market reductions (see Sections 3.2.2 and 2.3.5.8). Foundations of theory, principles, and heuristics allow for a better understanding of increasingly complex systems and decisions in the face of uncertainty (see Section 1.4). MBSE in support of Digital Engineering is standard practice and is integrated with other modeling and simulation as well as digital enterprise functions (see Section 5.4).

5.6 FUTURE OF SE

The primary focus of this handbook is the state-of-the-good-practice in SE. This section highlights some emerging areas, looking toward the future of SE. INCOSE's Systems Engineering Vision (2022) is an excellent resource. In addition, the SE Body of Knowledge (2023) is continually updated to reflect both the state-of-the-practice and the state-of-the-art in SE.

INCOSE's Future of Systems Engineering (FuSE) is a systems community initiative to realize the INCOSE Vision 2035 (2022) and to evolve the instruction, practice, and perception of SE to:

- Position the discipline to leverage new technologies in collaboration with allied fields,
- Enhance SE's ability to solve the emerging challenges, and

- 知识表示和沉浸式技术；

- 产品（系统）建模；

- 基于模型的系统工程（MBSE）实施方法和途径；

- 大规模虚拟样机和虚拟产品综合；

- 基础理论、原则和启发式方法；

- 支持数字工程的 MBSE。

知识表示和沉浸式虚拟现实技术（以深度融入或沉浸为特征）能够在跨越整个生命周期的虚拟环境中高效地共享人类对系统的理解。系统建模构成了数字复杂组织体系以产品为中心的主干，它结合了以模型为中心的方法来综合技术、计划、业务、监管和治理关切（见 3.2.1 节）。基于模型的方法和复杂的基于模型的途径超出了产品建模的范围，包括体系和复杂组织体系级建模与分析（见 4.2.1 节）。基于综合模型的大规模虚拟样机和虚拟产品综合可以显著缩短上市时间（见 3.2.2 节和 2.3.5.8 节）。基础理论、原则和启发式方法基础允许更好地理解面对不确定性的日益复杂的系统和决策（见 1.4 节）。支持数字工程的 MBSE 是标准实践，与其他建模和仿真以及数字复杂组织体系功能综合在一起（见 5.4 节）。

5.6　系统工程的未来

本手册的主要重点是介绍系统工程的最佳实践。本节重点介绍一些新兴领域，展望系统工程的未来。INCOSE 的系统工程愿景（2022）是一个很好的资料。此外，系统工程知识体（2023）不断更新，以反映系统工程的实践状态和最新技术。

INCOSE 的未来系统工程（FuSE）是一项系统群体倡议，旨在实现 INCOSE 愿景 2035（2022），并将系统工程的指导、实践和认知发展为：

- 定位学科，与相关领域合作利用新技术；

- 增强系统工程解决新挑战的能力；

- Promote SE as essential for achieving success and delivering value in the engineering of socio-cyber-physical systems and SoSs at scale and subject to non-deterministic influences and effects.

An important aspect of SE is to keep current on emerging trends, technologies, and challenges when considering both the SoI and the SE processes themselves. While performing SE, the practitioner needs to consider advances in computing, communications, software, human systems integration, and algorithms such as augmented intelligence and Machine Learning (ML) for both use in systems and SE. Leveraging these technologies will increase the capabilities of systems and the SE practitioner. By scale, we mean the challenges in applying SE from smaller (e.g., miniaturization of electronics) through larger scales (e.g., cloud-based systems with millions of users). With the exponential growth of scale and hyperconnectivity of systems and SoSs, scale is becoming even more important to the discipline of SE.

At an early 2019 FuSE workshop hosted by INCOSE, the terms Artificial Intelligence (AI) for SE and SE for AI were first used to describe the dual transformation envisioned for both the SE and AI disciplines. The "AI4SE" and "SE4AI" labels have quickly become symbols for an upcoming rapid evolutionary phase in the SE community. AI4SE applies AI and ML techniques to improve human-driven SE practices. This goal of "augmented intelligence" includes outcomes such as achieving scale in model construction and efficiency. Enhancing and assisting SE processes, methods, and tools, with tangible impacts on the quality of the engineered system as well as on the cycle time for the various life cycle activities, would be some of the primary focus areas of AI4SE (SEBoK, 2023).

The FuSE roadmap drives this evolution of SE to:

- Be increasingly adaptable, evolvable, and fit for purpose,
- Account for human abilities and needs as an integral system element and human interactions with systems and SoSs,
- Be more responsive in resolving increasingly challenging societal needs, and
- Realize and enhance the INCOSE Vision 2035 (2022) and other visionary statements.

Greater understanding of the inter-coupled technical, economic, social, and environmental systems will provide the basis for significantly increased involvement of SE practitioners in the policy arena. In this expanded role, SE practitioners will also make important contributions to the design of viable systems and transition pathways supporting global sustainability transformation. The scope of SE will widen to recognize and include policy, legal, economic, and environmental specializations.

- 促进系统工程成为受到不确定性影响和作用的大规模社会—赛博—物理系统和体系工程取得成功和交付价值的必要条件。

系统工程的一个重要方面是，保持对 SoI 和系统工程流程最新的趋势、技术和挑战的了解。在执行系统工程时，实践者需要考虑在系统和系统工程中共同使用的计算、通信、软件、人—系统综合和诸如增强智能与机器学习（ML）算法方面的进步。利用这些技术将提高系统和系统工程实践者的能力。就规模而言，我们指的是从较小规模（例如，电子设备的小型化）到较大规模（例如，拥有数百万用户的基于云的系统）应用系统工程的挑战。随着系统和体系的规模和超连通性的指数级增长，规模对于系统工程学科来说变得更加重要。

在由 INCOSE 主办的 2019 年初的 FuSE 研讨会上，术语人工智能用于系统工程和系统工程用于人工智能首次被用来描述系统工程和 AI 学科所设想的双重转变。"AI4SE"和"SE4AI"标签已迅速成为系统工程社区即将到来的快速进化阶段的标志。AI4SE 应用 AI 和机器学习（ML）技术来改进人类驱动的系统工程实践。"增强智能"的目标包括实现模型构建的规模和效率等成果。加强和协助系统工程流程、方法和工具，对工程系统的质量以及各种生命周期活动的周期时间产生切实影响，将是 AI4SE 的一些主要关注领域（SEBoK，2023）。

未来系统工程（FuSE）路线图推动系统工程的这一演进，以：

- 具有更强的适应性、进化性和针对性；

- 解决将人的能力和需要视为一个完整的系统元素，以及人与系统和体系的交互的问题；

- 更加积极地解决越来越具挑战性的社会需要；

- 落实和完善《INCOSE 愿景 2035（2022）》等前瞻性声明。

更好地理解相互耦合的技术、经济、社会和环境系统，将为系统工程实践者在政策领域更广泛的参与奠定基础。在这一扩展的角色中，系统工程实践者还将为设计支持全球可持续性转型的可行系统和过渡路径做出重要贡献。系统工程的范围将扩大，以认识和涵盖政策、法律、经济和环境等专业。

6 CASE STUDIES

Real-world examples that draw from diverse industries and types of systems are provided throughout this handbook, and in this part, five case studies have been selected to illustrate the diversity of systems to which Systems Engineering (SE) principles and practices can be applied: medical therapy equipment, a bridge, a breach of a cybersecurity system, a redesign of a high-tech medical system for low-tech maintenance, and autonomous vehicles. They represent examples of failed and successful systems.

6.1 CASE 1: RADIATION THERAPY—THE THERAC-25

Background Therac-25, a dual-mode medical linear accelerator (LINAC), was developed by the medical division of the Atomic Energy Commission Limited (AECL) of Canada, starting in 1976. A completely computerized system became commercially available in 1982. This new machine could be built at lower production cost, resulting in lower prices for the customers. However, a series of tragic accidents led to the recommended recall and discontinuation of the system.

The Therac-25 was a medical LINAC, or particle accelerator, capable of increasing the energy of electrically charged atomic particles. LINACs accelerate charged particles by introducing an electric field to produce particle beams (i.e., radiation), which are then focused by magnets. Medical LINACs are used to treat cancer patients by exposing malignant cells to radiation. Since malignant tissues are more sensitive than normal tissues to radiation exposure, a treatment plan can be developed that permits the absorption of an amount of radiation that is fatal to tumors but causes relatively minor damage to surrounding tissue.

Six accidents involving enormous radiation overdoses to patients took place between 1985 and 1987. Tragically, three of these accidents resulted in the death of the patients. This case is ranked in the top ten worst software-related incidents on many lists. Details of the accidents and analysis of the case are available from many sources, including Jacky (1989) and Leveson and Turner (1993).

INCOSE Systems Engineering Handbook: A Guide for System Life Cycle Processes and Activities, Fifth Edition.

Edited by David D. Walden, Thomas M. Shortell, Garry J. Roedler, Bernardo A. Delicado, Odile Mornas, Yip Yew-Seng, and David Endler.

© 2023 John Wiley & Sons Ltd. Published 2023 by John Wiley & Sons Ltd.

6 案例研究

本手册提供了取材于不同行业和不同类型系统的真实示例。本章选择了五个案例研究来阐明 SE 原理和实践可应用于多样化的系统：医疗设备、桥梁、自动驾驶汽车、赛博安全系统的攻击，为了低技术维护而对高技术医疗系统的重新设计。它们代表了失败和成功系统的范例。

6.1 案例 1：放射治疗——THERAC-25

案例背景　Therac-25 双模式医用直线加速器（LINAC）由加拿大原子能有限公司（AECL）医疗部门于 1976 年开始开发。完全计算机化的系统于 1982 年开始在市面上销售。这种新型机器的生产成本较低，从而对客户的销售价格也较低。然而，一系列不幸的事故导致系统被建议召回并且停止生产。

Therac-25 是一种医用 LINAC 或粒子加速器，能够增加带电原子粒子的能量。LINAC 通过引入电场产生粒子束（即辐射）来加速带电粒子，然后磁铁将带电粒子聚集到一起。医用 LINAC 通过将恶性细胞暴露于放射线下来治疗癌症患者。由于恶性组织对放射性照射比正常组织更敏感，能形成允许吸收适量辐射的治疗计划，这种辐射可以杀死肿瘤，但会对外围组织造成相对轻微的损伤。1985 年到 1987 年期间，发生了六起涉及对患者放射剂量过多的事故。可悲的是，其中的三起事故导致患者死亡。此案例在多个与软件事故有关的排行中名列前十。此案例的事故和分析的详细资料可从多个来源获得，包括 Jacky（1989），Leveson 和 Turner（1993）。

CASE STUDIES

278 *Approach* Therac-25 was a revolutionary design compared to its predecessors, Therac-6 and Therac-20, both with exceptional safety records. It was based on a double-pass concept that allowed a more powerful accelerator to be built into a compact and versatile machine. AECL designed Therac-25 to fully utilize the potential of software control. While Therac-6 and Therac-20 were built as stand-alone machines and could be operated without a computer, Therac-25 depended on a tight integration of software and hardware. In the new, tightly coupled system, AECL used software to monitor the state of the machine and to ensure its proper operations and safety. Previous versions had included independent circuits to monitor the status of the beam as well as hardware interlocks that prevented the machine from delivering radiation doses that were too high or from performing any unsafe operation that could potentially harm the patient. In Therac-25, AECL decided not to duplicate these hardware interlocks since the software already performed status checks and handled all the malfunctions. This meant that the Therac-25 software had far more responsibility for safety than the software in the previous models. If, in the course of treatment, the software detected a minor malfunction, it would pause the treatment. In this case, the procedure could be restarted by pressing a single "proceed" key. Only if a serious malfunction was detected was it required to completely reset the treatment parameters to restart the machine.

The software for Therac-25 was developed from the Therac-20's software, which was developed from the Therac-6's software, a brownfield, or legacy, development (see Section 4.3.2). One programmer, over several years, evolved the Therac-6 software into the Therac-25 software. A stand-alone, real-time operating system was added along with application software written in assembly language and tested as a part of the Therac-25 system operation. In addition, significant adjustments had been made to simplify the operator interface and minimize data entry, since initial operators complained that it took too long to enter a treatment plan.

At the time of its introduction to market in 1982, Therac-25 was classified as a Class II medical device. Since the Therac-25 software was based on software used in the earlier Therac-20 and Therac-6 models, Therac-25 was approved by the federal Food and Drug Administration under Premarket Equivalency.

Conclusions The errors were introduced in the concept and early development stages, when the decisions were made to create the software for Therac-25 using the modification of existing software from the two prior machines. The consequences of these actions were difficult to assess at the time, because the starting point (software from Therac-6) was a poorly documented product and no one except the original software developer could follow the logic (Leveson and Turner, 1993).

实现方法 与其前身 Therac-6 和 Therac-20 相比（两者都具有优异的安全记录），Therac-25 是一次革命性设计。Therac-25 基于双程概念，可将功能更强的加速器设计成小型通用机器。AECL 设计了 Therac-25 以全面发挥软件控制的潜力。Therac-6 和 Therac-20 被设计成独立的机器，不使用计算机即可运行，而 Therac-25 依赖于软件和硬件的紧密综合。在全新的紧密耦合系统中，AECL 使用软件监控机器的状态并确保机器的恰当运行和安全性。先前版本包括用于监控射束状态的独立回路，以及硬件互锁装置，用于防止机器发射过大的放射剂量，或防止机器执行任何可能伤害到患者的不安全操作。在 Therac-25 中，AECL 决定不复制这些硬件互锁装置，因为软件已经对所有故障进行了状态检查和处理。这意味着 Therac-25 软件比先前型号中的软件承担更多的安全职责。如果治疗过程中软件检测到较小的故障，可暂停治疗。在这种情况下，可通过单独按下"继续"键重新启动程序。只有检测到严重的故障时，才需要完全重置治疗参数以重新启动机器。

Therac-20 的软件是从 Therac-6 的软件开发而来的，Therac-25 的软件是从 Therac-20 的软件开发而来的，这是一个对老软件的改造开发方法，一个程序经过多年的时间从 Therac-6 软件演进成 Therac-25 软件。单机实时操作系统和以汇编语言编写的应用软件经测试作为 Therac-25 系统运行的一部分。另外，由于最初的操作者抱怨输入治疗计划需要花费很长时间，因此对系统进行了重大调整以简化操作界面并将数据输入最小化。

1982 年 Therac-25 上市时，被分类为第二类医疗设备。由于 Therac-25 软件是基于早期的 Therac-20 和 Therac-6 模型中使用的软件开发的，按照上市前有效性原则，Therac-25 由美国联邦药品管理局批准。

结论 在决定采用修改先前两类机器原有软件创建 Therac-25 软件时，在概念阶段和早期开发阶段就引入了错误。这些行动的后果在那时很难评估，因为起点（来自 Therac-6 的软件）是文档记录很差的产品，且除了最初的软件开发者没有人能理解它的逻辑（Leveson 和 Turner,1993）。

CASE STUDIES

The issues from the Therac case are, unfortunately, still relevant, as evidenced by similar deaths for similar reasons in 2007 upon the introduction of new LINAC-based radiation therapy machines (Bogdanich, 2010).

6.2 CASE 2: JOINING TWO COUNTRIES—THE ØRESUND BRIDGE

Background The Øresund Region is composed of eastern Denmark and southern Sweden and since 2000 has been linked by the Øresund Bridge. The area includes two major cities, Copenhagen and Malmö, has a population of three million, and counts as Europe's eighth largest economic center. One fifth of the total Danish and Swedish Gross National Product (GNP) is produced in the region. The official name of the bridge is translated "the Øresund Connection" to underscore the full integration of the region. For the first time ever, Sweden is joined permanently to the mainland of Europe by a 10-minute drive or train ride. The cost for the entire Øresund Connection construction project was calculated at 30.1 billion DKK (3 billion USD), and the investment is expected to be paid back by 2035.

The Øresund Bridge is the world's largest composite structure, has the longest cable-stayed bridge span in the world carrying motorway and railway traffic, and boasts the highest freestanding pylons. The 7.9 km (5 miles)-long bridge crosses the international navigation route between the Baltic Sea and the North Sea. A cable-stayed high bridge rises 57 m (160 ft) above the surface of the sea, with a main span of 490 m (0.3 miles). Both the main span and the approach bridges are constructed as a two-level composite steel-concrete structure. The upper deck carries a four-lane motorway, and the lower deck carries a two-track railway for both passenger trains and freight trains. The rest of the distance is spanned by the artificial island Peberholm ("Pepper" islet, named to complement the Saltholm islet to the north) and a tunnel on the Danish side that is the longest immersed concrete tunnel in the world. Since completion, Peberholm has become a natural habitat for colonies of rare birds, one of the largest of its kind in Denmark and Sweden.

Nations other than Denmark and Sweden also contributed to this project. Canada provided a floating crane, aptly named Svanen (the swan), to carry prefabricated bridge sections out to the site and place them into position. Forty-nine steel girders for the approach bridges were fabricated in Cádiz, Spain. A specially designed catamaran was built to handle transportation of the foundations for the pylons, which weighed 19,000 tons each.

不幸的是，引入新的基于 LINAC 的放射治疗机后类似原因导致的类似死亡的证据表明，Therac 案例中的问题仍然存在（Bogdanich，2010）。

6.2 案例 2：连接两个国家——厄勒海峡大桥

案例背景　厄勒海峡区域是由丹麦东部地区和瑞典南部地区组成的，自 2000 年起由厄勒海峡大桥连接起来。该区域包括哥本哈根和马尔默两大城市，拥有 300 万人口，是欧洲第八大经济中心。丹麦和瑞典的全部国民生产总值（GNP）的五分之一来自该区域。大桥的官方名称被翻译为"厄勒海峡连接"，以强调区域的完全整合。瑞典首次实现了与欧洲大陆的永久性连接，开车或乘火车只需 10 分钟即可到达欧洲大陆。整个厄勒海峡连接桥的建造项目的成本预计为 301 亿丹麦克朗（30 亿美元），预期到 2035 年能收回投资。

厄勒海峡大桥是世界上最大的复合结构，具有世界上最长的斜拉桥跨度，可承载高速公路和铁路运输，拥有最高的独立式索塔。7.9 千米（5 英里）长的桥横跨波罗的海和北海之间的国际航行路线。高斜拉索桥比海平面高 57 米（160 英尺），主跨 490 米（0.3 英里）。主跨和引桥被建成双层复合钢混凝土结构。上层桥面承载四车道高速公路，下层桥面承载客运列车和货运列车的双轨铁路。其余的跨度则位于"佩博霍尔姆"（又名 Pepper 岛，用以在北部地区作为萨尔特岛的补充）人工岛上，以及丹麦一侧的隧道中——世界上最长的沉埋式混凝土隧道。佩博霍尔姆岛完工后，成为珍稀鸟类集群的天然栖息地，也是丹麦和瑞典最大的这类岛屿之一。

丹麦和瑞典以外的其他国家也对该项目做出了贡献。加拿大提供了名为天鹅（Svanen）的浮式起重机，用于现场承载预制桥段并将其放置于适当位置。在西班牙加迪斯省制造了 49 个引桥钢梁。一艘特殊设计的双体船被制造用于搬运桥塔底座，每个底座重达 19000 吨。

CASE STUDIES

Approach As noted in the many histories of the bridge, the development stage of the project began with well-defined time, budget, and quality constraints. The design evolved over more than seven years, from start to delivery of final documentation and maintenance manuals. More than 4,000 drawings were produced. The consortium dealt with changes, as necessary, using a combination of technical competence and stakeholder cooperation. Notably, there were no disputes and no significant claims against the owners at the conclusion, and this has been attributed to the spirit of partnership.

What is not often reported is that the success of the development stage is clearly based on the productive, focused, creative effort in the concept stage that began when the royal families of Denmark and Sweden finally agreed in 1990 to move ahead with a bridge project connecting their two countries. That SE effort shaped the approach to the project with well-defined time, budget, and quality constraints at the transition to the development stage. During the concept stage, the SE team also recognized that the concerns of environmental groups would—and should—impact the approach to the construction of the bridge. The owners took a creative approach by inviting the head of a key environmental group to be part of the board of directors.

From the beginning of the development stage, the owners defined comprehensive requirements and provided definition drawings as part of the contract documents to ensure a project result that not only fulfilled the quality requirements on materials and workmanship but also had the envisioned appearance. The contractor was responsible for the detailed design and for delivering a quality-assured product in accordance with the owners' requirements. The following are representative of the requirements levied at the start of the project:

Schedule: Design life, 100 years; construction time, 1996-2000

Railway: Rail load, International Union of Railways (UIC) 71; train speed, 200 km/h

Motorway: Road axle load, 260 kN; vehicle speed, 120 km/h

Ambient environment: Wind speed (10 min), 61 m/s; wave height, 2.5 m; ice thickness, 0.6 m; temperature, +/− 27°C

Ship impact: To pylons, 560 MN; to girder, 35 MN

In addition to established requirements, this project crossed national boundaries and was thereby subject to the legislations of each country. Technical requirements were based on the Eurocodes, with project-specific amendments made to suit the national standards of both countries. Special safety regulations were set up for the working conditions, meeting the individual safety standards of Denmark and Sweden.

实现方法 正如许多的桥梁历史所指出，项目的开发阶段从定义良好的时间、预算和质量约束开始。设计从项目启动一直到最终文件和维护手册的交付经历了七年之久，产生了 4000 多张图样。必要时，联合企业通过结合技术能力和利益相关方合作来处理各种变更。很明显，项目结束时其与所有者没有任何纠纷和重大索赔，这归于各方的合作精神。

通常没有被报道的是，开发阶段的成功很明显是基于概念阶段中富有成效的、聚焦的、创造性的工作，该工作在丹麦和瑞典两个王室家族最终于 1990 年在推动连接他们两国的桥梁项目上达成一致时开始。该 SE 工作在向开发阶段的转移中形成了具有定义良好的时间、预算和质量约束的项目方法。在概念阶段期间，SE 团队还意识到环境组织的担忧，将会并且应该影响对桥梁施工的方法。所有者通过邀请关键环境组织的领导作为理事会的一员来采取创造性的方法。

从开发阶段一开始，所有者定义全面的需求并提供定义图作为合同文件的一部分，以确保项目结果不仅符合材料和工艺上的质量要求，还具有预期的外观。承包商负责按照所有者的需求进行详细设计并交付质量合格的产品。以下是项目开始阶段制定的典型需求：

进度：设计寿命 100 年；施工时间从 1996 年到 2000 年。

铁路：轨道载重，国际铁路联盟（UIC）71；列车速度 200 千米/时。

高速公路：道路轴载 260 千牛；车速 120 千米/时。

周围环境：风速（10 分钟）61 米/秒；浪高 2.5 米；冰厚 0.6 米；温度 +/–27 摄氏度。

船舶撞击：索塔 560 兆牛；梁 35 兆牛。

除了已确定的需求外，该项目跨越国界，因此同时受每个国家法律的管辖。技术需求基于欧洲标准，项目特有的修正文件符合丹麦和瑞典两个国家的标准。为工作条件设立了特殊的安全规则，从而符合丹麦和瑞典各自的安全标准。

CASE STUDIES

The railway link introduced yet another challenge. In Denmark, the rail traffic is right-handed, as on roadways, whereas the trains in Sweden pass on the left-hand side. The connection needed to ensure a logical transition between the two systems, including safety aspects. In addition, the railway power supply differs between the two countries; thus, it was necessary to develop a system that could accommodate power supply for both railway systems and switch between them on the fly.

The design of a major cable-stayed bridge with approach spans for both road and railway traffic involves several disciplines, including, but not limited to, geotechnical engineering, aerodynamics, foundation engineering, wind tunnel tests, design of piers and pylons, design of composite girders, design of cables and anchorages, design of structural monitoring system, ship impact analysis, earthquake analysis, analysis of shrinkage and creep of concrete, ice load analysis, fatigue analysis, pavement design, mechanical systems, electrical systems, comfort analysis for railway passengers, traffic forecast, operation and maintenance aspects, analysis of construction stages, risk analysis for construction and operation, quality management, and environmental studies and monitoring.

280 Comprehensive risk analyses were carried out in connection with the initial planning studies, including specification of requirements to secure all safety aspects. Important examples of the results of these studies for the Øresund Bridge were as follows:

Navigation span was increased from 330 to 490 m.

The navigation channel was realigned and deepened to reduce ship groundings.

Pier protection islands were introduced to mitigate bridge/ship accidents.

Risks were considered in a systematic way, using contemporary risk analysis methods such as functional safety analysis using fault tree and "what-if" techniques. Three main issues were considered under the design-build contract:

General identification and assessment of construction risks

Ship collision in connection with realignment of navigation channel

Risks in connection with 5-year bridge operation by contractor

A fully quantified risk assessment of the human safety and traffic delay risks was carried out for a comprehensive list of hazards, including fire, explosion, train collisions and derailments, road accidents, ship collisions and groundings, aircraft collisions, environmental loads beyond design basis, and toxic spillages. An example of a consequence of this analysis was the provision of passive fire protection on the tunnel walls and ceilings.

铁路连接也引入另一个挑战。在丹麦，铁路运输与道路交通一样靠右侧行驶，而瑞典的列车靠左侧行驶。两个国家的铁路连接需要确保两个系统之间的逻辑转换，包括安全方面。另外，两个国家之间的铁路电力供应不同，因此有必要开发一种系统以适应两种铁路系统的电力供应，并且可在高速行驶中互相切换。

用于公路和铁路运输的具有多个引桥的大型斜拉桥的设计涉及多个学科，包括但不限于：岩土工程学、空气动力学、基础工程学、风洞试验、桥墩和索塔的设计、组合梁设计、缆绳和锚固件的设计、结构监测系统的设计、船舶撞击分析、地震分析、混凝土收缩和蠕变的分析、冰负载分析、疲劳分析、路面设计、机械系统、电气系统、铁路乘客舒适度分析、交通预测、运行和维护、施工阶段分析、施工和运行的风险分析、质量管理以及环境的研究和监测。

结合最初的计划研究，包括保证所有安全方面的需求规范，进行了全面的风险分析。厄勒海峡大桥研究结果的重要示例如下：

航道跨度由 330 米增加到 490 米。

对航道进行改线和加深，以减少船舶搁浅。

引入桥墩保护岛，以减少桥梁/船舶事故。使用现代风险分析方法，如采用了故障树和"what-if（假设）"技术的功能安全分析，以系统化的方式对风险进行考虑。

按照设计—施工合同考虑以下三个主要问题：

施工风险的一般性识别和评估。

关于航道重新调整的船舶碰撞问题。

与承包商五年桥梁运营相关的风险。

项目开展了人身安全风险和交通延误风险的全面量化风险评估，总结出全面的危害列表，包括：火灾、爆炸、列车碰撞和脱轨、公路交通事故、船舶碰撞和搁浅、飞机碰撞、超出设计基础的环境负荷以及有毒物质泄漏。该分析结果的一个示例是在隧道侧壁和隧道顶部提供被动防火保护。

CASE STUDIES

Both Denmark and Sweden are proud of being among the cleanest industrial countries in the world. Their citizens, and therefore the politicians, would not allow for any adverse environmental impact from the construction or operation of a bridge. The Great Belt and Øresund Strait both constitute corridors between the salty Kattegat and the sweeter water of the Baltic Sea. Any reduction in water exchange would reduce the salt content and, therefore, the oxygen content of the Baltic Sea and would alter its ecological balance. The Danish and Swedish authorities decided that the bridge should be designed in such a way that the flow through of water, salt, and oxygen into the Baltic was not affected. This requirement was designated the zero solution. To limit impacts on the local flora and fauna in Øresund during the construction, the Danish and Swedish authorities imposed a restriction that the spillage of seabed material from dredging operations should not exceed 5% of the dredged amounts. The zero solution was obtained by modeling with two different and independent hydrographical models.

In total, 18 million cubic meters of seabed materials were dredged. All dredged materials were reused for reclamation of the artificial peninsula at Kastrup and the artificial island, Peberholm. A comprehensive and intensive monitoring of the environment was performed to ensure and document the fulfillment of all environmental requirements. In their final status report from 2001, the Danish and Swedish authorities concluded that the zero solution as well as all environmental requirements related to the construction of the link had been fulfilled. Continual monitoring of eel grass and common mussels showed that, after a general but minor decline, populations had recovered by the time the bridge was opened. Overall, the environment paid a low price at both Øresund and the Great Belt because it was given consideration throughout the planning and construction stages of the bridges.

Conclusions This award-winning bridge is the subject of numerous articles and a doctoral thesis, where details of the construction history and collaboration among all the stakeholders are provided (Jensen, 2014; Nissen, 2006; Skanska, 2013). This project provides a clear example of the benefit of a solid concept stage where the management team was able to resist the customer-driven temptation to jump prematurely into the development stage.

丹麦和瑞典都以位于全世界最洁净的工业国家之列而自豪。两个国家的公民乃至政治家都不准许桥梁的施工或运行带来任何不利于环境的影响。大贝尔特桥和厄勒海峡构成卡特加特海峡咸水和波罗的海淡水之间的走廊。减少水体交换会降低含盐量，因此会改变波罗的海的含氧量继而改变其生态平衡。丹麦和瑞典当局决定在桥梁设计时应确保流入波罗的海的水、盐和氧气的流量不受影响。这一要求被指定为"零方案"。为限制施工期间对厄勒海峡当地的植物群和动物群的影响，丹麦和瑞典当局限制疏浚操作中海底物质泄漏量不应超过疏浚量的5%。通过用两个不同的独立水文地理模型进行建模得出"零方案"。

项目总计疏浚海底物质1800万立方米。所有疏浚物质重新用于围垦卡斯特鲁普的人工半岛和人工岛"佩博霍尔姆"。开展全面深入的环境监测以确保所有环境需求的满足并进行记录。在2001年的最终状态报告中，丹麦和瑞典的当局总结说"零方案"和与"连接"施工有关的所有环境需求已被满足。对鳗草和常见贻贝的持续监控表明其种群经过普遍但略微的衰退之后，在大桥开放时得以恢复。总之，由于在大桥的计划阶段和施工阶段都考虑到环境问题，厄勒海峡大桥和大贝尔特桥的环境代价很低。

结论 这座获奖的桥梁是众多文章和博士论文的主题，其中提供了所有利益相关方之间的施工历史和合作细节（Jensen，2014；Nissen，2006；Skanska，2013）。这个项目提供了一个明确的例子，说明了扎实的概念阶段的好处，在这个阶段，管理团队能够抵制客户驱动的诱惑避免过早进入开发阶段。

CASE STUDIES

6.3 CASE 3: CYBERSECURITY CONSIDERATIONS IN SYSTEMS ENGINEERING—THE STUXNET ATTACK ON A CYBER-PHYSICAL SYSTEM

Background As our world becomes increasingly digital, the issue of cybersecurity is a factor that the SE practitioner needs to consider. Both hardware and software systems are increasingly at risk for disruption or damage caused by threats taking advantage of digital technologies. Stuxnet, a cyber-attack on Iran's nuclear capabilities discovered in 2010, illustrates the need for the SE practitioner to be comprehensive in application of secure design principles and methods for assessing and avoiding vulnerabilities, and rigorous in mitigation of attack potential (Failliere, 2011; Langner, 2012).

This case study discusses a high degree of attack sophistication previously unseen— malware complexity at military-grade performance, nearly no side effects, and pinpoint accuracy. However, though the creation and deployment of Stuxnet were expensive undertakings, the strategy, tactical methods, and code mechanisms became openly available for others to reuse and build upon at much less expense. Cyber-physical system attacks are becoming increasingly prevalent, and SE must consider the implications of cybersecurity to reduce the vulnerabilities.

Iran's Natanz nuclear fuel enrichment plant (FEP) is a military-hardened facility, with a security fence surrounding a complex of buildings, which are in turn each protected by a series of concrete walls. The complex contains several "cascade halls" for the production of enriched uranium in gas centrifuges. This facility was further hardened with a roof of several meters of reinforced concrete and covered with a thick layer of earth.

Each of the cascade halls is a cyber-physical system, with an industrial control system (ICS) of programmable logic controllers (PLCs), computers, an internal network with no connections to the outside world, and capacity for thousands of centrifuges. Though the internal network is isolated from the outside world by an "air gap," possible vulnerabilities still include malicious insider collusion, non-malicious insider insertion of memory devices brought in from the outside, visiting service technicians, and supply chain intervention. It has been suggested that all of these breech vectors may have played a role in the massive centrifuge damage that began occurring in 2009 and continued at least through 2010.

Malware, now known as Stuxnet, was introduced into the ICS of at least one of the cascade halls and managed to take surreptitious control of the centrifuges, causing them to spin periodically and repeatedly at rates damaging to sustained physical operation. The net effect of the attack is still unclear, but at a minimum, it ranged from disruption of the production process up to potential permanent damage to the affected centrifuges.

6.3 案例3：系统工程中的网络安全考虑——对赛博物理系统的STUXNET攻击

案例背景　随着我们的世界变得日益数字化，赛博安全问题是系统工程实践者需要考虑到的一个因素。硬件和软件系统都日益面临着利用数字技术的威胁所造成的扰乱或损坏的风险。Stuxnet，于2010年发现的对伊朗核能力的赛博攻击，说明了系统工程实践者需要全面应用安全设计原则和方法来评估和避免系统的弱点，以及缜密地预防潜在的攻击。

此案例的研究论述了前所未见的攻击复杂性程度——军事级表现上的恶意软件复杂性的新水平，几乎没有负面影响并且精确度高。然而，尽管Stuxnet的创建和部署是昂贵的负担，但现在策略、战术方法和代码机制对其他人公开可用，能够以很少的费用复用并基于其构建。赛博物理系统攻击变得日益普遍，SE必须考虑赛博安全的意义以减少脆弱性。

伊朗的纳坦兹核燃料浓缩厂（FEP）是一个军事强化设施，围绕建筑群具有安保防护装置，这些建筑进一步受一系列混凝土墙的保护。该建筑群包含若干"串联的大厅"，用于在气体离心机中生产浓缩铀。该工厂使用由几米厚钢筋混凝土制成的屋顶进一步强化，并在上面盖有一层厚厚的土。

诸多串联大厅的每一个都是一个赛博物理系统，其具有可编程逻辑控制器（PLC）的工业控制系统（ICS）、计算机、与外界不连接的内部网络以及成千个离心机的容量。尽管"安全隔离网闸"将内部网络与外界隔离，但可能的脆弱性仍然包括恶意的内部合谋，从外部引入的存储设备的非恶意内部插入，来访的服务技术人员和供应链介入。有人说所有这些攻击向量在2009年开始发生的、持续到至少2010年的离心机大规模损坏中也许发挥了作用。

现在被称为Stuxnet的恶意软件，被引入到至少是多个串联大厅中之一的ICS中并设法对离心机采取秘密控制，导致离心机以对持续物理运行不利的速率定期反复旋转。该攻击的净效应尚不清楚，但范围至少包括生产流程中断甚至严重到对受影响的离心机造成潜在的永久损坏。

CASE STUDIES

Approach Many characteristics of Stuxnet were unprecedented and stand as the inflection point that ushered in a new era of system attack methodology and cyber-physical system targeting. Illuminating forensic analysis of the Stuxnet code was conducted by several well-known cybersecurity firms, with detailed postmortems covered in two documents from the Institute for Science and International Security (Albright, et al., 2010, 2011). This analysis is beneficial in expanding the risk landscape that the SE practitioner should consider during design. Below are some concepts that are concerned in the context of Stuxnet:

Knowing what to do (intelligence)—To be successful, a threat has to be able to take advantage of the targeted system(s). It is uncertain how the perpetrators knew what specific devices were employed in what configuration at Natanz; but after the Stuxnet code was analyzed, Natanz was clearly identified as the target. Stuxnet infected many sites other than Natanz, but it would only activate if that site was configured to certain specific system specifications. The perpetrators needed specific system configuration information to know how to cause damage and also to know how to single out the target among many similar but not identical facilities elsewhere. The SE practitioner needs to consider that adversaries will attempt to gain intelligence on a system and must consider methods to prevent this.

Crafting the code—A zero-day attack is one that exploits a previously unknown vulnerability in a computer application, one that developers have had no time to address and patch. Stuxnet attacked Windows systems outside the FEP using a variety of zero-day exploits and stolen certificates to get proper insertion into the operating system and then initiated a multistage propagation mechanism that started with Universal Serial Bus (USB) removable media infected outside the FEP and ended with code insertion into the ICS inside the FEP. SE practitioners need to be prepared for many different attack vectors (including internal threats) and must consider them during system design.

Jumping the air gap—It was widely believed that Stuxnet crossed the air gap on a USB removable media device, which had been originally infected on a computer outside of the FEP and carried inside. But it was also suggested that the supply chain for PLCs and PLC maintenance personnel may have been at least two additional attack vectors. Whatever the methods, the air gap was crossed multiple times. USB removable media could have also affected a bidirectional transfer of information, sending out detailed intelligence about device types connected to the FEP network subsequently relayed to remote servers outside of the control of the facility. The SE practitioner always needs to remember that threats to the system are both inside and outside the system boundary.

实现方法 Stuxnet 的许多特性是前所未见的，是开创系统攻击方法论和赛博物理系统目标定位的一个新时代的转折点。几家著名的网络安全公司对 Stuxnet 代码进行了启发性取证分析，并在两份文件中涵盖了来自科学与国际安全研究所的详细事后调查（Albright 等，2010，2011）。该分析有益于系统工程实践者在设计期间考虑扩大风险的范围。下面是 Stuxnet 中涉及的一些概念：

知道该做什么（情报）——为取得成功，一种威胁必须能够利用目标系统。不能确定作恶者是如何知晓哪些特定装置用于纳坦兹的何种构型配置的；但对 Stuxnet 代码进行分析后，纳坦兹被明确地识别为攻击目标。Stuxnet 感染了纳坦兹以外的许多地点，但它仅激活按照某些特定系统规范配置的地点。作恶者需要特定系统构型配置信息以知晓如何导致破坏，以及知晓如何在其他地方的许多类似但不相同的工厂之间挑选出攻击目标。系统工程实践者需要考虑到对手会尝试获得系统的情报，且必须考虑到阻止的方法。

周密编制代码——零日攻击是利用对计算机应用程序中先前未知的且开发者没有时间解决和修补的弱点的一种攻击。Stuxnet 使用各种零日攻击攻击 FEP 外部的 Windows 系统，利用盗取的证书侵入操作系统，然后启动多级繁殖机制，从通用串行总线（USB）可移动介质在 FEP 外部感染开始，最终将代码植入 FEP 内。系统工程实践者需要为许多不同的攻击向量（包括内部威胁）做好准备，且必须在系统设计期间予以考虑。

跳过安全隔离网闸——人们普遍相信 Stuxnet 跨越了 USB 可移动介质设备上的安全隔离网闸，该设备最初在 FEP 外部的计算机上被感染并携带到内部。但至少还有 PLC 供应链和 PLC 维护人员可能是两个另外的攻击向量。不管是什么方法，网闸都被跨越了很多次。USB 可移动介质还可能被双向信息传递影响，将连接到 FEP 网络的设备类型的详细情报发送出来，然后被转发到超出工厂控制范围的远程服务器上。系统工程实践者始终需要牢记系统的威胁同时存在于系统边界的内部和外部。

CASE STUDIES

282 *Dynamic updating*—Analysis shows that the attack code, once inserted, could be updated and changed over time, perhaps to take advantage of new knowledge or to implement new objectives. Stuxnet appears to have been continuously updated, with new operational parameters reintroduced as new air gap crossings occur. The SE practitioner needs to prepare for situations after a successful attack has occurred.

Conclusions As the complexity and technology of systems change, the SE practitioner's perspective needs to adjust accordingly. The increasing use of digital-based technologies in system design offers enormous benefits to everyone. However, the introduction of digital technologies also brings different risks than previously dealt with by SE. The case study earlier illustrates a point in time behind us, and the adversarial community continues to evolve new methods. The lesson of this case study is that the SE practitioner needs to understand the threats toward their system(s), be cognizant that attacks can and will occur, and be proactive in protecting their system(s). Robust and dynamic system security needs full engagement of SE (see Section 3.1.12). A database that the SE practitioners should be aware of is maintained by the National Institute of Standards and Technology (NIST, 2012).

6.4 CASE 4: DESIGN FOR MAINTAINABILITY—INCUBATORS

Note: This case study is excerpted from "Where Good Ideas Come From: The Natural History of Innovation" (Johnson, 2010).

Background In the late 1870s, a Parisian obstetrician named Stephane Tarnier was visiting the Paris Zoo where they had farm animals. While there, he conceived the idea of adapting a chicken incubator to use for human newborns, and he hired "the zoo's poultry raiser to construct a device that would perform a similar function for human newborns." At the time, infant mortality was staggeringly high "even in a city as sophisticated as Paris. One in five babies died before learning to crawl, and the odds were far worse for premature babies born with low birth weights." Tarnier installed his incubator for newborns at Maternité de Paris and embarked on a quick study of 500 babies. "The results shocked the Parisian medical establishment: while 66 percent of low-weight babies died within weeks of birth, only 38 percent died if they were housed in Tarnier's incubating box.... Tarnier's statistical analysis gave newborn incubation the push that it needed: within a few years the Paris municipal board required that incubators be installed in all the city's maternity hospitals."

动态更新——分析表明，入侵的攻击代码可能被更新并随时间推移而变化，可能利用新信息或达到新目标。Stuxnet 似乎不断更新，在出现新的网闸跨越时会再引入新的运行参数。系统工程实践者需要为一次成功攻击的出现做好应对的准备。

结论 随着系统复杂性和技术的变化，系统工程实践者的视角需要相应地调整。系统设计中基于数字化的技术的日益增加给每个人都提供了巨大的好处。然而，数字化技术的引入还带来了与系统工程先前所处理的风险不同的风险。先前的案例研究展示了我们过去某一时间点的状况，而敌对群体则在不断演进出新的方法。此案例研究的教训是，系统工程实践者需要理解他们的系统所面临的威胁，需要认识到攻击能够并且即将出现，需要积极保护他们的系统。鲁棒和动态系统安保需要系统工程的全面参与（见 3.1.12 节）。系统工程实践者应当知道的一个数据库由（美国）国家标准与技术研究院来维护（NIST，2012）。

6.4 案例 4：可维护性设计——保育箱

注：本案例研究摘自《伟大创意的诞生：创新的自然史》（Johnson，2010）。

案例背景 在 19 世纪 70 年代末，名为 Stephane Tarnier 的巴黎产科医师游览拥有农场动物的巴黎动物园。在那里，他构思了使小鸡孵化器适用于人类新生儿的这一想法，他雇用了"动物园的饲养员来构造一种能够对人类新生儿执行类似功能的装置"。那时，"即使在如巴黎一样技术先进的城市中，婴儿死亡率也高得惊人。五分之一的婴儿在学习爬行之前就死亡了，出生时体重低的早产儿情况就更糟"。Tarnier 为巴黎出生的新生儿安装了他的保育箱，并快速研究了 500 名婴儿。"结果震惊了巴黎医疗机构：66% 的低体重婴儿在出生几周之内死亡，如果将他们放在 Tarnier 的保育箱中，仅 38% 的婴儿死亡……Tarnier 的统计分析为新生儿培育提供了所需的推动力：在几年内，巴黎市政委员会要求将保育箱安装在城市所有的产科医院中。"

CASE STUDIES

"Modern incubators, supplemented with high-oxygen therapy and other advances, became standard equipment in all American hospitals after the end of World War II, triggering a spectacular 75 percent decline in infant mortality rates between 1950 and 1998."... "In the developing world, however, the infant mortality story remains bleak. Whereas infant deaths are below ten per thousand births throughout Europe and the United States, over a hundred infants die per thousand (births) in countries like Liberia and Ethiopia, many of them premature babies that would have survived with access to incubators. But modern incubators are complex, expensive things. A standard incubator in an American hospital might cost more than $40,000 (about €30,000). But the expense is arguably the smaller hurdle to overcome. Complex equipment breaks, and when it breaks, you need the technical expertise to fix it. You also need replacement parts. In the year that followed the 2004 Indian Ocean tsunami, the Indonesian city of Meulaboh received eight incubators from a range of international relief organizations. By late 2008, when an MIT professor named Timothy Prestero visited the hospital, all eight were out of order, the victims of power surges and tropical humidity, along with the hospital staff's inability to read the English repair manual. The Meulaboh incubators were a representative sample: some studies suggest that as much as 95% of medical technology donated to developing countries breaks within the first 5 years of use."

Approach "Prestero had a vested interest in those broken incubators, because the organization he founded, Design that Matters, had been working for several years on a scheme for a more reliable, and less expensive, incubator, one that recognized complex medical technology was likely to have a very different tenure in a developing world context than it would in an American or European hospital. Designing an incubator for a developing country wasn't just a matter of creating something that worked; it was also a matter of designing something that would break in a non-catastrophic way. You couldn't guarantee a steady supply of spare parts, or trained repair technicians. So instead, Prestero and his team decided to build an incubator out of parts that were already abundant in the developing world. The idea had originated with a Boston doctor named Jonathan Rosen, who had observed that even the smaller towns of the developing world seemed to be able to keep automobiles in working order. The towns might lack air conditioning and laptops and cable television, but they managed to keep their Toyota 4Runners on the road. So, Rosen approached Prestero with an idea: What if you made an incubator out of automobile parts?"

"现代保育箱，辅以高氧疗法及其他先进技术，在第二次世界大战结束后成为所有美国医院的标准设备，使得在1950年和1998年之间婴儿死亡率明显下降75%。"……"然而在发展中国家，婴儿死亡率的故事仍不乐观。尽管整个欧洲和美国的新生婴儿死亡率低于千分之十，但像利比里亚和埃塞俄比亚这样的国家每1000名婴儿（新生儿）中有超过100名死亡，其中许多婴儿是早产儿，如果有机会使用保育箱就能够幸存。但现代保育箱是复杂、昂贵的东西。美国医院的标准保育箱可能要花费40000美元（约30000欧元）以上。但该费用还可以说是需要克服的较小障碍。复杂的设备损坏时，你需要技术专家来修理它，你还需要替换零件。在2004年印度洋海啸的第二年，印度尼西亚米拉务从一系列的国际救援组织收到了八个保育箱。到2008年年底，当名为Timothy Prestero的MIT教授参观医院时，八个保育箱都出现故障，原因是电涌和热带潮湿，以及医务人员没有阅读英文维修手册的能力。米拉务保育箱是一个典型案例：一些研究表明，捐赠给发展中国家的医疗技术产品，差不多95%在使用的前五年内损坏。"

实现方法 "Prestero对于那些损坏的保育箱很有兴趣，因为他建立的名为'设计很重要'的组织已多年致力于更可靠且更便宜的保育箱方案，该组织意识到，与美国或欧洲医院相比，发展中国家的复杂医疗技术可能具有截然不同的使用期。为发展中国家设计保育箱不只是关系到创造出有用东西的问题；它还关系到设计出的东西以非灾难性方式损坏。你无法保证备件的稳定供应或受过训练的维修技术人员。所以，与之相反，Prestero和他的团队决定用发展中国家中已经很多的零件构建保育箱。这个想法源自名为Jonathan Rosen的波士顿医生，他发现即使是发展中国家的较小城镇似乎也能够使汽车正常工作。这些城镇可能缺乏空调、笔记本电脑和有线电视，但他们能设法驾驶丰田4Runner越野车在路上行驶。因此Rosen与Prestero商量这一想法：如果用汽车零件制造保育箱将会怎么样？"

CASE STUDIES

283   "Three years after Rosen suggested the idea, the Design that Matters team introduced a prototype device called NeoNurture. From the outside, it looked like a streamlined modern incubator, but its guts were automotive. Sealedbeam headlights supplied the crucial warmth; dashboard fans provided filtered air circulation; door chimes sounded alarms. You could power the device via an adapted cigarette lighter, or a standard-issue motorcycle battery. Building the NeoNurture out of car parts was doubly efficient, because it tapped both the local supply of parts themselves and the local knowledge of automobile repair. These were both abundant resources in the developing world context, as Rosen liked to say. You didn't have to be a trained medical technician to fix the NeoNurture; you didn't even have to read the manual. You just needed to know how to replace a broken headlight."

Conclusions   Sometime the highest technology solution is not the best. SE practitioners need to consider issues like maintainability and logistics at the project outset in the concept and development stages. It is too late to address these in later stages.

6.5 CASE 5: ARTIFICIAL INTELLIGENCE IN SYSTEMS ENGINEERING—AUTONOMOUS VEHICLES

Note: Much of the information in this case study is derived from the United States National Transportation Safety Board (NTSB) report on automation (2019a). Page numbers are indicated.

Background   On March 18, 2018, a pedestrian walking a bicycle was fatally struck by a 2017 Volvo XC90 Uber vehicle operating an Automated Driving System (ADS) then under development by Uber's Advanced Technologies Group (ATG). The Volvo's advanced driver assistance system was disabled to prevent conflicts with its radar which operated on the same frequency as the radar for Uber's ATG ADS (p. 15).

At the time of the pedestrian fatality, the ATG-ADS had used one lidar and eight radars to measure distance; several cameras for detecting vehicles, pedestrians, reading traffic lights, and classifying detected objects; and various sensors that had been recently calibrated for telemetry, positioning, monitoring of people and objects, communication, acceleration, and angular rates. It also had a human-machine interface (HMI) tablet and a Global Positioning System (GPS) used solely to assure that the car was on an approved and pre-mapped route before engaging the ADS. The ADS allowed the vehicle to operate at a maximum speed of 45 mph (p. 7), to travel only on urban and rural roads, and under all lighting and weather conditions except for snow accumulation. The ADS system was easily disengaged; until then, almost all of its data was recorded, with the exception noted below of lost data occurred whenever an alternative determination of an object was made by ADS (e.g., shifting from an "object" in the road to an oncoming "vehicle" ahead).

"Rosen 提出这个想法三年后,'设计很重要'团队推出了名为 NeoNurture 的产品原型装置。从外表上,它看起来像一个流线型现代保育箱,但其内部零件是汽车的。封闭式前罩灯提供至关重要的热量;仪表板风扇提供过滤空气的循环流通;车门蜂鸣器发出警报。你可以通过改造的点烟器或标准版摩托车电池为该装置供电。用汽车零件构建 NeoNurture 具有双重有效性,因为其既利用了零件本身的本地供应,也利用了汽车修理的本地知识。这些是发展中国家的丰富资源,正如 Rosen 喜欢说的。你不必一定是受过培训的医疗技术人员,才能够修理 NeoNurture;你甚至不必阅读手册。你只需要知晓如何更换损坏的前照灯即可。"

结论 有时高技术方案不是最好的方案。系统工程实践者需要在项目开始时的概念阶段就考虑到诸如可维护性和可保障性这样的问题。在后续阶段再去考虑这些问题为时已晚。

6.5 案例 5：系统工程中的人工智能——自动驾驶汽车

注：本案例研究中的大部分信息来自美国国家运输安全委员会（NTSB）关于自动化的报告（2019a）。页码已标明。

案例背景 2018 年 3 月 18 日,一名推着自行车的行人,被一辆 2017 款沃尔沃 XC90 优步（Uber）汽车撞死,该车当时使用的是优步先进技术集团（ATG）开发的自动驾驶系统（ADS）。沃尔沃的高级驾驶员辅助系统被禁用,以防止与其雷达发生冲突,该雷达的工作频率与优步 ATG ADS 的雷达相同（第 15 页）。

在行人死亡事故发生时,ATG-ADS 使用了一个激光雷达和八个雷达来测量距离;多个摄像头用于检测车辆、行人、读取交通信号灯,并对检测到的物体进行分类;以及多种最近校准的传感器,用于遥测、定位、监视人员和物体、通信、加速度和角速率。它还有一个人机界面（HMI）平板电脑和一个全球定位系统（GPS）,仅用于确保在使用 ADS 之前,车辆处于已批准和预先规划的路线上。ADS 允许车辆以 45 英里/时的最大速度运行（第 7 页）,仅在城市和农村道路上行驶,并且在除积雪以外的所有照明和天气条件下行驶。ADS 系统很容易断开连接;在断开连接之前,几乎所有的数据都被记录下来,但以下所述的数据丢失除外,即只要 ADS 将某个物体判断为另一个物体时,就会丢失数据（例如,从道路上的"物体"切换到前方迎面而来的"车辆"）。

CASE STUDIES

Approach Designing the interactions of a human and a machine to form into a team (or system) that also acts autonomously requires significant shifts in thinking, modeling, and practice. This begins with changing the unit of analysis from individual humans or programmable machines to teams.

The ADS constructed a virtual environment from the objects that its sensors detected, tracked, classified, and then prioritized based on fusion processes (p. 8). ADS predicted and detected any perceived object's goals and paths as part of its classification system. However, if classifications were made and then changed, as happened in this case (e.g., from "object" to "vehicle" and back to "object"), the prior tracking history was discarded. A flaw since corrected. Also, pedestrians outside of a crosswalk were not assigned a predicted track. Another flaw since corrected.

When ADS detected an emergency (p. 9), it suppressed taking any action for one second to avoid false alarms. After the one second delay, the car's self-braking or evasion could begin. Another major flaw since corrected (p. 15). If a collision could not have been avoided, an auditory warning was to be given to the operator at the same time that the vehicle was to be slowed (in this case, the vehicle may have also begun to slow because an intersection was being approached).

As shown in Figure 6.1, using the recorded data to replay the accident, before impact: Radar first detected the pedestrian 5.6 seconds; Lidar made its first detection at 5.2 seconds, classified the object as unknown and static, changed to a static vehicle at 4.2 seconds on a path predicted to be a miss, reclassified to "other" and static but back again to vehicle between 3.7 to 2.7 seconds, each re-classification discarding its previous prediction history for that object; then a bicycle, but static and a miss at 2.6 seconds; then unknown, static and a miss at 1.5 seconds; then classified the object a bicycle and an unavoidable hazard at 1.2 seconds, the categorization of a hazard immediately initiating "action suppression;" after the 1 seconds pause, finally an auditory alert was sounded at 0.2 seconds; the operator took control at 0.02 seconds before impact; and the operator selected brakes at 0.7 seconds after impact.

The ADS failed to correctly predict the detected object's path, and only determined it to be a hazard at 1.2 seconds before impact, causing any action to be suppressed for one second but, and as a consequence of the impact anticipated in the shortened time-interval remaining before impact, exceeding the ADS design specifications for braking, and thus not enacted; after this self-imposed one second delay, an auditory alert was sounded (p. 12). For almost 20 minutes before impact, the HMI presented no requests for its human operator's input (p. 13), likely contributing to the human operator's sense of complacency.

实现方法　设计人与机器的交互以形成一个能自主行动的团队（或系统），这需要在思维、建模和实践方面进行重大转变。这始于将分析单位从单个人或可编程机器转变为团队。

ADS 利用其传感器探测到的物体构建了一个虚拟环境，对物体进行跟踪、分类，然后根据融合流程确定优先次序（第 8 页）。ADS 预测并检测任何感知对象的目标和路径，作为其分类系统的一部分。但是，如果进行了分类，然后进行了更改，如本例所述（例如，从"物体"变为"车辆"，再变回"物体"），则先前的跟踪历史记录将被丢弃。这是一个在事故发生后已纠正的缺陷。此外，不在人行横道上的行人没有被分配预测轨迹。这是另一个在事故发生后已纠正的缺陷。

当 ADS 检测到紧急情况时（第 9 页），它会在一秒钟内禁止采取任何行动，以避免误报。在一秒钟的延迟后，汽车可以开始自动刹车或躲避。这是又一个在事故发生后已经被纠正的重大缺陷（第 15 页）。如果无法避免碰撞，则应在车辆减速的同时向操作员发出听觉警告（在这种情况下，车辆也可能因为接近交叉口而开始减速）。

如图 6.1 所示，使用记录的数据重现事故，碰撞前：雷达在碰撞前 5.6 秒第一次探测到行人；激光雷达在 5.2 秒前首次探测到，将目标分类为未知和静态；在 4.2 秒前预测为会错过的静态车辆，在 3.7 秒前重新分类为"其他"和静态，但到 2.7 秒前再次变回车辆，每次重新分类都会丢弃其之前对该目标的预测历史；然后在 2.6 秒前变为一辆静止的且会错过的自行车；然后在 1.5 秒前，分类为未知且静止且会错过；然后在 1.2 秒前将物体分类为自行车和不可避免的危险，危险分类立即启动"行动抑制"；在 1 秒的停顿后，最后在碰撞前 0.2 秒时发出听觉警报；操作员在撞击前 0.02 秒接管了控制；碰撞后 0.7 秒，操作员选择刹车。

ADS 未能正确预测检测到的物体的路径，仅在碰撞前 1.2 秒确定其为危险，因为任何行动都被抑制了 1 秒，于是撞击在剩余的极短时间内即将发生，这超出了 ADS 刹车的设计规格，导致刹车行动并未实际执行；在这一自我设定的一秒钟延迟后，系统发出了听觉警报（第 12 页）。在撞击前的近 20 分钟内，HMI 没有对其人工操作员的输入提出任何请求（第 13 页），这可能导致人工操作员的疏忽大意。

CASE STUDIES

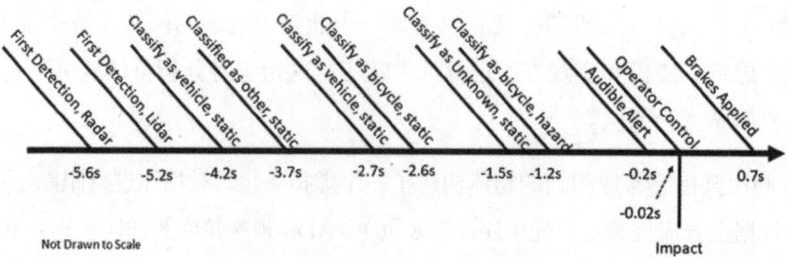

FIGURE 6.1 Timeline of vehicle impact. From NTSB (2019a). Used with permission. All other rights reserved.

Conclusions The following lessons can be taken from this case study:

- The operator was distracted by their personal cell phone; the pedestrian's blood indicated that they were impaired from drugs and that they violated Arizona State's policy by jaywalking.

- The indecisiveness of the ADS was partly attributed to the pedestrian not being in a crosswalk, a feature the system was not designed to address (p. 12), since corrected.

- Uber had inadequate safety risk assessments of its procedures, ineffective oversight in real-time of its vehicle operators to determine whether they were being complacent and exhibited overall an inadequate safety culture (p. vi; see also NTSB, 2019b).

- The Uber ADS was functionally limited, unable to correctly classify the object as a pedestrian, to predict their path, or to adequately assess its risk until almost impact.

- The ADS's decision to suppress action for one second to avoid false alarms increased the risk of driving on the roads and prevented the brakes from being applied immediately to avoid a hazardous situation.

- By disconnecting the Volvo car's own safety systems, Uber increased risk by eliminating the redundant safety systems for its ADS, since corrected (p. vii).

According to NTSB's decision, although the National Highway Traffic Safety Administration (NHTSA) had published a third version of its automated vehicles policy, NHTSA provided no means to a self-driving company of evaluating its vehicle's ADS to meet national or State safety regulations, or to provide a company with the detailed guidance to design an adequate ADS to operate safely. NTSB recommended that safety assessment reports submitted to NHTSA, voluntary at the time of NTSB's final report, be made mandatory (p. viii) and uniform across all states (e.g., Arizona had taken no action by the time of NTSB's final report).

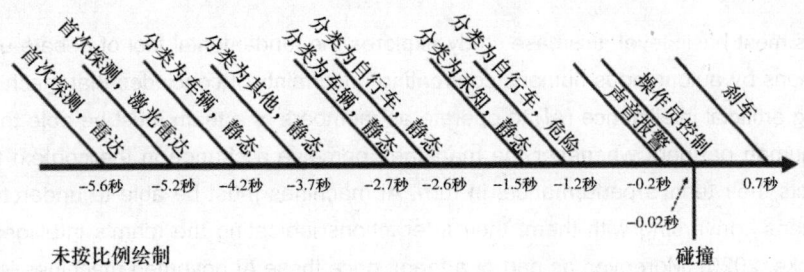

图 6.1 车辆碰撞时间轴。源自 NTSB（2019a）。经许可后使用。版权所有。

结论 从本案例研究中可以得出以下教训：

- 操作员因为个人手机分心；行人的血液检测显示他们因药物影响而受妨害，并且他们违反了亚利桑那州的交通政策，进行了横穿马路行为。
- ADS 的决策迟疑部分归因于行人不在人行横道上，这是系统设计时没有考虑的情形（第 12 页），这一问题已经得到了修正。
- 优步对其程序的安全风险评估不足，对其车辆操作者的实时监督不力，无法确定他们是否疏忽大意，并且总体上表现出不充分的安全文化（第 vi 页；另见 NTSB，2019b）。
- 优步的 ADS 功能有限，无法将物体正确分类为行人，无法预测其路径，或在几乎发生撞击之前无法充分评估其风险。
- ADS 决定抑制行动一秒钟，以避免误报警，这增加了在道路上行驶的风险，并导致在危险情况发生时无法立即刹车。
- 优步通过断开沃尔沃汽车自身的安全系统，去除了对其 ADS 而言冗余的安全系统，从而增加了风险，这一问题后来已经得到了纠正（第 vii 页）。

根据 NTSB 的决定，尽管国家公路交通安全管理局（NHTSA）发布了第三版的自动驾驶车辆政策，但 NHTSA 没有向自动驾驶公司提供评估其车辆 ADS 是否符合国家或州安全法规的方法，也没有向公司提供详细的指导，以设计一个能够安全运行的足够好的 ADS。NTSB 建议当时（TNSB 提交最终报告时）自愿提交给 NHTSA 的安全评估报告改为强制提交，并在所有州统一执行（第 viii 页）（例如，亚利桑那州在 NTSB 提交最终报告时没有采取任何行动）。

CASE STUDIES

285   At its most basic level, this case study explores the fundamental tool of debate used for eons by autonomous humans confronting uncertainty. It concludes that machines using artificial intelligence (AI) to operate as members of a team must be able to tell its human partners whenever the machines perceive a change in the context that affects their team's performance; in turn, AI machines must be able to understand humans conversing with them, their interactions indicating the team's intelligence (Cooke, 2020). Moreover, as part of a team, once these AI governed machines learn what humans want them to learn, they will know when the human members of their team are either complacent or malicious in the human's performance of their roles (Lawless, et al., 2017), a capability not yet available in real time, but possibly over the next five years (Sofge, et al., 2019).

From a human-machine team's perspective, the Uber car was a poor team player (Lawless, 2019). Human teams are autonomous. The operator and vehicle operated independently of each other. Facing uncertain situations, the NTSB report confirmed that no single human or machine agent can determine context alone. Resolving uncertainty requires at a minimum a state of shared interdependence to build context, to adapt to rapid changes in context, and, overall, to operate safely and ethically autonomous human-machine systems. We also know from Cummings (2015) that the best science teams are fully interdependent. Cooke (2020) locates a team's intelligence in the interdependent interactions among its teammates. And to reduce uncertainty in an autonomous system necessitates that human and machine teammates are able to explain to each other, however imperfectly, their view of reality in causal terms (Pearl, 2002; Pearl and Mackenzie, 2018).

As SE moves into the future with the design and operation of autonomous human-machine teams and systems, an interdependence among the parts of a team not only makes the parts reactive to the presence of each other, but it also allows for the team to emerge as a single unit, increasing the team's performance. SE practitioners must be cognizant of the benefits and downfalls of AI and autonomy.

6.6 OTHER CASE STUDIES

Additional case studies can be found in other sources. The SEBoK maintains a set of case studies identified as "implementation examples" (https://www.sebokwiki.org/wiki/Systems_Engineering_Implementation_Examples). The SEBoK case studies span domains including defense systems, information systems, management systems, medical systems, space systems, transportation systems, and utility systems.

在其最基本的层面上，本案例研究探讨了人类一直以来使用的基本工具在采用自动化时面对不确定性存在的争论。它的结论是，使用人工智能（AI）的机器作为团队成员必须能够在机器感知到影响其团队表现的环境变化时告知其人类合作伙伴；反过来，AI 机器必须能够理解人类与它们的对话，它们的互动表明了团队的智能（Cooke，2020）。此外，作为团队的一部分，一旦这些由 AI 控制的机器学习到人类想要它们学习的东西，它们就会知道团队中的人类成员在履行其角色时是疏忽的还是恶意的（Lawless 等，2017），这一能力当前尚未实现，但可能会在未来五年内实现（Sofge 等，2019）。

从人机团队的角度来看，优步汽车是一个糟糕的团队（Lawless，2019）。人类团队是自主的，操作员和车辆相互独立运作。面对不确定的情况，NTSB 的报告证实，没有任何一个人或机器代理能够单独确定情境。解决不确定性至少需要一种共享的相互依赖状态，以构建共同的情境理解，适应情境的快速变化，并且总体上安全和合乎伦理地操作自主的人机系统。我们还从 Cummings（2015）处了解到，最好的科学团队是完全相互依赖的。Cooke（2020）将团队的智能定位在其团队成员之间相互依赖的互动中。为了减少自主系统处的不确定性，人类和机器的团队成员必须能够相互解释他们对现实情境的因果关系看法，无论这种解释多么不完善（Pearl，2002；Pearl 和 Mackenzie，2018）。

随着 SE 向未来迈进，涉及设计和操作自主人机团队和系统时，团队各部分之间的相互依赖不仅使各部分对彼此的存在做出回应，还促进了团队作为一个整体单元的形成，提高团队的整体表现。SE 实践者必须认识到 AI 和自主性的好处和坏处。

6.6 其他案例研究

其他案例研究可在其他来源中找到。SEBoK 维护了一组名为"实施示例"的案例研究（https://www.sebokwiki.org/wiki/Systems_Engineering_Implementation_Examples）。SEBoK 案例研究涉及防务系统、信息系统、管理系统、医疗系统、航天系统、运输系统和公共设施系统等领域。

REFERENCES

APPENDIX A: REFERENCES（参考文献）

ABET (2017). Principles of Diversity and Inclusion website, *The Accreditation Board for Engineering and Technology*. Retrieved from https://www.abet.org/about-abet/diversity-equity-and-inclusion.

Abuzied, H., Senbel, H., Awad, M., and Abbas, A. (2020). A Review of Advances in Design for Disassembly with Active Disassembly Applications, *Engineering Science and Technology, an International Journal*, 23(3), 618-624.

Adkins, H., Beyer, B., Blankinship, P., Lewandowski, P., Oprea, A., and Stubblefield, A. (2020). *Building Secure & Reliable Systems, Best Practices for Designing, Implementing and Maintaining Systems,* O'Reilly Media, Inc.

Akroyd-Wallis, K. (2018). Agile Systems Engineering Guide, *The UK Chapter of the International Council on Systems Engineering (INCOSE UK)*.

Alavi, M. and Leidner, D. E. (1999). Knowledge Management Systems: Issues, Challenges, and Benefits, *Communications of the Association for Information Systems*, 1(2), 7.

Albright, D., Brannan, P., and Walrond, C. (2010). Did Stuxnet Take Out 1,000 Centrifuges at the Natanz Enrichment Plant? *Institute for Science and International Security*. Retrieved from http://isis-online.org/isis-reports/detail/did-stuxnet-take-out-1000-centrifuges-at-the-natanz-enrichment-plant 10 March 2023.

Albright, D., Brannan, P., and Walrond, C. (2011). Stuxnet Malware and Natanz: Update of ISIS December 22, 2010 Report. *Institute for Science and International Security*. Retrieved from http://isis-online.org/uploads/isis-reports/documents/stuxnet_update_15Feb2011. pdf 10 March 2023.

Alexander, C., Ishikawa, S., Silverstein, M., Jacobson, M., Fiksdahl-King, I., and Angel, S. (1977). *A Pattern Language*, Oxford University Press.

Alwi, S., Manan, Z., Klemeš, J., and Huisingh, D. (2014). Sustainability engineering for the future, *Journal of Cleaner Production*, 71, 1-10.

ANSI/AIAA G-043B (2018). *Guide to the Preparation of Operational Concept Documents*, The American National Standards Institute and The American Institute of Aeronautics and Astronautics.

ANSI/EIA 632 (2003). *Processes for Engineering a System*, The American National

REFERENCES

Standards Institute and The Electronic Industries Alliance.

ANSI/GEIA-STD-0009 (2008). *Reliability Program Standard for Systems Design, Development, and Manufacturing,* The American National Standards Institute and The Government Electronics and Information Technology Association.

Anx, Q. (2021). The DevSecOps Cultural Transformation, *PagerDuty Blog.* Retrieved from https://www.pagerduty.com/blog/devsecops-ops-guide/ 10 March 2023.

Arnold, S. and Lawson, H. (2003). Viewing Systems from a Business Management Perspective: The ISO/IEC 15288 Standard, *Systems Engineering*, 7(3), 229-242.

ARP 4754A (2010). *Aerospace Recommended Practice ARP4754A, Guidelines for Development of Civil Aircraft and Systems,* SAE International.

Asare, P., Broman, D., Lee, E., Torngren, M., and Sunder, S. (2012). *Cyber-Physical Systems - a concept map, Cyber-Physical Systems.* Retrieved from https://ptolemy.berkeley.edu/projects/cps 10 March 2023.

ASQ (2007). *Quality Progress, In Quality Glossary, American Society for Quality.* Retrieved from https://asq.org 10 March 2023.

Avraamidou, S., Baratsas, S., Tian, Y., and Pistikopoulos, E. (2020). Circular Economy-A challenge and an opportunity for Process Systems Engineering, *Computers & Chemical Engineering*, 133, 106629.

Axehill, J., Herzog, E., Tingström, J., and Bengtsson, M. (2021). From Brownfield to Greenfield Development - Understanding and Managing the Transition, *Proceedings of the 31st Annual International Symposium of the International Council on Systems Engineering,* The International Council on Systems Engineering (INCOSE).

Axelsson, J. (2020). Achieving System-of-Systems Interoperability Levels Using Linked Data and Ontologies, *Proceedings of the 30th Annual International Symposium of the International Council on Systems Engineering,* The International Council on Systems Engineering (INCOSE).

Baley, K. and Belcham, D. (2010). *Brownfield Application Development in .NET,* Manning Publishing.

INCOSE Systems Engineering Handbook: A Guide for System Life Cycle Processes and Activities, Fifth Edition.

Edited by David D. Walden, Thomas M. Shortell, Garry J. Roedler, Bernardo A. Delicado, Odile Mornas, Yip Yew-Seng, and David Endler.

© 2023 John Wiley & Sons Ltd. Published 2023 by John Wiley & Sons Ltd.

REFERENCES

Banach, Z. (2019). What is DevSecOps: How to integrate security into DevOps, *Invicti Web Security Blog.* Retrieved from https://www.invicti.com/blog/web-security/what-is-devsecops/ 10 March 2023.

Barnard, R. (2008). What Is Wrong with Reliability Engineering? *Proceedings of the 18th Annual International Symposium of the International Council on Systems Engineering,* The International Council on Systems Engineering (INCOSE).

Bass, L., Clements, P., and Kazman, R. (2012). *Software Architecture in Practice*, Third Edition. Addison-Wesley Professional.

Becker, O., Ben-Ashe, J., and Ackerman, I. (2000). A Method for Systems Interface Reduction Using N2 Charts, *Systems Engineering*, 3(1), 27-37.

Beery, P. and Paulo, E. (2019). Application of model-based systems engineering concepts to support mission engineering, *Systems*, 7(3), 44. Retrieved from https://www.mdpi.com/2079-8954/7/3/44 10 March 2023.

Bernus, P. (1999). GERAM - Generalized Enterprise Reference - Architecture and Methodology, *IFIP-IFAC Task Force on Architectures for Enterprise Integration.* Retrieved from http://dx.doi.org/10.13140/RG.2.2.35937.33120 10 March 2023.

Bidanda, B. (2022). *Maynard's Industrial and Systems Engineering Handbook*, Sixth Edition. McGraw Hill.

Biomimicry Institute. (2022). Biomimicry Toolbox website, *The Biomimicry Institute.* Retrieved from https://toolbox.biomimicry.org 10 March 2023.

Birman, K. (2012). *Guide to Reliable Distributed Systems: Building High-Assurance Applications and Cloud-Hosted Services,* Springer.

Blanchard, B. (1967). Cost Effectiveness, System Effectiveness, Integrated Logistics Support, and Maintainability, *IEEE Transactions on Reliability*, 163(3), 117-126

Blanchard, B. (2004). *Logistics Engineering and Management*, Sixth Edition. Pearson Prentice Hall.

Blanchard, B. and Fabrycky, W. (2011). *Systems Engineering and Analysis*, Fifth. Prentice Hall.

Bobinis, J., Haimowitz, J., Tuttle, P., Garrison, C., Mitchell, T., and Klingberg, J. (2013). Affordability Considerations: Cost Effective Capability, *Proceedings of the 23rd Annual International Symposium of the International Council on Systems Engineering*, The International Council on Systems Engineering (INCOSE).

REFERENCES

Boehm, B. (1987). A spiral model of software development and enhancement, *ACM SIGSOFT Software Engineering Notes*, 11(4), 14-24.

Boehm, B., Lane, J., Koolmanojwong, S., and Turner, R. (2014). *The Incremental Commitment Spiral Model: Principles and Practices for Successful Systems and Software*, Addison-Wesley Professional.

Boehm, B. and Turner, R. (2004). *Balancing Agility and Discipline*, Addison-Wesley.

Boehm-Davis, D., Durso, F., and Lee, J. (2015). *APA Handbook of Human Systems Integration*, American Psychological Association.

Bogdanich, W. (2010). *Radiation Offers New Cures, and Ways to Do Harm*, The New York Times.

Bonnet, S., Voirin, J.-L., Exertier, D., and Normand, V. (2017). Modeling system modes, states, configurations with Arcadia and Capella: Method and tool perspectives, *Proceedings of the 27th Annual International Symposium of the International Council on Systems Engineering*, The International Council on Systems Engineering (INCOSE).

Boy, G. (2013). *Orchestrating Human-Centered Design*, Springer.

Boy, G. (2020). *Human Systems Integration: From Virtual to Tangible*, CRC Press - Taylor & Francis Group.

Bradley, J., Hughes, M., and Schindel, W. (2010). Optimizing Delivery of Global Pharmaceutical Packaging Solutions, Using Systems Engineering Patterns, *Proceedings of the 20th Annual International Symposium of the International Council on Systems Engineering*, The International Council on Systems Engineering (INCOSE).

Brtis, J. S. (2016). *How to Think About Resilience, MITRE Technical Report*, MITRE Corporation.

Brtis, J. S. (2020). Loss-Driven Systems Engineering (LDSE), *INSIGHT*, 23(4), The International Council on Systems Engineering (INCOSE).

Brtis, J. S. and McEvilley, M. A. (2019). Systems Engineering for Resilience, *MITRE Technical Report*, The MITRE Corporation.

Buede, D. and Miller, W. (2016). *The Engineering Design of Systems: Models and Methods*, Third Edition. John Wiley & Sons.

Cabrera, D., Cabrera, L., and Powers, E. (2015). A unifying theory of systems thinking

REFERENCES

with psychosocial applications, *Systems Research and Behavioral Science*, 32, 534-545.

Calvo-Amodio, J. and Rousseau, D. (2019). The Human Activity System: Emergence from Purpose, Boundaries, Relationships, and Context, *Procedia Computer Science*, 153, 91-99.

Cantwell. (2021). Aviation Safety Whistleblower Report, *U.S. Senate Committee on Commerce, Science, and Transportation*.

Carayon, P., Schoofs Hundt, A., Karsh, B.-T., Gurses, A., Alvarado, C., Smith, M., and Flatley Brennan, P. (2006). Work system design for patient safety: The SEIPS model, *Quality and Safety in Health Care*, 15(Suppl 1), i50-i58.

Carpenter, S., Delugach, H., Etzkorn, L., Fortune, J., Utley, D., and Virani, S. (2010). The Effect of Shared Mental Models on Team Performance, *Industrial Engineering Research Conference*, Cancun, Mexico, Institute of Industrial Engineers.

Chapman, W., Bahill, A., and Wymore, A. (1992). *Engineering Modeling and Design*, CRC Press. Retrieved from https://doi.org/10.1201/9780203757314.

Checkland, P. (1999). *Systems Thinking, Systems Practice*, John Wiley.

Choi, S., Suh, E., and Park, C. (2020). Value chain and stakeholder-driven product platform design, *Systems Engineering*, 23(3), 312-326. Retrieved from https://doi:10.1002/sys.21527.

Clausing, D. and Frey, D. (2005). Improving System Reliability by Failure Mode Avoidance including Four Concept Design Strategies, *Systems Engineering*, 8(3), 245-261.

Cloutier, R., DiMario, M., and Pozer, H. (2009). Net Centricity and Systems of Systems, in M. Jamshidi (Ed.) *Systems of Systems Engineering*, CRC Press/Taylor & Francis Group.

CMMI (2018). *Capability Maturity Model Integration (CMMI®) for Development V2.0, the CMMI Institute, a subsidiary of the Information Systems Audit and Control Association (ISACA)*. Retrieved from https://cmmiinstitute.com/cmmi/dev 10 March 2023.

CMU/SEI (2000). *ATAM - Architecture Tradeoff Analysis Method - TR-004 ESC-TR-2000-004, the Software Engineering Institute at Carnegie Mellon University*. Retrieved from https://resources.sei.cmu.edu/asset_files/TechnicalReport/2000_005_001_13706. pdf 10 March 2023.

REFERENCES

Conrow, E. (2003). *Effective Risk Management*, Second Edition. American Institute of Aeronautics and Astronautics, Inc.

Cook, C. and Unewisse, M. (2019). *A SoS Approach for Engineering Capability Programs*. Retrieved from https://doi.org/10.1002/j.2334-5837.2017.00342.x 10 March 2023.

Cook, D. and Schindel, W. (2015). Utilizing MBSE Patterns to Accelerate System Verification, *Proceedings of the 25th Annual International Symposium of the International Council on Systems Engineering*, The International Council on Systems Engineering (INCOSE).

Cooke, N. (2020). Effective human-artificial intelligence teaming, *Proceedings of the AAAI Spring Symposium*, Stanford, CA.

Crosby, P. (1979). *Quality Is Free: The Art of Making Quality Certain*, McGraw Hill.

Cross, N. (2000). *Engineering Design Methods - Strategies for Product Design*. Chichester UK: Wiley. Third edition.

CST (2020). *A Systems Approach to Delivering Net Zero: Recommendations From The Prime Minister's Council For Science And Technology, the UK Council for Science and Technology*. Retrieved from https://assets.publishing.service.gov.uk/government/uploads/system/uploads/attachment_data/file/910446/cst-net-zero-report-30-january-2020.pdf 10 March 2023.

Cullen, T. (1990). *The Public Inquiry into the Piper Alpha Disaster*, HMSO.

Cummings, J. (2015). *Team Science successes and challenges, National Science Foundation Sponsored Workshop on Fundamentals of Team Science & Science of Team Science*, Bethesda MD.

Dahmann, J. (2014). System of Systems Pain Points. *Proceedings of the 24th Annual International Symposium of the International Council on Systems Engineering*, The International Council on Systems Engineering (INCOSE).

Dahmann, J., Rebovich, G., Lane, J., Lowry, R., and Baldwin, K. (2011). An Implementer's View of Systems Engineering for Systems of Systems, *IEEE Systems Conference*, April 4-7, 2011, Montreal, Canada, p. 212-217.

Daskin, M. (2010). *Service Science*, John Wiley & Sons, Inc.

DAU (1993). *Committed Life Cycle Cost against Time*, US Defense Acquisition University.

REFERENCES

DAU (2022). *Glossary*, US Defense Acquisition University. Retrieved from https://www.dau.edu/glossary/Pages/Glossary.aspx 10 March 2023.

Defoe, J. (1993). An Identification of Pragmatic Principles, *Final Report, Systems Engineering Practice Working Group, Subgroup on Pragmatic Principles*, National Council on Systems Engineering (NCOSE) WMA Chapter.

Dekker, S. (2014). *Safety Differently: Human Factors for a New Era*, Second Edition. Routledge.

Delicado, B., Salado, A., and Mompó, R. (2018). Conceptualization of a T-Shaped engineering competency model in collaborative organizational settings: Problem and status in the Spanish aircraft industry, *Systems Engineering*, 21, 534-554, Retrieved from https://doi.org/10.1002/sys.21453.

Deming, W. (1986). *Out of the Crisis, Massachusetts Institute of Technology Center for Advanced Engineering Study.*

Dennis, A., Wixom, B., and Tegarden, D. (2020). *Systems Analysis and Design: An Object-Oriented Approach with UML*, Sixth Edition. John Wiley & Sons.

Desapriya, E., Kerr, J., Hewapathirane, D., Peiris, C., Mann, B., Gomes, N., Peiris, K., Scime, G., and Jones, J. (2012). Bull Bars and Vulnerable Road Users, *Traffic Injury Prevention*, 13, 86-92, Retrieved from http://dx.doi.org/10.1080/15389588.2011.624143.

DoDAF (2010). *DoD Architecture Framework, Version 2.02*, US Department of Defense. Retrieved from https://dodcio.defense.gov/Library/DoD-Architecture-Framework.

Domingue, J., Fensel, D., Davies, J., Gonzalez-Cabero, R., and Pedrinaci, C. (2009). The Service Web: A Web of Billions of Services, in G. Tselentis, et al. (Ed.) *Toward the Future Internet—A European Research Perspective*, IOS Press. Retrieved from https://doi.org/10.3233/978-1-60750-007-0-203.

Donovan, J. and Prabhu, K. (2017). *Building the Network of the Future: Getting Smarter, Faster and More Flexible with a Software Centric Approach*, CRC Press.

Dorst, K. (2015). *Frame Innovation: Create New Thinking by Design.* Cambridge MA: MIT Press.

Dove, R. and LaBarge, R. (2014). Fundamentals of Agile Systems Engineering - Part 1. *Proceedings of the 24th Annual International Symposium of the International Council on Systems Engineering*, The International Council on Systems Engineering (INCOSE).

REFERENCES

Dove, R. and Schindel, W. (2017). Case Study: Agile SE Process for Centralized SoS Sustainment at Northrop Grumman, *Proceedings of the 27th Annual International Symposium of the International Council on Systems Engineering*, The International Council on Systems Engineering (INCOSE).

Dove, R. and Schindel, W. (2019). Agile Systems Engineering Life Cycle Model for Mixed Discipline Engineering, *Proceedings of the 29th Annual International Symposium of the International Council on Systems Engineering*, The International Council on Systems Engineering (INCOSE).

Dove, R., Schindel, W., and Garlington, K. (2018). Case Study: Agile Systems Engineering at Lockheed Martin Aeronautics Integrated Fighter Group, *Proceedings of the 28th Annual International Symposium of the International Council on Systems Engineering*, The International Council on Systems Engineering (INCOSE).

Dove, R., Schindel, W., and Hartney, R. (2017). Case Study: Agile Hardware/Firmware/Software Product Line Engineering at Rockwell Collins, *Proceedings 11th Annual IEEE International Systems Conference*. Retrieved from https://ieeexplore.ieee.org/document/7934807/authors#authors 10 March 2023.

Dove, R., Schindel, W., and Scrapper, C. (2016). Agile Systems Engineering Process Features Collective Culture, Consciousness, and Conscience at SSC Pacific Unmanned Systems Group. *Proceedings of the 26th Annual International Symposium of the International Council on Systems Engineering*, The International Council on Systems Engineering (INCOSE).

DSMC (1983). *Systems Engineering Management Guide*, US Defense Systems Management College.

Edwards, W., Miles Jr., R., and Von Winterfeldt, D. (2007). *Advances in Decision Analysis: From Foundations to Applications,* Cambridge University Press.

Elm, J. and Goldenson, D. (2012). The Business Case for Systems Engineering Study: Results of the Systems Engineering Effectiveness Study, *The Software Engineering Institute at Carnegie Mellon University*. Retrieved from http://resources.sei.cmu.edu/library/asset-view.cfm?assetID=34061.

Eppinger, S. and Browning, T. (2012). *Design Structure Matrix Methods and Applications*, MIT Press.

EPRS (2016). *The European Parliament Research Service website*. Retrieved from https://www.europarl.europa.eu/at-your-service/en/stay-informed/research-and-analysis 10 March 2023.

REFERENCES

Estefan, J. (2008). *Survey of Model Based Systems Engineering (MBSE) Methodologies*, Rev. B, Section 3.2, NASA Jet Propulsion Laboratory.

Evans, D. (2014). Styles of Architecting - A smarter approach to architecting the Defence Enterprise, *Niteworks White Paper*. Retrieved from Styles of architecting: a smarter approach to architecting the Defence Enterprise (white paper) - GOV.UK (www.gov.uk) 10 March 2023.

FAA (2014). *FAA Systems Engineering Manual*, US Federal Aviation Administration.

Fagen, M. (1978). *A History of engineering and science in the Bell System: National Service in War and Peace (1925-1975)*, Bell Telephone Laboratories (Author), M. Fagen (Editor).

Failliere, N. (2011). *W32, Stuxnet Dossier, Version 1.4*. Retrieved from https://archive.org/details/w32_stuxnet_dossier 10 March 2023.

Fairley, R. (2019). *Systems Engineering of Software-Enabled Systems*, John Wiley & Sons, Inc.

Firesmith, D., Capell, P., Falkenthal, D., Hammons, C., Latimer IV, T., and Merendino, T. (2008). *Method Framework for Engineering System Architectures (MFESA)*, Auerbach Publications.

Fishman, G. (1997). *Monte Carlo: Concepts, Algorithms, and Applications*, pp. 1-4. Retrieved from http://www.sei.cmu.edu/library/assets/quality-assess.pdf.

Forsberg, K. (1995). If I Could Do That, Then I Could ...: Systems Engineering in a Research and Development Environment, *Proceedings of the 5th Annual International Symposium of the International Council on Systems Engineering*, The International Council on Systems Engineering (INCOSE).

Forsberg, K. and Mooz, H. (1991). The Relationship of System Engineering to the Project Cycle, *Proceedings of the 1st Annual Symposium of the National Council on Systems Engineering*, The National Council on Systems Engineering (NCOSE).

Forsberg, K., Mooz, H., and Cotterman, H. (2005). *Visualizing Project Management*, Third Edition. John Wiley & Sons, Inc.

Fossnes, T. (2005). Lessons from Mt. Everest Applicable to Project Leadership, *Proceedings of the 15th Annual International Symposium of the International Council on Systems Engineering*, The International Council on Systems Engineering (INCOSE).

Friedland, B. (2012). *Control System Design*, Dover Publications.

REFERENCES

Fries, M. and Paal, B. (2019). *Smart contracts.* Retrieved from http://library.oapen.org/handle/20.500.12657/24858 10 March 2023.

Frost, S. (2016). *Compound Eye Sensor for Real-time Aircraft Wing Deflection Measurement*, American Institute of Aeronautics and Astronautics.

Gallup Report (2017). *State of the Global Workplace - Gallup Report.* Retrieved from https://www.gallup.com/home.aspx 10 March 2023.

Gallup Report (2020). *State of the Global Workplace - Gallup Report.* Retrieved from https://www.gallup.com/workplace/285818/state-american-workplace-report.aspx 10 March 2023.

Gamma, E., Helm, R., Johnson, R., and Vlissides, J. (1995). *Design Patterns: Elements of Reusable Object-Oriented Software*, Addison-Wesley Publishing Company.

GAO (2008). *Best Practices—Increased Focus on Requirements and Oversight Needed to Improve DOD's Acquisition Environment and Weapon System Quality*, US Government Accountability Office. Retrieved from https://www.gao.gov/new.items/d08294.pdf 10 March 2023.

Garlan, D. and Shaw, M. (1994). *Advances in Software Engineering and Knowledge Engineering*, Volume 1.

Garlan, D. and Shaw, M. (1996). *Advances in Software Engineering and Knowledge Engineering*, Volume 2.

Gartner (2022). *Gartner Glossary.* Retrieved from https://www.gartner.com/en/information-technology/glossary/ie-information-engineering 10 March 2023.

Gass, S. and Harris, C. (2001). *Encyclopedia of Operations Research and Management Science*, xli Journal of the Operational Research Society.

Gebhardt, A. and Hötte, J.-S. (2016). *Additive Manufacturing: 3D Printing for Prototyping and Manufacturing*, Hanser Publications.

GEIA HB649A (2016). *Configuration Management Standard Implementation Guide*, The Government Electronics and Information Technology Association.

Geissdoerfer, M., Pieroni, M., Pigosso, D., and Soufani, K. (2020). Circular business models: A review, J*ournal of Cleaner Production*, 277, 123741.

Gilb, T. and Graham, D. (1993). *Software Inspection*, Addison-Wesley-Longman.

Goode, H. and Machol, R. (1957). *System Engineering; An Introduction to the Design*

REFERENCES

of Large-scale Systems, McGraw-Hill.

Grady, J. O. (1994). *System Integration.* Boca Raton, FL: CRC Press.

Gregg, S., Scharadin, R., and Clements, P. (2015). The More You Do, the More You Save: The Superlinear Cost Avoidance Effect of Systems and Software Product Line Engineering, *Proceedings of the Software Product Line Conference*, Nashville.

Griffin, M. (2010). How do we fix system engineering? *Proceedings of the 61st International Astronautical Congress*, Prague, CZ.

Guariniello, C., Raz, A. K., Fang, Z., and DeLaurentis, D. (2020). System-of-systems tools and techniques for the analysis of cyberphysical systems, *Systems Engineering*, 23(4), 480-491. Retrieved from https://incose.onlinelibrary.wiley.com/doi/10.1002/sys.21539.

Gupta, J. and Sharma, S. (2004). *Creating Knowledge Based Organizations*, Ida Group Publishing.

Haberfellner, R. and de Weck, O. (2005). Agile SYSTEMS ENGINEERING versus AGILE SYSTEMS Engineering, *Proceedings of the 15th Annual International Symposium of the International Council on Systems Engineering*, The International Council on Systems Engineering (INCOSE).

Hall, A. (1962). *A Methodology for Systems Engineering*, Van Nostrand.

Hallman, C. (2022). *50 Cognitive Biases to be Aware of so You Can be the Very Best Version of You*. Retrieved from https://www.titlemax.com/discovery-center/lifestyle/50-cognitive-biases-to-be-aware-of-so-you-can-be-the-very-best-version-of-you 10 March 2023.

Hammond, D. (2003). *The Science of Synthesis: Exploring the Social Implications of General Systems Theory*, University Press of Colorado.

Harding, A. and Pickard, A. (2019). Towards a More Diverse INCOSE, *INSIGHT*, 22(3), The International Council on Systems Engineering (INCOSE).

Haskins, C. (2021). Systems Engineering for Sustainable Development Goals, *Sustainability*, 13(18), 10293.

He, B., Pan, Q., and Deng, Z. (2018). Product carbon footprint for product life cycle under uncertainty, *Journal of Cleaner Production*, 187, 459-472.

Henshaw, M. (2016). Systems of Systems, Cyber-Physical Systems, the Internet-of-Things... Whatever Next?, *INSIGHT*, 19(3), The International Council on Systems

REFERENCES

Engineering (INCOSE).

Hidden, A. (1989). *Investigation into the Clapham Junction Railway Accident*, HMSO.

Hoehne, O. (2020). Case Study: Achieving System Integration through Interoperability in a large System of Systems (SoS), *Proceedings of the 30th Annual International Symposium of the International Council on Systems Engineering*, The International Council on Systems Engineering (INCOSE).

Hoeller, N., Farnsworth, M., Jacobs, S., Chirazi, J., Mead, T., Goel, A., and Salustri, F. (2016). A Systems View of Bio-inspiration: Bridging the Gaps, *INSIGHT*, 19(1), The International Council on Systems Engineering (INCOSE).

Honour, E. (2013). Systems Engineering Return on Investment, Ph.D. Thesis, *Defense and Systems Institute*, University of South Wales. Retrieved from https://incose.onlinelibrary.wiley.com/doi/10.1002/j.2334-5837.2010.tb01150.x 10 March 2023.

Hopkins, R. and Jenkins, K. (2008). *Eating the IT Elephant: Moving from Greenfield Development to Brownfield*, IBM Press/Pearson.

Howard, R. (1968). The Foundations of Decision Analysis, *IEEE Transactions on Systems Science and Cyberntics*, 4(3), 211-219. Retrieved from https://doi.org/10.1109/TSSC.1968.300115.

Hudson, P. (2001). *Safety Management and Safety Culture: The Long, Hard and Winding Road, Occupational Health & Safety Management Systems*.

ICE (2023). *Proceedings of the Institution of Civil Engineers - Engineering Sustainability*, The Institution of Civil Engineers. Retrieved from https://www.icevirtuallibrary.com/toc/jensu/current 10 March 2023.

IEC 60601 (2020). *Medical device safety*, The International Electrotechnical Commission.

IEC 62196 (2022). *Plugs, Socket-Outlets, Vehicle Connectors And Vehicle Inlets - Conductive Charging Of Electric Vehicles (Multipart Standard)*, The International Electrotechnical Commission.

IEC 62304 (2006). *Medical Device software - Software life cycle processes,* The International Electrotechnical Commission.

IEC 62366 (2015). *Application of usability engineering to medical devices*, The International Electrotechnical Commission.

IEC 62402 (2019). *Obsolescence management*, The International Electrotechnical

REFERENCES

Commission.

IEEE 1517 (2010). *IEEE Standard for Information Technology - System and Software Life Cycle Processes - Reuse Processes*, The Institute of Electrical and Electronics Engineers.

IEEE 610.12 (1990). *IEEE Standard Glossary of Software Engineering Terminology*, The Institute of Electrical and Electronics Engineers. Retrieved from https://doi.org/10.1109/IEEESTD.1990.101064.

IEEE 828 (2012). *IEEE Standard for Configuration Management in Systems and Software Engineering*, The Institute of Electrical and Electronics Engineers.

IEEE Reliability Society (2023). *IEEE Reliability Society website*, The Institute of Electrical and Electronics Engineers. Retrieved from https://rs.ieee.org 10 March 2023.

IISE (2022). *The Industrial and Systems Engineering Body of Knowledge (ISEBoK)*, The Institute of Industrial and Systems Engineers. Retrieved from https://www.iise.org/details.aspx?id=43631 10 March 2023.

INCOSE Automotive SE Vision (2020). *INCOSE Automotive SE Vision 2025*, The International Council on Systems Engineering (INCOSE).

INCOSE Code of Ethics (2023). *INCOSE Code of Ethics website*, The International Council on Systems Engineering (INCOSE). Retrieved from https://www.incose.org/about-incose/Leadership-Organization/code-of-ethics 10 March 2023.

INCOSE Complexity Primer (2021). *INCOSE Complexity Primer*, The International Council on Systems Engineering (INCOSE).

INCOSE Definitions (2019). *INCOSE Definitions*, The International Council on Systems Engineering (INCOSE).

INCOSE GtNR (2022). *INCOSE Guide to Needs and Requirements*, The International Council on Systems Engineering (INCOSE).

INCOSE GtVV (2022). *INCOSE Guide to Verification and Validation*, The International Council on Systems Engineering (INCOSE).

INCOSE GtWR (2022). *INCOSE Guide to Writing Requirements*, The International Council on Systems Engineering (INCOSE).

INCOSE HSI Primer (2023). *Human Systems Integration Primer,* The International Council on Systems Engineering (INCOSE).

REFERENCES

INCOSE Innovation Ecosystem (2022). *Adaptive, Learning Ecosystems: Introduction to the Innovation Ecosystem S*Pattern,* Version 1.0, The International Council on Systems Engineering (INCOSE).

INCOSE MBSE Wiki (2022). *INCOSE MBSE Wiki website*, The International Council on Systems Engineering (INCOSE). Retrieved from http://www.omgwiki.org/MBSE/doku.php 10 March 2023.

INCOSE NS Primer (2023). *Natural Systems And The Systems Engineering Process: A Primer*, The International Council on Systems Engineering (INCOSE).

INCOSE Measurement Primer (2010). *Systems Engineering Measurement Primer, A Basic Introduction to Measurement Concepts and Use for Systems Engineering*, The International Council on Systems Engineering (INCOSE).

INCOSE NRM (2022). *INCOSE Needs and Requirements Manual*, The International Council on Systems Engineering (INCOSE).

INCOSE OOSEM (2022). *INCOSE OOSEM Working Group website*, The International Council on Systems Engineering (INCOSE). Retrieved from https://www.incose.org/incose-member-resources/working-groups/transformational/object-oriented-se-method 10 March 2023.

INCOSE PLE Primer (2019). *INCOSE PLE Primer*, The International Council on Systems Engineering (INCOSE).

INCOSE PMGtSEMfPS (2015). *Project Manager's Guide to Systems Engineering Measurement for Project Success, A Basic Introduction to Systems Engineering Measures for Use by Project Managers*, The International Council on Systems Engineering (INCOSE).

INCOSE S*MBSE (2022) *Minimal S*Models: A Primer.* The International Council on Systems Engineering (INCOSE).

INCOSE S*MCP (2019). *The Model Characterization Pattern: A Universal Characterization & Labeling S*Pattern for All Models, V1.9.3*, The International Council on Systems Engineering (INCOSE).

INCOSE S*Patterns Primer (2022). *An MBSE S*Patterns Primer, Version 1.0*, The International Council on Systems Engineering (INCOSE).

INCOSE SE Principles (2022). *INCOSE SE Principles*, The International Council on Systems Engineering (INCOSE).

INCOSE SECAG (2023). *INCOSE Systems Engineering Competency Assessment*

REFERENCES

Guide, The International Council on Systems Engineering (INCOSE), Wiley.

INCOSE SECF (2018). INCOSE SE Competency Framework, The International Council on Systems Engineering (INCOSE).

INCOSE SETDB (2021). INCOSE *Systems Engineering Tools Database*, The International Council on Systems Engineering (INCOSE).

INCOSE Value Report (2021). *INCOSE Value Strategic Initiative Report*, The International Council on Systems Engineering (INCOSE).

INCOSE Vision 2020 (2007). *Systems Engineering Vision 2020*, The International Council on Systems Engineering (INCOSE).

INCOSE Vision 2035 (2022). *Systems Engineering Vision 2035*, The International Council on Systems Engineering (INCOSE).

INCOSE, PSM, NDIA, SERC, OSD R&E, AIA, and Aerospace (2022). *Practical Software and Systems Measurement (PSM) Digital Engineering Measurement Framework*, The International Council on Systems Engineering, Practical Software & Systems Measurement Support Center, The National Defense Industrial Association, Systems Engineering Research Center, US Office of the Secretary of Defense Research & Engineering, The Aerospace Industries Association, and The Aerospace Corporation.

INFORMS (2022). *Institute for Operations Research and the Management Sciences website*. Retrieved from https://www.informs.org 10 March 2023.

IOGP (2021). *International Association of Oil & Gas Producers website.* Retrieved from https://www.iogp.org 10 March 2023.

ISO 10007 (2017). *Quality management - Guidelines for configuration management*, The International Organization for Standardization.

ISO 10303-233 (2012). *Industrial automation systems and integration — Product data representation and exchange - Part 233: Application protocol: Systems engineering*, The International Organization for Standardization.

ISO 13008 (2022). *Information and documentation — Digital records conversion and migration process*, The International Organization for Standardization.

ISO 13485 (2016). *Medical devices — Quality management systems — Requirements for regulatory purposes*, The International Organization for Standardization.

REFERENCES

ISO 14000 (2015). *ISO 14001 and related standards Environmental management*, The International Organization for Standardization.

ISO 14001 (2015). *Environmental management systems — Requirements with guidance for use*, The International Organization for Standardization.

ISO 14971 (2019). *Medical devices — Application of risk management to medical devices*, The International Organization for Standardization.

ISO 15704 (2019). *Enterprise modelling and architecture — Requirements for enterprise-referencing architectures and methodologies*, The International Organization for Standardization.

ISO 17757 (2019). *Earth-moving machinery and mining — Autonomous and semi-autonomous machine system safety,* The International Organization for Standardization.

ISO 21347 (2005). *Space systems — Fracture and damage control*, The International Organization for Standardization.

ISO 22367 (2020). *Medical laboratories — Application of risk management to medical laboratories*, The International Organization for Standardization.

ISO 26262 (2018). *Road vehicles — Functional safety (Multi-part Standard)*, The International Organization for Standardization.

ISO 27000 (2018). *Series of standards for information security matters*, The International Organization for Standardization.

ISO 8930 (2021). *General principles on reliability for structures — Vocabulary,* The International Organization for Standardization.

ISO 9000 (2015). *Quality management*, The International Organization for Standardization.

ISO 9001 (2015). *Quality management — Requirements*, The International Organization for Standardization.

ISO Guide 73 (2009). *Risk management — Vocabulary*, The International Organization for Standardization.

ISO/IEC 17799 (2005). *Information technology — Security techniques — Code of practice for information security management,* The International Organization for Standardization and The International Electrotechnical Commission.

ISO/IEC 19759 (2015). *Software Engineering — Guide to the software engineering*

REFERENCES

body of knowledge (SWEBOK), The International Organization for Standardization and The International Electrotechnical Commission.

ISO/IEC 19970-1 (2017). *Information Technology - IT Asset Management - Part 1: IT Asset Management Systems - Requirements,* The International Organization for Standardization and The International Electrotechnical Commission.

ISO/IEC 2382 (2015). *Information technology — Vocabulary,* The International Organization for Standardization and The International Electrotechnical Commission.

ISO/IEC 29110 (2016). *Systems and Software Engineering Standards and Guides for Very Small Entities (VSEs) (Multi-part set),* The International Organization for Standardization and The International Electrotechnical Commission.

ISO/IEC 31000 (2018). *Risk management*, The International Organization for Standardization and The International Electrotechnical Commission.

ISO/IEC 31010 (2019). *Risk management - Risk assessment techniques,* The International Organization for Standardization and The International Electrotechnical Commission.

ISO/IEC 33060 (2020). *Process Assessment - Process Assessment Model for System Life Cycle Processes*, The International Organization for Standardization and The International Electrotechnical Commission.

ISO/IEC Guide 51 (2014). *Safety Aspects — Guidelines for their Inclusion in Standards*, The International Organization for Standardization and The International Electrotechnical Commission.

ISO/IEC/IEEE 12207 (2017). *Systems and Software Engineering - Software Life Cycle Processes*, The International Organization for Standardization, The International Electrotechnical Commission, and The Institute of Electrical and Electronics Engineers.

ISO/IEC/IEEE 15026 (2019). *Systems and Software Engineering - Systems and Software Assurance (Multi-Part Standard)*, The International Organization for Standardization, The International Electrotechnical Commission, and The Institute of Electrical and Electronics Engineers.

ISO/IEC/IEEE 15288 (2023). *Systems and Software Engineering - System Life Cycle Processes*, The International Organization for Standardization, The International Electrotechnical Commission, and The Institute of Electrical and Electronics Engineers.

REFERENCES

ISO/IEC/IEEE 15289 (2019). *Systems and Software Engineering - Content of Life Cycle Information Items (Documentation)*, The International Organization for Standardization, The International Electrotechnical Commission, and The Institute of Electrical and Electronics Engineers.

ISO/IEC/IEEE 15939 (2017). *Systems and Software Engineering - Measurement Process*, The International Organization for Standardization, The International Electrotechnical Commission, and The Institute of Electrical and Electronics Engineers.

ISO/IEC/IEEE 16085 (2021). *Systems and Software Engineering - Life Cycle Processes - Risk Management*, The International Organization for Standardization, The International Electrotechnical Commission, and The Institute of Electrical and Electronics Engineers.

ISO/IEC/IEEE 16326 (2019). *Systems and Software Engineering - Life Cycle Processes - Project Management*, The International Organization for Standardization, The International Electrotechnical Commission, and The Institute of Electrical and Electronics Engineers.

ISO/IEC/IEEE 21839 (2019). *Systems and software engineering - System of systems (SoS) considerations in life cycle stages of a system*, The International Organization for Standardization, The International Electrotechnical Commission, and The Institute of Electrical and Electronics Engineers.

ISO/IEC/IEEE 21840 (2019). *Systems and software engineering - Guidelines for the utilization of ISO/IEC/IEEE 15288 in the context of system of systems (SoS)*, The International Organization for Standardization, The International Electrotechnical Commission, and The Institute of Electrical and Electronics Engineers.

ISO/IEC/IEEE 21841 (2019). *Systems and software engineering — Taxonomy of systems of systems*, The International Organization for Standardization, The International Electrotechnical Commission, and The Institute of Electrical and Electronics Engineers.

ISO/IEC/IEEE 24641 (2022) *Systems and Software Engineering — Methods and Tools for Model-Based Systems and Software Engineering, The International Organization for Standardization*, The International Electrotechnical Commission, and The Institute of Electrical and Electronics Engineers.

ISO/IEC/IEEE 24748-1 (2018). *Systems and Software Engineering - Life Cycle Management - Part 1: Guidelines for Life Cycle Management,* The International

REFERENCES

Organization for Standardization, The International Electrotechnical Commission, and The Institute of Electrical and Electronics Engineers.

ISO/IEC/IEEE 24748-2 (2018). *Systems and Software Engineering - Life Cycle Management - Part 2: Guidelines for the Application of ISO/IEC/IEEE 15288 (System Life Cycle Processes)*, The International Organization for Standardization, The International Electrotechnical Commission, and The Institute of Electrical and Electronics Engineers.

ISO/IEC/IEEE 24748-4 (2016). *Systems and Software Engineering - Life Cycle Management - Part 4: Systems Engineering Planning*, The International Organization for Standardization, The International Electrotechnical Commission, and The Institute of Electrical and Electronics Engineers.

ISO/IEC/IEEE 24748-5 (2017). *Systems and Software Engineering - Life cycle Management - Part 5: Software Development Planning*, The International Organization for Standardization, The International Electrotechnical Commission, and The Institute of Electrical and Electronics Engineers.

ISO/IEC/IEEE 24748-6 (2016). *Systems and software engineering - Life cycle management - Part 6: System integration engineering*, The International Organization for Standardization, The International Electrotechnical Commission, and The Institute of Electrical and Electronics Engineers.

ISO/IEC/IEEE 24748-7 (2019). *Systems and software engineering - Life cycle management - Part 7: Application of systems engineering on defense programs*, The International Organization for Standardization, The International Electrotechnical Commission, and The Institute of Electrical and Electronics Engineers.

ISO/IEC/IEEE 24748-8/IEEE15288.2 (2014). *Systems and Software Engineering - Life Cycle Management - Part 8: Technical Reviews and Audits on Defense Programs*, The International Organization for Standardization, The International Electrotechnical Commission, and The Institute of Electrical and Electronics Engineers.

ISO/IEC/IEEE 24765 (2017). *Systems and Software Engineering - Vocabulary*, The International Organization for Standardization, The International Electrotechnical Commission, and The Institute of Electrical and Electronics Engineers.

ISO/IEC/IEEE 26550 (2015). *Software and Systems Engineering - Reference Model for Product Line Engineering and Management*, The International Organization for Standardization, The International Electrotechnical Commission, and The Institute of

REFERENCES

Electrical and Electronics Engineers.

ISO/IEC/IEEE 26580 (2021). *Software and Systems Engineering - Methods and Tools for the Feature-Based Approach to Software and Systems Product Line Engineering*, The International Organization for Standardization, The International Electrotechnical Commission, and The Institute of Electrical and Electronics Engineers.

ISO/IEC/IEEE 29148 (2018). *Systems and Software Engineering - Life Cycle Processes - Requirements Engineering*, The International Organization for Standardization, The International Electrotechnical Commission, and The Institute of Electrical and Electronics Engineers.

ISO/IEC/IEEE 42010 (2022). *Systems and Software Engineering - Architecture Description*, The International Organization for Standardization, The International Electrotechnical Commission, and The Institute of Electrical and Electronics Engineers.

ISO/IEC/IEEE 42020 (2019). *Software, Systems and Enterprise - Architecture Processes*, The International Organization for Standardization, The International Electrotechnical Commission, and The Institute of Electrical and Electronics Engineers.

ISO/IEC/IEEE 42030 (2019). *Software, Systems and Enterprise - Architecture Evaluation Framework*, The International Organization for Standardization, The International Electrotechnical Commission, and The Institute of Electrical and Electronics Engineers.

ISO/PAS 19450 (2015). *Automation systems and integration — Object-Process Methodology (OPM)*, The International Organization for Standardization.

ISO/SAE 21434 (2021). *Road vehicles — Cybersecurity engineering*, The International Organization for Standardization and SAE International.

ISO/TS 16949 (2009). *Quality management systems — Particular requirements for the application of ISO 9001:2008 for automotive production and relevant service part organizations*, The International Organization for Standardization.

Jackson, M. (2003). *Systems Thinking: Creative Holism for Managers*, Wiley.

Jackson, M. (2019). *Critical Systems Thinking and the Management of Complexity*, Wiley.

Jackson, M. and Keys, P. (1984). Towards a system of systems methodologies, *Journal of the Operational Research Society*, 35, 473-486.

REFERENCES

Jackson, S. and Ferris, T. (2013). Resilience Principles for Engineered *Systems, Systems Engineering*, 19(2), 152-164.

Jackson, S. and Ferris, T. (2016). *Proactive and Reactive Resilience: A Comparison of Perspectives.* Retrieved from https://www.academia.edu/34079700/Proactive_and_Reactive_Resilience_A_Comparison_of_Perspectives 10 March 2023.

Jacky, J. (1989). Programmed for Disaster, *The Sciences*, 29, 22-27.

Jensen, J. (2014). *The Øresund Bridge—Linking Two Nations.* Retrieved from https://www.cowi.dk 10 March 2023.

Johnson, S. (2010). *Where Good Ideas Come From: The Natural History of Innovation*, New York, NY: Riverhead Books.

Journal of Cleaner Production (2023). *Journal of Cleaner Production website.* Retrieved from www.journals.elsevier.com/journal-of-cleaner-production 10 March 2023.

Journal of Environmental Management (2023). *Journal of Environmental Management website.* Retrieved from www.sciencedirect.com/journal/journal-of-environmental-management 10 March 2023.

Journal of Organizational Behavior (2004). *Journal of Organizational Behavior*, 25, 439-459, Wiley.

Juran, J. (1974). *Quality Control Handbook*, Third Edition. McGraw-Hill.

Kagermann, H., Wahlster, W., and Helbig, J. (2013). *Securing the Future of German Manufacturing Industry: Recommendations for Implementing the Strategic Initiative INDUSTRIE 4.0, Final Report of the INDUSTRIE 4.0 Working Group, Vol. 4.*

Kaposi, A. and Myers, M. (2001). *Systems for All*, Imperial College Press.

Keeney, R. (2002). Common Mistakes in Making Value Trade-Offs, *Operations Research*, 50(6), 935-945.

Keeney, R. and Gregory, R. (2005). Selecting Attributes to Measure the Achievement of Objectives, *Operations Research*, 15(1), 1-11.

Kemp, D. (2010). So what is "in service systems engineering"?. *Proceedings of the 20th Annual International Symposium of the International Council on Systems Engineering,* The International Council on Systems Engineering (INCOSE).

Kemp, D. and O'Neil, M. (2018). Breaking Casandra's Curse: Understanding Unsafe

Mental Models to Build a Safe Systems Engineering Culture, *Proceedings of the 28th Annual International Symposium of the International Council on Systems Engineering*, The International Council on Systems Engineering (INCOSE).

Kennedy, L. (2005). *Keeping the promise: A work ethic for doing things right, QMI Books.* Retrieved from https://qualitymanagementinstitute.com/lk/biolk2.aspx.

Krueger, C. (2022). From Systems Engineering to System Family Engineering, *Proceedings of the 32nd Annual International Symposium of the International Council on Systems Engineering*, The International Council on Systems Engineering (INCOSE).

Kumar, A. (2020). Delivering System Value: A Systematic Approach, in G. Metcalf, et al. (Eds.), *Handbook of Systems Sciences*, Springer. Retrieved from https://doi.org/10.1007/978-981-13-0370-8_21-1.

Kurtz, C. and Snowden, D. (2003). The new dynamics of strategy: Sense-making in a complex and complicated world, *IBM Systems Journal*, 42, 462-483.

LAI (2013). *Lean Enterprise Value Phase 1, The Massachusetts Institute of Technology Lean Advancement Initiative*. Retrieved from https://dspace.mit.edu/handle/1721.1/1785 10 March 2023.

Langley, M., Robitaille, S., and Thomas, J. (2011). Toward a New Mindset: Bridging the Gap Between Program Management and Systems Engineering, *PM Network*, 25(9),24-26. Retrieved from http://www.pmi.org 10 March 2023.

Langner, R. (2012). Stuxnet Deep Dive, SCADA *Security Scientific Symposium (S4)*. Retrieved from. https://www.youtube.com/watch?v=zBjmm48zwQU 10 March 2023.

Lano, R. (1977). *The N^2 Chart*, TRW, Inc.

Larman, C. and Basili, V. (2003). Iterative and Incremental Development: A Brief History, *IEEE Software*, 36(6), 47-56.

Lawless, W. (2019). The Interdependence of Autonomous Human-Machine Teams: The Entropy of Teams, But Not Individuals, *Advances Science, Entropy*, 21(12), 1195.

Lawless, W., Mittu, R., Sofge, D., and Russell, S. (2017). *Autonomy and Artificial Intelligence: A Threat or Savior?* Springer.

Lawson, B. (1997). How Designers Think - The Design Process Demystified. Oxford: Architectural Press. Third edition.

REFERENCES

Lee, E. (2015). The Past, Present and Future of Cyber-Physical Systems: A Focus on Models, *Sensors*, 15(3), 4837-4869. Retrieved from http://www.mdpi.com/1424-8220/15/3/4837 10 Mar.

LEfMEP (2012). *The Guide to Lean Enablers for Managing Engineering Programs, Version 1.0. Joint MIT PMI INCOSE Community of Practice on Lean in Program Management.* Retrieved from http://hdl.handle.net/1721.1/70495.

Leveson, N. (1995). *Safeware: System Safety and Computers*, Addison Wesley.

Leveson, N. (2011). *Engineering a Safer World*, MIT Press.

Leveson, N. and Turner, C. (1993). An Investigation of the Therac-25 Accidents, *IEEE Computer*, 26(7), 18-41.

Lewis, T. (2019). Communication, Chapter 5 in *Critical Infrastructure Protection in Homeland Security: Defending a Networked Nation*, Third Edition. Wiley, 102-122.

Li, M. and Vitanyi, P. (2009). *An Introduction to Kolmogorov Complexity and Its Applications*, Third edition. Springer-Verlag, 102.

Long, J. (2000). COTS: What You Get (In Addition to the Potential Development Savings), *Proceedings of the 10th Annual International Symposium of the International Council on Systems Engineering,* The International Council on Systems Engineering (INCOSE).

Lu, J. (2019). *A Framework for Cyber-physical System Tool-chain Development: A Service-oriented and Model-based Systems Engineering Approach*, KTH Royal Institute of Technology. Retrieved from https://kth.diva-portal.org/smash/get/diva2:1316044/FULLTEXT01.pdf.

Lustig, I., Dietrich, B., Johnson, C., and Dziekan, C. (2010). *The Analytics Journey*, Oxford University Press.

Maier, M. (1998). Architecting Principles for Systems of Systems, *Systems Engineering*, 1(4), 267-284.

Maier, M. W. and Rechtin, E. (2009). *The Art of Systems Architecting*, Third Edition. CRC Press.

Martin, J. (1996). *Systems Engineering Guidebook: A Process for Developing Systems and Products*, CRC Press.

Martin, J. (2003). On the Use of Knowledge Modeling Tools and Techniques to Characterize the NOAA Observing System Architecture, *Proceedings of the 13th*

REFERENCES

Annual International Symposium of the International Council on Systems Engineering, The International Council on Systems Engineering (INCOSE).

Martin, J. (2005). Using an Enterprise Architecture to Assess the Societal Benefits of Earth Science Research, *Proceedings of the 15th Annual International Symposium of the International Council on Systems Engineering*, The International Council on Systems Engineering (INCOSE).

Martin, J., Conklin, J., Evans, J., Robinson, C., Doggrell, L., and Diehl, J. (2004). The Capability Integration Framework: A New Way of doing Enterprise Architecture, *Proceedings of the 14th Annual International Symposium of the International Council on Systems Engineering*, The International Council on Systems Engineering (INCOSE).

McDermott, T., Folds, D., and Hallo, L. (2020). Addressing Cognitive Bias in Systems Engineering Teams, *Proceedings of the 30th Annual International Symposium of the International Council on Systems Engineering*, The International Council on Systems Engineering (INCOSE).

McDonough, W. (2013). McDonough Innovations: Design for the Ecological Century. Retrieved from http://www.mcdonough.com. 10 March 2023.

McGarry et al. (2001). Practical Software Measurement: Objective Information for Decision Makers

McManus, H. (2005). *Product Development Transition to Lean (PDTTL) Roadmap, LAI Release Beta, Massachusetts Institute of Technology Lean Advancement Initiative.*

McNicholas, R. (2021). Application of PLE to US Army Live Training, *Momentum2021 Symposium*. Retrieved from https://vimeo.com/548839826 10 March 2023.

MDPI (2023).*Sustainability Journal website, Multidisciplinary Digital Publishing Institute (MDPI).* Retrieved from https://www.mdpi.com/journal/sustainability 10 March 2023.

MIL-HDBK-61 (2020). *Configuration Management Guidance*, US Department of Defense.

Miller, G. (1956). The Magical Number Seven, Plus or Minus Two: Some Limits on our Capacity for Processing Information, *Psychological Review*, 63(2), 81.

Minsky, M. (1965). Models, Minds, Machines, *Proceedings of the IFIP Congress*, pp. 45-49.

REFERENCES

NAFEMS (2021). *NAFEMS Resource Centre website, The International Association for Engineering Modelling, Analysis and Simulation (NAFEMS)*. Retrieved from https://www.nafems.org/publications/resource_center 10 March 2023.

NAFEMS and INCOSE (2019). *What is Systems Modeling and Simulation, The International Association for Engineering Modelling, Analysis and Simulation (NAFEMS) WT10 and The International Council on Systems Engineering Systems (INCOSE) Modeling and Simulation Working Group (SMSWG)*. Retrieved from https://www.nafems.org/publications/resource_center/wt10 10 March 2023.

NAO (2008). *Chinook Mk3 Helicopters, NAO Report HC 512 2007-08*, UK Ministry of Defence, National Audit Office.

NASA (2003). *Columbia Accident Investigation Report*, US National Aeronautic and Space Administration.

NASA (2007a). *NASA Pilot Benchmarking Initiative: Exploring Design Excellence Leading to Improved Safety and Reliability, Final Report*, US National Aeronautic and Space Administration.

NASA (2007b). *NASA Systems Engineering Handbook*, US National Aeronautic and Space Administration.

NASA JPL (2013). *ON-OFF Adhesive Grippers for Earth Orbit*, US National Aeronautic and Space Administration, Jet Propulsion Laboratory. Retrieved from https://www.nasa.gov/sites/default/files/files/A_Parness-Gecko_Like_Adhesives_for_InSpace_Inspection.pdf 10 March 2023.

NASA JPL (2014). *Gecko Grippers Get a Microgravity Test Flight*, US National Aeronautic and Space Administration, Jet Propulsion Laboratory. Retrieved from https://www.nasa.gov/jpl/tech/gecko-grippers-microgravity-flight 10 March 2023.

NASA JPL (2015). *Gecko Grippers Moving On Up*, US National Aeronautic and Space Administration, Jet Propulsion Laboratory. Retrieved from https://www.nasa.gov/jpl/gecko-grippers-moving-on-up 10 March 2023.

NATO (2018). *NATO Architecture Framework (NAF), Version 4*, the North Atlantic Treaty Organization.

NDIA, INCOSE, and PSM (2011). *System Development Performance Measurement Report*, National Defense Industrial Association, The International Council on Systems Engineering, and Practical Software & Systems Measurement Support Center.

REFERENCES

Nejib, P., Yakabovicz, E., and Beyer, D. (2017). System Security Engineering: What Every System Engineer Needs to Know, *Proceedings of the 27th Annual International Symposium of the International Council on Systems Engineering*, The International Council on Systems Engineering (INCOSE).

Nissen, J. (2006). The Øresund Link, The Arup Journal, 31(2), 37-41.

NIST NVB (2012). National Vulnerability Database, Version 2.2, *US National Institute of Standards and Technology, Computer Science Division*.

NIST SP 500-230 (1996). *Application Portability Profile (APP): The U.S. Government's Open System Environment Profile, Version 3.0*, US National Institute of Standards and Technology Special Publication.

NIST SP 800-53 (2020). Security and Privacy Controls for Information Systems and Organizations, US National Institute of Standards and Technology Special.

NIST SP 800-128 (2019). *Guide for Security-Focused Configuration Management of Information Systems*, US National Institute of Standards and Technology Special Publication.

NIST SP 800-160 Vol. 1 (2022). *Systems Security Engineering: Considerations for a Multidisciplinary Approach in the Engineering of Trustworthy Secure Systems, Rev 1*, US National Institute of Standards and Technology Special Publication.

NIST SP 800-160 Vol. 2 (2021). *Developing Cyber-Resilient Systems: A Systems Security Engineering Approach*, US National Institute of Standards and Technology Special Publication.

Noorani, R. (2008). *Rapid Prototyping: Principles and Applications*, Wiley.

NTSB (2019a). *Vehicle Automation Report*, US National Transportation Safety Board.

NTSB (2019b). *Inadequate Safety Culture Contributed to Uber Automated Test Vehicle Crash - NTSB Calls for Federal Review Process for Automated Vehicle Testing on Public Roads*, US National Transportation Safety Board.

NTSB (2019c). *Accident Report, Collision Between Vehicle Controlled by Developmental Automated Driving System and Pedestrian*, Tempe, AZ: US National Transportation Safety Board. March 18, 2018, NTSB/HAR-19/03, PB2019-101402.

O'Connor, P. and Kleyner, A. (2012). *Practical Reliability Engineering*, Fifth Edition. John Wiley & Sons, Inc.

REFERENCES

OASIS (2012). *Reference Architecture Foundation for Service Oriented Architecture (SOA-RAF), Version 1.0, OASIS Open TC 01.*

Oberndorf, T., Brownsword, L., and Sledge, C. (2000). *An Activity Framework for COTS-Based Systems, CMU/SEI-2000-TR-010,* The Software Engineering Institute (SEI) at Carnegie Mellon University.

OMG MBSE Wiki (2023). *OMG MBSE Wiki, MBSE Events and Related Meetings website.* Retrieved from http://www.omgwiki.org/MBSE/doku.php?id=mbse:methodology 10 March 2023.

OMG SysML™ (2021). *Systems Modeling Language (SysML).* Retrieved from https://omgsysml.org 10 March 2023.

OMG TOGAF (2023). *TOGAF - The Open Group Architecture Framework.* Retrieved from http://www.opengroup.org/togaf 10 March 2023.

OMG UAF (2023). *Unified Architecture Framework.* Retrieved from http://www.omg.org/uaf 10 March 2023.

Oppenheim, B. (2004). Lean Product Development Flow, *Systems Engineering*, 7(4), 352-376.

Oppenheim, B. (2011). *Lean for Systems Engineering with Lean Enablers for Systems Engineering*, Wiley.

Oppenheim, B. (2021). *Lean Healthcare Systems Engineering Process for Clinical Environments, A Step-by-step Process for Managing Workflow and Care Improvement Projects*, Routledge, Taylor & Francis Group, Productivity Press.

Oxford (2020). *Oxford English Dictionary*, Oxford University Press.

Parnell, G. (2016). *Trade-off Analytics: Creating and Evaluating the Tradespace*, Wiley & Sons.

Parnell, G., Bresnick, T., Tani, S., and Johnson, E. (2013). *Handbook of Decision Analysis*, John Wiley & Sons, Inc.

Parnell, G., Kenley, C., Specking, E., and Pohl, E. (2022). Systems Engineering and Industrial Engineering, *Proceedings of the 32nd Annual International Symposium of the International Council on Systems Engineering*, The International Council on

REFERENCES

Systems Engineering (INCOSE).

Paté-Cornell, M. (1990). Organizational Aspects of Engineering System Safety: The Case of Offshore Platforms, *Science*, 250.

Pax Water Technologies (2022). *Biomimicry website, Pax Water Technologies*. Retrieved from https://www.paxwater.com/biomimicry 10 March 2023.

Pearce, O., Murry, N., and Broyd, T. (2012). Halstar: Systems engineering for sustainable development, Proceedings of the Institution of Civil Engineers, *Engineering Sustainability*, 165(2), 129-140, Thomas Telford Ltd.

Pearl, J. (2002). Reasoning with Cause and Effect, *AI Magazine*, 23(1), 95-95. Retrieved from https://doi.org/10.1609/aimag.v23i1.1612.

Pearl, J. and Mackenzie, D. (2018). AI can't reason why, *Wall Street Journal*. Retrieved from https://www.wsj.com/articles/ai-cant-reason-why-1526657442.

Peterson, T. (2019). Systems Engineering: Transforming Digital Transformation, *Proceedings of the 29th Annual International Symposium of the International Council on Systems Engineering*, The International Council on Systems Engineering (INCOSE).

Petersen, T. and Sutcliffe, P. (1992). Systems engineering as applied to the Boeing 777, AIAA 92-1010, *AIAA Aerospace Design Conference*, Irvine, CA.

Pineda, R. (2010). *Understanding Complex Systems of Systems Engineering, Fourth General Assembly Cartagena Network of Engineering*, Metz, France.

PMI (2013). *The Standard for Program Management*, Third Edition, Project Management Institute.

PMI (2016). *Requirements Management: A Practice Guide*, Project Management Institute.

PMI (2017). *PMI Standard for Portfolio Management*, Fourth Edition, Project Management Institute.

PMI (2021). *Project Management Body of Knowledge (PMBOK®)*, Project Management Institute.

PMI (2022). *Situation Context Framework (SCF)*, Project Management Institute.

REFERENCES

Pragmatic 365 (2023). *Pragmatic Enterprise Architecture Framework (PEAF) website.* Retrieved from https://www.pragmatic365.org/peaf-intro.asp 10 March 2023.

PSM (2003). *Practical Software and Systems Measurement (PSM) Guide, Version 4.0c, Practical Software and System Measurement Support Center.* Retrieved from https://www.psmsc.com/psmguide.asp 10 March 2023.

PSM, NDIA, and INCOSE (2021). *Continuous Iterative Development Measurement Framework, Practical Software & Systems Measurement Support Center, National Defense Industrial Association, and The International Council on Systems Engineering.*

Quade, E. and Boucher, W. (1968). *Systems Analysis and Policy Planning: Applications in Defense, RAND R-439-PR (Abridged).*

Rasoulkahni, K. (2018). Resilience as an emergent property of human infrastructure dynamics; A multi-agent simulation model for characterizing regime shifts and tipping point behaviours in infrastructure systems, *Plos One*, 13.

Raworth, K. (2017). *Doughnut Economics: Seven Ways to Think like a 21st-Century Economist*, Random House.

Raz, A., Wood, P., Mockus, L., and DeLaurentis, D. (2020). System of systems uncertainty quantification using machine learning techniques with smart grid application, *Systems Engineering*, 23(6), 770-782.

Rebentisch, E. (2017). *Integrating Program Management and Systems Engineering: Methods, Tools, and Organizational Systems for Improving Performance*, Wiley.

Rebovich, G. and White, B. (2011). *Enterprise Systems Engineering: Advances in the Theory and Practice*, CRC Press.

Roedler, G. (2010). Knowledge Management Position, *Proceedings of the 20th Annual International Symposium of the International Council on Systems Engineering*, The International Council on Systems Engineering (INCOSE).

Roedler, G. and Jones, C. (2005). *INCOSE Technical Measurement Guide*, The International Council on Systems Engineering.

Roedler, G., Rhodes, D., Schimmoler, H., and Jones, C. (2010). *Systems Engineering Leading Indicators Guide, v2.0, Massachusetts Institute of Technology,* The

REFERENCES

International Council on Systems Engineering, and Practical Software & Systems Measurement Support Center.

Rogers, E. and Mitchell, S. (2021). MBSE delivers significant return on investment in evolutionary development of complex SoS, *Systems Engineering*, 24(6), 385-408.

Rosen, M. (2012). Engineering sustainability: A technical approach to sustainability, *Sustainability*, 4(9), 2270-2292.

Rouse, W. (2009). Engineering the Enterprise as a System, in A. Sage & W. Rouse (Eds.), *Handbook of Systems Engineering and Management*, Second Edition. John Wiley & Sons, Inc.

Rousseau, D. (2018a). A framework for understanding systems principles and methods, *INSIGHT*, 21(3), The International Council on Systems Engineering (INCOSE).

Rousseau, D. (2018b). Three general systems principles and their derivation: Insights from the philosophy of science applied to systems concepts, in Madni, et al. (Eds.) *Disciplinary convergence in systems engineering research* (pp. 665-681). Springer International Publishing. Retrieved from https://link.springer.com/book/10.1007/978-3-319-62217-0 10 March 2023.

Rousseau, D., Billingham, J., and Calvo-Amodio, J. (2018). Systemic Semantics: A Systems Approach to Building Ontologies and Concept Maps, Systems, 6(3).

Rousseau, D., Billingham, J., and Calvo-Amodio, J. (2019). Systemic virtues as a foundation for a general theory of design elegance, *Systems Research and Behavioural Science*, 36(5), 656-667.

Rousseau, D., Pennotti, M., and Brook, P. (2022). Systems Engineering's Evolving Guidelines. *Report of the INCOSE Bridge Team presented on January 31, 2022 to the INCOSE Systems Science Working Group meeting*, The International Council on Systems Engineering, published on the SSWG's Google Drive. Retrieved from https://drive.google.com/file/d/1JibL44sUh0ztefZQ5Rfy4kGiodXIy63n/view 10 March 2023.

Royce, W. (1970). Managing the Development of Large Software Systems, *Proceedings of IEEE WESCON*, pp. 1-9.

REFERENCES

SAE 1001 (2018). *Integrated Project Processes for Engineering a System*, SAE International. (Note: Replaced ANSI/EIA 632).

SAE-EIA 649C (2019). *Configuration Management Standard*, SAE International and The Electronic Industries Alliance.

Salado, A. and Kannan, H. (2018). A mathematical model of verification strategies, *Systems Engineering*, 21(6), 593-608.

Salter, K. (2003). Presentation Given at the Jet Propulsion Laboratory, *US National Aeronautic and Space Administration, Jet Propulsion Laboratory.*

Schindel, W. (2005). Requirement Statements Are Transfer Functions: An Insight from Model-Based Systems Engineering), *Proceedings of the 15th Annual International Symposium of the International Council on Systems Engineering*, The International Council on Systems Engineering (INCOSE).

Schindel, W. (2010). Failure Analysis: Insights from Model-Based Systems Engineering, *Proceedings of the 20th Annual International Symposium of the International Council on Systems Engineering*, The International Council on Systems Engineering (INCOSE).

Schindel, W. (2011). What Is the Smallest Model of a System? *Proceedings of the 21st Annual International Symposium of the International Council on Systems Engineering,* The International Council on Systems Engineering (INCOSE).

Schindel, W. (2012). Integrating Materials, Process & Product Portfolios: Lessons from Pattern-Based Systems Engineering, *Proceedings of the Society for the Advancement of Material and Process Engineering*, Society for Advancement of Material and Process Engineering.

Schindel, W. (2013). System Interactions: Making the Heart of Systems More Visible, *Proceedings of the INCOSE 2013 Great Lakes Regional Conference on Systems Engineering,* The International Council on Systems Engineering (INCOSE).

Schindel, W. (2016). Got Phenomena? Science-Based Disciplines for Emerging Systems Challenges, *Proceedings of the 26th Annual International Symposium of the International Council on Systems Engineering,* The International Council on Systems Engineering (INCOSE).

REFERENCES

Schindel, W. (2020). System Patterns in Engineering and Science, in G. Metcalf, et al. (Eds.), *Handbook of System Sciences*, Springer Nature.

Schindel, W. (2022a). Pattern-Based Methods and MBSE, in A. Madni, et al. (Eds.), *Handbook of Model-Based Systems Engineering*, Springer. Retrieved from https://doi.org/10.1007/978-3-030-27486-3_73-1.

Schindel, W. (2022b). Realizing the Value Promise of Digital Engineering: Planning, Implementing, and Evolving the Ecosystem, *INSIGHT*, 25(1), The International Council on Systems Engineering (INCOSE).

Schindel, W. and Dove, R. (2016). Introduction to the INCOSE Agile Systems Engineering Life Cycle Management (ASELCM) Pattern, *Proceedings of the 26th Annual International Symposium of the International Council on Systems Engineering*, The International Council on Systems Engineering (INCOSE).

Schindel, W. and Peterson, T. (2013). Introduction to Pattern-Based Systems Engineering (PBSE): Leveraging MBSE Techniques, *Proceedings of the 23rd Annual International Symposium of the International Council on Systems Engineering*, The International Council on Systems Engineering (INCOSE).

Schindel, W. and Smith, V. (2002). Results of Applying a Families-of-Systems Approach to Systems Engineering of Product Line Families, *Technical Report 2002-01-3086*, SAE International.

Schlager, K. (1956). Systems engineering - Key to modern development, *IRE Transactions of Professional Group Engineering Management*, 3, 64-66.

Seacord, R., Plakosh, D., and Lewis, G. (2003). *Modernizing Legacy Systems*, Pearson.

SEBoK (2023). Guide to the Systems Engineering Body of Knowledge (SEBoK) website, *The International Council on Systems Engineering (INCOSE), the IEEE Systems Council, and Stevens Institute of Technology*. Retrieved from https://sebokwiki.org/wiki/Guide_to_the_Systems_Engineering_Body_of_Knowledge_(SEBoK) 10 March.

Senge, P. (1990). *The Fifth Discipline: The Art & Practice of the Learning Organization*, Crown Business.

REFERENCES

SEVOCAB (2023). *SEVOCAB: Software and Systems Engineering Vocabulary website, The Institute of Electrical and Electronics Engineers Computer Society*, The International Organization for Standardization, and The International Electrotechnical Commission.

Shafaat, A. and Kenley, C. (2020). Model-based design of project systems, *Modes, and States, Systems Engineering*, 23(2), 165-176.

Sharma, R., Jabbour, C., and Lopes de Sousa Jabbour, A. (2020). Sustainable manufacturing and industry 4.0: What we know and what we don't, *Journal of Enterprise Information Management*, Retrieved from, https://doi.org/10.1108/JEIM-01-2020-0024.

Siegel, N. (2019). *Engineering Project Management*, John Wiley and Sons, Inc.

Sillitto, H. (2010). Design Principles for Ultra-Large Scale (ULS) Systems, *Proceedings of the 20th Annual International Symposium of the International Council on Systems Engineering*, The International Council on Systems Engineering (INCOSE).

Sillitto, H. and Dori, D. (2017). Defining 'System': A Comprehensive Approach, *Proceedings of the 27th Annual International Symposium of the International Council on Systems Engineering*, The International Council on Systems Engineering (INCOSE).

Skanska (2013). *Øresund Bridge: Improving Daily Life for Commuters, Travelers, and Frogs*, The Skanska Group.

Slack, R. (1998). *Application of Lean Principles to the Military Aerospace Product Development Process, Master of Science—Engineering and Management Thesis*, Massachusetts Institute of Technology.

Snowden, D. and Boone, M. (2007). A Leader's Framework for Decision Making, *Harvard Business Review*, 85(11), 68-76.

Sofge, D., Mittu, R., and Lawless, W. (2019). AI Bookie Bet: How likely is it that an AI-based system will self-authorize taking control from a human operator? *AI Magazine*, 40(3), 79-84.

Sowa, J. and Zachman, J. (1992). Extending and formalizing the framework for

REFERENCES

information systems architecture, *IBM Systems Journal*, 31(3), 590-616.

Specking, E., Parnell, G., Pohl, E., and Buchanan, R. (2018). Early Design Space Exploration with Model-Based System Engineering and Set-Based Design, *Systems*, 6(4), 45.

Spohrer, J. (2011). Service Science: Progress & Direction, *International Joint Conference on Service Science*, Taipei, Chinese Taiwan.

Suh, N. (2001). Axiomatic Design: Advances and Applications, Oxford University Press

Studor, G. (2016). What is NASA's Interest in Natural Systems? *INSIGHT*, 19(1), The International Council on Systems Engineering (INCOSE).

Taleb, N. (2018). *Skin in the Game: Hidden Asymmetries in Daily Life*, Random House.

Tapscott, D. and Tapscott, A. (2018). *Blockchain Revolution: How the Technology Behind Bitcoin and Other Cryptocurrencies Is Changing the World*, Portfolio.

Thaler, R. and Sunstein, C. (2008). *Nudge: Improving Decisions About Health, Wealth, and Happiness*, Penguin Books.

Tortorella, M. (2015). *Reliability, Maintainability, and Supportability: Best Practices for Systems Engineers*, John Wiley & Sons.

Toyota (2009). *Toyota Production System: Just in Time—Productivity Improvement,* Toyota. Retrieved from https://global.toyota/en/company/vision-and-philosophy/production-system 10 March 2023.

Tuttle, P. and Bobinis, J. (2013). Specifying Affordability, *Proceedings of the 23rd Annual International Symposium of the International Council on Systems Engineering*, The International Council on Systems Engineering (INCOSE).

Tversky, A. and Kahneman, D. (1974). Judgment under Uncertainty: Heuristics and Biases, *Science*, 185(4157), 1124-1131.

Tyson, B., Albert, C., and Brownsword, L. (2003). *Interpreting Capability Maturity Model Integration (CMMI) for COTS-Based Systems, Technical Report CMU/SEI-2003-TR-022,* The Software Engineering Institute at Carnegie Mellon University.

REFERENCES

UAM (2022). *The Unified Architecture Method (UAM) website.* Retrieved from https://www.unified-am.com 10 March 2023.

Urwick, L. (1956). The Manager's Span of Control, *Harvard Business Review*.

US Army (1997). *Army Technical Architecture, Version 4.9.5X, Draft*, US Department of the Army.

US DoD (2021). *DoD Dictionary of Military and Related Terms*, US Department of Defense.

Van De Ven, M., Talik, J., and Hulse, J. (2012). An Introduction to Applying Systems Engineering to In-Service Systems, *Proceedings of the 22nd Annual International Symposium of the International Council on Systems Engineering*, The International Council on Systems Engineering (INCOSE).

Velcro (2023). *A Mind-Blowing Biomimicry Example, Velcro Brand.* Retrieved from https://www.velcro.com/news-and-blog/2020/07/a-mind-blowing-biomimicry-examples 10 March 2023.

von Bertalanffy, L. (1950). The Theory of Open Systems in Physics and Biology, Science, 111(2872), 23-29.

von Bertalanffy, L. (1968). *General System Theory: Foundations, Development, Applications*, Braziller.

von Bertalanffy, L. (1969). The theory of open systems in physics and biology, in F. Emery (Ed.), *Systems Thinking*, 70-85, Penguin.

von Bertalanffy, L. (1971). *General System Theory*, Penguin.

VV&A (2021). *Verification, Validation, & Accreditation (VV&A), US DoD Modeling and Simulation Enterprise.* Retrieved from https://vva.msco.mil 10 March 2023.

Walden, D. (2007). YADSES: Yet Another Darn Systems Engineering Standard, *Proceedings of the 17th Annual International Symposium of the International Council on Systems Engineering,* The International Council on Systems Engineering (INCOSE).

Walden, D. (2019). Brownfield Systems Development: Moving from the Vee Model to the N Model for Legacy Systems, *Proceedings of the 29th Annual International*

REFERENCES

Symposium of the International Council on Systems Engineering, The International Council on Systems Engineering (INCOSE).

Warfield, J. (2006). *An Introduction to Systems Science*, World Scientific Publishing Company.

Wasson, C. (2016). *System Engineering Analysis, Design, and Development: Concepts, Principles, and Practices*, Second Edition, John Wiley & Sons, Inc.

Watson, I. O. T. (2017). *Descriptive, Predictive, Prescriptive: Transforming Asset and Facilities Management with Analytics*, Software Group, IBM Corporation.

Watson, M. (2020). *Engineering Elegant Systems: Theory of Systems Engineering, NASA_TP_20205003644, NASA*, Washington, D.C., August 2020.

Watson, M., Mesmer, B., Roedler, G., Rousseau, D., Gold, R., Calvo-Amodio, J., Jones, C., Miller, W., Long, D., Lucero, S., Russell, R., Sedmak, A., and Verma, D. (2019). Systems Engineering Principles and Hypotheses, *INSIGHT*, 21(1), The International Council on Systems Engineering (INCOSE).

White, R. and Tantsura, J. (2016). *Navigating Network Complexity*, Addison Wesley.

Womack, J. and Jones, D. (1996). *Lean Thinking*, Simon & Schuster.

Wood, R., Zhu, J., and Liu, G. (2023). *Journal of Industrial Ecology*. Retrieved from https://onlinelibrary.wiley.com/journal/1530929010 March 2023.

Wymore, A. (1993). *Model-Based Systems Engineering*, CRC Press.

Xu, T. and Zhou, Y. (2015). Systems Approaches to Tackling Configuration Errors: A Survey, *ACM Computing Survey*, 47(4), 41.

APPENDIX B: ACRONYMS

Note: Other acronyms may be defined as used under their respective appendices. Abbreviations used for references are described in Appendix A. Abbreviations used for the system life cycle processes are described in Appendix D.

A_a	Achieved availability
A_i	Inherent availability
A_o	Operational availability
ADS	Automated Driving Systems
AECL	Atomic Energy Commission Limited [Canada]
AF	Architecture Framework
AI	Artificial Intelligence
AIAA	American Institute of Aeronautics and Astronautics [United States]
ALARP	As low as reasonably practicable
ALT	Accelerated Life Testing
ANSI	American National Standards Institute [United States]
API	American Petroleum Institute
API	Application programming interface
ARAP	As Resilient as Practicable
ARP	Aerospace Recommended Practice
ASEP	Associate Systems Engineering Professional [INCOSE]
ASOT	Authoritative Source of Truth
ASQ	American Society for Quality
ATAM	Architecture tradeoff analysis method
AWG	Automotive Working Group [INCOSE]
BIT	Built-In Test
CAD	Computer-aided design
CAIV	Cost as an independent variable

附录 B：首字母缩写词

注：其他首字母缩写词会在各自附录中定义。附录 A 介绍了参考文献中使用的缩写。系统生命周期流程中使用的缩写在附录 D 中说明。

A_a	实现可用性
A_i	固有可用性
A_o	运行可用性
ADS	自动驾驶系统
AECL	原子能有限公司［加拿大］
AF	架构框架
AI	人工智能
AIAA	美国国家航空航天管理局［美国］
ALARP	合理可行的最低水平
ALT	加速寿命试验
ANSI	美国国家标准协会［美国］
API	美国石油学会
API	应用编程接口
ARAP	可行的强韧性
ARP	航空航天所推荐的实践
ASEP	助理级系统工程专业人员［INCOSE］
ASOT	权威真相源
ASQ	美国质量学会
ATAM	架构权衡分析方法
AWG	汽车工作组
BIT	内置测试
CAD	计算机辅助设计
CAIV	成本作为独立变量

ACRONYMS

306	CBA	Cost-benefit analysis
	CBS	Cost Breakdown Structure
	CCB	Configuration Control Board
	CE	Conformité Européenne [EU]
	CE	Cost Effectiveness
	CEA	Cost-effectiveness analysis
	CFD	Computational Fluid Dynamics
	CI	Configuration Item
	CI/CD	Continuous Integration/Continuous Delivery
	CM	Configuration Management
	CMMI®	Capability Maturity Model® Integration [CMMI Institute]
	COCOMO	Constructive Cost Model
	ConOps	Concept of operations
	COSYSMO	Constructive Systems Engineering Cost Model
	COTS	Commercial off-the-shelf
	CPS	Cyber-physical system
	CRB	Configuration Review Board
	CSEP	Certified Systems Engineering Professional [INCOSE]
	DANSE	Designing for Adaptability and evolutioN in System of Systems Engineering
	DAU	Defense Acquisition University [United States]
	DD	Data Dictionary
	DE	Digital Engineering
	DevOps	Development, Operations
	DevSecOps	Development, Security, Operations
	DFD	Data flow diagrams
	DFM	Design For Manufacturing
	DFT	Design For Testability
	DFX	Design For X
	DMSMS	Diminishing manufacturing sources and material shortages

CBA	成本—效益分析
CBS	成本分解结构
CCB	构型配置控制委员会
CE	欧洲合格证［欧洲］
CE	成本有效性
CEA	成本—有效性分析
CFD	计算流体力学
CI	构型配置项
CI/CD	持续综合／持续交付
CM	构型配置管理
CMMI®	能力成熟度模型®综合［CMMI 研究所］
COCOMO	构造性成本模型
ConOps	运行意图
COSYSMO	构造性系统工程成本模型
COTS	商用货架产品
CPS	赛博物理系统
CRB	构型配置评审委员会
CSEP	认证的系统工程专业人员［INCOSE］
DANSE	体系工程中的适应性和进化设计
DAU	国防军需大学［美国］
DD	数据字典
DE	数字工程
DevOps	开发、运行
DeveSecOps	开发、安保、运行
DFD	数据流程图
DFM	可制造性
DFT	可测试性
DFX	X 设计
DMSMS	制造资源减少及材料短缺

ACRONYMS

	DoD	Department of Defense [United States]
	DoDAF	Department of Defense Architecture Framework [United States]
	DSM	Design Structure Matrix
	DT	Design Thinking
	DTC	Design to cost
	EIA	Electronic Industries Alliance
	EPD	Environmental Product Declaration
	ESEP	Expert Systems Engineering Professional [INCOSE]
	EU	European Union
	FAA	Federal Aviation Administration [United States]
	FBS	Functional Breakdown Structure
	FCA	Functional configuration audit
	FD/FI	Failure detection/Failure isolation or Fault Detection/Fault Isolation
	FEA	Finite Element Analysis
	FEP	Fuel enrichment plant
	FFBD	Functional flow block diagram
	FMEA	Failure Mode and Effects Analysis
	FMECA	Failure modes, effects, and criticality analysis
	FTA	Fault tree analysis
	FuSE	Future of Systems Engineering [INCOSE]
	G&A	General and administrative
	GAO	Government Accountability Office [United States]
	GEIA	Government Electronics & Information Technology Association
	GERAM	Generalized Enterprise Reference Architecture and Methodology
	GNP	Gross national product
	GPS	Global Positioning System
	GRIP	Governance for Railway Investment Projects
	HALT	Highly accelerated life testing
	HCD	Human-Centered Design
	HFE	Human factors engineering

DoD	国防部［美国］	
DoDAF	美国国防部架构框架［美国］	
DSM	设计结构矩阵	
DT	设计思维	
DTC	面向成本的设计	
EIA	电子工业联盟	
EPD	环境产品声明	
ESEP	专家级系统工程专业人员［INCOSE］	
EU	欧盟	
FAA	美国联邦航空管理局	
FBS	功能分解结构	
FCA	功能构型配置审核	
FD/FI	故障检测/故障隔离	
FEA	有限元分析	
FEP	燃料浓缩厂	
FEBD	功能流块图	
FMEA	故障模式和影响分析	
FMECA	故障模式、影响与危害性分析	
FTA	故障树分析	
FuSE	未来系统工程	
G&A	一般及行政管理	
GAO	政府问责局［美国］	
GEIA	政府电子工业联盟	
GERAM	通用复杂组织体系参考架构和方法	
GNP	国民生产总值	
GPS	全球定位系统	
GRIP	铁路投资项目治理	
HALT	高加速寿命试验	
HCD	以人为中心的设计	
HFE	人因工程	

ACRONYMS

HITL	Human-in-the-loop
HMI	Human Machine Interface
HPC	High Performance Computing
HSI	Human systems integration
IAD	Interface Agreement Document
IC	Initial cost
ICD	Interface Control Document
ICS	Industrial control system
ICSM	Incremental Commitment Spiral Model
ICWG	Interface Control Working Group
IDD	Interface Definition Document
IE	Industrial engineering
IEC	International Electrotechnical Commission
IEEE	The IEEE [formerly the Institute of Electrical and Electronics Engineers]
IISE	Institute of Industrial and Systems Engineers
ILS	Integrated logistics support
INCOSE	International Council on Systems Engineering
INFORMS	Institute for Operations Research and the Management Sciences
IoT	Internet of Things
IPAL	INCOSE Product Asset Library [INCOSE]
IPDT	Integrated Product Development Team
IPO	Input-process-output
IPT	Integrated Product Team
ISEBoK	Industrial and SE Body of Knowledge
ISO	International Organization for Standardization
IT	Information technology
ITS	Intelligent Transportation System
JAXA	Japan Aerospace Exploration Agency [Japan]
JERG	JAXA Engineering Requirement, Guideline [Japan]

HITL	人在回路	
HMI	人机界面	
HPC	高性能计算	
HIS	人系统综合	
IAD	接口协议文档	
IC	初始成本	
ICD	接口控制文档	
ICS	工业控制系统	
ICSM	增量承诺螺旋模型	
ICWG	接口控制工作组	
IDD	接口定义文档	
IE	工业工程	
IEC	国际电工委员会	
IEEE	电气与电子工程师协会	
IISE	工业与系统工程师协会	
ILS	综合后勤支持	
INCOSE	国际系统工程委员会	
INFORMS	运筹学与管理科学协会	
IoT	物联网	
IPAL	INCOSE 产品资产库 [INCOSE]	
IPDT	综合产品开发团队	
IPO	输入—流程—输出	
IPT	综合产品团队	
ISEBoK	工业和系统工程知识体	
ISO	国际标准化组织	
IT	信息技术	
ITS	智能交通系统	
JAXA	日本航空航天局	
JERG	JAXA 工程需求指南 [日本]	

ACRONYMS

	KM	Knowledge management
	KPP	Key Performance Parameter
	LAI	Lean Advancement Initiative
	LCA	Life cycle assessment
	LCC	Life cycle cost
	LCIA	Life cycle impact assessment
308	LCM	Life cycle management
	LCO	Life cycle optimization
	LDSE	Loss-Driven Systems Engineering
	LEfMEP	Lean Enablers for Managing Engineering Programs
	LINAC	Linear accelerator
	LORA	Level of Repair Analysis
	MA&S	Modeling, analysis, and simulation
	MaaS	Mobility as a Service
	MBSE	Model-based systems engineering
	MFESA	Method Framework for Engineering System Architectures
	MIT	Massachusetts Institute of Technology [USA]
	ML	Machine Learning
	MODA	Multiple objective decision approach
	MOE	Measure of effectiveness
	MOP	Measure of performance
	MTBF	Mean time between failure
	MTTR	Mean time to repair
	MVP	Minimum viable product
	N^2	N-squared diagram
	NAF	NATO Architecture Framework
	NAFEMS	The International Association for the Engineering Modelling, Analysis and Simulation Community
	NASA	National Aeronautics and Space Administration [United States]
	NCOSE	National Council on Systems Engineering (INCOSE, pre-1995)

KM	知识管理	
KPP	关键性能参数	
LAI	精益推进计划	
LCA	生命周期评估	
LCC	生命周期成本	
LCIA	生命周期影响评估	
LCM	生命周期管理	
LCO	生命周期优化	
LDSE	损失驱动的系统工程	
LEfMEP	管理工程项目的精益使能项	
LINAC	直线加速器	
LORA	系统级维修分析	
MA&S	建模、分析和仿真	
MaaS	出行即服务	
MBSE	基于模型的系统工程	
MFESA	工程系统架构的方法框架	
MIT	麻省理工学院［美国］	
ML	机器学习	
MODA	多目标决策方法	
MOE	有效性测量	
MOP	性能测量	
MTBF	平均无故障时间	
MTTR	平均维修时间	
MVP	最小可行产品	
N^2	N 方	
NAF	北约架构框架	
NAFEMS	工程建模、分析与仿真国际协会	
NASA	国家航空航天局［美国］	
NCOSE	国家系统工程委员会（1995 年前）	

ACRONYMS

309	NCS	Network-Centric Systems
	NDI	Non-developmental item
	NDIA	National Defense Industrial Association [United States]
	NIH	Not Invented Here
	NIST	National Institute of Standards and Technology [United States]
	O&G	Oil and Gas
	OBS	Organizational Breakdown Structure
	OEM	Original Equipment Manufacturer
	OMG	Object Management Group
	OOSEM	Object-Oriented Systems Engineering Method
	OpsCon	Operational concept
	OR	Operations Research
	PBS	Product Breakdown Structure
	PCA	Physical configuration audit
	PEAF	Pragmatic Enterprise Architecture Framework
	PESTEL	Political, Economic, Social, Technological, Environmental, and Legal
	PHS&T	Packaging, handling, storage, and transportation
	PLC	Programmable logic controller
	PLE	Product line engineering
	PLM	Product line management
	PMBoK	Project Management Body of Knowledge [PMI]
	PMI	Project Management Institute
	PMP	Project Management Plan
	PPP	Public-Private Partnership
	PSM	Practical Software and Systems Measurement
	QA	Quality assurance
	QC	Quality characteristics
	QC	Quality control
	QM	Quality management

NCS	以网络为中心的系统
NDI	非开发项目
NDIA	国防工业协会［美国］
NIH	未在此处发明
NIST	美国国家标准技术局
O&G	石油和天然气
OBS	组织分解结构
OEM	原始设备制造商
OMG	对象管理组
OOSEM	面向对象的系统工程方法
OpsCon	运行概念
OR	运筹学
PBS	产品分解结构
PCA	物理构型配置审核
PEAF	实用复杂组织体系架构框架
PESTEL	政治、经济、社会、技术、环境和法律
PHS&T	包装、搬运、储存和运输
PLC	可编程逻辑控制器
PLE	产品线工程
PLM	产品生命周期管理
PMBoK	项目管理知识体
PMI	项目管理协会
PMP	项目管理计划
PPP	公私合作关系
PSM	实用软件和系统测量
QA	质量保证
QC	质量特性
QC	质量控制
QM	质量管理

ACRONYMS

R&D	Research and development
RAM	Reliability, availability, and maintainability
RBD	Reliability block diagram
RCM	Reliability-centered maintenance
RFP	Request for proposal
RFQ	Request for quotation
RMP	Risk management plan
ROI	Return on investment
SAE	SAE International [formerly the Society of Automotive Engineers]
SAFe	Scaled agile framework
SaMDs	Software as Medical Devices
SBD	Set-Based Design
SC	Sustainment cost
SCF	Situation Context Framework
SCM	Supply chain management
SE	System effectiveness
SE	Systems engineering
SEBoK	Guide to the Systems Engineering Body of Knowledge
SECAG	Systems Engineering Competency Assessment Guide [INCOSE]
SECF	Systems Engineering Competency Framework [INCOSE]
SEH	Systems Engineering Handbook [INCOSE]
SEIPS	Systems Engineering Intervention for Patient Safety
SEIT	Systems Engineering and Integration Team
SEMP	Systems Engineering Management Plan
SEMS	Systems Engineering Master Schedule
SEP	Systems Engineering Plan
SEQM	System Engineering Quality Management
SLA	Service-level agreement
SMSWG	Systems Modeling and Simulation Working Group [NAFEMS and INCOSE]
SoI	System of interest

R&D		研究与开发
RAM		可靠性、可用性和可维护性
RBD		可靠性块图
RCM		以可靠性为中心的维护
RFP		邀标书
RFQ		报价申请书
RMP		风险管理计划
ROI		投资回报
SAE		国际汽车工程师学会［之前称为美国汽车工程师学会］
SAFe		大规模敏捷框架
SaMDs		软件即医疗设备
SBD		基于集合的设计
SC		维持成本
SCF		情境背景框架
SCM		供应链管理
SE		系统有效性
SE		系统工程
SEBoK		系统工程知识体指南
SECAG		系统工程胜任力评估指南
SECF		系统工程胜任力框架
SEH		系统工程手册［INCOSE］
SEIPS		患者安全性系统工程干预
SEIT		系统工程综合团队
SEMP		系统工程管理计划
SEMS		系统工程主进度表
SEP		系统工程计划
SEQM		系统工程质量管理
SLA		服务水平协议
SMSWG		系统建模与仿真工作组
SoI		所感兴趣之系统

ACRONYMS

	SoS	System of systems
	SOW	Statement of work
	SPC	Statistical Process Control
	SROI	Social return on investment
	SSE	System Security Engineering
	STEM	Science, technology, engineering, and mathematics
	STPA	System-theoretic process analysis
	SWaP	Size, weight, and power
	SWE	Software engineering
	SWOT	Strengths, Weaknesses, Opportunities, Threats
	SysML™	Systems Modeling Language [OMG]
	TADSS	Training Aids, Devices, Simulators, and Simulations
	TCO	Total cost of ownership
	TOC	Total ownership cost
310	TOGAF	The Open Group Architecture Framework [The Open Group]
	TOP	Technology, Organization, People
	TOWS	Threats, Opportunities, Weaknesses, and Strengths
	TP	Transaction-processing
	TPM	Technical performance measure
	TLI	Technical Leadership Institute [INCOSE]
	TR	Technical report
	TRL	Technology readiness level
	UAF	Unified Architecture Framework
	UAM	Unified Architecture Method
	UI	User Interface
	UIC	International Union of Railways
	UK	United Kingdom
	UL	Underwriters Laboratory [United States and Canada]
	US/USA	United States/ United States of America
	USB	Universal Serial Bus

SoS	体系	
SOW	工作说明书	
SPC	统计过程控制	
SROI	社会投资回报	
SSE	系统安保工程	
STEM	科学、技术、工程和数学	
STPA	系统论的流程分析	
SWaP	尺寸、重量和功率	
SWE	软件工程	
SWOT	优势、劣势、机会和威胁	
SysML™	系统建模语言［OMG］	
TADSS	培训辅助装置、设备、仿真器和仿真	
TCO	拥有总成本	
TOC	总拥有成本	
TOGAF	开放组织架构框架	
TOP	技术、组织、人员	
TOWS	威胁、机会、劣势和优势	
TP	事务处理	
TPM	技术性能测度	
TLI	技术领导力学院［INCOSE］	
TR	技术报告	
TRL	技术准备水平	
UAF	统一架构框架	
UAM	统一架构方法	
UI	用户界面	
UIC	国际铁路联盟	
UK	英国	
UL	保险商实验室［美国和加拿大］	
US/USA	美国	
USB	通用串行总线	

ACRONYMS

USD	US dollars [United States]
UX	User Experience or User eXperience
V&V	Verification and Validation or Verify and Validate
VSE	Very Small Entities or Very Small Enterprises
VV&A	Verification, validation, and accreditation
WBS	Work Breakdown Structure
WG	Working group
WLC	Whole Life Cost
WP	Work package
WPA	Work Process Analysis
XP	Extreme Programming
ZD	Zero Defect
ZDA	Zero Defect Attitude

USD	美元［美国］	
UX	用户体验	
V&V	验证和确认	
VSE	极小型复杂组织体系	
VV&A	验证、确认和认可	
WBS	工作分解结构	
WG	工作组	
WLC	全生命周期成本	
WP	工作包	
WPA	工作流程分析	
XP	极限编程	
ZD	零缺陷	
ZDA	零缺陷态度	

TERMS AND DEFINITIONS

APPENDIX C: TERMS AND DEFINITIONS

Note: Terms that carry meanings consistent with general dictionary definitions are not included in this glossary. Sources of definitions are as indicated. Other related terms can be found in ISO/IEC/IEEE 24765 (2017) *and* SEVOCAB (2023). *Definitions of the typical inputs and outputs on the IPO diagrams can be found in Appendix E.*

Term	Definition
Ability	A term used in human resource management denoting an acquired or natural capacity or talent that enables an individual to perform a particular task successfully. (INCOSE SECF)
Acquirer	The stakeholder that acquires or procures a product or service from a supplier. (ISO/IEC/IEEE 15288, 2023)
Activity	A set of cohesive tasks of a process. (ISO/IEC/IEEE 15288, 2023)
Agile systems-engineering	An SE process using agile approach.
Agile-systems engineering	An engineering process producing agile systems.
Agreement	The mutual acknowledgment of terms and conditions under which a working relationship is conducted. (ISO/IEC/IEEE 15288, 2023)
Architect	See System architect.
Architecture	See System architecture.
Artifact	Work product that is produced and used during a project to capture and convey information. (ISO/IEC/IEEE 15288, 2023)
Attribute	An attribute of a system (or system element) is an observable characteristic or property of the system (or system element).
Baseline	An agreed-to description of the attributes of a product at a point in time, which serves as a basis for defining change. (EIA-649C, 2019)
Behavior	The way in which one acts or conducts oneself, especially towards others. (INCOSE SECF)
Black box	Black box represents an external view of the system (attributes). Also referred to as opaque box.
Brownfield SE	Development of "to-be" system or system elements in the presence of existing or legacy "as-is" system or system elements. Note: A brownfield approach is usually used to extend, improve, or replace a system that is in use or to reuse system elements that will not be impacted by the desired changes. The new system architecture must take into account the existing system elements and functions, which impose constraints on the overall system definition.

INCOSE Systems Engineering Handbook: A Guide for System Life Cycle Processes and Activities, Fifth Edition.

Edited by David D. Walden, Thomas M. Shortell, Garry J. Roedler, Bernardo A. Delicado, Odile Mornas, Yip Yew-Seng, and David Endler.

© 2023 John Wiley & Sons Ltd. Published 2023 by John Wiley & Sons Ltd.

附录 C：术语和定义

注意：含义与一般字典定义一致的术语不包括在本术语表中。定义的来源如下所示。其他相关术语可在 ISO/IEC/IEEE 24765（2017）和 SEVOCAB（2023）中找到。IPO 图表中典型输入和输出的定义见附录 E。

术语	定义
能力	人力资源管理中的一个术语，指一种使个人能够成功完成特定任务的后天或天赋的资质或才能。（INCOSE SECF）
采办方	从供应商处采办或采购产品或服务的利益相关方。（ISO/IEC/IEEE 15288, 2023）
活动	一个流程中紧密衔接的任务集合。（ISO/IEC/IEEE 15288, 2023）
敏捷的系统工程	采用敏捷实施方法的系统工程流程
敏捷系统的工程	产生敏捷系统的工程流程
协议	相互认可的条款或条件，并据此使工作关系得以实施。（ISO/IEC/IEEE 15288, 2023）
架构师	见系统架构师
架构	见系统架构
制品	在项目期间制作和使用的工作产品，用于获取和传递信息。（ISO/IEC/IEEE 15288, 2023）
属性	系统（或系统元素）的属性是系统（或系统元素）的可观测特征或属性
基线	在某一个时间点商定的产品属性的描述，作为定义变化的基础。（EIA - 649C, 2019）
行为	一个人的行为举止，尤其是对他人的行为举止。（INCOSE SECF）
黑盒	黑盒代表系统（属性）的外部视图。也称为不透明盒
棕地系统工程	在现有或遗留的"现状"系统或系统要素的基础上开发"未来"系统或系统要素。注："棕地"方法通常用于扩展、改进或替换正在使用的系统，或重新使用不会受到预期变更影响的系统元素。新的系统架构必须考虑到现有的系统元素和功能，这些元素和功能会对整个系统定义造成限制

TERMS AND DEFINITIONS

(Continued)

Term	Definition
Capability	An expression of a system, product, function, or process ability to achieve a specific objective under stated conditions.
Commonality	(Of a product line) refers to functional and non-functional characteristics that can be shared with all member products within a product line. (ISO/IEC/IEEE 26550, 2015)
Competence	The measure of specified ability to do something well. (INCOSE SECF)
Competency	An observable, measurable set of skills, knowledge, abilities, behaviors, and other characteristics an individual needs to successfully perform work roles or occupational functions. Competencies are typically required at different levels of proficiency depending on the specific work role or occupational function. Competencies can help ensure individual and team performance aligns with the organization's mission and strategic direction. (INCOSE SECF)
Configuration item (CI)	A system, system element, or artifact designated for configuration management. Customer See Acquirer.
Decision gate	A decision gate is an approval event (may be associated with a review). Entry and exit criteria are established for each decision gate; continuation beyond the decision gate is contingent on the agreement of decision makers.
Design constraints	The boundary conditions, externally or internally imposed, for the SoI within which the organization must remain when executing the processes during the concept and development stages.
Engineered System	A system designed or adapted to interact with an anticipated operational environment to achieve one or more intended purposes while complying with applicable constraints. (INCOSE Definitions, 2019)
Enterprise	A purposeful combination of interdependent resources that interact with each other to achieve business and operational goals. (Rebovich and White, 2011)
Environment	The surroundings (natural or man-made) in which the SoI is utilized and supported or in which the system is being developed, produced, and retired.
Facility	The physical means or equipment for facilitating the performance of an action, for example, buildings, instruments, and tools.
Failure	The event in which any part of a system or system element does not perform as required by its specification. Note: The failure may occur at a value in excess of the minimum required in the specification, that is, past design limits or beyond the margin of safety.
Functional configuration audit (FCA)	An evaluation to ensure that the product meets baseline functional and performance capabilities. (Adapted from ISO/IEC/IEEE 15288, 2023)

术语和定义

（续）

术语	定义
能力	在申明的条件下达成特定目标的系统、产品、功能或流程能力的表述
共通性	（产品线的共通性）指的是产品线范围内可与所有成员产品共享的功能特征和非功能特征。（ISO/IEC/IEEE 26550, 2015）
才能	对做好某件事的具体能力的衡量。（INCOSE SECF）
胜任力	个人成功履行工作角色或职业职能所需的一套可观察、可测量的技能、知识、能力、行为和其他特征。根据具体的工作角色或职业职能，胜任力通常要求达到不同的熟练程度。胜任力有助于确保个人和团队的绩效符合组织的使命和战略方向。（INCOSE SECF）
构型配置项（CI）	指定进行配置管理的系统、系统要素或人工制品
客户	见采办方
决策门	决策门是一个审批事件（常常与评审会议相关）。为每个决策门建立了进入和退出准则；决策门以外的延续取决于决策者们的协议
设计约束	外部或内部施加给 SoI 的边界条件，在概念和开发阶段中实施流程时，组织必须保持这些边界条件
工程系统	一个系统，其设计或调整旨在与预期的运行环境互动，以实现一个或多个预期目的，同时遵守适用的限制条件。（INCOSE 定义, 2019）
复杂组织体系	为达到业务和运行目标而彼此交互的、相互依赖的资源的有目的的组合。（Rebovich 和 White, 2011）
环境	周围的事物（天然的或人造的），SoI 在其中使用并得到支持或者系统在其中开发、生产和退役
设施	用于辅助行动执行的物理手段或设备，如建筑物、仪器和工具
故障	物品的任意部分没按规范的要求而实施的事件。注意：失效可能在数值超过规范的最低要求（即超过设计限制或超出安全裕度）时出现
功能构型配置审核（FCA）	一种评价，以确保产品满足基线功能能力和性能能力。（改编自 ISO/IEC/IEEE 15288, 2023）

TERMS AND DEFINITIONS

(Continued)

Term	Definition
Greenfield SE	Development of a system for a new environment and set of user scenarios and requirements. Note: A greenfield approach typically has no significant legacy constraints or dependencies within the system boundary. However, it is rare that there are no constraints or dependencies from external interfaces or enabling systems.
Human factors	The systematic application of relevant information about human abilities, characteristics, behavior, motivation, and performance.
Interface	A shared boundary between two systems or system elements, defined by functional characteristics, common physical interconnection characteristics, signal characteristics, or other characteristics, as appropriate. (Adapted from ISO/IEC 2382, 2015)
IPO diagram	Figures in this handbook that provide a high-level view of the process of interest. The diagram summarizes the process activities and their typical inputs and typical outputs from/to other processes or external actors.
Knowledge	A body of information applied directly to the performance of a function. (INCOSE SECF)
Life cycle cost (LCC)	The total cost of a system over its entire life. Note: It includes all costs associated with the system and its use in the concept, development, production, utilization, support, and retirement stages.
Life cycle model	A framework of processes and activities concerned with the life cycle, which also acts as a common reference for communication and understanding. (ISO/IEC/IEEE 15288, 2023)
Measure	Variable to which a value is assigned as the result of measurement. (ISO/IEC/IEEE 15939, 2017)
Measurement	Set of operations having the object of determining a value of a measure. (ISO/IEC/IEEE 15939, 2017)
Measures of effectiveness (MOEs)	Measures that define the acquirer's key indicators of achieving the mission needs for performance, suitability, and affordability across the life cycle.
Measures of performance (MOPs)	Measures to assess whether the system meets design or performance requirements and has the capability to achieve operational objectives.
N^2 diagrams	Graphical representation used to define the internal operational relationships or external interfaces of the SoI.
Need statement	The result of a formal transformation of one or more life cycle concepts into an agreed-to expectation for an entity to perform some function or possess some quality. (INCOSE GtWR, 2022)
Operator	See User.
Organization	Person, or a group of people, and facilities with an arrangement of responsibilities, authorities, and relationships. (Adapted from ISO 9001, 2015)

（续）

术语	定义
绿地系统工程	针对新的环境和用户场景及需求开发系统。注：绿地实施方法通常在系统边界内没有显著的遗留限制或依赖关系。但是，没有外部接口或使能系统的限制或依赖的情况很少见
人因	有关人员能力、特征、行为、动机和绩效等相关信息的系统化应用
接口	两个功能单元之间的共享边界，由功能特征、共同物理互联特征、信号特征或其他特征定义。（改编自 ISO/IEC 2382, 2015）
IPO 图	本手册中提供了关于受关注流程的高层级视角的图。该图总结了流程活动及其中来自/去到外部参与者的输入和输出
知识	直接应用于履行某项功能的一整套信息
生命周期成本（LCC）	在系统的全生命周期内采办和拥有系统的总成本。它包括与系统及其在概念、开发、生产、使用、保障和退役阶段中的使用相关的所有成本
生命周期模型	与生命周期相关的流程和活动的框架，亦可用作沟通和理解的公共参照。（ISO/IEC/ IEEE 15288, 2023）
测度	测量结果赋值的变量。（ISO/IEC/IEEE 15939, 2017）
测量	以确定测度值为目标的一组行动。（ISO/IEC/ IEEE 15939, 2017）
有效性测度（MOEs）	定义采办方在整个生命周期内完成任务所需的性能、适用性和经济性的关键指标的测度
性能测度	评估系统是否符合设计或性能需求，是否有能力达到运行目标的测度
N^2 图	用于定义 SoI 的内部运行关系或外部接口的图形表示
需要声明	将一个或多个生命周期概念形式化地转化为对实体执行某些功能或具备某些质量的一致预期的结果。（INCOSE GtWR, 2022）
操作人员	见使用人员
组织	具有职责、权限和关系设置安排的个人或群体与设施。（改编自 ISO 9001, 2015）

TERMS AND DEFINITIONS

(Continued)

Term	Definition
Performance	A quantitative measure characterizing a physical or functional attribute relating to the execution of a process, function, activity, or task; performance attributes include quantity (how many or how much), quality (how well), timeliness (how responsive, how frequent), and readiness (when, under which circumstances).
Physical configuration audit (PCA)	An evaluation to ensure that the operational system conforms to the operational and configuration documentation. (Adapted from ISO/IEC/IEEE 15288, 2023)
Process	A set of interrelated or interacting activities that transforms inputs into outputs. (Adapted from ISO 9001, 2015)
Product line	Group of products or services sharing a common, managed set of features that satisfy specific needs of a selected market or mission. (ISO/IEC/IEEE 24765, 2017)
Project	An endeavor with defined start and finish criteria undertaken to create a product or service in accordance with specified resources and requirements. (ISO/IEC/IEEE 15288, 2023)
Proof of concept	A realization of an idea or technology to demonstrate its feasibility.
Quality Characteristics	Inherent characteristic of a product, process, or system related to a requirement. (ISO/IEC/IEEE 15288, 2023)
Requirement statement	The result of a formal transformation of one or more needs or parent requirements into an agreed-to obligation for an entity to perform some function or possess some quality. (INCOSE GtWR, 2022)
Resource	An asset that is utilized or consumed during the execution of a process. (ISO/IEC/IEEE 15288, 2023)
Return on investment	Ratio of revenue from output (product or service) to development and production costs, which determines whether an organization benefits from performing an action to produce something. (ISO/IEC/IEEE 24765, 2017)
Reuse	The use of an asset in the solution of different problems. (IEEE 1517, 2010)
Skills	An observable competence to perform a learned psychomotor act.
Stage	A period within the life cycle of an entity that relates to the state of its description or realization. Note: Typical life cycle stages include concept, development, production, utilization, support, and retirement.
Stakeholder	A party having a right, share, or claim in a system or in its possession of characteristics that meet that party's needs and expectations.
Supplier	An organization or an individual that enters into an agreement with an acquirer for the supply of a product or service. (ISO/IEC/IEEE 15288, 2023)
System	An arrangement of parts or elements that together exhibit behavior or meaning that the individual constituents do not. (INCOSE Definitions, 2019)

（续）

术语	定义
性能	与流程、功能、活动或任务执行相关的物理或功能属性的定量测度；性能属性包括数量（多少）、品质（怎么样）、时间性（响应如何、频度如何）及准备度（何时，在何种情况下）
物理构型配置审核（PCA）	一种评价，以确保运行的系统或产品符合运行文件和构型文件的要求。（改编自 ISO/IEC/IEEE 15288, 2023）
流程	将输入转变为输出的相互关联或相互作用的活动的集合。（改编自 ISO 9001, 2015）
产品线	产品或服务的群组，这些产品或服务共享一组受管理的、满足所选市场或任务的特定需要的公共特点的集合。（ISO/IEC/IEEE 24765, 2017）
项目	按照特定的资源和需求创建产品或服务所付出的具有明确定义的开始与完成准则的努力。（ISO/IEC/IEEE 15288, 2023）
概念验证	某个想法或技术的实现，以验证其可行性
质量特性	与需求相关的产品、流程或系统的固有特性。（ISO/IEC/IEEE 15288, 2023）
需求声明	将一个或多个需要或上级需求形式化地转化为实体履行某种功能或具备某种质量的约定义务的结果。（INCOSE GtWR，2022）
资源	在流程执行期间被使用或消耗的资产。（ISO/IEC/ IEEE 15288, 2023）
投资回报	来自输出（产品或服务）的收入与开发和生产成本的比率，该比率确定组织是否受益于实施产生某些事物的活动。（ISO/IEC/IEEE 24765, 2017）
复用	在不同问题的解决方案中使用同一种资产。（IEEE 1517, 2010）
技能	可观察到的完成所学心理运动行为的能力
阶段	实体生命周期内的某一时期，与其描述或实现状态相关
利益相关方	在满足其需要和期望的某一系统或其拥有的特征中具有权利、份额或要求权的一方
供应商	与采办方签订协议以供应产品或服务的组织或个人。（ISO/IEC/IEEE 15288, 2023）
系统	组成部分或元素的编排，这些组成部分或元素共同表现出个体所不具备的行为或意义。（INCOSE 定义, 2019）

TERMS AND DEFINITIONS

(Continued)

Term	Definition
System architect	The person, team, or organization responsible for a system's architecture, for coordinating engineering effort towards devising solutions to complex problems, and overseeing their implementations.
System architecture	The fundamental concepts or properties of an entity in its environment and governing principles for the realization and evolution of this entity and its related life cycle processes. (ISO/IEC/IEEE 42020, 2019)
System element	Member of a set of elements that constitutes a system. (ISO/IEC/IEEE 15288, 2023)
System life cycle	The evolution with time of a SoI from conception to retirement.
System of interest (SoI)	The system whose life cycle is under consideration. (ISO/IEC/IEEE 15288, 2023)
System of systems	A SoI whose system elements are themselves systems; typically, these entail large-scale interdisciplinary problems with multiple, heterogeneous, distributed systems.
Systems engineering	A transdisciplinary and integrative approach to enable the successful realization, use, and retirement of engineered systems, using systems principles and concepts, and scientific, technological, and management methods. (INCOSE Definitions, 2019)
Tailoring	The manner in which any selected issue is addressed in a particular project. Tailoring may be applied to various aspects of the project, including project documentation, processes, and activities performed in each life cycle stage, the time and scope of reviews, analysis, and decision making consistent with all applicable statutory requirements.
Technical performance measures (TPMs)	Measures to assess design progress, compliance to performance requirements, or technical risks and provide visibility into the status of important project technical parameters to enable effective management, thus enhancing the likelihood of achieving the technical objectives of the project.
Trade-off	Decision-making actions that selects from various alternatives on the basis of net benefit to the stakeholders.
User	An individual who, or an organization that, contributes to the functionality of a system and draws on knowledge, skills, and procedures to contribute to the function. Individual who or group that benefits from a system during its utilization.
Validation	Confirmation, through the provision of objective evidence, that the requirements for a specific intended use or application have been fulfilled. (ISO/IEC/IEEE 15288, 2023)
Value	A measure of worth (e.g., benefit divided by cost) of a specific product or service by a customer, and potentially other stakeholders. (McManus, 2005)
Variability	(Of a product line) refers to characteristics that may differ among members of the product line. (ISO/IEC/IEEE 26550, 2015)
Verification	Confirmation, through the provision of objective evidence, that specified requirements have been fulfilled. (ISO/IEC/IEEE 15288, 2023)
Waste	Work that adds no value to the product or service in the eyes of the customer. (Womack and Jones, 1996)
White box	White box represents an internal view of the system (attributes and structure of the elements). Also referred to as transparent box.

（续）

术语	定义
系统架构师	负责系统架构的个人、团队或组织，负责协调工程工作，为复杂问题设计解决方案，并监督其实施
系统架构	实体在其环境中的基本概念或属性，以及实现和演化该实体及其相关生命周期流程的指导原则。（ISO/IEC/IEEE 42020, 2019）
系统元素	构成系统的一个元素集合中的成员。（ISO/IEC/IEEE 15288, 2023）
系统生命周期	SoI 从概念到退役随时间的演进
所感兴趣之系统（SoI）	全生命周期都在考虑之中的系统。（ISO/IEC/IEEE 15288, 2023）
系统之系统	系统元素本身也是系统的 SoI；这些系统之系统通常带来大规模的跨学科问题，包括多重与异构的分布式系统
系统工程	一种跨学科的综合实施方法，旨在利用系统原理和概念以及科学的、技术的和管理的方法，使工程系统能够成功实现、使用和退役。（INCOSE 定义, 2019）
剪裁	在特殊项目中应对任何选定项目的方式。剪裁可适用于项目的各个方面，包括项目文件编制、在生命周期每个阶段执行的流程和活动以及符合所有适用法定要求的评审、分析和决策的时间与范围
技术性能测度（TPMs）	评估设计进度、性能需求符合性或技术风险的测度，提供重要的项目技术参数状况的可见性，以便进行有效管理，从而提高达到项目技术目标的可能性
权衡	决策行动，根据利益相关方的净利益从各种要求和备选解决方案中进行选择
用户	对系统功能性做出贡献的个人或组织，并利用知识、技能和程序对功能做出贡献。在系统使用过程中受益的个人或团体
确认	通过客观证据的提供，证实某一特定的使用或应用的需求已经得到实现。（ISO/IEC/IEEE 15288, 2023）
价值	客户和潜在的其他利益相关方对特定产品或服务的意义（如收益除以成本）的度量
可变性	产品线的可变性指的是在产品线成员间可能有所不同的特征。（ISO/IEC/IEEE 26550, 2015）
验证	通过客观证据的提供，证实规定的需求已经得到实现。（ISO/IEC/IEEE 15288, 2023）
浪费	在客户眼中不能为产品或服务增加价值的工作。（Womack 和 Jones, 1996）
白盒	白盒表示系统的内部视图（元素的属性和结构）。也称为透明盒

APPENDIX D: N² DIAGRAM OF SYSTEMS ENGINEERING PROCESSES

Note: Figure D.1 in this appendix provides an N2 diagram (see Section 3.2.4) of the typical inputs and outputs that appear in the IPO diagrams in this handbook. The off-diagonal squares represent the typical inputs/outputs shared by the processes that intersect at a given square. Outputs flow horizontally, inputs flow vertically, and the diagram can be read in a clockwise fashion. These typical inputs and outputs represent "a" way that the SE processes can be performed, but not necessarily "the" way that they must be performed. The absence of a relationship between any two processes does not preclude tailoring to create a relationship. Definitions of the typical inputs and outputs on the IPO diagrams can be found in Appendix E.

The system life cycle processes are placed on the diagonal, abbreviated as follows:

Abbreviation	Life Cycle Process	Handbook Section
ACQ	Acquisition	2.3.2.1
SUP	Supply	2.3.2.2
LCMM	Life Cycle Model Management	2.3.3.1
INFRAM	Infrastructure Management	2.3.3.2
PM	Portfolio Management	2.3.3.3
HRM	Human Resource Management	2.3.3.4
QM	Quality Management	2.3.3.5
KM	Knowledge Management	2.3.3.6
PP	Project Planning	2.3.4.1
PAC	Project Assessment and Control	2.3.4.2
DM	Decision Management	2.3.4.3
RM	Risk Management	2.3.4.4
CM	Configuration Management	2.3.4.5
INFOM	Information Management	2.3.4.6

INCOSE Systems Engineering Handbook: A Guide for System Life Cycle Processes and Activities, Fifth Edition.

Edited by David D. Walden, Thomas M. Shortell, Garry J. Roedler, Bernardo A. Delicado, Odile Mornas, Yip Yew-Seng, and David Endler.

© 2023 John Wiley & Sons Ltd. Published 2023 by John Wiley & Sons Ltd.

附录 D：系统工程流程的 N^2 图

注：本附录中的图 D.1 提供了本手册 IPO 图中出现的典型输入和输出的 N^2 图（见 3.2.4 节）。非对角线正方形表示在给定正方形处相交的流程共享的典型输入/输出。输出水平流动，输入垂直流动，图表可以顺时针阅读。这些典型的输入和输出表示可以执行系统工程流程的"一种"方式，但不一定是执行系统工程流程的"唯一"方式。任何两个流程之间没有关系并不妨碍剪裁以创建关系。IPO 图表中典型输入和输出的定义见附录 E。

对角线上的系统生命周期流程的缩写如下：

缩写	生命周期流程	手册章节
ACQ	采办	2.3.2.1
SUP	供应	2.3.2.2
LCMM	生命周期模型管理	2.3.3.1
INFRAM	基础设施管理	2.3.3.2
PM	项目组合管理	2.3.3.3
HRM	人力资源管理	2.3.3.4
QM	质量管理	2.3.3.5
KM	知识管理	2.3.3.6
PP	项目规划	2.3.4.1
PAC	项目评估和控制	2.3.4.2
DM	决策管理	2.3.4.3
RM	风险管理	2.3.4.4
CM	构型配置管理	2.3.4.5
INFOM	信息管理	2.3.4.6

N² DIAGRAM OF SYSTEMS ENGINEERING PROCESSES

(Continued)

Abbreviation	Life Cycle Process	Handbook Section
MEAS	Measurement	2.3.4.7
QA	Quality Assurance	2.3.4.8
BMA	Business or Mission Analysis	2.3.5.1
SNRD	Stakeholder Needs and Requirements Definition	2.3.5.2
SRD	System Requirements Definition	2.3.5.3
SAD	System Architecture Definition	2.3.5.4
DD	Design Definition	2.3.5.5
SA	System Analysis	2.3.5.6
IMPL	Implementation	2.3.5.7
INT	Integration	2.3.5.8
VER	Verification	2.3.5.9
TRAN	Transition	2.3.5.10
VAL	Validation	2.3.5.11
OPER	Operation	2.3.5.12
MAINT	Maintenance	2.3.5.13
DISP	Disposal	2.3.5.14
TLR	Tailoring	4.1

In addition to the individual system life cycle processes, the following are also placed on the diagonal, abbreviated as follows:

Abbreviation	Name	Description
EXT	External	External represents those typical inputs and outputs that come from, or go to, beyond the set of system life cycle processes (i.e., they do not come from, or go to, another system life cycle process). Note that these can be either internal (e.g., Organization strategic plan) or external (e.g., Applicable laws and regulations) to the organization.
CTL	Controls	Controls represent those typical inputs and outputs that control, or limit, the execution of the system life cycle processes. They either come in as an external (EXT) typical input or from one or more life cycle processes. They go into every system life cycle process and are shown in Figure 2.11.
ENAB	Enablers	Enablers represent those typical inputs and outputs that enable, or assist in, the execution of the system life cycle processes. They either come in as an external (EXT) typical input or from one or more life cycle processes. They go into every system life cycle process and are shown in Figure 2.11.
SIT	Situational	Situational represents those typical inputs and outputs that are situational with respect to the execution of the system life cycle processes (i.e., they are invoked when needed). They can come from any life cycle process. They go into a select number of system life cycle processes, specifically: Decision Management, Risk Management, Configuration Management, Information Management, and System Analysis.

(续)

缩写	生命周期流程	手册章节
MEAS	测量	2.3.4.7
QA	质量保证	2.3.4.8
BMA	业务或使命任务分析	2.3.5.1
SNRD	利益相关方需要和需求定义	2.3.5.2
SRD	系统需求定义	2.3.5.3
SAD	架构定义	2.3.5.4
DD	设计定义	2.3.5.5
SA	系统分析	2.3.5.6
IMPL	实施	2.3.5.7
INT	综合	2.3.5.8
VER	验证	2.3.5.9
TRAN	转移	2.3.5.10
VAL	确认	2.3.5.11
OPER	运行	2.3.5.12
MAINT	维护	2.3.5.13
DISP	处置	2.3.5.14
TLR	剪裁	4.1

除了单个系统生命周期流程外，对角线上还放置了以下内容，缩写如下：

缩写	名字	描述
EXT	外部	外部代表那些来自或流向系统生命周期流程集之外的典型输入和输出（即它们不是来自或流向另一个系统生命周期流程）。请注意，这些输入和输出既可以是组织内部的（如组织战略规划），也可以是组织外部的（如适用的法律法规）
CTL	控制	控制是指控制或限制系统生命周期流程执行的典型输入和输出。它们或者作为外部（EXT）典型输入，或者来自一个或多个生命周期流程。它们进入每个系统生命周期流程，如图2.11所示
ENAB	使能项	使能项代表那些能够或协助执行系统生命周期流程的典型输入和输出。它们或者作为外部（EXT）典型输入，或者来自一个或多个生命周期流程。它们进入每个系统生命周期流程，如图2.11所示
SIT	情境的	情境输入和输出是指与系统生命周期流程的执行有关的典型输入和输出（即在需要时调用）。它们可以来自任何生命周期流程。它们进入特定数量的系统生命周期流程，特别是决策管理、风险管理、构型配置管理、信息管理和系统分析

N² DIAGRAM OF SYSTEMS ENGINEERING PROCESSES

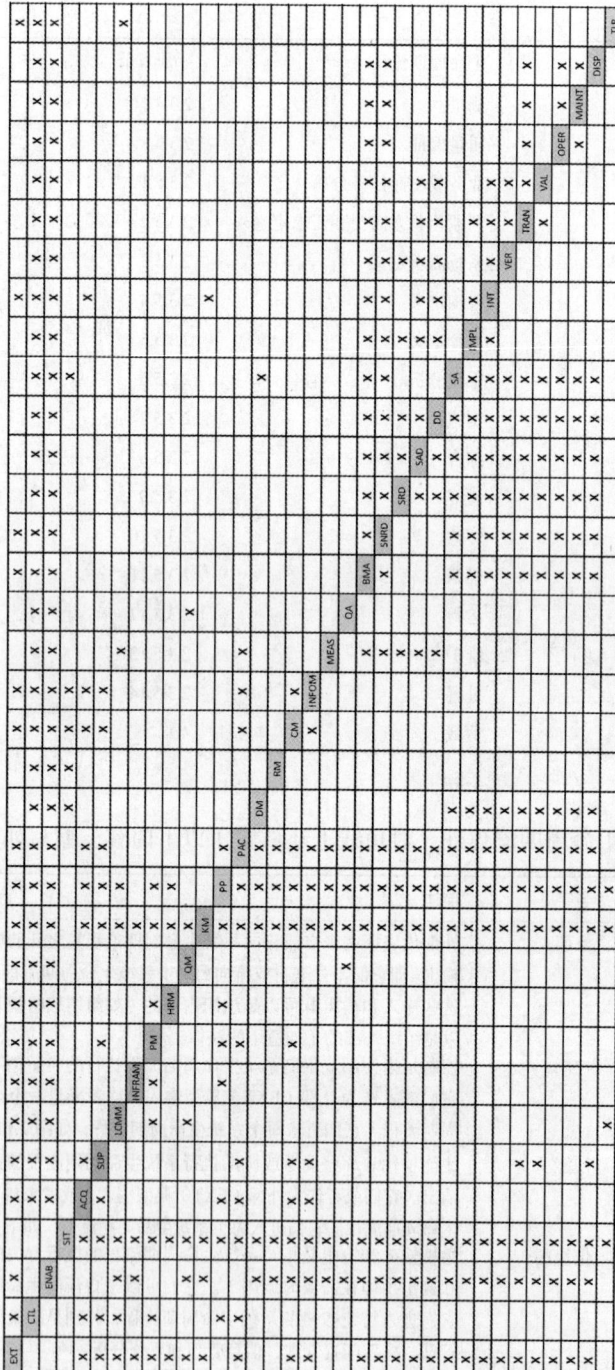

FIGURE D.1 Input/output relationships between the various SE processes. INCOSE SEH original figure created by Shortell, Walden, and Yip. Usage per the INCOSE Notices pages. All other rights reserved.

EXT	X	X		X	X	X	X	X	X	X	X	X	X			X	X			X	X						X							X
	CTL			X	X	X	X	X	X	X	X	X	X	X	X	X	X	X	X	X	X	X	X	X	X	X	X	X	X	X	X	X	X	X
		ENAB		X	X	X	X	X	X	X	X	X	X	X	X	X	X	X	X	X	X	X	X	X	X	X	X	X	X	X	X	X	X	X
			SIT											X	X	X	X								X									
X	X		X	ACQ	X						X	X	X			X	X										X							
X	X		X	X	SUP			X			X	X	X			X	X																	
X	X	X	X			LCMM					X	X						X																X
X		X	X				INFRAM				X																							
X	X		X			X	X	PM	X		X	X																						
X			X						HRM		X	X																						
X		X	X			X				QM	X								X															
X		X	X								KM																X							
	X		X	X			X	X	X		X	PP	X																					
X	X		X	X	X			X			X	X	PAC			X	X	X																
		X	X								X	X	X	DM											X									
		X	X								X	X	X		RM																			
X		X	X	X	X			X			X	X	X			CM	X																	
X		X	X	X	X						X	X	X			X	INFOM																	
		X	X								X	X	X					MEAS																
		X	X							X	X	X	X						QA															
X		X	X								X	X	X					X		BMA	X	X	X	X	X	X	X	X	X	X	X	X	X	
X		X	X								X	X	X					X		X	SNRD	X	X	X	X	X	X	X	X	X	X	X	X	
X		X	X								X	X	X					X				SRD	X	X		X		X						
X		X	X								X	X	X					X				X	SAD	X		X	X	X	X	X				
X		X	X								X	X	X					X				X	X	DD		X	X	X	X	X				
X		X	X								X	X	X	X						X	X	X	X	X	SA									
X		X	X								X	X	X	X						X	X	X	X	X	X	IMPL	X		X					
X		X	X								X	X	X	X						X	X	X	X	X	X	X	INT	X	X	X				
X		X	X								X	X	X	X						X	X	X	X	X	X			VER	X	X				
X		X	X		X						X	X	X	X						X	X	X	X	X	X				TRAN	X	X	X	X	
X		X	X		X						X	X	X	X						X	X	X	X	X	X				X	VAL				
X		X	X								X	X	X	X						X	X	X	X	X	X						OPER	X	X	
X		X	X								X	X	X	X						X	X	X	X	X	X						X	MAINT	X	
X		X	X		X						X	X	X	X						X	X	X	X	X	X								DISP	
			X			X					X	X																						TLR

图 D.1　系统工程流程的输入 / 输出关系。INCOSE SEH 原始图由 Shortell、 Walden 和 Yip 创建。按照 INCOSE 通知页使用。版权所有。

APPENDIX E: INPUT/OUTPUT DESCRIPTIONS

Note: This appendix is a alphabetical list of all the typical inputs and outputs that appear in the IPO diagrams in this handbook. Sources of descriptions are as indicated. These typical inputs and outputs represent "a" way that the SE processes can be performed, but not necessarily "the" way that they must be performed. Other related terms and definitions can be found in Appendix B.

Typical Input/Output	Description
Accepted system or system element	System or system element (product or service) accepted by an acquirer from a supplier consistent with the delivery conditions of the supply agreement.
Acquired system or system element	System or system element (product or service) delivered to the acquirer from a supplier consistent with the delivery conditions of the acquisition agreement.
Acquisitio agreement	Mutual acknowledgment of terms and conditions under which a working relationship is conducted between an acquirer and a supplier. (Adapted from ISO/IEC/IEEE 15288, 2023).
Acquisition need	Identified need that cannot be met within the organization encountering the need or a need that can be met in a more economical way by a supplier.
Acquisition payment	Payments or other compensations for an acquired system.
Acquisition records/artifacts	Permanent, readable form of data, information, or knowledge related to acquisition.
Acquisition report	An account prepared for interested parties in order to communicate the status, results, and outcomes of the acquisition activities.
Acquisition strategy/approach	Approaches, schedules, resources, and specific considerations required to perform acquisition.

INCOSE Systems Engineering Handbook: A Guide for System Life Cycle Processes and Activities, Fifth Edition.
Edited by David D. Walden, Thomas M. Shortell, Garry J. Roedler, Bernardo A. Delicado, Odile Mornas, Yip Yew-Seng, and David Endler.
© 2023 John Wiley & Sons Ltd. Published 2023 by John Wiley & Sons Ltd.

附录 E：输入/输出描述

注：本附录按字母顺序列出了本手册 IPO 图表中出现的所有典型输入和输出。说明的来源已标明。这些典型的输入和输出代表了可以执行系统工程流程的"一种"方式，但是必须执行的"唯一"方式。其他相关术语和定义见附录 B。

典型的输入/输出	描述
已接受的系统或系统元素	采办方从供应商处接受的符合供应协议交货条件的系统或系统元素（产品或服务）
采办的系统或系统元素	供应商按照采办协议的交付条件向采办方交付的系统或系统元素（产品或服务）
采办协议	采办方和供应商之间建立工作关系所依据的相互承认的条款和条件。（改编自 ISO/IEC/IEEE 15288，2023）
采办需要	组织内遇到的但不能被满足的需要，或能以更经济的方式由供应商满足的需要
采办支付	采办的系统的付款或其他补偿
采办记录/制品	与采办有关的永久可读取形式的数据、信息或知识
采办报告	为有关方准备的一份记述报告，以便沟通采办活动的状态、结果和成果
采办策略/实施方法	采办系统元素所要求的实施方法、进度、资源和特定的考虑因素

INPUT/OUTPUT DESCRIPTIONS

(Continued)

Typical Input/Output	Description
Agreements	Agreements from all applicable life cycle processes, including: acquisition agreement and supply agreement.
Alternative solution classes	Identifies and describes the classes of solutions that may address the problem or opportunity.
Analysis situations	Analyses that arise from any stakeholder. Can originate from any life cycle process.
Applicable laws and regulations	International, national, or local laws or regulations.
Breakdown structures	Hierarchical representations of project aspects into smaller components providing the necessary frameworks to accomplish the project objectives and create the required deliverables.
Business or mission analysis records/artifacts	Permanent, readable form of data, information, or knowledge related to business or mission analysis.
Business or mission analysis report	An account prepared for interested parties in order to communicate the status, results, and outcomes of the business or mission analysis activities.
Business or mission analysis strategy/approach	Approaches, schedules, resources, and specific considerations required to perform business or mission analysis.
Business plan	The overall organization business plan, including the business objectives.
Candidate items for configuration management	Items for configuration control. Can originate from any life cycle process.
Candidate items for information management	Items for information control. Can originate from any life cycle process.
Candidate risks and opportunities	Risks and opportunities that arise from any stakeholder. Can originate from any life cycle process.
Change request	Identified anomaly, required, or recommended enhancement to a project, from the time an idea is recorded until the disposition by a designated change authority. (Adapted from ISO/IEC/IEEE 24765, 2017).
Concept of operations (ConOps)	At the organization level, addresses the leadership's intended way of operating the organization (ISO/IEC/IEEE 29148, 2018).
Configuration baseline	Configuration information formally designated at a specific time during the life of a product, product component, service, or service component. (Adapted from ISO/IEC/IEEE 24765, 2017).
Configuration management records/artifacts	Permanent, readable form of data, information, or knowledge related to configuration management.
Configuration management report	An account prepared for interested parties in order to communicate the status, results, and outcomes of the configuration management activities.

输入／输出描述

（续）

典型的输入／输出	描述
协议	所有来自适用生命周期流程的协议，包括采办协议和供应协议
备选解决方案类别	识别和描述可应对问题或机会的解决方案的类别
分析情况	来自任何利益相关方的分析。可源于任何生命周期流程
适用法律和法规	国际、国家或当地法律或法规
分解结构	将项目各方面分层表示为较小的组成部分，为达到项目目标和创建所需的交付成果提供必要的框架
业务或任务分析记录／制品	与业务或任务分析有关的永久可读取形式的数据、信息或知识
业务或任务分析报告	为有关各方编写的说明，以传达业务或任务分析活动的状态、结果和成果
业务或任务分析策略／实施方法	执行业务或任务分析所需的实施方法、进度、资源和特定考虑因素
业务计划	组织的总体业务计划，包括业务目标
构型配置管理的备选项	构型配置控制项。可源于任何生命周期流程
信息管理的备选项	信息控制项。可源于任何生命周期流程
候选风险和机会	来源于任何利益相关方的风险和机会。可源于任何生命周期流程
变更请求	从一个想法被记录到指定的变更机构进行处置的整个过程中，所发现的项目异常、所需的或建议的改进。（改编自 ISO/IEC/IEEE 24765，2017）
运行意图（ConOps）	在组织层面，实现领导层希望的组织运作方式。（ISO/IEC/IEEE 29148，2018）
构型配置基线	在产品、产品组件、服务或服务组件生命周期中的特定时间正式指定的配置信息。（改编自 ISO/IEC/IEEE 24765，2017）
构型配置管理记录／制品	与构型管理有关的永久可读取形式的数据、信息或知识
构型配置管理报告	为有关方准备的一份记述报告，以便沟通构型管理活动的状态、结果和成果

INPUT/OUTPUT DESCRIPTIONS

(Continued)

Typical Input/Output	Description
Configuration management strategy/approach	Approaches, schedules, resources, and specific considerations required to perform configuration management.
Configuration management system	System used to support and enable configuration management.
Configuration verification and audit report	Provides results of configuration management verifications and audits to ensure adequate traceability, control, and visibility. It includes evaluation criteria.
Constraints on solution	Externally imposed limitation on the system, its design, or implementation or on the process used to develop or modify a system. (ISO/IEC/IEEE 29148, 2018).
Critical performance measurement data	Data provided for the identified system-of-interest measurement needs.
Critical performance measurement needs	Identified information needs of the decision makers with respect to system-of-interest expectations.
Customer satisfaction inputs	Responses to customer satisfaction surveys or other instruments.
Decision management records/artifacts	Permanent, readable form of data, information, or knowledge related to decision management.
Decision management report	An account prepared for interested parties in order to communicate the status, results, and outcomes of the decision management activities.
Decision management strategy/approach	Approaches, schedules, resources, and specific considerations required to perform decision management.
Decision register	A repository that supports the availability for use and communication of all relevant decision information in a timely, complete, valid, and, if required, confidential manner.
Decision situations	Decisions that arise from any stakeholder. Can originate from any life cycle process.
Design definition records/artifacts	Permanent, readable form of data, information, or knowledge related to design definition.
Design definition report	An account prepared for interested parties in order to communicate the status, results, and outcomes of the design definition activities.
Design definition strategy/approach	Approaches, schedules, resources, and specific considerations required to perform design definition.
Disposal procedure	Presents an ordered series of steps to perform disposal.
Disposal records/artifacts	Permanent, readable form of data, information, or knowledge related to disposal.
Disposal report	An account prepared for interested parties in order to communicate the status, results, and outcomes of the disposal activities.
Disposal strategy/approach	Approaches, schedules, resources, and specific considerations required to perform disposal.

输入 / 输出描述

（续）

典型的输入 / 输出	描述
构型配置管理策略 / 实施方法	执行构型配置管理所需的实施方法、进度、资源和特定考虑因素
构型配置管理系统	用于支持和启动构型配置管理的系统
构型配置验证和审核报告	提供构型配置管理验证和审核的结果，以确保充分的可追溯性、控制和可见性。它包括评估准则
方案约束	对系统、其设计或实施以及对用于开发或修改系统的过程施加的外部限制。（ISO/IEC/IEEE 29148，2018）
关键绩效测量数据	为已确定的所感兴趣之系统的测量需要提供数据
关键绩效测量需要	确定决策者在所感兴趣之系统预期方面的信息需求
客户满意度输入	对客户满意度调查或其他手段的响应
决策管理记录 / 制品	与决策管理有关的永久性可读形式的数据、信息或知识
决策管理报告	为有关方准备的一份记述报告，以便沟通决策管理活动的状态、结果和成果
决策管理策略 / 实施方法	执行决策管理所要求的实施方法、进度、资源和特定考量
决策登记	支持及时、完整、有效并在必要时保密地提供和交流所有相关决策信息的信息库
决策情况	可能来源于任何利益相关方的决策，可源于任何生命周期流程
设计定义记录 / 制品	与设计定义有关的永久可读取形式的数据、信息或知识
设计定义报告	为有关方准备的一份记述报告，以便沟通设计定义活动的状态、结果和成果
设计定义策略 / 实施方法	执行设计定义所需的实施方法、进度、资源和特定考虑因素
处置程序	提出一系列有序的处置步骤
处置记录 / 制品	与处置有关的永久可读取形式的数据、信息或知识
处置报告	为有关方准备的一份记述报告，以便沟通处置活动的状态、结果和成果
处置策略 / 方法	执行处置所需的实施方法、进度、资源和特定考虑因素

INPUT/OUTPUT DESCRIPTIONS

(Continued)

324

Typical Input/Output	Description
Disposed system	System (product or service) that has been deactivated, disassembled, and removed from operations and been properly disposed.
Enabling systems	External systems that facilitate the life cycle activities of the SoI but are not a direct element of the operational environment.
Human resource management records/artifacts	Permanent, readable form of data, information, or knowledge related to human resource management.
Human resource management report	An account prepared for interested parties in order to communicate the status, results, and outcomes of the human resource management activities.
Human resource management strategy/approach	Approaches, schedules, resources, and specific considerations required to perform human resource management.
Implementation records/artifacts	Permanent, readable form of data, information, or knowledge related to implementation.
Implementation report	An account prepared for interested parties in order to communicate the status, results, and outcomes of the implementation activities.
Implementation strategy/approach	Approaches, schedules, resources, and specific considerations required to perform implementation.
Information management records/artifacts	Permanent, readable form of data, information, or knowledge related to information management.
Information management report	An account prepared for interested parties in order to communicate the status, results, and outcomes of the information management activities.
Information management strategy/approach	Approaches, schedules, resources, and specific considerations required to perform information management.
Information register	A repository that supports the availability for use and communication of all relevant project information artifacts in a timely, complete, valid, and, if required, restricted manner.
Infrastructure management records/artifacts	Permanent, readable form of data, information, or knowledge related to infrastructure management.
Infrastructure management report	An account prepared for interested parties in order to communicate the status, results, and outcomes of the infrastructure management activities.
Infrastructure management strategy/approach	Approaches, schedules, resources, and specific considerations required to perform infrastructure management.
Installation procedure	Presents an ordered series of steps to perform transition.
Installed system	System (product or service) that has been installed in its operational environment.

（续）

典型的输入/输出	描述
已处置的系统	系统（产品或服务）已停用、拆卸、停止运行并得到妥善处理
使能系统	促进SoI生命周期活动的外部系统，但不是运行环境的直接要素
人力资源管理记录/制品	与人力资源管理有关的永久可读取形式的数据、信息或知识
人力资源管理报告	为有关方准备的一份记述报告，以便沟通人力资源管理活动的状态、结果和成果
人力资源管理策略/实施方法	执行人力资源管理所需的实施方法、进度、资源和特定考虑因素
实施记录/制品	与实施有关的永久可读取形式的数据、信息或知识
实施报告	为有关方准备的一份记述报告，以便沟通实施活动的状态、结果和成果
实施策略/实施方法	执行实施所需的实施方法、进度、资源和特定考虑因素
信息管理记录/制品	与信息管理有关的永久可读取形式的数据、信息或知识
信息管理报告	为有关方准备的一份记述报告，以便沟通信息管理活动的状态、结果和成果
信息管理策略/实施方法	执行信息管理所需的实施方法、进度、资源和特定考虑因素
信息登记	支持及时、完整、有效并在必要时加以限制地交流所有相关项目信息制品的信息库
基础设施管理记录/制品	与基础设施管理有关的永久可读取形式的数据、信息或知识
基础设施管理报告	为有关方准备的一份记述报告，以便沟通基础设施管理活动的状态、结果和成果。包括成本、用法、停工时间/响应测度等
基础设施管理策略/实施方法	执行基础设施管理所需的实施方法、进度、资源和特定考虑因素
安装程序	提出一系列有序的转移步骤
已安装的系统	已安装在运行环境中的系统（产品或服务）

INPUT/OUTPUT DESCRIPTIONS

(Continued)

	Typical Input/Output	Description
325	Integrated system or system element	System or system element (product or service) that has been aggregated from system elements.
	Integration procedure	Presents an ordered series of steps to perform integration.
	Integration records/artifacts	Permanent, readable form of data, information, or knowledge related to integration.
	Integration report	An account prepared for interested parties in order to communicate the status, results, and outcomes of the integration activities.
	Integration strategy/approach	Approaches, schedules, resources, and specific considerations required to perform integration.
	Knowledge management records/artifacts	Permanent, readable form of data, information, or knowledge related to knowledge management.
	Knowledge management report	An account prepared for interested parties in order to communicate the status, results, and outcomes of the knowledge management activities.
	Knowledge management strategy/approach	Approaches, schedules, resources, and specific considerations required to perform knowledge management.
	Knowledge management system	System used to support and enable knowledge management.
	Life cycle concepts	Articulation and refinement of the various life cycle concepts consistent with the stakeholder needs. Typical concepts include: acquisition concept; deployment concept; operational concept (OpsCon); support concept; retirement concept.
	Life cycle model management records/artifacts	Permanent, readable form of data, information, or knowledge related to life cycle model management.
	Life cycle model management report	An account prepared for interested parties in order to communicate the status, results, and outcomes of the life cycle model management activities.
	Life cycle model management strategy/approach	Approaches, schedules, resources, and specific considerations required to perform life cycle model management.
	Life cycle models	Framework of processes and activities concerned with the life cycle that can be organized into stages, acting as a common reference for communication and understanding. (ISO/IEC/IEEE 15288, 2023)
	Maintained and sustained system	System (product or service) that has been maintained for use in its operational environment.
	Maintenance and logistics procedure	Presents an ordered series of steps to perform maintenance.
	Maintenance and logistics records/artifacts	Permanent, readable form of data, information, or knowledge related to maintenance.

输入/输出描述

（续）

典型的输入/输出	描述
综合的系统或系统元素	由系统元素聚合而成的系统或系统元素（产品或服务）
综合程序	提出一系列有序的综合步骤
综合记录/制品	与综合有关的永久可读取形式的数据、信息或知识
综合报告	为有关方准备的一份记述报告，以便沟通综合活动的状态、结果和成果
综合策略/实施方法	执行综合所需的实施方法、进度、资源和特定考虑因素
知识管理记录/制品	与知识管理有关的永久可读取形式的数据、信息或知识
知识管理报告	为有关方准备的一份记述报告，以便沟通知识管理活动的状态、结果和成果
知识管理策略/实施方法	执行知识管理所需的实施方法、进度、资源和特定考虑因素
知识管理系统	用于支持和启动知识管理的系统
生命周期概念	根据利益相关方的需要，阐明并完善各种生命周期概念。典型的概念包括：采办概念、部署概念、运行概念（OpsCon）、支持概念、退役概念
生命周期模型管理记录/制品	与生命周期模型管理有关的永久可读取形式的数据、信息或知识
生命周期模型管理报告	为有关方准备的一份记述报告，以便沟通生命周期模型管理活动的状态、结果和成果
生命周期模型管理策略/实施方法	执行生命周期模型管理所需的实施方法、进度、资源和特定考虑因素
生命周期模型	与生命周期有关的流程和活动框架，可按阶段组织，作为交流和理解的共同参考。（ISO/IEC/IEEE 15288，2023）
维护和维持的系统	在运行环境中维护使用的系统（产品或服务）
维护和后勤程序	提出一系列有序的维护步骤
维护和后勤记录/制品	与维护有关的永久可读取形式的数据、信息或知识

INPUT/OUTPUT DESCRIPTIONS

(Continued)

Typical Input/Output	Description
Maintenance and logistics report	An account prepared for interested parties in order to communicate the status, results, and outcomes of the maintenance activities.
Maintenance and logistics strategy/approach	Approaches, schedules, resources, and specific considerations required to perform maintenance.
Measurement data	Measurement data from all applicable life cycle processes, including: critical performance measurement data, organizational measurement data, and project measurement data.
Measurement needs	Measurement needs from all applicable life cycle processes, including: critical performance measurement needs, organizational measurement needs, and project measurement needs.
Measurement records/artifacts	Permanent, readable form of data, information, or knowledge related to measurement.
Measurement register	A repository that supports the availability for use and communication of all relevant measures in a timely, complete, valid, and, if required, confidential manner.
Measurement report	An account prepared for interested parties in order to communicate the status, results, and outcomes of the measurement activities.
Measurement strategy/approach	Approaches, schedules, resources, and specific considerations required to perform measurement.
Operation procedure	Presents an ordered series of steps to perform operation.
Operation records/artifacts	Permanent, readable form of data, information, or knowledge related to operation.
Operation report	An account prepared for interested parties in order to communicate the status, results, and outcomes of the operation activities.
Operation strategy/approach	Approaches, schedules, resources, and specific considerations required to perform operation.
Operational system	System (product or service) being used in its operational environment.
Organization infrastructure	Resources, facilities, personnel, and/or services that support the organization.
Organization infrastructure needs	Identified organizational infrastructure needs.
Organization lessons learned	Organizational-related lessons learned. Results from an evaluation or observation of an implemented corrective action that contributed to improved performance or increased capability. A lesson learned also results from an evaluation or observation of a positive finding that did not necessarily require corrective action other than sustainment.
Organization policies	High-level direction at the organizational level consistent with the organization's strategies.(Adapted from ISO/IEC/IEEE 15289, 2019)
Organization portfolio direction and constraints	Organization direction and constraints related to the project portfolio.
Organization procedures	Presents an ordered series of steps to perform a process, activity, or task for an organization.(Adapted from ISO/IEC/IEEE 15289, 2019)
Organization processes	Set of interrelated or interacting activities that transform inputs into outputs for an organization. (Adapted from ISO/IEC/IEEE 15288, 2023)

输入/输出描述

（续）

典型的输入/输出	描述
维护和后勤报告	为有关方准备的一份记述报告，以便沟通维护活动的状态、结果和成果
维护和后勤策略/实施方法	执行维护所需的实施方法、进度、资源和特定考虑因素
测量数据	来自所有适用生命周期流程的测量数据，包括：关键绩效测量数据、组织测量数据和项目测量数据
测量需要	来自所有适用生命周期流程的测量需要，包括：关键绩效测量需要、组织测量需要和项目测量需要
测量记录/制品	与测量有关的永久可读取形式的数据、信息或知识
测量登记	支持及时、完整、有效并在必要时保密地使用和交流所有相关测度的信息库
测量报告	为有关方准备的一份记述报告，以便沟通测量活动的状态、结果和成果
测量策略/实施方法	执行测量所需的实施方法、进度、资源和特定考虑因素
运行程序	提出一系列有序的运行步骤
运行记录/制品	与运行有关的永久可读取形式的数据、信息或知识
运行报告	为有关方准备一份记述报告，以便沟通运行活动的状态、结果和成果
运行策略/实施方法	执行运行所需的实施方法、进度、资源和特定考虑因素
运行的系统	在其运行环境中使用的系统（产品或服务）
组织基础设施	支持组织的资源、设施、人员和/或服务
组织基础设施需要	识别的组织基础设施需要
吸取的组织教训	吸取的与组织有关的教训。来自对已实施的有助于改进性能或提高能力的纠正措施的评价或观察。吸取的教训亦来自对不要求纠正的积极结果的评价或观察
组织方针	与组织战略相一致的组织层面的高层指导。（改编自 ISO/IEC/IEEE 15289，2019）
组织项目组合方向与约束	与项目组合有关的组织方向和制约因素
组织程序	提出一系列有序的步骤，以执行组织的流程、活动或任务。（改编自 ISO/IEC/IEEE 15289，2019）
组织流程	将一个组织的投入转化为产出的一系列相互关联或相互作用的活动。（改编自 ISO/IEC/IEEE 15288，2023）

INPUT/OUTPUT DESCRIPTIONS

(Continued)

Typical Input/Output	Description
Organization reports	Reports from all applicable organization life cycle processes, including: life cycle model management report, infrastructure management report, portfolio management report, human resource management report, quality management report, and knowledge management report.
Organization strategic plan	The overall organization strategy, including the business mission or vision and strategic goals and objectives.
Organization strategies/approaches	Strategies/approaches for all applicable organization life processes, including: life cycle model management strategy/approach, infrastructure management strategy/approach, portfolio management strategy/approach, human resource management strategy/approach, quality management strategy/approach, and knowledge management strategy/approach.
Organization tailoring strategy/approach	Organization's specific strategy and approach to tailoring required to incorporate new or updated external standards.
Organizational measurement data	Data provided for the identified organizational measurement needs.
Organizational measurement needs	Identified information needs of the decision makers with respect to organizational expectations.
Other validated artifacts	Artifacts that are validated
Other verified artifacts	Artifacts that are verified
Portfolio management records/artifacts	Permanent, readable form of data, information, or knowledge related to portfolio management.
Portfolio management report	An account prepared for interested parties in order to communicate the status, results, and outcomes of the portfolio management activities.
Portfolio management strategy/approach	Approaches, schedules, resources, and specific considerations required to perform portfolio management.
Problem or opportunity statement	Description of the problem or opportunity. Should be derived from the organization strategy and provide enough detail to understand the gap or new capability that is being considered
Project assessment and control records/artifacts	Permanent, readable form of data, information, or knowledge related to project assessment and control.
Project assessment and control strategy/approach	Approaches, schedules, resources, and specific considerations required to perform project assessment and control.
Project authorization	Authorization from the organization to proceed per the agreed-to project plan.
Project authorization request	Request from the project to the organization to authorize the project.

（续）

典型的输入/输出	描述
组织报告	来自所有适用生命周期流程的报告，包括：生命周期模型管理报告、基础设施管理报告、投资组合管理报告、人力资源管理报告、质量管理报告和知识管理报告
组织战略计划	总体组织战略，包括业务任务或愿景以及战略目标和目的
组织策略/实施方法	所有适用组织生命过程的策略/实施方法，包括：生命周期模型管理策略/实施方法、基础设施管理策略/实施方法、项目组合管理策略/实施方法、人力资源管理策略/实施方法、质量管理策略/实施方法和知识管理策略/实施方法
组织剪裁策略/实施方法	组织根据新的或更新的外部标准调整所需的具体策略和实施方法
组织测量数据	为已确定的组织测量需要提供数据
组织测量需要	确定决策者在组织期望方面的信息需要
其他确认的制品	经过确认的制品
其他验证的制品	经过验证的制品
项目组合管理记录/制品	与项目组合管理有关的永久可读取形式的数据、信息或知识
项目组合管理报告	为有关方准备的一份记述报告，以便沟通项目组合管理活动的状态、结果和成果
项目组合管理策略/实施方法	执行项目组合管理所需的实施方法、进度、资源和特定考虑因素
问题或机会声明	问题或机会的描述。应来自组织策略并提供足够详细的说明以理解考虑中的差距或新能力
项目评估和控制记录/制品	与项目评估和控制有关的永久可读取形式的数据、信息或知识
项目评估和控制策略/实施方法	执行项目评估和控制所需的实施方法、进度、资源和特定考虑因素
项目批准	组织被批准按照商定的项目计划开展工作
项目批准请求	项目向组织提出的项目批准申请

INPUT/OUTPUT DESCRIPTIONS

(Continued)

Typical Input/Output	Description
Project budget	Estimate of the costs associated with a particular project. Includes labor, infrastructure, acquisition, and enabling system costs along with reserves for risk management.
Project constraints	Externally imposed limitation on the project developing or modifying a system. (ISO/IEC/IEEE 29148, 2018)
Project control request	Project directives based on action required due to deviations from the project plan. If assessments are associated with a decision gate, a decision to proceed or not to proceed, is taken.
Project decision gate/review result	Decision gate and review artifacts that are expected through conduct of the decision gate or technical review and that can be considered elements of exit criteria. (Adapted from ISO/IEC/IEEE 24748-8, 2019)
Project direction	Organizational direction to the project. Includes sustainment of projects meeting objectives and redirection or termination of projects not meeting objectives.
Project human resource needs	Identified human resource needs of the project.
Project infrastructure	Resources, facilities, personnel, and/or services that support the project.
Project infrastructure needs	Identified infrastructure needs of the project.
Project lessons learned	Project-related lessons learned. Results from an evaluation or observation of an implemented corrective action that contributed to improved performance or increased capability. A lesson learned also results from an evaluation or observation of a positive finding that did not necessarily require corrective action other than sustainment.
Project measurement data	Data provided for the identified project measurement needs.
Project measurement needs	Identified information needs of the decision makers with respect to project expectations.
Project objectives	The objectives or goals for the project.
Project planning records/artifacts	Permanent, readable form of data, information, or knowledge related to project planning.
Project portfolio	Collection of projects that addresses the strategic objectives of the organization. (ISO/IEC/IEEE 12207, 2017)
Project procedures	Procedures from all applicable life cycle processes, including: integration procedure, verification procedure, installation procedure, validation procedure, operation procedure, maintenance and logistics procedure, and disposal procedure.
Project reports	Reports from all applicable project life cycle processes, including: acquisition report, supply report, decision management report, risk management report, configuration management report, configuration verification and audit report, information management report, measurement report, quality assurance report, quality assurance evaluation report, business or mission analysis report, stakeholder needs and requirements definition report, system requirements definition report, system architecture definition report, system architecture assessment report, design definition report, system design assessment report, system analysis report, implementation report, integration report, verification report, transition report, validation report, operation report, maintenance and logistics report, and disposal report.

输入／输出描述

（续）

典型的输入／输出	描述
项目预算	与特定项目相关的成本估算。包括人工、基础设施、购置和使能系统成本以及风险管理准备金
项目约束	对开发或修改系统的项目施加的外部限制。（ISO/IEC/IEEE 29148，2018）
项目控制请求	根据偏离项目计划所需的行动发出项目指令。如果评估与决策门相关联，则会做出继续或不继续的决定
项目决策门／评审结果	通过开展决策门或技术评审而预期的、可被视为退出准则要素的决策门和评审制品。（改编自 ISO/IEC/IEEE 24748-8，2019）
项目指导	组织对项目的指导包括达到评估准则的项目的维持和未达到评估准则的项目的重定向或终止
项目人力资源需要	确定项目的人力资源需要
项目基础设施	支持项目的资源、设施、人员和／或服务
项目基础设施需要	确定项目的基础设施需要
吸取项目的教训	吸取的与项目有关的教训。来自对已实施的有助于改进性能或提高能力的纠正措施的评价或观察。吸取的教训亦来自对不要求纠正的积极结果的评价或观察
项目性能测度数据	为识别的项目测量需要提供的数据
项目性能测度需要	确定决策者在项目预期方面的信息需求
项目目标	项目的目标或目的
项目规划记录／工件	与项目规划有关的永久可读取形式的数据、信息或知识
项目组合	达到组织战略目标的项目集。（ISO/IEC/IEEE 12207，2017）
项目程序	来自所有适用生命周期流程的程序，包括：综合程序、验证程序、安装程序、确认程序、运行程序、维护和后勤程序以及处置程序
项目报告	来自所有适用项目生命周期流程的报告，包括：采购报告、供应报告、决策管理报告、风险管理报告、构型配置管理报告、配置验证和审核报告、信息管理报告、测量报告、质量保证报告、质量保证评估报告、业务或任务分析报告、利益相关者需要和需求定义报告、系统需求定义报告、系统架构定义报告、系统架构评估报告、设计定义报告、系统设计评估报告、系统分析报告、实施报告、综合报告、验证报告、转移报告、确认报告、运行报告、维护和后勤报告以及处置报告

INPUT/OUTPUT DESCRIPTIONS

(Continued)

Typical Input/Output	Description
Project schedule	A linked list of a project's milestones, activities, and deliverables with intended start and finish dates May include a top-level milestone schedule and multiple levels (also called tiers) of schedules of increasing detail and task descriptions with completion criteria and work authorizations.
Project status report/ dashboard	Provides results of monitoring the execution of the defined plan or processes for internal or external distribution. It includes a summary of decisions, monitoring results, action items, process or performance data, and recorded process improvements. It assesses the degree of adherence to the plans. (Adapted from ISO/IEC/IEEE 15289, 2019)
Project strategies/ approaches	Strategies/approaches for all applicable project life processes, including: acquisition strategy/approach, supply strategy & approach, project assessment and control strategy/approach, decision management strategy/approach, risk management strategy/approach, configuration management strategy/approach, information management strategy/ approach, measurement strategy/approach, quality assurance strategy/ approach, business or mission analysis strategy/approach, stakeholder needs and requirements definition strategy/approach, system requirements definition strategy/approach, system architecture definition strategy/approach, design definition strategy/approach, system analysis strategy/approach, implementation strategy/approach, integration strategy/ approach, verification strategy/approach, transition strategy/approach, validation strategy/approach, operation strategy/approach, maintenance and logistics strategy/approach, and disposal strategy/approach.
Project tailoring strategy/ approach	Project's specific strategy and approach to tailoring required to incorporate new or updated life cycle models.
Qualified personnel	Individuals equipped to perform duties on behalf of the organization, including officers, employees, and contractors. (Adapted from ISO/IEC/IEEE 24765, 2017)
Quality assurance corrective action	Action to eliminate the cause or reduce the likelihood of recurrence of a detected project nonconformity or other undesirable situation. (Adapted from ISO/IEC 19770-1, 2017)
Quality assurance evaluation report	Provides results of quality assurance evaluations. It includes evaluation criteria. (Adapted from ISO/IEC/IEEE 15289, 2019)
Quality assurance records/ artifacts	Permanent, readable form of data, information, or knowledge related to quality assurance.
Quality assurance report	An account prepared for interested parties in order to communicate the status, results, and outcomes of the quality assurance activities.
Quality assurance strategy/ approach	Approaches, schedules, resources, and specific considerations required to perform quality assurance.
Quality assurance system	System used to support and enable quality assurance.
Quality management corrective action	Action to eliminate the cause or reduce the likelihood of recurrence of a detected organizational nonconformity or other undesirable situation. (Adapted from ISO/IEC 19770-1, 2017)
Quality management criteria and methods	Rules on which a judgment or decision can be based, or by which an organization can be evaluated. (Adapted from ISO/IEC/IEEE 15289, 2019)
Quality management evaluation report	Provides results of quality management evaluations. It includes evaluation criteria. (Adapted from ISO/IEC/IEEE 15289, 2019)

（续）

典型的输入 / 输出	描述
项目进度	带有预期的开始时间和结束时间的项目里程碑、活动和可交付物的链接表。可包括顶层里程碑进度以及使用完成准则和工作授权来增加细节和任务描述的多层级（亦称为多层）进度
项目状态报告 / 仪表板	提供既定计划或流程执行情况的监测结果，供内部或外部分发。它包括决策摘要、监测结果、行动项目、流程或绩效数据以及记录的流程改进。它评估计划的执行程度。（改编自 ISO/IEC/IEEE 15289, 2019）
项目策略 / 实施方法	所有适用项目生命过程的策略 / 实施方法，包括：采购策略 / 实施方法、供应策略 / 实施方法、项目评估和控制策略 / 实施方法、决策管理策略 / 实施方法、风险管理策略 / 实施方法、构型配置管理策略 / 实施方法、信息管理策略 / 实施方法、测量策略 / 实施方法、质量保证策略 / 实施方法、业务或任务分析策略 / 实施方法、利益相关方需要和需求定义策略 / 实施方法、系统需求定义策略 / 实施方法、系统架构定义策略 / 实施方法、设计定义策略 / 实施方法、系统分析策略 / 实施方法、实施策略 / 实施方法、综合策略 / 实施方法、验证策略 / 实施方法、转移策略 / 实施方法、确认策略 / 实施方法、运行策略 / 实施方法、维护和后勤策略 / 实施方法以及处置策略 / 实施方法
项目剪裁策略 / 实施方法	为纳入新的或更新的生命周期模型而需要调整的项目具体策略 / 实施方法
有资质的人员	有能力代表组织履行职责的个人，包括官员、雇员和承包商。（改编自 ISO/IEC/IEEE 24765, 2017）
质量保证纠正措施	消除已发现的项目不符合项或其他不良情况的原因，或降低其再次发生的可能性的行动。（改编自 ISO/IEC 19770-1, 2017）
质量保证评价报告	提供质量保证评价的结果。其中包括评价准则。（改编自 ISO/IEC/IEEE 15289, 2019）
质量保证记录 / 制品	与质量保证有关的永久可读取形式的数据、信息或知识
质量保证报告	为有关方准备的一份记述报告，以便沟通质量保证活动的状态、结果和成果
质量保证策略 / 实施方法	执行质量保证所需的实施方法、进度、资源和特定考虑因素
质量保证系统	用于支持和启动质量保证的系统
质量管理纠正措施	消除已发现的组织不合规或其他不良情况的原因，或降低其再次发生的可能性的行动。（改编自 ISO/IEC 19770-1, 2017）
质量管理准则和方法	判断或决策所依据的规则，或评估一个组织所依据的规则。（改编自 ISO/IEC/IEEE 15289, 2019）
质量管理评价报告	提供质量管理评价结果。其中包括评价准则。（改编自 ISO/IEC/IEEE 15289, 2019）

INPUT/OUTPUT DESCRIPTIONS

(Continued)

Typical Input/Output	Description
Quality management records/artifacts	Permanent, readable form of data, information, or knowledge related to quality management.
Quality management report	An account prepared for interested parties in order to communicate the status, results, and outcomes of the quality management activities.
Quality management strategy/approach	Approaches, schedules, resources, and specific considerations required to perform quality management.
Quality management system	System used to support and enable quality management.
Records/artifacts	Records from all applicable life cycle processes, including: acquisition records/artifacts, supply records/artifacts, life cycle model management records/artifacts, infrastructure management records/artifacts, portfolio management records/artifacts, human resource management records/artifacts, quality management records/artifacts, knowledge management records/artifacts, project planning records/artifacts, project assessment and control records/artifacts, decision management records/artifacts, risk management records/artifacts, configuration management records/artifacts, information management records/artifacts, measurement records/artifacts, quality assurance records/artifacts, business or mission analysis records/artifacts, stakeholder needs and requirements definition records/artifacts, system requirements definition records/artifacts, system architecture definition records/artifacts, design definition records/artifacts, system analysis records/artifacts, implementation records/artifacts, integration records/artifacts, verification records/artifacts, transition records/artifacts, validation records/artifacts, operation records/artifacts, maintenance and logistics records/artifacts, disposal records/artifacts, tailoring records/artifacts.
Request for supply	Acquirer's request for information and commitments needed from the supplier that are required to be included in the potential supplier's proposal. It announces the acquirer's intention to potential bidders to acquire a specified system or system element (product or service). (Adapted from ISO/IEC/IEEE 15289, 2019)
Requirements imposed on enabling systems	Identified requirements for enabling systems of the system-of-interest.
Reused system or system element	System or system element (product or service) reused by an organization consistent with its system element requirements.
Risk management records/artifacts	Permanent, readable form of data, information, or knowledge related to risk management.
Risk management report	An account prepared for interested parties in order to communicate the status, results, and outcomes of the risk management activities.
Risk management strategy/approach	Approaches, schedules, resources, and specific considerations required to perform risk management.
Risk register	A repository that supports the availability for use and communication of all relevant risk information in a timely, complete, valid, and, if required, confidential manner.
Source documents	External documents relevant to the particular stage of the system of interest.
Stakeholder identification	List of individuals or organizations having a right, share, claim, or interest in a system or in its possession of characteristics that meet their needs and expectations. (Adapted from ISO/IEC/IEEE 15288, 2023)

输入 / 输出描述

（续）

典型的输入 / 输出	描述
质量管理记录 / 制品	与质量管理有关的永久可读取形式的数据、信息或知识
质量管理报告	为有关方准备的一份记述报告，以便沟通质量管理活动的状态、结果和成果
质量管理策略 / 实施方法	执行质量管理所需的实施方法、进度、资源和特定考虑因素
质量管理系统	用于支持和启动质量管理的系统
记录 / 制品	所有适用生命周期流程的记录，包括：采购记录 / 制品、供应记录 / 制品、生命周期模型管理记录 / 制品、基础设施管理记录 / 制品、项目群管理记录 / 制品、人力资源管理记录 / 制品、质量管理记录 / 制品、知识管理记录 / 制品、项目规划记录 / 制品、项目评估和控制记录 / 制品、决策管理记录 / 制品、风险管理记录 / 制品、构型配置管理记录 / 制品、信息管理记录 / 制品、测量记录 / 制品、质量保证记录 / 制品、业务或任务分析记录 / 制品、利益相关者需要和需求定义记录 / 制品、系统需求定义记录 / 制品、系统架构定义记录 / 制品、设计定义记录 / 制品、系统分析记录 / 制品、实施记录 / 制品、综合记录 / 制品、验证记录 / 制品、转移记录 / 制品、确认记录 / 制品、运行记录 / 制品、维护和后勤记录 / 制品、处置记录 / 制品、剪裁记录 / 制品
供应请求	采办方要求供应商提供潜在供应商建议书中必须包含的信息和承诺。它向潜在投标人宣布采办方有意采办指定的系统或系统元素（产品或服务）。（改编自 ISO/IEC/IEEE 15289，2019）
对使能系统的需求	确定对所感兴趣之系统的使能系统的需求
重复使用的系统或系统元素	一个组织根据其系统要素需求重复使用的系统或系统要素（产品或服务）
风险管理记录 / 制品	与风险管理有关的永久可读取形式的数据、信息或知识
风险管理报告	为有关方准备的一份记述报告，以便沟通风险管理活动的状态、结果和成果
风险管理策略 / 实施方法	执行风险管理所需的实施方法、进度、资源和特定考虑因素
风险登记	支持及时、完整、有效并在必要时保密地使用和交流所有相关风险信息的信息库
源文件	与所感兴趣之系统的采购活动的特殊阶段有关的外部文件。与组织策略和方针相关的源文件中包含的书面指令
利益相关方识别	对某一系统或该系统拥有的满足其需要和期望的特性拥有权利、份额、主张或利益的个人或组织清单。（改编自 ISO/IEC/IEEE 15288，2023）

INPUT/OUTPUT DESCRIPTIONS

(Continued)

Typical Input/Output	Description
Stakeholder needs and requirements	Structured collection of the requirements [characteristics, context, concepts, constraints and priorities] of the stakeholder and the relationship to the external environment. (ISO/IEC/IEEE 29148, 2018)
Stakeholder needs and requirements definition records/artifacts	Permanent, readable form of data, information, or knowledge related to stakeholder needs and requirements definition.
Stakeholder needs and requirements definition report	An account prepared for interested parties in order to communicate the status, results, and outcomes of the stakeholder needs and requirements definition activities.
Stakeholder needs and requirements definition strategy/approach	Approaches, schedules, resources, and specific considerations required to perform stakeholder needs and requirements definition.
Standards	This handbook and relevant industry, country, military, acquirer, and other specifications and standards. Includes new knowledge from industry sponsored knowledge networks.
Supplied system or system element	System or system element (product or service) delivered from a supplier to an acquirer consistent with the delivery conditions of the supply agreement.
Supply agreement	Mutual acknowledgment of terms and conditions under which a working relationship is conducted between a supplier and an acquirer. (Adapted from ISO/IEC/IEEE 15288, 2023)
Supply payment	Payments or other compensations for the supplied system.
Supply records/artifacts	Permanent, readable form of data, information, or knowledge related to supply.
Supply report	An account prepared for interested parties in order to communicate the status, results, and outcomes of the supply activities.
Supply response	Prepared by a potential supplier to support the offer of a contract bid, including cost, schedule, risk statements, methodology to satisfy the request for supply, experiences and capabilities, any recommendations to tailor the request for supply or contract, and the signature of the supplier's approving authority. Informally, may be prepared within an organization. (Adapted from ISO/IEC/IEEE 15289, 2019)
Supply strategy/approach	Approaches, schedules, resources, and specific considerations required to perform supply.
System analysis records/artifacts	Permanent, readable form of data, information, or knowledge related to system analysis.
System analysis report	An account prepared for interested parties in order to communicate the status, results, and outcomes of the system analysis activities.
System analysis request	A request to conduct a system analysis.

输入 / 输出描述

（续）

典型的输入 / 输出	描述
利益相关方需要和需求	利益相关方的需求［特征、背景环境、概念、限制和优先级］以及与外部环境的关系的结构化集合。（ISO/IEC/IEEE 29148，2018）
利益相关方需要和需求定义记录 / 制品	与利益相关方需要和需求定义有关的永久可读取形式的数据、信息或知识
利益相关方需要和需求定义报告	为有关方准备的一份记述报告，以便沟通利益相关方需要和需求定义活动的状态、结果和成果
利益相关方需要和需求定义策略 / 实施方法	执行利益相关方需要和需求定义所需的实施方法、进度、资源和特定考虑因素
标准	本手册和相关的行业、国家、军用、采办方规范和标准以及其他规范和标准。包括来自于行业资助知识网络的新知识
所供应的系统或系统元素	供应商按照供应协议的交付条件向采办方交付的系统或系统元素（产品或服务）
供应协议	供应商和采办方之间建立工作关系所依据的相互承认的条款和条件。（改编自 ISO/IEC/IEEE 15288，2023）
供应款项	供应的系统的款项或其他补偿
供应记录 / 制品	与供应有关的永久可读取形式的数据、信息或知识
供应报告	为有关方准备一份记述报告，以便沟通供应活动的状态、结果和成果
供应响应	潜在供应商为支持合同投标报价而编写的文件，包括成本、进度、风险声明、满足供应要求的方法、经验和能力、任何调整供应要求或合同的建议，以及供应商批准机构的签名。非正式情况下，可在组织内部编写。（改编自 ISO/IEC/IEEE 15289，2019）
供应策略 / 实施方法	执行供应所需的实施方法、进度、资源和特定考虑因素
系统分析记录 / 制品	与系统分析有关的永久可读取形式的数据、信息或知识
系统分析报告	为有关方准备的一份记述报告，以便沟通系统分析活动的状态、结果和成果
系统分析请求	进行系统分析的请求

INPUT/OUTPUT DESCRIPTIONS

(Continued)

Typical Input/Output	Description
System analysis strategy/approach	Approaches, schedules, resources, and specific considerations required to perform system analysis.
System architecture assessment report	Provides results of system architecture assessments. It includes evaluation criteria. (Adapted from ISO/IEC/IEEE 15289, 2019)
System architecture definition records/artifacts	Permanent, readable form of data, information, or knowledge related to system architecture definition.
System architecture definition report	An account prepared for interested parties in order to communicate the status, results, and outcomes of the system architecture definition activities.
System architecture definition strategy/approach	Approaches, schedules, resources, and specific considerations required to perform system architecture definition.
System architecture description	The fundamental conception of a system-of-interest in terms of its purpose, system qualities (such as feasibility, performance, safety, and interoperability), constraints, and design decisions and rationale. Identification of the architecture's stakeholders and the stakeholders' architecture-related concerns. (Adapted from ISO/IEC/IEEE 15289, 2019)
System architecture rationale	Rationale for architecture selection, technological/technical system element selection, and allocation between system requirements and architectural entities.
System design assessment report	Provides results of system design assessments. It includes evaluation criteria. (Adapted from ISO/IEC/IEEE 15289, 2019)
System design characteristics	Design attributes or distinguishing features that pertain to a measurable description of a product or service. (ISO/IEC/IEEE 15288, 2023)
System design description	Describes the design of a system or element. (Adapted from ISO/IEC/IEEE 24765, 2017)
System design rationale	Rationale for design selection, system element selection, and allocation between system requirements and system elements. Includes rationale of major selected implementation options and enablers.
System element	System element (product or service) implemented consistent with its system element requirements.
System element description	Applies the system architecture description to the low-level system configuration items and elements. It is at a level of detail to permit design, implementation, and test. (Adapted from ISO/IEC/IEEE 15289, 2019)
System interface definition	Description of the interfaces between systems and system elements. (Adapted from ISO/IEC/IEEE 24765, 2017)
System requirements	Structured collection of the requirements [functions, performance, design constraints, and other attributes] for the system and its operational environments and external interfaces. (ISO/IEC/IEEE 29148, 2018)
System requirements definition records/artifacts	Permanent, readable form of data, information, or knowledge related to system requirements definition.
System requirements definition report	An account prepared for interested parties in order to communicate the status, results, and outcomes of the system requirements definition activities.

（续）

典型的输入/输出	描述
系统分析策略/实施方法	执行系统分析所需的实施方法、进度、资源和特定考虑因素
系统架构评估报告	提供系统架构评估结果。其中包括评估准则。（改编自 ISO/IEC/IEEE 15289，2019）
系统架构定义记录/制品	与系统架构定义有关的永久可读取形式的数据、信息或知识
系统架构定义报告	为有关方准备的一份记述报告，以便沟通系统架构定义活动的状态、结果和成果
系统架构定义策略/实施方法	执行系统架构定义所需的实施方法、进度、资源和特定考虑因素
系统架构描述	从目的、系统质量（如可行性、性能、安全性和互操作性）、制约因素以及设计决策和理由等方面对相关系统进行基本构思。确定架构的利益相关方和利益相关方对架构的关切。（改编自 ISO/IEC/IEEE 15289，2019）
系统架构基本原理	架构选择、科技/技术系统元素选择以及系统要求与架构实体之间分配的理由
系统设计评估报告	提供系统设计评估结果。其中包括评估准则。（改编自 ISO/IEC/IEEE 15289，2019）
系统设计特征	与产品或服务的可测量描述相关的设计属性或显著特征。（ISO/IEC/IEEE 15288，2023）
系统设计描述	描述系统或系统元素的设计。（改编自 ISO/IEC/IEEE 24765，2017）
系统设计基本原理	设计选择、系统元素选择以及系统需求和系统元素之间分配的理由。包括主要选定实施方案和使能因素的理由
系统元素	系统元素（产品或服务）的实施符合其系统元素需求
系统元素描述	将系统架构描述应用于底层系统配置项目和元素。其详细程度允许进行设计、实施和测试。（改编自 ISO/IEC/IEEE 15289，2019）
系统接口识别	描述系统和系统元素之间的接口。（改编自 ISO/IEC/IEEE 24765，2017）
系统需求	系统及其运行环境和外部接口的需求[功能、性能、设计限制和其他属性]的结构化集合。（ISO/IEC/IEEE 29148，2018）
系统需求定义记录/制品	与系统需求定义有关的永久可读取形式的数据、信息或知识
系统需求定义报告	为有关方准备的一份记述报告，以便沟通系统需求定义活动的状态、结果和成果

INPUT/OUTPUT DESCRIPTIONS

(Continued)

Typical Input/Output	Description
System requirements definition strategy/approach	Approaches, schedules, resources, and specific considerations required to perform system requirements definition.
System viewpoints, views, and models	Definitions of viewpoints to document the procedures for creating, interpreting, analyzing, and evaluating architectural data. One or more views of the system. Each architectural view is a representation of the complete system from the perspective of one or more system concerns, for its stakeholders. (Adapted from ISO/IEC/IEEE 15289, 2019)
Systems engineering management plan (SEMP)	Presents how the project processes and activities are executed to assure the project's successful completion, and the quality of the deliverable product or service. (Adapted from ISO/IEC/IEEE 15289, 2019)
Tailoring records/artifacts	Permanent, readable form of data, information, or knowledge related to tailoring.
Traceability mapping	Records the relationship between two or more artifacts of the development process (e.g., requirements, functions, system elements, verifications, and validations, tasks). (Adapted from ISO/IEC/IEEE 24765, 2017)
Trained personnel	Trained individuals or organizations that perform the operation, maintenance, or other functions of or for a system.
Training materials	Materials for the provision of formal and informal learning activities. (Adapted from ISO/IEC/IEEE 24765, 2017)
Transition records/artifacts	Permanent, readable form of data, information, or knowledge related to transition.
Transition report	An account prepared for interested parties in order to communicate the status, results, and outcomes of the transition activities.
Transition strategy/approach	Approaches, schedules, resources, and specific considerations required to perform transition.
Validated stakeholder needs and requirements	Set of stakeholder needs and requirements that have been validated.
Validated system	System (product or service) that has been validated.
Validated system architecture and design	System architecture and design that has been validated.
Validation criteria	The validation criteria (the measures to be assessed), who will perform validation activities, and the validation environments of the system-of-interest.
Validation procedure	Presents an ordered series of steps to perform validation.
Validation records/artifacts	Permanent, readable form of data, information, or knowledge related to validation.
Validation report	An account prepared for interested parties in order to communicate the status, results, and outcomes of the validation activities.
Validation strategy/approach	Approaches, schedules, resources, and specific considerations required to perform validation.

输入 / 输出描述

（续）

典型的输入 / 输出	描述
系统需求定义策略 / 实施方法	执行系统需求定义所需的实施方法、进度、资源和特定考虑因素
系统视角、视图、模型	视角的定义，用于记录创建、解释、分析和评估架构数据的程序。一个或多个系统视图。每个架构视图都是从一个或多个系统透视的关切角度，为利益相关方呈现完整的系统。（改编自 ISO/IEC/IEEE 15289，2019）
系统工程管理计划	提出如何执行项目流程和活动，以确保项目顺利完成以及交付产品或服务的质量。（改编自 ISO/IEC/IEEE 15289，2019）
剪裁记录 / 制品	与剪裁有关的永久可读取形式的数据、信息或知识
可追溯性映射	记录开发过程中两个或多个制品（如需求、功能、系统元素、验证和确认、任务）之间的关系。（改编自 ISO/IEC/IEEE 24765，2017）
经培训的人员	执行系统操作、维护或其他功能的训练有素的个人或组织
培训资料	提供形式化和非形式化学习活动的材料。（改编自 ISO/IEC/IEEE 24765，2017）
转移记录 / 制品	与转移有关的永久可读取形式的数据、信息或知识
转移报告	为有关方准备的一份记述报告，以便沟通转移活动的状态、结果和成果
转移策略 / 实施方法	执行转移所需的实施方法、进度、资源和特定考虑因素
确认的利益相关方需要和需求	经过确认的利益相关方需要和需求集
已确认的系统	经过确认的系统（产品或服务）
确认的系统架构和设计	经过确认的系统架构和设计
确认准则	确认准则（要评估的测度）、谁来执行确认活动以及所感兴趣的系统的确认环境
确认程序	提出一系列有序的确认步骤
确认记录 / 制品	与确认有关的永久可读取形式的数据、信息或知识
确认报告	为有关方准备的一份记述报告，以便沟通确认活动的状态、结果和成果
确认策略 / 实施方法	执行确认所需的实施方法、进度、资源和特定考虑因素

INPUT/OUTPUT DESCRIPTIONS

(Continued)

Typical Input/Output	Description
Variance/deviation/waiver request	Request, temporary or permanent, to accept a configuration item or other designated item which, during production or after having been submitted for inspection, is found to depart from specified requirements, but is nevertheless considered suitable for use as is or after rework by an approved method. (Adapted from ISO/IEC/IEEE 24765, 2017)
Verification criteria	The verification criteria (the measures to be assessed), who will perform verification activities, and the verification environments of the system-of-interest.
Verification procedure	Presents an ordered series of steps to perform verification.
Verification records/artifacts	Permanent, readable form of data, information, or knowledge related to verification.
Verification report	An account prepared for interested parties in order to communicate the status, results, and outcomes of the verification activities.
Verification strategy/ approach	Approaches, schedules, resources, and specific considerations required to perform verification.
Verified system	System (product or service) that has been verified.
Verified system architecture and design	System architecture and design that has been verified.
Verified system requirements	Set of system requirements that have been verified.

输入 / 输出描述

（续）

典型的输入 / 输出	描述
变更 / 偏离 / 豁免请求	临时或永久请求接受在生产过程中或在送检后发现与规定要求不符，但仍被认为是适合按原样使用或以经批准的方法返工后使用的配置物品或其他指定物品。（改编自 ISO/IEC/IEEE 24765，2017）
验证准则	验证准则（要评估的测度）、谁来执行验证活动以及所感兴趣的系统的验证环境
验证程序	提出一系列有序的确认步骤
验证记录 / 制品	与验证有关的永久可读取形式的数据、信息或知识
验证报告	为有关方准备的一份记述报告，以便沟通验证活动的状态、结果和成果
验证策略 / 实施方法	执行验证所需的实施方法、进度、资源和特定考虑因素
已验证的系统	经过验证的系统（产品或服务）
已验证的系统架构和设计	经过验证的系统架构和设计
已验证的系统需求	经过验证的系统需求集

APPENDIX F: ACKNOWLEDGMENTS

The INCOSE Systems Engineering Handbook Fifth Edition editorial team owes a debt of gratitude to all the contributors to prior editions (versions 1, 2, 2A, 3.n, and 4). Tim Robertson led the effort to create Version 1 of the handbook. Version 2 was led by: James Whalen, ESEP and Richard Wray, ESEP. Version 3 was led at various times by: Kevin Forsberg, ESEP; Terje Fossnes, ESEP; Douglas Hamelin; Cecilia Haskins, ESEP; Michael Krueger, ESEP; and David Walden, ESEP. The Fourth Edition was led by David Walden, ESEP. The framework they provided gave a solid basis for moving ahead with this edition. This revision reflects changes to the previous version based on three primary objectives: first, to reflect the updated ISO/IEC/IEEE 15288:2023 standard; second, to reflect the state-of-the-good-practice based on inputs from the relevant INCOSE Working Groups (WGs); and third, reflect changes suggested by the INCOSE community.[1]

A great deal of effort and enthusiasm was provided by the key authors, many of whom also serve as INCOSE WG Chairs or SEBoK authors. We acknowledge them in alphabetical order: Juan Amenabar, ESEP; Randy Anway; James Armstrong, ESEP; Albertyn Barnard; William Bearden, CSEP; Peter Bernus; Dawn Beyer; Mike Boardman; Guy André Boy; Barclay Brown, ESEP; Dale Brown; Jeffrey Brown; Christopher Browne, CSEP; John Brtis, CSEP; Javier Calvo-Amodio; Yann Chazal; Cindy Chen; John Clark, CSEP; Daniel Cobb, CSEP; Peter Coleman; Iain Cunningham; Kenneth Cureton; Cihan Dagli; Judith Dahmann; Alain Dauron; Hans Peter de Koning; William Donaldson; Rick Dove; Rod Dreisbach; Adrianna D'Souza, CSEP; Daniel Eisenberg; Richard Fairley; Paul Frenz, ESEP; Sanford Friedenthal; Jean-Luc Garnier; Donald Gelosh, ESEP; Peter Graham, ASEP; Alan Harding; Cecilia Haskins, ESEP; Porter Haskins, CSEP; Michael Henshaw; David Hetherington; Oliver Hoehne, CSEP; Adam Hulse, CSEP; Mike Jackson; Scott Jackson; Chamara

---

INCOSE Systems Engineering Handbook: A Guide for System Life Cycle Processes and Activities, Fifth Edition.

Edited by David D. Walden, Thomas M. Shortell, Garry J. Roedler, Bernardo A. Delicado, Odile Mornas, Yip Yew-Seng, and David Endler.

© 2023 John Wiley & Sons Ltd. Published 2023 by John Wiley & Sons Ltd.

附录 F：致谢

INCOSE 系统工程手册第 5 版编辑团队对之前版本（版本 1、2、2A、3.n 和 4）的所有贡献者表示感谢。Tim Robertson 领导了创建手册第 1 版的工作。第 2 版由 James Whalen，ESEP 和 Richard Wray，ESEP 领导。第 3 版在不同时期由下列人员领导：Kevin Forsberg，ESEP；Terje Fossnes，ESEP；Douglas Hamelin；Cecilia Haskins，ESEP；Michael Krueger，ESEP；David Walden，ESEP。第 4 版由 David Walden，ESEP 领导。他们提供的框架为这个版本的开发提供了坚实的基础。本次修订反映了基于以下三个主要目标对前一版本所做的修改：第一，反映更新的 ISO/IEC/IEEE 15288：2023 标准；第二，反映基于 INCOSE 相关工作组意见的最新实践状况；第三，反映 INCOSE 社区建议的变化。

主要作者付出了巨大的努力和热情，其中许多人同时担任 INCOSE 工作组主席或 SEBoK 作者。我们对下列人员表示感谢（按名字首字母顺序排列）：Juan Amenabar，ESEP；Randy Anway；James Armstrong，ESEP；Albertyn Barnard；William Bearden，CSEP；Peter Bernus；Dawn Beyer；Mike Boardman；Guy André Boy；Barclay Brown，ESEP；Dale Brown；Jeffrey Brown；Christopher Browne，CSEP；John Brtis，CSEP；Javier Calvo-Amodio；Yann Chazal；Cindy Chen；John Clark，CSEP；Daniel Cobb，CSEP；Peter Coleman；Iain Cunningham；Kenneth Cureton；Cihan Dagli；Judith Dahmann；Alain Dauron；Hans Peter de Koning；William Donaldson；Rick Dove；Rod Dreisbach；Adrianna D'Souza，CSEP；Daniel Eisenberg；Richard Fairley；Paul Frenz，ESEP；Sanford Friedenthal；Jean-Luc Garnier；Donald Gelosh，ESEP；Peter Graham，ASEP；Alan Harding；Cecilia Haskins，ESEP；Porter Haskins，CSEP；Michael Henshaw；David Hetherington；Oliver Hoehne，CSEP；Adam Hulse，CSEP；Mike Jackson；Scott Jackson；Chamara Johnson，CSEP；John Juhasz；Alexander Karl；David Kaslow；Tami Katz，ESEP；Duncan Kemp；Bob Kenley，ESEP；Grace Kennedy，CSEP；Larry Kennedy；Ron Kenett；Bill Klimack，CSEP；Alain Kouassi，

ACKNOWLEDGMENTS

Johnson, CSEP; John Juhasz; Alexander Karl; David Kaslow; Tami Katz, ESEP; Duncan Kemp; Bob Kenley, ESEP; Grace Kennedy, CSEP; Larry Kennedy; Ron Kenett; Bill Klimack, CSEP; Alain Kouassi, CSEP; Charles Krueger; Eric Krueger; Anand Kumar; William Lawless; Alejandro Levi, CSEP; Ivan Mactaggart; Ray Madachy; Robert Malins; Thomas Manley, CSEP; James Martin; Sean McCoy, CSEP; Dorothy McKinney; Curt McNamara; William Miller; Ricardo Moraes; Perri Nejib, ESEP; Meaghan O'Neil; Bohdan Oppenheim; Gregory Parnell, CSEP; Bob Parro; Tasha Penner, CSEP; Michael Pennotti; Troy Peterson, CSEP; Andrew Pickard; Edward Pohl; Stephen Powley; Tim Rabbets; Susan Ronning, ASEP; Larri Rosser, ASEP; David Rousseau; Jean-Claude Roussel, ESEP; Gary Rushton; Michael Ryan; Frank Salvatore, ESEP; Bill Scheible, ESEP; William Schindel, CSEP; Christopher Schreiber; Zane Scott, ASEP; Dr. Alice F. Squires, ESEP-ACQ; Dr. Tina P. Srivastava; Kim Stansfield; Jack Stein; Drew Stovall; Bob Swarz; Corrie Taljaard; Maurice Theobald; Sergey Tozik; Hubertus Tummescheit; Laura Uden, CSEP; Christopher Unger, ESEP; Ricardo Valerdi; Marcel van de Ven, CSEP; Harry van der Velde, CSEP; Andreas van Zyl; Michael Vinarcik, ESEP; Charles Wasson, ESEP; Michael Watson; Louis Wheatcraft; Clifford Whitcomb; Raymond Wolfgang, CSEP; Hazel Woodcock, ESEP; Edward Yakabovicz; Michael Yokell, ESEP; Lori Zipes, ESEP; and Avigdor Zonnenshain. We also acknowledge the INCOSE UK Energy Systems Interest Group, the INCOSE-PMI Alliance, ISO, and NAFEMS for their support.

The INCOSE Technical Operations reviews were led by TJ Ferrell and facilitated by Molly Kovaka. The reviews generated excellent comments that significantly improved the handbook. Other individual and group reviewers also generated useful review comments. Space prevents us from acknowledging them individually. We also thank the INCOSE Corporate Advisory Board (CAB), the INCOSE Certification Advisory Group (CAG), and the specific and anonymous reviewers who provided comments on the Fourth Edition. Their inputs were much appreciated.

The editors thank Vitech, A Zuken Company, for the use of their GENESYS™ tool, which was used to create an underlying process model that helped ensure consistency in the handbook IPO diagrams. We also thank Jama for the use of their Connect® tool to help manage the significant number of handbook requirements. The editors also thank Taylor Riethle for her graphical support with key handbook figures and the Wiley team for their editorial support.

CSEP；Charles Krueger；Eric Krueger；Anand Kumar；William Lawless；Alejandro Levi，CSEP；Ivan Mactaggart；Ray Madachy；Robert Malins；Thomas Manley，CSEP；James Martin；Sean McCoy，CSEP；Dorothy McKinney；Curt McNamara；William Miller；Ricardo Moraes；Perri Nejib，ESEP；Meaghan O'Neil；Bohdan Oppenheim；Gregory Parnell，CSEP；Bob Parro；Tasha Penner，CSEP；Michael Pennotti；Troy Peterson，CSEP；Andrew Pickard；Edward Pohl；Stephen Powley；Tim Rabbets；Susan Ronning，ASEP；Larri Rosser，ASEP；David Rousseau；Jean-Claude Roussel，ESEP；Gary Rushton；Michael Ryan；Frank Salvatore，ESEP；Bill Scheible，ESEP；William Schindel，CSEP；Christopher Schreiber；Zane Scott，ASEP；Dr. Alice F. Squires，ESEP-ACQ；Dr. Tina P. Srivastava；Kim Stansfield；Jack Stein；Drew Stovall；Bob Swarz；Corrie Taljaard；Maurice Theobald；Sergey Tozik；Hubertus Tummescheit；Laura Uden，CSEP；Christopher Unger，ESEP；Ricardo Valerdi；Marcel van de Ven，CSEP；Harry van der Velde，CSEP；Andreas van Zyl；Michael Vinarcik，ESEP；Charles Wasson，ESEP；Michael Watson；Louis Wheatcraft；Clifford Whitcomb；Raymond Wolfgang，CSEP；Hazel Woodcock，ESEP；Edward Yakabovicz；Michael Yokell，ESEP；Lori Zipes，ESEP；和 Avigdor Zonnenshain。我们也感谢 INCOSE 英国能源系统兴趣小组、INCOSE-PMI 联盟、ISO 和 NAFEMS 的支持。

INCOSE 技术操作评审由 TJ Ferrell 领导，Molly Kovaka 协助。评审形成了非常好的意见，极大地改进了手册的质量。其他个人和小组评审者也产生了有用的评审意见。篇幅所限，我们无法逐一感谢他们。我们还要感谢 INCOSE 企业咨询委员会（CAB）、INCOSE 认证咨询小组（CAG），以及对第 4 版提出意见的特定和匿名评审人。非常感谢他们的意见。

编者为使用 Zuken 公司旗下的 Vitech 公司的 GENESYS™ 工具而向其表示感谢，该工具创建了一个基础流程模型，有助于确保手册 IPO 图表的一致性。我们还要为使用 Jama 公司的 Connect® 工具向其表示感谢，该工具帮助我们管理大量的手册需求。编者还要感谢 Taylor Riethle 为手册关键数据提供的图表支持，

ACKNOWLEDGMENTS

Any errors introduced as part of the editorial process rest with the editors, not the contributors.

We apologize if we unintentionally omitted anyone from these lists.

Gratefully,

David D. Walden, ESEP

Thomas M. Shortell, CSEP

Garry J. Roedler, ESEP

Bernardo A. Delicado, ESEP

Odile Mornas, ESEP

Yip Yew-Seng, CSEP

David Endler, ESEP

以及 Wiley 团队提供的编辑支持。

在编著过程中引入的任何错误都由编者负责，而不是贡献者。

如果我们无意中遗漏了这些名单中的任何人，在此致以歉意。

敬上，

David D. Walden，ESEP

Thomas M. Shortell，CSEP

Garry J. Roedler，ESEP

Bernardo A. Delicado，ESEP

Odile Mornas，ESEP

Yip Yew-Seng，CSEP

David Endler，ESEP

COMMENT FORM

APPENDIX G: COMMENT FORM

Comments and suggestions from users of the handbook are welcome. Please make sure your inputs are actionable by following the suggested format below.[2]

Reviewed document:	INCOSE SE Handbook Fifth Edition
Name of submitter:	Given FAMILY (given name and family name)
Date submitted:	DD-MMM-YYYY
Contact info:	john.doe@anywhere.com (email address)
Type of submission:	Individual or Group
Group name and number of contributors:	INCOSE XYZ WG (if applicable)
Comments:	Detailed comments with reference to document section, paragraph, etc. Please include detailed recommendations, as shown in the table below

Send comments to: info@incose.org

Comment ID (if multiple comments, sequential for your set of comments)	Category (TH, TL, E, G—see below)	Section number (e.g., 3.4.2.1)	Specific reference (e.g., paragraph, line, figure, table)	Issue, comment, and rationale (rationale must make comment clearly evident and supportable)	Proposed change/ new text (mandatory entry, must be substantial to increase the odds of acceptance)

TH, technical high; TL, technical low; E, editorial; G, general

INCOSE Systems Engineering Handbook: A Guide for System Life Cycle Processes and Activities, Fifth Edition.

Edited by David D. Walden, Thomas M. Shortell, Garry J. Roedler, Bernardo A. Delicado, Odile Mornas, Yip Yew-Seng, and David Endler.

© 2023 John Wiley & Sons Ltd. Published 2023 by John Wiley & Sons Ltd.

附录 G：意见表

欢迎手册用户提出意见和建议。请确保您的意见和建议具有可操作性，请按照以下建议的格式提出。

评审的文档：	INCOSE 系统工程手册 v5.0
提交者姓名：	姓名（名字和姓氏）
提交日期：	DD - MMM - YYYY
联系方式：	john.doe@anywhere.com（电子邮件地址）
提交形式：	个人 / 团体
团体名称和贡献者数量：	INCOSE XYZ 工作组（如果适用）
意见：	关于文档章节、段落等的详细意见，请提供详细建议，如下表所示。

将意见发送至 info@incose.org

意见 ID（如果有多条意见，请按顺序填写您的意见集）	类别(TH, TL, E, G—见下）	章节号（例如，3.4.2.1）	特定参考（如段、行、图、表）	问题、意见和基本原理（基本原理的阐述必须是清晰、明显和言之有据的）	建议性变更 / 新文本强制性输入（对于提高接受机会是非常重要的）

TH，技术性高；TL，技术性低；E，编辑；G，一般

INDEX

Note: Index only shows primary entries for commonly used terms.

accessibility, see reliability, availability, maintainability (RAM)

acquirer, see also supplier, 2, 3, 5, 33, 44–50, 65, 76, 89, 97, 106, 114–115, 128, 140, 145–152, 168, 176–179, 203, 252, 253, 311, 313, 321, 330–331

acquisition process, 45–48

adaptability, *see* agility

aerospace, *see* commercial aerospace systems

affordability, 97, 130, 160–165, 313

aggregate, 135–137, 181, 205–206, 238, 325

agile, 21, 29, 38–39, 72, 90, 137, 165–168, 188–189, 221–224, 274, 309, 311

agility, 161, 165–168, 181, 223, 274^3

agreement(s), 44–51, 60, 65, 70–71, 74, 76, 86, 107, 145, 148, 179, 202–203, 216, 218, 232, 237, 311, 321–322, 331

allocate/allocation, 43–44, 48, 56–63, 70, 74, 83, 99, 112–117, 121–128, 144, 174, 198, 203, 221, 232, 233, 252–253, 257, 267–268, 332

analysis, *see also* inspection, demonstration, and test, 131, 136, 139, 142, 147

architect, 20, 191, 311, 314

architecture, 2, 4, 8, 9, 42–44, 74, 78, 101, 115, 118–129, 137, 142, 150–151, 166–167, 178, 180–182, 198, 201, 203–205, 206–208, 212, 230, 232, 237, 243–244, 252,254, 268, 311, 314, 332–334

architecture definition, see system architecture definition

INCOSE Systems Engineering Handbook: A Guide for System Life Cycle Processes and Activities, Fifth Edition.

Edited by David D. Walden, Thomas M. Shortell, Garry J. Roedler, Bernardo A. Delicado, Odile Mornas, Yip Yew-Seng, and David Endler.

© 2023 John Wiley & Sons Ltd. Published 2023 by John Wiley & Sons Ltd.

索引

（原书页码，见偶数页左侧标注）

注：索引只显示常用术语的主要条目。

可访问性，见 可靠性、可用性和可维护性（RAM）

采办方，另见 供应商，2，3，5，33，44–50，65，76，89，97，106，114–115，128，140，145–152，168，176–179，203，252，253，311，313，321，330–331

采办流程，45–48

适应性，见 敏捷性

太空，见 商业太空系统

可承受性，97，130，160–165，313

聚集，135–137，181，205–206，238，325

敏捷，21，29，38–39，72，90，137，165–168，188–189，221–224，274，309，311

敏捷性，161，165–168，181，223，274

协议，44–51，60，65，70–71，74，76，86，107，145，148，179，202–203，216，218，232，237，311，321–322，331

分配（动词）/分配（名词），43–44，48，56–63，70，74，83，99，112–117，121–128，144，174，198，203，221，232，233，252–253，257，267–268，332

分析，另见 检验、演示和测试，131，136，139，142，147

架构师，20，191，311，314

架构，2，4，8，9，42–44，74，78，101，115，118–129，137，142，150–151，166–167，178，180–182，198，201，203–205，206–208，212，230，232，237，243–244，252，254，268，311，314，332–334

架构定义，见 系统架构定义

INDEX

architecture framework, 120–123, 206–208, 305

artificial intelligence (AI), 5, 170, 249, 275, 283–285, 305

assessment, 18, 20, 52–54, 59, 61–62, 64, 75–78, 81, 86, 98, 114–115, 120, 123, 126, 129, 132, 185, 189–190, 195, 204, 208, 217, 243–244, 261, 280, 332

associate systems engineering professional (ASEP), xxii, 305

attribute, 9, 14, 66, 109, 114–117, 127, 162, 266, 311, 313

audits, *see also* reviews, 31–33, 54, 72–73, 76–78, 89–90, 132–134, 248–249, 252, 313–314, 323

automotive systems, 245–247, 282–285

availability, *see* reliability, availability, maintainability (RAM)

baseline, 31–32, 35–36, 74, 89–90, 105, 110, 114, 117, 131, 133, 136, 140, 148, 200, 204, 218, 312, 322

behavioral architecture, see functional architecture

benchmark, 53–54

bias, 17–18, 110–111, 112, 230

big data-driven systems, see internet of things (IoT)

biomedical and healthcare systems, 248–249

biomimicry, 213

black box, *see also* white box, 9, 13, 200, 312

blank sheet, *see* greenfield

boundary, 8, 10, 21, 113, 120–121, 166, 203–204, 245, 281

brainstorming, 86, 125

breakdown structures, 13, 71–75, 174, 269, 322

brownfield, *see also* greenfield, 145, 229, 230, 259, 278, 312

business or mission analysis process, 103–107

business requirements, 103–107, 252

case studies, 277–285

certified systems engineering professional (CSEP), xxii, 306

索引

架构框架，120–123，206–208，305

人工智能（AI），5，170，249，275，283–285，305

评估，18，20，52–54，59，61–62，64，75–78，81，86，98，114–115，120，123，126，129，132，185，189–190，195，204，208，217，243–244，261，280，332

助理级系统工程专业人员（ASEP），xxii，305

属性，9，14，66，109，114–117，127，162，266，311，313

审核，另见 评审，31–33，54，72–73，76–78，89–90，132–134，248–249，252，313–314，323

汽车系统，245–247，282–285

可用性，见 可靠性、可用性和可维护性（RAM）

基线，31–32，35–36，74，89–90，105，110，114，117，131，133，136，140，148，200，204，218，312，322

行为架构，见 功能架构基准，53–54

偏差，17–18，110–111，112，230

大数据驱动系统，见 物联网（IoT）

生物医学和医疗卫生系统，248–249

仿生学，213

黑盒，另见 白盒，9，13，200，312

空白纸，见 绿地

边界，8，10，21，113，120–121，166，203–204，245，281

头脑风暴，86，125

分解结构，13，71–75，174，269，322

棕地，另见 绿地，145，229，230，259，278，312

业务或任务分析，103–107

业务需求，103–107，252

案例研究，277–285

认证的系统工程专业人员（CSEP），xxii，306

INDEX

change control, 35, 56, 91, 117

changeability, *see* agility

clean sheet, *see* greenfield

cognitive bias *see* bias

commercial off-the-shelf (COTS), 69–70, 122, 134, 231–232, 238, 251, 258

commercial aerospace systems, 8, 246, 249–250

compatibility, see interoperability

competence, 171, 242, 161–262, 312, 314

competency, 21, 62, 226, 242, 261–263, 312

complexity, xix, 2, 5–6, 9–10, 15, 20–24, 33–35, 53, 170, 195, 203, 210, 216, 218, 220, 226, 229, 234, 238, 243, 245–247, 249, 250–251, 253, 255, 257–258, 262, 281–282

concept of operations (ConOps), *see also* operational concept (OpsCon) and life cycle concepts, 104, 106, 108, 152, 154, 182–183, 223, 244, 322

concept stage, 26–28, 222, 278

concurrency, see also iteration and recursion, xxiii, 25, 30, 35, 39, 42–44, 101–103, 110, 112, 115, 145, 152, 154, 176, 192–193, 203, 215, 222, 269

configuration/change control board (CCB), 89, 117

configuration item (CI), 88–89, 155, 312, 322

configuration management process, 87–90

connectivity, see interoperability

consensus, 45, 110, 197

constraint, 3–4, 9, 14, 19, 43, 45, 71–73, 89, 101, 103–105, 107–111, 113–116, 118–123, 125–127, 131, 132–133, 134–137, 139–140, 147–149, 152, 155, 156–157, 160–165, 175, 178, 183–184, 195, 222, 228, 229, 232, 237, 239–240, 244, 262, 272, 279, 312, 323, 326, 328

context, 8–15, 17–20, 21–24, 45, 73–75, 80, 82–83, 86, 88, 101–102, 104–105, 108, 110–111, 117, 119–120, 144–145, 159, 161–163, 168, 192, 204, 207, 212, 220, 224, 237–238, 252, 253

contract(s)/subcontract(s), *see also* agreement, 11, 44–45, 46–48, 50, 91, 99, 115, 139, 145, 147–148, 157, 203, 208, 226, 228, 251, 252–253, 279–280

索引

变更控制，35，56，91，117

可变性，见 敏捷性

空白纸，见 绿地

认知偏差 见 偏差

商用货架产品（COTS），69–70，122，134，231–232，238，251，258

商业航天系统，8，246，249–250

兼容性，见 互操作性

才能，171，242，161–262，312，314

胜任力，21，62，226，242，261–263，312

复杂性，xix，2，5–6，9–10，15，20–24，33–35，53，170，195，203，210，216，218，220，226，229，234，238，243，245–247，249，250–251，253，255，257–258，262，281–282

运行意图（ConOps），另见 运行概念（OpsCon）和 生命周期概念，104，106，108，152，154，182–183，223，244，322

概念阶段，26–28，222，278

并行，另见 迭代和递归，xxiii，25，30，35，39，42–44，101–103，110，112，115，145，152，154，176，192–193，203，215，222，269

构型控制委员会（CCB），89，117

构型配置项（CI），88–89，155，312，322

构型配置管理流程，87–90

连接性，见 互操作性

共识，45，110，197

约束，3–4，9，14，19，43，45，71–73，89，101，103–105，107–111，113–116，118–123，125–127，131，132–133，134–137，139–140，147–149，152，155，156–157，160–165，175，178，183–184，195，222，228，229，232，237，239–240，244，262，272，279，312，323，326，328

背景环境，8–15，17–20，21–24，45，73–75，80，82–83，86，88，101–102，104–105，108，110–111，117，119–120，144–145，159，161–163，168，192，204，207，212，220，224，237–238，252，253

合同/分包合同，另见 协议，11，44–45，46–48，50，91，99，115，139，145，147–148，157，203，208，226，228，251，252–253，279–280

INDEX

cost as an independent variable (CAIV), 162

cost breakdown structure (CBS), see breakdown structures

cost effectiveness, *see* affordability

cost estimating, 16, 160–165, 253

coupling, 19, 208

coupling matrix, *see also* N^2 diagram, 136, 205–206

customer, *see* acquirer

cyber-physical systems (CPS), 180, 228, 233–235, 266, 275

cybersecurity, *see* security

decision gates, *see also* reviews, 25–27, 29–31, 47, 51, 72–73, 75, 252, 312

decision management process, 78–81

decisions, *see* also trade study/trade-off study, 14, 15–16, 17–18, 19, 25–26, 29–31, 42–44, 45–47, 49, 56–57, 59, 61, 63, 76–77, 78–81, 90, 93–98, 105, 114, 119–123, 126, 129–131, 163–164, 167, 170, 175, 178, 184–185, 187, 189, 191, 192, 195–196, 217–218, 220, 223, 231–232, 234, 238–239, 241, 249, 263, 268, 269, 270, 271–272, 275, 278, 284, 323

defense systems, 4, 8, 27, 31, 91, 97, 173, 206–207, 246, 250–251, 256, 285

demonstration, *see also* inspection, analysis, and test, 131, 136, 139, 142, 147

derivation/derived, 9, 94–95, 97–98, 114–115, 123, 132, 149, 154, 178–179, 188, 228, 267

design definition, 124–129

design for X (DFX), see also quality characteristics and approaches, 127, 159

design structure matrix (DSM), *see also* N^2 diagram, 205

design thinking, 127, 170, 212

design to cost (DTC), 165

desirability, *see* human systems integration (HSI)

development models, see life cycle model approaches

development stage, 26–28, 35, 222

DevOps, 38, 90, 221

索引

成本作为独立变量（CAIV），162

成本分解结构（CBS），见 分解结构

成本效益，见 可承受性

成本估算，16，160–165，253

耦合，19，208

耦合矩阵，另见 N^2 图，136，205–206

客户，见采办方

赛博物理系统（CPS），180，228，233–235，266，275

网络安全，见 安保

决策门，另见 评审，25–27，29–31，47，51，72–73，75，252，312

决策管理流程，78–81

决策，另见 权衡研究，14，15–16，17–18，19，25–26，29–31，42–44，45–47，49，56–57，59，61，63，76–77，78–81，90，93–98，105，114，119–123，126，129–131，163–164，167，170，175，178，184–185，187，189，191，192，195–196，217–218，220，223，231–232，234，238–239，241，249，263，268，269，270，271–272，275，278，284，323

防务系统，4，8，27，31，91，97，173，206–207，246，250–251，256，285

证明，另见 检验、分析和测试，131，136，139，142，147

推演/推导，9，94–95，97–98，114–115，123，132，149，154，178–179，188，228，267

设计定义，124–129

X 设计（DFX），另见 质量特性和实施方法，127，159

设计结构矩阵（DSM），另见 N^2 图，205

设计思维，127，170，212

面向成本的设计（DTC），165

可取性，见 人与系统综合（HSI）

开发模型，见 生命周期模型实施方法

开发阶段，26–28，35，222

开发、运行，38，90，221

INDEX

DevSecOps, 38, 90, 221

digital engineering, 5, 81, 93, 95–96, 170, 226, 273–274, 275

digital twin, 11, 175, 193, 202, 228, 234, 273

disposability, *see* sustainability

disposal process, 156–158

diversity, equity, and inclusion (DEI), 265–266

domains/industries/sectors, 244–259

effectiveness, 51–54, 67, 71–72, 75, 83, 87, 89, 96–97, 99, 101, 111, 118, 121–122, 131–132, 161–164, 173, 178, 189, 209

element, *see* system element

emergence and emergent properties/behaviors, 5, 9–10, 15, 21–23, 70, 118, 123, 129, 151, 169–170, 186, 210, 212, 213, 230, 235, 237–238, 240, 245

enabling system, see also interfacing system and interoperating system, 2, 8, 10–11, 16, 19, 26, 28, 33, 56–57, 63, 72, 99, 103–105, 107–111, 113–114, 118–119, 122, 125–126, 130, 132, 134, 135–137, 139–140, 143, 145, 147–148, 152, 154, 155–156, 157–158, 159, 170, 175, 191, 203, 243, 254–255, 267, 268, 324

engineered system, 3, 11–12

enterprise, *see* also organization/organizational, 8, 11–12, 44, 60, 82, 88, 96, 106, 118, 122–123, 124, 206–208, 219, 223, 226, 241–244, 273, 275, 312

environment, 2–3, 8, 9, 10, 11–12, 14, 15, 16, 17, 19, 21, 22, 28, 33, 48, 69, 84, 88, 101, 103, 104–106, 107– 111, 115, 119, 122, 129, 132, 136–137, 142, 143, 144, 146–147, 149–152, 154–155, 156–158, 159, 161, 165–166, 168–169, 171, 173–174, 176–179, 180–182, 184–185, 186–189, 192–193, 202, 204, 206–207, 213–214–215, 221–222, 230, 231, 233–234, 238, 240, 241–242, 244, 248, 250, 272, 273, 276, 279–280, 312

environmental engineering/impact, *see* sustainability

ergonomics, see human systems integration (HSI)

estimating, 28, 50, 53, 71–73, 83–84, 131, 164–165, 168, 177, 179, 239, 261, 272

ethics, 234, 262, 263, 264–265

开发、安保、运行，38，90，221

数字工程，5，81，93，95–96，170，226，273–274，275

数字孪生，11，175，193，202，228，234，273

可处置性，见 可持续性

处置流程，156–158

多样性、公平性和包容性（DEI），265–266

领域/产业/行业，244–259

有效性，51–54，67，71–72，75，83，87，89，96–97，99，101，111，118，121–122，131–132，161–164，173，178，189，209

元素，见 系统元素

涌现性和涌现属性/行为，5，9–10，15，21–23，70，118，123，129，151，169–170，186，210，212，213，230，235，237–238，240，245

使能系统，另见 接口系统和互操作系统，2，8，10–11，16，19，26，28，33，56–57，63，72，99，103–105，107–111，113–114，118–119. 122，125–126，130，132，134，135–137，139–140，143，145，147–148，152，154，155–156，157–158，159，170，175，191，203，243，254–255，267，268，324

工程系统，3，11–12

复杂组织体系，另见 组织/组织的，8，11–12，44，60，82，88，96，106，118，122–123，124，206–208，219，223，226，241–244，273，275，312

环境，2–3，8，9，10，11–12，14，15，16，17，19，21，22，28，33，48，69，84，88，101，103，104–106，107–111，115，119，122，129，132，136–137，142，143，144，146–147，149–152，154–155，156–158，159，161，165–166，168–169，171，173–174，176–179，180–182，184–185，186–189，192–193，202，204，206–207，213–214–215，221–222，230，231，233–234，238，240，241–242，244，248，250，272，273，276，279–280，312

环境工程/影响，见 可持续性

工效，见 人与系统综合（HSI）

估算，28，50，53，71–73，83–84，131，164–165，168，177，179，239，261，272

道德，234，262，263，264–265

INDEX

evaluation criteria, 162, 208

evolutionary, *see also* incremental and sequential, 21, 29, 33–39, 77, 96, 137, 222, 235, 249, 256, 275

evolvability, *see* agility

expert systems engineering professional (ESEP), 306

extensibility, *see* agility

failure, 17, 20, 29, 30, 45, 50, 65, 75, 100, 101, 151, 155–156, 161, 171, 174–175, 176–180, 181, 186–187, 208–211, 266, 269, 312

failure modes, and effects, [and criticality] analysis (FMEA/FMECA), 86, 174, 178, 180, 204

family of systems (FoS)/system family, *see* product line engineering (PLE)/product lines

flexibility, *see* agility

flow-down/flow-up, 115, 193, 221

functional analysis, 8, 88–89, 105–106, 110, 113, 129–131, 133, 134, 159, 166–167, 174, 186–187, 193, 202, 205, 231–232, 233, 238, 239, 266

functional architecture, *see also* physical architecture, 8, 14, 74, 120–121, 124, 126–129, 136–137, 192, 212, 253

functional flow block diagram (FFBD), 204–205,

functional tree/functional breakdown structure (FBS), *see* breakdown structures

future of SE (FuSE), 275–276

gates, *see* decision gate

greenfield, *see also* brownfield, 145, 229–230, 313

habitability, see human systems integration (HSI)

hardware engineering (HWE), 16, 38–39, 267–268, 278

hazard, 124, 169, 186–189, 284

healthcare, see biomedical and healthcare systems

heuristics, see systems engineering heuristics

hierarchy, 12–13, 21, 32, 35, 42–44, 115, 117, 129, 137, 211, 221

评价准则，162，208

演进式，另见 渐进式和顺序式，21，29，33–39，77，96，137，222，235，249，256，275

演进性，见 敏捷性

专家级系统工程专业人员（ESEP），306

可扩展性，见 敏捷性

故障，17，20，29，30，45，50，65，75，100，101，151，155–156，161，171，174–175，176–180，181，186–187，208–211，266，269，312

故障模式、影响与危害性分析（FMEA/FMECA），86，174，178，180，204

系统族（FoS）/系统族，见 产品线工程（PLE）/产品线

柔性，见 敏捷性

向下流/向上流，115，193，221

功能分析，8，88–89，105–106，110，113，129–131，133，134，159，166–167，174，186–187，193，202，205，231–232，233，238，239，266

功能架构，另见 物理架构，8，14，74，120–121，124，126–129，136–137，192，212，253

功能流程方块图（FFBD），204–205，

功能树/功能分解结构（FBS），见 分解结构

未来系统工程（FuSE），275–276

门，见 决策门

绿地，另见 棕地，145，229–230，313

宜居性，见 人与系统综合（HSI）

硬件工程（HWE），16，38–39，267–268，278

危害，124，169，186–189，284

医疗卫生，见 生物医学和医疗卫生系统

启发式方法，见 系统工程启发式方法

层次结构，12–13，21，32，35，42–44，115，117，129，137，211，221

INDEX

horizontal integration, *see also* vertical integration, 10, 14, 44, 90, 110, 124, 137, 203, 218

horizontal traceability, *see also* vertical traceability, 201

human-centered design, *see* human systems integration (HSI)

human-computer interaction (HCI), *see* human systems integration (HSI)

human factors, *see* human systems integration (HSI)

human-machine interface (HMI), see human systems integration (HSI)

human resource management process, 60–63

human systems integration (HSI), 131, 134, 168–171, 201, 212, 249, 255

–ilities, see quality characteristics and approaches

implementation, 132–134

incremental, see also evolutionary and sequential, 28, 31, 33–39, 48, 65, 77, 96, 118, 137, 144–145, 156, 170, 193, 198, 222, 229, 245, 248, 249, 256, 267

incremental commit spiral model (ICSM), 31, 37

industrial engineering (IE), 270–271

information assurance (IA), see security

information management process, 91–93

infrastructure, 54–57, 72–73, 75, 166–167, 174, 175, 234

infrastructure management process, 54–57

infrastructure systems, 251–253

innovation ecosystem, 11–12, 211–212

input-process-output (IPO) diagram, 40, 42, 204, 313

inspection, see also analysis, demonstration, and test, 131, 136, 139, 142, 147

integrated logistics support, see logistics

integration, 134–137

interchangeability, *see* reliability, availability, maintainability (RAM)

interface, 8, 10–11, 89–90, 107–108, 114–115, 119–121, 123–124, 125–127, 130–131, 134–137, 166–167, 172, 197, 204–206, 231, 232–233, 238, 250, 253, 266–268, 313

横向综合，另见 纵向综合，10，14，44，90，110，124，137，203，218

横向可追溯性，另见 纵向可追溯性，201

以人为中心的设计，见 人与系统综合（HSI）

人机交互（HCI），见 人与系统综合（HSI）

人因，见 人与系统综合（HSI）

人机界面（HMI），见 人与系统综合（HSI）

人力资源管理流程，60–63

人与系统综合（HSI），131，134，168–171，201，212，249，255

–性，见 质量特性和实施方法

实施，132–134

增量，另见 进化式和顺序式，28，31，33–39，48，65，77，96，118，137，144–145，156，170，193，198，222，229，245，248，249，256，267

增量承诺螺旋模型（ICSM），31，37

工业工程（IE），270–271

信息保证（IA），见 安保

信息管理流程，91–93

基础设施，54–57，72–73，75，166–167，174，175，234

基础设施管理流程，54–57

基础设施系统，251–253

创新生态，11–12，211–212

输入—流程—输出（IPO）图，40，42，204，313

检验，另见 分析、演示和测试，131，136，139，142，147

综合后勤支持，见 后勤

综合，134–137

可互换性，见 可靠性、可用性和可维护性（RAM）

接口，8，10–11，89–90，107–108，114–115，119–121，123–124，125–127，130–131，134–137，166–167，172，197，204–206，231，232–233，238，250，253，266–268，313

INDEX

interfacing system, *see also* enabling system and interoperating system, 8, 10–11, 108, 136, 148, 152

international council on systems engineering (INCOSE), ix, xix

international organization for standardization (ISO), ix, xxi, xxiii, 3–4

internet of things (IoT), 172, 234–235, 238–239

interoperability, 124, 161, 171–172, 197–198, 209, 240, 248, 249, 251, 254, 256

interoperating system, *see also* enabling system and interfacing system, 8, 10–11, 19, 148

ISO/IEC/IEEE 15288, ix, xxi, xxiii, 3, 41

iteration, *see also* concurrency and recursion, xxiii, 15, 32, 35, 37, 39, 42–44, 72, 95–96, 101–103, 106, 110, 112, 115, 118, 128, 132, 170, 192–194, 203, 211, 215, 221–222, 238, 266

key performance parameters (KPPs), 80, 97

knowledge management process, 67–70

leadership, 2, 66, 229, 237, 263–264, 265

leading indicators, 95–97

lean, 224–226

legacy, see brownfield

lessons learned, 20, 47, 50, 54, 67–70, 136, 225, 239, 252, 326, 328

life cycle concepts, xxiii, 25–33, 175, 202–203, 325

life cycle cost (LCC), *see also* affordability, 7, 38, 132, 158, 160–165, 169, 173, 180, 231–232, 262, 313

life cycle model approaches, 33–36, 77, 110, 221

life cycle model management process, 51–54

life cycle processes, 39–158

life cycle stages, 25–29, 51, 164, 215, 222–223, 314

logical architecture, see functional architecture

logistics, 106, 154–156, 171, 172–175, 178–180, 230, 251, 283

loss-driven systems engineering, 191

索引

接口系统，另见 使能系统和互操作系统，8, 10–11, 108, 136, 148, 152

国际系统工程委员会（INCOSE），ix, xix

国际标准组织（ISO），ix, xxi, xxiii, 3–4

物联网（IoT），172, 234–235, 238–239

互操作性，124, 161, 171–172, 197–198, 209, 240, 248, 249, 251, 254, 256

互操作系统，另见 使能系统和接口系统，8, 10–11, 19, 148

ISO/IEC/IEEE 15288, ix, xxi, xxiii, 3, 41

迭代，另见 并行和递归，xxiii, 15, 32, 35, 37, 39, 42–44, 72, 95–96, 101–103, 106, 110, 112, 115, 118, 128, 132, 170, 192–194, 203, 211, 215, 221–222, 238, 266

关键性能参数（KPPs），80, 97

知识管理流程，67–70

领导，2, 66, 229, 237, 263–264, 265

领先指标，95–97

精益，224–226

遗留，见 棕地

经验教训，20, 47, 50, 54, 67–70, 136, 225, 239, 252, 326, 328

生命周期概念，xxiii, 25–33, 175, 202–203, 325

生命周期成本（LCC），另见 可承受性，7, 38, 132, 158, 160–165, 169, 173, 180, 231–232, 262, 313

生命周期模型实施方法，33–36, 77, 110, 221

生命周期模型管理流程，51–54

生命周期流程，39–158

生命周期阶段，25–29, 51, 164, 215, 222–223, 314

逻辑架构，见 功能架构

后勤，106, 154–156, 171, 172–175, 178–180, 230, 251, 283

损失驱动的系统工程，191

INDEX

maintainability, see reliability, availability, maintainability (RAM)

maintenance process, 154–156

manufacturability/producibility, 175

margin, 20, 48, 98, 151, 246

measurement process, 93–98

measures of effectiveness (MOEs), 80, 95, 97, 131–132, 313

measures of performance (MOPs), 80, 95, 97, 131–132, 313

medical/medical devices, see biomedical and healthcare systems

minimum viable product (MVP), 38

mission analysis see business or mission analysis

mode, *see also* state, 8–9, 14, 117, 120, 148, 182–184, 236

model, *see also* simulation, 11–12, 19, 21, 24, 33–39, 40, 51–53, 118–123, 124–128, 129–131, 137, 141, 150, 175, 192–201, 208–211, 238–239, 273, 274–275, 313

model-based systems engineering (MBSE), 5, 90, 96, 143, 151, 202, 209–211, 219–221, 228, 273, 274–275

modularity, *see* agility

N^2 diagram, 205–206, 252, 313, 317–319

natural systems, see biomimicry

non-developmental item (NDI), *see also* commercial off-the-shelf (COTS), 69

object-oriented systems engineering method (OOSEM), 219–221

oil and gas systems, 187, 253–254

opaque box, see black box operation, 152–154

operational concept (OpsCon), *see also* concept of operations (ConOps), 28, 106, 108, 131, 148, 152–154, 170, 182–183, 325

operations research (OR), 270, 271–272

opportunity, *see also* risk, 27, 35, 44, 59, 78, 81–87, 103–107, 132, 242–244, 265, 327

opportunity management process, *see* risk management process

索引

可维护性, 见 可靠性、可用性和可维护性 (RAM)

维护流程, 154–156

可制造性/可生产性, 175

边际, 20, 48, 98, 151, 246

测量流程, 93–98

有效性测度 (MOEs), 80, 95, 97, 131–132, 313

性能测度 (MOPs), 80, 95, 97, 131–132, 313

医疗/医疗设备, 见 生物医学和医疗卫生系统

最小可行产品 (MVP), 38

任务分析, 见 业务或任务分析

模式, 另见 状态, 8–9, 14, 117, 120, 148, 182–184, 236

模型, 另见 仿真, 11–12, 19, 21, 24, 33–39, 40, 51–53, 118–123, 124–128, 129–131, 137, 141, 150, 175, 192–201, 208–211, 238–239, 273, 274–275, 313

基于模型的系统工程 (MBSE), 5, 90, 96, 143, 151, 202, 209–211, 219–221, 228, 273, 274–275

模块化, 见 敏捷性

N^2 图, 205–206, 252, 313, 317–319

自然系统, 见 仿生学

非开发项目, 另见 商用货架产品 (COTS), 69

面向对象的系统工程方法 (OOSEM), 219–221

石油和天然气系统, 187, 253–254

不透明盒, 见 黑盒运行, 152–154

运行概念 (OpsCon), 另见 运行意图 (ConOps), 28, 106, 108, 131, 148, 152–154, 170, 182–183, 325

运筹学 (OR), 270, 271–272

机会, 另见 风险, 27, 35, 44, 59, 78, 81–87, 103–107, 132, 242–244, 265, 327

机会管理流程, 见 风险管理流程

INDEX

organization/organizational, *see also* enterprise, 16, 19, 44–50, 51–70, 168–171, 215–219, 241–243, 274–275, 313

organizational breakdown structure (OBS), *see* breakdown structures

patterns, 11–12, 21–22, 67–69, 83, 116, 119–120, 123, 141–142, 166, 184, 195, 198–199, 206, 208–212, 222–223, 264

physical architecture, *see also* functional architecture, 4, 8–9, 74, 78, 101–102, 118–124, 127, 132–133, 134–137, 166–167, 182, 198, 201, 203–205, 206–208, 220–221, 226–228, 230, 232, 233, 237, 252, 254, 267–268

physical model, 192, 196, 201

portfolio management process, 57–60

power and energy systems, 254–255

process, 51–54, 70–75, 215–219

producibility, see manufacturability/producibility

product line engineering (PLE)/product lines, 37, 58–59, 67–69, 117, 123, 164, 180, 209–211, 224, 226–229, 312, 314–315

product tree/product breakdown structure (PBS), *see* breakdown structures

production stage, 26–28, 222

professional competencies, *see also* soft skills, 40, 261–263

professional development, 62

project/program, 60, 226, 241–242, 268–270

project assessment and control process, 75–78

project dashboard, *see* status report/dashboard

project management (PM), 11–12, 44, 56, 58–60, 66, 70, 72–73, 85, 95, 111, 118, 223–224, 226, 268–271

project planning process, 71–75

prototyping, 5, 21, 28, 59, 69, 121, 128, 134, 136–137, 170, 200–201, 252, 275

qualification, 120, 130, 151

quality assurance process, 98–101

组织/组织的，另见 复杂组织体系，16，19，44–50，51–70，168–171，215–219，241–243，274–275，313

组织分解结构（OBS），见 分解结构

模式，11–12，21–22，67–69，83，116，119–120，123，141–142，166，184，195，198–199，206，208–212，222–223，264

物理架构，另见功能架构，4，8–9，74，78，101–102，118–124，127，132–133，134–137，166–167，182，198，201，203–205，206–208，220–221，226–228，230，232，233，237，252，254，267–268

物理模型，192，196，201

项目组合管理流程，57–60

电力和能源系统，254–255

流程，51–54，70–75，215–219

可生产性，见 可制造性/可生产性

产品线工程（PLE）/产品线，37，58–59，67–69，117，123，164，180，209–211，224，226–229，312，314–315

产品树/产品分解结构（PBS），见 分解结构

生产阶段，26–28，222

职业胜任力，另见 软技能，40，261–263

专业开发，62

项目/项目集，60，226，241–242，268–270

项目评估和控制流程，75–78

项目仪表板，见 状态报告/仪表板

项目管理（PM），11–12，44，56，58–60，66，70，72–73，85，95，111，118，223–224，226，268–271

项目规划流程，71–75

原型构建，5，21，28，59，69，121，128，134，136–137，170，200–201，252，275

鉴定，120，130，151

质量保证流程，98–101

INDEX

quality characteristics and approaches, 159–192

quality management process, 63–66

reconfigurability, *see agility*

recursion, *see also* iteration, concurrency, and recursion, xxiii, 35, 39, 42–44, 102, 110, 112, 115, 117, 118, 132, 137, 142, 192, 207, 215, 221, 314

reliability, availability, maintainability (RAM), 176–180

repairability, *see* reliability, availability, maintainability (RAM)

requirements, 19, 33–39, 101–117, 138–143, 146–152, 201–206

resilience, 180–184

retirement stage, 26–27, 29, 158, 222–223

return on investment (ROI), 5–6, 163

reuse, 13, 36, 44, 67–70, 117, 123, 134, 156–157, 167, 184–185, 201, 206, 218, 220, 226, 233, 245–246, 273, 314

reviews, *see also* audits and decision gates, 29, 31–33, 48, 52, 54, 58–59, 72, 76–78, 117, 126, 133, 252

risk, *see also* opportunity (and safety in biomedical and healthcare), xix, 2, 16, 18, 19, 25–26, 28, 29–30, 32–33, 35–36, 37, 38, 47–48, 50–51, 71–74, 75–78, 81–87, 94–97, 106, 112, 116–117, 130–132, 135–137, 140,149, 169, 171, 185–189, 190, 195, 201, 215–219, 220, 231–232, 248, 253, 265

risk management process, 81–87

robustness, *see* resilience

S*, 11–12, 208–212

safety, *see also* risk, 185–189

scalability, *see* agility

scenario, 107–109, 148–149, 170, 182–184, 192–193

security, 190–191

sensitivity analysis, 69, 81, 129, 131, 272

sequential, *see also* evolutionary and incremental, 8, 25, 30, 31, 33–39, 42, 221–222, 249, 254, 256

service systems, 239–240

质量特性和实施方法，159–192

质量管理流程，63–66

可重构性，见 敏捷性

递归，另见 迭代、并行和递归，xxiii，35，39，42–44，102，110，112，115，117，118，132，137，142，192，207，215，221，314

可靠性、可用性和可维护性（RAM），176–180

可维修性，见 可靠性、可用性和可维护性（RAM）需求，19，33–39，101–117，138–143，146–152，201–206

强韧性，180–184

退役阶段，26–27，29，158，222–223

投资回报（ROI），5–6，163

重用，13，36，44，67–70，117，123，134，156–157，167，184–185，201，206，218，220，226，233，245–246，273，314

评审，另见 审核 和 决策门，29，31–33，48，52，54，58–59，72，76–78，117，126，133，252

风险，另见 机会（及生物医学和医疗卫生中的安全），xix，2，16，18，19，25–26，28，29–30，32–33，35–36，37，38，47–48，50–51，71–74，75–78，81–87，94–97，106，112，116–117，130–132，135–137，140，149，169，171，185–189，190，195，201，215–219，220，231–232，248，253，265

风险管理流程，81–87

鲁棒性，见 强韧性

S*，11–12，208–212

安全性，另见 风险，185–189

可扩展性，见 敏捷性

场景，107–109，148–149，170，182–184，192–193

安保性，190–191

灵敏度分析，69，81，129，131，272

顺序式，另见 进化式和增量式，8，25，30，31，33–39，42，221–222，249，254，256

服务系统，239–240

INDEX

similarity, 142

simulation, *see also* model, 141–142, 150, 192–201, 272

soft skills, *see also* professional competencies, 262–263

software engineering (SWE), 9, 16, 38–39, 90, 266–267, 278

software intensive systems, 198, 203, 232–233, 257, 266–267

space/aerospace systems, 8, 27, 31, 38, 69, 97, 151, 174, 224, 246, 249–250, 255–257, 285

specialty engineering, *see* quality characteristics and approaches

spiral, 31, 37, 229

stakeholder needs and requirements definition process, 107–112

standards, 3–4, 172, 197, 215–219, 247, 248, 249, 251, 256–257, 263

state, *see also* mode, 4, 8–9, 14, 179, 181–184, 210, 243, 278

status report/dashboard, 49, 58, 75–78, 329

supplier, *see also* acquirer, 3, 5, 33, 44–49, 65, 76–77, 89, 106, 114–115, 142, 148–151, 153, 168, 175, 178, 195, 203–204, 231, 245, 247, 252, 253, 311, 314, 321, 330–331

supply process, 48–50

support stage, 26–27, 29, 222, 250, 266

supportability *see* logistics

survivability, *see* resilience

sustainability, 184–185

SysML *see* Systems Modeling Language (SysML)

system (definition), 2–3

system analysis, 79, 109, 120, 129–132, 193, 204, 267, 331–332

system analysis process, 129–132

system architecture definition process, 118–124

system element, 2–3, 8–9, 12–14, 19, 26, 35–36, 43, 44–48, 68–69, 78–81, 101, 112, 115–117, 118–124, 125–128, 132–137, 142, 151, 156–158, 201–206, 223–224, 230, 231–232, 314

相似性，142

仿真，另见 模型，141–142，150，192–201，272

软技能，另见 职业胜任力，262–263

软件工程（SWE），9，16，38–39，90，266–267，278

软件密集系统，198，203，232–233，257，266–267

空间/航天系统，8，27，31，38，69，97，151，174，224，246，249–250，255–257，285

专业工程，见 质量特性和实施方法

螺旋，31，37，229

利益相关方需要和需求定义流程，107–112

标准，3–4，172，197，215–219，247，248，249，251，256–257，263

阶段，另见 模式，4，8–9，14，179，181–184，210，243，278

状态报告/仪表板，49，58，75–78，329

供应商，另见 采办方，3，5，33，44–49，65，76–77，89，106，114–115，142，148–151，153，168，175，178，195，203–204，231，245，247，252，253，311，314，321，330–331

供应流程，48–50

支持阶段，26–27，29，222，250，266

可支持性 见 后勤

可生存性，见 强韧性

可持续性，184–185

SysML，见 系统建模语言（SysML）

系统（定义），2–3

系统分析，79，109，120，129–132，193，204，267，331–332

系统分析流程，129–132

系统架构定义流程，118–124

系统元素，2–3，8–9，12–14，19，26，35–36，43，44–48，68–69，78–81，101，112，115–117，118–124，125–128，132–137，142，151，156–158，201–206，223–224，230，231–232，314

INDEX

system(s) engineer, *see* systems engineering practitioner

system of interest (SoI), 8, 10–12, 13

system of systems (SoS), 234, 235–238

system requirements definition process, 112–117

system science/systems thinking, xxii, 1, 21–24, 66, 127, 170, 238, 253

systems engineering (definition), 1–2

systems engineering and integration team (SEIT), 137

systems engineering body of knowledge (SEBoK), guide to, xxi, xxiii

systems engineering heuristics, 20–21

systems engineering management plan (SEMP), 31, 71–73, 77, 88, 97, 118, 139, 147, 176, 333

systems engineering practitioner, xix, xxi-xxii, 261–266

systems engineering principles, 17–20

Systems Modeling Language (SysML), 4–5, 220–221, 228

tailoring, 215–219

taxonomy, 68, 130, 165, 181–182, 196, 236

team, 1, 63, 87, 230, 241, 262–265

technical performance measures (TPMs), 72, 80, 95, 97–98, 131–132, 137, 315

telecommunications systems, 257–258

test, *see also* inspection, analysis, and demonstration, 131, 136, 139, 142, 147

testability, *see* reliability, availability, maintainability (RAM)

testing, *see* verification

tools, xxii, 5, 23, 51, 197–198, 274

traceability, 67, 81, 87–90, 105, 107–108, 110–112, 113–114, 117, 121, 126, 131, 133,136–137, 140, 145, 148, 153, 155, 188–189, 191, 195–196, 198, 201–202, 333

trade study/trade-off study, see also decision management, 27–28, 43, 44, 48, 79–81, 87, 90, 94, 104, 115, 118, 120, 123, 126, 128, 130, 132, 161–162, 164–165, 170–171, 172–173, 178, 193, 195, 204, 208, 210, 231, 233, 265, 315

training, 52, 54, 61–63, 106, 133–134, 144, 152,155, 171, 173–174, 187, 193, 262

系统工程师，见 系统工程实践者

所感兴趣之系统（SoI），8，10–12，13

体系（SoS），234，235–238

系统需求定义流程，112–117

系统科学 / 系统思维，xxii，1，21–24，66，127，170，238，253

系统工程（定义），1–2

系统工程综合团队（SEIT），137

系统工程知识体指南（SEBoK），xxi，xxiii

系统工程启发式方法，20–21

系统工程管理计划（SEMP），31，71–73，77，88，97，118，139，147，176，333

系统工程实践者，xix，xxi-xxii，261–266

系统工程原则，17–20

系统建模语言（SysML），4–5，220–221，228

剪裁，215–219

分类法，68，130，165，181–182，196，236

团队，1，63，87，230，241，262–265

技术性能测度（TPMs），72，80，95，97–98，131–132，137，315

电信系统，257–258

试验，另见 检验、分析和演示，131，136，139，142，147

可测试性，见 可靠性、可用性和可维护性（RAM）

测试，见 验证

工具，xxii，5，23，51，197–198，274

可追溯性，67，81，87–90，105，107–108，110–112，113–114，117，121，126，131，133，136–137，140，145，148，153，155，188–189，191，195–196，198，201–202，333

权衡研究 / 权衡研究，另见 决策管理，27–28，43，44，48，79–81，87，90，94，104，115，118，120，123，126，128，130，132，161–162，164–165，170–171，172–173，178，193，195，204，208，210，231，233，265，315

培训，52，54，61–63，106，133–134，144，152，155，171，173–174，187，193，262

INDEX

transdisciplinary, 1, 21–23, 168, 274

transformation, 96, 101–103, 109, 111, 115, 125, 138, 185, 192, 194, 197, 228, 273,274, 275–276

transition, 143–145

transparent box, *see* white box

transportation systems, 258–259

tree(s), *see* breakdown structures

trustworthiness, *see* security

uncertainty, xix, 2, 15–16, 17–18, 19, 48, 51, 59, 79, 81, 82, 84, 106, 112, 120, 129–131, 165, 192, 198, 201, 221–222, 239, 244, 272, 275, 281, 285

usability, *see* human systems integration (HSI)

user, *see* operator

user eXperience (UX), *see* human systems integration (HSI)

user interface (UI), *see* human systems integration (HSI)

utilization stage, 26–28, 145, 222

validation, 146–152

value, xxii, 5, 7–8, 9, 14, 15–16, 17–19, 22, 36, 53, 66, 72, 77, 80–82, 85–87, 95, 97–98, 104–105, 109–110, 120, 123–124, 126, 128, 129–131, 160–164, 170, 173–175, 181, 183–184, 185, 191, 192–195, 208–210, 212, 224–225, 226–229, 239, 240, 241–243, 265, 272, 275, 313, 315

value robustness, *see* affordability

variable, 9, 14, 20, 129, 131, 210, 239, 313

variability, 58, 226–229, 315

Vee model, 35–36, 222, 256

verification, 138–143

vertical integration, *see also* horizontal integration, 10, 14, 44, 90, 124, 137, 203, 218

vertical traceability, see also horizontal traceability, 201

very small enterprise (VSE), 4, 219

跨学科，1，21–23，168，274

转型，96，101–103，109，111，115，125，138，185，192，194，197，228，273，274，275–276

转移，143–145

透明盒，见 白盒

运输系统，258–259

树，见 分解结构

可信度，见 安保

不确定性，xix，2，15–16，17–18，19，48，51，59，79，81，82，84，106，112，120，129–131，165，192，198，201，221–222，239，244，272，275，281，285

可用性，见 人与系统综合（HSI）

用户，见 操作人员

用户体验（UX），见 人与系统综合（HSI）

用户接口（UI），见 人与系统综合（HSI）

使用阶段，26–28，145，222

确认，146–152

价值，xxii，5，7–8，9，14，15–16，17–19，22，36，53，66，72，77，80–82，85–87，95，97–98，104–105，109–110，120，123–124，126，128，129–131，160–164，170，173–175，181，183–184，185，191，192–195，208–210，212，224–225，226–229，239，240，241–243，265，272，275，313，315

价值鲁棒性，见 可承受性

变量，9，14，20，129，131，210，239，313

变异性，58，226–229，315

Vee 模型，35–36，222，256

验证，138–143

纵向综合，另见 横向综合，10，14，44，90，124，137，203，218

纵向可追溯性，另见 横向可追溯性，201

极小型复杂组织体系（VSE），4，219

INDEX

views and viewpoints, 8–9, 14, 16, 17, 19, 23–24, 26–27, 70, 77–78, 84, 97, 110–112, 118–129, 137, 168, 176, 180, 182, 189, 190, 195–198, 201, 205, 206–208, 238, 265, 333

vision, 1, 3, 4–5, 22, 192, 219, 245, 264, 275–276

waste, 97, 156–158, 184–185, 224–226, 229, 230, 255, 315

white box, *see also* black box, 9, 200, 315

work breakdown structure (WBS), *see* breakdown structures

视图和视角，8–9，14，16，17，19，23–24，26–27，70，77–78，84，97，110–112，118–129，137，168，176，180，182，189，190，195–198，201，205，206–208，238，265，333

愿景，1，3，4–5，22，192，219，245，264，275–276

浪费，97，156–158，184–185，224–226，229，230，255，315

白盒，另见 黑盒，9，200，315

工作分解结构（WBS），见 分解结构